SOMETHING ABOUT THE AUTHOR®

Something about
the Author *was named
an "Outstanding
Reference Source,"*
the highest honor given
by the American
Library Association
Reference and Adult
Services Division.

ISSN 0276-816X

something ABOUT THE AUTHOR®

**Facts and Pictures about Authors
and Illustrators of Books for Young People**

volume 193

GALE
CENGAGE Learning·

Detroit • New York • San Francisco • New Haven, Conn • Waterville, Maine • London

GALE
CENGAGE Learning

Something about the Author, Volume 193

Project Editor: Lisa Kumar

Editorial: Dana Ferguson, Amy Elisabeth Fuller, Michelle Kazensky, Jennifer Mossman, Joseph Palmisano, Mary Ruby, Marie Toft

Permissions: Mollika Basu, Kelly Quin, Tracie Richardson

Imaging and Multimedia: Leitha Etheridge-Sims, John Watkins

Composition and Electronic Capture: Amy Darga

Manufacturing: Drew Kalasky

Product Manager: Janet Witalec

For product information and technology assistance, contact us at **Gale Customer Support, 1-800-877-4253.**
For permission to use material from this text or product, submit all requests online at **www.cengage.com/permissions.**
Further permissions questions can be emailed to **permissionrequest@cengage.com**

Gale
27500 Drake Rd.
Farmington Hills, MI, 48331-3535

LIBRARY OF CONGRESS CATALOG CARD NUMBER 62-52046

ISBN-13: 978-1-4144-2165-0
ISBN-10: 1-4144-2165-6

ISSN 0276-816X

This title is also available as an e-book.
ISBN-13: 978-1-4144-5739-0
ISBN-10: 1-4144-5739-1
Contact your Gale sales representative for ordering information.

Printed in the United States of America
1 2 3 4 5 6 7 12 11 10 09 08

Contents

Authors in Forthcoming Volumes vii

Introduction ix

SATA Product Advisory Board xi

Illustrations Index 223

Author Index 255

A

Abadzis, Nick 1965- 1

Allen, Thomas B. 1929- 2

Allen, Thomas Benton
  See Allen, Thomas B. 2

Allen, Tom
  See Allen, Thomas B. 2

Amado, Elisa 8

Archer, Lily 1981- 10

Austin, Carrie
  See Seuling, Barbara 174

B

Bailey, Len 12

Banyai, Istvan 13

Bidner, Jenni 1963- 17

Bradley, Timothy J. 18

Burleigh, Robert 1936- 19

Burnett Bossi, Lisa 26

Burns, Loree Griffin 26

C

Caple, Kathy 28

Catlow, Nikalas
  See Catlow, Niki 29

Catlow, Niki 1975- 29

Chien, Catia 30

Chien-min, Lin
  See Rumford, James 165

Clayman, Deborah Paula
  See Da Costa, Deborah 33

Clippinger, Carol 30

Crocker, Carter 31

D

Da Costa, Deborah 33

De Mari, Silvana 1953- 33

Denise, Christopher 1968- 34

Dubosarsky, Ursula 1961- 37

E

Engle, Margarita 1951- 42

Erskine, Kathryn 43

G

Griffin, Peni R. 1961- 45

Griffin, Peni Rae Robinson
  See Griffin, Peni R. 45

H

Halpin, Brendan 1968- 50

Heiligman, Deborah 1958- 52

Hest, Amy 1950- 55

Hill, Susanna Leonard 1965- 61

Hobbs, Valerie 1941- 63

Hokenson, Terry 1948- 67

J

Jahn-Clough, Lisa 1967- 69

Johnson, Stacie
  See Myers, Walter Dean 131

K

Kingsley, Kaza 74

Kline, Suzy 1943- 74
  Autobiography Feature 81

Kraft, Erik P. 98

Authors in Forthcoming Volumes

Below are some of the authors and illustrators that will be featured in upcoming volumes of *SATA*. These include new entries on the swiftly rising stars of the field, as well as completely revised and updated entries (indicated with *) on some of the most notable and best-loved creators of books for children.

Peter Abrahams ∎ Known for his critically acclaimed crime novels *Nerve Damage, End of Story,* and *Lights Out,* Abrahams has turned to a younger readership with his "Echo Falls" mystery novels. In *Down the Rabbit Hole* readers meet Ingrid Levin-Hill, a fan of famous literary sleuth Sherlock Holmes as well as a likeable eight grader with a love of soccer. Using the skills of deduction espoused by Holmes, Ingrid tracks down mysteries in her rural New England town, teaming up with best friend Joey in *Behind the Curtain* to expose the local drug-selling ring that has hooked her star-athlete older brother on steroids.

Terence Blacker ∎ In addition to writing such well-received young-adult novels as *Homebird, The Angel Factory,* and *Boy2Girl,* Blacker is well known on both sides of the Atlantic for his picture books and his quirky and popular "Ms Wiz" series of middle-grade novels. In *Homebird* a British teen flees from boarding school after meeting with violence from a vicious bully, while *The Angel Factory* introduces a boy who discovers that he is not only adopted, but that his seemingly normal parents are actually extraterrestrials. Gender bending is at the crux of *Boy2Girl,* as a California teen takes a dare to live as a girl after moving in with his British cousin, then realizes that his new identity has surprising benefits.

Stephen L. Buchmann ∎ An associate professor of entomology at the University of Arizona in Tucson, Buchmann is also an amateur beekeeper and founder of the environmentally-focused The Bee Works. Drawing on his interest in bees and their habitat, his book *The Forgotten Pollinators* was among the first books to raise awareness regarding environmental threats to the pollination cycle, and he also presents an admiring tribute to the honey bee in *Letters from the Hive: An Intimate History of Bees, Honey, and Humankind.* In his picture book *The Bee Tree* he teams up with artist Paul Mirocha and coauthor Diana Cohn to share with young children the excitement of a honey hunt in rural Malaysia.

*Leo and Diane Dillon ∎ One of the best-known husband-and-wife teams in children's literature, the Dillons are noted illustrators and artists. Since the 1960s, their bold drawings and illustrations have ranged from the highly realistic to the abstract, and they have contributed to science fiction, literary classics, and folktales by numerous authors. In addition to creating award-winning illustrations for picture books such as Sharon Bell Mathis's *The Hundred Penny Box* and Virginia Hamilton's *The People Could Fly: American Black Folktales*, they have also produced honored original picture books such as *Jazz on a Saturday Night*. The Dillons are the only illustrators to have received consecutive Caldecott medals, considered the highest illustration achievement in children's literature.

*E.L. Konigsburg ∎ An impressive figure in children's literature, Konigsburg is the only author to have had two books on the Newbery list at the same time. The Connecticut-based writer is the author of the modern childhood classic *From the Mixed-up Files of Mrs. Basil E. Frankweiler,* as well as award-winning novels such as *Jennifer, Hecate, Macbeth, William McKinley, and Me, Elizabeth,* and *The View from Saturday.* Known for her witty, often self-illustrated texts, she has carved out a unique niche with her writing, whether drawing on her own experiences or exploring medieval and Renaissance worlds. Konigsburg focuses on recent history in *The Mysterious Edge of the Heroic World* in her story of two sixth graders who team up to help organize the possessions of an eccentric and elderly neighbor. Combining Holocaust history with a contemporary mystery, the story also showcases Konigsburg's characteristic focus on the rich rewards to be gained in multigenerational friendships.

Laura McNeal ∎ A former journalist, McNeal is one half of the writing team of Laura and Tom McNeal, the authors of novels, short stories, and essays. Their critically acclaimed young-adult novels include *Crushed, Zipped,* and *Crooked.* In another imaginative novel, *The Decoding of Lana Morris,* McNeal and her husband inject fantasy into their story of a preteen artist who buys an antique drawing kit that transforms the artwork she then creates into reality.

Diane Purkiss ∎ Purkiss is a fellow and tutor of English at Keble College, Oxford, where her research focuses on such serious areas of study as Renaissance drama and the English Civil War. Apart from her academic work, Purkiss is one half of Tobias Druitt, pseudonymous author of the "Corydon" fantasy novels for young readers. The other half of Tobias Druitt is Michael Dowling, Purkiss's son, who was eight years old when Druitt's first novel, *Corydon and the Island of Monsters,* was written. Based on characters from Greek mythology, the "Corydon" books introduce readers to an orphaned shepherd who, outcast because of a birth defect that left him with a goat's hoof instead of a foot, teams up with classical monsters such as Medusa, Minotaur, and Sphinx to battle Perseus, Zeus, and a disjointed army of Greek heroes.

*R.L. Stine ∎ With hundreds of millions of books in print—some bearing the titles *The Howler, When Good Ghouls Go Bad,* and *Twister*—Stine is the world's undisputed top-selling children's author. While criticized by some, his novels in the "Fear Street," "Goosebumps," and "Nightmare Room" series have made avid bookworms out of even reluctant readers. His "Fear Street" series illustrates the captivating quality of Stine's literary stew: likeable and realistic teen characters, a seemingly normal small town, and a horrific threat that results in at least one untimely and gruesome end.

*Lynne Truss ▌ Truss learned the importance of proper punctuation as a young child, and she has observed its misuse during her career as a critic, journalist, and novelist. Her book *Eats, Shoots and Leaves: The Zero Tolerance Approach to Punctuation* sold millions of copies in her native Britain as well as in the United States, inspiring a series of books designed to inspire children with an interest in correct communication. *Eats, Shoots and Leaves: Why, Commas Really DO Make a Difference!* echoes the lessons of her bestseller, mixing humorous cartoon art with amusing instances of how the lack of a comma can transform sense into non-sense.

*Jane Yolen ▌ Spanning genres from fiction and poetry to biography, criticism, and books on the art of writing, Yolen is particularly well known for her history-based fiction for young readers, as well as for fantasy novels such as those in her "Pit Dragon" series. A natural storyteller, she also incorporates music and oral folklore in compilations of international songs, rhymes, and stories. Now often working in collaboration with her three grown children, Yolen is perhaps best known for creating original folk and fairy tales and fables that feature a surprising twist and a strong moral core. She has received special recognition for her literary fairy tales, which combine familiar fantasy motifs with contemporary elements and philosophical themes.

Introduction

Something about the Author (*SATA*) is an ongoing reference series that examines the lives and works of authors and illustrators of books for children. *SATA* includes not only well-known writers and artists but also less prominent individuals whose works are just coming to be recognized. This series is often the only readily available information source on emerging authors and illustrators. You'll find *SATA* informative and entertaining, whether you are a student, a librarian, an English teacher, a parent, or simply an adult who enjoys children's literature.

What's Inside *SATA*

SATA provides detailed information about authors and illustrators who span the full time range of children's literature, from early figures like John Newbery and L. Frank Baum to contemporary figures like Judy Blume and Richard Peck. Authors in the series represent primarily English-speaking countries, particularly the United States, Canada, and the United Kingdom. Also included, however, are authors from around the world whose works are available in English translation. The writings represented in *SATA* include those created intentionally for children and young adults as well as those written for a general audience and known to interest younger readers. These writings cover the entire spectrum of children's literature, including picture books, humor, folk and fairy tales, animal stories, mystery and adventure, science fiction and fantasy, historical fiction, poetry and nonsense verse, drama, biography, and nonfiction. Obituaries are also included in *SATA* and are intended not only as death notices but also as concise overviews of people's lives and work. Additionally, each edition features newly revised and updated entries for a selection of *SATA* listees who remain of interest to today's readers and who have been active enough to require extensive revisions of their earlier biographies.

Autobiography Feature

Beginning with Volume 103, many volumes of *SATA* feature one or more specially commissioned autobiographical essays. These unique essays, averaging about ten thousand words in length and illustrated with an abundance of personal photos, present an entertaining and informative first-person perspective on the lives and careers of prominent authors and illustrators profiled in *SATA*.

Two Convenient Indexes

In response to suggestions from librarians, *SATA* indexes no longer appear in every volume but are included in alternate (odd-numbered) volumes of the series, beginning with Volume 57.

SATA continues to include two indexes that cumulate with each alternate volume: the Illustrations Index, arranged by the name of the illustrator, gives the number of the volume and page where the illustrator's work appears in the current volume as well as all preceding volumes in the series; the Author Index gives the number of the volume in which a person's biographical sketch, autobiographical essay, or obituary appears in the current volume as well as all preceding volumes in the series.

These indexes also include references to authors and illustrators who appear in *Gale's Yesterday's Authors of Books for Children, Children's Literature Review,* and *Something about the Author Autobiography Series.*

Easy-to-Use Entry Format

Whether you're already familiar with the *SATA* series or just getting acquainted, you will want to be aware of the kind of information that an entry provides. In every *SATA* entry the editors attempt to give as complete a picture of the person's life and work as possible. A typical entry in *SATA* includes the following clearly labeled information sections:

PERSONAL: date and place of birth and death, parents' names and occupations, name of spouse, date of marriage, names of children, educational institutions attended, degrees received, religious and political affiliations, hobbies and other interests.

ADDRESSES: complete home, office, electronic mail, and agent addresses, whenever available.

CAREER: name of employer, position, and dates for each career post; art exhibitions; military service; memberships and offices held in professional and civic organizations.

MEMBER: professional, civic, and other association memberships and any official posts held.

AWARDS, HONORS: literary and professional awards received.

WRITINGS: title-by-title chronological bibliography of books written and/or illustrated, listed by genre when known; lists of other notable publications, such as plays, screenplays, and periodical contributions.

ADAPTATIONS: a list of films, television programs, plays, CD-ROMs, recordings, and other media presentations that have been adapted from the author's work.

WORK IN PROGRESS: description of projects in progress.

SIDELIGHTS: a biographical portrait of the author or illustrator's development, either directly from the biographee—and often written specifically for the *SATA* entry—or gathered from diaries, letters, interviews, or other published sources.

BIOGRAPHICAL AND CRITICAL SOURCES: cites sources quoted in "Sidelights" along with references for further reading.

EXTENSIVE ILLUSTRATIONS: photographs, movie stills, book illustrations, and other interesting visual materials supplement the text.

How a *SATA* Entry Is Compiled

SATA editors examine a wide variety of published sources to gather information for an entry. Biographical and bibliographic sources are consulted, as are book reviews, feature articles, published interviews, and material sometimes obtained from the biographee's family, publishers, agent, or other associates. Whenever possible, the author or illustrator is sent a copy of the entry to check for accuracy and completeness.

Entries that have not been verified by the biographees or their representatives are marked with an asterisk (*).

Contact the Editor

We encourage our readers to examine the entire *SATA* series. Please write and tell us if we can make *SATA* even more helpful to you. Give your comments and suggestions to the editor:

Editor
Something about the Author
Gale, Cengage Learning
27500 Drake Rd.
Farmington Hills MI 48331-3535

Toll-free: 800-877-GALE
Fax: 248-699-8070

Something about the Author Product Advisory Board

The editors of *Something about the Author* are dedicated to maintaining a high standard of excellence by publishing comprehensive, accurate, and highly readable entries on a wide array of writers for children and young adults. In addition to the quality of the content, the editors take pride in the graphic design of the series, which is intended to be orderly yet inviting, allowing readers to utilize the pages of *SATA* easily and with efficiency. Despite the longevity of the *SATA* print series, and the success of its format, we are mindful that the vitality of a literary reference product is dependent on its ability to serve its users over time. As literature, and attitudes about literature, constantly evolve, so do the reference needs of students, teachers, scholars, journalists, researchers, and book club members. To be certain that we continue to keep pace with the expectations of our customers, the editors of *SATA* listen carefully to their comments regarding the value, utility, and quality of the series. Librarians, who have firsthand knowledge of the needs of library users, are a valuable resource for us. The *Something about the Author* Product Advisory Board, made up of school, public, and academic librarians, is a forum to promote focused feedback about *SATA* on a regular basis. The nine-member advisory board includes the following individuals, whom the editors wish to thank for sharing their expertise:

Eva M. Davis
Youth Department Manager,
Ann Arbor District Library,
Ann Arbor, Michigan

Joan B. Eisenberg
Lower School Librarian,
Milton Academy,
Milton, Massachusetts

Francisca Goldsmith
Teen Services Librarian,
Berkeley Public Library,
Berkeley, California

Susan Dove Lempke
Children's Services Supervisor,
Niles Public Library District,
Niles, Illinois

Robyn Lupa
Head of Children's Services,
Jefferson County Public Library,
Lakewood, Colorado

Victor L. Schill
Assistant Branch Librarian/Children's Librarian,
Harris County Public Library/Fairbanks Branch,
Houston, Texas

Caryn Sipos
Community Librarian,
Three Creeks Community Library,
Vancouver, Washington

Steven Weiner
Director,
Maynard Public Library,
Maynard, Massachusetts

SOMETHING ABOUT THE AUTHOR

ABADZIS, Nick 1965-

Personal

Born 1965, in Sweden; married; children: one daughter.

Addresses

Home—London, England.

Career

Writer and artist. Editorial consultant for children's magazines in London, England. Developer of cartoon Web sites for clients, including British Broadcasting Corporation.

Awards, Honors

UK Comic Art Award, 1994, for *Hugo Tate: O America*; Royal Television Society Award, 1999, for best Web site; Great Graphic Novel citation and Top-Ten Graphic Novel citation, both Young Adult Library Services Association, Book for the Teen Age selection, New York Public Library, and Cybil Award nomination, all 2007, and two Eisner Award nominations and National Cartoonists' Society Division Award nomination, both 2008, all for *Laika*.

Writings

GRAPHIC NOVELS

Hugo Tate: O America (originally serialized in *Deadline* magazine), Atomeka Press, 1993.

(With Paul Johnson) *Children of the Voyager*, Marvel (New York, NY), 1993.

(With Duncan Fegredo) *Millennium Fever*, DC/Vertigo (New York, NY), 1995.

The Amazing Mr Pleebus, Orchard (London, England), 1996.

The Freaky Beastie of Hill Road School, Orchard (London, England), 1997.

The Magic Skateboard, Orchard (London, England), 1998.

Voyage to Planet Voon, Orchard (London, England), 1999.

Oscar y Oso, Mary Glasgow, 1999.

Comme un poisson dans l'eau, Mary Glasgow, 2000.

The Dangerous Planet, Heinemann (London, England), 2000.

The Pyramid of Doom, Heinemann (London, England), 2001.

The Dog from Outer Space, Heinemann (London, England), 2002.

Blottvoomer's Volcano, Behemoth, 2002.

Laika, First Second (New York, NY), 2007.

Author and artist of comic strip *Cora's Breakfast,* serialized in London *Guardian,* and *The Trial of the Sober Dog,* serialized in London *Times,* both 2008. Author, with Michael Coleman, of comic strip *Angels FC,* issues 1 through 15, 1998-2004. Author of self-published short titles *Landscape of Possibilities* and *Listening, Not Hearing,* both 2004. Contributor to *Project: Superior,* AdHouse, 2005; contributor to London *Times, Independent on Sunday, TimeOut, Punch, Sunday Correspondent, Radio Times,* and the BBC.

Sidelights

Born in Sweden of Greek and English parents, Nick Abadzis is a writer and illustrator of comics and graphic novels. His serialized comic strip *Hugo Tate* first brought Abadzis a measure of international attention in the early 1990s, and he has since been cited for his work with dominant American comics publishers Marvel and DC. Throughout the 1990s and early 2000s, however, Abadzis focused primarily on creating comics for children's publishers in the United Kingdom while also working as an editor and creative consultant.

When independent comics publisher First Second launched, one of the early projects the publishing house solicited was *Laika,* a full-color graphic novel by Abadzis. *Laika* recounts the story of the stray Russian dog who became the first creature ever to travel into outer space. More historical fiction than biography, due to the few records available that document Laika's life, the novel gives readers an idea of the people who were involved in the early Soviet space movement. It also avoids any easy answers to questions about the morality of sending a dog into space for the sole purpose of scientific advancement. Noting that Laika does not speak in the story, Brian Heater wrote in the *Daily Crosshatch* online that by retelling the dog's story Abadzis gives Laika a voice: "The first living creature to enter the earth's orbit found her medium, in the form of Nick Abadzis."

Laika begins as the stray dog is caught and sent to the Institute of Aviation Medicine. Her trained behavior and ability to withstand a higher G-force than the other canines make her the obvious choice when the scientists select a dog to send into space. "Abadzis's artwork genuinely captures the Cold War atmosphere," wrote Sarah Krygier in *School Library Journal,* the critic comparing the author's "youth-friendly textual take on the politically dangerous USSR" to Marjane Satrapi's *Persepolis,* a graphic novel that provided a similar perspective on the complicated politics of Iran. Noting the book's historical detail, Roger Sabin wrote in the London *Observer* that Abadzis's "research has resulted in one of the most atmospheric historical graphic novels yet produced." A *Publishers Weekly* critic deemed the graphic novel "a standout, not just for its sympathetic point of view but for its refusal to Disnify or anthropomorphize the undeniably cute dog at its heart," and a *Kirkus Reviews* contributor described *Laika* as "a luminous masterpiece filled with pathos and poignancy."

"I often have an amorphous idea of what a story could turn out like—a sort of story goal, if you like," Abadzis told Tom Spurgeon in an interview for *Comics Reporter* online. "But any one thing during the process can change that and make the creative outcome totally different from how you thought it would be." Abadzis also commented on the end of the creative process, particularly with regard to *Laika*: "Whenever you finish a comics project and look back at it with the benefit of hindsight, there are always things you'd change. I'd have liked some extra pages to allow chapter two a little more room to breathe. . . . In the end, I just went with what I had and tried to make it accessible and make it flow. I hope it still managed to draw [readers] . . . in."

Biographical and Critical Sources

PERIODICALS

Booklist, September 1, 2007, Jesse Karp, review of *Laika,* p. 107.

Bulletin of the Center for Children's Books, October, 2007, Elizabeth Bush, review of *Laika,* p. 70.

Guardian (London, England), February 9, 2008, review of *Laika,* p. 19.

Kirkus Reviews, August 1, 2007, review of *Laika.*

Library Journal, January 1, 2008, Martha Cornog, review of *Laika,* p. 71.

Observer (London, England), November 25, 2007, "Posy Simmonds Updates Hardy While Nick Abadzis Is Drawn to a High-flying Dog," p. 29.

Publishers Weekly, October 1, 2007, review of *Laika,* p. 60.

School Library Journal, November, 2007, Sarah Krygier, review of *Laika,* p. 155.

ONLINE

Comics Reporter Online, http://www.comicsreporter.com/ (September 1, 2007), Tom Spurgeon, interview with Abdazis.

Daily Crosshatch Online, http://thedailycrosshatch.com/ (October 29, 2007), Brian Heater, interview with Abadzis.

First Second Web site, http://www.firstsecondbooks.com/ (October 6, 2008), "Nick Abadzis."

Nick Abadzis Web log, http://nickabadzis.my-expressions. com (October 5, 2008).

Nick Abadzis Home Page, http://www.nickabadzis.com (October 6, 2008).*

*   *   *

ALLEN, Thomas B. 1929-
(Thomas Benton Allen, Tom Allen)

Personal

Born March 20, 1929, in Bridgeport, CT; son of Walter Leo (a salesman) and Elizabeth Allen; married Florence "Scottie" MacBride (a potter), June 5, 1950; children: Christopher, Constance, Roger. *Education:* Attended Fairfield University, 1947-49; University of Bridgeport, B.A. (journalism), 1955. *Politics:* Democrat. *Religion:* Unitarian Universalist.

Addresses

Home and office—Bethesda, MD. *Agent*—Carl Brandt, 1501 Broadway, New York, NY 10036. *E-mail*—tballen@tballen.com.

Career

Journalist and author. Bridgeport Herald, Bridgeport, CT, reporter, 1946-52, 1953-63; New York Daily News, New York, NY, feature writer, 1956-63; Chilton Book Co., Philadelphia, PA, managing editor for trade books, 1963-65; National Geographic Book Service, Washington, DC, editor, beginning 1965, associate chief editor, 1974-81; freelance writer, 1981—. Montgomery College, instructor in freshman English, 1969-70; instructor at Writers Center, Bethesda, MD. Consultant and on-screen speaker for Documedia series *Secrets of War,* History Channel. *Military service:* U.S. Navy, journalist, 1952-53.

Member

Authors Guild, National Press Club, Bethesda Writer's Center (founder and former member of board of directors).

Awards, Honors

Notable Book of the Year designation, *New York Times,* 1981, for *Rickover;* New York Public Library Reference Book of the Year selection, 1991, for *World War II: America at War 1941-1945;* Eller Prize in Naval History (with Norman Polmar), 1995, for article in *Naval Institute Proceedings;* Notable Book designation, American Library Association, 2001, for *Remember Pearl Harbor;* Gold Award, Art Directors' Club, 2002, for interactive Web feature on Pearl Harbor; New York Public Library 100 Titles for Reading and Sharing citation.

Writings

(Under name Tom Allen; with Harold W. McCormick and William E. Young) *Shadows in the Sea: The Sharks, Skates, and Rays,* Chilton (Radnor, PA), 1963, new edition, Lyons & Burford (Branford, CT), 1996.

The Quest: A Report on Extraterrestrial Life, Chilton (Philadelphia, PA), 1965.

(Editor and contributor) *Vacationland U.S.A.,* National Geographic Society (Washington, DC), 1970.

(With others) *Living in Washington: A Moving Experience,* Westover (Richmond, VA), 1972.

(Editor) *The Marvels of Animal Behavior,* National Geographic Society (Washington, DC), 1972.

The Last Inmate (novel), Charterhouse (New York, NY), 1973.

Vanishing Wildlife of North America, National Geographic Society (Washington, DC), 1974.

(Editor and contributor) *We Americans: Celebrating a Nation, Its People, and Its Past,* National Geographic Society (Washington, DC), 1975, millennium edition edited with Charles O. Hyman, 1999.

A Short Life (novel), Putnam (New York, NY), 1978.

(Editor and contributor) *Wild Animals of North America,* National Wildlife Society (Washington, DC), 1979.

(Editor and contributor) *Images of the World,* National Geographic Society (Washington, DC), 1981.

(Coauthor) *America's Wildlife Sampler,* National Wildlife Federation (Vienna, VA), 1982.

(With Norman Polmar) *Rickover: Controversy and Genius* (biography), Simon & Schuster (New York, NY), 1982, reprinted, Potomac Books (Washington, DC), 2007.

(With Caroline Hottenstein) *Field Guide to the Birds of North America,* National Geographic Society (Washington, DC), 1983.

(With Karen Jensen and Philip Kopper) *Earth's Amazing Animals,* National Wildlife Federation (Washington, DC), 1983.

(With Norman Polmar) *Ship of Gold* (novel), Macmillan (New York, NY), 1987.

War Games: The Secret World of the Creators, Players, and Policy Makers Rehearsing World War III Today, McGraw-Hill (New York, NY), 1987.

Guardian of the Wild: The Story of the National Wildlife Federation, 1936-1986, University of Indiana Press (Bloomington, IN), 1987.

(Editor) *America's Hidden Wilderness,* National Geographic Society (Washington, DC), 1988.

(With Norman Polmar) *Merchants of Treason: America's Secrets for Sale,* Macmillan (New York, NY), 1988.

(With Bob Devine and Donald Dale Jackson) *Treasures of the Tide,* National Wildlife Federation (Washington, DC), 1990.

(With Norman Polmar) *World War II: Americans at War, 1941-1945,* Random House (New York, NY), 1991, revised as *World War II: The Encyclopedia of the War Years, 1941-1945,* 1996.

(With Norman Polmar and F. Clifton Berry) *CNN: War in the Gulf,* Turner (Atlanta, GA), 1991.

The Blue and the Gray, National Geographic Society (Washington, DC), 1992.

(With William S. Cohen) *Murder in the Senate,* Doubleday (New York, NY), 1992.

CNN Guide to the 1992 Election: Change vs. Trust, Turner (Atlanta, GA), 1992.

Possessed: The True Story of an Exorcism, Doubleday (New York, NY), 1993, revised edition, Iuniverse. com, 1999.

Offerings at the Wall: Artifacts from the Vietnam Veterans Memorial Collection, Turner (Atlanta, GA), 1995.

(With Norman Polmar) *Code-Name: Downfall: The Secret Plan to Invade Japan—and Why Truman Dropped the Bomb,* Simon & Schuster (New York, NY), 1995, published as *Why Truman Dropped the Atomic Bomb on Japan: Code Downfall: The Secret Plan to Invade Japan,* Ross & Perry (Washington, DC), 2001.

(With Norman Polmar) *Spy Book: The Encyclopedia of Espionage,* Random House (New York, NY), 1997, revised and updated edition published as *The Encyclopedia of Espionage,* Gramercy (New York, NY), 1998, second edition, Random House (New York, NY), 2004.

Animals of Africa, Hugh Lauter Levin Associates (New York, NY), 1997.

America from Space, Firefly Books (Buffalo, NY), 1998.

The Shark Almanac: A Fully Illustrated Natural History of Sharks, Skates, and Rays, Lyons Press (New York, NY), 1999.

The Washington Monument: It Stands for All, Discovery Books (New York, NY), 2000.

Shark Attacks: Their Causes and Avoidance, Lyons Press (New York, NY), 2001.

Remember Pearl Harbor: American and Japanese Survivors Tell Their Stories, National Geographic Society (Washington, DC), 2001.

(Editor, with T.J. Cornell) *War and Games,* Boydell (Rochester, NY), 2002.

(With Paul Dickson) *The Bonus Army: An American Epic,* Walker (New York, NY), 2004.

George Washington, Spymaster: How America Outspied the British and Won the Revolutionary War, illustrated by Cheryl Harness, National Geographic (Washington, DC), 2004.

Harriet Tubman, Secret Agent: How Daring Slaves and Free Blacks Spied for the Union during the Civil War, illustrated by Carla Bauer, National Geographic (Washington, DC), 2006.

Remember Valley Forge: Patriots, Tories, and Redcoats Tell Their Stories, National Geographic (Washington, DC), 2007.

Declassified: Fifty Top Secret Documents That Change History, National Geographic (Washington, DC), 2008.

(With son, Roger MacBride Allen) *Mr. Lincoln's High-Tech War: How the North Used the Ironclads, Telegraph, Railroads, High-powered Weapons, and More to Win the Civil War,* National Geographic (Washington, DC), 2009.

Associate editor and contributor to *Guide to U.S. National Parks,* National Geographic Society (Washington, DC), 1990. Contributor to books published by National Geographic Society, including *Greece and Rome: Builders of Our World,* 1968, *The Age of Chivalry,* 1969, *Wilderness U.S.A.,* 1972, *The World of the American Indian,* 1974, *Our Continent,* 1976, *Visiting Our Past,* 1977, *Ancient Egypt,* 1978, *Romance of the Sea,* 1980, *Journey to China,* 1982, and *England and Ireland,* 1985.

Contributing editor to periodicals, including *Seapower* and *National Geographic.* Contributor to periodicals, including *New York Times Magazine, American History, Military History Quarterly, Traveller, Washington Post, Naval Institute Proceedings, Smithsonian, Washingtonian, U.S. Naval Proceedings, Popular Science Annual, Chicago Tribune-New York Daily News,* and Syndicate and Field Enterprises Syndicate. Author of film scripts for National Geographic Educational Film Division. Contributor to Web sites, including those operated by National Geographic, Discovery, Kodak, National Portrait Gallery, and Central Intelligence Agency.

Author's books have been translated into Spanish, French, Catalan, Russian, German, Scandinavian, and Japanese.

Adaptations

A Short Life was adapted as the television film *The Plutonium Incident; Murder in the Senate* was optioned for film by Tri-Star. *Possessed* was adapted as a film of the same name for Showtime; was the basis for the documentary *In the Grip of Evil,* broadcast on the Discovery Channel; and was recorded as an audiobook.

Sidelights

In addition to writing a number of books focusing on military history, Thomas B. Allen has penned novels and collaborated on works with fellow author Norman Polmar and others. Through his sixteen-year career with the National Geographic Society, he has also edited books that have entertained and informed a generation of young Americans, among them *Vacationland U.S.A.* and *Wild Animals of North America. We Americans: Celebrating a Nation, Its People, and Its Past,* which Allen also edited, has remained in print since its first publication in 1975 and was released in a special edition to mark the millennium. Of this edition, coedited with Charles O. Hyman, *Booklist* contributor Gilbert Taylor noted that "patriotism presides over this gallery of historical images." Taylor went on to praise the editors for their choice of "eminent historians and writers . . . to give context to the pictures."

Born in Bridgeport, Connecticut, in 1929, Allen has been writing professionally since he was fifteen years old, and even in his fiction has always grounded his writing in facts. Referring to himself as a "generalist," he once told *SATA:* "I started being a generalist as a newspaper reporter whose beat was what my editor called 'general assignment.' Since then, much of my work, particularly in *National Geographic* magazine, is on assignment: I cover a subject and write about it, working against a deadline and limited to a certain number of words." "I sometimes think an assignment writer is similar to an actor in a troupe," added Allen: "There is a script and a way to deliver it. Tonight it's *Hamlet,* tomorrow night it's *Death of a Salesman*—to name two of my favorite plays."

Working at the National Geographic Society allowed Allen the chance to gain expertise in many areas of nature study. *Vanishing Wildlife of North America,* which he wrote in 1974, presents readers of all ages a "comprehensive, profusely illustrated account of the myriad problems" facing the birds, fish, and other creatures whose habitats are threatened by the growing U.S. and Canadian population and advancing technology, according to *Library Journal* reviewer Lola Dudley. Including 109 creatures listed as endangered by the U.S. government, the book describes the conflict between biologists and businessmen, developers, and farmers, and "comments on the lack of concern over the fate of lesser creatures" such as small reptiles, according to a contributor to *Booklist.* Allen has continued to publish books on environmental topics since leaving the prestigious magazine to become a freelance writer in 1981. *Guardian of the Wild: The Story of the National Wildlife Federation, 1936-1986* is one such work; it was de-

scribed by a *Booklist* critic as an "inspiring chronology of the hard-won battle for the environment" that was then being waged by the world's largest conservation organization.

Many of Allen's books focus on his main interest: military history. *War Games: The Secret World of the Creators, Players, and Policy Makers Rehearsing World* *War III Today* reveals the way the U.S. government calculated the potential risk of engagement following World War II. Beginning with a history of war gaming, which has its roots in nineteenth-century Germany, the book discusses the computer-enhanced role-playing and simulation exercises used by the armed forces and other agencies in determining the potential outcome of an at-

Cover of Thomas B. Allen's **Remember Pearl Harbor,** *a picture-book history of the famous World War II incident.* (Photograph copyright © by Stuart N. Hedley. Reproduced by permission.)

tack by perceived enemy powers. "Book writing calls for skills somewhat similar to those needed for assignment writing," Allen explained to *SATA:* "Learn about the topic, figure out how to deliver the topic to a reader, and then write in clear English." In *War Games,* he did just that, according to critics. A *Kirkus Reviews* contributor praised the book as "an exactly documented, commendably measured briefing that raises disturbing questions about the games geopolitical and military strategists play far from the bloody realities of battle."

Remember Pearl Harbor: American and Japanese Survivors Tell Their Stories draws on Allen's skills as a journalist and interviewer in presenting what a *Kirkus Reviews* critic described as "a handsome title that will appeal to WWII buffs." Using interviews of the men and women who survived the "day of infamy"—December 7, 1941—and its aftermath, he created an "effective narrative" that presents readers with "powerful tales of warfare, destruction, and patriotism," according to Andrew Medlar in *School Library Journal.* From Japanese bomber pilots training for the attack in Japan to the harbor in Hawai'i where the USS *Arizona* sank after the aerial bombardment of the U.S. fleet, *Remember Pearl Harbor* offers readers a "complex view of events . . . in a conflict that swept people up—and nearly swept them away," in the words of *Booklist* contributor Randy Meyer.

Unable to use his interviewing skills for *Remember Valley Forge: Patriots, Tories, and Redcoats Tell Their Stories,* Allen turned to primary documents to capture the same feel for the Revolutionary War that *Remember Pearl Harbor* presented for World War II. The text offers the voices of famous patriots, including John Adams and George Washington, but also presents the viewpoints of little-known participants. "It is the smooth-flowing narrative's balanced mixture of the well known and obscure that makes the volume so inviting," wrote Sheila Fiscus in her *School Library Journal* review. Kay Weisman, writing in *Booklist,* considered *Remember Pearl Harbor* an "excellent" reference for classroom use and "a perfect introduction for those planning a visit to the site."

Allen focused on another area of military history in the non-traditional biographies *George Washington, Spymaster: How the Americans Outspied the British and Won the Revolutionary War* and *Harriet Tubman, Secret Agent: How Daring Slaves and Free Blacks Spied for the Union during the Civil War.* Although each book includes the personal story of the biographical subject, they also provide a context for the use of espionage during the wars they discuss. Each features tools used by spies, including invisible ink and secret codes, and the text is accompanied by period reproductions of paintings, archival images, and maps. "Allen presents the facts with a gleeful edge, clearly enjoying his subject and writing with vigor," wrote Joyce Burner Adams in her *School Library Journal* review of *George Washington, Spymaster.* Carolyn Phelan, writing in *Booklist,*

Cover of Allen's biography Harriet Tubman, Secret Agent, *which features contemporary images of the well-known former slave and American abolitionist.* (National Geographic, 2006. Illustrations copyright © 2006 by Carla Bauer. Reproduced by permission.)

called the same book "handsome, unusual, [and] intriguing." In *Booklist* Hazel Rochman found *Harriet Tubman, Secret Agent* to be "an excellent resource for students' research," while Elizabeth M. Reardon concluded in *School Library Journal* that Allen's "small book contains a lot of fascinating information."

Allen has joined fellow writer Norman Polmar on several projects, including the award-winning *Rickover: Controversy and Genius,* a biography of Russian-born naval engineer Hyman George Rickover, who helped design the first nuclear submarine; *Spy Book: The Encyclopedia of Espionage;* and *Code-Name Downfall: The Secret Plan to Invade Japan—and Why Truman Dropped the Bomb. Code-Name Downfall* discusses the development of the plan to invade Japan in the aftermath of the bombing of Pearl Harbor on December 7, 1941. Aerial bombing, poison gas, anthrax, and ultimately the atomic bomb were discussed by General Marshall, General MacArthur, and others in the planning stages of a full-scale attack on the Japanese mainland, and Allen and Polmar clearly show that the danger of atomic weaponry was not then fully realized by the Allied command. In arguing that U.S. President Harry S Truman sought the best way to end the war with the least amount of American casualties, *Code-Name Downfall* sets forth what a *Publishers Weekly* contributor called "a convincing case to settle a long-running controversy," while in *Booklist,* Gilbert Taylor noted that the coau-

thors' "encompassing narrative . . . constitutes the war's unwritten final chapter." Both *Code-Name Downfall* and *Rickover* have been republished in current editions.

Allen collaborates with Paul Dickson on *The Bonus Army: An American Epic.* The book covers the two-month period in 1932 when 45,000 World War I veterans descended on Washington, DC, to demand the cash bonus payment they had been promised for their wartime service. Due to the Great Depression and the looming war in Europe and Asia, the U.S. government did not comply with its promise, deferring this payment until 1945 and dispersing the assembly of veterans with military force. The incident eventually led to the creation of the G.I. Bill of Rights. Jay Freeman, writing in *Booklist,* called *The Bonus Army* an "agreeably written and often moving account."

As a practitioner of both fiction and nonfiction, Allen sees little difference between the two: "to me, there is no difference in style and little difference in approach," he once explained. "Words are words; English is English." His novel *A Short Life* reflects this, based as it is on an actual incident involving the illegal dispersal of radioactive substances. "This, for me, is the best kind of writing," noted Allen: "'factual fiction' which can shed light on a vital current issue." *A Short Life* is based on the story of Karen Silkwood, a young woman who met an untimely death in the 1970s after she publicized the fact that she and her coworkers were exposed to high levels of radiation at a nuclear facility. In *School Library Journal,* Janet Leonberger praised Allen for the creation of "dramatically paced scenes" which "evoke a mood of paranoia and terror."

Allen's other forays into fiction include *The Last Inmate* and *Ship of Gold,* the latter a thriller based on World War II salvage operations that was written in collaboration with Polmar. *The Last Inmate* follows the release of a psychotic killer in a story that "by virtue of both logic and imagination proves gripping from start to finish," according to a *Publishers Weekly* contributor. In *Ship of Gold* an attempt to raise a sunken Japanese freighter results in murder, causing an ex-Central Intelligence Agency operative to be put on the case. A *Publishers Weekly* reviewer praised *Ship of Gold* as "plausibly scary and great, whiz-bang fun," while in *Library Journal,* Brian Alley called deemed the book "a gripping thriller complete with believable characters . . . and an exceptionally clever plot."

As a professional author and editor, Allen views clarity as the most important aspect of his work. The rules are "all in what passes for my writer's bible: *The Elements of Style* by William Strunk, Jr. and E.B. White." He still considers himself a student of writing, even "after more than fifty years. And I hope to keep on learning." In addition to writing, Allen has taught writing at the Writer's Center, which serves the Washingtion, DC, area.

Biographical and Critical Sources

PERIODICALS

America, February 1, 1986, David Tomlinson, review of *Rickover: Controversy and Genius,* p. 76.

American History, August, 2000, review of *We Americans: Celebrating a Nation, Its People, and Its Past,* p. 67.

Booklist, May 15, 1974, review of *Vanishing Wildlife of North America,* p. 1021; April 15, 1978, review of *A Short Life,* p. 1322; June 15, 1987, review of *War Games: The Secret World of the Creators, Players, and Policy Makers Rehearsing World War III Today,* p. 1542; November 15, 1987, review of *Guardian of the Wild: The Story of the National Wildlife Federation,* p. 516; March 15, 1988, review of *Merchants of Treason: America's Secrets for Sale,* p. 1206; December 15, 1992, Gilbert Taylor, review of *Murder in the Senate,* p. 717; June 1, 1993, Lindsay Throm, review of *Possessed: The True Story of an Exorcism,* p. 1737; June 1, 1995, Gilbert Taylor, review of *Offerings at the Wall: Artifacts from the Vietnam Veterans Memorial Collection* and *Code-Name Downfall: The Secret Plan to Invade Japan,* p. 1722; April 15, 1997, review of *Spy Book: The Encyclopedia of Espionage,* p. 1453; November 15, 1998, Mary Carroll, review of *America from Space,* p. 561; May 15, 1999, Nancy Bent, review of *The Shark Almanac,* p. 1651; March, 2000, review of *We Americans,* p. 1193; June 1, 2000, Mary Carroll, review of *The Washington Monument: It Stands for All,* p. 1840; September 1, 2001, Randy Meyer, review of *Remember Pearl Harbor: American and Japanese Survivors Tell Their Stories,* p. 93; April 15, 2004, review of *George Washington, Spymaster: How the Americans Outspied the British and Won the Revolutionary War,* p. 1440; January 1, 2005, Jay Freeman, review of *The Bonus Army: An American Epic,* p. 808; December 1, 2006, Hazel Rochman, review of *Harriet Tubman, Secret Agent: How Daring Slaves and Free Blacks Spied for the Union during the Civil War,* p. 36; December 15, 2007, Kay Weisman, review of *Remember Valley Forge: Patriots, Tories, and Redcoats Tell Their Stories,* p. 42.

Bulletin of the Atomic Scientists, June, 1988, Andrew Goldberg, review of *War Games,* p. 48.

Business Week, May 9, 1988, Morton A. Reichek, review of *Merchants of Treason,* p. 24.

Childhood Education, spring, 2002, Gina Hoagland, review of *Remember Pearl Harbor,* p. 171.

Choice, October, 1987, E. Lewis, review of *War Games,* p. 376; June, 1988, K.B. Sterling, review of *Guardian of the Wild,* p. 1576.

Discover, August, 2001, review of *Shark Attacks: Their Causes and Avoidance,* p. 78.

International Affairs, autumn, 1988, Michael Nicholson, review of *War Games,* p. 662.

Journal of American History, March, 1997, Sanho Tree, review of *Code-Name Downfall,* p. 1475.

Journal of Asian Studies, February, 1996, Joseph A. Yager, review of *Code-Name Downfall,* p. 121.

Kirkus Reviews, December 15, 1977, review of *A Short Life,* p. 1329; May 1, 1987, review of *War Games,* p.

683; February 1, 1987, review of *Ship of Gold,* p. 148; January 15, 1988, review of *Merchants of Treason,* p. 97; May 15, 1993, review of *Possessed,* p. 631; July 15, 2001, review of *Remember Pearl Harbor,* p. 1020.

Library Journal, August, 1973, Ronald L. Coombs, review of *The Last Inmate,* pp. 2330-2331; June 1, 1974, Lola Dudley, review of *Vanishing Wildlife of North America,* p. 1557; April 1, 1987, Brian Alley, review of *Ship of Gold,* p. 160; July, 1987, Zachary T. Irwin, review of *War Games,* p. 82; December, 1987, James R. Karr, review of *Guardian of the Wild,* p. 123; May 1, 1988, Richard B. Finnegan, review of *Merchants of Treason,* p. 82; February 1, 1992, Raymond L. Puffer, review of *World War II: America at War, 1941-1945,* p. 82; May 1, 1993, Randall M. Miller, review of *The Blue and the Gray,* p. 98; June 15, 1993, Richard S. Watts, review of *Possessed,* p. 71; November 15, 1996, Jean E. Crampon, review of *Shadows in the Sea,* p. 85; April 15, 1997, Stephen W. Green, review of *Spy Book,* p. 72; March 1, 1998, Nancy J. Moeckel, review of *Animals of Africa,* p. 117; June 1, 1999, Judith Barnett, review of *The Shark Almanac,* p. 100; June 15, 2000, Thomas K. Fry, review of *The Washington Monument,* p. 102; January 1, 2005, William D. Pederson, review of *The Bonus Army,* p. 127.

Los Angeles Times Book Review, June 4, 1995, Charles Solomon, review of *Offerings at the Wall,* p. 15.

Marine Fisheries Review, fall, 1988, review of *Guardian of the Wild,* p. 218.

National Parks, January-February, 1993, Bruce Craig, review of *The Blue and the Gray,* p. 41.

New Statesman, August 11, 1995, Glyn Ford, review of *Code-Name Downfall,* p. 38.

New York Review of Books, September 21, 1995, Ian Buruma, review of *Code-Name Downfall,* p. 26.

New York Times Book Review, July 30, 1995, Michael R. Beschloss, review of *Code-Name Downfall,* pp. 10-11.

Oceans, November-December, 1987, Philip Kopper, review of *Ship of Gold,* p. 62.

Pacific Historical Review, August, 1991, Dian Olson Belanger, review of *Guardian of the Wild,* p. 420; August, 1996, Roger Dingman, review of *Code-Name Downfall,* p. 500.

People, September 6, 1993, Louisa Emrelino, review of *Possessed,* p. 28.

Publishers Weekly, June 18, 1973, review of *The Last Inmate,* p. 63; April, 1978, review of *A Short Life,* p. 100; February 13, 1987, review of *Ship of Gold,* p. 79; May 1, 1987, review of *War Games,* p. 57; February 12, 1988, review of *Merchants of Treason,* p. 74; November 9, 1992, review of *Murder in the Senate,* p. 76; May 24, 1993, review of *Possessed,* p. 73; May 15, 1995, review of *Code-Name Downfall,* p. 61; November, 1999, review of *The Shark Almanac,* pp. 182-183; September, 2001, review of *Remember Pearl Harbor,* p. 237.

School Library Journal, April, 1978, Janet Leonberger, review of *A Short Life,* p. 100; November, 1997, Margaret Tice, review of *Spy Book,* p. 142; September, 2001, Andrew Medlar, review of *Remember Pearl Harbor,* p. 237; May, 2004, Joyce Adams Burner, review of

George Washington, Spymaster, p. 160; February, 2007, Elizabeth M. Reardon, review of *Harriet Tubman, Secret Agent,* p. 130; February, 2008, Sheila Fiscus, review of *Remember Valley Forge,* p. 130.

Time, December 9, 1996, Jesse Birnbaum, review of *Spy Book,* p. 86.

Washington Post Book World, December 29, 1996, review of *The Shark Almanac,* p. 12.

Western Historical Quarterly, August, 1989, William E. Brown, review of *Guardian of the Wild,* p. 337.

ONLINE

Houghton Mifflin Web Site, http://www.eduplace.com/ (September 15, 2008), "Thomas B. Allen."

Random House Web site, http://www.randomhouse.com/ (September 15, 2008), "Thomas B. Allen."

Thomas B. Allen Home Page, http://tballen.com (September 15, 2008).

*   *   *

ALLEN, Thomas Benton
See ALLEN, Thomas B.

*   *   *

ALLEN, Tom
See ALLEN, Thomas B.

*   *   *

AMADO, Elisa

Personal
Born in Guatemala.

Addresses
Home—Toronto, Ontario, Canada.

Career
Writer and translator.

Awards, Honors
New Horizons Prize, Bologna Children's Book Fair, 2007, for *Sun Stone Days;* Américas Award Commended designation, 2008, for *Tricycle.*

Writings

Barrilete: A Kite for the Day of the Dead, photographs by Joya Hairs, Douglas & McIntyre (Toronto, Ontario, Canada), 1999.

Primas, illustrated by Louis Garay, Libros Tigrillos (Toronto, Ontario, Canada), 2003, published as *Cousins,* Groundwood Books (Toronto, Ontario, Canada), 2004.

(Author of text) Ianna Andréadis, *Sun Stone Days,* Groundwood Books (Toronto, Ontario, Canada), 2005.

Tricycle, illustrated by Alfonso Ruano, Groundwood Books (Toronto, Ontario, Canada), 2007.

TRANSLATOR

Antonio Skármeta, *The Composition,* illustrated by Alfonso Ruano, Groundwood Books (Toronto, Ontario, Canada), 2000.

María Elena Maggi, *The Great Canoe,* illustrated by Gloria Calderón, Douglas & McIntyre (Toronto, Ontario, Canada) 2001.

(With Veronica Uribe) *Buzz Buzz Buzz,* illustrated by Gloria Calderón, Douglas & McIntyre (Toronto, Ontario, Canada) 2001.

Jorge Argueta, *Trees Are Hanging from the Sky,* illustrated by Rafael Yockteng, Groundwood Books (Toronto, Ontario, Canada), 2003.

Jorge Argueta, *Zipitio,* illustrated by Gloria Calderón, Groundwood Books (Toronto, Ontario, Canada), 2003.

Jorge Luján, *Rooster = Gallo,* illustrated by Manuel Monroy, Groundwood Books (Toronto, Ontario, Canada), 2004.

Antonio Ramírez, *Napi Goes to the Mountain,* illustrated by Domi, Groundwood Books (Toronto, Ontario, Canada), 2004.

Jorge Luján, *Tarde de Invierno = Winter Afternoon,* illustrated by Mandana Sadat, Groundwood Books (Toronto, Ontario, Canada), 2006.

Sandra Comino, *Morning Glory,* Groundwood Books (Toronto, Ontario, Canada), 2006.

Jorge Luján, *Sky Blue Accident,* illustrated by Piet Grobler, Groundwood Books (Toronto, Ontario, Canada), 2007.

Jorge Argueta, *Alfredito Flies Home,* illustrated by Luis Garay, Groundwood Books (Toronto, Ontario, Canada), 2007.

Natalia Toledo, *Light Foot = Pies Ligeros,* Groundwood Books (Toronto, Ontario, Canada), 2007.

Menena Cottin and Rosana Faría, *The Black Book of Colors,* Groundwood Books (Toronto, Ontario, Canada), 2008.

Teresa Cárdenas, *Oloyou,* illustrated by Margarita Sada, Groundwood Books (Toronto, Ontario, Canada), 2008.

Mireille Levert, *Tulip and Lupin Forever,* Groundwood Books (Toronto, Ontario, Canada), 2009.

Sidelights

Elisa Amado is a native of Guatemala who now lives and works in eastern Canada. In addition to writing stories for the early grades based upon her own multicultural experiences, she has also served as a translator for both Spanish and Zapotec authors who craft tales for young children. In her dual roles as writer and translator, Amado has expanded the number of Central American folk tales available to an English-speaking audience.

Amado's picture book *Barrilete: A Kite for the Day of the Dead* introduces youngsters to the Guatemalan practice of constructing and flying huge kites as part of the celebrations for Dio del los Muertos, or Day of the Dead. Her tale, illustrated with black-and-white photographs, follows a boy named Juan as he creates a kite in honor of his deceased grandfather—the person who taught Juan the fine art of kite-making. The book also describes other Day of the Dead traditions, some of which originated with the Mayan Indians. To quote Gillian Engberg in *Booklist,* Amado and her photographer "use one boy's excitement to personalize the area's culture and its exceptional craft." A reviewer for *Resource Links* deemed *Barrilete* a "useful addition" to children's literature "depicting life in other countries and . . . different cultures."

Cousins tackles the issue of multiculturalism through the eyes of a little girl. Although she lives with her Latin-American father and American grandmother, the girl is drawn to the home of her paternal grandmother, Abuela Adela, who follows the Roman Catholic traditions of her homeland. Jealousy erupts as the girl watches her cousin prepare for an elaborate first communion ceremony. Ann Welton noted in *School Library Journal* that the story's simplicity of narrative proves to be an "excellent discussion starter" on the issues of youngsters torn between two cultures. A *Kirkus Reviews* critic likewise noted that the book's "issues are sure to spark reflection and discussion."

Amado wrote the text for the elaborate *Sun Stone Days,* an award-winning book based on the ancient Aztec calendar. The Aztec month consisted of twenty days, each represented by a different animal or symbol. The civilization's calendrical information was recorded on a large "Sun Stone" from which archeologists have learned about the Aztec dating system. In addition to Ianna Andréadis's illustrations of each symbol, Amado provides a text in English, Spanish, and Nahuatl, the last the language of the ancient Aztec people. In *Resource Links,* Tanya Boudreau called *Sun Stone Days* "a nice presentation of a record from the past," and a *Kirkus Reviews* correspondent cited it for its "handsome presentation."

The great gulf between rich and poor can be a difficult topic to explain to very young children, but Amado takes on the task in *Tricycle,* illustrated by Alfonso Ruano. When the central character, Margarita, climbs a tree in her yard, she can see beyond the protected grounds of her affluent home. Margarita spies on two very poor children living nearby and watches as they steal her tricycle. Later when she hears her family discussing thievery, Margarita concocts a story to cover up the theft she has witnessed. In *Kirkus Reviews,* a critic called the book "a discussion-starter if ever there was one." Linda Berezowski in *Resource Links* thought that the book should be reserved for more mature children but that it provides "a provocative story that confronts complicated social issues."

In addition to writing her own books, Amado has translated numerous picture books by Latin American authors. Sometimes the English translations also include the Spanish original, as in *Rooster = Gallo,* and *Sky Blue Accident = Accidente Celeste,* both by Jorge Luján. These bilingual books are "easily read in both languages," to quote Denise Parrott in *Resource Links,* making them useful for older students learning Spanish as well as youngsters who are just eager for a story.

Biographical and Critical Sources

PERIODICALS

Booklist, February 1, 2000, Gillian Engberg, review of *Barrilete: A Kite for the Day of the Dead,* p. 1024; April 1, 2007, Hazel Rochman, review of *Tricycle,* p. 55; March 1, 2008, Gillian Engberg, review of *Alfredito Flies Home,* p. 72.

Horn Book, March-April, 2004, Joanna Rudge Long, review of *Rooster = Gallo,* p. 173.

Kirkus Reviews, March 1, 2004, review of *Rooster = Gallo,* p. 226; March 15, 2004, review of *Cousins,* p. 265; March 1, 2007, review of *Sun Stone Days,* p. 215; March 1, 2007, review of *Sky Blue Accident = Accidente Celeste,* p. 227; May 1, 2007, review of *Tricycle.*

Resource Links, February, 2000, review of *Barrilete,* p. 13; October, 2004, Carroll Chapman, review of *Cousins,* p. 1; October, 2004, Denise Parrott, review of *Rooster = Gallo,* p. 6; October, 2007, Linda Berezowski, review of *Tricycle,* p. 2; October, 2007, Tanya Boudreau, review of *Sun Stone Days,* p. 1.

School Library Journal, May, 2004, Ann Welton, review of *Cousins,* p. 100; September, 2004, Ann Welton, review of *Rooster = Gallo,* p. 197; June, 2007, Lucinda Snyder Whitehurst, review of *Tricycle,* p. 92; July, 2007, Mary Elam, review of *Sky Blue Accident = Accidente Celeste,* p. 80.

ONLINE

Groundwood Books Web site, http://www.groundwood books.com/ (September 8, 2008), "Elisa Amado."*

*   *   *

ARCHER, Lily 1981-

Personal

Born 1981.

Addresses

Home and office—New York, NY.

Career

Writer.

Writings

The Poison Apples, Feiwel & Friends (New York, NY), 2007.

Sidelights

The Poison Apples, the debut novel by New York-based writer Lily Archer, updates the classic evil stepmother fairy tale. In Archer's revisioning, three girls of different backgrounds find themselves attending an exclusive Massachusetts boarding school after their home lives are disrupted by the entrance of new stepmothers. Molly, Alice, and Reena discover their shared troubles, christen themselves the Poison Apples, and begin to methodically plot a fitting revenge.

A critic for *Kirkus Reviews* wrote of *The Poison Apples* that the girls "are not really mean enough to exact the punishment they want," but that the plotting and complaints should appeal to young audiences. Gillian Engberg wrote in *Booklist* that while some of Archer's "characters and situations fit neatly into stock categories, [her] . . . story's predictability and exaggerated,

Cover of Lily Archer's young-adult novel The Poison Apples, *featuring artwork by Rich Deas.* (Illustration copyright © 2007 by Rich Deas. Reproduced by permission of St. Martin's Press.)

made-for-teen-film scenarios won't deter readers." Also enthusiastic, a *Publishers Weekly* reviewer dubbed *The Poison Apples* "a wickedly funny debut."

Biographical and Critical Sources

PERIODICALS

Booklist, October 15, 2007, Gillian Engberg, review of *The Poison Apples,* p. 44.

Bulletin of the Center for Children's Books, November, 2007, Karen Coates, review of *The Poison Apples,* p. 127.

Kirkus Reviews, September 15, 2007, review of *The Poison Apples.*

Kliatt, September, 2007, Claire Rosser, review of *The Poison Apples,* p. 6.

Publishers Weekly, July 30, 2007, review of *The Poison Apples.*

School Library Journal, September, 2007, Miram Lang Budin, review of *The Poison Apples,* p. 190.

ONLINE

Macmillan Web site, http://us.macmillan.com/ (September 28, 2008), "Lily Archer."*

*   *   *

AUSTIN, Carrie
See SEULING, Barbara

B

BAILEY, Len

Personal

Married; children: three sons. *Education:* Trinity College (Deerfield, IL), B.A.

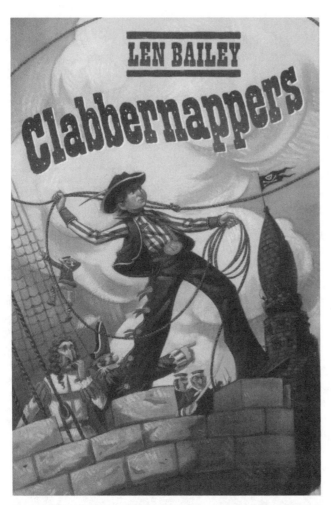

Cover of Len Bailey's middle-grade fantasy novel Clabbernappers, *featuring artwork by Brett Helquist.* (Copyright © by Brett Helquist. Reproduced by permission.)

Addresses

Home—Metro Chicago, IL. *Agent*—Tracy Grant, Leona Literary Agency, P.O. Box 835, Highland Park, IL 60035.

Career

Voice-over actor and author. Has also worked as a bag-pipe player.

Writings

Clabbernappers, Starscape (New York, NY), 2005.
Fantasms, Starscape (New York, NY), 2007.

Sidelights

Len Bailey is a professional radio-commercial and voice-over actor as well as the author of the fantasy novels *Clabbernappers* and *Fantasms*. Bailey studied journalism in college, earning a scholarship in that field, but did not pursue writing professionally until he began to focus on fiction for younger readers. In addition to writing and acting, he has also worked as a bag-piper and, during college, was a member of the National Collegiate Athletics Association National Champion soccer team. Although he also enjoys golf, Bailey acknowledged on the Macmillan Web site that "his best 'wood' is his pencil."

The idea for *Clabbernappers* came to Bailey while he was playing a game of chess on his computer. In the story, eleven-year-old Danny Ray, a junior-division rodeo champion, steps through a magical doorway and into a land inhabited by chess pieces. Given the task of rescuing the captured queen of Eliador from across the Checkered Sea, Danny finds himself combating pirates and staving off man-eating ghosts while on the biggest adventure of his life. "Action is paramount in the imaginatively told tale, which is filled with near misses and

Cover of Bailey's middle-grade novel Fantasms, *featuring artwork by* *Paul Hess.* (Illustration copyright © by Paul Hess. Reproduced by permission.)

close calls," wrote Cindy Welch in a *Booklist* review of *Clabbernappers.* Jessi Platt, writing for *School Library Journal,* noted that while Bailey's vocabulary might be too difficult for some readers in the novel's targeted age group, the novel is "interesting and wonderfully written." A *Publishers Weekly* critic predicted that readers who enjoyed Danny's "plucky cowboy attitude . . . and over-the-top dialect will find this a fun, fast read."

Part of a planned series, *Fantasms* chronicles Danny's second adventure in the enchanted land of Eliador. In this sequel to *Clabbernappers,* Princess Amber has been captured by fantasms: powerful, shapeshifting monsters that are poised to take over all of Eliador unless Amber is rescued. The princess herself faces an awful fate if she cannot be freed: her life will be forfeit. Unfortunately, Danny has just suffered a defeat back home in Oklahoma: a disastrous bull ride has robbed him of his confidence, and in order to defeat the fantasms, he must face his own doubts. Some of the characters who helped him in *Clabbernappers* have also returned, but they, too, have changed, and some are not as trustworthy as they were before. "There's more than enough adventure to capture the imagination of any young YA," wrote Lesley Farmer in *Kliatt.* While a *Kirkus Reviews* con-

tributor commented that *Fantasms* falls short of the standards set by *Clabbernappers,* the critic added that "Bailey's imagination remains fertile and his language sumptuous."

Biographical and Critical Sources

PERIODICALS

Booklist, January 1, 2005, Cindy Welch, review of *Clabbernappers,* p. 856.
Kirkus Reviews, February 1, 2007, review of *Fantasms,* p. 119.
Kliatt, March, 2007, Lesley Farmer, review of *Fantasms,* p. 8.
Publishers Weekly, March 7, 2005, review of *Clabbernappers,* p. 68.
School Library Journal, June, 2005, Jessi Platt, review of *Clabbernappers,* p. 147; June, 2007, Walter Minkel, review of *Fantasms,* p. 138.

ONLINE

Macmillan Web site, http://us.macmillan.com/ (October 6, 2008), "Len Bailey."*

*   *   *

BANYAI, Istvan

Personal
Born in Budapest, Hungary; immigrated to United States, 1981; naturalized U.S. citizen; married; children: one son.

Addresses
Home—New York, NY; CT. *Agent*—Betsy Hillman, P.O. Box 77644, San Francisco, CA 94107; betsy@betsyhillman.com. *E-mail*—ibanyai@sbcglobal.net.

Career
Artist, designer, and animator. Has produced cover art for Sony, Verve, and Capitol Records; creator of animated short films for Nickelodeon and MTV Europe.

Awards, Honors
Children's Choice Award, International Reading Association, for *Zoom.*

Writings

SELF-ILLUSTRATED

Zoom, Viking (New York, NY), 1995.
Re-Zoom, Viking (New York, NY), 1995.

R.E.M.: Rapid Eye Movement, Viking (New York, NY), 1997.

Minus Equals Plus, introduction by Kurt Andersen, Harry Abrams (New York, NY), 2001.

Among Istvan Banyai's self-illustrated picture books is* Rezoom, *which features detailed cartoon art.

The Other Side, Chronicle Books (San Francisco, CA), 2005.

ILLUSTRATOR

Eve Feldman, *A Giant Surprise,* Raintree Publishers (Milwaukee, WI), 1989.

Mark Ciabattari, *Dreams of an Imaginary New Yorker Named Rizzoli,* Dutton (New York, NY), 1990.

Tom Dalzell, *The Slang of Sin,* Merriam-Webster (Springfield, MA), 1998.

Carl Sandburg, *Poems for Children Nowhere Near Old Enough to Vote,* compiled and with an introduction by George and Willene Hendrick, Knopf (New York, NY), 1999.

Linda Sue Park, *Tap Dancing on the Roof: Sijo* (poems), Clarion Books (New York, NY), 2007.

Barbara Kerley, *Greetings from Planet Earth,* Scholastic (New York, NY), 2007.

Contributor to *Atlantic Monthly, Time, New Yorker, Playboy,* and *Rolling Stone.*

Sidelights

Hungarian-born American illustrator and animator Istvan Banyai has produced a number of surrealistic wordless picture books, including *Zoom* and *The Other Side.* In the words of *New York Times Book Review* contributor David Small, Banyai "likes to makes pictures that whip the viewer into a fury of fast-paced looking. His books make us feel like someone caught in a sudden rush of traffic. They draw us into a world in constant flux. Abrupt change and reversals are the order of the day."

Born in Budapest, Hungary, Banyai immigrated to the United States in 1981 and made his mark as an editorial cartoonist, with his work appearing in such publications as the *Atlantic Monthly, Time,* and *Rolling Stone.* He also created cover art for Sony and Verve Records as well as animated films for Nickelodeon and MTV Europe.

Banyai's picture-book debut, *Zoom,* appeared in 1995. Playing with the readers's sense of perspective, the work opens with a close-up of a rooster's comb; each successive illustration pulls back from the previous picture to reveal a larger scene. Viewers learn, for example, that the rooster is actually part of a toy farm set that is pictured on the cover of a magazine, and that the youngster holding the magazine is shown to be the focus of a cruise-line poster plastered on the side of a bus. "Not a story, but an 'idea' book," noted *Booklist* reviewer Carolyn Phelan, *Zoom* "makes the viewer ask, 'What am I really seeing here?'" In *Horn Book,* Martha V. Parravano praised the work, remarking that "the layout is ingenious" and noting that the "concept and the book design are distinctive." Comparing Banyai's illustrations to the art found in such comic strips as Hal Foster's "Prince Valiant," a *Publisher Weekly* contribu-

tor called *Zoom* "a startling experience"; "Readers are in for a perpetually surprising—and even philosophical—adventure." In *Re-Zoom,* a companion volume, Banyai "toys not only with spatial relations but with time and with cultural referents," a *Publishers Weekly* critic wrote.

In his next wordless picture book, *R.E.M.: Rapid Eye Movement,* Banyai "does an ingenious job of invoking the hauntingly alternative reality of dreams," according to Michael Cart in *Booklist.* The work features a series of images in which ordinary objects undergo unusual transformations. "Banyai cleverly mixes the fantastic and the familiar," noted Cathryn M. Mercier in *Horn Book,* and a *Publishers Weekly* reviewer commented that he "questions perception on every page, prompting readers either to make up stories for each scene or simply to draw inspiration from his cinematic way of thinking."

Banyai's *The Other Side* presents contrasting perspectives on a host of quirky scenarios; readers spying a small, red triangle turn the page to reveal a chick pecking at the paper on "the other side." Small applauded the illustrator's graphite sketches and computer-enhanced colors, stating that Banyai "blends the machine's lines so discreetly with his own precise freehand drawing style that it is often difficult to tell one from another. The results, always compelling, are often astonishing."

Banyai has also provided the artwork for titles by other authors, including *Poems for Children Nowhere Near Old Enough to Vote,* a compilation of verse by beloved American poet Carl Sandburg, and *Tap Dancing on the Roof: Sijo,* a collection of poems by Linda Sue Park. In the former, which contains Sandburg's previously unpublished verse, Banyai's "playful ink drawings and computer graphics pick up the comedy," remarked a *Publishers Weekly* reviewer. Park's *Tap Dancing on the Roof* contains twenty-seven sijo, traditional Korean poems similar in form to haiku. "Banyai's illustrations enhance the collection with an extra element of wit and imaginative freedom," noted *Horn Book* contributor Deirdre F. Baker.

Biographical and Critical Sources

BOOKS

Banyai, Istvan, *Minus Equals Plus,* introduction by Kurt Andersen, Harry Abrams (New York, NY), 2001.

PERIODICALS

Booklist, February 1, 1995, Carolyn Phelan, review of *Zoom,* p. 1007; July, 1997, Michael Cart, review of *R.E.M.: Rapid Eye Movement,* p. 1821; September 1,

Banyai's unique, high-contrast cartoon art is collected in his book **The Other Side.**

1999, Hazel Rochman, review of *Poems for Children Nowhere Near Old Enough Vote,* p. 136; August, 2001, Regina Schroeder, review of *Minus Equals Plus,* p. 2070; December 1, 2005, Jennifer Mattson, review of *The Other Side,* p. 45; December 1, 2007, Jennifer Mattson, review of *Tap Dancing on the Roof: Sijo,* p. 45.

Horn Book, September-October, 1995, Martha V. Parravano, review of *Zoom,* p. 585; January-February, 1996, Lolly Robinson, review of *Re-Zoom,* p. 59; May-June, 1997, Cathryn M. Mercier, review of *R.E.M.,* p. 302; November-December, 2005, Lolly Robinson, review of *The Other Side,* p. 702; September-October, 2007, Deirdre F. Baker, review of *Tap Dancing on the Roof,* p. 595.

Star Tribune (Minneapolis, MN), June 17, 2001, Robert Armstrong, "Illustrator Masters Art for the 22nd Century," review of *Minus Equals Plus,* p. F15.

New York Times Book Review, May 16, 1999, Sean Kelly, review of *Poems for Children Nowhere Near Old Enough Vote;* November 13, 2005, David Small, review of *The Other Side,* p. 20.

Publishers Weekly, December 19, 1994, review of *Zoom,* p. 53; July 17, 1997, review of *Re-Zoom,* p. 228; April 14, 1997, review of *R.E.M.,* p. 73; April 12, 1999, review of *Poems for Children Nowhere Near Old Enough Vote,* p. 75; May 14, 2001, review of *Minus Equals Plus,* p. 71; October 24, 2005, review of *The Other Side,* p. 56; October 15, 2007, review of *Tap Dancing on the Roof,* p. 61.

School Library Journal, January, 2006, Carol L. MacKay, review of *The Other Side,* p. 90.

ONLINE

Istvan Banyai Home Page, http://www.ist-one.com (August 10, 2008).*

*   *   *

BIDNER, Jenni 1963-

Personal

Born 1963. *Education:* Rochester Institute of Technology, B.S.

Addresses

Home and office—WI.

Career

Editor, author, and photographer. Former editor of *Petersen's Photographic* magazine and *Outdoor & Travel Photography;* currently works as an instructor at Better-Photo.com. Volunteer search-and-rescue dog handler.

Awards, Honors

Henry Bergh Award for Nonfiction Children's Book of the Year, American Society for the Prevention of Cruelty to Animals, 2007, for *Is My Dog a Wolf?*

Writings

Great Photos with the Advanced Photo System, Kodak Books (Rochester, NY), 1996.

The Lighting Cookbook: Foolproof Recipes for Perfect Glamour, Portrait, Still Life, and Corporate Photographs, Amphoto Books (New York, NY), 1997.

Digital Photography, Silver Pixel Press (Rochester, NY), 1998.

Yearbook Photography, Eastman Kodak (Rochester, NY), 1998.

Digital Photography: A Basic Guide to New Technology, Silver Pixel Press (Rochester, NY), 2000.

Digital Camera Basics: Getting the Most from Your Digital Camera, Silver Pixel Press (Rochester, NY), 2002.

(With Meleda Wegner) *The Best of Nature Photography: Images and Techniques from the Pros,* Amherst Media (Buffalo, NY), 2003.

Making Family Websites: Fun and Easy Ways to Share Memories, Lark Books (New York, NY), 2003.

(With Eric Bean) *Complete Guide for Models: Inside Advice from Industry Pros,* Lark Books (New York, NY), 2004.

The Kids' Guide to Digital Photography: How to Shoot, Save, Play with, and Print Your Digital Photos, Lark Books (New York, NY), 2004.

Amphoto's Complete Book of Photography: How to Improve Your Pictures with a Film or Digital Camera, Amphoto Books (New York, NY), 2004.

(With Eric Bean) *Lighting Cookbook for Fashion and Beauty: Foolproof Recipes for Taking Perfect Portraits,* Amphoto Books (New York, NY), 2005.

Is My Dog a Wolf?: How Your Pet Compares to Its Wild Cousin, Lark Books (New York, NY), 2006.

Kodak Most Basic Book of Digital Printing, Lark Books (New York, NY), 2006.

Love Your Dog Pictures: How to Photograph Your Dog with Any Camera, Watson-Guptill (New York, NY), 2006.

Is My Cat a Tiger?: How Your Pet Compares to Its Wild Cousins, Lark Books (New York, NY), 2006.

Dog Heroes: Saving Lives and Protecting America, Lyons (Guilford, CT), 2006.

Capture the Portrait: How to Create Great Digital Photos, Lark Books (New York, NY), 2008.

Contributor of articles to periodicals including *Petersen's Photographic.*

Sidelights

Jenni Bidner is a Wisconsin-based photographer and writer who brings decades of experience to her position as an instructor at BetterPhotos.com as well as to her published books. Sharing her leisure time with her two dogs, Ajax and Yukon, Bidner also works as a K-9 handler with a volunteer search-and-rescue unit around Chicago.

Bidner's affection for dogs has inspired her choice of subject matter for much of her writing. In *Is My Dog a Wolf?: How Your Pet Compares to Its Wild Cousin,* for

example, she discusses the similarities and differences between man's best friend and its wild relative. Complete with "terrific black-and-white and color photographs—some filling up the pages, others in snapshot form," according to Ilene Cooper in *Booklist,* the book answers questions about typical canine behaviors, such as licking the faces of humans. Bidner's follow up book, *Is My Cat a Tiger?: How Your Pet Compares to Its Wild Cousins,* continues in the same vein, this time focusing on felines. Carolyn Phelan, reviewing *Is My Cat a Tiger?* for *Booklist,* predicted that "most children will learn something new from this attractive, accessible guide to cats."

In addition to books on animal habits, Bidner has written numerous books on photography, providing instruction to children, novices, and aspiring photographers and models. In *The Kids' Guide to Digital Photography: How to Shoot, Save, Play with, and Print Your Digital Photos* she "introduces sophisticated technical material in enthusiastic language that is kid-friendly without being condescending," according to *Booklist* contributor Gillian Engberg. Bidner reaches out to adult photographers with books such as *Amphoto's Complete Book of Photography: How to Improve Your Pictures with a Film or Digital Camera* and the many "How to" articles she has contributed to *Petersen's Photographic.*

Biographical and Critical Sources

PERIODICALS

Booklist, December 15, 2003, Barbara Jacobs, review of *Making Family Websites: Fun and Easy Ways to Share Memories,* p. 714; January 1, 2005, Gillian Engberg, review of *The Kids' Guide to Digital Photography: How to Shoot, Save, Play with, and Print Your Digital Photos,* p. 837; September 1, 2006, Irene Cooper, review of *Is My Dog a Wolf?: How Your Pet Compares to Its Wild Cousin,* p.122; January 1, 2007, Carolyn Phelan, review of *Is My Cat a Tiger?: How Your Pet Compares to Its Wild Cousins,* p. 84.
Kliatt, January, 2005, Nola Theiss, review of *Amphoto's Complete Book of Photography: How to Improve Your Pictures with a Film or Digital Camera,* p. 36.
Library Bookwatch, June, 2005, review of *Complete Guide for Models: Inside Advice from Industry Pros.*
School Library Journal, May, 2005, Jodi Kearns, review of *The Kids' Guide to Digital Photography,* p. 143; October, 2006, Cynde Suite, review of *Is My Dog a Wolf?,* p. 132; May, 2007, Kara Schaff, review of *Is My Cat a Tiger?,* p. 114.
Science and Children, September, 2007, Martha Svatek, review of *Is My Cat a Tiger?,* p. 70.

ONLINE

BetterPhoto.com, http://www.betterphoto.com/ (October 6, 2008), "Jenni Bidner."

Jenni Bidner Home Page, http://www.jennibidner.com (October 6, 2008).*

* * *

BRADLEY, Timothy J.

Personal

Male.

Addresses

E-mail—raptoryx13@mac.com.

Career

Designer, illustrator, and author. Freelance designer, beginning 1988; assistant artist to Syd Mead, 1989; graphic designer and artist for screenwriter J.F. Lawton, 1991-93; graphic and storyboard artist for television; 1993; Dinamation, illustrator, beginning 1994, senior art director, 1998; Hasbro, project designer, 1998; Universal Studios' Jurassic Park Institute, Web site designer and illustrator, 2001; designer of giftware, educational products, and toys for clients including Hasbro, Universal, and Upper Deck.

Writings

SELF-ILLUSTRATED; FOR CHILDREN

The Care and Feeding of Dinosaurs, Millbrook Press (Brookfield, CT), 2000.
Paleo Sharks: Survival of the Strangest, Chronicle Books (San Francisco, CA), 2007.
Paleo Bugs: Survival of the Creepiest, Chronicle Books (San Francisco, CA), 2008.

Sidelights

Timothy J. Bradley's vivid imagination has helped him become a successful designer and illustrator for such large companies as Hasbro and Universal. Specializing in dinosaurs and other prehistoric creatures, Bradley's use of vivid colors has set him apart from other artists. As he remarked about his experience as a toy designer for *Transformer Toys* online, "I have always liked the idea of taking my two-dimensional drawings and seeing them realized in three dimensions. A concept can go from existing on a flat piece of paper to something you can hold in your hand. I always get a kick out of seeing a product I designed hanging in a store—that's really fun." Bradley has designed toys for Hasbro's Transformers, Star Wars, and Jurassic Park toy lines.

In addition to designing toys, Bradley also creates informative books for children and young adults. His approach to writing and illustrating books such as *Paleo*

Bugs: Survival of the Creepiest involves a good deal of research to ensure that the text and illustrations in his books are scientifically accurate. As the author/illustrator told an online interviewer for the *Transformer Toys* Web site, "Sharks don't fossilize well at all, and neither do insects, so I had to deal with paleontologists to make sure my art and text reflected what is known about those creatures. I actually visited with a paleontologist at the London Natural History Museum for *Paleo Bugs,* and got to look at their collection of ancient arthropod fossils they keep in the 'back rooms' of the museum." In *Science Books and Films,* Nathan Dubosky noted of *Paleo Bugs* that Bradley's "nimble prose" makes the book easy to read even for younger children, and the "abundant, colorful illustrations are well crafted, fascinating, and compelling," and a *Horn Book* contributor wrote that the book's "bug-human comparisions are particularly effective."

Danielle F. Ford, reviewing *Paleo Sharks: Survival of the Strangest* for *Horn Book,* complimented Bradley's treatment of his subject, noting that the author/illustrator's "chronologic tour of extinct shark species employs a smart design and sharp graphics." A *Kirkus Reviews* contributor also commended the book, concluding that Bradley's "introduction to extinct sharks and their relatives is a definite goosebump-raiser."

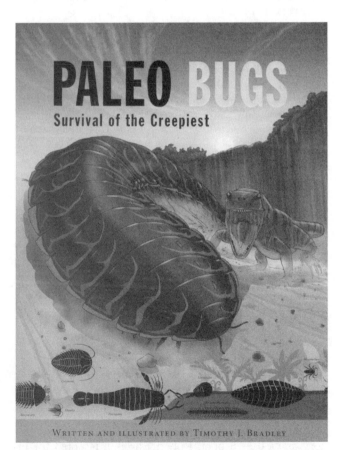

Cover of Timothy J. Bradley's unique self-illustrated nonfiction book **Paleo Bugs,** *a study of insects in the age of the dinosaurs.* (Chronicle Books, 2008. Copyright © 2008 by Timothy J. Bradley. All rights reserved. Reproduced by permission.)

Biographical and Critical Sources

PERIODICALS

Booklist, April 1, 2007, GraceAnne A. DeCandido, review of *Paleo Sharks: Survival of the Strangest,* p. 44.
Horn Book, September, 2008, review of *Paleo Bugs: Survival of the Creepiest;* July-August, 2007, Danielle F. Ford, review of *Paleo Sharks,* p. 410.
Kirkus Reviews, May, 2008, review of *Paleo Bugs;* September-October, 2008, Nathan Dubowsky, review of *Paleo Bugs,* p. 204.
School Library Journal, June, 2007, Patricia Manning, review of *Paleo Sharks,* p. 166; July, 2008, Ellen Heath, review of *Paleo Bugs.*
Science Books and Film, May, 2008, review of *Paleo Bugs;* March 15, 2007, review of *Paleo Sharks,* p. 44.

ONLINE

Timothy J. Bradley Home Page, http://web.mac.com/raptoryx13 (September 1, 2008).
JP Toys Web site, http://www.jptoys.com/ (September 1, 2008), interview with Bradley.
Transformer Toys Web site, http://www.transformertoys.co.uk/ (September 1, 2008), interview with Bradley.

*   *   *

BURLEIGH, Robert 1936-

Personal

Born January 4, 1936, in Chicago, IL; married; children: three. *Education:* Graduated from DePauw University, 1957; University of Chicago, M.A. 1962.

Addresses

Home and office—Chicago, IL. *E-mail*—roburleigh@earthlink.net.

Career

Author and artist. Worked for Society of Visual Education as a writer and artist. *Exhibitions:* Work has appeared in solo exhibitions, under pseudonym Burleigh Kronquist, at ARC Gallery, Chicago, IL, 1988; Southport Gallery, Chicago, 1988, 1995; Artemisia Gallery, Chicago, 1992, 1994; University Club, Chicago, 1994; IDAO Gallery, Chicago, 1998, 1999, 2000; DePauw University Gallery, Greencastle, IN, 2002; O.K. Harris Works of Art, New York, NY, 2001, 2005; Riverside Arts Center, Riverside, IL, 2006. Work has appeared in group exhibitions at Randolph Street Gallery, Chicago, IL, 1988; University of Nebraska Gallery, Omaha, NE, 1989; Greater Lafayette Art Museum, Lafayette, IN, 1992; Harper College Gallery, Palatine, IL, 2000; Ukrainian Institute of Art, Chicago, 2001, 2004; and Cumberland Gallery, Nashville, TN, 2004.

Member

Society of Children's Book Writers and Illustrators.

Awards, Honors

Orbis Pictus Award, 1992, for *Flight;* Notable Children's Book selection, American Library Association, Children's Choice selection, International Reading Association/Children's Book Council, and 100 Titles for Reading and Sharing selection and Books for the Teen Age selection, both New York Public Library, all for *Hoops.*

Writings

A Man Named Thoreau, illustrated by Lloyd Bloom, Atheneum (New York, NY), 1985.

Flight: The Journey of Charles Lindbergh, illustrated by Mike Wimmer, Philomel (New York, NY), 1991.

Who Said That? Famous Americans Speak, illustrated by David Catrow, Holt (New York, NY), 1997.

Hoops (picture book), illustrated by Stephen T. Johnson, Silver Whistle (San Diego, CA), 1997.

Home Run: The Story of Babe Ruth, illustrated by Mike Wimmer, Silver Whistle (San Diego, CA), 1998.

Black Whiteness: Admiral Byrd Alone in the Antarctic, illustrated by Walter Lyon Krudop, Atheneum (New York, NY), 1998.

It's Funny Where Ben's Train Takes Him, illustrated by Joanna Yardley, Orchard (New York, NY), 1999.

Hercules, illustrated by Raul Colón, Silver Whistle (San Diego, CA), 1999.

Edna, illustrated by Joanna Yardley, Orchard (New York, NY), 2000.

Messenger, Messenger, illustrated by Barry Root, Atheneum (New York, NY), 2000.

Lookin' for Bird in the Big City, illustrated by Marek Los, Harcourt (San Diego, CA), 2001.

I Love Going through This Book, illustrated by Dan Yaccarino, HarperCollins (New York, NY), 2001.

Goal (picture book), illustrated by Stephen T. Johnson, Harcourt (San Diego, CA), 2001.

Chocolate: Riches from the Rainforest, Abrams (New York, NY), 2002.

Pandora, illustrated by Raul Colón, Harcourt (San Diego, CA), 2002.

The Secret of the Great Houdini, illustrated by Leonid Gore, Simon & Schuster (New York, NY), 2002.

Into the Air: The Story of the Wright Brothers' First Flight (picture-book biography), illustrated by Bill Wylie, Silver Whistle (San Diego, CA), 2002.

Into the Woods: John James Audubon Lives His Dream, illustrated by Wendell Minor, Atheneum (New York, NY), 2003.

(Editor) *Earth from Above for Young Readers,* photographs by Yann Arthus Bertrand, illustrated by David Giraudon, Abrams (New York, NY), 2003.

(Editor) *Volcanoes: Journey to the Crater's Edge,* photographs by Philippe Bourseiller, illustrated by David Giraudon, Abrams (New York, NY), 2003.

(Editor) *The Sea: Exploring Life on an Ocean Planet,* photographs by Philip Plisson, illustrated by Emmanuel Cerisier, Abrams (New York, NY), 2003.

Amelia Earhart: Free in the Skies, illustrated by Bill Wylie, Silver Whistle (San Diego, CA), 2003.

Langston's Train Ride, illustrated by Leonard Jenkins, Orchard (New York, NY), 2004.

American Moments: Scenes from American History, illustrated by Bruce Strachan, Holt (New York, NY), 2004.

Seurat and La Grande Jatte: Connecting the Dots, Abrams (New York, NY), 2004.

(With Tiki and Ronde Barber) *By My Brother's Side,* illustrated by Barry Root, Simon & Schuster (New York, NY), 2004.

(With Tiki and Ronde Barber) *Game Day,* illustrated by Barry Root, Simon & Schuster (New York, NY), 2005.

Toulouse-Lautrec: The Moulin Rouge and the City of Light, Abrams (New York, NY), 2005.

(With Tiki and Ronde Barber) *Teammates,* illustrated by Barry Root, Simon & Schuster (New York, NY), 2006.

Paul Cézanne: A Painter's Journey, Abrams (New York, NY), 2006.

(With Jorge Posada) *Play Ball!,* Simon & Schuster (New York, NY), 2006.

Tiger of the Snows: Tenzing Norgay: The Boy Whose Dream Was Everest, illustrated by Ed Young, Atheneum (New York, NY), 2006.

Stealing Home: Jackie Robinson: Against the Odds, illustrated by Mike Wimmer, Simon & Schuster (New York, NY), 2007.

Napoleon: The Story of the Little Corporal, Abrams (New York, NY), 2007.

Fly, Cher Ami, Fly!: The Pigeon Who Saved the Lost Battalion, illustrated by Robert MacKenzie, Abrams (New York, NY), 2008.

Abraham Lincoln Comes Home, illustrated by Wendell Minor, Holt (New York, NY), 2008.

Clang-Clang! Beep-Beep!: Listen to the City, illustrated by Beppe Giacobbe, Simon & Schuster (New York, NY), 2009.

One Giant Leap, illustrated by Mike Wimmer, Philomel (New York, NY), 2009.

OTHER

(With Mary Jane Gray) *Basic Writing Skills,* Society for Visual Education (Chicago, IL), 1976.

The Triumph of Mittens: Poems, Boardwell-Kloner (Chicago, IL), 1980.

Colonial America, illustrated by James Seward, Doubleday (Garden City, NY), 1992.

Also writer and producer of over one hundred filmstrips and cassettes on educational subjects.

Sidelights

A writer of informational books of biography and history as well as a poet, Robert Burleigh is noted for introducing complex historical topics to young readers in an accessible and effective manner. Using a picture book format, the author presents facts about his sub-

jects—most often notable Americans such as Henry David Thoreau, Charles Lindbergh, Harry Houdini, Admiral Richard Byrd, and Jackie Robinson—in simple language and present-tense narration. Burleigh favors clipped, staccato texts in both his prose and his poetry, a style credited with expressing the ideas, drama, and importance of each of his topics in an evocative fashion. Reviewers also note the successful marriage of the author's texts with the illustrations of such artists as Lloyd Bloom, Ed Young, and Wendell Minor.

Nineteenth-century writer and philosopher Henry David Thoreau is the subject of Burleigh's first biography, *A Man Named Thoreau.* Considered a balanced overview of Thoreau's life and influence, the book addresses its subject's time at Walden Pond, his love for nature, his literary works, and his civil disobedience, among other topics. Burleigh presents Thoreau and his ideas by combining biographical facts with quotes from the philosopher's popular work *Walden.* Writing in *School Library Journal,* Ruth Semrau called *A Man Named Thoreau* a book that "unfolds new pleasures on every page" and deemed it an "exquisitely simple introduction to a difficult subject." David E. White observed in *Horn Book* that the quotations "interspersed throughout the text . . . are beneficial in capturing the essence of this noted figure." A reviewer for the *Bulletin of the Center for Children's Books* declared that to "have simplified concepts so much without distortion is a gift to the younger reader or listener."

In his picture book *Flight: The Journey of Charles Lindbergh,* Burleigh describes Lindbergh's famous non-stop

In **Flight,** *Mike Wimmer's illustrations bring to life Robert Burleigh's story about the life of famed aviator Charles Lindbergh.* (Illustration copyright © 1991 by Mike Wimmer. All rights reserved. Used by permission of Philomel Books, a Division of Penguin Young Readers Group, a Member of Penguin Group (USA) Inc., 345 Hudson St., New York, NY 10014.)

flight from New York to Paris in 1927. Basing his text on the famed pilot's memoir *The Spirit of St. Louis,* Burleigh focuses on Lindbergh's journey undertaken at age twenty-five. Once again, the author is credited with successfully conveying a sophisticated concept, in this case the difficulty of, in the words of *New York Times Book Review* contributor Signe Wilkinson, "staying awake, alert and in charge of a plane and one's life for two days and a very long, lonely night before sleep" to an audience "too young to appreciate what pulling an all-nighter feels like." *Horn Book* reviewer Ann A. Flowers remarked that the text conveys Lindbergh's bravery, the drain on him personally, and the primitive state of his plane, all in "completely convincing detail." Burleigh's use of the present tense "keeps the reader in suspense from the moment the plane takes off until [its arrival in] Paris," the critic added, concluding that the book is a "pioneer example of the 'right stuff,' splendidly and excitingly presented." Burleigh's use of sentence fragments and single-sentence paragraphs "conveys the excitement of Lindbergh's historic flight," noted a critic in *Kirkus Reviews,* who called *Flight* a book "that brings new life to one of the stories of the century." Burleigh received the Orbis Pictus Award in 1992 for this work.

Shifting to sports, Burleigh crafts a picture-book look at one of baseball's most widely known heroes in *Home Run: The Story of Babe Ruth,* while in two picture books of poetry, *Hoops* and *Goal,* he describes basketball and soccer in verses that simulate the action of the players and capture the excitement of the game. Filled with tactile imagery, *Hoops* and *Goal* outline the way the game feels to its players. "An ode to the game for older children, veteran players, and NBA fans," declared a *Publishers Weekly* reviewer of *Hoops,* adding that Burleigh's "book will give language to teenagers' experience both on and off the court." A *Kirkus Reviews* critic noted that *Goal* uses soccer as a frame "to demonstrate the power of teamwork to achieve success," and concluded that Burleigh's book is "a real winner."

In his picture book *Black Whiteness: Admiral Byrd Alone in the Antarctic,* Burleigh retells the explorer's incredible six-month stay alone in the Antarctic. Based on Byrd's daily journal, *Black Whiteness* includes detailed descriptions of Byrd's enduring hardships—sub-zero temperatures, continuous darkness with limited lighting equipment, and loneliness. "Burleigh's spare prose eloquently captures the spartan surroundings in which Byrd conducted daily meteorological studies," observed a critic in *Kirkus Reviews,* who concluded that the explorer's story is "severe, often depressing, and always riveting." A similar adventurous hero can be found in *Into the Woods: John James Audubon Lives His Dream.* Burleigh uses rhyming couplets to communicate Audubon's decision to give up a job in business in order to wander through the wilderness, painting and drawing the sights to be seen during his adventures. A *Publishers Weekly* reviewer wrote of *Into the Woods*

that Audubon's "philosophy wafts through the volume like a summer breeze." A *Kirkus Reviews* critic called the book a "tribute" to Audubon and a "feast for bird lovers."

Burleigh is as comfortable writing about big cities as he is about wilderness explorers. *Messenger, Messenger* follows a bike messenger through his busy day, from waking up in his book-filled apartment to making deliveries throughout the city. At the book's end, the tired worker returns to his flat to be warmly greeted by his cat. Writing in *Booklist,* Gillian Engberg felt that the picture book "beautifully captures the energizing pulse of urban life and satisfying work." In *Lookin' for Bird in the Big City,* a teenaged Miles Davis, trumpet in hand, makes music on the city streets as he goes in search of his hero, Charlie Parker. Once again, Burleigh employs poetic language and rhythms to convey the flavor of jazz music and the enthusiasm Davis feels for it. "Words and art harmonize in this creatively imagined account," observed a *Publishers Weekly* reviewer. *School Library Journal* contributor Mary Elam concluded that *Lookin' for Bird in the Big City* offers "a lovely and lyrical look at this all-American art form."

Cover of Burleigh's picture-book biography **Napoleon,** *which features contemporary images of the nineteenth-century French emperor and his age.*
(Painting by Jacques-Louis David. Abrams Books for Young Readers, an imprint of Harry N. Abrams, Inc., 2007. Copyright © 2007 by Robert Burleigh. Reproduced by permission. All rights reserved.)

Jazz musician Miles Davis is the subject of Burleigh's picture book **Lookin' for Bird in the Big City,** *featuring artwork by Marek Los.* (Harcourt 2001.
Illustrations copyright © 2001 by Marek Los. All rights reserved. Reproduced by permission of Houghton Mifflin Harcourt Publishing Company.)

Ancient Greece abounds with mythical tales about superhuman exploits and misadventures. Burleigh has brought two of these to younger readers with his *Hercules* and *Pandora.* In *Hercules,* the hero tests his mettle against supernatural challenges, culminating in his descent to the underworld to battle the three-headed dog, Cerberus. In *Booklist* Ilene Cooper liked the fact that *Hercules* uses "language that draws on the strength of its subject yet speaks in the lilt of poetry." In her *Booklist* review, Stephanie Zvirin felt that *Hercules* would inspire young readers to search for other ancient myths about Hercules and other Greek gods, calling the book a "beautiful retelling."

Pandora puts a human face to the curious woman who, according to Greek myth, unleashed all the world's ills by opening a container. In his version of the story, Burleigh uses verse to illuminate how Pandora's curiosity becomes an obsession, despite her understanding of the danger she faces opening the jar. In a *School Library Journal* review of the work, Patricia Lothrop-Green praised "the graceful drama that unfolds" in the story,

concluding: "This Pandora is tempting." Gillian Engberg of *Booklist* found *Pandora* to be "another fine retelling of a Greek myth."

Burleigh offers middle-grade readers a detailed look at a favorite confection in *Chocolate: Riches from the Rainforest.* This illustrated book covers many aspects of chocolate, from its history as a food of the Maya and Aztecs to its journey from cacao pod to candy bar. The author writes about the slave labor once used in the cacao and sugar industries, and about how Milton Hershey revolutionized the sale of milk chocolate from his factory in Pennsylvania. In a *School Library Journal* review, Augusta R. Malvagno praised the "delightful" book for its "kaleidoscope of fascinating information," while a contributor to *Kirkus Reviews* concluded that *Chocolate* is "a well-conceived and executed work on a subject of great interest."

Some critics have particularly praised Burleigh's *The Secret of the Great Houdini.* Here he explores Houdini's escape from a trunk hurled into deep water from the point of view of a youngster named Sam and his Uncle Ezra, who have joined a crowd to watch the feat.

While Sam and Uncle Ezra anxiously await Houdini's escape, Uncle Ezra tells Sam about Houdini's childhood and hardscrabble youth. Sam can hardly concentrate on what his uncle is saying, so terrified is he of the possibility that Houdini will drown. "Burleigh achieves immediacy by writing his poetic text in the present tense," observed Marianne Saccardi in *School Library Journal.* "Houdini is a fascinating figure for all ages," maintained a *Kirkus Reviews* critic. "This snapshot of one incredible feat . . . may spur further exploration, and inspiration." In her *Booklist* review, Gillian Engberg declared that the work "captures the mystique of its famous subject."

In *Langston's Train Ride,* Burleigh chronicles a significant episode in the life of Harlem Renaissance writer Langston Hughes—a cross-country train ride during which he composed his famous poem "The Negro Speaks of Rivers." Wendy Lukehart, writing in *School Library Journal,* applauded the "well-crafted, first-person narration," and a *Publishers Weekly* contributor

stated that the work may prompt readers "to reach out for their dreams." Burleigh's *Tiger of the Snows: Tenzing Norgay: The Boy Whose Dream Was Everest* was described as "a stunning and lyrical ode to a contemplative man and his amazing achievement" by *School Library Journal* reviewer Be Astengo. The work examines the life of the Nepalese Sherpa who joined Sir Edmund Hillary as one of the first men to climb Mount Everest. In *Stealing Home: Jackie Robinson: Against the Odds,* Burleigh offers biographical information about the man who broke Major League Baseball's color barrier and depicts an electrifying moment from the 1955 World Series. "Burleigh's text features vivid, sharp images," noted GraceAnne A. DeCandido in *Booklist.*

Burleigh, who paints under the pseudonym Burleigh Kronquist, has also produced picture book biographies of celebrated French artists, illustrated with reproductions of their paintings. Henri de Toulouse-Lautrec, the diminutive nineteenth-century painter, printmaker,

Burleigh teams up with artist Raul Colón to tell a classic story of curiosity rewarded in the picture book **Pandora.** (Harcourt, Inc., 2002. Illustration copyright © 2002 by Raul Colón. Reproduced by permission of Houghton Mifflin Harcourt Publishing Company.)

In Stealing Home *Burleigh joins artist Mike Wimmer in capturing a highlight in the career of baseball great Jackie Robinson.* (Illustration copyright © 2007 by Mike Wimmer. All rights reserved. Reprinted with the permission of Simon & Schuster Books Young Readers, an imprint of Simon & Schuster Children's Publishing Division.)

draftsman, and illustrator, is the subject of *Toulouse-Lautrec: The Moulin Rouge and the City of Light.* "Burleigh confidently celebrates Lautrec's work and skill," observed Steev Baker in *School Library Journal.* In *Paul Cézanne: A Painter's Journey,* Burleigh examines the life of the famed post-impressionist. According to Regan McMahon in the *San Francisco Chronicle,* "Burleigh's excellent work is a complex portrait of a complex man, driven to paint no matter what other people thought of him and his art."

"While the subjects vary," Burleigh remarked on his home page, "my books are linked philosophically, stylistically and structurally by my wish to capture where possible the emotional intensity—the essence—of whatever the subject is."

Biographical and Critical Sources

PERIODICALS

Booklist, February 1, 1999, Stephanie Zvirin, review of *It's Funny Where Ben's Train Takes Him,* p. 979; August, 1999, Ilene Cooper, review of *Hercules,* p. 2050; March 15, 2000, Carolyn Phelan, review of *Edna,* p. 1377; May 15, 2000, Gillian Engberg, review of *Messenger, Messenger,* p. 1742, and Stephanie Zvirin, review of *Hercules,* p. 1758; February 15, 2001, Bill Ott, review of *Lookin' for Bird in the Big City,* p. 1152; June 1, 2001, Marta Segal, review of *I Love Going through This Book,* p. 1888; June 1, 2002, Gillian Engberg, review of *Pandora,* p. 1711; July, 2002, Gillian Engberg, review of *The Secret of the Great Houdini,* p. 1854; January 1, 2003, Julie Cummins, review of *Into the Woods: John James Audubon Lives His Dream,* p. 874; September 15, 2004, Hazel Rochman, review of *Langston's Train Ride,* p. 238; March 1, 2005, Carolyn Phelan, review of *Toulouse-Lautrec: The Moulin Rouge and the City of Light,* p. 1194;

February 15, 2006, Gillian Engberg, review of *Paul Cézanne: A Painter's Journey,* p. 94; June 1, 2006, Gillian Engberg, review of *Tiger of the Snows: Tenzing Norgay: The Boy Whose Dream Was Everest,* p. 97; December 15, 2006, GraceAnne A. DeCandido, review of *Stealing Home: Jackie Robinson: Against the Odds,* p. 49; June 1, 2007, Hazel Rochman, review of *Napoleon: The Story of the Little Corporal,* p. 94.

Bulletin of the Center for Children's Books, December, 1985, review of *A Man Named Thoreau,* p. 63.

Horn Book, March, 1986, David E. White, review of *A Man Named Thoreau,* pp. 215-216; November, 1991, Ann A. Flowers, review of *Flight: The Journey of Charles Lindbergh,* p. 752.

Kirkus Reviews, August 15, 1991, review of *Flight,* p. 1086; December 1, 1997, review of *Black Whiteness: Admiral Byrd Alone in the Antarctic,* p. 1773; February 1, 2001, review of *Goal,* p. 180; March 1, 2002, review of *Chocolate: Riches from the Rainforest,* p. 330; May 1, 2002, review of *Pandora,* p. 650; June 15, 2002, review of *The Secret of the Great Houdini,* p. 876; January 1, 2003, review of *Into the Woods,* p. 58; September 15, 2004, review of *By My Brother's Side,* p. 909, and *Langston's Train Ride,* p. 911; February 1, 2006, review of *Paul Cézanne,* p. 128; March 1, 2006, review of *Play Ball!,* p. 237; May 15, 2006, review of *Tiger of the Snows,* p. 514; May 1, 2007, review of *Stealing Home;* May 15, 2007, review of *Napoleon;* June 15, 2008, review of *Abraham Lincoln Comes Home;* August 15, 2008, review of *Fly, Cher Ami, Fly!: The Pigeon Who Saved the Lost Battalion.*

New York Times Book Review, January 26, 1992, Signe Wilkinson, review of *Flight,* p. 21.

Publishers Weekly, October 6, 1997, review of *Hoops,* p. 83; August 9, 1999, review of *Hercules,* p. 352; May 14, 2001, review of *Lookin' for Bird in the Big City,* p. 82; June 19, 2000, review of *Messenger, Messenger,* p. 54; June 4, 2001, review of *I Love Going through This Book,* p. 79; April 1, 2002, review of *Pandora,* p. 83; June 3, 2002, review of *The Secret of the Great Houdini,* p. 88; December 2, 2002, review of *Into the Woods,* p. 52; January 3, 2005, review of *Langston's Train Ride,* p. 54; January 9, 2006, review of *Play Ball!,* p. 53; December 11, 2006, review of *Stealing Home,* p. 69; June 5, 2006, review of *Tiger of the Snows,* p. 64.

San Francisco Chronicle, January 29, 2006, Regan McMahon, "Touchdown Teamwork," review of *Game Day,* p. M6; June 25, 2006, "An Artist's Life Is No Easy Path," p. M4.

School Library Journal, January, 1986, Ruth Semrau, review of *A Man Named Thoreau,* p. 64; October, 1999, Nina Lindsay, review of *Hercules,* p. 135; April, 2000, Kate McClelland, review of *Edna,* p. 92; April, 2001, Lee Bock, review of *Goal,* p. 129; June, 2001, Marianne Saccardi, review of *I Love Going through This Book,* p. 104, and Mary Elam, review of *Lookin' for Bird in the Big City,* p. 104; April, 2002, Augusta R. Malvagno, review of *Chocolate,* p. 129; May, 2002, Patricia Lothrop-Green, review of *Pandora,* p. 134; July, 2002, Marianne Saccardi, review of *The Secret*

of the Great Houdini, p. 85; September, 2002, Dona Ratterree, review of *Into the Air,* p. 241; January, 2003, Laurie von Mehren, review of *Earth from Above for Young Readers,* p. 150; February, 2003, Robyn Walker, review of *Into the Woods,* p. 128; November, 2004, Ann M. Holcomb, review of *By My Brother's Side,* p. 122; December, 2004, Wendy Lukehart, review of *Langston's Train Ride,* p. 127; May, 2005, Steev Baker, review of *Toulouse-Lautrec,* p. 146; January, 2006, Mary Hazelton, review of *Game Day,* p. 116; May, 2006, Marilyn Taniguchi, review of *Play Ball!,* p. 97; June, 2006, Be Astengo, review of *Tiger of the Snows,* p. 134; November, 2006, Rachel G. Payne, review of *Teammates,* p. 117; January, 2007, Marilyn Taniguchi, review of *Stealing Home,* p. 114; July, 2007, Ann W. Moore, review of *Napoleon,* p. 113.

Teacher Librarian, June, 2000, Jessica Higgs, review of *Hercules,* p. 54.

ONLINE

Robert Burleigh Home Page, http://robertburleigh.com (August 10, 2008).

Burleigh Kronquist Web site, www.burleighkronquist.com/ (August 10, 2008).

* * *

BURNETT BOSSI, Lisa

Personal

Married; husband's name Adrian; children: Lila, Clara. *Education:* Bowdoin College, B.A. (fine art and art history).

Addresses

Home—Brunswick, ME. *E-mail*—lisa@bossigosline. com.

Career

Illustrator, graphic designer, and residential color consultant. Ambledance Studios (workshop), San Francisco, CA, cofounder with Andrea Alban Gosline.

Illustrator

Andrea Alban Gosline and Ame Mahler Beanland, *Mother's Nature: Timeless Wisdom for the Journey into Motherhood,* Conari Press (Berkeley, CA), 1999.

Andrea Alban Gosline, *Ten Little Wishes: A Baby Animal Counting Book,* HarperCollins (New York, NY), 2007.

Andrea Alban Gosline, *January's Child: The Birthday Month Book,* Scholastic (New York, NY), 2007.

Andrea Alban Gosline, *The Happiness Tree: Celebrating the Gifts of Trees We Treasure,* Feiwel & Friends (New York, NY), 2008.

Andrea Alban Gosline, *BAByC;s: An Alphabet of Little Surprises,* HarperCollins (New York, NY), 2009.

Also illustrator of journals and greeting cards.

Biographical and Critical Sources

PERIODICALS

Booklist, February 1, 2007, Hazel Rochman, review of *Ten Little Wishes: A Baby Animal Counting Book,* p. 49.

Kirkus Reviews, December 1, 2006, review of *January's Child: The Birthday Month Book,* p. 1220.

School Library Journal, March, 2007, Linda Staskus, review of *Ten Little Wishes,* p. 162.

ONLINE

BossiGosline Web site, http://www.bossigosline.com (September 15, 2008), "Lisa Burnett Bossi."

Macmillan Web site, http://us.macmillan.com/ (September 15, 2008), interview with Burnett Bossi.*

* * *

BURNS, Loree Griffin

Personal

Married Gerry Burns; children: three children. *Education:* Worcester Polytechnic Institute, B.S. (biology); University of Massachusetts, Ph.D. (biochemistry).

Addresses

Home—MA. *E-mail*—lgb@loreeburns.com.

Career

Scientist and author.

Awards, Honors

Orbis Pictus Recommended designation, SB & F Prize for Excellence in Science Books finalist, American Library Association Notable Book designation, International Reading Association Children's Book Award designation, and *Horn Book* Honor Book designation, all 2008, all for *Tracking Trash.*

Writings

Tracking Trash: Flotsam, Jetsam, and the Science of Motion, Houghton Mifflin (Boston, MA), 2007.

Sidelights

Drawing on her lifelong love of both science and the men and women who have made it their career, Loree Griffin Burns wrote *Tracking Trash: Flotsam, Jetsam,*

and the Science of Motion to introduce young readers to an unusual scientist. An oceanographer, Dr. Curt Ebbesmeyer studies the path that lost or discarded man-made items take after falling into the world's waterways. Ebbesmeyer's study of this flotsam—which encompasses such amazing things as sneakers and LEGO pieces and the thousands of rubber ducks that were swept overboard and left to float from the Pacific all the way through the Arctic and into the Atlantic Ocean—joins several others in generating the data that has helped marine biologists safeguard fragile habitats and protect seagoing creatures from the threats posed by unnatural objects. Burns illustrates *Tracking Trash* with numerous photographs that help bring to life Ebbesmeyer's work and also inspire interest in young readers.

In his review of *Tracking Trash* for the *New York Times Book Review,* Hank Green wrote that Burns' book features "scientists doing science," but with "a bit of detective novel thrown in as well." In *Booklist* Carolyn Phelan noted the inclusion of a comprehensive glossary and notes, a section titled "What You Can Do," and a list of study resources, called *Tracking Trash* "a unique and often fascinating book on ocean currents, drifting trash, and the scientists who study them." Praising the author's "well-written narration," Esther Keller added in *School Library Journal* that the book "will get readers thinking and possibly acting" on the problem of ocean pollution. Burns grounds her text with what *Horn Book* critic Betty Carter described as "solid scientific explanations" which include terms such as "charting, latitude and longitude, currents, waves, tides, and gyres." *Tracking Trash* is part of the "Scientists in the Field" series, an award-winning group of books that seeks to inspire an interest in pursuing scientific careers.

Biographical and Critical Sources

PERIODICALS

Audubon, May-June, 2007, Julie Leibach, review of *Tracking Trash: Flotsam, Jetsam, and the Science of Motion,* p. 94.

Booklist, April 1, 2007, Carolyn Phelan, review of *Tracking Trash,* p. 38.

Bulletin of the Center for Children's Books, May, 2007, Elizabeth Bush, review of *Tracking Trash,* p. 362.

Horn Book, March-April, 2007, Betty Carter, review of *Tracking Trash,* p. 211.

Kirkus Reviews, March 1, 2007, review of *Tracking Trash,* p. 217.

New York Times Book Review, October 14, 2007, Hank Green, "Notes on a Sick Planet."

School Library Journal, December, 2007, Kathleen Baxter, review of *Tracking Trash,* p. 28.

Voice of Youth Advocates, February, 2007, Michele Winship, review of *Tracking Trash,* p. 550.

Wildlife Conservation, July-August, 2007, review of *Tracking Trash.*

ONLINE

Loree Griffin Burns Home Page, http://www.loreeburns.com (September 15, 2008).

C

CAPLE, Kathy

Personal
Married.

Addresses
Home—Cambridge, MA.

Career
Author, illustrator, and children's and teen services librarian.

Writings

SELF-ILLUSTRATED

Inspector Aardvark and the Perfect Cake, Windmill/ Wanderer (New York, NY), 1980.
The Biggest Nose, Houghton Mifflin (Boston, MA), 1985.
The Purse, Houghton Mifflin (Boston, MA), 1986.
Harry's Smile, Houghton Mifflin (Boston, MA), 1987.
The Coolest Place in Town, Houghton Mifflin (Boston, MA), 1990.
Fox and Bear, Houghton Mifflin (Boston, MA), 1992.
The Wimp, Houghton Mifflin (Boston, MA), 1994.
Starring Hillary, Carolrhoda (Minneapolis, MN), 1999.
Well Done, Worm!, Candlewick (Cambridge, MA), 2000.
Hillary to the Rescue, Carolrhoda (Minneapolis, MN), 2000.
The Friendship Tree, Holiday House (New York, NY), 2000.
Wow, It's Worm!, Candlewick (Cambridge, MA), 2001.
Worm Gets a Job, Candlewick (Cambridge, MA), 2004.
Termite Trouble, Candlewick (Cambridge, MA), 2005.
Duck and Company, Holiday House (New York, NY), 2007.

Sidelights
When Kathy Caple was growing up, her dream was to become a dancer. However, during her free time she found herself drawing rather than practicing her plié.

As Caple noted on the Walker Books Web site, "I enjoyed doodling in my notebook, and making up stories in my head. I didn't really figure out how to write the stories down, as well as illustrate them, until much later." As an adult, Caple has figured it out, and more than a dozen self-illustrated titles for young readers are the result.

Caple's picture books typically depict a universal problem faced by children, all seen through the eyes of animal characters. Dealing with themes from bullying to friendship to tackling odd jobs, her tales are populated with sheep, pigs, ducks, and worms. Three hippo siblings struggle over who gets to play in their kiddie pool on a hot summer day in *The Coolest Place in Town.* Comparing Caple's work to Marc Brown's "Arthur" books, a *Publishers Weekly* critic cited the "snappy dialogue [and] . . . simple but clever plot" in the summertime-themed picture book.

Two pig siblings deal with bullies in Caple's humorous picture book *The Wimp.* Arnold is picked on by two school bullies, and his sister Rose calls him a wimp, until she starts to be the focus of teasing as well. Eventually, Arnold figures out a non-violent way to trick the bullies into ending their bullying ways. According to Hazel Rochman, writing in *Booklist,* readers "will laugh with sympathy at Arnold's humiliation even as they rejoice in his sweet triumph." Caple "is especially skilled at painting [Arnold's] reactions," wrote a contributor to *Publishers Weekly.*

One of Caple's popular characters is Hillary the cat, a would-be actress who goes on an ill advised diet in *Starring Hillary.* Although Hillary's sister tells her that she cannot succeed at her audition unless she is skinny, the dieting makes the cat nervous and sleepless until she sees the performance of a rotund actress built more like herself and gains the courage she needs to ace her audition. While writing that Caple's message is perhaps too obvious, a *Publishers Weekly* concluded that the author/illustrator's "art captures Hillary's spunk and determination." In *Hillary to the Rescue,* the cat again sees

how being different can be good. When she and her friends from the drama club go into the city in the winter to see a performance, only Hillary wears her heavy winter clothing. She gets too hot in the car and has to remove some layers, but when the car gets stuck in a ditch, she has the warm clothing needed to go for help. Ilene Cooper, writing in *Booklist,* noted that Caple's "pen-and-watercolor illustrations are well drawn and laugh-aloud funny."

Several of Caple's books feature vignettes or short chapters rather than a single story. *Fox and Bear* features four stories about a pair of friends as they go camping and have other short adventures. A *Publishers Weekly* critic noted that the emotions of Caple's two characters "are portrayed with immediacy through the action and pictures, never merely related in the text." *The Friendship Tree* uses the same structure and shows the friendship of two sheep over four seasons as the pair enjoys the forest outside their homes. When one tree is struck by lightning, the neighboring sheep buys her friend a small potted pine tree to plant the next spring. "Caple's soft illustrations depict the changing seasons and emphasize the quiet mood of the episodic plot," wrote a contributor to *Horn Book.* A *Publishers Weekly* contributor noted that the "whisper-soft words and pictures" in *The Friendship Tree* "say a lot about kindness."

Another animal-centered story by Caple, *Duck and Rat* is the tale of two booksellers who serve a diverse community of animal customers. Here "Caple's ink-and-gouache pictures furnish funny, easily interpreted scenes of retail life," wrote a contributor to *Kirkus Reviews.*

Featuring a series of vignettes, *Well Done, Worm!* introduces another of Caple's recurring characters. In one story, Worm illustrates shape concepts by turning himself into a triangle, a circle, and a square; in another short tale, he paints a picture. Worm's interest in painting continues in *Worm Gets a Job,* in which he has to earn money in order to enter an art competition. All of his jobs, from babysitting to housecleaning, become disasters, and Worm ultimately loses the job he is good at: creating signs for a store. Luckily, the contest judges see Worm's discarded signs and award him a prize in the competition. "Each of Worm's mishaps is depicted with amusing exaggeration," wrote Linda L. Walkins in *School Library Journal.*

Biographical and Critical Sources

PERIODICALS

Booklist, June 1, 1994, Hazel Rochman, review of *The Wimp,* p. 1835; February 15, 2000, Carolyn Phelan, review of *The Friendship Tree,* p. 1123; October 1, 2000, Hazel Rochman, review of *Well Done, Worm!,* p. 351; November 15, 2000, Ilene Cooper, review of *Hillary to the Rescue,* p. 646.

Bulletin of the Center for Children's Books, October, 2007, Hope Morrison, review of *Duck and Company,* p. 76.
Horn Book, July, 2000, review of *The Friendship Tree,* p. 453.
Kirkus Reviews, May 15, 2004, review of *Worm Gets a Job,* p. 489; September 1, 2007, review of *Duck and Company.*
Publishers Weekly, June 21, 1985, review of *The Biggest Nose,* p. 104; February 9, 1990, review of *The Coolest Place in Town,* p. 60; March 9, 1992, review of *Fox and Bear,* p. 56; August 8, 1994, review of *The Wimp,* p. 434; March 8, 1999, review of *Starring Hillary,* p. 68; February 14, 2000, review of *The Friendship Tree,* p. 197.
School Library Journal, September, 1980, Holly Sanhuber, review of *Inspector Aardvark and the Perfect Cake,* p. 56; April, 2000, Linda M. Kenton, review of *The Friendship Tree,* p. 92; December, 2000, Piper L. Nyman, review of *Hillary to the Rescue,* p. 104; March, 2001, Christina F. Renaud, review of *Well Done, Worm!,* p. 194; July, 2004, Linda L. Walkins, review of *Worm Gets a Job,* p. 68.

ONLINE

Scholastic Web site, http://www.scholastic.com/ (October 6, 2008), "Kathy Caple."
Walker Books Web site, http://www.walker.co.uk/ (October 6, 2008), "Kathy Caple."*

*   *   *

CATLOW, Nikalas
See CATLOW, Niki

*   *   *

CATLOW, Niki 1975-
(Nikalas Catlow)

Personal

Born 1975, in Stockport, Cheshire, England. *Education:* Cambridge School of Art, M.A. (children's book illustration).

Addresses

Home—England. *E-mail*—n@catlow.biz.

Career

Illustrator and animator. Formerly worked in theatre and in advertising.

Illustrator

Matthew Morgan and Samantha Barnes, *Children's Miscellany: Useless Information That's Essential to Know,* Buster Books (London, England), 2004, Chronicle Books (San Francisco, CA), 2005.

Dominique Enright, *How to Be the Best at Everything,* Buster Books (London, England), 2004, expanded with Guy Macdonald as *The Boys' Book: How to Be the Best at Everything,* 2006, Scholastic (New York, NY), 2007.

(With Paul Middlewick) Elizabeth Medley, *Are You a Superstar?,* Buster Books (London, England), 2004.

Dominique Enright, *Children's Miscellany, Volume 2,* Buster Books (London, England), 2005, published as *Children's Miscellany Too: More Useless Information That's Essential to Know,* Chronicle Books (San Francisco, CA), 2006.

Dominique Enright, *Children's Miscellany, Volume 3,* Buster Books (London, England), 2006.

Rob Eastaway, *How to Remember (Almost) Everything, Ever!,* Wizard (Thriplow, England), 2007.

Mind Your Own Business: A File of Super Secret Stuff, Wizard (Thriplow, England), 2007.

Author and illustrator of *Doodles to Do, Do You Doodle?,* and *Oodles of Doodles.* Also illustrator of puzzle books, including *The Kids' Book of Sudoku, The Kids' Book of Kakuro, The Kids' Book of Hanjie,* and *The Kids' Book of Number Puzzles.*

Biographical and Critical Sources

PERIODICALS

Kirkus Reviews, July 15, 2007, review of *The Boys' Book: How to Be the Best at Everything.*

ONLINE

Niki Catlow Home Page, http://www.catlow.biz (September 15, 2008).*

* * *

CHIEN, Catia

Personal

Born in São Paulo, Brazil; immigrated to United States. *Education:* Attended college. *Hobbies and other interests:* Swing dancing, making soup.

Addresses

Home—P.O. Box 1290, Tustin, CA 92781. *E-mail*—gatapuff@yahoo.com.

Career

Illustrator and animator. *Exhibitions:* Work included in exhibitions in California and Chicago, IL.

Illustrator

Suzanne Selfors, *To Catch a Mermaid,* Little, Brown (New York, NY), 2007.

Dashka Slater, *The Sea Serpent and Me,* Houghton Mifflin (Boston, MA), 2008.

Contributor to books, including *Princess Alyss of Wonderland,* by Frank Beddor, Dial (New York, NY), 2007. Creator of comics, including "Tumbleweed." Contributor to "Flight" and "Belle and Sebastian" cartoon anthologies.

Biographical and Critical Sources

PERIODICALS

Kirkus Reviews, July 15, 2007, review of *To Catch a Mermaid.*

Publishers Weekly, September 3, 2007, review of *To Catch a Mermaid,* p. 59.

School Library Journal, September, 2007, Elizabeth Bird, review of *To Catch a Mermaid,* p. 208.

ONLINE

Catia Chien Home Page, http://www.catiachien.com (September 15, 2008).

GUU Press Web site, http://www.guupress.com/ (February 1, 2007), Byron Tsang, interview with Chien.*

* * *

CHIEN-MIN, Lin
See RUMFORD, James

* * *

CLAYMAN, Deborah Paula
See Da COSTA, Deborah

* * *

CLIPPINGER, Carol

Personal

Female. *Hobbies and other interests:* Tennis.

Addresses

Home—CO. *Agent*—Chudney Agency, 72 N. State Rd., Ste. 501, Briarcliff Manor, NY 10510.

Career

Writer.

Writings

Open Court, Knopf (New York, NY), 2007.

Sidelights

Carol Clippinger taps her deep insight into the world of the tennis circuit in her debut young-adult novel, *Open Court*. In the novel, readers meet Holloway "Hall" Braxton, a thirteen-year-old tennis prodigy who is facing some very difficult decisions. Holly has been competing since she was six, and in order to advance to the professional tennis circuit she needs to attend a tennis academy. Her parents are supportive, but are feeling the strain of paying for equipment and tournaments even before the expensive tennis academy's fliers start arriving. When Holly's training partner, Janie, suffers a mental breakdown that causes her to question whether she wants to continue in the sport, pressures begin to mount for Hall. Questioning whether she still has the mental and competitive edge she needs to continue, the teen weathers a setback at the tennis academy and reconfirms her belief that she does have the inner drive needed to win.

According to *School Library Journal* reviewer Roxanne Myers Spencer, Clippinger's tale presents "the ever-present and relentless demands of the game, creating a

Cover of Carol Clippinger's novel Open Court, *which focuses on the life of an up-and-coming teenage tennis star.* (Copyright © 2007 by Carol Clippinger. All rights reserved. Used by permission of Alfred A. Knopf, an imprint of Random House Children's Books, a division of Random House, Inc.)

tension and rhythm that will capture readers' attention to the finish, just as a good tennis match should." A *Kirkus Reviews* contributor predicted that *Open Court* will appeal to "fans of tennis and readers who have experienced the similar pressures."

Biographical and Critical Sources

PERIODICALS

Bulletin of the Center for Children's Books, July-August, 2007, Deborah Stevenson, review of *Open Court,* p. 458.
Kirkus Reviews, May 15, 2007, review of *Open Court.*
School Library Journal, July, 2007, Roxanne Myers Spencer, review of *Open Court,* p. 99.
Voice of Youth Advocates, June, 2007, Mary Ann Harlan, review of *Open Court,* p. 139.*

*   *   *

CROCKER, Carter

Personal
Male.

Addresses
Home and office—CA.

Career
Writer. Scriptwriter and story editor for television programs, including *Disney's Winnie the Pooh: Seasons of Giving, The New Adventures of Winnie the Pooh,* 1988-90, *Darkwing Duck,* 1991, *Winnie the Pooh: Seasons of Giving,* 1999, and *Horseland,* 2006-07.

Awards, Honors
Daytime Emmy for Outstanding Animated Program, 1990, for *The New Adventures of Winnie the Pooh;* Daytime Emmy for Outstanding Children's Animated Program nominee, 2006, for *Baby Looney Tunes.*

Writings

FOR CHILDREN

The Tale of the Swamp Rat, Philomel Books (New York, NY), 2003.

Author of television scripts for programs, including *Madame's Place,* 1982; *The New Adventures of Winnie the Pooh,* 1988-90; *Goof Troop,* 1992; *Boo to You Too!*

Winnie the Pooh, 1996; *Pooh's Grand Adventure: The Search for Christopher Robin,* 1997; *Disney's Belle's Magical World* and *Young Hercules,* both 1998; *Winnie the Pooh: A Valentine for You, Winnie the Pooh: Seasons of Giving, A Very Goofy Christmas,* and *Mickey's Once upon a Christmas,* all 1999; *Nine Dog Christmas,* 2001; *Little People: Big Discoveries, Return to Never Land,* and *Sabrina the Teenage Witch in: Friends Forever,* all 2002; *New Girl in Town* and *The Jungle Book 2,* 2003; *A Hair A-Faire* and *Trollz,* both 2005; *You Can' Judge a Girl by Her Limo, Horseland, Merlin, l'enchanteur, Barney and Friends, Welcome, Cousin Riff: Special Skills, Barney: Let's Make Music, Strawberry Shortcake: The Sweet Dreams Movie, Winnie the Pooh: Wonderful Word Adventure,* and *Winnie the Pooh: Shapes and Sizes,* all 2006; *Barney: Dino-mite Birthday,* 2007; and *Hi! I'm Riff!,* and *Barney: Animal ABC's,* both 2008.

Sidelights

Carter Crocker has worked extensively in television and film, bringing many favorite children's characters to life, including Barney and Winnie the Pooh. Crocker's career has spanned several decades, beginning as an assistant story editor and eventually winning a Daytime Emmy award for his work in television. Turning to writing, his well-received picture book, *The Tale of the Swamp Rat* invites children into a new world and brings several interesting characters to life.

The Tale of the Swamp Rat is set in an unusual location: a Florida swamp. Told by a tiny creature named Little Mole, the story focuses on the main character, Ossie, a swamp rat whose small size makes him very vulnerable. After Ossie's parents and siblings meet an untimely death—they are, eaten by Mr. Took, the rattlesnake—the rat finds himself fighting to survive on his own. A very old alligator, Uncle Will, takes care of Oddir, letting the rat rest on his back while predators stay at bay. Through the alligator, Ossie learns about the history of the swamp, including tales of Native Americans, runaway slaves, and poachers. He also finds love with the beautiful Emma, but Prophet Bubba, a misguided and ill-intentioned stork, begins to spread rumors about the rat. While dealing with these rumors, Ossie must also fend off Mr. Took and find a way to help his friends deal with a local drought.

Booklist contributor John Green wrote of *The Tale of the Swamp Rat* that Crocker's "writing is uncommonly evocative, and this is the kind of folkloric fiction that kids can treasure." Susan Oliver, reviewing the book for *School Library Journal,* praised the story's main character. "With Southern flavor, adventure, and environmental drama, Ossie's tale of finding his own way in the world will hit close to home for many," the critic concluded. A *Kirkus Reviews* writer deemed *The Tale of the Swamp Rat* entertaining as well as educational, adding that "readers may enjoy Crocker's low-key brand of humor and non-preachy philosophizing." In *Publishers Weekly* a reviewer concluded of the book that "the real joy here is simply spending time with these memorable characters."

Biographical and Critical Sources

PERIODICALS

Booklist, November 1, 2003, John Green, review of *The Tale of the Swamp Rat,* p. 608.
Kirkus Reviews, September 15, 2003, review of *The Tale of the Swamp Rat,* p. 1172.
Publishers Weekly, September 8, 2003, review of *The Tale of the Swamp Rat,* p. 77.
School Library Journal, October, 2003, Susan Oliver, review of *The Tale of the Swamp Rat,* p. 162.

ONLINE

Internet Movie Database, http://www.imdb.com/ (September 1, 2008), "Carter Crocker."*

D

Da COSTA, Deborah
[A pseudonym]
(Deborah Paula Clayman)

Personal
Born in Jersey City, NJ; married; husband's name Warren; children: Anthony, Danit (daughter). *Education:* Ohio State University, B.A. (international studies), B.S. (education); M.A. (anthropology); Columbia University, M.A. (remedial reading), Ph.D. (developmental psychology). *Hobbies and other interests:* Traveling, animal welfare causes, reading, spending time with family.

Addresses
Home—MD. *E-mail*—debbie@deborahdacosta.com.

Career
Psychologist, educator, and author of books for children. Former teacher of elementary school, Adams City, CO, and Montclair, NJ; educational consultant; former high-school teacher; currently freelance writer; teacher of writing and presenter at conferences.

Awards, Honors
Notable Book for Younger Readers designation, Jewish Theological Seminary, Notable Children's Book of Jewish Content designation, Association of Jewish Libraries, and Children's Literature Choice selection, all 2002, all for *Snow in Jerusalem;* Notable Children's Book of Jewish Content designation, Association of Jewish Libraries, 2007, for *Hanukkah Moon.*

Writings

Snow in Jerusalem, illustrated by Cornelius Van Wright and Ying-Hwa Hu, Albert Whitman (Morton Grove, IL), 2001.

Hanukkah Moon, illustrated by Gosia Mocz, Kar-Ben Publishing (Minneapolis, MN), 2007.

Author's work has been translated into Italian.

Biographical and Critical Sources

PERIODICALS

Booklist, October 15, 2001, Stephanie Zvirin, review of *Snow in Jerusalem,* p. 400; September 15, 2007, Kay Weisman, review of *Hanukkah Moon,* p. 80.
Bulletin of the Center for Children's Books, October, 2007, Elizabeth Bush, review of *Hanukkah Moon,* p. 80.
Kirkus Reviews, September 1, 2001, review of *Snow in Jerusalem,* p. 1288.
Publishers Weekly, November 5, 2001, review of *Snow in Jerusalem,* p. 68; October 29, 2007, review of *Hanukkah Moon,* p. 56.
School Library Journal, December, 2001, Amy Lilien-Harper, review of *Snow in Jerusalem,* p. 98.

ONLINE

Deborah Da Costa Home Page, http://www.deborahdacosta.com (September 15, 2008).

*   *   *

De MARI, Silvana 1953-

Personal
Born 1953, in Caserta, Italy.

Addresses
Home—Turin, Italy.

Career
Writer, novelist, psychotherapist, and physician. Psychotherapist in private practice. Worked as a surgeon in Italy and Ethiopia.

Awards, Honors

Best Children's Books of 2006, *Kirkus Reviews,* for *The Last Dragon.*

Writings

NOVELS

L'ultima stella a destra della luna, Salani, 2000.
The Last Dragon (published in Italian as *L'ultimo orco*), translated by Shaun Whiteside, Miramax Books/ Hyperion Books for Children (New York, NY), 2004.
La bestia y la bella, Grupo Editorial Norma, 2005.
El ultimo elfo (title means "The Last Elf"), Grupo Editorial Norma, 2005.

Contributor of short stories to periodicals and magazines.

Sidelights

Silvana De Mari is a physician, psychotherapist, and surgeon who has worked in both Europe and Africa. De Mari is also the author of several novels, most with a lighthearted and heroic fantasy element. In *The Last Dragon,* kindhearted and gentle Yorsh is the last elf surviving in a harsh, cold, always rainy world where humans hate him simply because he is an elf. An encounter with a hot-tempered human woman, Sajra, turns out to be beneficial, however, as the woman's sympathy is aroused by the little elf's plight. The two decide to search for a drier, more comfortable place in which to live, and during their travels they meet a third companion, Monser, a hunter who joins their search. When they enter the human city of Daligar, they are captured and imprisoned. Facing death by hanging, they manage to escape, but not before Yorsh divines his destiny using an inscription on the wall that states that when the last dragon and last elf come together, the world will be saved. Inspired to begin a search for the last dragon, Yorsh and his companions take up the perilous quest. Meanwhile, in a concurrent story, the destiny of a young orphaned human girl develops and soon becomes intertwined in Yorsh's prophecy. Tragedy befalls the group of comrades, and Yorsh discovers that "prophecies are for people who don't want to control their own destiny," in the words of a *Publishers Weekly* reviewer.

De Mari "takes common fantasy elements and combines them in a unique way in this stirring, subtly post-apocalyptic fantasy," observed Anita L. Burkham in a *Horn Book* review of *The Last Dragon.* "At times hilarious, at times poignant, and always entertaining," the story of Yorsh's determined quest "will grip young fantasy fans," commented *Booklist* reviewer Sally Estes, and a contributor to *Kirkus Reviews* called the book a "wise, warmhearted fairytale." The story's "satisfying, poignant ending does not disappoint," remarked a *Kliatt*

contributor. *School Library Journal* critic Sarah Couri concluded of *The Last Dragon* that "young fantasy fans will appreciate the many humorous touches and get caught up in this tale of strength and sacrifice."

Biographical and Critical Sources

PERIODICALS

Booklist, November 1, 2006, Sally Estes, review of *The Last Dragon,* p. 53.
Horn Book, November-December, 2006, Anita L. Burkam, review of *The Last Dragon,* p. 707; January-February, 2007, review of *The Last Dragon,* p. 12.
Kirkus Reviews, October 1, 2006, review of *The Last Dragon,* p. 1012.
Kliatt, November, 2006, review of *The Last Dragon,* p. 8.
Publishers Weekly, December 18, 2006, review of *The Last Dragon,* p. 64.
School Library Journal, January 1, 2007, Sarah Couri, review of *The Last Dragon,* p. 126.

ONLINE

Festivaletteratura Web site, http://www.festivaletteratura.it/ (April 24, 2007), biography of Silvana De Mari.*

* * *

DENISE, Christopher 1968-

Personal

Born 1968, in Ashland, MA; son of a corporate executive; married October, 1999; wife's name Anika. *Education:* Attended St. Lawrence University; Rhode Island School of Design, B.F.A. (illustration), 1990.

Addresses

Home—Providence, RI. *E-mail*—christopher@christopherdenise.com.

Career

Children's book illustrator. Designer of posters and greeting cards.

Member

Children's Book Council.

Writings

ILLUSTRATOR

Robert P. Denise, *Hiking the Colorado Trail: A Guide to Short and Long Hiking Trips along the Colorado Trail,* Lothlorien Press (Fort Collins, CO), 1993.

(And adapter) Petr Nikolaevich Polevoi, *The Fool of the World and the Flying Ship* (based on a Russian folktale), Philomel (New York, NY), 1994.

Brian Jacques, *The Great Redwall Feast,* Philomel (New York, NY), 1996.

Jane Yolen, *The Sea Man,* Philomel (New York, NY), 1997.

Susan Canizares, *Little Raccoon Catches a Cold,* Scholastic (New York, NY), 1998.

Caron Lee Cohen, *Digger Pig and the Turnip* ("Green Light Readers" series), Harcourt (San Diego, CA), 2000.

Lucy Floyd, *Rabbit and Turtle Go to School* ("Green Light Readers" series), Harcourt (New York, NY), 2000.

Brian Jacques, *A Redwall's Winter's Tale,* Philomel (New York, NY), 2001.

Phyllis Root, *Oliver Finds His Way,* Candlewick Press (Cambridge, MA), 2002.

Joy Cowley, *The Wishing of Biddy Malone,* Philomel (New York, NY), 2004.

Brian Jacques, *The Redwall Cookbook,* Philomel (New York, NY), 2005.

Anika Denise, *Pigs Love Potatoes,* Philomel (New York, NY), 2007.

Susan Milord, *If I Could: A Mother's Promise,* Candlewick Press (Cambridge, MA), 2008.

David Elliott, *Knitty Kitty,* Candlewick Press (Cambridge, MA), 2008.

Kristy Dempsey, *Me with You,* Philomel (New York, NY), 2009.

Contributor of illustrations to textbooks published by D.C. Heath and to Web sites and newspapers.

Works featuring Denise's illustrations have been translated into Spanish.

Sidelights

Christopher Denise began his illustrating career after graduating from the Rhode Island School of Design, starting in newspapers and quickly finding his way into children's book illustration. From his first published book, titled *Hiking the Colorado Trail,* Denise has gone on to contribute illustrations to books by several popular authors, among them Phyllis Root, Jane Yolen, and Brian Jacques. In addition, he has collaborated with his wife, Anika Denise, on the humorous counting book *Pigs Love Potatoes,* which features what *School Library Journal* contributor Maryann H. Owen described as "charming acrylic and charcoal pictures of a cozy household and a happy family." A *Kirkus Reviews* writer cited the "delightful details" in the artwork for the couple's collaborative effort, while in *Publishers Weekly* a critic cited the book's "main draw" Denise's "soft, smudged colors and . . . keen, loving eye for domestic detail."

Born in the United States, Denise grew up in New England and spent several years in Ireland as a youth, where his father was then working. Not inclined to sports, the

Christopher Denise contributes his detailed animal paintings to books such as Phyllis Root's **Oliver Finds His Way.** (Illustration copyright © 2002 by Christopher Denise. Reproduced by permission of the publisher Candlewick Press, Inc., Somerville, MA.)

young Denise developed an interest and talent in drawing. A degree from the prestigious Rhode Island School of Design came next, followed by a stint showing his portfolio to various New York publishers. Denise's artwork quickly caught the eye of an editor at Philomel, and he soon had a book contract.

Working primarily in oil pastel, charcoal, and pencil, Denise gravitates toward texts that feature animal characters. His first book of fiction, an adaptation of a Russian folktale titled *The Fool of the World and the Flying Ship,* is enlivened by the mice, rabbits, and badgers who, garbed in nineteenth-century Eastern-European folk costumes, inhabit the story of a simpleton who wins the hand of a princess by searching the world for a flying ship. Praising Denise's unique approach and his "lush," "luxurious palette," Denise Anton Wright noted in a *School Library Journal* review that *The Fool of the World and the Flying Ship* effectively showcases Denise's "considerable talent as an artist." Remarking favorably upon the story's "energetic cadence," a *Kirkus Reviews* critic also had praise for the picture book, noting in particular the author/illustrator's whimsical touch and "elegant, rather dark, and mysterious" artwork.

From his picture-book debut, Denise has gone on to become a popular illustrator of texts by an assortment of children's book writers. Brian Jacques' popular "Redwall" epic, which focuses on the animal inhabitants of Redwall Abbey, includes *The Great Redwall Feast* and

A Redwall Winter's Tale, both of which feature illustrations by Denise and are more geared toward younger readers than Jacques' adventure-filled "Redwall" novels. The novels and picture books feature series' characters Tubspike the hedgehog, Bulbrock Badger, and Matthais, the Warrior Mouse. Denise brings to life all the characters introduced in Jacques' rhyming picture-book text, drawing young listeners into a simple, rural world wherein animals are cared for by a kindly country abbot. In *Booklist,* Sally Estes commented that the "engaging" artwork by Denise brings life to "the ebullient characters and tumultuous preparations" recounted in *The Great Redwall Feast.* Also writing in *Booklist,* Kay Weisman claimed that "Denise's appealing, cozy illustrations perfectly capture the feel" of Jacques' text for *A Redwall Winter's Tale.* In another book in the series, *The Redwall Cookbook,* Denise makes his characteristic contribution to Jacques' text by creating what *School Library Journal* critic Joyce Adams Burner described as "gorgeously rendered and finely detailed" illustrations.

Other books featuring artwork by Denise include *Digger Pig and the Turnip,* Carol Lee Cohen's adaptation of "The Little Red Hen," which is enhanced by colored-pencil illustrations described by *Booklist* contributor Ilene Cooper as "old-fashioned yet jaunty." In *Oliver Finds His Way* by Phyllis Root, Denise "alternates close-up portraits with panoramic view to bring a fresh poignancy" to Root's story about a young bear cub who wanders too far from home while playing, according to a *Publishers Weekly* contributor. Using what *School Library Journal* contributor Kathleen Simonetta described as "a darker palette to bring home the scariness of the situation," both author and illustrator resolve the story of a lost child through a happy ending that will reassure young listeners. David Elliott's humorous *Knitty Kitty* is enlivened by Denise's "vibrant, old-school acrylic-and-ink pictures," according to one *Publishers Weekly* critic, while another reviewer wrote that the artist "harnesses firefly flashes of other-worldliness in his glowing, truly enchanting faerie scenes" for Joy Cowley's fanciful picture book *The Wishing of Biddy Malone.*

Biographical and Critical Sources

PERIODICALS

Booklist, April 1, 1994, Carolyn Phelan, review of *The Fool of the World and the Flying Ship,* p. 1453; October 15, 1996, Sally Estes, review of *The Great Redwall Feast,* p. 424; February 1, 2000, Ilene Cooper, review of *Digger Pig and the Turnip,* p. 1123; September 1, 2001, Kay Weisman, review of *A Redwall Winter's Tale,* p. 106; January 1, 2004, Carolyn Phelan, review of *The Wishing of Biddy Malone,* p. 872; June 1, 2007, Carolyn Phelan, review of *Pigs Love Potatoes,* p. 84; March 1, 2008, Jennifer Mattson, review of *If I Could: A Mother's Promise,* p. 73.

The books Denise has illustrated for popular fantasy writer Brian Jacques include the picture book **A Redwall Winter's Tale.** (Illustration copyright © 2001 by Christopher Denise. All rights reserved. Reproduced by permission of Puffin Books, a division of Penguin Putnam Books for Young Readers.)

Denise teams up with wife Anika Denise to create the humorous picture book **Pigs Love Potatoes.**

Kirkus Reviews, March 1, 1994, review of *The Fool of the World and the Flying Ship,* p. 302; June 1, 2007, review of *Pigs Love Potatoes;* August 1, 2008, review of *Knitty Kitty.*

Publishers Weekly, March 21, 1994, review of *The Fool of the World and the Flying Ship,* p. 71; July 4, 1994, "Flying Starts" (interview with Denise), pp. 36-41; August 19, 2002, review of *Oliver Finds His Way,* p. 87; January 5, 2004, review of *The Wishing of Biddy Malone,* p. 60; June 11, 2007, review of *Pigs Love Potatoes,* p. 58; March 24, 2008, review of *If I Could,* p. 69; June 30, 2008, review of *Knitty Kitty,* p. 183.

School Library Journal, June, 1994, Denise Anton Wright, *The Fool of the World and the Flying Ship,* p. 118; September, 2001, Susan L. Rogers, review of *A Redwall Winter's Tale,* p. 190; October, 2002, Kathleen Simonetta, review of *Oliver Finds His Way,* p. 126; March, 2004, Miriam Lang Budin, review of *The Wishing of Biddy Malone,* p. 155; January, 2006, Joyce Adams Burner, review of *The Redwall Cookbook,* p. 153; July, 2007, Maryann H. Owen, review of *Pigs Love Potatoes,* p. 74; May, 2008, Susan E. Murray, review of *If I Could,* p. 103.

ONLINE

Christopher Denise Home Page, http://www.christopherdenise.com (September 15, 2008).

Redwall Abbey: The Official Redwall Web Site, http://www.redwall.org/ (January 26, 2004), "Meet the Illustrator: Christopher Denise."*

*   *   *

DUBOSARSKY, Ursula 1961-

Personal

Born June 25, 1961, in Sydney, New South Wales, Australia; daughter of Peter (a writer and politician) and Verna (a writer) Coleman; married Avi Dubosarsky, December 17, 1987; children: Maisie, Dover, Bruno. *Education:* Sydney University, B.A. (with honors), 1982, Dip. Ed., 1989; Macquarie University, Ph.D., 2007.

Addresses

Home—Sydney, New South Wales, Australia. *E-mail*—dubosar@optusnet.com.au.

Career

Writer. Australian Public Service, Canberra, Australian Capital Territory, Australia, researcher, 1983-84; *Reader's Digest* magazine, Sydney, New South Wales, Australia, freelance researcher, 1986—. Formerly worked as a teacher of French.

Awards, Honors

Notable Book designation, Children's Book Council of Australia (CBCA), for *High Hopes, Zizzy Zing, Bruno and the Crumhorn,* and *Black Sails White Sails;* New South Wales commendation for Family Therapy Award,

1990, for *High Hopes;* CBCA Young Readers Award shortlist, 1994, for *The Last Week in December,* and 2001, for *The Game of the Goose;* New South Wales State Literary Award, and Victorian Premier's Award for Children's Literature, both 1994, and CBCA Award for Older Readers shortlist, 1995, all for *The White Guinea-Pig;* New South Wales State Ethnic Affairs Commission Award, 1995, and Royal Blind Society Talking Book Award shortlist, inclusion in United Nations White Raven library collection, and CBCA Honour Book designation, all 1996, all for *The First Book of Samuel;* Queensland Premier's Literary Award shortlist, 2001, for *The Game of the Goose,* and 2003, for *Abyssinia*; South Australian Festival Award for Literature (Young Adult), and Ethel Turner Prize shortlist, New South Wales Premier's Literary Awards, both 2004, both for *Abyssinia*; Ethel Turner Prize, and Victorian Premier's Literary Award, both 2006, both for *Theodora's Gift*; Queensland Premier's Award, 2006, White Ravens International Catalogue Honor Book citation, CBCA Book of the Year designation, and Ethel Turner Prize, all 2007, all for *The Red Shoe.*

Writings

Maisie and the Pinny Gig, illustrated by Roberta Landers, Macmillan (South Melbourne, Victoria, Australia), 1989.

High Hopes, Penguin (New York, NY), 1990.

Zizzy Zing, Angus & Robertson (North Ryde, New South Wales, Australia), 1991.

The Last Week in December, Puffin (Ringwood, Victoria, Australia), 1993.

The White Guinea-Pig, Viking (Ringwood, Victoria, Australia), 1994, Viking (New York, NY), 1995.

The First Book of Samuel, Viking (New York, NY), 1995.

Bruno and the Crumhorn, Viking (Ringwood, Victoria, Australia), 1996.

Black Sails White Sails, Penguin (Ringwood, Victoria, Australia), 1997.

The Strange Adventures of Isador Brown ("Aussie Bites" series), illustrated by Paty Marshall-Stace, Puffin (Ringwood, Victoria, Australia), 1998.

Honey and Bear, illustrated by Ron Brooks, Viking (Ringwood, Victoria, Australia), 1998.

My Father Is Not a Comedian!, Puffin (Ringwood, Victoria, Australia), 1999.

The Game of the Goose, illustrated by John Winch, Penguin (Ringwood, Victoria, Australia), 2000.

The Even Stranger Adventures of Isador Brown ("Aussie Bites" series), illustrated by Paty Marshall-Stace, Puffin (Ringwood, Victoria, Australia), 2000.

The Two Gorillas ("Aussie Nibbles" series), illustrated by Mitch Vane, Puffin (Ringwood, Victoria, Australia), 2001.

Fairy Bread ("Aussie Nibbles" series), Puffin (Ringwood, Victoria, Australia), 2001.

The Magic Wand, Puffin (Camberwell, Victoria, Australia), 2002.

Special Days with Honey and Bear, illustrated by Ron Brooks, Puffin (Camberwell, Victoria, Australia), 2002.

Abyssinia, Viking (Ringwood, Victoria, Australia), 2003.

Isador Brown's Strangest Adventures of All, illustrated by Mitch Vane, Puffin (Camberwell, Victoria, Australia), 2003.

How to Be a Great Detective, Puffin (Camberwell, Victoria, Australia), 2004.

Theodora's Gift, Penguin (Camberwell, Victoria, Australia), 2005.

Rex, illustrated by David Mackintosh, Roaring Brook Press (New Milford, CT), 2005.

The Red Shoe, Allen & Unwin (Crows Nest, New South Wales, Australia), 2006, Roaring Brook Press (New Milford, CT), 2007.

The Puppet Show, illustrated by Mitch Vane, Puffin (Camberwell, Victoria, Australia), 2006.

The Word Spy: Come and Discover the Secrets of the English Language, illustrated by Tohby Riddle, Penguin (Camberwell, Victoria, Australia), 2008.

Jerry, illustrated by Patricia Mullins, Puffin (Camberwell, Victoria, Australia), 2008.

Sidelights

Australian author Ursula Dubosarsky is noted for penning young-adult novels that, while sometimes humorous, also reveal a dark side. In award-winning books such as *Zizzy Zing, High Hopes, The White Guinea-Pig, The First Book of Samuel,* and *Black Sails White Sails,* she introduces readers to vivid characters who are involved in closely wrought incidents. Gaining in popularity even among U.S. readers who are sometimes unfamiliar with the "Australianisms" scattered throughout her books, Dubosarsky has continued to reveal her talent as a writer through both her compelling protagonists and her use of language. Noting that she "writes with extraordinary clarity and simplicity," *Viewpoint* contributor Robyn Sheahan-Bright added that Dubosarsky's books "are timeless . . . and ageless in their appeal." Moreover, the critic added, the Australian author "loves to empathize with children. She gives us their angst and their fearlessness; their poignant attempts to understand the frailties of adults who act in ways which are impenetrable to them." Difficult to classify by genre, according to Sheahan-Bright, Dubosarsky's stories "are enigmatic and original and boundaries definitely don't suit them."

Born in Sydney, New South Wales, Australia, Dubosarsky was raised by parents who were both writers, and as a child she enjoyed books by Maurice Sendak, Enid Blyton, and other imaginative authors. Graduating from Sydney University in 1982, she spent two years in Canberra as a researcher for the Australian Public Service while writing in the evenings. She lived for a year on an Israeli kibbutz where she met her Argentine-born husband. Returning to Sydney in 1986, Dubosarsky worked as a researcher for *Reader's Digest,* married, and began raising her three children.

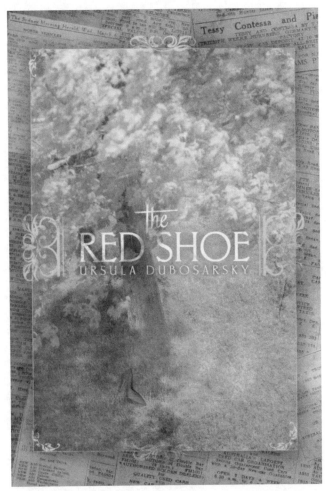

Cover of Ursula Dubosarsky's cold-war-era novel **The Red Shoe,** *a story set in Australia during the mid-1950s.* (Roaring Brook Press, 2006. Tree photo copyright © by Corbis. All rights reserved. Reprinted by permission of Henry Holt & Company, LLC.)

Dubosarsky's first published picture book, *Maisie and the Pinny Gig,* tells the story of a young girl and her imaginary friend, Pinny Gig. Also for young readers are several books in the "Aussie Bites" series of beginning readers, among them *The Strange Adventures of Isador Brown* and its sequels, *The Even Stranger Adventures of Isador Brown* and *Isador Brown's Strangest Adventures of All.* Part of the "Aussie Nibbles" series of readers, Dubosarsky's *The Two Gorillas* is a "highly entertaining" story about how a pair of stuffed gorillas are treated by their rambunctious owner, according to *Magpies* reviewer Debbie Mulligan.

In *Rex,* another title designed for young readers, Dubosarsky chronicles the adventures of Rex, the chameleon class pet, as he goes home with each student. As the classmates take care of Rex in turn, each chronicles his or her adventures, and the pictures that accompany the student's words are drawn in a childlike style. Rather than just staying at the student's home, the chameleon is often taken to movies or restaurants; in one case, he is dressed up to play with a little girl's Barbie dolls. Through the children's imaginations, Rex is transformed from a humble chameleon to a powerful dino-

saur. "Dubosarsky writes open-ended comments and questions that leave Rex's true nature up to the reader," noted a contributor to *Publishers Weekly.* Noting the short phrases the author uses to describe the experiences of the story's young characters, Randall Enos concluded in *Booklist* that in *Rex* Dubosarsky's "text clearly reflects a child's point of view."

High Hopes is one of many novels Dubosarsky has written for older readers. The novel focuses on twelve-year-old Julia. The preteen's concern over her widowed father's new girlfriend leads her to bake a "poisoned" cake—one with an entire bottle of vanilla in it—in an effort to derail the romance. Although her harmless plot fails, Julia eventually accepts her father's need for companionship and reconciles herself to the addition of a stepmother to the family. Reviewing *High Hopes* for *Voice of Youth Advocates,* Andrea Davidson deemed it a "funny, offbeat novel about growing up, remarriage, and family ups and downs," praising in particular Dubosarsky's "very skillful writing." In *Horn Book* Ellen Fader described the novel as "breezy" and "with realistic underpinnings that will please fans of contemporary fiction," while Adrian Jackson concluded his assessment of *High Hopes* in *Books for Keeps* by praising the author's "lovely confidence in the story telling" and her "clever blending of the comic and serious."

The mysterious letter at the heart of Dubosarsky's *Zizzy Zing* leads young Phyllis back in time to 1938 and into the most horrifying summer of her life. Dubosarsky cut her teeth on this mystery novel, which she wrote years before the publication of her first two books. As she worked on the book, Dubosarsky knew only that she wanted to create a murder mystery where the child was the detective; what she ended up with was perhaps a bit more of a ghost story than mystery, teaching her that the best stories are sometimes as much a surprise to the writer as they are to the reader.

Abyssinia, like *Zizzy Zing,* is a mystery novel that involves time shifting. In the story, sisters Mary and Grace live in rural Australia, where a dollhouse is one of their few playthings. As Dubosarsky's story unfolds, readers learn that there is a strange connection between the stories the girls concoct for their dolls and their own lives, a connection that becomes alarmingly clear when one of the girls disappears.

Written in the third person, *The White Guinea-Pig* introduces Geraldine, who while reluctantly taking care of her friend's guinea pig for six weeks, finds her life suddenly falling apart. Her bankrupt father is selling their house; her older sister is emotionally crumbling under relationship problems; and her cute neighbor, Ezra, appears to be guarding an awful secret. *Booklist* contributor Chris Sherman felt that the "surreal quality" of the novel "sets it apart from the usual crop of middle-school problem novels about families," while Deborah Stevenson, writing in the *Bulletin of the Center for Children's Books,* noted that with *The White Guinea-*

Pig Dubosarsky creates "a story of humor and notable eccentricity" that is sure to be appreciated by "readers with particularly offbeat literary tastes."

The First Book of Samuel is inspired by the Biblical story of Samuel. In it, the main character disappears on his twelfth birthday, leaving family members trying to piece together his life using the scraps of information available to them. Reviewing the novel for *Magpies,* Jo Goodman observed that "every word, every nuance is carefully judged." *Bruno and the Crumhorn,* another middle-grade novel by Dubosarsky, is about a boy taking lessons on the crumhorn, a musical instrument dating back to the fourteenth century that has an embarrassing honking sound. Val Randall, writing in *Books for Keeps,* called *Bruno and the Crumhorn* "a whimsical story peopled with eccentric characters," then went on to note that the "narrative has a dry, whacky humour." Reviewing that same novel in *Magpies,* Anne Hanzl called *Bruno and the Crumhorn* "a 'hoot' of a story full of sly humour, and interesting, quirky characters."

In *My Father Is Not a Comedian!* Dubosarsky showcases her humorous take on adult life from a nine year old's point of view. In the first-person novel, Claudie is determined to waste no time in beginning her literary career and she decides to start by writing about her family and friends. Her disgruntlement at not having her story about a singing cactus acknowledged by a literary magazine—as well as her slightly off-kilter interpretations of adult activities—fuels the novel's subtle humor, according to *Australian Book Review* contributor Ruthe Starke. Starke called Claudie "a keen but tolerant observer" and cited *My Father Is Not a Comedian!* as proof that Dubosarsky "is one of the funniest writers around." In *Magpies,* Joan Zahnleiter offered a similar opinion, writing that the dramatic Claudie, the ostensible author of the book, "knows how to hold her audience, with tantalising chapter headings and hooks in the ends of chapters. . . . She is quite a character."

Rather than using time travel to bring her readers into the past, Dubosarsky wrote her award-winning novel *The Red Shoe* as straight historical fiction. Set in 1954, the novel describes the lives of three sisters: fifteen-year-old Elizabeth, eleven-year-old Frances, and six-year-old Matilda. Told in the third person, the text focuses on Matilda's perspective, particularly the little girl's fantasies about the mysterious neighbors living in the large house next door. When Matilda makes a connection between a newsreel she sees about a Russian diplomat who defected to Australia and her neighbors, she tells another neighbor that they are surrounded by spies. *The Red Shoe* includes excerpts from actual 1954 newspaper articles, giving readers a deeper picture into time and place. Calling the novel "honest" and "poignant," a critic for *Publishers Weekly* added that "Dubosarsky proves masterful in conjuring and connecting images" such as that surrounding the titular red shoes. Deirdre F. Baker, writing in *Horn Book,* noted that the

narrative tells three different coming-of-age stories simultaneously, "evoking the concerns and sensibilities of each with affection, humor, and insight."

Although most of Dubosarsky's stories take many months to make it from idea to finished manuscript, there are notable exceptions. She once described the process of writing her book *Honey and Bear* to *SATA:* "I was suffering a great deal from sleeplessness. One night lying there staring at the dark feeling rather desperate, the very first story of *Honey and Bear,* which is called 'Good Idea, Bad Idea,' came into my head, word for word, virtually as it appears on the page today. It was as though the characters of Honey the bird and Bear the bear and their life together dropped down from heaven, in just the right voice. In fact, all five of the little stories in Honey and Bear came to me that very night. Then, at last, feeling both very excited and content, I fell asleep.

"When I woke up, I remembered my nocturnal visitors, and I was both happy and nervous—altogether too nervous to rush to the word processor to write them down! What if they were no good? I walked around for several days keeping the stories a secret in my head, like someone who has witnessed something strange and is in two minds about telling anyone about it. Finally, about a week later, I sat down and typed the stories out. Wonderful to relate, I seemed to have remembered them all—every word.

"I had never had what you might call a creative experience quite like that—one that came like something given, and brought its creator so much pleasure in the process. . . . For me, the book feels like a blessing; writing it was one of those experiences which . . . comes to a writer perhaps once in a lifetime. And I am so grateful for it."

Biographical and Critical Sources

BOOKS

St. James Guide to Young-Adult Writers, 2nd edition, St. James Press (Detroit, MI), 1999.

PERIODICALS

Australian Book Review, September, 1999, Ruth Starke, review of *My Father Is Not a Comedian!,* pp. 42-43.
Booklist, August, 1991, Mary Romano Marks, review of *High Hopes,* pp. 2146-2147; July, 1995, Chris Sherman, review of *The White Guinea-Pig,* p. 1878; November 15, 2006, Randall Enos, review of *Rex,* p. 52.
Books for Keeps, May, 1991, Adrian Jackson, review of *High Hopes,* pp. 14-15; September, 1996, Val Randall, review of *Bruno and the Crumhorn,* p. 16.
Bulletin of the Center for Children's Books, June, 1995, Deborah Stevenson, review of *The White Guinea-Pig,* p. 107.

Economist, November 26, 1994, review of *The White Guinea-Pig,* p. 102.

Horn Book, September-October, 1991, Ellen Fader, review of *High Hopes,* p. 596; May-June, 2007, Deirdre F. Baker, review of *The Red Shoes,* p. 281.

Kirkus Reviews, August 1, 2006, review of *Rex,* p. 784; May 1, 2007, review of *The Red Shoe.*

Magpies, July, 1993, Robyn Sheahan, review of *The Last Week in December,* p. 34; May, 1995, Jo Goodman, review of *The First Book of Samuel,* p. 32; May, 1996, Anne Hanzl, review of *Bruno and the Crumhorn,* p. 42; July, 1999, Joan Zahnleiter, review of *My Father Is Not a Comedian!,* p. 33; March, 2001, Debbie Mulligan, review of *The Even Stranger Adventures of Isador Brown* and *The Two Gorillas,* p. 29; May, 2002, review of *Special Days with Honey and Bear,* p. 28; September, 2002, review of *The Magic Wand,* p. 30; May, 2003, review of *Abyssinia,* p. 16; March, 2008, Lyn Linning, review of *The Word Spy: Come and Discover the Secrets of the English Language,* p. 34.

Observer (London, England), November 20, 1994, review of *The White Guinea-Pig,* p. 12.

Publishers Weekly, September 11, 2006, review of *Rex,* p. 54; March 26, 2007, review of *The Red Shoe,* p. 94.

School Librarian, spring, 2007, Lucinda Jacob, review of *The Magic Wand,* p. 18.

School Library Journal, September, 2006, Grace Oliff, review of *Rex,* p. 171; June, 2007, Suzanne Gordon, review of *The Red Shoe,* p. 142.

Viewpoint, summer, 2000, Robyn Sheahan-Bright, review of *The Game of the Goose.*

Voice of Youth Advocates, October, 1991, Andrea Davidson, review of *High Hopes,* p. 226.

ONLINE

Achuka Web site, http://www.achuka.co.uk/ (September 28, 2008), interview with Dubosarsky.

Penguin Australia Web site, http://www.penguin.com.au/ (September 28, 2008), "Ursula Dubosarsky."

Ursula Dubosarsky Home Page, http://www.ursuladubosarsky.com (September 28, 2008).*

E-G

ENGLE, Margarita 1951-

Personal

Born September 2, 1951, in Pasadena, CA; daughter of Martin (an artist) and Eloisa (a quilter) Mondrus; married Curtis E. Engle (a research biologist), 1978; children: Victor, Nicole. *Ethnicity:* "Cuban-American" *Education:* California State Polytechnic University, B.S., 1974; Iowa State University, M.S., 1977; doctoral study at University of California, Riverside, 1983. *Politics:* "Human rights advocate." *Religion:* Christian. *Hobbies and other interests:* Horsemanship, western equitation, trail riding.

Addresses

Agent—Julie Castiglia, 1155 Camino Del Mar, Ste. 510, Del Mar, CA 92014.

Career

Botanist, poet, novelist, and journalist. California State Polytechnic University, Pomona, associate professor of agronomy, 1978-82.

Member

Pen USA West, Amnesty International, Freedom House of Human Rights, Freedom to Write Committee.

Awards, Honors

CINTAS fellow, Arts International, 1994-95; San Diego Book Award, 1996, for *Skywriting;* Willow Review Poetry Award, 2005; Americas Award, Consortium of Latin American Studies Programs, 2007, Pura Belpré Award, American Library Association, 2008, and International Reading Association Children's Book Award and Teachers' Choice award, all for *The Poet Slave of Cuba.*

Writings

Singing to Cuba (adult novel), Arte Público Press (Houston, TX), 1993.

Skywriting: A Novel of Cuba (adult novel), Bantam (New York, NY), 1995.

The Poet Slave of Cuba: A Biography of Juan Francisco Manzano (nonfiction for children), illustrated by Sean Qualls, Henry Holt (New York, NY), 2006.

The Surrender Tree: Poems of Cuba's Struggle for Freedom (for young adults), Henry Holt (New York, NY), 2008.

Tropical Secrets: Holocaust Refugees in Cuba, Henry Holt (New York, NY), 2009.

Contributor to periodicals, including *Atlanta Review, Bilingual Review, California Quarterly, Caribbean Writer, Hawai'i Pacific Review,* and *Nimrod.*

Sidelights

The author of adult novels as well as books for young readers, Cuban-American writer Margarita Engle fell in love with reading and writing as a young child. While growing up, her mother instilled her with a love for Cuba, telling the young Engle many stories of her homeland. Despite Engle's love of stories and poetry, she decided to go to school to study agronomy and botany, a form of rebellion as well as a way to connect with the wilderness she had been missing while growing up in Los Angeles. She became a professor of agronomy and married Curtis Engle, an agricultural entomologist. While raising her two children, she revisited her love of writing, submitting her haiku and having it published, as well as writing editorial columns for news organizations. After a trip to Cuba in 1991, thirty years after she had last visited as a child, Engle was inspired to write two adult novels about Cuba: *Singing to Cuba* and *Skywriting: A Novel of Cuba.*

While traveling in Cuba, Engle learned the story of Juan Franciso Manzano, a Cuban slave who became a well-known poet. She struggled for years to write a historical novel about Manzano, but the words never came. Eventually, she changed directions, writing a biography of Manzano in the form of poetry. A *Kirkus Reviews* contributor called *The Poet Slave of Cuba: A Biography of Juan Francisco Manzano,* which won the Americas

Margarita Engle contributes folk-style art to Sean Qualls' picture-book biography **The Poet Slave of Cuba.** (Illustration © 2006 by Sean Qualls. Reprinted by permission of Henry Holt & Company, LLC.)

Award and the Pura Belpré Award, a "powerful and accessible biography." Engle "achieves an impressive synergy between poetry and biography," wrote a critic for *Publishers Weekly.* Commenting on Engle's depiction of Manzano telling himself stories while being beaten by his owners, Hazel Rochman wrote in *Booklist* that "today's readers will hear the stories . . . and never forget them," while in *School Library Journal* Carol Jones Collins concluded that *The Poet Slave of Cuba* "should be read by young and old, black and white, Anglo and Latino."

Like *The Poet Slave of Cuba, The Surrender Tree* is a story told in poetry that focuses on the life of a Cuban slave. Rosa la Bayamesa was born into slavery, but after she was freed by her owner she became a rebel, fighting for Cuban independence from Spain. She worked as a nurse, healing the wounded on both sides of the conflict. "*The Surrender Tree* is hauntingly beautiful, revealing pieces of Cuba's troubled past through the poetry of hidden moments," wrote Jill Heritage Maza in *School Library Journal,* commenting on the small details in Engle's poetry that illuminate the larger story. Jane Lopez-Santillana, writing in *Horn Book,* called Engle's poetry "haunting," and a *Kirkus Reviews* contributor concluded that "young readers will come away inspired by these portraits of courageous ordinary people."

Engle once noted: "I write to express my hopes, passions, fears, and beliefs. I write to communicate, explore, and understand. Usually I am haunted by a theme, or by characters, a setting, or events. Until I have experimented with them, I do not understand them clearly. I go through a slow process of trial and error, false starts, wrong turns, and humbling misjudgments. For every one hundred publishable pages, I have discarded perhaps a thousand pages of 'error.' The process is emotionally exhausting, but I know I am always striving to be honest about the general themes of freedom and faith, and about specific tales of the search for freedoms, both personal and political. I have been deeply influenced by the suffering of my relatives in Cuba and by my love for the island, despite its desperation."

Biographical and Critical Sources

PERIODICALS

Booklist, February 15, 2006, Hazel Rochman, review of *The Poet Slave of Cuba: A Biography of Juan Francisco Manzano,* p. 95; March 15, 2008, Hazel Rochman, review of *The Surrender Tree: Poems of Cuba's Struggle for Freedom,* p. 53.

Fresno Bee (Fresno, CA), February 18, 2008, Felicia Cousart Matlosz, "Paying Homage to a Poet."

Horn Book, July-August, 2006, Lelac Almagor, review of *The Poet Slave of Cuba,* p. 459; July-August, 2008, Jane Lopez-Santillana, review of *The Surrender Tree,* p. 465.

Kirkus Reviews, March 15, 2006, review of *The Poet Slave of Cuba,* p. 289; March 15, 2008, review of *The Surrender Tree.*

MELUS, spring, 1998, Gisele M. Requeña, "The Sounds of Silence: Remembering and Creating in Margarita Engle's *Singing to Cuba,* p. 147.

Publishers Weekly, June 5, 1995, review of *Skywriting,* p. 52; April 17, 2006, review of *The Poet Slave of Cuba,* p. 190.

School Library Journal, April, 2006, Carol Jones Collins, review of *The Poet Slave of Cuba,* p. 154; June, 2008, Jill Heritage Maza, review of *The Surrender Tree,* p. 158.

ONLINE

Macmillan Web site, http://us.macmillan.com/ (October 2, 2008), "Margarita Engle."

Poet Seers Web site, http://www.poetseers.org/ (October 2, 2008), Margarita Engle, "Layers of Time."*

*   *   *

ERSKINE, Kathryn

Personal

Born in the Netherlands; married; children: one daughter. *Hobbies and other interests:* Traveling, exploring, walking, spending time with family and friends, playing games, fencing.

Addresses

Home and office—VA. *E-mail*—Kathryn@kathrynerskine.com.

Career

Writer. Formerly worked as an attorney.

Member

Society of Children's Book Writers and Illustrators.

Awards, Honors

Best Books for Young Adults selection, and Quick Picks for Reluctant Readers selection, both American Library Association, both 2008, both for *Quaking*.

Writings

Quaking (novel), Philomel Books (New York, NY), 2007.

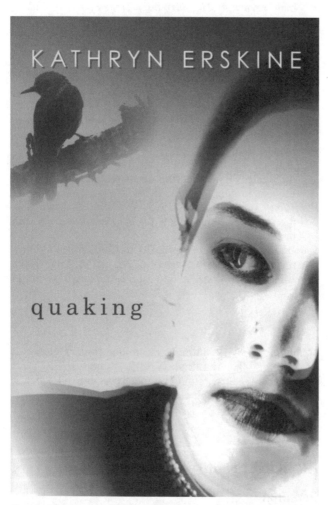

Cover of Kathryn Erskine's young-adult novel Quaking, *in which a foster teen is introduced to the Quaker faith and begins to examine her moral beliefs.* (Philomel Books, 2007. Cover photo of bird copyright © by Getty Images. Cover photo of girl copyright © by Lawrence Manning/Corbis. Reproduced by permission of Philomel Books, a division of Penguin Putnam Books for Young Readers.)

Adaptations

Quaking was adapted as an audio book.

Sidelights

Kathryn Erskine's critically acclaimed debut novel, *Quaking,* examines themes of patriotism, idealism, and faith. Set against the backdrop of the War in Iraq, Erskine's story centers on fourteen-year-old Matilda (known as Matt), a suspicious, withdrawn girl who has been shuttled from one foster home to another since being taken from her abusive father years earlier. "I was concerned about why we were in Iraq and how people respond to war and violence in general," Erskine related in an interview on the *Jessica M. Burkhart* Web log. "That's why I didn't make [*Quaking*] . . . Iraq-specific, but it obviously speaks to our current situation. I also wanted to relate the issue of violence in war to a more personal level. Matt is going through her own post-traumatic stress syndrome. War or violence in any form has powerful effects on individuals and society."

When Matt is sent to live with Sam and Jessica Fox, a Quaker couple raising a disabled young boy, she slowly finds herself drawn to their pacifist beliefs. Matt's adjustment to her new life is complicated, however, by her encounters with a staunchly pro-war civics teacher and a school bully, and she grows concerned about her foster parents when the local churches are vandalized by protesters. Erksine "enfolds the political issues into a deeper focus on the characters' personal stories," noted Francisca Goldsmith in *Booklist,* and Janis Flint-Ferguson, writing in *Kliatt,* stated that *Quaking* "gives a balanced look at the ramifications of violent actions, both on a personal and a national level." In a *TeensReadToo.com* interview with Jennifer Wardrip, Erskine described *Quaking* as "a story of finding peace, no matter where you've been or where you're going."

Biographical and Critical Sources

PERIODICALS

Booklist, May 1, 2007, Francisca Goldsmith, review of *Quaking,* p. 82.
Horn Book, July-August, 2007, Lauren Adams, review of *Quaking,* p. 393.
Kirkus Reviews, July 1, 2007, review of *Quaking.*
Kliatt, July, 2007, Janis Flint-Ferguson, review of *Quaking,* p. 14.
Publishers Weekly, June 4, 2007, review of *Quaking,* p. 50.
School Library Journal, July, 2007, Kathleen Isaacs, review of *Quaking,* p. 101.

ONLINE

Jessica M. Burkhart Web log, http://jessicaburkhart.blogspot.com/ (February 22, 2008), "Author Visit: Kathryn Erskine."

Kathryn Erskine Home Page, http://www.kathrynerskine. com (August 10, 2008).

Kathryn Erskine Web log, http://kathyerskine.blogspot.com (August 10, 2008).

TeensReadToo, http://teensreadtoo.com/ (August 10, 2008), Jennifer Wardrip, interview with Erskine.*

*   *   *

GRIFFIN, Peni R. 1961-
(Peni Rae Robinson Griffin)

Personal

Born July 11, 1961, in Harlingin, TX; daughter of William Jay (retired Air Force) and Sandra Sue (a Methodist lay pastor) Robinson; married Michael David Griffin (a programmer for Bexar county), July 13, 1987; stepchildren: Morgan Leigh. *Education:* Attended Trinity University, 1979-80, and University of Texas at San Antonio, 1982-84. *Politics:* "All systems fail eventually, and ours is going." *Religion:* "Agnostic." *Hobbies and other interests:* "Exploring the Net with a 'Computer Gothic' in view; always reading history, archaeology, mysteries; gardening."

Addresses

Home and office—1123 W. Magnolia Ave., San Antonio, TX 78201.

Career

Writer. City Public Service, San Antonio, TX, clerk, 1985-89; Manpower Temporary Services, San Antonio, temporary worker, 1990; ASCO, production assistant, 1991-95; Eckmann, Groll, Runyan & Waters, Inc., word processor, 1996—.

Member

Society of Children's Book Writers and Illustrators, Science Fiction Writers of America.

Awards, Honors

Third place, *Twilight Zone* magazine writing contest, 1986, for "Nereid"; second place, National Society for Arts and Letters (San Antonio branch) short story contest, 1988, for "The Truth in the Case of Eliza Mary Muller, by Herself"; Edgar Allen Poe Award nominee, Mystery Writers of America, 1993, for *The Treasure Bird;* Best Western Juvenile Fiction Award finalist, Golden Spur Awards, 1993, for *The Switching Well; The Ghost Sitter* Edgar Award nomination, Anthony Award nomination, and William Allen White Award, all 2004, all for *The Ghost Sitter.*

Writings

FOR YOUNG PEOPLE

Otto from Otherwhere (fantasy), McElderry/Macmillan (New York, NY), 1990.

Peni R. Griffin (Photograph by Michael D. Griffin. Reproduced by permission.)

A Dig in Time (fantasy), McElderry/Macmillan (New York, NY), 1991.

Hobkin (fantasy), McElderry/Macmillan (New York, NY), 1992.

The Treasure Bird (mystery), McElderry/Macmillan (New York, NY), 1992.

The Switching Well (fantasy), McElderry/Macmillan (New York, NY), 1993.

The Brick House Burglars (mystery), McElderry/ Macmillan (New York, NY), 1994.

The Maze (fantasy), Margaret K. McElderry (New York, NY), 1994.

Vikki Vanishes (mystery), Margaret K. McElderry (New York, NY), 1995.

Margo's House (fantasy), Margaret K. McElderry (New York, NY), 1996.

The Ghost Sitter, Dutton (New York, NY), 2001.

The Music Thief, Holt (New York, NY), 2002.

11,000 Years Lost (fantasy), Amulet (New York, NY), 2004.

Author's works have been translated into Italian.

OTHER

Contributor to magazines, including *Dragon, Fantasy Macabre, Figment, Isaac Asimov's Science Fiction Magazine, Leading Edge, Magazine of Fantasy and Science Fiction, Pandora, Pulphouse, Realms of Fantasy, Space and Time,* and *Twilight Zone.* Cntributor to *Stay True: Short Stories for Strong Girls,* edited by Marilyn Singer, Scholastic, 1998.

Sidelights

Peni R. Griffin, who writes fantasy and mystery novels for young people, gained a reputation for her work by the publication of her fourth book. "Communication—singing and speaking—is important in Griffin's novels," wrote a *Kirkus Reviews* critic in a review of *The Treasure Bird,* a juvenile novel published in 1992. In another review of the same book, Deborah Stevenson wrote in the *Bulletin of the Center for Children's Books* that "Griffin's Texas settings are always atmospheric." Carolyn Cushman, writing in *Locus,* concluded in a review of the work that Griffin "has a knack" for "giving . . . [an] otherworldly twist" to the concerns of preteens.

Griffin once told *SATA* that writing comes naturally to her. "I have been absorbing stories through my skin since the hour I was born," she explained, "and an untold story is only half a story. Being an Air Force brat helped. Crossing the broad, apparently empty landscape of Mid-America, my brain had plenty of leisure to absorb and get to work on the implied stories of the houses, the landmark names, and the historical markers

Cover of Griffin's middle-grade mystery The Treasure Bird, *featuring artwork by Scott Gladden.* (Illustration copyright © 1994 by Scott Gladden. Reproduced by permission of Puffin, a division of Penguin Putnam, Inc.)

we passed. Arriving at a new town, it was easier to infiltrate the world of a new library than of a new school. Books don't reject you, don't let you down, and they make the world so much broader than the scope of one little life. Louisa May Alcott never lied to me. Anne Frank died, but the diary preserved her alive. Words were Helen Keller's road out of lonely, silent darkness."

Griffin attended college in Texas and began to write, working day jobs only when necessary. She came up with the idea for her first book, *Otto from Otherwhere,* when her husband told her about a lake covered with fog, that "looked as if you could walk out across it into another world. I knew at once what people in that other world looked like." *Otto from Otherwhere* begins as ten-year-old Ahto is leading the family sheep home. He gets lost in a bank of mist and steps into the world we know. There, Paula and her brother, riding to school, are also encountering fog. The children run into, and then befriend Ahto, whom they call Otto, and he very quickly learns to speak English (with a southern accent). Claiming that Otto is a cousin from Brazil, Paula takes him to school. Because he looks different, with holes for his nose and ears, and has no hair or pinkies, the children avoid him. Meanwhile, Otto grows lonely for his old world, replete with music. After the school's music teacher discovers Otto's beautiful voice, the children begin to change their minds about him.

Griffin's "*E.T.*-style plot is likely to ensnare readers," predicted Barbara Elleman in a *Booklist* review of *Otto from Otherwhere.* While many critics noted the theme of accepting others for who they are, not what they look like, Annette Curtis Klause commented in *School Library Journal* that "readers are not beaten over the head with the theme," while Stevenson described the book as "a cozy and wish-fulfilling venture into science fantasy."

Griffin's second book "came bursting out of my head in about six months. . . . The idea of two children having an archaeological dig in their back yard and literally digging up the past took hold of me and made me write it." *A Dig in Time* is set in contemporary times where twelve-year-old Nan and her brother Tim live with their grandmother in San Antonio while their parents are out of the country on an archaeological dig. When the children decide to work on their own dig in the backyard and find their grandfather's pipe, Tim utters a poem that magically transports them through time to the moment of their grandfather's death. Nan and Tim then travel to other important and meaningful moments in family history, including their parents' wedding. They explain their activities to their parents upon their return, and, with their mother, take one last trip through time. A *Kirkus Reviews* critic described Griffin as a "powerful storyteller" and asserted that "few illustrate the continuity of place and family so well" in stories about time travel. Roger Sutton concluded in the *Bulletin of the*

Cover of Griffin's Switching Well, *a spine-tingling mystery featuring cover art by Scott Gladden.* (Illustration copyright © 1994 by Scott Gladden. Reproduced by permission of Puffin, a division of Penguin Putnam Inc.)

Center for Children's Books that *A Dig in Time* "would be a good introduction for those readers put off by the more arcane reaches of the genre."

Hobkin begins as two girls—bearing names changed to Kay and Liza—are running away from their abusive stepfather. Although the younger sister, Liza, does not know it, the abuse Kay has suffered has been sexual, and Kay wants to protect Liza. When the sisters find an abandoned house, they tell those they meet that it belongs to a relative and they make it their home. Kay finds a job in the West Texas town, and Liza stays home to cook and clean (a difficult task in a place without running water or heat). It is not long until a brownie, Hobkin, makes himself known to Liza and helps her work in different ways. As readers learn, Hobkin followed a woman from England years ago to the house. By the end of the story, the brownie is finally released to make his own way in the world, and the girls' mother comes to live with them.

"Kay and Liza are fully realized, by turns resourceful or frightened," wrote a *Kirkus Reviews* critic in a re-

view of *Hobkin.* According to Zena Sutherland, writing in the *Bulletin of the Center for Children's Books,* the fantasy of Hobkin and the story of the girls' lives works: "It's the seamless blending that is impressive." As Edith S. Tyson observed in her review of the novel for the *Voice of Youth Advocates,* Griffin's "mixture of stark realism with fantasy may remind some people of some of the books of Madeleine L'Engle," and *Booklist* critic Deborah Abbott commented that *Hobkin* "offers an interesting variation on the survival theme."

Vikki Vanishes is another of Griffin's books that treats serious young-adult issues, but this one adds mystery. Sixteen-year-old Vikki and her nine-year-old half-sister Nikki have lived their lives without their respective fathers. Now, when Vikki's father reappears and takes her for a ride, Nikki is jealous. Then the man attempts to abuse his daughter, prompting Vikki to disappear. Nikki is the only one who has some idea what has happened to Vikki, but the adults ignore her. According to a *Kirkus Reviews* critic, *Vikki Vanishes* is "tightly written" and builds "dramatic tension until the girls are reunited." Although Anne O'Malley wrote in *Booklist* that Griffin's novel suffers from less than fully fleshed-out characters, she considered *Vikki Vanishes* "a well-plotted, tension-mounting survival story with a satisfying conclusion."

Fantasy works to the advantage of another girl with a serious problem in *Margo's House.* The father in this novel is near death when, magically, his spirit and his daughter Margo's make their way into Sis and Butch, two dolls he made for Margo. Margo and her father, as Sis and Butch, move in creaky doll bodies from the handmade doll house and through the large family house, dodging the family's scary pet cat to save Margo's father.

Maintaining a beloved home is difficult in *The Treasure Bird.* In this mystery by Griffin, when Jessy and her family move to a house in Texas, they are uncertain that they will be able to pay the taxes on the house. Jessy and her stepbrother, along with a parrot, search for a hidden treasure by piecing together a message found in some inherited samplers. According to Renee Steinberg in *School Library Journal, The Treasure Bird* "deals with loyalty, trust, love, and family" as well as treasure.

The Brick House Burglars, another of Griffin's mysteries, is "full of excitement," according to *School Library Journal* contributor Suzanne Hawley. Four adolescent girls set up a club, and, in the process of protecting their meeting place in San Antonio, foil the plans of criminals. A *Kirkus Reviews* critic found that Griffin provides "some realities of urban living" in her novel, and Hazel Rochman noted in *Booklist* that the author's "lively voice . . . captures the immediacy of the community in all its rich diversity."

One of Griffin's books treats historical San Antonio as well as the contemporary city. *Switching Well* is the

Cover of Griffin's middle-grade mystery novel The Ghost Sitter, *featuring artwork by Rob Wood.* (Illustration copyright © 2001 by Rob Wood. Reproduced by permission of Puffin Books, a division of Penguin Putnam Books for Young Readers.)

story of two girls—one living in 1891 and one living in 1991—who wish themselves into the past and future. As a *Kirkus Reviews* critic noted, the girls' stories unfold in "alternating chapters, using parallel experiences." The characters, confused and lost, are eventually taken in by each other's families. According to *School Library Journal* contributor Bruce Anne Shook, the fantasy/historical fiction features "plucky, intelligent characters who are believable and easy to like."

Griffin combines mystery and ghost stories with *The Ghost Sitter.* Noting that many ghost stories focus either on ghosts being humorous or horrifying, the author wanted to use the contemporary idea of ghosts as confused and harmless. "This story takes the assumptions of modern ghost belief, primarily that ghosts don't understand that they're dead and must be helped to 'move on' toward some unspecified place they're supposed to be," Griffin explained in an online interview with Cynthia Leitich Smith for *Cynsations.* Told from the alternating perspectives of a ghost who was killed in a fireworks accident fifty years before and Charlotte, the young girl who now moves into the ghost's room and

decides to help her, *The Ghost Sitter* is "a suitable choice for kids who really don't want to be scared but love ghost stories," according to Marta Segal in *Booklist.* A critic for *Horn Book* felt that the mystery—as solved by Charlotte and her new neighbor and friend Shannon, the "just-scary-enough-ghost girl"—combines with the theme of sisterhood to bring *The Ghost Sitter* to a "resoundingly satisfying conclusion."

The Music Thief is set in a gritty urban environment, as eleven-year-old Alma is grieving for both her dead abuela and a local singer she idolized who was killed in a drive-by-shooting. To escape her crowded and noisy home life—one of her siblings is a high-school drop out with a child, and the other is a drug dealer—Alma creeps into the home of a neighbor, a music teacher who is gone during the day, and listens to the music collection. She carefully picks up after herself, leaving no trace, until one day when her brother follows her and begins burglarizing the house. Her brother's actions leave Alma with a difficult choice: does she protect her brother, or protect the house that has been her refuge? Griffin "observes without moralizing, allowing readers a clearer view of choices in their own lives," wrote a contributor to *Kirkus Reviews.* Noting that the book does not conclude with an easy resolution, Elizabeth Fernandez wrote in *School Library Journal* that *The Music Thief* "leaves readers earnestly wishing that Alma can find and stay on the right track."

Griffin spent several years doing the research for *11,000 Years Lost,* in order to accurately depict life in the American Pleistocene era among the mammoth hunters. "It took me ten years off and on to do, was researched twice and substantially re-written three times, has lots of lovely backup material (map, family tree, glossary, etc.), and is even a fun read," she explained to Leitich Smith. "I've never been prouder of anything in my life." The story begins when Esther Aragones finds an Ice Age spearhead. While helping an archaeologist at the dig site, thie girl suddenly finds herself back in the Pleistocene era with no way to get home. Fortunately, she is taken in by mammoth hunters and struggles to learn their language and customs while also looking for a way home. "Along with sheer adventure, Griffin works in a touch of mysticism and an appreciation for the natural world," wrote Sally Estes in her *Booklist* review. A *Kirkus Reviews* contributor wrote that *11,000 Years Lost* contains "likable characters [that] populate a fully realized world."

Griffin once told *SATA* that her work is as essential to her as breathing. She also finds that writing fiction is important for another reason. "You don't reach people by talking to them straight. You reach them by telling stories, and letting them work out the truth for themselves, the same way you're doing as you write. It's simple."

Biographical and Critical Sources

PERIODICALS

Booklist, May 1, 1990, Barbara Elleman, review of *Otto from Otherwhere,* pp. 1702-1704; March 15, 1992, Deborah Abbott, review of *Hobkin,* p. 1378; June 1, 1993, p. 1812; March 1, 1994, Hazel Rochman, review of *The Brick House Burglars,* p. 1259; May 15, 1995, Anne O'Malley, review of *Vikki Vanishes,* p. 1639; September 1, 1996, Ilene Cooper, review of

Cover of Griffin's time-travel novel **11,000 Years Lost,** *featuring artwork by Bert Kitchen.* (Amulet Books, an imprint of Harry N. Abrams, Inc., 2004. Illustration copyright © by Bert Kitchen. Reproduced by permission. All rights reserved.)

Margo's House, p. 130; August, 2001, Marta Segal, review of *The Ghost Sitter,* p. 2120; November 1, 2004, Sally Estes, review of *11,000 Years Lost,* p. 484.

Bulletin of the Center for Children's Books, July-August, 1990, Deborah Stevenson, review of *Otto from Otherwhere,* pp. 264-265; October, 1991, Roger Sutton, review of *A Dig in Time,* p. 38; June, 1992, Zena Sutherland, review of *Hobkin,* p. 261; February, 1993, Deborah Stevenson, review of *The Treasure Bird,* p. 177.

Horn Book, May, 2001, review of *The Ghost Sitter,* p. 323.

Kirkus Reviews, April 1, 1991, review of *A Dig in Time,* p. 471; April 15, 1992, review of *Hobkin,* p. 537; November 1, 1992, review of *The Treasure Bird,* p. 1375; April 15, 1993, review of *Switching Well,* p. 529; February 1, 1994, review of *The Brick House Burglars,* pp. 143-144; May 1, 1995, review of *Vikki Vanishes,* p. 634; September 15, 2002, review of *The Music Thief,* p. 1390; November 15, 2004, review of *11,000 Years Lost,* p. 1089.

Locus, May, 1993, Carolyn Cushman, review of *Switching Well,* p. 58.

School Library Journal, August, 1990, Annette Curtis Klause, review of *Otto from Otherwhere,* pp. 146-148; November, 1992, Renee Steinberg, review of *The Treasure Bird,* p. 91; June, 1993, Bruce Anne Shook, review of *Switching Well,* p. 106; June, 1994, Suzanne Hawley, review of *The Brick House Burglars,* p. 128; June, 2001, Eva Mitnick, review of *The Ghost Sitter,* p. 149; December, 2002, Elizabeth Fernandez, review of *The Music Thief,* p. 140; December, 2004, Karen T. Bilton, review of *11,000 Years Lost,* p. 146.

Voice of Youth Advocates, June, 1992, Edith S. Tyson, review of *Hobkin,* pp. 94-95.

ONLINE

Peni R. Griffin Home Page, http://users.idworld.net/griffin (October 2, 2008).

Cynsations, http://cynthialeitichsmith.blogspot.com/ (October 8, 2005), Cynthia Leitich Smith, interview with Griffin.*

* * *

GRIFFIN, Peni Rae Robinson
See GRIFFIN, Peni R.

H

HALPIN, Brendan 1968-

Personal

Born 1968, in Cincinnati, OH; married Kirsten Shanks (deceased); married Suzanne Demarco; children: (first marriage) Rowen (daughter); (second marriage) Casey (son), Kylie (daughter). *Education:* University of Pennsylvania, B.A., 1990; Tufts University, M.A., 1993; attended University of Edinburgh, 1998-99. *Hobbies and other interests:* Playing guitar, vegetarian cooking, music, Muppets, fudge, public education, Harry Potter, reading.

Addresses

Home—Boston, MA. *Agent*—Douglas Stewart, Sterling Lord Literistic, Inc., 65 Bleecker St., 12th Fl., New York, NY 10012. *E-mail*—brendan@brendanhalpin.com.

Career

Writer, novelist, memoirist, and educator. High school English teacher in Boston, MA, for ten years; writer.

Writings

It Takes a Worried Man (memoir), Villard (New York, NY), 2002.
Losing My Faculties: A Teacher's Story, Villard (New York, NY), 2003.
Donorboy (novel), Villard (New York, NY), 2004.
Long Way Back (novel), Villard (New York, NY), 2006.
How Ya Like Me Now, Farrar, Straus & Giroux (New York, NY), 2007.
Dear Catastrophe Waitress (novel), Villard (New York, NY), 2007.

Sidelights

Brendan Halpin's first book, *It Takes a Worried Man,* tells of his late wife, Kirsten Shanks, who was thirty-two when she was diagnosed with stage-four breast cancer that had metastasized to her spine. Halpin kept a journal about their shared struggle in coping with the disease. The title is taken from lyrics by the country group the Carter Family. "His prose is breezy, his attitudes hip, but he vividly describes real anguish and fears," noted a *Kirkus Reviews* contributor. Halpin writes of Kirsten's chemotherapy, his difficult relations with his mother and Kirsten's parents, a medical establishment he perceives as being indifferent, and his parenting of his and Kristen's young daughter, Rowen. Although his own faith falters, Halpin acknowledges the kindness of the congregation of their Unitarian church. Angela Culbertson reviewed the journal-turned-memoir for *City Beat* online, calling it "mostly upbeat and funny, but never fake. Of course there are moments where Halpin admits to bouts of tears—but, make no mistake, *It Takes a Worried Man* is definitively bittersweet."

Halpin was teaching high school English in Boston at the time of his wife's illness, and in his second memoir, *Losing My Faculties: A Teacher's Story,* he describes how he went from job to job in urban schools while he tried to find a position in the city's public school system. There he felt he could influence children who had greater needs. He writes of his frustration at being unable to control a roomful of rowdy students and of academically challenged students who amazed him with their interpretation of poetry. He eventually taught at a charter school but was frustrated by the inappropriately rigid administration and bureaucracy. A *Publishers Weekly* contributor concluded of *Losing My Faculties* that "this chronicle provides an irreverent yet earnest look at the vocation its author clearly loves."

After ten years of teaching, Halpin became a full-time writer. His fiction debut, *Donorboy,* is the story of a fourteen-year-old girl and her first meeting with her father. After Rosalind's two moms are killed in an accident, her sperm-donor father, Sean Cassidy, tries to take over. Sean tells Rosalind about how and why she was conceived and about himself through e-mails. The story unfolds through Roz's diary entries, as well as e-mails

and text messages to their friends as well as each other. Their mutual loneliness becomes apparent, as well as Roz's confusion over her sexual identity and grief for the lesbian couple who raised her. Eventually, as father and daughter continue to communicate, they become closer. *Booklist* contributor Hazel Rochman commented that *Donorboy* "presents contemporary voices that are funny, tender, defiant, and immediate."

Francis Kelly loses his oncologist wife, Lourdes, in *Long Way Back,* a novel described by a *Kirkus Reviews* critic as "boy meets God, boy gets girl, boy loses girl and God, all to a soundtrack by Dee Dee Ramone." Fran's story is told by his sister Clare, who describes their childhood and his religious experience, which eventually leads Frances to be a youth-group leader for their diocese. After brother and sister finish college and are on their own, their parents, devout Catholics, move to South America to do missionary work. Clare, who becomes a nurse, marries, and has children; she speculates as to whether Francis should have entered the priesthood, but he marries Lourdes, then loses her. His faith is then shaken when the cardinal for whom he works becomes involved in a pedophilia scandal. Francis retreats into the punk rock music of his youth, joins a gay band, and gets a tattoo. Clare, who has been the glue holding the family together even as she faces problems in her own life, continues to support her little brother. In a *Booklist* review, Joanne Wilkinson commented on "Halpin's skill for mixing the sacred with the profane."

In *How Ya Like Me Now,* young Eddie has suffered tragedy as his father dies and his alcoholic mother enters a residential treatment program. Eddie's aunt and uncle take him in, and he lives with them and his cousin, Alex, in Boston. Eddie is allowed to attend the same charter school as Alex, and within this supportive, creative atmosphere, the boy thrives academically, socially, and personally. As the story progresses, he and his cousin become the closest of friends, and Alex's gregariousness and Eddie's studiousness counterpoint each other to both boys' benefit. When Eddie's mother is released from her treatment program, however, his newfound life of success and contentment is about to crumble, as his mother wants to take him back home and start over again. "Halpin does an excellent job of baring Eddie's emotions and his inner conflict about his mom," observed Anthony C. Doyle in *School Library Journal.* "This short novel about a suburban boy fitting into an inner-city charter school has charm and humor," commented *Kliatt* reviewer Claire Rosser. A *Kirkus Reviews* contributor named *How Ya Like Me Now* an "interesting exploration of serious issues, presented in a lighthearted tone."

Dear Catastrophe Waitress is a "funny and unlikely story about mending broken hearts," commented a *Publishers Weekly* reviewer. The story concerns Philippa Strange and Mark Norris. A punk-rock princess just graduated from high school, Philippa divides her time between Cincinnati, where she lives with her alcoholic mother, and London, where she cohabitates with her rock-n-roll boyfriend. After Philippa cheats one time too many, her boyfriend immortalizes her lack of faithfulness in a song that becomes a hit, making the young woman an unlikely celebrity. Mark, recently graduated from college, has a similar experience when his ex-girlfriend also has a hit with a song, "Two-Minute Man," that explores his sexual malfunctions. As Mark pursues his career as an elementary school teacher, he also wends his way in and out of emotionally harrowing relationships. Elsewhere, the now-pregnant Philippa changes her name and takes up permanent residence in the United States in an attempt to evade an abusive boyfriend. Halpin "writes sweetly about young men and women trying to carve out a decent life in contemporary times," commented a *Kirkus Reviews* critic. Joanne Wilkinson, writing in *Booklist,* called Halpin "an insightful observer of contemporary relationships," and named *Dear Catastrophe Waitress* a "funny and touching, if somewhat predictable, tribute to the brokenhearted."

Biographical and Critical Sources

BOOKS

Halpin, Brendan, *It Takes a Worried Man* (memoir), Villard Books (New York, NY), 2002.
Halpin, Brendan, *Losing My Faculties: A Teacher's Story,* Villard Books (New York, NY), 2003.

PERIODICALS

Book, September-October, 2003, Steve Wilson, review of *Losing My Faculties,* p. 87.
Booklist, January 1, 2002, Vanessa Bush, review of *It Takes a Worried Man,* p. 782; September 1, 2003, Terry Glover, review of *Losing My Faculties,* p. 29; July, 2004, Hazel Rochman, review of *Donorboy,* p. 1817; November 1, 2005, Joanne Wilkinson, review of *Long Way Back,* p. 24; January 1, 2007, Joanne Wilkinson, review of *Dear Catastrophe Waitress,* p. 54.
Kirkus Reviews, January 1, 2002, review of *It Takes a Worried Man,* p. 29; June 15, 2003, review of *Losing My Faculties,* p. 845; July 1, 2004, review of *Donorboy,* p. 596; November 1, 2005, review of *Long Way Back,* p. 1158; December 1, 2006, review of *Dear Catastrophe Waitress,* p. 1189; April 15, 2007, review of *How Ya Like Me Now.*
Kliatt, May 1, 2007, Claire Rosser, review of *How Ya Like Me Now,* p. 12.
Library Journal, January, 2002, Bette-Lee Fox, review of *It Takes a Worried Man,* p. 141; August, 2003, Leroy Hommerding, review of *Losing My Faculties,* p. 98.
Publishers Weekly, December 17, 2001, review of *It Takes a Worried Man,* p. 71; June 23, 2003, review of *Losing My Faculties,* p. 56; August 9, 2004, review of

Donorboy, p. 233; October 3, 2005, review of *Long Way Back,* p. 47; November 27, 2006, review of *Dear Catastrophe Waitress,* p. 29.

School Library Journal, July 1, 2007, Anthony C. Doyle, review of *How Ya Like Me Now,* p. 103.

ONLINE

BBC News Web site, http://news.bbc.co.uk/ (July 11, 2002), "Breast Cancer: A Husband's Tale," review of *It Takes a Worried Man.*

Bookreporter.com, http://www.bookreporter.com/ (February 28, 2006), Shannon Bloomstran, review of *It Takes a Worried Man.*

Brendan Halpin Home Page, http://www.brendanhalpin. com (August 27, 2007).

Brendan Halpin Web log, http://brendanhalpin.typepad. com/ (August 27, 2007).

City Beat, http:// www.citybeat.com/ (August 27, 2007), Angela Culbertson, review of *It Takes a Worried Man.*

University of Pennsylvania Gazette Online, http://www. upenn.edu/gazette/ (August 27, 2007), interview with Halpin.*

*   *   *

HEILIGMAN, Deborah 1958-

Personal

Born April 24, 1958, in Allentown, PA; daughter of Nathan (a physician) and Helen Heiligman; married Jonathan Weiner (an author), May 29, 1982; children: Aaron, Benjamin. *Education:* Brown University, A.B. (religious studies), 1980. *Religion:* Jewish.

Addresses

Home—Macguncie, PA. *E-mail*—deborah@deborah-heiligman.com.

Career

Author of children's books. Scholastic Inc., New York, NY, editor, 1981-85.

Member

Authors Guild, Authors League of America, Society of Children's Book Writers and Illustrators.

Awards, Honors

Distinguished Alumnus award, Allen High School, 1993; Best in Category Award, Educational Press Association, for article in *Zillions* magazine; Notable Children's Trade Book in the Field of Social Studies, National Council for the Social Studies/Children's Book Council (CBC), 1995, for *Barbara McClintock: Alone in Her Field,* and 1998, for *The New York Public Library Kid's Guide to Research;* Best Book designation, Bank Street School of Education Book Committee, 1997, for *On the Move;* Outstanding Science Trade Book designation, 2002, for *Honeybees;* National Science Teachers Association/CBC, for *Celebrate Diwali, Celebrate Thanksgiving, Celebrate Ramadan,* and *Celebrate Hanukkah;* Sydney Taylor Book Award Notable Book designation, Association of Jewish Libraries, for *Celebrate Hanukkah, Celebrate Passover,* and *Celebrate Rosh Hashannah and Yom Kippur.*

Writings

FOR CHILDREN

Into the Night, illustrated by Melissa Sweet, Harper & Row (New York, NY), 1990.

Barbara McClintock: Alone in Her Field, illustrated by Janet Hamlin, Scientific American Books for Young Readers (New York, NY), 1994.

Mary Leakey: In Search of Human Beginnings, illustrated by Janet Hamlin, Scientific American Books for Young Readers (New York, NY), 1995.

Pockets, illustrated by Suzanne Duranceau, Hyperion (New York, NY), 1995.

On the Move, illustrated by Lizzy Rockwell, HarperCollins (New York, NY), 1996.

From Caterpillar to Butterfly, illustrated by Bari Weissman, HarperCollins (New York, NY), 1996.

Mike Swan, Sink or Swim, illustrated by Chris L. Demarest, First Choice Chapter Books (New York, NY), 1998.

The Story of the Titanic, illustrated by James Watling, Random House (New York, NY), 1998.

The New York Public Library Kid's Guide to Research, illustrated by David Cain, Scholastic (New York, NY), 1998, also published as *The Kid's Guide to Research,* 1999.

Too Perfect, illustrated by Deborah Kogan Ray, Grosset & Dunlap (New York, NY), 1999.

The Mysterious Ocean Highway: Benjamin Franklin and the Gulf Stream, Raintree Steck-Vaughn (Austin, TX), 2000.

Honeybees, illustrated by Carla Golembe, National Geographic Society (Washington, DC), 2002.

Babies: All You Need to Know, illustrated by Laura Freeman, National Geographic Society (Washington, DC), 2002.

Earthquakes, Scholastic (New York, NY), 2002.

High Hopes: A Photobiography of John F. Kennedy, National Geographic Society (Washington, DC), 2003.

Fun Dog, Sun Dog, Marshall Cavendish (New York, NY), 2005.

Charles and Emma: The Darwins' Leap of Faith, Henry Holt (New York, NY), 2008.

Cool Dog, School Dog, illustrated by Tim Bowers, Marshall Cavendish (New York, NY), 2009.

Contributor to magazines, including *Ladies' Home Journal, Sesame Street Parents Guide,* and *Parents.* Con-

tributor to anthologies, including *Don't Cramp My Style: Stories about That Time of the Month,* edited by Lisa Rowe Fraustino, Simon & Schuster (New York, NY), 2004.

"HOLIDAYS AROUND THE WORLD" SERIES; FOR CHILDREN

Celebrate Hanukkah: With Lights, Latkes, and Dreidels, National Geographic Society (Washington, DC), 2006.

Celebrate Thanksgiving, National Geographic Society (Washington, DC), 2006.

Celebrate Diwali: With Sweets, Lights, and Fireworks, National Geographic Society (Washington, DC), 2006.

Celebrate Ramadan and Eid al-Fitr, National Geographic Society (Washington, DC), 2006.

Celebrate Rosh Hashanah and Yom Kippur: With Honey, Prayers, and the Shofar, National Geographic Society (Washington, DC), 2007.

Celebrate Passover, National Geographic Society (Washington, DC), 2007.

Celebrate Independence Day, National Geographic Society (Washington, DC), 2007.

Celebrate Easter: With Colored Eggs, Flowers, and Prayer, National Geographic Society (Washington, DC), 2007.

Celebrate Christmas, National Geographic Society (Washington, DC), 2007.

Celebrate Halloween: With Pumpkins, Costumes, and Candy, National Geographic Society (Washington, DC), 2007.

Sidelights

A former children's book editor, Deborah Heiligman is the author of both fiction and nonfiction titles for younger readers. From biographies such as *Barbara McClintock: Alone in Her Field, High Hopes: A Photobiography of John F. Kennedy,* and *Charles and Emma: The Darwins' Leap of Faith,* to books about insects, titles for emergent readers, and a series about holidays throughout the world, Heiligman ranges widely in her focus. *Charles and Emma,* in particular, combines many

Deborah Heiligman's picture book **Honeybees** *features brilliantly colored collage art by Carla Golembe.* (National Geographic Society, 2002. Illustration copyright © 2002 by Carla Golembe. Reproduced by permission.)

of Heiligman's interests, as she once explained to *SATA:* "Religion, science, a good story, and the most important connections between people."

Like many people who eventually become writers, Heiligman loved books from an early age. One of the first books she checked out from the library, a picture book titled *What Is a Butterfly?,* "told me everything I wanted to know about how a caterpillar becomes a butterfly," the author once recalled. As her mother read the text to her, Heiligman entered "a whole new world," as she explained. "I wanted to explore every nook and cranny. I kept reading nonfiction, and then branched out into fiction, longer books, encyclopedias, and magazines. While I was growing up, I had many friends and did all kinds of wonderful things. But the one anchor in my life was always my love of reading. Reading was like magic for me. I found, too, that I loved to write, and that I was pretty good at it."

Inspired by another memorable event from the author's childhood, *High Hopes* captures the all-too-brief life of the beloved political leader whose assassination occurred during Heiligman's childhood. The author "is almost in awe of her subject," concluded *Booklist* critic Hazel Rochman in a review of the well-illustrated picture-book biography of thirty-fifth U.S. president John F. Kennedy, while Lucinda Whitehurst maintained in *School Library Journal* that *High Hopes* "successfully captures the spirit that makes Kennedy ala enduring figure in our history."

After graduating from Brown University in 1980, Heiligman married and worked for New York City publisher Scholastic for several years before striking out on her own. "The magic came full circle . . . [in 1995]," she explained, "when an editor asked me to write a picture book on how a caterpillar turns into a butterfly! I had long been searching for my first butterfly book, but it was out of print. So I was able to write my own!" Writing this first book was also a personal experience; it was written shortly after Heiligman's mother passed away. "I poured into it memories of her, and all of my books, and the wonders of the world, and of life. From a funny-looking caterpillar comes a beautiful Painted Lady butterfly. And life comes full circle too, as I dedicated *From Caterpillar to Butterfly* to my first son, Aaron, who loves books even more than I do, if that is possible."

Heiligman concentrates on nonfiction in her writings, and she shares her knowledge of research tools to readers in *The New York Public Library Kid's Guide to Research.* Geared to students in grades four through eight, this "short and complete" title, to quote Edith Ching in *School Library Journal,* gives practical advice on note taking, interviewing, evaluating Internet sources, and conducting surveys, as well on as using secondary sources.

Turning her attention to older readers, Heiligman spins an historical science mystery in *The Mysterious Ocean*

Highway: Benjamin Franklin and the Gulf Stream, which traces the development of scientific investigation into this powerful ocean current from Franklin's discoveries in the eighteenth century to the work of contemporary scientists. Writing in *Appraisal,* Linda de Lyon praised the book's "scientifically accurate" and "concise" information and Robert Newman deemed *The Mysterious Ocean Highway* "a well written and fascinating tale of discovery and mapping."

Heiligman's storytelling talent is tapped in a number of books for emergent readers, among them *Honeybees, Babies: All You Need to Know,* and the amusing *Fun Dog, Sun Dog. Honeybees* is an information-packed book featuring "fascinating details" about the secret life of bees, according to *Booklist* critic Carolyn Phelan. Although Edith Ching, writing in *School Library Journal,* pointed out several flaws in the work, she called *Honeybees* an "attractive addition" to children's nonfiction choices. *Babies* is also packed with "interesting information," according to *School Library Journal* contributor Martha Topol, and a *Kirkus Reviews* commentator described the book as "a satisfying introduction" to infants and an "upbeat and fun" resource for families expecting a new member. *Fun Dog, Sun Dog,* which pairs a simple rhyming story about a golden retriever and her boy during a day at the beach with illustrations by Tim Bowers, prompted *Booklist* critic Julie Cummins to predict that "kids will relish this clever sharing and caring

Cover of Heiligman's nonfiction picture book Celebrate Diwali, *which focuses on the Indian holiday.* (National Geographic Society, 2006. Cover photograph copyright © by AFP/Getty Images. Reproduced by permission.)

story." In *School Library Journal,* Catherine Callegari praised *Fun Dog, Sun Dog* for featuring "a repetitive and effective singsong text that is catchy and enjoyable to read."

Featuring highly illustrated profiles of familiar holidays such as Christmas, Hannukah, and Halloween as well as Diwali, Eid al-Fitr, and Yom Kippur, Heiligman's "Holidays around the World" books "balance historical perspective with contemporary cultural significance," according to *School Library Journal* contributor Julie R. Ranelli. In each volume in the series, the author describes the history and purpose of the special day in question, including local celebration customs in various countries. Also writing in *School Library Journal,* Amanda Moss described *Celebrate Halloween: With Pumpkins, Costumes, and Candy* as a "warm, informational book [that is] perfect for sharing aloud or enjoying individually," the critic adding that Heiligman's reassuring text "will calm any fears." In *Celebrate Hannukah: With Lights, Latkes, and Dreidels,* celebrations everywhere from Israel and India to Peru and Uganda are described, all in a text that *Booklist* critic Kay Weisman deemed "succinct and appropriate for reading aloud." Featuring a "beautiful explanation of the Jewish High Holy Days," according to a *Kirkus Reviews* writer, *Celebrate Rosh Hashanah and Yom Kippur* incorporates important prayer rituals in a multicultural volume that features what the critic described as "a colorful, clean photographic design."

Biographical and Critical Sources

PERIODICALS

Appraisal, spring-summer-fall, 2000, Linda de Lyon Friel, review of *The Mysterious Ocean Highway: Benjamin Franklin and the Gulf Stream,* p. 39; spring-summer-fall, 2000, Robert Newman, review of *The Mysterious Ocean Highway,* p. 39.

Booklist, October 1, 1998, Mary Ellen Quinn, review of *The New York Public Library Kid's Guide to Research,* p. 362; October 15, 1999, Hazel Rochman, review of *The Mysterious Ocean Highway,* p. 437; May 1, 2002, Carolyn Phelan, review of *Honeybees,* p. 1529; October 1, 2002, Kathy Broderick, review of *Babies: All You Need to Know,* p. 328; November 15, 2003, Hazel Rochman, review of *High Hopes: A Photobiography of John F. Kennedy,* p. 595; May 1, 2005, Julie Cummins, review of *Fun Dog, Sun Dog,* p. 1590; October 15, 2006, Kay Weisman, review of *Celebrate Hanukkah: With Lights, Latkes, and Dreidels,* p. 77; March 15, 2007, Ilene Cooper, review of *Celebrate Passover,* p. 45.

Bulletin of the Center for Children's Books, September, 2002, review of *Honeybees,* p. 19; October, 2002, review of *Babies,* p. 59.

Kirkus Reviews, August 15, 2002, review of *Babies,* p. 1225; June 1, 2007, review of *Celebrate Rosh Hashanah and Yom Kippur.*

Publishers Weekly, July 27, 1998, review of *The New York Public Library Kid's Guide to Research,* p. 79.

Reading Teacher, October, 1997, review of *From Caterpillar to Butterfly,* p. 152.

School Library Journal, February, 1999, Edith Ching, review of *The New York Public Library Kid's Guide to Research,* p. 119; May, 2002, Edith Ching, review of *Honeybees,* p. 138; October, 2002, Martha Topol, review of *Babies,* p. 146; April, 2004, Lucinda Whitehurst, review of *High Hopes,* p. 170; May, 2005, Catherine Callegari, review of *Fun Dog, Sun Dog,* p. 85; January, 2007, Julie R. Ranelli, review of *Celebrate Diwali,* p. 118; August, 2007, Heidi Estrin, review of *Celebrate Independence Day,* p. 98; September, 2007, Angela Moss, review of *Celebrate Halloween: With Pumpkins, Costumes, and Candy,* p. 183.

ONLINE

Deborah Heiligman Home Page, http://www.deborah heiligman.com (September 15, 2008).

*   *   *

HEST, Amy 1950-

Personal

Born April 28, 1950, in New York, NY; daughter of Seymour Cye (a businessman) and Thelma (a teacher) Levine; married Lionel Hest (a lawyer), May 19, 1977; children: Sam, Kate. *Education:* Hunter College of the City University of New York, B.A., 1971; C.W. Post College of Long Island University, M.L.S., 1972.

Addresses

Home and office—New York, NY. *E-mail*—amy@amy hest.com.

Career

New York Public Library, New York, NY, children's librarian, 1972-75; Viking Press, Inc., New York, NY, assistant editor, 1977; full-time writer, 1977—. Teaches at Bank Street College of Education and New York University.

Member

Society of Children's Book Writers and Illustrators.

Awards, Honors

Sydney Taylor Honor Book Award, for *Love You, Soldier;* Boston Globe/Horn Book Award, 1996, for *In the Rain with Baby Duck;* Parents' Choice Gold Award, Sydney Taylor Honor Book Award, Christopher Award, Notable Children's Trade Book in the Field of Social Studies designation, National Council for the Social Studies (NCSS)/Children's Book Council (CBC), and Notable Book designation, International Reading Asso-

ciation (IRA), all for *When Jessie Came across the Sea;* Oppenheim Toy Portfolio Gold Award, for *Off to School, Baby Duck!, Baby Duck and the Cozy Blanket, Don't You Fell Well, Sam?, Guess Who, Baby Duck!,* and *You Can Swim, Baby Duck;* Notable Book for Children designation, American Library Association (ALA), Notable Children's Trade Book in the Field of Social Studies designation, NCSS/CBC, and Christopher Award, all for *The Purple Coat;* Christopher Award, for *Kiss Good Night;* Teachers' Choice selection, IRA, and Oppenheim Toy Portfolio Gold Award, both for *Make the Team, Baby Duck!;* Parents' Choice Awards Silver Honor designation, and Teacher's Choice Award, IRA, both for *Mr. George Baker;* Notable Book for Children designation, ALA, for *Remembering Mrs. Rossi.*

Writings

FOR CHILDREN

Maybe Next Year . . ., Morrow (New York, NY), 1982.

The Crack-of-Dawn Walkers, illustrated by Amy Schwartz, Puffin (New York, NY), 1984.

Pete and Lily, Morrow (New York, NY), 1986.

The Purple Coat, illustrated by Amy Schwartz, Four Winds Press (New York, NY), 1986.

The Mommy Exchange, illustrated by DyAnne DiSalvo-Ryan, Four Winds Press (New York, NY), 1988.

Getting Rid of Krista, illustrated by Jacqueline Rogers, Morrow (New York, NY), 1988.

The Midnight Eaters, illustrated by Karen Gundersheimer, Aladdin Books (New York, NY), 1989.

Travel Tips from Harry: A Guide to Family Vacations in the Sun, illustrated by Sue Truesdell, Morrow (New York, NY), 1989.

Where in the World Is the Perfect Family?, Clarion (New York, NY), 1989.

The Best-Ever Good-Bye Party, illustrated by DyAnne DiSalvo-Ryan, Morrow (New York, NY), 1989.

The Ring and the Window Seat, illustrated by Deborah Haeffele, Scholastic (New York, NY), 1990.

Fancy Aunt Jess, illustrated by Amy Schwartz, Morrow (New York, NY), 1990.

A Sort-Of Sailor, illustrated by Lizzy Rockwell, Four Winds Press (New York, NY), 1990.

Love You, Soldier, Four Winds Press (New York, NY), 1991.

Pajama Party, illustrated by Irene Trivas, Morrow (New York, NY), 1992.

The Go-Between, illustrated by DyAnne DiSalvo-Ryan, Four Winds Press (New York, NY), 1992.

Nana's Birthday Party, illustrated by Amy Schwartz, Morrow (New York, NY), 1993.

Weekend Girl, illustrated by Harvey Stevenson, Morrow (New York, NY), 1993.

Nannies for Hire, illustrated by Irene Trivas, Morrow (New York, NY), 1994.

Ruby's Storm, illustrated by Nancy Cote, Four Winds Press (New York, NY), 1994.

Rosie's Fishing Trip, illustrated by Paul Howard, Candlewick Press (Cambridge, MA), 1994.

How to Get Famous in Brooklyn, illustrated by Linda Dalal Sawaya, Four Winds Press (New York, NY), 1994.

The Private Notebook of Katie Roberts, Age Eleven (sequel to *Love You, Soldier*), illustrated by Sonja Lamut, Candlewick Press (Cambridge, MA), 1995.

In the Rain with Baby Duck, illustrated by Jill Barton, Candlewick Press (Cambridge, MA), 1995.

Party on Ice, illustrated by Irene Trivas, Morrow (New York, NY), 1995.

Jamaica Louise James, illustrated by Sheila White Stanton, Candlewick Press (Cambridge, MA), 1996.

Baby Duck and the Bad Eyeglasses, illustrated by Jill Barton, Candlewick Press (Cambridge, MA), 1996.

The Babies Are Coming, illustrated by Chloe Cheese, Crown (New York, NY), 1997.

You're the Boss, illustrated by Jill Barton, Candlewick Press (Cambridge, MA), 1997.

When Jessie Came across the Sea, illustrated by P.J. Lynch, Candlewick Press (Cambridge, MA), 1997.

The Great Green Notebook of Katie Roberts: Who Just Turned Twelve on Monday, illustrated by Sonja Lamut, Candlewick Press (Cambridge, MA), 1998.

Gabby Growing Up, illustrated by Amy Schwartz, Simon & Schuster (New York, NY), 1998.

Off to School, Baby Duck!, illustrated by Jill Barton, Candlewick Press (Cambridge, MA), 1999.

Mabel Dancing, illustrated by Christine Cavenier, Candlewick Press (Cambridge, MA), 2000.

The Friday Nights of Nana, illustrated by Claire A. Nivola, Candlewick Press (Cambridge, MA), 2001.

Kiss Good Night, illustrated by Anita Jeram, Candlewick Press (Cambridge, MA), 2001.

Don't You Feel Well, Sam?, illustrated by Anita Jeram, Candlewick Press (Cambridge, MA), 2002.

Baby Duck and the Cozy Blanket, illustrated by Jill Barton, Candlewick Press (Cambridge, MA), 2002.

Make the Team, Baby Duck!, illustrated by Jill Barton, Candlewick Press (Cambridge, MA), 2002.

Guess Who, Baby Duck!, illustrated by Jill Barton, Candlewick Press (Cambridge, MA), 2003.

You Can Do It, Sam, illustrated by Anita Jeram, Candlewick Press (Cambridge, MA), 2003.

Mr. George Baker, illustrated by Jon J. Muth, Candlewick Press (Cambridge, MA), 2004.

You Can Swim, Baby Duck!, illustrated by Jill Barton, Candlewick Press (Cambridge, MA), 2005.

Remembering Mrs. Rossi, illustrated by Heather Maione, Candlewick Press (Cambridge, MA), 2007.

The Dog Who Belonged to No One, illustrated by Amy Bates, Abrams (New York, NY), 2008.

One Day with Little Chick, illustrated by Anita Jeram, Candlewick Press (Cambridge, MA), 2009.

Sidelights

An award-winning author of picture books and juvenile novels, Amy Hest is known for her sensitive and insightful depictions of family relationships. Many of her books, including *The Purple Coat* and the "Baby Duck" series, focus on youngsters and their grandparents, al-

though parents, annoying siblings, and fabulous aunts also make frequent appearances. Additionally, several of her tales are set in New York City and illustrate how love and support of family and friends can get one through trying times as well as the ordinary ups and downs of everyday existence. According to a contributor in *The Essential Guide to Children's Books and their Creators,* "Hest has created a notable body of work reflecting childhood concerns about home and family, with specific details that illuminate universal truths."

Hest grew up in a small suburban community about an hour's drive from New York City. As a child, her favorite things to do were biking, reading, and spying. "I spied on everyone, and still do," Hest said in a Four Winds Press publicity release. "All writers, I suspect, are excellent spies. At least they ought to be. My parents took me to the city quite often, and by the time I was seven, I was certain of one thing, that I would one day live there. Many years later, after graduating from library school, I moved to the Upper West Side of Manhattan, and I live here still, with my husband and two children, Sam and Kate."

Hest often uses her children's names for the main characters in her books. *Maybe Next Year,* her first published book, features a twelve year old named Kate who lives with her grandmother on the Upper West Side of New York City. Two major events unfold in Kate's life during the course of the story, and she must sort out her feelings about both. First, Mr. Schumacher, a widower friend of her grandmother's, moves in to share their apartment. Kate also has to decide whether she is ready and willing to audition for the National Ballet Summer School, as her best friend, Peter, feels she should.

In *The Crack-of-Dawn-Walkers,* Hest again portrays a young girl's relationship with a grandparent. Every other Sunday, Sadie gets to go with Grandfather on his traditional morning walk. On the other Sundays, her little brother gets to spend time alone with Grandfather. Millie Hawk Daniel, in a review for the *New York Times Book Review,* praised Hest's combination of the two themes, "the validity of intergenerational camaraderie and the understanding that each child needs his or her own private time with a grandparent."

Children and their grandparents are the primary focus of several more of Hest's books. Dubbed by Ellen Feldman a "triumph of imagination, resourcefulness and hope" in the *New York Times Book Review, The Purple Coat* tells how Gabrielle and her mother go on their annual trip to Grampa's tailor shop so that Gabby can get a new coat. Up until now, Grampa has always made Gabby a navy blue coat with buttons and a half belt in the back, just the way Mama likes it. This time, Gabby wants a purple coat, but Mama says no. Fashioning an imaginative reversible coat, Grampa manages to please them both.

Hest and illustrator Amy Schwartz also team up in *Gabby Growing Up,* in which the eponymous protagonist, now eight or nine years old, has knitted mittens to give to Grampa for his birthday. When she and her mother come to Manhattan to meet him at a skating rink, Gabby first gets a new hairdo among other surprises en route. Now worries arise as to whether Grampa will like Gabby's new braidless look and the bright orange mittens she has knitted for him. As with *The Purple Coat,* reviewers responded warmly to this intergenerational tale. "Hest and Schwartz lovingly recreate postwar New York City," wrote a reviewer for *Publishers Weekly,* "but the issues they address are timeless. . . in this "thoughtful, effective collaboration." Writing in *Booklist,* Ilene Cooper felt that *Gabby Growing Up* has something for both adults and children: "Although the setting may evoke nostalgia for adults, Gabby's story of universal hopes and worries will easily appeal to today's children," she noted. and Virginia Golodetz, reviewing *Gabby Growing Up* in *School Library Journal,* wrote that "art and text together tell a totally satisfying story of a youngster making choices about herself, with the love and support of her family."

A young girl's relationship with her grandmother is explored in both *The Midnight Eaters* and *The Go-Between.* In the former, Samantha Bluestein and her ill-but-recovering Nana share a bedroom, a cold midnight snack, and some warm conversation in what Heide Piehler called in *School Library Journal* an adept portrayal of "the special love and understanding between generations." *The Go-Between* is also the story of granddaughter-grandmother roommates, as Lexi and Gran share a room and enjoy looking out the window at the bustling New York City street below. There, they spy Murray Singer, who runs the newsstand and used to be a good friend of Gran's. Lexi plays matchmaker until she fears that Gran's budding romance with Murray may change her own cherished relationship. All ends happily, however, in this story which a *Publishers Weekly* reviewer wrote "blends nostalgia and contemporary family dynamics."

New York City plays a particularly large role in two of Hest's books about grandparents. In *The Weekend Girl,* Sophie's parents take a "private, no-kid" vacation, leaving Sophie and her dog to spend the weekend with Gram and Grampa. Although Sophie is sad to be without her parents, she enjoys her grandparents' special surprise of a picnic and concert in Central Park. The city streets and a brewing storm are the background against which Ruby must make her way to keep a checkers date with Grandpa in *Ruby's Storm.* This book not only explores the intergenerational relationship, but also conveys what Joyce Richards called in *School Library Journal* the "allegorical message that nurturing family relationships often means weathering storms along the way."

Aunts provide nurturing family relationships in Hest's *Fancy Aunt Jess* and *The Ring and the Window Seat.*

The title character of *Fancy Aunt Jess* has luxurious blonde hair, dresses stylishly, and loves to host her niece Becky at sleepovers in her Brooklyn apartment. Whenever anyone questions Aunt Jess about her unmarried status, she replies that she is waiting for someone special, someone who will give her goose bumps. Goose bumps appear when she meets the father of Becky's new friend. Eleanor K. MacDonald wrote in *School Library Journal* that this story of a special friendship would "appeal to any child who has pondered the mysteries of adult romance."

Another aunt is featured in *The Ring and the Window Seat,* Hest's "low-key introduction" to the story of the Holocaust, according to Leone McDermott in *Booklist.* In this graceful tale, Annie's Aunt Stella recalls a birthday she had many years ago. Stella had been saving her money to buy a beautiful golden ring, but one day a carpenter knocked on her door, asking for work. As he was building a window seat for Stella, he told her how he needed the work so he could earn money to send for his daughter, who was hiding from the Nazis. After she heard this, Stella silently slipped her ring money into the carpenter's bag. A few weeks later, she unexpectedly received a gift of a golden ring from the carpenter's daughter. Now, Stella passes the ring on to Annie as a special birthday surprise.

Hest's focus shifts from relatives to friends and their relationships in *Pete and Lily.* These two twelve-year-old girls, neighbors in the same apartment building in New York, form an "Anti-Romance Mission" when Pete—whose real name is Patricia—finds out that her mother and Lily's father have begun dating. Cynthia Percak Infantino praised the author's "convincing portrait of adolescent jealousy" in a *School Library Journal* review by noting that the book also shows the "need to let go of the past and adapt to life's changes." *Getting Rid of Krista* also deals with the themes of jealousy and adaptation. When eight-year-old Gillie's father loses his job, her big sister Krista has to come back home from college. Gillie wants her self-centered, preening sister out of the house as soon as possible. With the help of her best friend and a coincidental meeting with a famous Broadway producer, Gillie gets her wish.

In all of Hest's books, an underlying theme is the incredible variety of family relationships that exist in society. Large families, small families, single-parent families, and families with step-parents and step-siblings are all seen as having their own special charm, as well as their own special difficulties. Another type of special family arrangement is depicted in *Where in the World Is the Perfect Family?,* in which complicated problems face eleven-year-old Cornie Blume. Cornie is adjusting well to the joint-custody arrangement of her divorced parents, shuttling between the East and West sides of New York. But then Cornie's father announces that his new wife is about to have a baby and her mother begins mentioning a possible move to California. Roger Sutton noted in the *Bulletin of the Center for Children's Books*

that these complications give the story "texture" and that "Cornie's a likable, one-of-us heroine whom readers will enjoy."

While the problems in *The Mommy Exchange* are not quite as complex as Cornie's situation in *Where in the World Is the Perfect Family?,* they do demonstrate that families have their good and bad points. Hest's story compares and contrasts two families who live in the same apartment building: Jessica lives upstairs with her parents and her twin siblings while Jason lives downstairs, in peace and quiet with his mother and father. The two friends envy each other's lives, and they decide to make a weekend switch. After they each experience how the other lives, Jessica and Jason discover the blessings their own environments have to offer. Hest continues the young duo's friendship in *The Best-Ever Good-Bye Party,* as the two children adapt to the fact that Jason is moving away. Jason seems to be looking forward to the move, which hurts Jessica's feelings, and the two have a fight the day before the move. However, at the good-bye party arranged by Jessica's mother, Jason and Jessica realize that they are still best friends despite everything.

Hest examines loss and renewal in *Remembering Mrs. Rossi,* "a peek inside a story that no one wants to live,

Heather Maione creates cartoon art for Amy Hest's heartwarming picture book Remembering Mrs. Rossi. (Illustration copyright © 2007 by Heather Maione. Reproduced by permission of the publisher, Candlewick Press, Inc., Somerville, MA.)

but that many will want to understand," according to *Horn Book* reviewer Robin Smith. When Annie's mother, a dedicated teacher, passes away unexpectedly, the eight year old must reconstruct her life with the help of her father and a scrapbook put together by Mrs. Rossi's students. According to *Booklist* critic Kay Weisman, the author "imbues her characters with warmth, humor, and realistic imperfections," and a *Publishers Weekly* reviewer noted, "Readers of this fine novel will find the spirited, resilient Annie another character—just like her mother—well worth remembering."

The ups and downs of friendship take the stage in *Pajama Party* and *Nannies for Hire,* which focus on three best friends, eight-year-old Casey and her pals Jenny and Kate. In *Pajama Party,* the girls decide to have their own pajama party when they are excluded from Casey's thirteen-year-old sister's party. Although Kate gets homesick and does not make it through her first night away from home, all ends happily when the girls are reunited in the morning with special breakfast treats. In what Hanna B. Zeiger characterized in *Horn Book* as "a warm-hearted tale of friendship," *Nannies for Hire* finds the three friends collaborating on a baby-sitting job taking care of Jenny's new baby sister. Not surprisingly, things do not go quite as smoothly as planned, and at the end of what becomes a very stressful day, all three girls appreciate why Jenny's Mom has been so tired and frazzled lately.

A youngster and his elderly neighbor share a love of learning in *Mr. George Baker,* "a gentle tale of intergenerational and interracial friendship," observed a contributor in *Kirkus Reviews.* Each day Harry, a first-grader, boards the school bus with George, a former jazz drummer who is taking reading lessons at Harry's school. "Harry narrates the story in short articulate sentences that present an uncomplicated picture of two unlikely friends," noted *School Library Journal* reviewer Carolyn Janssen. Writing in *Booklist,* Gillian Engberg called *Mr. George Baker* "a simple, sweet, moving portrait of a natural friendship between seniors and children."

In addition to picture books, Hest also writes middle-grade novels. Her most popular books of this type feature a young Jewish girl, Katie, who lives in New York City and Texas during the 1940s. In the first "Katie" book, *Love You, Soldier,* Katie sees the world change from her seventh to tenth birthdays as World War II affects everyone around her, and she worries about her father, who is fighting overseas. She and her mother pore over his letters and try to keep a sense of normalcy on the home front. When a childhood friend of her mother's moves in, also waiting for a husband to return from the war, Katie helps out with the woman's new baby. Sadly, one day the long-dreaded telegram arrives to tell nine-year-old Katie and her mom that Katie's father will not be coming home. Critical praise greeted the publication of *Love You, Soldier.* "Hest's book offers another viewpoint of the hardships of World

Hest's picture book **Mr. George Baker** *features artwork by Jon J. Muth.* (Illustration copyright © 2004 by Jon J. Muth. All rights reserved. Reproduced by permission of the publisher, Candlewick Press, Inc., Somerville, MA.)

War II in the United States," wrote Phyllis Kennemer in a *School Library Journal* review, while *Horn Book* contributor Mary M. Burns dubbed the novel a "small gem," concluding, "It isn't often that a story accessible to younger readers has the emotional impact of a much more complex novel. Amy Hest's *Love You, Soldier* belongs in that category."

Katie's story continues in *The Private Notebook of Katie Roberts, Age Eleven,* in which the preteen fills the pages of a leather notebook with images of her new life in Texas. Her mother is now married to Sam Gold, and the family now lives on Sam's ranch. Katie's diary records her nervousness at entering a new school, her ups when she becomes editor of the class paper, and her downs when she learns of her mother's pregnancy and ponders her place in this new blended family. A reviewer for *Publishers Weekly* called Katie an "unusually exuberant narrator" and noted that the young narrator's humorous takes on life "will win readers as (Katie) surmounts hurdle after hurdle." Writing in *Booklist,* Chris Sherman felt that fans of *Love You, Soldier* "will be delighted with this sequel" and called Katie a "captivating, outspoken protagonist whose concerns will be familiar to many children." In *Horn Book* Burns had high praise for the novel, noting that unlike most sequels it stands up well on its own; moreover it distinguishes Hest "as a remarkable writer for a difficult au-

dience." "So lifelike is her characterization," added Burns, "that the reader feels impelled to slip into the narrative to offer (Katie) . . . a bit of advice." Burns deemed *The Private Notebook of Katie Roberts, Age Eleven* a "finely crafted story" made even better by the "lively line drawings" of illustrator Sonja Lamut.

Katie's third outing, *The Great Green Notebook of Katie Roberts: Who Just Turned Twelve on Monday,* finds the protagonist entering the seventh grade in Texas. Her new notebook was sent to her by a former New York neighbor, and in it she continues to record her feelings about her life. In this installment, readers learn of her infatuation with David, her frustration when she is prohibited from wearing lipstick to school, and her on-again, off-again friendship with fellow student Rudy, an Italian immigrant. Katie still misses her biological father and has fears that her stepfather's new business—a diner—will not succeed. *Booklist* contributor Michael Cart called Katie an "engaging presence" and characterized her parents as "likable and sympathetic." Burns also had positive things to say about the journal-novel, calling Katie "a believable, dauntless character, with just the right mix of sass and sympathy." A *Kirkus Reviews* critic deemed *The Great Green Notebook of Katie Roberts* a "rollicking story that balances humor and pre-adolescent angst with the larger canvas of post-WWII America."

Writing for younger readers, Hest has teamed up with illustrator Jill Barton on several "Baby Duck" picture books, chronicling the adventures and misadventures of this young quacker. Her first outing, *In the Rain with Baby Duck,* blends family and weather when Baby Duck—no fan of rain—must navigate puddles to get to Grampa's home on the other side of town. There she learns that her mother did not much like the rain either as a youngster. "Preschoolers will love the large, bright pages with the funny pencil and watercolor illustrations of the duck family," wrote *Horn Book* reviewer Hanna Zeiger, "and they will easily identify with the joy of splashing in puddles (with boots on)." Spectacles give Baby Duck problems in *Baby Duck and the Bad Eyeglasses,* a story that one again depicts a loving relationship between grandfather and grandchild. Here Grampa is able to convince Baby Duck that wearing her new glasses is not only simply okay but actually good for her. More praise greeted this addition to the series. *Booklist* contributor Ilene Cooper wrote that "Hest and Barton combine their considerable talents in a delightful story," while in *Horn Book* Maeve Visser Knoth felt that readers "will be delighted to encounter (Baby Duck) again."

The arrival of a new sibling provides the inspiration for *You're the Boss, Baby Duck.* No longer the youngest in the family, Baby Duck is unsure how she feels about her new sister, Hot Stuff, but a visit to Grampa helps to set things right again. This oft-written-about topic is given a new twist by Hest and Barton, according to *Booklist* contributor Cooper; "Baby is just so ducky," the critic quipped, "that anything she appears in is hardly run-of-the-mill." The first day of school is at the heart of *Off to School, Baby Duck!,* and Baby Duck is none too happy about the prospect. Once again, however, it is a talk with understanding Grampa that reassures her that things will be fine. Cooper, reviewing *Off to School, Baby Duck!,* called the young protagonist a "trailblazer of sorts" for introducing young readers to the pleasures of rain, eyeglasses, a new sibling, and school. While there are many books which deal with the subject, "familiar situations seem new, fresh, and very real when Baby is in the middle of them," Cooper noted. In *Guess Who, Baby Duck!* Grampa has just the cure for the youngster's head cold: a photo album with pictures of Baby Duck's first bath, first steps, and first birthday party. According to *School Library Journal* contributor Rachel G. Payne, the work "beautifully taps into the heart" of the "Baby Duck" series, "the youngster's special relationship with her loving grandfather."

Hest has also written a number of books inspired by her son, Sam. In *Kiss Good Night* a cub finds countless ways to keep Mrs. Bear in his room until she remembers a special bedtime ritual. *Don't You Feel Well, Sam?* concerns Mrs. Bear's efforts to coax her youngster into taking a foul-tasting cough syrup for his cold. A critic in *Publishers Weekly* praised the author's "soothingly rhythmic and repetitive prose," and Gillian Engberg, writing in *Booklist,* called the work "a quiet, shining story of things made better." In *You Can Do It, Sam,* Mrs. Bear encourages her son to help her deliver tasty treats to the neighbors. "Endearing characters add to the sweetness and fulfillment that younger children will identify with," wrote a *Kirkus Reviews* contributor.

Before Hest began writing children's books, she worked for several years as a children's librarian, and then in the children's book departments of several major publishing houses. "All my life, though, I secretly wanted to write children's books," she wrote in her publicity release. "'What? You?' This nasty little voice in the back of my head simply laughed at me. 'What in the world would someone like YOU have to say? Don't you get it, Amy, you're the least exciting person in the universe! Go away and let the writers do the writing!'

"It took me a long time—and I won't tell you how many years—to smash that voice to smithereens . . . but smash it I did, and I'm not a bit sorry. Having done that, I was able to get on with it, with the writing. Amazing! I DID find something to write about, and every single day I find something more."

Biographical and Critical Sources

PERIODICALS

Silvey, Anita, editor, *The Essential Guide to Children's Books and Their Creators,* Houghton Mifflin (Boston, MA), 2002.

PERIODICALS

Booklist, January 15, 1991, Leone McDermott, review of *The Ring and the Window Seat,* p. 1063; July, 1995, Chris Sherman, review of *The Private Notebook of Katie Roberts, Age Eleven,* p. 1879; August, 1996, Ilene Cooper, review of *Baby Duck and the Bad Eyeglasses,* p. 1905; September 1, 1997, Ilene Cooper, review of *You're the Boss, Baby Duck!,* p. 133; January 1, 1998, Ilene Cooper, review of *Gabby Growing Up,* pp. 822-823; November 15, 1998, Michael Cart, review of *The Great Green Notebook of Katie Roberts: Who Just Turned Twelve on Monday,* p. 590; September 15, 1999, Ilene Cooper, review of *Off to School, Baby Duck!,* p. 259; October 1, 2001, Gillian Engberg, review of *Kiss Good Night,* p. 325, and Carolyn Phelan, review of *The Friday Nights of Nana,* p. 334; November 15, 2002, Gillian Engberg, review of *Don't You Feel Well, Sam?,* p. 602; November 1, 2003, Abby Nolan, review of *You Can Do It, Sam,* p. 501; March 1, 2004, Carolyn Phelan, review of *Guess Who, Baby Duck!,* p. 1195; September 1, 2004, Gillian Engberg, review of *Mr. George Baker,* p. 132; January 1, 2007, Kay Weisman, review of *Remembering Mrs. Rossi,* p. 102.

Bulletin of the Center for Children's Books, November, 1989, Roger Sutton, review of *Where in the World Is the Perfect Family?,* pp. 59-60.

Horn Book, September-October, 1991, Mary M. Burns, review of *Love You, Soldier,* pp. 591-592; May-June, 1994, Janna B. Zeiger, review of *Nannies for Hire,* pp. 339-340; September-October, 1995, Mary M. Burns, review of *The Private Notebooks of Katie Roberts, Age Eleven,* pp. 599-600; March-April, 1996, Hanna B. Zeiger, review of *In the Rain with Baby Duck,* pp. 188-189; September-October, 1996, Maeve Visser Knoth, review of *Baby Duck and the Bad Eyeglasses,* pp. 577-578; January-February, 1999, Mary M. Burns, review of *The Great Green Notebook of Katie Roberts,* p. 62; May-June, 2007, Robin Smith, review of *Remembering Mrs. Rossi,* p. 283.

Kirkus Reviews, August 15, 1998, review of *The Great Green Notebook of Katie Roberts;* October 1. 2003, review of *You Can Do It, Sam,* p. 1224; July 15, 2004, review of *Mr. George Baker,* p. 686; July 15, 2008, review of *The Dog Who Belonged To No One.*

New York Times Book Review, May 13, 1984, Millie Hawk Daniel, review of *The Crack-of-Dawn-Walkers,* pp. 20-21; November 9, 1986, Ellen Feldman, review of *The Purple Coat,* p. 60.

Publishers Weekly, June 5, 1995, review of *The Private Notebook of Katie Roberts, Age Eleven,* p. 64; December 1, 1997, review of *Gabby Growing Up,* p. 53; July 22, 2002, review of *Don't you Feel Well, Sam?,* p. 176; September 6, 2004, review of *Mr. George Baker,* p. 62; February 12, 2007, review of *Remembering Mrs. Rossi,* p. 86.

School Library Journal, August, 1986, Cynthia Percak Infantino, review of *Pete and Lily,* p. 92; October, 1989, Heide Piehler, review of *The Midnight Eaters,* p. 86; June, 1990, Eleanor K. MacDonald, review of *Fancy Aunt Jess,* p. 100; August, 1991, Phyllis K. Kennemer, review of *Love You, Soldier,* p. 166; April, 1994, Joyce Richards, review of *Ruby's Storm,* p. 106; March, 1998, Virginia Golodetz, review of *Gabby Growing Up,* p. 180; September, 1999, Kathleen M. Kelly MacMillan, review of *Off to School, Baby Duck!,* p. 183; October, 2001, Amy Lilien-Harper, review of *The Friday Nights of Nana,* p. 120; November, 2001, Susan Weitz, review of *Kiss Good Night,* p. 124; September, 2002, Kathleen Simonetta, review of *Don't You Feel Well, Sam?,* p. 193; October, 2003, Kathy Krasniewicz, review of *You Can Do It, Sam,* p. 126; May, 2004, Rachel G. Payne, review of *Guess Who, Baby Duck!,* p. 114; September, 2004, Carolyn Janssen, review of *Mr. George Baker,* p. 162; March, 2007, Linda Ward-Callaghan, review of *Remembering Mrs. Rossi,* p. 173.

ONLINE

Amy Hest Home Page, http://www.amyhest.com (August 10, 2008).

Candlewick Press Web site, http://www.candlewick.com/ (August 10, 2008), "Amy Hest."

OTHER

Four Winds Publicity Release, 1993, "Amy Hest."*

* * *

HILL, Susanna Leonard 1965-

Personal

Born April 14, 1965, in New York, NY; daughter of Edwin Deane (a lawyer) and Judith (a lawyer) Leonard; married Eric J. Hill (a teacher and musician), April 21, 1990; children: three. *Ethnicity:* "Caucasian." *Education:* Middlebury College, B.A., 1987; Columbia University, M.A., M.Ed., 1991. *Hobbies and other interests:* Reading, running, horseback riding, hiking, piano, puzzles and games of all kinds.

Addresses

Home—Poughquag, NY. *Agent*—Liza Voges, Kirchoff/Wohlberg, 866 United Nations Plaza, New York, NY 10017. *E-mail*—slhill65@msn.com.

Career

Self-employed educational therapist, 1990-97; freelance writer, 1997—.

Member

Society of Children's Book Writers and Illustrators, Authors Guild, Authors League of America, Southwest Writers.

Awards, Honors

First Place, Southwest Writers Children's Picture Book Contest, 2005, for *Not Yet, Rose;* first place, Seven Hills Contest for Writers, 2005, for collection of three

stories; Children's Picks listee, Book Sense, 2005, and Feminist Books for Youth List, Amelia Bloomer Project, 2006, both for *Punxsutawney Phyllis;* first place, CNW/FFWA Florida State Writing Competition, 2006, for "The One-Hour Bicycle"; first place, CNW/FFWA Florida State Writing Competition, 2007, for "The Sisters Club"; first place, Seven Hills Contest for Writers, 2007, for "Gone Fishin'."

Writings

FOR CHILDREN

The House That Mack Built, illustrated by Ken Wilson-Max, Little Simon (New York, NY), 2002.
Taxi!, Little Simon (New York, NY), 2005.

Punxsutawney Phyllis, illustrated by Jeffrey Ebbeler, Holiday House (New York, NY), 2005.
No Sword Fighting in the House, illustrated by True Kelley, Holiday House (New York, NY), 2007.
Not Yet, Rose, illustrated by Nicole Rutten, Eerdmans (Grand Rapids, MI), 2008.

Sidelights

Susanna Leonard Hill, a former educational therapist who worked with dyslexic students, is the author of a number of picture books for children. Hill's first published book, *The House That Mack Built,* appeared in 2002. "*The House That Mack Built* was inspired by my son, who loved construction vehicles when he was two or three years old," the author once told *SATA.* "We had books that showed pictures of construction vehicles and

Susanna Leonard Hill takes a unique twist on a popular U.S. tradition in her picture book **Punxsutawney Phyllis,** *featuring artwork by Jeffrey* ***Ebbeler.***

told about what jobs they did, but nothing with parts that moved or that showed how a bunch of equipment could work together to complete a project. So I wrote one."

Hill later wrote *Punxsutawney Phyllis,* a feminist take on Groundhog Day. The work follows the efforts of young Phyllis, the niece of celebrated forecaster Punxsutawney Phil, to follow in her uncle's footsteps. After Phil stubbornly predicts another six weeks of winter, Phyllis tries unsuccessfully to convince him that the signs of an early spring are all around. "*Punxsutawney Phyllis* was inspired by two things," Hill explained to *SATA.* "There is much talk on the radio where I live on Groundhog Day about Punxsutawney Phil making his prediction. One Groundhog Day I was driving my children to nursery school, listening to Phil's prediction, and I thought—why should Phil always by a boy? A girl could do the job just as well! Also, where I live, winter seems very long. I thought, it's my story, I can make anything I want happen, so how about an early spring for once?"

In *No Sword Fighting in the House,* two brothers take their horseplay outdoors, and in the process they trample their mother's daffodils, jeopardizing her chance to win a gardening competition. According to Hill, *"No Sword Fighting in the House* was inspired by my children's play and by a situation that I think is common in all families: the intentional or unintentional miscommunication between grownups and kids." Reviewing the tale in the *Bulletin of the Center for Children's Books,* Deborah Stevenson commented that "readers will revel at the sardonic and absurd wit mustered in the spare prose," and a *Kirkus Reviews* contributor described *No Sword Fighting in the House* as "a quick and amusing read."

Hill once told *SATA:* "I write because I love to write. I can't not write. There is something so exciting about a blank page, full of possibilities, waiting for whatever story you dream up. I like to write stories that will entertain children or touch them in some meaningful way, that will encourage in them the same love of reading that I have always enjoyed.

"My work is particularly influenced by my own childhood and by my children. Everything is new to children. The world is full of wonder, full of things to learn and do and experience for the first time, and hence full of ideas for stories.

"Sometimes an idea comes full-blown to my mind, and I just write it. More often I get a piece of an idea—a character, a setting, a problem—and I have to let it sit in the back corner of my mind for a while to simmer until I get the rest of the story together and it becomes something that works. Once I have written a story, I try to put it aside for a while and forget about it, so I can come back to it later with a fresh perspective and see if it still works or whether it needs tweaking. A lot of the

writing process is about the working in your mind that takes place before you ever set pen to paper (or fingers to keyboard)."

Biographical and Critical Sources

PERIODICALS

Booklist, May 1, 2007, Todd Morning, review of *No Sword Fighting in the House,* p. 98.
Bulletin of the Center for Children's Books, March, 2007, Deborah Stevenson, review of *No Sword Fighting in the House.*
Kirkus Reviews, March 15, 2007, review of *No Sword Fighting in the House.*
School Library Journal, October, 2005, Linda Staskus, review of *Punxsutawney Phyllis,* p. 116; August, 2007, Danielle Nicole Du Puis, review of *No Sword Fighting in the House,* p. 81.

ONLINE

Susanna Leonard Hill Home Page, http://www.susannahill. com (August 10, 2008).*

*   *   *

HOBBS, Valerie 1941-

Personal

Born April 18, 1941, in Metuchen, NJ; daughter of Herbert Trevor Evans and Alise (a painter) Minney; married Gary Johnson, 1962 (divorced, 1973); married Jack Hobbs (a teacher), June 18, 1978; children: (first marriage) Juliet. *Education:* University of California, Santa Barbara, B.A., 1968, M.A., 1978. *Politics:* Democrat. *Hobbies and other interests:* Golf, hiking, travel, poker.

Addresses

Home and office—Santa Barbara, CA. *Agent*—Barbara Markowitz, 117 North Mansfield Ave., Los Angeles, CA 90036. *E-mail*—valhobbs@cox.net.

Career

Writer. High school English teacher on the Hawaiian island of Oahu, 1971-74; University of California, Santa Barbara, lecturer in writing, 1981-2001, professor emeritus, beginning 2001. Speaker on writing topics at schools and seminars.

Member

PEN Center West, Society of Children's Book Writers and Illustrators, South Coast Writing Project.

Awards, Honors

Best Books for Young Adults selection, American Library Association, 1995, for *How Far Would You Have Gotten If I Hadn't Called You Back?;* Teen Choice

Valerie Hobbs (Reproduced by permission.)

Award, International Reading Association, for *Get It While It's Hot. Or Not;* One Hundred Titles for Reading and Sharing inclusion, New York Public Library, 1999, for *Carolina Crow Girl,* and 2007, for *Anything but Ordinary;* Best Books of the Year selection, Bank Street College of Education, for *Charlie's Run;* PEN/Norma Klein Award for "emerging voice of literary merit in American children's literature," 1999; Quick Pick for Reluctant Readers selection, American Library Association, for *Letting Go of Bobby James; or, How I Found Myself of Steam by Sally Jo Walker;* named Judy Goddard Arizona Library Association Young Adult Author of the Year, 2003; Distinguished Book of the Year selection, Children's Literature Council of Southern California, and Henry Bergh Award, American Society for the Prevention of Cruelty to Animals, both for *Defiance.*

Writings

How Far Would You Have Gotten If I Hadn't Called You Back?, Orchard Books (New York, NY), 1995.
Get It While It's Hot. Or Not, Orchard Books (New York, NY), 1996.

Carolina Crow Girl, Farrar, Straus (New York, NY), 1999.
Charlie's Run, Frances Foster Books (New York, NY), 2000.
Tender, Farrar, Straus (New York, NY), 2001.
Sonny's War, Farrar, Straus (New York, NY), 2002.
Stefan's Story, Farrar, Straus (New York, NY), 2003.
Letting Go of Bobby James; or, How I Found Myself of Steam by Sally Jo Walker, Farrar, Straus (New York, NY), 2004.
Call It a Gift (adult fiction), University of Nevada Press (Reno, NV), 2005.
Defiance, Farrar, Straus (New York, NY), 2005.
Sheep, Farrar, Straus (New York, NY), 2006.
Anything but Ordinary, Farrar, Straus (New York, NY), 2007.

Work represented in anthologies, including *California Childhoods,* edited by Gary Soto, 1987. Contributor of stories to magazines, including *Northeast Corridor, Chrysalis, American Fiction, New Renaissance,* and *Kansas Quarterly.*

Sidelights

Valerie Hobbs did not set out to write novels for young adults, but ever since critics praised her 1995 coming-of-age story *How Far Would You Have Gotten If I Hadn't Called You Back?,* she has been respected as an author of fiction for teens. At the rate of approximately one book per year, Hobbs crafts character-driven tales about young people on the verge of adulthood who are forced to make serious decisions about the direction their lives will take. Often her young protagonists are confronted with circumstances beyond their control: the death of a guardian or a boyfriend, parental divorce, or physical disability. How they deal with these challenges forms the core of Hobbs's works. *Horn Book* contributor Jeannine M. Chapman observed that in Hobbs's novels, "the confusion of adolescence is truthfully rendered," and a *Publishers Weekly* reviewer credited Hobbs with "a keen understanding of adolescent moods and concerns."

Hobbs keenly recalls the defining moment of her own young adulthood. When she was in high school, her parents relocated the family from New Jersey to California, separating her not only from friends and beloved activities, but also from the urban surroundings in which she had grown up. This experience provides the catalyst for Hobbs's debut novel, *How Far Would You Have Gotten If I Hadn't Called You Back?* The story of a young woman with a love of both racing cars and the men who drive them, the book has drawn praise from critics for its original and sensitive portrait of a teen-ager struggling to find herself amidst a sea of contradictory influences. The title comes from an expression often used by the author's father; the plot comes from the incidents in her own childhood that probably prompted her father's question.

In *How Far Would You Have Gotten If I Hadn't Called You Back?,* sixteen-year-old Bronwyn Lewis seeks to carve an unconventional life for herself. Growing up in

the late 1950s, in a generation where young women her age chose role models like Doris Day and Donna Reed and looked forward to marriage and a future of domesticity, Bronwyn prefers to be behind the wheel of a dragster. Like her creator, the fictional Bronwyn has moved from urban New Jersey to rural California at age fifteen. Her interests and hobbies are different than those of the teens in her new town, and fitting in at her new high school has been almost impossible. The fact that her family is now poor and her out-of-work dad has already attempted suicide makes Bronwyn feel even more withdrawn. Finally, a friendship with Lanie, a pretty but poor young woman from the "wild side" of town, allows Bronwyn a way in to a peer group. She falls behind in school, dumps her interest in playing classical piano for rock 'n' roll, and starts dating, drinking, and hanging out with the drag-racing crowd. A sexual fling with the much older racer known as J.C. is interrupted by a budding love affair with the mature and far-more-suitable Will, but when Will leaves for his first year at West Point, Bronwyn returns to her old ways, with tragic consequences.

Cover of Hobbs's middle-grade novel **How Far Would You Have Gotten If I Hadn't Called You Back?,** *featuring artwork by Jon Weiman.*
(Orchard Books, 1995. Illustration copyright © 1995 by Jon Weiman. Reproduced by permission of the illustrator.)

Calling Bronwyn "a believable and realistic voice," Joel Shoemaker praised *How Far Would You Have Gotten If I Hadn't Called You Back?* in his review for *School Library Journal,* noting that the novel's "themes are subtly evoked and life's lessons are learned the hard way." *Booklist* reviewer Stephanie Zvirin called the novel "an enticing coming-of-age story," asserting that Hobbs "manipulates the elements (including the sex) with energy, confidence, and surprise."

Hobbs's second novel, *Get It While It's Hot. Or Not,* focuses on friendships and teen sexual relationships. Megan, Mia, Elaine, and Kit have been fast friends since eighth grade, but as they begin their junior year of high school they find themselves beset with problems. Kit is pregnant and confined to bed, and Megan is being pressured for sex by a boyfriend. Megan's response to her situation is to write a piece on sexual issues for the school newspaper, but the principal bars its publication. According to Marcia Mann in *Voice of Youth Advocates,* readers of *Get It While It's Hot. Or Not* "relate to Megan's struggle to define the boundaries of friendship and her responsibilities to her family and community." Janice M. Del Negro, writing in the *Bulletin of the Center for Children's Books,* observed that young-adult readers would likely find the "friends, group dynamics and the contemporary themes appealing." In *Horn Book* Lauren Adams called *Get It While It's Hot. Or Not* "well paced and highly readable, taking on serious issues with humor and intelligence."

Both *Carolina Crow Girl* and *Stefan's Story* explore the lives of two unique individuals. Carolina, the heroine of *Carolina Crow Girl,* lives in an old school bus with her single mother and baby sister. When she saves a crow that has been abandoned by its mother, her enthusiasm for the fledgling leads to a friendship with Stefan Millington Crouch, a wealthy boy who is confined to a wheelchair. Stefan's family offers Carolina a chance to escape her poverty, but just as she realizes her crow will need its freedom, she rejects the offer and remains with her mother. *Booklist* contributor Lauren Peterson found *Carolina Crow Girl* to be "a deeply moving story with rich, complex characters," and a *Publishers Weekly* critic deemed it "sensitive in its explorations of friendships."

In a sequel, *Stefan's Story,* Stefan travels by himself to Oregon to attend Carolina's mother's wedding and finds that his feelings for Carolina are deepening from friendship into something more serious. For her part, Carolina is embroiled in a controversy that pits local logging interests against environmentalists and fishermen as preparations are made to cut down a local old-growth forest. Hobbs does not settle for easy answers in this novel, as Stefan confronts his disabilities and Carolina sees both sides of the logging dispute. According to Cindy Darling Codell in *School Library Journal,* the author "gives proper balance to the economic pressures of the issue." Writing for *Booklist,* Hazel Rochman

commented of *Stefan's Story* that "the wonder of this story is the fusion of the small things with exciting action."

Hobbs explores the plight of urban runaways in *Charlie's Run.* Charlie, always a model son, decides to run away from home in protest of his parents' impending separation. He intends his absence to be short, but when he falls in with the volatile Doo, he finds himself in Los Angeles, living on the streets. A *Publishers Weekly* reviewer praised the novel as "an emotionally complex rendition of a familiar story," adding that Hobbs's "energetic, honest storytelling" moves the novel along. Connie Tyrrell Burns in *School Library Journal* likewise admired the "fast-moving plot, complex and appealing characters" in a book she characterized as "a sure winner," and a *Horn Book* critic deemed *Charlie's Run* "a compelling story, convincingly told."

Tender once again addresses the issues of lifestyle change and adjustment to a new household. Here Olivia Trager is uprooted when her beloved grandmother dies. Forced to move from Manhattan to rural California, Olivia must live with a father who abandoned her at birth. Gradually Olivia's fury gives way to acceptance, particularly after she begins to help her father with his deep-sea-diving expeditions. In *School Library Journal* correspondent Francisca Goldsmith liked Olivia's strength and personality, adding that the book draws readers in "immediately and inextricably." In her *Booklist* review of *Tender*, Debbie Carton found Hobbs's characters "wonderfully human and fully realized," commending the story for its "loving undertones that will linger."

Hobbs was a college student during the Vietnam War era, and her brother was drafted to serve in the conflict. *Sonny's War* draws upon personal experience as Hobbs crafts a tale of a teenager whose brother is in Southeast Asia while she participates in anti-war protests. She delves into the morally complex issues surrounding the Vietnam War as young Cory becomes disillusioned by the actions of a beloved schoolteacher who goes too far during a violent protest. The war's toll on individuals is also portrayed, as Cory's brother returns with wounds both physical and psychological. Miriam Lang Budin noted in *School Library Journal* that *Sonny's War* reveals "the ambiguities and tensions driving the nation and individual citizens during this difficult time." In her review for *Horn Book,* Martha V. Parravano called *Sonny's War* "a convincing, affecting novel," noting that the central character "is as real as real, completely believable in all her teenage vulnerability and sharp-eyed observation."

Letting Go of Bobby James; or, How I Found Myself of Steam by Sally Jo Walker concerns a newlywed sixteen-year-old who is abandoned in Florida by her abusive husband. Virtually penniless, Sally Jo—known as Jody—finds a job as a waitress in Jackson Beach, and she quickly bonds with her older coworkers, who be-

come her surrogate family. When Bobby arrives in town, Jody must decide if reconciliation is the wisest course. "Hobbs handles tough subjects with a light hand," wrote *Horn Book* contributor Jennifer M. Brabander, and *Booklist* critic Ilene Cooper stated that the narrative "shines with Jody's simple, but never simplistic, insights." *Letting Go of Bobby James* "is an excellent tale of inspiration, self-reliance, and making lemonade of life's lemons," noted James Blasingame in the *Journal of Adolescent & Adult Literacy.* "Hobbs carefully and gently handles adult issues in such a way that this novel would be appropriate reading for any young person old enough to understand Jody's plight."

Defiance centers on Toby Steiner, an eleven-year-old cancer survivor hoping to spend a carefree summer in the country. When Toby discovers a new lump in his side, he dreads the thought of returning to the hospital and decides not to tell his parents. Instead, he finds solace in his newfound friendship with elderly neighbor Pearl Rhodes Richardson, a celebrated poet who is nearly blind. "Without morbidity, Hobbs ranges between tart and poignant, sorrowful rage and hope," Deirdre F. Baker stated in *Horn Book,* and *School Library Journal* contributor Marie Orlando observed that in *Defiance* the author "keeps the focus on Toby's conflicted feelings, ultimately celebrating the source of strength he and Pearl become to one another."

In *Sheep,* a work for younger readers, a border collie drifts from one home to another after a fire destroys the California ranch where he has learned to herd. "The classic foundling story is beautifully told in the dog's simple, first-person voice," remarked Rochman in *Booklist.* A pair of social misfits are the focus of *Anything but Ordinary,* a critically acclaimed young-adult novel. Best friends throughout high school, New Jersey teenagers Winifred Owens and Bernie Federman make plans to attend the same college, but Bernie's life falls apart after his mother dies unexpectedly. Winifred eventually heads to school in California and undergoes a remarkable personal transformation. When Bernie arrives on campus, he is startled by her new look and attitude. *Anything but Ordinary* "captures the headiness of college life, the thrill of intellectual discovery, and the ups and downs of first love," noted Kathleen Isaacs in *Booklist,* and a *Publishers Weekly* critic stated that Hobbs "covers the years with smooth pacing, always keeping her protagonists front and center."

In an interview with *Authors and Artists for Young Adults (AAYA),* Hobbs said she writes about growing up under pressure because she wants young adults to know that they are not alone in their troubles. "I think I write to share some feelings I've had and some feelings I think a lot of people have, so when they read them there might be a moment of recognition when they say 'I'm not the only one who feels this way,' or 'I'm OK, and I can get through this,'" she said. "I remember the teenage years being very stressful and thinking I was the only one going through certain things. When I talk

to teenagers now, they seem to feel that way, too. I think it gives you courage to see that somebody else went through similar situations and made it to the other side. I realize that's a part of why I write—to share common feelings."

Biographical and Critical Sources

BOOKS

Authors and Artists for Young Adults, Volume 28, Gale (Detroit, MI), 1999.

PERIODICALS

ALAN Review, winter, 2004, Jim Blasingame, "Caring about the Topic: An Interview with Valerie Hobbs."

Booklist, October 1, 1995, Stephanie Zvirin, review of *How Far Would You Have Gotten If I Hadn't Called You Back?,* p. 304; February 15, 1999, Lauren Peterson, review of *Carolina Crow Girl,* p. 1070; August, 2001, Debbie Carton, review of *Tender,* p. 2107; November 1, 2002, Hazel Rochman, review of *Sonny's War,* p. 484; September 15, 2003, Hazel Rochman, review of *Stefan's Story,* p. 236; July, 2004, Ilene Cooper, review of *Letting Go of Bobby James; or How I Found Myself of Steam,* p. 1834; August, 2005, Michael Cart, review of *Defiance,* p. 2028; February 1, 2006, Hazel Rochman, review of *Sheep,* p. 50; April 15, 2007, Kathleen Isaacs, review of *Anything but Ordinary,* p. 38.

Bulletin of the Center for Children's Books, November, 1996, Janice M. Del Negro, review of *Get It While It's Hot. Or Not,* p. 99.

Horn Book, December, 1996, Lauren Adams, review of *Get It While It's Hot,* p. 744; March, 2000, review of *Charlie's Run,* p. 195; September, 2001, Jeannine M. Chapman, review of *Tender,* p. 584; November-December, 2002, Martha V. Parravano, review of *Sonny's War,* p. 760; September-October, 2004, Jennifer M. Brabander, review of *Letting Go of Bobby James; or How I Found My Self of Steam,* p. 586; September-October, 2005, Deirdre F. Baker, review of *Defiance,* p. 580.

Journal of Adolescent & Adult Literacy, October, 2004, James Blasingame, review of *Letting Go of Bobby James, or How I Found My Self of Steam,* p. 170, and interview with Hobbs, p. 176.

Publishers Weekly, December 18, 1995, Nathalie Op de Beeck, "Flying Starts: Three Children's Novelists Talk about Their Fall '95 Debuts," pp. 28-30; March 15, 1999, review of *Carolina Crow Girl,* p. 60; February 7, 2000, review of *Charlie's Run,* p. 86; August 27, 2001, review of *Tender,* p. 86; July 19, 2004, review of *Letting Go of Bobby James; or How I Found My Self of Steam,* p. 163; April 24, 2006, review of *Sheep,* p. 61; February 12, 2007, review of *Anything but Ordinary,* p. 87.

School Library Journal, October, 1995, Joel Shoemaker, review of *How Far Would You Have Gotten If I Hadn't Called You Back?,* p. 155; March, 2000, Connie Tyr-

rell Burns, review of *Charlie's Run,* p. 238; September, 2001, Francisca Goldsmith, review of *Tender,* p. 225; November, 2002, Miriam Lang Budin, review of *Sonny's War,* p. 168; August, 2003, Cindy Darling Codell, review of *Stefan's Story,* p. 160; September, 2004, Roxanne Myers Spencer, review of *Letting Go of Bobby James; or How I Found My Self of Steam,* p. 208; September, 2005, Marie Orlando, review of *Defiance,* p. 205; March, 2006, Lee Bock, review of *Sheep,* p. 192; March, 2007, Jennifer Barnes, review of *Anything but Ordinary,* p. 212.

Voice of Youth Advocates, December, 1995, C. Allen Nichols, review of *How Far Would You Have Gotten If I Hadn't Called You Back?,* p. 302; December, 1996, Marcia Mann, review of *Get It While It's Hot,* p. 270.

ONLINE

Valerie Hobbs Home Page, http://www.valeriehobbs.com (August 10, 2008).

Macmillan Web site, http://us.macmillan.com/ (August 10, 2008), "Valerie Hobbs."*

*   *   *

HOKENSON, Terry 1948-

Personal

Born 1948; children: one daughter. *Hobbies and other interests:* Camping, genealogy, reading, bicycling.

Addresses

Home—Minneapolis, MN. *E-mail*—hokenson@thewin terroad.com.

Career

Writer. Has worked as a carpenter and an attorney.

Writings

The Winter Road (young-adult novel), Front Street (Ashville, NC), 2006.

Sidelights

Terry Hokenson's first novel, *The Winter Road,* is a work for young adults. It follows the adventures of seventeen-year-old Willa, who makes a foolhardy decision that has long-term results. When her uncle is too drunk to make the trip safely, Willa decides to take her uncle's plane without permission and fly his winter supply route. Although Willa is a licensed pilot, she crashes during the flight, and finds herself stranded in the snowy Canadian wilderness.

Jennifer Mattson, in a review for *Booklist,* remarked of *The Winter Road* that "the mortal challenges Willa faces make for a gripping narrative, one sharpened by vis-

ceral details." Vicky Smith, in a contribution for *Horn Book,* commented that "readers may well feel they've gone through a whole survival course with her." Sharon Morrison, writing for *School Library Journal,* noted that beyond being a story of survival, *The Winter Road* is "a well-written, thoughtful book about a girl's desperate efforts to gain her father's approval."

Hokenson once commented: "*The Winter Road* is based on a story I wrote for my daughter when she was eleven years old. I told her a tale of a young woman using her wits to survive a great challenge. While I had long enjoyed letter writing, journaling and travel writing, this was the first fiction I attempted to publish. I am drawn toward the existential struggles of emerging adults, and to settings of outdoor adventure. While I wrote the core of *The Winter Road* "off the top of my head" and researched the details later, the process is reversed for my current work in progress. I've done a lot of research and undertaken field trips first, to acquire the materials of the setting (immigrant farm life in central Minnesota in 1880), and am constructing the story later. In both cases, the story is dashed off in a careless heat, while the organization and refinement follow.

"I was surprised to learn how very long one may spend refining a story, learning how to write, learning how to tell a tale. Eudora Welty is one of my favorite authors. The power of her craft is striking, yet invisible.

"I want my books to provide young people, including those inhabiting older adults, with an engaging adventure that is both entertaining and existentially productive."

Biographical and Critical Sources

PERIODICALS

Booklist, June 1, 2006, Jennifer Mattson, review of *The Winter Road,* p. 60.
Children's Bookwatch, June, 2006, review of *The Winter Road.*
Horn Book, May-June, 2006, Vicky Smith, review of *The Winter Road,* p. 319.
Kirkus Reviews, May 1, 2006, review of *The Winter Road,* p. 461.
Library Media Connection, November-December, 2006, Donna Steffan, review of *The Winter Road,* p. 74.
Publishers Weekly, May 29, 2006, review of *The Winter Road,* p. 60.
School Library Journal, May, 2006, Sharon Morrison, review of *The Winter Road,* p. 128.

ONLINE

Winter Road Web site, http://www.thewinterroad.com/ (February 28, 2007), author biography.

J

JAHN-CLOUGH, Lisa 1967-

Personal

Last name pronounced "Yahn-Clow"; born March 3, 1967, in Wakefield, RI; daughter of Garrett C. Clough (a zoologist) and Elena Jahn (an artist). *Education:* Hampshire College, B.A., 1988; Emerson College, M.F. A., 1993.

Addresses

E-mail—jahnclough@aol.com.

Career

Writer, illustrator, and teacher. Emerson College, Boston, MA, teacher of writing and children's literature, 1994-2004; Maine College of Art, interim chair of illustration program, 2004-08; Hamline University, low-residency faculty in writing for children and young adults, 2007; teacher of writing for children and young adults, Vermont College. Teacher of writing at conferences and workshops, including Children's Museum of Maine, Boston Public Library, Stonecoast Writer's Conference, Portland, ME, and Company of Writers, Cambridge, MA. Judge, Emerging Writer Award, PEN American Center, 2002.

Lisa Jahn-Clough (Reproduced by permission of Lisa Jahn-Clough.)

Writings

Country Girl, City Girl (young-adult novel), Houghton Mifflin (Boston, MA), 2004.
Me, Penelope (young-adult novel), Houghton Mifflin (Boston, MA), 2007.

SELF-ILLUSTRATED

Alicia and Her Happy Way of Life, Arm-in-Arm Press (Boston, MA), 1991.
Alicia's Evil Side, Arm-in-Arm Press (Boston, MA), 1992.

Alicia Has a Bad Day, Houghton Mifflin (Boston, MA), 1994.
My Happy Birthday Book!, Houghton Mifflin (Boston, MA), 1996.
ABC Yummy, Houghton Mifflin (Boston, MA), 1997.
1 2 3 Yippie, Houghton Mifflin (Boston, MA), 1998.
My Friend and I, Houghton Mifflin (Boston, MA), 1999.
Missing Molly, Houghton Mifflin (Boston, MA), 2000.
Simon and Molly plus Hester, Houghton Mifflin (Boston, MA), 2001.
Alicia's Best Friends, Houghton Mifflin (Boston, MA), 2003.

On the Hill, Houghton Mifflin (Boston, MA), 2004.
Little Dog, Houghton Mifflin (Boston, MA), 2006.

ILLUSTRATOR

Carol Snyder, *We're Painting,* HarperFestival (New York, NY), 2002.
Laurie Friedman, *A Big Bed for Jed,* Dial Books (New York, NY), 2002.

Sidelights

Lisa Jahn-Clough has turned a lifelong interest in reading and writing into a career as an author and illustrator of children's books. An avid writer and artist since the age of four, when she was handed her first paintbrush by her mother and dictated her first story to her father, Jahn-Clough considers the art of creating books to be her primary means of expression. Supplementing her writing and drawing with several jobs, including teaching, Jahn-Clough wrote, illustrated, and self-published several children's picture books before *Alicia Has a Bad Day* was picked up by Boston publisher Houghton Mifflin and released in 1994.

Writing for children is especially important to Jahn-Clough because, as she once told *SATA,* "I recall my own youth vividly, both the warmth and the suffering, and feel that I have something to say to children of all ages." Raised on a small farm in Rhode Island by her zoologist father and artist mother, Jahn-Clough and her older brother grew up around all sorts of animals in an environment that encouraged creativity. "There was an entire wall in our kitchen plastered from top to bottom with [our] artwork," she recalled.

Cover of Jahn-Clough's self-illustrated picture book **Alicia Has a Bad Day,** *featuring graphic, child-friendly art.* (Illustration copyright © 1994 by Lisa Jahn-Clough. Reprinted by permission of Houghton Mifflin Harcourt Publishing Company. All rights reserved.)

Although determined to make writing a large part of her life, Jahn-Clough's start in publishing would be hard work. As she once explained to *SATA:* "In 1990 I wrote and illustrated a small book (literally small, approximately three inches by four inches with black and white drawings and hand-written text, tied with ribbon) called *Alicia and Her Happy Way of Life.* It describes Alicia and her seemingly relentless happiness and delight in the world. After several friends pointed out that not even Alicia could be happy all the time, I felt I needed to explore Alicia's other moods. Thus came *Alicia Has a Bad Day.*

"I wrote and illustrated four books about the character Alicia and self-published them. . . . I marketed them from 1990 to 1993 with some regional success, mostly in Maine where I grew up." Although Jahn-Clough enjoyed writing her books, having *Alicia Has a Bad Day* published by a mainstream publishing house like Houghton Mifflin marked a turning point in her career. "Although I learned a great deal about the field, about publishing, about marketing, and about believing in my work and myself from this experience . . . self-publishing is not something I advocate," she told *SATA.* "Although it was exciting, it was also a lot of work and produced very little money. Having my work out there and knowing others were reading it was my main motivation. It is incredibly gratifying to have your work reach other people."

Alicia Has a Bad Day features a character that its author calls "sort of an alter-ego. . . . She is a strong, spunky, independent child who is not afraid of her own emotions, although she does not always understand them." A happy person by nature, Alicia wakes up on the "wrong side of the bed" one morning. When her dog, Neptune, does not even lick her face like he usually does, it puts her further out of sorts. She tries to shake off her bad mood by writing about it, playing her favorite music really loud and dancing, and going out to play. Of course, it rains; she gives up and crawls back into bed. Finally, Neptune cheers her up with a doggy kiss, and Alicia's day gets better. A *Publishers Weekly* contributor observed that "Jahn-Clough's simplistic brushwork, roughly hewn in straight-from-the-tube colors, wryly conveys surliness."

Jahn-Clough's spunky heroine returns in *Alicia's Best Friends.* In the work, Alicia is put on the spot when her four closest pals demand that she choose one of them as her favorite. She resolves the situation by acknowledging that each friend is special to her in a particular way. Jahn-Clough "once again presents a complex aspect of friendship in a way children will understand," wrote Ellen Mandel in *Booklist.* A *Kirkus Reviews* contributor stated that "the brightly hued illustrations sparkle with the energy and vivacity of Alicia's personality," and Gay Lynn Van Vleck, reviewing the book in *School Library Journal,* wrote that "childlike, multicultural cartoon paintings prove highly successful in using color to evoke mood."

Jahn-Clough tells a story of two good friends in her self-illustrated picture book Missing Molly.

New neighbors have their budding friendship tested in *My Friend and I.* Here a young girl, the story's narrator, has fun playing with the boy who has moved in next door, until the pair argue and she damages his new stuffed animal. Together, the children come up with a solution that repairs both the toy and their budding relationship. "The understated message that friendship includes sorrow and forgiveness makes this a solid choice" for children, according to Anne Knickerbocker in *School Library Journal.* A *Publishers Weekly* critic remarked that Jahn-Clough "never betrays her narrator's perspective, neither in the text nor in her paintings," and *Booklist* contributor Hazel Rochman stated of *My Friend and I* that "young preschoolers will like the bright, simple, childlike illustrations."

Jahn-Clough introduces the characters of Molly and Simon in *Missing Molly.* The two best friends love to play hide-and-seek, but Simon complains that Molly makes the game too easy by always hiding in the same place. During one of Simon's visits Molly is nowhere to be found, and a mysterious, strangely dressed girl who appears at the door joins in the search. After Simon fails to locate his friend, the stranger reveals her secret: she is really Molly in disguise. Ilene Cooper, reviewing *Missing Molly* in *Booklist,* remarked that "the search that turns silly will tickle listeners." In *School Library Journal,* Lisa Dennis noted that there is "an engaging element of fantasy implied in the illustrations."

In *Simon and Molly plus Hester* "both story and illustrations capture a child's misgivings about change and

being left out," according to Wanda Meyers-Hines in *School Library Journal.* Simon and Molly do everything together, but new neighbor Hester has her own interests. When Molly invites Hester to play, Simon feels threatened. Molly comes up with the solution: she suggests that Simon teach Hester how to ride a two-wheeler, and Hester agrees to show Simon how to fold a paper airplane.

On the Hill is written in more of a folktale style than Jahn-Clough's previous picture books. Camille and Franzi live on opposite sides of the same hill, and though they love their homes and their animals, they are lonely. One day, they decide to explore the hill and find each other. Realizing that their homes are too small to share, they come up with a unique solution: they take their homes apart and combine them. "Cheery, cartoonish, childlike paintings illustrate this simple, satisfying tale," wrote Sally R. Dow in *School Library Journal.* The illustrations inject "a comfy feel as well as a subtle note of humor," according to a *Publishers Weekly* contributor, and a *Kirkus Reviews* contributor credited Jahn-Clough's art with "evok[ing] an unspecified time and place that feels very old and yet abiding and comforting."

In another tale of friends coming together, *Little Dog,* a street dog finds a home with an artist, whose work he inspires to be more cheerful. As Jahn-Clough's story progresses, Rosa and Little Dog find joy in friendship, and the illustrations become brighter and more cheerful. "Children will revel in the joy Little Dog and Rosa derive from one another," wrote Randall Enos in a *Booklist* review of the picture book.

Along with her illustrated books for young children, Jahn-Clough is also the author of the young-adult novels *Country Girl, City Girl* and *Me, Penelope.* In the first, teens Phoebe and Melita spend a summer together in Maine, where Phoebe lives and where Melita, a New Yorker, has been shipped while her mother stays in a clinic. Their friendship blossoms over the summer, complicated by Phoebe's growing romantic attraction to Melita. "The author's descriptions of Phoebe's colliding emotions ring true," wrote a contributor to *Publishers Weekly. Me, Penelope* is also a coming-of-age story that features developing sexuality. Lopi longs to leave high school and her complex relationship with her mother, and so she plans to graduate early. She also struggles to cope with her guilt over the car accident that killed her brother ten years before, and like many teens her age she longs to find fulfillment in a sexual relationship. While noting Lopi's self-involved narration, Myrna Marler complimented the novel's "lively prose, humorous situations, and certain quirks in the plot that surprise." Claire E. Gross, reviewing *Me, Penelope* for *Horn Book,* called Lopi's narration "at once brutally cynical and achingly naive."

Jahn-Clough has also illustrated works for other writers. Featuring a text by Laurie Friedman, *A Big Bed for Jed* tells of the difficulties a young boy faces when he switches from his crib to a larger bed. Jed refuses to sleep in his new bed because he is certain he will fall out of it, and his family's efforts to convince him otherwise simply aren't working. Finally, Jed's sister comes up with an ingenious plan that helps settle him in. According to Rosalyn Pierini in *School Library Journal,* Jahn-Clough's artwork does a "great job of conveying the disproportionate sense of scale Jed experiences as he feels dwarfed, overwhelmed, and intimidated by this developmental challenge." Cooper stated that the artist's "pen-and-gouache illustrations, set against bright backgrounds, have the carefree look of kids' own drawings."

Discussing the themes of her books on her home page, Jahn-Clough stated: "We all deal with the same things the kids in my books do: having bad days and not knowing why, wanting something someone else has, missing people, or being jealous or insecure that we aren't loved enough. The great thing about making my own books is that I can create an ending that is logical and happily resolved! I love that part of it." It is hard for her to choose between which she likes better: writing or illustrating. "The writing allows me to convey something with words that has been in my head. If I can express that without being too wordy or analytical or boring it feels great! The art is very playful for me and seems to come with less brain work. I can listen to the radio or to music while I paint, even talk on the phone sometimes, but when I write I have to shut everything out and be in my own thoughts. Both have their appeal."

Biographical and Critical Sources

PERIODICALS

Booklist, April 1, 1997, Julie Corsaro, review of *ABC Yummy,* pp. 1337-1338; March 15, 1998, Hazel Rochman, review of *1 2 3 Yippie,* p. 1249; April 15, 1999, Hazel Rochman, review of *My Friend and I,* p. 1536; February 1, 2000, Ilene Cooper, review of *Missing Molly,* p. 1029; September 1, 2001, Ellen Mandel, review of *Simon and Molly plus Hester,* p. 115; January 1, 2002, Ilene Cooper, review of *A Big Bed for Jed,* p. 864; August, 2002, Cynthia Turnquest, review of *We're Painting,* pp. 1976-1977; March 15, 2003, Ellen Mandel, review of *Alicia's Best Friends,* p. 1332; November 15, 2004, GraceAnne A. DeCandido, review of *Country Girl, City Girl,* p. 574; April 15, 2006, Randall Enos, review of *Little Dog,* p. 52; April 1, 2007, Heather Booth, review of *Me, Penelope,* p. 40.

Horn Book, February 9, 2004, review of *On the Hill,* pp. 80-81; May-June, 2007, Claire E. Gross, review of *Me, Penelope,* p. 284.

Kirkus Reviews, February 15, 2003, review of *Alicia's Best Friends,* p. 309; February 15, 2004, review of *On the Hill,* p. 180; October, 2004, review of *Country Girl, City Girl,* p. 1007; April, 2006, review of *Little Dog,* p. 349; April 1, 2007, review of *Me, Penelope.*

Kliatt, March, 2007, Myrna Marler, review of *Me, Penelope,* p. 15.

Publishers Weekly, August 29, 1994, review of *Alicia Has a Bad Day,* p. 79; January 22, 1996, review of *My Happy Birthday Book,* p. 72; February 8, 1999, review of *My Friend and I,* p. 212; March 27, 2000, review of *Missing Molly,* p. 80; January 7, 2002, review of *A Big Bed for Jed,* p. 63; October 6, 2003, review of *My Friend and I,* p. 87; February 9, 2004, review of *On the Hill,* pp. 81-82; December 6, 2004, review of *Country Girl, City Girl,* p. 60; May 29, 2006, review of *Little Dog,* p. 58; May, 2007, review of *Me, Penelope,* p. 62.

School Library Journal, October, 1994, Margaret C. Howell, review of *Alicia Has a Bad Day,* pp. 91-92; June, 1996, Lisa Marie Gangemi, review of *My Happy Birthday Book,* pp. 100-101; June, 1997, Lisa Dennis, review of *ABC Yummy,* pp. 92-93; July, 1998, Meg Stackpole, review of *1 2 3 Yippie,* p. 76; May, 1999, Anne Knickerbocker, review of *My Friend and I,* pp. 90-91; April, 2000, Lisa Dennis, review of *Missing Molly,* p. 107; September, 2001, Wanda Meyers-Hines, review of *Simon and Molly plus Hester,* p. 191; July, 2002, Rosalyn Pierini, review of *A Big Bed for Jed,* p. 90; March, 2003, Gay Lynn Van Vleck, review of *Alicia's Best Friends,* p. 196; May, 2004, Sally R. Dow, review of *On the Hill,* p. 114; November, 2004, Faith Brautigam, review of *Country Girl, City Girl,* p. 146; May, 2006, Susan Weitz, review of *Little Dog,* p. 90; July, 2007, Diane P. Tuccillo, review of *Me, Penelope,* p. 104.

ONLINE

Berkeley Beacon Online, http://www.berkeleybeacon.com/ (November 15, 2001), Megan Petersen, "Illustrations in Learning."

Houghton Mifflin Web site, http://www.houghtonmifflinbooks.com/ (September 30, 2008), "Lisa Jahn-Clough."

Lisa Jahn-Clough Home Page, http://www.lisajahnclough.com (September 30, 2008).

*   *   *

JOHNSON, Stacie
See MYERS, Walter Dean

K

KINGSLEY, Kaza

Personal

Born in Cleveland, OH. *Hobbies and other interests:* Traveling, movies.

Addresses

Home—Cincinnati, OH. *E-mail*—kazakingsley@fuse. net.

Career

Writer, artist, and singer.

Writings

Erec Rex: The Dragon's Eye (novel), illustrated by Melvyn Grant, Firelight Press (Cincinnati, OH), 2006.

Sidelights

In her first fantasy novel, *Erec Rex: The Dragon's Eye,* Kaza Kingsley tells the story of young Erec Rex, who finds a secret door in Grand Central Station that leads to a magical world. Erec is out to save his kidnapped mother whom he can see and speak to anytime he wants through a pair of magic eyeglasses. In the process of trying to rescue his mother and discover the real villains, Erec and his friend Bethany find themselves participating in a series of contests that will decide who will be the rulers of three magical kingdoms.

"Entertaining magics and magical gear, along with polished vignettes from Grant, animate familiar fantasy tropes in this seriocomic debut," reported a *Kirkus Reviews* contributor in a review of *Erec Rex.* Other reviewers also had praise for the novel, a contributor to the *Watcher* online calling it "an entertaining book" in which "the characters are riveting." In *Fantasy Novel Review,* online critic Sherryl King-Wilds referred to *Erec Rex* as "a fun, fascinating book that makes you want to chill out for a while and just read." Like several other critics, King-Wilds also acknowledged the book's debt to the extremely successful "Harry Potter" fantasy series by J.K. Rowling, but pointed out that *The Dragon's Eye* "stands on its own!"

Biographical and Critical Sources

PERIODICALS

Kirkus Reviews, October 1, 2006, review of *Erec Rex: The Dragon's Eye,* p. 1017.

ONLINE

Erec Rex Web site, http:// www.erecrex.com (April 19, 2007).
Fantasy Novel Review Online, http:// www.fantasynovel review.com/ (April 19, 2007), Sherryl King-Wilds, review of *Erec Rex.*
Watcher Online, http:// www.readthewatcher.org/ (April 19, 2007), review of *Eric Rex.*

* * *

KLINE, Suzy 1943-

Personal

Born August 27, 1943, in Berkeley, CA; daughter of Harry C. (in real estate) and Martha S. (a substitute school teacher) Weaver; married Rufus O. Kline (a college teacher, newspaper correspondent, and children's author), October 12, 1968; children: Jennifer, Emily. *Education:* Attended Columbia University; University of California, Berkeley, B.A., 1966; California State College (now University), Hayward, Standard Elemen-

Suzy Kline (Reproduced by permission.)

tary Credential, 1967. *Politics:* Democrat. *Religion:* Presbyterian. *Hobbies and other interests:* Writing, walking, dancing, sports, reading, movies and plays, spending time with grandchildren, traveling with her husband.

Addresses

Home—Willington, CT. *E-mail*—Suzy@SuzyKline.com.

Career

Author and educator. Elementary schoolteacher in Richmond, CA, 1968-71; Southwest School, Torrington, CT, elementary teacher, 1976-2000. University of Connecticut, Storrs, graduate instructor in teaching children's literature, 2001-03. Presenter at schools and workshops.

Member

Society of Children's Book Writers and Illustrators, PEN, New England Reading Association, Connecticut Education Association, Torrington Education Association.

Awards, Honors

Best Books designation, *Christian Science Monitor,* 1985, and West Virginia Children's Book Award, 1987-88, for *Herbie Jones;* International Reading Association

Children's Choice Awards, 1986, for *Herbie Jones,* 1987, for *What's the Matter with Herbie Jones?,* 1989, for *Horrible Harry in Room 2-B,* 1990, for *Orp,* and 1991, for *Orp and the Chop Suey Burgers;* School District Teacher of the Year Award, State of Connecticut, 1987; Probus Educator of the Year Award, 1988.

Writings

FOR CHILDREN

Shhhh!, illustrated by Dora Leder, Albert Whitman (Morton Grove, IL), 1984.

Don't Touch!, illustrated by Dora Leder, Albert Whitman (Morton Grove, IL), 1985.

Ooops!, illustrated by Dora Leder, Albert Whitman (Morton Grove, IL), 1987.

The Hole Book, illustrated by Laurie Newton, Putnam (New York, NY), 1989.

Molly's in a Mess ("Molly Zander" series), illustrated by Diana Cain Blumenthal, Putnam (New York, NY), 1999.

Molly Gets Mad ("Molly Zander" series), illustrated by Diana Cain Blumenthal, Putnam (New York, NY), 2001.

"HERBIE JONES" SERIES

Herbie Jones, illustrated by Richard Williams, Putnam (New York, NY), 1985.

What's the Matter with Herbie Jones?, illustrated by Richard Williams, Putnam (New York, NY), 1986.

Herbie Jones and the Class Gift, illustrated by Richard Williams, Putnam (New York, NY), 1987.

Herbie Jones and the Monster Ball, illustrated by Richard Williams, Putnam (New York, NY), 1988.

Herbie Jones and Hamburger Head, illustrated by Richard Williams, Putnam (New York, NY), 1989.

The Herbie Jones Reader's Theater, illustrated by Richard Williams, Putnam (New York, NY), 1992.

Herbie Jones and the Dark Attic, illustrated by Richard Williams, Putnam (New York, NY), 1992.

Herbie Jones and the Birthday Showdown, illustrated by Carl Cassler, Putnam (New York, NY), 1993.

Herbie Jones Moves On, illustrated by Richard Williams, Putnam (New York, NY), 2003.

Herbie Jones Sails into Second Grade, illustrated by Sami Sweeten, Putnam (New York, NY), 2006.

Herbie Jones and the Second Grade Slippers, illustrated by Sami Sweeten, Putnam (New York, NY), 2006.

"HORRIBLE HARRY" SERIES

Horrible Harry in Room 2-B, illustrated by Frank Remkiewicz, Viking (New York, NY), 1988.

Horrible Harry and the Green Slime, illustrated by Frank Remkiewicz, Viking (New York, NY), 1989.

Horrible Harry and the Ant Invasion, illustrated by Frank Remkiewicz, Viking (New York, NY), 1989.

Horrible Harry's Secret, illustrated by Frank Remkiewicz, Viking (New York, NY), 1990.

Horrible Harry and the Christmas Surprise, illustrated by Frank Remkiewicz, Viking (New York, NY), 1991.

Horrible Harry and the Kickball Wedding, illustrated by Frank Remkiewicz, Viking (New York, NY), 1992.

Horrible Harry and the Dungeon, illustrated by Frank Remkiewicz, Viking (New York, NY), 1996.

Horrible Harry and the Purple People, illustrated by Frank Remkiewicz, Viking (New York, NY), 1997.

Horrible Harry and the Drop of Doom, illustrated by Frank Remkiewicz, Viking (New York, NY), 1998.

Horrible Harry Moves Up to Third Grade, illustrated by Frank Remkiewicz, Viking (New York, NY), 1998.

Horrible Harry Goes to the Moon, illustrated by Frank Remkiewicz, Viking (New York, NY), 2000.

Horrible Harry at Halloween, illustrated by Frank Remkiewicz, Viking (New York, NY), 2000.

Horrible Harry Goes to Sea, illustrated by Frank Remkiewicz, Viking (New York, NY), 2001.

Horrible Harry and the Dragon War, illustrated by Frank Remkiewicz, Viking (New York, NY), 2002.

Horrible Harry and the Mud Gremlins, illustrated by Frank Remkiewicz, Viking (New York, NY), 2003.

Horrible Harry and the Holidaze, illustrated by Frank Remkiewicz, Viking (New York, NY), 2003.

Horrible Harry and the Locked Closet, illustrated by Frank Remkiewicz, Viking (New York, NY), 2004.

Horrible Harry and the Goog, illustrated by Frank Remkiewicz, Viking (New York, NY), 2005.

Horrible Harry Takes the Cake, illustrated by Frank Remkiewicz, Viking (New York, NY), 2006.

Horrible Harry and the Triple Revenge, illustrated by Frank Remkiewicz, Viking (New York, NY), 2006.

Horrible Harry Cracks the Code, illustrated by Frank Remkiewicz, Viking (New York, NY), 2007.

Horrible Harry Bugs the Three Bears, illustrated by Frank Remkiewicz, Viking (New York, NY), 2008.

Horrible Harry and the Dead Letters, illustrated by Amy Wummer, Viking (New York, NY), 2008.

"ORP" SERIES

Orp, Putnam (New York, NY), 1989.

Orp and the Chop Suey Burgers, Putnam (New York, NY), 1990.

Orp Goes to the Hoop, Putnam (New York, NY), 1991.

Who's Orp's Girlfriend?, Putnam (New York, NY), 1992.

Orp and the FBI, Putnam (New York, NY), 1995.

"MARY MARONY" SERIES

Mary Marony and the Snake, illustrated by Blanche Sims, Putnam (New York, NY), 1992.

Mary Marony Hides Out, illustrated by Blanche Sims, Putnam (New York, NY), 1993.

Mary Marony, Mummy Girl, illustrated by Blanche Sims, Putnam (New York, NY), 1994.

Mary Marony and the Chocolate Surprise, illustrated by Blanche Sims, Putnam (New York, NY), 1995.

Marvin and the Mean Words, illustrated by Blanche Sims, Putnam (New York, NY), 1997.

Marvin and the Meanest Girl, illustrated by Blanche Sims, Putnam (New York, NY), 2000.

"SONG LEE" SERIES

Song Lee in Room 2-B, illustrated by Frank Remkiewicz, Viking (New York, NY), 1993.

Song Lee and the Hamster Hunt, illustrated by Frank Remkiewicz, Viking (New York, NY), 1994.

Song Lee and the Leech Man, illustrated by Frank Remkiewicz, Viking (New York, NY), 1995.

Song Lee and the "I Hate You" Notes, illustrated by Frank Remkiewicz, Viking (New York, NY), 1999.

Also author of plays for local elementary school. Contributor to *Instructor* magazine.

Adaptations

Several of Kline's books have been adapted as audiobooks. James Larson adapted *Horrible Harry in Room 2B* and *Horrible Harry Moves Up to Third Grade* for a touring stage production, 2008.

Sidelights

As a former elementary schoolteacher, Suzy Kline knows a lot about kids, and as a writer she has inspired young children with a love of reading that she hopes they will retain throughout their lives. Her award-winning chapter books feature endearing and realistic characters such as third grader Herbie Jones; second-grade stutterer Mary Marony; a basketball-crazy middle schooler who answers to the nickname "Orp"; Horrible Harry, the rambunctious nemesis of his second-and third-grade teachers; and Song Lee, the object of Harry's affections. Kline also has a sure-fire ability to create true-to-life plots, which she relates using plenty of down-to-earth humor. Her "characters are all well defined, with their own unique personalities finely drawn," noted Cheryl Cufari in an appraisal of one of Kline's books for *School Library Journal*. Pat Leach, reviewing a book from the "Mary Marony" series in the same periodical, added that "Kline understands the dynamics of relationships in the primary grades." Observing the long-running popularity of Kline's stories, Carolyn Phelan noted in *Booklist* of the publication of *Horrible Harry Bugs the Three Bears* that "not many series reach the 20-year mark, but [Kline's "Horrible Harry" series] . . . is still going strong."

Kline was born in Berkeley, California, in 1943, and her first foray into writing occurred at age eight, when she wrote a series of letters to her ailing grandfather in Indiana. After high school she attended Columbia University for a year before transferring to the University of California, Berkeley, to earn her bachelor's degree in

1966 and her teaching credentials the following year. In 1968 Kline got a job teaching in an elementary school in Richmond, California, where she remained for three years. She also married Rufus O. Kline, a local college teacher and writer, and together they had two daughters. In 1976 the Kline family moved to New England, and they have made their home in Connecticut ever since.

Kline's first titles for children were picture books. In 1984's *Shhhh!*, an energetic, chatty youngster lists all the people who tell her to pipe down during the day, until she tiptoes out of doors to make all the noise she possibly can before she settles down to being quiet again. Called "delightful" by *School Library Journal* contributor Lisa Redd, *Shhhh!* portrays "a situation common to all children." *Don't Touch!* finds young Dan similarly reprimanded: sharp edges, hot pans, wet paint, and the like are barriers to his curiosity. Finally, he gets hold of some modeling clay, which he can touch to his heart's content in this picture book that Joan McGrath noted in *School Library Journal* should be "satisfying to kids who are constantly admonished to keep hands off."

Kline introduced the first of her popular elementary-school characters in *Herbie Jones*. A reluctant reader, Herbie tries to get out of the "slow" class while finding that causing trouble seems to impress his peers. Finally, he sets his mind on his schoolwork, and his grades start to climb. *Booklist* contributor Ilene Cooper offered a favorable assessment of Kline's "shrewd depictions of childhood concerns," and added that Herbie is joined by "a fine supporting cast of characters." *What's the Matter with Herbie Jones?* finds Kline's young hero in a romantic muddle as he falls head over heels for Annabelle Louisa Hodgekiss. When his friends catch him reading poetry and being seen with a GIRL in public, they take swift—and humorous—action to save their comrade in a book that Cooper called "a fun read."

Other books featuring the popular third grader include *Herbie Jones and the Monster Ball*, "another sure winner," according to a *Publishers Weekly* reviewer, and *Herbie Jones and the Dark Attic*. In *Herbie Jones and the Monster Ball*, Herbie tries out for the local baseball team coached by his favorite uncle, while he is bumped up to an attic bedroom when Grandpa comes for a long-term visit in *Herbie Jones and the Dark Attic*. Kline has expanded the elementary-grader's saga by returning to his second-grade years in chapter books such as *Herbie Jones Sails into Second Grade*, which finds the boy relieved to find a likeable male teacher at the head of the class and happy to make a new student friend. Youngsters "venturing into chapter books will also enjoy Herbie's previous home-and-school-centered adventures," assured Phelan in her *Booklist* review of *Herbie Jones Sails into Second Grade*.

In *Horrible Harry in Room 2-B*, readers meet the impish Harry as seen through the eyes of his best friend, Doug. Dubbed "horrible" in a lighthearted way, Harry loves to play practical jokes, especially when they prompt screams of terror from second-grade girls. Kline illustrates each of Harry's antics in short chapters; in *Horrible Harry and the Green Slime*, he not only concocts some nasty green slime, but drapes the school with spider webs and gets involved in other mischief, fitting "comfortably into the genre of light classroom realism," according to Betsy Hearne in the *Bulletin of the Center for Children's Books*. *Horrible Harry's Secret* teams Harry with fellow classmate Song Lee, a Korean girl who has a water frog that eats liver—a sure-fire magnet for second-grade boys. Harry is attracted to more than the frog, however, and falling for Song Lee sends him into a tizzy. "Harry's appeal is that he's both 'gross' and vulnerable," according to *Booklist* contributor Hazel Rochman, who found Kline's classroom tales full of kid charm. Commenting on *Horrible Harry and the Kickball Wedding*, Rochman stated that "Kline evokes the farce of the classroom, and just a glimpse of the hurt, too." In *Horrible Harry and the Drop of Doom*, Song Lee invites Harry, Doug, and some of their classmates on a trip to Mountainside Amusement Park; Harry is delighted until his archnemesis, Sidney, tells him about one of the rides, which features a thirteen-storey elevator drop. As the tale continues to play out in what *Booklist* critic Kay Weisman deemed a "breezy text," Harry, who was once stuck inside an elevator, has to face his fears.

Harry and his classmates "loop together," and all end up in the same third-grade class as their adventures continue. In *Horrible Harry Moves Up to the Third Grade*, Harry must again confront Sidney when Sidney kills Harry's pet spider. "Harry's many fans will clamor for this enjoyable story," assured *Booklist* contributor Lauren Peterson. Harry disappoints his classmates by not dressing as something scary in *Horrible Harry at Halloween*. He explains that he is LAPD Sergeant Joe Friday of the popular television program *Dragnet*, and when one of his classmates realizes part of her costume is missing, it is up to Harry to solve the mystery. "Harry's detective work is delicious," praised Rochman in her review of the story for *Booklist*. Class 3-B goes on a riverboat trip in *Horrible Harry Goes to Sea*, and everything goes swimmingly until Song Lee discovers that Sidney is missing. The class scrambles to make sure that the boy has not gone overboard, prompting Ashley Larsen to write in *School Library Journal* that fans will "enjoy the class's exploits." Also reviewing *Horrible Harry Goes to Sea*, Phelan predicted in her *Booklist* review that readers will "happily climb aboard" to spend more time with Class 3-B.

In *Horrible Harry and the Dragon War*, Harry and Song Lee agree to work on a project on dragons together, only to realize that they have completely different ideas about dragons. When Harry calls Song Lee's dragon "stupid," their fight begins. Karen Hutt, writing in *Booklist*, commented that "Kline perfectly captures the difficulties of learning about differing opinions." A contributor to *Kirkus Reviews* praised the author for allow-

ing "the young protagonists to solve their own problems . . . with light adult intervention, good intentions, and gentle forgiveness."

In *Horrible Harry and the Mud Gremlins,* Harry is at his troublemaking again. When Sidney tries to get Class 3-B to tease Harry for wearing a necklace, Harry explains that the charm he is wearing is actually a minimicroscope, with which he can see the kingdom of mushrooms. He offers to show his classmates, but in order to do this they have to sneak off school grounds during recess, which is against the rules. The children follow anyway, and when their teacher asks where all the mud came from after recess Harry tells her a lie. Now his classmates must decide whether they should support Harry's fib or tell their teacher the truth. A contributor to *Kirkus Reviews* called *Horrible Harry and the Mud Gremlins* "another winner," and Rochman deemed Kline's chapter book "one of the best" in the "Horrible Harry" series.

Room 3-B celebrates the winter holidays in *Horrible Harry and the Holidaze,* but Harry does not seem to be himself. Friend Doug begins to worry when Harry's crush on Song Lee appears to have faded, but when the teacher finds out that Harry's great-grandfather has gone to live in a nursing home, she takes the whole class to visit, which cheers the boy up considerably. "The depiction of Harry's sadness . . . is sensitive," commented Phelan. Harry also makes appearances in *Horrible Harry and the Goog* and *Horrible Harry Cracks the Code,* a "simply written" tale featuring drawings by Frank Remkiewicz that, paired together, "vividly portray elementary-school life," according to Phelan.

Song Lee has several books in which she is not just the object of Harry's affections, but is the focus of the story. In *Song Lee and the Hamster Hunt,* she brings a pet to school and someone leaves the cage door open. "Amusing characterizations, snappy dialogue, and a happy ending" distinguish this book, according to a *Kirkus Reviews* critic. Although Song Lee is shy, her sensitivity to animals and troubled classmates surfaces in *Song Lee in Room 2B,* prompting Maggie McEwen to remark in *School Library Journal* that "Kline has an exceptional talent for capturing the language, humor, and group dynamics of a primary-grade classroom." In *Song Lee and the Leech Man,* Sidney tattles on Song Lee, and Harry vows to avenge his friend. When Harry's practical joke on Sidney fails, Harry ends up falling in the pond, covered with leeches. "Song Lee comes to the rescue and saves the day," wrote April Judge in *Booklist.* In *Song Lee and the "I Hate You Notes,"* someone is sending hate notes to Song Lee, even though she is the nicest person in the class. Although she is hurt by the notes, she gets her revenge in a very creative and unhurtful way.

Orville Rudemeyer Pygenski, Jr., survives elementary school only with the use of a nickname, Orp. When he starts an "I hate my name" club during the summer va-

cation after sixth grade, he realizes that he is not alone in wishing his parents had been a little less creative when he was born. In *Orp Goes to the Hoop,* the young teen decides that a good way to avoid chores is to join the middle-school basketball team. Ultimately, he becomes one of the team's star players, balancing his new sport with a long-distance romance with a girl named Jenny Lee. Orp's social life gets complicated in *Who's Orp's Girlfriend?* when two different girls at school catch the boy's eye, while longtime pen-pal Jenny Lee announces that she is coming for a visit. "Kline's gentle humor, well-paced plot, and likeable characters" are "just right" for middle-school readers, wrote *Booklist* contributor Chris Sherman. *Orp and the FBI* profiles Orp and his private detective agency, Famous Bathtub Investigators (FBI), and his rival, sister Chloe's CIA (Chloe's Investigation Agency). "The plot develops smoothly . . . [and] the level of suspense is maintained," commented *School Library Journal* contributor Carol Torrance, the critic deeming *Orp and the FBI* "a fun addition" to Kline's entertaining series.

Kline's first heroine to have her own series was second grader Mary Marony. In *Mary Marony and the Snake,* Mary fears being teased because of her speech impediment: she stutters. Her fears are realized when at least one student, mean Marvin Higgins, makes her school day miserable. Fortunately, with the help of a speech teacher, Mary gets her stutter under control. When she is the only one in her class brave enough to pick up a snake that has gotten loose in the classroom, Marvin's taunts can do little to tarnish her reputation among her classmates. "Any child who's been teased (that is, any child) will enjoy Mary's triumph," Roger Sutton asserted, while *School Library Journal* contributor Gale W. Sherman suggested: "Make room on the shelves for this one—young readers will love it."

In the entertaining *Mary Marony, Mummy Girl,* Halloween is around the corner and Mary wants to be a mummy—but where to find a costume? Without permission, she rips up her bedsheet, which works fine as a costume but makes her mom more than a little upset. Kline's spunky protagonist is "resourceful," dealing with both her stutter and "other challenges in a positive manner," maintained Elaine Lesh Morgan, describing the book in *School Library Journal. Mary Marony and the Chocolate Surprise,* hailed by *Booklist* critic Stephanie Zvirin as "one of Kline's best," raises the moral question of whether cheating is always wrong. In *Marvin and the Mean Words,* bully Marvin takes the spotlight, learning what it feels like to be the target of someone's taunting. Rochman noted that "Kline's touch is light," and praised the reality of her classroom scenarios. Marvin returns in *Marvin and the Meanest Girl,* in which he squares off against girl-bully, Lucy Tinker. The taunting escalates until Marvin learns that Lucy's grandmother has just died, and she is being mean to cover up her own hurt. "The school action is fast, the talk is lively," wrote Rochman in *Booklist.*

Third-grader Molly Zander's series began in 1999 with *Molly's in a Mess.* The stories are narrated by Molly's best friend Morty, the more-cautious of the pair. In her first adventure, Molly gets in trouble for accidentally knocking off the principal's hairpiece. When she and Morty explain, Molly is forgiven, but she nonetheless seeks revenge on Florence, the girl who told on her. Though Molly manages to embarrass Florence in front of the whole class, she and Florence both learn some lessons about how to treat their peers, and eventually become friends. A reviewer for *Publishers Weekly* noted that *Molly's in a Mess* "exhibits her usual flair for elementary school antics." In *Molly Gets Mad,* it looks like her friendship with Morty might be over. The two friends have an ice-skating race, which Molly wins, but only because Morty breaks his ankle in the process. When Molly becomes sullen when no one congratulates her as the winner, Morty tells her she is a poor sport and realizes too late that he may never be able to make things right. However, the friendship flickers back to life when Morty cheers Molly on during a game of hockey. "The real action here is off the rink," commented Pat Leach in a *School Library Journal* review of *Molly Gets Mad,* and *Booklist* critic Ellen Mandel praised Kline's depiction of "Molly's humorous and true-to-life antics."

"Most of my stories have been inspired by the classroom, my family and my childhood," Kline once commented. "Everyday life is full of stories if we just take the time to write them." Since her retirement from teaching in 2000, Kline has been able to travel from her native New England and devote more time to visiting students in other parts of the United States; as she once noted, "I always take my pocket notebook with me and jot down things that inspire me to write a new story." For example, she credits "some wonderful custodians and teachers" she met during her career for providing details on story and settings for *Horrible Harry and the Goog,* an installment in her popular series that finds Herbie's cat Goog prowling the South School teachers' lounge, teachers' restroom, and boiler room.

"I think I could go on forever writing about Herbie Jones and Horrible Harry and Song Lee," Kline added. "To me, these series are about family, friendships, and the classroom, three things that are so close to my heart. Most of all, I am blessed with a strong Christian faith, and that has made all the difference in my life."

Biographical and Critical Sources

PERIODICALS

Booklist, August, 1985, Ilene Cooper, review of *Herbie Jones,* p. 1666; December 1, 1986, Ilene Cooper, review of *What's the Matter with Herbie Jones?,* p. 579; December 1, 1990, Hazel Rochman, review of *Horrible Harry's Secret,* p. 751; October 1, 1992, Hazel Rochman, review of *Horrible Harry and the Kickball Wedding,* p. 327; August, 1993, Chris Sherman, review of *Who's Orp's Girlfriend?,* p. 2062; November 15, 1994, Kay Weisman, review of *Mary Marony, Mummy Girl,* pp. 601-602; April 15, 1995, Mary Harris Veeder, review of *Orp and the FBI,* p. 1500; October 1, 1995, April Judge, review of *Song Lee and the Leech Man,* p. 316; December 1, 1995, Stephanie Zvirin, review of *Mary Marony and the Chocolate Surprise,* p. 636; April 1, 1997, Hazel Rochman, review of *Marvin and the Mean Words,* p. 1334; February 15, 1998, Kay Weisman, review of *Horrible Harry and the Drop of Doom,* p. 1012; October 15, 1998, Lauren Peterson, review of *Horrible Harry Moves Up to Third Grade,* p. 422; May 1, 1999, Hazel Rochman, review of *Song Lee and the "I Hate You" Notes,* p. 1594; August, 1999, Lauren Peterson, review of *Molly's in a Mess,* p. 2058; September 15, 2000, Hazel Rochman, review of *Horrible Harry at Halloween,* p. 241; November 1, 2000, Hazel Rochman, review of *Marvin and the Meanest Girl,* p. 540; September 1, 2001, Ellen Mandel, review of *Molly Gets Mad,* p. 106; December 1, 2001, Carolyn Phelan, review of *Horrible Harry Goes to Sea,* p. 643; June 1, 2002, Karen Hutt, review of *Horrible Harry and the Dragon War,* p. 1740; March 15, 2003, Hazel Rochman, review of *Horrible Harry and the Mud Gremlins,* p. 1327; September 1, 2003, Carolyn Phelan, review of *Horrible Harry and the Holidaze,* p. 134; May 1, 2004, Stephanie Zvirin, review of *Horrible Harry and the Locked Closet,* p. 1499; April 15, 2005, Hazel Rochman, review of *Horrible Harry and the Goog,* p. 1456; February 1, 2006, Hazel Rochman, review of *Horrible Harry Takes the Cake,* p. 55; August 1, 2006, Carolyn Phelan, review of *Herbie Jones Sails into Second Grade,* p. 95; May 1, 2007, Carolyn Phelan, review of *Horrible Harry Cracks the Code,* p. 49; February 1, 2008, Carolyn Phelan, review of *Horrible Harry Bugs the Three Bears,* p. 40.

Bulletin of the Center for Children's Books, October, 1984, review of *Shhhh!,* p. 29; December, 1985, review of *Don't Touch!,* pp. 70-71; December, 1986, review of *What's the Matter with Herbie Jones?,* pp. 70-71; May, 1989, Betsy Hearne, review of *Horrible Harry and the Green Slime,* p. 227; July-August, 1991, review of *Orp Goes to the Hoop,* pp. 266-267; June, 1992, Roger Sutton, review of *Mary Marony and the Snake,* pp. 266-267.

Kirkus Reviews, July 15, 1994, review of *Song Lee and the Hamster Hunt,* p. 987; September 15, 2001, review of *Horrible Harry Goes to Sea,* p. 1360; April 15, 2002, review of *Horrible Harry and the Dragon War,* p. 572; February 1, 2003, review of *Horrible Harry and the Mud Gremlins,* p. 233; June 1, 2006, review of *Herbie Jones Sails into Second Grade,* p. 575.

Publishers Weekly, October 30, 1987, review of *What's the Matter with Herbie Jones?,* p. 72; September 8, 1988, review of *Herbie Jones and the Monster Ball,* p. 135; March 3, 1997, review of *Marvin and the Mean Words,* p. 76; August 2, 1999, review of *Molly's in a Mess,* p. 84; November 1, 1999, review of *Orp,* p. 86; Septem-

ber 25, 2000, review of *Horrible Harry at Halloween,* p. 65; June 9, 2003, review of *Herbie Jones Moves On,* p. 54.

School Library Journal, February, 1985, Lisa Redd, review of *Shhhh!,* p. 66; February, 1986, Joan McGrath, review of *Don't Touch,* p. 76; March, 1988, Dudley B. Carlson, review of *Herbie Jones and the Class Gift,* p. 192; April, 1989, Hayden E. Atwood, review of *Orp,* pp. 102-103; December, 1992, Cheryl Cufari, review of *Herbie Jones and the Dark Attic,* p. 85; April, 1993, Gale W. Sherman, review of *Mary Marony and the Snake,* p. 98; July, 1993, Julie Tomlianovich, review of *Who's Orp's Girlfriend?,* p. 86; September, 1993, Maggie McEwen, review of *Song Lee in Room 2B,* pp. 209-210; November, 1993, Cynthia Cordes, review of *Mary Marony Hides Out,* p. 85; September, 1994, review of *Song Lee and the Hamster Hunt,* p. 187; December, 1994, Elaine Lesh Morgan, review of *Mary Marony, Mummy Girl,* p. 77; May, 1995, Carol Torrance, review of *Orp and the FBI,* p. 108; December, 1995, Suzanne Hawley, review of *Song Lee and the Leech Man,* p. 83; May, 1997, Elisabeth Palmer Abarbanel, review of *Marvin and the Mean Words,* p. 102; September, 1997, Carrie A. Guarria, review of *Horrible Harry and the Purple People,* p. 184; August, 1998, Suzanne Hawley, review of *Horrible Harry and the Drop of Doom,* p. 142; September, 1998, Linda Binder, review of *Horrible Harry Moves Up to Third Grade,* p. 175; June, 1999, Pat Leach, review of *Song Lee and the "I Hate You" Notes,* p. 99; August, 1999, Maggie McEwen, review of *Molly's in a Mess,* p. 138; February, 2000, Pat Leach, review of *Horrible Harry Goes to the Moon,* p. 96; September, 2000, Janie Schomberg, review of *Horrible Harry at Halloween,* p. 202; August, 2001, Pat Leach, review of *Molly Gets Mad,* p. 155; November, 2001, Ashley Larsen, review of *Horrible Harry Goes to Sea,* p. 127; August, 2002, Laurie von Mehren, review of *Horrible Harry and the Dragon War,* p. 159; October, 2003, Eva Mitnick, review of *Horrible Harry and the Holidaze,* p. 65; November, 2004, Kristina Aaronson, review of *Horrible Harry and the Locked Closet,* p. 108; July, 2005, Lynda S. Poling, review of *Horrible Harry and the Goog,* p. 75; May, 2006, Diane Eddington, review of *Horrible Harry Takes the Cake,* p. 92; August, 2006, Kate Kohlbeck, review of *Herbie Jones and the Second Grade Slippers,* p. 90.

ONLINE

Suzy Kline Home Page, http://www.suzykline.com (April 15, 2008).

Autobiography Feature

Suzy Kline

Kline contributed the following autobiographical essay to *SATA:*

Some Autobiographical Reflections . . . about My Motivations for Writing, together with Notes about the People and Experiences That Shaped My Writing, and the Rewards I Get From It

The most important thing I own as a writer is my pocket notebook. I carry it with me all the time. When I was teaching for twenty-seven years, there were days when I would say, "Ohhhh . . . that would make a great story!" And then I would write down one or two words. That's all I had time for. But let me tell you, those one or two words I recorded during my school year became seeds for stories I wrote in the summer. I'd like to share a few story seeds from my old pocket notebooks. I'll begin with the one that motivated me to write the very first "Horrible Harry" book in 1988.

Stub Pencil

Twenty-five years ago, when I was teaching second grade at Southwest School in Torrington, Connecticut, I had a student named Robert. Every week Robert walked into my classroom he had a new complaint. This particular week it was the pencil sharpener. "It's so bad," he said, "I'm bringing my own." I said "Fine." And he did. It was a very small, white, plastic pencil sharpener that enabled him to sharpen his pencil shorter than anyone else. The day of our spelling test, Robert was writing with a pencil stub not much bigger than my wedding ring. "Robert!" I said. "Do you want a new pencil?" And he said, "No thank you, Mrs. Kline. I like writing with stubs." After he had taken his spelling test (and he had gotten 100 percent too!), I asked if I could see it more closely. And that's when Robert said, "Mrs. Kline, it's yours."

I know that pencil stub was the best gift I ever got from one of my students. I took it home and set it next to my typewriter. There's a story here, I thought. I'm making up a character and I'll name him Harry after my dad (because my grandfather told me my dad was mischievous when he was young. One example of that was my dad putting a cow pattie in my grandfather's mailbox!) Then I picked up the pencil stub, and thought. Harry does something with these. . . . he makes scary people!

He uses all the scraps from the classroom floor like bits of clay and erasers, broken crayons, pieces of used construction paper. Harry's motive? To bring Doom to Room 2B with his Invasion of the Stub Pencils. Harry loves to scare people just for fun.

Sometimes I get letters from readers and they ask me if I ever had a Horrible Harry in my classroom. I sure did—every year! Some years I had two or three. But the truth is that although the Harrys could drive me nuts sometimes, they always made class more fun. And I loved each one!

(P.S. I keep Robert's stub pencil in a small box and share it with schools when I visit.)

Purple Hanger

One particular week, my students were coming to school earlier and earlier. On Monday, they arrived five minutes before the bell. I thought . . . maybe they love school and can't wait to get here. That was not the reason. Tuesday, my students were racing up the hall ten minutes before the bell. What was going on? I looked around our classroom. We had three frog tanks but there were no eggs yet. Wednesday, when a handful of students showed up fifteen minutes before the bell, I stepped out into the hallway and found out why.

I was teaching at a school that was one hundred years old, and we still had the original wooden hangers! The previous week, one of my wooden hangers broke so I brought one from home. One purple plastic hanger. I

Robert's Stub Pencil, a prized possession. (Reproduced by permission.)

put it on the rack with the other twenty wooden hangers. The reason why my students were racing down the hall was because they wanted to be the person to hang their jacket on the purple hanger! I immediately took out my notebook and wrote down two words, "purple hanger."

The following summer I wrote the book *Horrible Harry and the Purple People.* It all started with the color purple. The purple hanger was the seed for that manuscript. I usually have a muse, too, when I'm writing. This time it was the writer Lewis Carroll. I had been reading his book *Alice in Wonderland* to my class that year. "The Purple Party" at the end of *Horrible Harry and the Purple People* was definitely inspired by the Mad Hatter's Tea Party and explains why the theme—imagination—permeates the entire book.

Orange Sticker

Now that I'm a grandmother and not teaching anymore, I get a lot of my ideas from schools that I visit, and from my grandchildren. Two years ago when I would ask my grandson Jake how school was going, he always talked about an orange sticker. "What was that?" I asked. I knew he didn't get one and he was not happy about that. Jake explained to me that in his school cafeteria one person in each class found an orange sticker under their milk carton. That lucky person got a prize from the cook! I knew Harry, who was then developing an interest in detective work, would love to figure out who got an orange sticker in his class. But how? A mathematical code! I mentioned it once before in *Horrible Harry and the Dungeon.* Mr. Scooghammer is the suspension teacher and teaches Harry about the Fibonacci numbers. It would be easy to say that Mrs. Thunderburke, the cook, was taking a college math course and was going to use a special code. Harry would try to crack it! The orange sticker was the first seed for *Horrible Harry Cracks the Code,* which came out in 2007. The second seed for this book was . . .

The Ketchup Lady

When I was making an author visit at the Helen Keller School in Franklin, Massachusetts, I had the good fortune to meet Terry Fenton. She was a volunteer mother who helped out in the cafeteria. The kids called her the "Ketchup Lady." When I asked her why, she said she would walk around holding a large container of ketchup. If a kid was eating nicely she would squirt a ketchup happy-face on his plate. I was so charmed! It had to happen at Harry's school! I drew a picture of a ketchup happy-face in my pocket notebook! Now I knew the cafeteria setting for *Horrible Harry Cracks the Code* was going to be fun.

Chemistry Lesson

My daughter Jennifer came home from high school chemistry one day and said, "Mom, we made this great substance in class today. It's two states of matter." "Two?" I said. "How could that be?" And she showed me. We went to the sink and she got out some cornstarch and water. The ratio was two parts cornstarch to one part water. After she stirred it, she lifted some with her spoon and let it drip onto a plate. The substance flowed like a slimy liquid, but when it landed, it turned solid. It was so cool!

At the time, I was working on a chapter about Harry doing demonstration talks with his class. I didn't know what Harry would do. But I sure did now. He would make slime! And probably make it green. And that's how this story seed—a chemistry lesson—gave birth to *Horrible Harry and the Green Slime.* The author who inspired me for this book was E.B. White and his book *Charlotte's Web.* I read White's masterpiece to my class every year, and we so loved the character Charlotte, we had our own cobweb invasion, just like in Room 2B.

The Monster Ball

My husband's brother Doug came to visit us one summer for two weeks. He ended up staying with us for seven years. He moved up to the attic and made a face on a basketball. He called it the Monster Ball and pretended it could talk. When he came down to the breakfast table, he would bring the Monster Ball and pretend to be listening to it. Jennifer and Emily, my two daughters, would ask, "What did the Monster Ball say?"

Uncle Doug, the inspiration for Uncle Dwight in **Herbie Jones and the Monster Ball** (Reproduced by permission.)

Uncle Doug would say, "Just a minute, he's not through talking yet." And then, after a quiet moment, he would say something like, "The Monster Ball says that even though it's raining you're going to have a great day at school."

I decided to use this Monster Ball in my book *Herbie Jones and the Monster Ball*. And of course Uncle Dwight was based on our eccentric Uncle Doug. The six years that my husband coached Little League for Jennifer and Emily's teams provided lots of details for the baseball parts of the story.

Carl Sandburg's Poem, "Fog"

I have always loved Carl Sandburg's poetry. In the book *What's the Matter with Herbie Jones?* I had Herbie team up with Annabelle to write poetry. It was a great opportunity to use some of Sandburg's poems, like "Fog." Herbie was inspired by Sandburg too. That's why he wrote this gem, which I included in the book:

A daddy longlegs
comes across the sealing
It sits looking
over the bedroom
on its haunches
and then walks on.

Another poem below that Herbie penned is actually one I wrote in the third grade when I was on a Sunday drive with my parents. My maiden name was Weaver.

Let's go home.
Someones on the phone.
Lift up the reseaver
It's Mr. Weaver
Lets go home.

Yellow Scarf

One spring I spent a week visiting Cherokee Bend Elementary School in Mountain Brook, Alabama. While I was waiting for the fifth graders to settle in on the gym floor, a girl sitting in the second row had this very long yellow scarf on. I leaned over and said, "I like your scarf." She said thank you and then pointed out that it wasn't a regular scarf. I asked what she meant by that and she said, "It's actually magic. You can put your hand in it, and if you like, slip it over your head and wear it as a dress. "Really!" I said. I was so impressed. I got one just like it and set it down next to my computer. Which one of my characters would use this?, I thought. Annabelle of course! She is the character who is very much like my younger daughter, Emily. Emily has OCD [obsessive-compulsive disorder] and many times needs to do things a certain way. When Emily bought a paperback book at the bookstore, she would check every seam to make sure she got the most perfect one. I decided Annabelle would wear that yellow scarf the first day of school and tie it a special way.

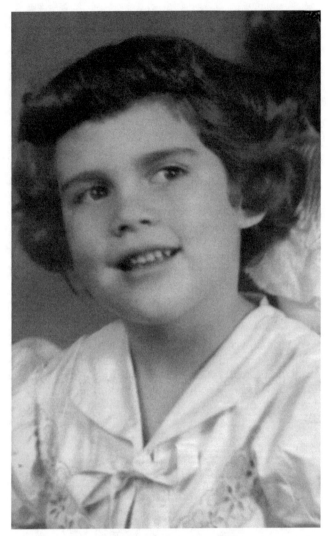

Suzy at age seven, a stutterer (Reproduced by permission.)

As I typed, I didn't know what was going to happen next, but I knew a lot about that scarf. It was very long and would probably dangle on the desk behind her. Raymond Martin would be sitting there and be very nervous about coming to a new school and not reading very well. The scarf helped move the story! I began writing what Ray did with it, and how Annabelle responded. This episode was one of several in *Herbie Jones Sails into Second Grade*.

Haunted Bathrooms

During Halloween one year, the children were saying the bathrooms in our school basement were haunted. That seed turned out to be a wonderful one. I wrote the chapter "Haunted Bathrooms" for my first "Herbie Jones" book in 1985, *Herbie Jones*. The character, Herbie, is a lot like my husband, Rufus, who nearly flunked first grade but went on to earn his doctorate. Herbie is that underachiever who had lots of potential. Again, I was inspired by E.B. White and quoted Charlotte talking about being a spider.

My Stuttering

Many times an experience I have had is the seed for a story. When I was in elementary school, I had a stuttering problem. I especially couldn't say words that started with "W." It was tough because my name was Susie Weaver. I went to a speech therapist at Marin Elementary School. Actually, I had two wonderful ones: Doris Maier and Francis Clarke. They had me repeat very short phrases, and then would praise me for doing it. Pretty soon I got to sentences, and then longer ones. Their support and loving dedication made a huge difference in my speaking. Now I speak to schools all over the United States and I have them to thank for that!

I decided to have a character named Mary Marony who stuttered on M words. And like me, she would have someone who made fun of her, Marvin! A boy named Freddy always made fun of me! He would say, "Hi Su-su-suzie We-we-weaver!" I knew exactly how it felt to be teased like that.

When you write about a real situation, you usually change a few things, and I did in this case. But I also used other real experiences in writing *Mary Marony and the Snake,* like the snake that slithered away. It happened in my own classroom. My student Patrick Hickey brought a garter snake to school in a terrarium

Kline reading to her grandchildren, (left to right) Saylor, Gabby, Mikenna, and Jake (Reproduced by permission.)

and it escaped! Our janitor, Mr. Beausoleil, found the snake the next morning in the basement under the teachers' soda machine!

Charlie and the Chocolate Factory

Many times a story seed for me is another book. I love reading aloud to my grandchildren! Sometimes we read for over an hour! I always read aloud to my class. And when I taught Children's Literature at the University of Connecticut, Storrs, a few years ago, I read aloud to my graduate students. It's so powerful to hear the story. It's one of the most important things a teacher can do. Some of my favorite read-alouds were *Stone Fox, Charlotte's Web, My Father's Dragon, Velveteen Rabbit, Ramona Quimby, Age 8, The Phantom Tollbooth, Philip Hall Likes Me, I Reckon, Maybe,* and *Charlie and the Chocolate Factory.*

One year when I finished reading *Charlie and the Chocolate Factory,* the kids were so disappointed that it was over that I decided to extend it with a special activity. I put twenty-four small chocolate bars on a round yellow table and asked the children to each choose one. In five of those bars was a golden ticket. I told my students, "If you find a golden ticket in your chocolate bar, you're not going to Charlie's Chocolate Factory; you're having lunch with me tomorrow in our classroom. We'll have pizza and chat about the book." Well, my class loved the idea!

Now, as it happened, the five winners were the five students least likely to want to participate in a book talk. But because it was a "prize," it must have held a special value. Boy was I surprised with the results! It was one of the most enlightening experiences I had as a teacher. Maybe it was the small numbers and extra attention; I don't know. But the conversation and joy we shared over that book was priceless. And it was shared with the most reluctant of readers!

At the time, I was thinking about writing another book about Mary Marony. I immediately gave the unwritten book a title, *Mary Marony and the Chocolate Surprise,* and so the chocolate candy bar with the golden ticket became the most important story prop. I think it was my best "Mary Marony" book too, because it deals with cheating and all the suffering it causes.

Earwig Report

I love reading the letters I get from readers. I feel really bad that I can't answer them as often as I would like. Sometimes I get months behind in my correspondence. But . . . each one I do read is a gem.

One in particular was from Ethan D. Fitz of Hilliard Elementary School in Westlake, Ohio. Ethan loved earwigs and did research on them. When I was visiting his school, the librarian mentioned to me that there was a boy very much like Harry at her school. Ethan loved

"Southwest School teacher friends with whom I get together every year. In 2007 we met in Corea, Maine": (left to right) Donna Graham, Mary Ann Boulanger, Pat Matey, me, and Cindy Gelzinis (Reproduced by permission.)

slimy, creepy, crawly things just like Harry in my books. So I asked to see Ethan. Ethan told me how he climbed up in his maple tree in the backyard after a rain and, using a dangling rope, caught earwigs! I was fascinated. He said he could send me his study on them. I told him I would love to read it. Ethan mailed that delightful report to me and that report was the seed for my 2008 book, *Horrible Harry Bugs the Three Bears.* In the book, Harry is into earwigs! He digs one up just under the school fence and calls it Edward.

I had Miss Mackle reading fairy tales to her class in that book because I love them. When I was teaching in college, I shared the ten elements of a fairy tale with my graduate students. I had a few of my characters discover them in the story. A writer has to be careful not to be didactic! I'm listing all ten just in case a *SATA* reader is interested in writing a fairy tale like Miss Mackle's class.

If a story has four of these elements it may be considered to be a fairy tale:

1. Starts with "Once upon a time . . ."
2. Ends with ". . . happily ever after."
3. Objects and/or animals talk
4. Good character
5. Evil character
6. Royalty and/or a castle
7. A lesson to be learned
8. Uses the numbers 3 or 7
9. Magical event
10. A task to be done, a quest, or a problem to be solved

Snack Attack!

When I was visiting Quaker Hill Elementary in Waterford, Connecticut, I bumped into a giant apple in the hallway. It was the gym teacher, dressed up in a huge red costume! The school was trying to encourage healthy snacks and this giant apple would suddenly appear in a classroom and see how many kids were eating nutritious snacks. What a great story seed! I used it in my book *Horrible Harry and the Triple Revenge.* Another seed for this same book was Pajama Day at North Boulevard School in Pompton Plains, New York. It got me thinking about what kind of pajamas Harry might wear, and when I came up with the answer, I knew what trick Harry would play on Sidney for a second revenge!

The Light-bulb Necklace

When I was writing *Horrible Harry's Secret,* I couldn't think of what love gift Harry would give to Song Lee.

It was a real writer's block. It was late December and almost time for our school break. One of my students, Joey Fasciano, approached me with a gift. "Merry Christmas, Mrs. Kline," he said. I smiled and said "You didn't have to do that." And Joe responded, "Well, Mom was going to throw it out anyway." I opened it up and there was a light-bulb necklace. They were small christmas-tree lights, all dead, and strung together. I absolutely loved it! "Would you mind if I used your gift in my next chapter?" I asked. "Sure!" Joe answered. My students have been a wonderful resource for me. It's why I always dedicated my "Horrible Harry" books to them while I was teaching. Each year, I listed their names to show my appreciation.

My Fifth-Grade Wedding

When I was ten, I married Randy Heinrich in the tennis court. He gave me a pretend ring and I wore it around my neck on a string. When I was having lunch with my editor in New York City, I happened to mention this and she said she got married in kindergarten! Maybe it was time for Harry to get married, I thought! So I wrote the manuscript "Horrible Harry Gets Married" and read it to my students. After recess, Mary Anne Boulanger, the other second-grade teacher, told me that my students had a mock wedding out on the playground. I was charmed! She asked if I had read them a story about a wedding, and I said "Yes, my new manuscript." "Well," Mary Anne said, "I wonder if it ended the way your story did though. Right in the middle of the ceremony, a boy ran by and shouted 'KICKBALL GAME!,' and the guy playing Harry took off!" I just laughed. No. My story did not end that way, but I was going to rewrite the ending that night. Thanks to my students, my story became more realistic. And I changed the title to *Horrible Harry and the Kickball Wedding*.

Justin O. Schmidt's Pain Index

I often ask my husband, Rufus, for a good source when I want to learn something. I was writing *Song Lee and the Leechman* and I wanted to find out a few fascinating facts about insects. Rufus suggested I take a look at

Kline and husband, Rufus Kline (Reproduced by permission.)

Justin O. Schmidt's *Pain Index*. He was a scientist who did fieldwork on insect bites. He went out and got bitten by all kinds of insects! Then he charted their sting—how much it hurt and for how long. I loved it! Harry and his classmates would be fascinated with this new information! I could have Professor Guo, who was leading Harry's class on a field trip to a local pond, share some of it. This seed also helped me to show the ribbing Harry and Sidney often engage in.

Green Smorgasbord

Every year on St. Patrick's Day, my class would have a green smorgasbord. It was amazing what my students would bring for it: grapes, green peppers, snap beans, green-colored hard-boiled eggs!, lime Jello, pistachio pudding, a jar of pickles, green-onion potato chips, green cookies, and green-frosted cupcakes. While they were eating, I would read from *The Wizard of Oz* about the Emerald City where everything was green! It was such a special day I decided to use it as the backdrop of a conflict between Mary and Song Lee. Song Lee, Ida, and Doug get to go to the school kitchen because their green items need refrigeration. When they put their items in the refrigerator, they see Harry's ants! "Don't tell anyone," Mrs. Funderburke says. "Harry wants his ants to be a surprise." Keeping this secret from Mary causes a real conflict between the girls and provided the friction needed for the chapter, "Green with Envy" in *Song Lee in Room 2B*.

*

Questions

I always enjoy the questions I get when readers write to me, and when I visit their school. Below are the popular ones and some of my favorites. I have made my answers more elaborate for *SATA* readers!

Q: Who helps you write?

A: My editors, and especially my husband, Rufus. I wouldn't be an author today if it weren't for him. He loves to read and write himself, and is a natural editor. He'll ask me a question or give me frank criticism that really helps me rewrite the story. Rufus has always been great with one-liners. When I finish a book, I often ask Ruf to title it for me because I'm not very good at thinking of titles. *Herbie Jones and the Monster Ball* was originally called *Herbie Jones and His Uncle*. You can see how the former title is much better—that was Rufus's idea. And when I wrote a story about Harry being afraid to go on an elevator ride very much like the Tower of Terror at Disney World, Ruf named it for me: The Drop of Doom. It was so good I used it for my title, *Horrible Harry and the Drop of Doom*. My first published chapter book, *Herbie Jones* (1985), was dedicated to Rufus because he helped me with it so much.

"Our engagement photograph," 1968 (Reproduced by permission.)

And, he is a lot like Herbie, an underachiever. Rufus nearly flunked first grade but went on to earn his Ph.D. in anthropology at the University of California at Davis. On October 12, 2008, we will celebrate our 40th wedding anniversary. He's the love of my life.

Q: How long does it take to write a book?

A: It depends. My first book was published in 1984. It took me one night to write. It was a two-page, double-spaced manuscript for a picture book called *SHHHH!* I must have said, "Shhhh!" a hundred times that day to my class, and when I got home and was having dinner with my family, Jennifer said, "Pass the green beans, please." My response was "Shhhh!"

"Do you have a problem?" Jen asked me. Yes, I thought! I was on automatic with that word. I went to my desk and wrote *SHHHH!* that very night.

Now *Herbie Jones and the Dark Attic* took me four years! My editor told me, "Suzy you have the setting: the attic. You have the characters: Herbie, Annabelle, and Raymond." You have to have something happen in that attic that's scary! Four years later, I came up with two things: one I made up, and the other really happened. A water rat had come up into our attic and terrified me! I changed the animal for the book and made it a raccoon which turned out to really move the story along.

Q: What is your favorite book you wrote?

A: My favorite book was the hardest one to write, *What's the Matter with Herbie Jones?* It's the story about a third-grade boy who falls in love with Anna-

"At Jennifer's bridal shower, 1995. Mom was eighty-five then." (Left to right: Emily, Kline, Mom, Jennifer) (Reproduced by permission.)

belle Louisa Hodgekiss for a day and a half. There was one chapter called "Herbie in the Soup" that I had to rewrite twenty-seven TIMES! When I told my beloved editor, Ann O'Connell, that I had written it already twenty-six times, she said to do it again. The chapter was flat, and not funny. Her criticism was very helpful (although I gritted my teeth when I was doing all those rewrites!). I think that this book is one of my very best, and I think it was because I spent so much time rewriting it.

Q: How do you get published?

A: It's kind of like a rough roller-coaster ride. It took me three years and 127 rejections before I got my first book published in 1984. But I could see some progress when my rejections got longer. The first six months I got postcards with no name on it, and no comments. Then in December of 1981, I got a rejection with my name on it and I was thrilled! The editor, Ann Schwartz, said that although she didn't want my manuscript, "Phoebe at Twelve," she wanted to see more of my work. I taped her letter on the bathroom tile right next to our bathtub and read the last two lines over and over. They inspired me to keep trying. Then I got a two-page

rejection with criticism from Beverly Horowitz at Dial, so I knew I was making progress. Once I got a letter from an editor saying he liked my manuscript, "Emily's Birthday Party," adding it might even make a good series. Two days later, I got a letter from the same editor saying he was fired, and they weren't taking any of his ideas. So "Emily's Birthday Party" never got published. There are lots of ups and downs, but if you have written a good story, and you don't give up, you might just get it published.

Q: How important is not giving up?

A: It's everything! I have one important example of this from my college days. I was at UC at Davis during the winter semester of 1962. I was taking an eight o'clock psychology class. That first day when I walked into the large lecture hall, I noticed Rufus, my future husband, sitting in the second row with a few buddies. His head was buried in his hands. He looked just like Rodin's *The Thinker,* meditating over some dilemma. My two friends, Betty and Janet, followed me to the front row. I wanted to nab those seats right in front of him. Every day, we sat in the same seats. It's kind of a quirky thing that people would do that, but we did it in those days.

During those next two months, I found out several things about him. Rufus was very witty and would make loud comments that would elicit laughter from the class and even the professor sometimes. I knew he was not only brilliant but funny. It was love at first sight for me. Not for Rufus. After a couple of feeble attempts to get his attention—Like, could I borrow a pencil? etc.—I decided to take the bull by the horns. Our Malcolm Hall Dorm dance was coming up and I wanted to ask Rufus, a complete stranger, to it! If it wasn't for another friend, Phyllis, I wouldn't have done it. She stood in the phone booth with me and kept encouraging me to call. How did I get Rufus's number, you ask? It wasn't easy, but in 1962, you could go to the Student Co-op on the green at Davis and look up any student's address and phone by going through white index cards. There were long trays of them! All I knew was that the "thinker's" first name was Rufus, so I went through every card until I came to the K's. I finally found the first Rufus. The card said "Rufus Kline," so I took a chance.

I remember the conversation very well. I think I had practiced it for an hour.

"Are you the Rufus in Psychology 1A Class?"

"Yes," a deep voice replied rather hesitantly.

"Hi, my name is Susie Weaver, you don't know me, but I sit in front of you."

Rufus was quiet for a moment. "Are you the blonde?"

"No." (That was Janet Kluge.)

Then Ruf said, "Are you the redhead?"

I said no again. (That was Betty Calloway.)

"I'm the tall brunette in the middle," I explained.

The next silence must have been a full minute. I was dying!

Then, when I asked him, he mumbled, "Okay."

It was divine! Really! I was so excited. We went to the dance and had a wonderful time. He gave me a beautiful wrist corsage of yellow roses and I saved it. What followed was a five-year courtship—and it weathered my going back to Berkeley to get my degree, and my one year in New York City. I saved every letter Ruf wrote and I still have them tied together.

After I finished my senior year at Berkeley and got my teaching credential at Cal State, Hayward, we got married. It was kind of a spur-of-the-moment thing. Ruf was working on his doctorate in anthropology at UC Davis and his used red MG broke down. I was driving a used yellow Mustang that zipped around just fine, and I think that made Ruf think about setting a date. He needed a car. "Do you want to get married next Satur-

day?" After six years of dating and wondering if we ever were going to tie the knot, hearing those decisive words were terrific. I didn't care if it meant no big wedding, no guest list. The main character, Rufus Kline, was going to be there and that's all I cared about. I am so glad I didn't give up! If I had, I wouldn't have been an author, or given birth to Emily and Jennifer, or had my five precious grandchildren: Jake, Mikenna, Gabby, Saylor, and Holden. So when it came time to face 127 rejections, I had some practice persevering.

Q: Which book was Harry the horriblest?

A: (I don't think there is such a word as horriblest, but I loved this question from a fifth-grade girl.) I had to think about this one. Finally, I came up with my answer. It had to be *Horrible Harry and the Mud Gremlins* because he got his friends to break a school rule: leaving the playground!

The seed for this book was the hole in our school fence! It had been there for three years. It was just big enough for one child to squeeze through. It presented a dilemma for me as a teacher too. When we played kickball, sometimes someone would kick the ball over the fence. Since I only had one red rubber ball, I discretely asked one of my students to crawl through the hole and retrieve it from the empty lot. It was usually just a few yards away. This experience made me think about Harry and his friends. How would they respond to a hole in the fence?

"Our five precious grandkids," 2007 (Reproduced by permission.)

At the same time I was mulling this over in my mind, I took a group hike through at state park in Connecticut looking for fungi. When we came across the stinkhorn mushrooms, I stopped in my tracks! Harry would LOVE these putrid-smelling specimens! That would be the reason why Harry would crawl through the hole in the fence and break a school rule: to see the kingdom of mushrooms growing behind the white oak tree! When Doug saw them, I would have him say, "It was like nothing we had ever seen before. Ten mushrooms poked through the earth like white thumbs wearing olive green helmets."

Q: Why did you give Harry a fear of elevators?

A: My sister Nancy, who I adore, has a terrible fear of elevators. She got stuck in one once and had a panic attack. That was it! She will walk up nine flights of stairs rather than ride in one now. I have a fear of heights; it's very hard for me to ride a plane so I always drive or take a train when I visit schools.

We all have little fears, so I knew Harry would have one too. The "fear of elevators" came to me one summer when I took a mother-daughter trip to Disney World with Emily. She said, "Mom you're fifty, you've never been to Disney World. It would be a lot of fun. You could talk to your students about going on the Tower of Terror. They would be impressed!" The Tower of Terror? It took me all week to get up the nerve to ride that thing. I was petrified with fear. You can see that in my souvenir photo. I'm sitting in the back row leaning on Emily!

When I survived dropping thirteen floors and got my breath back, I decided Harry would have to experience something like this. I would say he got stuck on an elevator when he was four, and the one thing he couldn't do was ride elevators! I could have Song Lee having her end-of-the-year party at an amusement park so Harry would have to face his fear. I loved writing *Horrible Harry and the Drop of Doom* because I had a chance to show how friendships help us through difficult times. Song Lee's support and encouragement made all the difference to Harry.

Q: How come you usually have science in your "Horrible Harry" books?

A: Because I LOVE science! It was one of my favorite subjects to teach when I was a teacher. Science is Harry's favorite subject too (besides recess and lunch). Harry loves smelly, slimy, creepy, crawling, horrible

"October, 2000, when Mom was ninety. I brought her home often. We had a ramp built onto the house so we could wheel her in." (Reproduced by permission.)

things. That often is what science is about! I've listed ten "Harry" books below that feature a particular topic:

1. *Horrible Harry and the Green Slime*—States of Matter
2. *Horrible Harry and the Ant Invasion*—Study of Ants and Ant Behavior
3. *Horrible Harry and the Dungeon*—Study of Monarch Butterflies
4. *Horrible Harry Moves Up to Third Grade*—Spider Studies and Rocks and Minerals
5. *Horrible Harry Goes to the Moon*—Moon Studies
6. *Horrible Harry at Halloween*—Water Experiments
7. *Horrible Harry and the Mud Gremlins*—Study of Mushrooms/Fungi
8. *Horrible Harry and the Locked Closet*—Study of Volcanoes
9. *Horrible Harry Takes the Cake*—Animal Studies
10. *Horrible Harry Bugs the Three Bears*—Earwig Studies

Q: Do you have children?

A: Yes I do. Two beloved daughters. Both of them were great scholars and athletes, and graduated from the University of Connecticut where they met their husbands. Jennifer is married and lives in Bedford, New Hampshire, with her husband, Matt DeAngelis, and their two wonderful children, Jake and Gabby. Emily is married to Victor Hurtuk and lives ten minutes from my house, in Tolland, Connecticut. They have three beautiful children: Mikenna, Saylor, and Holden.

Q: Do you have pets?

A: Five cats. Hoag is our ginger cat. Deja and Vu are twin brothers that were orphaned at a barn. Teeter is grey and white and very old. Our newest is a kitten, Eve. We got her on Christmas Eve.

Q: Have you written a book about any of your cats?

A: Yes. Tux. Tux was with us for over fifteen years. He only had one eye. He got caught in a dumpster and had to have surgery, but he did just fine afterwards getting around. Tux inspired me to write *Horrible Harry and the Goog*. Goog was really our cat Tux.

Q: What is the name of your favorite team in sports?

A: UConn! My husband and I have season tickets for the football games and we always follow them when they go to bowl games. We don't miss a UConn basketball game either! Go Huskies!

Q: Why do you have Harry's grandfather in a nursing home?

A: When my mother and dad got older, they lived in the downstairs apartment of our house on Hoffman Street in Torrington, Connecticut. It was wonderful having them participate in our daily family life. Mom helped watch Jennifer and Emily after school when I

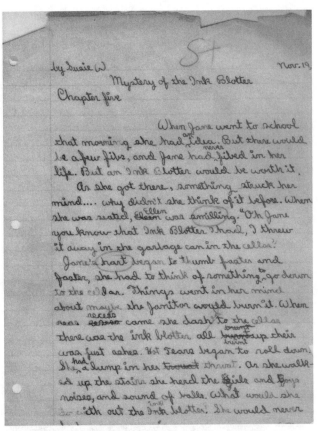

Original, corrected copy of Kline's ongoing saga "Mystery of the Ink Blotter," 1953 (Reproduced by permission.)

was teaching. She also took care of Dad, who was in a wheelchair. After Dad died, Mom continued to be independent until she was ninety. It was too hard for her to be alone, so we chose a nursing home nearby us in Willington, Connecticut.

During the years 2001-2007, I visited Mom several times a week. Mom helped me think through so many things, even when she was almost ninety-seven! She was my first best friend. I kept a notebook of our conversations. I got to know Mansfield Manor pretty well. I saw firsthand how Mom would light up when I walked into her room. She enjoyed playing Bingo and winning a prize, listening to piano concerts there, and having cheese-and-cracker snacks, but none of those things could compare to having family or a friend visit.

I am so thankful she held each of my five grandchildren in her arms, and every Halloween got to see Kenna and Saylor and Holden's costumes. I also know the heartache that comes with that kind of a living situation. A nursing home is nothing like home. Granddad Spooger is at Shady Glen. Harry's Wednesday visits make his day. Harry appreciates his Granddad Spooger; he is one of his best friends. Friendship has no age requirements.

Q: When did you first start writing chapter books?

A: When I was in the fifth grade at Marin School in Albany, California, I had my favorite teacher in elementary school, Mr. Vance Teague. I was fortunate to have

"Mr. Robert Ruebman, instructor in seniors honors English at Albany High School, Albany, California, 1961—my favorite all-time teacher!" (Reproduced by permission.)

him for two years: fifth and sixth grade. He was very innovative. Every Wednesday at ten o'clock, we got to write on anything for a whole forty minutes. I couldn't wait for Wednesdays, and every Wednesday I wrote a chapter about "The Missing Ink Blotter." I never got an E for excellent, or an O for outstanding, I always got S+'s. But my teacher did something very special when we finished our stories. He asked us to read them aloud over a microphone so every word could be heard. When it was my turn, I could tell by the way my classmates were listening that some day I would be an author. I thank Mr. Teague for making me feel like that.

When I was at Albany High School and took seniors honors English, I had Mr. Robert Ruebman. He was the teacher I adored. He would read great literature and poetry aloud, and encouraged us to read and write on our own. I dedicated my book *Who's Orp's Girlfriend?* to him.

Q: Did you really know a Horrible Harry?

A. Yes. My dad. And I loved him very much. Every three weeks or so, my dad would leave a note by the phone that said, "Gone Fishing. Harry." Mom would

wince and for a while be very angry. She thought he was being a "Horrible Harry" those times, not choosing to give her advance notice. Dad loved going to Clear Lake Oaks, California, to fish. It was a three-hour drive from our house. Once in a great while he would take us. He always stayed at Indian Beach, which had six cabins near the water. He'd stop off first at the bait shop and get a bucket of minnows and a white carton of night crawlers. Then he'd fish on the pier for hours, saving every croppie, blue gill, catfish, and bass to bring home in a bucket of ice for a fish fry. We didn't use plastic bags then. Newspaper mostly. I loved sitting next to Dad when we fished. We'd keep our eye peeled on our red bobbers. We rarely said anything. We just sat quietly together.

Dad was just the opposite of Mom. She was deep, loved conversation, music, and literature. Dad was uncomplicated, very simple, very much in the now like Horrible Harry. My dad and Horrible Harry live in the present moment. The red bobber was what was important, not what happened years ago. I felt so special being able to share Dad's fishing moments. I would watch him scrape the scales of each fish he caught on a wooden table at the pier. He would scoop out the "innards" as he called them and plop them into a barrel. It was smelly and

"The original Harry, my dad, who earned a basketball scholarship to Wabash College, Indiana, in 1929" (Reproduced by permission.)

Dad and Mom, 1955 (Reproduced by permission.)

disgusting. When one of the fish was pregnant and he scooped out yellow eggs, I would turn away and feel bad. Dad said he was sad too, and then moved on.

Dad looked a lot like Clark Gable or a present-day George Clooney. He was a very handsome man named Harry Weaver, son of David Weaver, the farmer. His friends called him Buck. I know Mom was infatuated with him. She had met Dad at a card party in Fairmount, Indiana. They were playing bridge. It was love at first sight for Mom. They dated off and on. She wrote to him at Wabash College when she was at the University of Michigan. During the Depression in 1934, Dad was driving an ice truck and he delivered ice to all the houses in her neighborhood. On one particular day, she ran out and asked him to marry her, but she put it in more of a business proposition. She said she needed someone to run her farm since her mom and dad were gone. Dad said, "Sounds fine to me." And then later that night he called and asked to speak to Mrs. Weaver. Mom said she was completely charmed. They were married for forty-eight years until he died in 1982.

When I was in third grade, I started writing regularly to my grandfather in Fairmount, Indiana. I wrote mostly about his son, "Harry," my dad. I would write about his Sundays mowing the lawn while Mom and my sister

Nancy and I would go to church. When we came home, he would be sitting on the stoop smoking a Pall Mall cigarette (Ugh!). Sometimes I would "sit on a house" with Dad on the weekends. We would set up all the saw horses along the way that had a sign pointing to OPEN HOUSE. Since the homes were usually empty, Dad would bring a chair for himself, and I would sit on the floor. Dad brought our Philco radio so we could listen to the old radio shows, and they were wonderful. I LOVED those afternoons listening to *Amos and Andy, Francis the Talking Mule, Our Miss Brooks, Lux Radio Theater, Tarzan,* and *Dennis the Menace.* My Aunt Walneta told me that my weekly letters to Granddad made him live a few more years. That made me feel awfully good; it also made me realize the rewards of writing.

Q: Herbie Jones and Raymond Martin both come from families with money problems. Did your family have money problems too?

A: Mom and Dad always had money problems. I know that's why my characters Herbie Jones and Raymond Martin had them. It was the lifestyle I grew up with. My parents were real-estate salesmen and had a very hard time selling houses regularly. During the dry spells, Mom and Dad got very creative with their cooking. Dad made a wonderful pot of navy beans with a ham

bone. Mom made Indiana spaghetti go a long way—that was the kind that was put in a casserole and served over several meals.

Mom became a very good knitter too. She knit me a beautiful maroon suit when I was in kindergarten at Vista Primary School. I remember my teacher sent me to the principal just so he could see how beautiful it was. Mom got a second job as a substitute teacher. I remember her keeping a cardboard file of activities for each month. She also worked part time as a clerk at Hinks on Shattuck Avenue in Berkeley. When she didn't have customers in her linen department, she was supposed to fold the towels. Some nights she would come home with teary eyes. Her manager had criticized her for not folding them neat enough and Mom was afraid of losing her job.

During the time I passed from third grade to fourth to fifth and finally sixth, Mom saved enough pennies to buy a used piano and some sheet music. I remember every tune she played from that Sigmund Romberg album: "Deep in My Heart, Dear," "I Bring a Love Song," "Softly as a Morning Sunrise," and "Wanting You." I remember being eleven in 1954, sitting next to her at the piano, and singing our hearts out together.

"Best friend Terry Chaplin and me at Donner Lake" (Reproduced by permission.)

When Mom was very young growing up in South Whitley, Indiana, she had a baby grand piano and lived in a mansion. Her dad was a banker and was president of the Farmers Bank in town. But when the Depression hit, her family lost the bank and had to pay back all its shareholders. My granddad had died the year before in a car accident—in those days they didn't have stop signs, and as he was chugging along, a car sideswiped him. He never recovered. Neither did my grandmother. She was so devastated by the financial loss and the loss of her husband that she took her own life. I knew when Mom sang those Sigmund Romberg songs, she was dealing with the sadness of having lost her parents and her South Whitley homestead.

Q: Do you have a theme you use a lot in your writing?

A: Yes. A good friendship endures all things. The reason why I write about friendship so much in my "Horrible Harry," "Herbie Jones," and "Mary Marony" books is because I have such vivid memories of my own friendships as a young girl. A strong friendship helps weather the toughest of times, the most painful moments, and hurtful acts. Harry and Doug's friendship lasts because they forgive each other. Herbie and Raymond accept one another with all their warts and weaknesses! Song Lee and Mary and Ida make time for each other. All of them encourage each other's interests.

I met Terry Chaplin in third grade in 1951. She's the best listener I know. And a true, loyal friend. We continue to be best friends today! She and I both went to Marin Elementary School in Albany, California, and then Albany High, and the University of California at Berkeley. Over the years we shared our marriages, her divorce, the death of my son to SIDS [sudden infant death syndrome], and the joyful, sometimes painful growing years of our children.

Terry and I would go to her house a couple of times a week to play a game of Clue, eat tomato sandwiches, and sip Cokes. It was such a treat to have my very own bottle. Terry's dad worked at the Coca Cola plant in Oakland and he was always bringing home a case of Coke. My family couldn't afford such delicacies as a six pack of soda.

Terry's mom and dad kept a tally of our growing height on their kitchen wall. There was something very comforting about that. I would watch the dark pencil marks go up big notches every year. I would stand with my heels pressed against the wall, and Mr. Chaplin would put a book on my head and make a mark just below it. We started when I was five foot and finished nine years later with a measurement of five foot nine and a half—almost five foot ten! Terry was an inch and a half shorter, but considered tall too. It wasn't until we left for Berkeley that they decided to paint their walls.

Every summer I went with the Chaplins for a two-week vacation. Sometimes another dear friend, Kathy Moulton, would come too. It was so exciting! We camped

"Cheerleading days at Albany High (I'm in the middle)" (Reproduced by permission.)

out at Donner Lake, Lake Tahoe, Shasta Mountain, Mt. Lassen, and along the Pacific Ocean near the Redwoods. At night, I would make up stories and Terry and Kathy would laugh. I learned about the different smells of manzanita, sequoia, redwoods, and Jeffrey pines. I learned to identify paper birches and quaking aspens. We took walks with the rangers and learned about the history of each area. At night we had a campfire and watched the sparks make their way to the sky scene of a thousand stars! We always spotted the North Star, the big dipper and the little dipper, and Orion's belt. Like Harry, my friends and I shared a love for science.

I lived in Albany, California, at 1038 Peralta Street. Most of the time, though, my friends and I played at Terrace Park. There was a huge hedge in my backyard that separated my house from the park. After we made a hole in it, we had a secret passageway to the best play yard in the world. A slide, teeter-totter, jungle gym, and sand! And then there were picnic tables for bag lunches on Saturdays, and a huge green lawn for kickball and baseball, and near the Recreation Hut was a tetherball where I practiced daily winding that ball around the pole. Inside the hut was a constant ongoing contest of some kind—in ping pong or checkers or chess, and I loved learning about each one. In the summer, the small dugout pool in the cement was filled with water no more that three and a half feet deep, but we thought it was our own private pool!

On rainy days, I would write with my friend Robin McConahy. She and I wrote a novel together in seventh grade, and felt very good about that. Sometimes we would take turns reading it aloud. Robin and I have kept in touch over the years and we still visit one an-

other today. She's a retired high-school counselor and grandmother now.

When I was at Albany High School in Albany, California, I met a girl who became my other best friend, Charla Pinkham. She was two years older than me, a pom-pom girl, and starred in the Junior Class Play. We had the same gym period and took the same typing class. I loved her honesty, humor, and enthusiasm. She and her friends were responsible for getting me elected to cheerleader. We all ran in groups but were voted individually, and after my group came out to do a cheer at our school assembly, she and her friends shouted "Vote for Susie Weaver!" They even had made signs. I was the only girl in my group to win, and I owe that largely to Charla. I loved being a cheerleader. We didn't have girls' basketball teams like Mom did when she was in Indiana. She was high-point girl at South Whitley High, and Dad had gotten a basketball scholarship to Wabash. There was no girls' team in the late 1950s at Albany High. You had a choice of four things if you were a girl: Be in the rooting section, be a majorette, be a pom-pom girl or be a cheerleader. I chose the last one. I remember losing my voice after several games, but I was always loving it, and felt like we really did help our Cougars win games.

I've been blessed with good friends throughout my life. When I taught at Southwest School, I made friendships that will last a lifetime. I get together regularly with my teacher friends. They're like sisters to me. Once a year, we have an overnight visit, usually at my house. This year, 2008, will be our eighth reunion!

Q: Sometimes you have a character pray when he's in a jam. Like when Herbie prayed about his dog, Hamburger Head, and Horrible Harry and Doug prayed about their teacher moving to Oklahoma. Is faith important to you?

A: Yes. When I was sixteen I was walking along the beach at Honeymoon State Park in Oregon. When I came to a tall redwood, I stopped for a while. There was so much light. I felt God's presence, and said, "Lord, take my life, and make it yours. Fill me with your love and your strength. Use me where ever I go." When I was growing up, Mom would drive my sister and me to the First Presbyterian Church in Berkeley to hear Dr. Munger speak. He was such an inspirational speaker. After Dr. Munger, there was Dr. MooMaw, and then Dr. Palmer. Listening to these ministers each week made Jesus' words come alive for me. I began collecting favorite passages from the Bible and lines from spiritual writers for a special notebook I keep close by. Here are some of my inspirational favorites:

"Nothing can separate you from the love of our lord," Romans 8:38-39

"Always be thankful," Colossians 3:15

"It's not what you do but how much love you put into it that matters," Mother Teresa

"My friend Charla (center) and sister Nancy (right) visiting me in Torrington at my old house, 1993" (Reproduced by permission.)

Q: What are the rewards of writing for you?

A: When I get a letter from a parent or teacher that tells me my books were the ones that turned their children on to reading, I just beam! That means so much to me! If my stories can grab a reluctant reader, I am thrilled. And when I go to schools and get a chance to talk with children, I am amazed to see how many have read my books and love my characters. It's a joy to see how they respond to my books with their own writing and art. I can't believe that I actually get paid for what I love doing so much. Writing!

Q: Anything new happening with your books?

A: Yes! I am very excited that James Larson, artistic director for the award-winning Omaha Theater Company and Rose Theater, is bringing "Horrible Harry" stories to the stage in 2008! His national touring company will produce *Horrible Harry in Room 2B* and *Horrible Harry Moves Up to Third Grade*. Children from schools all over the United States will be able to see these stories acted out on stage! I am just thrilled and can't wait to see the production when it comes to Connecticut in 2008. I always thought Horrible Harry and Herbie Jones

would make great live theater. It's an honor to have Dr. Larson include Horrible Harry among his long list of wonderful live productions.

And . . . the "Horrible Harry" books have a new artist, Amy Wummer! I think she brings new energy and a fresh look to the series. Frank Remkiewicz, my beloved illustrator of twenty-two "Horrible Harry" books, will be leaving. His illustrations have created loveable characters and realistic settings. I will always be one of his fans! Although I was saddened by his departure, I understand his need for more time. Frank told me that he loved working on the art for the series but that it had gotten to be too time consuming. I wish him the very best on his new projects!

Q: Has there ever been a mistake in one of your books?

A: Yes! I can think of several right away! I have Mr. Jeffrey Oppenheim's second-grade class in Las Vegas to thank for letting me know about the first one. They wrote to me via my Web site, and I was so happy to respond. I mentioned their names in the paperback reprint of *Horrible Harry Goes to the Moon*. They were absolutely right! Alan Shepard was the only astronaut to

play golf on the moon. Neil Armstrong and Buzz Aldrin didn't get a chance! If you have a hardbound copy in your library, it may not have been corrected.

The other mistakes were with the art and I have a fourth-grade girl from Michigan to thank for one keen observation. She asked why the pink note on the cover of *Song Lee and the "I Hate You" Notes* was not folded into eighths like the text said. I looked at the cover and my eyes BULGED! The interior art was correct. The pink notes were folded into eighths, but the one on the cover was folded in 12ths! Horrors! And it still has not been changed.

The other art error was really my fault. When *Herbie Jones and the Monster Ball* came out I called my editor right away. That Monster Ball on the cover didn't look like a monster! It had a big smiling face. The kind I would make on a child's spelling paper. My editor told me that I didn't describe the Monster Ball in the text, which was true! I write a lot of dialogue. That's what I love! But this time, my NOT describing the Monster Ball cost me a little. The artist, Richard Williams, obviously felt the Monster Ball was a kind being and so drew him like that. And he's a wonderful artist that I respect very much. The original Monster Ball that Uncle Doug created (see above *Monster Ball*) had an eye patch, and drool, and glaring eyebrows. So writers, when you have a certain picture in your mind about something in your story, be sure to describe it.

Q: Do you have any disappointments about your books?

A: Only a few. I am sorry that the Herbie Jones Readers' Theater went out of print. I loved creating those plays from the first "Herbie Jones" books. When I visit schools, I always use a skit with the teachers. My one consolation is that Scholastic Books has printed a dozen of them and uses it as a bonus for teachers. At least teachers who request it can get it. I'm happy about that!

And I'm disappointed that my "Orp" books went out of print. The reviews for those books were wonderful! Orp was an ordinary seventh grader who started an "I Hate My Name Club," created a booth for a school fair that was unique, made chop-suey burgers at a cooking contest, led a basketball team to victory, and tried unsuccessfully to have two girlfriends. He also did some detective work about the strange happenings in a vacant house next door. I'm hopeful one day they might be reprinted.

Q: What are you working on now?

A: I just finished *Horrible Harry and the Dead Letters,* which Amy Wummer is currently illustrating. It will be out in late 2008. The story seed for this book was a visit I made to Byron Bergen Elementary in Bergen, New York. I got to meet a dedicated librarian, Joyce Cullum, who kept a real big blue mailbox in her library. The children had special jobs managing the mail at By-

ron Bergen, and I could just see Song Lee and Mary and Doug and Harry and ZuZu and Ida and Sidney jumping into that activity. The author who inspired me for this book was Eileen Spinelli and her book *If You Want to Find Golden.* Harry discovers poetry! This was the poem he wrote for the color brown:

"If You Want to Find Brown" by Harry Spooger

If you want to find brown,
go barefoot on a farm after it rains.
Step in the mud and
Wiggle your toes!
Feel the muck
Ooze between your piggies and moo twice!
If you want to find brown.

And I just finished writing something for Dan Gutman's *Let's Save the Planet by 100 Authors.* The title may change before it goes to press, but the idea is wonderful. We need to exchange ideas about how we can preserve our planet and eliminate waste. I read some of the entries by other authors and they were great! It was a project I was happy to participate in.

Q: What tips do you have for struggling writers?

A. I have two. First, carry a notebook and collect your own story seeds. Write down one or two words about something you notice, or think is really fascinating. Keep your notebook in your pocket so it's always

"Ruf and me at my teacher's retirement party," June, 2000 (Reproduced by permission.)

handy. Who knows what might inspire you? Each one of you has your own unique voice so your story seeds will be different from someone else's.

Second, read a lot of books. We learn so much from other authors, and many times they can inspire us to write. When I read Rhoda Blumberg's essay on "The Truth about Dragons," I was inspired to write *Horrible Harry and the Dragon War*. I didn't know there were two kinds of dragons. I loved reading about them! There was the dangerous European one that spits fire and green smoke, drinks blood, and kidnaps maidens. Then there was the Asian dragon that sips cream, munches on bamboo, and brings good luck! I knew which dragon Harry and Song Lee would like. It was the beginning of a story about a friendship that gets tested.

*   *   *

KRAFT, Erik P.

Personal

Male. *Education:* Vermont College, M.F.A., 2000.

Addresses

Home—Box 230508, Astor Station, Boston, MA 02123. *E-mail*—erik@erikpcraft.com.

Career

Author and illustrator. Columbia University, New York, NY, adjunct assistant professor. Previously worked as a vacuum salesman.

Writings

Chocolatina, illustrated by Denise Brunkus, BridgeWater Books (Mahwah, NJ), 1998.
(And illustrator) *Lenny and Mel,* Simon & Schuster (New York, NY), 2002.
(And illustrator) *Lenny and Mel's Summer Vacation,* Simon & Schuster (New York, NY), 2003.
(And illustrator) *Lenny and Mel: After-School Confidential,* Simon & Schuster (New York, NY), 2004.
Miracle Wimp (young-adult novel), Little, Brown (New York, NY), 2007.

Children's book reviewer for *Boston Book Review.*

Sidelights

"I always wanted to be a writer, once I realized that was even a possibility," author and illustrator Erik P. Kraft told an online interviewer for the *Powells Web site.* Although it took some time for Kraft to reach his chosen profession—including a stint working as a vacuum-cleaner salesman—he now works as a writer

and illustrator of books for children and young adults, as well as serving as an adjunct associate professor at Columbia University.

With *Lenny and Mel,* Kraft introduces two recurring characters in his chapter books. Twin brothers, Lenny and Mel get summer odd jobs, celebrate holidays with wacky antics, and investigate after-school clubs for their middle-school paper. *Lenny and Mel* follows the pair through the American holiday cycle, introducing concepts like the "Leftover Fairy" who visits after Thanksgiving. While describing the chapters as uneven, Shannon R. Pearce noted in her *School Library Journal* review that in *Lenny and Mel* "there are moments of laugh-out-loud hilarity." Calling the pair descendants of characters from books by Jon Scieszka or James Marshall, Roger Sutton wrote in *Horn Book* that Kraft's "humor is absurd and unashamedly obvious," while a *Kirkus Reviews* contributor observed that "the author goes more for droll humor than cheap laffs or grossness." Recommending *Lenny and Mel* to students more prone to pulling pranks than reading, a *Publishers Weekly* contributor added that "Kraft's deadpan cartoon-panel drawings . . . may well get even nonreaders in on the laughs."

In *Lenny and Mel's Summer Vacation* the twins are busy looking for part-time work during the summer while also hoping to avoid writing book reports for their mother. Eventually, the boys wind up on a family vacation to a ramshackle cabin. Anne Knickerbocker, writing in *School Library Journal,* compared Kraft's book to Dav Pilkey's "Captain Underpants" series and called *Lenny and Mel's Summer Vacation* "light summertime fare." A *Publishers Weekly* contributor noted that the author's illustrations heighten "the caper's goofy good fun."

The twins' adventures continue in *Lenny and Mel: After-School Confidential,* as they take on an assignment to write an article about after-school clubs. Mel hopes to uncover a conspiracy, but the twins are limited by their assignment to stick with facts. Ultimately, the boys find little to interest them in reality, and "their pithy reports, reproduced along with Kraft's evocatively unambitious line drawings, reflect [their attitude] to a tee," according to a *Kirkus Reviews* contributor.

In *Miracle Wimp* Kraft leaves behind the middle-school setting of Lenny and Mel and introduces high-school sophomore Tom Mayo, a nerd planted squarely at the bottom of the social ladder. To make matters worse, Tom is accidentally enrolled in wood shop instead of his preferred computer animation class, and his counselor refuses to fix his schedule. As the teen navigates the perils of dating and driver's ed, he manages to survive high school one day at a time. A *Kirkus Reviews* contributor called *Miracle Wimp* "as sly and dry as [Kraft's] Lenny and Mel series." Discussing Tom's first-person narrative in *Miracle Wimp, Booklist* contributor Kathleen Isaacs noted that the teen "perfectly captures the

The adventures of Eric P. Kraft's sweet-toothed heroine in his debut picture book Chocolatina *are brought to life in artwork by Denise Brunkus.* (Illustration copyright © 1998 by Denise Brunkus. Reproduced by permission of Scholastic, Inc.)

insecurity and self-consciousness of his age." A contributor to *Publishers Weekly* felt that while *Miracle Wimp* might not appeal to girls, boys who enjoy stories "infused with slapstick and sarcasm . . . will find [Kraft's] . . . virtually plotless book a quick and entertaining read."

Biographical and Critical Sources

PERIODICALS

Booklist, June 1, 2007, Kathleen Isaacs, review of *Miracle Wimp,* p. 58.

Bulletin of the Center for Children's Books, June, 2003, review of *Lenny and Mel's Summer Vacation,* p. 408.

Horn Book, May-June, 2002, Roger Sutton, review of *Lenny and Mel,* p. 333.

Kirkus Reviews, January 1, 2002, review of *Lenny and Mel,* p. 48; June 15, 2004, review of *Lenny and Mel: After-School Confidential,* p. 578; July 15, 2007, review of *Miracle Wimp.*

Kliatt, July, 2007, Myrna Marler, review of *Miracle Wimp,* p. 18.

Publishers Weekly, January 21, 2002, review of *Lenny and Mel,* p. 90; August 20, 2007, review of *Miracle Wimp,* p. 70.

School Library Journal, February, 2002, Shannon R. Pearce, review of *Lenny and Mel,* p. 107; August, 2003, Anne Knickerbocker, review of *Lenny and Mel's Summer Vacation,* p. 135.

Tribune Books (Chicago, IL), June 29, 2003, review of *Lenny and Mel's Summer Vacation,* p. 5.

Voice of Youth Advocates, October, 2007, David Goodale, review of *Miracle Wimp,* p. 332.

ONLINE

Columbia University Web site, http://www.app.cc.columbia.edu/ (October 6, 2008), "Erik P. Kraft."

Erik P. Craft Home Page, http://www.erikpkraft.com (October 6, 2008).

Powells Web site, http://www.powells.com/ (October 6, 2008), interview with Kraft.*

L

LAYBOURN, Emma

Personal
Born in England; children: two. *Hobbies and other interests:* Walking.

Career
Writer. Has also worked as librarian and classroom assistant for special-needs children.

Writings

Robopop, illustrated by Nick Sharratt, Yearling (London, England), 1997.

Monster Shoes, illustrated by Georgien Overwater, Corgi Pups (London, England), 1999.

Megamouse, Andersen Press (London, England), 2001.

Mummy Mania, Andersen Press (London, England), 2002.

Clone Rangers, Andersen Press (London, England), 2003.

Minus Magic, Andersen Press (London, England), 2006, published as *Missing Magic,* Dial Books for Young Readers (New York, NY), 2007.

Dungeon Dragon, Andersen Press (London, England), 2008.

Sidelights
Emma Laybourn has published several fantasy books for children in the United Kingdom while also working as a librarian and classroom assistant for special-needs children. In 2007 her novel *Minus Magic* crossed the Atlantic and now entertains readers under its new title, *Missing Magic.* In this novel, Laybourn describes the adventures of Ned, an ordinary eleven year old growing up in a family with special magical powers. At the urging of his uncle Kelver, Ned enrolls in Leodwych, a private boarding school where the other students comfortably use magic to complete their assignments—and

also to torment Ned, who cannot retaliate because he cannot do magic. Frustrated and alienated, the boy nearly leaves the school, but when he and a few fellow

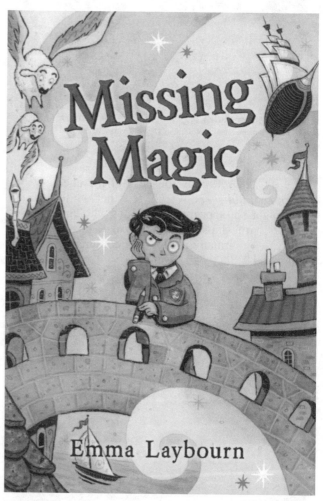

Cover of Emma Laybourn's easy-reading Missing Magic, *featuring artwork by Adam McCauley.* (Illustration copyright © 2007 by Adam McCauley. Cover design by Tony Sahara. Reproduced by permission of Dial, a division of Penguin Putnam Books for Young Readers.)

students are abducted by evil Necromancers, he must fight to save himself and the others caught in the net. In the process, Ned learns why he has no magical abilities and takes steps to regain his lost talents.

Some reviewers recognized the thematic similarity between *Missing Magic* and the popular "Harry Potter" series by J.K. Rowling. As a *Kirkus Reviews* contributor put it, Laybourn's novel is a "younger read" that will appeal to elementary school students who may not be ready for the Potter books. The same reviewer cited *Missing Magic* for containing "lots of humorous school scenes" and a narrator who uses his wits to overcome adversity. According to Corinda J. Humphrey in *School Library Journal*, Laybourn's plot "goes against convention" by creating a world in which magic does not solve every problem. Kathleen Isaacs, reviewing the work in *Booklist*, described Ned as an "engaging character who copes manfully with his difference," and a *Publishers Weekly* critic commended Laybourn for combining "heaps of humor and a strong moral message."

Biographical and Critical Sources

PERIODICALS

Booklist, July 1, 2007, Kathleen Isaacs, review of *Missing Magic*, p. 62.
Kirkus Reviews, June 1, 2007, review of *Missing Magic*.
Publishers Weekly, June 18, 2007, review of *Missing Magic*, p. 54.
School Librarian, spring, 2002, review of *Megamouse*, p. 33; spring, 2003, review of *Mummy Mania*, p. 34.
School Library Journal, September, 2007, Corinda J. Humphrey, review of *Missing Magic*, p. 202.

ONLINE

Random House Web site, http://www.randomhouse.co.uk/ (September 7, 2008), author biography.*

*   *   *

LEE, Suzy

Personal

Born in Seoul, South Korea; children: Sahn. *Education:* Seoul National University, B.F.A., 1996; Camberwell College of Arts, M.A., 2001.

Addresses

Home and office—Singapore.

Career

Artist, author, and illustrator of children's books. Founder of Hintoki Press. *Exhibitions:* Illustrations have been featured in exhibitions in the United States, South Korea, Germany, France, and England.

Awards, Honors

Most Beautiful Swiss Books selection, Swiss Federal Office of Culture, 2003, for *La revanche des lapins;* Notable Children's Book in the Language Arts selection, National Council of Teachers of English, 2008, for *The Zoo;* Gold Medal, Original Art, Society of Illustrators, 2008, for *Wave.*

Writings

SELF-ILLUSTRATED

La revanche des lapins (title means "The Revenge of the Rabbits"), Editions la Joie de Lire (Geneva, Switzerland), 2003.
Mirror, Edizioni Corraini (Mantova, Italy), 2003.
Action Korean Alphabet, Chondung Books (Seoul, South Korea), 2006.
The Black Bird, Chondung Books (Seoul, South Korea), 2007.
The Zoo, Kane/Miller (La Jolla, CA), 2007.
Wave, Chronicle Books (San Francisco, CA), 2008.

Contributor to *Mis primeras 80,000 palabras* (title means "My First 80,000 Words"), edited by Vicente Ferrer, Media Vaca (Valencia, Spain), 2002. Author and illustrator of short story "The Rabbit Hole," published in *Gunzo* literary magazine, 2005.

ILLUSTRATOR

Uwe Timm, *Run Rudi!*, Changbi (Seoul, South Korea), 1999.
Seok Baek, *Deaf Raccoon*, Woongjin (Seoul, South Korea), 1999.
(And adaptor) Lewis Carroll, *Alice in Wonderland*, Edizioni Corraini (Mantova, Italy), 2002.
Brothers Grimm, *Little Red Riding Hood*, translated by Ho-Sang Jo, Woongjin (Seoul, South Korea), 2004.
Seung-Yeon Moon, *The Naked Painters*, Chondung Books (Seoul, South Korea), 2005.
Jung-Sun Park, *Open the Door!*, BIR (Seoul, South Korea), 2008.

Sidelights

South Korean artist Suzy Lee has created paintings exhibited around the world as well as illustrations for picture books published in several countries. Lee has been cited by several critics for her limited use of text; instead she concentrates on artwork to communicate her message to the reader. "I tend to think in visual images," the illustrator explained in an online interview with Chronicle Books. "Often a story comes in a visual form at first. And the story built by the series of pictures usually does not need to have any words added later on. Some stories are best told without words."

In 2007, Lee entered the U.S. children's picture-book market with the publication of *The Zoo*, a nearly wordless tale about a young girl's outing with her parents.

As the family walks through the zoo, the somber illustrations depict cages empty of animals. Spotting a colorful peacock, the young girl leaves her parents behind to chase after it, leading her to more vibrantly colored creatures with whom she enjoys her visit. By story's end, the missing girl's parents discover her asleep on a park bench, and all of the animals wish her a colorful goodbye as the reunited family departs. Writing in *Kirkus Reviews,* a contributor described Lee's artwork as "wonderfully detailed, patterned and angular, with much to look at with delight," while *School Library Journal* reviewer Lucinda Snyder Whitehurst recommended *The Zoo* as a "sophisticated picture book" for "older readers who are willing to explore its complicated visual images."

In *Wave,* Lee "perfectly captures a child's day at the beach," observed *School Library Journal* critic Kim T. Ha. In the book a young girl conquers her own fear of the thundering water and befriends a flock of seagulls during a day at the beach. Using only shades of blue and gray in this wordless picture book, Lee engages the young girl in a slow dance with the sea, with the sea eventually sending a large wave that briefly submerges the surprised youngster. However, as the water from the giant wave recedes, the sea reveals seashell treasures to the delight of the girl. According to *New York Times Book Review* critic Becca Zerkin, the author/illustrator "portrays a universal childhood experience of carefree adventure," and a reviewer in *Publishers Weekly* deemed *Wave* "a book whose rewards multiply with rereading."

Biographical and Critical Sources

PERIODICALS

Kirkus Reviews, February 1, 2007, review of *The Zoo,* p. 125; May 1, 2008, review of *Wave.*
New York Times Book Review, July 13, 2008, Becca Zerkin, review of *Wave.*
Publishers Weekly, May 5, 2008, review of *Wave,* p. 62.
School Library Journal, June, 2007, Lucinda Snyder Whitehurst, review of *The Zoo,* p. 110; May, 2008, Kim T. Ha, review of *Wave,* p. 102.

ONLINE

Chronicle Books Web site, http://www.chroniclebooks.com/ (September 22, 2008), interview with Lee.
Suzy Lee Home Page, http://www.suzyleebooks.com (September 22, 2008).*

*   *   *

LICHTMAN, Wendy 1946-

Personal

Born April 7, 1946, in Buffalo, NY; daughter of Irving and Lenore Lichtman; married Jeff Mandel (a physician), June 23, 1977; children: Lev Lichtman Mandel.

Education: University of Michigan, B.A., 1966; California State University, Sonoma (now Sonoma State University), M.A., 1974.

Addresses

Home—Berkeley, CA. *E-mail*—wlichtman@aol.com.

Career

John F. Kennedy University, Orinda, CA, adjunct professor of psychology, beginning 1975; writer. Has tutored middle school students in mathematics.

Writings

Blew and the Death of the Mag, illustrated by Diane Mayers, Freestone Publishing (Albion, CA), 1975.
The Boy Who Wanted a Baby, illustrated by Vala Rae Williams, Feminist Press (Old Westbury, NY), 1982.
Telling Secrets, Harper & Row (New York, NY), 1986.
Do the Math: Secrets, Lies, and Algebra, Greenwillow Books (New York, NY), 2007.
Do the Math: The Writing on the Wall, Greenwillow Books (New York, NY), 2008.

Contributor to periodicals, including *Washington Post, New York Times, San Francisco Chronicle,* and *Good Housekeeping.*

Sidelights

Wendy Lichtman combines her expertise in the field of mathematics with her ability to write for young adults in her novels *Do The Math: Secrets, Lies, and Algebra,* and *Do the Math: The Writing on the Wall.* Lichtman hopes that these novels will encourage students to embrace algebra through an immersion in its practical aspects. Both books are set in middle school, where the heroine, Tess, applies mathematical formulas to everything from her changing level of crush on a boy to her choice of a dress for the formal dance. Mainly Tess uses math to solve mysteries, including a suspicious suicide that may actually have been a murder. Lichtman "researched" her math novels by drawing upon her own past experiences, by working in the classroom with a local middle school teacher, and by helping individual students improve their algebra skills.

A *Kirkus Reviews* contributor suggested that Lichtman's math novels could help struggling middle schoolers to "appreciate the accessibility of arithmetic" through the author's "lucid descriptions and drawings." Laura Lutz, writing in *School Library Journal,* cited *Do the Math: Secrets, Lies, and Algebra* for the "interesting premise" that mathematics can help bring control to troubling situations. Lutz also felt that Lichtman "skillfully captures the teenage voice."

Lichtman was inspired to write her math novels after reading about the work of Dr. Robert Moses, an educator who emphasizes the importance of acquiring math

skills at an early age. On *Powells.com* she explained that she uses her books to reach out to readers who are unenthusiastic about mathematics. "Thirteen-year-old kids are too old and too cool to say that they feel hopeless about their skills—they just say that they hate the subject," she noted. "The more I hung out with these students, the more I understood that my job in writing . . . was to try to get under their 'I hate math' radar."

Biographical and Critical Sources

PERIODICALS

Bulletin of the Center for Children's Books, June, 1986, review of *Telling Secrets,* p. 188; September, 2007, Cindy Welch, review of *Do the Math: Secrets, Lies, and Algebra,* p. 35.
Kirkus Reviews, June 1, 2007, review of *Do the Math: Secrets, Lies, and Algebra.*
Publishers Weekly, June 27, 1986, review of *Telling Secrets,* p. 94.
School Library Journal, September, 1986, Susan F. Marcus, review of *Telling Secrets,* p. 144; December, 2007, Laura Lutz, review of *Do The Math: Secrets, Lies, and Algebra,* p. 134.
Voice of Youth Advocates, August, 1986, review of *Telling Secrets,* p. 146.

ONLINE

Wendy Lichtman Home Page, http://www.wendylichtman. com (September 8, 2008).
Education Oasis, http://www.educationoasis.com/ (September 8, 2008), "Math as Metaphor: A Conversation with Author Wendy Lichtman."
Powells.com, http://www.powells.com/ (September 8, 2008), Wendy Lichtman, "Math and *Fiction?* Math and *Social Change?*"

*   *   *

LOREY, Dean 1967-

Personal

Born November 17, 1967, in Oscoda, MI; married; wife's name Elizabeth; children: Chris, Alex. *Education:* Graduated from New York University.

Addresses

Home—Calabasas, CA. *Agent*—William Morris Agency, 151 El Camino Dr., Beverly Hills, CA 90212. *E-mail*—dean@deanlorey.com.

Career

Screenwriter, producer, director, and author. Television work includes: *413 Hope St.,* Fox, co-executive producer, 1997; *My Wife and Kids,* ABC, co-executive pro-

ducer, 2001-03, executive producer, 2003-05, director, 2003-05; *Arrested Development,* Fox, co-executive producer, 2005-2006. Actor in films, including *Jason Goes to Hell* and *Major Payne.*

Member

Writers Guild of America, Screen Actors Guild, Directors Guild of America.

Awards, Honors

Writers Guild of America Award nominations, 2005 and 2006, and Emmy Award nomination for Outstanding Comedy Series, 2006, all for *Arrested Development.*

Writings

"NIGHTMARE ACADEMY" SERIES

Nightmare Academy, illustrated by Brandon Dorman, HarperCollins (New York, NY), 2007, published as *Nightmare Academy, Book One: Monster Hunters,* HarperCollins (New York, NY), 2008.
Nightmare Academy, Book Two: Monster Madness, illustrated by Brandon Dorman, HarperCollins (New York, NY), 2008.

SCREENPLAYS

My Boyfriend's Back, Touchstone Pictures, 1993.
(With Jay Hugely) *Jason Goes to Hell: The Final Friday,* New Line Cinema, 1993.
(With Damon Wayans and Gary Rosen) *Major Payne,* Universal, 1995.

TELEVISION SERIES

413 Hope St., Fox, 1997.
My Wife and Kids, American Broadcast Company (ABC), 2004-05.
Arrested Development, Fox, 2005-06.

Adaptations

Nightmare Academy was optioned for film by Universal Studios.

Sidelights

Dean Lorey, a producer and screenwriter who worked on the Emmy Award-winning television show *Arrested Development,* is the creator of the popular "Nightmare Academy" series of horror novels for middle-grade readers. Lorey has also written the screenplays for such films as *Jason Goes to Hell: The Final Friday* and *Major Payne,* and he served as a producer and writer for the sitcom *My Wife and Kids.*

Born in Michigan, Lorey grew up in Conyers, Georgia. "I pretty much always wrote since I was about eight years old," he told Jennifer Wardrip in a *TeensReadToo* online interview. "I *loved* writing short stories—usually about things coming out of swamps to drag people to their doom (I never claimed to be a normal eight year old)." Lorey attended film school at New York University; his big break came after a friend showed one of his screenplays to a producer in Los Angeles. A blend of comedy and horror, the story about a high school student who returns from the grave to attend prom was filmed as *My Boyfriend's Back.* Lorey later cowrote the script for *Jason Goes to Hell,* the ninth film in the iconic "Friday the 13th" series.

Lorey has enjoyed a successful collaboration with comedian Damon Wayans. The pair coauthored the 1995 film *Major Payne,* in which Wayans plays Major Benson Payne, a former Marine Corps commander making the difficult adjustment to civilian life. Hired as an instructor at a prep school, Payne soon finds himself befuddled and amused by his pint-sized charges. "The clash of hard-nosed Marine training and youthful antics are the grist of the film's comedy," noted *Variety* reviewer Leonard Klady, who added that the screenwriters "wisely do not tamper much with the pic's essential strength—its core idea." Lorey also served as a writer, director, and executive producer on *My Wife and Kids,* a family comedy featuring Wayans as a suburban husband and father of three.

In 2005 Lorey joined the crew of *Arrested Development,* a critically acclaimed television sitcom that revolves around the antics of the dysfunctional and incompetent members of the Bluth family. *San Francisco Chronicle* reviewer Tim Goodman dubbed *Arrested Development* "one of the most hysterically ridiculous half hours on television," and Robert Bianco, writing in *USA Today,* called the series "heaven-sent for anyone who has longed for something, anything, a little outside the comedy norm."

After the cancellation of *Arrested Development,* Lorey began work on the first of his "Nightmare Academy" titles. Discussing his inspiration for the series, the author told *Columbus Dispatch* interviewer Kevin Joy, "I had tons of nightmares as a kid—and the only good part about nightmares is waking up and realizing they're not real. So I got to thinking, What if your nightmares have real and terrible consequences?" Lorey's debut, published as *Nightmare Academy, Book One: Monster*

Hunters, centers on Charlie Benjamin, a youngster who possesses an incredible power: the ability to summon creatures from the netherworld through his dreams. A contributor in *Kirkus Reviews.* praised the story, describing it as "*Men in Black* for kids."

Lorey has garnered praise for his work in two seemingly unrelated genres. As he views it, "Comedy and horror aren't really all that different—they're both out to get you on a gut level, to make you scream or make you laugh," he remarked to Joy. "I just want to be as entertaining as I possibly can."

Biographical and Critical Sources

PERIODICALS

Columbus Dispatch (Columbus, OH), Kevin Joy, "Scary Dreams of Childhood Spook Author's Imagination."

Kirkus Reviews, July 15, 2007, review of *Nightmare Academy.*

Publishers Weekly, August 14, 2006, Michelle Kung, "Fright Night," p. 26.

San Francisco Chronicle, October 31, 2003, Tim Goodman, "Latest Fox Comedy *Arrested Development* Is So Funny It's Doomed."

School Library Journal, December, 2007, Sharon Senser McKellar, review of *Nightmare Academy,* p. 135.

USA Today, October 31, 2003, Robert Bianco, "*Development:* Not Your Father's Family Sitcom, Thankfully."

Variety, March 20, 1995, Leonard Klady, review of *Major Payne.*

Washington Post, August 14, 1993, Richard Harrington, review of *Jason Goes to Hell: The Final Friday;* March 24, 1995, Rita Kempley, review of *Major Payne.*

ONLINE

Dean Lorey Home Page, http://www.deanlorey.com (August 10, 2008).

Dean Lorey Web log, http://deanlorey.livejournal.com (August 10, 2008).

ReelViews Web site, http://www.reelviews.net/ (August 10, 2008), James Berardinelli, review of *My Boyfriend's Back.*

TeensReadToo.com, http://www.teensreadtoo.com/ (August 10, 2008), Jennifer Wardrip, interview with Lorey.

M

MacDONALD, Suse 1940-

Personal

Given name rhymes with "news"; born March 3, 1940, in Evanston, IL; married Stuart G. MacDonald (an architect) July 14, 1962; children: Alison Heath, Ripley Graeme. *Education:* Attended Chatham College, 1958-60; University of Iowa, B.A., 1962; also attended Radcliffe College, Art Institute, and New England School of Design.

Addresses

Home—P.O. Box 25, South Londonderry, VT 05155. *Agent*—Phyllis Wender, 3 E. 48th St., New York, NY 10017. *E-mail*—suse@susemacdonald.com.

Career

Caru Studios, New York, NY, textbook illustrator, 1964-69; MacDonald & Swan Construction, South Londonderry, VT, architectural designer, 1969-76; author and illustrator, 1976—.

Member

Society of Children's Book Writers and Illustrators, Authors Guild.

Awards, Honors

Child Study Association of America's Children's Books of the Year inclusion, and American Booksellers Association Pick of the List, both 1986, and Caldecott Honor designation, American Library Association, and Golden Kite Award, Society of Children's Book Writers and Illustrators, both 1987, all for *Alphabatics;* Gold Medal in preschool category, National Parenting Publication Awards, 1997, and Missouri Building Block Award nomination, 1998, both for *Nanta's Lion.*

Writings

SELF-ILLUSTRATED

Alphabatics, Bradbury (New York, NY), 1986.
(With Bill Oakes) *Numblers,* Dial (New York, NY), 1988.

Suse MacDonald (Reproduced by permission.)

(With Bill Oakes) *Puzzlers,* Dial (New York, NY), 1989.
(With Bill Oakes) *Once upon Another,* Dial (New York, NY), 1990.
Space Spinners, Dial (New York, NY), 1991.
Sea Shapes, Harcourt (San Diego, CA), 1994.
Nanta's Lion: A Search-and-Find Adventure, Morrow (New York, NY), 1995.
Peck, Slither, and Slide, Harcourt (San Diego, CA), 1997.

Elephants on Board, Harcourt (San Diego, CA), 1999.

Look Whooo's Counting, Scholastic (New York, NY), 2000.

Here a Chick, Where a Chick?, Scholastic (New York, NY), 2004.

(Adapter) Edward Lear, *A Was Once an Apple Pie,* Orchard (New York, NY), 2005.

Fish, Swish! Splash, Dash!: Counting Round and Round, Little Simon (New York, NY), 2007.

Alphabet Animals: A Slide-and-Peek Adventure, Simon & Schuster (New York, NY), 2008.

ILLUSTRATOR

Hank de Zutter, *Who Says a Dog Goes Bow-wow?,* Doubleday (New York, NY), 1993.

Jean Marzollo, *I Love You: A Rebus Poem,* Scholastic (New York, NY), 2000.

Jean Marzollo, *I See a Star,* Scholastic (New York, NY), 2002.

Sidelights

Children's book author and illustrator Suse MacDonald has a unique graphic style. Familiar shapes—whether they be letters, numbers, or other symbols—limber up and transform into new objects, stretching young imaginations in the process. Among MacDonald's works for children are the Caldecott Honor award-winning *Alphabatics,* as well as *Sea Shapes, Elephants on Board,* and *Peck, Slither, and Slide,* the last a guessing game about animals and their habitats. Seeking to expand her audience's visual sense, MacDonald finds the process of illustrating children's fiction to be full of opportunities and challenges for expanding creativity.

Born in 1940, MacDonald grew up in Glencoe, Illinois, a suburb of Chicago. Her father, a professor at Northwestern University, took his family during the summer months to an old farm in Weston, Vermont, where MacDonald enjoyed swimming and collecting specimens in the pond, horseback riding, and investigating the mysteries of an old barn in which she kept a playhouse, several forts, and numerous catwalks and perches. She also worked at the local summer theater handling the box office, pounding nails, and painting sets.

By the time MacDonald graduated from high school and enrolled at Chatham College in Pittsburgh, Penn-

MacDonald's self-illustrated picture book Peck, Slither, and Slide *reflects her interest in even the chilliest parts of the natural world.* (Copyright © 1997 by Suse MacDonald. Reproduced by permission of Harcourt, Inc.)

MacDonald's brightly colored collage art pairs with her simple, child-friendly text in the concept book Sea Shapes. (Copyright © 1994 by Suse MacDonald. Reproduced by permission of Houghton Mifflin Harcourt Publishing Company.)

sylvania, she was certain she wanted to be an artist. During her junior year in college she transferred to the art school at the University of Iowa, where she received her B.A. in 1962. During MacDonald's college years her classes were limited to fine-art techniques and art appreciation, because the concept of studying "commercial" art was not deemed appropriate for an academic institution. So the building blocks of her degree consisted of a traditional art curriculum: life drawing, print-making, sculpture, and painting. While each of these areas of study intrigued her, MacDonald was a pragmatic young woman and had difficulty envisioning where such expertise would fit into a future career.

Married to Stuart MacDonald shortly after completing her bachelor's degree, Suse and her husband settled in New York City, where she hoped to get a job using her artistic talents. However, competition for art-oriented jobs was fierce, and it took several years before she landed a position. In 1964, she accepted a job illustrating textbooks at Manhattan-based Caru Studios.

In 1969 the MacDonalds decided they needed a change from fast-paced city life. They moved to the MacDonald family farm in Vermont and ran a construction company for ten years, during which time they raised their two children. When their second child entered first grade, MacDonald decided to return to school and study illustration. She drove between Vermont and Boston for four years and attended classes at Radcliffe, the Art Institute, and the New England School of Art and Design. "It's hard to pinpoint the time when I decided that children's book illustration was the field in which I wanted to concentrate my energies," she later recalled. "My interests always seemed to lean in that direction."

While enrolled in a class in children's book writing and illustration at Radcliffe College, Macdonald became serious about children's books. By writing and illustrating several stories, she learned how to make sketched and colored "dummies," which are the first stage of life for a picture book. After completing her studies, she and

two other artists bought an old house in South Londonderry, Vermont, renovated it, and created five artists' studios: one for each of the women and two for rental. MacDonald assembled a portfolio of her illustrations and began to look for work, in both advertising and the children's book field. Her first assignments were paper sculpture for advertising. These jobs kept her going financially as she began to make the rounds of the publishers.

The idea for MacDonald's first book, *Alphabatics,* emerged while she was enrolled in a typography course. Working with letter forms, she discovered a technique for manipulating their shapes in various ways. Intrigued by the process, she felt there were possibilities for a book. Bradbury Press saw the possibilities as well, and *Alphabatics* was published in 1986, to positive reviews and many awards. "*Alphabatics* relates the shape of each letter in the alphabet to an object whose name starts with that letter," MacDonald once explained. "By changing the letter's shape, it evolves into something which is familiar but exciting to a child. This removes the alphabet from the adult world of letters on pages and brings it into the child's world of action and visual image." Margaret Hunt, in a review in *School Librarian,* noted: "Very few alphabet books . . . can be said to be as versatile and imaginative as this . . . one."

Encouraged by the success of her first book, MacDonald followed *Alphabatics* with several other books in which familiar shapes transform into something else. In *Numblers,* one of several books MacDonald created with fellow artist/author Bill Oakes, the numbers one to ten evolve into familiar objects. *School Library Journal* contributor Judith Gloyer deemed *Numblers* "a stretch for the imagination and an enjoyable way to introduce children to numbers."

In *Sea Shapes* ocean-dwelling creatures are distilled into geometric shapes: triangle, diamond, heart, circle, and oval. Each creature is described in a section of "sea facts" which provides information about each animal's behavior and physical characteristics. *Horn Book* reviewer Margaret A. Bush praised MacDonald's use of "shades of blue, green, and tan [that] illuminate the watery terrain and complement warm, unconventional tones of pink, orange, and purple."

MacDonald has used her cut-paper artistry to illustrate several narrative tales for young listeners. In her picture book *Space Spinners,* spider sisters Kate and Arabelle become the first arachnids to survive space travel, spinning a beautiful web during a NASA space voyage. Calling MacDonald's collages "a wonder," *Booklist* contributor Abbott maintained that *Space Spinners* "blasts off with a lively story line and first-rate artwork."

Nanta's Lion: A Search-and-Find Adventure takes young listeners to Africa, where a Maasai girl goes in search of a lion that has stolen cattle from her small village. A "search and find" story, *Nanta's Lion* allows readers to participate in Nanta's search by hiding the lion figure amid the African landscape; Nanta never finds her lion but readers certainly do. Equally challenging is *Peck, Slither, and Slide,* which provides clues about ten different animals, each characterized by a different action verb. The word "Build" pairs with a depiction of beavers in a stream, while "Wade" finds the long legs of the initial picture attached to pink flamingoes on the next page. Comparing MacDonald's cut-tissue-paper work to that of popular illustrator Eric Carle, a *Kirkus* reviewer praised the "simple, uncluttered wildlife scenes" in *Peck, Slither, and Slide,* while *School Library Journal* contributor Kate McClelland praised the "engaging art and inventive format" of a work that *Bulletin of the Center for Children's Books* critic Elizabeth Bush hailed as "an enticing gallery of animals on the move."

Look Whooo's Counting and *Alphabet Animals: A Slide-and-Peek Adventure* both contain a seek-and-find element. In *Look Who's Counting,* each page shows an increasing number of animals, and the numeral itself is used to form part of the animal's body. A bat's crooked wing is in the shape of the number seven, and a ram's horns form the shape of the number six. In addition, the owl narrator's wing feathers reveal the numbers from previous pages, so young learners can keep track of the numbers they've already seen. "Young audiences should have a fine time plumbing the subtle beauty and humor," wrote a contributor to *Publishers Weekly.* Kathie Meizner concluded in her *School Library Journal* review, "This is an owlishly clever approach to counting and looking at number shapes." *Alphabet Animals* is both an alphabet book and a puzzle or guessing game. Each animal hints at the uppercase letter of the alphabet that begins its name. The book contains moving parts, so that young readers can pull out cards with hints to the animal or letter's identity. "A coup of concept, color and construction," concluded a contributor to *Kirkus Reviews.*

Here a Chick, Where a Chick? is another of MacDonald's titles with moving parts. The story begins as the hens of the chicken coop search for a missing chick. Each page features different animals—not the hiding chick—hidden under flaps that readers can lift. The animal entourage grows as all of the animals join in the hunt for the chick. "MacDonald's illustrations are the main attraction," wrote a contributor to *Publishers Weekly.* Describing the repeated refrain of the title and the response of the uncovered animals with their appropriate noises, Be Astengo wrote in *School Library Journal* that "the narrative and animal sounds invite participation."

MacDonald returns to an under-the-sea setting in her counting book *Fish, Swish! Splash, Dash!: Counting Round and Round.* After guiding readers in a count upward to ten, the book then encourages readers to flip the volume upside down and count backward down from ten to one; the underwater setting allows images to be viewed in either direction without confusion. Joy

Fleishhacker, writing in *School Library Journal,* called *Fish, Swish! Splash, Dash!* "a fun book for beginning counters that will be enjoyed again and again," and a *Kirkus Reviews* contributor wrote that "the clever construction of this counting book guarantees a repeat audience."

In addition to her self-illustrated titles, MacDonald has provided illustrations for other authors, including Jean Marzollo. Their first book together, *I Love You: A Rebus Poem,* has text and small illustrations on one page and a full spread of illustration, demonstrating the ac-

tions described, on the other. Their second collaboration, *I See a Star,* shows children preparing for a Christmas pageant. MacDonald "provides humorous asides in her illustrations with the pageant participants getting into minor mischief," noted a contributor to *Kirkus Reviews.*

MacDonald has also adapted the work of nineteenth-century humorist Edward Lear. Accompanying Lear's popular limericks with her signature illustrations, *A Was Once an Apple Pie,* bringing the famous poet's work to a generation of new readers. The original alphabet poem

Cover of MacDonald's self-illustrated **Fish, Swish! Splash, Dash!,** *an aquatic-themed counting book.* (Illustration copyright © 2007 by Suse MacDonald.. All rights reserved. Reprinted by permission of Little Simon, an imprint of Simon & Schuster Children's Publishing Division.)

MacDonald's illustration project for other writers include creating art for Jean Marzollo's **I Love You: A Rebus Poem.** (Scholastic, 2000. Illustration copyright © 2000 by Suse MacDonald. Reproduced by permission.)

is nonsensical, and features many objects young readers might not be familiar with, which MacDonald replaced with new refrains for the appropriate letters. Noting that MacDonald's illustrations keep early characters, such as the bear representing the letter B, interacting with further letters, a *Publishers Weekly* critic felt the artist "skillfully counterbalances the ruminative nature of the verse." Although Karin Snelson wrote in *Booklist* that the substitutions in the text might bother some purists, she concluded that "nonpurist book lovers and preschool storytime readers, embrace this colorful introduction to Lear's classic poem." Teresa Pfeifer, writing for *School Library Journal,* deemed MacDonald's illustrations "a perfect match for Lear's sheer daring," and a *Kirkus Reviews* contributor described *A Was Once an Apple Pie* "an upbeat trip from A to Z."

As she noted on her home page, one of MacDonald's greatest joys as an author/illustrator has been "encouraging my readers to go beyond their usual stopping points and make their own artistic discoveries." "Children are inventors," she added. "They just need situations that bring out that quality of inventiveness. In my books I create those opportunities."

Biographical and Critical Sources

PERIODICALS

Booklist, September 15, 1989, Deborah Abbott, review of *Puzzlers,* p. 186; December 15, 1991, Deborah Abbott, review of *Space Spinners,* p. 770; March 15, 1999, Ilene Cooper, review of *Elephants on Board,* p. 1334; December 15, 1999, Hazel Rochman, review of *I Love You: A Rebus Poem,* p. 787; October 15, 2000, Gillian Engberg, review of *Look Whooo's Counting,* p. 445; October 15, 2002, Carolyn Phelan, review of *I See a Star,* p. 412; August, 2005, Karin Snelson, review of *A Was Once an Apple Pie,* p. 2034.

Bulletin of the Center for Children's Books, June, 1997, Elizabeth Bush, review of *Peck, Slither, and Slide,* pp. 366-367.

Horn Book, November-December, 1994, Margaret A. Bush, review of *Sea Shapes,* p. 722.

Kirkus Reviews, August 15, 1989, review of *Puzzlers,* p. 1247; April 15, 1997, review of *Peck, Slither, and Slide,* pp. 643-644; November 1, 2002, review of *I See a Star,* p. 1621; August 1, 2005, review of *A Was Once an Apple Pie,* p. 852; June 1, 2007, review of *Fish, Swish! Splash, Dash!*; May 1, 2008, review of *Alphabet Animals: A Slide-and-Peek Adventure.*

Publishers Weekly, January 3, 2000, review of *I Love You,* p. 74; October 16, 2000, review of *Look Whooo's Counting,* p. 75; February 9, 2004, review of *Here a Chick, Where a Chick?,* p. 79; August 15, 2005, review of *A Was Once an Apple Pie,* p. 56.

School Library Journal, November, 1988, Judith Gloyer, review of *Numblers,* p. 92; August, 1989, Margaret Hunt, review of *Alphabatics,* p. 100; April, 1997, Kate McClelland, review of *Peck, Slither, and Slide,* p. 128; December, 2000, Kathie Meizner, review of *Look Whooo's Counting,* p. 114; October, 2002, Susan Patron, review of *I See a Star,* p. 61; June, 2004, Be Astengo, review of *Here a Chick, Where a Chick?,* p. 114; August, 2005, Teresa Pfeifer, review of *A Was Once an Apple Pie,* p. 99; June, 2007, Joy Fleishhacker, review of *Fish, Swish! Splash, Dash!,* p. 114.

ONLINE

Scholastic Web site, http://www2.scholastic.com/ (October 2, 2008), "Suse MacDonald."

Suse MacDonald Home Page, http://www.susemacdonald.com (September 29, 2008).

Albert Marrin (Reproduced by permission.)

*   *   *

MARRIN, Albert 1936-

Personal

Born July 24, 1936, in New York, NY; son of Louis and Frieda Marrin; married Yvette Rappaport, November 22, 1959. *Education:* City College (now City College of the City University of New York), B.A., 1958; Yeshiva University, M.Ed., 1959; Columbia University, M.A., 1961, Ph.D., 1968. *Hobbies and other interests:* Travel in Europe.

Addresses

Home—Bronx, NY. *Agent*—Toni Mendez, Inc., 141 E. 56th St., New York, NY 10022.

Career

William Howard Taft High School, New York, NY, social studies teacher, 1959-68; Yeshiva University, New York, NY, assistant professor of history, 1968-78, professor and chairman of history department, beginning 1978; writer, 1968—. Visiting professor, Yeshiva University, 1967-68, and Touro College, 1972-74.

Member

Western Writers of America.

Awards, Honors

Notable Children's Trade Book selection, National Council for Social Studies (NCSS)/Children's Book Council, and *Boston Globe/Horn Book* Honor Book designation, both 1985, both for *1812: The War Nobody Won;* Western Heritage Award for best juvenile nonfiction book, National Cowboy Hall of Fame, and Spur Award, Western Writers of America, both 1993, both for *Cowboys, Indians, and Gunfighters: The Story of the Cattle Kingdom; Boston Globe/Horn Book* Honor Book designation, 1994, and Dorothy Canfield Fisher Children's Book Award, and Association of Christian Public School Teachers and Administrators Honor Award, both 1995, all for *"Unconditional Surrender": U.S. Grant and the Civil War;* Children's Book Guild/*Washington Post* Nonfiction Award for contribution to children's literature, 1995; Jefferson Cup Award, 1998, for *Commander in Chief;* Best Books for Young Adults citation, Young Adult Library Services Association, 2000, for *Terror of the Spanish Main; Boston Globe/Horn Book* Honor Book designation, and Parents' Choice Award, both 2000, and Carter G. Woodson Book Award, NCSS, and Best Western Juvenile Nonfiction designation, Western Writers of America, both 2001, all for *Sitting Bull and His World;* James Madison Book Award, 2005, for *Old Hickory;* Best Book of the Year citation, American Library Association, 2005, for *The Great Adventure: Theodore Roosevelt and the Rise of*

Modern America; James Madison Honor Book Award, 2007, for *Saving the Buffalo*; James Madison Book Award for Lifetime Achievement, 2008.

Writings

FOR CHILDREN; NONFICTION

Overlord: D-Day and the Invasion of Europe, Atheneum (New York, NY), 1982.

The Airman's War: World War II in the Sky, Atheneum (New York, NY), 1982.

Victory in the Pacific, Atheneum (New York, NY), 1983, reprinted, Beautiful Feet Books (Sandwich, MA), 2003.

War Clouds in the West: Indians and Cavalrymen, 1860-1890, Atheneum (New York, NY), 1984.

The Sea Rovers: Pirates, Privateers, and Buccaneers, Atheneum (New York, NY), 1984.

The Secret Armies: Spies, Counterspies, and Saboteurs in World War II, Atheneum (New York, NY), 1985.

1812: The War Nobody Won, Atheneum (New York, NY), 1985.

The Yanks Are Coming: The United States in the First World War, Atheneum (New York, NY), 1986.

Aztecs and Spaniards: Cortes and the Conquest of Mexico, Atheneum (New York, NY), 1986.

Struggle for a Continent: The French and Indian Wars, 1690-1760, Atheneum (New York, NY), 1987.

Hitler, Viking (New York, NY), 1987, reprinted, Beautiful Feet Books (Sandwich, MA), 2002.

The War for Independence: The Story of the American Revolution, Atheneum (New York, NY), 1988.

Stalin: Russia's Man of Steel, Viking (New York, NY), 1988, published as *Stalin,* Beautiful Feet Books (Sandwich, MA), 2002.

Inca and Spaniard: Pizarro and the Conquest of Peru, Atheneum (New York, NY), 1989.

Mao Tse-tung and His China, Viking (New York, NY), 1989.

Napoleon and the Napoleonic Wars, Viking (New York, NY), 1990.

The Spanish-American War, Atheneum (New York, NY), 1991.

America and Vietnam: The Elephant and the Tiger, Viking (New York, NY), 1992, reprinted, Beautiful Feet Books (Sandwich, MA), 2002.

Cowboys, Indians, and Gunfighters: The Story of the Cattle Kingdom, Atheneum (New York, NY), 1993.

"Unconditional Surrender": U.S. Grant and the Civil War, Atheneum (New York, NY), 1993.

Virginia's General: Robert E. Lee and the Civil War, Atheneum (New York, NY), 1994.

The Sea King: Sir Francis Drake and His Times, Atheneum (New York, NY), 1995.

Plains Warrior: Chief Quanah Parker and the Comanche, Atheneum (New York, NY), 1996.

Empires Lost and Won: The Spanish Heritage in the Southwest, Atheneum (New York, NY), 1997.

Commander in Chief: Abraham Lincoln and the Civil War. Dutton (New York, NY), 1997.

Terror of the Spanish Main: Sir Henry Morgan and His Buccaneers, Dutton (New York, NY), 1999.

Sitting Bull and His World, Dutton (New York, NY), 2000.

George Washington and the Founding of a Nation, Dutton (New York, NY), 2001.

Secrets from the Rocks: Dinosaur Hunting with Roy Chapman Andrews, Dutton (New York, NY), 2002.

Dr. Jenner and the Speckled Monster: The Story of the Conquest of Smallpox, Dutton (New York, NY), 2002.

Old Hickory: Andrew Jackson and the American People, Dutton (New York, NY), 2004.

Oh Rats!, The Story of Rats and People, illustrated by C.B. Mordan, Dutton (New York, NY), 2006.

Saving the Buffalo, Scholastic (New York, NY), 2006.

The Great Adventure: Theodore Roosevelt and Modern America, Dutton (New York, NY), 2007.

Years of Dust: The Story of the Dust Bowl, Dutton (New York, NY), 2009.

FOR ADULTS; NONFICTION

War and the Christian Conscience: Augustine to Martin Luther King, Jr., Gateway (Chicago, IL), 1971.

The Last Crusade: The Church of England in the First World War, Duke University Press (Durham, NC), 1974.

Nicholas Murray Butler: An Intellectual Portrait, Twayne (Boston, MA), 1976.

Sir Norman Angell, Twayne (Boston, MA), 1976.

Adaptations

Victory in the Pacific and *The Secret Armies* were both adapted for audio by Recorded Books, 2001; *The Airman's War, Commander in Chief,* and *Overlord: D-Day and the Invasion of Europe* were recorded as audio books by Recorded Books, 2002; and *George Washington and the Founding of a Nation* was adapted as an audio book by Recorded Books, 2003.

Sidelights

Albert Marrin is a professor of history who has attempted to make the past accessible to young readers via the many award-winning books he has authored. In books such as *1812: The War Nobody Won, Cowboys, Indians, and Gunfighters: The Story of the Cattle Kingdom,* and *Years of Dust: The Story of the Dust Bowl,* Marrin weaves an intriguing tapestry of U.S. history by focusing on dramatic moments and famous personalities. In biographies of world political figures from Napoleon Bonaparte to Adolph Hitler, Marrin has also interpreted the events of a larger world stage for juvenile readers. Additionally, his books on World Wars I and II provide introductions to many aspects of those struggles. "Without much in the way of fireworks, Albert Marrin is quietly establishing himself as one of the main chroniclers of American history for young people," Deborah Stevenson wrote in the *Bulletin for the Center of Chil-*

dren's Books. For many years, Marrin's books for young readers complemented his academic duties as chair of the history department at New York's Yeshiva University.

One of Marrin's first books intended for a young audience, *Victory in the Pacific,* is indicative of the author's approach to history. Writing in *Voice of Youth Advocates,* Michael Wessells commented on the author's "straightforward account," an account highlighted by "lucid capsule descriptions of selected topics" interspersed in the otherwise chronologically organized narrative which follows the war through major battles, from Pearl Harbor to Midway and Guadalcanal and the bombing of Japan. Marrin's treatment, anecdotal rather than detailed, will appeal, the reviewer noted, to "hi/lo readers." Kate M. Flanagan, writing in *Horn Book,* cited Marrin's "fast-paced" accounts of various battles and his ability to present a balanced narration that looks at history from both sides of the conflict in order to "provide an understanding of the warrior heritage that made the Japanese such a formidable enemy."

Cover of Marrin's middle-grade biography Hitler, *featuring artwork by Viqui Maggio.* (Illustration copyright © 1987 by Viqui Maggio. Reproduced by permission of Penguin Putnam Inc., and Toni Mendez, Inc.)

Marrin has dealt with various other aspects of World War II, from the invasion of Europe by the Allies to a history of spies and a study of the air war. With *The Yanks Are Coming,* he also examined U.S. involvement in World War I. His concentration on military subjects enhances an even more domestic topic in his *War Clouds in the West: Indians and Cavalrymen, 1860-1890,* which chronicles, battle by battle, the thirty-year war of destruction of the Plains Indians and Apache by the U.S. Cavalry. "The breadth of coverage," along with detailed diagrams and photos "all recommend this book for general readers," noted George Gleason in a *School Library Journal* review. In *Horn Book* Nancy C. Hammond called Marrin's book a "dramatic readable account" featuring enlightening cultural and historical perspectives on the struggle, such as the pressures ensuing from commercial demands for buffalo brought on by a new hide-tanning process.

The history of the Native Americans of the Great Plains also figures in several titles by Marrin: *Cowboys, Indians, and Gunfighters, Sitting Bull and His World, Plains Warrior: Chief Quanah Parker and the Comanche,* and *Saving the Buffalo.* The award-winning *Cowboys, Indians, and Gunfighters* presents a history of the Old West that ranges from the earliest Spanish settlers, who introduced horses and cattle to the region, to the growing struggle between buffalo and cattle for the open range. Divided into six chronological chapters, the book includes what *School Library Journal* critic Julie Halverstadt described as "minority viewpoints" that encompass the contributions of African-American and Mexican cowboys. *Cowboys, Indians, and Gunfighters* serves as "a dynamic look at one of the most exciting and dangerous periods in U.S. history," Halverstadt concluded.

With *Plains Warrior,* Marrin focuses on the Comanche and their losing battle in the nineteenth century for their traditional life on the Great Plains. Providing at once an overview of Comanche history as well as a dramatic representation of the last tragic years of fighting under Chief Quanah Parker, son of a kidnaped settler, *Plains Warrior* "brings the period to life," according to a reviewer in the *Bulletin of the Center for Children's Books.* The reviewer also praised Marrin for his even-handed treatment of both parties in the battle. While noting that Marrin's "vivid writing occasionally strays into sensationalism," *Horn Book* contributor Mary M. Burns praised *Plains Warrior* for building on both the "major differences between the Comanche and the white points of view and the tragedy inherent in those differences." In *Booklist,* Chris Sherman commented favorably on Marrin's use of "vivid description" and "compelling anecdotes" in telling his "engrossing" story.

In *Sitting Bull and His World,* Marrin frames his biography of the Lakota warrior within "both the nature and substance of one man's resistance to and witness of his nation's enthnocide," according to a contributor to *Horn Book. Saving the Buffalo,* told in "characteristically robust prose," according to *School Library Journal* con-

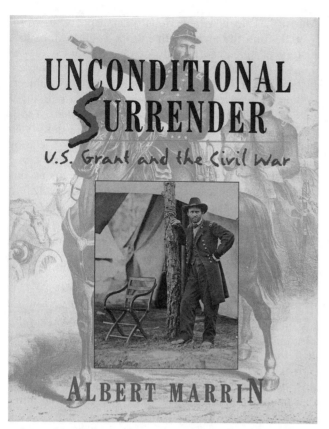

Cover of Marrin's fully illustrated biography "Unconditional Surrender": U.S. Grant and the Civil War. (Atheneum Books for Young Readers, 1994. Matthew Brady, photographer. Copyright © by National Portrait Gallery/Art Resource, New York. Reproduced by permission of Art Resource, New York.)

tributor John Peterson, covers the near-extinction of America's bison at the hands of both big game hunters and a deliberate attempt to slaughter the creatures to gain advantage over American Indian populations.

Going further into the past, Marrin investigates a conflict between Europeans and Native Americans in the New World—the wars between the British and French and their Indian allies—in *Struggle for a Continent: The French and Indian Wars, 1690-1760.* Here the author once again demonstrates his use of accurate research as well as his skillful use of anecdote to create a "retelling of history that young people find accessible and appealing," according to Elizabeth S. Watson in *Horn Book.* Paula Nespeca Deal, writing in the *Voice of Youth Advocates,* called *Struggle for a Continent* a "fascinating, easy to read overview" in which Marrin brings to life a little-understood battle for power by using "vivid details of the cultural and social background." Deal also pointed out that Marrin includes the accomplishments of women in the struggle.

A logical chronological companion piece to *Struggle for a Continent, The War for Independence: The Story of the American Revolution* provides a "detailed account" of the American war for independence, according to Anne Frost in the *Voice of Youth Advocates.* "This engrossing narrative gives the reader rare insight," Frost wrote, dubbing *The War for Independence* "highly rec-

ommended." Marrin divides his narrative into eight chapters, dealing with various topics such as causes, spies, naval battles, and the front-line skirmishes along the frontier. A contributor in *Kirkus Reviews* remarked particularly on Marrin's use of details that "engage the reader's senses," and a *Bulletin of the Center for Children's Books* reviewer called the work a "spirited and thoughtful account."

Marrin turns to the U.S. Civil War with titles profiling generals on opposing sides. *"Unconditional Surrender": U.S. Grant and the Civil War* uses Union General Ulysses S. Grant to focus on the war years, then includes information about the general before and after that conflict. The historian confines his chronicle to the battles and strategies that Grant was personally involved in. Thus, although Gettysburg and Bull Run are not included, detailed accounts of Shiloh and Petersburg are set forth, studded with a plethora of facts and anecdotes. Neither Grant's racism nor his drinking are glossed over in Marrin's account, and the extensive bibliography appended "will be much appreciated by both history students and Civil War buffs," concluded Elizabeth M. Reardon in her *School Library Journal* review of *"Unconventional Surrender."*

A view from the other side of the battle lines is provided in *Virginia's General: Robert E. Lee and the Civil War.* Beginning with a brief account of the subject's life before and after the U.S. Civil War, it focuses on the war years through the Confederate general's eyes as well as through the eyes of a score of other witnesses. The extensive use of quotations from Lee and his generals, as well as plentiful detail, provides a "vivid picture of the war, its participants, and its effects," according to Deborah Stevenson in the *Bulletin of the Center for Children's Books.* Carolyn Phelan, writing in *Booklist,* concluded that *Virginia's General* is "well researched and readable," and Connie Allerton noted in the *Voice of Youth Advocates* that Marrin tells "an exciting story."

Marrin extends his series on the U.S. Civil War with a volume focusing on President Abraham Lincoln: *Commander in Chief: Abraham Lincoln and the Civil War.* Patricia A. Moore, writing in *Kliatt,* considered this book to be "an outstanding addition to a crowded field."

With *The Spanish-American War* and *America and Vietnam: The Elephant and the Tiger,* Marrin tackles two other bloody chapters in U.S. history. In *The Spanish-American War* he creates "a fine sense of intimacy in his text," according to Margaret A. Bush in *Horn Book,* the book detailing the events leading up to the war U.S. President McKinley did not want. Raymond E. Houser, writing in the *Voice of Youth Advocates,* called *The Spanish-American War* "a good YA history," and a contributor in *Kirkus Reviews* labeled the same work "fresh (and timely)."

Marrin's history of America's longest war, *America and Vietnam,* was praised for its even handedness and also

criticized for its bias, demonstrating the deep rifts that still exist among historians as a result of that conflict. Initially, Marrin provides an overview of Vietnamese history as one of struggle, beginning with Chinese control of the nation and continuing through the French colonial system, occupation by the Japanese, renewed conflict with the French, and growing U.S. involvement. The book offers a lengthy account of the early life of Ho Chi Minh, the leader who established Communism in the northern regions of Vietnam following World War II, then focuses on the U.S. presence in and the ensuing war. "Marrin covers the Vietnam Conflict in a sweeping fashion," according to Raymond E. Houser in *Voice of Youth Advocates.* Calling *America and Vietnam* "remarkably even handed," Margaret A. Bush wrote in *Horn Book* that "if a YA reader had but one book to read on this subject, this should be the one."

Marrin's biographies on world leaders include portraits of Hitler, Stalin, Mao Tse-tung, Sir Henry Morgan, and Napoleon, as well as books on the influence of Spain in the Americas. A *Kirkus Reviews* critic deemed *Hitler* "a dramatic account" that includes such timely topics as the White Rose resistance group and the fate of Dr. Josef Mengele. Margaret A. Bush, writing in *Horn Book,* termed the work a "riveting account that is informative, illuminating, and inescapably painful." *Stalin* was dubbed "another fine biography" by Elizabeth S. Watson in *Horn Book,* while in *Mao Tse-tung and His China* Marrin interweaves Mao's life with the history of China from 1911 to the emperor's death. From Mao's troubled childhood through the Long March and the days of the Cultural Revolution, the book traces the major turning points in the life of one of China's most controversial leaders.

With *Napoleon and the Napoleonic Wars* Marrin takes on a project that has been attempted by many other biographers. He puts Napoleon's life into the context of the man's times through what Margaret Miles described as his "particular talent for selecting an incident or anecdote" that sums up an individual in her *Voice of Youth Advocates* review. In *Terror of the Spanish Main: Sir Henry Morgan and His Buccaneers* Marrin treats readers to "a narrative of epic proportions," in the opinion of *Horn Book* reviewer Mary M. Burns. Beginning with

C.B. Mordan creates dramatic pen-and-ink illustrations for Marrin's fascinating picture-book history Oh, Rats! (Illustration copyright © 2006 by C.B. Mordan. Reproduced by permission of Dutton Children's Books, a division of Penguin Putnam Books for Young Readers.)

a history of Spain on the high seas, the author focuses on the Welsh-born Morgan, who built his career from that of lowly pirate to almost-respectable businessman, creating a book Burns dubbed "addictive reading." In *Booklist* Randy Meyer praised Marrin for doing "a top-notch job of bringing [the seventeenth-century Jamaican] setting to life, describing colonial life in all its grit and glory."

Like Marrin's work on Abraham Lincoln, *George Washington and the Founding of a Nation* presents what *School Library Journal* contributor Steven Engelfried called an "engaging" portrait of both Washington and the times in which he lived. Covering General Washington's military campaigns in detailed fashion, the book captures Washington's courage and character by including the words of his contemporaries. Although, as Engelfried pointed out, the author "clearly admires his subject," he "carefully discusses [Washington's] . . . flaws and errors . . . [and] raises questions and presents different views," among them questions about Washington's ownership of slaves. Washington becomes, through Marrin's lens, "a man of his time," according to *Booklist* reviewer Randy Meyer, "one who could never reconcile his public philosophy of freedom with his private actions."

Marrin places other presidents in their historical contexts in the books *Old Hickory: Andrew Jackson and the American People* and *The Great Adventure: Theodore Roosevelt and the Rise of Modern America.* The former shows Jackson as both a product and a shaper of his times, and a man of many contradictions: he adopted a Native American child but brought about the legislation that led to the Trail of Tears. "Marrin lets readers judge the worth of Jackson the man as well as Jackson the general and president," wrote Betty Carter in her *Horn Book* review. Jane G. Connor, writing for *School Library Journal,* found *Old Hickory* to be "written in an engaging style and with a wealth of detail."

The Great Adventure ties the presidency of Theodore Roosevelt to the shaping of the role of the executive branch in modern America. Like Jackson, Roosevelt was a man of many contradictions: he was a big-game hunter who was an environmental conservationist, and though he loathed violence, he staunchly supported U.S. involvement in World War I. "Martin does justice to his subject's complex nature," wrote Denise Ryan in *School Library Journal.* A *Publishers Weekly* contributor considered the book "an engaging account," and John Peters, writing in *Booklist,* felt that *The Great Adventure* will "give serious history students a solid grounding in the man's times, career, and forceful character."

With *Inca and Spaniard: Pizarro and the Conquest of Peru, Aztecs and Spaniards: Cortes and the Conquest of Mexico,* and *Empires Lost and Won: The Spanish Heritage in the Southwest,* Marrin focuses on Spanish incursions in the New World and the clash of cultures that such incursions brought about. Kathryn Pierson

commented in the *Bulletin of the Center for Children's Books* that Marrin's novelistic treatment of *Inca and Spaniard,* rather than limiting the research value of his book, "has probably enhanced its appeal," while Zena Sutherland wrote in the *Bulletin of the Center for Children's Books* that *Aztecs and Spaniards* is "as dramatic as fiction but well-grounded in fact."

Moving away from large-scale world events, *Dr. Jenner and the Speckled Monster: The Search for the Smallpox Vaccine* describes not only Jenner's quest to end the smallpox disease, but also the history of the virus. Marrin "ably weaves in the scientific, religious, social, and cultural forces at work in Jenner's day without ever muddying his main story line," according to a critic for *Kirkus Reviews.* Kay Weisman, writing in *Booklist,* called *Dr. Jenner and the Speckled Monster* "a fascinating, eminently readable social history."

Explorations in the Gobi Desert set the scene in *Secrets from the Rocks: Dinosaur Hunting with Roy Chapman Andrews.* Andrews organized expeditions in Mongolia and in his search for fossils became one of the most renowned dinosaur hunters in paleontology—possibly even the inspiration behind famous movie character Indiana Jones. Marin's title "includes compelling details of danger and triumph and offers scientific and political background," according to Ellen Heath in *School Library Journal,* while Betty Carter, writing for *Horn Book,* considered *Secrets from the Rocks* "an exciting story of exploration, adventure, and scientific inquiry."

Marrin sometimes narrows his focus in order to reveal a larger picture of history, as he does in *Oh, Rats!: The Story of Rats and People.* Discussing both the biology of the rat and its relationship with humans throughout history, the book also celebrates rats as "champions of survival." As Kitty Flynn wrote in *Horn Book:* "Love rats or hate them, this book will leave readers with a greater respect for rats' intelligence and perseverance." A *Kirkus Reviews* contributor reacted to the work similarly, writing that "even the most rat-o-phobic reader will emerge with a heightened appreciation for the hardy rodent." Noting that the format of *Oh, Rats!* is different than in his previous books, *School Library Journal* critic Margaret Bush believed the book's style and topic to be "one that he has clearly enjoyed, as will a wide variety of nonfiction readers and animal fans."

Biographical and Critical Sources

BOOKS

Children's Literature Review, Volume 53, Gale (Detroit, MI), 1999.

PERIODICALS

Booklist, February 1, 1983, Ilene Cooper, review of *Overlord: D-Day and the Invasion of Europe,* p. 725; June 15, 1983, review of *Victory in the Pacific,* p. 1340;

December 15, 1994, Carolyn Phelan, review of *Virginia's General: Robert E. Lee and the Civil War,* p. 746; June 1, 1996, Chris Sherman, review of *Plains Warrior,* p. 1723; January 1, 1998, review of *Commander-in-Chief Abraham Lincoln and the Civil War,* p. 744; January 1-15, 1999, Randy Meyer, review of *Terror of the Spanish Main,* p. 849; January 1, 2001, Randy Meyer, review of *George Washington and the Founding of a Nation,* p. 951; April 15, 2002, Gillian Engberg, review of *Secrets from the Rocks: Dinosaur Hunting with Roy Chapman,* p. 1400; November 15, 2002, Kay Weisman, review of *Dr. Jenner and the Speckled Monster: The Search for the Smallpox Vaccine,* p. 603; December 1, 2004, John Peters, review of *Old Hickory: Andrew Jackson and the American People,* p. 645; July 1, 2006, John Peters, review of *Oh, Rats!: The Story of Rats and People,* p. 53; September 1, 2007, John Peters, review of *The Great Adventure: Theodore Roosevelt and the Rise of Modern America,* p. 102.

Bulletin of the Center for Children's Books, April, 1986, Zena Sutherland, review of *Aztecs and Spaniards: Cortes and the Conquest of Mexico,* p. 153; April, 1988, review of *The War for Independence: The Story of the American Revolution,* p. 161; February, 1990, Kathryn Pierson, review of *Inca and Spaniard: Pizarro and the Conquest of Peru,* p. 142; March, 1994, Deborah Stevenson, review of *"Unconditional Surrender": U.S. Grant and the Civil War,* p. 227; January, 1995, Deborah Stevenson, review of *Virginia's General,* p. 173; May, 1996, review of *Plains Warrior: Chief Quanah Parker and the Comanche,* p. 308; December, 1999, Deborah Stevenson, "True Blue."

Horn Book, April, 1983, Kate M. Flanagan, review of *Victory in the Pacific,* p. 184; March-April, 1985, Nancy C. Hammond, review of *War Clouds in the West: Indians and Cavalrymen, 1860-1890,* pp. 195-196; April, 1986, Zena Sutherland, review of *Aztecs and Spaniards,* pp. 153-154; September-October, 1987, Margaret A. Bush, review of *Hitler,* p. 630; January-February, 1988, Elizabeth S. Watson, review of *Struggle for a Continent: The French and Indian Wars, 1690-1760,* p. 87; March-April, 1989, Elizabeth S. Watson, review of *Stalin,* p. 234; January, 1990, p. 89; July-August, 1991, Margaret A. Bush, review of *The Spanish-American War,* p. 481; September-October, 1991, Elizabeth S. Watson, review of *Napoleon and the Napoleonic Wars,* p. 617; September-October, 1992, Margaret A. Bush, review of *America and Vietnam: The Elephant and the Tiger,* pp. 600-601; September, 1996, Mary M. Burns, review of *Plains Warrior,* p. 621; March, 1999, Mary M. Burns, review of *Terror of the Spanish Main,* p. 227; July, 2000, review of *Sitting Bull and His World,* p. 474; July-August, 2002, Betty Carter, review of *Secrets from the Rocks,* p. 486; November-December, 2002, Betty Carter, review of *Dr. Jenner and the Speckled Monster,* p. 777; November-December, 2004, Betty Carter, review of *Old Hickory,* p. 730; September-October, 2006, Kitty Flynn, review of *Oh, Rats!,* p. 608; January-February, 2008, Betty Carter, review of *The Great Adventure,* p. 114.

Kirkus Reviews, May 15, 1987, review of *Hitler,* pp. 796-797; April 15, 1988, review of *The War for Independence, p. 621; February 15, 1991, review of *The Spanish-American War,* p. 250; April 1, 1992, review of *America and Vietnam,* p. 463; March 1, 2002, review of *Secrets from the Rocks,* p. 339; September 1, 2002, review of *Dr. Jenner and the Speckled Monster,* p. 1314; November 15, 2004, review of *Old Hickory,* p. 1091; July 15, 2006, review of *Oh, Rats!,* p. 727.

Kliatt, May, 2003, Penelope Power, review of *George Washington and the Founding of a Nation,* p. 33, and Patricia A. Moore, review of *Commander-in-Chief,* p. 38.

New York Times Book Review, February 25, 1990, Marsha L. Wagner, review of *Mao Tse-tung and His China,* p. 33; August 17, 1997, review of *Empires Lost and Won,* p. 19; August 13, 2000, review of *Sitting Bull and His World,* p. 16.

Publishers Weekly, December 10, 2007, "Presidential Prose," p. 57.

School Library Journal, March, 1985, George Gleason, review of *War Clouds in the West,* p. 180; August, 1993, Julie Halverstadt, review of *Cowboys, Indians, and Gunfighters: The Story of the Cattle Kingdom,* p. 199; July, 1994, Elizabeth M. Reardon, review of *"Unconditional Surrender,"* p. 1122; July, 2000, review of *Sitting Bull and His World,* p. 15; January, 2001, Steven Engelfried, review of *George Washington and the Founding of a Nation,* p. 150; April, 2002, Ellen Heath, review of *Secrets from the Rocks,* p. 178; December, 2004, Jane G. Connor, review of *Old Hickory,* p. 164; August, 2006, Margaret Bush, review of *Oh, Rats!,* p. 140; December, 2006, John Peters, review of *Saving the Buffalo,* p. 166; December, 2007, Denise Ryan, review of *The Great Adventure,* p. 155.

Voice of Youth Advocates, October, 1983, Michael Wessells, review of *Victory in the Pacific,* p. 226; October, 1987, Paula Nespeca Deal, review of *Struggle for a Continent,* p. 189; June, 1988, Anne Frost, review of *The War for Independence,* p. 103; June, 1991, Raymond E. Houser, review of *The Spanish-American War,* p. 127; October, 1991, Margaret Miles, review of *Napoleon and the Napoleonic Wars,* p. 265; June, 1992, Raymond E. Houser, review of *America and Vietnam,* p. 130; April, 1995, Connie Allerton, review of *Virginia's General,* p. 50; August, 1996, review of *The Sea King,* p. 181; February, 1998, review of *Empires Lost and Won,* p. 365.

ONLINE

Albert Marrin Home Page, http://www.albertmarrin.com (October 1, 2008).

James Madison Award Web site, http://www.jamesmadison bookaward.org/ (October 1, 2008), profile of Marrin.*

*   *   *

MATHEWS, Ellie 1946(?)-

Personal

Born c. 1946; married Carl Youngmann (a medical devices consultant). *Education:* Graduated from University of Washington. *Religion:* Society of Friends (Quaker).

Addresses

Home and office—Seattle, WA; and Port Townsend, WA. *E-mail*—web_mail@elliemathews.com.

Career

Author, illustrator, software designer, and cartographer. Organizer of writers' retreats.

Awards, Honors

Fishtrap Writer's Conference fellowship (Enterprise, OR), 1997; grand prize, Pillsbury Bake-Off, 1998; Seattle Artists Program for Literary Artists grant, 1998; Milkweed Prize for Children's Literature, 2007, for *The Linden Tree.*

Writings

Ambassador to the Penguins: A Naturalist's Year aboard a Yankee Whaleship, Godine (Boston, MA), 2003.

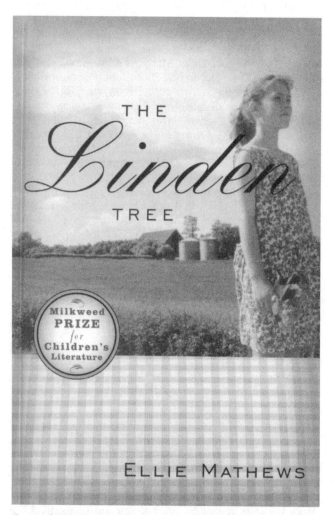

Cover of Ellie Mathews' coming-of-age novel The Linden Tree, *in which a girl comes to deal with her mother's death in rural 1940s Iowa.* (Milkweed Press, 2007. Cover design by Brad Norr. Cover photos copyright © by Corbis. Reproduced by permission.)

The Linden Tree, Milkweed Editions (Minneapolis, MN), 2007.
The Ungarnished Truth: A Cooking Contest Memoir, Berkley Books (New York, NY), 2008.

Also author of *The Presentation Design Book,* Ventura Press. Contributor of short fiction and poetry to anthologies, including *Friends Bulletin, FlipSide, Fishtrap Anthology,* 1998; *Cicada, Cricket,* and *Tidepools.*

Sidelights

Previous to starting her career in children's books, Ellie Mathews spent many years in the field of graphic illustration working in a wide variety of areas, from developing computer software to creating maps for government and private agencies. In 2003, she refocused her creative talents on writing and published her first children's book, *Ambassador to the Penguins: A Naturalist's Year aboard a Yankee Whaleship.* A biographical title, the book chronicles the exploits of ornithologist Robert Cushman Murphy after he joined a whaling expedition to the Antarctic.

Mathews addresses a young-adult audience in her novel *The Linden Tree.* Set on a farm in Iowa in the late 1940s, *The Linden Tree* offers "a timeless, heartfelt story of family, loss, and love," according to *Booklist* reviewer Heather Booth. The story portrays the events that unfold after nine-year-old Katie Sue Hanson unexpectedly loses her mother to meningitis. With her older sister and brother, Katie Sue struggles emotionally, leading her father to ask his late wife's sister for help. Initially, Aunt Katherine's presence is welcoming for the grieving children, but as time progresses, Katie Sue begins to have mixed feelings for the woman taking her mother's place. Recommending *The Linden Tree* for teens who have also suffered the loss of a loved one, *School Library Journal* critic Christi Voth concluded that Mathews' "honest account of a family's journey of grieving and healing is well portrayed." Several critics favorably noted the book's well-drawn characters, *Kliatt* contributor Marissa Elliott finding Katie Sue "believable and honest, lovable even in her anger."

In addition to her efforts in literature and illustration, Mathews has also demonstrated her creative ability in the kitchen, winning the top prize in the 1998 Pillsbury Bake-Off and taking home one million dollars for her recipe. Although she had entered cooking contests before, the author admitted to Minneapolis *Star Tribune* contributor Lee Svitak Dean that she entered her recipe for Salsa Couscous Chicken on a whim, having prepared the dish only twice before. Ten years after the contest, Mathews reflected on this competitive cooking experience with *The Ungarnished Truth: A Cooking Contest Memoir.* In the book, the author recounts her brief appearances on national televisions shows along with her feelings about becoming a grandmother just days after her victory. Mathews also reflects on her life after winning such a notable prize, telling Kristen

Cover of Mathews' memoir The Ungarnished Truth, *in which her life is transformed by a winning recipe.* (Berkley Books, 2008. Jacket photos copyright © by Masterfile. All rights reserved. Used by permission of Penguin Group (USA), Inc.)

Browning-Blas in the *Denver Post,* "We all see plenty of media moments where people win huge money prizes like mine, people struck with extraordinary good luck the way I was." However, the author observed, the media offers little information about what happens to those individuals after their brief moment of fame. By publishing *The Ungarnished Truth,* Mathews told Browning-Blas she attempted to put her win into the "context" of her life. "Over the years, people have been as interested—if not more interested—in what it all meant to me, whether the experience changed me, than in how I dreamed up a chicken recipe." Writing in *Kirkus Reviews,* a critic suggested that fans of television cooking shows "will eat up Mathews's pleasantly fluffy tale of culinary triumph."

Biographical and Critical Sources

PERIODICALS

Booklist, May 1, 2007, Heather Booth, review of *The Linden Tree,* p. 92.

Denver Post, April 16, 2008, Kristen Browning-Blas, "Her Award Was Just the First Chapter," p. D1.

Kirkus Reviews, May 1, 2007, review of *The Linden Tree*; December 15, 2007, review of *The Ungarnished Truth: A Cooking Contest Memoir.*

Kliatt, May, 2007, Janis Flint-Ferguson, review of *The Linden Tree,* p. 16; November, 2007, Marissa Elliott, review of *The Linden Tree,* p. 19.

Publishers Weekly, January 14, 2008, review of *The Ungarnished Truth,* p. 50.

School Library Journal, September, 2007, Christi Voth, review of *The Linden Tree,* p. 204.

Seattle Times, April 9, 2008, Karen Gaudette, "A Memoir in Getting Lucky with Holy Grail of Cook-Offs" (interview with Mathews), p. C1.

Star Tribune (Minneapolis, MN), April 10, 2008, Lee Svitak Dean, "Go behind the Bake-off Scene," p. 8T.

ONLINE

Ellie Mathews Home Page, http://elliemathews.home.att. net (September 23, 2008).*

*   *   *

McGRORY, Anik

Personal

Married; husband's name Glenn; children: Noel, Solenn. *Education:* Attended Rhode Island School of Design. *Hobbies and other interests:* Travel.

Addresses

Home—Tarrytown, NY. *E-mail*—zefyr@hotmail.com.

Career

Illustrator and author of picture books.

Member

Society of Children's Book Writers and Illustrators.

Awards, Honors

Don Freeman Memorial grant-in-aid, Society of Children's Book Writers and Illustrators, 2003.

Writings

SELF-ILLUSTRATED

Mouton's Impossible Dream, Harcourt (San Diego, CA), 2000.
Kidogo, Bloomsbury (New York, NY), 2005.

ILLUSTRATOR

Barbara Diamond Goldin, *A Mountain of Blintzes,* Harcourt (San Francisco, CA), 2001.

Sneed B. Collard, III, *Animals Asleep,* Houghton Mifflin (Boston, MA), 2004.

Mike Downs, *You See a Circus, I See . . .,* Charlesbridge (Watertown, MA), 2005.

Linda Ashman, *Desmond and the Naughtybugs,* Dutton (New York, NY), 2006.

Johanna Hurwitz, *Mostly Monty,* Candlewick Press (Cambridge, MA), 2007.

Sidelights

Children's author and illustrator Anik McGrory has provided artwork for texts by a variety of authors, including Barbara Diamond Goldin, Mike Downs, and Sneed B. Collard, III. McGrory's detailed watercolors have been credited for adding an extra dimension to each story she illustrates. For instance, in *A Mountain of Blintzes,* Goldin's tale about a family preparing for Shavuot, *School Library Journal* contributor Teri Markson highlighted the "bright, friendly palette and endearing pink-cheeked characters" featured in McGrory's art, suggesting that "the illustrations tell an amusing story within a story." In his *Booklist* review, John Peters wrote

Among Anik McGrory's illustration projects is **Mostly Monty,** *a picture book by popular writer Johanna Hurwitz.* (Illustration copyright © 2007 by Anik McGrory. All rights reserved. Reproduced by permission of the publisher, Candlewick Press, Inc., Somerville, MA.)

that Down's narrative in *You See a Circus, I See . . .* "is considerably heightened by McGrory's splashy scenes" about life under the big top.

McGrory earned additional praise for the art she created to accompany Collard's *Animals Asleep,* a picture book offering young readers information about the resting habits of numerous creatures. According to *Booklist* critic Carolyn Phelan, the illustrations "offer graceful, well-composed depictions of beasts, birds, and butterflies in a series of beautifully lit settings." Similarly, a *Kirkus Reviews* writer claimed that McGrory's "softly colored, detailed watercolor paintings enhance the text," making *Animals Asleep* "good for bedtime."

Teaming up with author Linda Ashman, McGrory created the artwork for *Desmond and the Naughtybugs,* a story about a little boy who struggles to behave. In general, Desmond is a well-behaved child, but occasionally the Naughtybugs appear, causing much mayhem. For instance, the presence of Squirmies causes Desmond to become restless at a restaurant, while a Pesky influences the boy to mishandle the apples at the supermarket. Fortunately, Desmond's parents have the Gigglies to fight the Naughtybugs, restoring harmony in the family. Reviewing the book in *School Library Journal,* Andrea Tarr concluded that "McGrory's charming illustrations add a whimsical touch."

In McGrory's first self-illustrated picture book, *Mouton's Impossible Dream,* a sheep named Mouton hopes to fly in a hot-air balloon. Watching her owners labor on such a flying machine, Mouton decides that she, too, would like to soar into the sky. To do so, he enlists the help of feathered farm animals Canard and Cocorico, a duck and rooster, respectively. Eventually, the threesome takes flight as part of a test to see if living creatures can travel safely in the balloon. "Lavish, beautifully composed watercolors are the strength of this pleasing story," claimed *Booklist* critic Gillian Engberg, and a *Horn Book* contributor suggested that the author/illustrator offers children an interesting look at history "through Mouton's highly sympathetic personality and through her light, atmospheric watercolors."

McGrory's next solo effort, *Kidogo,* is a story about a little elephant's search to find a creature smaller than himself. Setting out alone through the African wilderness, Kidogo looks high and low, yet encounters no one. Only when he begins itching does he realize a creature smaller than he exists: ants. Happy to finally be the largest, the growing elephant helps the insects as they lead him back to his family. Calling *Kidogo* a "sweet, enchanting story," *School Library Journal* reviewer Rebecca Sheridan found McGrory's "poetic text*rdquo; to be "perfectly matched with pencil-and-watercolor illustrations."

Biographical and Critical Sources

PERIODICALS

Booklist, June 1, 2000, Gillian Engberg, review of *Mouton's Impossible Dream,* p. 1910; March 1, 2001,

Karen Simonetti, review of *A Mountain of Blintzes,* p. 1287; March 1, 2004, Carolyn Phelan, review of *Animals Asleep,* p. 1190; April 1, 2005, John Peters, review of *You See a Circus, I See . . .,* p. 1365; June 1, 2007, Suzanne Harold, review of *Mostly Monty,* p. 82.

Horn Book, May, 2000, review of *Mouton's Impossible Dream,* p. 297.

Kirkus Reviews, March 1, 2004, review of *Animals Asleep,* p. 220; September 1, 2005, review of *Kidogo,* p. 978; December 15, 2005, review of *Desmond and the Naughtybugs,* p. 1317.

Publishers Weekly, May 8, 2000, review of *Mouton's Impossible Dream,* p. 220; February 28, 2005, review of *You See a Circus, I See . . .,* p. 65.

School Library Journal, April, 2000, Grace Oliff, review of *Mouton's Impossible Dream,* p. 108; April, 2001, Teri Markson, review of *A Mountain of Blintzes,* p. 108; May, 2004, Nancy Call, review of *Animals Asleep,* p. 192; April, 2005, Bina Williams, review of *You See a Circus, I See . . .,* p. 96; September, 2005, Rebecca Sheridan, review of *Kidogo,* p. 177; January, 2006, Andrea Tarr, review of *Desmond and the Naughtybugs,* p. 90; July, 2007, Donna Atmur, review of *Mostly Monty,* p. 77.

ONLINE

Anik McGrory Home Page, http://www.anikmcgrory.com (September 23, 2008).*

* * *

McHENRY, E.B. 1963(?)-

Personal

Born c. 1963, in PA. *Education:* Philadelphia College of Art, B.F.A., 1985; attended Moore College of Art and Design.

Addresses

Home—San Francisco, CA. *E-mail*—info@poodlena. com.

Career

Author, illustrator, and commercial artist. Formerly worked in educational software development for firms, including Adobe Software. *Exhibitions:* Work exhibited at galleries, including Dolan/Maxwell Gallery, Philadelphia, PA.

Writings

SELF-ILLUSTRATED

Poodlena, Bloomsbury (New York, NY), 2004.

Has Anyone Seen Winnie and Jean?, Bloomsbury (New York, NY), 2007.

Contributor of illustrations to periodicals, including *Philadelphia Daily News* and *Philadelphia Inquirer.* Contributed artwork to educational software projects.

Sidelights

After spending the early portion of her professional career as a fine and commercial artist, E.B. McHenry turned her creative energies to writing and illustrating children's books. Growing up just outside of Philadelphia, Pennsylvania, she graduated from the Philadelphia College of Art with a degree in painting and began producing work for art galleries as well as illustrations for magazines and newspapers. A move to California's Bay Area in the mid-1990s led to a position creating illustrations for software developers. In 2004, McHenry further shifted her focus, writing and illustrating her first picture book for children, *Poodlena.*

Living a pampered life in a metropolitan high-rise apartment, Poodlena spends much of her day being groomed by her owner so she will look the part of the most sophisticated canine in the dog park. At the park, Poodlena takes special care not to muss her carefully sculpted pink fur, even if it means keeping away from other dogs so they cannot damage her beloved coiffure. However, after a rainfall makes the dog park a muddy mess, the treasured pooch is accidentally pushed into the mud, where she discovers the joy of getting dirty. Writing in *School Library Journal,* Sally R. Dow noted that McHenry's "illustrations done . . . in bubble-gum shades complement the rhyming text," while *Booklist* critic Ilene Cooper credited much of the book's appeal to pictures that "have a retro feel and conjure up visions of a 1950s New York."

Dogs reappear in McHenry's second book, *Has Anyone Seen Winnie and Jean?* This time adventurous corgis Winnie and Jean escape from their comfortable suburban backyard and embark on a week-long expedition. The duo visit a golf course, crash a barbecue, and forage for food from a vending machine. Meanwhile, the dog's owners, a heartbroken brother and sister, search for the pair, eventually enlisting the aid of the police, who help the children and dogs reunite. "The big draw of this rhyming picture book are the gouache illustrations," noted *Booklist* critic Kristen McKulski, the critic adding that McHenry's art presents an interesting contrast between the carefree pets and the worried children. In *School Library Journal* Linda L. Walkins also found much merit in McHenry's artwork, suggesting that the "richly colored" pictures "enhance the narrative, lending an old-fashioned air and a bit of humor to the tale."

Biographical and Critical Sources

PERIODICALS

Booklist, May 1, 2004, Ilene Cooper, review of *Poodlena,* p. 1563; June 1, 2007, Kristen McKulski, review of *Has Anyone Seen Winnie and Jean?,* p. 80.

Kirkus Reviews, May 1, 2007, review of *Has Anyone Seen Winnie and Jean?*

Publishers Weekly, May 24, 2004, review of *Poodlena,* p. 62.

School Library Journal, November, 2004, Sally R. Dow, review of *Poodlena,* p. 112; July, 2007, Linda L. Walkins, review of *Has Anyone Seen Winnie and Jean?,* p. 81.

A courageous puppy rescue is the subject of E.B. McHenry's self-illustrated picture book **Has Anyone Seen Winnie and Jean?** (Bloomsbury Children's Books, 2007. Copyright © 2007 by E.B. McHenry. All rights reserved. Reproduced by permission.)

ONLINE

E.B. McHenry Home Page, http://www.poodlena.com
    (September 24, 2008).*

*   *   *

MEDINA, Nico 1982-

Personal

Born June 5, 1982, in Orlando, FL; partner of Billy
Merrell (a poet). *Education:* University of Florida, B.A.,
2004.

Addresses

Home—New York, NY. *E-mail*—nico@nicomedina.com.

Career

Author and editor. Gleim Publications, Gainesville, FL,
proofreader, 2001-04; Viking Children's Books, New
York, NY, associate production editor, 2004—; writer,
2005—.

Awards, Honors

Popular Paperback for Young Adults selection, American Library Association, and Books for the Teen Age
selection, New York Public Library, both 2008, both for
The Straight Road to Kylie.

Writings

The Straight Road to Kylie, Simon Pulse (New York, NY),
    2007.
Fat Hoochie Prom Queen, Simon Pulse (New York, NY),
    2008.

Sidelights

Nico Medina, a copyeditor of children's books, is the
author of the 2007 novel *The Straight Road to Kylie,* "a
well-written, thought-provoking, and welcome twist on
the coming-out story," observed *School Library Journal*
contributor Johanna Lewis. Medina, who came out during his freshman year at the University of Florida, began work on his story in the winter of 2005 after join-
ing a novel-writing group. As he told *Watermark*
interviewer John Sullivan, "I wrote it for fun and I
wrote it 'real,' never thinking of it as becoming a resource for GLBT teens. But I guess that in doing that,
I've made it sort of a resource in itself."

Set in the author's hometown of Orlando, Florida, *The
Straight Road to Kylie* centers on Jonathan Parish, a
gay high school senior who drunkenly sleeps with one
of his best girlfriends at a party. When rumors spread

that Jonathan is straight and available, he is approached
by the wealthy and glamorous Laura Schulberg. She offers Jonathan a trip to London to see his favorite pop
star, Kylie Minogue, in concert, if he pretends to be her
boyfriend. Jonathan's decision to accept Laura's bribe
causes friction with his best friends, however, and the
situation is further complicated when he develops feelings for a new guy. *The Straight Road to Kylie* "packs
slick, Gossip-Girl-Goes-to-Orlando language stylings
with realistic yet over-the-top situations," noted a *Kirkus
Reviews* contributor, and Olivia Duran remarked in *Kliatt* that the novel "explores the many facets of friendships and romantic relationships."

Medina's second novel, *Fat Hoochie Prom Queen,* concerns the rivalry between Margarita "Madge" Diaz, a
flamboyant, overweight teen, and Bridget Benson, a
perky cheerleader. Describing the work to Rhonda
Stapleton on the *Fictionistas* Web log, the author stated:
"I won't give anything much away except that these
two girls have one UGLY history, and during a heated
argument at a house party, they decide there's only one
way to end their rivalry: be named prom queen, and the
other backs off for good."

Biographical and Critical Sources

PERIODICALS

Kirkus Reviews, May 1, 2007, review of *The Straight Road
    to Kylie.*
Kliatt, September, 2007, Olivia Durant, review of *The
    Straight Road to Kylie,* p. 25.
School Library Journal, July, 2007, Johanna Lewis, re-
    view of *The Straight Road to Kylie,* p. 106.

ONLINE

Fictionistas Web log, http://fictionistas.blogspot.com/ (May
    14, 2008), Rhonda Stapleton, interview with Medina.
Nico Medina Home Page, http://nicomedina.com (August
    10, 2008).
TeensReadToo.com, http://teensreadtoo.com/ (August 10,
    2008), Jennifer Wardrip, interview with Medina.
Watermark Online, http://www.watermarkonline.com/ (July
    12, 2007), John Sullivan, interview with Medina.*

*   *   *

MEYER, Stephenie 1973-

Personal

Born 1973, in CT; married; husband's name Christiaan
"Pancho" (an auditor); children: Gabe, Seth, Eli. *Education:* Brigham Young University, B.A.

Addresses

Home—Cave Creek, AZ. *Agent*—c/o Jodi Reamer, 21
W. 26th St., New York, NY 10010; jreamerwritershouse.
com.

Career
Author.

Awards, Honors
Editor's Choice selection, *New York Times,* and Top Ten Best Books for Young Adults and Top Ten Books for Reluctant Readers listee, both American Library Association, all 2005, all for *Twilight.*

Writings

"TWILIGHT" SERIES

Twilight, Little, Brown (New York, NY), 2005.
New Moon, Little, Brown (New York, NY), 2006.
Eclipse, Little, Brown (New York, NY), 2007.
Breaking Dawn, Little, Brown (New York, NY), 2008.

OTHER

The Host, Little, Brown (New York, NY), 2007.

Contributor to *Prom Nights from Hell,* HarperTeen (New York, NY), 2007.

Adaptations
Twilight has been adapted as a major motion picture, Summit Entertainment, 2008.

Sidelights
Stephenie Meyer is the creator of the phenomenally successful "Twilight" series about a teenaged vampire. The four books in the series—*Twilight, New Moon, Eclipse,* and *Breaking Dawn*—have sold millions of copies and found their way onto bestseller lists across the United States. Often compared to books by bestselling novelist Anne Rice, and with sales reminiscent of British author J.K. Rowling, Meyer's romantic vampire novels have attracted throngs of teenage readers. As Cindy Dobrez noted in *Booklist,* Meyer's "Twilight" books "began as a simple vampire series and quickly became a megaselling publishing phenomenon."

Meyer was born in Connecticut in 1973. Her family moved to Phoenix, Arizona, when she was four years old. "I am the second of six children," the author told Cynthia Leitich Smith in a *Cynsations* online interview. "I think that coming from such a large family has given me a lot of insight into different personality types—my siblings sometimes crop up as characters in my stories." After winning a National Merit Scholarship, Meyer attended Brigham Young University in Provo, Utah.

Meyer got married and gave birth to three sons before she embarked on a writing career. As she told Smith: "I have a husband and three young sons who all are slightly bewildered with my sudden career shift from mommy to writer. A lifelong reader, I didn't start writing until I was twenty-nine, but once I began typing I've never been able to stop." Meyer's entry into the world of vampire literature began as the result of a dream she had on June 2, 2003. As she explained to William Morris of *A Motley Vision* online: "It was a conversation between a boy and a girl which took place in a beautiful, sunny meadow in the middle of a dark forest. The boy and the girl were in love with each other, and they were discussing the problems involved with that love, seeing that she was human and he was a vampire. The boy was more beautiful than the meadow, and his skin sparkled like diamonds in the sun. He was so gentle and polite, and yet the potential for violence was very strong, inherent to the scene." Meyer recorded her dream later that day, and she continued writing the rest of the summer, finishing her manuscript in August.

Almost overnight, *Twilight* propelled Meyer into the ranks of top-selling writers for teenage readers. The vampire love story features teen narrator Isabella "Bella" Swan and her love interest, Edward Cullen. Bella has just moved from Phoenix to the small town of

Cover of Stephenie Meyer's novel New Moon, *the second volume in her "Twilight" series.* (Little, Brown, 2006. Jacket photo copyright © by John Grant/ Getty Images. Reproduced by permission.)

Forks, Washington, and is now living with her police chief-father. The first day at her new school she is attracted to Edward, a vampire who has trained himself to feed on animal, rather than human, blood. Trouble soon arises in the form of another group of vampires who have no such restraint. While the novel concerns vampires, the story is more romance than horror. Amanda Craig noted on her Web site that *Twilight* is the "chaste yet intensely erotic description of a teenager's love-affair with a vampire." Referring to the novel's romantic story, Meyer told Rick Margolis in the *School Library Journal:* "I do like to say it's a vampire book for people who don't like vampire books."

Twilight won critical praise from many quarters. A *Publishers Weekly* contributor, for example, called it a "riveting first novel, propelled by suspense and romance in equal parts," as well as a "tantalizing debut." Similarly, Hillias J. Martin, writing in the *School Library Journal,* called the book "realistic, subtle, succinct, and easy to follow, [a novel that] will have readers dying to sink their teeth into it." "*Twilight* builds to a dramatic and suspenseful second half, not to mention a nail-biting conclusion," according to online reviewer Linda M. Castellitto in *BookPage.* For *Booklist* contributor Ilene Cooper, *Twilight* is a "dark romance [that] seeps into the soul."

In *New Moon* Bella loses her vampire lover only to be courted by a teen who is an incipient werewolf. The Cullens move from town, fearful that they cannot control themselves and that they may do harm to Bella. Months later she comes out of her depression and strikes up a friendship with a Native American named Jacob. Meanwhile, she is also pursued by an evil vampire whose presence triggers the lycanthropy in Jacob's genes. While all this is happening, Edward is seemingly determined to die at the hands of an Italian vampire cult. *Booklist* contributor Cindy Dobrez predicted that "teens will relish this new adventure and hunger for more," while *Kliatt* reviewer Claire Rosser similarly concluded that young readers "will be eager to share [Bella's] passion and her adventures."

Eclipse finds Bella faced with a difficult choice. She must decide whether to become, like Edward, a vampire or to stay human. Bella knows that her choice will spark a war between the vampires and the werewolves. Meanwhile, Seattle is being terrorized by a serial killer and a female vampire is out for revenge. When Bella is placed in danger, Edward and Jacob find themselves forging an unlikely alliance to save her. Norah Piehl noted in *TeenReads.com* that, "since Meyer's books have always been more of a love story than a vampire series, . . . many readers will appreciate *Eclipse*'s more firm grounding in reality, largely focusing on character realization rather than on melodramatic, metaphysical conflicts." "The supernatural elements," wrote a critic for *Publishers Weekly,* "accentuate the ordinary human dramas of growing up." "Just like the first two novels,"

Cover of Meyer's popular novel Twilight, *in which romance disrupts the life of a vampire living under the radar in the Pacific Northwest.* (Little, Brown, 2005. Cover photograph copyright © by Roger Hagadone. Reproduced by permission.)

Janis Flint-Ferguson wrote in *Kliatt,* "this one is hard to put down as it draws the reader into heart pounding gothic romance tinged with mythic horror."

The much-anticipated conclusion to the series, *Breaking Dawn,* appeared in 2008. Having exchanged their wedding vows, Bella and Edward embark on a romantic honeymoon, after which Edward will transform his bride into a vampire. The pair is unprepared for Bella's surprise pregnancy, however, and complications arise during the delivery of their half-human/half-vampire baby. Surprisingly, the initial response to the novel from Meyer's legions of fans was one of disappointment. "Meyer's trouble may have been the simplicity of her romance saga," wrote *Chicago Tribune* critic Patrick T. Reardon. "The core questions had to do with whether Bella and her vampire boyfriend would have sex and whether Bella would become a vampire." Reardon added that "however Meyer answered them, it seems clear now in retrospect that she was bound to disappoint some major segment of her readership, the majority of whom are teenage girls." Still, *Breaking Dawn* received a number of positive reviews. "Many readers

seem to be on a honeymoon high," noted Carol Memmott in *USA Today,* and *Time* contributor Lev Grossman described the novel as "a wild but satisfying finish to the ballad of Bella and Edward."

Meyer's books have attracted a great number of devoted fans. In Pasadena, California, a "vampire prom" was held, just like the prom that Bella and Edward attend in *Twilight.* Tickets for the event sold out in seven hours, so a second prom, held later the same day, was added. Hundreds of fans, mostly girls, showed up at both events and, over the course of several hours, Meyer autographed some 1,000 copies of her books. On the eve of *Breaking Dawn*'s publication, hundreds of bookstores across the nation held vampire-themed parties.

Speaking with Gregory Kirschling in *Entertainment Weekly,* Meyer explained the appeal of her vampire books: "I think some of it's because Bella is an everygirl. She's not a hero, and she doesn't know the difference between Prada and whatever else is out there. She doesn't always have to be cool, or wear the coolest clothes ever. She's normal. And there aren't a lot of girls in literature that are normal."

In addition to her "Twilight" series, Meyer has also written a science-fiction thriller titled *The Host.* The work concerns a race of parasitic aliens that inhabit their human hosts and work for the betterment of the planet, eliminating war and curing disease. Some individuals resist the invasion, however, including Melanie Stryder, a seventeen year old who is captured and taken over by a soul named "Wanderer." What remains of Melanie's consciousness exerts a powerful influence over the alien, and Wanderer journeys to a desert stronghold to locate the teenager's family and friends. Critics praised Meyer's decision to feature an alien protagonist, *Booklist* contributor Jennifer Mattson commenting that "the view of the apocalypse from the vantage point of one of its horsemen makes for propulsive reading." According to Karen E. Brooks-Reese in *School Library Journal,* "Questions of what defines humanity and love add a philosophical angle to an engaging and entertaining title."

Success has not drastically changed Meyer's life. "In my everyday, normal life, it's just something I don't think about very much," Meyer told Cecelia Goodnow in the *Seattle Post-Intelligencer.* Asked by Smith if she had any advice for budding authors, Meyer stated, "If you love to write, then write. Don't let your goal be having a novel published, let your goal be enjoying your stories. However, if you finish your story and you want to share it, be brave about it. Don't doubt your story's appeal." She concluded, "If I would have realized that the stories in my head would be as intriguing to others as they were to me, I would probably have started writing sooner."

Biographical and Critical Sources

PERIODICALS

Advertising Age, August 11, 2008, Nat Ives, "Making Release of *Breaking Dawn* One for the Books," p. 7.

Arizona Republic, October 17, 2005, Kathy Cano Murillo, "A Vampire Bit Her with Writing Bug."

Booklist, November 15, 2005, Ilene Cooper, review of *Twilight,* p. 58; July 1, 2006, Cindy Dobrez, review of *New Moon,* p. 51; September 15, 2007, Michael Cart, "Everlasting Love," p. 58, and Cindy Dobrez, review of *Eclipse,* p. 74; March 1, 2008, Jennifer Mattson, review of *The Host,* p. 29.

BookPage, October, 2005, Linda M. Castellitto, "Dreams of High School Vampires Inspire a Toothsome Debut."

Business Week, August 11, 2008, Heather Green, "Harry Potter with Fangs—and a Social Network," p. 44.

Chicago Tribune, August 12, 2008, Patrick T. Reardon, "Breaking down *Breaking Dawn.*"

Entertainment Weekly, August 10, 2007, Gregory Kirschling, "The Q&A: Stephenie Meyer's 'Twilight' Zone," p. 74; May 9, 2008, Jeff Giles, "Alien Nation," p. 68; July 18, 2008, Karen Valby and Kate Ward, "The Vampire Empire," p. 22, and Nicole Sperling, "*Twilight* Hits Hollywood," p. 28; August 15, 2008, Kate Ward, "Out for Blood, Twilight Fans Bite Back at the New Book," p. 8, and Jennifer Reese, review of *Breaking Dawn,* p. 68.

Globe & Mail (Toronto, Ontario, Canada), September 8, 2007, review of *Eclipse,* p. D18.

Journal of Adolescent & Adult Literacy, April, 2006, James Blasingame, review of *Twilight,* p. 628.

Kirkus Reviews, September 15, 2005, review of *Twilight,* p. 1031; July 15, 2006, review of *New Moon,* p. 727; March 1, 2008, review of *The Host.*

Kliatt, September, 2005, Michele Winship, review of *Twilight,* p. 11; September, 2006, Claire Rosser, review of *New Moon,* p. 15; November, 2006, Michele Winship, review of *Twilight,* p. 29; November, 2007, Janis Flint-Ferguson, review of *Eclipse,* p. 12.

Maclean's, July 28, 2008, Brian Bethune, "Love at First Bite," p. 53.

Miami Herald, September 8, 2007, Sue Corbett, "The Hero's Tall, Dark and Toothsome."

New York Times Book Review, February 12, 2006, Elizabeth Spires, review of *Twilight,* p. 17; August 12, 2007, Liesl Schillinger, review of *Eclipse,* p. 19.

People, September 8, 2008, Bob Meadows and Kari Lydersen, "Stephenie Meyer Written in Blood," p. 90.

Phoenix New Times, July 12, 2007, Megan Irwin, "Charmed: Stephenie Meyer's Vampire Romance Novels Made a Mormon Mom an International Sensation."

Publishers Weekly, December 8, 2003, John F. Baker, "LB Preempts 'Anne Rice for Teens,'" p. 12; July 18, 2005, review of *Twilight,* p. 207; October 31, 2005, Jennifer M. Brown, "*Twilight* in Translation," p. 28; July 17, 2006, review of *New Moon,* p. 159; July 23, 2007, Rachel Deahl, "Little, Brown Has Big Plans for

Meyer"; August 20, 2007, review of *Eclipse,* p. 69; March 31, 2008, review of *The Host,* p. 42; August 11, 2008, Sam Nelson, "Breaking Trust?," p. 5.

School Library Journal, October, 2005, Rick Margolis, "Love at First Bite: Stephenie Meyer Talks about Vampires, Teen Love, and Her First Novel, *Twilight,*" p. 37, and Hillias J. Martin, review of *Twilight,* p. 166; August, 2006, Hillias J. Martin, review of *New Moon,* p. 125; June, 2008, Karen E. Brooks-Reese, review of *The Host,* p. 171.

Seattle Post-Intelligencer, August 6, 2007, Cecelia Goodnow, "Stephenie Meyer's Forks-based Saga of Teen Vampire Love Is Now a Global Hit."

Time, May 5, 2008, Lev Grossman, "The Next J.K. Rowling?," p. 49; August 18, 2008, Lev Grossman, review of *Breaking Dawn,* p. 65.

USA Today, August 16, 2007, Bob Minzesheimer, "Vampire Tale Takes Bite out of 'Potter,'" p. 1D; August 7, 2008, Carol Memmott, "*Dawn* Fans Light up over Saga's End," p. 1D.

Virginian Pilot, August 12, 2007, Edward Nowatka, "Teen Series on Vampires Eclipses Rivals," p. E5.

Voice of Youth Advocates, October, 2005, Angelica Delgado, review of *New Moon.*

Wall Street Journal, August 10, 2007, Jeffrey A. Trachtenberg, "Booksellers Find Life after Harry in a Vampire Novel," p. B1.

ONLINE

Amanda Craig Web site, http://www.amandacraig.com/ (January, 2006), "A Quick Bite—Vampires Resurgent."

Cynsations, http://cynthialeitichsmith.blogspot.com/ (March 27, 2006), Cynthia Leitich Smith, interview with Meyer.

Motley Vision Web site, http://www.motleyvision.org/ (October 26, 2005), William Morris, interview with Meyer.

Stephenie Meyer Home Page, http://www.stepheniemeyer.com (September 10, 2008).

TeenReads.com, http://www.teenreads.com/ (March 20, 2008), reviews of *Twilight, Eclipse,* and *New Moon.**

* * *

MILLER, Kate 1948-

Personal

Born 1948; married.

Addresses

Home—Stillwater, NY.

Career

Artist and poet.

Awards, Honors

Cybils Award finalist, 2007, and International Reading Association Children's and Young Adults Book Award Notable Book designation, 2008, both for *Poems in Black and White.*

Writings

(Self-illustrated) *Poems in Black and White,* Wordsong (Honesdale, PA), 2007.

Biographical and Critical Sources

PERIODICALS

Booklist, April 1, 2007, Hazel Rochman, review of *Poems in Black and White,* p. 51.

Bulletin of the Center for Children's Books, April, 2007, Deborah Stevenson, review of *Poems in Black and White,* p. 339.

Kirkus Reviews, February 15, 2007, review of *Poems in Black and White.*

Publishers Weekly, March 5, 2007, review of *Poems in Black and White,* p. 60.

School Library Journal, May, 2007, Teresa Pfeifer, review of *Poems in Black and White,* p. 160.*

* * *

MOORE, Perry

Personal

Born in Virginia Beach, VA; partner of Hunter Hill (a writer and filmmaker). *Education:* University of Virginia, B.A.

Addresses

Home—New York, NY. *Agent*—Merrilee Heifetz, Writers House, 21 W. 26th St., New York, NY 10010.

Career

Author, film producer, screenwriter, and director of feature films. Worked in talent and development for cable television, including MTV and VH1; former producer of television program *The Rosie O'Donnell Show;* Walden Media, Los Angeles, CA, developer of films, including *I Am David* and *North to Freedom.* Executive producer of feature films, including *The Chronicles of Narnia: The Lion, the Witch, and the Wardrobe, The Chronicles of Narnia: Prince Caspian, The Chronicles of Narnia: The Voyage of the Dawn Treader,* and *Lake City.* White House intern during Clinton administration.

Awards, Honors

Lambda Award for best young-adult book, 2008, for *Hero.*

Writings

The Chronicles of Narnia: The Lion, the Witch, and the Wardrobe: The Official Illustrated Movie Companion, HarperSanFrancisco (San Francisco, CA), 2005.
Hero (young-adult novel), Hyperion (New York, NY), 2007.

Co-author with Hunter Hill, and director, *Lake City* (screenplay).

Adaptations

Hero was optioned for production as a feature film.

Sidelights

Perry Moore's busy life includes funding, writing, and directing films—most notably the popular "Chronicles of Narnia" film series based on the books by C.S. Lewis, for which he has served as executive producer. Nevertheless, Moore has found time to write the Lambda Award-winning young-adult novel *Hero,* about a young gay man with superpowers. Moore was inspired to write the novel after observing that most mainstream U.S. comics have dealt harshly with gay superheroes or have simply avoided them altogether. In an interview posted on his home page, Moore explained: "Every other barrier has been broken in comics: race, gender, class, physical challenges. But gay characters remain few and far between. . . . I wrote *Hero* with the sincere and passionate intention of telling the traditional hero's journey, and turning it on its ear by creating a hero unlike any we've ever seen before."

Moore grew up reading comic books, and as an adult he has continued to purchase several each week. He was galvanized to work on *Hero* when the Marvel Comics character Northstar was killed in an *X-Men* installment. Northstar was one of the few gay heroes in the comics world. "I found this to be disturbing, to say the least," Moore recalled. "I'm a real big believer . . . that the pen is mightier than the sword. So I became more determined than ever to write *Hero* and have it connect with audiences everywhere."

Moore's father also provided inspiration. A Vietnam War veteran, the elder Moore's ongoing efforts to deal with the trauma of war impressed his son. In *Hero,* Thom Creed, the central character, has a father who was a superhero but somehow became disgraced and embittered by the experience. As a teen, Thom must deal with his own budding superpowers, as well as his sexual orientation and his father's consequent disapproval. At first, Thom hides his superpowers and his sexual identity from his dad and from the wider world. Eventually, however, he performs a heroic task and is invited to join the League, a prestigious organization that provides training and support for superheroes. Thom appreciates his position in the League, but when he comes out as gay he is stripped of his membership. Determined to continue fighting crime, he forms his own team of cast-off heroes and continues his quest for justice.

Dylan Thomarie praised *Hero* in a review for *School Library Journal,* calling Moore's novel "tactful, interesting, and well-developed." According to George Gene Gustines in the *New York Times, Hero* "is not a saccharine fairy tale with male superheroes in matching capes flying arm in arm. Thom struggles with feelings of shame. He's the target of ugly slurs. . . . But things work out relatively well for him."

Moore plans to write sequels to his debut novel, even as he meets responsibilities for further installments in the "Chronicles of Narnia" film series. As he told a *Newsarama* online interviewer, the message of *Hero* "is that gay, straight, black, white, young or old, the very thing that makes you different isn't a bad thing. If you embrace it, it can be the most empowering thing in your life."

Biographical and Critical Sources

PERIODICALS

Booklist, August, 2007, Jennifer Mattson, review of *Hero,* p. 63.
Horn Book, September-October, 2007, Claire E. Gross, review of *Hero,* p. 582.
Kirkus Reviews, August 15, 2007, review of *Hero.*
New York Times, September 3, 2007, George Gene Gustines, "A Novelist's Superhero Is out to Right Wrongs."
People, November 19, 2007, Melody S. Wells, "Perry Moore," p. 121.
Publishers Weekly, September 10, 2007, review of *Hero,* p. 62.
School Library Journal, September, 2007, Dylan Thomarie, review of *Hero,* p. 204.

ONLINE

Newsarama Online, http://www.newsarama.com/ (July 24, 2007), interview with Moore; (August 18, 2008) interview with Moore; (August 20, 2008) interview with Moore.
Perry Moore Web site, http://www.perrymoorestories.com (September 8, 2008).*

* * *

MURAWSKI, Darlyne A.

Personal

Education: Art Institute of Chicago, M.F.A.; University of Texas, Ph.D.

Addresses

Home—Arlington, MA.

Career

Writer, botanist, and nature photographer. Former research biologist and teacher at University of Georgia, University of Massachusetts, and Harvard University.

Awards, Honors

Alfred Eisenstaedt Awards for nature photography, 1998, 1999; Communications Arts award of Excellence for nature photography, 2001.

Writings

(Contributor) M. Lowman and N. Nadkarni, editors, *Forest Canopies,* Academic Press (New York, NY), 1995.

The World of Reptiles: Ranger Rick Science Spectacular, Newbridge Communications, Inc., 1997.

Bug Faces, National Geographic Society (Washington, DC), 2000.

Spiders and Their Webs, National Geographic Society (Washington, DC), 2004.

Animal Faces, Sterling Publishing (New York, NY), 2005.

Face to Face with Caterpillars, National Geographic Society (Washington, DC), 2007.

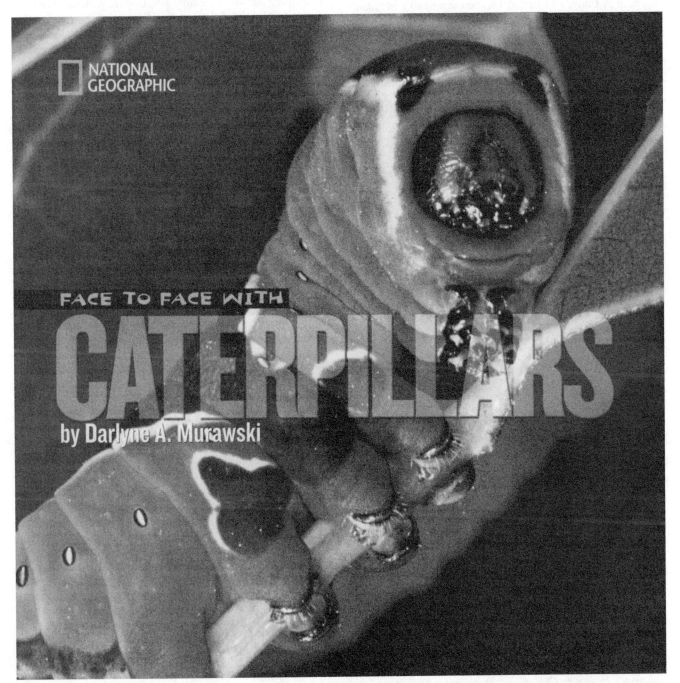

Cover of Darlyne A. Murawski's nonfiction picture book Face to Face with Caterpillars. (Jacket copyright © 2007 by National Geographic Society. Reproduced by permission.)

Contributor to popular magazines and scholarly journals, including *Ecology, Conservation Biology, Biotropica, American Journal of Botany, Journal of Heredity, Selbyana, Journal of Tropical Ecology, Plant Species Biology, Plant Science Tomorrow, Oecologia,* and *Heredity.* Contributor of wildlife photography to calendars and magazines, including *National Geographic.*

Sidelights

Few people find their life's calling at the age of five, but Darlyne A. Murawski did just that. While flipping through a medical book, she discovered highly detailed photographs of the many parasites that live on—or in—the human body. Fascinated by the complexity of these tiny creatures, she embarked on a study of insects that eventually dovetailed with her interest in fine-art photography. Now a trained botanist with a Ph.D. in biology, Murawski is best known for her vivid photographs of insects, spiders, caterpillars, and unusual animals. These photos can be enjoyed by young readers through her books, which include *Bug Faces, Spiders and Their Webs, Animal Faces,* and *Face to Face with Caterpillars.*

Murawski's graduate work included photographing butterflies in rain forests and other locations, and her book *Face to Face with Caterpillars* draws on this by presenting extreme close-ups of butterflies' larval stage. In the work she combines bright pictures with facts about each species and an overview of the entire butterfly life cycle. Nancy Call, writing in *School Library Journal,* called the book "attractive, well written, and fascinating." A *Kirkus Reviews* critic cited *Face to Face with Caterpillars* for its "spectacular close-up views" adding that the format makes "intriguing reading and viewing."

Bug Faces and *Animal Faces* feature full-page color photographs of some unusual creatures that children may never have seen before. The animals Murawski presents include common ones such as squirrels, but also crabs, sloths, and lizards—all photographed from extreme close-up. Cassandra A. Lopez, writing in *School Library Journal,* found *Animal Faces* to be "a delightful walk on the wild side," while in the same periodical Edith Ching described *Bug Faces* as "visually appealing." Ching also thought that Murawski's work "encourages youngsters to make up-close and personal observations." According to Hazel Rochman in her *Booklist* review of *Bug Faces,* "the immediate effect is both yucky and beautiful."

Spiders and Their Webs also combines Murawski's vivid photographs with fast facts about spiders and their habits. According to *Booklist* correspondent Gillian Engberg, the book invites "reluctant children to move beyond spiders' creepy reputation." Writing in *School Library Journal,* Karey Wehner appreciated *Spiders and Their Webs* for its "marvelous pictures, clear text, and fresh approach to a popular subject."

Murawski received her first camera as a gift from her parents when she was ten years old. In order to photograph insects in such extreme close-up, she has developed macro lenses and has even attached her cameras to microscopes. "I have to be careful, though," she said in an interview with *Science World.* "Shine too much light on them, and the bugs fry."

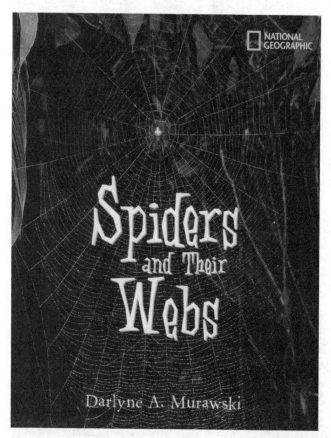

Murawski's fascinating close-up photographs are a highlight of her picture book Spiders and Their Webs. (National Geographic, 2004. Illustration by Mark Burrier. Reproduced by permission.)

Biographical and Critical Sources

PERIODICALS

Booklist, November 15, 2000, Hazel Rochman, review of *Bug Faces,* p. 644; December 1, 2004, Gillian Engberg, review of *Spiders and Their Webs,* p. 668.

Kirkus Reviews, September 15, 2004, review of *Spiders and Their Webs,* p. 917; May 1, 2007, review of *Face to Face with Caterpillars.*

School Library Journal, November, 2000, Edith Ching, review of *Bug Faces,* p. 146; March, 2005, Karey Wehner, review of *Spiders and Their Webs,* p. 196; March, 2006, Cassandra A. Lopez, review of *Animal Faces,* p. 199; June, 2007, Nancy Call, review of *Face to Face with Caterpillars,* p. 175.

Science World, September 6, 1999, "Hot Job: Photo 'Bug' Lady."

Darlyne A. Murawski Home Page, http://www.darlyne
murawski.com (September 28, 2008).*

*   *   *

MYERS, Walter Dean 1937-
(Stacie Johnson, Walter M. Myers)

Personal

Born Walter Milton Myers, August 12, 1937, in Martinsburg, WV; son of George Ambrose and Mary Myers; raised from age three by Herbert Julius (a shipping clerk) and Florence (a factory worker) Dean; married (marriage dissolved); married Constance Brendel, June 19, 1973; children: (first marriage) Karen, Michael Dean; (second marriage) Christopher. *Education:* Attended City College of the City University of New York; Empire State College, B.A., 1984.

Addresses

Home—Jersey City, NJ. *E-mail*—mailbox@walterdean-myers.net.

Walter Dean Myers (Photograph by David Godlis. Reproduced by permission of Walter Dean Myers.)

Career

New York State Department of Labor, New York, NY, employment supervisor, 1966-70; Bobbs-Merrill Co., Inc. (publisher), New York, NY, senior trade books editor, 1970-77; full-time writer, beginning 1977. Teacher of creative writing and black history on a part-time basis in New York, NY, 1974-75; worked variously as a post-office clerk, inter-office messenger, and an interviewer at a factory. *Military service:* U.S. Army, 1954-57.

Member

PEN, Harlem Writers Guild.

Awards, Honors

Council on Interracial Books for Children Award, 1968, for *Where Does the Day Go?;* Children's Book of the Year, Child Study Association of America (CSAA), 1972, for *The Dancers;* Notable Book designation, American Library Association (ALA), 1975, and Woodward Park School Annual Book Award, 1976, both for *Fast Sam, Cool Clyde, and Stuff;* Best Books for Young Adults designation, ALA, 1978, for *It Ain't All for Nothin',* and 1979, for *The Young Landlords;* Coretta Scott King Award, 1980, for *The Young Landlords;* Best Books for Young Adults designation, ALA, 1981, and Notable Children's Trade Book in the Field of Social Studies designation, National Council for Social Studies/Children's Book Council, 1982, both for *The Legend of Tarik;* runner-up, Edgar Allan Poe Award, and Best Books for Young Adults designation, ALA,

1982, both for *Hoops;* Parents' Choice Award, Parents' Choice Foundation, 1982, for *Won't Know till I Get There,* 1984, for *The Outside Shot,* and 1988, for *Fallen Angels;* New Jersey Institute of Technology Authors Award, 1983, for *Tales of a Dead King;* Coretta Scott King Award, 1985, for *Motown and Didi;* Children's Book of the Year, CSAA, 1987, for *Adventure in Granada;* Parents' Choice Award, 1987, for *Crystal;* New Jersey Institute of Technology Authors Award and Best Books for Young Adults designation, ALA, 1988, Coretta Scott King Award, 1989, and Children's Book Award, South Carolina Association of School Librarians, 1991, all for *Fallen Angels;* Notable Book and Best Books for Young Adults designations, ALA, both 1988, both for *Me, Mop, and the Moondance Kid;* Notable Book designation, ALA, 1988, and Newbery Medal Honor Book designation, ALA, 1989, both for *Scorpions;* Parents' Choice Award, 1990, for *The Mouse Rap;* Golden Kite Award Honor Book, and Jane Addams Award Honor Book designation, both 1991, and Coretta Scott King Award, and Orbis Pictus Award Honor Book designation, both 1992, all for *Now Is Your Time! The African-American Struggle for Freedom;* Parents' Choice Award, 1992, for *The Righteous Revenge of Artemis Bonner; Boston Globe/Horn Book* Award Honor Book, 1992, and Coretta Scott King Award Honor Book, and Newbery Medal Honor Book designation, both 1993, all for *Somewhere in the Darkness;* Jeremiah Ludington Award, Educational Paperback Association, 1993, for "18 Pine St." series; CRABberry Award, 1993, for *Malcolm X: By Any Means Necessary;* Margaret A. Edwards Award, ALA/*School*

Library Journal, 1994, for contributions to young adult literature; Coretta Scott King Award, 1997, for *Slam!;* *Boston Globe/Horn Book* Award Honor Book designation, 1997, for *Harlem: A Poem;* Michael Printz Award, and Coretta Scott King Award Honor Book designation, both ALA, both 2000, both for *Monster;* Lee Bennett Hopkins Poetry Award, International Reading Association, 2005, for *Here in Harlem;* May Hill Arbuthnot Honor Lecture Award, ALA, 2009; several child-selected awards.

Writings

FICTION; FOR CHILDREN AND YOUNG ADULTS

Fast Sam, Cool Clyde, and Stuff, Viking (New York, NY), 1975.

Brainstorm, photographs by Chuck Freedman, F. Watts (New York, NY), 1977.

Mojo and the Russians, Viking (New York, NY), 1977.

Victory for Jamie, Scholastic (New York, NY), 1977.

It Ain't All for Nothin', Viking (New York, NY), 1978.

The Young Landlords, Viking (New York, NY), 1979.

The Golden Serpent, illustrated by Alice and Martin Provensen, Viking (New York, NY), 1980.

Hoops, Delacorte (New York, NY), 1981.

The Legend of Tarik, Viking (New York, NY), 1981.

Won't Know till I Get There, Viking (New York, NY), 1982.

The Nicholas Factor, Viking (New York, NY), 1983.

Tales of a Dead King, Morrow (New York, NY), 1983.

Motown and Didi: A Love Story, Viking (New York, NY), 1984.

The Outside Shot, Delacorte (New York, NY), 1984.

Sweet Illusions, Teachers & Writers Collaborative, 1986.

Crystal, Viking (New York, NY), 1987, reprinted, Harper-Trophy (New York, NY), 2001.

Scorpions, Harper (New York, NY), 1988.

Me, Mop, and the Moondance Kid, illustrated by Rodney Pate, Delacorte (New York, NY), 1988.

Fallen Angels, Scholastic (New York, NY), 1988.

The Mouse Rap, HarperCollins (New York, NY), 1990.

Somewhere in the Darkness, Scholastic (New York, NY), 1992.

Mop, Moondance, and the Nagasaki Knights, Delacorte (New York, NY), 1992.

The Righteous Revenge of Artemis Bonner, HarperCollins (New York, NY), 1992.

The Glory Field, Scholastic (New York, NY), 1994.

Darnell Rock Reporting, Delacorte (New York, NY), 1994.

Shadow of the Red Moon, illustrated by son Christopher Myers, Scholastic (New York, NY), 1995.

Sniffy Blue, Ace Crime Detective: The Case of the Missing Ruby and Other Stories, illustrated by David J.A. Sims, Scholastic (New York, NY), 1996.

Slam!, Scholastic (New York, NY), 1996.

The Journal of Joshua Loper: A Black Cowboy, Atheneum (New York, NY), 1999.

The Journal of Scott Pendleton Collins: A World War II Soldier, Normandy, France, 1944, Scholastic (New York, NY), 1999.

Monster, illustrated by Christopher Myers, HarperCollins (New York, NY), 1999.

The Blues of Flats Brown, illustrated by Nina Laden, Holiday House (New York, NY), 2000.

145th Street: Short Stories, Delacorte Press (New York, NY), 2000.

Patrol: An American Soldier in Vietnam, illustrated by Ann Grifalconi, HarperCollins (New York, NY), 2001.

The Journal of Biddy Owens and the Negro Leagues, Scholastic (New York, NY), 2001.

Three Swords for Granada, illustrated by John Speirs, Holiday House (New York, NY), 2002.

Handbook for Boys, illustrated by Matthew Bandsuch, HarperCollins (New York, NY), 2002.

A Time to Love: Stories from the Old Testament, illustrated by Christopher Myers, Scholastic (New York, NY), 2003.

The Beast, Scholastic (New York, NY), 2003.

The Dream Bearer, HarperCollins (New York, NY), 2003.

Shooter, HarperTempest (New York, NY), 2004.

Southern Fried, St. Martin's Minotaur (New York, NY), 2004.

Autobiography of My Dead Brother, HarperTempest/Amistad (New York, NY), 2005.

Street Love, HarperTempest/Amistad (New York, NY), 2006.

Harlem Summer, Scholastic (New York, NY), 2007.

What They Found: Love on 145th St. (short stories), Wendy Lamb Books (New York, NY), 2007.

Game, HarperTeen (New York, NY), 2008.

Sunrise over Fallujah (sequel to *Fallen Angels*), Scholastic (New York, NY), 2008.

Dope Stick, HarperTeen/Amistad (New York, NY), 2009.

Creator and editor of "18 Pine Street" series of young-adult novels, Bantam, beginning 1992. Work represented in anthologies, including *What We Must SEE: Young Black Storytellers,* Dodd, 1971, and *We Be Word Sorcerers: Twenty-five Stories by Black Americans.*

"ARROW" SERIES

Adventure in Granada, Viking (New York, NY), 1985.

The Hidden Shrine, Viking (New York, NY), 1985.

Duel in the Desert, Viking (New York, NY), 1986.

Ambush in the Amazon, Viking (New York, NY), 1986.

JUVENILE NONFICTION

The World of Work: A Guide to Choosing a Career, Bobbs-Merrill (New York, NY), 1975.

Social Welfare, F. Watts (New York, NY), 1976.

Now Is Your Time! The African-American Struggle for Freedom, HarperCollins (New York, NY), 1992.

A Place Called Heartbreak: A Story of Vietnam, illustrated by Frederick Porter, Raintree (Austin, TX), 1992.

Young Martin's Promise (picture book), illustrated by Barbara Higgins Bond, Raintree (Austin, TX), 1992.

Malcolm X: By Any Means Necessary, Scholastic (New York, NY), 1993.

One More River to Cross: An African-American Photograph Album, Harcourt (New York, NY), 1995.

Turning Points: When Everything Changes, Troll Communications (Matwah, NJ), 1996.

Toussaint L'Ouverture: The Fight for Haiti's Freedom, illustrated by Jacob Lawrence, Simon & Schuster (New York, NY), 1996.

Amistad: A Long Road to Freedom, Dutton (New York, NY), 1998.

At Her Majesty's Request: An African Princess in Victorian England, Scholastic (New York, NY), 1999.

Malcolm X: A Fire Burning Brightly, illustrated by Leonard Jenkins, HarperCollins (New York, NY), 2000.

The Greatest: Muhammad Ali, Scholastic (New York, NY), 2001.

Bad Boy: A Memoir, HarperCollins (New York, NY), 2001.

USS Constellation: Pride of the American Navy, Holiday House (New York, NY), 2004.

I've Seen the Promised Land: The Life of Dr. Martin Luther King, Jr., illustrated by Leonard Jenkins, HarperCollins (New York, NY), 2004.

Antarctica: Journeys to the South Pole, Scholastic (New York, NY), 2004.

(With William Miles) *The Harlem Hellfighters: When Pride Met Courage,* HarperCollins (New York, NY), 2006.

Ida B. Wells: Let the Truth Be Told, HarperCollins (New York, NY), 2008.

PICTURE BOOKS

(Under name Walter M. Myers) *Where Does the Day Go?,* illustrated by Leo Carty, Parents Magazine Press, 1969.

The Dragon Takes a Wife, illustrated by Ann Grifalconi, Bobbs-Merrill (New York, NY), 1972.

The Dancers, illustrated by Anne Rockwell, Parents Magazine Press, 1972.

Fly, Jimmy, Fly!, illustrated by Moneta Barnett, Putnam (New York, NY), 1974.

The Black Pearl and the Ghost; or, One Mystery after Another, illustrated by Robert Quackenbush, Viking (New York, NY), 1980.

Mr. Monkey and the Gotcha Bird, illustrated by Leslie Morrill, Delacorte (New York, NY), 1984.

The Story of the Three Kingdoms, illustrated by Ashley Bryan, HarperCollins (New York, NY), 1995.

How Mr. Monkey Saw the Whole World, illustrated by Synthia Saint James, Bantam (New York, NY), 1996.

Harlem: A Poem, illustrated by Christopher Myers, Scholastic (New York, NY), 1997.

Jazz, illustrated by Christopher Myers, Holiday House (New York, NY), 2006.

Amiri and Odette: A Dance for Two, illustrated by Javaka Steptoe, Scholastic (New York, NY), 2009.

POETRY

Brown Angels: An Album of Pictures and Verse, HarperCollins (New York, NY), 1993.

Remember Us Well: An Album of Pictures and Verse, HarperCollins (New York, NY), 1993.

Glorious Angels: A Celebration of Children, HarperCollins (New York, NY), 1995.

Angel to Angel: A Mother's Gift of Love, HarperCollins (New York, NY), 1998.

Blues Journey, illustrated by Christopher Myers, Holiday House (New York, NY), 2003.

Here in Harlem: Poems in Many Voices, Holiday House (New York, NY), 2004.

UNDER NAME STACIE JOHNSON

Sort of Sisters, Delacorte (New York, NY), 1993.
The Party, Delacorte (New York, NY), 1993.
The Prince, Delacorte (New York, NY), 1993.

Contributor of articles and fiction to books and to periodicals, including *Alfred Hitchcock Mystery Magazine, Argosy, Black Creation, Black World, Boy's Life, Ebony, Jr.!, Espionage, Essence, McCall's, National Enquirer, Negro Digest,* and *Scholastic;* also contributor of poetry to university reviews and quarterlies.

Adaptations

The Young Landlords was made into a film by Topol Productions. *Mojo and the Russians* was made into a videorecording by Children's Television International, Great Plains National Instructional Television Library, 1980. Demco Media released videos of *Fallen Angels* and *Me, Mop, and the Moondance Kid* in 1988, *Scorpions* in 1990, and *The Righteous Revenge of Artemis Bonner* in 1996. *Darnell Rock Reporting* was released on video in 1996. *Harlem: A Poem* was released as a combination book and audio version in 1997. *Scorpions* was adapted as a sound recording in 1998.

Sidelights

Deemed "a giant among children's and young adult authors" by Frances Bradburn in the *Wilson Library Bulletin,* Walter Dean Myers ranks among the best-known contemporary American writers for children and teens. An author of African-American descent, Myers is credited with helping to redefine the image of blacks in juvenile literature through award-winning books such as *The Glory Field, Monster,* and *Somewhere in the Darkness.*

During the 1960s and 1970s African-American writers such as Alice Childress, Lucille Clifton, Eloise Greenfield, Virginia Hamilton, and Sharon Bell Mathis sought to provide realistic storylines and well-rounded portrayals of black characters in books for younger readers. As a member of this group, Myers distinguished himself by bringing both humor and poignancy to his work, as well by creating books with special appeal to boys; in addition, he is considered the only prominent male writer of the group to have consistently published books of quality. A versatile and prolific author, Myers has

written realistic and historical fiction, mysteries, adventure stories, fantasies, nonfiction, poetry, and picture books. Praised for his contributions to several genres, he is perhaps best known for his books geared for readers in middle school and high school, stories that range from farcical, lighthearted tales for preteens to powerful, moving novels for older adolescents. Myers stresses the more positive aspects of black urban life in his works; often setting his stories in his boyhood home of Harlem, he is acknowledged for depicting the strength and dignity of his characters without downplaying the harsh realities of their lives.

Although he features both young men and women as protagonists, Myers is noted for his focus on young black males. His themes often include the relationship between fathers and sons as well as the search for identity and self-worth in an environment of poverty, drugs, gangs, and racism. Although his characters confront difficult issues, Myers stresses survival, pride, and hope in his works, which are filled with love and laughter and a strong sense of possibility for the future of their protagonists. Lauded for his understanding of the young, Myers is acclaimed as the creator of believable, sympathetic adolescent characters; he is also praised for creating realistic dialogue, some of which draws on rap music and other aspects of black culture.

Calling Myers "a unique voice," Rudine Sims Bishop wrote in *Presenting Walter Dean Myers* that the author is significant "because he creates books that appeal to young adults from many cultural groups. They appeal because Myers knows and cares about the things that concern his readers and because he creates characters . . . readers are happy to spend time with." R.D. Lane noted in the *African American Review* that the author "celebrates children by weaving narratives of the black juvenile experience in ways that reverse the effects of mediated messages of the black experience in public culture. . . . Myers's stratagem is revolutionary: the intrinsic value to black youth of his lessons stands priceless, timeless, and class-transcendent." In her entry in the *Dictionary of Literary Biography,* Carmen Subryan concluded that "Myers's books demonstrate that writers can not only challenge the minds of black youths but also emphasize the black experience in a nondidactic way that benefits all readers."

Born Walter Milton Myers in Martinsburg, West Virginia, Myers lost his mother, Mary Green Myers, at age two, during the birth of his younger sister Imogene. Since his father, George Ambrose Myers, was struggling economically, Walter and two of his sisters were informally adopted by family friends Florence and Herbert Dean; Myers has written about surrogate parenting in several of his stories, including *Won't Know Till I Get There* and *Me, Mop, and the Moondance Kid.*

The Dean family moved to Harlem when Myers was about three years old. He recalled in *Something about the Author Autobiography Series (SAAS),* "I loved Harlem. I lived in an exciting corner of the renowned Black

capital and in an exciting era. The people I met there, the things I did, have left a permanent impression on me." When he was four years old Myers was taught to read by his foster mother; his foster father sat the boy on his knee and told him "endless stories." As the author later wrote in *Children's Books and Their Creators,* "Somewhere along the line I discovered that books could be part of a child's world, and by the time I was nine I found myself spending long hours reading in my room. The books began to shape new bouts of imagination."

When not reading, Myers enjoyed playing sports, especially stickball, baseball, and basketball, and sports provide the background for young-adult novels such as *Hoops, The Outside Shot,* and *Slam!* At school, he enjoyed classwork but found that a speech impediment caused him some difficulty. His fellow classmates would laugh at him and, as a result, he would fight back; consequently, he was often suspended from school. When Myers was in fifth grade, as he recalled in *SAAS,* "a marvelous thing happened." Made to sit at the back of the class for fighting, he was reading a comic book during a math lesson when the teacher, Mrs. Conway, caught him. Mrs. Conway, who was known for her meanness, surprised Walter by saying that if he was going to read, he might as well read something decent and brought him a selection of children's books; Myers remembered Asbjornsen and Moe's *East of the Sun and West of the Moon,* a collection of Norwegian folktales, as a turning point in his appreciation of literature. Mrs. Conway also required her students to read aloud in class. In order to avoid some of the words that he had trouble speaking, she suggested that Walter write something for himself to read.

After junior high, Myers attended Stuyvesant High School, a school for boys that stressed academic achievement. Although he struggled somewhat due to the school's focus on science, he met another influential teacher, Bonnie Liebow, who interviewed each of her students and made up individualized reading lists for them. Myers's list included works by such European authors as Emile Zola and Thomas Mann. Liebow also told Myers that he was a gifted writer, inspiring him to consider writing as a career.

Despite this encouragement, as a teen Myers realized that writing "had no practical value for a Black child," as he recalled. "These minor victories did not bolster my ego. Instead, they convinced me that even though I was bright, even though I might have some talent, I was still defined by factors other than my ability." In addition, Myers was depressed by the fact that he would not be able to attend college due to his family's financial status. Consequently, he wrote in *SAAS,* he began "writing poems about death, despair, and doom" and began "having doubts about everything in my life."

When not writing or working odd jobs, Myers hung out in the streets: "I was steeped in the mystique of the semi-hoodlum," he recalled in *SAAS.* He acquired a sti-

letto and acted as a drug courier; he also became a target for one of the local gangs after intervening in a fight between three gang members and a new boy in the neighborhood. Finally, influenced by the war poems of British writer Rupert Brooke, Myers joined the army at age seventeen in order to, as he wrote in *SAAS*, "hie myself off to some far-off battlefield and get killed. There, where I fell, would be a little piece of Harlem."

In *Bad Boy: A Memoir,* Myers recounts his childhood, then takes the reader through his adolescence—during which he often skipped school and sometimes made deliveries for drug dealers—and to his beginnings as a writer. Rochman said of this work that "the most beautiful writing is about Mama: how she taught him to read, sharing *True Romance* magazines." "The author's growing awareness of racism and of his own identity as a black man make up one of the most interesting threads" of *Bad Boy,* wrote Miranda Doyle in *School Library Journal.* Myers' "voice and heart are consistently heard and felt throughout," concluded a *Horn Book* contributor.

Myers's army experience was less than the glorious adventure promised by the poetry he had read; he went to radio-repair school and spent most of his time playing basketball. "I also learned several efficient ways of killing human beings," he later recalled. In addition, as he told Bishop in *Presenting Walter Dean Myers,* "I learned something about dying. I learned a lot about facilitating the process, of making it abstract." During his military service, Myer also developed the strong antiwar attitude that would later become part of his young-adult novel *Fallen Angels,* the story of a young black soldier in Vietnam.

After three years in the U.S. Army, Myers returned home to his parents, who had by now moved to Morristown, New Jersey. Then he returned to Harlem, where he took an apartment and began to work at becoming a professional writer. In what he recalled as his "starving artist period," Myers wrote poetry and read books about the Bohemian life by such authors as George Orwell and André Gide; he also lived on two dollars a week from unemployment compensation and lost fifty pounds. While working briefly for the U.S. Post Office, he married Joyce, a woman he later called "wonderful, warm, beautiful, religious, caring."

Even after becoming a father—two of his three children, Karen and Michael, are from his first marriage— Myers continued to try to live a romantic lifestyle. While working odd jobs in a factory and an office, he played bongos with a group of jazz musicians, some of whom were into heroin and cocaine, and wrote jazz-based poetry, some of which was published in Canada. He also began to be published in African-American magazines such as the *Negro Digest* and the *Liberator* as well as in men's magazines such as *Argosy* and *Cavalier.* During this time, his first marriage collapsed.

In 1961, Myers enrolled in a writing class with author Lajos Egri, who told him that he had a special talent. A few years later, he attended City College of the City University of New York as a night student, but dropped out. At a writer's workshop at Columbia University led by novelist John Oliver Killens, he was recommended for a new editorial position at the publishing house Bobbs-Merrill and became an acquisitions editor. In 1968, he won first prize in a contest for black writers sponsored by the Council on Interracial Books for Children and a year later his picture-book text was published by Parents' Magazine Press as *Where Does the Day Go?*

Where Does the Day Go? features Steven, a small black boy whose father takes him and a group of children of various races for an evening walk in the park. When Steven wonders where the day goes, his friends each provide imaginative opinions of their own. Finally, Steven's dad explains that day and night are different, just like people, and that the times of day are caused by the rotation of the Earth. "Integration, involvement, and togetherness are all deftly handled," noted Mary Eble in *School Library Journal,* while Zena Sutherland, Dianne L. Monson, and May Hill Arbuthnot claimed in *Children and Books* that the story has "other strong values in addition to its exploration of the mystery of night and day." The critics noted that *Where Does the Day Go?* "explains natural phenomena accurately, and it presents an exemplary father."

After the publication of his first book, Myers changed his name from Walter Milton Myers to "one that would honor my foster parents, Walter Dean Myers." He also remarried, and he and his wife Connie had a son, Christopher, now an artist who has illustrated several of his father's works. In 1972, Myers published *The Dragon Takes a Wife,* a picture book that some considered controversial. The story features Harry, a lonely dragon who cannot fight, and Mabel May, the African-American fairy who helps him. In order to acquire a wife, Harry must defeat a knight in battle. When Mabel May turns into a dragon to show Harry how to fight, Harry falls in love with her, defeats the knight, and wins her hand, not to mention a good job at the post office.

Other picture books by Myers include several in which he teams up with son Christopher Myers. In *Jazz,* Myers "creates a scintillating paean to jazz," claimed a *Publishers Weekly* critic. Compared to other authors who struggle to capture the spirit of the music form in text, *Booklist* reviewer Bill Ott found *Jazz* "an absolutely airtight melding of words and pictures that is perfectly accessible to a younger audience." Through a series of poems accompanied by brightly colored illustrations, the pair chronicles the evolution of the music form, from fast-paced New Orleans jazz to bebop, so clearly "readers will find music coming irresistibly into their heads," suggested Roger Sutton in *Horn Book.*

The Blues of Flats Brown is a children's picture book about a dog that flees to Memphis and has a hit record. The pup's success angers former owner A.J. Grubbs, who follows him on to New York. "Myers's shaggy

fantasy has the slow-and-easy pacing of a lazy Southern afternoon," wrote a *Publishers Weekly* reviewer. "Myers beautifully conveys the blues' unique roots and the way the music bestows comfort, catharsis, and healing," said Shelle Rosenfeld in *Booklist*.

In 1975, Myers published his first novel for young adults, *Fast Sam, Cool Clyde, and Stuff*. Set in a Harlem neighborhood much like the one in which its author grew up, the story describes a group of young teens who take a positive approach to living in a difficult environment. The story is narrated by eighteen-year-old Stuff, who recalls the year that he was thirteen and formed a sort of anti-gang, the Good People, with his best friends Fast Sam and Cool Clyde plus five other boys and girls from the neighborhood. The Good People have several hilarious adventures, including one where Sam and Clyde—who is dressed as a girl—win a dance contest. However, they also deal with such problems as mistaken arrest and the deaths of one of their fathers and a friend who has turned to drugs. The children survive, both through their inner strength and the fellowship of their friends, who are dependable and respectful of one another. Writing in *English Journal*, Alleen Pace Nilsen called *Fast Sam, Cool Clyde, and Stuff* "a rich, warm story about black kids in which Myers makes the reader feel so close to the characters that ethnic group identification is secondary." In *Horn Book*, Paul Heins noted that "the humorous and ironic elements of the plot give the book the flavor of a Harlem *Tom Sawyer* or *Penrod*."

In 1977, after leaving Bobbs-Merrill, Myers became a full-time writer. *It Ain't All for Nothin'*, a young-adult novel published the next year, is considered the first of his more serious, thought-provoking works. The novel features twelve-year-old Tippy, a motherless Harlem boy who has been living with his loving, principled grandmother since he was a baby. When she goes into a nursing home, Tippy moves in with his father Lonnie, an ex-con who makes his living by stealing and who beats his son viciously. Lonely and afraid, Tippy begins drinking whiskey. When Lonnie and his pals rob a store, he coerces Tippy into participating. Bubba, a member of the group, is shot during the heist; in order to save Bubba and save himself, Tippy calls the police and turns in his father. At the end of the novel, Tippy goes to live with Mr. Roland, a kind man who has befriended him.

It Ain't All for Nothin' was praised by Steven Matthews in *School Library Journal* as "a first-rate read," and by a critic in *Kirkus Reviews* as "like Tippy—a winner." Although questioning "how many children are really going to 'drop a dime' on their father?," Ashley Jane Pennington concluded in her review for *Interracial Books for Children Bulletin* that *It Ain't All for Nothin'* "is a devastating book which needed to be written." *Motown and Didi: A Love Story*, a highly praised sequel, features two of the peripheral characters from *It Ain't All for Nothin'* and includes a strong anti-drug message as well as the theme that love can conquer all.

"It is a tale that is as thought-provoking as it is entertaining...."
—*The New York Times*

Cover of Myers' wartime novel Fallen Angels, *which is set in Vietnam during the Tet Offensive of 1967.* (Illustration copyright © 1988 by Jim Dietz. Reproduced by permission of Scholastic, Inc.)

Shooter focuses on the events leading up to and following a school shooting. Ironically, many reviewers compared the book to the real-life and well-publicized Columbine school tragedy, which occurred months prior to *Shooter*'s publication. The novel is told through a unique narrative approach: the book consists of police reports, news articles, a journal, and other "real-life" documentation of the event. For its dark subject matter and its unique narration, *Shooter* has often been compared with *Monster*. Of *Shooter*, Lauren Adams wrote in *Horn Book* that Myers's "exacting look at the many possible players and causes in the events makes for a compelling story." A *Publishers Weekly* reviewer praised the author for his handling of a controversial subject in which "no one is completely innocent and no one is entirely to blame." The reviewer concluded, "Readers will find themselves racing through the pages, then turning back to pore over the details once more."

Although Myers turns to a lighter subject in *Game*, he still explores serious themes through the first-person perspective of Drew, a seventeen year old from Harlem

who hopes to earn a college basketball scholarship and play at the professional level. Like several of the author's earlier novels, *Game* features an African-American male from the inner city who reflects on the urban environment around him and questions his place in it. In addition to narrating Drew's struggle to chart his future, Myers includes "tautly choreographed game sequences that . . . bristle with the electricity of the sport," noted a *New York Times Book Review* critic. Predicting the book will appeal to readers who enjoyed *Monster* and *Slam,* a *Kirkus Reviews* contributor wrote that *Game* offers readers "a sensitive portrait of a likable young man, his family, city and dreams."

The middle-grade novels *Scorpions* and *Fallen Angels* are considered among Myers' best. In *Scorpions* twelve-year-old Jamal lives in Harlem with his mother and younger sister. He is approached to take the place of his older brother Randy, who is in jail for killing a man, as the leader of his gang, the Scorpions. At first, Jamal refuses; however, he is fascinated with the gun that Randy's friend Mack gives him and is searching for a way to help his family raise the money for Randy's appeal. Jamal and his best friend Tito, a sensitive Puerto Rican boy, join the Scorpions, who are dealing cocaine. During a confrontation, Jamal is defended by Tito, who uses the gun Mack had given Jamal to kill to protect his friend. Marcus Crouch wrote in *Junior Bookshelf* that Myers "writes with great power, capturing the cadences of black New York, and keeps a firm hold on his narrative and his emotions. He is a fine story-teller as well as a social critic and, I suspect, a moralist." *Bulletin of the Center for Children's Books* contributor Roger Sutton noted that Myers's "compassion for Tito and Jamal is deep; perhaps the book's seminal achievement is the way it makes us realize how young, in Harlem and elsewhere, twelve years old really is."

Fallen Angels describes the horrors of the Vietnam War from the perspective of Richie Perry, a seventeen-year-old African American who has joined the U.S. Army as a way to make life easier for his mother and younger brother at home in Harlem. During the course of a year, Richie experiences fear and terror as he fights in the war; he burns the bodies of American soldiers because they cannot be carried and—with a rifle at his head—shoots a North Vietnamese soldier in the face; finally, after being wounded twice, he is sent home. Underscoring the novel, which includes rough language and gallows humor, is a strong antiwar message; Myers also addresses such issues as racial discrimination within the service and the conditions faced by the Vietnamese people. Calling Myers "a writer of skill, maturity, and judgment," Ethel L. Heins maintained in *Horn Book* that, "With its intensity and vividness in depicting a young soldier amid the chaos and the carnage of war, the novel recalls Stephen Crane's *The Red Badge of Courage.*" W. Keith McCoy, writing in *Voice of Youth Advocates,* commented that "Everything about this book rings true," while Mary Veeder, writing in Chicago's *Tribune Books,* noted that *Fallen Angels* "may be the best novel for young adults I've read this year."

Myers wrote *Fallen Angels* as a tribute to his brother Sonny, who was killed on his first day as a soldier in Vietnam; he also based much of the book on his own experience in the U.S. Army. In discussing both *Fallen Angels* and *Scorpions* with Kimberly Olson Fakih in *Publishers Weekly,* Myers called these books "a departure" and "very serious, probing work." He concluded: "Not that the others didn't address serious issues, too, but the new ones were more difficult to write." Also inspired by the war, *A Place Called Heartbreak: A Story of Vietnam* is a well-received biography of Colonel Fred V. Cherry, an African-American Air Force pilot who was held as a prisoner of the North Vietnamese for nearly eight years.

In *Sunrise over Fallujah,* Myers returns to the family depicted in his award-winning *Fallen Angels.* While the first book spoke about the horrors of the Vietnam War, *Sunrise over Fallujah* focuses on the Second Gulf War in Iraq. Enlisting after the terrorist attacks of September 11, 2001, Robin, the nephew of Richie from *Fallen Angels,* narrates his experiences in the army through a series of letters he sends home during his time in Iraq. Initially assigned to a Civil Affairs unit working to gain the cooperation of Iraqi citizens, Robin struggles to comprehend the collateral bloodshed occurring as the

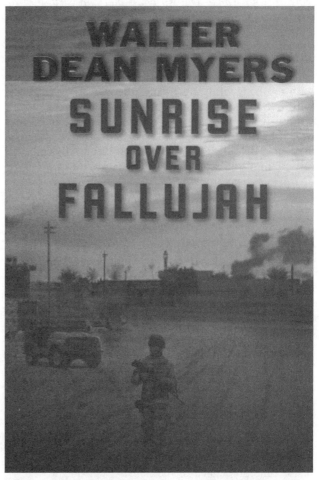

Cover of **Sunrise over Fallujah,** *Myers' novel about the American servicemen and women serving in Operation Iraqi Freedom.* (Illustration copyright © 2008 by Tim O'Brien. Reproduced by permission of Scholastic, Inc.)

conflict progresses as well as deal with the constant threat to his life from Iraqis fighting against the presence of American troops in their country. By experiencing first hand the horrors of war similar to those his uncle endured, the young soldier finally understands why Uncle Richie kept silent about his experiences in the jungles of Southeast Asia a generation earlier. Writing in *School Library Journal,* Diane P. Tuccillo thought the author avoids editorializing about the war and instead offers an "expert portrayal of a soldier's feelings and perspectives . . . allow[ing] the circumstances to speak for themselves." Several reviewers also commended Myers for his efforts to write about the war, as few novels for teens exist on the subject. In light of this lack of material, a *Kirkus Reviews* writer deemed *Sunrise over Fallujah* "an important volume, covering much ground and offering much insight," while a *Publishers Weekly* critic suggested that Myers has written "the novel that will allow American teens to grapple intelligently and thoughtfully with the war in Iraq."

In addition to his fiction, Myers has written several highly praised informational books for children and young people in which he characteristically outlines the fight for freedom by people of color; he has also written biographies of such figures as Toussaint L'Ouverture, Martin Luther King, and Malcolm X. In *Now Is Your Time! The African-American Struggle for Freedom* Myers recounts the history of black Americans through both overviews and profiles of individuals. "What happens," wrote a critic in *Kirkus Reviews,* "when a gifted novelist chooses to write the story of his people? In this case, the result is engrossing history with a strong unifying theme, the narrative enriched with accounts of outstanding lives." Michael Dirda, writing in the *Washington Post Book World,* added that Myers "writes with the vividness of a novelist, the balance of a historian, and the passion of an advocate. He tells a familiar story and shocks us with it all over again." Writing in *Voice of Youth Advocates,* Kellie Flynn noted that *Now Is Your Time!* "is alive and vital—with breathing biographical sketches and historic interpretations like rabbit punches."

With *Amistad: A Long Road to Freedom* Myers tells the dramatic story of the captive Africans who mutinied against their captors on the slave ship *Amistad* in the late 1830s. The book recounts the hellish journey on the ship and the forced landing in Connecticut as well as the landmark trial and the struggle of the West Africans to return home. Writing in *Booklist,* Hazel Rochman stated that "the narrative is exciting, not only the account of the uprising but also the tension of the court arguments about whether the captives were property and what their rights were in a country that banned the slave trade but allowed slavery." Gerry Larson added in a review for *School Library Journal* that, "with characteristic scholarship, clarity, insight, and compassion, Myers presents readers with the facts and the moral and historical significance of the *Amistad* episode."

A longtime collector of historical photographs and documents depicting the lives and culture of African Americans, Myers has used his own art to illustrate several of his informational books. The photos and letters from the author's collection have also inspired several of his works, including volumes of original poetry on black children and mothers and the biography *At Her Majesty's Request: An African Princess in Victorian England.* Published in 1999, this work reconstructs the life of Sarah Forbes Bonetta, a child of royal African descent who became a goddaughter of Queen Victoria as well as a British celebrity. Saved from a sacrificial rite in Dahomey by English sea captain Frederick E. Forbes, orphaned Sarah—named after her rescuer and his ship— was brought to England as a gift for Queen Victoria from the Dahomian king who slaughtered her family. Victoria provided the means for Sarah—nicknamed Sally—to be educated as a young woman of privilege in a missionary school in Sierra Leone. Sally, who often returned to England to visit her benefactor, eventually married a West African businessman and named her first-born child Victoria. Eventually returning with her husband to Africa, she taught in missionary schools until she died of tuberculosis at the age of thirty-six.

Working from a packet of letters he discovered in a London bookstore, Myers tells Sally's story, which he embellishes with quotes from Queen Victoria's diary, newspapers, and other memoirs of the time. As a critic in *Kirkus Reviews* commented, "This vividly researched biography will enthrall readers, and ranks among Myers's best writing." Calling *At Her Majesty's Request* a "fascinating biography" and a "moving and very humane portrait of a princess," a reviewer in *Publishers Weekly* concluded that Myers "portrays a young woman who never truly belongs."

Myers's second book about Malcolm X, *Malcolm X: A Fire Burning Brightly,* focuses on the stages of Malcolm's life and contains Leonard Jenkins's artwork, "full-color montage illustrations, in acrylic, pastel, and spray paint . . . like mural art, with larger-than-life individual portraits set against the crowded streets and the swirl of politics," wrote *Booklist* contributor Rochman, who noted that nearly every page contains a quote from speeches or writings. Myers chronicles Malcolm's childhood, his time in the Charlestown State Prison, his conversion to Islam, leadership of the Black Muslims until his break with Black Muslim leader Elijah Muhammad, and his pilgrimage to Mecca prior to his assassination in 1965.

In *The Greatest: Muhammad Ali,* Myers documents the life of the boxer born Cassius Clay, moving from Ali's childhood in segregated St. Louis to his Olympic win in 1960 and his success as a world-class athlete. Myers then relates the athlete's commitment as a Black Muslim and his political activism as a conscientious objector during the Vietnam War. Myers also reports on Ali's major fights against Sonny Liston, Joe Frazier, and George Foreman. *Horn Book* contributor Jack Forman felt the book "is more a portrait of Ali's character and cultural impact than a narrative of his life." "This is finally a story about a black man of tremendous cour-

age," wrote Bill Ott in *Booklist,* "the kind of universal story that needs a writer as talented as Myers to retell it for every generation." Khafre K. Abif added in *Black Issues Book Review* that in *The Greatest* Myers "inspires a new generation of fans by exposing the hazards Ali faced in boxing, the rise of a champion, and now his battle against Parkinson's disease."

Myers's nonfiction title *USS Constellation* relates the entire story of the famous ship, from construction to war victories to encounters with slave ships to crew training. The book is complemented by first-person accounts, along with illustrations and charts. Carolyn Phelan, writing in *Booklist,* praised *USS Constellation* as a "well-researched" volume, calling it a "unique addition to American history collections." In *Publishers Weekly,* a reviewer praised Myers book as a"meticulously researched, fast-flowing chronicle," and applauded *USS Constellation* for offering "a larger view of the shaping of America." Betty Carter, writing in *Horn Book,* noted that the first-person accounts "lend authenticity while personalizing events."

In *Here in Harlem: Poems in Many Voices,* Myers presents over fifty poems that explore the streets of Harlem through the experiences of dozens of characters. He "treats readers to a tour of Harlem's past and present," remarked a *Publishers Weekly* contributor, by covering a wide variety of settings, including a church, hair salons, and restaurants. Accompanying the poems are period photographs of Harlem, offering readers a visual context to the poems, which vary in style from free verse to conversational. In *Booklist* Carolyn Phelan dubbed *Here in Harlem* "a colorful and warmly personal portrayal of Harlem," before going on to predict, "this unusual book will be long remembered."

"Children and adults," wrote Myers in *SAAS,* "must have role models with which they can identify"; therefore in his writing he has attempted to "deliver images upon which [they] could build and expand their own worlds." In an interview with Roger Sutton for *School Library Journal,* Myers noted that writing about the African-American experience is fraught with complexity and difficulties. "Very often people want more from books than a story," the author explained; "they want books to represent them well. This is where I get the flak."

Commenting on the question of writing primarily for a black audience, Myers stated: "as a black person you are always representing the race. . . . So what you have to do is try to write it as well as you can and hope that if you write the story well enough, people won't be offended." Myers sees an element of racism in the notion that black authors must write about "black subjects" for a primarily black audience. Likewise, he views the controversy surrounding the question of whether whites should write about the black experience as "a false issue." "I think basically you need to write what you believe in."

Myers teams up with son Christopher Myers on the music-driven picture book Jazz. (Illustration copyright © 2006 by Christopher Myers. Reproduced by permission of Holiday House, Inc.)

Writing in *SAAS,* Myers stated that he feels the need to show young blacks "the possibilities that exist for them that were never revealed to me as a youngster; possibilities that did not even exist for me then." He continued: "As a Black writer I want to talk about my people. . . . I want to tell Black children about their humanity and about their history and how to grease their legs so the ash won't show and how to braid their hair so it's easy to comb on frosty winter mornings. The books come. They pour from me at a great rate. . . . There is always one more story to tell, one more person whose life needs to be held up to the sun."

Biographical and Critical Sources

BOOKS

Bishop, Rudine Sims, *Presenting Walter Dean Myers,* Twayne, 1991.
Dictionary of Literary Biography, Volume 33: *Afro-American Fiction Writers after 1955,* Gale (Detroit, MI), 1984, pp. 199-202.
Something about the Author Autobiography Series, Gale (Detroit, MI), 1986, pp. 143-156.

PERIODICALS

African American Review, spring, 1988, R.H. Lane, "Keepin It Real: Walter Dean Myers and the Promise of African-American Children's Literature," p. 125.

Black Issues Book Review, May, 2001, Khafre K. Abif, review of *The Greatest: Muhammad Ali,* p. 80.

Booklist, February 15, 1998, Hazel Rochman, "Some Versions of *Amistad,*" p. 1003; February 15, 2000, Hazel Rochman, review of *Malcolm X: A Fire Burning Brightly,* p. 1103; March 1, 2000, Shelle Rosenfeld, review of *The Blues of Flats Brown,* p. 1242; January 1, 2001, Bill Ott, review of *The Greatest,* p. 952; May 1, 2001, Hazel Rochman, review of *Bad Boy: A Memoir,* p. 1673; July, 2004, Carolyn Phelan, review of *USS Constellation,* p. 1841; November 1, 2004, Carolyn Phelan, review of *Here in Harlem: Poems in Many Voices,* p. 480; February 1, 2006, Jennifer Hubert, review of *The Harlem Hellfighters: When Pride Met Courage,* p. 62; September 1, 2006, Bill Ott, review of *Jazz,* p. 127; October 1, 2006, Hazel Rochman, review of *Street Love,* p. 52; February 1, 2007, Michael Cart, review of *Harlem Summer,* p. 56; July 1, 2007, Hazel Rochman, review of *What They Found: Love on 145th Street,* p. 61; February 1, 2008, Gillian Engberg, review of *Game,* p. 51; February 15, 2008, Jennifer Mattson, review of *Sunrise over Fallujah,* p. 76.

Bulletin of the Center for Children's Books, July-August, 1988, review of *Scorpions,* p. 235.

English Journal, March, 1976, Alleen Pace Nilsen, "Love and the Teenage Reader," pp. 90-92.

Horn Book, August, 1975, Ethel L. Heins, review of *Fallen Angels,* pp. 503-504; July-August, 1988, Paul Heins, review of *Fast Sam, Cool Clyde, and Stuff,* pp. 388-389; May, 2000, review of *Malcolm X: A Fire Burning Brightly,* p. 336; January, 2000, Jack Forman, review of *The Greatest,* p. 115; July, 2001, review of *Bad Boy,* p. 473; May-June, 2004, Lauren Adams, review of *Shooter,* p. 335; July-August, 2004, Betty Carter, review of *USS Constellation,* p. 469; November-December, 2006, Roger Sutton, review of *Jazz,* p. 735, and Claire E. Gross, review of *Street Love,* p. 722; May-June, 2007, Roger Sutton, review of *Harlem Summer,* p. 286; May-June, 2008, Betty Carter, review of *Sunrise over Fallujah,* p. 324.

Interracial Books for Children Bulletin, Volume 10, number 4, 1979, Ashley Jane Pennington, review of *It Ain't All for Nothin',* p. 18.

Junior Bookshelf, August, 1990, Marcus Crouch, review of *Scorpions,* pp. 190-191.

Kirkus Reviews, March 1, 1972, review of *The Dragon Takes a Wife,* p. 256; October 15, 1978, review of *It Ain't All for Nothin',* p. 1143; October 1, 1991, review of *Now Is Your Time!,* p. 1537; December 15, 1998, review of *At Her Majesty's Request: An African Princess in Victorian England,* p. 1802; November 15, 2005, review of *The Harlem Hellfighters,* p. 1235; December 15, 2007, review of *Game;* April 1, 2008, review of *Sunrise over Fallujah.*

Kliatt, July, 2005, KaaVonia Hinton, review of *Autobiography of My Dead Brother,* p. 14; March, 2007, Paula Rohrlick, review of *Harlem Summer,* p. 17; January, 2008, Paula Rohrlick, review of *Game,* p. 11; May, 2008, Paula Rohrlick, review of *Sunrise over Fallujah,* p. 15.

New York Times Book Review, April 19, 1972, Nancy Griffin, review of *The Dragon Takes a Wife,* p. 8; October 21, 2001, Kermit Frazier, review of *Bad Boy,* p. 31; May 11, 2008, review of *Game* and *Sunrise over Fallujah,* p. 26.

Publishers Weekly, February 26, 1988, "Walter Dean Myers," p. 117; February 8, 1999, review of *At Her Majesty's Request,* p. 215; January 24, 2000, review of *The Blues of Flats Brown,* p. 311; March 22, 2004, review of *Shooter,* p. 87; June 28, 2004, review of *USS Constellation,* p. 52; November 15, 2004, review of *Here in Harlem,* p. 61; September 19, 2005, review of *Autobiography of My Dead Brother,* p. 68; August 7, 2006, review of *Jazz,* p. 57; March 26, 2007, review of *Harlem Summer,* p. 94; April 21, 2008, review of *Sunrise over Fallujah,* p. 59.

School Librarian, August, 1990, Allison Hurst, review of *Fallen Angels,* pp. 118-119.

School Library Journal, April 15, 1970, Mary Eble, review of *Where Does the Day Go?,* p. 111; October, 1978, Steven Matthews, review of *It Aint' All for Nothin',* p. 158; May, 1998, Gerry Larson, review of *Amistad: A Long Road to Freedom,* p. 158; March, 2000, Karen James, review of *The Blues of Flats Brown,* p. 210; May, 2001, Miranda Doyle, review of *Bad Boy,* p. 169; December, 2001, Kathleen Baxter, review of *The Greatest,* p. 39; April, 2005, Nina Lindsay, review of *Here in Harlem,* p. 57; August, 2005, Francisca Goldsmith, review of *Autobiography of My Dead Brother,* p. 132; March, 2007, Hillias J. Martin, review of *Harlem Summer,* p. 216; August, 2007, Chris Shoemaker, review of *What They Found: Love on 145th Street,* p. 122; April, 2008, Diane P. Tuccillo, review of *Sunrise over Fallujah,* p. 146; February, 2008, Richard Luzer, review of *Game,* p. 122.

Teaching and Learning Literature, September-October, 1998, Ellen A. Greever, "Making Connections in the Life and Works of Walter Dean Myers," pp. 42-54.

Tribune Books (Chicago, IL), November 13, 1988, Mary Veeder, "Some Versions of *Fallen Angels,*" p. 6.

USA Today, April 24, 2008, Bob Minzesheimer, "The Somber Realities of War Cross Generations," interview with Myers, p. 7D.

Voice of Youth Advocates, August, 1988, W. Keith McCoy, review of *Fallen Angels,* p. 133; February, 1992, Kellie Flynn, review of *Now Is Your Time!,* p. 398.

Washington Post Book World, March 8, 1992, Michael Dirda, review of *Now Is Your Time!,* p. 11.

Wilson Library Bulletin, January, 1993, Frances Bradburn, review of *The Righteous Revenge of Artemis Bonner,* p. 88.

ONLINE

Walter Dean Myers Home Page, http://www.walterdean myers.net (October 15, 2008).

National Public Radio Web site, http://www.npr.org/ (August 19, 2008), Juan Williams, "Walter Dean Myers: A 'Bad Boy' Makes Good."*

*   *   *

MYERS, Walter M.
See MYERS, Walter Dean

O-P

O'BRIEN, Patrick 1960-

Personal

Born 1960; son of Charles M. O'Brien, Jr. (a U.S. Navy officer); married; wife's name Allison; children: Alex. *Education:* Graduated from University of Virginia, 1982; attended art school at Virginia Commonwealth University.

Addresses

Home and office—Baltimore, MD. *Office*—2010 Clipper Park Rd., Studio 109, Baltimore, MD, 21211. *E-mail*—pat@patrickobrienstudio.com.

Career

Painter, author, and illustrator. Freelance illustrator, 1986—; clients include Discovery Channel, Smithsonian, and American Museum of Natural History. Work has appeared on posters, videocassette boxes, greeting cards, and billboards; paintings have been commissioned for National Geographic Television, Navy Federal Credit Union, U.S. Coast Guard, and Exxon Mobil. Also worked at a naval architecture firm. *Exhibitions:* Work included in permanent collection at Mazza Museum, Findlay, OH. Solo exhibitions include "New York in the Age of Sail," Union League Club, New York, NY, 2008.

Awards, Honors

Award of Excellence, Mystic International Marine Art Exhibition; Teacher's Choice Award, International Reading Association, for *The Mutiny on the Bounty.*

Writings

SELF-ILLUSTRATED

The Making of a Knight: How Sir James Earned His Armor, Charlesbridge (Watertown, MA), 1998.

Gigantic!: How Big Were the Dinosaurs?, Holt (New York, NY), 1999.
The Hindenburg, Holt (New York, NY), 2000.
Steam, Smoke, and Steel: Back in Time with Trains, Charlesbridge (Watertown, MA), 2000.
The Great Ships, Walker (New York, NY), 2001.
Megatooth, Holt (New York, NY), 2001.
Mammoth, Holt (New York, NY), 2002.
Fantastic Flights: One Hundred Years of Flying on the Edge, Walker (New York, NY), 2003.
Duel of the Ironclads: The Monitor vs. the Virginia, Walker (New York, NY), 2003.
The Mutiny on the Bounty, Walker (New York, NY), 2007.
Sabertooth, Holt (New York, NY), 2008.

ILLUSTRATOR

Marilyn Singer, *A Wasp Is Not a Bee,* Holt (New York, NY), 1995.
Carol A. Amato, *Captain Jim and the Killer Whales* Barron's (Hauppage, NY), 1995.
Carol A. Amato, *The Bald Eagle: Free Again!,* Barron's (Hauppage, NY), 1996.
Julie Thompson and Brownie Macintosh, *A Pirate's Life for Me!: A Day Aboard a Pirate Ship,* Charlesbridge (Watertown, MA), 1996.
Brenda Z. Guiberson, *Teddy Roosevelt's Elk,* Holt (New York, NY), 1997.
Marilyn Singer, *Bottoms Up!,* Holt (New York, NY), 1997.
Carol A. Amato, *On the Trail of the Grizzly,* Barron's (Hauppage, NY), 1997.
Sharon Katz, *The Wandering Gorilla,* Wildlife Conservation Society (New York, NY), 1999.
K.S. Rodriguez, *Pteranodon,* Steadwell Books (Austin, TX), 2000.
K.S. Rodriguez, *Stegosaurus,* Steadwell Books (Austin, TX), 2000.
K.S. Rodriguez, *Tyrannosaurus Rex,* Steadwell Books (Austin, TX), 2000.
Alex Bandon, *The Travels of Marco Polo,* Steadwell Books (Austin, TX), 2000.
Joanne Mattern, *The Travels of Ferdinand Magellan,* Steadwell Books (Austin, TX), 2000.

Joanne Mattern, *The Travels of Henry Hudson,* Steadwell Books (Austin, TX), 2000.

Lara Bergen, *The Travels of Francisco Pizarro,* Steadwell Books (Austin, TX), 2000.

Lara Bergen, *The Travels of Lewis and Clark,* Steadwell Books (Austin, TX), 2000.

Debbie Crisfield, *The Travels of Hernán Cortés,* Steadwell Books (Austin, TX), 2000.

Audrey B. Baird, *Storm Coming!* (poems), Wordsong (Honesdale, PA), 2001.

Deborah Crisfield, *The Travels of Juan Ponce de León,* Steadwell Books (Austin, TX), 2001.

Joanne Mattern, *The Travels of John and Sebastian Cabot,* Steadwell Books (Austin, TX), 2001.

Joanne Mattern, *The Travels of Samuel de Champlain,* Steadwell Books (Austin, TX), 2001.

Joanne Mattern, *The Travels of Vasco da Gama,* Steadwell Books (Austin, TX), 2001.

Lara Bergen, *The Travels of Sieur de La Salle,* Steadwell Books (Austin, TX), 2001.

Audrey B. Baird, *A Cold Snap!: Frosty Poems,* Wordsong (Honesdale, PA), 2002.

Melinda Lilly, *The Boston Tea Party,* Rourke Publishing (Vero Beach, FL), 2003.

Kevin O'Malley, *Captain Raptor and the Moon Mystery,* Walker (New York, NY), 2005.

Kevin O'Malley, *Captain Raptor and the Space Pirates,* Walker (New York, NY), 2007.

Contributor of paintings to periodicals, including *Artist's* and *Naval History.*

Sidelights

Patrick O'Brien, a highly regarded fine artist specializing in historic subjects, has written and illustrated several works for children, including *Fantastic Flights: One Hundred Years of Flying on the Edge* and *The Mutiny on the Bounty.* O'Brien has also provided the artwork for such titles as *Storm Coming!,* a poetry collection by Audrey B. Baird, and *Captain Raptor and the Moon Mystery,* an adventure tale by Kevin O'Malley.

O'Brien first self-illustrated title, *The Making of a Knight: How Sir James Earned His Armor,* appeared in

Patrick O'Brien's love of the history of seafaring is evident in the detailed paintings he creates for his book **The Great Ships.** (Walker & Company, 2001. Copyright © 2001 by Patrick O'Brien. Reproduced by permission.)

1998. Set in fifteenth-century England, the work concerns young James, a lowly page who grows up to become first a squire and then a knight. According to a *Publishers Weekly* reviewer, O'Brien's story "works well here to hold interest and provide cohesiveness to the many nuggets of information served up," and *Booklist* contributor Carolyn Phelan stated that his "richly colored and dramatically lit oil paintings sensitively portray James as he grows from boy to man."

In *The Hindenburg* chronicles the development of the great German airship that exploded over a New Jersey airfield in 1937. "O'Brien's lifelike watercolor and gouache paintings pack as much drama as the story he tells," noted a contributor in *Publishers Weekly,* and a *Horn Book* critic stated that O'Brien's "economical prose explains the basic science of dirigible flight but also captures the haunting beauty" of the dirigible. The author/illustrator looks at the achievements of the Wright Brothers, Amelia Earhart, Chuck Yeager, and other aviation pioneers in *Fantastic Flights.* O'Brien's "text is concise and readable; the colorful illustrations depict inspiring views of the planes and spacecraft in flight," observed Jeffrey A. French in *School Library Journal.*

The son of a retired U.S. Navy commander, O'Brien has written and illustrated a number of book with nautical themes. In *The Great Ships,* he presents the stories behind seventeen of the world's most historically significant vessels, including a Viking Gokstad ship, the *Titanic,* and the *Nautilus,* the last a nuclear-powered submarine. According to Phelan, O'Brien's "paintings often feature dramatic effects of light on sea, sky, and sail." The author explores the 1862 sea battle that changed the course of naval warfare in *Duel of the Ironclads: The Monitor vs. the Virginia,* wherein his "clear and lively writing, dramatic watercolor and gouache illustrations, maps, and handsome, large-format design combine to make an appealing volume," observed a contributor in *Kirkus Reviews.* In *The Mutiny on the Bounty,* O'Brien recounts the famous confrontation between ship captain William Bligh and his second-in-command, Fletcher Christian, in 1787. Phelan stated that the "handsome artwork sets the story's tone, defines the period, and brings the characters to life."

O'Brien has examined prehistoric subjects in self-illustrated works such as *Mammoth* and *Sabertooth.* In the former, he traces the evolution of the great Ice Age creature. O'Brien's pictures "are realistically clear and help make this an enticing offering," observed Dona Ratterree in *School Library Journal. Sabertooth* provides an introduction to the ferocious cat, and features "realistic watercolor and gouache illustrations [that] lend eye-catching glamour to the captionlike text," as Patricia Manning commented in *School Library Journal.*

O'Brien has also drawn praise for his contributions to works by other authors. Audrey B. Baird's *Storm Coming!* contains verse about lightning, fog, and wind.

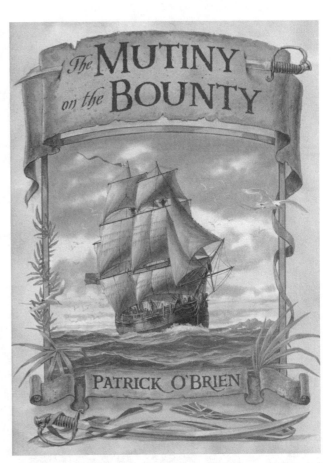

One of the most compelling stories of life on the high seas is recounted by O'Brien in his The Mutiny on the Bounty. (Walker & Company, 2007. Copyright © 1997 by Patrick O'Brien. Reproduced by permission.)

O'Brien illustrator captures "much of the poetry's imagery in pale-toned watercolors," remarked *School Library Journal* critic John Peters. In Kevin O'Malley's *Captain Raptor and the Moon Mystery,* a crew of space-traveling dinosaurs find adventure and danger. O'Brien's "naturalistic watercolors parody museum murals of dinosaurs, while his outer-space images recall the pulp covers of sixties sci-fi," wrote a *Publishers Weekly* critic in a review of the entertaining middle-grade novel.

Biographical and Critical Sources

PERIODICALS

Baltimore Sun, December 27, 2006, Tom Pelton, "Engaged in a Depiction of War: Painter Mixes History, Art to Re-create a Momentous Revolutionary War Battle."

Booklist, October 15, 1995, April Judge, review of *A Wasp Is Not a Bee,* p. 409; September 15, 1997, John Peters, review of *Teddy Roosevelt's Elk,* p. 237; August, 1998, Carolyn Phelan, review of *The Making of a Knight: How Sir James Earned His Armor,* p. 2007; June 1, 1999, Denia Hester, review of *Gigantic! How Big Were the Dinosaurs?,* p. 1833; September 1, 2000,

The war ships that arose due to nineteenth-century advancements in technology are the focus of O'Brien's **Duel of the Ironclads.** (Walker & Company, 2003. Copyright © 2003 by Patrick O'Brien. Reproduced by permission.)

Connie Fletcher, review of *The Hindenburg,* p. 110; March 15, 2001, Stephanie Zvirin, review of *Storm Coming!,* p. 1394; January 1, 2002, Carolyn Phelan, review of *The Great Ships,* p. 854; September 15, 2002, GraceAnne A. DeCandido, review of *A Cold Snap! Frosty Poems,* p. 229; December 1, 2002, Carolyn Phelan, review of *Mammoth,* p. 686; March 15, 2003, Carolyn Phelan, review of *Duel of the Ironclads: The Monitor vs. the Virginia,* p. 1323; Septem-

ber 1, 2003, Todd Morning, review of *Fantastic Flights: One Hundred Years of Flying on the Edge,* p. 119; January 1, 2007, Carolyn Phelan, review of *The Mutiny on the Bounty,* p. 90; September 1, 2007, Todd Morning, review of *Captain Raptor and the Space Pirates,* p. 124.

Horn Book, September, 2000, review of *The Hindenburg,* p. 598; March-April, 2007, Betty Carter, review of *The Mutiny on the Bounty,* p. 215.

Kirkus Reviews, October 1, 2001, review of *The Great Ships,* p. 1430; November 15, 2002, review of *Mammoth,* p. 1700; February 15, 2003, review of *Duel of the Ironclads,* p. 313; June 15, 2003, review of *Fantastic Flights,* p. 862; May 15, 2008, review of *Sabertooth.*

Publishers Weekly, June 22, 1998, review of *The Making of a Knight,* p. 90; October 16, 2000, review of *The Hindenburg,* p. 76; March 7, 2005, review of *Captain Raptor and the Moon Mystery,* p. 68.

School Library Journal, August, 2000, Steven Engelfried, review of *Steam, Smoke, and Steel: Back in Time with Trains,* p. 173; October, 2000, Steve Clancy, review of *The Hindenburg,* p. 150; December, 2000, Ann Welton, review of *The Travels of Marco Polo,* p. 130; June, 2001, John Peters, review of *Storm Coming!,* p. 133, and Judith Constantinides, review of *Megatooth,* p. 140; September, 2001, Be Astengo, review of *The Great Ships,* p. 252; November, 2002, Dona Ratterree, review of *Mammoth,* p. 146; December, 2002, Sally R. Dow, review of *A Cold Snap!,* p. 116; March, 2003, Susan Shaver, review of *The Boston Tea Party,* p. 220; May, 2003, Nina Lindsay, review of *Duel of the Ironclads,* p. 175; November, 2003, Jeffrey A. French, review of *Fantastic Flights,* p. 164; April, 2005, Joy Fleishhacker, review of *Captain Raptor and the Moon Mystery,* p. 108; March, 2007, Ann Joslin, review of *The Mutiny on the Bounty,* p. 200; September, 2007, Mary Jean Smith, review of *Captain Raptor and the Space Pirates,* p. 224; July, 2008, Patricia Manning, review of *Sabertooth,* p. 91.

ONLINE

Patrick O'Brien Home Page, http://www.patrickobrienstu dio.com (August 10, 2008).

Charlesbridge Web site, http://www.charlesbridge.com/ (August 10, 2008), "Patrick O'Brien."*

*   *   *

O'CONNOR, Barbara 1950-

Personal

Born November 9, 1950, in Greenville, SC; daughter of William (a food broker) and Harriet (a homemaker) Lawrence; married William O'Connor (a risk manager), 1984; children: Grady. *Education:* University of South Carolina, B.A., 1972.

Addresses

Home—Duxbury, MA. *Agent*—Barbara Markowitz, P.O. Box 41709, Los Angeles, CA 90041-0709. *E-mail*—barbaraoconnor@mac.com.

Career

Children's book author.

Member

Society of Children's Book Writers and Illustrators.

Awards, Honors

Best books citation, *Family Fun* magazine, 1997, summer reading showcase citation, Children's Book Council, and Popular Paperbacks for Young Adults citation, American Library Association (ALA), 2003, all for *Beethoven in Paradise;* Best Books citation, Bank Street College School of Education, 1999, Dolly Gray Book Award, 2000, and Notable Book citation, ALA, 2000, all for *Me and Rupert Goody;* Gold Award, Parents' Choice, Best Books citation, Bank Street College School of Education, and Best Children's Book citation, *Child* magazine, all 2001, and Cream of the Crop designation, Maine Regional Library System, and Massachusetts Book Award, both 2002, all for *Moonpie and Ivy;* Gold Award, Parents' Choice, and Best of the Best citation, Chicago Public Library, both 2003, both for *Fame and Glory in Freedom, Georgia;* Recommended Award, Parent's Choice, for *Taking Care of Moses* and *How to Steal a Dog;* Silver Award, Parent's Choice, for *Greetings from Nowhere.*

Writings

FICTION

Beethoven in Paradise, Frances Foster Books (New York, NY), 1997.

Me and Rupert Goody, Frances Foster Books (New York, NY), 1999.

Moonpie and Ivy, Frances Foster Books (New York, NY), 2001.

Fame and Glory in Freedom, Georgia, Frances Foster Books (New York, NY), 2003.

Taking Care of Moses, Frances Foster Books (New York, NY), 2004.

How to Steal a Dog, Frances Foster Books (New York, NY), 2007.

Greetings from Nowhere, Frances Foster Books (New York, NY), 2008.

The Small Adventure of Popeye and Elvis, Farrar, Straus & Giroux (New York, NY), 2009.

NONFICTION

Mammolina: A Story about Maria Montessori, illustrated by Sara Campitelli, foreword by Margot Waltuch, Carolrhoda Books (Minneapolis, MN), 1993.

Barefoot Dancer: The Story of Isadora Duncan, Carolrhoda Books (Minneapolis, MN), 1994.

The Soldier's Voice: The Story of Ernie Pyle, Carolrhoda Books (Minneapolis, MN), 1996.

The World at His Fingertips: A Story about Louis Braille, illustrated by Rochelle Draper, Carolrhoda Books (Minneapolis, MN), 1997.

Katherine Dunham: Pioneer of Black Dance, Carolrhoda Books (Minneapolis, MN), 2000.

Leonardo da Vinci: Renaissance Genius, Carolrhoda Books (Minneapolis, MN), 2003.

Sidelights

Books by middle-grades author Barbara O'Connor fall into two categories: novels that are frequently set in small towns in the author's native South, and biographies of famous figures such as dancers Isadora Duncan and Katherine Dunham, journalist Ernie Pyle, and painter and inventor Leonardo da Vinci. "I enjoy writing biographies because I like reading about people's lives and I like to research (I really do!)—and I like turning facts about a life into a story about a life," O'Connor wrote on her home page. "I love writing novels because I can let my imagination run wild."

Critics have noted that O'Connor's enjoyment of and commitment to doing research is evident in each of her biographies. Reviewing her book *Leonardo da Vinci: Renaissance Genius* for *School Library Journal,* Kristen Oravec praised O'Connor's "outstanding writing" and noted that her "thorough research is evident in both the text and the several appendices." In *Booklist* Carolyn Phelan praised another biography by O'Connor, *Katherine Dunham: Pioneer of Black Dance,* as "solid," while *School Library Journal* contributor Janet Woodward deemed the same volume "accessible" to its intended readership.

O'Connor's novel *Beethoven in Paradise* is set in the Paradise Trailer Park in South Carolina, where twelve-year-old Martin Pittman lives with his emotionally abusive father. Martin's father thinks that the boy is a "sissy britches" because Martin prefers music to more macho activities like baseball. "All my life I ain't never had nothing but disappointments," Martin's father tells his son, "and you're just the icing on the cake." However, Martin's chain-smoking grandmother Hazeline, his lonely neighbor, Wylene, and the new girl at school, Sybil, all support the boy's desire to be a musician. Wylene helps him to get a violin which, in what *Booklist* critic Hazel Rochman called a "dramatic resolution," Martin's father smashes. Martin, however, refuses to be cowed, and with the help of his friends he gets a second, less-breakable instrument: a saxophone. Critics noted the particularly Southern feel of the book; "the power of this novel is in the hard-scrabble portrait of the people and the place," Rochman declared, while a *Publishers Weekly* reviewer noted that O'Connor "has an instinctive feel for the local speech and its rhythms."

Me and Rupert Goody also features a protagonist who does not quite fit in with her relatives. Jennalee Helton's immediate family is large and disorganized, so much so that there are not enough beds to go around. The girl prefers to spend her time with a neighbor, Uncle Beau—no actual relation—who lets her help out in his general store and pays her in candy bars. When a mentally challenged young African-American man named Rupert Goody arrives in town and claims to be Uncle Beau's long-lost son, Jennalee is afraid the newcomer will replace her in Uncle Beau's heart. Meanwhile, the townsfolk also have a hard time accepting Rupert, since Uncle Beau is white, and eventually a

growing tide of racism provokes Jennalee into defending the young man. "How this stubborn but winning protagonist travels from complete resentment to acceptance of her rival for Uncle Beau's affections is a journey readers won't want to miss," concluded a *Publishers Weekly* contributor. Calling *Me and Rupert Goody* a "gutsy, heartwarming novel," Shelley Townsend-Hudson added in *Booklist* that O'Connor's novel "ultimately shows the capacity for love in the human heart."

Pearl, the protagonist of *Moonpie and Ivy,* is also searching for stability and love. Pearl's biological mother, Ruby, dumps the girl with her Aunt Ivy in rural Georgia, because she claims to need time off from being a mother. Now Pearl and Ivy struggle with their relationship, both knowing that Ruby will eventually come to reclaim her daughter. At first Pearl rebuffs Aunt Ivy's friendly overtures, not wanting to get attached, but when she finally overcomes her fear it is her aunt who pulls back. Ivy's unwillingness to take Pearl completely into her heart is made even harder on the girl when another child, the abandoned Moon, is about to be taken in by Aunt Ivy and her new husband.

Reviewing *Moonpie and Ivy,* critics again praised the novel's realistic evocation of the South. "O'Connor's gritty descriptions of the characters and scenery," wrote a *Horn Book* contributor, "vividly evoke the environment as Pearl experiences it," while Katie O'Dell noted in *School Library Journal* that "the rural Georgia setting is fully realized through gentle and descriptive prose." "There is no happy ending and no message," Rochman added in her *Booklist* review, "just the heartrending drama of Pearl's struggle to change and her search for home."

"Readers dealing with acceptance issues will find solace in" *Fame and Glory in Freedom, Georgia,* maintained *School Library Journal* contributor Jean Gaffney. Burdette "Bird" Weaver, the protagonist of O'Connor's novel, is a sixth grader with two dreams in life: to experience "just one short day of fame and glory" in the small town where she is generally ignored, and to go to Disney World. A school spelling bee offers Bird both, if she can win. The spelling bee is a team event, and Bird, encouraged by her neighbor Miss Delphine, decides to partner with another social outcast, a new boy in town named Harlem Tate. Harlem is an incredible speller, but he inexplicably runs off of the stage in the middle of the contest. Again following Miss Delphine's encouragement, Bird decides not to dismiss her new friend and tries to get him to tell her what happened. She eventually learns that Harlem has poor eyesight and could not read the writing on the chalkboard at the event. Bird's role as narrator was praised by several critics; her "original voice has charm, grit, and spunkiness," commented a *Kirkus Reviews* contributor, while the girl's "conversations with empathetic Miss Delphine" were viewed by a *Publishers Weekly* critic as effective in revealing "Bird's humor and [the] big heart beneath her rough edges."

O'Connor once again deals with racial issues in *Taking Care of Moses*. After a newborn African-American baby is left on the doorsteps of a Baptist church in rural South Carolina, two women in the community struggle over who should have custody of the child. One of the women, the white, childless wife of the church's minister, wants to keep the child as her own, while the other woman, a black foster parent, believes the child should remain with a family of his own race. Only eleven-year-old Randall knows the identity of the abandoned child's mother, but revealing his secret would cause much hardship among members of his community. As townspeople argue over the baby named Moses, Randall must struggle to reach the right decision about his important knowledge. Several reviewers applauded the author's ability to create believable characters and realistic dialogue in *Taking Care of Moses*. *Booklist* critic Carolyn Phelan suggested that O'Connor not only creates "characters whose idiosyncrasies make them believable," but also develops "memorable, convincing portrayals of interracial friendships and spats." The author also earned praise for her ability to create an engaging story, *Horn Book* contributor Christine M. Hepperman writing that "particularly satisfying is how the narrative resolutely avoids easy answers." In *Kirkus Reviews* a critic dubbed *Taking Care of Moses* "a well-developed, intriguing short novel with a suspenseful clue-filled story line."

In *How to Steal a Dog* "O'Connor once again smoothly balances challenging themes with her heroine's strength and sense of humor," declared a reviewer in *Publishers Weekly*. After her father abandons the family, Georgina Hayes finds herself living with her mother and younger brother in the family car, evicted from their apartment. As her mother works two jobs to earn enough money to find another place to live, Georgina becomes inspired by a poster offering a reward for a lost dog. The young girl carefully formulates a plan to kidnap the pet of a seemingly wealthy woman, hoping to earn a generous reward when she returns the dog. The scheme begins to unravel, however, as a sensitive homeless man influences Georgina to reconsider her actions. Writing in *School Library Journal*, Robyn Gioia suggested that O'Connor's "gentle storytelling carries a theme of love and emphasizes what is really right in the world." *Horn Book* critic Kitty Flynn also commented favorably on the author's narrative skills, writing that she "knows how to spin a touching story."

The stories of four different families combine in *Greetings from Nowhere*, another novel for teens. Upon the death of her husband, Aggie Duncan decides to sell the motel she and her late husband owned in the Smoky Mountains of North Carolina. Coming to purchase the hotel is Clyde Dover, a man whose wife has recently left him and their daughter, Willow. Two other individuals staying as guests at the hotel—an older boy on his way to military school and an adopted girl searching for more information about her recently deceased biological mother—round out O'Connor's collection of characters as they interact with each other in life-changing ways. "Fans of O'Connor's many award-winning books . . . will find *Greetings from Nowhere* endearing, poignant, and even funny," predicted *Christian Science Monitor* contributor Augusta Scattergood. Writing in *School Library Journal*, Kim Dare concluded that "O'Connor's knack for well-developed characters and feisty protagonists is evident" in *Greetings from Nowhere*, "as is her signature Southern charm."

O'Connor once told *SATA*: "I love young people and I love writing, so it was only natural that I combined the two. I set my fiction in the South because I consider the South my 'heart's home.' I grew up there, so I know the details that make a story rich in character and setting.

"I often find myself drawn to the troubled child, the outcast child, the spunky misfit. Those are the kids who find their way into my stories.

"I don't write to teach a lesson. I write to take kids to new places, to introduce them to new characters, to show them the potential of the human heart—and sometimes to take them to a familiar and safe place.

"My advice to aspiring writers?

"1. Read.

"2. Never be afraid to write something that's not very good. You can always make it better.

"3. Make friends with a librarian."

Biographical and Critical Sources

BOOKS

O'Connor, Barbara, *Beethoven in Paradise*, Frances Foster Books (New York, NY), 1997.
O'Connor, Barbara, *Moonpie and Ivy*, Frances Foster Books (New York, NY), 2001.
O'Connor, Barbara, *Fame and Glory in Freedom, Georgia*, Frances Foster Books (New York, NY), 2003.

PERIODICALS

Book, July, 2001, Kathleen Odean, review of *Moonpie and Ivy*, p. 81.
Booklist, April 1, 1993, Kay Weisman, review of *Mammolina: A Story about Maria Montessori*, p. 1426; July, 1994, Mary Harris Veeder, review of *Barefoot Dancer: The Story of Isadora Duncan*, p. 1941; September 1, 1996, Denia Hester, review of *The Soldier's Voice: The Story of Ernie Pyle*, p. 123; April 15, 1997, Hazel Rochman, review of *Beethoven in Paradise*, p. 1430; November 1, 1999, Shelley Townsend-Hudson, re-

view of *Me and Rupert Goody,* p. 530; May 15, 2000, Carolyn Phelan, review of *Katherine Dunham: Pioneer of Black Dance,* p. 1740; May 1, 2001, Hazel Rochman, review of *Moonpie and Ivy,* p. 1682; July, 2003, Carolyn Phelan, review of *Fame and Glory in Freedom, Georgia,* p. 1887; August, 2004, Carolyn Phelan, review of *Taking Care of Moses,* p. 1936; March 15, 2007, Stephanie Zvirin, review of *How to Steal a Dog,* p. 49; January 1, 2008, Carolyn Phelan, review of *Greetings from Nowhere,* p. 80.

Book Report, November-December, 1997, Esther Sinofsky, review of *Beethoven in Paradise,* p. 40.

Christian Science Monitor, March 18, 2008, Augusta Scattergood, "*Greetings from Nowhere* Speaks to Young Readers," p. 15.

Horn Book, September, 1999, review of *Me and Rupert Goody,* p. 615; May, 2001, review of *Moonpie and Ivy,* p. 333; July-August, 2003, Kitty Flynn, review of *Fame and Glory in Freedom, Georgia,* p. 465; November-December, 2004, Christine M. Hepperman, review of *Taking Care of Moses,* p. 715; May-June, 2007, Kitty Flynn, review of *How to Steal a Dog,* p. 286.

Kirkus Reviews, May 1, 2003, review of *Fame and Glory in Freedom, Georgia,* p. 681; October 1, 2004, review of *Taking Care of Moses,* p. 966; March 15, 2007, review of *How to Steal a Dog;* February 1, 2008, review of *Greetings from Nowhere.*

Kliatt, May, 2004, Claire Rosser, review of *Moonpie and Ivy,* p. 22.

Language Arts, November, 2002, Junko Yokota and Mingshui Cai, review of *Moonpie and Ivy,* p. 150.

Publishers Weekly, March 3, 1997, review of *Beethoven in Paradise,* p. 76; September 27, 1999, review of *Beethoven in Paradise,* p. 107; December 13, 1999, review of *Me and Rupert Goody,* p. 84; January 22, 2001, review of *Moonpie and Ivy,* p. 325; May 12, 2003, review of *Fame and Glory in Freedom, Georgia,* p. 67; April 2, 2007, review of *How to Steal a Dog,* p. 57.

School Library Journal, April, 1993, Christine A. Moesch, review of *Mammolina,* p. 137; August, 1996, L.R. Little, review of *The Soldier's Voice,* p. 158; April, 1997, Lauralyn Persson, review of *Beethoven in Paradise,* p. 140; October, 1997, Jane Claes, review of *The World at His Fingertips: A Story about Louis Braille,* p. 121; October, 1999, Renee Steinberg, review of *Me and Rupert Goody,* p. 156; July, 2000, Janet Woodward, review of *Katherine Dunham,* p. 120; May, 2001, Katie O'Dell, review of *Moonpie and Ivy,* p. 157; November, 2002, Kristen Oravec, review of *Leonardo da Vinci: Renaissance Genius,* p. 190; June, 2003, Jean Gaffney, review of *Fame and Glory in Freedom, Georgia,* p. 148; October, 2004, Lauralyn Persson, review of *Taking Care of Moses,* p. 173; May, 2007, Robyn Gioia, review of *How to Steal a Dog,* p. 140; March, 2008, Kim Dare, review of *Greetings from Nowhere,* p. 208.

ONLINE

Barbara O'Connor Home Page, http://www.barboconnor.com (September 15, 2008).

PARKER-REES, Guy

Personal

Born in Zimbabwe; married; children: three. *Education:* York University, B.A. (with honours); Hertfordshire University, diploma (art therapy).

Addresses

Home—Brighton, England. *E-mail*—guy@guyparker-rees.com.

Career

Illustrator of children's books, 1989—. Founder of "Art Attack" (mural-painting cooperative); has worked as art teacher in hospitals and as an art therapist in a social services day center.

Awards, Honors

Sheffield Book Award, Dundee Book Award, and Portsmouth Book award, all for *Spookyrumpus* and *Giraffes Can't Dance* by Giles Andreae; Blue Peter Book Award shortlist, 2002, for *Giraffes Can't Dance,* and 2003, for *Quiet!* by Paul Bright.

Writings

SELF-ILLUSTRATED

No Such Thing as Monsters, David Bennett (St. Albans, England), 1993.
Little Lost Jim, Walker (London, England), 1999.

ILLUSTRATOR

Sue Limb, *Mr Loopy and Mrs Snoopy,* Orchard Books (London, England), 1989.
Kenneth Oppel, *Galactic Snapshots,* Hamish Hamilton (London, England), 1993.
Julia Feast and others, editors, *Preparing for Reunion: Adopted People, Adoptive Parents, and Birth Parents Tell Their Stories,* Children's Society (London, England), 1994.
David Parkinson, *The Case of the Pigeon's Pyjamas,* Oxford University Press (Oxford, England), 1994.
Philip Wooderson, *Teacher's Pet,* Orchard Books (London, England), 1995.
Vivian French, *Morris in the Apple Tree,* Collins Children's Books (London, England), 1995.
Vivian French, *Morris the Mouse Hunter,* Collins Children's Books (London, England), 1995.
Alecia McKenzie, *When the Rain Stopped in Natland,* Longman (Harlow, England), 1995.
Andrew Matthews, *The Smugglers of Crab Cove,* Orchard Books (London, England), 1995.
Andrew Matthews, *Super Spy, Miskin Snythely,* Orchard Books, 1995.

Andrew Matthews, *The Great Gold Train Robbery,* Orchard Books (London, England), 1995.

Andrew Matthews, *The Chocolate Bunny Plot,* Orchard Books (London, England), 1995.

Valerie Wilding, *Prince Vince and the Hot Diggory Dogs,* Hodder Children's Books (London, England), 1995.

Valerie Wilding, *Prince Vince and the Case of the Smelly Goat,* Hodder Children's Books (London, England), 1995.

Clare Bevan, *The Shoe Box Millionaire,* Macdonald Young (Hove, England), 1996.

Clive Gifford, *The Really Useless Spy School,* Hodder Children's Books (London, England), 1996.

Enid Blyton, *Bimbo and Topsy,* Bloomsbury (London, England), 1997.

Enid Blyton, *Best Stories for Five Year Olds,* Bloomsbury (London, England), 1997.

Mary Hooper, *Slow Down Sally,* World International (Handforth, England), 1997.

Anita Naik, *Friends or Enemies?,* Hodder Children's Books (London, England), 1997.

Julie Bertagna, *The Ice-Cream Machine,* Mammoth Books (London, England), 1998.

Jan Burchett and Sarah Vogler, *The Terrible Trainer,* Bloomsbury (London, England), 1998.

Jan Burchett and Sarah Vogler, *The Cup Final,* Bloomsbury (London, England), 1998.

Frank Flynn, *Glumf,* Ginn (Aylesbury, England), 1998.

Michaela Morgan, *Dexter's Dinosaurs,* Oxford University Press (Oxford, England), 1998.

Peter Wastall, *Old MacDonald's Recorder Book,* Boosey & Hawkes (London, England), 1998.

Jan Burchett and Sarah Vogler, *Ghost Striker,* Bloomsbury Children's Books (London, England), 1999.

Giles Andreae, *Giraffes Can't Dance,* Orchard Books (London, England), 1999, Orchard Books (New York, NY), 2001.

Alan Durant, *Big Bad Bunny,* Orchard Books (London, England), 2000, Dutton Children's Books (New York, NY), 2001.

Geraldine Taylor, *My Secret Book of Rules,* Ladybird (London, England), 2001.

Tony Mitton, *Down by the Cool of the Pool,* Orchard Books (London, England), 2001, Orchard Books (New York, NY), 2002.

Julia Jarman, *Flying Friends,* Scholastic (New York, NY), 2002.

Julia Jarman, *Owl's Big Mistake,* Scholastic (London, England), 2002.

Julia Jarman, *Mole's Useful Day,* Scholastic (London, England), 2002.

Tony Mitton, *Bumpus Jumpus Dinosaurumpus!,* Orchard Books (London, England), 2003, published as *Dinosaurumpus!,* Orchard Books (New York, NY), 2003.

Julia Jarman, *Rabbit Helps Out,* Scholastic (London, England), 2003.

Giles Andreae, *K Is for Kissing a Cool Kangaroo,* Orchard Books (New York, NY), 2003.

Paul Bright, *Quiet!,* Orchard Books (New York, NY), 2003.

Tony Payne and Jan Payne, *The Hippo-NOT-amus,* Orchard Books (New York, NY), 2004.

Roger McGough and Brian Patten, *The Monsters' Guide to Choosing a Pet,* Penguin Books (London, England), 2004.

Tony Mitton, *Spooky Hour,* Orchard Books (New York, NY), 2004.

Tony Mitton, *Spookyrumpus,* Orchard Books (London, England), 2004.

Richard M.N. Waring, *Ducky Dives In!,* Barron's Educational Series (Hauppage, NY), 2004.

Tony Mitton, *Come to Tea on Planet Zum-Zee,* Orchard Books (London, England), 2005.

Giles Andreae, *The Chimpanzees of Happytown,* Orchard Books (New York, NY), 2006.

Tony Mitton, *Playful Little Penguins,* Walker Books (New York, NY), 2007.

Tony Mitton, *All Afloat on Noah's Boat!,* Orchard Books (New York, NY), 2007.

Karen Wallace, *Thunderbelle's Party,* Orchard Books (London, England), 2007.

Karen Wallace, *Thunderbelle's Spooky Night,* Orchard Books (London, England), 2007.

Karen Wallace, *Thunderbelle's New Home,* Orchard Books (London, England), 2007.

Karen Wallace, *Thunderbelle's Bad Mood,* Orchard Books (London, England), 2007.

Ian Whybrow, *Along Came a Bedtime,* Orchard Books (London, England), 2007.

The humorous cartoon art of Guy Parker-Rees is a perfect complement to Tony Mitton's story for **Down by the Cool of the Pool.** (Orchard Books, 2002. Illustration copyright © 2001 by Guy Parker-Rees. All rights reserved. Reproduced by permission Scholastic, Inc.)

Karen Wallace, *Thunderbelle's Beauty Parlour,* Orchard Books (London, England), 2008.

Karen Wallace, *Thunderbelle's Flying Machine,* Orchard Books (London, England), 2008.

Karen Wallace, *Thunderbelle Goes to the Movies,* Orchard Books (London, England), 2008.

Karen Wallace, *Thunderbelle's Song,* Orchard Books (London, England), 2008.

Contributor to books, including *What's That Noise?,* Ladybird (London, England), 2001; *The Orchard Book of Favourite Rhyme and Verse,* Orchard Books (London, England), 2001; *A Poem a Day,* Orchard Books, 2001; and *With Love,* Orchard Books, 2004.

Sidelights

Guy Parker-Rees is a British artist known for his bright, comic-infused illustrations of animals, monsters, and exotic landscapes. Parker-Rees became a freelance illustrator in 1989 after working as a mural painter and art therapist. He has since provided drawings and paintings to more than fifty children's books published in England and America. In *School Library Journal,* Anna Walls described Parker-Rees's work as "brimming with color, action, and humor."

Most of Parker-Rees's books have been published in the United Kingdom, but more and more of them are making the transit across the Atlantic to the United States. Among these are *Big Bad Bunny* by Alan Durant and *All Afloat on Noah's Boat!* by Tony Mitton. Set in a brightly colored Wild West, *Big Bad Bunny* follows a bad-tempered rabbit as he demands money from more peace-loving animals. In the end, Bad Bunny meets his match and agrees to return all the loot. Connie Fletcher, writing in *Booklist,* liked Parker-Rees's "eyepopping" colors that "bring the desert backdrop to comical life."

In *All Afloat on Noah's Boat!* the tightly packed animals become ever crankier until Noah decides to give a talent show. Each species showcases his or her special abilities, cheering all the others in the process. A *Kirkus Reviews* critic found the book to be a "particularly buoyant version of the world's best-known cruise."

Many of the stories Parker-Rees illustrates are written in rhyme, and some reviewers have noted that the singsong prose and bright visuals make the books appropriate for active story hour reading. Mitton's *Dinosaurumpus!,* for instance, features a cast of stomping, dancing, leaping dinosaurs that revel in their exuberance. According to a *Kirkus Reviews* contributor, the book's paintings "resound and bounce on a glowing color palette." In her *Booklist* review of the same title, Gillian Engberg felt that Parker-Rees's "color-saturated cartoonlike artwork . . . shows the humor and farce" of the story. Parker-Rees strikes a similar lighthearted mood in his artwork for another rhyming story by Mitton, *Down by the Cool of the Pool,* in which farm animals dance to the waterhole and then roll into it en masse. To quote a *Publishers Weekly* correspondent, Parker-Rees's ani-

Parker-Rees teams up with the writing team of Tony and Jan Payne in creating the engaging picture book The Hippo-NOT-amus. (Illustration copyright © 2003 by Guy Parker-Rees. Reproduced by permission of the publisher, Orchard Books, an imprint of Scholastic, Inc.)

mals "radiate an infectious silliness." A *Kirkus Reviews* writer also liked the "wacky romp of a tale," with its "electrically jazzy artwork."

One of Parker-Rees's most popular titles is a collaboration with writer Giles Andreae titled *Giraffes Can't Dance.* Drawing sneers and jeers from the other jungle creatures, Gerald the giraffe tries to overcome his clumsiness and join in the dance. He achieves success when he discovers the perfect music for his taste. In *Publishers Weekly,* a reviewer noted that Parker-Rees's art "exudes a fun, party vibe." Another Parker-Rees animal who challenges convention is Portly the hippopotamus, the star of *The Hippo-NOT-amus* by Tony Payne and Jan Payne. Dissatisfied with his dull life in the mud wallow, Portly sets out to re-invent himself by mimicking other wildlife. Needless to say, he finds it difficult to be like a bat or a giraffe. Be Astengo maintained in *School Library Journal* that Portly's "multifaceted personality is well illustrated."

"'Exuberance is beauty,'once noted by William Blake, is one of my favourite quotations and it sums up what I aspire to with my illustrations," Parker-Rees told *SATA.* "I do think it's very difficult to handle strong colours in a sensitive way, and it's something I struggle with a lot in order to get across the sense of explosive awe I feel for this wonderful world of ours. I'm sorry to say that

it's all too often something that fades with age. We stop looking at the real beauty of the world around us and those funny apes that have taken it over.

"I particularly like painting animals because they never make the reader feel excluded. There isn't that faint awareness the reader and child might feel that the people in the story don't look like the people in 'my' family. Everyone loves animas and maybe has enough DNA in common to identify with them!

"I'm lucky enough to work with some of the best poets writing for children at the moment and often the images just leap from the page as I read the stories for the first time. All I have to do is jot them down.

"Although I love illustrating big bold feelings, I particularly like capturing the subtler moments, maybe a little character looking on from the sidelines, small gestures of contact between characters going on in the background, the one who's a little bit left behind and running to catch up, the one who's finding it all a bit too much! All those feelings a child might see and recognize from their own lives.

"I do love my job!"

Biographical and Critical Sources

PERIODICALS

Booklist, May 1, 2001, Connie Fletcher, review of *Big Bad Bunny,* p. 1689; January 1, 2003, Gillian Engberg, review of *Dinosaurumpus!,* p. 908.
Kirkus Reviews, May 1, 2002, review of *Down by the Cool of the Pool,* p. 662; March 1, 2003, review of *Dinosaurumpus!,* p. 393; July 1, 2004, review of *Spooky Hour,* p. 634; May 1, 2007, review of *All Afloat on Noah's Boat!*
Publishers Weekly, September 10, 2001, review of *Giraffes Can't Dance,* p. 91; April 15, 2002, review of *Down by the Cool of the Pool,* p. 62; January 6, 2003, review of *Dinosaurumpus!,* p. 57; May 14, 2007, review of *All Afloat on Noah's Boat!,* p. 58.
School Library Journal, February, 2001, Sue Sherif, review of *Big Bad Bunny,* p. 99; October, 2001, Kathleen Simonetta, review of *Giraffes Can't Dance,* p. 104; July, 2002, Elaine Morgan, review of *Down by the Cool of the Pool,* p. 96; March, 2003, Dona Ratterree, review of *Dinosaurumpus!,* p. 200; December, 2003, Anna DeWind Walls, review of *K Is for Kissing a Cool Kangaroo,* p. 102; December, 2003, Andrea Tarr, review of *Quiet!,* p. 104; August, 2004, Catherine Threadgill, review of *Spooky Hour,* p. 90; September, 2004, Be Astengo, review of *The Hippo-NOT-a-mus,* p. 177; May, 2007, Kathy Piehl, review of *All Afloat on Noah's Boat!,* p. 104; December, 2007, Catherine Callegari, review of *Playful Little Penguins,* p. 96.

ONLINE

Guy Parker-Rees Home Page, http://www.guyparkerrees.com (September 8, 2008).

Orchard Books Web site, http://www.orchardbooks.co.uk/ (September 8, 2008), "Guy Parker-Rees."

*   *   *

PEDERSEN, Janet

Personal

Married; children: one son. *Education:* Art Center College of Design, graduate.

Addresses

Home—Brooklyn, NY. *E-mail*—janettom@earthlink.net.

Career

Children's book author and illustrator. *Exhibitions:* Work included in Society of Illustrators "Original Art Show."

Writings

SELF-ILLUSTRATED

Millie in the Meadow, Candlewick Press (Cambridge, MA), 2003.
Millie Wants to Play, Candlewick Press (Cambridge, MA), 2004.
Pino and the Signora's Pasta, Candlewick Press (Cambridge, MA), 2005.
Houdini the Amazing Caterpillar, Clarion Books (New York, NY), 2008.

ILLUSTRATOR

Ferida Wolff, *A Weed Is a Seed,* Houghton Mifflin (Boston, MA), 1996.
Vincent Courtney, *Virtual Fred and the Big Dip,* Random House (New York, NY), 1997.
Karen Wagner, *A Friend like Ed,* Walker (New York, NY), 1998.
Joanne Rocklin, *Jake and the Copycats,* Yearling First Choice Chapter Book (New York, NY), 1998.
Karen Wagner, *Bravo, Mildred and Ed,* Walker (New York, NY), 2000.
Jackie French Koller, *Baby for Sale,* Marshall Cavendish (New York, NY), 2002.
Eileen Spinelli, *Bath Time,* Marshall Cavendish (New York, NY), 2003.
Toni Teevin, *What to Do? What to Do?,* Clarion Books (New York, NY), 2006.
Cece Meng, *The Wonderful Thing about Hiccups,* Clarion Books (New York, NY), 2007.
Alison Jackson, *Thea's Tree,* Dutton Children's Books (New York, NY), 2008.
Irene Breznak, *Sneezy Louise,* Random House (New York, NY), 2009.

Sidelights

Janet Pedersen began her career illustrating children's books after graduating with honors from the Art Center College of Design. Her signature style, which involves expressive watercolors, won her accolades in the profession and led to her inclusion in the prestigious "Original Art Show" hosted by the Society of Illustrators. After creating art for many books by other writer, Pedersen decided to write and illustrate her own books, and has since produced books that include *Millie in the Meadow* and *Houdini the Amazing Caterpillar.*

One of the first books Pedersen illustrated, Jackie French Kroller's *Baby for Sale,* finds that that big-brother rabbit Peter has finally had enough of his toddler baby sister Emily after Emily throws his prize baseball cap into the toilet. Wheeling her around the neighborhood, Peter attempts to sell the rambunctious baby bunny to other families, but she does such annoying things as poop in her diapers at the most inopportune moments. After narrowly saving Emily when she tries to toddle out into the street, Peter realizes that his little sister is not so annoying after all. In *Kirkus Reviews* a critic praised Pedersen's expressive artwork, writing that her paintings cast "her all-rabbit cast in fine-lined, pale watercolors, capturing both Peter's irritation and Emily's innate cuteness." Lauren Peterson, writing in *Booklist* observed that the "humorous watercolor illustrations depict Emily in all her naughty glory," and in *School Library Journal* Rosalyn Pierini asserted that the "sweet . . . family story" in *Baby for Sale* "is well matched by humorous cartoon illustrations with child appeal."

Eileen Spinelli's humorous *Bath Time* follows the adventures of a mother penguin as she tries to get her energetic son into the bathtub. While penguins normally

Janet Pedersen introduces young children to a group of kind-hearted farmyard friends in her self-illustrated **Millie Wants to Play.** (Copyright © 2004 by Janet Pedersen. All rights reserved. Reproduced by permission of the publisher Candlewick Press, Inc., Somerville, MA.)

take to water, this young bird has a hard time settling down and getting clean. After scampering around the house collecting all sorts of toys to play with in the tub, the penguin finds that there is no room left for him. A *Kirkus Reviews* contributor praised Pedersen's art for *Bath Time,* writing that her "lightly smudged and simply lined drawings are an amusing pairing with the rhyming text." Carolyn Phelan, writing in *Booklist,* concluded that the artist's contributions, done "in charcoal pencil with watercolor and gouache, reflects the innocent and lightly humorous tone of the verse."

In Toni Teevin's *What to Do? What to Do?* a lonely village woman named Sophie gets tired of talking to all the objects in her house. One day, she starts feeding the neighboring birds with her delicious homemade bread. Soon, she is inundated by birds and, after visiting a fortune-teller, decides to use the bread to feed her human neighbors instead. In *Horn Book,* Vicky Smith wrote that "Pedersen's loose line-and-watercolor illustrations are a perfect complement to [Tevin's] . . . text." Carolyn Janssen, reviewing the book for *School Library Journal,* noted that "the light, airy watercolors reflect her bright outlook," while a *Kirkus Reviews* critic described the illustrator's watercolor images as "light as air and cartoon-silly. . . . Ever so clever and charming." Gillian Engberg, writing in *Booklist,* similarly concluded that Pedersen's "appealing illustrations capture the tall-tale action and expressive characters with spidery, ink lines and bright paint washes."

Pedersen's first original self-illustrated book, *Millie in the Meadow,* introduces readers to Millie, a spindly-legged calf as she discovers an artist sketching in her pasture. Curiously, the calf keeps guessing the subject of each of the artist's sketches until, at last, he draws her. In *Kirkus Reviews* a critic predicted that "young readers will enjoy guessing the animals from the descriptions" provided in Pedersen's text. A *Publishers Weekly* reviewer also praised *Millie in the Meadow,* finding that Pederen's "unprepossessing tale of a cow with a toddler attitude teaches animal attributes as it goes along." Karin Snelson, writing in *Booklist,* believes that "the inquisitive, long-lashed, tail-swishing Millie will win the hearts of preschoolers."

Millie returns in *Millie Wants to Play!,* as she journeys through her meadow, awaiting the morning noises made by the other animals that signal that it is time to play. Donna Marie Wagner wrote in her *School Library Journal* review that *Millie Wants to Play!* will engage younger readers as they identify each animal by the noises it makes. She dubbed the book "a delightful read for one-on-one sharing or for storytime," while *Booklist* critic Ilene Cooper wrote that Pedersen's *Millie Wants to Play!* serves up "much good humor and spunk."

Another original picture book by Pedersen, *Pino and the Signora's Pasta* follows a homeless cat in Rome who is tired of the pasta served to him every day by the Signora. Traveling around the city, the kitty samples a variety of different cuisine, trips a waiter, and is thrown out of a restaurant. Finding that nothing is as good as the Signora's pasta, Pino realizes that the reason is because the woman's food is full of love. Shawn Brommer, writing in *School Library Journal,* wrote that "Pedersen's text is bouncy and the humorous dialogue gives depth to the feline protagonist," while Cooper dubbed *Pino and the Signora's Pasta* "full of life."

Biographical and Critical Sources

PERIODICALS

Booklist, September 15, 1998, Kathleen Squires, review of *A Friend like Ed,* p. 241; September 1, 2002, Lauren Peterson, review of *Baby for Sale,* p. 136; March 15, 2003, Carolyn Phelan, review of *Bath Time,* p. 1334; April 1, 2003, Karin Snelson, review of *Millie in the Meadow,* p. 1404; April 1, 2004, Ilene Cooper, review of *Millie Wants to Play!,* p. 1369; September 1, 2005, Ilene Cooper, review of *Pino and the Signora's Pasta,* p. 145; May 1, 2006, Gillian Engberg, review of *What to Do? What to Do?,* p. 94.
Horn Book, May-June, 2006, Vicky Smith, review of *What to Do?,* p. 305.
Kirkus Reviews, August 1, 2002, review of *Baby for Sale,* p. 1134; February 15, 2003, review of *Millie in the Meadow,* p. 314; March 1, 2003, review of *Bath Time,* p. 398; February 15, 2004, review of *Millie Wants to Play!,* p. 183; August 15, 2005, review of *Pino and the Signora's Pasta,* p. 920; June 15, 2006, review of *What to Do?,* p. 638.
Publishers Weekly, September 21, 1998, review of *A Friend like Ed,* p. 85; April 15, 1996, review of *A Weed Is a Seed,* p. 67; August 12, 2002, review of *Baby for Sale,* p. 299; January 6, 2003, review of *Millie in the Meadow,* p. 57; March 3, 2003, review of *Bath Time,* p. 74.
School Library Journal, September, 2002, Rosalyn Pierini, review of *Baby for Sale,* p. 196; September, 2000, Karen Land, review of *Bravo, Mildred and Ed!,* p. 210; May, 2004, Donna Marie Wagner, review of *Millie Wants to Play!,* p. 121; September, 2005, Shawn Brommer, review of *Pino and the Signora's Pasta,* p. 184; July, 2006, Carolyn Janssen, review of *What to Do?,* p. 87; November, 2007, Linda M. Kenton, review of *The Wonderful Thing about Hiccups.*

ONLINE

Houghton Mifflin Web site, http://www.houghtonmifflinbooks.com/ (September 25, 2008), "Janet Pedersen."
I-Spot Web site, http://www.theispot.com/ (September 1, 2008), "Janet Pedersen."

*   *   *

PETROSINO, Tamara

Personal

Female. *Education:* Rhode Island School of Design, B.F.A. (illustration), 1998.

Addresses

Agent—Herman Agency, 350 Central Park W., New York, NY 10025. *E-mail*—hello@tamarapetrosino.com.

Career

Illustrator and graphic designer. Formerly worked for an illustrator's design studio and a publishing company.

Illustrator

Donna Kosow, *Rabbit Stew,* Grosset & Dunlap (New York, NY), 1999.

Arthur Bloch, *Murphy's Law: What Else Can Go Wrong in the 21st Century!* (for adults), Price Stern Sloan, 1999.

Margo Linn, *The Worst Haircut Ever!,* Scholastic (New York, NY), 2002.

Donna Jo Napoli and Marie Kane, *Rocky: The Cat Who Barks,* Dutton (New York, NY), 2002.

Jayne Harvey, *Cat Show,* Grosset & Dunlap (New York, NY), 2003.

Gail Herman, *Sam's First Library Card,* Grosset & Dunlap (New York, NY), 2003.

Stephen Krensky, *There Once Was a Very Odd School, and Other Lunch-Box Limericks,* Dutton (New York, NY), 2004.

Coleen Murtagh Paratore, *How Prudence Proovit Proved the Truth about Fairy Tales,* Simon & Schuster (New York, NY), 2004.

Mark Shulman, *AA Is for Aardvark,* Sterling Publishing (New York, NY), 2005.

Wendy Wax, *Class Picture Day,* Grosset & Dunlap (New York, NY), 2005.

David Crawley, *Cat Poems,* Wordsong (Honesdale, PA), 2005.

Harriet Ziefert, *No Plain Hair!,* Sterling Publishing (New York, NY), 2006.

Mark Shulman, *A Is for Zebra,* Sterling Publishing (New York, NY), 2006.

Jacqueline Horsfall, *Kid's Kookiest Knock-Knocks,* Sterling Publishing (New York, NY), 2006.

Siobhan Ciminera, *The Spookiest Jack O'Lantern Ever!,* Grosset & Dunlap (New York, NY), 2007.

Siobhan Ciminera, *The Funniest Bunny Ever!,* Grosset & Dunlap (New York, NY), 2007.

Siobhan Ciminera, *The Coolest Snowman Ever!,* Grosset & Dunlap (New York, NY), 2007.

David Crawley, *Dog Poems,* Wordsong (Honesdale, PA), 2007.

Siobhan Ciminera, *The Silliest Valentine Ever!,* Grosset & Dunlap (New York, NY), 2007.

Tamara Petrosino contributes her quirky cartoon art to Dave Crawley's simply titled and feline-inspired Cat Poems. (Boyds Mills Press, 2005. Illustration copyright © 2005 by Tamara Petrosino. Reproduced by permission.)

In **Dog Poems** *Petrosino and Crawley reunite to pay homage to another sector of the animal kingdom.* (Wordsong, 2007. Illustration copyright © 2007 by Tamara Petrosino. All rights reserved. Reproduced by permission.)

Sidelights

Quirky animal characters take center stage in the colorful cartoon art of Tamara Petrosino. Since earning her degree at the prestigious Rhode Island School of Design, Petrosino has created illustrations that highlight a number of children's books. In addition to collaborating with author Dave Crawley on *Dog Poems* and *Cat Poems,* her work also brings to life texts by Donna Jo Napoli, Harriet Ziefert, Stephen Krensky, Mark Shulman, and Siobhan Ciminera. Reviewing her work for Krensky's *There Once Was a Very Odd School,* Kay Weisman noted in *Booklist* that "Petrosino's colorful, cartoon-like illustrations extend the humor of the rhymes, sometimes in surprising ways." "Exaggerated facial expressions and body language are used to great effect" in her work for Napoli's *Rocky: The Cat Who Barked,* concluded Lauren Peterson in a *Booklist* review.

An illustrated collection of humorous poems about cats, Crawley's simply titled *Cat Poems* "addresses feline types and idiosyncrasies with unapologetic adoration," according to a *Publishers Weekly* reviewer. Petrosino's cartoon illustrations track Crawley's twenty-four-poem tour of cat breeds, from Devon rex and Persian to Siamese, and range "from full-spread compositions to . . . very clever vignettes" rendered in comic-book style, wrote the *Publishers Weekly* critic. In *School Library Journal,* Shawn Brommer concluded of *Cat Poems* that "Petrosino's watercolor illustrations match the mood of the light verse," and a *Kirkus Reviews* contributor concluded that Crawley's "rollicking rhymed tributes" to the feline species team well with the illustrator's "simple, vivacious cartoon portraits."

Author and illustrator team up again for *Dog Poems,* in which Petrosino's "comic ink-and-watercolor illustra-

tions perfectly reflect the lighthearted mood" of Crawley's verse. Here the focus is exclusively canine and strays from poodles to sheepdogs to pups of a fiercer nature. In *Kirkus Reviews* a reviewer praised the "additional comic touches" Petrosino gives to Crawley's "casual, humorous" poems and remarked that the illustrator includes "dog owners of varying ethnicities." Writing that "there's lots of humor packed in the poems," *Booklist* contributor Ilene Cooper added that Petrosino's illustrations for *Dog Poems* "has a bounce all its own."

Praised by a *Publishers Weekly* contributor for its "silly, often inventive pages," *AA Is for Aardvark* pairs Petrosino with the equally whimsical Schulman. As its title suggests, the book focuses on words containing repeated letters, from "Boo" to "Yummy." In *School Library Journal* Steven Engelfried commented on the collaborators' "inventive approach" and added that the artist's "playful" images "depict a large cast of characters interacting in . . . humorous settings." While Schulman's wordplay is designed to engage beginning readers, "the farce of [Petrosino's] . . . pictures will appeal to young children," predicted *Booklist* critic Hazel Rochman in a review of the author and illustrator's equally unconventionally titled companion volume *A Is for Zebra*.

Biographical and Critical Sources

PERIODICALS

Booklist, March 1, 2002, Lauren Peterson, review of *Rocky: The Cat Who Barks*, p. 1143; June 1, 2004, GraceAnne A. DeCandido, review of *How Prudence Proovit Proved the Truth about Fairy Tales*, p. 1744; September 1, 2004, Kay Weisman, review of *There Once Was a Very Odd School, and Other Lunch-Box Limericks* p. 117; March 15, 2006, Hazel Rochman, review of *A Is for Zebra*, p. 51; September 1, 2007, Ilene Cooper, review of *Dog Poems*, p. 121.

Kirkus Reviews, December 15, 2001, review of *Rocky*, p. 1761; June 1, 2004, review of *How Prudence Proovit Proved the Truth about Fairy Tales*, p. 540; March 15, 2005, review of *Cat Poems*, p. 349; July 15, 2007, review of *Dog Poems*.

Publishers Weekly, December 10, 2001, review of *Rocky*, p. 69; July 5, 2004, review of *How Prudence Proovit Proved the Truth about Fairy Tales*, p. 55; March 14, 2005, review of *Cat Poems*, p. 67; November 14, 2005, review of *AA Is for Ardvark*, p. 68.

School Library Journal, March, 2002, Cathie E. Bashaw, review of *Rocky*, p. 198; December, 2003, Lisa Smith, review of *Cat Show*, p. 114; July, 2004, Grace Oliff, review of *How Prudence Proovit Proved the Truth about Fairy Tales*, p. 84; August, 2004, Doris Losey, review of *There Once Was a Very Odd School, and Other Lunch-Box Limericks*, p. 110; June, 2005, Shawn Brommer, review of *Cat Poems*, p. 136; February, 2006, Steven Engelfried, review of *AA Is for Aardvark*, p. 109; August, 2007, Donna Cardon, review of *Dog Poems*, p. 97.

ONLINE

Tamara Petrosino Home Page, http://www.tamarapet rosino.com (September 15, 2008).

* * *

PINKNEY, Sandra L. 1965-

Personal

Born 1965, in Vahalla, NY; daughter of Alfred (a presser) and Frances (an insurance adjuster) McRae; married Myles C. Pinkney (a photographer); children: Myles "Leon" Jr., Charnelle-Rene, Rashad. *Education:* State University of New York, Empire State College, C.D.A. (early childhood education); attended Duchess Community College. *Religion:* Baptist. *Hobbies and other interests:* Running, softball, singing, acting, crocheting, and collecting angels.

Addresses

Home—30 Spring St., Poughkeepsie, NY 12601. *Agent*—Sheldon Fogelman, 10 E. 40th St., New York, NY 10016.

Career

Author and educator. Lil' Praiser's Christian Day-Care, Poughkeepsie, NY, director, 1996—.

Member

National Association for the Education of Young Children, National Black Child Development Institute.

Awards, Honors

Image Award for Outstanding Children's Literary Works, National Association for the Advancement of Colored People, for *Shades of Black: A Celebration of Our Children*, 2001.

Writings

Shades of Black: A Celebration of Our Children, photographs by husband Myles C. Pinkney, Scholastic (New York, NY), 2000.

A Rainbow All around Me, photographs by Myles C. Pinkney, Scholastic (New York, NY), 2002.

Read and Rise, photographs by Myles C. Pinkney, foreword by Maya Angelou, Scholastic (New York, NY), 2006.

I Am Latino: The Beauty in Me, photographs by Myles C. Pinkney, Little, Brown (New York, NY), 2007.

Sidelights

Sandra L. Pinkney is the award-winning author of picture books such as *Shades of Black: A Celebration of Our Children*, all illustrate with color photographs by

Sandra L. Pinkney (Reproduced by permission.)

her husband, Myles C. Pinkney. Her books celebrate diversity by displaying photographs of children from many ethnicities. They encourage children to appreciate multicultural environments and emphasize the fun of reading. Through her work, Pinkney joins the clan headed by her husband's parents, prominent children's-book creators Jerry and Gloria Pinkney.

In *Shades of Black* Pinkney describes the many different skin, eye, and hair tones of African-American children, both verbally and visually. "I came up with the idea for the book while sitting down in the library and reading a book on how to write poetry," she once told *SATA*. "It started out 'I like chocolate.' I thought to myself, 'Yeah, I like chocolate.' It went on to say, 'Chocolate is sweet.' I thought again, 'Yeah, it is sweet. Hey! I could write this.' . . . But I can't write about chocolate. That's been done, I told myself. I looked around and looked at my hands and said, 'I am black.' I realized I could write about how I am black and differences and beauty in the black race." While Tammy K. Baggett, writing in *School Library Journal*, praised *Shades of Black* as "vivid," a *Kirkus Reviews* critic wrote that its "patterned text [is] full of rich vocabulary." Pinkney's work "can certainly be appreciated by children of any color," concluded *Booklist* reviewer Denia Hester.

A Rainbow All around Me features a wider multiethnic cast, as youngsters of all shades represent each of the colors of the rainbow. Green refers not to eye color, but to objects alongside the child pictured, such as grass and Granny Smith apples. "Kids will enjoy reading the jazzy lyrical text," predicted a contributor to *Black Is-*

sues Book Review. In *Kirkus Reviews* a contributor observed that Myles Pinkney's photographs "take center stage," but added that Sandra's "spare text with a poetic beat carries the reader from page to page." In *Booklist* Shelley Townsend-Hudson concluded that in *A Rainbow All around Me* "the message of racial awareness and tolerance is well served."

The Pinkneys created *Read and Rise* as a contribution to a program designed by Scholastic and the National Urban League to promote reading. Particularly geared toward African-American youngsters, the book emphasizes the power of reading and the fun it can bring. The children pictured read about professions and adventures, then have similar adventures themselves, dressing up as firefighters, astronauts, or ballerinas. "Powerful verbs match the vivid portrayal of children succeeding," wrote Alexa L. Sandman in *School Library Journal*, while Julie Cummins noted in *Booklist* that *Read and Rise* serves as "an effective tool for encouraging reading for every child."

With *I Am Latino: The Beauty in Me* the Pinkneys celebrate Latino culture, showing family members, foods, and dances. Sandra's text is paired with Spanish-language translations of simple phrases ranging from goodbye/adios and sister/hermana, to more complex food names like banana milkshake/batido de plantano.

In **Shades of Black** *Sandra L. Pinkney teams up with husband and photographer Myles C. Pinkney.* (Scholastic, 2000. Photograph copyright © 2000 by Myles C. Pinkney. Reproduced by permission of Scholastic, Inc.)

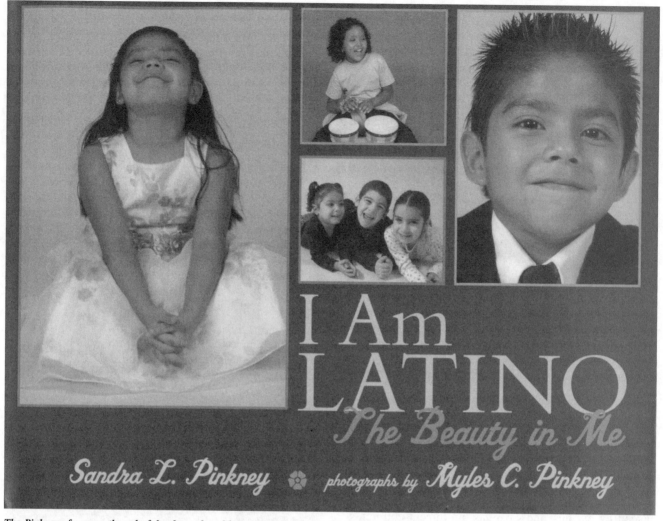

The Pinkneys focus on the colorful culture shared by many young Americans in the collaborative picture book I Am Latino. (Little, Brown & Company, 2007. Photograph copyright © 2007 by Myles C. Pinkney. All rights reserved. Reproduced by permission.)

"Readers will take pleasure in this quiet, joyful book," Melissa Christy Buron predicted in her favorable *School Library Journal* review.

Pinkney once told *SATA:* "My favorite time to write is early in the morning, 4:00 a.m. before the birds get up. I believe that is when God gives me my greatest inspirations. I enjoy writing poetry, but I also enjoy writing short stories and inspirational stories."

Biographical and Critical Sources

PERIODICALS

Black Issues Book Review, March-April, 2002, Lynda Jones, review of *A Rainbow All around Me,* p. 68.

Booklist, November 1, 2000, Denia Hester, review of *Shades of Black: A Celebration of Our Children,* p. 548; February 1, 2002, Shelley Townsend-Hudson, review of *A Rainbow All around Me,* p. 948; February 1, 2006, Julie Cummins, review of *Read and Rise,* p. 70.

Bulletin of the Center for Children's Books, January, 2001, review of *Shades of Black,* p. 193.

Kirkus Reviews, December 1, 2000, review of *Shades of Black;* December 1, 2001, review of *A Rainbow All around Me,* p. 1689; December 1, 2005, review of *Read and Rise,* p. 1278; June 1, 2007, review of *I Am Latino: The Beauty in Me.*

Language Arts, September, 2002, Daniel L. Darigan, "Sorting out the Pinkneys," pp. 75-80.

Publishers Weekly, November 20, 2000, "Excursions in Diversity," p. 70; January 28, 2002, review of *A Rainbow All around Me,* p. 293.

School Library Journal, December, 2000, Tammy K. Baggett, review of *Shades of Black,* p. 135; March, 2002, Grace Oliff, review of *A Rainbow All around Me,* p. 198; January, 2006, Alexa L. Sandman, review of *Read and Rise,* p. 112; July, 2007, Melissa Christy Buron, review of *I Am Latino,* p. 83.

ONLINE

Calvin College Web site, http://www.calvin.edu/ (April 6, 2006), Myrna Anderson, "Pinkneys Make Festival a Family Affair."

* * *

PORTER, Pamela 1956-

Personal

Born 1956, in NM; married; children: Cecilia, Drew.

Addresses

Home and office—Sidney, British Columbia, Canada.

Career

Author.

Awards, Honors

Governor General's Literary Award for Children's Fiction, 2005, Canadian Children's Literature Award, and Geoffrey Bilson Award for Historical Fiction for Young People, both 2006, and Silver Birch Award nomination, and Rocky Mountain Book Award shortlist, both 2007, all for *The Crazy Man;* Jane Addams Award, Jane Addams Peace Association, 2006.

Writings

JUVENILE FICTION

Sky, illustrated by Mary Jane Gerber, Groundwood Books (Toronto, Ontario, Canada), 2004.
The Crazy Man, Groundwood Books (Toronto, Ontario, Canada), 2005.
Stones Call Out, Coteau Books (Regina, Saskatchewan, Canada), 2006.
Yellow Moon, Apple Moon, illustrated by Matt James, Groundwood Books (Toronto, Ontario, Canada), 2008.

OTHER

Poems for the Luminous World, Frog Hollow Press (Victoria, British Columbia, Canada), 2002.

Also author of lyrics for *Songs for the Journey of Remembrance* (sound recording).

Sidelights

Award-winning young-adult writer Pamela Porter takes her inspiration from the significant settings in her life. Her adopted country of Canada, as well as her native state of New Mexico, figures prominently in her work. Porter's skill at weaving fact and fiction into inspirational narratives is considered a hallmark of her fiction, which includes the novels *The Crazy Man* and *Stones Call Out.*

Porter's first book for middle-grade readers, *Sky,* is based on a first-person account of the major floods that washed over the northwestern United States in 1964. The novel focuses on eleven-year old Georgia, who lives with her grandparents in Blackfoot Nation territory in Montana. After days of rain, the family narrowly escapes a flood that destroys their home and barn. Taking shelter in a local school, the girl and her grandparents become the focus of mistreatment and prejudice when their Caucasian neighbors receive better treatment than they do. Returning home to clean up the rubble that is all that remains of her grandparents' home, Georgia discovers that a young foal has escaped the calamity. She turns all her energy into saving the foal, which she names Sky, and through her caring actions Georgia turns a tragic situation into something positive. Susan P. Bloom, reviewing *Sky* for *Horn Book,* asserted that readers will be "won over by Georgia's forthright personality and fresh, first-person voice." Kristen Oravec, writing in *School Library Journal,* believed that Porter's "simple tale elegantly showcases a girl's story, of triumph over adversity."

Porter's award-winning novel *The Crazy Man* was based on the family wheat farm in rural Saskatchewan where her husband was raised. In the novel, which is set in the mid-1960s, twelve-year-old Emaline endures an accident in which she loses a leg. Distraught by this tragedy, the girl's newly widowed mother must now hire Angus, a man from the local mental hospital, to help put in the new crop. Finding Angus to be an odd but gentle man, Emaline befriends him and finds jobs to keep him busy around the farm. Although she is confused that Angus is feared by many in town, when the man saves a local girl from tragedy, Emaline is reassured about human nature. Martha V. Parravano, writing in *Horn Book,* called *The Crazy Man* "a touching portrait of a real-seeming girl, set in a well-delineated time and place." *School Library Journal* critic Julie Webb noted that, "subtle in its themes and organization," Porter's novel "is pure pleasure, offering lessons about love, loyalty, and loss." In *Resource Links,* Angela Thompson praised the verse novel, asserting that "what makes this book interesting is the format, a story written as poetry." Vikki VanSickle, writing in *Canadian Review of Materials,* concluded of *The Crazy Man* that in this "deceptively simple" novel "Porter explores large issues such as prejudice, fear, and disability with grace and honesty," studding his story with "beautiful, shining moments of hope."

Featuring artwork by Matt James, Porter's picture book *Yellow Moon, Apple Moon* was inspired by a family story. "One night late in summer when I was cleaning up the kitchen after dinner, I looked out of the window and saw the great harvest moon rising just beyond the hills over the valley . . .," she recalled on the Groundwood Books Web site. "We all watched in awe, quietly, when little Drew said, 'Yellow moon. Apple moon.'" This phrase, woven into a New Mexico lullaby Porter had heard as a child, became the core of the picture

book. A *Kirkus Reviews* writer praised *Yellow Moon, Apple Moon,* writing that "verbal and visual images of nighttime guarantee safe passage to dreamland." Jessica Kelley, writing in *Quill & Quire,* concluded that the picture book "has its own brand of charm, and many young readers will identify with the contented child sleeping peacefully under the moon."

Biographical and Critical Sources

PERIODICALS

Canadian Review of Materials, December 9, 2005, Vikki VanSickle, review of *The Crazy Man.*

Horn Book, January-February, 2005, Susan P. Bloom, review of *Sky,* p. 97; January-February, 2006, Martha V. Parravano, review of *The Crazy Man,* p. 86.

Kirkus Reviews, February 15, 2008, review of *Yellow Moon, Apple Moon.*

Quill & Quire, March, 2008, Jessica Kelley, review of *Yellow Moon, Apple Moon.*

Resource Links, February, 2005, Elaine Rospad, review of *Sky,* p. 20; December, 2005, Angela Thompson, review of *The Crazy Man,* p. 35.

School Library Journal, April, 2005, Kristen Oravec, review of *Sky,* p. 108; December, 2005, Julie Webb, review of *The Crazy Man,* p. 152.

ONLINE

Groundwood Books Web site, http://www.groundwood books.com/ (September 25, 2008), interview with Porter.

R

ROGERS, Sherry

Personal
Married. *Education:* Foothill College, B.S. (graphic design/graphic arts).

Addresses
Home—Rocklin, CA. *Agent*—Chris Tugeau, 3009 Margaret Jones La., Williamsburg, VA 23185. *E-mail*—sr@ sherry-rogers.com.

Career
Digital illustrator. Former graphic designer and technical illustrator; illustrator of children's books, 2004—.

Member
Picture Book Artists, Society of Children's Book Writers and Illustrators.

Illustrator
Katherine Rawson, *If You Were a Parrot,* Sylvan Dell Publishing (Mt. Pleasant, SC), 2006.

Charline Profiri, *Counting Little Geckos,* RGU Group (Tempe, AZ), 2006.

Terri Fields, *Burro's Tortillas,* Sylvan Dell Publishing (Mt. Pleasant, SC), 2007.

Susan K. Mitchell, *Kersplatypus,* Sylvan Dell Publishing (Mt. Pleasant, SC), 2008.

Barbara Mariconda, *Sort It Out!,* Sylvan Dell Publishing (Mt. Pleasant, SC), 2008.

Kimberly Hutmacher, *Paws, Claws, Hands, and Feet,* Sylvan Dell Publishing (Mt. Pleasant, CA), 2009.

Bettina Restrepo, *Moose and Magpie,* Sylvan Dell Publishing (Mt. Pleasant, CA), 2009.

Also illustrator of educational materials for McGraw Hill and Oxford University Press.

Biographical and Critical Sources

PERIODICALS

Kirkus Reviews, July 1, 2006, review of *If You Were a Parrot,* p. 681; May 15, 2007, review of *Burro's Tortillas.*
Publishers Weekly, February 11, 2008, review of *Kersplatypus,* p. 68.
School Library Journal, December, 2006, Kathleen Whalin, review of *If You Were a Parrot,* p. 114; August, 2008, Patricia Manning, review of *Kersplatypus,* p. 99.

ONLINE

Sherry Rogers Home Page, http://www.sherry-rogers.com (September 15, 2008).*

* * *

ROSENTHAL, Marc 1949-

Personal
Born 1949; married; wife's name Eileen; children: Willem. *Education:* Graduated from Princeton University, 1971; State University of New York, M.F.A., 1978. *Hobbies and other interests:* Ashtanga yoga, cooking, eating.

Addresses
Home and office—Lenox, MA. *Agent*—Gerald & Cullen Rapp, 420 Lexington Ave., New York, NY, 10170; inforappart.com. *E-mail*—marc@marc-rosenthal.com.

Career
Designer, sequential artist, and book illustrator. Worked as a graphic designer and illustrator for Milton Glaser, New York, NY; freelance illustrator, 1983—; clients in-

clude AT&T and McCann-Erickson. Creator of Earth 2U (traveling exhibition on geography for children), with Smithsonian Institution and National Geographic Society.

Writings

SELF-ILLUSTRATED

Phooey!, Joanna Cotler Books (New York, NY), 2007.

ILLUSTRATOR

Paul Rosenthal, *Where on Earth: A Geografunny Guide to the Globe,* Knopf (New York, NY), 1992.

Kate Banks, *Peter and the Talking Shoes,* Knopf (New York, NY), 1994.

Mem Fox, *The Straight Line Wonder,* Mondo (Greenvale, NY), 1996.

Daniil Kharms, *First, Second,* translated from the Russian by Richard Pevear, Farrar, Straus & Giroux (New York, NY), 1996.

Paul Rosenthal, *Yo, Aesop!: Get a Load of These Fables,* Simon & Schuster (New York, NY), 1997.

David Schiller, *The Runaway Beard,* Workman Publishing (New York, NY), 1998.

Samuel Marshak, *The Absentminded Fellow,* translated from the Russian by Richard Pevear, Farrar, Straus & Giroux (New York, NY), 1999.

Michael Abrams and Jeffrey Winters, *Dr. Broth and Ollie's Brain-boggling Search for the Lost Luggage: Across Time and Space in Eighty Puzzles,* Fireside (New York, NY), 2000.

Andrea Zimmerman and David Clemesha, *Dig!,* Harcourt (Orlando, FL), 2004.

Contributor to *Little Lit Two: Strange Stories for Strange Kids,* edited by Art Spiegelman and Françoise Mouly, RAW (New York, NY), 2001. Contributor to periodicals, including *Time, Newsweek, Fortune, New Yorker,* and *Atlantic Monthly.*

Sidelights

Marc Rosenthal is a designer, sequential artist, and illustrations whose work has appeared in such publications as *Time, Newsweek,* and the *New Yorker.* He has also provided the art for several critically acclaimed children's books, including *First, Second* by Russian author Daniil Kharms and *Dig!* by the husband-and-wife team of Andrea Zimmerman and David Clemesha. Rosenthal has also produced a self-illustrated title, *Phooey!*

Rosenthal's first picture book, *Where on Earth: A Geografunny Guide to the Globe,* was a collaboration with his brother, author Paul Rosenthal. The work fea-

tures a variety of humorous mnemonic devices to help young readers learn geographical terms. "Cartoony illustrations extend the academic antics," a contributor in *Publishers Weekly* observed. The duo have also teamed up on *Yo, Aesop!: Get a Load of These Fables,* which includes zany retellings of well-known tales. Rosenthal's "pen-and-ink and watercolor illustrations elevate the tales with a 1940s color scheme and imaginative perspectives," remarked a *Publishers Weekly* critic, and Susan Dove Lempke, writing in *Booklist,* stated that Rosenthal's "illustrations are zippy and bold in shades of green, orange, and yellow, accentuated with black ink lines."

Rosenthal served as the illustrator for *Peter and the Talking Shoes,* a cumulative tale by Kate Banks. According to Ilene Cooper in *Booklist,* "Gasoline Alley-style cartoon characters cavort through a funny retro-world where unusual shapings and offbeat perspectives will catch kids' attention." Mem Fox addresses themes of individuality and identity in *The Straight Line Wonder,* about a straight black line that decides to experiment with curves, much to the shock of its friends. "Rosenthal's bouncy artwork catches the story's frisky flavor," observed Lempke, and a *Publishers Weekly* reviewer commented that the illustrator "succeeds in attributing the thick black lines with personality through a shock of wild hair, wire-rim spectacles or a bright baseball cap."

Originally published in a Russian children's magazine in the 1930s, Kharms's text for *First, Second* follows a group of companions traveling through a fantastical landscape. *Booklist* contributor Hazel Rochman praised the "brightly colored cartoon-style pictures that extend the exaggeration and cheerful innocence of the nonsense world." *The Absentminded Fellow,* a story by Russian author Samuel Marshak that was first published in 1928, follows the misadventures of an amusing but befuddled soul. "Defying gravity and exuding antic glee, Rosenthal's figures hurl themselves across [the] pages" of this story, Joanna Rudge Long announced in a *Horn Book* review.

In *Dig!,* Zimmerman and Clemesha depict a day in the life of Mr. Rally, a construction worker, and his loyal dog, Lightning. According to *New York Times Book Review* critic Jess Bruder, in *Dig!* Rosenthal's "illustrations in ink and watercolor are full of action and small surprises," and a *Publishers Weekly* contributor noted that the book's "simple, good-humored art harks back to classic picture books with the appealing old-fashioned feel of Margaret Bloy Graham or Virginia Lee Burton."

Rosenthal's authorial debut, *Phooey!* centers on a bored youngster who unwittingly triggers a series of riotous events in his town. The action is more old-time movie than modern picture book," noted Robin Smith in her *Horn Book* review of the original work. "In his pliable

line drawings, sunny watercolor palette and quaint town setting," a *Publishers Weekly* critic wrote, "Rosenthal salutes '30s and '40s comic strips and children's classics."

Rosenthal, who worked for designer Charles Eames and illustrator Milton Glaser earlier in his career, believes that those artists greatly influenced his own aesthetic. As he told an interviewer on the *HarperCollins* Web site, "I feel that all of our experiences shape us, and enrich our creative life. For example, in college, I studied architecture, and, at one point in my life, worked as a carpenter. The appreciation I developed for building, and for how things fit together, can be seen directly in *Phooey!* I studied design and was involved with filmmaking. Both of these disciplines are present in all of my work."

Biographical and Critical Sources

PERIODICALS

Booklist, April 1, 1994, Ilene Cooper, review of *Peter and the Talking Shoes*, p. 1457; April 15, 1996, Hazel Rochman, review of *First, Second*, p. 1445; October 15, 1997, Susan Dove Lempke, review of *Straight Line Wonder*, p. 414; April, 1998, Susan Dove Lempke, review of *Yo, Aesop!: Get a Load of These Fables*, p. 1322; July, 1999, Susan Dove Lempke, review of *The Absentminded Fellow*, p. 1952; May 15, 2004, Gillian Engberg, review of *Dig!*, p. 1627; July 1, 2007, Hazel Rochman, review of *Phooey!*, p. 66.

Horn Book, September-October, 1996, Lauren Adams, review of *First, Second*, p. 580; March-April, 1999, Joanna Rudge Long, review of *The Absentminded Fellow*, p. 198; September-October, 2007, Robin Smith, review of *Phooey!*, p. 561.

New York Times Book Review, September 19, 2004, Jess Bruder, review of *Dig!*, p. 16.

Publishers Weekly, November 9, 1992, review of *Where on Earth: A Geografunny Guide to the Globe*, p. 88; March 11, 1996, review of *First, Second*, p. 62; August 18, 1997, review of *Straight Line Wonder*, p. 93; March 23, 1998, review of *Yo, Aesop!*, p. 99; May 3, 1999, review of *The Absentminded Fellow*, p. 75; May 10, 2004, review of *Dig!*, p. 57; July 23, 2007, review of *Phooey!*, p. 66.

School Library Journal, July, 2004, Marian Creamer, review of *Dig!*, p. 90; September, 2007, Julie R. Ranelli, review of *Phooey!*, p. 174.

ONLINE

HarperCollins Web site, http://www.harpercollinschildrens.com/ (September 10, 2008), "A Q&A with the Creator of *Phooey!*"

Marc Rosenthal Home Page, http://www.marc-rosenthal.com (September 10, 2008).*

RUBIN, Vicky 1964-

Personal

Born 1964, in NJ. *Education:* Barnard College, bachelor's degree; University of Massachusetts at Amherst, M.A. (art education).

Addresses

Home—Brooklyn, NY. *E-mail*—vicky_rubin@yahoo.com; kartoonia@aol.com.

Career

Author and illustrator of children's books. Formerly worked as a teacher, proofreader, and hand model.

Writings

Ralphie and the Swamp Baby, Henry Holt (New York, NY), 2004.

The Three Swingin' Pigs, illustrated by Rhode Montijo, Henry Holt (New York, NY), 2007.

Sidelights

Vicky Rubin created the humorous and engaging illustrations for her first book for children, *Ralphie and the Swamp Baby*. This story about accepting a new sibling focuses on Ralphie, a young alligator who worries that his parents will have no time for him once their new egg hatches. Although he attempts to return the egg to the nest of a local stork, the young alligator winds up rescuing his potential sibling, learning an important lesson about the deep well of parental love in the process. In *Publishers Weekly* a critic described *Ralphie and the Swamp Baby* as a "perceptive tale about sibling rivalry" and cited Rubin's "chipper ink-and-watercolor" illustrations for adding to the story's "cozy" and reassuring mood.

A "jazzed-up version" of the well-known story of the Three Little Pigs, *The Three Swingin' Pigs* introduces Ella the scat singer, Satch the sax player, and Mo the bass player. These three porcine beboppers are headlining the Big Pig Gig when the villainous Wolfie shows up. While the sharp-toothed wolf hopes to make up for his inability to capture the pigs' three uncles, Satch, Mo, and Ella must convince him that their toe-tapping tunes are more tasty than they are. "Full of porker-inspired puns and clever repartee," *The Three Swingin' Pigs* is a "fast-paced tale [that] has definite appeal," wrote *School Library Journal* critic Maura Bresnahan, and in *Kirkus Reviews* a critic concluded that "Rubin's skit-scat-skedoodle words" transform her updated fairy tale into "a hand-clapping, foot-stomping romp."

Rubin's love of pairing text and illustration goes back to her childhood, when she was an avid artist, writer, and reader. As she explained to *SATA,* "I like to draw animal characters as stand-ins for humans because they have extra ways of expressing emotions, such as ears and tails. I feel that strong characters are the key to good stories. My first published works for children were humorous poems in *Cricket* and *Spider* magazines. I think magazines are a good way to get started in publishing and I continue to do work for magazines as well as books. I also enjoy doing author visits in schools."

Rubin works on new projects from her home in Brooklyn, New York. She has a multicultural background; her mother is from mainland China and her father is from the United States. She likes to travel and lived for a year in China. "I believe all people are creative," she maintained, "and they should pay attention to that part of themselves."

Biographical and Critical Sources

PERIODICALS

Kirkus Reviews, April 15, 2007, review of *The Three Swingin' Pigs.*

Publishers Weekly, May 24, 2004, review of *Ralphie and the Swamp Baby,* p. 61; May 28, 2007, review of *The Three Swingin' Pigs,* p. 62.

School Library Journal, June, 2007, Maura Bresnahan, review of *The Three Swingin' Pigs,* p. 122.

ONLINE

ChildrensIllustrators.com, http://www.childrensillustrators.com/ (September 15, 2008), "Vicky Rubin."

Vicky Rubin Home Page, http://vickyrubin.com (September 15, 2008).

Cover of Vicky Rubin's The Three Swingin' Pigs, *featuring artwork by Rhode Montijo.*

RUMFORD, James 1948-
(Lin Chien-min)

Personal

Born August 13, 1948, in CA; son of Sydney (a salesman) and Audrey (a store clerk) Rumford; married Carol Drollinger (an office manager), 1969; children: Jonathan. *Education:* University of California-Irvine, B.A. (French literature), 1970; University of Hawaii, M.A. (English as a second language), 1976. *Hobbies and other interests:* Foreign languages, travel.

Addresses

Home—Honolulu, HI. *E-mail*—Kauhau@lava.net.

Career

Author and illustrator. Peace Corps, 1971-75; Fulbright lecturer, 1977-81; Manoa Press (publisher), owner, 1986—; writer and illustrator, 1996—.

Member

Honolulu Printmakers, Society of Children's Book Writers and Illustrators.

Awards, Honors

Charlotte Zolotow Award, 2004, for *Calabash Cat and His Amazing Journey;* Robert F. Sibert Honor Book citation, and Jane Addams Children's Book Award, both 2005, and Normal A. Sugarman Award, Cleveland Public Library, 2006, all for *Sequoyah: The Cherokee Man Who Gave His People Writing.*

Writings

SELF-ILLUSTRATED

The Cloudmakers, Houghton Mifflin (Boston, MA), 1996.
The Island-below-the-Star, Houghton Mifflin (Boston, MA), 1998.
When Silver Needles Swam: A Story of Tutu's Quilt, Manoa (Honolulu, HI), 1998.
Seeker of Knowledge: The Man Who Deciphered Egyptian Hieroglyphs, Houghton Mifflin, (Boston, MA), 2000.
Traveling Man: The Journey of Ibn Battuta, 1325-1354, Houghton Mifflin (Boston, MA), 2001.
Ka-hala-o-puna: The Beauty of Manoa, Manoa Press (Honolulu, HI), 2001.
There's a Monster in the Alphabet, Houghton Mifflin (Boston, MA), 2002.
Calabash Cat and His Amazing Journey, Houghton Mifflin (Boston, MA), 2003.
Nine Animals and the Well, Houghton Mifflin (Boston, MA), 2003.
Dog-of-the-Sea-Waves (bilingual English and Hawaiian), Houghton Mifflin (Boston, MA), 2004.

Sequoyah: The Cherokee Man Who Gave His People Writing, Houghton Mifflin (Boston, MA), 2004.
Beowulf: A Hero's Tale Retold, Houghton Mifflin (Boston, MA), 2007.
Don't Touch My Hat!, Alfred A. Knopf (New York, NY), 2007.
Silent Music: A Story of Baghdad, Roaring Brook Press (New York, NY), 2008.
Chee-lin: A Giraffe's Journey, Houghton Mifflin (Boston, MA), 2008.

OTHER

(Translator and commentator) Tsung-mu Wang, *An Essay on Paper: Observations Made by Wan Zongmu at the Imperial Paper Mill at Jade Mountain,* Manoa (Honolulu, HI), 1993.
(Under pseudonym Lin Chien-min) Wu Wei-yun, *Cloudmaker: A Translation of a Page from the T'ang chi'i shuo, Strange Stories from the T'ang Dynasty,* Manoa (Honolulu, HI), 1996.
(Co-illustrator) Martha G. Alexander, *Max and the Dumb Flower Picture,* Charlesbridge Publishers (Watertown, MA), 2009.

Author's books have been translated into Hawaiian.

Sidelights

The self-illustrated picture books of James Rumford, which have won awards for their originality, sometimes include texts in more than one language. With the exception of his books on Hawaii, Rumford tends not to repeat himself, moving through projects that illuminate ancient and modern cultures in the United States and throughout the globe. Through titles such as *Calabash Cat and His Amazing Journey, Dog-of-the-Sea-Waves, Sequoyah: The Cherokee Man Who Gave His People Writing,* and *Silent Music,* to name just a few, the author/illustrator introduces young readers to serious topics through a combination of story, artwork, and elements of native languages and lore. As Rumford once told *SATA,* "Each book has been a new and rewarding experience. Writing and illustrating children's books—I can't think of a better way to spend the rest of my life."

In *The Cloudmakers* Rumford explains how the secret of papermaking traveled from the Chinese world to Arabia in the eighth century A.D., according to Arab legend. As the story starts, a Chinese grandfather and his grandson are captured in Turkestan during a battle with troops of the Sultan of Samarkand. In a bid to win their freedom, the young man brags that his grandfather can make clouds, and when challenged to do so, they produce a billowing piece of paper. Adding poetry and drama to the process, Young Wu describes each step "as if the end product will actually be a cloud," observed Margaret A. Chang in *School Library Journal.* Rumford's "lyrical watercolor paintings perfectly complement the spare, engaging text," remarked a critic for *Kirkus Reviews,* while Julie Corsaro concluded in

Booklist that Rumford's "smoothly written text and . . . soft, atmospheric watercolors" in *The Cloudmakers* "encourage children to use their imaginations."

In *The Island-below-the-Star* Rumford reimagines the discovery of the Hawaiian Islands by Polynesian explorers before the time of recorded history. In the story, five brothers, each with a unique talent, leave home in search of a certain star and the island that lies beneath it. The youngest is a stowaway; when his brothers' skill with the wind, currents, stars, and waves cannot save them after a storm blows their ship far off course, the youngest brother's skill with birds aids them in reaching the island of their quest. "Told with the spare formulaic structure of a folktale," *The Island-below-the-Star* "has the appeal of a youthful adventure while it uses the five brothers to tell the story of the migration of a whole people," observed Sally Margolis in *School Library Journal*.

The five Polynesian brothers from *The Island-below-the-Star* return in *Dog-of-the-Sea-Waves*. This time, the youngest brother shirks his duties in favor of caring for an injured sea lion washed up on the beach. The four older brothers berate the boy for laziness, but the sea lion proves to be a devoted friend when a crisis later erupts. To quote Gillian Engberg in *Booklist*, Rumford's "attention to Hawaiian culture and language is a rare treat." Harriet Fargnoli in *School Library Journal* also maintained that *Dog-of-the-Sea-Waves* gives its audience "a taste of Hawaii's diverse flora and fauna."

Both *Traveling Man: The Journey of Ibn Battuta, 1325-1354* and *Calabash Cat and His Amazing Journey* feature footloose characters who set out to explore the world. Ibn Battuta is an actual historical figure: he was a Muslim scholar who spent nearly thirty years traversing the Eastern hemisphere, from Tangiers to China and back again. Rumford's take on the tale includes stylized calligraphic passages from Battuta's actual diaries, as well as maps and landscape renderings. "This is the sort of book you keep handling as you read, tilting and turning it so as not to miss a phrase as the text winds its way across mountains, seas and deserts," wrote Laura Shapiro in the *New York Times Book Review*. Shapiro deemed Rumford's "dazzling" book "a fine testament to the lure of the road in any age," and Nina Lindsay wrote in *School Library Journal* that the author/illustrator's account of Battuta's journey will please "readers intrigued by the ancient past."

Calabash Cat and His Amazing Journey strikes a more whimsical tone, as Calabash Cat sets out to located the end of the world. As he sojourns, he seeks the aid of various other animals, all of whom assure the cat that he has reached his journey's end when they can no longer help him. The horse, for instance, stops at the edge of the grassy field bordering the jungle and declares it the end of the world—once inside the jungle, a tiger escorts Calabash Cat further yet before claiming that the world's end has been reached. As Susan Dove

Lempke observed in *Horn Book*, the book suggests that "different parts of the world tend to see things from their own unique perspectives." In *Booklist* Michael Cart called *Calabash Cat and His Amazing Journey* "a lovely . . . book, with multigenerational appeal."

Rumford won several awards and citations for *Sequoyah*. Tall and slender in format, the book explains how Cherokee Chief Sequoyah experimented with symbols until he created a unique writing for the people of his nation. Using a simple narrative tone and illustrations that incorporate Cherokee translations, Rumford helps readers to understand not only the Cherokee culture but also how alphabets are devised. In *School Library Journal*, Sean George called *Sequoyah* "one of those rare gems of read-aloud nonfiction," and a *Publishers Weekly* reviewer praised Rumford's bilingual text as "economical yet lyrically told" and set off by illustrations characterized by a "pleasingly subtle, rough-hewn texture."

The ancient epic *Beowulf* is both complex and violent, not necessarily good fare for children, but in *Beowulf: A Hero's Tale Retold* Rumford meets the challenge of bringing the famous story to life for younger readers. The author decided to infuse his text with Anglo-Saxon words wherever possible in order to evoke the feel of the original work. According to Charles McGrath in the *New York Times Book Review*, the result is "a not-bad approximation . . . easily comprehensible to readers in, say, the fourth and fifth grades." A *Publishers Weekly* reviewer called the epic retelling "a very skillful presentation," and *Horn Book* contributor Martha P. Parravano deemed *Beowulf* "superb on all counts."

At the commencement of the Iraq War, Rumford was inspired to write a children's book from the point of view of a youngster caught in the violence in Baghdad. In *Silent Music: A Story of Baghdad*, Ali, the central character, retreats into the solace of calligraphy while the war rages, drawing strength from the tales of his hero, Yakut, who did the same when the Mongols invaded the same region in the thirteenth century. According to Joy Fleishhacker in *School Library Journal*, *Silent Music* "sheds light on life in war-torn Iraq and builds empathy for those caught in the crossfire." In *Horn Book* Robin L. Smith concluded of the book that, "told plainly and without bathos, this is one story of how people use art to find understanding."

Rumford's self-illustrated books for preschoolers included *Nine Animals and the Well* and *Don't Touch My Hat!* A counting book, *Nine Animals and the Well* introduces one animal after another, as each successive creature carries more items than the animal preceding it. All become greedy when they learn that the last of the nine animals has nine coins. In *Don't Touch My Hat!* Sheriff John is convinced that his toughness comes from his cowboy hat—until one night when he arrives at a brawl wearing one of his wife's prissy bonnets. "Hat's off to

James Rumford brings to life a young boy's love of his Arabic culture in his self-illustrated picture book **Silent Music.** (Roaring Brook Press, 2008. Copyright © 2008 by James Rumford. All rights reserved. Reprinted by permission of Henry Holt & Company, LLC.)

this one!" exclaimed a *Kirkus Reviews* critic, while a *Publishers Weekly* reviewer called *Don't Touch My Hat!* a "romp of a read."

In an online interview with the *Internationalist,* Rumford explained how he chooses the topics he covers in his children's literature: "I'm writing books that I would've wanted to read when I was in 2nd or 3rd or 4th grade," he said. "I was sorely disappointed at how shallow most of the books were. I wanted to know more. So I'm writing those kinds of books now."

Biographical and Critical Sources

PERIODICALS

Booklist, September 15, 1996, Julie Corsaro, review of *The Cloudmakers,* p. 250; December 1, 2002, Carolyn Phelan, review of *There's a Monster in the Alphabet,* p. 670; October 15, 2003, Michael Cart, review of *Calabash Cat and His Amazing Journey,* p. 420; June 1, 2004, Gillian Engberg, review of *Dog-of-the-Sea-*

Waves, p. 1748; October 15, 2004, Carolyn Phelan, review of *Sequoyah: The Cherokee Man Who Gave His People Writing,* p. 402; December 15, 2006, Julie Cummins, review of *Don't Touch My Hat!,* p. 51; August, 2007, Ian Chipman, review of *Beowulf: A Hero's Tale Retold,* p. 67; April 15, 2008, Gillian Engberg, review of *Silent Music: A Story of Baghdad,* p. 51.

Horn Book, January-February, 2002, Margaret A. Bush, review of *Traveling Man: The Journey of Ibn Battuta, 1325-1354,* p. 106; May-June, 2003, Susan P. Bloom, review of *Nine Animals and the Well,* p. 337; November-December, 2003, Susan Dove Lempke, review of *Calabash Cat and His Amazing Journey,* p. 734; May-June, 2004, Margaret A. Bush, review of *Dog-of-the-Sea-Waves,* p. 321; November-December, 2004, Margaret A. Bush, review of *Sequoyah,* p. 730; March-April, 2007, Christine M. Heppermann, review of *Don't Touch My Hat!,* p. 189; July-August, 2007, Martha P. Parravano, review of *Beowulf,* p. 412; March-April, 2008, Robin L. Smith, review of *Silent Music,* p. 210.

Kirkus Reviews, June 15, 1996, review of *The Cloudmakers,* p. 904; March 1, 1998, review of *The Island-below-the-Star,* p. 343; September 15, 2003, review of

Calabash Cat and His Amazing Journey, p. 1181; May 1, 2004, review of *Dog-of-the-Sea-Waves,* p. 448; October 15, 2004, review of *Sequoyah,* p. 1013; December 15, 2006, review of *Don't Touch My Hat!,* p. 1272; July 1, 2007, review of *Beowulf;* February 15, 2008, review of *Silent Music;* July 15, 2008, review of *Chee-Lin: A Giraffe's Journey.*

New York Times Book Review, November 18, 2001, Laura Shapiro, "Pilgrims' Progress: The Stories of Two Celebrated Islamic Travelers, One of Them a Scholar and the Other One a King," p. 27; June 17, 2007, Charles Mcgrath, review of *Beowulf,* p. 17.

Publishers Weekly, April 21, 2003, review of *Nine Animals and the Well,* p. 62; November 8, 2004, review of *Sequoyah,* p. 55; February 5, 2007, review of *Don't Touch My Hat!,* p. 58; August 13, 2007, review of *Beowulf,* p. 67; March 10, 2008, review of *Silent Music,* p. 80.

School Library Journal, September, 1996, Margaret A. Chang, review of *The Cloudmakers,* p. 189; June, 1998, Sally Margolis, review of *The Island-below-the-Star,* p. 121; October, 2004, Nina Lindsay, review of *There's a Monster in the Alphabet,* p. 150; October, 2004, Harriett Fargnoli, review of *Dog-of-the-Sea-Waves,* p. 128; October, 2004, Sean George, review of *Sequoyah,* p. 150; January, 2007, Julie Roach, review of *Don't Touch My Hat!,* p. 108; August, 2007, Susan Scheps, review of *Beowulf,* p. 138; April, 2008, Joy Fleishhacker, review of *Silent Music,* p. 121.

ONLINE

Houghton Mifflin Web site, http://www.houghtonmifflin books.com/ (September 8, 2008), "James Rumford."

Internationalist Online, http://www.intmag.org/ (April 12, 2007), "Exposing America to the World, One Child at a Time."

Scholastic Web site, http://www2.scholastic.com/ (September 8, 2008), "James Rumford."*

S

SCHMIDT, Gary D. 1957-

Personal

Born April 14, 1957, in Hicksville, NY; son of Robert H. (a bank vice president) and Jeanne A. (a teacher) Schmidt; married Anne E. Stickney (a writer), December 22, 1979; children: James, Kathleen, Rebecca, David, Margaret, Benjamin. *Education:* Gordon College, B.A., 1979; University of Illinois at Urbana-Champaign, M.A., 1981, Ph.D., 1985. *Religion:* Christian Reformed. *Hobbies and other interests:* Gardening.

Addresses

Home and office—Alto, MI. *Office*—Department of English, Calvin College, 1795 Knollcrest Circle, Grand Rapids, MI 49546. *E-mail*—schg@calvin.edu.

Career

Author and educator. Calvin College, Grand Rapids, MI, professor of English, 1985—, department head, 1991-97.

Member

Children's Literature Association, Early English Text Society, Phi Kappa Phi, Phi Alpha Chi.

Awards, Honors

Honorable mention, Book Award Committee, Children's Literature Association, 1993, for *Robert McCloskey;* Best Books for Young Adults citation, American Library Association (ALA), 1997, for *The Sin Eater;* Newbery Honor Book designation, ALA, Michael L. Printz Honor Book designation, ALA, and Gustavus Myers Outstanding Book designation, all 2005, all for *Lizzie Bright and the Buckminster Boy;* Newbery Honor Book designation, 2008, for *The Wednesday Wars.*

Writings

JUVENILE

John Bunyan's Pilgrim's Progress, illustrated by Barry Moser, Eerdmans (Grand Rapids, MI), 1994.

Gary D. Schmidt (Photograph by Myrna Anderson. Courtesy of Gary Schmidt.)

Robert Frost, illustrated by Henri Sorensen, Sterling Publishing (New York, NY), 1994.

The Sin Eater (novel), Dutton (New York, NY), 1996.

The Blessing of the Lord, illustrated by Dennis Nolan, Eerdmans (Grand Rapids, MI), 1997.

William Bradford: Pilgrim of Answerable Courage, Eerdmans (Grand Rapids, MI), 1997.

Anson's Way (novel), Clarion Books (New York, NY), 1999.

William Bradford: Plymouth's Faithful Pilgrim, Eerdmans (Grand Rapids, MI), 1999.

Saint Ciaran: The Tale of a Saint of Ireland, illustrated by Todd Doney, Eerdmans (Grand Rapids, MI), 2000.

(Editor, with Frances Schoonmaker Bolin and Brod Bagert) *The Blackbirch Treasury of American Poetry,* Blackbirch Press (Woodbridge, CT), 2001.

Mara's Stories, Henry Holt (New York, NY), 2001.

Straw into Gold (novel), Clarion Books (New York, NY), 2001.

The Wonders of Donal O'Donnell: A Folktale of Ireland, Henry Holt (New York, NY), 2002.

The Great Stone Face: A Tale by Nathaniel Hawthorne, illustrated by Bill Farnsworth, Eerdmans (Grand Rapids, MI), 2002.

Lizzie Bright and the Buckminster Boy (novel), Clarion Books (New York, NY), 2004.

First Boy (novel), Holt (New York, NY), 2005.

The Wednesday Wars (novel), Clarion Books (New York, NY), 2007.

Trouble (novel), Clarion Books (New York, NY), 2008.

FOR ADULTS

Supplementary Essays for College Writers, Prentice-Hall (Englewood Cliffs, NJ), 1988, third edition, 1993.

(Editor, with Charlotte F. Otten) *The Voice of the Narrator in Children's Literature: Insights from Writers and Critics,* Greenwood Press (Westport, CT), 1989.

Robert McCloskey, Twayne (Boston, MA), 1990.

Hugh Lofting, Macmillan (New York, NY), 1992.

(Editor, with Donald R. Hettinga) *Sitting at the Feet of the Past: Retelling the North American Folktale for Children,* Greenwood Press (Westport, CT), 1992.

(Editor, with William J. Vande Kopple) *Communities of Discourse: The Rhetoric of Disciplines* (includes instructor's manual), Prentice-Hall (Englewood Cliffs, NJ), 1993.

Katherine Paterson, Macmillan (New York, NY), 1994.

The Iconography of the Mouth of Hell: Eighth-Century Britain to the Fifteenth Century, Susquehanna University Press (Cranbury, NJ), 1995.

Robert Lawson, Macmillan (New York, NY), 1997.

(With Carol Winters) *Edging the Boundaries of Children's Literature,* Allyn & Bacon (Boston, MA), 2001.

(Editor, with Susan M. Felch) *Winter: A Spiritual Biography of the Season,* illustrated by Barry Moser, Skylight Paths Publishing (Woodstock, VT), 2003.

(Editor, with Susan M. Felch) *Autumn: A Spiritual Biography of the Season,* illustrated by Barry Moser, Skylight Paths Publishing (Woodstock, VT), 2004.

A Passionate Usefulness: The Life and Literary Labors of Hannah Adams, University of Virginia Press (Charlottesville, VA), 2004.

(With Lawrence Kushner) *In God's Hands,* Jewish Lights Publishing (Woodstock, VT), 2005.

(Editor, with Susan M. Felch) *Summer: A Spiritual Biography of the Season,* illustrated by Barry Moser, Skylight Paths Publishing (Woodstock, VT), 2005.

(Editor, with Susan M. Felch) *Spring: A Spiritual Biography of the Season,* illustrated by Mary Azarian, Skylight Paths Publishing (Woodstock, VT), 2006.

(Editor, with Susan M. Felch) *The Emmaus Readers: Listening for God in Contemporary Fiction,* Paraclete Press (Brewster, MA), 2008.

Contributor to books, including *Text and Matter: New Critical Perspectives of the Pearl Poet,* edited by Robert J. Blanch, Miriam Miller, and Julian Wasserman, Whitston (Troy, NY), 1991. Contributor of articles, essays, stories, poems, and reviews to journals, including *Christian Home and School, Lion and the Unicorn, Studies in American Humor, Christian Educators Journal,* and *Martha's KidLit Newsletter.* Guest editor, *Children's Literature Association Quarterly,* 1989.

Adaptations

Several of Schmidt's works have been adapted as audio books.

Sidelights

Gary D. Schmidt has blended a career as a professor of English with one that involves writing both for children and adults. Schmidt's fiction and nonfiction children's books span genres from young adult and middle grade novels to picture books, and they deal with topics from biography to suicide. His novels include *The Sin Eater, Anson's Way,* and *Lizzie Bright and the Buckminster Boy,* while in other books, including *The Blessing of the Lord: Stories from the Old and New Testaments* and *Saint Ciaran: The Tale of a Saint of Ireland,* Schmidt mixes religious themes with biographical tales and retellings.

Schmidt's first books were for adults, but after writing a few biographies of children's writers, including *Robert McCloskey* and *Katherine Paterson,* he turned his hand to writing his own children's books. Ilene Cooper, reviewing Schmidt's biography of Paterson in *Booklist,* commented that he does "an excellent job of chronicling" the life of the two-time Newbery-Award-winning author. Schmidt once told *SATA:* "My first two children's books, the retelling of *Pilgrim's Progress* and *The Sin Eater,* both came out of my own past. *Pilgrim's Progress* had been with me some fifteen years before I finally turned to a retelling. It seemed to me that there were strong reasons why children would have turned this into a child's story back in the seventeenth and eighteenth centuries, and I was not convinced that those reasons no longer pertained in the late twentieth century. I wrote the retelling thinking of my own early responses to the book, cutting out the parts that bored and that struck discordant notes."

Schmidt's retelling of *Pilgrim's Progress* "is much more accessible than the original version," according to *School Library Journal* contributor Kate Hegarty Bouman, voicing a common response to the work. Bouman noted that Schmidt's "mix of both historical periods and ethnic groups is a fascinating way to extend the text spatially and temporally." A reviewer for *Publishers Weekly* similarly praised Schmidt's "masterly rendition" as "a treasure sure to delight young and old."

Schmidt's first young-adult novel was *The Sin Eater*. "For *The Sin Eater*, I reached back into my own family's past and that of my wife," the author later explained. "The house is not the same as, but is like a real house in Brunswick, Maine. Though the action of the novel itself is not based on real events, the responses of the characters mirror responses that I have had in my past to not dissimilar events and people. The places around the farmhouse are all real, though drawn from sites in upper New York state, the Catskill Mountains, the White Mountains of New Hampshire, and Cape Cod."

In *The Sin Eater*, middle-schooler Cole and his father move in with Cole's maternal grandparents in rural New Hampshire after Cole's mother dies of cancer. Cole delights in his new surroundings and in the village lore and tales of ancestry told him by his grandparents and other locals. His father, however, remains grief-stricken and ultimately commits suicide. "A work laden with atmosphere and meaning, this is a promising debut from an author who captures with admirable accuracy both the dark and light of life," asserted a *Kirkus Reviews* critic. A *Publishers Weekly* reviewer also found Schmidt's novel "engrossing," adding that the plot forms a "point of departure for a profound and lyrical meditation on life and the importance of shared history."

The Blessing of the Lord: Stories from the Old and New Testaments includes retellings from "unusual perspectives," as Shelley Townsend-Hudson commented in *Booklist*. Schmidt retells the stories of Jonah, Deborah, Barak, Peter, and others, with a twist that gives the "often tired old tales . . . new life," according to Townsend-Hudson. A *Publishers Weekly* reviewer praised the "dramatic spin" Schmidt gives to these tales.

Further religious and spiritual matters are served up in *William Bradford: Plymouth's Faithful Pilgrim* and *Saint Ciaran: The Tale of Saint of Ireland*. The former biography, intended for older readers, looks at the guiding light of the Plymouth Colony, painting "a warm and cohesive picture of William Bradford's role in that colony's foundation and growth," as a critic for *Kirkus Reviews* observed. Bradford, an orphan from early childhood, embraced Puritan ideals as a teenager and ultimately led a group of Separatists on a perilous mission to found a colony in the New World. Schmidt uses Bradford's own writings as well as contemporary journals and prints to take the reader back into the religious beliefs of those early colonists. "The author clearly presents Bradford's religious views and shows how those beliefs affected his life and actions and those of the Pilgrims," wrote Elaine Fort Weischedel in a *School Library Journal* review.

Saint Ciaran is a picture book intended for younger readers. "In mouth-filling cadences of Gaelic . . . Schmidt tells the story of the sixth-century Irish saint," noted GraceAnne A. DeCandido in *Booklist*. Growing up a spiritual child, Ciaran went to Rome and discovered the Catholic faith in the city's churches. Sent back to Ireland by St. Patrick, he founded a religious community that attracted Christians from all over the island. DeCandido called *Saint Ciaran* a "beautiful picture book for older children," and Kathleen Kelly MacMillan, writing in *School Library Journal*, deemed the book a "gently moving tribute to a lesser-known saint."

Schmidt demonstrates the variety of his prose styles in the novels *Anson's Way* and *Straw into Gold*. Again using Ireland for a setting, this time in the eighteenth century, *Anson's Way* features a young Anson Granville Staplyton who follows his family calling and joins the Staffordshire military, the Fencible. Dreaming of glory, he is sent to Ireland as a mere drummer to help keep the peace. When he sees his fellow soldiers persecuting the locals, Anson begins to have mixed loyalties. When he meets an Irish hedge master—a person who illegally teaches the Irish their forbidden language and culture—he soon befriends some of the Irish rebels. Ultimately, Anson is forced to choose between his comrades in arms and his new Irish friends. This book "realistically portrays not only the tragedies of war but also the battle between heart and mind of a young soldier," as *Booklist* writer Shelle Rosenfeld remarked. Janice M. Del Negro, reviewing the title in *Bulletin of the Center for Children's Books*, also praised this "complex action/adventure novel" with its "shifting moral center." "Replete with drama and action," wrote Hilary Crew in *Voice of Youth Advocates*, "Schmidt's story presents a side of Irish history that is frequently marginalized in textbooks."

In his middle-grade novel *Straw into Gold*, Schmidt spins a new twist in the old Rumpelstiltskin tale, extending it to see what could have happened. In Schmidt's rendering, young Tousle leaves his forest cottage with his magical father, Da, to travel to the city and view the king's procession. He becomes separated from his father and then surprises himself by calling out for mercy for some rebels facing execution. One other voice raised against the execution is that of the queen herself. The king will spare the lives only if Tousle and a blind young rebel, Innes, are able solve the riddle the king sets for them: "What fills a hand fuller than a skein of gold?" "So begins a suspenseful quest that adds surprising twists and turns to the traditional fairy tale," wrote *Booklist* critic Frances Bradburn. *School Library Journal* reviewer Ginny Gustin was also beguiled by the tale, calling *Straw into Gold* a "fantasy-flavored quest."

Based on actual events, *Lizzie Bright and the Buckminster Boy* was named a John Newbery Honor Book and a Michael L. Printz Honor Book. Set in 1912, the novel centers on Turner Ernest Buckminster, III, the son of a minister in Phippsburg, Maine, and his unlikely friendship with Lizzie Bright Griffin, who lives on nearby Malaga Island, which was settled by former slaves. Fearful that the impoverished community will hurt tour-

ism, the town elders force the island's residents from their homes, despite Turner's efforts to intervene. Writing in *Booklist*, Hazel Rochman called *Lizzie Bright and the Buckminster Boy* a "haunting combination of fact and fiction that has a powerful and tragic climax," and *School Library Journal* contributor Connie Tyrrell Burns remarked that the "novel will leave a powerful impression on readers."

In *First Boy*, fourteen-year-old Cooper Jewett decides to stay on his family's New Hampshire dairy farm after the death of his grandfather, who had raised Cooper. Soon, however, the teen is followed by black sedans, a barn on the farm burns to the ground, and a U.S. presidential candidate takes a strong interest in his life. "Cooper is an entirely appealing protagonist," noted Vicky Smith in *Horn Book*, and Rochman described *First Boy* as "a poignant account of one boy's search for home."

The Wednesday Wars, set in 1967 against the backdrop of the Vietnam War, concerns Holling Hoodhood, a seventh grader who spends every Wednesday afternoon alone with his demanding teacher, Mrs. Baker, while his schoolmates attend religious classes. The pair finds common ground, however, when they begin reading the plays of William Shakespeare, and the educator becomes a positive force in Holling's life, in contrast to his often neglectful parents. Writing in *Kliatt*, Paula Rohrlick called *The Wednesday Wars* "a marvelous read, both achingly funny and deeply affecting," and *School Library Journal* critic Joel Shoemaker stated that the author "explores many important themes, not the least of which is what makes a person a hero."

The members of an affluent New England family find their privileged lives irrevocably altered by tragedy in *Trouble*, a work that examines loss, responsibility, and reconciliation. When Franklin Smith, a rugby star, is struck and killed by a car driven by his classmate, a Cambodian refugee named Chay Chouan, the residents of Blythbury-by-the-Sea react with anger toward the nearby immigrant community. According to Kate McClelland in *School Library Journal*, Schmidt's novel contains "compassionate examinations of the passage from childhood to adulthood and of the patterns of common experience that mark and unite us as humans."

"Teaching children's literature as I do, I have the opportunity to read many of the extraordinary children's books published each year," Schmidt once noted in *SATA*. "But teaching also means that I need to balance each day between my family, my writing, and my students. This, especially when the care of a hundred-fifty-year-old farm is thrown into the balance, becomes a delicate act. It means that I can spend one to three hours a day on my writing, but that's all. Afterwards, there are other worlds to turn to.

"Working at a college also means that I combine several levels of writing. . . . At the same time [as writing for children], I work on books that are slightly more ar-

cane: a study of the medieval image of the mouth of hell and a biography of an eighteenth-century female historian. For me, these two very different kinds of writing (both creative, but one more scholarly than the other) help keep each project exciting rather than burdensome, even though there are the days when neither seems to have much energy."

"In thinking about my own work in children's literature, it seems to me that I am interested in showing the beatific and terrible complexities of our lives." Schmidt concluded for *SATA*. "I have had one reader tell me that *The Sin Eater* was sadder and funnier than he thought it would be. It seems to me that our lives are just that: often sadder and funnier than we ever thought they would be. They are also more beatific than we have any reason to expect, and my hope is to show that in the context of a world that is often dark."

Biographical and Critical Sources

PERIODICALS

Booklist, May 1, 1994, Ilene Cooper, review of *Katherine Paterson*, p. 1611; December 1, 1994, Hazel Rochman, review of *Robert Frost*, p. 669; November 1, 1996, Ilene Cooper, review of *The Sin Eater*, p. 491; November 1, 1997, Shelley Townsend-Hudson, review of *The Blessing of the Lord*, p. 469; April 1, 1999, Shelle Rosenfeld, review of *Anson's Way*, p. 1428; April 1, 2000, GraceAnne A. DeCandido, review of *Saint Ciaran: The Tale of a Saint of Ireland*, p. 1459; August, 2001, Frances Bradburn, review of *Straw into Gold*, p. 2108; October 1, 2002, Kay Weisman, review of *The Great Stone Face: A Tale by Nathaniel Hawthorne*, p. 327; May 15, 2004, Hazel Rochman, review of *Lizzie Bright and the Buckminster Boy*, p. 1629; September 15, 2005, Hazel Rochman, review of *First Boy*, p. 60; March 1, 2008, Ian Chipman, review of *Trouble*, p. 61.

Bulletin of the Center for Children's Books, May, 1999, Janice M. Del Negro, review of *Anson's Way*, pp. 327-328.

Horn Book, November-December, 2004, Betty Carter, review of *Lizzie Bright and the Buckminster Boy*, p. 717; September-October, 2005, Vicky Smith, review of *First Boy*, p. 589; July-August, 2007, Betty Carter, review of *The Wednesday Wars*, p. 403; May-June, 2008, Robin L. Smith, review of *Trouble*, p. 326.

Kirkus Reviews, September 1, 1996, review of *The Sin Eater*, p. 1328; June 1, 1998, review of *William Bradford*, p. 816.

Kliatt, September, 2005, Paula Rohrlick, review of *First Boy*, p. 14; May, 2007, Paula Rohrlick, review of *The Wednesday Wars*, p. 19; March, 2008, Ashleigh Larsen, review of *Trouble*, p. 19.

New York Times Book Review, December 16, 2007, Tanya Lee Stone, "Starting out in the '60s," review of *The Wednesday Wars*, p. 23.

Publishers Weekly, December 19, 1994, review of *John Bunyan's Pilgrim's Progress,* pp. 54-55; October 14, 1996, review of *The Sin Eater,* p. 84; August 25, 1997, review of *The Blessing of the Lord,* p. 66; March 1, 1999, review of *Anson's Way,* p. 70; April 10, 2000, review of *Saint Ciaran,* p. 95; March 31, 2008, review of *Trouble,* p. 62.

School Library Journal, December, 1994, Kate Hegarty Bouman, review of *Pilgrim's Progress,* p. 130; October, 1997, Patricia Pearl Dole, review of *The Blessing of the Lord,* p. 154; April, 1999, Starr E. Smith, review of *Anson's Way,* p. 12; June, 1999, Elaine Fort Weischedel, review of *William Bradford,* p. 153; August, 2000, Kathleen Kelly MacMillan, review of *Saint Ciaran,* p. 175; August, 2001, Ginny Gustin, review of *Straw into Gold,* p. 188; November, 2002, Grace Oliff, review of *The Great Stone Face,* p. 135; May, 2004, Connie Tyrrell Burns, review of *Lizzie Bright and the Buckminster Boy,* p. 157; October, 2005, Connie Tyrrell Burns, review of *First Boy,* p. 173; July, 2007, Joel Shoemaker, review of *The Wednesday Wars,* p. 110; April, 2008, Kate McClelland, review of *Trouble,* p. 148.

Voice of Youth Advocates, June, 1998, Kathleen Beck, review of *The Sin Eater,* p. 103; August, 1999, Hilary Crew, review of *Anson's Way,* pp. 185-186.

ONLINE

Calvin Spark Web site, http://www.calvin.edu/publications/spark/ (spring, 2006), Myrna DeVries Anderson, "Opening The Book That Is Gary Schmidt: Award-Winning Author, Supportive Colleague and Dedicated Father Are Chapters in the Life of This Calvin English Professor."

Miss Erin Web log, http://misserinmarie.blogspot.com/ (May 23, 2008), "SBBT Interview: Gary D. Schmidt."

Publishers Weekly Online, http://www.publishersweekly.com/ (May 3, 2007), Sue Corbett, "Children's Bookshelf Talks with Gary Schmidt."

Random House Web site, http://www.randomhouse.com/ (September 10, 2008), "A Conversation with Gary D. Schmidt."*

*   *   *

SELFORS, Suzanne 1963-

Personal

Born 1963, in Munich, Germany; daughter of Conrad (a teacher) and Marilyn (a real-estate broker); married children: Walker, Isabelle. *Education:* Attended Bennington College; Occidental College, B.A. (cum laude); University of Washington, 1990, M.A.

Addresses

Office—P.O. Box 10414, Bainbridge Island, WA 98110. *Agent*—Michael Bourret, Dystel & Goderich Literary Management, mbourret@dystel.com. *E-mail*—mail@suzanneselfors.com.

Career

Writer. Has worked variously as a prep cook, children's photographer, salesperson, receptionist, gardener, video producer, television-station sales assistant, organic flower grower, and marketing director.

Writings

To Catch a Mermaid, illustrated by Catia Chien, Little, Brown (New York, NY), 2007.

Saving Juliet, Walker & Company (New York, NY), 2008.

Fortune's Magic Farm, Little, Brown (New York, NY), 2009.

Coffeehouse Angel, Walker & Company (New York, NY), 2009.

Adaptations

Saving Juliet was adapted as a play by the Bainbridge Performing Arts, 2008.

Sidelights

In 2002, at the age of thirty-nine, Suzanne Selfors saw her youngest child safely off to school, then realized that she would have a few hours each day to finally pursue her dream of becoming a writer. Five years later her first picture book, *To Catch a Mermaid,* saw publication, and she followed that success with the young-adult novel *Saving Juliet.* Writing, the author stated on her home page, is "hard, hard work. Most non-writers don't realize that. It's lonely work, sometimes tedious work, sometimes exhilarating work. You should want it in a compulsive way. Talent helps but determination is mandatory."

Born on an army base in Munich, Germany, Selfors was raised in Bainbridge Island, Washington, where she now lives. "I was a happy kid," she remarked to *Cynsations* online interviewer Cynthia Leitich Smith. "I was fairly happy in my teen years too, though I limited myself to a smaller group of friends." Selfors discovered a love for the theater during those years after being cast as Mercutio in her school's production of William Shakespeare's *Romeo and Juliet.* "High school was all about performing for me, in plays and in dance productions," she told Smith. "My parents started having marriage problems, and so being in plays was a way to get out of the house."

Selfors later studied dance and art at Bennington College before earning a degree in theater from Occidental College. She eventually completed a master's degree in communications from the University of Washington and worked at a number of jobs, including children's photographer, video producer, and organic flower grower, before becoming a full-time mom. Selfors told Smith that reading to her two children helped inspire her to try her hand at writing. "I loved what I was reading and

realized that there was this huge Renaissance going on in children's literature," the author told Smith. "Every time I went to a bookstore, I'd start in the adult section, find nothing I wanted to read, and then ended up in the kids' section with an armful of books. I wanted to be a part of it."

The idea for *To Catch a Mermaid,* came to Selfors while she jogged through a park in Vancouver, British Columbia, Canada. "The tide was out, exposing beautiful tide pools," she stated on the *Class of 2k7* Web site. "Lots of kids were playing in the pools, delighting at the things they discovered. I realized that one of the universal joys of childhood is discovering things. What would be a neater thing to discover in a tide pool than a baby mercreature? And so, the story was born." *To Catch a Mermaid* concerns sixth-grader Boomerang "Boom" Broom and his dysfunctional family. When Boom unwittingly brings home an ill-tempered baby mermaid in a bucket of seafood, the creature places a curse upon his household, and Boom's sister, Mertyle, comes down with a bad case of Ick Disease. "Selfors has conjured up great characters and settings, and her narrative voice never falters," Elizabeth Bird remarked in *School Library Journal.* Despite its humorous narrative, "Selfors's adventure also subtly explores serious themes like grief, adversity and misfortune," noted a *Publishers Weekly* contributor.

In *Saving Juliet,* the family of seventeen-year-old Mimi Wallingford owns a financially unsound Shakespearean theater in New York City, and Mimi is pressured to carry on the family tradition to rescue the theater. When Mimi is cast as Juliet, she finds herself transported to sixteenth-century Verona where she meets the star-crossed daughter of the Capulets. Mimi decides to reinvent Shakespeare's tale, giving Juliet a satisfying resolution to her predicament. Selfors' "dialogue is lively," Jennifer Hubert commented in *Booklist,* and Mimi "is an honest, savvy narrator," noted a *Publishers Weekly* reviewer.

Selfors plans to write additional fantasy tales. "I adore the process of writing for middle grade readers," she remarked on the *Class of 2k7* Web site. "Why? Because they are still willing to believe that all sorts of crazy things are possible. They don't have all those hormones getting in the way. They don't yet need romance. They just want great adventure."

Biographical and Critical Sources

PERIODICALS

Booklist, January 1, 2008, Jennifer Hubert, review of *Saving Juliet,* p. 61.
Kirkus Reviews, July 15, 2007, review of *To Catch a Mermaid;* January 15, 2008, review of *Saving Juliet.*

Publishers Weekly, September 3, 2007, review of *To Catch a Mermaid,* p. 59; February 4, 2008, review of *Saving Juliet,* p. 58.
School Library Journal, September, 2007, Elizabeth Bird, review of *To Catch a Mermaid,* p. 208; March, 2008, Kathleen E. Gruver, review of *Saving Juliet,* p. 210.

ONLINE

Class of 2k7 Web site, http://www.classof2k7.com/ (September 2, 2008), "Debut Author Interviews: Suzanne Selfors."
Cynsations Web log, http://cynthialeitichsmith.blogspot.com/ (September 2, 2008), Cynthia Leitich Smith, interview with Selfors.
Suzanne Selfors Home Page, http://www.suzanneselfors.com (September 10, 2008).

*   *   *

SEULING, Barbara 1937-
(Carrie Austin, Bob Winn, a joint pseudonym)

Personal

Surname pronounced "Soo-ling"; born July 22, 1937, in Brooklyn, NY; daughter of Kaspar Joseph (a postman) and Helen Veronica (a homemaker) Seuling. *Education:* Attended Hunter College (now Hunter College of the City University of New York), 1955-57, Columbia University, 1957-59, School of Visual Arts, and New School for Social Research; also studied art and illustration privately. *Hobbies and other interests:* Movies, travel, reading, music.

Addresses

Home and office—New York, NY. *Office— Agent*—Miriam Altshuler Literary Agency, 5e Old Post Rd. North, Red Hook, NY 12571. *E-mail*—aplbrk@aol.com.

Career

Freelance writer and illustrator, 1968—. Has worked for an investment firm, for Columbia University, and at General Electric Co. exhibit at 1964 New York World's Fair. Dell Publishing Co., New York, NY, children's book editor, 1965-71; J.B. Lippincott Co., New York, NY, children's book editor, 1971-73. The Manuscript Workshop, Landgrove, VT, director, 1982—. Lecturer, teacher, and consultant on children's books and writing for children. Consultant to New York Foundling Hospital and Soros Foundation's Step-by-Step program in Moscow, Russia, and Budapest, Hungary.

Member

Society of Children's Book Writers and Illustrators (member, board of directors).

Awards, Honors

Award from American Institute of Graphic Arts, 1979, for *The Teeny Tiny Woman: An Old English Ghost Story;* Christopher Award, 1979, for *The New York Kid's Book;* first place, Harold Marshall Solstad Prize, Cameron University Children's Short Story Competition, 1982.

Writings

ILLUSTRATOR

Wilma Thompson, *That Barbara!,* Delacorte (New York, NY), 1969.

Nan Hayden Agle, *Tarr of Belway Smith,* Seabury Press (New York, NY), 1969.

Stella Pevsner, *Break a Leg!,* Crown (New York, NY), 1969.

Antonia Barber, *The Affair of the Rockerbye Baby,* Delacorte (New York, NY), 1970.

Stella Pevsner, *Footsteps on the Stairs,* Crown (New York, NY), 1970.

Moses L. Howard, *The Ostrich Chase,* Holt (New York, NY), 1974.

Melinda Green, *Bembelman's Bakery,* Parents' Magazine Press (New York, NY), 1978.

SELF-ILLUSTRATED; NONFICTION

Freaky Facts, Xerox Education Publications (Middletown, CT), 1972.

More Freaky Facts, Xerox Education Publications (Middletown, CT), 1973.

The Last Legal Spitball and Other Little-known Facts about Sports, Doubleday (New York, NY), 1975.

Abracadabra!: Creating Your Own Magic Show from Beginning to End, Messner (New York, NY), 1975.

You Can't Eat Peanuts in Church and Other Little-known Laws, Doubleday (New York, NY), 1975.

The Loudest Screen Kiss and Other Little-known Facts about the Movies, Doubleday (New York, NY), 1976.

The Last Cow on the White House Lawn and Other Little-known Facts about the Presidency, Doubleday (New York, NY), 1978.

You Can't Count a Billion Dollars and Other Little-known Facts about Money, Doubleday (New York, NY), 1979.

You Can't Show Kids in Underwear and Other Little-known Facts about Television, Doubleday (New York, NY), 1982.

Elephants Can't Jump and Other Freaky Facts about Animals, Dutton/Lodestar (New York, NY), 1985.

You Can't Sneeze with Your Eyes Open and Other Freaky Facts about the Human Body, Dutton/Lodestar (New York, NY), 1986.

The Man in the Moon Is Upside Down in Argentina and Other Freaky Facts about Geography, Ivy Books/Ballantine (New York, NY), 1991.

Too Cold to Hatch a Dinosaur and Other Freaky Facts about Weather, Ivy Books/Ballantine (New York, NY), 1993.

PUZZLE AND ACTIVITY BOOKS

Monster Mix, Xerox Education Publications (Middletown, CT), 1975.

Monster Madness, Xerox Education Publications (Middletown, CT), 1976.

(With Winnette Glasgow) *Fun with Crafts,* Xerox Education Publications (Middletown, CT), 1976.

Dinosaur Puzzles, Xerox Education Publications (Middletown, CT), 1976.

Did You Know?, Xerox Education Publications (Middletown, CT), 1977.

Monster Puzzles, Xerox Education Publications (Middletown, CT), 1978.

(With Winnette Glasgow; under joint pseudonym Bob Winn), *Christmas Puzzles,* Scholastic (New York, NY), 1980.

Valentine Puzzles, Xerox Education Publications (Middletown, CT), 1980.

Space Monster Puzzles, Xerox Education Publications (Middletown, CT), 1980.

Goblins and Ghosts, Xerox Education Publications (Middletown, CT), 1980.

Scary Hairy Fun Book, Xerox Education Publications (Middletown, CT), 1981.

My Secrets, Xerox Education Publications (Middletown, CT), 1984.

SELF-ILLUSTRATED; FICTION; FOR CHILDREN

(Reteller) *The Teeny Tiny Woman: An Old English Ghost Tale,* Viking (New York, NY), 1976.

The Great Big Elephant and the Very Small Elephant, Crown (New York, NY), 1977.

The Triplets, Houghton Mifflin/Clarion (Boston, MA), 1980.

Just Me, Harcourt (New York, NY), 1982.

NONFICTION; FOR CHILDREN

(Editor and contributor) *The New York Kid's Book,* Doubleday (New York, NY), 1979.

Stay Safe, Play Safe: A Book about Safety Rules, illustrated by Kathy Allert, Golden Books (New York, NY), 1985.

(With Winnette Glasgow) *Fun Facts about People around the World,* illustrated by Leslie Connor, Xerox Education Publications (New York, NY), 1986.

It Is Illegal to Quack like a Duck, and Other Freaky Laws, illustrated by Gwenn Seuling, Dutton/Lodestar (New York, NY), 1988.

Natural Disasters, Kidsbooks (Chicago, IL), 1994.

Bugs That Go Blam!, and Other Creepy Crawly Trivia, Willowisp (Worthington, OH), 1995.

To Be a Writer: A Guide for Young People Who Want to Write and Publish, Twenty-first Century Books (New York, NY), 1997.

Winter Lullaby, illustrated by Greg Newbold, Browndeer Press (San Diego, CA), 1998.

Drip! Drop!: How Water Gets to Your Tap, illustrated by Nancy Tobin, Holiday House (New York, NY), 2000.

Spring Song, illustrated by Greg Newbold, Harcourt (San Diego, CA), 2001.

From Head to Toe: The Amazing Human Body and How It Works, illustrated by Edward Miller, Holiday House (New York, NY), 2002.

Flick a Switch: How Electricity Gets to Your Home, illustrated by Nancy Tobin, Holiday House (New York, NY), 2003.

Say It with Music: The Life and Legacy of Jane Froman, Boxing Day Books (Princeton, IL), 2007.

Ancient Coins Were Shaped like Hams and Other Freaky Facts about Coins, Bills, and Counterfeiting, illustrated by Matthew Skeens, Picture Window Books (Minneapolis, MN), 2008.

Cows Sweat through Their Noses and Other Freaky Facts about Animal Habits, Characteristics, and Homes, illustrated by Matthew Skeens, Picture Window Books (Minneapolis, MN), 2008.

Earth Is like a Giant Magnet and Other Freaky Facts about Planets, Oceans, and Volcanoes, illustrated by Matthew Skeens, Picture Window Books (Minneapolis, MN), 2008.

One President Was Born on Independence Day and Other Freaky Facts about the Twenty-sixth through Forty-third Presidents, illustrated by Matthew Skeens, Picture Window Books (Minneapolis, MN), 2008.

Some Porcupines Wrestle and Other Freaky Facts about Animal Antics and Families, illustrated by Matthew Skeens, Picture Window Books (Minneapolis, MN), 2008.

Three Presidents Died on the Fourth of July and Other Freaky Facts about the First Twenty-five Presidents, illustrated by Matthew Skeens, Picture Window Books (Minneapolis, MN), 2008.

Your Skin Weighs More than Your Brain and Other Freaky Facts about Your Skin, Skeleton, and Other Body Parts, illustrated by Matthew Skeens, Picture Window Books (Minneapolis, MN), 2008.

It Never Rains in Antarctica and Other Freaky Facts about Climate, Land, and Nature, illustrated by Matthew Skeens, Picture Window Books (Minneapolis, MN), 2009.

There Are Millions of Millionaires and Other Freaky Facts about Earning, Saving, and Spending, illustrated by Matthew Skeens, Picture Window Books (Minneapolis, MN), 2009.

You Blink Twelve Times a Minute and Other Freaky Facts about the Human Body, illustrated by Matthew Skeens, Picture Window Books (Minneapolis, MN), 2009.

FICTION; FOR CHILDREN

What Kind of Family Is This?: A Book about Stepfamilies, illustrated by Ellen Dolce, Golden Books (New York, NY), 1985.

I'm Not So Different: A Book about Handicaps, illustrated by Pat Schories, Golden Books (New York, NY), 1986.

Who's the Boss Here?: A Book about Parental Authority, illustrated by Eugenie, Golden Books (New York, NY), 1986.

Boo the Ghost Has a Party, Xerox Educational Publications (Middletown, CT), 1986.

Boo the Ghost and the Robbers, Xerox Educational Publications (Middletown, CT), 1987.

Boo the Ghost and the Magic Hat, Xerox Education Publications (Middletown, CT), 1988.

(Under pseudonym Carrie Austin) *Julie's Boy Problem* ("Party Line" series), Berkeley (New York, NY), 1990.

(Under pseudonym Carrie Austin) *Allie's Wild Surprise* ("Party Line" series), Berkeley (New York, NY), 1990.

Whose House?, illustrated by Kay Chorao, Harcourt (San Diego, CA), 2004.

"ROBERT" SERIES; FOR CHILDREN

Oh No, It's Robert, illustrated by Paul Brewer, Cricket Books (Chicago, IL), 1999.

Robert and the Attack of the Giant Tarantula, illustrated by Paul Brewer, Scholastic (New York, NY), 1999.

Robert and the Great Pepperoni, illustrated by Paul Brewer, Cricket Books (Chicago, IL), 2002.

Robert and the Weird and Wacky Facts, illustrated by Paul Brewer, Cricket Books (Chicago, IL), 2002.

Robert and the Back-to-School Special, illustrated by Paul Brewer, Cricket Books (Chicago, IL), 2002.

Robert and the Lemming Problem, illustrated by Paul Brewer, Cricket Books (Chicago, IL), 2003.

Robert and the Three Wishes, illustrated by Paul Brewer, Cricket Books (Chicago, IL), 2003.

Robert and the Great Escape, illustrated by Paul Brewer, Cricket Books (Chicago, IL), 2003.

Robert and the Terrible Secret, illustrated by Paul Brewer, Cricket Books (Chicago, IL), 2004.

Robert Takes a Stand, illustrated by Paul Brewer, Cricket Books (Chicago, IL), 2004.

Robert Finds a Way, illustrated by Paul Brewer, Cricket Books (Chicago, IL), 2005.

Robert and the Practical Jokes, illustrated by Paul Brewer, Cricket Books (Chicago, IL), 2006.

Robert and the Happy Endings, illustrated by Paul Brewer, Cricket Books (Chicago, IL), 2007.

Robert Goes to Camp, illustrated by Paul Brewer, Cricket Books (Chicago, IL), 2007.

OTHER

How to Write a Children's Book and Get It Published, Scribner (New York, NY), 1984, 3rd edition, Wiley (Hoboken, NJ), 2004.

Contributor to books and periodicals for and about children, including *Cricket, Ladybug,* and *Once upon a Time.*

Sidelights

The author and illustrator of fiction, nonfiction, and picture books for young readers and the illustrator of works by such writers as Stella Pevsner and Antonia Barber, Barbara Seuling is well known for her "Freaky Facts" books, as well as for her "Robert" series about an el-

ementary school boy and his humorous escapades in the classroom. The informational "Freaky Facts" books, organized thematically, provide middle graders with little-known facts, myths, and legends on such subjects as sports, law, money, television, geography, the weather, the human body, and the presidency. Reflecting the author's fascination with her subjects, the "Freaky Facts" books are generally considered both edifying and entertaining.

Seuling is also the author of individual volumes of middle-grade nonfiction on such topics as natural disasters, safety, and creating a magic show. In addition, she has written books on the art of writing and being published and has edited a popular guide to New York City for children. As the creator of picture books for preschoolers and early readers, Seuling is the author and illustrator of a well-received retelling of an English folktale; works that address such topics as friendship and individuality; and three stories about Boo, a ghost. For older children, she has written bibliotherapy titles on being handicapped, adjusting to a new stepfamily, and establishing personal independence with parents as well as two stories for middle graders published under the pseudonym of Carrie Austin. Seuling is also the creator of activity books on some of children's favorite subjects, such as monsters, ghosts, dinosaurs, crafts, and holidays.

"My early years," Seuling explained in her essay in *Something about the Author Autobiography Series* (*SAAS*), "were the part of my childhood that left the deepest impression, and it is where I feel most connected." Born and raised in the Bensonhurst section of Brooklyn, New York, she was the middle child and

In **The Teeny, Tiny Woman** *Barbara Seuling highlights her retelling of a traditional tale with unique, detailed art.* (Copyright © 1976 by Barbara Seuling. All rights reserved. Reproduced by permission of Viking Penguin, a division of Penguin Putnam, Inc.)

only girl in her family, which also included two brothers. Her parents, Kaspar and Helen Seuling, were influential figures in Barbara's decision to create books for children. "My mother," Seuling explained, "passed on to me her love of reading, of fairy tales and mythology and stories in general. . . . While my mother filled my head with a love of books, it was my father who fostered the magic and wonder in our childhood, especially around the holidays." Her father, Seuling recalled, "had a unique, witty [writing] style. I like to think I inherited some of my feeling for writing from him."

Growing up in the richly varied area of Bensonhurst, Seuling absorbed neighborhood life as well as the stories passed on by members of her family. "I didn't know then, of course," she recalled in *SAAS*, "that I was collecting details—the colors, the sounds, the language, the sights, the emotions, of my world—and that I would later use them as a writer and artist." She was also greatly influenced by the popular culture of the time: radio shows like "Gangbusters," "The Green Hornet," and "Inner Sanctum"; the comics; and movies, which, Seuling wrote, "left a great impression on me, and it's no wonder that one of my freaky fact books—*The Loudest Screen Kiss and Other Little-known Movie Facts*—is about them."

While Seuling was developing her love of story, she was also establishing her talent as an artist. "I showed talent for drawing as soon as I could hold a pencil," she recalled. "For a long time, my talent for drawing became an important part of my identity. My family was close, but never showed affection openly. The praise and encouragement I received through my drawing, however, seemed to make up for that, giving me a sense of importance. All through my school years, my skill in drawing served as a kind of reminder to an otherwise not-very-confident youngster that I was really good at something." In addition to her interest in art, Seuling was developing a love of nature, fostered by the summers she spent outside of New York City. "These summers," she wrote, "instilled in me a deep love of the country and of space and time to explore and discover the natural world. They balanced my view so that I did not grow up thinking city life was the only life."

In grade school, Seuling was, she recalled, a "good student, if rather passive." In junior high, she experienced some difficulties, both social and academic—"I just wasn't ready for all the changes in my life, physical and social, happening all at once." However, she made some friends and learned to cope with her problem subjects, science and algebra. In addition, she was voted wittiest in her class, claiming, she once told *SATA,* "I've been clowning around ever since." In the summer between junior high and high school, Seuling went to Indiana to live with one of her cousins, an experience that helped her to gain self-confidence. "My trip to Indiana—seeing a slice of another way of life," she recalled, "set off something inside of me. . . . I didn't know what I wanted, but it seemed to be outside school, even outside Brooklyn. I began to question what I

would do with my life, what I might accomplish. I wanted to see so much of the world, do so much, be *useful.*" By the time Seuling reached high school, there "was certainly none of the trauma that junior high had for me," she wrote in *SAAS.*

At fourteen, Seuling saw the movie *With a Song in My Heart,* the story of singer Jane Froman, who learned to walk again after surviving a plane crash that occurred while she was traveling as part of the USO. Froman's "strength and courage," wrote Seuling, "became my model for all that a person could be." Becoming a member of the Jane Froman fan club, Seuling met Froman in person and became friends with her. "It was through Jane," Seuling wrote, "that I began writing." Becoming the assistant editor of the Froman fan club journal, she wrote and illustrated stories and edited features. "I developed my love for editing at this point," she recalled

in *SAAS,* "and while I still didn't think of myself as a writer, I was becoming one. I was, at that time, more confident in my abilities as an artist." The editor of the fan club journal, Winnette Glasgow, has remained Seuling's lifelong friend and has collaborated with her on several works.

Seuling attended night school at Hunter College in the Bronx while working at an insurance company during the day; at nineteen, she changed jobs and schools, taking a position at Columbia University, which offered free college credits as a benefit. She took a room with a single mother in exchange for part-time child-care help. Struggling with the balance of work and school, Seuling decided to take a full-time position as the office manager of an investment company. In charge of hiring temporary help, she hired Winnette Glasgow and Nancy Garden, a budding writer who later became a successful

Seuling's text for **Spring Song** *is brought to life in stylized artwork by Greg Newbold.* (Gulliver Books, 2001. Illustration copyright © 2001 by Greg Newbold. Reproduced by permission.)

children's author. Seuling and Garden collaborated on a tale for young readers—"a long story about a bookworm," Seuling remembers—with Garden doing the text and Seuling the pictures. When the investment company went bankrupt, Seuling found a position at Dell Publishing Company as a secretary in the adult trade department; when Dell created a new department for children's books, Seuling transferred into it. Working with editor Lee Hoffman, she began to learn about the craft of editing and about the principles of successful writing for children. Seuling then became an assistant children's book editor and also began writing her own works. Her first book, *Freaky Facts,* was written for the Weekly Reader Book Club and published in paperback. *Freaky Facts* compiles hundreds of humorous and outrageous facts on a wide range of subjects, from, Seuling wrote in *SAAS,* "language and hair to animal behavior and diseases." This compilation, she continued, "came from my own love of the strange and fascinating. As a child I had devoured Ripley's *Believe It or Not* in the Sunday funnies and later on in paperback books. . . . I knew strange and funny facts would entertain kids, and I could illustrate them humorously as well. This little book began a long trail of fact books for me that has not stopped yet."

While creating her own books, Seuling continued to work at Dell with Lee Hoffman's successor, George Nicholson. "My association with children's books and publishing," she wrote in *SAAS,* "only whetted my appetite for illustrating. George liked some samples of my drawings that I showed him, and he gave me a middle grade novel to illustrate. My illustrations were mentioned in a couple of reviews, and my career as an illustrator was started." Seuling showed Nicholson, who had moved from Dell to Viking, her first ideas for a version of the English folktale "The Teeny Tiny Woman." When she had completed the book, Nicholson accepted it for publication. *The Teeny Tiny Woman: An Old English Ghost Tale* is a picture-book version of the ghost story in which a small woman in a miniature house finds a small bone on top of a tiny grave. When she gets home, the woman puts the bone in some soup and hears a voice saying, "Give me my bone." She does not give up the bone; instead, she tells the voice to take it. Seuling illustrates the tale in soft pencil with rosy overlays and incorporates hand-lettering into her drawings. A critic in *Publishers Weekly* noted that this "just-for-fun ghost story . . . is embellished with exuberant pictures," while a *School Library Journal* reviewer called *The Teeny Tiny Woman* "a fine new retelling" in which "gentle pencil drawings soften the scare so even the most timid beginning readers will enjoy this."

In *SAAS,* Seuling wrote: "Of all I have written, the work I love best is in picture books. Picture books offer the greatest challenges and bring the most satisfaction. . . . Every word must count, so I have to choose my words carefully, and to hone and polish for the best

Kay Chorao creates detailed images of the natural world that reflect elements of Seuling's story in **Whose House?** (Gulliver Books, 2004. Illustration copyright © 2004 by Kay Chorao. Reproduced by permission of Houghton Mifflin Harcourt Publishing Company.)

effect. This has made me a better writer in all forms, not just in picture books."

Seuling based her next picture book, *The Great Big Elephant and the Very Small Elephant,* on her friendship with Glasgow. Seuling describes this book, which is comprised of three gentle stories illustrated in ink and watercolor that stress the affection of her title characters for each other, as "a picture storybook about two friends who are opposite personalities and who see things differently but who ultimately get along by contributing what they each do best." A contributor in *Publishers Weekly* said that Seuling "tells and shows with equal skill in three stories of friendship. . . . Seuling has given beginners a funny, enduring, and altogether lovely book." *The Great Big Elephant* has received comparisons to Arnold Lobel's "Frog and Toad" books and James Marshall's "George and Martha" series. For example, a reviewer in the *Bulletin of the Center for Children's Books* stated that although *The Great Big Elephant* "hasn't the tenderness of the Lobel stories or the humor of the Marshall books, . . . it's adequate, both in writing style and as a testament to the give-and-take of friendship."

Several of Seuling's picture books have personal identity as their theme. In *The Triplets,* sisters Pattie, Mattie, and Hattie, who have been dressed and treated alike since birth, sequester themselves in their room and

refuse to emerge until they are recognized as individuals. A contributor in *Kirkus Reviews* noted that the book contained "an obvious problem-solution contrivance, but there is some zip in the specific examples and in the author's simple two-color cartoons," while *Horn Book* reviewer Kate M. Flanagan noted the "guileless text" and that the illustrations of the "three round-faced triplets, though identical in appearance, exhibit subtle but distinct differences in facial expressions and mannerisms."

In the easy reader *Just Me,* Seuling depicts a little girl who, over a three-day period, imagines herself as a horse (with hooves made by blocks on her feet), a dragon (with a jump rope for a tale), and a robot (with a box for a body); finally, she decides to just be herself when her supportive mother says, "I like you best of all." According to *Booklist* reviewer Judith Goldberger, "With this unimposing set of first-person stories, Seuling shines a true yet carefully framed mirror on the younger reader," while a reviewer in *School Library Journal* noted that the "blend of real life and imagination in both text and pictures will strike a chord within any child who's ever . . . been sent to his room for refusing to go against dragon nature and 'be nice.'"

While contributing books to other genres, Seuling continues to write and illustrate her nonfiction collections of arcane information. One of the earliest "Freaky Facts" titles, *You Can't Eat Peanuts in Church and Other Little-known Laws,* is a collection of obscure and offbeat laws gathered from around the United States and illustrated in cartoon-like line drawings that underscore the incongruous nature of the laws. Writing in *School Library Journal,* Linda Kochinski called *You Can't Eat Peanuts in Church and Other Little-known Laws* "[just] the ticket for upper elementary and junior high trivia buffs." Seuling's research for *The Last Cow on the White House Lawn and Other Little-known Facts about the Presidency,* a collection of facts, firsts, and unique accomplishments, took the author to the Library of Congress, where she investigated the diaries and journals of presidents from George Washington to Jimmy Carter as well as their families and staffs. As *Booklist* reviewer Denise M. Wilms claimed, Seuling's "historical hodgepodge is entertaining, to say the least," while a *Publishers Weekly* critic wrote that "trivia fans have taken to Seuling's other books. . . . They may do the same for her new collection."

In *Elephants Can't Jump and Other Freaky Facts about Animals,* Seuling organizes her information in eleven categories such as eating habits, dwellings, and reproduction and enhances her facts with humorous line drawings. *Appraisal* reviewer Althea L. Phillips predicted that "trivia enthusiasts with an interest in animals will devour this book," while Nancy Murphy, writing in the same publication, noted that Seuling provides "a fresh outlook on some familiar bits of knowledge." In *School Library Journal* Mavis D. Arizzi commented: "These unusual bits of information just might inspire

some students to do further research into the characteristics of various animals." With *You Can't Sneeze with Your Eyes Open and Other Freaky Facts about the Human Body,* Seuling covers, in the words of *Appraisal* reviewer Renee E. Blumenkrantz, "amusing and amazing facts" about the body in general, body systems and functions, the brain, birth, death, disease, medical practices, and unusual beliefs. She notes that cricket chirps can be used to determine temperature and that badgers play leap frog in *Some Porcupines Wrestle and Other Freaky Facts about Animal Antics and Families,* a work that presents "factual information in a quick, colorful format," according to *School Library Journal* contributor Cynde Suite.

Looking back on the "Freaky Facts" books, Seuling wrote, "I was fast becoming known for these books, and it worried me that I would be considered the Queen of Trivia instead of a bona fide writer of children's books, so I tried to steer away from them for a while. Every time I thought I had done my last freaky fact book, however, something came along to persuade me to do another one. . . . From the feedback I've received over the years . . . I'd say that these books, with their short readable bits of funny or fascinating information, have turned more than a few reluctant readers onto reading, and that pleases me enormously." Yet Seuling could not resist writing more fact books, and has added such titles as *Drip! Drop!: How Water Gets to Your Tap, From Head to Toe: The Amazing Human Body and How It Works,* and *Flick a Switch: How Electricity Gets to Your Home,* to her roster of nonfiction treats.

Further works for younger children include the companion picture book titles *Winter Lullaby* and *Spring Song,* both illustrated by Greg Newbold. The pair celebrates the seasons through lyrical texts, using a question-and-answer format. In the first title, Seuling tells what happens as winter approaches, employing literary techniques such as "subtle alliteration and assonance as well as rhyme," which, according to Peg Solonika of *School Library Journal,* "work well for reading aloud." *Winter Lullaby* is "a picture-perfect conclusion to a frosty night," commented *Booklist* reviewer Ellen Mandel. Spring gets a similar treatment in *Spring Song.* Although "sometimes clumsy" in the view of a *Publishers Weekly* contributor, the text presents "a joyful introduction to the creatures of the woodland forest, mountain range, meadow, and marshland." In a more-recent title with an environmental theme, *Whose House?,* Seuling looks at a variety of animal abodes through the eyes of an imaginative youngster. "Light humor and a comforting message give this lots of child appeal," wrote Ilene Cooper in *Booklist.*

According to *Booklist* critic Todd Morning, Seuling's "Robert" series of easy readers are known for "a fast-moving plot, short chapters, and witty writing." Geared to readers in grades two through four, they also feature familiar characters and situations, such as the desire for

a dog or for stress-free recognition from a teacher. Reviewing *Robert and the Back-to-School Special*, a *Kirkus Reviews* critic praised Seuling's command of a "tight plot and realistic situations," predicting that "young readers will identify with and root" for the young protagonist. Seuling examines themes of identity and self-reliance in *Robert and the Lemming Problem*. "The message is positive, and the plot has solid child appeal," wrote Shelle Rosenfeld in *Booklist*. Accompanying Seuling's humorous stories are pen-and-ink drawings by Paul Brewer, which "create satisfying visual interest," wrote Janie Schomberg in a *School Library Journal* review of *Robert and the Great Pepperoni*.

Other reviewers saw much to like about the "Robert" books, including a *Kirkus Reviews* contributor who appreciated the "familiar and comforting" and yet "goofy but believable situations" in *Robert and the Weird and Wacky Facts*. In that work, Seuling combined her long-held penchant for interesting tidbits and her likeable Robert character when Robert tries to enter a television trivia contest; Morning applauded the "easy-to-read text, . . . fast-moving plot, short chapters, and witty writing." The youngster helps his best friend run for class president and questions his grandmother about her love of furs in *Robert Takes a Stand*. "Humor abounds," observed *School Library Journal* critic Andrea Tarr. A series of pranks is at the center of *Robert and the Practical Jokes*, a "well-plotted story grounded in the details of everyday life," as *Booklist* contributor Carolyn Phelan noted. The affable third-grader befriends a hearing impaired classmate in *Robert and the Happy Endings*, a tale written "with a fine-tuned perception of children's concerns," Phelan observed.

In addition to working as an author, illustrator, and editor, Seuling has been a teacher at the Bank Street College, the Manuscript Workshop, and the Institute for Children's Literature, among other places, and has become recognized as an authority on writing for children. She is eager to share her insight with would-be writers and in 1984 wrote *How to Write a Children's Book and Get It Published*, which she revised and expanded in a 2004 edition. A member of the Society of Children's Book Writers and Illustrators' board of advisors, Seuling noted on her home page that "writing is a tough game. You have to keep proving yourself and you can never take the next success for granted. In spite of that, I continue to love my work."

Biographical and Critical Sources

BOOKS

Seuling, Barbara, *Just Me*, Harcourt (New York, NY), 1982.

Seuling, Barbara, essay in *Something about the Author Autobiography Series*, Volume 24, Gale (Detroit, MI), 1997.

PERIODICALS

Appraisal, fall, 1985, Nancy Murphy and Althea L. Phillips, reviews of *Elephants Can't Jump and Other Freaky Facts about Animals*, pp. 35-36; fall, 1987, Renee E. Blumenkrantz and John R. Pancella, reviews of *You Can't Sneeze with Your Eyes Open and Other Freaky Facts about the Human Body*, pp. 49-50.

Booklist, September 1, 1978, Denise M. Wilms, review of *The Last Cow on the White House Lawn and Other Little-known Facts about the Presidency*, p. 53; June 15, 1982, Judith Goldberger, review of *Just Me*, p. 1372; September 1, 1998, Ellen Mandel, review of *Winter Lullaby*, p. 123; July, 1999, Kay Weisman, review of *Oh No, It's Robert*, p. 1947; April 15, 2001, Carolyn Phelan, review of *Spring Song*, p. 1566; April 1, 2002, Todd Morning, review of *Robert and the Weird and Wacky Facts*, p. 1329; January 1, 2003, Carolyn Phelan, review of *Robert and the Back-to-School Special*, p. 893; April 1, 2003, Shelle Rosenfeld, review of *Robert and the Lemming Problem*, p. 1398; September 1, 2003, Roger Leslie, review of *Flick a Switch: How Electricity Gets to Your Home*, p. 126; December 1, 2003, Ilene Cooper, review of *Robert and the Great Escape*, p. 669; April 1, 2003, Shelle Rosenfeld, review of *Robert and the Lemming Problem*, p. 1398; April 1, 2004, Jennifer Locke, review of *Robert Takes a Stand*, p. 1364; May 1, 2004, Ilene Cooper, review of *Whose House?*, p. 1564; May 1, 2006, Carolyn Phelan, review of *Robert and the Practical Jokes*, p. 82; January 1, 2007, Carolyn Phelan, review of *Robert and the Happy Endings*, p. 81.

Bulletin of the Center for Children's Books, October, 1997, review of *The Great Big Elephant and the Very Small Elephant*, pp. 36-37; July, 1999, Janice M. DelNegro, review of *Oh No, It's Robert* p. 400.

Horn Book, August, 1976, Virginia Haviland, review of *The Teeny Tiny Woman: An Old English Ghost Tale*, pp. 591-592; April, 1980, Kate M. Flanagan, review of *The Triplets*, p. 400; January-February, 2002, Betty Carter, review of *Robert and the Great Pepperoni*, pp. 83-84; July-August, 2002, Betty Carter, review of *Robert and the Weird and Wacky Facts*, pp. 471-472; July-August, 2004, Betty Carter, review of *Robert Takes a Stand*, p. 460; July-August, 2006, Betty Carter, review of *Robert and the Practical Jokes*, p. 450.

Kirkus Reviews, July 15, 1978, pp. 752-753; April 1, 1980, review of *Triplets*, p. 437; February 15, 2001, review of *Spring Song*, p. 265; March, 2002, review of *Robert and the Weird and Wacky Facts*, p. 246; August 15, 2002, review of *From Head to Toe: The Amazing Human Body and How It Works*, p. 1236; October 1, 2002, review of *Robert and the Back-to-School Special*, p. 1481; March 1, 2003, review of *Robert and the Lemming Problem*, p. 398.

Publishers Weekly, April 12, 1976, review of *The Teeny Tiny Woman*, p. 66; June 13, 1977, review of *The Great Big Elephant and the Very Small Elephant*, p. 108; May 15, 1978, review of *The Last Cow on the White House Lawn and Other Little-known Facts about the Presidency*, p. 104; October 5, 1998, review of *Winter Lullaby*, p. 88; June 14, 1999, review of *Oh*

No, It's Robert, p. 70; February 26, 2001, review of *Spring Song,* p. 84; September 6, 2002, review of *From Head to Toe,* p. 71.

School Library Journal, October, 1975, Linda Kochinski, review of *You Can't Eat Peanuts in Church and Other Little-known Laws,* p. 101; May, 1976, review of *The Teeny Tiny Woman,* p. 75; May, 1982, review of *Just Me,* p. 80; August, 1982, p. 122; March, 1985, Mavis D. Arizzi, review of *Elephants Can't Jump and Other Freaky Facts about Animals,* p. 171; February, 1987, Denise L. Moll, review of *You Can't Sneeze with Your Eyes Open and Other Freaky Facts about the Human Body,* p. 84; September, 1998, Peg Solonika, review of *Winter Lullaby,* p. 198; July, 1999, Linda Beck, review of *Oh No, It's Robert,* p. 80; February, 2001, Ellen Heath, review of *Drip! Drop!,* p. 115; May, 2001, Helen Foster, review of *Spring Song,* p. 135; October, 2001, Janie Schomberg, review of *Robert and the Great Pepperoni,* p. 131; July, 2002, John Sigwald, review of *Robert and the Weird and Wacky Tales,* pp. 98-99; November, 2002, Dona Ratterree, review of *From Head to Toe,* p. 148; November, 2003, Lynda Ritterman, review of *Flick a Switch,* p. 130; December, 2003, Tina Zubak, review of *Robert and the Lemming Problem,* p. 126; January, 2004, Shelley B. Sutherland, review of *Robert and the Great Escape,* p. 106; April, 2004, Andrea Tarr, review of *Robert Takes a Stand,* p. 124; August, 2004, Elaine Lesh Morgan, review of *Whose House?,* p. 93; April, 2005, Robyn Walker, review of *Robert Finds a Way,* p. 112; March, 2006, Alison Grant, review of *Robert and the Practical Jokes,* p. 202; June, 2007, Michelle Easley Bridges, review of *Robert and the Happy Endings,* p. 123; June, 2008, Cynde Suite, reviews of *One President Was Born on Independence Day and Other Freaky Facts about the Twenty-sixth through Forty-third Presidents* and *Some Porcupines Wrestle and Other Freaky Facts about Animal Antics and Families,* p. 131.

ONLINE

Barbara Seuling Home Page, http://www.barbaraseuling. com (September 10, 2008).

*   *   *

SHAPIRO, Jody Fickes 1940-

Personal

Born December 25, 1940, in Detroit, MI; married Perry Shapiro (a professor of economics); children: David, Michael; (step children) Mark, Jon, Carol, and Tom Fickes; Elizabeth, Sam, and Sarah Shapiro. *Education:* Wayne State University, degree, 1961; Peabody College, M.L.S., 1964; also attended University of Michigan.

Addresses

Home—Ventura, CA. *E-mail*—jody@jodyfickesshapiro. com.

Career

Writer. Librarian in Oak Ridge, TN, 1964; children's librarian in Glendora, CA, 1966-78; Adventures for Kids (children's bookstore), owner, 1979-2006; author of children's books, 2003—.

Awards, Honors

Charles S. Haslam Award for Excellence in Bookselling, American Booksellers Association, 2002; Lucile Micheels Pannell Award for excellence in children's bookselling, Women's National Book Association, 1994; Dorothy C. McKenzie Award for Distinguished Contribution to the Field of Children's Literature, Children's Literature Council of Southern California, 2006.

Writings

Up, Up, Up! It's Apple Picking Time, illustrated by Kitty Harvill, Holiday House (New York, NY), 2003.
Family Lullaby, illustrated by Cathie Felstead, Greenwillow Books (New York, NY), 2007.

Contributor to books, including *Great Books I Have Read,* by Bev Armstrong, Learning Works (Santa Barbara, CA), 1998. Book column editor for *The Gifted Education Communicator* (newsletter).

Sidelights

After working much of her career as a children's librarian and owner of a children's bookstore in California, Jody Fickes Shapiro began penning her own books for the youngest reader in 2003 with the publication of *Up, Up, Up! It's Apple Picking Time.* Throughout her years as a librarian and bookseller, "children's book ideas were always in the back of my mind but I was too busy reading other people's books to write my own," Shapiro related on her home page. However, seeing the need for a title set outside the typical Midwestern orchard, the author used her family's experience helping relatives on a California apple ranch to write *Up, Up, Up!* The book follows the activities of a family visiting their grandparents' orchard, collecting fallen apples for cider, picking fresh apples to sell, and preparing others for pie. Reviewing the picture book in *School Library Journal,* Linda M. Kenton described *Up, Up, Up!* as "a pleasant addition to harvest units and storytimes."

Shapiro's picture book *Family Lullaby* features "repeated words and design [to] create a lullaby to family love," a *Kirkus Reviews* critic remarked. In the book, each member of the family contributes to the nurturing of the youngest child, with dad burping, mom feeding, and grandpa playing with the happy baby. According to a *Publishers Weekly* contributor, in *Family Lullaby* Shapiro offers "a deserving testament to the extended family at the core of a child's universe."

During an interview with Sally Lodge for *Publishers Weekly,* Shapiro explained the differences in writing her first two children's books. While working on *Up, Up,*

Up! she viewed her manuscript "more as a bookseller than an author." However, Shapiro noted, "once I got the writing bug I decided to try other books as well," moving into picture books and books for readers in the middle grades. As for the career transition that has drawn her into writing children's literature, the former librarian and bookseller remarked to Lodge: "There is still plenty of material in my brain and more books that I would love to get out of my system and out into the world. . . . It's fun to be wearing a new hat at this stage of my life."

Biographical and Critical Sources

PERIODICALS

Kirkus Reviews, August 15, 2003, review of *Up, Up, Up! It's Apple Picking Time,* p. 1079; April 15, 2007, review of *Family Lullaby.*
Publishers Weekly, September 15, 2003, review of *Up, Up, Up!,* p. 64; September 29, 2003, Sally Lodge, "Making the Leap: A Trio of Booksellers Don Authors' Caps" (interview), p. 24; May 21, 2007, review of *Family Lullaby,* p. 53.
School Library Journal, September, 2003, Linda M. Kenton, review of *Up, Up, Up!,* p. 190; July, 2007, Amy Lilien-Harper, review of *Family Lullaby,* p. 84.

ONLINE

Jody Fickes Shapiro Home Page, http://www.jodyfickes shapiro.com (October 17, 2008).

*   *   *

SHARENOW, Robert

Personal

Married; children: two daughters. *Education:* Brandeis University, graduate; New York University, M.A. (American studies).

Addresses

Home and office—New York, NY.

Career

Author and producer of television programming. A&E (television network), vice president, 2003-07, senior vice president of nonfiction and alternative programming, 2007—. Executive producer of History Channel television series *The Week in History;* co-creator of *Extreme History with Roger Daltrey.*

Awards, Honors

American Library Association Best of the Best Books for Young Adults designation, for *My Mother the Cheerleader.*

Writings

JUVENILE FICTION

My Mother the Cheerleader, Laura Geringer Books (New York, NY), 2007.

Also author of screenplay *Stephen Crane's The Monster.*

Sidelights

Robert Sharenow has spent much of his career producing reality-based television. He has been responsible for such popular shows as *Dog the Bounty Hunter* and *Criss Angel: Mind Freak.* Inspired by reading another interesting nonfiction story, *Travels with Charley,* by John Steinbeck, Sharenow decided to write a novel based on some of the events Steinbeck experienced. In an interview on *Harpercollins.com,* Sharenow commented that "on some level, I've always wanted to be a writer (although the desire wasn't fully expressed until I got out of college). I've always been awed by books and have been drawn to libraries and bookstores."

Written in the early morning hours and on business trips, *My Mother the Cheerleader* is set in 1960. As a group of white mothers dubbed "The Cheerleaders" protest school integration in New Orleans, their protests threaten a six-year-old black girl who is trying to attend their local school. Susan Riley, writing in *School Library Journal,* noted that Sharenow's "powerfully written . . . coming-of-age story [is] flamed by a historical event." Hazel Rochman praised the author's fiction debut in *Booklist,* concluding that "readers will be held fast by the history told from the inside as adult Louise remembers the vicious role of ordinary people." A *Publishers Weekly* reviewer predicted that *My Mother the Cheerleader* will hold the attention of young adults: "Teens should remain riveted right through the devastating conclusion to Sharenow's promising work of historical fiction." A *Kirkus Reviews* contributor asserted that the novel "provides an unflinching look at the violence and hatred that permeated" the civil rights era of the mid-twentieth century.

On the HarperCollins Web site, Sharenow asserted that "it was quite flattering hearing that some readers assumed the book was written by a female author because of the authenticity of my narrator's voice. To some degree fiction writing is an act of persuasion. I try to convince readers that my characters and situations are as real as they can possibly be." Giving advice to future authors, Sharenow concluded to Laughran: "Just write whatever you are passionate about. Don't try to write what you think is cool or what you think you're supposed to write. I had no direct connection to the subjects of my book. I'm not a 13-year-old girl. I'm not from New Orleans. And I wasn't even born when the book takes place. Yet, I was inspired to write that story. Follow your passion."

Biographical and Critical Sources

PERIODICALS

Booklist, July 1, 2007, Hazel Rochman, review of *My Mother the Cheerleader,* p. 61.
Kirkus Reviews, April 1, 2007, review of *My Mother the Cheerleader.*
Kliatt, May, 2007, Myrna Marler, review of *My Mother the Cheerleader,* p. 20.
Publishers Weekly, May 28, 2007, review of *My Mother the Cheerleader,* p. 65.
School Library Journal, July, 2007, Susan Riley, review of *My Mother the Cheerleader,* p. 110.

ONLINE

A & E Web site, http://www.aetn.com/ (September 25, 2008).
CableU Web site, http://www.cableu.tv/cableu (September 1, 2008), interview with Sharenow.
HarperCollins Web site, http://www.harpercollins.com/ (September 1, 2008), interview with Sharenow.*

* * *

SIY, Alexandra

Personal

Born in Clarksville, NY; married; children. *Education:* Attended University of Colorado; State University of New York at Plattsburgh, B.A. (biology); State University of New York at Albany, M.S. (science education).

Addresses

Home and office—NY. *E-mail*—alex@alexandrasiy.com.

Career

Writer. Taught high school biology in New Haven, CT; has also worked as a janitor, waitress, bookkeeper, swimming teacher, secretary, lifeguard, landscaper, copywriter, and research technician.

Member

Authors Guild.

Awards, Honors

Parents' Choice Silver Honor designation, 2001, for *Footprints on the Moon;* three books in "Global Villages" series earned Notable Trade Books in the Field of Social Studies designations, National Council for the Social Studies/Children's Book Council; Outstanding Science Trade Book Selectors' Choice, National Science Teachers Association, Orbis Pictus Honor Book designation, and finalist, American Association for the Advancement of Science/Subaru Science Books & Films Prize for Excellence in Science Books, all 2006, all for *Mosquito Bite;* One Hundred Titles for Reading and Sharing designation, New York Public Library, Outstanding Science Trade Book Selectors' Choice, National Science Teachers Association, and Best of the Best designation, Chicago Public Library, all 2007, all for *Sneeze!*

Writings

Footprints on the Moon, Charlesbridge (Watertown, MA), 2001.
(And photographer) *Mosquito Bite,* electron microphotographs by Dennis Kunkel, Charlesbridge (Watertown, MA), 2005.
(And photographer) *Sneeze!,* electron microphotographs by Dennis Kunkel, Charlesbridge (Watertown, MA), 2007.
One Tractor: A Counting Book, illustrated by Jacqueline Rogers, Holiday House (New York, NY), 2008.

Contributor to anthologies, including *Sports Shorts* and *What a Song Can Do.*

"CIRCLE OF LIFE" SERIES; NONFICTION

Ancient Forests, Dillon Press (New York, NY), 1991.
Arctic National Wildlife Refuge, Dillon Press (New York, NY), 1991.
Hawaiian Islands, Dillon Press (New York, NY), 1991.
Native Grasslands, Dillon Press (New York, NY), 1991.
The Great Astrolabe Reef, Dillon Press (New York, NY), 1992.
The Brazilian Rain Forest, Dillon Press (New York, NY), 1992.

"GLOBAL VILLAGES" SERIES; NONFICTION

The Efe: People of the Ituri Rain Forest, Dillon Press (New York, NY), 1993.
The Waorani: People of the Ecuadoran Rain Forest, Dillon Press (New York, NY), 1993.
The Penan: People of the Borneo Jungle, Dillon Press (New York, NY), 1993.
The Eeyou: People of Eastern James Bay, Dillon Press (New York, NY), 1993.

Sidelights

A former high school biology teacher, Alexandra Siy is the author of a number of award-winning nonfiction books, including *Mosquito Bite* and *Sneeze!,* both fea-

turing black-and-white photographs by Siy and electron microphotographs by Dennis Kunkel. In addition, Siy has written *One Tractor: A Counting Book,* a work for early readers.

In *Mosquito Bite,* a group of children playing hide-and-seek on a summer night are hunted by a female Culex pipiens mosquito. As Siy describes one child's search for his friends, she also provides detailed information about the mosquito's life cycle and development as well as the health problems the insect poses. The work garnered strong reviews, and several critics complimented the pairing of Siy's narrative and Kunkel's digitally colored micrographs. According to a contributor in

Kirkus Reviews, Kunkel's photos "make irresistible eye candy—rendered even more fascinating by Siy's clear, specific descriptions," and Patricia Manning, writing in *Booklist,* remarked that the work "is fascinating for its photography and the informative text and captions."

Siy examines nine causes of sneezing and describes the body parts responsible for the explosive reflex in *Sneeze!,* a "lively, charming, beautifully designed and illustrated book," according to Christopher Arlyn in *Science and Children.* The work includes Siy's photographs of children in mid-sneeze, as well as Kunkel's micrographs of pollen grains, the flu virus, and other irritants. A *Kirkus Reviews* critic stated that *Sneeze!* "has

Cover of Alexandra Siy's picture book Sneeze!, *which gives readers a microscopic view of something we all do.* (Photograph copyright © 2007 by Alexandra Siy. Illustration copyright © 2007 by Dennis Kunkel. Used by permission of Charlesbridge Publishing, Inc. All rights reserved.)

Jacqueline Rogers contributes the artwork to Siy's rural-themed picture book **One Tractor.** (Illustration copyright © 2008 by Jacqueline Rogers. Reproduced by permission of Holiday House, Inc.)

it all—from explosive humor and drama to fascinating pictures," and Anne Chapman Callaghan in *School Library Journal* commented that Siy's "text is chatty and inviting."

A youngster engages in a series of wild adventures in *One Tractor,* a "clever one-to-ten counting book," according to a contributor in *Kirkus Reviews.* Inspired by a set of toys, the boy battles a fire and builds a road with the help of his mouse pal and a trio of pirates. Siy's tale allows young readers "an opportunity to rec-

ognize the kind of imaginative play they engage in every day," Hazel Rochman noted in her *Booklist* review of *One Tractor.*

Biographical and Critical Sources

PERIODICALS

Booklist, June 1, 2005, Karin Snelson, review of *Mosquito Bite,* p. 1802; July 1, 2007, Hazel Rochman, review of *Sneeze!,* p. 47; March 1, 2008, Hazel Rochman, review of *One Tractor: A Counting Book,* p. 73.

Horn Book, September-October, 2005, Danielle J. Ford, review of *Mosquito Bite,* p. 608; November-December, 2007, Danielle J. Ford, review of *Sneeze!,* p. 702.

Kirkus Reviews, June 15, 2005, review of *Mosquito Bite,* p. 691; June 15, 2007, review of *Sneeze!;* January 15, 2008, review of *One Tractor.*

School Library Journal, December, 2005, Patricia Manning, review of *Mosquito Bite,* p. 134; September, 2007, Anne Chapman Callaghan, review of *Sneeze!,* p. 220; February, 2008, Ieva Bates, review of *One Tractor,* p. 96.

Science and Children, January, 2008, Christopher Arlyn, review of *Sneeze!,* p. 67.

ONLINE

Alexandra Siy Home Page, http://www.alexandrasiy.com (September 10, 2008).

Charlesbridge Web site, http://www.charlesbridge.com/ (September 10, 2008), "Alexandra Siy."*

*   *   *

SLADE, Christian 1974-

Personal

Born 1974, in NJ; married Ann Borowski; children: Kate, Nate. *Education:* Syracuse University, M.A., 2005.

Addresses

Home and office—Winter Garden, FL. *Agent*—Mendola Artists Reps, Ltd., 420 Lexington Ave., Penthouse, New York, NY 10170. *E-mail*—christianslade@earthlink.net.

Career

Author and illustrator. Animation illustrator for Disney; freelance illustrator.

Writings

SELF-ILLUSTRATED; FOR CHILDREN

(With wife, Ann Borowski-Slade) *Korgi,* Slade Studio (Winter Garden, FL), 2005, revised as *Korgi Book 1: Sprouting Wings,* Top Shelf Comics, 2007.

(With Ann Borowski-Slade) *Penny's Day Out,* Slade Studio (Winter Garden, FL), 2006.

Korgi Book 2: The Cosmic Collector, Top Shelf Comics, 2008.

ILLUSTRATOR

Joni Sensel, *Reality Leak,* Holt (New York, NY), 2007.

Sally Rogan, *The Daring Adventures of Penhaligon Brush,* Alfred A. Knopf (New York, NY), 2007.

Nathaniel Lachenmeyer, *The Decoy,* Mitten Press (Ann Arbor, MI), 2007.

Kate Wharton, *What Does Mrs. Claus Do?,* Tricycle Press (Berkeley, CA), 2008.

Sidelights

Illustrator and animator Christian Slade has a somewhat unusual source of inspiration for his first major book: his wife's two dogs. As he explained to *Comicon.com* interviewer Chris Beckett, "it actually started when I first got my two Welsh Corgis, Penny and Leo. . . . I feel that the Welsh Corgi is one of the coolest animals in the world. Their design is adorable and their attitude is often hilarious. They are also loyal and caring, like many intelligent dogs. These critters helped me cast my main characters for *Korgi.* The [book] . . . developed because I have always enjoyed sci-fi and fantasy. I imagined *Korgi* for years, but after I chose it as my fi-

Christian Slade creates detailed artwork for S. Jones Rogan's middle-grade novel **The Daring Adventures of Pehaligon Brush.** (Illustration copyright © 2007 by Christian Slade. Used by permission of Alfred A. Knopf, an imprint of Random House Children's Books, a division of Random House, Inc.)

nal thesis project for my Master's Degree, that kicked things forward into development."

A silent—wordless—graphic novel, *Korgi* draws readers into the Korgi Hollow world. In it, human-like fairies named Mollies live alongside the magical Korgis, which look remarkably like Corgi dogs. The story follows the antics of Ivy and her Korgi, Sprout. Speaking with interviewer Zack Smith for *Newsarama.com,* Slade admitted that Sprout's mischievous antics were definitely influenced by his own dog: "There was a tree at our dog park with a forked trunk. For some reason, someone kept putting dog biscuits in the tree. Leo was always smart enough to smell out the cookies and try to jump into the center of the open trunk of the tree containing the hidden treats. It is one of the cutest things I've ever seen. I sketched out his mannerisms trying to leap up with his short legs in my sketchbook."

Critics greeted *Korgi* with enthusiasm. Noting the difficulty of engaging a viewer in a wordless story, a *Publishers Weekly* reviewer added that "Slade's illustrations are so expressive and full of life that the pages radiate the feelings of his characters." Douglas P. Davey, writing in *School Library Journal* also found that the illustrations convey the sense of the story, indicating that *Korgi* is "funny, thrilling, and scary in all the right places."

In addition to *Korgi,* Slade has also created artwork for texts by others. His work on Sally Rogan's *The Daring Adventures of Penhaligon Brush,* about a crafty fox whose antics in a seaside town bring up memories of swashbuckling tales, was praised by several critics. In *Kirkus Reviews* a critic wrote of the book that Slade's "appealing, detailed drawings add a touch of warmth, adventure and fun."

Biographical and Critical Sources

PERIODICALS

Booklist, November 15, 2007, Todd Morning, review of *The Daring Adventures of Penhaligon Brush,* p. 43.
Design Week, April 18, 2008, "Illustrated Woodland Fantasy."
Kirkus Reviews, March 15, 2007, review of *Reality Leak;* September 1, 2007, review of *The Daring Adventures of Penhaligon Brush.*
Publishers Weekly, April 9, 2007, review of *Korgi,* p. 38; September 24, 2007, review of *The Daring Adventures of Penhaligon Brush,* p. 71.
School Library Journal, May, 2007, Steven Engelfried, review of *Reality Leak,* p. 144; November, 2007, Nicki Clausen-Grace, review of *The Daring Adventures of Penhaligon Brush,* p. 136; March, 2008, Douglas P. Davey, review of *Korgi,* p. 227.

ONLINE

Christian Slade Home Page, http://www.sladestudio.com (September 1, 2008).
Christian Slade Web log, http://www.korgihollow.blogspot. com (September 1, 2008).
Comicon Web site, http://www.comicon.com (September 22, 2008), Chris Beckett, review of *Korgi* and interview with Slade.
I-Spot Web site, http://www.theispot.com/ (September 1, 2008), "Christian Slade."
Mitten Press Web site, http://www.mittenpress.com/ (September 1, 2008), "Christian Slade."
Newsarama Web site, http://www.forum.newsarama.com/ (September 1, 2008), Zack Smith, "Talking to Christian Slade about *Korgi.*"
Ten Speed Press Web site, http://www.tenspeed.com/ (September 1, 2008), "Christian Slade."
Top Shelf Comix Web site, http://www.topshelfcomix.com/ (September 1, 2008), "Christian Slade."*

*   *   *

SMITH, James Noel 1950-

Personal

Born 1950; married Michele Warner (an artist); children: two.

Addresses

Home—Unicoi, TN. *Agent*—Friend and Johnson, 39 W. 19th St., No. 606, New York, NY 10011. *E-mail*—james@jamesnoelsmith.com.

Career

Illustrator.

Writings

ILLUSTRATOR

Susan J. Tweit, *Seasons on the Pacific Coast: A Naturalist's Notebook,* Chronicle Books (San Francisco, CA), 1999.
Paul Coelho, *The Alchemist,* HarperOne (New York, NY), 2006.
Shannon Hale, *Book of a Thousand Days,* Bloomsbury (New York, NY), 2007.

OTHER

The Decline of Galveston Bay: A Profile of Government's Failure to Control Pollution in an Endangered American Estuary (nonfiction), Conservation Foundation (Washington, DC), 1972.
(Editor) *Environmental Quality and Social Justice in Urban America; An Exploration of Conflict and Concord among Those Who Seek Environmental Quality and Those Who Seek Social Justice* (conference proceedings), Conservation Foundation (Washington, DC), 1974.

Contributor to periodicals, including *Conde Nast Traveler, Atlantic Monthly, National Geographic, Travel and Leisure, Departures,* and *Food and Wine.*

Biographical and Critical Sources

ONLINE

Friend & Johnson Web site, http://www.friendandjohnson. com/ (September 15, 2008), "James Noel Smith."
James Noel Smith Home Page, http://www.jamesnoelsmith. com (September 15, 2008).*

*   *   *

SMITH, Roland 1951-

Personal

Born November 30, 1951, in Portland, OR; married, wife's name Marie; children: (stepchildren) Bethany, Shawn, Niki. *Education:* Attended Portland State University.

Addresses

Home—Wilsonville, OR. *Agent*—Barbara Kouts, P.O. Box 560, Bellport, NY 11713. *E-mail*—roland@rolandsmith.com.

Career

Zoologist and author. Zoo keeper and senior research biologist at Portland Zoo, Portland, OR, and Point Defiance Zoo, Tacoma, WA, for twenty years; American Zoo Association, red wolf species coordinator, for twelve years; member of U.S. Fish & Wildlife Services Red Wolf Recovery Team. Has appeared on national and local television shows, including *National Geographic, Audubon, Discover the World of Science,* and *Northwest Wild.*

Awards, Honors

Outstanding Trade Books for Children designation, and *Bulletin of the Center for Children's Books* Blue Ribbon Book, both 1990, both for *Sea Otter Rescue;* Notable Children's Trade Book in the Field of Social Studies, and Notable Books for a Global Society, Children's Literature and Reading Specialist Interest Group of the International Reading Association (IRA), both 1996, and Young Readers Choice Award nomination, 1998, all for *Thunder Cave;* Notable Science Trade Books for Children, National Science Teachers Association/Children's Book Council (CBC), and Children's Choices list, IRA/CBC, both 1997, both for *Journey of the Red Wolf;* IRA Children's Choice Award, 1998, IRA Young Adult Choice, and Bank Street College of Edu-

Roland Smith (Reproduced by permission.)

cation Children's Books of the Year designation, both 1999, Nebraska Golden Sower Award, and Florida Sunshine Book Award, both 2000, and Novel of the Year, Jason Project, all for *Jaguar;* Quick Picks for Reluctant Young Adult Readers designation, American Library Association (ALA), and Bank Street College of Education Best Children's Books of the Year designation, all 1999, all for *Sasquatch;* Bank Street College of Education Best Children's Books of the Year designation, and Children's Literature Choice List, both 1999, both for *In the Forest with the Elephants;* Pacific Northwest Booksellers Association Children's Book Award, 1999, and Beacon of Freedom Award, 2002, both for *The Captain's Dog;* Mark Twain Book Award, 2003-04, Maud Hart Lovelace Award, 2004-05, and Nevada Young Readers Award, and North Dakota Flickertail Award, all for *Zach's Lie;* Books for the Teen Age list, New York Public Library, 2006, for *Jack's Run;* Black-eyed Susan Award, 2006-07, Colorado Children's Book Award, 2007, Nevada Young Readers Award, 2007, and South Carolina Junior Book Award, and Mark Twain Book Award, both 2007-08, all for *Cryptid Hunters;* Best Books for Young Adults designation and Quick Picks for Reluctant Young Adult Readers designation, both ALA, Books for the Teen Age listee, New York Public Library, and National Outdoor Book Award, all 2008, all for *Peak;* Best Books for Young Adults designation, ALA, 2009, for *Elephant Run;* nominations for numerous state reading awards.

Writings

NOVELS

Thunder Cave, Hyperion (New York, NY), 1995.
Amy's Missing, YS Press, 1996.
Jaguar, Hyperion (New York, NY), 1997.
Sasquatch, Hyperion (New York, NY), 1998.
The Captain's Dog: My Journey with the Lewis and Clark Tribe, Harcourt (San Diego, CA), 1999.
The Last Lobo, Hyperion (New York, NY), 1999.
Zach's Lie, Hyperion (New York, NY), 2001.
Cryptid Hunters, Hyperion (New York, NY), 2005.
Jach's Run, Hyperion (New York, NY), 2005.

NONFICTION

Sea Otter Rescue: The Aftermath of an Oil Spill, photographs by the author, Cobblehill Books, 1990.
Primates in the Zoo, photographs by William Muñoz, Millbrook Press (New York, NY), 1992.
Snakes in the Zoo, photographs by William Muñoz, Millbrook Press (New York, NY), 1992.
Inside the Zoo Nursery, photographs by William Muñoz, Cobblehill Books (New York, NY), 1993.
Cats in the Zoo, photographs by William Muñoz, Millbrook Press (New York, NY), 1994.
Whales, Dolphins, and Porpoises in the Zoo, photographs by William Muñoz, Millbrook Press (New York, NY), 1994.
African Elephants, photographs by Gerry Ellis, Lerner (Minneapolis, MN), 1995.
(And photographer) *Journey of the Red Wolf,* Cobblehill Books (New York, NY), 1996.
Vultures, photographs by Lynn M. Stone, Lerner (Minneapolis, MN), 1997.
(With Michael J. Schmidt) *In the Forest with the Elephants,* Harcourt (San Diego, CA), 1998.
(With wife, Marie Smith) *B Is for Beaver: An Oregon Alphabet,* illustrated by Michael Roydon, Sleeping Bear Press (Chelsea, MI), 2003.
(With Marie Smith) *E Is for Evergreen: A Washington Alphabet,* illustrated by Linda Holt Ayriss, Sleeping Bear Press (Chelsea, MI), 2004.
Z Is for Zookeeper: A Zoo Alphabet, illustrated by Henry Cole, Sleeping Bear Press (Chelsea, MI), 2005.
(With wife, Marie Smith) *N Is for Our Nation's Capital: A Washington, DC, Alphabet,* illustrated by Barbara Gibson, Sleeping Bear Press (Chelsea, MI), 2005.
Peak, Harcourt (Orlando, FL), 2005.
Elephant Run, Harcourt (Orlando, FL), 2007.
(With wife, Marie Smith) *W Is for Waves: An Ocean Alphabet,* illustrated by John Megahan, Harcourt (Orlando, FL), 2008.
I, Q, Sleeping Bear Press (Chelsea, MI), 2008.

Contributor of photography to *National Geographic.*

Adaptations

Thunder Cave has been optioned as a television movie by RHI with a screenplay by Smith and Hunter Clarke. Several of Smith's books have been adapted for audio.

Sidelights

Roland Smith is a zookeeper turned children's author who has carved a niche for himself both in nonfiction and fiction with such award-winning titles as *Sea Otter Rescue: The Aftermath of an Oil Spill, Journey of the Red Wolf, Cryptid Hunters.* and *Peak.* Blending action and adventure with accurate scientific detail, Smith's fiction has been praised by critics and applauded by young-adult readers, while his nonfiction works are marked by readability and feature detailed insider information told in an accessible manner. "When you read his books," a *Storyworks* writer noted of Smith's work, "you almost feel like you're inside the story, seeing through the eyes of his characters."

Born in Portland, Oregon, Smith formed a love of reading and writing early in life. As he stated in a *Scholastic* interview, "When I was five, my parents got me an old manual typewriter for Christmas and it was my favorite possession. I spent hours in my room clacking away. Even before I knew how to read, I always loved books. I used to go down to my parents' library, pull books off the shelf and sniff them. I just loved the smell of books for some reason, and this hasn't diminished."

Cover of Smith's Sasquatch, *featuring artwork by Dan Brown.* (Copyright © 1998 by Roland Smith. Reprinted by permission of Hyperion Books for Children. All rights reserved.)

After graduating from high school, Smith attended Portland State University, studying English and biology. A work-study program led to part-time work at the Portland's children's zoo, which he thought might provide some interesting material to write about. Instead, the program led to a more-than-twenty-year career in zoo keeping, first at Portland's main zoo, and then at the Point Defiance Zoo in Tacoma, Washington, where Smith became general curator and assistant director, as well as senior research biologist.

While at Point Defiance, Smith became involved in a project to reintroduce the near-extinct red wolf into former habitats in North Carolina, South Carolina, and Mississippi. Functioning as species coordinator and studbook keeper for the U.S. Fish and Wildlife Service's Red Wolf Recovery Team, he helped oversee the breeding of the last pairs of the endangered wolf, which were brought to Washington State for that purpose. Once enough litters of new wolves had been born, they were then placed back into the wild, bearing radio transmitters in collars to help with tracking. This successful project served as the basis of one of Smith's most popular nonfiction titles, *Journey of the Red Wolf.*

Working in Alaska to help save endangered animals from the 1989 Exxon *Valdez* oil spill led to another title, *Sea Otter Rescue.* Such work led to appearances and interviews on local and national television shows, such as *National Geographic, Audubon,* and *Discover the World of Science.* Additionally, in his professional capacity, Smith authored numerous professional papers and presented them at meetings and conferences of scientific organizations as well as to the general public.

While working as a zookeeper and research biologist, Smith never lost his love of writing, and he spent time early each morning teaching himself the basics of the writing craft. He also read voraciously, up to four books a week, and was a steady consumer of how-to writing books and other information about the publishing world. A chance meeting with well-known children's writer Dorothy Hinshaw Patent led to the publication of his first title in 1990, *Sea Otter Rescue.* Smith's long-time dream finally became a reality.

With color photographs by the author, this first book provides readers with an "in-depth view of the special care given to 342 sea otters after the Exxon *Valdez* oil spill," according to *Booklist* reviewer Deborah Abbott, who went on to note that the book "reflects the complexity of the operation, which was exacerbated by the geography." Smith recounts in detail how the sea otters were affected by the oil spill, and how they were cleaned and taken care of. "With the environment a top priority of the 1990s, this is an especially useful resource," concluded Abbott. A writer for *Kirkus Reviews* felt Smith's book is unlike "many perfunctory treatments of current events" in that it is written and photographed "by an expert with in-depth knowledge of the *Valdez* oil spill and its effect on wildlife." The same

Cover of Smith's novel adventure novel **Jaguar,** *a sequel to* **Thunder Cave** *that finds Jacob in the jungles of Brazil.* (Cover design by Stephanie Bart-Horvath. Hyperion, 1997. Reprinted by permission of Hyperion Books for Children. All rights reserved.)

writer continued, "Smith is an experienced zoologist whose writing and color photographs are both clear and immediate, involving readers in the fate of the sea otters by describing individual animals as well as general rescue operations." A reviewer for *Faces: People, Places, and Cultures* found the book "fascinating."

With his first book, Smith created a space for himself in children's literature: eco-books told from an insider's perspective. He has continued to mine this rich vein in more recent nonfiction and fiction titles. Approaching his new career in a pragmatic manner, Smith realized that he had to find new topics or new ways to talk about old topics in order to be able to ultimately support his family with words. Sticking with nonfiction at first, he contracted behind-the-scenes zoo books with Millbrook Press and Cobblehill Books. In 1992 his *Primates in the Zoo* and *Snakes in the Zoo* were published, followed by *Inside the Zoo Nursery* in 1993, and *Cats in the Zoo* and *Whales, Dolphins and Porpoises in the Zoo* in 1994.

Reviewing the first two titles, *Booklist* contributor Stephanie Zvirin wrote that "Smith's conversational

tone" will help make the books "especially appealing to middle graders." Zvirin noted that both books "supply excellent perspectives on how the animals are cared for in a zoo environment." Karey Wehner wrote in *School Library Journal* that the texts for both Smith's "New Zoo" series books "are straightforward, well organized, and contain some interesting anecdotes." Wehner predicted that "Smith's titles will appeal most to youngsters who want to know the nitty-gritty details on zoo routines."

With *Inside the Zoo Nursery* Smith uses the rescue of a newborn baboon as a dramatic narrative thread to connect information on zoo medical facilities. *Horn Book* critic Elizabeth S. Watson noted that the author creates "an extremely readable and engaging text that provides excellent information about the complex procedures followed in a zoo nursery." Ruth M. McConnell, writing in *School Library Journal,* called the book a "clear, competent presentation, illustrated with captivating, full-color photographs of the baby animals."

Publication of these early titles and their reception by reviewers and readers encouraged Smith to leave zoo keeping behind and make writing his full-time profes-

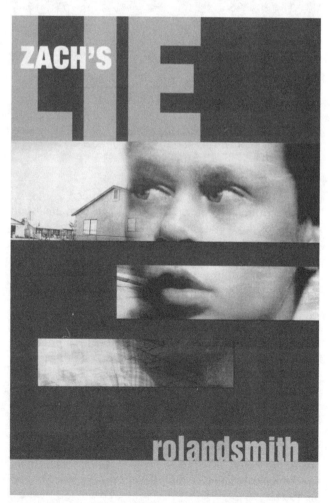

A young teen's life goes into a tailspin when his family enters the witness-protection program in Smith's novel Zach's Lie. (Hyperion, 2001. Reprinted by permission of Hyperion Books for Children. All rights reserved.)

sion. Other nonfiction titles have followed, including several books for the Lerner "Early Bird Nature Series": *African Elephants* and *Vultures.* In *Journey of the Red Wolf* he recounts the efforts to save the rare red wolf from extinction. In a *Booklist* review, Ellen Mandel commented, "Smith delivers behind-the-scenes details about the species-saving effort, generously illustrating his fascinating account with intimate color photographs." Employing dramatized fact, the author recounts the arduous task that confronted the team of men and women who labored to save the red wolf. Roger Sutton, writing in the *Bulletin of the Center for Children's Books,* found Smith's fictionalizing technique somewhat confusing, noting that it is "not always clear what really happened." Barbara Murphy, on the other hand, wrote in *School Library Journal* that "Smith's straightforward style conveys firsthand knowledge."

A 1996 trip to Burma (present-day Myanmar) with fellow zoologist Michael J. Schmidt led to a book on the plight of the Asian elephant, *In the Forest with the Elephants.* Focusing on the Myanmar Forest, where a third of Asia's remaining 35,000 elephants live, Smith and Schmidt tell the story of Won Lin and his elephant, Toe Lai, who have developed a working partnership in harvesting wood. These techniques of partnership may ultimately not only save the dwindling population of elephants, but also the forest. Patricia Manning, writing in *School Library Journal,* called the book an "informative and rich cultural experience," while *Horn Book* contributor Mary Ann Burns concluded that a "strong ecological theme runs throughout the book, which documents this complex enterprise and relationship between humans and nature."

Moving to fiction, Smith's first novel, *Thunder Cave,* recounts the adventures of young Jacob Lansa, the half-Italian, half-Native American son of a biologist. When Jacob's mother is killed, his stepfather wants to send the boy off to relatives, but Jacob has a better idea: he goes to Kenya to find his biologist father, who is doing field research on African elephants. There Jacob hooks up with a Masai trying to bring rain to his drought-ridden country, an experience that helps the boy understand his Hopi roots. Jacob also battles poachers who threaten local elephants with extinction in his adventuresome quest to find his father.

"Sparkling detail and vivid realism are keys to *Thunder Cave*'s success," noted Thomas S. Owens in a review for *Five Owls.* "A boy wanting a dad, elephants eluding capture, and an African exploring tradition combine to create a guaranteed, feel-good thriller." Sutton commented in *Bulletin of the Center for Children's Books* that *Thunder Cave* "is precisely the kind of book people are thinking of when they ask for a 'boys' book.'"

As with his nonfiction, Smith plays on ecological themes with his debut novel. He also approaches fiction

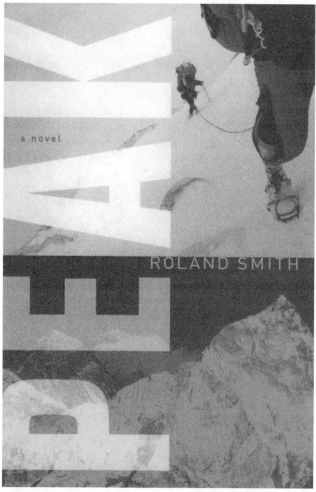

Cover of Smith's novel **Peak,** *which takes a thrill-seeking teen on a mountain-climbing adventure of a lifetime.* (Harcourt, Inc., 2007. Jacket photographs: (climbers) copyright © by Galen Rowell/Corbis; (mountains) copyright © by Gordon Wiltsie/National Geographic/Getty Images. Reproduced by permission of Houghton Mifflin Harcourt Publishing Company.)

with the mind of a scientist: for the early drafts of *Thunder Cave* he consulted over 2,000 index cards with bits of information ranging from plot twists to facts about Africa.

Smith reprises his protagonist Jacob Lansa in *Jaguar,* as the boy follows his dad to Brazil, where the biologist is setting up a jaguar preserve. Jacob's journey upriver to join his father is beset by danger and violence, and once again he comes face to face with those despoiling nature for their own selfish gain. *Booklist* reviewer Kay Weisman noted that, "While Smith's ecological message . . . comes through loud and clear, the book's strength lies in strong characterization . . . vivid local color, and high adventure." A contributor to *Kirkus Reviews* called Smith's sequel to *Thunder Cave* a "first-rate adventure about greed, mutual dependence, and family," while Janet Woodward commented in *School Library Journal* that "this fast-paced adventure and survival tale blends enough action, suspense, and legend to keep readers interested until the end."

In *The Last Lobo* Jacob tracks his missing grandfather from the nursing home the elderly man quietly left to the Hopi village of Walpi, in Arizona. Grandfather is happy in the village, surrounded by relatives and friends, and Jacob decides to stay with him for a time. While there, the teen soon becomes involved with trying to save the area's last remaining lobo, or Mexican wolf, from hunters determined to earn a bounty for killing the creature. Frances Bradburn, in her review of the novel for *Booklist,* called *The Last Lobo* "another exciting outdoor adventure."

Smith tackles the Sasquatch or "Bigfoot" legend in the aptly titled *Sasquatch.* Again, a father-son relationship is at the center of Smith's adventure novel in which Dylan must keep his somewhat erratic father in line after his mother leaves for Egypt. The job is made more difficult when the boy's father joins a team hunting the Sasquatch on Washington State's volcanic Mount St. Helens. Dylan joins another team shadowing his father's group, but soon begins to wonder if his father is crazy after all; the Sasquatch may be more of a reality than he has ever imagined. *Booklist* critic Lauren Peterson dubbed *Sasquatch* "a first-rate thriller," while Elaine E. Knight concluded in *School Library Journal* that with its "exciting climax set amid Mount Saint-Helens's eruption, this fast-moving, suspenseful story provides lots of action and appeal."

In *Zach's Lie* Smith tells the story of Jack Osborne, a thirteen year old whose family must enter the witness-protection program after his father is arrested for drug trafficking. The family members take on new names, something that Jack—now named Zach Granger—finds difficult to do. He also finds it hard to adjust to their new home in a small town in Nevada. Trying to hide from drug-cartel assassins, the family must keep quiet about its past life. However, when Zach has his diary stolen and begins to see incriminating lines from the book appearing on the classroom blackboard at school, the information soon leads the criminals to Zach's family. "The reader will be caught up in a vicarious fear for the family's safety," according to Phyllis LaMontagne in *Kliatt.* Debbie Carton, reviewing *Zach's Lie* for *Booklist,* believed that "Zach's well-depicted emotional turmoil about his once-beloved father lends depth" to the story. A critic for *Publishers Weekly* concluded that "readers are sure to be caught up in Zach's suspenseful adventure."

In *Jack's Run,* a sequel to *Zach's Lie,* the Osborne family again faces great danger. After Jack's older sister, Joanne, reveals the whereabouts of her parents while appearing on national television, criminal drug czar Alonzo Aznar kidnaps Jack and Joanne and transports them to his hideaway in Argentina. Although some critics noted that aspects of the plot strain credibility, the novel received generally strong reviews. "The action is nonstop and the characters are compelling," observed a contributor in *Kirkus Reviews,* and Carolyn Phelan, writing in *Booklist,* stated that *Jack's Run* will appeal to readers "who crave plot-driven fiction full of action and danger."

In *Cryptid Hunters,* Smith tells of the field of cryptozoology, or the study of animals that may or may not really exist. Creatures like the Loch Ness Monster and Bigfoot are examples of the type. When cryptozoologist Tobias Wolfe takes his orphaned niece Grace and nephew Marty to hunt for a rumored dinosaur in the jungles of the Congo, they find themselves hopelessly lost. Worse, the devilish Dr. Blackwood is also after the dinosaur for his own purposes and will stop at nothing. While trying to locate the elusive dinosaur and avoid Dr. Blackwood, the orphans also untangle a hidden family secret. Todd Morning wrote in *Booklist* that "the action is nonstop" in Smith's "well-paced jungle adventure."

A fourteen-year-old daredevil is the focus of *Peak,* "a thrilling, multifaceted adventure story," according to Morning. The son of a noted mountain climber and expedition leader, Peak Marcello is arrested while attempting to scale a New York City skyscraper. Bailed out of jail by his estranged father, the teen is sent to Tibet, where his dad hopes to reinvigorate his business by making Peak the youngest person ever to climb Mount Everest. "A well-crafted plot and exotic setting give [*Peak*] . . . great appeal to survival adventure fans," noted *School Library Journal* contributor Vicki Reutter, and a *Publishers Weekly* reviewer similarly noted that the "nifty plotting, gripping story line and Peak's assured delivery give those who join this expedition much to savor."

Smith has also written historical fiction, but with a naturalist's eye for detail. In *The Captain's Dog: My Journey with the Lewis and Clark Tribe,* he treats the Lewis and Clark expedition from a dog's point of view, telling the story from the perspective of Seaman, a Newfoundland pup who becomes the companion of Meriwether Lewis. "The canine's perspective, both fresh and original, is most effective," a critic for *Publishers Weekly* noted. Helen Rosenberg, in her review of the title for *Booklist,* called Smith's book a "marvelous piece of historical fiction."

Set during World War II, *Elephant Run* concerns fourteen-year-old Nick Freestone, a British youth sent to his father's teak plantation in Burma. When the Japanese invade and take both Nick and his father prisoner, the teen attempts to escape with the help of a Buddhist monk and a Burmese girl. A *Kirkus Reviews* critic described the work as an "adventure tale that is also a family story," and in *School Library Journal* Rita Soltan commented that Smith's novel "is filled with intrigue, danger, surprising plot twists, and suspense."

As Smith noted on his home page, "My writing led me to animals and my work with animals led me back to writing. It's funny how things work out. I spent over twenty years working with animals. Now I'm going to spend the next twenty years writing about animals . . . as well as a few other things."

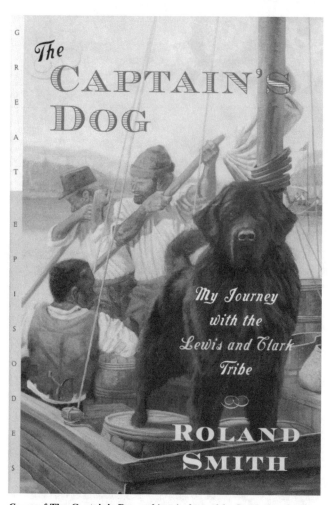

Cover of **The Captain's Dog,** *a historical novel by Smith that features cover art by Bryn Barnard.* (Gulliver Books, a division of Harcourt, 1999. Illustration by Bryn Barnard. Reproduced by permission of Houghton Mifflin Harcourt Publishing Company.)

Biographical and Critical Sources

PERIODICALS

Booklist, September 15, 1990, Deborah Abbott, review of *Sea Otter Rescue: The Aftermath of an Oil Spill,* p. 158; October 15, 1992, Stephanie Zvirin, review of *Primates in the Zoo,* p. 427; May 1, 1996, Ellen Mandel, review of *Journey of the Red Wolf,* p. 1504; May 15, 1997, Kay Weisman, review of *Jaguar,* p. 1576; April 15, 1998, Lauren Peterson, review of *Sasquatch,* pp. 1446-1447; October 15, 1999, Helen Rosenberg, review of *The Captain's Dog: My Journey with the Lewis and Clark Tribe,* p. 429; December 1, 1999, Frances Bradburn, review of *The Last Lobo,* p. 696; May 15, 2001, Debbie Carton, review of *Zach's Lie,* p. 1754; February 1, 2005, Todd Morning, review of *Cryptid Hunters,* p. 962; August, 2005, Carolyn Phelan, review of *Jack's Run,* p. 2030; April 1, 2007, Todd Morning, review of *Peak,* p. 49; February 15, 2008, Jennifer Mattson, review of *Elephant Run,* p. 82.

Bulletin of the Center for Children's Books, June, 1995, Roger Sutton, review of *Thunder Cave,* p. 359; Febru-

ary, 1996, Roger Sutton, review of *Journey of the Red Wolf,* p. 20; January, 2005, Krista Hutley, review of *Cryptid Hunters,* p. 227.

Faces: People, Places, and Cultures, February, 2005, review of *Sea Otter Rescue,* p. 47.

Five Owls, September-October, 1995, Thomas S. Owens, review of *Thunder Cave,* p. 18.

Horn Book, January-February, 1993, Elizabeth S. Watson, review of *Inside the Zoo Nursery,* p. 99; March-April, 1998, Mary M. Burns, review of *In the Forest with the Elephants,* p. 2371; May-June, 2007, Vicky Smith, review of *Peak,* p. 290.

Kirkus Reviews, November, 1990, review of *Sea Otter Rescue,* p. 71; May 15, 1997, review of *Jaguar,* p. 808; December 15, 2004, review of *The Cryptid Hunters,* p. 1208; August 1, 2005, review of *Jack's Run,* p. 858; May 1, 2007, review of *Peak;* September 1, 2007, review of *Elephant Run;* July 1, 2008, review of *I, Q.*

Kliatt, March, 2004, Phyllis LaMontagne, review of *Zach's Lie,* p. 22; May, 2007, Paula Rohrlick, review of *Peak,* p. 20.

Publishers Weekly, December 13, 1999, review of *The Captain's Dog,* p. 83; June 25, 2001, review of *Zach's Lie,* p. 73; February 14, 2005, review of *Cryptid Hunters,* p. 77; June 4, 2007, review of *Peak,* p. 51.

School Library Journal, November, 1990, p. 133; December, 1992, Karey Wehner, review of *Primates in the Zoo,* p. 130; June, 1993, Ruth M. McConnell, review of *Inside the Zoo Nursery,* p. 126; May, 1995, pp. 122-123; August, 1995, p. 138; May, 1996, Barbara B. Murphy, review of *Journey of the Red Wolf,* p. 126; June, 1997, Janet Woodward, review of *Jaguar,* p. 128; March, 1998, pp. 191-192; April, 1998, Patricia Manning, review of *In the Forest with the Elephants,* p. 154; June, 1998, Elaine E. Knight, review of *Sasquatch,* p. 153; June, 2001, Vicki Reutter, review of *Zach's Lie,* p. 156; August, 2005, Pamela K. Bomboy, review of *N Is for Our Nation's Capital: A Washington, DC Alphabet,* p. 118; December, 2005, Emily Garrett, review of *Jack's Run,* p. 155; June, 2007, Vicki Reutter, review of *Peak,* p. 160; January, 2008, Rita Soltan, review of *Elephant Run,* p. 126.

Storyworks, September, 2000, "Meet Roland Smith," p. 14.

Voice of Youth Advocates, October, 2004, Michael Levy, review of *Cryptid Hunters,* p. 320.

ONLINE

Roland Smith Home Page, http://www.rolandsmith.com (September 10, 2008).

Scholastic Web site, http://www2.scholastic.com/ (September 10, 2008), Roland Smith, "From the Zoo to Kenya: My Journey as a Writer."*

* * *

STEINHARDT, Bernice

Personal

Born in Belgium; daughter of Max and Esther Nisenthal Krinitz.

Addresses

Office—Art and Remembrance, 5505 Connecticut Ave. NW, No. 131, Washington, DC 20015-2601.

Career

Author. Worked in a variety of positions for U.S. Government Accountability Office (GAO); founder, Esther Project and Art and Remembrance.

Awards, Honors

One Hundred Best Books inclusion, New York Public Library, 2005, for *Memories of Survival.*

Writings

FOR YOUNG ADULTS

(With mother, Esther Nisenthal Krinitz) *Memories of Survival,* illustrated by Krinitz, Hyperion (New York, NY), 2005.

Sidelights

The daughter of a Holocaust survivor, Bernice Steinhardt grew up with her mother's unique story of survival informing her life. Esther Nisenthal Krinitz escaped death in the concentration camps of Nazi Germany by running away with her sister and posing as a Catholic farm girl. The sisters evaded the Nazis for the duration of World War II, laboring for local farmers, but were never to see the rest of their family again. Years later, when she was fifty years old, Krinitz began to use her skills as a seamstress to create striking pieces of art that depicted her wartime experiences.

Inspired by her mother's work, Steinhardt formed the nonprofit organization Art and Remembrance to showcase these textiles, as well as other works of art that feature similar themes. As she remarked on her organization's Web site, "Art and Remembrance aims to use [the power of personal narrative in various forms of art] . . . to illuminate the effects of war, intolerance, and other forms of social injustice on its victims. By bringing to light the works of those who have told the stories of their struggles in art, our organization aims to serve as a force for peace and social justice. By allowing audiences, especially children, to see and feel war and injustice through the eyes and hearts of its victims, we hope to create a sympathy and compassion great enough to change people's perceptions forever."

Working together with Steinhardt, Krinitz tells her story in *Memories of Survival.* Brought to life by reproductions of her unique artwork, mother and daughter evoke Krinitz's own idyllic childhood, her persecution as a Jew during the Holocaust, and her emergence from the war. Reviewing the powerful tale, Robin Smith wrote in

Horn Book that "Esther's strong memories and clear storytelling move the heartbreaking tale forward and leave the reader stunned." Rachel Kamin, writing in

School Library Journal, also praised *Memories of Survival,* indicating that "the intricate, multifaceted artwork uniquely illustrates the horrors of the Holocaust." A

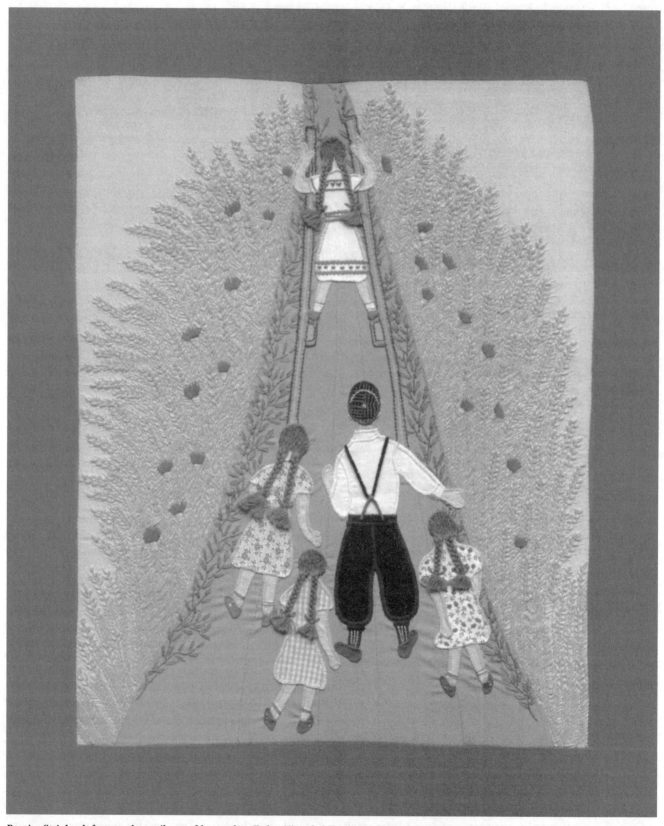

Bernice Steinhardt features the textile art of her mother, Esther Nisenthal Krinitz, in the book Memories of Survival.

Kirkus Reviews writer also found the work to be remarkable, writing that Steinhardt's narrative adds clarity by "highlighting the increasingly difficult environment Jews faced with the impending dangers of Nazi rule." A *Publishers Weekly* reviewer deemed the illustrated memoir powerful and full of difficult emotions, a work that "also stand[s] as one woman's testimony to hope, endurance and the unquenchable passion to bear witness."

Biographical and Critical Sources

PERIODICALS

Horn Book, November-December, 2005, Robin Smith, review of *Memories of Survival,* p. 737.
Kirkus Reviews, October 1, 2005, review of *Memories of Survival,* p. 1082.
Publishers Weekly, October 10, 2005, review of *Memories of Survival,* p. 61.
School Library Journal, November, 2005, Rachel Kamin, review of *Memories of Survival,* p. 165; March, 2006, John Peters, review of *Memories of Survival,* p. 90.

ONLINE

Art and Remembrance Web site, http://www.artandremembrance.org/ (September 22, 2008).
Nextbook Web site, http://www.nextbook.org/ (January 16, 2007), Tessa DeCarlo, "A Stitch in Time: Seamstress Esther Nisenthal Krinitz Used the Tools of Her Trade to Capture the Horrors of War."*

*   *   *

STEVENS, Janet 1953-

Personal

Born January 17, 1953, in Dallas, TX; daughter of Jack (a naval officer) and Frances Stevens; married Ted Habermann (a research scientist); children: Lindsey, Blake. *Education:* University of Colorado, B.F.A., 1975. *Hobbies and other interests:* Mountain biking, camping, hiking, skiing.

Addresses

Home and office—Boulder, CO. *E-mail*—rhinoink@aol.com.

Career

Children's book illustrator and writer, 1979—. Has worked in advertising, textile design, and architectural illustration.

Awards, Honors

Parents Choice Award, 1987, and Notable Children's Trade Book in the Field of Social Studies citation, National Council for Social Studies/Children's Book Coun-

Janet Stevens (Photo courtesy of Janet Stevens.)

cil, both for *The Three Billy Goats Gruff;* Caldecott Honor citation, and Notable Books for Children citation, both American Library Association (ALA), both 1996, Parents' Choice Honor Award, and American Bookseller Association (ABA) Pick of the Lists citation, all for *Tops and Bottoms;* ABA Book of the Year Honor Book designation, and Notable Books for Children citation, ALA, both 1998, both for *To Market, to Market;* Best Children's Book selection, *Child* magazine, 2001, Notable Book selection, National Council of Teachers of English, and Notable Books for Children citation, ALA, all for *And the Dish Ran away with the Spoon.* Stevens's books have been named International Reading Association Children's Choice selections, and have received several state children's choice book awards.

Writings

SELF-ILLUSTRATED

From Pictures to Words: A Book about Making a Book, Holiday House (New York, NY), 1995.
(With sister, Susan Stevens Crummel) *Shoe Town,* Harcourt (San Diego, CA), 1999.
(With Susan Stevens Crummel) *Cook-a-Doodle-Doo!,* Harcourt (San Diego, CA), 1999.
(With Susan Stevens Crummel) *My Big Dog,* Random House (New York, NY), 1999.
(With Susan Stevens Crummel) *And the Dish Ran away with the Spoon,* Harcourt (San Diego, CA), 2001.
(With Susan Stevens Crummel) *Jackalope,* Harcourt (San Diego, CA), 2003.
(With Susan Stevens Crummel) *Plaidypus Lost,* Holiday House (New York, NY), 2004.

(With Susan Stevens Crummel) *The Great Fuzz Frenzy*, Harcourt (San Diego, CA), 2005.

(With Susan Stevens Crummel) *My Big Dog*, Golden Books (New York, NY), 2005.

(With Susan Stevens Crummel) *Help Me, Mr. Mutt! Expert Answers for Dogs with People Problems*, Harcourt (San Diego, CA), 2008.

RETELLER; SELF-ILLUSTRATED

Animal Fair, Holiday House (New York, NY), 1981.

Hans Christian Andersen, *The Princess and the Pea*, Holiday House (New York, NY), 1982.

Aesop, *The Tortoise and the Hare*, Holiday House (New York, NY), 1984.

Hans Christian Andersen, *The Emperor's New Clothes*, Holiday House (New York, NY), 1985.

The House That Jack Built: A Mother Goose Nursery Rhyme, Holiday House (New York, NY), 1985.

Goldilocks and the Three Bears, Holiday House (New York, NY), 1986.

Aesop, *The Town Mouse and the Country Mouse*, Holiday House (New York, NY), 1987.

The Three Billy Goats Gruff, Harcourt (San Diego, CA), 1987.

Hans Christian Andersen, *It's Perfectly True*, Holiday House (New York, NY), 1988.

Aesop, *Androcles and the Lion*, Holiday House (New York, NY), 1989.

How the Manx Cat Lost Its Tail, Harcourt (San Diego, CA), 1990.

Jakob Ludwig and Wilhelm Karl Grimm, *The Bremen Town Musicians*, Holiday House (New York, NY), 1992.

Coyote Steals the Blanket: An Ute Tale, Holiday House (New York, NY), 1993.

Tops and Bottoms, Harcourt (San Diego, CA), 1995.

Old Bag of Bones: A Coyote Tale, Holiday House (New York, NY), 1996.

ILLUSTRATOR

Myra Cohen Livingston, editor, *Callooh! Callay! Holiday Poems for Young Readers*, Atheneum (New York, NY), 1978.

Marjorie Sharmat, *Twitchell the Wishful*, Holiday House (New York, NY), 1981.

Marjorie Sharmat, *Lucretia the Unbearable*, Holiday House (New York, NY), 1981.

Ida Lutrell, *Not like That, Armadillo*, Harcourt (New York, NY), 1982.

Steven Kroll, *The Big Bunny and the Easter Eggs*, Holiday House (New York, NY), 1982.

Edward Lear, *The Owl and the Pussycat*, Holiday House (New York, NY), 1983.

Marjorie Sharmat, *Sasha the Silly*, Holiday House (New York, NY), 1984.

Sheila Turnage, *Trout the Magnificent*, Harcourt (San Diego, CA), 1984.

Arnold Adoff, *The Cabbages Are Chasing the Rabbits*, Harcourt (San Diego, CA), 1985.

Paul Levitt and others, *The Weighty Word Book*, Bookmakers Guild/University of Colorado Foundation (Longmont, CO), 1985, reprinted, University of New Mexico Press (Albuquerque, NM), 2009.

Steven Kroll, *The Big Bunny and the Magic Show*, Holiday House (New York, NY), 1986.

Squire D. Rushnell, *Little David's Adventures*, Word (Waco, TX), 1986.

Eric Kimmel, reteller, *Anansi and the Moss-covered Rock*, Holiday House (New York, NY), 1988.

Edward Lear, *The Quangle Wangle's Hat*, Harcourt (San Diego, CA), 1988.

Brent Ashabranner, *I'm in the Zoo, Too*, Dutton (New York, NY), 1989.

Barbara Shook Hazen, *Wally, the Worry-Warthog*, Clarion Books (Boston, MA), 1990.

Eric Kimmel, *Nanny Goat and the Seven Little Kids*, Holiday House (New York, NY), 1990.

Polly Robertus, *The Dog Who Had Kittens*, Holiday House (New York, NY), 1991.

Eric Kimmel, reteller, *Anansi Goes Fishing*, Holiday House (New York, NY), 1992.

Margery Cuyler, *Buddy Bear and the Bad Guys*, Houghton Mifflin (Boston, MA), 1993.

Eric Kimmel, reteller, *Anansi and the Talking Melon*, Holiday House (New York, NY), 1995.

Kathryn Lasky, *The Gates of the Wind*, Harcourt (San Diego, CA), 1995.

Anne Miranda, *To Market, to Market*, Harcourt (San Diego, CA), 1997.

Susan Stevens Crummel, *Tumbleweed Stew*, Harcourt (San Diego, CA), 2000.

Eric Kimmel, reteller, *Anansi and the Magic Stick*, Holiday House (New York, NY), 2001.

Coleen Salley, *Epossumondas*, Harcourt (San Diego, CA), 2002.

Coleen Salley, *Why Epossumondas Has No Hair on His Tail*, Harcourt (San Diego, CA), 2004.

Coleen Salley, *Epossumondas Saves the Day*, Harcourt (San Diego, CA), 2006.

Eric Kimmel, reteller, *Anansi's Party Time*, Holiday House (New York, NY), 2008.

Adaptations

The Tortoise and the Hare was narrated by Gilda Radner and televised on *Reading Rainbow*, Public Broadcasting System, 1985.

Sidelights

Bringing to life such well-loved storybook characters as Anansi the spider, Epossumondas, and Jackalope, children's book illustrator and writer Janet Stevens creates artwork for numerous books written by prominent authors. She has illustrated her own retellings of traditional stories, and has collaborated with her sister and fellow author Susan Stevens Crummel as well. Using artistic media such as pastel crayon, pencil, color pencil, and watercolor, Stevens is especially noted for her humorous illustrations that feature likeable animals. Her work as an illustrator has been described by *Booklist* re-

viewer Denise M. Wilms as "strong, showing a sense of movement, composition, and drama similar to that found in [noted illustrator Paul] Galdone's most successful works."

Stevens was born in 1953, in Dallas, Texas, but was raised in such places as Virginia, Rhode Island, Florida, and Hawaii because her father was a career naval officer. After finishing high school, she earned a degree in fine arts from the University of Colorado, graduating in 1975. Involved since then in such creative endeavors as advertising, textile design, and illustrations for architects, Stevens has translated her early love of drawing into a career that has filled her life.

Stevens illustrated her first children's book, the anthology *Callooh! Callay! Holiday Poems for Young Read-*

ers, in 1978, after being inspired by a workshop she attended. An editor at New York City publishing company Holiday House liked her work so much that she offered Stevens a contract. *Animal Fair* followed in 1981, a traditional nursery song that Stevens both illustrated and adapted as a read-aloud picture book. Michele Slung commented in the *New York Times Book Review* that the illustrations in the book display "such an array of inventiveness" that the reader might believe they "somehow have a life of their own."

Numerous other retellings have followed, including versions of such classic children's stories as *The Princess and the Pea, The Emperor's New Clothes*—where Stevens casts a rotund porker in the starring role—and *Goldilocks and the Three Bears.* Her imaginative retell-

The picture book **To Market, to Market,** *with a text by Anne Miranda, is among the many books Stevens has illustrated.* (Illustration copyright © 1997 by Janet Stevens. Reproduced by permission of Houghton Mifflin Harcourt Publishing Company.)

Eric A. Kimmel's folk-tale retelling Anansi and the Talking Melon *is given a humorous slant in Stevens' detailed art.* (Illustration copyright © 1994 by Janet Stevens. Reproduced by permission of Holiday House, Inc.)

ing of *The Bremen Town Musicians,* originally written by one of the Brothers Grimm, has been particularly praised as a book worthy of a prominent spot during story time. Using watercolor and pastel on textured handmade paper, Stevens tells of the adventures of the four old animals who set out together for the city of Bremen in hopes of becoming musicians. "That Stevens can pull off chaos without clutter is a real tribute to her powers of composition and design," noted Betsy Hearne in the *Bulletin of the Center for Children's Books.*

In *How the Manx Cat Lost Its Tail,* Stevens presents the explanation for an entire breed of tailless felines by showing Noah slamming the door on his favorite pet just as the cat scurries into the Ark at the last minute— the Manx cat's bad timing costs it one of its nine lives in addition to a tail. Hearne praised the "rollicking details" of the artist's double-page spreads, while Kathy Piehl commented in *School Library Journal* that Stevens's watercolors "create dramatic tension" by con-

trasting the coming rainstorm with "the anxious and skittish expressions of the animals."

Similarly, in *Coyote Steals the Blanket: An Ute Tale,* Stevens introduces readers to the folklore of the Ute Indians with her characteristic action-filled and animal-packed illustrations. "I go where I want, I do what I want, and I take what I want," announces the defiant Coyote, and his daredevil attitude ends up getting him into trouble. "A scruffier, more scraggly Coyote would be hard to find," noted Janice Del Negro in *Booklist,* praising *Coyote Steals the Blanket* as useful for "reading aloud, reading alone, and storytelling." A *Kirkus Reviews* critic applauded Stevens's "briskly informal, well-honed telling" and found her illustrations create "an outstanding setting for a lively, sagacious, well-sourced tale."

Several fables by Aesop, including *The Town Mouse and the Country Mouse, Androcles and the Lion,* and

The Tortoise and the Hare, have also been brought to new life through Stevens's colorful artwork and updated adaptation. Despite the criticism from some reviewers that Aesop's classic stories contain a compactness and simplicity that can not be improved upon in their appeal to children, Stevens's *The Tortoise and the Hare* was honored by being showcased on the Public Broadcasting System's popular *Reading Rainbow* television series. In addition to providing both text and pictures to these old tales, Stevens has also illustrated several stories by other authors, from Edward Lear's classic nineteenth-century rhymes *The Owl and the Pussycat* and *The Quangle Wangle's Hat* to Eric A. Kimmel's retellings of the African Anansi the Spider trickster tales and Arnold Adoff's humorous 1985 work *The Cabbages Are Chasing the Rabbits.*

Another trickster tale is the focus of Stevens's picture book *Tops and Bottoms,* recipient of a Caldecott Honor citation. A clever Hare, noting that rich but lazy Bear sleeps through the growing season, offers to work Bear's land in exchange for half of the crops—and Bear can even choose which half, tops or bottoms. When Bear chooses tops, Hare outwits his landlord by planting carrots and beets; when Bear then selects bottoms, Hare raises lettuce and celery. "Stevens retells the story with vigor and humor," Susan Dove Lempke noted in her *Bulletin of the Center for Children's Books* review, "but the artwork is the real star." The critic added that the vertical, top-to-bottom positioning of the illustrations creates "an ingenious twist." *Horn Book* contributor Ellen Fader similarly praised the artist's "bold, well-composed watercolor, pencil, and gesso illustrations," and concluded that "the story contains enough sly humor and reassuring predictability to captivate listeners."

Stevens uses anthropomorphism—endowing animals with human characteristics—in approaching her work as an illustrator. In *From Pictures to Words: A Book about Making a Book* she even uses animal characters to describe how she comes up with the idea for each new story. In fact, "Stevens barely has time to introduce herself before the text is taken over by a cast of imaginary animals clad in colorful clothing," according to Joy Fleishhacker in *School Library Journal.* "We need to be in a book," her animal characters demand of the illustrator at the start of her day in the studio. "We want something exciting to do. We need places to go, people to meet. We're like actors without a stage, burgers without buns, aliens without spaceships!" Faced with pitiful entreaties such as these, Stevens launches into a step-by-step guide to the way a children's picture book is constructed—setting, plot, cast of characters, and the development of a problem and solution that comprise the basics of dramatic tension. She portrays the creative task of bookmaking in a way that inspires young writers and concludes by encouraging them to try their hand at the process as well. "I hope I always have the opportunity to create books for children," Stevens once said, "so that my animal characters will have homes."

Stevens has also enjoyed success as an illustrator of books by others, including *To Market, to Market* by Anne Miranda. In this story, readers follow the adventures of a dedicated shopper as she travels between her kitchen and the hectic activity of the market in an increasingly harried effort to complete her grocery shopping. A *Kirkus Reviews* critic noted that Stevens brings "hilarity to scenes that combine acrylics, oil pastels, and colored pencil with photo and fabric collage elements." In *Horn Book* Marilyn Bousquin found that Stevens's illustrations help to draw readers into the text, commenting that the pictures "evoke the reckless feeling of being caught—like the increasingly disheveled shopper—in the loop of this rhyme."

Beginning in 1999, Stevens began collaborating with her sister, Susan Stevens Crummel. Their third book, *My Big Dog,* tells the story of a family cat who is accustomed to ruling the roost. When a new puppy comes along, though, the cat thinks they cannot be friends and decides to run away. After a series of adventures, the dog comes to rescue him, and the two go home together. A reviewer for *Publishers Weekly* called the story an "irresistible tale," and praised Stevens's effectiveness at showing the cat's inner life through illustrations. In a review for *School Library Journal,* however, Martha Topol noted that the cat's moping might cause "readers' interest and sympathy . . . to wane."

Several of the Stevens sisters' joint efforts have taken place in the world of nursery rhymes and expanded or retold familiar stories. *Cook-a-Doodle-Doo!* tells the story of a rooster, the great-grandson of the Little Red Hen, who sets out to make a strawberry shortcake from a recipe in his great-grandmother's cookbook. In an echo of the Little Red Hen story, the first few animals he asks for help refuse, saying, "Not I," but he soon finds enthusiastic, if somewhat inept (and unusual), helpers in Turtle, Iguana, and Pig. The animals learn about teamwork as well as about cooking and following a recipe, and readers can make their own strawberry shortcake with the recipe and cooking tips provided. A critic for *Kirkus Reviews* felt that "though entertaining, the story is not seamless in its many functions," but praised Stevens' "hilarious illustrations." Hazel Rochman, writing in *Booklist,* called *Cook-a-Doodle-Doo!* a "gloriously illustrated picture book . . . with parody and puns and nonsense slapstick that kids will love."

Another continuation and expansion of a familiar story can be found in *And the Dish Ran away with the Spoon.* One evening, Dish and Spoon run away and do not return, and Cat, Dog, and Cow must go find them and bring them back for the next evening's reading of their rhyme. They make their way through an enchanted landscape filled with literary landmarks, visual puns, and other well-known characters. As Carolyn Phelan wrote in *Booklist,* "children who know their nursery rhymes . . . will best appreciate" this rich picture book. A reviewer for *Horn Book* called it "an inventive, amusing farce that blends elements of Gilbert and Sullivan with

Monty Python and Mel Brooks." Several reviewers praised the illustrations but pointed out that young children may not understand the puns and double meanings. However, as Rosalyn Pierrini wrote in a *School Library Journal* review, "those sophisticated enough to get it will love it."

One of the Stevens sisters' collaborations resulted in the publication of *Jackalope,* the story of a jackrabbit who wants to be fierce. His fairy godrabbit gives him horns, but they come with a Pinocchio-type curse, and the entrance of Coyote into the tale adds further conflict. Stevens' unique illustrations for this tale combine watercolors and colored pencils with photographs and collage. Although a critic for *Kirkus Reviews* called *Jackalope* "a labored slog through a confused tall-fairytale landscape," other critics had more positive reactions. A *Publishers Weekly* reviewer remarked favorably upon "the double ending, the puns, and the artwork," and Cris Riedel, writing for *School Library Journal,* found that "the nutty plot, sympathetic characters, and handsome illustrations make for a roaring good time."

Dogs looking for advice are the focus of the sisters' *Help Me, Mr. Mutt! Expert Answers for Dogs with People Problems.* Dog counselor Mr. Mutt offers solutions for the pets who write to him about their problems, such as owners who put their pooches on diets or neglect to take their animals on long walks. Much to the annoyance of "The Queen," Mr. Mutt's feisty feline counterpart, many of the canine's suggestions include denigrating cats, leading to an eventual run-in between the two parties. "Art and text work seamlessly," thought *Booklist* critic Stephanie Zvirin, who predicted the title would appeal to readers young and old. In a review for *School Library Journal,* Maura Bresnahan commented favorably on the book's "multi-layered story" and suggested that *Help Me, Mr. Mutt!* would most likely be enjoyed by "more sophisticated readers who will recognize the amount of effort that went into this creative venture."

A pig-tailed preschooler receives a special present, a stuffed animal made from an old plaid shirt, from her grandmother in *Plaidypus Lost,* but consistently loses it during her daily activities. Every time the girl realizes her toy has gone missing, she sets everyone in motion to find it, promising not to ever lose Plaidypus again. However, the youngster continues to forget the creature, leaving the toy in a lake and even accidentally throwing Plaidypus out the car window. While a few critics expressed reservations about the book's "aggressive, over-designed pages," as a *Kirkus Reviews* contributor described them, other critics found the layout an appealing feature of *Plaidypus Lost.* Writing in *Booklist,* Jennifer

Stevens teams up with sister and writer Susan Stevens Crummel on the humorous picture book **And the Dish Ran Away with the Spoon.** (Illustration copyright © 2001 by Janet Stevens. Reproduced by permission of Houghton Mifflin Harcourt Publishing Company.)

Mattson thought the author/illustrator's use of "digitally collaged elements . . . add[ed] texture without cluttering the clean, open compositions." A *Publishers Weekly* reviewer also found the artwork appealing: "Set against crisp white space, Stevens's watercolors capture the heroine's personality."

Stevens and Crummel continued their use of unusual page layouts in *The Great Fuzz Frenzy,* inviting readers to view vertical and horizontal illustrations on fold-out pages. When a bright green tennis ball falls into a prairie dog burrow, the underground rodents fall in love with the colorful fuzz, adorning themselves with it until they pluck the ball bare. The scarcity of the fuzz not only leads to a war among the prairie dogs but also causes one of them to forget about nearby predators. "Only the Stevens sisters could create such an over-the-top tale about fuzz," remarked Julie Cummins in *Booklist,* while a *Publishers Weekly* critic claimed Stevens "endows her furry cast with winning goofiness." Other reviewers also found delight in the author/illustrator's depiction of fuzz, with *School Library Journal* contributor Lisa Gangemi Kropp suggesting that Stevens' "marvelously rendered mixed-media illustrations . . . capture the true fuzzy nature and greenish glow of the ball."

In 2002, Stevens illustrated the first of Coleen Salley's books about the hapless possum Epossumondas, using the author herself as the model for the animal protagonist's human mother. In *Epossumondas,* readers are introduced to the title character, and to his often misguided attempts to follow the advice of his Mama. *School Library Journal* contributor Jane Marino praised Salley's text and took note of Stevens's "delightful watercolor and colored-pencil art." A *Kirkus Reviews* critic commented that while readers familiar with Salley's work as a storyteller will recognize "her signature tale . . . it is the lively, outsize illustrations that spark the story."

More tales about Epossumondas have followed, including *Why Epossumondas Has No Hair on His Tail* and *Epossumondas Saves the Day.* In the former, the young possum wants to know why his tail is skinny, pink, and hairless, unlike most other animals. To explain why, Mama Possum shares with Epossumondas a story about his great-great-grandfather who forgot to share stolen persimmons with his friend Hare. Angered by papa possum's greediness, the rabbit informs the owner of the persimmon tree, a bear, the identity of the thief. Bear catches the marsupial by his tail, stretching the once fluffy ball into a long, hair-free whip. "Stevens' signature mixed-media illustrations humorously concoct the delightful fun," claimed *Booklist* critic Julie Cummins. Other reviewers thought the book's pairing of text and colorful illustrations make the title a natural selection for reading aloud to children. Wrote Joanna Rudge Long in *Horn Book,* "Stevens's big, boisterous illustrations

fairly leap off the page, nicely suiting them for the group-sharing the tale demands."

When Mama Possum runs out of "sody sallyraytus," or baking soda, in *Epossumondas Saves the Day,* the lovable possum must find a way to the store or else he will not have biscuits for his birthday treat. Though a dangerous snapping turtle has devoured everyone his mother sent before him, Epossumondas uses his wits to escape the same fate and rescue his family from the hungry turtle. "Stevens's art is right in the comic spirit of things," wrote Long in a *Horn Book* review, while *School Library Journal* contributor Lee Bock found "Stevens's hilarious mixed-media illustrations . . . a perfect match for the narrative."

Stevens once told *SATA:* "I treasure humor a great deal, and enjoy drawing animals in people situations. Facial expressions, clothing, movement, and accessories help make the animals become distinct personalities. Putting the diaper on Epossumondas brought him to life for me, and gave him his individuality; similarly, Jack doesn't need his glasses when he's transformed into Jackalope.

"I've always loved to draw and read—and I love children—so what a great combination for a career in illustrating and writing children's books!"

Biographical and Critical Sources

BOOKS

McElmeel, Sharron L., *An Author a Month (for Dimes),* Volume 3, Teacher Ideas Press (Englewood, CO), 1993.

Stevens, Janet, *Coyote Steals the Blanket: An Ute Tale,* Holiday House (New York, NY), 1993.

Stevens, Janet, *From Pictures to Words: A Book about Making a Book,* Holiday House (New York, NY), 1995.

Stevens, Janet, and Susan Stevens Crummel, *Cook-a-Doodle-Doo!,* Harcourt (San Diego, CA), 1999.

PERIODICALS

Booklist, October 1, 1984, Denise M. Wilms, review of *The Tortoise and the Hare,* p. 251; April 1, 1993, Janice Del Negro, review of *Coyote Steals the Blanket,* p. 1428; January 1, 1999, Kathleen Squires, review of *My Big Dog,* p. 891; April 15, 1999, Hazel Rochman, review of *Cook-a-Doodle-Doo!,* p. 1530; May 15, 1999, Stephanie Zvirin, review of *Shoe Town,* p. 1705; April 1, 2001, Carolyn Phelan, review of *And the Dish Ran away with the Spoon,* p. 1472; September 1, 2004, Julie Cummins, review of *Why Epossumondas Has No Hair on His Tail,* p. 135; September 1, 2005, Julie Cummins, review of *The Great Fuzz Frenzy,* p. 146.

Bulletin of the Center for Children's Books, October, 1990, Betsy Hearne, review of *How the Manx Cat Lost Its Tail,* p. 47; November, 1992, Betsy Hearne, review of *The Bremen Town Musicians,* p. 73; April, 1995, Susan Dove Lempke, review of *Tops and Bottoms,* p. 287; March 15, 2004, Jennifer Mattson, review of *Plaidypus Lost,* p. 1311; March 15, 2008, Stephanie Zvirin, review of *Help Me, Mr. Mutt! Expert Answers for Dogs with People Problems,* p. 55.

Horn Book, May, 1995, Ellen Fader, review of *Tops and Bottoms,* p. 337; November-December, 1997, Marilyn Bousquin, review of *To Market, to Market,* p. 671; July, 2001, review of *And the Dish Ran away with the Spoon,* p. 444; January-February, 2005, Joanna Rudge Long, review of *Why Epossumondas Has No Hair on His Tail,* p. 85; November-December, 2006, Joanna Rudge Long, review of *Epossumondas Saves the Day,* p. 729.

Kirkus Reviews, April 15, 1993, review of *Coyote Steals the Blanket,* p. 537; October 15, 1997, review of *To Market, to Market;* March 15, 1999, review of *Cook-a-Doodle-Doo!,* p. 457; August 1, 2002, review of *Epossumondas,* p. 1142; April 1, 2003, review of *Jackalope,* p. 541; February 15, 2004, review of *Plaidypus Lost,* p. 186; August 1, 2004, review of *Why Epossumondas Has No Hair on His Tail,* p. 748; August 1, 2005, review of *The Great Fuzz Frenzy,* p. 859; October 15, 2006, review of *Epossumondas Saves the Day,* p. 1079; March 1, 2008, review of *Help Me, Mr. Mutt!*

New York Times Book Review, April 26, 1981, Michele Slung, review of *Animal Fair,* p. 66.

Publishers Weekly, December 7, 1998, review of *My Big Dog,* p. 58; January 13, 2003, review of *Jackalope,* p. 60; February 9, 2004, review of *Plaidypus Lost,* p. 81; July 18, 2005, review of *The Great Fuzz Frenzy,* p. 204; April 21, 2008, review of *Help Me, Mr. Mutt!,* p. 56.

School Library Journal, May, 1990, Kathy Piehl, review of *How the Manx Cat Lost Its Tail,* p. 101; July, 1995, Joy Fleishhacker, review of *From Pictures to Words,* p. 75; January, 1999, Martha Topol, review of *My Big Dog,* p. 102; May, 1999, Sharon R. Pearce, review of *Shoe Town,* p. 85; May, 2001, Rosalyn Pierrini, review of *And the Dish Ran away with the Spoon,* p. 136; September, 2002, Jane Marino, review of *Epossumondas,* p. 217; July, 2003, Cris Riedel, review of *Jackalope,* p. 108; May, 2004, Julie Roach, review of *Plaidypus Lost,* p. 125; September, 2004, Grace Oliff, review of *Why Epossumondas Has No Hair on His Tail,* p. 179; September, 2005, Lisa Gangemi Kropp, review of *The Great Fuzz Frenzy,* p. 186; December, 2006, Lee Bock, review of *Epossumondas Saves the Day,* p. 116; May, 2008, Maura Bresnahan, review of *Help Me, Mr. Mutt!,* p. 110.

ONLINE

Janet Stevens Home Page, http://www.janetstevens.com (September 15, 2008).*

STORACE, Patricia

Personal

Born in Mobile, AL. *Education:* Attended Barnard College and University of Cambridge.

Addresses

Home—New York, NY.

Career

Poet, journalist, and travel writer.

Awards, Honors

Notable Book citation, *New York Times,* 1996, for *Dinner with Persephone;* Whiting Award, 1996, for poetry; Best of the Best citation, Chicago Public Library, and Best Book citation, New York Public Library, both 2007, both for *Sugar Cane: A Caribbean Rapunzel.*

Writings

Heredity, Beacon Press (Boston, MA), 1987.
Dinner with Persephone, Pantheon Books (New York, NY), 1996.
Sugar Cane: A Caribbean Rapunzel, illustrated by Raul Colón, Hyperion Books for Children (New York, NY), 2007.

Contributor to periodicals, including *New York Review of Books, Paris Review,* and *Condé Nast Traveler.* Contributor to books, including *The Condé Nast Traveler Book of Unforgettable Journeys: Great Writers on Great Places,* Penguin Books (New York, NY), 2007; and *Arvon* (poetry anthology).

Sidelights

Patricia Storace is a poet and travel writer. In 1996 she received a prestigious Whiting Award for her verse, some of which is collected in her book *Heredity.* More recently Storace has received attention for her first children's book, *Sugar Cane: A Caribbean Rapunzel.* The book re-tells the fairy tale of Rapunzel, setting it on a lush Caribbean island and modernizing its influences, if not necessarily its plot.

Sugar Cane begins with a pregnant mother who craves sugar. Her husband, a humble fisherman, searches for and finds a field of cane. Only after he has stolen some does the fisherman discover that the field belongs to a "conjure-woman" named Madame Fate. The evil Madame Fate arrives on the child's first birthday and locks the unfortunate little girl in a tall tower with no stairs. Left to her own devices, the girl learns to sing with the help of ghosts who helpfully introduce her to the music of vastly different eras. In the meantime her hair grows

Patricia Storace tells a familiar story from a unique cultural perspective in Sugar Cane: A Caribbean Rapunzel, *featuring art by Raul Colón.* (Illustration copyright © 2007 by Raul Colón. Reproduced by permission of Hyperion Books for Children. All rights reserved.)

ever longer as she contemplates the view from her tower, visited by her only friend, a green monkey. Finally her talent attracts the notice of a young man who helps her to escape. They marry, and she is reunited with her overjoyed parents.

Although *Sugar Cane*'s story line is recognizable, Storace brings the tale new variety through the setting, the choice of musical preferences, and through her poetic sensibilities. To quote Gillian Engberg in *Booklist,* Storace "writes with a poet's command of rhythm, sound, and imagery." A *Kirkus Reviews* contributor likewise cited the work for its "lyrical" and "glimmering" prose, finding the story "a dreamlike tribute" to its original source. According to Mary Jean Smith in *School Library Journal,* Storace's "lovely book begs to be read out loud."

Storace is also the author of *Dinner with Persephone,* an account of a year the author spent traveling through Greece. The title refers to an ancient Greek goddess, but in Storace's book, "Persephone" is actually a favorite dessert at an ice cream shop. The author delights in her problems mastering the nuances of the Greek language, and she is particularly interested in how the modern Greeks react to their past history as a cradle of Western civilization. Phoebe-Lou Adams, writing in the *Atlantic Monthly,* described *Dinner with Persephone* as

"unusual and delightful . . . a splendid book." In *Booklist* Donna Seaman concluded that the work reads like "a fountain on a sunny day: bright, melodic, and entrancing."

Storace lives in New York City, where she continues to write poetry for adults and essays for periodicals such as the *New York Review of Books* and *Condé Nast Traveler.* Her collection *Heredity* drew comparisons with such famous poets as Hart Crane, Marianne Moore, Elizabeth Bishop, and Walt Whitman from Sherrod Santos, who critiqued the work for the *New York Times Book Review.* Santos called *Heredity* "rich, erudite and unintimidated," concluding with praise for "the healthy audacity that led Ms. Storace to attempt such a grand and expansive first book."

Biographical and Critical Sources

PERIODICALS

Atlantic Monthly, November, 1996, Phoebe-Lou Adams, review of *Dinner with Persephone,* p. 121.
Booklist, October 15, 1996, Donna Seaman, review of *Dinner with Persephone,* p. 403; July 1, 2007, Gillian Engberg, review of *Sugar Cane: A Caribbean Rapunzel,* p. 61.
Bulletin of the Center for Children's Books, October, 2007, review of *Sugar Cane,* p. 113.
Kirkus Reviews, June 15, 2007, review of *Sugar Cane.*
New York Times Book Review, November 8, 1987, Sherrod Santos, "Small Moments of Grace and Change."
Publishers Weekly, August 19, 1996, review of *Dinner with Persephone,* p. 44.
School Library Journal, July, 2007, Mary Jean Smith, review of *Sugar Cane,* p. 86.

ONLINE

Boston University Web site, http://www.bu.edu/ (September 8, 2008), "Patricia Storace."
Hyperion Books for Children Web site, http://www.hyperionbooksforchildren.com/ (September 8, 2008), author biography.*

*   *   *

van HAERINGEN, Annemarie

Addresses
Home—Netherlands.

Career
Author and illustrator of children's books, 1985—. *Exhibitions:* Work exhibited in the Netherlands and elsewhere, including Eric Carle Museum of Picture Book Art, Amherst, MA, and UBS Gallery, New York, NY, both 2005.

Awards, Honors

Gouden Penseel awards for best children's book illustration (Netherlands), 1999, for *Malmok,* 2000 for *De Prinses met de Lange Haren,* and 2005, for *Beer Is op Vlinder;* Austrian children's and youth book award, 2003, for *Kleine Ezel en jarige Jakkie.*

Writings

SELF-ILLUSTRATED

Kattesprongen en Reuzestappen, Lemniscaat (Rotterdam, Netherlands), 1985.

Op Hoge Poten, Leopold (Amsterdam, Netherlands), 1994.

(With Sjoerd Kuyper) *Malmok,* Leopold (Amsterdam, Netherlands), 1999.

De Prinses met de Lange Haren, Leopold (Amsterdam, Netherlands), 2000.

Beer Is op Vlinder (title means "Bear Fancies Butterfly"), [Netherlands], 2004.

ILLUSTRATOR

Hanna Kraan, *Verhalen Vande Boze Heks,* Lemniscaat [Netherlands], 1995, published as *Tales of the Wicked Witch,* Front Street (Arden, NC), 1995.

Hanna Kraan, *Boze Heks Is Weer Bezig,* [Netherlands], 1995, translation by Wanda Boeke published as *The Wicked Witch Is at It Again!,* Front Street (Arden, NC), 1997.

Hanna Kraan, *Bloemen voor de Boze Heks,* [Netherlands], translation by Wanda Boeke published as *Flowers for the Wicked Witch,* Front Street (Asheville, NC), 1998.

Rindert Kromhout, *Kleine Ezel en Jarige Jakkie,* Leopold (Amsterdam, Netherlands), 2003, translation by Marianne Martens published as *Little Donkey and the Birthday Present,* North-South Books (New York, NY), 2007.

Rindert Kromhout, *Kleine Ezel en de Oppas,* [Netherlands], translation by Marianne Martens published as *Little Donkey and the Baby-Sitter,* North-South Books (New York, NY), 2006.

Sidelights

Annemarie van Haeringen is one of the Netherlands' best-known children's book illustrators. A three-time winner of the Gouden Penseel award—the Netherlands' most prestigious prize for illustrators—van Haeringen creates pencil-and-color cartoons that are equally suited to animal characters acting like humans, and humans themselves, particularly princesses and witches. According to Gay Lynn Van Vleck in *School Library Journal,* van Haeringen's works "are captivating in their simplicity and amusing details." Several books featuring van Haeringen's art have been translated into En-

Annemarie van Haeringen contributes gently colored ink drawings to **Little Donkey and the Birthday Present,** *one of several stories by Rindert Kromhout.* (Illustration copyright © 2001 by Annemarie van Haeringen. Used with permission of North-South Books, Inc., New York.)

glish and published in America, and her stylized artwork has been cited as a principal part of their Transatlantic appeal.

Van Haeringen's art appears in the picture books by Hanna Kraan: *Tales of the Wicked Witch, The Wicked Witch Is at It Again,* and *Flowers for the Wicked Witch.* The witch of these books is not particularly wicked, and she is also somewhat inept with her magic. Rather than fearing her wrath, the forest animals alternately pull tricks on the witch and woo her with gifts, ignoring her threats to turn them into pine cones. Each book contains short stories that intertwine but can also be read individually. In *Booklist,* Stephanie Zvirin described *Tales of the Wicked Witch* as "a simple charmer that never turns saccharine," and a *Publishers Weekly* reviewer felt that van Haeringen's art "injects a refreshing note of whimsy" into Kraan's tale.

Little Donkey, a popular van Haeringen character, is introduced to American readers in *Little Donkey and the Baby-Sitter* and *Little Donkey and the Birthday Present,* both featuring a text by Rindert Kromhout. In the first book, the crafty donkey bamboozles his baby-sitter, who seems perfectly content to allow him to act out. In the second, Little Donkey faces a dilemma when he chooses a birthday gift for a friend—he likes the gift so much he does not want to give it away. A *Publishers Weekly* contributor noted that van Haeringen's illustrations for *Little Donkey and the Baby-Sitter* "bubble with a knowing playfulness," and a *Kirkus Reviews*

critic concluded that her artwork for *Little Donkey and the Birthday Present* is "vastly appealing."

Biographical and Critical Sources

PERIODICALS

Booklist, January 1, 1996, Stephanie Zvirin, review of *Tales of the Wicked Witch,* p. 834; September 15, 1997, Susan Dove Lempke, review of *The Wicked Witch Is at It Again,* p. 235; November 15, 1998, GraceAnne A. DeCandido, review of *Flowers for the Wicked Witch,* p. 591; May 1, 2007, Hazel Rochman, review of *Little Donkey and the Birthday Present,* p. 98.

Kirkus Reviews, February 15, 2007, review of *Little Donkey and the Birthday Present.*

Publishers Weekly, December 11, 1995, review of *Tales of the Wicked Witch,* p. 71; April 10, 2006, review of *Little Donkey and the Baby-Sitter,* p. 70.

School Library Journal, July, 2006, Gay Lynn Van Vleck, review of *Little Donkey and the Baby-Sitter,* p. 81; April, 2007, Kristen M. Todd, review of *Little Donkey and the Birthday Present,* p. 110.

ONLINE

Foundation for the Production and Translation of Dutch Literature Web site, http://www.nlpvf.nl/ (September 8, 2008), "Austrian Children's Book Prizes 2003"; "Gouden Penseel 2005 for Annemarie van Haeringen."*

W

WASHBURN, Lucia

Personal
Married David Washburn.

Addresses
Home—Petaluma, CA. *Agent*—Bernadett Szost, Portfolio Solutions, 136 Jameson Hill Rd., Clinton Corners, NY 12514.

Career
Illustrator.

Illustrator
Jennifer Armstrong, *Sunshine, Moonshine,* Random House (New York, NY), 1995.

Look to the North: A Wolf Pup Diary, HarperCollins (New York, NY), 1997.

Virginia Kroll, *Motherlove,* Dawn Publications (Nevada City, CA), 1998.

Kathleen Weidner Zoehfeld, *Dinosaur Babies,* HarperCollins (New York, NY), 1999.

Pegi Deitz Shea, *I See Me!,* HarperFestival (New York, NY), 2000.

Kathleen Weidner Zoehfeld, *Terrible Tyrannosaurs,* HarperCollins (New York, NY), 2001.

Kathleen Weidner Zoehfeld, *Dinosaurs Big and Small,* HarperCollins (New York, NY), 2002.

Kathleen Weidner Zoehfeld, *Did Dinosaurs Have Feathers?,* HarperCollins (New York, NY), 2004.

Kathleen Weidner Zoehfeld, *Dinosaur Tracks,* HarperCollins (New York, NY), 2007.

Ginjer L. Clarke, *Cheetah Cubs,* HarperCollins (New York, NY), 2007.

Kristin Ostby, *A Baby Panda Is Born,* Grosset & Dunlap (New York, NY), 2008.

Biographical and Critical Sources

PERIODICALS

Booklist, April 15, 1997, Carolyn Phelan, review of *Look to the North: A Wolf Pup Diary,* p. 1435; May 1, 1997, Carolyn Phelan, review of *Sunshine, Moonshine,* p. 1502; November 15, 1999, Carolyn Phelan, review of *Dinosaur Babies,* p. 632; May 15, 2000, Carolyn Phelan, review of *I See Me!,* p. 1749; February 1, 2001, Denia Hester, review of *Terrible Tyrannosaurs,* p. 1054; July, 2002, Carolyn Phelan, review of *Dinosaurs Big and Small,* p. 1852; January 1, 2004, Carolyn Phelan, review of *Did Dinosaurs Have Feathers?,* p. 879; December 1, 2006, Hazel Rochman, review of *Dinosaur Tracks,* p. 63.

Horn Book, March-April, 2007, Danielle J. Ford, review of *Dinosaur Tracks,* p. 217.

Kirkus Reviews, April 1, 2002, review of *Dinosaurs Big and Small,* p. 502; January 1, 2004, review of *Did Dinosaurs Have Feathers?,* p. 43; March 1, 2007, review of *Dinosaur Tracks,* p. 235.

Publishers Weekly, April 7, 1997, review of *Look to the North,* p. 91.

School Library Journal, July, 2002, Patricia Manning, review of *Dinosaurs Big and Small,* p. 112; February, 2004, Jean Lowery, review of *Did Dinosaurs Have Feathers?,* p. 140.*

*   *   *

WATSON, C.G.

Personal
Married; husband's name Tom; children: two. *Hobbies and other interests:* Writing, playing and listening to music, reading, in-line skating, learning new languages, bike riding, connecting with people.

Addresses
Home—CA. *E-mail*—carrie@cgwatson.com.

Career
Writer and educator. Teaches high school Spanish in CA. Has also worked as a songwriter and musician.

Awards, Honors

Cybils nomination, 2007, and Quick Picks For Reluctant Young Adult Readers selection, American Library Association, and Edgar Award nomination, Mystery Writers of America, both 2008, all for *Quad.*

Writings

Quad (novel), Razorbill (New York, NY), 2007.

Sidelights

C.G. Watson is the author of *Quad,* her debut work of young adult fiction. The novel concerns a school shooting spree that takes the life of a teenage girl. "I never wanted to write a book like *Quad,*" the author stated in an interview with Becky Laney on the *Becky's Book Reviews* Web site. "But I'm a high school teacher, and a couple of years ago, I watched helplessly as one of my classes systematically dismantled certain kids with a campaign of meanness, teasing and isolation so cruel, I

Cover of C.G. Watson's young-adult thriller Quad, *which focuses on a tragic school shooting and the bullying that motivated it.* (Razorbill, 2007. Jacket photo copyright © by Rosanne Olson/Jupiter Images. Reproduced by permission of Razorbill, a division of Penguin Putnam Books for Young Readers.)

was afraid it would end in tragedy. And they wouldn't listen to my interventions, which came off as flimsy, even funny to them. I felt like I needed to find another way for them to get the message. Not long after that, the first draft of *Quad* was born."

In the novel, six students from disparate backgrounds find themselves trapped in the school store after gunshots ring out. As the teens attempt to determine the shooter's identity, suspicion immediately falls on Stone, a bullying football player. The chapters, written from the perspective of the students in the school's various cliques, "describe their thinking in a way with which readers can empathize," observed Corinda J. Humphrey in *School Library Journal.*

Parents and teachers can help prevent the type of situation described in her novel, Watson maintains, telling Laney, "We simply can't let negative comments, name-calling, or hurtful, isolating language go unchallenged, ever. Not at home, not at school. And we need to lead by example. Sometimes I think that parents and other caring adults underestimate their value in the eyes of our children—especially our teens."

Biographical and Critical Sources

PERIODICALS

Bulletin of the Center for Children's Books, July-August, 2007, Deborah Stevenson, review of *Quad,* p. 489.
Kirkus Reviews, May 1, 2007, review of *Quad.*
School Library Journal, August, 2007, Corinda J. Humphrey, review of *Quad,* p. 128.
Voice of Youth Advocates, June, 2007, Vikki Terrile, review of *Quad,* p. 155.

ONLINE

Becky's Book Reviews Web site, http://blbooks.blogspot. com/ (November 19, 2007), Becky Laney, interview with Watson.
C.G. Watson Home Page, http://www.cgwatson.com (August 10, 2008).
C.G. Watson Web log, http://antiquecarrot.typepad.com/(August 10, 2008).
Class of 2k7 Web site, http://classof2k7.com/ (August 10, 2008), "C.G. Watson."*

*   *   *

WATT, Mélanie 1975-

Personal

Born August 20, 1975, in Trois-Rivières, Québec, Canada; daughter of John (a senior manager at Petro-Canada) and Francine (a retired administrative assis-

tant) Watt. *Education:* C.E.G.E.P. Marie-Victorin (Québec, Canada), diploma in graphic design, 1997; University of Québec—Montreal, B.A. (graphic design), 2000. *Hobbies and other interests:* Music, art, design.

Addresses

Home and office—Montréal, Québec, Canada. *E-mail*—melanie_watt@hotmail.com.

Career

Author and illustrator.

Member

Canadian Society of Children's Authors, Illustrators, and Performers, Association des illustrateurs et illustratrices du Québec, Cooperative Children's Book Center.

Awards, Honors

Ruth and Sylvia Schwartz Children's Book Award for Picture Book; two Blue Spruce awards; Amelia Frances Howard-Gibbon Illustrator's Award; International Honor Book designation, Society of School Librarians, 2001, Our Choice List, Cooperative Children's Book Center, 2002, and Children's Choices designation, International Reading Association/Children's Book Council, 2002, all for *Leon the Chameleon;* Outstanding Children's Book Award shortlist, Animal Behavior Society, 2003, for *Where Does a Tiger Heron Spend the Night?;* Notable Book designation, American Library Association; Bronze Award for picture book, Independent Publishers; Cybils award; NCTE Notable Children's Book in Language Arts designation; North Carolina Children's Book Award for Picture Book, 2008, for *Scaredy Squirrel.*

Writings

SELF-ILLUSTRATED

Leon the Chameleon, Kids Can Press (Toronto, Ontario, Canada), 2001.

Learning with Animals (boxed set; contains *Numbers, Opposites, Colors, Shapes,* and *The Alphabet,* Kids Can Press (Toronto, Ontario, Canada), 2003.

Augustine, Kids Can Press (Toronto, Ontario, Canada), 2006.

Scaredy Squirrel, Kids Can Press (Toronto, Ontario, Canada), 2006.

Scaredy Squirrel Makes a Friend, Kids Can Press (Toronto, Ontario, Canada), 2007.

Chester, Kids Can Press (Toronto, Ontario, Canada), 2007.

Scaredy Squirrel at the Beach, Kids Can Press (Toronto, Ontario, Canada), 2007.

Chester's Back, Kids Can Press (Toronto, Ontario, Canada), 2008.

Scaredy Squirrel at Night, Kids Can Press (Toronto, Ontario, Canada), 2009.

ILLUSTRATOR

Margaret Carney, *Where Does a Tiger Heron Spend the Night?,* Kids Can Press (Toronto, Ontario, Canada), 2002.

Sharon Jennings, *Bearcub and Mama,* Kids Can Press (Toronto, Ontario, Canada), 2005.

Sidelights

Canadian author and illustrator Mélanie Watt has produced several highly regarded books for children, including *Leon the Chameleon, Augustine,* and the works in the "Scaredy Squirrel" series.

Born in Québec, Canada, in 1975, Watt had a passion for drawing at an early age. "Classmates often asked me to sketch little cartoon characters on pieces of paper or on the back of their hands," she once explained to *SATA.* "I later developed my art by drawing portraits in pencil." In college, Watt took business administration classes for two years before realizing that she needed a change. Entering a graphic design program, she eventually enrolled in the bachelor's program at the University of Québec. Watt began her first picture book for children, *Leon the Chameleon,* in 1999, her final year as a student. "We had to make a book about colour," she recalled. "It was up to us to decide what the content would be. Having always been interested in children's books, I decided to make one that would teach complementary colours in a fun and simple way. I had a great time thinking up a story for little Leon, in fact, I think I spent more time on the storyline than working on the actual illustrations."

With the encouragement of her teacher, Michéle Lemieux, Watt translated her story into English and submitted it to Kids Can Press, where it was quickly accepted. Praised by *Quill & Quire* contributor Jessica Higgs as "not only a lesson on the interaction of colour but a celebration of being different," *Leon the Chameleon* focuses on a little chameleon who doesn't blend into the background like his other chameleon friends. Instead, he turns the *opposite* color of his environment. It is hard to hide a problem like this—when hiding behind something yellow, Leon turns bright purple—and soon everyone is aware that young Leon is somehow different. In addition to praise for her sensitive storyline, Watt received kudos for her use of "vibrant, eye-popping primary and complementary colors" in illustrations that make *Leon the Chameleon* a "visually effective choice for children just learning colors," according to *Booklist* contributor Shelle Rosenfeld.

One of the aspects of the book that intrigued the publisher was Watt's inclusion of an appendix providing an introduction to color theory via a color wheel. "This is certainly a fine way to extend the book," maintained

Kathryn McNaughton in her review of the "absolutely delightful" *Leon the Chameleon* for *Resource Links,* "and children will enjoy experimenting with paints or gels which can help them see how colours are mixed."

A shy little penguin is the subject of *Augustine,* another self-illustrated title. When Augustine's father takes a new job at the North Pole, Augustine must adjust to a new home and a new school, and she uses her artistic abilities to make friends. Critics applauded the book's unusual layout, which incorporates references to such celebrated painters as Salvador Dali and Leonardo Da Vinci. According to *School Library Journal* contributor Andrea Tarr, Watt's "acrylic-and-pencil artwork is naturally childlike, an effective touch," and Carolyn Phelan, writing in *Booklist,* noted that the "distinctive, vividly colored illustrations create eye-catching effects."

Watt has also created a number of popular works featuring a neurotic squirrel. "I knew for a long time that I wanted to write a book about fearing the unknown," she stated in an interview on the *Cybils* Web site. "I grew up in a family that was sometimes a little too overly cautious. I had my mind set on exploring this

Mélanie Watt tells a humorous tale that plays out in her entertaining cartoon art for **Scaredy Squirrel.** (Illustration copyright © 2006 by Mélanie Watt. Used by permission of Kids Can Press, Ltd., Toronto.)

subject and expressing how fear stops us from discovering our talents and capabilities." Watt introduces her anxious protagonist in *Scaredy Squirrel,* "a tongue-in-cheek tale that may help to prod anxious readers out of their hidebound routines," wrote *Booklist* contributor John Peters. Worried about everything from poison ivy to Martians, Scaredy bails from his tree after spotting a "killer" bee and discovers—much to his surprise—that he is really a flying squirrel. "With his iconic nervous grin and over-the-top punctiliousness, Scaredy Squirrel is an endearing character," noted Payne, Rachel G. Payne remarked in *School Library Journal,* and *Horn Book* reviewer Kitty Flynn observed that Watt's "casual, child-friendly illustrations and tongue-in-cheek text have a lot of fun with Scaredy and his story."

In *Scaredy Squirrel Makes a Friend* the phobic critter, who is wary of companions with teeth, decides to make the acquaintance with a goldfish in a nearby fountain. When a playful pooch interrupts the proceedings, however, Scaredy tries to avoid harm by playing dead. Watt's "playfully varied page designs add liveliness to a lighthearted story that doesn't take itself too seriously," Flynn stated. Scaredy's efforts to acquire a seashell are the focus of *Scaredy Squirrel at the Beach.* "In appealing, flat colors, Watt's cartoon-style pictures (full spread and graphic-novel-style panels) add joke after joke," Stephanie Zvirin commented in *Booklist.*

In *Chester,* Watt does battle with a plump, egotistical feline who tries to take over the book. As the author attempts to pen a story about a country mouse, Chester the cat enters the tale and, marker in hand, begins to disrupt the narrative. "This sidesplitting metafiction offers further proof of Wart's extravagantly fresh, cheeky voice," observed a contributor in *Publishers Weekly.* *Chester's Back,* a sequel, finds the self-centered cat bathing in his own glory. A *Publishers Weekly* critic applauded Watt's portrayal of the feisty title character, remarking that young readers will be "tickled by his ongoing battle of wits with his owner/ creator."

Watt's advice to budding picture-book creators is to "have a good message to tell. Then find a way to tell it by choosing the best possible character and setting to explore it. Think like a kid again and have fun creating."

Biographical and Critical Sources

PERIODICALS

Booklist, April 1, 2001, Shelle Rosenfeld, review of *Leon the Chameleon,* p. 1480; February 15, 2005, Ilene Cooper, review of *Bearcub and Mama,* p. 1084; May 1, 2006, John Peters, review of *Scaredy Squirrel,* p. 94; November 15, 2006, Carolyn Phelan, review of *Augustine,* p. 55; June 1, 2008, Stephanie Zvirin, review of *Scaredy Squirrel at the Beach,* p. 92.

Childhood Education, winter, 2001, review of *Leon the Chameleon,* p. 112.

Guardian (London, England), September 12, 2006, Kate Agnew, review of *Scaredy Squirrel,* p. 6.

Horn Book, May-June, 2006, Kitty Flynn, review of *Scaredy Squirrel,* p. 305; May-June, 2008, Kitty Flynn, review of *Scaredy Squirrel at the Beach,* p. 275.

Kirkus Reviews, February 1, 2001, review of *Leon the Chameleon,* p. 191; February 15, 2005, review of *Bearcub and Mama,* p. 230; August 1, 2006, review of *Augustine,* p. 797; September 1, 2007, review of *Chester.*

Publishers Weekly, March 13, 2006, review of *Scaredy Squirrel,* p. 64; September 18, 2006, review of *Augustine,* p. 53; November 5, 2007, review of *Chester,* p. 63; June 30, 2008, review of *Chester's Back!,* p. 183.

Quill & Quire, May, 2001, Jessica Higgs, review of *Leon the Chameleon,* p. 32.

Resource Links, June, 2001, Kathryn McNaughton, review of *Leon the Chameleon,* p. 7; October, 2003, Kathryn McNaughton, review of "Learning with Animals" series, p. 10; June, 2005, Antonia Gisler, review of *Bearcub and Mama,* p. 5; April, 2006, Linda Ludke, review of *Scaredy Squirrel,* p. 13; February, 2007, Janneka Guise, review of *Augustine,* p. 62; June, 2007, Zoe Johnstone, review of *Scaredy Squirrel Makes a Friend,* p. 7; December, 2007, Rachelle Gooden, review of *Chester,* p. 14.

School Library Journal, April, 2001, Maura Bresnahan, review of *Leon the Chameleon,* p. 126; May, 2002, Lynn Dye, review of *Where Does a Tiger Heron Spend the Night,* p. 134; August, 2005, Rebecca Sheridan, review of *Bearcub and Mama,* p. 98; June, 2006, Rachel G. Payne review of *Scaredy Squirrel,* p. 128; November, 2006, Andrea Tarr, review of *Augustine,* p. 115; May, 2007, Susan Moorhead, review of *Scaredy Squirrel Makes a Friend,* p. 111; December, 2007, Maryann H. Owen, review of *Chester,* p. 102; May, 2008, review of *Scaredy Squirrel at the Beach,* p. 111.

Sunday Times (London, England), November 12, 2006, Nicolette Jones, review of *Scaredy Squirrel,* p. 56.

ONLINE

Cybils Web site, http://dadtalk.typepad.com/cybils/ (March 6, 2007), "An Interview with Mélanie Watt."

Cynsations Web log, http://cynthialeitichsmith.blogspot. com/ (May 12, 2006), Cynthia Leitich Smith, "Author-Illustrator Interview: Mélanie Watt on *Scaredy Squirrel.*"

Mélanie Watt Home Page, http://www.scaredysquirrel.com (September 10, 2008).*

*　　*　　*

WILKOWSKI, Sue

Personal

Married; husband's name Mario; children: Hannah, Mia, Brian.

Addresses

Home—Long Island, NY.

Career

Children's author. Also works as a summer-camp counselor.

Writings

Baby's Bris, illustrated by Judith Friedman, Kar-Ben Copies (Rockville, MD), 1999.
The Bad Luck Chair, illustrated by C.B. Decker, Dutton Children's Books (New York, NY), 2007.

Biographical and Critical Sources

PERIODICALS

Kirkus Reviews, July 1, 2007, review of *The Bad Luck Chair.*
School Library Journal, July, 2007, Elaine Lesh Morgan, review of *The Bad Luck Chair,* p. 87.

ONLINE

Sue Wilkowski Home Page, http://www.suewilkowski.com (September 25, 2008).*

*   *   *

WINN, Bob
See SEULING, Barbara

*   *   *

WOLF, J.M.
See WOLF, Joan M.

*   *   *

WOLF, Joan M. 1966-
(J.M. Wolf)

Personal

Born 1966. *Education:* Bachelor's degree (education); Hamline University, M.F.A. (writing). *Hobbies and other interests:* Reading, drawing, painting Ukranian eggs, knitting, spinning, playing piano.

Addresses

Home—Minneapolis, MN. *E-mail*—joan@joanmwolf.com.

Career

Author and educator. Elementary-school teacher in Minnesota.

Awards, Honors

Cybil Award nomination for Middle-Grade Fiction, and Society of Midland Authors Literary Competition finalist, both 2008, both for *Someone Named Eva.*

Writings

The Beanstalk and Beyond: Developing Critical Thinking through Fairy Tales, Teacher Ideas Press (Englewood, CO), 1997.
Someone Named Eva, Clarion Books (New York, NY), 2007.

UNDER NAME J.M. WOLF

Cinderella Outgrows the Glass Slipper, and Other Zany Fractured Fairy-Tale Plays, Scholastic Professional (New York, NY), 2002.
Journal Activities That Sharpen Students' Writing, Scholastic (New York, NY), 2005.
Leveled Read-Aloud Plays: U.S. Civil Holidays, Scholastic (New York, NY), 2007.

Sidelights

A teacher as well as a writer, Joan M. Wolf has worked with both children and adults in her native Minnesota and her first books focus on educating young writers. Her first young-adult novel, *Someone Named Eva,* began as an assignment in a graduate-level writing program. In writing the book Wolf drew on her own family history and she even traveled to the Czechoslovakian village of Lidice, where the central events of the novel actually took place. *Someone Named Eva* "was inspired by the tragedy of Lidice and the frightening realities of the Nazi Lebensborn program," explained Wolf on her home page. "Although the significant events that happen in the book did take place, Milada, and the other characters in the book are fictional characters created to relay those events."

Set in 1942, *Someone Named Eva* focuses on a young girl named Milada as tragedy enters her small Czech village. In avenging the work of members of the Czech resistance, the Nazis enter Litice and kill all the men and boys, sent women to the Ravensbruck concentration camp, and farmed out ten Aryan children to German families. With her blonde hair and blue eyes, eleven-year-old Milada is one of these children, and she soon travels far from Lidice to attend a repatriation school that teaches German and obedience to the Fatherland. Renamed the German-sounding Eva, Milada finds her old life slowly being pushed from her mind by

her school's determined teachers. Their goal, which is that of the Nazi's Lebensborn program, is simple: destroy Milada's memories through lies and brainwashing and transform her into a loyal Nazi.

Reviewing *Someone Named Eva* for *Kirkus Reviews,* a contributor predicted that Wolf's historical novel recounts a "little-known side of the Nazi era [that] will fascinate young readers." In *School Library Journal* Rachel Kamin was impressed with the novel and its focus on the effects of Hitler's war against Europe's Jews, writing that Wolf's "amazing, eye-opening story, masterfully written, is an essential part of World War II literature."

"I have always been interested in finding the 'story within the story,' Wolf explained on her home page. "I am fascinated by the way that ordinary people live through extraordinary historical events. I am also very interested in unearthing lesser known stories that are part of a larger well known historical event. I find it amazing to think that the big thing that we call 'history' is really made up of many individual stories. I want to be a recorder of those stories."

Wolf also shared some advice for beginning writers with *SATA:* "I have always loved writing stories and playing with words. There is something wonderful about being able to create stories that touch other people in some way. If you want to be a writer, I would encour-age you to read everything you can get your hands on. Reading is what helps create great writers. And, of course, you must write, write, write. Try to make writing a regular part of your life so that you can develop and practice your skill. I believe in the power of words and the power that writers have to help make the world a better place!"

Biographical and Critical Sources

PERIODICALS

Booklist, September 15, 2007, Hazel Rochman, review of *Someone Named Eva,* p. 63.

Kirkus Reviews, June 15, 2007, review of *Someone Named Eva.*

Publishers Weekly, July 30, 2007, review of *Someone Named Eva,* p. 83.

School Library Journal, September, 2007, Rachel Kamin, review of *Someone Named Eva,* p. 211.

ONLINE

Joan M. Wolf Home Page, http://www.joanmwolf.com (September 15, 2008).

Y-Z

YANCEY, Richard
(Rick Yancey)

Personal
Born in FL; married; wife's name Sandy; children: Jonathan, Joshua (stepsons), Jacob. *Education:* Roosevelt University, B.A.

Addresses
Home—Gainesville, FL. *Agent*—Brian DeFiore, DeFiore & Company, 72 Spring St., Ste. 304, New York, NY 10012.

Career
Internal Revenue Service, former revenue officer; columnist and theater critic for Lakeland, FL, *Ledger.* Also worked as a typesetter, drama teacher, actor, ranch hand, playwright, and telemarketer.

Member
Screenwriters Guild of America, Authors Guild.

Awards, Honors
Best Books for Children selection, *Publishers Weekly,* 2005, and Carnegie Medal nominee, Chartered Institute of Library and Information Professionals, 2006, both for *The Extraordinary Adventures of Alfred Kropp.*

Writings

A Burning in Homeland (novel), Simon & Schuster (New York, NY), 2003.
Confessions of a Tax Collector: One Man's Tour of Duty inside the IRS (memoir), HarperCollins (New York, NY), 2004.
The Highly Effective Detective: A Teddy Ruzak Novel, Thomas Dunne Books (New York, NY), 2006.

The Highly Effective Detective Goes to the Dogs, St. Martin's Minotaur (New York, NY), 2008.

Also author of screenplays, including *The Orbit of Venus* and *The Cricket.*

"ALFRED KROPP" SERIES; FOR YOUNG ADULTS; UNDER NAME RICK YANCEY

The Extraordinary Adventures of Alfred Kropp, Bloomsbury (New York, NY), 2005.
The Seal of Solomon, Bloomsbury (New York, NY), 2007.
The Thirteenth Skull, Bloomsbury (New York, NY), 2008.

Adaptations
The Extraordinary Adventures of Alfred Kropp was optioned for film by Warner Bros. Pictures, 2006.

Sidelights
A former employee of the Internal Revenue Service, Richard Yancey mines his experiences working for this much-maligned government agency in his memoir *Confessions of a Tax Collector: One Man's Tour of Duty inside the IRS.* Moving from fact to fiction, he has also written several adult novels in addition to penning the "Alfred Kropp" books for a younger readership, the latter published under the name Rick Yancey. "Yancey is an honest, uningratiating writer, whose characters are grittily convincing, though rarely charming," commented a *Publishers Weekly* critic in appraising the author's adult novel *A Burning in Homeland.*

A Burning in Homeland, a Southern gothic, begins in 1960 and reaches back to the 1940s in its complex storyline. Set in Homeland, Florida, Yancey's story is narrated by three characters: Robert Lee "Shiny" Parker, a precocious seven year old; Mavis, a Baptist preacher's wife; and Mavis's strange daughter, Sharon-Rose, all of whom come to live with the Parkers after the preacher's house suspiciously burns to the ground and its owner is hospitalized. In another part of town, Halley Martin re-

flects on the last twenty years he spent pining for Mavis while he was in prison for the murder of Walter Hughes, who was accused of raping Mavis. Through the help of Ned Jeffries, a young Baptist preacher from Homeland who acts as prison chaplain, Halley writes to Mavis. Once again, however, Halley loses his love: through her letters, Mavis reveals the reasons she has decided to marry Ned, even though she still loves Halley.

A *Kirkus Reviews* contributor dubbed *A Burning in Homeland* "a beguiling, old-fashioned tale of desperate love and cruelty." In *Booklist* Kaite Mediatore wrote of the novel: "Dripping with atmosphere and drama, it's a pleasure as guilty as a third helping of pecan pie." Valerie Sayers commented in the *New York Times Book Review* on the character of Shiny, writing that although his voice does not sound like that of a seven year old, "we suspend our disbelief because that voice is so appealing. Shiny wins us over because of his glorious anxiety, his crying fits and especially his terror of Mavis's daughter, Sharon-Rose, a great fictional misfit, a deter-

Cover of Richard Yancey's novel **The Highly Effective Detective**, *part of a series featuring an offbeat sleuth.* (St. Martin's Paperbacks, 2006. Reproduced by permission.)

mined pursuer of boys and a good comic foil to her mother, that faded object of desire." Sayers noted that Yancey includes black characters as servants and that a black named Elias first informs Halley of Mavis's rape, a reversal of the stereotypical scene, in which the black man is accused of rape and a white man takes the first steps toward revenge.

Geared for teen readers, Yancey's novel *The Extraordinary Adventures of Alfred Kropp* is the story of a sixteen-year-old boy who is involved in a scheme to steal Excalibur, the sword of King Arthur. Yancey described his relationship with the character in an interview posted on the Bloomsbury Publishing Web site: "Growing up, I often felt like an outcast, kind of a loner like Alfred. I feel connected to Alfred's story, because it was written at a time when I was going through some professional challenges (becoming a full-time writer)."

The Extraordinary Adventures of Alfred Kropp begins as the orphaned Alfred is sent to live with his Uncle Farrell, a security guard who works the nightshift. An extraordinarily large boy, Alfred frequently feels like a loser, performing poorly in school and in sports. Offered a million dollars to retrieve a sword, Uncle Farrell readily accepts the task and enlists the help of his reluctant nephew. Retrieving the sword turns out to be quite easy and Alfred readily gives the object to the evil Mogart. Upon becoming aware that he has actually handed over Excalibur, the famed weapon of King Arthur, to an evil ex-knight looking to rule the world, Alfred undertakes to help Bennacio, an ancestor to a knight of the Round Table, in his efforts to recapture the powerful weapon.

Many critics found Yancey's hero to be an endearing character and predicted that adventure fans will find *The Extraordinary Adventures of Alfred Kropp* a good choice. "Alfred's naivete and basic good nature . . . make this pageturner stand out in the crowded fantasy adventure genre," claimed a *Publishers Weekly* critic. *School Library Journal* contributor Hillias J. Martin similarly called the volume "lighthearted, entertaining, occasionally half-witted, but by and large fun," while *Booklist* reviewer Michael Cart described *The Extraordinary Adventures of Alfred Kropp* as "a white-knuckle, page-turning read."

Alfred returns in *The Seal of Solomon,* "a rip-roaring story that teens will love and won't be able to put down," according to June H. Keuhn in *School Library Journal.* When a fired member of the Office of Interdimensional Paradoxes and Extraordinary Phenomenon (OIPEP) steals one of King Solomon's rings along with a vessel said to contain trapped demons, OIPEP Operative Nine seeks the help of Alfred to track down the thief. Noting that *The Seal of Solomon* also works as a stand-alone title, *Booklist* contributor Todd Morning added that Yancey combines "action-packed scenes with tongue-in-cheek humor and occasional heart-on-sleeve sincerity" in Alfred's second adventure.

In 2006, Yancey also began a series of detective novels for adult readers. Left with a small inheritance, gumshoe Teddy Ruzak opens a private investigating agency in *The Highly Effective Detective: A Teddy Ruzak Novel,* despite having no training or experience in the field. Looking into a seemingly minor case of goslings killed by a speeding motorist, Ruzak stumbles upon a murder mystery involving a missing spouse. The book was described as "an adorably quixotic adventure from mystery first-timer Yancey" by a *Kirkus Reviews* critic. In *Publishers Weekly* a contributor also found much to like, suggesting that Yancey's "narrative takes unforeseen, utterly believable twists that wind to an extremely satisfying close."

Yancey's follow-up novel featuring Ruzak, *The Highly Effective Detective Goes to the Dogs,* also earned praise from reviewers as the unlicensed private investigator searches for the killer of a homeless man. As the only one who believes Cadillac Joe was murdered, Ruzak looks for the culprit in a second installment that is "even funnier than the first," according to *Booklist* reviewer David Pitt. Also finding *The Highly Effective Detective Goes to the Dogs* enjoyable, a contributor to *Publishers Weekly* predicted that the detective's "distinctive voice . . . will endear this surprisingly effective bumbler" to mystery fans.

Confessions of a Tax Collector recounts Yancey's twelve-year stint at the Internal Revenue Service working as a revenue officer (RO). Discussing actual cases in which identities have been protected, he describes how he confiscated property to satisfy back taxes owed to the government and examines what he describes as "the 'cowboy' attitude of the old days," before the Revenue Restructuring Act of 1998 cut back on the extreme tactics and harassment that RO's employed. Yancey also recounts the dangers he encountered in facing delinquent taxpayers and of his isolation and obsession with his job. The story has a happy ending, however. Yancey married his supervisor and then quit the job at about the time his writing career began to take off. *Library Journal* contributor Richard Drezen described the memoir as "an engaging insider's account of life inside the dreaded IRS."

Biographical and Critical Sources

BOOKS

Yancey, Richard, *Confessions of a Tax Collector: One Man's Tour of Duty inside the IRS* (memoir), HarperCollins (New York, NY), 2004.

PERIODICALS

Booklist, January 1, 2003, Kaite Mediatore, review of *A Burning in Homeland,* p. 854; November 15, 2003, David Pitt, review of *Confessions of a Tax Collector,* p. 546; August, 2005, Michael Cart, review of *The Extraordinary Adventures of Alfred Kropp,* p. 2019; March 15, 2006, David Pitt, review of *The Highly Effective Detective: A Teddy Ruzak Novel,* p. 32; May 15, 2007, Todd Morning, review of *The Seal of Solomon,* p. 54; June 1, 2008, David Pitt, review of *The Highly Effective Detective Goes to the Dogs,* p. 50.

Entertainment Weekly, July 21, 2006, Tina Jordan, review of *The Highly Effective Detective,* p. 74.

Kirkus Reviews, November 15, 2002, review of *A Burning in Homeland,* p. 1656; December 15, 2003, review of *Confessions of a Tax Collector,* p. 1444; May 15, 2006, review of *The Highly Effective Detective,* p. 501; July 1, 2008, review of *The Highly Effective Detective Goes to the Dogs.*

Library Journal, March 15, 2003, Rebecca Sturm Kelm, review of *A Burning in Homeland,* p. 118; December, 2003, Richard Drezen, review of *Confessions of a Tax Collector,* p. 134.

New York Times Book Review, March 2, 2003, Valerie Sayers, review of *A Burning in Homeland,* p. 30; April 5, 2004, Janet Maslin, review of *Confessions of a Tax Collector,* p. E8.

Publishers Weekly, December 2, 2002, review of *A Burning in Homeland,* p. 31; January 19, 2004, review of *Confessions of a Tax Collector,* p. 60; August 29, 2005, review of *The Extraordinary Adventures of Alfred Kropp,* p. 57; April 10, 2006, review of *The Highly Effective Detective,* p. 48; April 2, 2007, review of *The Seal of Solomon,* p. 57; June 23, 2008, review of *The Highly Effective Detective Goes to the Dogs,* p. 40.

School Library Journal, October, 2005, Hillias J. Martin, review of *The Extraordinary Adventures of Alfred Kropp,* p. 178; June, 2006, Francisca Goldsmith, review of *The Highly Effective Detective,* p. 192; June, 2007, June H. Keuhn, review of *The Seal of Solomon,* p. 165.

USA Today, April 12, 2004, Carol Knopes, "Ex-Repo Man for IRS Tells It with a Smile," review of *Confessions of a Tax Collector,* p. B11.

Washington Post, March 7, 2004, Nancy McKeon, "A Tax Dodger Meets the Man" (interview), p. F1.

ONLINE

Bloomsbury Publishing Web site, http://www.bloomsbury.com/ (August 27, 2005), "A Conversation with Rick Yancey."

BookPage, http:// www.bookpage.com/ (August 27, 2005), Harold Parker, review of *A Burning in Homeland.*

Children's Bookshelf, http://www.publishersweekly.com/ (April 5, 2007), Sue Corbett, "Children's Bookshelf Talks with Rick Yancey."

Houston Chronicle Online, http://www.chron.com/ (June 27, 2003), Melanie Danburg, review of *A Burning in Homeland.*

Rick Yancey Home Page, http://www.rickyancey.com (September 28, 2008).*

*   *   *

YANCEY, Rick
See YANCEY, Richard

ZAHARES, Wade

Personal

Male. *Education:* Graduated from Maryland Institute College of Art.

Addresses

Home and office—Lyman, ME. *Office*—Zahares Limited, P.O. Box 626, West Kennebunk, ME 04904. *E-mail*—wade@zahares.com.

Career

Artist and illustrator. Work has been commissioned by HBO and Cinemax; freelance artist for Philips Academy, Andover, MA, 1994—. *Exhibitions:* Work included in permanent collection at DeCordova Museum of Art, Lincoln, MA.

Awards, Honors

Best Illustrated Children's Book selection, 1998, *New York Times,* for *Window Music.*

Writings

SELF-ILLUSTRATED

(Compiler) *Big, Bad, and a Little Bit Scary: Poems That Bite Back!,* Viking (New York, NY), 2001.

ILLUSTRATOR

Anastasia Suen, *Window Music,* Viking (New York, NY), 1998.
Anastasia Suen, *Delivery,* Viking (New York, NY), 1999.
Marc Harshman and Cheryl Ryan, *Red Are the Apples,* Gulliver Books (San Diego, CA), 2001.
Pegi Deitz Shea, *Liberty Rising: The Story of the Statue of Liberty,* Holt (New York, NY), 2005.
Sharon Hart Addy, *Lucky Jake,* Houghton Mifflin (Boston, MA), 2007.

Contributor to periodicals, including *Los Angeles Times Magazine, Family Circle,* and *Sesame Street* magazine.

Sidelights

Wade Zahares, a fine artist noted for his work with soft pastels, has also illustrated several well-received children's books, including *Window Music* by Anastasia Suen and *Liberty Rising: The Story of the Statue of Liberty* by Pegi Deitz Shea. "I've been working pastels for 25 years," Zahares told Elaine Magliaro in an interview on the *Wild Rose Reader* Web log, adding, "I like the immediacy of the chalk and the flat soft look of the finished piece."

Zahares made his picture-book debut in 1998 with *Window Music,* which follows a young girl and her mother as they travel via train through evocative and often surreal terrain (the title refers to nineteenth-century railroad slang for passing scenery). Complimenting the illustrator's choice of colors, *Horn Book* reviewer Lolly Robinson stated that "People and objects have been simplified, allowing Zahares to concentrate on how light strikes shapes, casting shadows and bringing out the sculptural qualities of each object." According to *New York Times Book Review* contributor Robin Tzannes, Zahares "has used a rich, earthy palette with brilliant white accents. His drawings are full of life and will have strong appeal for children." Zahares also teamed with Suen on *Delivery,* a work that examines how taxis, airplanes, and trains take items from one place to another. "Zahares' effective use of simple lines ensures that the pages never appear cluttered," Kay Weisman stated in *Booklist.*

Shea's *Liberty Rising* focuses on the construction of the fabled statue located in New York Harbor. The book examines the contributions of Edouard de Laboulaye, who first conceived the idea for the monument; Frédéric-Auguste Bartholdi, who designed the statue; and Alexandre-Gustave Eiffel, who constructed the framework. "Zahares's illustrations add considerable drama to the story," remarked a critic in *Kirkus Reviews,* and Vicky Smith, writing in *Horn Book,* applauded Zahares's pictures, noting that they "employ dizzying perspectives that position the reader at ground level or far above the action."

A young gold miner and his father turn a handful of seed corn into a prosperous business with the help of their pet pig in *Lucky Jake,* a work by Sharon Hart Addy. "Using pastels in deep and heavy hues, solid shapes, and unusual perspectives," wrote *Booklist* contributor Ilene Cooper, Zahares "provides images that roll breathtakingly across the pages," and Susan Dove Lempke, critiquing the work in *Horn Book,* stated that the illustrator "draws in a style reminiscent of Thomas Hart Benton but with a contemporary intensity of color." Zahares's pastels lend "a bold contrast to the old-time tenor of the easygoing narrative and creating an unlikely, but lucky, pairing," a critic stated in *Publishers Weekly.*

Big, Bad, and a Little Bit Scary: Poems That Bite Back!, a collection featuring verse by Dick King-Smith, Russell Hoban, Eve Merriam, and others, focuses on some of the world's most menacing creatures. A reviewer in *Publishers Weekly* cited Zahares's "captivating illustrations, in a unifying palette of cool blue and green hues," and *School Library Journal* contributor Shawn Brommer noted that the illustrator spotlights the characteristics "that make the animals so fearsome, such as the barracuda's saw-blade teeth and the octopus's powerful tentacles."

Wade Zahares pairs his dramatic stylized art with poems about critters with teeth in his picture book **Big, Bad, and a Little Bit Scary.** (Illustration copyright © 2001 by Wade Zahares. Reproduced by permission of Viking, a division of Penguin Putnam Books for Young Readers.)

Biographical and Critical Sources

PERIODICALS

Booklist, September 1, 1999, Kay Weisman, review of *Delivery,* p. 144; August, 2005, Jennifer Mattson, review of *Liberty Rising: The Story of the Statue of Liberty,* p. 2020; April 15, 2007, Ilene Cooper, review of *Lucky Jake,* p. 52.

Horn Book, November, 1998, Lolly Robinson, review of *Window Music,* p. 720; September-October, 2005, Vicky Smith, review of *Liberty Rising,* p. 608; July-August, 2007, Susan Dove Lempke, review of *Lucky Jake,* p. 375.

Kirkus Reviews, August 1, 2005, review of *Liberty Rising,* p. 858; May, 2007, review of *Lucky Jake.*

New York Times Book Review, November 15, 1998, Robin Tzannes, "Little Engines That Could," review of *Window Music;* December 19, 1999, Linda Villarosa, review of *Delivery.*

Publishers Weekly, September 21, 1998, review of *Window Music,* p. 83; September 13, 1999, review of *Delivery,* p. 828; September 10, 2001, review of *Big, Bad, and a Little Bit Scary: Poems That Bite Back!,* p. 93; May 7, 2007, review of *Lucky Jake,* p. 58.

School Library Journal, October, 2001, Shawn Brommer, review of *Big, Bad, and a Little Bit Scary,* p. 136; October, 2005, Susan Lissim, review of *Liberty Rising,* p. 146; July, 2007, Ieva Bates, review of *Lucky Jake,* p. 66.

ONLINE

Wade Zahares Home Page, http://www.zahares.com (August 10, 2008).

Wild Rose Reader Web log, http://wildrosereader.blogspot.com/ (November 18, 2007), Elaine Magliaro, "Interview with Wade Zahares."*

*   *   *

ZOEHFELD, Kathleen Weidner 1954-

Personal

Born 1954. *Education:* Earned M.A. (English literature and creative writing).

Addresses

Home and office—Berkeley, CA.

Career

Writer and editor of children's books. Has worked with paleontologists at digs, including Craddock Ranch, TX, and Como Bluff, WY.

Awards, Honors

Notable Book citation, American Library Association, for *Dinosaur Parents, Dinosaur Young.*

Writings

Seal Pup Grows Up: The Story of a Harbor Seal, illustrated by Lisa Bonforte, Soundprints (Norwalk, CT), 1994.

What Lives in a Shell?, illustrated by Helen K. Davie, HarperCollins (New York, NY) 1994.

Great White Shark, Ruler of the Sea, illustrated by Steven James Petruccio, Soundprints (Norwalk, CT), 1995.

How Mountains Are Made, illustrated by James Graham Hale, HarperCollins (New York, NY), 1995.

What's Alive?, illustrated by Nadine Bernard Westcott, HarperCollins (New York, NY), 1995.

Ladybug at Orchard Avenue, illustrated by Thomas Buchs, Soundprints (Norwalk, CT), 1996.

Cactus Café: A Story of the Sonoran Desert, illustrated by Paul Mirocha, Soundprints (Norwalk, CT), 1997.

Happy New Year, Pooh!, illustrated by Robbin Cuddy, Disney Press (New York, NY), 1997.

Pooh Plays Doctor, illustrated by Robbin Cuddy, Disney Press (New York, NY), 1997.

Pooh Welcomes Winter, illustrated by Robbin Cuddy, Disney Press (New York, NY), 1997.

Pooh's Christmas Box, illustrated by Orlando de la Paz and Nancy Stevenson, Disney Press (New York, NY), 1997.

Pooh' First Day of School, illustrated by Robbin Cuddy, Disney Press (New York, NY), 1997.

Pooh's Mailbox, illustrated by Mike Peterkin, Disney Press (New York, NY), 1997.

Pooh's Neighborhood, illustrated by Robbin Cuddy, Disney Press (New York, NY), 1997.

What Is the World Made Of?: All about Solids, Liquids, and Gases, illustrated by Paul Meisel, HarperCollins (New York, NY), 1998.

(Adapter) Russell Schoeder, *Disney's Mulan* (based on the animated film), Disney Press (New York, NY), 1998.

Disney's Big Egg, Little Egg, illustrated by Jose Cardona and Fred Marvin, Mouse Works (New York, NY), 1998.

Disney's Have You Seen My Pot of Honey?: A Lift-the-Flap Book, illustrated by Orlando de la Paz, Mouse Works (New York, NY), 1998.

Disney's Where Are You, Pooh?: A Lift-the-Flap Book, illustrated by Nancy Stevenson, Mouse Works (New York, NY) 1998.

Don't Talk to Strangers, Pooh!, illustrated by Robbin Cuddy, Disney Press (New York, NY), 1998.

Pooh's Bad Dream, illustrated by Robbin Cuddy, Disney Press (New York, NY), 1998.

Pooh Stays Safe, Disney Press (New York, NY), 1998.

Pooh's Friends, illustrated by Studio Orlando, Mouse Works (New York, NY), 1998.

Pooh's Jingle Bells, illustrated by Robbin Cuddy, Disney Press (New York, NY), 1998.

Tigger's Moving Day, illustrated by Robbin Cuddy, Disney Press (New York, NY), 1999.

Pooh's Scrapbook, illustrated by Robbin Cuddy, Disney Press (New York, NY), 1999.

(Adapter) *Toy Story 2: Buzz's Story,* Disney Press (New York, NY), 1999.

Dinosaur Babies, illustrated by Lucia Washburn, HarperCollins (New York, NY), 1999.

Disney's Can You Find the Easter Eggs, Pooh?: A Lift-the-Flap Book, illustrated by Orlando de la Paz, Mouse Works (New York, NY), 1999.

Disney's Rub-a-Dub, Pooh, illustrated by Gus Alavezos, Mouse Works (New York, NY), 1999.

(Adapter) *Disney's Tarzan,* illustrated by Glenn Harrington, Judith Holmes Clarke, and Denise Shimabukuro, Disney Press (New York, NY), 1999.

Disney's Where Is the Heffalump?, illustrated by Nancy Stevenson, Mouse Works (New York, NY), 1999.

Disney's Winnie the Pooh's Big Book of First Words, illustrated by Josie Yee, Mouse Works (New York, NY), 1999.

Growing Up Stories (includes *Pooh's First Day of School, Happy New Year, Pooh!, Pooh Plays Doctor, Pooh's Bad Dream, Don't Talk to Strangers, Pooh!,* and *Pooh's Neighborhood*), illustrated by Robbin Cuddy, Disney Press (New York, NY), 1999.

Pooh Helps Out, illustrated by Robbin Cuddy, Disney Press (New York, NY), 1999.

Roo's New Baby Sitter, illustrated by Robbin Cuddy, Disney Press (New York, NY), 1999.

Walt Disney Pictures Presents Dinosaur Aladar's Story, illustrated by Judith Holmes Clarke and Brent Ford, Disney Press (New York, NY), 2000.

(With Jeff Corwin) *Jeff Corwin's Mystery of the Rainforest Chocolate Tree,* illustrated by Victor Vaccaro, Hyperion Books for Children (New York, NY), 2000.

Be Patient, Pooh, illustrated by Robbin Cuddy, Disney Press (New York, NY), 2000.

Disney's Pooh's Birthday Surprise, illustrated by Studio Orlando, Mouse Works (New York, NY), 2000.

(Adapter) *Disney's The Emperor's New Groove: The Junior Novelization,* Disney Press (New York, NY), 2000.

Fossil Fever, illustrated by Paulette Bogan, Golden Books (New York, NY), 2000.

Human Body, Scholastic (New York, NY), 2000.

Once upon a Time with Winnie the Pooh: A Disney Treasury of Favorite Nursery Tales and Rhymes, illustrated by Studio Orlando, Disney Press (New York, NY), 2000.

Pooh's Favorite Things about Spring, illustrated by Elisa Marrucchi, Disney Press (New York, NY), 2000.

(Adapter) *Toy Story 2: A Read-Aloud Storybook,* Mouse Works (New York, NY), 2000.

Where's Pooh?, illustrated by Nancy Stevenson, Random House (New York, NY), 2001.

Who's Hiding?, illustrated by Nancy Stevenson, Random House (New York, NY), 2001.

Time for School, Pooh, Random House (New York, NY), 2001.

Amazon Fever, illustrated by Paulette Bogan, Golden Books (New York, NY), 2001.

A Beary-Good Neighbor, illustrated by Robbin Cuddy, Random House (New York, NY), 2001.

Dinosaur Parents, Dinosaur Young: Uncovering the Mystery of Dinosaur Families, illustrated by Paul Carrick and Bruce Shillinglaw, Clarion Books (New York, NY), 2001.

Fall Leaves Change Colors, Scholastic (New York, NY), 2001.

From Tadpole to Frog, photographs by Dwight Kuhn, Scholastic Reference (New York, NY), 2001.

Hello, Spring!, illustrated by Robbin Cuddy, Random House (New York, NY), 2001.

More Growing Up Stories, illustrated by Robbin Cuddy, Disney Press (New York, NY), 2001.

Pooh Gets a Checkup, illustrated by Robbin Cuddy, Random House (New York, NY), 2001.

Terrible Tyrannosaurs, illustrated by Lucia Washburn, HarperCollins (New York, NY), 2001.

Dinosaurs Big and Small, illustrated by Lucia Washburn, HarperCollins (New York, NY), 2002.

Disney's Winnie the Pooh: Pooh Helps Out, McGraw-Hill (New York, NY), 2002.

Penguins, Scholastic (New York, NY), 2002.

Disney's Winnie the Pooh Storybook Collection, (includes *Pooh's First Day of School, Happy New Year, Pooh!, Say Ahhh, Pooh!, Don't Talk to Strangers, Pooh!, Pooh's Neighborhood, Tigger's Moving Day, Roo's New Baby-Sitter, Pooh Helps Out, Pooh's Scrapbook, Pooh Welcomes Winter,* and *Be Patient, Pooh*), illustrated by Robbin Cuddy, Disney Press (New York, NY), 2003.

Good Boy!: The Movie Novel, HarperFestival (New York, NY), 2003.

Shipwreck Fever, illustrated by Ilene Richard, Golden Books (New York, NY), 2003.

Spy Kids 3-D: Game Over: The Joke Book, HarperFestival (New York, NY), 2003.

Apples, Apples, illustrated by Christopher Santoro, Harper-Festival (New York, NY), 2004.

Did Dinosaurs Have Feathers?, illustrated by Lucia Washburn, HarperCollins (New York, NY), 2004.

Fossil Fever, illustrated by Paulette Bogan, Random House (New York, NY), 2004.

Pumpkin Time, illustrated by Christopher Santoro, Harper-Festival (New York, NY), 2004.

(With Bill Nye) *Bill Nye the Science Guy's Great Big Book of Tiny Germs,* Hyperion Books for Children (New York, NY), 2005.

Curious George, the Movie: A Junior Novel, Houghton Mifflin (Boston, MA), 2005.

Duma: The Movie Novel, HarperKidsEntertainment (New York, NY), 2005.

Robots: Rodney to the Rescue, HarperKidsEntertainment (New York, NY), 2005.

Amazon Fever, illustrated by Paulette Bogan, Random House (New York, NY), 2006.

Flicka: The Movie Novel, illustrated by Judy Katschke, HarperCollins (New York, NY) 2006.

Ice Age 2, the Meltdown (based on the movie), HarperKidsEntertainment (New York, NY), 2006.

Wild Lives: 100 Years of People and Animals at the Bronx Zoo, Alfred A. Knopf (New York, NY), 2006.

The Curse of King Tut's Mummy, illustrated by Jim Nelson, Random House (New York, NY), 2007.

Dinosaur Tracks, illustrated by Lucia Washburn, Collins (New York, NY), 2007.

Shrek the Third: The Junior Novel, HarperEntertainment (New York, NY), 2007.

Curious You: You're on Your Way!, illustrated by H.A. Rey, Houghton Mifflin (Boston, MA), 2008.

Finding the First T. Rex, illustrated by Jim Nelson, Random House (New York, NY), 2008.

Sidelights

Kathleen Weidner Zoehfeld earned a master's degree in creative writing and she has put it to use in her career as an author of books for young readers. While perhaps best known for her science-themed picture books, many on the topic of paleontology, Zoehfeld has also written dozens of "Winnie-the-Pooh" titles for preschoolers, most of them released by Walt Disney Corporation's publishing wing. Her novelizations of popular feature films such as *Shrek the Third: The Junior Novel,* round out the career of an extremely busy children's author.

After creating a geology class for college-level humanities majors, Zoehfeld discovered that she had a talent for explaining paleontology to non-specialists. She added to her theoretical knowledge by participating in fossil-collecting projects in Wyoming and Texas—a fossil-rich site in the latter state has been named in her honor. This immersion in dinosaur paleontology has produced an array of titles, including *Dinosaur Parents, Dinosaur Young: Uncovering the Mystery of Dinosaur Families, Dinosaurs Big and Small, Dinosaur Tracks, Did Dinosaurs Have Feathers?,* and *Terrible Tyrannosaurs.* Zoehfeld's books introduce budding readers to some of the cutting-edge research being done on dinosaurs, including evidence that challenges and extends scientific knowledge of the many extinct species—and possibly their modern-day descendants.

Dinosaur Parents, Dinosaur Young begins with the re-creation of an ancient Oviraptor family and then explores the fossil evidence of dinosaur nests, eggs, and parenting behavior. *School Library Journal* critic Carolyn Angus called the work an "inviting, thought-provoking book." In *Dinosaurs Big and Small,* Zoehfeld uses modern-day animals as comparisons for extinct dinosaurs. A Brachiosaurus, for instance, weighed as much as sixteen elephants, and a Seismosaurus would have been longer than four school buses placed in a line. Carolyn Phelan, writing in *Booklist,* praised *Dinosaurs Big and Small* as "well focused and very appealing." In her *School Library Journal* review of the same work, Patricia Manning predicted that Zoehfeld's book will "gather no shelf-sitter dust."

One way dinosaurs left proof of their passing is in the series of footprints that are now forged by time into the solid rock. In *Dinosaur Tracks* Zoehfeld explains how such fossil footprints were formed by reminding her readers how their feet leave impressions in the sand at a beach. She goes on to show how a seemingly simple line of footprints can reveal complex dinosaur behavior patterns. In *Horn Book* Danielle J. Ford noted that the book's text "is pitched at just the right level for younger readers." Another interesting area of dinosaur research covers the growing body of evidence that some dinosaurs had feathers. *Did Dinosaurs Have Feathers?* introduces school children to recent finds such as Siuosauropteryx while also emphasizing the growing body of knowledge surrounding the better-known Archaeopteryx. According to a contributor in *Kirkus Reviews,* "young dinosaur enthusiasts will love this fascinating information." Jean Lowery, writing in *School Library Journal,* called *Did Dinosaurs Have Feathers?* "a visually appealing, informative, and interesting read."

Zoehfeld's science books are not limited to paleontology. She has also written about topics as far ranging as germs, bacteria, and viruses, the care of zoo animals, and the basics of chemistry. *What Is the World Made Of?: All about Solids, Liquids, and Gases* explains the three types of matter through easy examples, while including simple experiments kids can perform. In *Horn Book* Margaret A. Bush wrote that Zoehfeld's book shares "fundamental science that will be appreciated by teachers and enjoyed by children."

In *The Curse of King Tut's Mummy,* the author re-tells the story of the discovery of an untouched ancient Egyptian tomb holding the remains of a young pharaoh. By centering the tale on Howard Carter, the principal archeologist at the King Tut discovery, Zoehfeld allows children to imagine how they might have felt if they were there. As Carole Phillips noted in *School Library Journal, The Curse of King Tut's Mummy* "will appeal to young readers in search of true adventure."

Wild Lives: A History of the People and Animals of the Bronx Zoo explores how various species of animals and birds are cared for, and how much the employees of the Bronx Zoo care about their charges. *School Library Journal* correspondent Rebecca Stine called *Wild Lives* "a detailed, beautifully illustrated book," and *Booklist* reviewer Carolyn Phelan described it as both "attractive" and "informative."

What Lives in a Shell? and *What's Alive?* introduce kindergarten-level children to basic biology. For instance, adults may take for granted the fact that trees are alive, but to children this seems much less evident. Zoehfeld explains how living things grow, and how they differ from nonliving things. Hazel Rochman, writing in *Booklist,* concluded that *What's Alive?* will "invite attention and help sort things out."

Biographical and Critical Sources

PERIODICALS

Booklist, August, 1994, Carolyn Phelan, review of *What Lives in a Shell?,* p. 2047; November 1, 2005, Hazel Rochman, review of *What's Alive?,* p. 476; November 1, 1998, Hazel Rochman, review of *What Is the World Made Of?: All about Solids, Liquids, and Gases,* p. 508; November 15, 1999, Carolyn Phelan, review of *Dinosaur Babies,* p. 632; May 15, 2000, Lauren Peterson, review of *Fossil Fever,* p. 1745; February 1, 2001, Denia Hester, review of *Terrible Tyrannosaurs,* p. 1054; April 15, 2001, Gillian Engberg, review of *Dinosaur Parents, Dinosaur Young: Uncovering the Mystery of Dinosaur Families,* p. 1549; July, 2002, Carolyn Phelan, review of *Dinosaurs Big and Small,* p. 1852; January 1, 2004, Carolyn Phelan, review of *Did Dinosaurs Have Feathers?,* p. 870; June 1, 2005, Carolyn Phelan, review of *Bill Nye the Science Guy's Great Big Book of Tiny Germs,* p. 1802; March 15, 2006, Carolyn Phelan, review of *Wild Lives: A History of the People and Animals of the Bronx Zoo,* p. 48; December 1, 2006, Hazel Rochman, review of *Dinosaur Tracks,* p. 63.

Horn Book, September-October, 1998, Margaret A. Bush, review of *What Is the World Made Of?,* p. 627; March-April, 2007, Danielle J. Ford, review of *Dinosaur Tracks,* p. 217.

Kirkus Reviews, April 1, 2002, review of *Dinosaurs Big and Small,* p. 502; January 1, 2004, review of *Did Dinosaurs Have Feathers?,* p. 43; December 1, 2006, review of *The Curse of King Tut's Mummy,* p. 1226; March 1, 2007, review of *Dinosaur Tracks,* p. 235.

School Library Journal, November, 2000, Holly T. Sneeringer, review of *Fossil Fever,* p. 138; May, 2001, Patricia Manning, review of *Terrible Tyrannosaurs,* p. 147; July, 2001, Carolyn Angus, review of *Dinosaur Parents, Dinosaur Young,* p. 134; July, 2002, Patricia Manning, review of *Dinosaurs Big and Small,* p. 112; February, 2004, Jean Lowery, review of *Did Dinosaurs Have Feathers?,* p. 140; July, 2005, Donna Marie Wagner, review of *Bill Nye the Science Guy's Great Big Book of Tiny Germs,* p. 91; June, 2006, Rebecca Stine, review of *Wild Lives,* p. 190; March, 2007, Carole Phillips, review of *The Curse of King Tut's Mummy,* p. 202.

ONLINE

HarperCollins Children's Web site, http://www.harpercollinschildrens.com/ (September 8, 2008), "Kathleen Weidner Zoehfeld."

Prehistoric CSI Web site, http://hmnspaleo.blogspot.com/ (November, 2007), "Kathleen Zoehfeld, Volunteer Team Member."*

Illustrations Index

(In the following index, the number of the *volume* in which an illustrator's work appears is given *before* the colon, and the *page number* on which it appears is given *after* the colon. For example, a drawing by Adams, Adrienne appears in Volume 2 on page 6, another drawing by her appears in Volume 3 on page 80, another drawing in Volume 8 on page 1, and so on and so on. . . .)

YABC

Index references to *YABC* refer to listings appearing in the two-volume *Yesterday's Authors of Books for Children,* also published by Gale, Cengage Learning. *YABC* covers prominent authors and illustrators who died prior to 1960.

A

Aas, Ulf *5:* 174
Abbe, S. van
See van Abbe, S.
Abel, Raymond *6:* 122; *7:* 195; *12:* 3; *21:* 86; *25:* 119
Abelliera, Aldo *71:* 120
Abolafia, Yossi *60:* 2; *93:* 163; *152:* 202
Abrahams, Hilary *26:* 205; *29:* 24, 25; *53:* 61
Abrams, Kathie *36:* 170
Abrams, Lester *49:* 26
Abulafia, Yossi *154:* 67; *177:* 3
Accardo, Anthony *191:* 3, 8
Accornero, Franco *184:* 8
Accorsi, William *11:* 198
Acs, Laszlo *14:* 156; *42:* 22
Adams, Adrienne *2:* 6; *3:* 80; *8:* 1; *15:* 107; *16:* 180; *20:* 65; *22:* 134, 135; *33:* 75; *36:* 103, 112; *39:* 74; *86:* 54; *90:* 2, 3
Adams, Connie J. *129:* 68
Adams, John Wolcott *17:* 162
Adams, Lynn *96:* 44
Adams, Norman *55:* 82
Adams, Pam *112:* 1, 2
Adams, Sarah *98:* 126; *164:* 180
Adamson, George *30:* 23, 24; *69:* 64
Addams, Charles *55:* 5
Addison, Kenneth *192:* 173
Addy, Sean *180:* 8
Ade, Rene *76:* 198
Adinolfi, JoAnn *115:* 42; *176:* 2
Adkins, Alta *22:* 250
Adkins, Jan *8:* 3; *69:* 4; *144:* 2, 3, 4
Adler, Peggy *22:* 6; *29:* 31
Adler, Ruth *29:* 29
Adlerman, Daniel *163:* 2
Adragna, Robert *47:* 145
Agard, Nadema *18:* 1
Agee, Jon *116:* 8, 9, 10; *157:* 4
Agre, Patricia *47:* 195
Aguirre, Alfredo *152:* 218
Ahl, Anna Maria *32:* 24
Ahlberg, Allan *68:* 6, 7, 9; *165:* 5
Ahlberg, Janet *68:* 6, 7, 9
Aicher-Scholl, Inge *63:* 127
Aichinger, Helga *4:* 5, 45
Aitken, Amy *31:* 34
Akaba, Suekichi *46:* 23; *53:* 127
Akasaka, Miyoshi *YABC 2:* 261

Akib, Jamel *181:* 13; *182:* 99
Akino, Fuku *6:* 144
Alain *40:* 41
Alajalov *2:* 226
Alborough, Jez *86:* 1, 2, 3; *149:* 3
Albrecht, Jan *37:* 176
Albright, Donn *1:* 91
Alcala, Alfredo *91:* 128
Alcantará, Felipe Ugalde *171:* 186
Alcorn, John *3:* 159; *7:* 165; *31:* 22; *44:* 127; *46:* 23, 170
Alcorn, Stephen *110:* 4; *125:* 106; *128:* 172; *150:* 97; *160:* 188; *165:* 48
Alcott, May *100:* 3
Alda, Arlene *44:* 24; *158:* 2
Alden, Albert *11:* 103
Aldridge, Andy *27:* 131
Aldridge, George *105:* 125
Aldridge, Sheila *192:* 4
Alejandro, Cliff *176:* 75
Alex, Ben *45:* 25, 26
Alexander, Ellen *91:* 3
Alexander, Lloyd *49:* 34
Alexander, Martha *3:* 206; *11:* 103; *13:* 109; *25:* 100; *36:* 131; *70:* 6, 7; *136:* 3, 4, 5; *169:* 120
Alexander, Paul *85:* 57; *90:* 9
Alexeieff, Alexander *14:* 6; *26:* 199
Alfano, Wayne *80:* 69
Aliki
See Brandenberg, Aliki
Allamand, Pascale *12:* 9
Allan, Judith *38:* 166
Alland, Alexandra *16:* 255
Allen, Gertrude *9:* 6
Allen, Graham *31:* 145
Allen, Jonathan *131:* 3, 4; *177:* 8, 9, 10
Allen, Joy *168:* 185
Allen, Pamela *50:* 25, 26, 27, 28; *81:* 9, 10; *123:* 4, 5
Allen, Rowena *47:* 75
Allen, Thomas B. *81:* 101; *82:* 248; *89:* 37; *104:* 9
Allen, Tom *85:* 176
Allender, David *73:* 223
Alley, R.W. *80:* 183; *95:* 187; *156:* 100, 153; *169:* 4, 5; *179:* 17
Allison, Linda *43:* 27
Allon, Jeffrey *119:* 174
Allport, Mike *71:* 55
Almquist, Don *11:* 8; *12:* 128; *17:* 46; *22:* 110

Aloise, Frank *5:* 38; *10:* 133; *30:* 92
Alsenas, Linas *186:* 2
Althea
See Braithwaite, Althea
Altschuler, Franz *11:* 185; *23:* 141; *40:* 48; *45:* 29; *57:* 181
Alvin, John *117:* 5
Ambrus, Victor G. *1:* 6, 7, 194; *3:* 69; *5:* 15; *6:* 44; *7:* 36; *8:* 210; *12:* 227; *14:* 213; *15:* 213; *22:* 209; *24:* 36; *28:* 179; *30:* 178; *32:* 44, 46; *38:* 143; *41:* 25, 26, 27, 28, 29, 30, 31, 32; *42:* 87; *44:* 190; *55:* 172; *62:* 30, 144, 145, 148; *86:* 99, 100, 101; *87:* 66, 137; *89:* 162; *134:* 160
Ames, Lee J. *3:* 12; *9:* 130; *10:* 69; *17:* 214; *22:* 124; *151:* 13
Amon, Aline *9:* 9
Amoss, Berthe *5:* 5
Amstutz, Andre *152:* 102
Amundsen, Dick *7:* 77
Amundsen, Richard E. *5:* 10; *24:* 122
Ancona, George *12:* 11; *55:* 144; *145:* 7
Anderson, Alasdair *18:* 122
Andersen, Bethanne *116:* 167; *162:* 189; *175:* 17; *191:* 4, 5
Anderson, Bob *139:* 16
Anderson, Brad *33:* 28
Anderson, C.W. *11:* 10
Anderson, Carl *7:* 4
Anderson, Catherine Corley *72:* 2
Anderson, Cecil *127:* 152
Anderson, David Lee *118:* 176
Anderson, Derek *169:* 9; *174:* 180
Anderson, Doug *40:* 111
Anderson, Erica *23:* 65
Anderson, Laurie *12:* 153, 155
Anderson, Lena *99:* 26
Anderson, Peggy Perry *179:* 2
Anderson, Sara *173:* 3
Anderson, Scoular *138:* 13
Anderson, Susan *90:* 12
Anderson, Tara *188:* 132
Anderson, Wayne *23:* 119; *41:* 239; *56:* 7; *62:* 26; *147:* 6
Andreasen, Daniel *86:* 157; *87:* 104; *103:* 201, 202; *159:* 75; *167:* 106, 107; *168:* 184; *180:* 247; *186:* 9
Andrew, Ian *111:* 37; *116:* 12; *166:* 2
Andrew, John *22:* 4
Andrews, Benny *14:* 251; *31:* 24; *57:* 6, 7; *183:* 8

Andrews, Vaughn *166:* 28
Anelay, Henry *57:* 173
Angel, Marie *47:* 22
Angelo, Valenti *14:* 8; *18:* 100; *20:* 232; *32:* 70
Anglund, Joan Walsh *2:* 7, 250, 251; *37:* 198, 199, 200
Anholt, Catherine *74:* 8; *131:* 7; *141:* 5
Anholt, Laurence *141:* 4
Anno, Mitsumasa *5:* 7; *38:* 25, 26, 27, 28, 29, 30, 31, 32; *77:* 3, 4; *157:* 10, 11
Antal, Andrew *1:* 124; *30:* 145
Antram, David *152:* 133
Apostolou, Christy Hale
    See Hale, Christy
Apple, Margot *33:* 25; *35:* 206; *46:* 81; *53:* 8; *61:* 109; *64:* 21, 22, 24, 25, 27; *71:* 176; *77:* 53; *82:* 245; *92:* 39; *94:* 180; *96:* 107; *152:* 4, 5; *162:* 192, 194; *173:* 44
Appleyard, Dev *2:* 192
Aragones, Sergio *48:* 23, 24, 25, 26, 27
Araneus *40:* 29
Arbo, Cris *103:* 4
Archambault, Matt *85:* 173; *138:* 19, 20; *143:* 33; *145:* 144; *179:* 103; *187:* 7
Archer, Janet *16:* 69; *178:* 156
Ardizzone, Edward *1:* 11, 12; *2:* 105; *3:* 258; *4:* 78; *7:* 79; *10:* 100; *15:* 232; *20:* 69,178; *23:* 223; *24:* 125; *28:* 25, 26, 27, 28, 29, 30, 31,33, 34, 35, 36, 37; *31:* 192, 193; *34:* 215, 217; *60:* 173; *64:* 145; *87:* 176; *YABC 2:* 25
Arena, Jill *176:* 49
Arenella, Roy *14:* 9
Argent, Kerry *103:* 56; *138:* 17; *158:* 134
Arisman, Marshall *162:* 50
Armer, Austin *13:* 3
Armer, Laura Adams *13:* 3
Armer, Sidney *13:* 3
Armitage, David *47:* 23; *99:* 5; *155:* 4
Armitage, Eileen *4:* 16
Armstrong, George *10:* 6; *21:* 72
Armstrong, Shelagh *102:* 114
Armstrong-Ellis, Carey *185:* 196
Arno, Enrico *1:* 217; *2:* 22, 210; *4:* 9; *5:* 43; *6:* 52; *29:* 217, 219; *33:* 152; *35:* 99; *43:* 31, 32, 33; *45:* 212, 213, 214; *72:* 72; *74:* 166; *100:* 169
Arnold, Alli *187:* 40, 41
Arnold, Caroline *174:* 5
Arnold, Emily *76:* 7, 9, 10
Arnold, Katya *115:* 11; *168:* 2, 3
Arnold, Tedd *116:* 14; *133:* 152; *160:* 5
Arnosky, Jim *22:* 20; *70:* 9, 10, 11; *118:* 3, 5; *160:* 8, 10; *189:* 5, 7, 8, 9, 10
Arnsteen, Katy Keck *105:* 97; *116:* 145
Arrowood, Clinton *12:* 193; *19:* 11; *65:* 210
Artell, Mike *89:* 8
Arting, Fred J. *41:* 63
Artzybasheff, Boris *13:* 143; *14:* 15; *40:* 152, 155
Aruego, Ariane *6:* 4
Aruego, José *4:* 140; *6:* 4; *7:* 64; *33:* 195; *35:* 208; *68:* 16, 17; *75:* 46; *93:* 91, 92; *94:* 197; *109:* 65, 67; *125:* 2, 3, 4, 5; *127:* 188; *143:* 25; *178:* 17, 19, 74; *188:* 166
Arzoumanian, Alik *177:* 12
Asare, Meshack *86:* 9; *139:* 19
Ascensios, Natalie *105:* 139
Asch, Frank *5:* 9; *66:* 2, 4, 6, 7, 9, 10; *102:* 18, 19,21; *154:* 12
Ashby, Gail *11:* 135
Ashby, Gil *146:* 4
Ashby, Gwynneth *44:* 26
Ashley, C.W. *19:* 197
Ashmead, Hal *8:* 70
Aska, Warabe *56:* 10
Assel, Steven *44:* 153; *77:* 22, 97
Astrop, John *32:* 56
Atene, Ann *12:* 18
Atherton, Lisa *38:* 198
Atkinson, Allen *60:* 5

Atkinson, J. Priestman *17:* 275
Atkinson, Janet *86:* 147; *103:* 138
Atkinson, Mike *127:* 74
Atkinson, Wayne *40:* 46
Attebery, Charles *38:* 170
Atwell, Debby *150:* 6
Atwood, Ann *7:* 9
Aubrey, Meg Kelleher *77:* 159
Auch, Herm *173:* 7, 8
Auch, Mary Jane *173:* 7
Augarde, Steve *25:* 22; *159:* 7
Austerman, Miriam *23:* 107
Austin, Margot *11:* 16
Austin, Robert *3:* 44
Austin, Virginia *81:* 205; *127:* 221
Auth, Tony *51:* 5; *192:* 18
Avendano, Dolores *158:* 74
Avedon, Richard *57:* 140
Averill, Esther *1:* 17; *28:* 39, 40, 41
Axeman, Lois *2:* 32; *11:* 84; *13:* 165; *22:* 8; *23:* 49; *61:* 116; *101:* 124
Axtel, David *155:* 110
Ayer, Jacqueline *13:* 7
Ayer, Margaret *15:* 12; *50:* 120
Ayers, Alan *91:* 58; *107:* 169
Ayliffe, Alex *95:* 164
Ayto, Russell *111:* 5; *112:* 54
Azarian, Mary *112:* 9, 10; *114:* 129; *117:* 171; *137:* 163; *171:* 4, 5; *181:* 161; *188:* 128

B

B.T.B.
    See Blackwell, Basil T.
Babbitt, Bradford *33:* 158
Babbitt, Natalie *6:* 6; *8:* 220; *68:* 20; *70:* 242, 243
Baca, Maria *104:* 5
Bacchus, Andy *94:* 87
Bacha, Andy *109:* 169
Bachem, Paul *48:* 180; *67:* 65; *144:* 206
Back, Adam *63:* 125
Back, George *31:* 161
Backes, Nick *190:* 72
Backhouse, Colin *78:* 142
Bacon, Bruce *4:* 74
Bacon, Paul *7:* 155; *8:* 121; *31:* 55; *50:* 42; *56:* 175; *62:* 82, 84
Bacon, Peggy *2:* 11, 228; *46:* 44
Baek, Matthew J. *169:* 95
Baer, Julie *161:* 2
Baicker-McKee, Carol *177:* 15; *180:* 215
Bailey, Peter *58:* 174; *87:* 221
Bailey, Sheila *155:* 11
Baker, Alan *22:* 22; *61:* 134; *93:* 11, 12; *146:* 6, 7, 10
Baker, Charlotte *2:* 12
Baker, Garin *89:* 65
Baker, Jeannie *23:* 4; *88:* 18, 19, 20
Baker, Jim *22:* 24
Baker, Joe *82:* 188; *111:* 55; *124:* 70
Baker, Keith *179:* 6, 7
Baker, Leslie *112:* 214; *132:* 103, 246; *180:* 74, 246
Baldacci, Rudy *184:* 9
Baldridge, Cyrus LeRoy *19:* 69; *44:* 50
Baldus, Zachary *152:* 231; *187:* 60
Balet, Jan *11:* 22
Balian, Lorna *9:* 16; *91:* 16
Balit, Christina *102:* 24; *159:* 9; *162:* 118, 119
Ballantyne, R.M. *24:* 34
Ballis, George *14:* 199
Balouch, Kristen *176:* 11
Baltzer, Hans *40:* 30
Banbery, Fred *58:* 15
Banfill, A. Scott *98:* 7; *112:* 59
Bang, Molly Garrett *24:* 37, 38; *69:* 8, 9, 10; *111:* 7,9, 10, 11; *140:* 11; *158:* 37, 38, 39
Banik, Yvette Santiago *21:* 136

Banner, Angela
    See Maddison, Angela Mary
Bannerman, Helen *19:* 13, 14
Bannon, Laura *6:* 10; *23:* 8
Bantock, Nick *74:* 229; *95:* 6
Banyai, Istvan *185:* 209; *193:* 14, 16
Baptist, Michael *37:* 208
Baracca, Sal *135:* 206
Baranaski, Marcin *182:* 113
Barasch, Lynne *126:* 16; *186:* 15
Barbarin, Lucien C., Jr. *89:* 88
Barbour, Karen *96:* 5; *74:* 209; *170:* 16
Bare, Arnold Edwin *16:* 31
Bare, Colleen Stanley *32:* 33
Barger, Jan *147:* 11
Bargery, Geoffrey *14:* 258
Barkat, Jonathan *149:* 177; *164:* 254; *181:* 106; *184:* 186
Barker, Carol *31:* 27
Barker, Cicely Mary *49:* 50, 51
Barkley, James *4:* 13; *6:* 11; *13:* 112
Barks, Carl *37:* 27, 28, 29, 30, 31, 32, 33, 34
Barling, Joy *62:* 148
Barling, Tom *9:* 23
Barlow, Gillian *62:* 20
Barlow, Perry *35:* 28
Barlowe, Dot *30:* 223
Barlowe, Wayne *37:* 72; *84:* 43; *105:* 5
Barnard, Bryn *88:* 53; *13:* 55; *169:* 13; *193:* 194
Barner, Bob *29:* 37; *128:* 33; *136:* 19, 20; *177:* 27
Barnes, Hiram P. *20:* 28
Barnes, Tim *137:* 28
Barnes-Murphy, Rowan *88:* 22
Barnett, Charles II *175:* 150
Barnett, Ivan *70:* 14
Barnett, Moneta *16:* 89; *19:* 142; *31:* 102; *33:* 30, 31, 32; *41:* 153; *61:* 94, 97
Barney, Maginel Wright *39:* 32, 33, 34; *YABC 2:* 306
Barnum, Jay Hyde *11:* 224; *20:* 5; *37:* 189, 190
Baron, Alan *80:* 3; *89:* 123
Barr, George *60:* 74; *69:* 64
Barragan, Paula S. *134:* 116; *186:* 158
Barrall, Tim *115:* 152
Barraud, Martin *189:* 38
Barrauds *33:* 114
Barrer-Russell, Gertrude *9:* 65; *27:* 31
Barret, Robert *85:* 134
Barrett, Angela *40:* 136, 137; *62:* 74; *75:* 10; *76:* 142; *144:* 137; *145:* 14
Barrett, Jennifer *58:* 149
Barrett, John E. *43:* 119
Barrett, Moneta *74:* 10
Barrett, Peter *55:* 169; *86:* 111
Barrett, Robert *62:* 145; *77:* 146; *82:* 35
Barrett, Ron *14:* 24; *26:* 35
Barron, John N. *3:* 261; *5:* 101; *14:* 220
Barrow, Ann *136:* 27
Barrows, Walter *14:* 268
Barry, Ethelred B. *37:* 79; *YABC 1:* 229
Barry, James *14:* 25
Barry, Katharina *2:* 159; *4:* 22
Barry, Robert E. *6:* 12
Barry, Scott *32:* 35
Bartenbach, Jean *40:* 31
Barth, Ernest Kurt *2:* 172; *3:* 160; *8:* 26; *10:* 31
Bartlett, Alison *101:* 88; *165:* 93
Barton, Byron *8:* 207; *9:* 18; *23:* 66; *80:* 181; *90:* 18, 19, 20, 21; *126:* 29, 30
Barton, Harriett *30:* 71
Barton, Jill *129:* 108; *135:* 120; *145:* 185, 189; *184:* 177
Bartram, Robert *10:* 42
Bartsch, Jochen *8:* 105; *39:* 38
Bascove, Barbara *45:* 73
Base, Graeme *101:* 15, 16, 17, 18; *162:* 8, 10, 12

Baseman, Gary *174:* 12
Bash, Barbara *132:* 9
Baskin, Leonard *30:* 42, 43, 46, 47; *49:* 125, 126, 128, 129,133; *173:* 120
Bass, Saul *49:* 192
Bassett, Jeni *40:* 99; *64:* 30
Basso, Bill *99:* 139; *189:* 134
Batchelor, Joy *29:* 41, 47, 48
Bate, Norman *5:* 16
Bates, Amy June *188:* 170; *189:* 27, 28
Bates, Leo *24:* 35
Batet, Carmen *39:* 134
Batherman, Muriel *31:* 79; *45:* 185
Battaglia, Aurelius *50:* 44
Batten, John D. *25:* 161, 162
Batten, Mary *162:* 14, 15
Battles, Asa *32:* 94, 95
Bauer, Carla *193:* 6
Bauer, Jutta *150:* 32
Bauernschmidt, Marjorie *15:* 15
Baum, Allyn *20:* 10
Baum, Willi *4:* 24, 25; *7:* 173
Bauman, Leslie *61:* 121
Baumann, Jill *34:* 170
Baumhauer, Hans *11:* 218; *15:* 163, 165, 167
Baxter, Glen *57:* 100
Baxter, Leon *59:* 102
Baxter, Robert *87:* 129
Bayer, Herbert *181:* 16
Bayley, Dorothy *37:* 195
Bayley, Nicola *40:* 104; *41:* 34, 35; *69:* 15; *129:* 33, 34, 35
Baylin, Mark *158:* 233
Baynes, Pauline *2:* 244; *3:* 149; *13:* 133, 135,137, 141; *19:* 18, 19, 20; *32:* 208, 213, 214; *36:* 105, 108; *59:* 12, 13, 14, 16, 17, 18, 20; *100:* 158, 159, 243; *133:* 3, 4
Beach, Lou *150:* 150
Beame, Rona *12:* 40
Bear's Heart *73:* 215
Beard, Dan *22:* 31, 32
Beard, J.H. *YABC 1:* 158
Bearden, Romare *9:* 7; *22:* 35
Beardshaw, Rosalind *169:* 22; *190:* 22
Beardsley, Aubrey *17:* 14; *23:* 181; *59:* 130, 131
Bearman, Jane *29:* 38
Beaton, Cecil *24:* 208
Beaton, Clare *125:* 28
Beauce, J.A. *18:* 103
Beaujard, Sophie *81:* 54
Beccia, Carlyn *189:* 29
Beck, Charles *11:* 169; *51:* 173
Beck, Ian *138:* 27; *182:* 150; *190:* 25
Beck, Ruth *13:* 11
Becker, Harriet *12:* 211
Beckett, Sheilah *25:* 5; *33:* 37, 38
Beckhoff, Harry *1:* 78; *5:* 163
Beckhorn, Susan Williams *189:* 32
Beckman, Kaj *45:* 38, 39, 40, 41
Beckman, Per *45:* 42, 43
Beddows, Eric *72:* 70
Bedford, F.D. *20:* 118, 122; *33:* 170; *41:* 220, 221,230, 233
Bee, Joyce *19:* 62
Bee, William *188:* 6
Beeby, Betty *25:* 36
Beech, Carol *9:* 149
Beech, Mark *192:* 122
Beek *25:* 51, 55, 59
Beeke, Tiphanie *177:* 127
Beekman, Doug *125:* 146, 148
Beerbohm, Max *24:* 208
Beeson, Bob *108:* 57
Begin, Maryjane *82:* 13
Beha, Philippe *172:* 85
Behr, Joyce *15:* 15; *21:* 132; *23:* 161
Behrens, Hans *5:* 97
Beier, Ellen *135:* 170; *139:* 47; *183:* 164
Beinicke, Steve *69:* 18
Beisner, Monika *46:* 128, 131; *112:* 127

Belden, Charles J. *12:* 182
Belina, Renate *39:* 132
Bell, Corydon *3:* 20
Bell, Graham *54:* 48
Bell, Julia *151:* 214
Bell, Julie *159:* 172; *165:* 18
Bell, Thomas P. *76:* 182
Bellamy, Glen *127:* 15
Beltran, Alberto *43:* 37
Bemelmans, Ludwig *15:* 19, 21; *100:* 27
Ben-Ami, Doron *75:* 96; *84:* 107; *108:* 132; *110:* 63; *159:* 157
Bendall-Brunello, John *150:* 4; *157:* 163; *185:* 3, 4
Benda, Wladyslaw T. *15:* 256; *30:* 76, 77; *44:* 182
Bender, Robert *77:* 162; *79:* 13; *160:* 23
Bendick, Jeanne *2:* 24; *68:* 27, 28
Benioff, Carol *121:* 42; *175:* 23
Benner, Cheryl *80:* 11
Bennett, Charles H. *64:* 6
Bennett, Erin Susanne *165:* 216
Bennett, F.I. *YABC 1:* 134
Bennett, James *146:* 240
Bennett, Jill *26:* 61; *41:* 38, 39; *45:* 54
Bennett, Rainey *15:* 26; *23:* 53
Bennett, Richard *15:* 45; *21:* 11, 12, 13; *25:* 175
Bennett, Susan *5:* 55
Benny, Mike *142:* 78
Benoit, Elise *77:* 74
Benson, Linda *60:* 130; *62:* 91; *75:* 101; *79:* 156; *134:* 129
Benson, Patrick *68:* 162; *147:* 17, 18, 19, 20
Bentley, Carolyn *46:* 153
Bentley, James *149:* 30
Bentley, Roy *30:* 162
Benton, Jim *172:* 22
Benton, Thomas Hart *2:* 99
Berelson, Howard *5:* 20; *16:* 58; *31:* 50
Berenstain, Jan *12:* 47; *64:* 33, 34, 36, 37, 38, 40, 42, 44; *135:* 25, 28, 31, 35
Berenstain, Stan *12:* 47; *64:* 33, 34, 36, 37, 38, 40, 42, 44; *135:* 25, 28, 31, 35
Berenzy, Alix *65:* 13; *73:* 6; *78:* 115
Berg, Joan *1:* 115; *3:* 156; *6:* 26, 58
Berg, Ron *36:* 48, 49; *48:* 37, 38; *67:* 72
Bergen, David *115:* 44
Berger, Barbara *77:* 14
Berger, Carin *185:* 6
Berger, William M. *14:* 143; *YABC 1:* 204
Bergherr, Mary *74:* 170; *151:* 123
Bergin, Mark *114:* 8, 9; *143:* 95; *160:* 26, 27
Bergstreser, Douglas *69:* 76
Bergum, Constance R. *121:* 14, 15
Bering, Claus *13:* 14
Berkeley, Jon *139:* 218
Berkowitz, Jeanette *3:* 249
Berman, Paul *66:* 14
Bernal, Richard *154:* 176
Bernadette
　　See Watts, Bernadette
Bernardin, James *112:* 24; *167:* 94
Bernasconi, Pablo *183:* 10, 11
Bernath, Stefen *32:* 76
Bernhard, Durga *80:* 13
Bernstein, Michel J. *51:* 71
Bernstein, Ted *38:* 183; *50:* 131
Bernstein, Zena *23:* 46
Berridge, Celia *86:* 63
Berrill, Jacquelyn *12:* 50
Berry, Erick
　　See Best, Allena
Berry, William D. *14:* 29; *19:* 48
Berry, William A. *6:* 219
Berson, Harold *2:* 17, 18; *4:* 28, 29, 220; *9:* 10; *12:* 19; *17:* 45; *18:* 193; *22:* 85; *34:* 172; *44:* 120; *46:* 42; *80:* 240
Bertholf, Bret *187:* 9; *189:* 32, 33
Berton, Patsy *99:* 16
Bertschmann, Harry *16:* 1

Besco, Don *70:* 99
Beskow, Elsa *20:* 13, 14, 15
Bess, Clayton *63:* 94
Best, Allena *2:* 26; *34:* 76
Betera, Carol *74:* 68
Bethell, Thomas N. *61:* 169
Bethers, Ray *6:* 22
Bettina
　　See Ehrlich, Bettina
Betts, Ethel Franklin *17:* 161, 164, 165; *YABC 2:* 47
Betz, Rudolf *59:* 161
Bewick, Thomas *16:* 40, 41, 43, 44, 45, 47; *54:* 150; *YABC 1:* 107
Beyer, Paul J. III *74:* 24
Bezencon, Jacqueline *48:* 40
Biamonte, Daniel *40:* 90
Bianchi, John *91:* 19
Bianco, Pamela *15:* 31; *28:* 44, 45, 46
Bible, Charles *13:* 15
Bice, Clare *22:* 40
Biedrzycki, David *186:* 170
Bierman, Don *57:* 184
Biggers, John *2:* 123
Biggs, Brian *192:* 38
Bileck, Marvin *3:* 102; *40:* 36, 37
Bilibin, Ivan *61:* 8, 9, 12, 13, 14, 15, 151, 152, 154, 162
Billington, Patrick *98:* 71
Billout, Guy *144:* 38, 39
Bimen, Levent *5:* 179
Binch, Caroline *81:* 18; *140:* 15, 16; *144:* 115
Binder, Hannes *169:* 163
Bing, Christopher *126:* 34
Binger, Bill *121:* 46
Binks, Robert *25:* 150
Binzen, Bill *24:* 47
Birch, Reginald *15:* 150; *19:* 33, 34, 35, 36; *37:* 196,197; *44:* 182; *46:* 176; *YABC 1:* 84; *2:* 34, 39
Birchall, Mark *123:* 188
Bird, Esther Brock *1:* 36; *25:* 66
Birdsong, Keith *167:* 85
Birkett, Rachel *78:* 206
Birling, Paul *109:* 30
Birmingham, Christian *132:* 243; *143:* 114
Birmingham, Lloyd P. *12:* 51; *83:* 13
Biro, Val *1:* 26; *41:* 42; *60:* 178; *67:* 23, 24; *84:* 242, 243
Bischoff, Ilse *44:* 51
Bishop, Gavin *97:* 17, 18; *144:* 42, 44
Bishop, Kathleen Wong *115:* 67
Bishop, Rich *56:* 43
Bite, I. *60:* 14
Bittinger, Ned *93:* 117
Bjorklund, Lorence *3:* 188, 252; *7:* 100; *9:* 113; *10:* 66; *19:* 178; *33:* 122, 123; *35:* 36, 37, 38, 39,41, 42, 43; *36:* 185; *38:* 93; *47:* 106; *66:* 194; *YABC 1:* 242
Bjorkman, Steve *91:* 199; *160:* 110
Black Sheep *164:* 100
Blackburn, Loren H. *63:* 10
Blackford, John *137:* 105; *180:* 36
Blackwell, Basil T. *YABC 1:* 68, 69
Blackwood, Gary L. *118:* 17
Blades, Ann *16:* 52; *37:* 213; *50:* 41; *69:* 21; *99:* 215
Blair, Jay *45:* 46; *46:* 155
Blaisdell, Elinore *1:* 121; *3:* 134; *35:* 63
Blake, Anne Catharine *189:* 71
Blake, Quentin *3:* 170; *10:* 48; *13:* 38; *21:* 180; *26:* 60; *28:* 228; *30:* 29, 31; *40:* 108; *45:* 219; *46:* 165, 168; *48:* 196; *52:* 10, 11, 12,13, 14, 15, 16, 17; *73:* 41, 43; *78:* 84, 86; *80:* 250, 251; *84:* 210, 211, 212; *87:* 177; *96:* 24, 26, 28; *124:* 79; *125:* 32, 34; *181:* 139
Blake, Robert J. *37:* 90; *53:* 67; *54:* 23; *160:* 28, 29
Blake, William *30:* 54, 56, 57, 58, 59, 60
Blanchard, N. Taylor *82:* 140

Blass, Jacqueline *8:* 215
Blazek, Scott R. *91:* 71
Bleck, Cathie *118:* 116
Blegvad, Erik *2:* 59; *3:* 98; *5:* 117; *7:* 131; *11:* 149; *14:* 34, 35; *18:* 237; *32:* 219; *60:* 106; *66:* 16, 17, 18, 19; *70:* 233; *76:* 18; *82:* 106; *87:* 45; *100:* 188; *129:* 125; *132:* 17, 18, 19, 20; *176:* 14; *YABC 1:* 201
Blessen, Karen *93:* 126
Bliss, Corinne Demas *37:* 38
Blitt, Barry *179:* 199; *187:* 13
Bloch, Lucienne *10:* 12
Blondon, Herve *129:* 48; *183:* 22
Bloom, Lloyd *35:* 180; *36:* 149; *47:* 99; *62:* 117; *68:* 231; *72:* 136; *75:* 185; *83:* 99; *108:* 19
Bloom, Suzanne *172:* 23, 24
Blossom, Dave *34:* 29
Blumenschein, E.L. *YABC 1:* 113, 115
Blumer, Patt *29:* 214
Blundell, Kim *29:* 36
Bluthenthal, Diana Cain *93:* 32; *104:* 106; *177:* 26
Blythe, Benjamin *128:* 7
Blythe, Gary *112:* 52; *181:* 166; *182:* 64; *185:* 7; *186:* 116, 117
Boake, Kathy *176:* 185
Board, Perry *171:* 99
Boardman, Gwenn *12:* 60
Bober, Richard *125:* 145; *132:* 40
Bobri *30:* 138; *47:* 27
Bock, Vera *1:* 187; *21:* 41
Bock, William Sauts *8:* 7; *14:* 37; *16:* 120; *21:* 141; *36:* 177; *62:* 203
Bodecker, N(iels) M(ogens) *8:* 13; *14:* 2; *17:* 55, 56, 57; *73:* 22, 23, 24
Boehm, Linda *40:* 31
Bogacki, Tomek *138:* 31, 32; *144:* 123
Bogdan, Florentina *107:* 43
Bohdal, Susi *22:* 44; *101:* 20
Bohlen, Nina *58:* 13
Boies, Alex *96:* 53
Bolam, Emily *101:* 216; *159:* 12
Bolian, Polly *3:* 270; *4:* 30; *13:* 77; *29:* 197
Bolle, Frank *87:* 100
Bollen, Roger *79:* 186; *83:* 16
Bolling, Vickey *114:* 44
Bollinger, Peter *101:* 7; *128:* 198; *172:* 26
Bolognese, Don *2:* 147, 231; *4:* 176; *7:* 146; *17:* 43; *23:* 192; *24:* 50; *34:* 108; *36:* 133; *71:* 24, 25; *103:* 131; *129:* 39, 40
Bolster, Rob *186:* 169
Bolton, A.T. *57:* 158
Bond, Arnold *18:* 116
Bond, Barbara Higgins *21:* 102
Bond, Bruce *52:* 97
Bond, Felicia *38:* 197; *49:* 55, 56; *89:* 170; *90:* 171; *126:* 37
Bond, Higgins *177:* 22, 23
Bonn, Pat *43:* 40
Bonners, Susan *41:* 40; *85:* 36; *94:* 99, 100; *151:* 105, 106
Bono, Mary *184:* 73
Bonsall, Crosby *23:* 6
Boon, Debbie *103:* 6; *144:* 188
Boon, Emilie *86:* 23, 24
Boone, Debbie *165:* 77
Boore, Sara *60:* 73
Bootman, Colin *155:* 13; *159:* 35; *174:* 192
Booth, Franklin *YABC 2:* 76
Booth, George *191:* 13
Booth, Graham *32:* 193; *37:* 41, 42
Borda, Juliette *102:* 188
Bordier, Georgette *16:* 54
Boren, Tinka *27:* 128
Borges, Jose Francisco *119:* 62
Borja, Robert *22:* 48
Born, Adolf *49:* 63
Bornstein, Ruth *14:* 44; *88:* 45, 46; *107:* 30
Borten, Helen *3:* 54; *5:* 24
Bosin, Blackbear *69:* 104

Bossom, Naomi *35:* 48
Bostock, Mike *83:* 221; *114:* 14; *188:* 205
Boston, Peter *19:* 42
Bosustow, Stephen *34:* 202
Boszko, Ron *75:* 47
Bottner, Barbara *14:* 46
Boucher, Joelle *41:* 138
Boulat, Pierre *44:* 40
Boulet, Susan Seddon *50:* 47
Bouma, Paddy *118:* 25; *128:* 16
Bour, Daniele *66:* 145
Bourke-White, Margaret *15:* 286, 287; *57:* 102
Boutet de Monvel, M. *30:* 61, 62, 63, 65
Bowen, Betsy *105:* 222
Bowen, Richard *42:* 134
Bowen, Ruth *31:* 188
Bower, Ron *29:* 33
Bowers, David *95:* 38; *115:* 20; *127:* 169, 170; *165:* 57
Bowers, Tim *185:* 35
Bowman, Claire *174:* 177
Bowman, Eric *151:* 23
Bowman, Leslie *85:* 203; *105:* 108; *116:* 76; *128:* 234; *182:* 24, 25
Bowman, Peter *146:* 214, 215; *150:* 115
Bowser, Carolyn Ewing *22:* 253
Boxall, Ed *178:* 28
Boyd, Aaron *158:* 242
Boyd, Patti *45:* 31
Boyle, Eleanor Vere *28:* 50, 51
Boynton, Sandra *57:* 13, 14, 15; *107:* 36, 37; *152:* 12, 13, 14
Bozzo, Frank *4:* 154
Brabbs, Derry *55:* 170
Brace, Eric *132:* 193, 194; *152:* 71; *184:* 195
Brackers de Hugo, Pierre *115:* 21
Bradford, June *158:* 138
Bradford, Ron *7:* 157
Bradley, David P. *69:* 105
Bradley, Richard D. *26:* 182
Bradley, William *5:* 164
Brady, Irene *4:* 31; *42:* 37; *68:* 191
Bragg, Michael *32:* 78; *46:* 31
Bragg, Ruth Gembicki *77:* 18
Brainerd, John W. *65:* 19
Braithwaite, Althea *23:* 12, 13; *119:* 16
Brak, Syd *146:* 187
Bralds, Braldt *90:* 28; *91:* 151
Bram, Elizabeth *30:* 67
Bramley, Peter *4:* 3
Brandenberg, Aliki *2:* 36, 37; *24:* 222; *35:* 49, 50, 51,52, 53, 54, 56, 57; *75:* 15, 17; *92:* 205; *113:* 18, 19, 20; *157:* 28; *156:* 111
Brandenburg, Alexa *75:* 19
Brandenburg, Jim *47:* 58; *150:* 212
Brandi, Lillian *31:* 158
Brandon, Brumsic, Jr. *9:* 25
Bransom, Paul *17:* 121; *43:* 44
Braren, Loretta Trezzo *87:* 193
Brassard, France *186:* 22
Braun, Wendy *80:* 17, 18
Brautigam, Don *115:* 175, 176
Brazell, Derek *75:* 105; *79:* 9
Breathed, Berkeley *86:* 27, 28, 29; *161:* 13, 14
Breckenreid, Julia *192:* 209
Breen, Steve *186:* 23
Brennan, Steve *83:* 230; *101:* 184
Brenner, Fred *22:* 85; *36:* 34; *42:* 34
Brett, Bernard *22:* 54
Brett, Harold M. *26:* 98, 99, 100
Brett, Jan *30:* 135; *42:* 39; *71:* 31, 32; *130:* 23, 24, 25, 26, 27; *171:* 15, 16
Brewer, Paul *106:* 115; *145:* 202
Brewer, Sally King *33:* 44
Brewster, Patience *40:* 68; *45:* 22, 183; *51:* 20; *66:* 144; *89:* 4; *97:* 30, 31
Brick, John *10:* 15
Brickman, Robin D. *131:* 88; *142:* 150; *155:* 18; *178:* 109; *184:* 32
Bridge, David R. *45:* 28
Bridgman, L.J. *37:* 77

Bridwell, Norman *4:* 37; *138:* 36, 37, 40
Brierley, Louise *91:* 22; *96:* 165; *183:* 51
Briggs, Harry *172:* 187
Briggs, Raymond *10:* 168; *23:* 20, 21; *66:* 29, 31, 32; *131:* 28, 29; *184:* 15, 16
Brigham, Grace A. *37:* 148
Bright, Robert *24:* 55
Brighton, Catherine *107:* 39
Brinckloe, Julie *13:* 18; *24:* 79, 115; *29:* 35; *63:* 140; *81:* 131
Brion *47:* 116
Brisley, Joyce L. *22:* 57
Brisson, James F. *110:* 60
Brittingham, Geoffrey *88:* 37
Brix-Henker, Silke *81:* 194
Brock, Charles E. *15:* 97; *19:* 247, 249; *23:* 224, 225; *36:* 88; *42:* 41, 42, 43, 44, 45; *100:* 189; *YABC 1:* 194, 196, 203
Brock, Emma *7:* 21
Brock, Henry Matthew *15:* 81; *16:* 141; *19:* 71; *34:* 115; *40:* 164; *42:* 47, 48, 49; *49:* 66
Brocksopp, Arthur *57:* 157
Broda, Ron *136:* 180; *174:* 123
Brodkin, Gwen *34:* 135
Brodovitch, Alexi *52:* 22
Bromhall, Winifred *5:* 11; *26:* 38
Bromley, Lizzy *159:* 179
Bronson, Linda *150:* 210; *174:* 133
Brooke, L. Leslie *16:* 181, 182, 183, 186; *17:* 15, 16, 17; *18:* 194
Brooker, Christopher *15:* 251
Brooker, Krysten *111:* 94; *140:* 28; *162:* 111; *175:* 108; *186:* 42, 225
Brooks, Erik *166:* 52; *182:* 30
Brooks, Karen Stormer *186:* 110
Brooks, Maya Itzna *92:* 153
Brooks, Ron *94:* 15
Brooks, S.G. *178:* 124
Broomfield, Maurice *40:* 141
Brotman, Adolph E. *5:* 21
Brown, Buck *45:* 48
Brown, Calef *179:* 18
Brown, Christopher *62:* 124, 125, 127, 128
Brown, Craig McFarland *73:* 28; *84:* 65
Brown, Dan *61:* 167; *115:* 183, 184; *116:* 28, 29; *193:* 190
Brown, David *7:* 47; *48:* 52
Brown, Denise *11:* 213
Brown, Don *172:* 29
Brown, Ford Madox *48:* 74
Brown, Hunter *191:* 111, 112
Brown, Judith Gwyn *1:* 45; *7:* 5; *8:* 167; *9:* 182, 190; *20:* 16, 17, 18; *23:* 142; *29:* 117; *33:* 97; *36:* 23, 26; *43:* 184; *48:* 201, 223; *49:* 69; *86:* 227; *110:* 188; *153:* 7
Brown, Kathryn *98:* 26
Brown, Lisa *187:* 175
Brown, Laurie Krasny *99:* 30
Brown, Marc (Tolon) *10:* 17, 197; *14:* 263; *51:* 18; *53:* 11, 12, 13, 15, 16, 17; *75:* 58; *80:* 24, 25, 26; *82:* 261; *99:* 29; *145:* 22, 23, 25, 27; *162:* 198
Brown, Marcia *7:* 30; *25:* 203; *47:* 31, 32, 33, 34, 35,36, 37, 38, 39, 40, 42, 43, 44; *YABC 1:* 27
Brown, Margery W. *5:* 32, 33; *10:* 3
Brown, Martin *101:* 43
Brown, Mary Barrett *97:* 74
Brown, Palmer *36:* 40
Brown, Paul *25:* 26; *26:* 107
Brown, Richard *61:* 18; *67:* 30
Brown, Rick *78:* 71; *150:* 154
Brown, Robert S. *85:* 33
Brown, Rod *157:* 142
Brown, Ruth *55:* 165; *86:* 112, 113; *105:* 16, 17, 18; *171:* 178
Brown, Trevor *99:* 160; *139:* 247; *189:* 206
Browne, Anthony *45:* 50, 51, 52; *61:* 21, 22, 23, 24, 25; *105:* 21, 22, 23, 25
Browne, Dik *8:* 212; *67:* 32, 33, 35, 37, 39

Browne, Gordon *16:* 97; *64:* 114, 116, 117, 119, 121
Browne, Hablot K. *15:* 65, 80; *21:* 14, 15, 16, 17, 18, 19,20; *24:* 25
Browne, Jane *165:* 222
Browning, Coleen *4:* 132
Browning, Mary Eleanor *24:* 84
Bruce, Robert *23:* 23
Brude, Dick *48:* 215
Bruel, Nick *166:* 41
Brule, Al *3:* 135
Brumbeau, Jeff *157:* 29
Bruna, Dick *43:* 48, 49, 50; *76:* 27, 28
Brundage, Frances *19:* 244
Brunhoff, Jean de *24:* 57, 58
Brunhoff, Laurent de *24:* 60; *71:* 35, 36, 37
Brunkus, Denise *84:* 50; *123:* 117; *178:* 209; *193:* 99
Brunson, Bob *43:* 135
Bryan, Ashley *31:* 44; *72:* 27, 28, 29; *107:* 92; *116:* 192; *132:* 24; *178:* 33, 34, 35
Bryant, Laura J. *176:* 36; *183:* 168
Bryant, Michael *93:* 74
Brychta, Alex *21:* 21
Bryer, Diana *107:* 121
Bryson, Bernarda *3:* 88, 146; *39:* 26; *44:* 185; *131:* 40
Buba, Joy *12:* 83; *30:* 226; *44:* 56
Buchanan, George *166:* 198
Buchanan, Lilian *13:* 16
Buchanan, Rachel *171:* 71
Bucholtz-Ross, Linda *44:* 137
Buchs, Thomas *40:* 38
Buck, Margaret Waring *3:* 30
Buckhardt, Marc *172:* 59
Buckley, Mike *166:* 180
Budwine, Greg *175:* 172
Buehner, Mark *104:* 12, 15; *105:* 160; *119:* 98; *157:* 188; *159:* 39, 40, 43; *192:* 111
Buehr, Walter *3:* 31
Buff, Conrad *19:* 52, 53, 54
Buff, Mary *19:* 52, 53
Bull, Charles Livingston *18:* 207; *88:* 175, 176
Bullen, Anne *3:* 166, 167
Bullock, Kathleen *77:* 24
Bumgarner-Kirby, Claudia *77:* 194
Burbank, Addison *37:* 43
Burchard, Peter Duncan *3:* 197; *5:* 35; *6:* 158, 218; *143:* 17
Burckhardt, Marc *94:* 48; *110:* 89
Burger, Carl *3:* 33; *45:* 160, 162
Burgeson, Marjorie *19:* 31
Burgess, Anne *76:* 252
Burgess, Gelett *32:* 39, 42
Burgess, Mark *157:* 31
Burke, Jim *179:* 19; *185:* 63
Burke, Phillip *95:* 117
Burkert, Nancy Ekholm *18:* 186; *22:* 140; *24:* 62, 63,64, 65; *26:* 53; *29:* 60, 61; *46:* 171; *YABC 1:* 46
Burkhardt, Bruce *142:* 86
Burkhardt, Melissa A. *142:* 86
Burleson, Joe *104:* 35; *172:* 139
Burn, Doris *6:* 172
Burn, Jeffrey *89:* 125; *152:* 132
Burn, Ted
  See Burn, Thomas E.
Burn, Thomas E. *151:* 41
Burnard, Damon *115:* 23
Burnett, Virgil *44:* 42
Burningham, John *9:* 68; *16:* 60, 61; *59:* 28, 29, 30,31, 32, 33, 35; *111:* 18, 19, 21; *160:* 37
Burns, Howard M. *12:* 173
Burns, Jim *47:* 70; *86:* 32; *91:* 197; *123:* 16
Burns, M.F. *26:* 69
Burns, Raymond *9:* 29
Burns, Robert *24:* 106
Burr, Dan *65:* 28; *108:* 134; *164:* 203; *182:* 68
Burr, Dane *12:* 2
Burra, Edward *YABC 2:* 68

Burrell, Galen *56:* 76
Burri, Rene *41:* 143; *54:* 166
Burridge, Marge Opitz *14:* 42
Burris, Burmah *4:* 81
Burroughs, John Coleman *41:* 64
Burroughs, Studley O. *41:* 65
Burton, Marilee Robin *46:* 33
Burton, Virginia Lee *2:* 43; *44:* 49, 51; *100:* 46, 47; *YABC 1:* 24; *147:* 56
Busoni, Rafaello *1:* 186; *3:* 224; *6:* 126; *14:* 5; *16:* 62, 63
Butchkes, Sidney *50:* 58
Butler, Geoff *94:* 20
Butler, Ralph *116:* 212
Butterfield, Ned *1:* 153; *27:* 128; *79:* 63
Butterworth, Ian *184:* 48, 49
Butterworth, Nick *106:* 43, 44; *149:* 34
Buxton, John *123:* 12
Buzelli, Christopher *105:* 149
Buzonas, Gail *29:* 88
Buzzell, Russ W. *12:* 177
Byard, Carole *39:* 44; *57:* 18, 19, 20; *60:* 60; *61:* 93, 96; *69:* 210; *78:* 246; *79:* 227
Byars, Betsy *46:* 35
Byfield, Barbara Ninde *8:* 18
Byfield, Graham *32:* 29
Bynum, Janie *176:* 50
Byrd, Robert *13:* 218; *33:* 46; *158:* 70
Byrd, Samuel *123:* 104

C

Cabat, Erni *74:* 38
Cabban, Vanessa *138:* 73; *176:* 39; *185:* 65
Cabrera, Jane *103:* 24; *152:* 27; *182:* 33, 34
Caddy, Alice *6:* 41
Cady, Harrison *17:* 21, 23; *19:* 57, 58
Caffrey, Aileen *72:* 223; *141:* 154
Cairns, Julia *177:* 37
Caldecott, Randolph *16:* 98, 103; *17:* 32, 33, 36, 38, 39; *26:* 90; *100:* 49, 50; *YABC 2:* 172
Calder, Alexander *18:* 168
Calderón, Gloria *179:* 5
Calderon, W. Frank *25:* 160
Caldwell, Ben *105:* 75; *149:* 60
Caldwell, Clyde *98:* 100; *116:* 39
Caldwell, Doreen *23:* 77; *71:* 41
Caldwell, John *46:* 225
Call, Greg *126:* 135; *165:* 49; *182:* 105, 163
Callahan, Kevin *22:* 42
Callahan, Philip S. *25:* 77
Callan, Jamie *59:* 37
Calvin, James *61:* 92
Camburn-Bracalente, Carol A. *118:* 22
Cameron, Chad *190:* 144
Cameron, Julia Margaret *19:* 203
Cameron, Scott *99:* 18
Camm, Martin *140:* 208, 209, 210
Campbell, Ann *11:* 43; *123:* 182; *183:* 68
Campbell, Bill *89:* 39
Campbell, Ken *126:* 143
Campbell, Robert *55:* 120
Campbell, Rod *51:* 27; *98:* 34
Campbell, Walter M. *YABC 2:* 158
Camps, Luis *28:* 120, 121; *66:* 35
Canga, C.B. *187:* 165
Cann, Helen *124:* 50; *141:* 78; *170:* 138; *179:* 22, 23
Cannon, Janell *78:* 25; *128:* 40
Canright, David *36:* 162
Cantone, AnnaLaura *182:* 146
Canty, Thomas *85:* 161; *92:* 47; *113:* 192; *134:* 60; *185:* 117
Canyon, Christopher *150:* 44; *151:* 112
Caporale, Wende *70:* 42
Capp, Al *61:* 28, 30, 31, 40, 41, 43, 44
Cappon, Manuela *154:* 64
Caras, Peter *36:* 64

Caraway, Caren *57:* 22
Caraway, James *3:* 200, 201
Carbe, Nino *29:* 183
Cares, Linda *67:* 176
Carigiet, Alois *24:* 67
Carle, Eric *4:* 42; *11:* 121; *12:* 29; *65:* 32,33, 34, 36; *73:* 63, 65; *163:* 55, 56
Carling, Amelia Lau *164:* 46
Carlino, Angela *168:* 43; *188:* 20
Carlson, Nancy L. *41:* 116; *56:* 25; *90:* 45; *144:* 48, 50
Carlluccio, Maria *175:* 129
Carmi, Giora *79:* 35; *149:* 40
Carpenter, Nancy *76:* 128; *86:* 173; *89:* 171; *131:* 186; *134:* 8; *138:* 215; *153:* 204; *159:* 93; *165:* 232
Carr, Archie *37:* 225
Carrick, Donald *5:* 194; *39:* 97; *49:* 70; *53:* 156; *63:* 15, 16, 17, 18, 19, 21; *80:* 131; *86:* 151; *118:* 24
Carrick, Malcolm *28:* 59, 60
Carrick, Paul *118:* 26
Carrick, Valery *21:* 47
Carrier, Lark *71:* 43
Carroll, Jim *88:* 211; *140:* 177; *153:* 99
Carroll, Lewis
  See Dodgson, Charles L.
Carroll, Michael *72:* 5
Carroll, Pamela *84:* 68; *128:* 214
Carroll, Ruth *7:* 41; *10:* 68
Carter, Abby *81:* 32; *97:* 121; *102:* 61; *163:* 139; *164:* 125; *184:* 22, 23; *191:* 85
Carter, Barbara *47:* 167, 169
Carter, David A. *114:* 24, 25; *170:* 42, 43
Carter, Don *124:* 54; *184:* 100; *192:* 43, 44, 45
Carter, Harry *22:* 179
Carter, Helene *15:* 38; *22:* 202, 203; *YABC 2:* 220, 221
Carter, Penny *173:* 91
Cartlidge, Michelle *49:* 65; *96:* 50, 51
Cartwright, Reg *63:* 61, 62; *78:* 26; *143:* 4
Cartwright, Shannon *176:* 81
Carty, Leo *4:* 196; *7:* 163; *58:* 131
Cary *4:* 133; *9:* 32; *20:* 2; *21:* 143
Cary, Page *12:* 41
Casale, Paul *71:* 63; *109:* 122; *136:* 28
Case, Sandra E. *16:* 2
Caseley, Judith *87:* 36; *159:* 47, 48, 49
Casilla, Robert *78:* 7; *167:* 124
Casino, Steve *85:* 193
Cassel, Lili
  See Wronker, Lili Cassel
Cassel-Wronker, Lili
  See Wronker, Lili Cassel
Cassels, Jean *8:* 50; *150:* 119; *173:* 37; *186:* 182
Cassen, Melody *140:* 51
Cassity, Don *104:* 24
Cassler, Carl *75:* 137, 138; *82:* 162
Casson, Hugh *65:* 38, 40, 42, 43
Castellon, Federico *48:* 45, 46, 47, 48
Castle, Jane *4:* 80
Castro, Antonio *84:* 71
Catalano, Dominic *94:* 79; *163:* 60, 61; *162:* 54
Catalanotto, Peter *63:* 170; *70:* 23; *71:* 182; *72:* 96; *74:* 114; *76:* 194, 195; *77:* 7; *79:* 157; *80:* 28, 67; *83:* 157; *85:* 27; *108:* 11; *113:* 30, 31, 33, 34, 36; *114:* 27, 28, 29; *117:* 53; *124:* 168; *159:* 54, 55
Catania, Tom *68:* 82
Cather, Carolyn *3:* 83; *15:* 203; *34:* 216
Catrow, David *117:* 179; *152:* 31, 33; *173:* 24
Cauley, Lorinda Bryan *44:* 135; *46:* 49
Cayard, Bruce *38:* 67
Cazet, Denys *52:* 27; *99:* 39, 40; *163:* 65, 66; *191:* 25, 27, 28
Ceccoli, Nicoletta *181:* 39; *188:* 99
Cecil, Randy *127:* 132, 133; *187:* 16, 17; *191:* 168
Cellini, Joseph *2:* 73; *3:* 35; *16:* 116; *47:* 103

Cepeda, Joe *90:* 62; *109:* 91; *134:* 172; *159:* 57, 58, 164
Chabrian, Debbi *45:* 55
Chabrian, Deborah *51:* 182; *53:* 124; *63:* 107; *75:* 84; *79:* 85; *82:* 247; *89:* 93; *101:* 197
Chagnon, Mary *37:* 158
Chalmers, Mary *3:* 145; *13:* 148; *33:* 125; *66:* 214
Chamberlain, Christopher *45:* 57
Chamberlain, Margaret *46:* 51; *106:* 89; *188:* 193
Chamberlain, Nigel *78:* 140
Chambers, C.E. *17:* 230
Chambers, Dave *12:* 151
Chambers, Jill *134:* 110
Chambers, Mary *4:* 188
Chambliss, Maxie *42:* 186; *56:* 159; *93:* 163, 164; *103:* 178; *186:* 33, 34
Champlin, Dale *136:* 124
Chan, Harvey *96:* 236; *99:* 153; *143:* 218; *179:* 144
Chandler, David P. *28:* 62
Chaney, Howard *139:* 27
Chang, Warren *101:* 209
Chapel, Jody *68:* 20
Chapman, C.H. *13:* 83, 85, 87
Chapman, Frederick T. *6:* 27; *44:* 28
Chapman, Gaynor *32:* 52, 53
Chapman, Jane *145:* 186; *150:* 56; *166:* 220; *174:* 202; *176:* 43, 44; *179:* 131
Chapman, Lynne *175:* 31
Chappell, Warren *3:* 172; *21:* 56; *27:* 125
Charles, Donald *30:* 154, 155
Charlip, Remy *4:* 48; *34:* 138; *68:* 53, 54; *119:* 29, 30
Charlot, Jean *1:* 137, 138; *8:* 23; *14:* 31; *48:* 151; *56:* 21
Charlot, Martin *64:* 72
Charlton, Michael *34:* 50; *37:* 39
Charmatz, Bill *7:* 45
Chartier, Normand *9:* 36; *52:* 49; *66:* 40; *74:* 220; *145:* 169; *168:* 91; *177:* 108
Chase, Lynwood M. *14:* 4
Chast, Roz *97:* 39, 40
Chastain, Madye Lee *4:* 50
Chateron, Ann *152:* 19
Chatterton, Martin *68:* 102; *152:* 19
Chau, Tungwai *140:* 35
Chauncy, Francis *24:* 158
Chayka, Doug *145:* 97; *177:* 150
Chee, Cheng-Khee *79:* 42; *81:* 224; *180:* 245
Chen, Chih-sien *90:* 226
Chen, Tony *6:* 45; *19:* 131; *29:* 126; *34:* 160
Chen, Yong *183:* 34
Cheney, T.A. *11:* 47
Cheng, Judith *36:* 45; *51:* 16
Chermayeff, Ivan *47:* 53
Cherry, David *93:* 40
Cherry, Lynne *34:* 52; *65:* 184; *87:* 111; *99:* 46, 47
Chesak, Lina *135:* 118
Chess, Victoria *12:* 6; *33:* 42, 48, 49; *40:* 194; *41:* 145; *69:* 80; *72:* 100; *92:* 33, 34; *104:* 167
Chessare, Michele *41:* 50; *56:* 48; *69:* 145
Chesterton, G.K. *27:* 43, 44, 45, 47
Chestnutt, David *47:* 217
Chesworth, Michael *75:* 24, 152; *88:* 136; *94:* 25; *98:* 155; *160:* 42
Chetham, Celia *134:* 34
Chetwin, Grace *86:* 40
Cheung, Irving *158:* 96
Chevalier, Christa *35:* 66
Chew, Ruth *7:* 46; *132:* 147
Chewning, Randy *92:* 206
Chichester Clark, Emma *72:* 121; *77:* 212; *78:* 209; *87:* 143; *117:* 37, 39, 40; *144:* 138; *156:* 24, 25
Chifflart *47:* 113, 127
Child, Lauren *119:* 32; *183:* 30, 31
Chin, Alex *28:* 54

Chitwood, Susan Tanner *163:* 16
Cho, Shinta *8:* 126
Chodos-Irvine, Margaret *52:* 102, 103, 107; *152:* 44
Choi, Yangsook *171:* 134; *173:* 135; *178:* 38, 39, 40
Chollat, Emilie *170:* 203
Chollick, Jay *25:* 175
Choma, Christina *99:* 169
Chomey, Steve *188:* 53
Chorao, Kay *7:* 200, 201; *8:* 25; *11:* 234; *33:* 187; *35:* 239; *69:* 35; *70:* 235; *123:* 174; *193:* 179
Chowdhury, Subrata *62:* 130; *162:* 22, 23
Christelow, Eileen *38:* 44; *83:* 198, 199; *90:* 57, 58; *184:* 26
Christensen, Bonnie *93:* 100; *153:* 67
Christensen, Gardell Dano *1:* 57
Christensen, James C. *140:* 226
Christiana, David *90:* 64; *135:* 13; *171:* 7
Christiansen, Per *40:* 24
Christie, R. Gregory *116:* 107; *127:* 20, 21; *162:* 179; *164:* 114; *165:* 137; *174:* 157; *179:* 172; *185:* 17, 18, 19
Christy, Howard Chandler *17:* 163, 164, 165, 168, 169; *19:* 186, 187; *21:* 22, 23, 24, 25
Chronister, Robert *23:* 138; *63:* 27; *69:* 167
Church, Caroline Jayne *179:* 27
Church, Frederick *YABC 1:* 155
Chute, Marchette *1:* 59
Chwast, Jacqueline *1:* 63; *2:* 275; *6:* 46, 47; *11:* 125; *12:* 202; *14:* 235
Chwast, Seymour *3:* 128, 129; *18:* 43; *27:* 152; *92:* 79; *96:* 56, 57, 58; *146:* 32, 33
Cieslawksi, Steve *101:* 142; *127:* 116; *158:* 169, 171; *190:* 174
Cinelli, Lisa *146:* 253
Cirlin, Edgard *2:* 168
Clairin, Georges *53:* 109
Clapp, John *105:* 66; *109:* 58; *126:* 7; *129:* 148; *130:* 165
Clark, Brenda *119:* 85; *153:* 55
Clark, David *77:* 164; *134:* 144, 145
Clark, Emma Chichester See Chichester Clark, Emma
Clark, Victoria *35:* 159
Clarke, Greg *169:* 134
Clarke, Gus *72:* 226; *134:* 31
Clarke, Harry *23:* 172, 173
Clarke, Peter *75:* 102
Claverie, Jean *38:* 46; *88:* 29
Clavis, Philippe Goossens *182:* 167
Clayton, Elaine *159:* 60
Clayton, Robert *9:* 181
Cleary, Brian P. *186:* 37
Cleaver, Elizabeth *8:* 204; *23:* 36
Cleland, T.M. *26:* 92
Clemens, Peter *61:* 125
Clement, Charles *20:* 38
Clement, Gary *186:* 79; *191:* 32
Clement, Janet *182:* 50
Clement, Rod *97:* 42
Clement, Stephen *88:* 3
Clementson, John *84:* 213
Clemesha, David *192:* 49, 50
Clevin, Jorgen *7:* 50
Clifford, Judy *34:* 163; *45:* 198
Clokey, Art *59:* 44
Clouse, Dennis *187:* 158
Clouse, James *84:* 15
Clouse, Nancy L. *78:* 31; *114:* 90
Clover, Peter *152:* 45
Cneut, Carll *156:* 166; *165:* 67
Coalson, Glo *9:* 72, 85; *25:* 155; *26:* 42; *35:* 212; *53:* 31; *56:* 154; *94:* 37, 38, 193
Cober, Alan E. *17:* 158; *32:* 77; *49:* 127
Cober-Gentry, Leslie *92:* 111
Cocca-Leffler, Maryann *80:* 46; *136:* 60; *139:* 193
Cochran, Bobbye *11:* 52
CoConis, Ted *4:* 41; *46:* 41; *51:* 104

Cocozza, Chris *87:* 18; *110:* 173; *111:* 149
Cockroft, Jason *152:* 20
Coerr, Eleanor *1:* 64; *67:* 52
Coes, Peter *35:* 172
Cogancherry, Helen *52:* 143; *69:* 131; *77:* 93; *78:* 220; *109:* 204; *110:* 129
Coggins, Jack *2:* 69
Cohen, Alix *7:* 53
Cohen, Miriam *155:* 23, 24
Cohen, Nancy R. *165:* 35
Cohen, Santiago *164:* 26
Cohen, Sheldon *105:* 33, 34; *166:* 46, 47
Cohen, Vincent O. *19:* 243
Cohen, Vivien *11:* 112
Coker, Paul *51:* 172
Colbert, Anthony *15:* 41; *20:* 193
Colby, C.B. *3:* 47
Cole, Babette *58:* 172; *96:* 63, 64; *155:* 29
Cole, Brock *68:* 223; *72:* 36, 37, 38, 192; *127:* 23; *136:* 64, 65
Cole, Gwen *87:* 185
Cole, Henry *178:* 120; *181:* 42, 43; *189:* 60
Cole, Herbert *28:* 104
Cole, Michael *59:* 46
Cole, Olivia H.H. *1:* 134; *3:* 223; *9:* 111; *38:* 104
Colin, Paul *102:* 59; *123:* 118; *126:* 152; *192:* 129
Collicott, Sharleen *98:* 39; *143:* 29, 30
Collier, Bryan *126:* 54; *151:* 166; *174:* 16, 17, 18
Collier, David *13:* 127
Collier, John *27:* 179
Collier, Steven *50:* 52
Collier-Morales, Roberta *168:* 61
Collins, Heather *66:* 84; *67:* 68; *81:* 40; *98:* 192, 193; *129:* 95, 96, 98
Collins, Matt *167:* 90
Collins, Ross *140:* 23, 24
Colman, Audrey *146:* 161
Colón, Raul *108:* 112; *113:* 5; *117:* 167; *134:* 112; *146:* 23; *159:* 92; *166:* 73; *180:* 107; *186:* 156; *190:* 6; *193:* 24, 205
Colonna, Bernard *21:* 50; *28:* 103; *34:* 140; *43:* 180; *78:* 150
Comport, Sally Wern *117:* 169; *169:* 104; *190:* 42
Conde, J.M. *100:* 120
Condon, Grattan *54:* 85 Condon, Ken *161:* 44
Cone, Ferne Geller *39:* 49
Cone, J. Morton *39:* 49
Conklin, Paul *43:* 62
Connolly, Howard *67:* 88
Connolly, Jerome P. *4:* 128; *28:* 52
Connolly, Peter *47:* 60
Conoly, Walle *110:* 224
Conover, Chris *31:* 52; *40:* 184; *41:* 51; *44:* 79
Contreras, Gerry *72:* 9
Converse, James *38:* 70
Conway *62:* 62
Conway, Michael *69:* 12; *81:* 3; *92:* 108
Cook, Ande *188:* 135
Cook, G.R. *29:* 165
Cook, Joel *108:* 160
Cookburn, W.V. *29:* 204
Cooke, Donald E. *2:* 77
Cooke, Tom *52:* 118
Coomaraswamy, A.K. *50:* 100
Coombs, Charles *43:* 65
Coombs, Deborah *139:* 175
Coombs, Patricia *2:* 82; *3:* 52; *22:* 119; *51:* 32, 33, 34, 35, 36, 37, 38, 39, 40, 42, 43
Cooney, Barbara *6:* 16, 17, 50; *12:* 42; *13:* 92; *15:* 145; *16:* 74, 111; *18:* 189; *23:* 38, 89, 93; *32:* 138; *38:* 105; *59:* 48, 49, 51, 52, 53; *74:* 222; *81:* 100; *91:* 25; *96:* 71, 72, 74; *100:* 149; *YABC2:* 10
Cooper, Elisha *157:* 38, 39

Cooper, Floyd 79: 95; *81:* 45; *84:* 82; *85:* 74; *91:* 118; *96:* 77, 78; *103:* 149; *144:* 54; *145:* 151; *159:* 198; *176:* 133, 134; *187:* 26, 27, 28, 29; *188:* 22
Cooper, Heather *50:* 39
Cooper, Helen *102:* 42, 43, 44
Cooper, Mario *24:* 107
Cooper, Marjorie *7:* 112
Cope, Jane *61:* 201; *108* 52
Copeland, Mark *180:* 12
Copelman, Evelyn *8:* 61; *18:* 25
Copley, Heather *30:* 86; *45:* 57
Corbett, Grahame *30:* 114; *43:* 67
Corbino, John *19:* 248
Corcos, Lucille *2:* 223; *10:* 27; *34:* 66
Corey, Robert *9:* 34
Corlass, Heather *10:* 7
Cornell, James *27:* 60
Cornell, Jeff *11:* 58
Cornell, Laura *94:* 179; *95:* 25
Corrigan, Barbara *8:* 37
Corrigan, Patrick *145:* 149
Corwin, Judith Hoffman *10:* 28
Corwin, Oliver *191:* 119
Cory, Fanny Y. *20:* 113; *48:* 29
Cosentino, Ralph *169:* 32
Cosgrove, Margaret *3:* 100; *47:* 63; *82:* 133
Costabel, Eva Deutsch *45:* 66, 67
Costanza, John *58:* 7, 8, 9
Costello, Chris *86:* 78
Costello, David F. *23:* 55
Côté, Geneviéve *184:* 37, 39
Cote, Nancy *126:* 139; *156:* 101; *174:* 101; *182:* 53, 54, 55
Cottenden, Jeff *190:* 45
Couch, Greg *94:* 124; *110:* 13; *162:* 31; *168:* 149
Councell, Ruth Tietjen *79:* 29
Courtney, Cathy *58:* 69, 144; *59:* 15; *61:* 20, 87
Courtney, R. *35:* 110
Counihan, Claire *133:* 106
Cousineau, Normand *89:* 180; *112:* 76
Cousins, Lucy *172:* 53, 54
Couture, Christin *41:* 209
Covarrubias, Miguel *35:* 118, 119, 123, 124, 125
Coville, Katherine *32:* 57; *36:* 167; *92:* 38
Covington, Neverne *113:* 87
Cowdrey, Richard *169:* 170; *178:* 205
Cowell, Cressida *140:* 39
Cowell, Lucinda *77:* 54
Cox *43:* 93
Cox, Charles *8:* 20
Cox, David *56:* 37; *90:* 63; *119:* 38
Cox, Palmer *24:* 76, 77
Cox, Steve *140:* 96
Coxe, Molly *69:* 44
Coxon, Michele *158:* 80
Crabb, Gordon *70:* 39
Crabtree, Judith *98:* 42
Craft, Kinuko *22:* 182; *36:* 220; *53:* 122, 123, 148,149; *74:* 12; *81:* 129; *86:* 31; *89:* 139; *127:* 27, 28, 29; *132:* 142; *139:* 38
Craig, Daniel *177:* 67; *180:* 11; *185:* 203
Craig, David *136:* 198
Craig, Helen *49:* 76; *62:* 70, 71, 72; *69:* 141; *94:* 42, 43, 44; *112:* 53; *135:* 101, 102
Crane, Alan H. *1:* 217
Crane, H.M. *13:* 111
Crane, Jack *43:* 183
Crane, Jordan *174:* 21
Crane, Walter *18:* 46, 47, 48, 49, 53, 54, 56, 57, 59, 60, 61; *22:* 128; *24:* 210, 217; *100:* 70, 71
Cravath, Lynne W. *98:* 45; *182:* 58, 59
Crawford, Denise *137:* 213
Crawford, Will *43:* 77
Credle, Ellis *1:* 69
Czernecki, Stefan *154:* 104; *178:* 68, 69
Crespi, Francesca *87:* 90

Cressy, Michael *124:* 55
Crews, Donald *32:* 59, 60; *76:* 42, 43, 44
Crews, Nina *97:* 49
Crichlow, Ernest *74:* 88; *83:* 203
Croft, James *150:* 57
Crofut, Bob *80:* 87; *81:* 47
Crofut, Susan *23:* 61
Croll, Carolyn *80:* 137; *102:* 52
Cross, Peter *56:* 78; *63:* 60, 65
Crowe, Elizabeth *88:* 144
Crowell, Pers *3:* 125
Cruikshank, George *15:* 76, 83; *22:* 74, 75, 76, 77, 78, 79,80, 81, 82, 84, 137; *24:* 22, 23
Crump, Fred H. *11:* 62
Cruz, Ray *6:* 55; *70:* 234; *123:* 173; *172:* 192
Csatari, Joe *44:* 82; *55:* 152; *63:* 25, 28; *102:* 58
Cuetara, Mittie *158:* 85
Cuffari, Richard *4:* 75; *5:* 98; *6:* 56; *7:* 13,84, 153; *8:* 148, 155; *9:* 89; *11:* 19; *12:* 55, 96,114; *15:* 51, 202; *18:* 5; *20:* 139; *21:* 197; *22:* 14, 192; *23:* 15, 106; *25:* 97; *27:* 133; *28:* 196; *29:* 54; *30:* 85; *31:* 35; *36:* 101; *38:* 171; *42:* 97; *44:* 92, 192; *45:* 212, 213; *46:* 36, 198; *50:* 164; *54:* 80, 136, 137, 145; *56:* 17; *60:* 63; *66:* 49, 50; *70:* 41; *71:* 132; *77:* 157; *78:* 58, 149; *79:* 120; *85:* 2, 152
Cugat, Xavier *19:* 120
Cumings, Art *35:* 160
Cummings, Chris *29:* 167
Cummings, Michael *159:* 142
Cummings, Pat *42:* 61; *61:* 99; *69:* 205; *71:* 57,58; *78:* 24, 25; *93:* 75; *107:* 49, 50; *164:* 259
Cummings, Richard *24:* 119
Cunette, Lou *20:* 93; *22:* 125
Cunningham, Aline *25:* 180
Cunningham, David *11:* 13
Cunningham, Imogene *16:* 122, 127
Cunningham, Kelley *176:* 159
Cupples, Pat *107:* 12; *126:* 109; *182:* 13
Curlee, Lynn *98:* 48; *141:* 39; *190:* 48
Currey, Anna *190:* 145
Curry, John Steuart *2:* 5; *19:* 84; *34:* 36; *144:* 126
Curry, Tom *127:* 131; *185:* 25, 26
Curtis, Bruce *23:* 96; *30:* 88; *36:* 22
Curtis, Neil *167:* 30
Cusack, Margaret *58:* 49, 50, 51
Cushman, Doug *65:* 57; *101:* 39, 40; *133:* 179; *157:* 45; *186:* 157
Cyrus, Kurt *132:* 39; *179:* 36, 37
Czechowski, Alicia *95:* 21; *171:* 37
Czernecki, Stefan *117:* 173

D

Dabcovich, Lydia *25:* 105; *40:* 114; *99:* 75, 76
Dacey, Bob *82:* 175; *152:* 65
d'Achille, Gino *127:* 175, 176
Dailey, Don *78:* 197
Dain, Martin J. *35:* 75
Dale, Penny *127:* 224; *151:* 57; *160:* 89
Dale, Rae *72:* 197
Daley, Joann *50:* 22
Dalton, Anne *40:* 62; *63:* 119
Daly, Deborah M. *74:* 213
Daly, Jim *103:* 60; *150:* 48
Daly, Jude *138:* 118, 119
Daly, Nicholas *37:* 53; *76:* 48, 49
Daly, Niki *107:* 15; *114:* 38, 39, 40; *164:* 86; *192:* 53
Daly, Paul *97:* 205
Dalziel, Brothers *33:* 113
D'Amato, Alex *9:* 48; *20:* 25
D'Amato, Janet *9:* 48; *20:* 25; *26:* 118
D'Amico, Steve *170:* 52
Danalis, Johnny *167:* 27
D'Andrea, Domenick *183:* 108

Daniel, Alan *23:* 59; *29:* 110; *76:* 50, 53, 55, 56; *153:* 76 *115:* 74; *134:* 70
Daniel, Lea *76:* 53, 55; *153:* 76
Daniel, Lewis C. *20:* 216
Daniels, Beau *73:* 4
Daniels, Steve *22:* 16
Daniels, Stewart *56:* 12
Dann, Bonnie *31:* 83
Dann, Penny *82:* 128
Danska, Herbert *24:* 219
Danyell, Alice *20:* 27
Darley, F.O.C. *16:* 145; *19:* 79, 86, 88, 185; *21:* 28,36; *35:* 76, 77, 78, 79, 80, 81; *YABC 2:* 175
Darling, Lois *3:* 59; *23:* 30, 31
Darling, Louis *1:* 40, 41; *2:* 63; *3:* 59; *23:* 30,31; *43:* 54, 57, 59; *121:* 53
Darrow, David R. *84:* 101
Darrow, Whitney, Jr. *13:* 25; *38:* 220, 221
Darwin, Beatrice *43:* 54
Darwin, Len *24:* 82
Dastolfo, Frank *33:* 179
Dauber, Liz *1:* 22; *3:* 266; *30:* 49
Daugherty, James *3:* 66; *8:* 178; *13:* 27, 28, 161; *18:* 101; *19:* 72; *29:* 108; *32:* 156; *42:* 84; *YABC 1:* 256; *2:* 174
d'Aulaire, Edgar Parin *5:* 51; *66:* 53
d'Aulaire, Ingri Parin *5:* 51; *66:* 53
Davalos, Felipe *99:* 197; *159:* 66; *174:* 163
Davenier, Christine *125:* 88; *127:* 32; *128:* 152; *179:* 39, 40
Davick, Linda *151:* 124
David, Jacques-Louis *193:* 22
David, Jonathan *19:* 37
Davidson, Kevin *28:* 154
Davidson, Raymond *32:* 61
Davie, Helen K. *77:* 48, 49
Davis, Allen *20:* 11; *22:* 45; *27:* 222; *29:* 157; *41:* 99; *47:* 99; *50:* 84; *52:* 105
Davis, Bette J. *15:* 53; *23:* 95
Davis, Dimitris *45:* 95
Davis, Hendon *151:* 122
Davis, Jack E. *145:* 139; *175:* 84, 85
Davis, Jim *32:* 63, 64
Davis, Katie *152:* 52, 53, 54
Davis, Lambert *110:* 23, 24; *176:* 58
Davis, Marguerite *31:* 38; *34:* 69, 70; *100:* 34; *YABC 1:* 126, 230
Davis, Nelle *69:* 191
Davis, Paul *78:* 214
Davis, Yvonne LeBrun *94:* 144
Davisson, Virginia H. *44:* 178
DaVolls, Andy *85:* 53
Dawson, Diane *24:* 127; *42:* 126; *52:* 130; *68:* 104
Day, Alexandra *67:* 59; *97:* 54; *166:* 65; *169:* 40
Day, Larry *169:* 88; *185:* 59
Day, Rob *94:* 110; *127:* 24
Dean, Bob *19:* 211
Dean, David *192:* 55
de Angeli, Marguerite *1:* 77; *27:* 62, 65, 66, 67, 69, 70, 72; *100:* 75, 76; *YABC 1:* 166
DeArmond, Dale *70:* 47
Deas, Michael *27:* 219, 221; *30:* 156; *67:* 134; *72:* 24; *75:* 155; *84:* 206; *88:* 124
Deas, Rich *191:* 87; *193:* 10
Debon, Nicolas *151:* 60; *177:* 46
de Bosschere, Jean *19:* 252; *21:* 4; *186:* 44, 45
De Bruyn, M(onica) G. *13:* 30, 31
Decker, C.B. *172:* 120
De Cuir, John F. *1:* 28, 29
Deeter, Catherine *74:* 110; *103:* 150; *137:* 50
Degen, Bruce *40:* 227, 229; *57:* 28, 29; *56:* 156; *75:* 229; *76:* 19; *81:* 36, 37; *92:* 26; *93:* 199; *97:* 56, 58, 59; *124:* 40; *147:* 39, 40, 41; *168:* 23
De Grazia *14:* 59; *39:* 56, 57
DeGrazio, George *88:* 40

deGroat, Diane *9:* 39; *18:* 7; *23:* 123; *28:* 200, 201; *31:* 58, 59; *34:* 151; *41:* 152; *43:* 88; *46:* 40, 200; *49:* 163; *50:* 89; *52:* 30, 34; *54:* 43; *63:* 5; *70:* 136; *71:* 99; *73:* 117,156; *77:* 34; *85:* 48; *86:* 201; *87:* 142; *90:* 72, 73, 143; *95:* 182; *111:* 123; *118:* 160; *126:* 8; *130:* 130; *138:* 93, 94; *169:* 46, 47
de Groot, Lee *6:* 21
Deines, Brian *110:* 139
DeJohn, Marie *89:* 78
Dekhteryov, B. *61:* 158
de Kiefte, Kees *94:* 107
Delacre, Lulu *36:* 66; *156:* 35
Delaney, A. *21:* 78
Delaney, Michael *180:* 16
Delaney, Molly *80:* 43
Delaney, Ned *28:* 68; *56:* 80; *102:* 11
DeLange, Alex Pardo *179:* 128
DeLapine, Jim *79:* 21
De La Roche Saint Andre, Anne *75:* 37
de Larrea, Victoria *6:* 119, 204; *29:* 103; *72:* 203; *87:* 199
Delessert, Étienne *7:* 140; *46:* 61, 62, 63, 65, 67, 68; *130:* 38, 39, 40, 41, 42; *179:* 46, 47, 48, 49; *YABC 2:* 209
Delezenne, Christine *186:* 126
DeLorenzo, Christopher *154:* 149
Delulio, John *15:* 54
DeLuna, Tony *88:* 95
Demarest, Chris L. *45:* 68, 69, 70; *73:* 172, 173, 176; *78:* 106; *82:* 48, 49; *89:* 212; *92:* 86; *128:* 57, 58; *175:* 46, 48
De Mejo, Oscar *40:* 67
Demi *11:* 135; *15:* 245; *66:* 129, 130; *89:* 216; *102:* 66, 67, 68
Denetsosie, Hoke *13:* 126; *82:* 34
Denise, Christopher *147:* 43, 44; *176:* 101; *193:* 35, 36, 37
Dennis, Morgan *18:* 68, 69; *64:* 89
Dennis, Wesley *2:* 87; *3:* 111; *11:* 132; *18:* 71, 72, 73, 74; *22:* 9; *24:* 196, 200; *46:* 178; *69:* 94, 96; *129:* 62
Denslow, W.W. *16:* 84, 85, 86, 87; *18:* 19, 20, 24; *29:* 211; *100:* 21
Denton, Kady MacDonald *110:* 82; *130:* 70; *181:* 54, 55, 56; *192:* 75
Denton, Terry *72:* 163; *174:* 26; *186:* 52
DePalma, Mary Newell *132:* 114; *139:* 75; *185:* 30, 31; *186:* 121
de Paola, Tomie *8:* 95; *9:* 93; *11:* 69; *25:* 103; *28:* 157; *29:* 80; *39:* 52, 53; *40:* 226; *46:* 187; *59:* 61, 62, 63, 64, 65, 66, 67, 68, 69, 71, 72, 74; *62:* 19; *108:* 63, 67, 68, 70; *155:* 62, 64, 66; *180:* 105
Deraney, Michael J. *77:* 35; *78:* 148
deRosa, Dee *70:* 48; *71:* 210; *91:* 78
Dervaux, Isabelle *111:* 117
DeSaix, Deborah Durland *180:* 15; *188:* 24
De Saulles, Tony *119:* 39
de Seve, Peter *146:* 261
Deshaprabhu, Meera Dayal *86:* 192
Desimini, Lisa *86:* 68; *94:* 47; *96:* 7; *104:* 107; *125:* 194; *131:* 180; *172:* 56
de St. Menin, Charles *70:* 17
Detmold, Edward J. *22:* 104, 105, 106, 107; *35:* 120; *64:* 5; *YABC 2:* 203
Detrich, Susan *20:* 133
Deutermann, Diana *77:* 175
DeVelasco, Joseph E. *21:* 51
de Veyrac, Robert *YABC 2:* 19
DeVille, Edward A. *4:* 235
de Visser, John *55:* 119
Devito, Bert *12:* 164
Devlin, Harry *11:* 74; *74:* 63, 65; *136:* 77, 78
Dewan, Ted *108:* 73; *157:* 55; *165:* 129
Dewar, Nick *133:* 122
Dewdney, Anna *184:* 43, 44
Dewey, Ariane *7:* 64; *33:* 195; *35:* 208; *68:* 16,17; *75:* 46; *93:* 91; *94:* 197; *109:* 65, 66, 67; *125:* 2, 3, 4, 5; *127:* 188; *143:* 25; *178:* 17, 19, 74; *188:* 166

Dewey, Jennifer (Owings) *58:* 54; *64:* 214; *65:* 207; *88:* 169; *103:* 45
Dewey, Kenneth *39:* 62; *51:* 23; *56:* 163
de Zanger, Arie *30:* 40
Diakité, Baba Wagué *174:* 28
Diamond, Donna *21:* 200; *23:* 63; *26:* 142; *35:* 83, 84, 85, 86, 87, 88, 89; *38:* 78; *40:* 147; *44:* 152; *50:* 144; *53:* 126; *69:* 46, 47, 48, 201; *71:* 133; *123:* 19
Dias, Ron *71:* 67
Diaz, David *80:* 213; *96:* 83, 84; *108:* 228; *110:* 29; *149:* 106; *150:* 63; *179:* 160; *184:* 95, 97; *189:* 51, 52, 53
Dibley, Glin *138:* 83; *141:* 128
DiCesare, Joe *70:* 38; *71:* 63, 106; *79:* 214; *93:* 147; *116:* 217; *143:* 111; *166:* 57
Dick, John Henry *8:* 181
Dickens, Frank *34:* 131
Dickey, Robert L. *15:* 279
Dickson, Mora *84:* 21
Didier, Sam *166:* 114
Dietz, James *128:* 223; *193:* 136
di Fate, Vincent *37:* 70; *90:* 11; *93:* 60; *109:* 219, 220
Di Fiori, Lawrence *10:* 51; *12:* 190; *27:* 97; *40:* 219; *93:* 57; *130:* 45
Digby, Desmond *97:* 180
Di Grazia, Thomas *32:* 66; *35:* 241
Dillard, Annie *10:* 32
Dillard, Sarah *136:* 186
Dillon, Corinne B. *1:* 139
Dillon, Diane *4:* 104, 167; *6:* 23; *13:* 29; *15:* 99; *26:* 148; *27:* 136, 201; *51:* 29, 48, 51, 52, 53, 54,55, 56, 57, 58, 59, 60, 61, 62; *54:* 155; *56:* 69; *58:* 127,128; *61:* 95; *62:* 27; *64:* 46; *68:* 3; *69:* 209; *74:* 89; *79:* 92; *86:* 89; *92:* 28, 177; *93:* 7, 210; *94:* 239, 240; *97:* 167; *106:* 58, 59,61, 64; *107:* 3; *139:* 246; *167:* 77; *189:* 202; *191:* 191
Dillon, Leo *4:* 104, 167; *6:* 23; *13:* 29; *15:* 99; *26:* 148; *27:* 136, 201; *51:* 29, 48, 51, 52, 53, 54,55, 56, 57, 58, 59, 60, 61, 62; *54:* 155; *56:* 69; *58:* 127,128; *61:* 95; *62:* 27; *64:* 46; *68:* 3; *69:* 209; *74:* 89; *79:* 92; *86:* 89; *92:* 28, 177; *93:* 7, 210; *94:* 239, 240; *97:* 167; *106:* 58, 59,61, 64; *107:* 3; *139:* 246; *167:* 77; *189:* 202; *191:* 191
Dillon, Sharon Saseen *59:* 179, 188
DiMaccio, Gerald *121:* 80
DiMaggio, Joe *36:* 22
DiMassi, Gina *169:* 17
Dinan, Carol *25:* 169; *59:* 75
Dines, Glen *7:* 66, 67
Dinesen, Thomas *44:* 37
Dinh, Pham Viet *167:* 184
Dinnerstein, Harvey *42:* 63, 64, 65, 66, 67, 68; *50:* 146
Dinsdale, Mary *10:* 65; *11:* 171
Dinyer, Eric *86:* 148; *109:* 163; *110:* 239; *124:* 11; *150:* 69; *170:* 4; *171:* 30
Dion, Nathalie *170:* 124
DiRocco, Carl *181:* 23
DiSalvo-Ryan, DyAnne *59:* 77; *62:* 185; *117:* 46; *144:* 64; *150:* 153; *186:* 162
Disney, Walt *28:* 71, 72, 73, 76, 77, 78, 79, 80, 81, 87, 88, 89,90, 91, 94
DiTerlizzi, Tony *105:* 7; *147:* 22; *154:* 31, 32, 33
Divito, Anna *83:* 159
Dixon, Don *74:* 17; *109:* 196
Dixon, Larry *127:* 125
Dixon, Maynard *20:* 165
Doares, Robert G. *20:* 39
Dobias, Frank *22:* 162
Dobrin, Arnold *4:* 68
Dobson, Steven Gaston *102:* 103
Dockray, Tracy *139:* 77
Docktor, Irv *43:* 70
Dodd, Ed *4:* 69
Dodd, Julie *74:* 73
Dodd, Lynley *35:* 92; *86:* 71; *132:* 45, 46, 47

Dodge, Bill *96:* 36; *118:* 7, 8, 9; *133:* 135
Dodgson, Charles L. *20:* 148; *33:* 146; *YABC 2:* 98
Dodson, Bert *9:* 138; *14:* 195; *42:* 55; *54:* 8; *60:* 49; *101:* 125
Dodson, Liz Brenner *105:* 117; *111:* 15
Dohanos, Stevan *16:* 10
Dolce, J. Ellen *74:* 147; *75:* 41
Dolch, Marguerite P. *50:* 64
Dolesch, Susanne *34:* 49
Dollar, Diane *57:* 32
Dolobowsky, Mena *81:* 54
Dolson, Hildegarde *5:* 57
Domanska, Janina *6:* 66, 67; *YABC 1:* 166
Domi *134:* 113
Dominguez, El *53:* 94
Domjan, Joseph *25:* 93
Domm, Jeffrey C. *84:* 69; *135:* 70
Donahey, William *68:* 209
Donahue, Dorothy *76:* 170
Donahue, Vic *2:* 93; *3:* 190; *9:* 44
Donald, Elizabeth *4:* 18
Donalty, Alison *149:* 195, 196, 197
Donato *85:* 59; *149:* 204; *191:* 19
Doney, Todd L.W. *87:* 12; *93:* 112; *98:* 135; *101:* 57; *104:* 40; *118:* 163; *135:* 162, 163; *151:* 18
Donna, Natalie *9:* 52
Donohue, Dorothy *95:* 2; *132:* 30; *176:* 54, 55; *178:* 77, 78, 79
Dooling, Michael *82:* 19; *105:* 55; *106:* 224; *125:* 135; *171:* 46; *172:* 12; *176:* 120
Doran, Ben-Ami *128:* 189
Dore, Gustave *18:* 169, 172, 175; *19:* 93, 94, 95, 96, 97, 98,99, 100, 101, 102, 103, 104, 105; *23:* 188; *25:* 197, 199
Doremus, Robert *6:* 62; *13:* 90; *30:* 95, 96, 97; *38:* 97
Dorfman, Ronald *11:* 128
Doriau *86:* 59; *91:* 152
Dorros, Arthur *78:* 42, 43; *91:* 28
Doruyter, Karel *165:* 105
dos Santos, Joyce Audy *57:* 187, 189
Doty, Roy *28:* 98; *31:* 32; *32:* 224; *46:* 157; *82:* 71; *142:* 7
Doucet, Bob *132:* 238; *169:* 159
Dougherty, Charles *16:* 204; *18:* 74
Doughty, Rebecca *177:* 174
Doughty, Thomas *118:* 31; *140:* 60
Douglas, Aaron *31:* 103
Douglas, Carole Nelson *73:* 48
Douglas, Goray *13:* 151
Dow, Brian *150:* 92
Dowd, Jason *132:* 51, 52; *164:* 244
Dowd, Vic *3:* 244; *10:* 97
Dowden, Anne Ophelia *7:* 70, 71; *13:* 120
Dowdy, Mrs. Regera *29:* 100
Downes, Belinda *180:* 29
Downing, Julie *60:* 140; *81:* 50; *86:* 200; *99:* 129
Doyle, Janet *56:* 31
Doyle, Richard *21:* 31, 32, 33; *23:* 231; *24:* 177; *31:* 87
Draper, Angie *43:* 84
Drath, Bill *26:* 34
Drawson, Blair *17:* 53; *126:* 65
Dray, Matt *177:* 47
Drescher, Henrik *105:* 60, 62, 63; *172:* 72
Drescher, Joan *30:* 100, 101; *35:* 245; *52:* 168; *137:* 52
Dressell, Peggy *186:* 41
Drew, Patricia *15:* 100
Drummond, V.H. *6:* 70
Drury, Christian Potter *105:* 97; *186:* 224
Dubanevich, Arlene *56:* 44
Dubois, Gerard *182:* 9
DuBurke, Randy *187:* 89
Ducak, Danilo *99:* 130; *108:* 214
Duchesne, Janet *6:* 162; *79:* 8
Duda, Jana *102:* 155
Dudash, Michael *32:* 122; *77:* 134; *82:* 149

Duer, Douglas *34:* 177
Duffy, Daniel Mark *76:* 37; *101:* 196; *108:* 147, 148
Duffy, Joseph *38:* 203
Duffy, Pat *28:* 153
Dugan, Karen *181:* 26
Dugin, Andrej *77:* 60
Dugina, Olga *77:* 60
Duke, Chris *8:* 195; *139:* 164
Duke, Kate *87:* 186; *90:* 78, 79, 80, 81; *192:* 21, 59, 60, 61, 63
Duke, Marion *165:* 87
Dulac, Edmund *19:* 108, 109, 110, 111, 112, 113, 114, 115, 117; *23:* 187; *25:* 152; *YABC 1:* 37; *2:* 147
Dulac, Jean *13:* 64
Dumas, Philippe *52:* 36, 37, 38, 39, 40, 41, 42, 43, 45; *119:* 40, 41, 42
Dunaway, Nancy *108:* 161
Dunbar, James *76:* 63
Dunbar, Polly *181:* 60, 61
Duncan, Beverly *72:* 92
Duncan, John *116:* 94
Dunn, H.T. *62:* 196
Dunn, Harvey *34:* 78, 79, 80, 81
Dunn, Iris *5:* 175
Dunn, Phoebe *5:* 175
Dunne, Jeanette *72:* 57, 173, 222
Dunnick, Regan *176:* 51; *178:* 83, 84
Dunnington, Tom *3:* 36; *18:* 281; *25:* 61; *31:* 159; *35:* 168; *48:* 195; *79:* 144; *82:* 230
Dunn-Ramsey, Marcy *117:* 131
Dunrea, Olivier *59:* 81; *118:* 53, 54; *124:* 43
Duntze, Dorothee *88:* 28; *160:* 76
Dupasquier, Philippe *86:* 75; *104:* 76; *151:* 63
DuQuette, Keith *90:* 83; *155:* 73, 74
Durham, Sarah *192:* 248
Duroussy, Nathalie *146:* 150
Durrell, Julie *82:* 62; *94:* 62
Dutz *6:* 59
Duvoisin, Roger *2:* 95; *6:* 76, 77; *7:* 197; *28:* 125; *30:* 101, 102, 103, 104, 105, 107; *47:* 205; *84:* 254
Dyer, Dale *141:* 71
Dyer, Jane *75:* 219; *129:* 28; *147:* 49, 50, 51; *168:* 121; *190:* 4; *191:* 57, 59, 60
Dypold, Pat *15:* 37

E

E.V.B.
  See Boyle, Eleanor Vere (Gordon)
Eachus, Jennifer *29:* 74; *82:* 201; *164:* 153
Eadie, Bob *63:* 36
Eagle, Bruce *95:* 119
Eagle, Ellen *82:* 121; *89:* 3
Eagle, Jeremy *141:* 71
Eagle, Michael *11:* 86; *20:* 9; *23:* 18; *27:* 122; *28:* 57; *34:* 201; *44:* 189; *73:* 9; *78:* 235; *85:* 43
Earl-Bridges, Michele *159:* 128
Earle, Edwin *56:* 27
Earle, Olive L. *7:* 75
Earle, Vana *27:* 99
Early, Lori *132:* 2; *186:* 4
Early, Margaret *72:* 59
East, Stella *131:* 223
Eastman, P.D. *33:* 57
Easton, Reginald *29:* 181
Eaton, Tom *4:* 62; *6:* 64; *22:* 99; *24:* 124
Ebbeler, Jeffrey *193:* 62
Ebel, Alex *11:* 89
Eberbach, Andrea *192:* 115
Ebert, Len *9:* 191; *44:* 47
Echevarria, Abe *37:* 69
Echo Hawk, Bunky *187:* 192
Eckersley, Maureen *48:* 62
Eckert, Horst *72:* 62
Ede, Janina *33:* 59

Edens, Cooper *49:* 81, 82, 83, 84, 85; *112:* 58
Edens, John *109:* 115
Edgar, Sarah E. *41:* 97
Edliq, Emily S. *131:* 107
Edrien *11:* 53
Edwards, Freya *45:* 102
Edwards, George Wharton *31:* 155
Edwards, Gunvor *2:* 71; *25:* 47; *32:* 71; *54:* 106
Edwards, Jeanne *29:* 257
Edwards, Linda Strauss *21:* 134; *39:* 123; *49:* 88, 89
Edwards, Michelle *152:* 62, 63
Edwards, Wallace *170:* 55
Egan, Tim *155:* 76, 77, 78
Egge, David *102:* 71
Eggenhofer, Nicholas *2:* 81
Eggleton, Bob *74:* 40; *81:* 190, 191; *105:* 6; *121:* 183; *149:* 203; *166:* 215
Egielski, Richard *11:* 90; *16:* 208; *33:* 236; *38:* 35; *49:* 91, 92, 93, 95, 212, 213, 214, 216; *79:* 122; *106:* 67, 68, 69; *134:* 135; *144:* 244; *163:* 82, 84
Ehlert, Lois *35:* 97; *69:* 51; *112:* 7; *113:* 208; *128:* 63, 64, 65; *172:* 77, 79, 80
Ehrlich, Bettina *1:* 83
Eitan, Ora *160:* 165
Eichenberg, Fritz *1:* 79; *9:* 54; *19:* 248; *23:* 170; *24:* 200; *26:* 208; *50:* 67, 68, 69, 70, 71, 72, 73,74, 75, 77, 79, 80, 81; *60:* 165; *100:* 137; *YABC 1:* 104, 105; *2:* 213
Einsel, Naiad *10:* 35; *29:* 136
Einsel, Walter *10:* 37
Einzig, Susan *3:* 77; *43:* 78; *67:* 155; *129:* 154
Eisner, Will *165:* 82, 83
Eitzen, Allan *9:* 56; *12:* 212; *14:* 226; *21:* 194; *38:* 162; *76:* 218
Eldridge, H. *54:* 109
Eldridge, Harold *43:* 83
Elgaard, Greta *19:* 241
Elgin, Kathleen *9:* 188; *39:* 69
Ellacott, S.E. *19:* 118
Elliot, David *192:* 26
Elliott, Mark *93:* 69; *105:* 108; *107:* 123; *140:* 53; *165:* 189; *173:* 67
Elliott, Sarah M. *14:* 58
Ellis, Dianne *130:* 208
Ellis, Jan Davey *88:* 50; *115:* 80
Ellis, Richard *130:* 47, 48
Ellison, Pauline *55:* 21
Elmer, Richard *78:* 5
Elmore, Larry *90:* 8
Elschner, Géraldine *183:* 38
Elwell, Tristan *110:* 39; *121:* 182; *127:* 46; *137:* 144; *141:* 173; *151:* 236; *158:* 264; *167:* 119, 120, 121; *169:* 20; *190:* 12
Elzbieta *88:* 80, 81
Emberley, Ed *8:* 53; *70:* 53, 54; *146:* 65, 69, 70
Emberley, Michael *34:* 83; *80:* 72; *119:* 47, 48; *147:* 100; *158:* 115; *189:* 62, 64
Emerling, Dorothy *104:* 27
Emery, Leslie *49:* 187
Emmett, Bruce *49:* 147; *80:* 175; *101:* 206
Emry-Perrott, Jennifer *61:* 57
Emshwiller, Ed *174:* 45
Endle, Kate *191:* 167
Engel, Diana *70:* 57
Engle, Mort *38:* 64
Englebert, Victor *8:* 54
English, Mark *101:* 207
Enik, Ted *142:* 39
Enos, Randall *20:* 183
Enright, Maginel Wright *19:* 240, 243; *39:* 31, 35, 36
Enrique, Romeo *34:* 135
Ensor, Barbara *180:* 30
Epstein, Stephen *50:* 142, 148
Erdogan, Buket *174:* 179
Erdrich, Louise *141:* 62
Erhard, Walter *1:* 152

Erickson, Phoebe *11:* 83; *59:* 85
Erikson, Mel *31:* 69
Eriksson, Eva *63:* 88, 90, 92, 93
Ering, Timothy Basil *131:* 100; *176:* 63, 64
Erlbruch, Wolf *181:* 66
Ernst, Lisa Campbell *47:* 147; *95:* 47; *154:* 46, 47, 48; *164:* 88
Esco, Jo *61:* 103
Escourido, Joseph *4:* 81
Escrivá, Viví *119:* 51; *181:* 36
Este, Kirk *33:* 111
Estep, David *73:* 57
Estes, Eleanor *91:* 66
Estoril, Jean *32:* 27
Estrada, Pau *74:* 76
Estrada, Ric *5:* 52, 146; *13:* 174
Etchemendy, Teje *38:* 68
Etheredges, the *73:* 12
Etienne, Kirk-Albert *145:* 184
Ets, Marie Hall *2:* 102
Ettlinger, Doris *171:* 98; *186:* 106
Eulalie *YABC 2:* 315
Evans, Greg *73:* 54, 55, 56; *143:* 40, 41
Evans, Katherine *5:* 64
Evans, Leslie *144:* 227
Evans, Shane W. *159:* 142; *160:* 190; *168:* 39; *188:* 88; *189:* 66, 67, 68
Everitt, Betsy *151:* 110
Ewart, Claire *76:* 69; *145:* 59, 60
Ewing, Carolyn *66:* 143; *79:* 52
Ewing, Juliana Horatia *16:* 92
Eyolfson, Norman *98:* 154

F

Fabian, Limbert *136:* 114
Facklam, Paul *132:* 62
Falconer, Ian *125:* 66; *179:* 59
Falconer, Pearl *34:* 23
Falkenstern, Lisa *70:* 34; *76:* 133; *78:* 171; *127:* 16; *191:* 151
Falls, C.B. *1:* 19; *38:* 71, 72, 73, 74
Falter, John *40:* 169, 170
Falwell, Cathryn *118:* 77; *137:* 185
Fancher, Lou *138:* 219; *141:* 64; *144:* 199; *177:* 51
Fanelli, Sara *89:* 63; *126:* 69
Faria, Rosana *150:* 143
Faricy, Patrick *185:* 182
Farmer, Andrew *49:* 102
Farmer, Peter *24:* 108; *38:* 75
Farnsworth, Bill *93:* 189; *116:* 147; *124:* 8; *135:* 52; *146:* 242, 243, 244; *182:* 176; *186:* 31, 83, 84, 85; *191:* 197
Farquharson, Alexander *46:* 75
Farrell, David *40:* 135
Farris, David *74:* 42
Fasolino, Teresa *118:* 145
Fatigati, Evelyn *24:* 112
Fatus, Sophie *182:* 74; *190:* 218
Faul-Jansen, Regina *22:* 117
Faulkner, Jack *6:* 169
Faulkner, Matt *161:* 174; *167:* 75
Fava, Rita *2:* 29
Fearnley, Jan *153:* 82, 83
Fearrington, Ann *146:* 80
Federspiel, Marian *33:* 51
Fedorov, Nickolai Ivanovich *110:* 102
Feelings, Tom *5:* 22; *8:* 56; *12:* 153; *16:* 105; *30:* 196; *49:* 37; *61:* 101; *69:* 56, 57; *93:* 74; *105:* 88
Fehr, Terrence *21:* 87
Feiffer, Jules *3:* 91; *8:* 58; *61:* 66, 67, 70, 74, 76,77, 78; *111:* 47, 48, 49, 50; *132:* 122; *157:* 62
Feigeles, Neil *41:* 242
Feldman, Elyse *86:* 7

Feller, Gene *33:* 130
Fellows, Muriel H. *10:* 42
Felstead, Cathie *116:* 85
Felts, Shirley *33:* 71; *48:* 59
Fennell, Tracy *171:* 69
Fennelli, Maureen *38:* 181
Fenton, Carroll Lane *5:* 66; *21:* 39
Fenton, Mildred Adams *5:* 66; *21:* 39
Ferguson, Peter *177:* 30, 31; *181:* 154
Ferguson, Walter W. *34:* 86
Fernandes, Eugenie *77:* 67
Fernandes, Stanislaw *70:* 28
Fernandez, Fernando *77:* 57
Fernandez, Laura *77:* 153; *101:* 117; *131:* 222; *170:* 119; *175:* 182
Ferrari, Alex *188:* 121
Ferrington, Susan *172:* 22
Fetz, Ingrid *11:* 67; *12:* 52; *16:* 205; *17:* 59; *29:* 105; *30:* 108, 109; *32:* 149; *43:* 142; *56:* 29; *60:* 34; *85:* 48; *87:* 146
Fiammenghi, Gioia *9:* 66; *11:* 44; *12:* 206; *13:* 57, 59; *52:* 126, 129; *66:* 64; *85:* 83; *91:* 161; *166:* 169
Fiedler, Joseph Daniel *96:* 42; *113:* 173; *129:* 164; *146:* 17; *159:* 68; *162:* 104
Field, Rachel *15:* 113
Fielding, David *70:* 124
Fieser, Stephen *152:* 36
Fine, Howard *145:* 159; *159:* 64; *165:* 134; *174:* 129; *181:* 68
Fine, Peter K. *43:* 210
Finger, Helen *42:* 81
Finlay, Winifred *23:* 72
Finney, Pat *79:* 215
Fiore, Peter *99:* 196; *125:* 139; *144:* 225; *160:* 169; *180:* 72
Fiorentino, Al *3:* 240
Firehammer, Karla *174:* 202
Firmin, Charlotte *29:* 75; *48:* 70
Firmin, Peter *58:* 63, 64, 65, 67, 68, 70, 71
Firth, Barbara *81:* 208; *127:* 218; *179:* 62
Fischel, Lillian *40:* 204
Fischer, Hans *25:* 202
Fischer-Nagel, Andreas *56:* 50
Fischer-Nagel, Heiderose *56:* 50
Fisher, Carolyn *154:* 50
Fisher, Chris *79:* 62; *158:* 248; *188:* 195
Fisher, Cynthia *117:* 45; *137:* 118
Fisher, Jeffrey *142:* 80
Fisher, Leonard Everett *3:* 6; *4:* 72, 86; *6:* 197; *9:* 59; *16:* 151, 153; *23:* 44; *27:* 134; *29:* 26; *34:* 87, 89, 90, 91, 93, 94, 95, 96; *40:* 206; *50:* 150; *60:* 158; *73:* 68, 70, 71, 72, 73; *176:* 71, 72, 73; *YABC 2:* 169
Fisher, Lois *20:* 62; *21:* 7
Fisher, Valorie *177:* 55
Fisk, Nicholas *25:* 112
Fitschen, Marilyn *2:* 20, 21; *20:* 48
Fitz-Maurice, Jeff *175:* 2
Fitzgerald, F.A. *15:* 116; *25:* 86, 87
Fitzhugh, Louise *1:* 94; *9:* 163; *45:* 75, 78
Fitzgerald, Joanne *157:* 153, 154
Fitzhugh, Susie *11:* 117
Fitzpatrick, Jim *109:* 130
Fitzpatrick, Marie-Louise *125:* 69, 70; *189:* 72, 73
Fitzsimmons, Arthur *14:* 128
Fix, Philippe *26:* 102
Flack, Marjorie *21:* 67; *100:* 93; *YABC 2:* 122
Flagg, James Montgomery *17:* 227
Flavin, Teresa *132:* 115; *186:* 119
Flax, Zeona *2:* 245
Fleetwood, Tony *171:* 51
Fleishman, Seymour *14:* 232; *24:* 87
Fleming, Denise *71:* 179; *81:* 58; *126:* 71, 72, 73; *173:* 52, 53
Fleming, Guy *18:* 41
Flesher, Vivienne *85:* 55
Fletcher, Claire *80:* 106; *157:* 159
Flint, Russ *74:* 80

Floate, Helen *111:* 163
Floca, Brian *155:* 88, 89; *190:* 10, 66, 67
Floethe, Richard *3:* 131; *4:* 90
Floherty, John J., Jr. *5:* 68
Flook, Helen *160:* 81
Flora, James *1:* 96; *30:* 111, 112
Florczak, Robert *166:* 51
Florian, Douglas *19:* 122; *83:* 64, 65; *125:* 71, 72, 74, 76; *128:* 130; *177:* 58, 60
Flory, Jane *22:* 111
Flower, Renee *125:* 109
Floyd, Gareth *1:* 74; *17:* 245; *48:* 63; *62:* 35,36, 37, 39, 40, 41; *74:* 245; *79:* 56
Fluchere, Henri A. *40:* 79
Flynn, Alice *183:* 2
Flynn, Barbara *7:* 31; *9:* 70
Fogarty, Thomas *15:* 89
Foley, Greg *190:* 69
Folger, Joseph *9:* 100
Folkard, Charles *22:* 132; *29:* 128, 257, 258
Foott, Jeff *42:* 202
Forberg, Ati *12:* 71, 205; *14:* 1; *22:* 113; *26:* 22; *48:* 64, 65
Ford, George *24:* 120; *31:* 70, 177; *58:* 126; *81:* 103; *107:* 91; *136:* 100
Ford, H.J. *16:* 185, 186
Ford, Jason *174:* 119
Ford, Pamela Baldwin *27:* 104
Fordham, John *168:* 160, 161
Foreman, Michael *2:* 110, 111; *67:* 99; *73:* 78, 79, 80,81, 82; *93:* 146; *135:* 55, 56, 57; *184:* 58, 59
Forrester, Victoria *40:* 83
Forsey, Chris *140:* 210
Fortnum, Peggy *6:* 29; *20:* 179; *24:* 211; *26:* 76, 77, 78; *39:* 78; *58:* 19, 21, 23, 27; *YABC 1:* 148
Fortune, Eric *191:* 52
Foster, Brad W. *34:* 99
Foster, Genevieve *2:* 112
Foster, Gerald *7:* 78
Foster, Jon *146:* 18
Foster, Laura Louise *6:* 79
Foster, Marian Curtis *23:* 74; *40:* 42
Foster, Sally *58:* 73, 74
Foucher, Adele *47:* 118
Foust, Mitch *168:* 50
Fowler, Jim *184:* 190
Fowler, Mel *36:* 127
Fowler, Richard *87:* 219
Fowles, Selley *165:* 127
Fox, Charles Phillip *12:* 84
Fox, Christyan *188:* 36
Fox, Jim *6:* 187
Fox-Davies, Sarah *76:* 150; *182:* 63
Frace, Charles *15:* 118
Frailey, Joy *72:* 108
Frame, Paul *2:* 45, 145; *9:* 153; *10:* 124; *21:* 71; *23:* 62; *24:* 123; *27:* 106; *31:* 48; *32:* 159; *34:* 195; *38:* 136; *42:* 55; *44:* 139; *60:* 39, 40, 41, 42, 43, 44, 46; *73:* 183
Frampton, David *85:* 72; *102:* 33; *139:* 182; *152:* 37; *189:* 171
Francois, Andre *25:* 117
Francoise
See Seignobosc, Francoise
Frank, Lola Edick *2:* 199
Frank, Mary *4:* 54; *34:* 100
Franke, Phil *45:* 91
Frankel, Alona *66:* 70
Frankel, Julie *40:* 84, 85, 202
Frankenberg, Robert *22:* 116; *30:* 50; *38:* 92, 94, 95; *68:* 111
Frankfeldt, Gwen *84:* 223; *110:* 92
Frankland, David *169:* 137; *182:* 164
Franklin, Ashton *165:* 144
Franklin, John *24:* 22
Franson, Leanne R. *111:* 57, 58; *151:* 7
Frascino, Edward *9:* 133; *29:* 229; *33:* 190; *48:* 80, 81, 82, 83, 84, 85, 86

Frasconi, Antonio *6:* 80; *27:* 208; *53:* 41, 43, 45, 47,48; *68:* 145; *73:* 226; *131:* 68
Fraser, Betty *2:* 212; *6:* 185; *8:* 103; *31:* 72,73; *43:* 136; *111:* 76
Fraser, Eric *38:* 78; *41:* 149, 151
Fraser, F.A. *22:* 234
Fraser, James *171:* 68
Fraser, Mary Ann *137:* 63
Frasier, Debra *69:* 60; *112:* 67; *182:* 81, 82, 83
Fraustino, Lisa Rowe *146:* 87
Frazee, Marla *72:* 98; *105:* 79, 80; *151:* 67, 68; *164:* 165; *171:* 190, 191; *187:* 53, 54,55, 56, 143
Frazetta, Frank *41:* 72; *58:* 77, 78, 79, 80, 81, 82, 83
Frazier, Craig *177:* 63
Freas, John *25:* 207
Fredrickson, Mark *103:* 33
Freeland, Michael J. *118:* 115
Freeman, Don *2:* 15; *13:* 249; *17:* 62, 63, 65, 67, 68; *18:* 243; *20:* 195; *23:* 213, 217; *32:* 155; *55:* 129
Freeman, Irving *67:* 150
Freeman, Laura *144:* 111
Freeman, Pietri *140:* 223
Freeman, Tom *167:* 118
Freeman, Tor *164:* 93
Fregosi, Claudia *24:* 117
Fremaux, Charlotte Murray *138:* 29; *141:* 95
French, Fiona *6:* 82, 83; *75:* 61; *109:* 170; *132:* 79, 80, 81, 82
French, Martin *163:* 4
Frendak, Rodney *126:* 97, 98
Freschet, Gina *175:* 73
Freynet, Gilbert *72:* 221
Friedman, Judith *43:* 197; *131:* 221
Friedman, Marvin *19:* 59; *42:* 86
Frinta, Dagmar *36:* 42
Frith, Michael K. *15:* 138; *18:* 120
Fritz, Ronald *46:* 73; *82:* 124
Fromm, Lilo *29:* 85; *40:* 197
Frost, A.B. *17:* 6, 7; *19:* 123, 124, 125, 126, 127, 128, 129,130; *100:* 119; *YABC 1:* 156, 157, 160; *2:* 107
Frost, Helen *183:* 51
Frost, Kristi *118:* 113
Frost, Michael *151:* 209
Froud, Brian *150:* 82, 83
Froud, Wendy *151:* 237
Fry, Guy *2:* 224
Fry, Rosalie *3:* 72; *YABC 2:* 180, 181
Fry, Rosalind *21:* 153, 168
Fryer, Elmer *34:* 115
Fuchs, Bernie *110:* 10; *162:* 46
Fuchs, Erich *6:* 84
Fuchshuber, Annegert *43:* 96
Fufuka, Mahiri *32:* 146
Fuge, Charles *144:* 91, 93
Fujikawa, Gyo *39:* 75, 76; *76:* 72, 73, 74
Fulford, Deborah *23:* 159
Fuller, Margaret *25:* 189
Fulweiler, John *93:* 99
Funai, Mamoru *38:* 105
Funk, Tom *7:* 17, 99
Furchgott, Terry *29:* 86
Furness, William Henry, Jr. *94:* 18
Furukawa, Mel *25:* 42
Fusari, Erika *164:* 227

G

Gaadt, David *78:* 212; *121:* 166
Gaadt, George *71:* 9
Gaber, Susan *99:* 33; *115:* 57, 58; *164:* 195; *169:* 61, 62, 63; *185:* 50, 51; *188:* 124
Gaberell, J. *19:* 236
Gabler, Mirko *99:* 71
Gackenbach, Dick *19:* 168; *41:* 81; *48:* 89, 90, 91, 92,93, 94; *54:* 105; *79:* 75, 76, 77

Gad, Victor *87:* 161
Gaetano, Nicholas *23:* 209
Gaffney-Kessell, Walter *94:* 219; *174:* 188
Gag, Flavia *17:* 49, 52
Gag, Wanda *100:* 101, 102; *YABC 1:* 135, 137, 138, 141, 143
Gagnon, Cecile *11:* 77; *58:* 87
Gal, Laszlo *14:* 127; *52:* 54, 55, 56; *65:* 142; *68:* 150; *81:* 185; *96:* 104, 105
Galazinski, Tom *55:* 13
Galdone, Paul *1:* 156, 181, 206; *2:* 40, 241; *3:* 42,144; *4:* 141; *10:* 109, 158; *11:* 21; *12:* 118, 210; *14:* 12; *16:* 36, 37; *17:* 70, 71, 72, 73, 74; *18:* 111, 230; *19:* 183; *21:* 154; *22:* 150, 245; *33:* 126; *39:* 136, 137; *42:* 57; *51:* 169; *55:* 110; *66:* 80, 82, 139; *72:* 73; *100:* 84
Gale, Cathy *140:* 22; *143:* 52
Gall, Chris *176:* 79, 80
Gallagher, Jack *187:* 100
Gallagher, S. Saelig *105:* 154
Gallagher, Sears *20:* 112
Galloway, Ewing *51:* 154
Galouchka, Annouchka Gravel *95:* 55; *182:* 40
Galster, Robert *1:* 66
Galsworthy, Gay John *35:* 232
Galvez, Daniel *125:* 182
Gamble, Kim *112:* 64, 65; *124:* 77; *183:* 40, 42, 43, 56, 57; *187:* 170
Gammell, Stephen *7:* 48; *13:* 149; *29:* 82; *33:* 209; *41:* 88; *50:* 185, 186, 187; *53:* 51, 52, 53, 54, 55, 56,57, 58; *54:* 24, 25; *56:* 147, 148, 150; *57:* 27, 66; *81:* 62, 63; *87:* 88; *89:* 10; *106:* 223; *126:* 2; *128:* 71, 73, 74, 77; *154:* 34
Gamper, Ruth *84:* 198
Gampert, John *58:* 94
Ganly, Helen *56:* 56
Gannett, Ruth Chrisman *3:* 74; *18:* 254; *33:* 77, 78
Gantschev, Ivan *45:* 32
Garafano, Marie *73:* 33
Garbot, Dave *131:* 106
Garbutt, Bernard *23:* 68
Garcia *37:* 71
Garcia, Manuel *74:* 145
Garcia-Franco, Rebecca *173:* 46
Gardiner, Lindsey *178:* 128; *186:* 137
Gardner, Earle *45:* 167
Gardner, Joan *40:* 87
Gardner, Joel *40:* 87, 92
Gardner, John *40:* 87
Gardner, Lucy *40:* 87
Gardner, Richard
    See Cummings, Richard
Gardner, Sally *171:* 177; *177:* 66, 68
Gargiulo, Frank *84:* 158
Garland, Michael *36:* 29; *38:* 83; *44:* 168; *48:* 78, 221, 222; *49:* 161; *60:* 139; *71:* 6, 11; *72:* 229; *74:* 142; *89:* 187; *93:* 183; *104:* 110; *131:* 55; *139:* 209; *168:* 56
Garland, Peggy *60:* 139
Garland, Sarah *62:* 45; *135:* 67, 68; *171:* 118
Garn, Aimee *75:* 47
Garner, Joan *128:* 170
Garneray, Ambroise Louis *59:* 140
Garnett, Eve *3:* 75
Garnett, Gary *39:* 184
Garns, Allen *80:* 125; *84:* 39; *165:* 231
Garófoli, Viviana *186:* 123
Garraty, Gail *4:* 142; *52:* 106
Garrett, Agnes *46:* 110; *47:* 157
Garrett, Edmund H. *20:* 29
Garrett, Tom *107:* 194
Garrick, Jacqueline *67:* 42, 43; *77:* 94
Garrison, Barbara *19:* 133; *104:* 146; *109:* 87
Garro, Mark *108:* 131; *128:* 210
Garvey, Robert *98:* 222
Garza, Carmen Lomas *80:* 211; *182:* 86
Garza, Xavier *184:* 64
Gates, Frieda *26:* 80

Gaughan, Jack *26:* 79; *43:* 185
Gaver, Becky *20:* 61
Gawing, Toby *72:* 52
Gay, Marie-Louise *68:* 76, 77, 78; *102:* 136; *126:* 76, 78, 81, 83; *127:* 55, 56; *179:* 70, 72, 73, 74
Gay, Zhenya *19:* 135, 136
Gaydos, Tim *62:* 201
Gazsi, Ed *80:* 48
Gazso, Gabriel *73:* 85
Geary, Clifford N. *1:* 122; *9:* 104; *51:* 74
Geary, Rick *142:* 44, 46
Gee, Frank *33:* 26
Geehan, Wayne *157:* 181
Geer, Charles *1:* 91; *3:* 179; *4:* 201; *6:* 168; *7:* 96; *9:* 58; *10:* 72; *12:* 127; *39:* 156,157, 158, 159, 160; *42:* 88, 89, 90, 91; *55:* 111, 116
Geerinck, Manuel *173:* 128
Gehm, Charlie *36:* 65; *57:* 117; *62:* 60, 138
Geis, Alissa Imre *189:* 77
Geisel, Theodor Seuss *1:* 104, 105, 106; *28:* 108, 109, 110,111, 112, 113; *75:* 67, 68, 69, 70, 71; *89:* 127, 128; *100:* 106, 107, 108
Geisert, Arthur *92:* 67, 68; *133:* 72, 73, 74; *165:* 97, 98; *171:* 64, 65
Geldart, William *15:* 121; *21:* 202
Genia *4:* 84
Gentry, Cyrille R. *12:* 66
Genzo, John Paul *136:* 74
George, Jean *2:* 113
George, Lindsay Barrett *95:* 57; *155:* 97, 98
Geraghty, Paul *130:* 60, 61
Gerard, Jean Ignace *45:* 80
Gerard, Rolf *27:* 147, 150
Gerber, Mark *61:* 105
Gerber, Mary Jane *112:* 124; *171:* 56
Gerber, Stephanie *71:* 195
Gerdstein, Mordecai *169:* 105
Gergely, Tibor *54:* 15, 16
Geritz, Franz *17:* 135
Gerlach, Geff *42:* 58
Gerrard, Roy *47:* 78; *90:* 96, 97, 98, 99
Gerritsen, Paula *177:* 69
Gershinowitz, George *36:* 27
Gerstein, Mordicai *31:* 117; *47:* 80, 81, 82, 83, 84, 85, 86; *51:* 173; *69:* 134; *107:* 122; *142:* 49, 52; *165:* 209; *176:* 119; *178:* 95, 97, 99
Gervase *12:* 27
Geter, Tyrone *146:* 249; *150:* 86
Getz, Arthur *32:* 148
Gévry, Claudine *188:* 47
Gewirtz, Bina *61:* 81
Giancola, Donato *95:* 146; *164:* 226
Gibbons, Gail *23:* 78; *72:* 77, 78, 79; *82:* 182; *104:* 65; *160:* 99, 100
Gibbs, Tony *40:* 95
Gibran, Kahlil *32:* 116
Gider, Iskender *81:* 193
Giebfried, Rosemary *170:* 135
Giesen, Rosemary *34:* 192, 193
Giffard, Hannah *83:* 70
Giguere, George *20:* 111
Gilbert, John *19:* 184; *54:* 115; *YABC 2:* 287
Gilbert, W.S. *36:* 83, 85, 96
Gilbert, Yvonne *116:* 70; *128:* 84; *149:* 119; *185:* 69; *192:* 25
Gilchrist, Jan Spivey *72:* 82, 83, 84, 85, 87; *77:* 90; *105:* 89, 91; *130:* 63, 64; *155:* 105, 107; *182:* 67
Giles, Will *41:* 218
Gili, Phillida *70:* 73
Gill, Margery *4:* 57; *7:* 7; *22:* 122; *25:* 166; *26:* 146, 147
Gillen, Denver *28:* 216
Gillette, Henry J. *23:* 237
Gilliam, Stan *39:* 64, 81
Gillies, Chuck *62:* 31
Gilliland, Jillian *87:* 58
Gillman, Alec *98:* 105
Gilman, Esther *15:* 124
Gilman, Phoebe *104:* 70, 71

Ginsberg, Sari *111:* 184
Ginsburg, Max *62:* 59; *68:* 194 *Girard, Roge 161:* 30
Girouard, Patrick *155:* 100
Giovanopoulos, Paul *7:* 104; *60:* 36
Giovine, Sergio *79:* 12; *93:* 118; *139:* 118
Githens, Elizabeth M. *5:* 47
Gladden, Scott *99:* 108; *103:* 160; *193:* 46, 47
Gladstone, Gary *12:* 89; *13:* 190
Gladstone, Lise *15:* 273
Glanzman, Louis S. *2:* 177; *3:* 182; *36:* 97, 98; *38:* 120, 122; *52:* 141, 144; *71:* 191; *91:* 54, 56
Glaser, Byron *154:* 59, 60
Glaser, Milton *3:* 5; *5:* 156; *11:* 107; *30:* 26; *36:* 112; *54:* 141; *151:* 70
Glass, Andrew *36:* 38; *44:* 133; *48:* 205; *65:* 3; *68:* 43, 45; *90:* 104, 105; *150:* 89
Glass, Marvin *9:* 174
Glasser, Judy *41:* 156; *56:* 140; *69:* 79; *72:* 101
Glattauer, Ned *5:* 84; *13:* 224; *14:* 26
Glauber, Uta *17:* 76
Gleeson, J.M. *YABC 2:* 207
Glegg, Creina *36:* 100
Glienke, Amelie *63:* 150
Gliewe, Unada *3:* 78, 79; *21:* 73; *30:* 220
Gliori, Debi *72:* 91; *138:* 82; *162:* 37; *189:* 79, 81, 82
Glovach, Linda *7:* 105
Gobbato, Imero *3:* 180, 181; *6:* 213; *7:* 58; *9:* 150; *18:* 39; *21:* 167; *39:* 82, 83; *41:* 137, 251; *59:* 177
Goble, Paul *25:* 121; *26:* 86; *33:* 65; *69:* 68, 69; *131:* 79, 80
Goble, Warwick *46:* 78, 79
Godal, Eric *36:* 93
Godkin, Celia *145:* 84, 86
Godfrey, Michael *17:* 279
Godon, Ingrid *166:* 163; *186:* 99
Goembel, Ponder *42:* 124
Goffe, Toni *61:* 83, 84, 85; *89:* 11; *90:* 124; *178:* 118
Goffstein, M.B. *8:* 71; *70:* 75, 76, 77
Golbin, Andre *15:* 125
Gold, Robert *166:* 151, 152
Goldfeder, Cheryl *11:* 191
Goldfinger, Jennifer P. *185:* 71
Goldsborough, June *5:* 154, 155; *8:* 92; *14:* 226; *19:* 139; *54:* 165
Goldsmith, Robert *110:* 77
Goldstein, Leslie *5:* 8; *6:* 60; *10:* 106
Goldstein, Nathan *1:* 175; *2:* 79; *11:* 41, 232; *16:* 55
Goldstrom, Robert *98:* 36; *145:* 51, 52
Golembe, Carla *79:* 80, 81; *136:* 91; *144:* 113; *193:* 53
Golin, Carlo *74:* 112
Gomez, Elena *188:* 122; *191:* 72
Gomez, Elizabeth *127:* 70; *133:* 76
Gomi, Taro *64:* 102; *103:* 74, 76
Gon, Adriano *101:* 112
Gonsalve, Ron *178:* 213
Gonzalez, Maya Christina *104:* 3; *136:* 92
Goodall, John S. *4:* 92, 93; *10:* 132; *66:* 92, 93; *YABC 1:* 198
Goodelman, Aaron *40:* 203
Goodenow, Earle *40:* 97
Goodfellow, Peter *62:* 95; *94:* 202
Goodman, Joan Elizabeth *50:* 86
Goodman, Vivienne *82:* 251; *146:* 181, 182
Goodnow, Patti *117:* 33
Goodwin, Harold *13:* 74
Goodwin, Philip R. *18:* 206
Goor, Nancy *39:* 85, 86
Goor, Ron *39:* 85, 86
Gorbachev, Valeri *89:* 96; *112:* 97; *143:* 63, 64; *184:* 66, 67, 68, 101

Gordon, Gwen *12:* 151
Gordon, Margaret *4:* 147; *5:* 48, 49; *9:* 79
Gordon, Mike *101:* 62, 63, 64
Gordon, Russell *136:* 204; *137:* 214
Gordon, Walter *138:* 9
Gore, Leonid *89:* 51; *94:* 74; *136:* 8; *158:* 117; *166:* 136; *168:* 36; *170:* 107; *181:* 94; *185:* 73
Gorecka-Egan, Erica *18:* 35
Gorey, Edward *1:* 60, 61; *13:* 169; *18:* 192; *20:* 201; *29:* 90, 91, 92, 93, 94, 95, 96, 97, 98, 99, 100; *30:* 129; *32:* 90; *34:* 200, *65:* 48; *68:* 24, 25; *69:* 79; *70:* 80, 82, 83, 84; *85:* 136; *127:* 62
Gorsline, Douglas *1:* 98; *6:* 13; *11:* 113; *13:* 104; *15:* 14; *28:* 117, 118; *YABC 1:* 15
Gorton, Julia *108:* 94; *178:* 81, 82
Gosfield, Josh *118:* 165, 166; *149:* 67
Gosner, Kenneth *5:* 135
Gosney, Joy *167:* 142
Gotlieb, Jules *6:* 127
Goto, Scott *115:* 86; *136:* 69
Gottlieb, Dale *67:* 162; *107:* 16; *149:* 6
Goudey, Ray *97:* 86
Gough, Alan *91:* 57
Gough, Philip *23:* 47; *45:* 90
Gould, Chester *49:* 112, 113, 114, 116, 117, 118
Gould, Jason *151:* 232
Gourbault, Martine *177:* 159
Govern, Elaine R. *26:* 94
Gower, Teri *102:* 184
Gowing, Toby *60:* 25; *63:* 33; *78:* 70, 252; *83:* 228; *86:* 187; *93:* 145; *108:* 133; *110:* 217; *184:* 125
Grabianski *20:* 144
Grabianski, Janusz *39:* 92, 93, 94, 95
Graboff, Abner *35:* 103, 104
Graef, Renee *61:* 188; *72:* 207
Grafe, Max *156:* 173; *178:* 237; *192:* 240
Graham, A.B. *11:* 61
Graham, Bob *101:* 66, 67, 68; *151:* 74, 75; *187:* 65, 67, 68, 70
Graham, Georgia *188:* 3; *190:* 75
Graham, L. *7:* 108
Graham, Margaret Bloy *11:* 120; *18:* 305, 307
Graham, Mark *88:* 208; *159:* 153; *182:* 3
Grahame-Johnstone, Janet *13:* 61
Grahame-Johnstone, Anne *13:* 61
Grainger, Sam *42:* 95
Gralley, Jean *166:* 86
Gramatky, Hardie *1:* 107; *30:* 116, 119, 120, 122, 123
Gran, Julie *168:* 118
Granahan, Julie *84:* 84
GrandPré, Mary *84:* 131; *109:* 199; *118:* 76; *180:* 65; *184:* 70, 71, 180; *192:* 87
Grandström, Brita *176:* 139
Grandville, J.J. *45:* 81, 82, 83, 84, 85, 86, 87, 88; *47:* 125; *64:* 10
Granger, Paul *39:* 153
Granström, Brita *162:* 35; *167:* 46
Grant, (Alice) Leigh *10:* 52; *15:* 131; *20:* 20; *26:* 119; *48:* 202
Grant, Gordon *17:* 230, 234; *25:* 123, 124, 125, 126; *52:* 69; *YABC 1:* 164
Grant, Melvyn *159:* 186, 187; *170:* 48, 49
Grant, Renee *77:* 40
Grant, Shirley *109:* 45
Graves, Elizabeth *45:* 101
Graves, Keith *167:* 89; *191:* 74
Gray, Harold *33:* 87, 88
Gray, Les *82:* 76; *83:* 232
Gray, Reginald *6:* 69
Greco, Tony *184:* 6
Greder, Armin *76:* 235
Green, Ann Canevari *62:* 48
Green, Eileen *6:* 97
Green, Elizabeth Shippen *139:* 109
Green, Jonathan *86:* 135; *105:* 109
Green, Ken *111:* 68

Green, Michael *32:* 216
Green, Robina *87:* 138
Green, Jonathan *157:* 105
Greene, Jeffrey *117:* 93
Greenaway, Kate *17:* 275; *24:* 180; *26:* 107; *41:* 222, 232; *100:* 115, 116; *YABC 1:* 88, 89; *2:* 131, 133, 136,138, 139, 141
Greenberg, Melanie Hope *72:* 93; *80:* 125; *101:* 174; *133:* 180; *186:* 189
Greenseid, Diane *178:* 106, 107
Greenstein, Elaine *150:* 100
Greenwald, Sheila *1:* 34; *3:* 99; *8:* 72
Greger, Carol *76:* 86
Gregorian, Joyce Ballou *30:* 125
Gregory, Emilian *177:* 146; *187:* 10
Gregory, Fran *130:* 4; *140:* 93
Gregory, Frank M. *29:* 107
Greiffenhagen, Maurice *16:* 137; *27:* 57; *YABC 2:* 288
Greiner, Robert *6:* 86
Gretter, J. Clemens *31:* 134
Gretz, Susanna *7:* 114
Gretzer, John *1:* 54; *3:* 26; *4:* 162; *7:* 125; *16:* 247; *18:* 117; *28:* 66; *30:* 85, 211; *33:* 235; *56:* 16
Grey, Mini *166:* 90; *192:* 71
Grey Owl *24:* 41
Gri *25:* 90
Grieder, Walter *9:* 84
Griesbach/Martucci *59:* 3
Grifalconi, Ann *2:* 126; *3:* 248; *11:* 18; *13:* 182; *46:* 38; *50:* 145; *66:* 99, 100, 101, 104, 106; *69:* 38; *70:* 64; *87:* 128; *90:* 53; *93:* 49; *128:* 48; *133:* 79, 81
Griffin, Gillett Good *26:* 96
Griffin, James *30:* 166
Griffin, John Howard *59:* 186
Griffin, Rachel *131:* 23
Griffith, Gershom *94:* 214
Griffiths, Dave *29:* 76
Griffiths, Dean *168:* 180; *169:* 182
Grimly, Gris *186:* 102; *192:* 112
Grimsdell, Jeremy *83:* 75
Grimwood, Brian *82:* 89
Gringhuis, Dirk *6:* 98; *9:* 196
Gripe, Harald *2:* 127; *74:* 98
Grisha *3:* 71
Grohmann, Susan *84:* 97
Gropper, William *27:* 93; *37:* 193
Gros *60:* 199
Grose, Helen Mason *YABC 1:* 260; *2:* 150
Grossman, Nancy *24:* 130; *29:* 101
Grossman, Robert *11:* 124; *46:* 39
Groth, John *15:* 79; *21:* 53, 54; *83:* 230
Grover, Lorie Ann *168:* 59
Grubb, Lisa *160:* 116
Grue, Lisa *187:* 193
Gruelle, Johnny *35:* 107
Gschwind, William *11:* 72
Guay-Mitchell, Rebecca *110:* 95, 96; *135:* 240; *180:* 76; *181:* 71, 73
Guback, Georgia *88:* 102
Guerguerion, Claudine *105:* 73
Guevara, Susan *97:* 87; *167:* 49
Guggenheim, Hans *2:* 10; *3:* 37; *8:* 136
Guhathaakurta, Ajanta *183:* 199
Guida, Lisa Chauncy *172:* 188
Guilbeau, Honore *22:* 69
Guillette, Joseph *137:* 37
Guisewite, Cathy *57:* 52, 53, 54, 56, 57
Gukova, Julia *95:* 104; *154:* 103; *168:* 195
Gundersheimer, Karen *35:* 240; *82:* 100
Gunderson, Nick *57:* 120
Gunnella *192:* 144
Gurney, James *76:* 97; *86:* 32
Gurney, John Steven *75:* 39, 82; *110:* 175; *143:* 67, 68; *169:* 172
Gusman, Annie *38:* 62
Gustafson, Scott *34:* 111; *43:* 40
Gustavson, Adam *104:* 10; *171:* 183; *176:* 87
Guthridge, Bettina *108:* 79; *186:* 92

Guthrie, R. Dale *64:* 143
Guthrie, Robin *20:* 122
Gutierrez, Akemi *172:* 87
Gutierrez, Alan *136:* 31, 32
Gutierrez, Rudy *97:* 162
Gutmann, Bessie Pease *73:* 93, 94
Gwynne, Fred *41:* 94, 95
Gyberg, Bo-Erik *38:* 131

H

Haas, Irene *17:* 77; *87:* 46; *96:* 117
Hack, Konrad *51:* 127
Hader, Berta H. *16:* 126
Hader, Elmer S. *16:* 126
Haeffele, Deborah *76:* 99
Haemer, Alan *62:* 109
Hafner, Marylin *22:* 196, 216; *24:* 44; *30:* 51; *35:* 95; *51:* 25, 160, 164; *86:* 16; *105:* 196; *121:* 93, 94; *149:* 208, 209; *179:* 82, 83, 84, 115; *190:* 200
Hagerty, Sean *62:* 181
Hague, Michael *32:* 128; *48:* 98, 99, 100, 101, 103, 105,106, 107, 108, 109, 110; *49:* 121; *51:* 105; *64:* 14, 15; *79:* 134; *80:* 91, 92; *83:* 135; *100:* 241; *102:* 29; *129:* 101, 103, 104; *185:* 80, 81, 82
Hair, Jonathan *115:* 135
Halas, John *29:* 41, 47, 48
Haldane, Roger *13:* 76; *14:* 202
Hale, Christy *79:* 124; *84:* 200; *114:* 201; *128:* 2, 3; *146:* 203; *158:* 243; *167:* 99; *179:* 87
Hale, Irina *26:* 97
Hale, James Graham *88:* 207
Hale, Kathleen *17:* 79; *66:* 114, 116, 118
Haley, Gail E. *43:* 102, 103, 104, 105; *78:* 65, 67; *136:* 106, 107
Hall, Amanda *96:* 110
Hall, Chuck *30:* 189
Hall, Douglas *15:* 184; *43:* 106, 107; *86:* 100; *87:* 82; *129:* 72
Hall, H. Tom *1:* 227; *30:* 210
Hall, Melanie *116:* 48, 49; *169:* 77, 78
Hall, Sydney P. *31:* 89
Hall, Tim *164:* 196
Hall, Vicki *20:* 24
Hallinan, P.K. *39:* 98
Hallman, Tom *98:* 166
Hally, Greg *101:* 200; *151:* 224
Halperin, Wendy Anderson *96:* 151; *125:* 96, 97, 98, 99; *139:* 22; *140:* 84
Halpern, Joan *10:* 25
Halpern, Shari *174:* 172
Halsey, Megan *96:* 172; *114:* 185; *180:* 8; *185:* 85
Halstead, Virginia *125:* 105
Halverson, Janet *49:* 38, 42, 44
Hallensleben, Georg *134:* 5, 6; *172:* 17
Hamanaka, Sheila *71:* 100
Hamann, Brad *78:* 151
Hamann, Sigune *104:* 115
Hamberger, John *6:* 8; *8:* 32; *14:* 79; *34:* 136; *88:* 78
Hamil, Tom *14:* 80; *43:* 163
Hamilton, Bill and Associates *26:* 215
Hamilton, Helen S. *2:* 238
Hamilton, J. *19:* 83, 85, 87
Hamilton, Laurie *116:* 210
Hamilton, Todd Cameron *84:* 15
Hamlin, Janet *97:* 136; *124:* 90; *137:* 157; *182:* 117
Hamlin, Louise *71:* 135
Hammond, Chris *21:* 37
Hammond, Elizabeth *5:* 36, 203
Hampshire, Michael *5:* 187; *7:* 110, 111; *48:* 150; *51:* 129
Hampson, Denman *10:* 155; *15:* 130
Hampton, Blake *41:* 244
Handford, Martin *64:* 105, 106, 107, 109

Handforth, Thomas *42:* 100, 101, 102, 103, 104, 105, 107
Handville, Robert *1:* 89; *38:* 76; *45:* 108, 109
Hane, Roger *17:* 239; *44:* 54
Haney, Elizabeth Mathieu *34:* 84
Hanke, Ted *71:* 10
Hankinson, Phil *181:* 164
Hanley, Catherine *8:* 161
Hann, Jacquie *19:* 144
Hanna, Cheryl *91:* 133
Hanna, Wayne A. *67:* 145
Hannon, Mark *38:* 37
Hansen, Gaby *159:* 11; *186:* 25
Hansen, Mia *149:* 76
Hanson, Joan *8:* 76; *11:* 139
Hanson, Peter E. *52:* 47; *54:* 99, 100; *73:* 21; *84:* 79; *116:* 144
Hansson, Gunilla *64:* 111, 112
Hardcastle, Nick *121:* 82; *175:* 185
Hardy, David A. *9:* 96; *119:* 74
Hardy, Paul *YABC 2:* 245 *Haring, Keith 145:* 65
Harlan, Jerry *3:* 96
Harlin, Greg *89:* 194; *103:* 82; *118:* 161; *121:* 167; *182:* 76
Harness, Cheryl *106:* 80; *131:* 87; *178:* 111
Harnischfeger *18:* 121
Harper, Arthur *YABC 2:* 121
Harper, Betty *126:* 90
Harper, Jamie *174:* 71
Harper, Piers *79:* 27; *105:* 102; *161:* 67
Harrington, Glenn *82:* 18; *94:* 66, 68; *185:* 118
Harrington, Jack *83:* 162
Harrington, Richard *5:* 81
Harris, Andrew N. *191:* 78
Harris, Jim *127:* 130; *183:* 4
Harris, John *83:* 25
Harris, Nick *86:* 177
Harris, Susan Yard *42:* 121
Harrison, Florence *20:* 150, 152
Harrison, Harry *4:* 103
Harrison, Jack *28:* 149
Harrison, Mark *105:* 157; *165:* 190
Harrison, Ted *56:* 73
Harsh, Fred *72:* 107
Harston, Jerry *105:* 143
Hart, Lewis *98:* 115
Hart, Thomas *181:* 165
Hart, William *13:* 72
Hartland, Jessie *171:* 80, 81; *186:* 165
Hartung, Susan Kathleen *150:* 107, 108; *173:* 106; *175:* 106; *192:* 78
Hartelius, Margaret *10:* 24
Hartshorn, Ruth *5:* 115; *11:* 129
Harvey, Amanda *145:* 44
Harvey, Bob *48:* 219
Harvey, Gerry *7:* 180
Harvey, Lisa *97:* 21
Harvey, Paul *88:* 74
Harvey, Roland *71:* 88; *123:* 63; *179:* 94
Hassall, Joan *43:* 108, 109
Hassell, Hilton *YABC 1:* 187
Hassett, John *162:* 59
Hasselriis, Else *18:* 87; *YABC 1:* 96
Hastings, Glenn *89:* 183
Hastings, Ian *62:* 67
Hauman, Doris *2:* 184; *29:* 58, 59; *32:* 85, 86, 87
Hauman, George *2:* 184; *29:* 58, 59; *32:* 85, 86, 87
Hausherr, Rosmarie *15:* 29
Hawkes, Kevin *78:* 72; *104:* 198; *105:* 197; *112:* 109; *126:* 87; *144:* 88; *149:* 210; *150:* 110, 135; *156:* 94; *164:* 35; *186:* 18; *190:* 197
Hawkins, Jacqui *112:* 86; *162:* 64
Hawkinson, John *4:* 109; *7:* 83; *21:* 64
Hawkinson, Lucy *21:* 64
Hawthorne, Mike *140:* 228
Haxton, Elaine *28:* 131

Haydock, Robert *4:* 95
Hayes, Geoffrey *26:* 111; *44:* 133; *91:* 85
Haynes, Max *72:* 107
Hays, Michael *73:* 207; *83:* 93; *139:* 197; *146:* 202, 250
Haywood, Carolyn *1:* 112; *29:* 104
Heale, Jonathan *104:* 117
Healy, Daty *12:* 143
Healy, Deborah *58:* 181, 182; *101:* 111
Heap, Sue *102:* 207; *150:* 113, 114; *187:* 84, 85, 86
Hearn, Diane Dawson *79:* 99; *113:* 13
Hearon, Dorothy *34:* 69
Heaslip, William *57:* 24, 25
Hechtkopf, H. *11:* 110
Heck, Ed *173:* 81
Hedderwick, Mairi *30:* 127; *32:* 47; *36:* 104; *77:* 86; *145:* 91, 93, 95
Hefferman, Phil *146:* 197
Hefter, Richard *28:* 170; *31:* 81, 82; *33:* 183
Hehenberger, Shelly *126:* 91
Heigh, James *22:* 98
Heighway, Richard *25:* 160; *64:* 4
Heighway-Bury, Robin *159:* 89
Heine, Helme *67:* 86; *135:* 91, 92
Heinly, John *45:* 113
Hellard, Susan *81:* 21
Hellebrand, Nancy *26:* 57
Heller, Linda *46:* 86
Heller, Ruth M. *66:* 125; *77:* 30, 32
Hellmuth, Jim *38:* 164
Helms, Georgeann *33:* 62
Helquist, Brett *142:* 203; *146:* 133, 134; *156:* 10; *173:* 25; *180:* 106; *187:* 90, 91; *193:* 12
Helweg, Hans *41:* 118; *50:* 93; *58:* 22, 26
Hemphill, Helen *179:* 95
Henba, Bobbie *90:* 195
Henderson, Dave *73:* 76; *75:* 191, 192, 193, 194; *82:* 4
Henderson, Douglas *103:* 68
Henderson, Kathy *55:* 32; *155:* 118
Henderson, Keith *35:* 122
Henderson, Meryl *127:* 58, 60; *169:* 81
Hendrix, John *187:* 133
Hendry, Linda *80:* 104; *83:* 83; *164:* 216
Hengeveld, Dennis *142:* 86
Henkes, Kevin *43:* 111; *108:* 106, 107, 108
Henneberger, Robert *1:* 42; *2:* 237; *25:* 83
Henriksen, Harold *35:* 26; *48:* 68
Henriquez, Celeste *103:* 137
Henriquez, Elsa *82:* 260
Henriquez, Emile F. *89:* 88
Henry, Everett *29:* 191
Henry, Matthew *117:* 58
Henry, Paul *93:* 121
Henry, Thomas *5:* 102
Hensel, *27:* 119
Henshaw, Jacqui *141:* 127
Henstra, Friso *8:* 80; *36:* 70; *40:* 222; *41:* 250; *73:* 100, 101
Henterly, Jamichael *93:* 4
Heo, Yumi *89:* 85, 86; *94:* 89, 90; *146:* 40, 137, 138; *163:* 227
Hepple, Norman *28:* 198
Herbert, Helen *57:* 70
Herbert, Jennifer *189:* 47
Herbert, Wally *23:* 101
Herbster, Mary Lee *9:* 33
Herder, Edwin *182:* 104
Herge
See Remi, Georges
Hermansen, Pal *133:* 113
Hermanson, Dennis *10:* 55
Hermes, Gertrude *54:* 161
Herr, Margo *57:* 191
Herr, Susan *83:* 163
Herriman, George *140:* 74, 75, 76, 77, 78
Herriman, Lisa *87:* 190
Herring, Michael *121:* 76; *182:* 103
Herrington, Roger *3:* 161
Herscovici, C. *165:* 240

Hescox, Richard *85:* 86; *90:* 30; *139:* 35
Heslop, Mike *38:* 60; *40:* 130
Hess, Lydia J. *85:* 17
Hess, Mark *111:* 146; *113:* 207
Hess, Paul *134:* 47; *166:* 133; *193:* 13
Hess, Richard *42:* 31
Hester, Ronnie *37:* 85
Heuser, Olga J. *121:* 116
Heusser, Sibylle *168:* 195
Heustis, Louise L. *20:* 28
Hewitson, Jennifer *74:* 119; *124:* 167
Hewitt, Kathryn *80:* 126; *149:* 105; *184:* 93
Hewitt, Margaret *84:* 112
Heyduck-Huth, Hilde *8:* 82
Heyer, Carol *74:* 122; *130:* 72, 73; *192:* 35
Heyer, Hermann *20:* 114, 115
Heyer, Marilee *102:* 108
Heyman, Ken *8:* 33; *34:* 113
Heyne, Ulrike *146:* 151
Heywood, Karen *48:* 114
Hickling, P.B. *40:* 165
Hickman, Stephen *85:* 58; *136:* 33; *171:* 128
Hierstein, Judy *56:* 40; *162:* 168
Higashi, Sandra *154:* 59, 60
Higginbottom, J. Winslow *8:* 170; *29:* 105, 106
Higgins, Chester *101:* 79
Higham, David *50:* 104
Hilb, Nora *176:* 8
Hildebrandt, Greg *8:* 191; *55:* 35, 36, 38, 39, 40, 42, 46; *172:* 110
Hildebrandt, Tim *8:* 191; *55:* 44, 45, 46
Hilder, Rowland *19:* 207
Hill, Eric *66:* 127, 128; *133:* 91
Hill, Gregory *35:* 190
Hill, Pat *49:* 120
Hillenbrand, Will *84:* 115; *92:* 76, 80; *93:* 131; *104:* 168; *128:* 137; *145:* 187; *146:* 184; *147:* 105, 106, 107; *152:* 59; *184:* 179
Hilliard, Richard *183:* 74
Hillier, Matthew *45:* 205
Hillman, Priscilla *48:* 115
Hills, Tad *113:* 4; *137:* 147; *173:* 83
Himler, Ronald *6:* 114; *7:* 162; *8:* 17, 84, 125; *14:* 76; *19:* 145; *26:* 160; *31:* 43; *38:* 116; *41:* 44, 79; *43:* 52; *45:* 120; *46:* 43; *54:* 44, 83; *58:* 180; *59:* 38; *68:* 146; *69:* 231; *70:* 98; *71:* 177, 178; *77:* 219; *79:* 212; *83:* 62; *89:* 5; *91:* 160; *92:* 91, 92, 93; *94:* 93; *95:* 69, 174, 194; *99:* 99, 112; *113:* 92; *118:* 114; *137:* 73, 74, 77, 167; *163:* 99; *165:* 138; *178:* 9, 220; *183:* 77, 79, 80, 81; *184:* 80, 83
Himmelman, John *47:* 109; *65:* 87; *94:* 96, 97; *159:* 85
Hinds, Bill *37:* 127, 130
Hines, Anna Grossnickle *51:* 90; *74:* 124; *95:* 78, 79,80, 81
Hines, Bob *135:* 149, 150
Hiroko *99:* 61
Hiroshige *25:* 71
Hirsh, Marilyn *7:* 126
Hiscock, Bruce *137:* 80, 81
Hissey, Jane *103:* 90; *130:* 81
Hitch, Jeff *99:* 206; *128:* 86
Hitz, Demi *11:* 135; *15:* 245; *66:* 129, 130; *152:* 94, 95
Hnizdovsky, Jacques *32:* 96; *76:* 187
Ho, Kwoncjan *15:* 132
Hoban, Lillian *1:* 114; *22:* 157; *26:* 72; *29:* 53; *40:* 105, 107, 195; *41:* 80; *69:* 107, 108; *71:* 98; *77:* 168; *106:* 50; *113:* 86; *136:* 118
Hoban, Tana *22:* 159; *104:* 82, 83, 85
Hobbie, Jocelyn *190:* 78
Hobbs, Leigh *166:* 95
Hoberman, Norman *5:* 82
Hobson, Sally *77:* 185
Hockerman, Dennis *39:* 22; *56:* 23
Hodgell, P.C. *42:* 114
Hodges, C. Walter *2:* 139; *11:* 15; *12:* 25; *23:* 34; *25:* 96; *38:* 165; *44:* 197; *45:* 95; *100:* 57; *YABC 2:* 62, 63

Hodges, David *9:* 98
Hodgetts, Victoria *43:* 132
Hofbauer, Imre *2:* 162
Hoff, Syd *9:* 107; *10:* 128; *33:* 94; *72:* 115,116, 117, 118; *138:* 114, 115
Hoffman, Rosekrans *15:* 133; *50:* 219; *63:* 97
Hoffman, Sanford *38:* 208; *76:* 174; *88:* 160, 161; *151:* 156
Hoffmann, Felix *9:* 109
Hoffnung, Gerard *66:* 76, 77
Hofsinde, Robert *21:* 70
Hogan, Inez *2:* 141
Hogan, Jamie *192:* 94
Hogarth, Burne *41:* 58; *63:* 46, 48, 49, 50, 52, 53, 54, 55,56
Hogarth, Paul *41:* 102, 103, 104; *YABC 1:* 16
Hogarth, William *42:* 33
Hogenbyl, Jan *1:* 35
Hogner, Nils *4:* 122; *25:* 144
Hogrogian, Nonny *3:* 221; *4:* 106, 107; *5:* 166; *7:* 129; *15:* 2; *16:* 176; *20:* 154; *22:* 146; *25:* 217; *27:* 206; *74:* 127, 128, 129, 149, 152; *127:* 99; *YABC 2:* 84, 94
Hokanson, Lars *93:* 111; *172:* 137
Hokusai *25:* 71
Hol, Colby *126:* 96
Holberg, Richard *2:* 51
Holbrook, Kathy *107:* 114
Holdcroft, Tina *38:* 109
Holden, Caroline *55:* 159
Holder, Heidi *36:* 99; *64:* 9
Holder, Jimmy *151:* 224
Holiday, Henry *YABC 2:* 107
Holl, F. *36:* 91
Holland, Brad *45:* 59, 159
Holland, Gay W. *128:* 105
Holland, Janice *18:* 118
Holland, Marion *6:* 116
Holldobler, Turid *26:* 120
Holliday, Keaf *144:* 236
Holling, Holling C. *15:* 136, 137
Hollinger, Deanne *12:* 116
Holm, Sharon Lane *114:* 84; *115:* 52
Holmes, B. *3:* 82
Holmes, Bea *7:* 74; *24:* 156; *31:* 93
Holmes, Dave *54:* 22
Holmes, Lesley *135:* 96
Holmgren, George Ellen *45:* 112
Holmlund, Heather D. *150:* 140
Holt, Norma *44:* 106
Holt, Pater *151:* 188
Holtan, Gene *32:* 192
Holub, Joan *149:* 72
Holyfield, John *149:* 231
Holz, Loretta *17:* 81
Hom, Nancy *79:* 195
Homar, Lorenzo *6:* 2
Homer, Winslow *128:* 8; *YABC 2:* 87
Honey, Elizabeth *112:* 95, 96; *137:* 93, 94
Honeywood, Varnette P. *110:* 68, 70
Hong, Lily Toy *76:* 104
Honigman, Marian *3:* 2
Honore, Paul *42:* 77, 79, 81, 82
Hood, Alun *69:* 145, 218; *72:* 41; *80:* 226; *87:* 4; *95:* 139
Hood, Susan *12:* 43
Hook, Christian *104:* 103
Hook, Frances *26:* 188; *27:* 127
Hook, Jeff *14:* 137; *103:* 105
Hook, Richard *26:* 188
Hooks *63:* 30
Hooper, Hadley *177:* 145
Hoover, Carol A. *21:* 77
Hoover, Russell *12:* 95; *17:* 2; *34:* 156
Hope, James *141:* 116
Hopkins, Chris *99:* 127
Hopman, Philip *178:* 184
Hoppin, Augustus *34:* 66
Horacek, Petr *163:* 117
Horder, Margaret *2:* 108; *73:* 75
Horen, Michael *45:* 121

Horne, Daniel *73:* 106; *91:* 153; *109:* 127; *110:* 232; *164:* 176
Horne, Richard *111:* 80
Horse, Harry *128:* 195; *169:* 86
Horvat, Laurel *12:* 201
Horvath, David *192:* 95
Horvath, Ferdinand Kusati *24:* 176
Horvath, Maria *57:* 171
Horwitz, Richard *57:* 174
Hotchkiss, De Wolfe *20:* 49
Hough, Charlotte *9:* 112; *13:* 98; *17:* 83; *24:* 195
Houlihan, Ray *11:* 214
House, Caroline *183:* 121
Housman, Laurence *25:* 146, 147
Houston, James *13:* 107; *74:* 132, 134, 135
Hovland, Gary *88:* 172; *171:* 148
Hoyt, Eleanor *158:* 231
How, W.E. *20:* 47
Howard, Alan *16:* 80; *34:* 58; *45:* 114
Howard, Arthur *165:* 111, 112; *190:* 5
Howard, J.N. *15:* 234
Howard, John *33:* 179
Howard, Kim *116:* 71
Howard, Paul *142:* 126, 129; *144:* 187
Howard, Rob *40:* 161
Howarth, Daniel *170:* 34
Howe, John *115:* 47; *176:* 106
Howe, John F. *79:* 101; *80:* 150
Howe, Phillip *79:* 117; *175:* 115
Howe, Stephen *1:* 232
Howell, Karen *119:* 123
Howell, Pat *15:* 139
Howell, Troy *23:* 24; *31:* 61; *36:* 158; *37:* 184; *41:* 76, 235; *48:* 112; *56:* 13; *57:* 3; *59:* 174; *63:* 5; *74:* 46; *89:* 188; *90:* 231; *95:* 97; *98:* 130; *99:* 189; *153:* 156, 157, 158; *176:* 104
Howes, Charles *22:* 17
Hoyt, Ard *145:* 141; *190:* 82
Hranilovich, Barbara *127:* 51
Hu, Ying-Hwa *116:* 107; *152:* 236; *173:* 171
Huang, Benrei *137:* 55
Huang, Zhong-Yang *117:* 30, 32
Hubbard, Woodleigh Marx *98:* 67; *115:* 79; *160:* 138
Hubley, Faith *48:* 120, 121, 125, 130, 131, 132, 134
Hubley, John *48:* 125, 130, 131, 132, 134
Hudak, Michal *143:* 74
Hudnut, Robin *14:* 62
Huerta, Catherine *76:* 178; *77:* 44, 45; *90:* 182
Huffaker, Sandy *10:* 56
Huffman, Joan *13:* 33
Huffman, Tom *13:* 180; *17:* 212; *21:* 116; *24:* 132; *33:* 154; *38:* 59; *42:* 147
Hughes, Arthur *20:* 148, 149, 150; *33:* 114, 148, 149
Hughes, Darren *95:* 44
Hughes, David *36:* 197
Hughes, Shirley *1:* 20, 21; *7:* 3; *12:* 217; *16:* 163; *29:* 154; *63:* 118; *70:* 102, 103, 104; *73:* 169; *88:* 70; *110:* 118, 119; *159:* 103
Hugo, Victor *47:* 112
Hull, Cathy *78:* 29
Hull, Richard *95:* 120; *123:* 175; *172:* 195
Hulsmann, Eva *16:* 166
Hume, Lachie *189:* 93
Hummel, Berta *43:* 137, 138, 139
Hummel, Lisl *29:* 109; *YABC 2:* 333, 334
Humphrey, Henry *16:* 167
Humphreys, Graham *25:* 168
Humphries, Tudor *76:* 66; *80:* 4; *124:* 4, 5
Huneck, Stephen *183:* 88, 89
Hunt, James *2:* 143
Hunt, Jonathan *84:* 120
Hunt, Paul *119:* 104; *129:* 135; *139:* 160; *173:* 112
Hunt, Robert *110:* 206, 235; *147:* 136, 137; *170:* 3
Hunt, Scott *190:* 143

Hunter, Anne *133:* 190; *178:* 150
Huntington, Amy *180:* 99
Hurd, Clement *2:* 148, 149; *64:* 127, 128, 129, 131, 133, 134,135, 136; *100:* 37, 38
Hurd, Peter *24:* 30, 31,; *YABC 2:* 56
Hurd, Thacher *46:* 88, 89; *94:* 114, 115, 116; *123:* 81, 82, 84
Hurlimann, Ruth *32:* 99
Hurst, Carol Otis *185:* 92
Hurst, Tracey *192:* 238
Hussar, Michael *114:* 113; *117:* 159
Hustler, Tom *6:* 105
Hutchins, Laurence *55:* 22
Hutchins, Pat *15:* 142; *70:* 106, 107, 108; *178:* 131, 132
Hutchinson, Sascha *95:* 211
Hutchinson, William M. *6:* 3, 138; *46:* 70
Hutchison, Paula *23:* 10
Hutton, Clarke *YABC 2:* 335
Hutton, Kathryn *35:* 155; *89:* 91
Hutton, Warwick *20:* 91
Huyette, Marcia *29:* 188
Hyatt, John *54:* 7
Hyatt, Mitch *178:* 162
Hyde, Maureen *82:* 17; *121:* 145, 146
Hyman, David *117:* 64
Hyman, Trina Schart *1:* 204; *2:* 194; *5:* 153; *6:* 106; *7:* 138, 145; *8:* 22; *10:* 196; *13:* 96; *14:* 114; *15:* 204; *16:* 234; *20:* 82; *22:* 133; *24:* 151; *25:* 79, 82; *26:* 82; *29:* 83; *31:* 37, 39; *34:* 104; *38:* 84, 100, 128; *41:* 49; *43:* 146; *46:* 91, 92, 93, 95, 96, 97, 98, 99, 100, 101, 102, 103, 104, 105,108, 109, 111, 197; *48:* 60, 61; *52:* 32; *60:* 168; *66:* 38; *67:* 214; *72:* 74; *75:* 92; *79:* 57; *82:* 95, 238; *89:* 46; *95:* 91, 92, 93; *100:* 33, 199; *132:* 12; *147:* 33, 35, 36; *167:* 58, 60; *177:* 189, 190

I

Ibarra, Rosa *147:* 91
Ibatoulline, Bagram *156:* 48; *174:* 33, 82
Ichikawa, Satomi *29:* 152; *41:* 52; *47:* 133, 134,135, 136; *78:* 93, 94; *80:* 81; *146:* 143, 145, 146
Ide, Jacqueline *YABC 1:* 39
Ilsley, Velma *3:* 1; *7:* 55; *12:* 109; *37:* 62; *38:* 184
Imai, Ayano *190:* 85, 86
in den Bosch, Nicole *150:* 204
Inga *1:* 142
Ingman, Bruce *134:* 50; *182:* 91, 92
Ingpen, Robert *109:* 103, 104; *132:* 138; *137:* 177; *166:* 103; *181:* 140
Ingraham, Erick *21:* 177; *84:* 256; *103:* 66
Inkpen, Mick *99:* 104, 105; *106:* 44
Innerst, Stacy *149:* 104
Innocenti, Roberto *21:* 123; *96:* 122; *159:* 111, 197
Inoue, Yosuke *24:* 118
Iofin, Michael *97:* 157
Iosa, Ann *63:* 189
Ipcar, Dahlov *1:* 124, 125; *49:* 137, 138, 139, 140, 141, 142,143, 144, 145; *147:* 122, 124, 126
Irvin, Fred *13:* 166; *15:* 143, 144; *27:* 175
Irving, Jay *45:* 72
Irving, Laurence *27:* 50
Isaac, Joanne *21:* 76
Isaacs, Gary *170:* 188
Isadora, Rachel *43:* 159, 160; *54:* 31; *79:* 106, 107,108; *121:* 100, 102; *165:* 116, 117
Ishmael, Woodi *24:* 111; *31:* 99
Ives, Ruth *15:* 257
Iwai, Melissa *149:* 233; *183:* 92

J

Jabar, Cynthia *101:* 201
Jackness, Andrew *94:* 237
Jackson, Julian *91:* 104, 106
Jackson, Michael *43:* 42
Jackson, Shelley *79:* 71; *99:* 109; *187:* 82
Jacob, Murv *89:* 30
Jacobi, Kathy *62:* 118
Jacobs, Barbara *9:* 136
Jacobs, Lou, Jr. *9:* 136; *15:* 128
Jacobsen, Laura *176:* 98; *177:* 85, 86
Jacobson, Rick *131:* 222; *170:* 119
Jacobus, Tim *79:* 140; *109:* 126; *129:* 180
Jacques, Robin *1:* 70; *2:* 1; *8:* 46; *9:* 20; *15:* 187; *19:* 253; *32:* 102, 103, 104; *43:* 184; *73:* 135; *YABC 1:* 42
Jaeggi, Yoshiko *186:* 184
Jaffee, Al *66:* 131, 132
Jagr, Miloslav *13:* 197
Jahn-Clough, Lisa *88:* 114; *152:* 104; *193:* 70, 71
Jahnke, Robert *84:* 24
Jainschigg, Nicholas *80:* 64; *91:* 138; *95:* 63; *99:* 25; *108:* 50; *171:* 41
Jakesavic, Nenad *85:* 102
Jakobsen, Kathy *116:* 83
Jakubowski, Charles *14:* 192
Jambor, Louis *YABC 1:* 11
James, Ann *73:* 50; *82:* 113; *158:* 61; *183:* 44
James, Brian *140:* 91
James, Curtis E. *182:* 93
James, Derek *35:* 187; *44:* 91; *61:* 133; *74:* 2; *80:* 57; *86:* 88; *130:* 30; *179:* 29
James, Gilbert *YABC 1:* 43
James, Harold *2:* 151; *3:* 62; *8:* 79; *29:* 113; *51:* 195; *74:* 90
James, Kennon *126:* 211
James, Robin *50:* 106; *53:* 32, 34, 35
James, Will *19:* 150, 152, 153, 155, 163
Janosch
  See Eckert, Horst
Janovitch, Marilyn *68:* 168
Janovitz, Marilyn *87:* 187; *130:* 198
Jansons, Inese *48:* 117
Jansson, Tove *3:* 90; *41:* 106, 108, 109, 110, 111, 113, 114
Jaques, Faith *7:* 11, 132, 133; *21:* 83, 84; *69:* 114,116; *73:* 170
Jaques, Frances Lee *29:* 224
Jauss, Anne Marie *1:* 139; *3:* 34; *10:* 57, 119; *11:* 205; *23:* 194
Jay, Alison *158:* 97, 98; *183:* 126, 127
Jeffers, Oliver *175:* 111
Jeffers, Susan *17:* 86, 87; *25:* 164, 165; *26:* 112; *50:* 132, 134, 135; *70:* 111, 112, 113; *137:* 107, 108, 109, 110, 111
Jefferson, Louise E. *4:* 160
Jenkin-Pearce, Susie *78:* 16
Jenkins, Debra Reid *85:* 202; *114:* 89; *173:* 134
Jenkins, Jean *98:* 79, 102
Jenkins, Leonard *157:* 169; *167:* 128; *189:* 96, 97; *190:* 89
Jenkins, Patrick *72:* 126
Jenkins, Steve *124:* 177; *154:* 90, 91, 92, 93; *185:* 194; *188:* 81, 82, 83, 84, 85, 86
Jenks, Aleta *73:* 117; *124:* 225
Jenkyns, Chris *51:* 97
Jensen, Bruce *95:* 39
Jensinius, Kirsten *56:* 58
Jeram, Anita *89:* 135; *102:* 122, 123; *129:* 112; *154:* 96, 97, 98; *164:* 154
Jernigan, E. Wesley *85:* 92
Jerome, Karen A. *72:* 194
Jeruchim, Simon *6:* 173; *15:* 250
Jeschke, Susan *20:* 89; *39:* 161; *41:* 84; *42:* 120
Jessel, Camilla *29:* 115
Jessell, Tim *159:* 3; *177:* 87; *181:* 95

Jeyaveeran, Ruth *182:* 100
Jiang, Cheng An *109:* 108
Jiang, Wei *109:* 108
Jimenez, Maria *77:* 158; *93:* 127
Jobling, Curtis *138:* 74
Jocelyn, Marthe *118:* 83; *137:* 219; *163:* 119, 120
Joerns, Consuelo *38:* 36; *44:* 94
John, Diana *12:* 209
John, Helen *1:* 215; *28:* 204
Johns, Elizabeth *127:* 33
Johns, Jasper *61:* 172
Johns, Jeanne *24:* 114
Johnson, Adrian *143:* 50
Johnson, Bruce *9:* 47
Johnson, Cathy *92:* 136
Johnson, Crockett
  See Leisk, David
Johnson, D. William *23:* 104
Johnson, D.B. *183:* 98, 139
Johnson, David *175:* 18; *191:* 91
Johnson, Gillian *119:* 175; *164:* 217
Johnson, Harper *1:* 27; *2:* 33; *18:* 302; *19:* 61; *31:* 181; *44:* 46, 50, 95
Johnson, Ingrid *37:* 118
Johnson, James Ralph *1:* 23, 127
Johnson, James David *12:* 195
Johnson, Jane *48:* 136
Johnson, Joel Peter *98:* 18; *128:* 111
Johnson, John E. *34:* 133
Johnson, Kevin *72:* 44
Johnson, Kevin Eugene *109:* 215
Johnson, Larry *47:* 56; *123:* 107; *159:* 203
Johnson, Layne *94:* 94
Johnson, Margaret S. *35:* 131
Johnson, Meredith Merrell *71:* 181; *83:* 158; *89:* 103; *104:* 88
Johnson, Milton *1:* 67; *2:* 71; *26:* 45; *31:* 107; *60:* 112; *68:* 96
Johnson, Pamela *16:* 174; *52:* 145; *62:* 140; *73:* 116; *85:* 64
Johnson, Paul Brett *83:* 95; *132:* 119
Johnson, Stephen T. *80:* 15; *131:* 35; *141:* 96; *145:* 40; *164:* 187; *175:* 32; *189:* 99, 100; *177:* 51
Johnson, Steve *138:* 219; *141:* 64; *144:* 199; *177:* 51
Johnson, William R. *38:* 91
Johnson-Petrov, Arden *115:* 206
Johnston, David McCall *50:* 131, 133
Johnston, Lynne *118:* 85, 87, 89
Johnstone, Anne *8:* 120; *36:* 89
Johnstone, Janet Grahame *8:* 120; *36:* 89
Jonas, Ann *50:* 107, 108, 109; *135:* 113
Jones, Bob *71:* 5; *77:* 199
Jones, Carol *5:* 131; *72:* 185, 186; *153:* 111, 112
Jones, Chuck *53:* 70, 71
Jones, Davy *89:* 176
Jones, Douglas B. *185:* 192
Jones, Elizabeth Orton *18:* 124, 126, 128, 129
Jones, Harold *14:* 88; *52:* 50
Jones, Holly *127:* 3
Jones, Jeff *41:* 64
Jones, Laurian *25:* 24, 27
Jones, Margaret *74:* 57
Jones, Noah Z. *182:* 37
Jones, Randy *131:* 104
Jones, Richard *127:* 222
Jones, Robert *25:* 67
Jones, Wilfred *35:* 115; *YABC 1:* 163
Jordan, Charles *89:* 58
Jordan, Jess *158:* 136
Jordan, Martin George *84:* 127
Jordan, Richard *84:* 36
Jorgenson, Andrea *91:* 111
Jorisch, Stéphane *153:* 56, 193; *177:* 29; *178:* 138, 139; *187:* 23
Joseph, James *53:* 88
Joudrey, Ken *64:* 145; *78:* 6
Joyce, William *72:* 131, 132, 133, 134; *73:* 227; *145:* 37

Joyner, Jerry *34:* 138
Juan, Ana *175:* 38; *179:* 111, 112
Jucker, Sita *5:* 93
Judge, Lita *192:* 99
Judkis, Jim *37:* 38
Juhasz, Victor *31:* 67
Jullian, Philippe *24:* 206; *25:* 203
Jung, Tom *91:* 217
Junge, Alexandra *183:* 37
Junge, Walter *67:* 150
Jupo, Frank *7:* 148, 149
Jurisch, Stephane *154:* 105
Justice, Martin *34:* 72

K

Kabatova-Taborska, Zdenka *107:* 153
Kachik, John *165:* 230
Kaczman, James *156:* 98
Kadair, Deborah Ousley *184:* 45, 89
Kahl, David *74:* 95; *97:* 35; *109:* 174; *110:* 213
Kahl, M.P. *37:* 83
Kahl, Virginia *48:* 138
Kahn, Katherine Janus *90:* 135
Kakimoo, Kozo *11:* 148
Kalett, Jim *48:* 159, 160, 161
Kalin, Victor *39:* 186
Kalman, Maira *96:* 131, 132; *137:* 115
Kalmenoff, Matthew *22:* 191
Kalow, Gisela *32:* 105
Kamen, Gloria *1:* 41; *9:* 119; *10:* 178; *35:* 157; *78:* 236; *98:* 82
Kaminsky, Jef *102:* 153
Kandell, Alice *35:* 133
Kane, Henry B. *14:* 90; *18:* 219, 220
Kane, Robert *18:* 131
Kanfer, Larry *66:* 141
Kappes, Alfred *28:* 104
Karalus, Bob *41:* 157
Karas, G. Brian *80:* 60; *99:* 179; *115:* 41; *118:* 50; *136:* 168; *145:* 166; *149:* 245; *159:* 65; *171:* 192; *178:* 142, 143
Karasz, Ilonka *128:* 163
Karlin, Eugene *10:* 63; *20:* 131
Karlin, Nurit *63:* 78; *103:* 110
Karpinski, Tony *134:* 160
Kasamatsu, Shiro *139:* 155
Kasparavicius, Kestutis *139:* 210
Kassian, Olena *64:* 94
Kastner, Jill *79:* 135; *117:* 84, 85
Kasuya, Masahiro *41:* 206, 207; *51:* 100
Kasza, Keiko *191:* 99, 100, 101, 102, 103
Katona, Robert *21:* 85; *24:* 126
Katz, Karen *158:* 123
Kauffer, E. McKnight *33:* 103; *35:* 127; *63:* 67
Kaufman, Angelika *15:* 156
Kaufman, Joe *33:* 119
Kaufman, John *13:* 158
Kaufman, Stuart *62:* 64; *68:* 226; *137:* 44
Kaufmann, John *1:* 174; *4:* 159; *8:* 43, 1; *10:* 102; *18:* 133, 134; *22:* 251
Kaye, Graham *1:* 9; *67:* 7, 8
Kaye, M.M. *62:* 95
Kazalovski, Nata *40:* 205
Keane, Bil *4:* 135
Kearney, David *72:* 47; *121:* 83
Keating, Pamel T. *77:* 37
Keats, Ezra Jack *3:* 18, 105, 257; *14:* 101, 102; *33:* 129; *57:* 79, 80, 82, 83, 84, 87
Keegan, Charles *166:* 211
Keegan, Marcia *9:* 122; *32:* 93
Keeler, Patricia A. *81:* 56; *183:* 102, 103
Keely, Jack *119:* 95
Keely, John *26:* 104; *48:* 214
Keen, Eliot *25:* 213
Keep, Richard C. *170:* 122

Keeping, Charles *9:* 124, 185; *15:* 28, 134; *18:* 115; *44:* 194, 196; *47:* 25; *52:* 3; *54:* 156; *69:* 123, 124; *74:* 56; *155:* 9
Keeter, Susan *168:* 46; *183:* 192
Keith, Eros *4:* 98; *5:* 138; *31:* 29; *43:* 220; *52:* 91, 92, 93, 94; *56:* 64, 66; *60:* 37; *79:* 93
Keleinikov, Andrei *65:* 101, 102
Kelen, Emery *13:* 115
Keller, A.J. *62:* 198
Keller, Arthur I. *26:* 106
Keller, Dick *36:* 123, 125
Keller, Holly *45:* 79; *76:* 118, 119, 120, 121; *108:* 137, 138, 140; *157:* 117, 118, 119
Keller, Katie *79:* 222; *93:* 108
Keller, Ronald *45:* 208
Kelley, Gary *183:* 105
Kelley, True *41:* 114, 115; *42:* 137; *75:* 35; *92:* 104, 105; *124:* 62; *130:* 100, 101; *179:* 120, 121, 122; *192:* 251
Kellogg, Steven *8:* 96; *11:* 207; *14:* 130; *20:* 58; *29:* 140, 141; *30:* 35; *41:* 141; *57:* 89, 90, 92,93, 94, 96; *59:* 182; *73:* 141; *77:* 129; *130:* 105, 106; *177:* 94, 95, 96, 97; *YABC 1:* 65, 73
Kelly, Billy *158:* 143
Kelly, Geoff *97:* 196; *112:* 25
Kelly, Irene *147:* 134
Kelly, Joseph *174:* 94
Kelly, Kathleen M. *71:* 109
Kelly, Laura *89:* 217
Kelly, True *163:* 87
Kelly, Walt *18:* 136, 137, 138, 139, 140, 141, 144, 145, 146, 148, 149
Kemble, E.W. *34:* 75; *44:* 178; *YABC 2:* 54, 59
Kemp-Welsh, Lucy *24:* 197; *100:* 214
Kendall, Jane *150:* 105; *186:* 109
Kendall, Peter *152:* 85
Kendrick, Dennis *79:* 213
Kennaway, Adrienne *60:* 55, 56; *171:* 88, 89
Kennedy, Doug *189:* 104
Kennedy, Paul Edward *6:* 190; *8:* 132; *33:* 120
Kennedy, Richard *3:* 93; *12:* 179; *44:* 193; *100:* 15; *YABC 1:* 57
Kent, Jack *24:* 136; *37:* 37; *40:* 81; *84:* 89; *86:* 150; *88:* 77
Kent, Rockwell *5:* 166; *6:* 129; *20:* 225, 226, 227,229; *59:* 144
Kenyon, Tony *81:* 201; *127:* 74
Kepes, Juliet *13:* 119
Kerins, Anthony *76:* 84
Kerr, Judity *24:* 137
Kerr, Phyllis Forbes *72:* 141
Kessler, Leonard *1:* 108; *7:* 139; *14:* 107, 227; *22:* 101; *44:* 96; *67:* 79; *82:* 123
Kest, Kristin *168:* 99; *173:* 23
Kesteven, Peter *35:* 189
Ketcham, Hank *28:* 140, 141, 142
Kettelkamp, Larry *2:* 164
Key, Alexander *8:* 99
Khalsa, Dayal Kaur *62:* 99
Kiakshuk *8:* 59
Kidd, Chip *94:* 23
Kidd, Richard *152:* 110
Kidd, Tom *64:* 199; *81:* 189; *185:* 173
Kiddell-Monroe, Joan *19:* 201; *55:* 59, 60; *87:* 174; *121:* 112
Kidder, Harvey *9:* 105; *80:* 41
Kidwell, Carl *43:* 145
Kieffer, Christa *41:* 89
Kiesler, Kate *110:* 105; *136:* 142
Kiff, Ken *40:* 45
Kilbride, Robert *37:* 100
Kilby, Don *141:* 144
Kim, Glenn *99:* 82
Kimball, Anton *78:* 114; *119:* 105
Kimball, Yeffe *23:* 116; *37:* 88
Kimber, Murray *171:* 91
Kimmel, Warren *176:* 112
Kincade, Orin *34:* 116
Kindersley, Barnabas *96:* 110

Kindred, Wendy *7:* 151
King, Colin *53:* 3
King, Robin *10:* 164, 165
King, Stephen Michael *141:* 31
King, Tara Calahan *139:* 172
King, Tony *39:* 121
Kingman, Dong *16:* 287; *44:* 100, 102, 104
Kingsley, Charles *YABC 2:* 182
Kingston, Julie *147:* 14
Kingston, Maxine Hong *53:* 92
Kinney, Jeff *187:* 97
Kipling, John Lockwood *YABC 2:* 198
Kipling, Rudyard *YABC 2:* 196
Kipniss, Robert *29:* 59
Kirchherr, Astrid *55:* 23
Kirchhoff, Art *28:* 136
Kirk, Daniel *153:* 115, 116, 117; *173:* 101
Kirk, David *117:* 88, 89; *161:* 97, 98
Kirk, Ruth *5:* 96
Kirk, Steve *170:* 37
Kirk, Tim *32:* 209, 211; *72:* 89; *83:* 49
Kirmse, Marguerite *15:* 283; *18:* 153
Kirsch, Vincent X. *124:* 207
Kirschner, Ruth *22:* 154
Kish, Ely *73:* 119; *79:* 2
Kitamura, Satoshi *62:* 102; *98:* 91; *101:* 147; *138:* 2; *143:* 83, 85, 86
Kiss, Andrew *168:* 115
Kitchel, JoAnn E. *133:* 32
Kitchen, Bert *70:* 126; *193:* 49
Kittelsen, Theodor *62:* 14
Kiuchi, Tatsuro *114:* 71
Kiwak, Barbara *172:* 135
Klahr, Susan *176:* 196
Klapholz, Mel *13:* 35
Klein, Bill *89:* 105
Klein, Robert *55:* 77
Klein, Suzanna *63:* 104
Kleinman, Zalman *28:* 143
Kleven, Elisa *173:* 96, 97
Kliban, B. *35:* 137, 138
Kline, Michael *127:* 66
Klise, M. Sarah *180:* 117, 118; *181:* 97
Knabel, Lonnie *73:* 103; *75:* 187, 228
Kneen, Maggie *140:* 139
Knight, Ann *34:* 143
Knight, Christopher *13:* 125
Knight, Hilary *1:* 233; *3:* 21; *15:* 92, 158, 159; *16:* 258, 259, 260; *18:* 235; *19:* 169; *35:* 242; *46:* 167; *52:* 116; *69:* 126, 127; *132:* 129; *YABC 1:* 168, 169, 172
Knorr, Peter *126:* 92, 93
Knotts, Howard *20:* 4; *25:* 170; *36:* 163
Knutson, Barbara *112:* 134
Knutson, Kimberley *115:* 90
Kobayashi, Ann *39:* 58
Kocsis, J.C.
  See Paul, James
Koehler, Hanne Lore *176:* 203
Koehn, Ilse *34:* 198; *79:* 123
Koelsch, Michael *99:* 182; *107:* 164; *109:* 239; *138:* 142; *150:* 94; *176:* 105; *187:* 63
Koering, Ursula *3:* 28; *4:* 14; *44:* 5; *64:* 140,141; *85:* 46
Koerner, Henry
  See Koerner, W.H.D.
Koerner, W.H.D. *14:* 216; *21:* 88, 89, 90, 91; *23:* 211
Koetsch, Mike *166:* 68
Koffler, Camilla *36:* 113
Kogan, Deborah Ray *161:* 101, 102
Koide, Yasuko *50:* 114
Kolado, Karen *102:* 228
Komoda, Kiyo *9:* 128; *13:* 214
Kompaneyets, Marc *169:* 92
Konashevich, Vladimir *61:* 160
Konashevicha, V. *YABC 1:* 26
Konigsburg, E.L. *4:* 138; *48:* 141, 142, 144, 145; *94:* 129, 130; *126:* 129, 130, 131
Kono, Erin Eitter *177:* 99
Kooiker, Leonie *48:* 148

Koonook, Simon *65:* 157
Koontz, Robin Michal *136:* 155
Koopmans, Loek *101:* 121
Kopelke, Lisa *154:* 107
Kopper, Lisa *72:* 152, 153; *105:* 135, 136
Korach, Mimi *1:* 128, 129; *2:* 52; *4:* 39; *5:* 159; *9:* 129; *10:* 21; *24:* 69
Koren, Edward *5:* 100; *65:* 65, 67
Kosaka, Fumi *164:* 130
Koscielniak, Bruce *99:* 122; *153:* 120, 121, 122
Koshkin, Alexander *92:* 180
Kossin, Sandy *10:* 71; *23:* 105
Kostin, Andrej *26:* 204
Kosturko, Bob *164:* 56
Kotzky, Brian *68:* 184
Kovacevic, Zivojin *13:* 247
Kovalski, Maryann *58:* 120; *84:* 88; *97:* 124, 125, 126; *158:* 3; *186:* 80
Krahn, Fernando *2:* 257; *34:* 206; *49:* 152
Kramer, Anthony *33:* 81
Kramer, David *96:* 162; *109:* 132; *150:* 220
Kramer, Frank *6:* 121
Krantz, Kathy *35:* 83
Kratter, Paul *139:* 65
Kraus, Robert *13:* 217; *65:* 113; *93:* 93, 94
Krause, Jon *176:* 62
Krauss, Trisha *174:* 10
Kredel, Fritz *6:* 35; *17:* 93, 94, 95, 96; *22:* 147; *24:* 175; *29:* 130; *35:* 77; *YABC 2:* 166, 300
Kreloff, Eliot *189:* 107, 108
Krementz, Jill *17:* 98; *49:* 41
Krenina, Katya *117:* 106; *125:* 133; *176:* 117
Kresin, Robert *23:* 19
Krieger, Salem *54:* 164
Kriegler, Lyn *73:* 29
Krinitz, Esther Nisenthal *193:* 196
Krommes, Beth *128:* 141; *149:* 136; *181:* 100, 101; *184:* 105; *188:* 125
Krone, Mike *101:* 71
Kronheimer, Ann *135:* 119
Krosoczka, Jarrett J. *155:* 142
Kruck, Gerald *88:* 181
Krupinski, Loretta *67:* 104; *102:* 131; *161:* 105, 106
Krupp, Robin Rector *53:* 96, 98
Krush, Beth *1:* 51, 85; *2:* 233; *4:* 115; *9:* 61; *10:* 191; *11:* 196; *18:* 164, 165; *32:* 72; *37:* 203; *43:* 57; *60:* 102, 103, 107, 108, 109
Krush, Joe *2:* 233; *4:* 115; *9:* 61; *10:* 191; *11:* 196; *18:* 164, 165; *32:* 72, 91; *37:* 203; *43:* 57; *60:* 102, 103, 107, 108, 109
Krych, Duane *91:* 43
Krykorka, Vladyana *96:* 147; *143:* 90, 91; *168:* 14
Kubick, Dana *165:* 91
Kubinyi, Laszlo *4:* 116; *6:* 113; *16:* 118; *17:* 100; *28:* 227; *30:* 172; *49:* 24, 28; *54:* 23; *167:* 149
Kubricht, Mary *73:* 118
Kucharik, Elena *139:* 31
Kuchera, Kathleen *84:* 5
Kuhn, Bob *17:* 91; *35:* 235
Kulikov, Boris *163:* 185; *185:* 23
Kulka, Joe *188:* 110
Kukalis, Romas *90:* 27; *139:* 37
Kuklin, Susan *63:* 82, 83, 84
Kunhardt, Dorothy *53:* 101
Kunhardt, Edith *67:* 105, 106
Kunstler, Mort *10:* 73; *32:* 143
Kurchevsky, V. *34:* 61
Kurczok, Belinda *121:* 118
Kurelek, William *8:* 107
Kuriloff, Ron *13:* 19
Kurisu, Jane *160:* 120
Kuskin, Karla *2:* 170; *68:* 115, 116; *111:* 116
Kutzer, Ernst *19:* 249
Kuzma, Steve *57:* 8; *62:* 93
Kuznetsova, Berta *74:* 45

Kvasnosky, Laura McGee *93:* 103; *142:* 83; *182:* 108
Kwas, Susan Estelle *179:* 116
Kyong, Yunmee *165:* 139

L

LaBlanc, Andre *24:* 146
Laboccetta, Mario *27:* 120
LaBrose, Darcie *157:* 134
Labrosse, Darcia *58:* 88; *108:* 77; *178:* 89
LaCava, Vince *95:* 118
Laceky, Adam *32:* 121
Lacis, Astra *85:* 117
Lacome, Julie *174:* 96, 97
La Croix *YABC 2:* 4
Ladwig, Tim *98:* 212; *117:* 76
La Farge, Margaret *47:* 141
LaFave, Kim *64:* 177; *72:* 39; *97:* 146; *99:* 172; *106:* 123; *149:* 126
Lafontaine, Roger *167:* 158
Lagarrigue, Jerome *136:* 102; *187:* 81
Laimgruber, Monika *11:* 153
Laite, Gordon *1:* 130, 131; *8:* 209; *31:* 113; *40:* 63; *46:* 117
Laliberté, Louise-Andrée *169:* 98
LaMarche, Jim *46:* 204; *61:* 56; *94:* 69; *114:* 22; *129:* 163; *162:* 78, 80
Lamb, Jim *10:* 117
Lambase, Barbara *101:* 185; *150:* 221; *166:* 234
Lambert, J.K. *38:* 129; *39:* 24
Lambert, Sally Anne *133:* 191
Lambert, Saul *23:* 112; *33:* 107; *54:* 136
Lambert, Stephen *109:* 33; *174:* 99
Lambo, Don *6:* 156; *35:* 115; *36:* 146
Lamontagne, Jacques *166:* 227
Lamut, Sonja *57:* 193
Lamut, Sonya *85:* 102
Landa, Peter *11:* 95; *13:* 177; *53:* 119
Landau, Jacob *38:* 111
Landis, Joan *104:* 23
Landon, Lucinda *79:* 31
Landshoff, Ursula *13:* 124
Landström, Lena *146:* 165, 166
Landström, Olof *146:* 166, 168; *170:* 22
Lane, Daniel *112:* 60
Lane, John R. *8:* 145
Lane, John *15:* 176, 177; *30:* 146
Lane, Nancy *166:* 74
Lang, G.D. *48:* 56
Lang, Gary *73:* 75
Lang, Jerry *18:* 295
Langdo, Bryan *186:* 187; *191:* 113, 114, 115
Lange, Dorothea *50:* 141
Langley, Jonathan *162:* 128
Langner, Nola *8:* 110; *42:* 36
Lanino, Deborah *105:* 148
Lantz, Paul *1:* 82, 102; *27:* 88; *34:* 102; *45:* 123
Larkin, Bob *84:* 225
Laroche, Giles *126:* 140; *146:* 81
LaRochelle, David *171:* 97
Larrecq, John *44:* 108; *68:* 56
Larsen, Suzanne *1:* 13
Larson, Gary *57:* 121, 122, 123, 124, 125, 126, 127
Larsson, Carl *35:* 144, 145, 146, 147, 148, 149, 150, 152, 153, 154
Larsson, Karl *19:* 177
Lartitegui, Ana G. *105:* 167
LaRue, Jenna *167:* 20
La Rue, Michael D. *13:* 215
Lasker, Joe *7:* 186, 187; *14:* 55; *38:* 115; *39:* 47; *83:* 113, 114, 115
Latham, Barbara *16:* 188, 189; *43:* 71
Lathrop, Dorothy *14:* 117, 118, 119; *15:* 109; *16:* 78, 79, 81; *32:* 201, 203; *33:* 112; *YABC 2:* 301

Lattimore, Eleanor Frances *7:* 156
Lauden, Claire *16:* 173
Lauden, George, Jr. *16:* 173
Laune, Paul *2:* 235; *34:* 31
Laure, Jason *49:* 53; *50:* 122
Lauter, Richard *63:* 29; *67:* 111; *77:* 198
Lavallee, Barbara *74:* 157; *92:* 154; *96:* 126; *145:* 193; *166:* 125, 126; *186:* 155; *192:* 172
Lave, Fitz Hugh *59:* 139
Lavis, Stephen *43:* 143; *87:* 137, 164, 165
Layton, Neal *152:* 120, 121; *182:* 65; *187:* 103, 105, 106
Lawrason, June *168:* 30
Lawrence, John *25:* 131; *30:* 141; *44:* 198, 200
Lawrence, Stephen *20:* 195
Lawson, Carol *6:* 38; *42:* 93, 131; *174:* 56; *189:* 89
Lawson, George *17:* 280
Lawson, Robert *5:* 26; *6:* 94; *13:* 39; *16:* 11; *20:* 100, 102, 103; *54:* 3; *66:* 12; *100:* 144, 145; *YABC 2:* 222, 224, 225, 227, 228, 229, 230, 231, 232, 233, 234, 235, 237, 238, 239, 240, 241
Layfield, Kathie *60:* 194
Lazare, Jerry *44:* 109; *74:* 28
Lazarevich, Mila *17:* 118
Lazarus, Claire *103:* 30
Lazarus, Keo Felker *21:* 94
Lazzaro, Victor *11:* 126
Lea, Bob *166:* 208
Lea, Tom *43:* 72, 74
Leacroft, Richard *6:* 140
Leaf, Munro *20:* 99
Leake, Donald *70:* 41
Leander, Patricia *23:* 27
Lear, Edward *18:* 183, 184, 185
Lear, Rebecca *149:* 46
Lebenson, Richard *6:* 209; *7:* 76; *23:* 145; *44:* 191; *87:* 153
Le Cain, Errol *6:* 141; *9:* 3; *22:* 142; *25:* 198; *28:* 173; *68:* 128, 129; *86:* 49
Lechon, Daniel *113:* 211
Leder, Dora *129:* 172
Ledger, Bill *181:* 58
Leduc, Bernard *102:* 36
Lee, Alan *62:* 25, 28
Lee, Bryce *99:* 60; *101:* 195
Lee, Chinlun *181:* 138; *182:* 112
Lee, Declan *191:* 20
Lee, Dom *83:* 118, 120; *93:* 123; *121:* 121, 126; *146:* 174, 175, 206, 207; *174:* 204
Lee, Doris *13:* 246; *32:* 183; *44:* 111
Lee, Hector Viveros *115:* 96
Lee, Jeanne M. *158:* 56
Lee, Jared *93:* 200; *157:* 229
Lee, Jody *81:* 121; *82:* 225; *91:* 155; *100:* 182
Lee, Jody A. *127:* 124, 126, 127
  See also Lee, Jody
Lee, Manning de V. *2:* 200; *17:* 12; *27:* 87; *37:* 102, 103, 104; *YABC 2:* 304
Lee, Marie G. *138:* 157
Lee, Paul *97:* 100; *105:* 72, 209; *109:* 177; *128:* 113
Lee, Robert J. *3:* 97; *67:* 124
Lee, Victor *96:* 228; *105:* 182; *140:* 196
Leech, Dorothy *98:* 76
Leech, John *15:* 59
Leedy, Loreen *84:* 142; *128:* 144, 145, 146; *175:* 125, 126, 127
Leeman, Michael *44:* 157
Leeming, Catherine *87:* 39
Lees, Harry *6:* 112
LeFever, Bill *88:* 220, 221
Legenisel *47:* 111
Legrand, Edy *18:* 89, 93
Lehman, Barbara *73:* 123; *170:* 130
Lehrman, Rosalie *2:* 180
Leichman, Seymour *5:* 107
Leighton, Clare *25:* 130; *33:* 168; *37:* 105, 106, 108, 109

Leisk, David *1:* 140, 141; *11:* 54; *30:* 137, 142, 143, 144
Leister, Brian *89:* 45; *106:* 37; *114:* 67; *149:* 236
Leloir, Maurice *18:* 77, 80, 83, 99
Lemaître, Pascal *144:* 175; *176:* 130; *189:* 135
Lemieux, Michele *100:* 148; *139:* 153
Lemke, Horst *14:* 98; *38:* 117, 118, 119
Lemke, R.W. *42:* 162
Lemon, David Gwynne *9:* 1
LeMoult, Adolph *82:* 116
Lenn, Michael *136:* 89
Lennon, John *114:* 100
Lennox, Elsie *95:* 163; *143:* 160
Lenski, Lois *1:* 144; *26:* 135, 137, 139, 141; *100:* 153, 154
Lent, Blair *1:* 116, 117; *2:* 174; *3:* 206, 207; *7:* 168, 169; *34:* 62; *68:* 217; *133:* 101; *183:* 60
Leonard, Richard *91:* 128
Leone, Leonard *49:* 190
Lerner, Carol *86:* 140, 141, 142
Lerner, Judith *116:* 138
Lerner, Sharon *11:* 157; *22:* 56
Leroux-Hugon, Helene *132:* 139
Leslie, Cecil *19:* 244
Lessac, Frane *80:* 182, 207; *96:* 182
Lessing, Erich *167:* 52; *173:* 60
Lester, Alison *50:* 124; *90:* 147, 148; *129:* 130
Lethcoe, Jason *191:* 116, 117
Le Tord, Bijou *49:* 156; *95:* 112
Leutz, Emanuel *165:* 27
Levai, Blaise *39:* 130
Levin, Ted *12:* 148
Levine, David *43:* 147, 149, 150, 151, 152; *64:* 11
Levine, Joe *71:* 88
Levine, Marge *81:* 127
Levinson, David *178:* 232
Levit, Herschel *24:* 223
Levstek, Ljuba *131:* 192; *134:* 216; *149:* 65; *168:* 180
Levy, Jessica Ann *19:* 225; *39:* 191
Levy, Lina *117:* 126
Lewin, Betsy *32:* 114; *48:* 177; *90:* 151; *91:* 125; *92:* 85; *115:* 105; *169:* 110, 111; *178:* 47; *186:* 188
Lewin, Ted *4:* 77; *8:* 168; *20:* 110; *21:* 99,100; *27:* 110; *28:* 96, 97; *31:* 49; *45:* 55; *48:* 223; *60:* 20, 119, 120; *62:* 139; *66:* 108; *71:* 12; *72:* 21; *74:* 226; *76:* 139, 140; *77:* 82; *79:* 87; *85:* 49, 177; *86:* 55; *88:* 182; *93:* 28, 29; *94:* 34, 182, 194; *99:* 156; *104:* 8; *115:* 123; *118:* 74; *119:* 114, 116; *131:* 54; *145:* 99; *165:* 151; *177:* 75; *178:* 42; *190:* 30; *192:* 86
Lewis, Allen *15:* 112
Lewis, E.B. *88:* 143; *93:* 109; *119:* 79; *124:* 113; *128:* 49; *151:* 167; *168:* 110; *173:* 121; *174:* 66; *176:* 7; *184:* 150; *185:* 191
Lewis, H.B. *170:* 124
Lewis, J. Patrick *162:* 83
Lewis, Jan *81:* 22
Lewis, Kim *136:* 165
Lewis, Richard W. *52:* 25
Lewis, Robin Baird *98:* 193
Leydon, Rita Floden *21:* 101
Li, Xiojun *187:* 172
Lichtenheld, Tom *152:* 125, 126
Lieblich, Irene *22:* 173; *27:* 209, 214
Lieder, Rick *108:* 197
Lies, Brian *92:* 40; *141:* 101; *150:* 138; *190:* 97, 98, 99
Liese, Charles *4:* 222
Life, Kay *79:* 49
Lifton, Robert Jay *66:* 154
Lightburn, Ron *86:* 153; *91:* 122
Lightfoot, Norman R. *45:* 47
Lignell, Lois *37:* 114
Lill, Debra *121:* 70

Lilly, Charles *8:* 73; *20:* 127; *48:* 53; *72:* 9,16; *77:* 98; *102:* 94
Lilly, Ken *37:* 224
Lim, John *43:* 153
Limona, Mercedes *51:* 183
Lin, Grace *143:* 217; *162:* 86, 87; *174:* 185
Lincoln, Patricia Henderson *27:* 27; *78:* 127
Lindahn, Ron *84:* 17
Lindahn, Val *84:* 17
Lindberg, Howard *10:* 123; *16:* 190
Lindberg, Jeffrey *64:* 77; *77:* 71; *79:* 54; *80:* 149; *174:* 109; *179:* 52
Linden, Seymour *18:* 200, 201; *43:* 140
Lindenbaum, Pija *144:* 143; *183:* 113
Linder, Richard *27:* 119
Lindman, Maj *43:* 154
Lindsay, Norman *67:* 114
Lindsay, Vachel *40:* 118
Lindstrom, Jack *145:* 118
Line, Les *27:* 143
Linell
    See Smith, Linell
Lionni, Leo *8:* 115; *72:* 159, 160, 161
Lipinsky, Lino *2:* 156; *22:* 175
Lippincott, Gary A. *70:* 35; *119:* 118
Lippman, Peter *8:* 31; *31:* 119, 120, 160
Lisi, Victoria *89:* 145
Lisker, Emily *169:* 114
Lisker, Sonia O. *16:* 274; *31:* 31; *44:* 113, 114
Lisowski, Gabriel *47:* 144; *49:* 157
Lissim, Simon *17:* 138
Little, Ed *89:* 145; *151:* 53
Little, Harold *16:* 72
Little, Mary E. *28:* 146
Littlewood, Karen *165:* 126
Litty, Julie *111:* 63
Litzinger, Rosanne *151:* 101; *176:* 118
Liu, Lesley *143:* 72
Lively, Lorna *19:* 216
Livingston, Susan *95:* 22
Liwska, Renata *164:* 113
Ljungkvist, Laura *180:* 120
Llerena, Carlos Antonio *19:* 181
Lloyd, Errol *11:* 39; *22:* 178
Lloyd, Megan *77:* 118; *80:* 113; *97:* 75; *117:* 94, 95; *189:* 121, 122
Lloyd, Sam *183:* 116, 117
Lo, Beth *165:* 154
Lo, Koon-chiu *7:* 134
Loates, Glen *63:* 76
Lobel, Anita *6:* 87; *9:* 141; *18:* 248; *55:* 85,86, 87, 88, 93, 104; *60:* 67; *78:* 263; *82:* 110; *96:* 157, 159; *101:* 84; *132:* 35; *162:* 93, 94
Lobel, Arnold *1:* 188, 189; *5:* 12; *6:* 147; *7:* 167, 209; *18:* 190, 191; *25:* 39, 43; *27:* 40; *29:* 174; *52:* 127; *55:* 89, 91, 94, 95, 97, 98, 99, 100, 101, 102,103, 105, 106; *60:* 18, 31; *66:* 181, 183; *75:* 57; *82:* 246; *136:* 146
Lobel, Gillian *190:* 21
Locker, Thomas *109:* 134
Lodge, Bernard *107:* 125, 126; *153:* 93
Loeb, Jeph *153:* 177
Lodge, Jo *112:* 119
Loefgren, Ulf *3:* 108
Loescher, Ann *20:* 108
Loescher, Gil *20:* 108
Loew, David *93:* 184; *171:* 120
Lofting, Hugh *15:* 182, 183; *100:* 161, 162
Lofts, Pamela *60:* 188
Loh, George *38:* 88
Lomberg, Jon *58:* 160
Lonette, Reisie *11:* 211; *12:* 168; *13:* 56; *36:* 122; *43:* 155
Long, Ethan *168:* 146; *178:* 12; *182:* 120, 121
Long, Laurel *162:* 135; *190:* 11
Long, Loren *99:* 176; *172:* 65; *182:* 78; *188:* 114, 115
Long, Melinda *152:* 128
Long, Miles *115:* 174
Long, Sally *42:* 184
Long, Sylvia *74:* 168; *132:* 63; *179:* 134

Longoni, Eduardo *73:* 85
Longtemps, Ken *17:* 123; *29:* 221; *69:* 82
Looser, Heinz *YABC 2:* 208
Lopez, Loretta *190:* 100
Lopshire, Robert *6:* 149; *21:* 117; *34:* 166; *73:* 13
Lord, John Vernon *21:* 104; *23:* 25; *51:* 22
Lorenz, Albert *40:* 146; *115:* 127
Loretta, Sister Mary *33:* 73
Lorraine, Walter H. *3:* 110; *4:* 123; *16:* 192; *103:* 119
Los, Marek *146:* 22; *193:* 23
Loss, Joan *11:* 163
Louderback, Walt *YABC 1:* 164
Lousada, Sandra *40:* 138
Louth, Jack *149:* 252; *151:* 191, 192
Love, Judy *173:* 43
Low, Joseph *14:* 124, 125; *18:* 68; *19:* 194; *31:* 166; *80:* 239
Low, William *62:* 175; *80:* 147; *112:* 194; *150:* 202; *169:* 175; *177:* 110; *192:* 27
Lowe, Vicky *177:* 130
Lowenheim, Alfred *13:* 65, 66
Lowenstein, Sallie *116:* 90, 91
Lowitz, Anson *17:* 124; *18:* 215
Lowrey, Jo *8:* 133
Lubach, Vanessa *142:* 152
Lubell, Winifred *1:* 207; *3:* 15; *6:* 151
Lubin, Leonard B. *19:* 224; *36:* 79, 80; *45:* 128, 129,131, 132, 133, 134, 135, 136, 137, 139, 140, 141; *70:* 95; *YABC2:* 96
Lucht, Irmgard *82:* 145
Ludwig, Helen *33:* 144, 145
Lufkin, Raymond *38:* 138; *44:* 48
Luhrs, Henry *7:* 123; *11:* 120
Lujan, Tonita *82:* 33
Lupo, Dom *4:* 204
Lustig, Loretta *30:* 186; *46:* 134, 135, 136, 137
Luthardt, Kevin *172:* 125, 126
Luxbacher, Irene *153:* 145
Luzak, Dennis *52:* 121; *99:* 142
Lydbury, Jane *82:* 98
Lydecker, Laura *21:* 113; *42:* 53
Lynch, Charles *16:* 33
Lynch, Marietta *29:* 137; *30:* 171
Lynch, P.J. *126:* 228; *129:* 110; *132:* 247; *183:* 64
Lyne, Alison Davis *188:* 118, 198
Lyon, Carol *102:* 26
Lyon, Elinor *6:* 154
Lyon, Fred *14:* 16
Lyon, Tammie *175:* 170
Lyons, Oren *8:* 193
Lyster, Michael *26:* 41

M

Maas, Dorothy *6:* 175
Maas, Julie *47:* 61
Macaulay, David *46:* 139, 140, 141, 142, 143, 144, 145, 147, 149, 150; *72:* 167, 168, 169; *137:* 129, 130, 131, 132
MacCarthy, Patricia *69:* 141
Macdonald, Alister *21:* 55
Macdonald, Roberta *19:* 237; *52:* 164
MacDonald, Norman *13:* 99
MacDonald, Suse *54:* 41; *109* 138; *130:* 156; *193:* 106, 107, 109, 110
Mace, Varian *49:* 159
Macguire, Robert Reid *18:* 67
Machetanz, Fredrick *34:* 147, 148
MacInnes, Ian *35:* 59
MacIntyre, Elisabeth *17:* 127, 128
Mack, Jeff *161:* 128
Mack, Stan *17:* 129; *96:* 33
Mackay, Donald *17:* 60
MacKaye, Arvia *32:* 119
Mackenzie, Stuart *73:* 213

MacKenzie, Garry *33:* 159
Mackie, Clare *87:* 134
Mackinlay, Miguel *27:* 22
MacKinstry, Elizabeth *15:* 110; *42:* 139, 140, 141, 142, 143,144, 145
MacLeod, Lee *91:* 167
Maclise, Daniel *YABC 2:* 257
Macnaughton, Tina *182:* 145
MacRae, Tom *181:* 112
Madden, Don *3:* 112, 113; *4:* 33, 108, 155; *7:* 193; *78:* 12; *YABC 2:* 211
Maddison, Angela Mary *10:* 83
Madsen, Jim *146:* 259; *152:* 237; *184:* 106
Maestro, Giulio *8:* 124; *12:* 17; *13:* 108; *25:* 182; *54:* 147; *59:* 114, 115, 116, 117, 118, 121, 123, 124, 125,126, 127; *68:* 37, 38; *106:* 129, 130, 131, 136, 137, 138
Maffia, Daniel *60:* 200
Maggio, Viqui *58:* 136, 181; *74:* 150; *75:* 90; *85:* 159; *90:* 158; *109:* 184; *193:* 113
Magnus, Erica *77:* 123
Magnuson, Diana *28:* 102; *34:* 190; *41:* 175
Magoon, Scott *181:* 104
Magovern, Peg *103:* 123
Maguire, Sheila *41:* 100
Magurn, Susan *91:* 30
Mahony, Will *37:* 120
Mahony, Will *85:* 116
Mahood, Kenneth *24:* 141
Mahurin, Matt *164:* 225; *175:* 95; *189:* 37
Maik, Henri *9:* 102
Maione, Heather *106:* 5; *178:* 8; *189:* 126, 127; *193:* 58
Maisto, Carol *29:* 87
Maitland, Antony *1:* 100, 176; *8:* 41; *17:* 246; *24:* 46; *25:* 177, 178; *32:* 74; *60:* 65, 195; *67:* 156; *87:* 131; *101:* 110
Majewski, Dawn W. *169:* 95
Mak, Kam *72:* 25; *75:* 43; *87:* 186; *97:* 24; *102:* 154; *149:* 195; *186:* 28
Makie, Pam *37:* 117
Maktima, Joe *116:* 191
Maland, Nick *99:* 77
Male, Alan *132:* 64
Malone, James Hiram *84:* 161
Malone, Nola Langner *82:* 239
Malone, Peter *191:* 121, 122, 123
Malsberg, Edward *51:* 175
Malvern, Corinne *2:* 13; *34:* 148, 149
Manchess, Gregory *165:* 241
Mancusi, Stephen *63:* 198, 199
Mandelbaum, Ira *31:* 115
Manders, John *138:* 152, 155; *188:* 171; *190:* 92
Manet, Edouard *23:* 170
Mangiat, Jeff *173:* 127
Mangurian, David *14:* 133
Manham, Allan *42:* 109; *77:* 180; *80:* 227
Manley, Matt *103:* 167; *117:* 98; *172:* 49
Manna, Giovanni *178:* 44
Manniche, Lise *31:* 121
Manning, Jane *96:* 203
Manning, Jo *63:* 154
Manning, Lawrence *191:* 153
Manning, Mick *176:* 139
Manning, Samuel F. *5:* 75
Mantel, Richard *57:* 73; *63:* 106; *82:* 255
Maraja *15:* 86; *YABC 1:* 28; *2:* 115
Marcellino, Fred *20:* 125; *34:* 222; *53:* 125; *58:* 205; *61:* 64, 121, 122; *68:* 154, 156, 157, 158, 159; *72:* 25; *86:* 184; *98:* 181; *118:* 129, 130, 131; *149:* 218
Marchesi, Stephen *34:* 140; *46:* 72; *50:* 147; *66:* 239; *70:* 33; *73:* 18, 114, 163; *77:* 47, 76,147; *78:* 79; *80:* 30; *81:* 6; *89:* 66; *93:* 21,130; *94:* 94; *97:* 66; *98:* 96; *114:* 115, 116
Marchiori, Carlos *14:* 60
Marciano, John Bemelmans *118:* 133; *167:* 110, 111, 112
Marcus, Barry David *139:* 248; *145:* 18

Margules, Gabriele *21:* 120
Mariana
   See Foster, Marian Curtis
Mariano, Michael *52:* 108
Marino, Dorothy *6:* 37; *14:* 135
Mario, Heide Stetson *101:* 202
Maris, Ron *71:* 123
Maritz, Nicolaas *85:* 123
Mark, Mona *65:* 105; *68:* 205; *116:* 213
Markham, R.L. *17:* 240
Marks, Alan *104:* 104; *109:* 182; *164:* 92; *185:* 134; *187:* 120, 121, 122
Marks, Cara *54:* 9
Marokvia, Artur *31:* 122
Marquez, Susan *108:* 121
Marrella, Maria Pia *62:* 116
Marriott, Pat *30:* 30; *34:* 39; *35:* 164, 165, 166; *44:* 170; *48:* 186, 187, 188, 189, 191, 192, 193; *91:* 92
Mars, W.T. *1:* 161; *3:* 115; *4:* 208, 225; *5:* 92, 105, 186; *8:* 214; *9:* 12; *13:* 121; *27:* 151; *31:* 180; *38:* 102; *48:* 66; *62:* 164, 165; *64:* 62; *68:* 229; *79:* 55
Marschall, Ken *85:* 29
Marsh, Christine *3:* 164
Marsh, James *73:* 137
Marsh, Reginald *17:* 5; *19:* 89; *22:* 90, 96
Marshall, Anthony D. *18:* 216
Marshall, Felicia *170:* 190
Marshall, James *6:* 160; *40:* 221; *42:* 24, 25, 29; *51:* 111, 112, 113, 114, 115, 116, 117, 118, 119, 120, 121; *64:* 13; *75:* 126, 127, 128, 129; *102:* 10, 12
Marshall, Janet *97:* 154
Marstall, Bob *55:* 145; *84:* 153, 170; *104:* 145; *154:* 166, 167, 168
Martchenko, Michael *50:* 129, 153, 155, 156, 157; *83:* 144,145; *154:* 137, 138, 139
Marten, Ruth *129:* 52
Martin, Charles E. *70:* 144
Martin, David Stone *24:* 232; *62:* 4
Martin, Fletcher *18:* 213; *23:* 151
Martin, Rene *7:* 144; *42:* 148, 149, 150
Martin, Richard E. *51:* 157; *131:* 203
Martin, Ron *32:* 81
Martin, Stefan *8:* 68; *32:* 124, 126; *56:* 33
Martin, Whitney *166:* 137
Martinez, Ed *58:* 192; *72:* 231; *77:* 33; *80:* 214; *167:* 123
Martinez, John *6:* 113; *118:* 13; *139:* 143
Martinez, Sergio *158:* 190
Martini, Angela *183:* 161
Martiniere, Stephan *171:* 130
Marton, Jirina *95:* 127, 128; *144:* 145
Martorell, Antonio *84:* 6; *97:* 161
Martucci, Griesbach *52:* 106
Marvin, Frederic *83:* 86
Marx, Robert F. *24:* 143
Marzollo, Jean *190:* 127
Masefield, Judith *19:* 208, 209
Masheris, Robert *78:* 51
Masiello, Ralph *186:* 171
Mason, George F. *14:* 139
Mason, Robert *84:* 96
Massey, Barbara *68:* 142
Massie, Diane Redfield *16:* 194
Massie, Kim *31:* 43
Mataya, David *121:* 66
Mathers, Petra *119:* 135; *163:* 104; *176:* 143, 144; *187:* 142
Mathewuse, James *51:* 143
Mathieu, Joseph *14:* 33; *39:* 206; *43:* 167; *56:* 180; *79:* 126; *94:* 147; *185:* 140
Matje, Martin *169:* 177, 178; *172:* 180
Matsubara, Naoko *12:* 121
Matsuda, Shizu *13:* 167
Matsuoka, Mei *192:* 135
Matte, L'Enc *22:* 183
Mattelson, Marvin *36:* 50, 51
Mattheson, Jenny *180:* 132
Matthews, F. Leslie *4:* 216

Matthews, Tina *190:* 130
Mattingly, David *71:* 76, 77; *82:* 64; *91:* 216, 217; *109:* 25
Matulay, Laszlo *5:* 18; *43:* 168
Matus, Greta *12:* 142
Maughan, William *181:* 31
Mauldin, Bill *27:* 23
Mauterer, Erin Marie *119:* 5
Mawicke, Tran *9:* 137; *15:* 191; *47:* 100
Mawson, Matt *74:* 115
Max, Peter *45:* 146, 147, 148, 149, 150
Maxie, Betty *40:* 135
Maxwell, John Alan *1:* 148
Mayan, Earl *7:* 193
Mayer, Danuta *117:* 103
Mayer, Marianna *32:* 132
Mayer, Mercer *11:* 192; *16:* 195, 196; *20:* 55, 57; *32:* 129, 130, 132, 133, 134; *41:* 144, 248, 252; *58:* 186; *73:* 140, 142, 143; *137:* 137, 138
Mayforth, Hal *166:* 77
Mayhew, James *85:* 121; *138:* 187; *149:* 140
Mayhew, Richard *3:* 106
Mayo, Gretchen Will *38:* 81; *84:* 166
Mays, Victor *5:* 127; *8:* 45, 153; *14:* 245; *23:* 50; *34:* 155; *40:* 79; *45:* 158; *54:* 91; *66:* 240
Mazal, Chanan *49:* 104
Maze, Deborah *71:* 83
Mazellan, Ron *75:* 97, 98
Mazetti, Alan *112:* 72
Mazille, Capucine *96:* 168
Mazza, Adriana Saviozzi *19:* 215
Mazzella, Mary Jo *82:* 165
Mazzetti, Alan *45:* 210
McAfee, Steve *135:* 146; *167:* 176; *191:* 84
McAlinden, Paul *112:* 128
McBride, Angus *28:* 49; *103:* 40
McBride, Will *30:* 110
McCaffery, Janet *38:* 145
McCallum, Graham *78:* 78
McCallum, Stephen *141:* 143; *156:* 5; *166:* 228
McCann, Gerald *3:* 50; *4:* 94; *7:* 54; *41:* 121
McCarthy, Dan *174:* 74
McCarthy, Linda *177:* 128
McCarthy, Meghan *168:* 134
McCauley, Adam *157:* 36; *184:* 199; *193:* 100
McCay, Winsor *41:* 124, 126, 128, 129, 130, 131; *134:* 77, 79
McClary, Nelson *1:* 111
McClintock, Barbara *57:* 135; *95:* 130; *146:* 190
McClintock, Theodore *14:* 141
McCloskey, Robert *1:* 184, 185; *2:* 186, 187; *17:* 209; *39:* 139, 140, 141, 142, 143, 146, 147, 148; *85:* 150, 151; *100:* 172, 173, 174
McClung, Robert *2:* 189; *68:* 166, 167
McClure, Gillian *31:* 132; *150:* 53
McConnel, Jerry *31:* 75, 187
McConnell, Mary *102:* 49
McCord, Kathleen Garry *78:* 236
McCormack, John *66:* 193
McCormick, A.D. *35:* 119
McCormick, Dell J. *19:* 216
McCrady, Lady *16:* 198; *39:* 127
McCrea, James *3:* 122; *33:* 216
McCrea, Ruth *3:* 122; *27:* 102; *33:* 216
McCue, Lisa *65:* 148, 149; *77:* 54; *80:* 132; *175:* 33; *177:* 133, 135
McCully, Emily Arnold *2:* 89; *4:* 120, 121, 146, 197; *5:* 2, 129; *7:* 191; *11:* 122; *15:* 210; *33:* 23; *35:* 244; *37:* 122; *39:* 88; *40:* 103; *50:* 30,31, 32, 33, 34, 35, 36, 37; *52:* 89, 90; *57:* 6; *62:* 3; *70:* 195; *86:* 82; *96:* 192; *97:* 93; *110:* 143,144; *117:* 47; *167:* 96
McCurdy, Michael *13:* 153; *24:* 85; *81:* 160; *82:* 157, 158; *86:* 125; *97:* 92; *117:* 178; *132:* 6; *147:* 159, 160
McCusker, Paul *99:* 19
McDaniel, Jerry *132:* 135

McDaniel, Preston *160:* 206; *170:* 139
McDermott, Beverly Brodsky *11:* 180
McDermott, Gerald *16:* 201; *74:* 174, 175; *163:* 150, 151
McDermott, Mike *96:* 187
McDonald, Jill *13:* 155; *26:* 128
McDonald, Mercedes *169:* 118
McDonald, Ralph J. *5:* 123, 195
McDonnell, Flora *146:* 199, 200
McDonnell, Patrick *179:* 153, 154
McDonough, Don *10:* 163
McElmurry, Jill *137:* 148; *163:* 141
McElrath-Eslick, Lori *129:* 145; *142:* 21; *173:* 123
McEntee, Dorothy *37:* 124
McEwan, Keith *88:* 116; *165:* 122, 123
McEwen, Katharine *169:* 34
McFall, Christie *12:* 144
McFeely, Daniel *160:* 213
McGaw, Laurie *109:* 243; *143:* 216
McGee, Barbara *6:* 165
McGee, Marni *163:* 153
McGillvray, Kim *158:* 171; *165:* 213; *186:* 183; *190:* 175
McGinley-Nally, Sharon *131:* 19
McGinnis, Robert *110:* 113; *177:* 80
McGovern, Tara *98:* 171
McGraw, Sheila *83:* 146
McGregor, Malcolm *23:* 27
McGrory, Anik *193:* 120
McGuirk, Leslie *152:* 159
McHale, John *138:* 190
McHenry, E.B. *193:* 122
McHugh, Tom *23:* 64
McIntosh, Jon *42:* 56
McKay, Donald *2:* 118; *32:* 157; *45:* 151, 152
McKean, Dave *150:* 71; *174:* 156
McKeating, Eileen *44:* 58
McKee, David *10:* 48; *21:* 9; *70:* 154, 155; *107:* 139, 140, 141; *134:* 218; *158:* 148, 149, 150, 151
McKee, Diana *109:* 185
McKelvey, Patrick *164:* 141
McKendry, Joe *170:* 136
McKeveny, Tom *164:* 60; *173:* 79
McKie, Roy *7:* 44
McKillip, Kathy *30:* 153
McKinney, Ena *26:* 39
McKinnon, James *136:* 75
McKowen, Scott *172:* 63
McLachlan, Edward *5:* 89
McLaren, Chesley *133:* 53
McLaren, Kirsty *123:* 99; *124:* 226
Mclean, Andrew *113:* 117, 118, 120, 121; *172:* 130, 131
Mclean, Janet *172:* 130
McLean, Meg *94:* 196
McLean, Sammis *32:* 197
McLean, Wilson *90:* 29; *113:* 195
McLoughlin, John C. *47:* 149
McLoughlin, Wayne *102:* 230; *134:* 178
McMahon, Robert *36:* 155; *69:* 169
McManus, Shawn *85:* 71
McMenemy, Sarah *156:* 139
McMillan, Bruce *22:* 184
McMullan, James *40:* 33; *67:* 172; *87:* 142; *99:* 63, 64; *189:* 133
McMullen, Nigel *146:* 177
McNeely, Tom *162:* 55
McNaught, Harry *12:* 80; *32:* 136
McNaughton, Colin *39:* 149; *40:* 108; *92:* 144, 145, 146; *134:* 104, 106
McNicholas, Maureen *38:* 148
McNicholas, Shelagh *173:* 61; *191:* 125, 126
McPhail, David *14:* 105; *23:* 135; *37:* 217, 218, 220,221; *47:* 151, 152, 153, 154, 155, 156, 158, 159, 160, 162, 163, 164; *71:* 211; *81:* 139, 140, 142; *86:* 123; *132:* 150; *140:* 129, 131, 132; *183:* 134, 135, 137; *189:* 132
McPhee, Richard B. *41:* 133

McPheeters, Neal *78:* 132; *86:* 90; *99:* 162; *111:* 141; *142:* 162
McQuade, Jacqueline *124:* 223
McQueen, Lucinda *28:* 149; *41:* 249; *46:* 206; *53:* 103
McQuillan, Mary *153:* 97
McVay, Tracy *11:* 68
McVicker, Charles *39:* 150
Mead, Ben Carlton *43:* 75
Meade, Holly *90:* 102; *94:* 101; *149:* 8; *151:* 107
Mecray, John *33:* 62
Meddaugh, Susan *20:* 42; *29:* 143; *41:* 241; *77:* 50; *84:* 173, 174, 175, 176, 177, 178; *125:* 160, 161, 162; *176:* 148, 149, 150, 151
Meehan, Dennis B. *56:* 144
Meents, Len W. *73:* 147, 150
Meers, Tony *99:* 113
Meisel, Paul *98:* 137; *124:* 18; *162:* 180; *179:* 16; *181:* 62
Melanson, Luc *149:* 229
Melendez, Francisco *72:* 180
Melnychuk, Monika *153:* 65
Melo, John *16:* 285; *58:* 203
Meloni, Maria Teresa *98:* 62
Meltzer, Ericka
    See O'Rourke, Ericka
Menasco, Milton *43:* 85
Menchin, Scott *188:* 129
Mendelson, Steven T. *86:* 154
Mendelssohn, Felix *19:* 170
Mendola, Christopher *88:* 223
Meng, Heinz *13:* 158
Merian, Maria Sibylla *140:* 88
Mero, Lee *34:* 68
Merrill, Frank T. *16:* 147; *19:* 71; *YABC 1:* 226, 229,273
Merriman, Rachel *98:* 108; *114:* 122; *149:* 142
Meryman, Hope *27:* 41
Meryweather, Jack *10:* 179
Meseldzija, Petar *168:* 97
Meserve, Jess *184:* 137
Messick, Dale *64:* 150, 151, 152
Meth, Harold *24:* 203
Meyer, Herbert *19:* 189
Meyer, Renate *6:* 170
Meyers, Bob *11:* 136
Meyers, Nancy *172:* 124
Meynell, Louis *37:* 76
Micale, Albert *2:* 65; *22:* 185
Miccuci, Charles *82:* 163; *144:* 150
Micich, Paul *164:* 163
Middleton, Jeffrey *177:* 173
Middleton-Sandford, Betty *2:* 125
Mieke, Anne *45:* 74
Mighell, Patricia *43:* 134
Miglio, Paige *101:* 203; *151:* 223
Mikolaycak, Charles *9:* 144; *12:* 101; *13:* 212; *21:* 121; *22:* 168; *30:* 187; *34:* 103, 150; *37:* 183; *43:* 179; *44:* 90; *46:* 115, 118, 119; *49:* 25; *78:* 121, 122, 205, 207; *81:* 4
Milelli, Pascal *129:* 66; *135:* 153; *187:* 45
Miles, Elizabeth *117:* 77
Miles, Jennifer *17:* 278
Milgrim, David *158:* 157; *187:* 125, 126, 128
Milhous, Katherine *15:* 193; *17:* 51
Millais, John E. *22:* 230, 231
Millar, H.R. *YABC 1:* 194, 195, 203
Millard, C.E. *28:* 186
Millard, Kerry *105:* 124
Miller, Don *15:* 195; *16:* 71; *20:* 106; *31:* 178
Miller, Edna *29:* 148
Miller, Edward *115:* 64; *183:* 140, 141
Miller, Frank J. *25:* 94
Miller, Grambs *18:* 38; *23:* 16
Miller, Ian *99:* 128
Miller, Jane *15:* 196
Miller, Marcia *13:* 233
Miller, Marilyn *1:* 87; *31:* 69; *33:* 157
Miller, Mitchell *28:* 183; *34:* 207
Miller, Phil *175:* 150

Miller, Shane *5:* 140
Miller, Virginia *81:* 206
Millman, Isaac *172:* 18
Mills, Elaine *72:* 181
Mills, Judith Christine *130:* 168, 169
Mills, Lauren *92:* 170
Mills, Yaroslava Surmach *35:* 169, 170; *46:* 114
Millsap, Darrel *51:* 102
Milone, Karen *89:* 169
Milord, Susan *147:* 163, 164
Milton, Debbie *162:* 161
Mims, Ashley *51:* 170
Miner, Julia *98:* 69
Minor, Wendell *39:* 188; *52:* 87; *56:* 171; *58:* 116; *62:* 56; *66:* 109; *74:* 93; *78:* 129; *94:* 67; *117:* 12, 13; *124:* 84, 86; *136:* 121; *164:* 168, 169; *170:* 71
Minter, Daniel *176:* 154; *179:* 177
Mirocha, Paul *81:* 133; *192:* 148
Misako Rocks! *192:* 149, 150
Mitchell, Judith *109:* 117
Mitchell, Mark *91:* 208
Mitchell, Tracy *190:* 15
Mitgutsch, Ali *76:* 161
Mitsuhashi, Yoko *45:* 153
Miyake, Yoshi *38:* 141
Mizumura, Kazue *10:* 143; *18:* 223; *36:* 159
Mochi, Ugo *8:* 122; *38:* 150
Mock, Paul *55:* 83; *123:* 32
Modarressi, Mitra *90:* 236; *126:* 168; *173:* 165, 166
Modell, Frank *39:* 152
Mogenson, Jan *74:* 183
Mohn, Susan *89:* 224
Mohr, Mark *133:* 201
Mohr, Nicholasa *8:* 139; *113:* 127
Molan, Christine *60:* 177; *84:* 183
Moldon, Peter L. *49:* 168
Molk, Laurel *92:* 150
Momaday, N. Scott *48:* 159
Mombourquette, Paul *112:* 91; *126:* 142
Monk, Julie *165:* 231; *191:* 96
Monks, Lydia *189:* 136, 137
Montgomery, Lucy *150:* 126
Montgomery-Higham, Amanda *169:* 131
Montiel, David *69:* 106; *84:* 145
Montijo, Rhode *193:* 164
Montresor, Beni *2:* 91; *3:* 138; *38:* 152, 153, 154,155, 156, 157, 158, 159, 160; *68:* 63
Montserrat, Pep *128:* 135; *181:* 119; *184:* 53
Moon, Carl *25:* 183, 184, 185
Moon, Eliza *14:* 40
Moon, Ivan *22:* 39; *38:* 140
Moore, Adrienne *67:* 147
Moore, Agnes Kay Randall *43:* 187
Moore, Cyd *117:* 107, 108; *159:* 137, 138; *186:* 148, 149, 151
Moore, Gustav *127:* 181, 182; *170:* 162, 163
Moore, Jackie *128:* 79
Moore, Janet *63:* 153
Moore, Margie *176:* 156
Moore, Mary *29:* 160
Moore, Patrick *184:* 121
Moore, Yvette *101:* 11, 12; *154:* 141
Mora, Giovanni *179:* 127; *184:* 11
Mora, Raul Mina *20:* 41
Moraes, Odilon *102:* 144
Morales, Yuyi *154:* 144
Moran, Rosslyn *111:* 26
Moran, Tom *60:* 100
Mordan, C.B. *193:* 115
Mordvinoff, Nicolas *15:* 179
Moreno, René King *169:* 59; *190:* 133, 209
Morgan, Barbara *169:* 116
Morgan, Jacqui *58:* 57
Morgan, Mary *114:* 133, 134, 135; *123:* 11
Morgan, Tom *42:* 157
Morgan, Pierr *173:* 148
Morgenstern, Michael *158:* 7, 57; *171:* 103; *174:* 60

Morice, Dave *93:* 142
Morin, Paul *73:* 132; *79:* 130; *88:* 140; *137:* 143
Moriuchi, Mique *177:* 203
Morozumi, Atsuko *110:* 155
Morrill, Leslie *18:* 218; *29:* 177; *33:* 84; *38:* 147; *42:* 127; *44:* 93; *48:* 164, 165, 167, 168, 169, 170,171; *49:* 162; *63:* 136, 180; *70:* 72; *71:* 70, 91,92; *72:* 228; *80:* 163, 164, 165; *90:* 121; *121:* 88; *178:* 117
Morrill, Rowena A. *84:* 16; *98:* 163
Morris *47:* 91
Morris, Frank *55:* 133; *60:* 28; *76:* 2
Morris, Harry O. *119:* 138
Morris, Jackie *128:* 194; *144:* 119; *151:* 146
Morris, Jennifer E. *179:* 157
Morris, Oradel Nolen *128:* 180
Morris, Tony *62:* 146; *70:* 97
Morrison, Bill *42:* 116; *66:* 170; *69:* 40
Morrison, Gordon *87:* 150; *113:* 93; *128:* 181, 182; *183:* 144, 145, 146
Morrison, Frank *169:* 162
Morrison, Taylor *159:* 144, 145; *187:* 131
Morrow, Gray *2:* 64; *5:* 200; *10:* 103, 114; *14:* 175
Morton, Lee Jack *32:* 140
Morton, Marian *3:* 185
Mosberg, Hilary *117:* 195; *118:* 164; *149:* 55
Moser, Barry *56:* 68, 117, 118, 119, 120, 121, 122, 123, 124; *59:* 141; *60:* 160; *79:* 91, 147, 149, 151, 152; *82:* 81; *90:* 118; *91:* 35; *95:* 210; *97:* 91, 93; *102:* 152; *126:* 4; *128:* 175; *133:* 141; *138:* 167, 171, 174; *153:* 205; *174:* 130; *185:* 152, 154
Moser, Cara *90:* 118; *138:* 167
Moses, Grandma *18:* 228
Moses, Will *178:* 170, 171
Moskof, Martin Stephen *27:* 152
Mosley, Francis *57:* 144
Moss, Donald *11:* 184
Moss, Geoffrey *32:* 198
Moss, Marissa *71:* 130; *104:* 127; *163:* 156
Most, Bernard *48:* 173; *91:* 142, 143; *134:* 120
Mowll, Joshua *188:* 133
Mowry, Carmen *50:* 62
Moxley, Sheila *96:* 174; *169:* 26
Moyers, William *21:* 65
Moyler, Alan *36:* 142
Mozley, Charles *9:* 87; *20:* 176, 192, 193; *22:* 228; *25:* 205; *33:* 150; *43:* 170, 171, 172, 173, 174; *YABC2:* 89
Mueller, Hans Alexander *26:* 64; *27:* 52, 53
Mugnaini, Joseph *11:* 35; *27:* 52, 53; *35:* 62
Mujica, Rick *72:* 67; *88:* 95; *111:* 53; *180:* 185
Mullen, Douglas *180:* 178
Muller, Robin *86:* 161
Muller, Steven *32:* 167
Muller, Jorg *35:* 215; *67:* 138, 139
Mulock, Julie *163:* 112
Mullins, Edward S. *10:* 101
Mullins, Patricia *51:* 68
Multer, Scott *80:* 108
Munari, Bruno *15:* 200
Munch, Edvard *140:* 143
Munowitz, Ken *14:* 148; *72:* 178, 179
Munro, Roxie *58:* 134; *136:* 177; *137:* 218; *184:* 133, 134
Munsinger, Lynn *33:* 161; *46:* 126; *71:* 92; *82:* 80; *89:* 218; *92:* 125; *94:* 157, 158, 159, 160; *98:* 196; *103:* 198; *142:* 143; *145:* 133, 134, 136; *153:* 203; *176:* 162; *177:* 140, 141, 142; *189:* 113, 114, 116, 117
Munson, Russell *13:* 9
Munster, Sebastian *166:* 107
Munoz, William *42:* 160
Munzar, Barbara *149:* 75
Murdocca, Salvatore *73:* 212; *98:* 132; *111:* 168; *157:* 228; *164:* 257
Murphy, Bill *5:* 138; *130:* 170
Murphy, Jill *37:* 142; *70:* 166; *142:* 132, 134

Murphy, Kelly *130:* 212; *143:* 119; *176:* 158; *190:* 135
Murphy, Tom *192:* 40
Murr, Karl *20:* 62
Murray, Joe *175:* 37
Murray, Ossie *43:* 176
Mussino, Attilio *29:* 131; *100:* 164
Mutchler, Dwight *1:* 25
Myers, Bernice *9:* 147; *36:* 75; *81:* 146, 147, 148
Muth, Jon J. *165:* 169; *167:* 109; *190:* 227; *193:* 59
Myers, Christopher *183:* 150; *193:* 139
Myers, Duane O. *99:* 145
Myers, Tim *147:* 168
Myers, V.G. *142:* 41
Myers, Lou *11:* 2

N

Nachreiner, Tom *29:* 182
Nacht, Merle *65:* 49
Nadler, Ellis *88:* 91
Nagle, Shane *180:* 223
Najaka, Marlies *62:* 101
Nakai, Michael *30:* 217; *54:* 29
Nakata, Hiroe *157:* 156; *162:* 30
Nakatani, Chiyoko *12:* 124
Narahashi, Keiko *77:* 188; *82:* 213; *115:* 142, 143, 144
Nascimbene, Yan *133:* 128; *173:* 132, 133
Nash, Lesa *87:* 135
Nash, Linell *46:* 175
Nash, Scott *130:* 36; *188:* 196
Naso, John *33:* 183
Nason, Thomas W. *14:* 68
Nasser, Muriel *48:* 74
Nast, Thomas *21:* 29; *28:* 23; *51:* 132, 133, 134, 135,136, 137, 138, 139, 141
Nasta, Vincent *78:* 185
Natale, Vincent *76:* 3; *78:* 125; *112:* 47; *166:* 81; *174:* 189; *185:* 212
Natchev, Alexi *96:* 177
Nathan, Charlott *125:* 151
Nathan, Cheryl *150:* 104; *186:* 112
Natti, Susanna *20:* 146; *32:* 141, 142; *35:* 178; *37:* 143; *71:* 49; *93:* 98; *125:* 166, 168; *126:* 228; *151:* 6; *178:* 8; *188:* 106
Navarra, Celeste Scala *8:* 142
Naylor, Penelope *10:* 104
Nazz, James *72:* 8
Nebel, M. *45:* 154
Neebe, William *7:* 93
Needler, Jerry *12:* 93
Neel, Alice *31:* 23
Neely, Beth *119:* 184
Neely, Keith R. *46:* 124
Neff, Leland *78:* 74
Negri, Rocco *3:* 213; *5:* 67; *6:* 91, 108; *12:* 159
Negrin, Fabian *174:* 125; *175:* 15
Neidigh, Sherry *128:* 53
Neilan, Eujin Kim *180:* 241
Neill, John R. *18:* 8, 10, 11, 21, 30; *100:* 22
Neilsen, Cliff *158:* 131; *177:* 112, 121
Neilsen, Terese *116:* 74
Nelson, Craig *62:* 151; 153; *183:* 86
Nelson, Gail White *68:* 140
Nelson, Jennifer *129:* 152
Nelson, Kadir *151:* 185; *154:* 146, 147; *157:* 189, 222; *181:* 122, 124
Nelson, S.D. *131:* 34; *181:* 126, 127
Ness, Evaline *1:* 164, 165; *2:* 39; *3:* 8; *10:* 147; *12:* 53; *26:* 150, 151, 152, 153; *49:* 30, 31, 32; *56:* 30; *60:* 113
Neubecker, Robert *170:* 143
Neville, Vera *2:* 182
Nevins, Daniel *191:* 173
Nevwirth, Allan *79:* 168

Newberry, Clare Turlay *1:* 170
Newbold, Greg *108:* 125; *145:* 199; *151:* 23; *193:* 178
Newfeld, Frank *14:* 121; *26:* 154
Newman, Andy *149:* 61
Newman, Ann *43:* 90
Newman, Barbara Johansen *191:* 137, 138
Newsham, Ian *143:* 162
Newsom, Carol *40:* 159; *44:* 60; *47:* 189; *65:* 29; *70:* 192; *80:* 36; *85:* 137, 138; *92:* 167; *191:* 82
Newsom, Tom *49:* 149; *71:* 13, 62; *75:* 156; *91:* 113
Newton, Jill *83:* 105
Ng, Michael *29:* 171
Ng, Simon *167:* 7
Nguyen, Vincent *189:* 49
Nicholson, William *15:* 33, 34; *16:* 48
Nickens, Bessie *104:* 153
Nicklaus, Carol *45:* 194; *62:* 132, 133
Nickle, John *181:* 128
Nickless, Will *16:* 139
Nicholas, Corasue *154:* 20
Nicolas *17:* 130, 132, 133; *YABC 2:* 215
Niebrugge, Jane *6:* 118
Nielsen, Jon *6:* 100; *24:* 202
Nielsen, Kay *15:* 7; *16:* 211, 212, 213, 215, 217; *22:* 143; *YABC 1:* 32, 33
Nielson, Cliff *95:* 207, 208; *105:* 58; *114:* 112; *124:* 12; *125:* 91, 92; *132:* 224; *135:* 187; *136:* 40; *137:* 168; *145:* 54; *149:* 28; *158:* 129; *165:* 64, 158; *168:* 169; *170:* 6; *175:* 114, 116; *187:* 75, 76
Niemann, Christoph *191:* 141
Nikola-Lisa, W. *180:* 180
Niland, Deborah *25:* 191; *27:* 156; *135:* 50; *172:* 143
Niland, Kilmeny *25:* 191; *75:* 143
Nino, Alex *59:* 145
Ninon *1:* 5; *38:* 101, 103, 108
Nissen, Rie *44:* 35
Nithael, Mark *158:* 237
Nivola, Claire A. *78:* 126; *140:* 147
Nixon, K. *14:* 152
Noble, Louise *61:* 170
Noble, Marty *97:* 168; *125:* 171
Noble, Trinka Hakes *39:* 162; *84:* 157
Noda, Takayo *168:* 143
Noguchi, Yoshie *30:* 99
Nolan, Dennis *42:* 163; *67:* 163; *78:* 189; *82:* 225; *83:* 26; *92:* 169, 170; *103:* 166; *111:* 35; *112:* 213; *127:* 171; *166:* 161
Noll, Sally *82:* 171
Nolte, Larry *121:* 63, 65
Nones, Eric Jon *61:* 111; *76:* 38; *77:* 177
Noonan, Daniel *100:* 224
Noonan, Julia *4:* 163; *7:* 207; *25:* 151; *91:* 29; *95:* 149
Norcia, Ernie *108:* 155; *140:* 47
Nordenskjold, Birgitta *2:* 208
Noreika, Robert *173:* 20
Norling, Beth *149:* 153, 154
Norman, Elaine *77:* 72, 176; *94:* 35; *136:* 63; *178:* 42
Norman, Mary *36:* 138, 147
Norman, Michael *12:* 117; *27:* 168
Northway, Jennifer *85:* 96
Nostlinger, Christiana *162:* 131
Novak, Linda *166:* 205
Novak, Matt *104:* 132, 133; *165:* 173, 174
Novelli, Luca *61:* 137
Nugent, Cynthia *106:* 189
Numeroff, Laura Joffe *28:* 161; *30:* 177
Nurse, Chris *164:* 91
Nussbaumer, Paul *16:* 219; *39:* 117
Nutt, Ken *72:* 69; *97:* 170
Nyce, Helene *19:* 219
Nygren, Tord *30:* 148; *127:* 164

O

Oakley, Graham *8:* 112; *30:* 164, 165; *84:* 188,189, 190, 191, 192
Oakley, Thornton *YABC 2:* 189
Oberheide, Heide *118:* 37
Obligado, Lilian *2:* 28, 66, 67; *6:* 30; *14:* 179; *15:* 103; *25:* 84; *61:* 138, 139, 140, 141, 143
Oblinski, Rafael *190:* 139
Obrant, Susan *11:* 186
O'Brien, Anne Sibley *53:* 116, 117; *155:* 115
O'Brien, John *41:* 253; *72:* 12; *89:* 59, 60; *98:* 16; *161:* 185; *169:* 16; *180:* 196
O'Brien, Patrick *193:* 142, 143, 144
O'Brien, Teresa *87:* 89
O'Brien, Tim *93:* 25; *136:* 94; *164:* 57; *169:* 57; *173:* 55; *175:* 86; *184:* 192; *191:* 134; *193:* 137
O'Clair, Dennis *127:* 25
O'Connor, George *183:* 153
Odell, Carole *35:* 47
Odem, Mel *99:* 164; *167:* 84, 87
O'Donohue, Thomas *40:* 89
Oechsli, Kelly *5:* 144, 145; *7:* 115; *8:* 83, 183; *13:* 117; *20:* 94; *81:* 199
Offen, Hilda *42:* 207
Ogden, Bill *42:* 59; *47:* 55
Ogg, Oscar *33:* 34
Ogle, Nancy Gray *163:* 144
Ohi, Ruth *90:* 175, 177; *131:* 63; *135:* 106; *175:* 107; *179:* 55
Ohlsson, Ib *4:* 152; *7:* 57; *10:* 20; *11:* 90; *19:* 217; *41:* 246; *82:* 106; *92:* 213
Ohtomo, Yasuo *37:* 146; *39:* 212, 213
O'Keefe, Jennifer *136:* 184
O'Kelley, Mattie Lou *36:* 150
Olbinski, Rafal *149:* 27; *158:* 77
Oliver, Isaac *171:* 182
Oliver, Jenni *23:* 121; *35:* 112
Oliver, Narelle *152:* 192
Oller, Erika *128:* 186; *134:* 126
Olschewski, Alfred *7:* 172
Olsen, Ib Spang *6:* 178, 179; *81:* 164
Olson, Alan *77:* 229
Olson-Brown, Ellen *183:* 154
Olugebefola, Ademola *15:* 205
O'Malley, Kevin *94:* 180; *106:* 8; *113:* 108; *136:* 70; *157:* 193; *191:* 146
O'Neil, Dan IV *7:* 176
O'Neill, Catharine *72:* 113; *84:* 78; *134:* 153
O'Neill, Jean *22:* 146
O'Neill, Martin *187:* 39
O'Neill, Michael J. *54:* 172
O'Neill, Rose *48:* 30, 31
O'Neill, Steve *21:* 118
Ono, Chiyo *7:* 97
Orbaan, Albert *2:* 31; *5:* 65, 171; *9:* 8; *14:* 241; *20:* 109
Orbach, Ruth *21:* 112
Orfe, Joan *20:* 81
Org, Ed *119:* 93
Ormai, Stella *72:* 129
Ormerod, Jan *55:* 124; *70:* 170, 171; *90:* 39; *132:* 172, 173, 174; *147:* 98
Ormsby, Virginia H. *11:* 187
O'Rourke, Ericka *108:* 216; *117:* 194; *111:* 142; *119:* 194; *137:* 152; *150:* 134; *167:* 64; *172:* 164; *188:* 163; *191:* 172
O'Rourke, Ericka Meltzer
  See O'Rourke, Ericka
Orozco, Jose Clemente *9:* 177
Orr, Forrest W. *23:* 9
Orr, N. *19:* 70
Ortiz, Vilma *88:* 158
Osborn, Cathy *152:* 232
Osborn, Robert *65:* 49
Osborne, Billie Jean *35:* 209
Osmond, Edward *10:* 111
O'Sullivan, Tom *3:* 176; *4:* 55; *78:* 195
Otani, June *124:* 42; *156:* 53

Otis, Rebecca *185:* 92
Ottley, Matt *147:* 221; *171:* 133
Otto, Svend *22:* 130, 141; *67:* 188, 189
Oudry, J.B. *18:* 167
Oughton, Taylor *5:* 23; *104:* 136
Overeng, Johannes *44:* 36
Overlie, George *11:* 156
Owens, Carl *2:* 35; *23:* 521
Owens, Gail *10:* 170; *12:* 157; *19:* 16; *22:* 70; *25:* 81; *28:* 203, 205; *32:* 221, 222; *36:* 132; *46:* 40; *47:* 57; *54:* 66, 67, 68, 69, 70, 71, 72, 73; *71:* 100; *73:* 64; *77:* 157; *80:* 32; *82:* 3; *99:* 226
Owens, Mary Beth *113:* 202, 203; *191:* 148, 149
Owens, Nubia *84:* 74
Oxenbury, Helen *3:* 150, 151; *24:* 81; *68:* 174, 175,176; *81:* 209; *84:* 213, 245; *129:* 56; *149:* 159; *184:* 181
Oz, Robin *88:* 167; *185:* 181

P

Padgett, Jim *12:* 165
Page, Homer *14:* 145
Page, Mark *162:* 70
Paget, Sidney *24:* 90, 91, 93, 95, 97
Paget, Walter *64:* 122
Paillot, Jim *173:* 89
Pajouhesh, Noushin *160:* 121
Pak *12:* 76
Pak, Yu Cha *86:* 174
Paladino, Lance *134:* 30
Palazzo, Tony *3:* 152, 153
Palecek, Josef *56:* 136; *89:* 158
Palen, Debbie *135:* 88
Palencar, John Jude *84:* 12, 45; *85:* 87; *92:* 187; *99:* 128; *110:* 204; *150:* 122; *171:* 86
Palin, Nicki *81:* 201; *89:* 161
Palladini, David *4:* 113; *40:* 176, 177, 178, 179, 181,224, 225; *50:* 138; *78:* 186
Pallarito, Don *43:* 36
Palmer, Carol *158:* 230
Palmer, Heidi *15:* 207; *29:* 102
Palmer, Jan *42:* 153; *82:* 161
Palmer, Judd *153:* 160, 161
Palmer, Juliette *6:* 89; *15:* 208
Palmer, Kate Salley *104:* 143; *154:* 169
Palmer, Lemuel *17:* 25, 29
Palmisciano, Diane *110:* 62; *162:* 26
Palmquist, Eric *38:* 133
Panesis, Nicholas *3:* 127
Panter, Gary *182:* 191
Panton, Doug *52:* 99
Paparone, Pamela *129:* 174
Papas, William *11:* 223; *50:* 160
Papin, Joseph *26:* 113
Papish, Robin Lloyd *10:* 80
Paradis, Susan *40:* 216
Paraquin, Charles H. *18:* 166
Paris, Peter *31:* 127
Parisi, Elizabeth B. *141:* 82; *164:* 57
Park, Nick *113:* 143
Park, Seho *39:* 110
Park, W.B. *22:* 189
Parker, Ant *82:* 87, 88; *104:* 121
Parker, Lewis *2:* 179
Parker, Nancy Winslow *10:* 113; *22:* 164; *28:* 47, 144; *52:* 7; *69:* 153; *91:* 171, 174; *132:* 175
Parker, Robert *4:* 161; *5:* 74; *9:* 136; *29:* 39
Parker, Robert Andrew *11:* 81; *29:* 186; *39:* 165; *40:* 25; *41:* 78; *42:* 123; *43:* 144; *48:* 182; *54:* 140; *74:* 141; *91:* 24; *111:* 115; *151:* 201; *154:* 156
Parker-Rees, Guy *149:* 145; *193:* 149, 150
Parkin, Trevor *140:* 151
Parkins, David *114:* 123; *146:* 176; *176:* 168; *192:* 107

Parkinson, Kathy *71:* 143; *144:* 234
Parkinson, Keith *70:* 66
Parks, Gordon, Jr. *33:* 228
Parnall, Peter *5:* 137; *16:* 221; *24:* 70; *40:* 78; *51:* 130; *69:* 17, 155; *136:* 22, 23, 24
Parnall, Virginia *40:* 78
Parow, Lorraine *158:* 127
Parr, Todd *134:* 139, 140; *179:* 163, 164, 165
Parrish, Anne *27:* 159, 160
Parrish, Dillwyn *27:* 159
Parrish, Maxfield *14:* 160, 161, 164, 165; *16:* 109; *18:* 12, 13; *YABC 1:* 149, 152, 267; *2:* 146, 149
Parry, David *26:* 156
Parry, Marian *13:* 176; *19:* 179
Partch, Virgil *45:* 163, 165
Pascal, David *14:* 174
Paschkis, Julie *177:* 153, 154
Pasquier, J.A. *16:* 91
Pasternak, Robert *119:* 53
Paterson, Diane *13:* 116; *39:* 163; *59:* 164, 165, 166,167; *72:* 51, 53; *129:* 175; *177:* 156, 157
Paterson, Helen *16:* 93
Patkau, Karen *112:* 123
Paton, Jane *15:* 271; *35:* 176
Patrick, John *139:* 190
Patrick, Pamela *90:* 160; *93:* 211; *105:* 12
Patrick, Tom *190:* 103
Patterson, Geoffrey *54:* 75
Patterson, Robert *25:* 118
Patti, Joyce *187:* 145, 146
Patz, Nancy *111:* 40; *154:* 161
Paul, James *4:* 130; *23:* 161
Paul, Korky *102:* 85
Paull, Grace *24:* 157; *87:* 127
Paulsen, Ruth Wright *79:* 160, 164; *189:* 146
Pavlov, Elena *80:* 49
Payne, Adam S. *135:* 166
Payne, C.F. *145:* 138, 140; *179:* 168
Payne, Joan Balfour *1:* 118
Payne, Tom *170:* 27
Payson, Dale *7:* 34; *9:* 151; *20:* 140; *37:* 22
Payzant, Charles *21:* 147
Peacock, Ralph *64:* 118
Peake, Mervyn *22:* 136, 149; *23:* 162, 163, 164; *YABC2:* 307
Pearson, Larry *38:* 225
Pearson, Tracey Campbell *64:* 163, 164, 167, 168, 169; *118:* 51; *156:* 169, 171, 172; *163:* 140
Peat, Fern B. *16:* 115
Peck, Anne Merriman *18:* 241; *24:* 155
Peck, Beth *66:* 242; *79:* 166; *80:* 136; *91:* 34; *95:* 9; *101:* 77; *164:* 197; *190:* 170
Pedersen, Janet *193:* 152
Pedersen, Judy *66:* 217; *121:* 36; *172:* 67
Pedersen, Vilhelm *YABC 1:* 40
Pederson, Sharleen *12:* 92
Pedlar, Elaine *161:* 45
Peek, Merle *39:* 168
Peet, Bill *2:* 203; *41:* 159, 160, 161, 162, 163; *78:* 158, 159, 160, 161
Peguero, Adrian *116:* 133
Peguero, Gerard *116:* 133
Pels, Winslow Pinney *55:* 126
Peltier, Leslie C. *13:* 178
Penberthy, Mark *171:* 78
Pendle, Alexy *7:* 159; *13:* 34; *29:* 161; *33:* 215; *86:* 62
Pendola, Joanne *76:* 203; *81:* 125; *105:* 181; *178:* 152, 153
Pene du Bois, William *4:* 70; *10:* 122; *26:* 61; *27:* 145, 211; *35:* 243; *41:* 216; *68:* 180, 181; *73:* 45
Penfound, David *102:* 185
Pennington, Eunice *27:* 162
Peppe, Mark *28:* 142
Peppe, Rodney *4:* 164, 165; *74:* 187, 188, 189
Pepper, Hubert *64:* 143
Percy, Graham *63:* 2

Pericoli, Matteo *178:* 177
Perini, Ben *173:* 77
Perkins, David *60:* 68
Perkins, Lucy Fitch *72:* 199
Perkins, Lynne Rae *172:* 146
Perl, Susan *2:* 98; *4:* 231; *5:* 44, 45, 118; *6:* 199; *8:* 137; *12:* 88; *22:* 193; *34:* 54, 55; *52:* 128; *YABC 1:* 176
Perrone, Donna *78:* 166
Perry, Marie Fritz *165:* 180
Perry, Patricia *29:* 137; *30:* 171
Perry, Roger *27:* 163
Perske, Martha *46:* 83; *51:* 108, 147
Persson, Stina *175:* 166
Pesek, Ludek *15:* 237
Petach, Heidi *149:* 166
Peters, David *72:* 205; *182:* 116
Petersen, Jeff *181:* 95
Petersham, Maud *17:* 108, 147, 148, 149, 150, 151, 152, 153
Petersham, Miska *17:* 108, 147, 148, 149, 150, 151, 152, 153
Peterson, Eric *109:* 125
Peterson, Nisse *99:* 27
Peterson, R.F. *7:* 101
Peterson, Russell *7:* 130
Petie, Haris *2:* 3; *10:* 41, 118; *11:* 227; *12:* 70
Petricic, Dusan *153:* 75, 76, 77; *170:* 12; *172:* 13; *176:* 170; *179:* 56
Petrides, Heidrun *19:* 223
Petrone, Valeria *159:* 160; *171:* 92; *186:* 173
Petrosino, Tamara *177:* 40; *193:* 154, 155
Petruccio, Steven James *67:* 159; *127:* 5
Pettingill, Ondre *64:* 181; *70:* 64
Peyo *40:* 56, 57
Peyton, K.M. *15:* 212
Pfeifer, Herman *15:* 262
Pfister, Marcus *83:* 165, 166, 167; *146:* 152; *150:* 160
Pfloog, Jan *124:* 60
Pham, LeUyen *160:* 48; *175:* 154, 156; *179:* 149
Phelan, Matt *182:* 160; *184:* 222
Phillips, Craig *70:* 151
Phillips, Douglas *1:* 19
Phillips, F.D. *6:* 202
Phillips, Louise *133:* 67
Phillips, Matt *184:* 173
Phillips, Thomas *30:* 55
Philpot, Glyn *54:* 46
Phiz
   See Browne, Hablot K.
Piatti, Celestino *16:* 223
Pica, Steve *115:* 181
Picarella, Joseph *13:* 147
Picart, Gabriel *121:* 165
Pichon, Liz *174:* 139
Pickard, Charles *12:* 38; *18:* 203; *36:* 152
Picken, George A. *23:* 150
Pickens, David *22:* 156
Pienkowski, Jan *6:* 183; *30:* 32; *58:* 140, 141, 142,143, 146, 147; *73:* 3; *87:* 156, 157; *131:* 189
Pignataro, Anna *163:* 220 *Pileggi, Steve 145:* 122
Pilkey, Dav *68:* 186; *115:* 164, 166; *166:* 173, 174, 175
Pimlott, John *10:* 205
Pincus, Harriet *4:* 186; *8:* 179; *22:* 148; *27:* 164, 165; *66:* 202
Pini, Wendy *89:* 166
Pinkett, Neil *60:* 8
Pinkney, Brian *81:* 184, 185; *94:* 107; *113:* 146, 147; *117:* 121, 166; *132:* 145; *158:* 108, 191; *160:* 189
Pinkney, Jerry *8:* 218; *10:* 40; *15:* 276; *20:* 66; *24:* 121; *33:* 109; *36:* 222; *38:* 200; *41:* 165, 166, 167, 168, 169, 170, 171, 173, 174; *44:* 198; *48:* 51; *53:* 20; *56:* 61, 68; *58:* 184; *60:* 59; *61:* 91; *71:* 146, 148, 149; *72:* 17; *73:*

149; *74:* 159,192; *75:* 45; *80:* 206; *81:* 44; *85:* 144; *95:* 50; *107:* 158, 159, 160; *108:* 164; *112:* 114, 115; *133:* 58
Pinkwater, Daniel Manus *46:* 180, 181, 182, 185, 188, 189, 190; *151:* 161 *76:* 178, 179, 180
Pinkwater, Manus *8:* 156; *46:* 180
   See also Pinkwater, Daniel Manus
Pinkwater, Jill *114:* 160, 161; *158:* 179; *188:* 143, 145, 146
Pinto, Ralph *10:* 131; *45:* 93
Pinon, Mark *74:* 22
Piven, Hanoch *173:* 142
Pistolesi *73:* 211
Pitcairn, Ansel *188:* 10
Pittman, Helena Clare *71:* 151
Pitz, Henry C. *4:* 168; *19:* 165; *35:* 128; *42:* 80; *YABC 2:* 95, 176
Pitzenberger, Lawrence J. *26:* 94
Pitzer, Susanna *181:* 131
Player, Stephen *82:* 190
Plecas, Jennifer *84:* 201; *106:* 124; *149:* 168
Ploog, Mike *180:* 19
Plowden, David *52:* 135, 136
Plume, Ilse *170:* 149
Plummer, William *32:* 31
Podevin, Jean François *184:* 185
Podwal, Mark *56:* 170, 173; *101:* 154, 155, 157; *149:* 176; *160:* 194
Pogany, Willy *15:* 46, 49; *19:* 222, 256; *25:* 214; *44:* 142, 143, 144, 145, 146, 147, 148
Pohrt, Tom *67:* 116; *104:* 80; *152:* 199
Poirson, V.A. *26:* 89
Polacco, Patricia *74:* 195, 196, 197, 198; *123:* 121, 122, 123; *180:* 189, 190, 191, 193, 194
Polgreen, John *21:* 44
Politi, Leo *1:* 178; *4:* 53; *21:* 48; *47:* 173,174, 176, 178, 179, 180, 181
Pollema-Cahill, Phyllis *123:* 126
Pollen, Samson *64:* 80
Polonsky, Arthur *34:* 168
Polseno, Jo *1:* 53; *3:* 117; *5:* 114; *17:* 154; *20:* 87; *32:* 49; *41:* 245
Pomaska, Anna *117:* 148
Pons, Bernadette *184:* 100
Ponter, James *5:* 204
Poole, Colin *111:* 27
Poortvliet, Rien *6:* 212; *65:* 165, 166, 167
Pope, Kevin *183:* 158
Popp, Wendy *72:* 122; *158:* 68
Poppel, Hans *71:* 154, 155
Porfirio, Guy *76:* 134
Portal, Colette *6:* 186; *11:* 203
Porter, George *7:* 181
Porter, Janice Lee *136:* 175; *164:* 37
Porter, John *113:* 47
Porter, Pat Grant *84:* 112; *125:* 101
Porter, Sue *146:* 246, 247
Porter, Walter *124:* 175
Posada, Mia *187:* 151
Posen, Michael *175:* 82
Posthuma, Sieb *150:* 163
Postma, Lidia *79:* 17
Potter, Beatrix *100:* 194, 195; *132:* 179, 180, 181, 182; *YABC 1:* 208, 209, 210, 212, 213
Potter, Giselle *117:* 123; *143:* 44; *144:* 170, 197; *149:* 7; *150:* 165; *187:* 152, 153; *190:* 198
Potter, Katherine *104:* 147; *171:* 135; *173:* 136
Potter, Miriam Clark *3:* 162
Poulin, Stephane *98:* 140, 141
Poullis, Nick *146:* 210
Powell, Constance Buffington *174:* 141
Powell, Gary *151:* 208
Powell, Ivan *67:* 219
Power, Margaret *105:* 122
Powers, Daniel *161:* 173
Powers, Richard M. *1:* 230; *3:* 218; *7:* 194; *26:* 186
Powledge, Fred *37:* 154
Powzyk, Joyce *74:* 214

Poydar, Nancy *96:* 149; *190:* 180, 181, 182
Pracher, Richard *91:* 166
Prachaticka, Marketa *126:* 126
Prange, Beckie *181:* 169
Prap, Lila *177:* 165
Prater, John *103:* 142, 143, 144; *149:* 172
Pratt, Charles *23:* 29
Pratt, George *116:* 208
Pratt, Pierre *150:* 73; *166:* 183; *168:* 172
Prebenna, David *73:* 174
Preiss-Glasser, Robin *123:* 176; *152* 40; *172:* 194
Press, Jenny *116:* 95
Preston, Mark *152:* 162
Pretro, Korinna *91:* 126
Price, Christine *2:* 247; *3:* 163, 253; *8:* 166
Price, Cynthia *118:* 156
Price, Edward *33:* 34
Price, Garrett *1:* 76; *2:* 42
Price, Hattie Longstreet *17:* 13
Price, Norman *YABC 1:* 129
Price, Willard *48:* 184
Priceman, Marjorie *81:* 171; *136:* 169; *156:* 200; *168:* 153, 154; *188:* 45
Priestley, Alice *168:* 33
Primavera, Elise *26:* 95; *58:* 151; *73:* 37; *80:* 79; *86:* 156; *105:* 161
Primrose, Jean *36:* 109
Prince, Alison *86:* 188, 189
Prince, Leonora E. *7:* 170
Pritchett, Shelley *116:* 148
Prittie, Edwin J. *YABC 1:* 120
Proimos, James *176:* 4
Proimos, John *173:* 144
Prosmitsky, Jenya *132:* 33
Provensen, Alice *37:* 204, 215, 222; *70:* 176, 177, 178, 180, *71:* 213; *147:* 184; *191:* 190
Provensen, Martin *37:* 204, 215, 222; *70:* 176, 177, 178, 180; *71:* 213; *191:* 190
Pucci, Albert John *44:* 154
Pudlo *8:* 59
Pulver, Harry, Jr. *129:* 159
Pulver, Robin *160:* 4
Punchatz, Don *99:* 57
Purdy, Susan *8:* 162
Pursell, Weimer *55:* 18
Purtscher, Alfons *97:* 6
Puskas, James *5:* 141
Pyk, Jan *7:* 26; *38:* 123
Pyle, Chuck *99:* 149; *191:* 83
Pyle, Howard *16:* 225, 226, 227, 228, 230, 231, 232, 235; *24:* 27; *34:* 124, 125, 127, 128; *59:* 132; *100:* 198

Q

Quackenbush, Robert *4:* 190; *6:* 166; *7:* 175, 178; *9:* 86; *11:* 65, 221; *41:* 154; *43:* 157; *70:* 185, 186; *71:* 137; *85:* 47; *92:* 148; *133:* 154, 164, 169
Qualls, Sean *177:* 167, 168; *193:* 43
Quennell, Marjorie (Courtney) *29:* 163, 164
Quidor, John *19:* 82
Quirk, John *62:* 170
Quirk, Thomas *12:* 81

R

Rackham, Arthur *15:* 32, 78, 214-227; *17:* 105, 115; *18:* 233; *19:* 254; *20:* 151; *22:* 129, 131, 132, 133; *23:* 175; *24:* 161, 181; *26:* 91; *32:* 118; *64:* 18; *100:* 9, 16, 203, 204; *YABC 1:* 25, 45, 55, 147; *2:* 103, 142, 173, 210
Racz, Michael *56:* 134
Raczka, Bob *191:* 155, 156

Radcliffe, Andrew *82:* 215
Rader, Laura *101:* 219
Radunsky, Vladimir *177:* 170; *192:* 30
Rafilson, Sidney *11:* 172
Raglin, Tim *125:* 24
Raible, Alton *1:* 202, 203; *28:* 193; *35:* 181; *110:* 207
Raine, Patricia *82:* 74; *88:* 154
Ramá, Sue *173:* 45; *185:* 186; *190:* 184
Ramhorst, John *117:* 11
Ramirez, Gladys *177:* 19
Ramsey, James *16:* 41
Ramsey, Marcy Dunn *82:* 11; *180:* 186
Ramus, Michael *51:* 171
Rand, Paul *6:* 188
Rand, Ted *67:* 9, 10, 121, 123; *74:* 190; *84:* 170; *103:* 170; *112:* 6; *114:* 73; *139:* 168; *143:* 194; *156:* 154; *161:* 9, 10
Randazzo, Tony *81:* 98
Randell, William *55:* 54
Rane, Walter *93:* 144; *143:* 109; *184:* 126
Rankin, Joan *163:* 40
Rankin, Laura *176:* 173, 174; *179:* 150
Ransome, Arthur *22:* 201
Ransome, James E. *74:* 137; *75:* 80; *84:* 181; *94:* 108; *117:* 115; *123:* 128, 129, 130; *158:* 101, 102; *159:* 205; *178:* 188, 189, 190
Rantz, Don *119:* 184
Rao, Anthony *28:* 126
Raphael, Elaine *23:* 192; *71:* 24, 25
Rappaport, Eva *6:* 190
Raschka, Chris *80:* 187, 189, 190; *97:* 211; *115:* 210; *117:* 151, 152, 153, 154; *143:* 195; *145:* 153; *166:* 190, 191; *170:* 114
Rash, Andy *158:* 178; *162:* 172
Raskin, Ellen *2:* 208, 209; *4:* 142; *13:* 183; *22:* 68; *29:* 139; *36:* 134; *38:* 173, 174, 175, 176, 177, 178,179, 180, 181; *60:* 163; *86:* 81
Rathmann, Peggy *93:* 32; *94:* 168; *157:* 212, 214
Ratkus, Tony *77:* 133
Ratzkin, Lawrence *40:* 143
Rau, Margaret *9:* 157
Raverat, Gwen *YABC 1:* 152
Ravid, Joyce *61:* 73
Ravielli, Anthony *1:* 198; *3:* 168; *11:* 143
Ravilious, Robin *77:* 169
Rawlins, Donna *72:* 198; *73:* 15, 129
Rawlins, Janet *76:* 79
Rawlings, Steve *143:* 139; *151:* 54
Rawlinson, Debbie *75:* 132
Ray, Deborah Kogan *8:* 164; *29:* 238; *50:* 112, 113; *62:* 119; *78:* 191
Ray, Jane *96:* 166; *97:* 104; *152:* 208; *190:* 221
Ray, Ralph *2:* 239; *5:* 73
Rayann, Omar *162:* 205; *186:* 29, 30
Rayevsky, Robert *64:* 17; *70:* 173; *80:* 204; *117:* 79; *190:* 187, 188
Raymond, Larry *31:* 108; *97:* 109
Rayner, Hugh *151:* 170
Rayner, Mary *22:* 207; *47:* 140; *72:* 191; *87:* 171, 172; *192:* 104
Rayner, Shoo
   See Rayner, Hugh
Raynes, John *71:* 19
Raynor, Dorka *28:* 168
Raynor, Paul *24:* 73
Rayyan, Omar *110:* 222; *112:* 17; *125:* 131
Razzi, James *10:* 127
Read, Alexander D. *20:* 45
Reader, Dennis *71:* 157
Reasoner, Charles *53:* 33, 36, 37
Reczuch, Karen *115:* 132; *145:* 131
Redlich, Ben *163:* 221
Reed, Joseph *116:* 139
Reed, Lynn Rowe *115:* 173; *171:* 146
Reed, Tom *34:* 171
Reeder, Colin *74:* 202; *77:* 113
Rees, Mary *134:* 219
Reese, Bob *60:* 135

Reeve, Philip *171:* 50
Reeves, Eira B. *130:* 173, 174; *141:* 151
Reeves, Rick *181:* 179
Regan, Dana *117:* 116
Regan, Laura *103:* 198; *153:* 206
Reichert, Renée *169:* 127
Reid, Barbara *82:* 178; *92:* 17; *93:* 169, 170
Reid, Stephen *19:* 213; *22:* 89
Reim, Melanie *104:* 151; *150:* 98
Reinert, Kirk *89:* 138
Reinertson, Barbara *44:* 150; *62:* 103
Reiniger, Lotte *40:* 185
Reisberg, Mira *119:* 2
Reisch, Jesse *158:* 130
Reiser, Lynn *81:* 175; *138:* 184; *180:* 200
Reiss, John J. *23:* 193
Relf, Douglas *3:* 63
Relyea, C.M. *16:* 29; *31:* 153
Remi, Georges *13:* 184
Remington, Frederic *19:* 188; *41:* 178, 179,
    180, 181, 183,184, 185, 186, 187, 188; *62:*
    197
Remkiewicz, Frank *67:* 102; *77:* 171; *80:* 130;
    113: 107; *152:* 116; *152:* 211, 212; *157:* 148
Rendon, Maria *116:* 141; 192; *134:* 152
Renfro, Ed *79:* 176
Renlie, Frank *11:* 200
Reschofsky, Jean *7:* 118
Rethi *60:* 181
Rethi, Lili *2:* 153; *36:* 156
Reusswig, William *3:* 267
Rex, Adam *156:* 172; *169:* 91; *186:* 178, 179
Rex, Michael *157:* 147; *191:* 159, 160
Rey, H.A. *1:* 182; *26:* 163, 164, 166, 167, 169;
    69: 172, 173, 174, 175; *86:* 195, 196, 197;
    100: 211; *YABC 2:* 17
Reynolds, Adrian *192:* 159, 160
Reynolds, Doris *5:* 71; *31:* 77
Reynolds, Peter H. *142:* 12; *179:* 175, 176
Rhead, Louis *31:* 91; *100:* 228
Rhodes, Andrew *38:* 204; *50:* 163; *54:* 76; *61:*
    123, 124; *87:* 200
Ribbons, Ian *3:* 10; *37:* 161; *40:* 76
Ricci, Regolo *93:* 22; *164:* 148
Rice, Elizabeth *2:* 53, 214
Rice, Eve *34:* 174, 175; *91:* 172
Rice, James *22:* 210; *93:* 173
Richards, Chuck *170:* 154
Richards, George *40:* 116, 119, 121; *44:* 179
Richards, Henry *YABC 1:* 228, 231
Richardson, Ernest *2:* 144
Richardson, Frederick *18:* 27, 31
Richardson, John *110:* 88
Richman, Hilda *26:* 132
Richmond, George *24:* 179
Riddell, Chris *114:* 170, 195; *166:* 179
Riddle, Tohby *74:* 204; *151:* 179
Riding, Peter *63:* 195
Rieniets, Judy King *14:* 28
Riger, Bob *2:* 166
Riggio, Anita *73:* 191; *85:* 63; *137:* 184; *172:*
    165
Riley, Jon *74:* 70
Riley, Kenneth *22:* 230
Riley-Webb, Charlotte *153:* 143
Rinaldi, Angelo *165:* 60, 69
Ringgold, Faith *71:* 162; *114:* 173, 174, 176;
    187: 160, 161, 163
Ringi, Kjell *12:* 171
Rios, Tere
    See Versace, Marie
Ripper, Charles L. *3:* 175
Ripplinger, Henry *117:* 31
Ritchie, William *74:* 183
Ritter, John *175:* 14
Ritz, Karen *41:* 117; *72:* 239; *87:* 125; *102:* 7;
    106: 6
Rivers, Ruth *178:* 193
Rivkin, Jay *15:* 230
Rivoche, Paul *45:* 125
Roach, Marilynne *9:* 158

Robbin, Jodi *44:* 156, 159
Robbins, Frank *42:* 167
Robbins, Ken *147:* 191, 192
Robbins, Ruth *52:* 102
Roberts, Cliff *4:* 126
Roberts, David *154:* 4, 6; *191:* 162
Roberts, Doreen *4:* 230; *28:* 105
Roberts, Jim *22:* 166; *23:* 69; *31:* 110
Roberts, Tony *109:* 195, 214
Roberts, W. *22:* 2, 3
Robins, Arthur *137:* 172; *151:* 225
Robinson, Aminah Brenda Lynn *86:* 205; *103:*
    55; *159:* 175
Robinson, Charles [1870-1937] *17:* 157, 171,
    172, 173, 175, 176; *24:* 207; *25:* 204; *YABC
    2:* 308, 309, 310, 331
Robinson, Charles *3:* 53; *5:* 14; *6:* 193; *7:*
    150; *7:* 183; *8:* 38; *9:* 81; *13:* 188; *14:* 248,
    249; *23:* 149; *26:* 115; *27:* 48; *28:* 191; *32:*
    28; *35:* 210; *36:* 37; *48:* 96; *52:* 33; *53:* 157;
    56: 15; *62:* 142; *77:* 41; *111:* 148
Robinson, Jerry *3:* 262
Robinson, Joan G. *7:* 184
Robinson, Lolly *90:* 227
Robinson, T.H. *17:* 179, 181, 182, 183; *29:*
    254
Robinson, W. Heath *17:* 185, 187, 189, 191,
    193, 195, 197, 199, 202; *23:* 167; *25:* 194;
    29: 150; *YABC 1:* 44; *2:* 183
Rocco, John *187:* 4; *188:* 151
Roche, Christine *41:* 98
Roche, Denis *99:* 184; *180:* 32
Roche, P.K. *57:* 151, 152
Rocker, Fermin *7:* 34; *13:* 21; *31:* 40; *40:*
    190,191
Rocklen, Margot *101:* 181
Rockwell, Anne *5:* 147; *33:* 171, 173; *71:* 166,
    167,168; *114:* 183, 184
Rockwell, Gail *7:* 186
Rockwell, Harlow *33:* 171, 173, 175
Rockwell, Lizzy *114:* 182; *162:* 182; *185:* 189
Rockwell, Norman *23:* 39, 196, 197, 199, 200,
    203, 204, 207; *41:* 140, 143; *123:* 47; *YABC
    2:* 60
Rockwood, Richard *119:* 75
Rodanas, Kristina *156:* 183, 184
Rodegast, Roland *43:* 100
Rodgers, Frank *69:* 177
Rodriguez, Albert G. *182:* 50
Rodriguez, Christina *184:* 12
Rodriguez, Joel *16:* 65
Rodriguez, Robert *145:* 145
Rodriguez-Howard, Pauline *177:* 18
Roeckelein, Katrina *134:* 223
Roennfeldt, Robert *66:* 243
Roever, J.M. *4:* 119; *26:* 170
Roffey, Maureen *33:* 142, 176, 177
Rogasky, Barbara *46:* 90
Rogé *173:* 160
Rogers, Carol *2:* 262; *6:* 164; *26:* 129
Rogers, Chris M. *150:* 59
Rogers, Forest *87:* 160; *101:* 76
Rogers, Frances *10:* 130
Rogers, Gregory *104:* 76; *126:* 57; *171:* 26
Rogers, Jacqueline *78:* 249; *80:* 34; *86:* 54
    103: 70; *115:* 72; *129:* 173; *131:* 57, 225;
    143: 211; *153:* 100; *193:* 186
Rogers, Sherry *191:* 66
Rogers, Walter S. *31:* 135, 138; *67:* 65, 168;
    100: 81
Rogers, William A. *15:* 151, 153, 154; *33:* 35
Rogoff, Barbara *95:* 20
Rohmann, Eric *103:* 152
Rojankovsky, Feodor *6:* 134, 136; *10:* 183; *21:*
    128,129, 130; *25:* 110; *28:* 42; *68:* 120
Rolfsen, Alf *62:* 15
Romain, Trevor *134:* 157
Roman, Barbara J. *103:* 171
Romas *114:* 111; *165:* 63
Romano, Robert *64:* 68
Romero, Alejandro *187:* 185

Roos, Maryn *168:* 198
Root, Barry *80:* 212; *90:* 196; *146:* 78; *156:*
    165; *159:* 161; *182:* 18, 172
Root, Kimberly Bulcken *86:* 72; *98:* 21; *108:*
    111; *127:* 114; *159:* 162; *176:* 134; *192:* 163
Roper, Bob *65:* 153
Roraback, Robin *111:* 156
Rorer, Abigail *43:* 222; *85:* 155
Rosales, Melodye *80:* 35
Rosamilia, Patricia *36:* 120
Rose, Carl *5:* 62
Rose, David S. *29:* 109; *70:* 120
Rose, Gerald *68:* 200, 201; *86:* 48
Rose, Ted *93:* 178
Rosenbaum, Jonathan *50:* 46
Rosenberg, Amye *74:* 207, 208
Rosenberry, Vera *87:* 22, 26; *144:* 212, 213;
    158: 120
Rosenblum, Richard *11:* 202; *18:* 18
Rosier, Lydia *16:* 236; *20:* 104; *21:* 109; *22:*
    125; *30:* 151, 158; *42:* 128; *45:* 214; *77:*
    227, 228
Rosing, Jens *85:* 142
Ross
    See Thomson, Ross
Ross, Christine *83:* 172, 173
Ross, Clare Romano *3:* 123; *21:* 45; *48:* 199
Ross, Dave *32:* 152; *57:* 108
Ross, Herbert *37:* 78
Ross, John *3:* 123; *21:* 45
Ross, Johnny *32:* 190
Ross, Larry *47:* 168; *60:* 62
Ross, Ruth *109:* 233
Ross, Tony *17:* 204; *56:* 132; *65:* 176, 177,
    179; *90:* 123; *123:* 186, 187, 190; *130:* 188,
    190, 191, 192; *132:* 242; *174:* 159; *176:* 181,
    182, 183
Rossetti, Dante Gabriel *20:* 151, 153
Rostant, Larry *180:* 221
Roth, Arnold *4:* 238; *21:* 133
Roth, Julie Jersild *180:* 206
Roth, Marci *135:* 223
Roth, R.G. *184:* 50
Roth, Rob *105:* 98; *146:* 41
Roth, Robert *176:* 159
Roth, Roger *61:* 128; *190:* 192
Roth, Stephanie *136:* 171, 172
Roth, Susan L. *80:* 38; *93:* 78; *134:* 165, 166;
    181: 145, 146
Rothenberg, Joani Keller *162:* 190, 191
Rothman, Michael *139:* 62; *184:* 34 *Rotman,
    Jeffrey L.* *145:* 30
Rotondo, Pat *32:* 158
Roughsey, Dick *35:* 186
Rouille, M. *11:* 96
Rounds, Glen *8:* 173; *9:* 171; *12:* 56; *32:* 194;
    40: 230; *51:* 161, 162, 166; *56:* 149; *70:*
    198, 199; *YABC 1:* 1, 2, 3; *112:* 163
Roundtree, Katherine *114:* 88; *168:* 102
Rowan, Evadne *52:* 51
Rowe, Eric *111:* 161
Rowe, Gavin *27:* 144; *72:* 47; *88:* 201
Rowe, John *132:* 70, 71; *180:* 126
Rowell, Kenneth *40:* 72
Rowen, Amy *52:* 143
Rowena *116:* 101
Rowland, Andrew *164:* 136
Rowland, Jada *83:* 73
Rowles, Daphne *58:* 24
Roy, Jeroo *27:* 229; *36:* 110
Royo *118:* 32; *144:* 105, 106, 108; *165:* 19;
    166: 166
Rubel, Nicole *18:* 255; *20:* 59; *81:* 66, 67; *95:*
    169, 170; *119:* 60; *135:* 177, 179, 180; *169:*
    68; *181:* 150
Rubel, Reina *33:* 217
Rud, Borghild *6:* 15
Ruddell, Gary *110:* 238; *116:* 207
Rudolph, Norman Guthrie *17:* 13
Rue, Leonard Lee III *37:* 164
Rueda, Claudia *183:* 170, 171

Ruelle, Karen Gray *126:* 193
Ruff, Donna *50:* 173; *72:* 203; *78:* 49; *80:* 120,121; *93:* 162; *164:* 121
Ruffins, Reynold *10:* 134, 135; *41:* 191, 192, 193, 194, 195, 196; *125:* 187, 188, 189; *162:* 197
Ruhlin, Roger *34:* 44
Ruiz, Art *95:* 154; *110:* 91
Rumford, James *193:* 167
Runnerstroem, Bengt Arne *75:* 161
Ruse, Margaret *24:* 155
Rush, Ken *98:* 74
Rush, Peter *42:* 75
Russell, Charles M. *167:* 171
Russell, E.B. *18:* 177, 182
Russell, Jim *53:* 134
Russell, P. Craig *80:* 196; *146:* 102; *162:* 186
Russo, Marisabina *84:* 51; *106:* 164; *151:* 183; *188:* 153, 154, 155, 156
Russo, Susan *30:* 182; *36:* 144
Russon, Mary *87:* 145
Ruth, Greg *183:* 125
Ruth, Rod *9:* 161
Rutherford, Alexa *110:* 108
Rutherford, Jenny *78:* 5
Rutherford, Meg *25:* 174; *34:* 178, 179; *69:* 73; *72:* 31
Rutland, Jonathan *31:* 126
Ruurs, Margriet *147:* 195
Ruzzier, Sergio *159:* 176, 177; *163:* 184
Ryan, Amy *188:* 50
Ryan, Will *86:* 134
Ryden, Hope *8:* 176
Rylant, Cynthia *112:* 170, 172
Rymer, Alta M. *34:* 181
Ryniak, Christopher *178:* 11
Rystedt, Rex *49:* 80

S

Saaf, Chuck *49:* 179
Saaf, Donald *101:* 220; *124:* 180
Sabaka, Donna R. *21:* 172
Sabin, Robert *45:* 35; *60:* 30; *99:* 161
Sabuda, Robert *170:* 166, 167, 168
Sacker, Amy *16:* 100
Saelig, S.M. *129:* 73; *173:* 59
Saffioti, Lino *36:* 176; *48:* 60
Saflund, Birgitta *94:* 2
Sagsoorian, Paul *12:* 183; *22:* 154; *33:* 106; *87:* 152
Sahara, Tony *168:* 106; *177:* 181; *178:* 228; *186:* 132
Sahlberg, Myron *57:* 165
Saidens, Amy *145:* 162; *191:* 131
Saint Exupery, Antoine de *20:* 157
Saint James, Synthia *152:* 220; *188:* 90
Saldutti, Denise *39:* 186; *57:* 178
Sale, Morton *YABC 2:* 31
Sale, Tim *153:* 177
Salerno, Steven *150:* 79; *176:* 188
Salter, George *72:* 128, 130
Saltzberg, Barney *135:* 184, 185
Saltzman, David *86:* 209
Salwowski, Mark *71:* 54
Salzman, Yuri *86:* 12
Sambourne, Linley *YABC 2:* 181
Sampson, Katherine *9:* 197
Samson, Anne S. *2:* 216
San Souci, Daniel *40:* 200; *96:* 199, 200; *113:* 171; *157:* 149; *170:* 69; *192:* 167, 168
Sancha, Sheila *38:* 185
Sanchez, Enrique O. *155:* 84
Sand, George X. *45:* 182
Sandberg, Lasse *15:* 239, 241
Sanders, Beryl *39:* 173

Sanderson, Ruth *21:* 126; *24:* 53; *28:* 63; *33:* 67; *41:* 48, 198, 199, 200, 201, 202, 203; *43:* 79; *46:* 36,44; *47:* 102; *49:* 58; *62:* 121, 122; *85:* 3; *109:* 207, 208, 209, 210; *172:* 157, 158
Sandia *119:* 74
Sandin, Joan *4:* 36; *6:* 194; *7:* 177; *12:* 145,185; *20:* 43; *21:* 74; *26:* 144; *27:* 142; *28:* 224, 225; *38:* 86; *41:* 46; *42:* 35; *59:* 6; *80:* 136; *94:* 188; *140:* 116; *153:* 179, 180
Sandland, Reg *39:* 215
Sandoz, Edouard *26:* 45, 47
Sanford, John *66:* 96, 97
Sankey, Tom *72:* 103
sano, Kazuhiko *153:* 208
Santat, Dan *188:* 160
Santore, Charles *54:* 139
Santoro, Christopher *74:* 215
Santos, Jesse J. *99:* 24
Sapieha, Christine *1:* 180
Saport, Linda *123:* 137, 138
Sara
    See De La Roche Saint Andre, Anne
Sardinha, Rick *175:* 151
Sarg, Tony *YABC 2:* 236
Sargent, Claudia *64:* 181
Sargent, Robert *2:* 217
Saris *1:* 33
Sarony *YABC 2:* 170
Sasaki, Goro *170:* 46
Sasek, Miroslav *16:* 239, 240, 241, 242
Sassman, David *9:* 79
Satty *29:* 203, 205
Sauber, Robert *40:* 183; *76:* 256; *78:* 154; *87:* 92
Saunders, Dave *85:* 163, 164, 165
Savadier, Elivia *84:* 50; *145:* 45; *164:* 206
Savage, Naomi *56:* 172
Savage, Steele *10:* 203; *20:* 77; *35:* 28
Savage, Stephen *174:* 182
Savio *76:* 4
Savitt, Sam *8:* 66, 182; *15:* 278; *20:* 96; *24:* 192; *28:* 98
Sawyer, Kem Knapp *84:* 228, 229
Say, Allen *28:* 178; *69:* 182, 183, 232; *110:* 194, 195,196; *161:* 154, 155
Sayles, Elizabeth *82:* 93; *105:* 155; *109:* 116; *180:* 64
Scabrini, Janet *13:* 191; *44:* 128
Scanlan, Peter *83:* 27; *153:* 165; *187:* 149
Scanlon, Paul *83:* 87
Scannell, Reece *105:* 105
Scarry, Huck *35:* 204, 205
Scarry, Richard *2:* 220, 221; *18:* 20; *35:* 193, 194, 195,196, 197, 198, 199, 200, 201, 202; *75:* 165, 167, 168
Schachner, Judith Byron *88:* 180; *92:* 163; *93:* 102; *142:* 82; *178:* 199, 200; *190:* 140
Schaeffer, Mead *18:* 81, 94; *21:* 137, 138, 139; *47:* 128
Schaffer, Amanda *90:* 206
Schanzer, Rosalyn *138:* 192, 193
Scharl, Josef *20:* 132; *22:* 128
Scheel, Lita *11:* 230
Scheffler, Axel *180:* 23, 24
Scheib, Ida *29:* 28
Schermer, Judith *30:* 184
Schick, Eleanor *82:* 210, 211; *144:* 222
Schick, Joel *16:* 160; *17:* 167; *22:* 12; *27:* 176; *31:* 147, 148; *36:* 23; *38:* 64; *45:* 116, 117; *52:* 5, 85; *104:* 159
Schields, Gretchen *75:* 171, 203
Schindelman, Joseph *1:* 74; *4:* 101; *12:* 49; *26:* 51; *40:* 146; *56:* 158; *73:* 40
Schindler, Edith *7:* 22
Schindler, S.D. *38:* 107; *46:* 196; *74:* 162; *75:* 172, 173; *99:* 133; *112:* 177; *118:* 185, 186; *121:* 71; *136:* 159; *143:* 45; *149:* 120; *156:* 30; *169:* 135; *171:* 161, 162, 163; *172:* 9; *186:* 163
Schlesinger, Bret *7:* 77

Schmid, Eleanore *12:* 188; *126:* 196, 197
Schmiderer, Dorothy *19:* 224
Schmidt, Bill *73:* 34; *76:* 220, 222, 224
Schmidt, Elizabeth *15:* 242
Schmidt, George Paul *132:* 122
Schmidt, Karen Lee *54:* 12; *71:* 174; *92:* 56; *94:* 190, 191; *127:* 103
Schmidt, Lynette *76:* 205
Schneider, Christine M. *171:* 165
Schneider, Howie *181:* 159
Schneider, Rex *29:* 64; *44:* 171
Schnurr, Edward *170:* 62
Schoberle, Cecile *80:* 200; *92:* 134
Schoenherr, Ian *32:* 83; *173:* 41
Schoenherr, John *1:* 146, 147, 173; *3:* 39, 139; *17:* 75; *29:* 72; *32:* 83; *37:* 168, 169, 170; *43:* 164, 165; *45:* 160, 162; *51:* 127; *66:* 196, 197, 198; *68:* 83; *72:* 240; *75:* 225; *88:* 176
Scholder, Fritz *69:* 103
Schomburg, Alex *13:* 23
Schongut, Emanuel *4:* 102; *15:* 186; *47:* 218, 219; *52:* 147, 148, 149, 150; *185:* 27
Schoonover, Frank *17:* 107; *19:* 81, 190, 233; *22:* 88,129; *24:* 189; *31:* 88; *41:* 69; *YABC 2:* 282, 316
Schories, Pat *164:* 210
Schottland, Miriam *22:* 172
Schramm, Ulrik *2:* 16; *14:* 112
Schreiber, Elizabeth Anne *13:* 193
Schreiber, Ralph W. *13:* 193
Schreiter, Rick *14:* 97; *23:* 171; *41:* 247; *49:* 131
Schroeder, Binette *56:* 128, 129
Schroeder, E. Peter *12:* 112
Schroeder, Ted *11:* 160; *15:* 189; *30:* 91; *34:* 43
Schrotter, Gustav *22:* 212; *30:* 225
Schubert, Dieter *101:* 167, 168
Schubert-Gabrys, Ingrid *101:* 167, 168
Schucker, James *31:* 163
Schuett, Stacey *72:* 137
Schulder, Lili *146:* 29
Schulke, Debra *57:* 167
Schulke, Flip *57:* 167
Schulz, Barbara *167:* 24
Schulz, Charles M. *10:* 137, 138, 139, 140, 141, 142; *118:* 192, 193, 194, 196, 199
Schutzer, Dena *109:* 32
Schwark, Mary Beth *51:* 155; *72:* 175
Schwartz, Amy *47:* 191; *82:* 100; *83:* 178, 179, 180,181; *129:* 107; *131:* 197, 198; *189:* 166, 168
Schwartz, Carol *124:* 41; *130:* 199
Schwartz, Charles *8:* 184
Schwartz, Daniel *46:* 37
Schwartz, Joanie *124:* 170
Schwartzberg, Joan *3:* 208
Schweitzer, Iris *2:* 137; *6:* 207
Schweninger, Ann *29:* 172; *82:* 246; *159:* 202; *168:* 166
Schwinger, Laurence *84:* 44; *91:* 61
Scofield, Penrod *61:* 107; *62:* 160
Scott, Anita Walker *7:* 38
Scott, Art *39:* 41
Scott, Frances Gruse *38:* 43
Scott, Julian *34:* 126
Scott, Roszel *33:* 238
Scott, Sally *87:* 27
Scott, Steve *166:* 230, 231; *171:* 93
Scott, Trudy *27:* 172
Scrace, Carolyn *143:* 95, 96
Scribner, Joanne *14:* 236; *29:* 78; *33:* 185; *34:* 208; *78:* 75; *164:* 237
Scrofani, Joseph *31:* 65; *74:* 225
Scroggs, Kirk *187:* 169
Seaman, Mary Lott *34:* 64
Searle, Ronald *24:* 98; *42:* 172, 173, 174, 176, 177, 179; *66:* 73, 74; *70:* 205, 206, 207
Searle, Townley *36:* 85
Sebree, Charles *18:* 65

Sedacca, Joseph M. *11:* 25; *22:* 36
Seder, Jason *108:* 102
Seeger, Laura Vaccaro *172:* 162
Seegmiller, Don *174:* 57
Seely, David *164:* 173
Seeley, Laura L. *97:* 105
Segal, John *178:* 202
Segar, E.C. *61:* 179, 181
Segur, Adrienne *27:* 121
Seibold, J. Otto *83:* 188, 190, 191; *149:* 212, 214, 215, 216
Seignobosc, Francoise *21:* 145, 146
Sejima, Yoshimasa *8:* 187
Selig, Sylvie *13:* 199
Seltzer, Isadore *6:* 18; *133:* 59
Seltzer, Meyer *17:* 214
Selven, Maniam *144:* 133
Selway, Martina *169:* 157
Selznick, Brian *79:* 192; *104:* 25; *117:* 175; *126:* 156; *134:* 171; *158:* 76, 78; *169:* 70; *171:* 172, 173; *191:* 106; *192:* 130
Sempe, Jean-Jacques *47:* 92; *YABC 2:* 109
Sendak, Maurice *1:* 135, 190; *3:* 204; *7:* 142; *15:* 199; *17:* 210; *27:* 181, 182, 183, 185, 186, 187, 189,190, 191, 192, 193, 194, 195, 197, 198, 199, 203; *28:* 181, 182; *32:* 108; *33:* 148, 149; *35:* 238; *44:* 180, 181; *45:* 97, 99; *46:* 174; *73:* 225; *91:* 10, 11 *YABC1:* 167; *113:* 163, 165, 167, 168; *118:* 153; *127:* 161
Senders, Marci *180:* 79
Sengler, Johanna *18:* 256
Senn, Steve *60:* 145
Seredy, Kate *1:* 192; *14:* 20, 21; *17:* 210
Sergeant, John *6:* 74
Servello, Joe *10:* 144; *24:* 139; *40:* 91; *70:* 130, 131; *146:* 159
Seton, Ernest Thompson *18:* 260-269, 271
Seuss, Dr.
  See Geisel, Theodor
Severin, John Powers *7:* 62
Sewall, Marcia *15:* 8; *22:* 170; *37:* 171, 172, 173; *39:* 73; *45:* 209; *62:* 117; *69:* 185, 186; *71:* 212; *90:* 232; *96:* 127; *102:* 101; *107:* 129; *119:* 176, 177, 178, 180
Seward, James *70:* 35
Seward, Prudence *16:* 243
Sewell, Helen *3:* 186; *15:* 308; *33:* 102; *38:* 189, 190, 191, 192
Seymour, Stephen *54:* 21
Sfar, Joann *182:* 183
Shachat, Andrew *82:* 179
Shahn, Ben *39:* 178; *46:* 193
Shalansky, Len *38:* 167
Shanks, Anne Zane *10:* 149
Shannon, David *57:* 137; *107:* 184; *112:* 216; *135:* 12; *152:* 223, 224, 225; *158:* 192
Sharp, Paul *52:* 60
Sharp, William *6:* 131; *19:* 241; *20:* 112; *25:* 141
Sharratt, Nick *102:* 207, 208; *104:* 163; *153:* 198; *175:* 176; *192:* 208
Shaw, Barclay *74:* 14, 16; *118:* 138
Shaw, Charles *21:* 135; *38:* 187; *47:* 124; *126:* 219
Shaw, Charles G. *13:* 200
Shaw-Smith, Emma *144:* 117
Shea, Edmund *56:* 19
Shearer, Ted *43:* 193, 194, 195, 196
Sheban, Chris *182:* 185; *190:* 102, 104
Shecter, Ben *16:* 244; *25:* 109; *33:* 188, 191; *41:* 77
Shed, Greg *74:* 94; *84:* 204; *129:* 149, 167: 91; *179:* 192
Sheeban, Chris *144:* 190; *158:* 163
Shefcik, James *48:* 221, 222; *60:* 141
Shefelman, Karl *58:* 168
Shefts, Joelle *48:* 210
Shein, Bob *139:* 189
Shekerjian, Haig *16:* 245
Shekerjian, Regina *16:* 245; *25:* 73

Sheldon, David *184:* 174; *185:* 204
Shelley, John *186:* 223
Shemie, Bonnie *96:* 207
Shenton, Edward *45:* 187, 188, 189; *YABC 1:* 218, 219, 221
Shepard, Ernest H. *3:* 193; *4:* 74; *16:* 101; *17:* 109; *25:* 148; *33:* 152, 199, 200, 201, 202, 203, 204, 205, 206,207; *46:* 194; *98:* 114; *100:* 111, 178, 179, 217, 219, 220,221; *YABC 1:* 148, 153, 174, 176, 180, 181
Shepard, Mary *4:* 210; *22:* 205; *30:* 132, 133; *54:* 150, 152, 153, 157, 158; *59:* 108, 109, 111; *100:* 246
Shepherd, Irana *171:* 112
Shepperson, Rob *96:* 153; *177:* 163; *178:* 204
Sherman, Theresa *27:* 167
Sherwan, Earl *3:* 196
Shields, Charles *10:* 150; *36:* 63
Shields, Leonard *13:* 83, 85, 87
Shiffman, Lena *139:* 167; *168:* 136
Shigley, Neil K. *66:* 219
Shillabeer, Mary *35:* 74
Shilston, Arthur *49:* 61; *62:* 58
Shimin, Symeon *1:* 93; *2:* 128, 129; *3:* 202; *7:* 85; *11:* 177; *12:* 139; *13:* 202, 203; *27:* 138; *28:* 65; *35:* 129; *36:* 130; *48:* 151; *49:* 59; *56:* 63, 65, 153
Shine, Andrea *104:* 165; *128:* 34
Shinn, Everett *16:* 148; *18:* 229; *21:* 149, 150, 151; *24:* 218
Shinn, Florence Scovel *63:* 133, 135
Shore, Robert *27:* 54; *39:* 192, 193; *YABC 2:* 200
Shortall, Leonard *4:* 144; *8:* 196; *10:* 166; *19:* 227, 228, 229, 230; *25:* 78; *28:* 66, 167; *33:* 127; *52:* 125; *73:* 12, 212
Shortt, T.M. *27:* 36
Shpitalnik, Vladimir *83:* 194
Shropshire, Sandy *170:* 191
Shtainments, Leon *32:* 161
Shulevitz, Uri *3:* 198, 199; *17:* 85; *22:* 204; *27:* 212; *28:* 184; *50:* 190, 191, 192, 193, 194, 195, 196,197, 198, 199, 201; *106:* 181, 182, 183; *165:* 203, 205; *166:* 138
Shulman, Dee *180:* 140
Shupe, Bobbi *139:* 80, 81
Shute, A.B. *67:* 196
Shute, Linda *46:* 59; *74:* 118
Siberell, Anne *29:* 193
Sibley, Don *1:* 39; *12:* 196; *31:* 47
Sibthorp, Fletcher *94:* 111, 112
Sidjakov, Nicolas *18:* 274
Siebel, Fritz *3:* 120; *17:* 145
Siebold, J. Otto *158:* 227
Siegel, Hal *74:* 246
Sieger, Ted *189:* 172
Siegl, Helen *12:* 166; *23:* 216; *34:* 185, 186
Silin-Palmer, Pamela *184:* 102
Sill, John *140:* 194; *141:* 157
Sills, Joyce *5:* 199
Silva, Simon *108:* 122
Silver, Maggie *85:* 210
Silveria, Gordon *96:* 44
Silverstein, Alvin *8:* 189
Silverstein, Shel *33:* 211; *92:* 209, 210
Silverstein, Virginia *8:* 189
Silvey, Joe *135:* 203
Simard, Remy *95:* 156
Simmons, Elly *110:* 2; *127:* 69; *134:* 181
Simon, Eric M. *7:* 82
Simon, Hilda *28:* 189
Simon, Howard *2:* 175; *5:* 132; *19:* 199; *32:* 163, 164, 165
Simont, Marc *2:* 119; *4:* 213; *9:* 168; *13:* 238,240; *14:* 262; *16:* 179; *18:* 221; *26:* 210; *33:* 189, 194; *44:* 132; *58:* 122; *68:* 117; *73:* 204, 205, 206; *74:* 221; *126:* 199, 200; *133:* 195; *164:* 128
Sims, Agnes *54:* 152

Sims, Blanche *44:* 116; *57:* 129; *75:* 179, 180; *77:* 92; *104:* 192; *152:* 117; *156:* 160; *160:* 70; *168:* 174, 175
Singer, Edith G. *2:* 30
Singer, Gloria *34:* 56; *36:* 43
Singer, Julia *28:* 190
Singh, Jen *178:* 146
Siomades, Lorianne *134:* 45
Simont, Marc *163:* 40
Siracusa, Catherine *68:* 135; *82:* 218
Sís, Peter *67:* 179, 181, 183, 184, 185; *96:* 96, 98; *106:* 193, 194, 195; *149:* 224, 226; *180:* 177; *192:* 180, 182
Sivard, Robert *26:* 124
Sivertson, Liz *116:* 84
Skardinski, Stanley *23:* 144; *32:* 84; *66:* 122; *84:* 108
Slack, Michael *185:* 108; *189:* 173, 174
Slackman, Charles B. *12:* 201
Slade, Christian *193:* 187
Slade, Paul *61:* 170
Slark, Albert *99:* 212
Slater, Rod *25:* 167
Slavin, Bill *182:* 14, 15
Sloan, Joseph *16:* 68
Sloane, Eric *21:* 3; *52:* 153, 154, 155, 156, 157, 158, 160
Sloat, Teri *164:* 231
Slobodkin, Louis *1:* 200; *3:* 232; *5:* 168; *13:* 251; *15:* 13, 88; *26:* 173, 174, 175, 176, 178, 179; *60:* 180
Slobodkina, Esphyr *1:* 201
Slonim, David *166:* 167, 168
Small, David *50:* 204, 205; *79:* 44; *95:* 189, 190, 191; *126:* 203, 204; *136:* 119; *143:* 201, 202, 203; *144:* 246; *150:* 5; *161:* 176; *183:* 181, 182, 183, 184
Small, W. *33:* 113
Smalley, Janet *1:* 154
Smedley, William T. *34:* 129
Smee, David *14:* 78; *62:* 30
Smee, Nicola *167:* 156
Smith, A.G., Jr. *35:* 182
Smith, Alvin *1:* 31, 229; *13:* 187; *27:* 216; *28:* 226; *48:* 149; *49:* 60
Smith, Andy *188:* 20
Smith, Anne Warren *41:* 212
Smith, Barry *75:* 183
Smith, Carl *36:* 41
Smith, Cat Bowman *146:* 39; *164:* 219
Smith, Craig *97:* 197; *172:* 175
Smith, Donald A. *178:* 7
Smith, Doris Susan *41:* 139
Smith, Douglas *189:* 159
Smith, Duane *171:* 152
Smith, E. Boyd *19:* 70; *22:* 89; *26:* 63; *YABC 1:* 4, 5, 240, 248, 249
Smith, Edward J. *4:* 224
Smith, Elwood H. *157:* 231; *181:* 79
Smith, Eunice Young *5:* 170
Smith, Gary *113:* 216
Smith, George *102:* 169
Smith, Howard *19:* 196
Smith, J. Gerard *95:* 42
Smith, Jacqueline Bardner *27:* 108; *39:* 197
Smith, Jay J. *61:* 119
Smith, Jeff *93:* 191
Smith, Jessie Willcox *15:* 91; *16:* 95; *18:* 231; *19:* 57, 242; *21:* 29, 156, 157, 158, 159, 160, 161; *34:* 65; *100:* 223; *YABC 1:* 6; *2:* 180, 185, 191, 311, 325
Smith, Jos. A. *52:* 131; *72:* 120; *74:* 151; *84:* 147, 148; *85:* 146; *87:* 96; *94:* 219; *96:* 97; *104:* 33; *108:* 126, 127, 128; *111:* 140; *136:* 145; *181:* 173
Smith, Kenneth R. *47:* 182
Smith, Kevin Warren *89:* 112
Smith, L.H. *35:* 174
Smith, Lane *76:* 211, 213; *88:* 115; *105:* 202, 203,204, 205; *131:* 207; *160:* 217, 221; *179:* 183, 184, 185, 186

Smith, Lee 29: 32
Smith, Linell Nash 2: 195
Smith, Maggie Kaufman 13: 205; 35: 191; 110: 158; 178: 226; 190: 204
Smith, Mavis 101: 219
Smith, Moishe 33: 155
Smith, Philip 44: 134; 46: 203
Smith, Ralph Crosby 2: 267; 49: 203
Smith, Robert D. 5: 63
Smith, Sally J. 84: 55
Smith, Susan Carlton 12: 208
Smith, Terry 12: 106; 33: 158
Smith, Virginia 3: 157; 33: 72
Smith, William A. 1: 36; 10: 154; 25: 65
Smith-Moore, J.J. 98: 147
Smolinski, Dick 84: 217
Smoljan, Joe 112: 201
Smollin, Mike 39: 203
Smyth, Iain 105: 207
Smyth, M. Jane 12: 15
Smythe, Fiona 151: 213
Smythe, Theresa 141: 37
Snair, Andy 176: 4
Sneed, Brad 125: 25; 191: 175, 176
Snyder, Andrew A. 30: 212
Snyder, Jerome 13: 207; 30: 173
Snyder, Joel 28: 163
So, Meilo 162: 201
Soentpiet, Chris K. 97: 208; 110: 33; 159: 184; 161: 10; 163: 130
Sofia 1: 62; 5: 90; 32: 166; 86: 43
Sofilas, Mark 93: 157
Sohn, Jiho 182: 78
Sokol, Bill 37: 178; 49: 23
Sokolov, Kirill 34: 188
Solbert, Ronni 1: 159; 2: 232; 5: 121; 6: 34; 17: 249
Solomon, Michael 174: 115
Solonevich, George 15: 246; 17: 47
Soma, Liana 81: 118
Soman, David 90: 122; 102: 126; 140: 120; 93; 188: 43, 89
Sommer, Robert 12: 211
Sorel, Edward 4: 61; 36: 82; 65: 191, 193; 126: 214
Sorensen, Henrik 62: 16
Sorensen, Svend Otto 22: 130, 141; 67: 188, 189
Sorra, Kristin 155: 80
Sostre, Maria 187: 36
Sotomayor, Antonio 11: 215
Souhami, Jessica 112: 128; 176: 193
Souza, Diana 71: 139
Sovak, Jan 115: 190
Soyer, Moses 20: 177
Spaenkuch, August 16: 28
Spafford, Suzy 160: 228
Spain, Valerie 105: 76
Spain, Sunday Sahara 133: 204
Spalenka, Greg 149: 69; 151: 228; 184: 195; 191: 21
Spanfeller, James 1: 72, 149; 2: 183; 19: 230, 231,232; 22: 66; 36: 160, 161; 40: 75; 52: 166; 76: 2
Sparks, Mary Walker 15: 247
Spears, Rick 182: 187
Speidel, Sandra 78: 233; 94: 178; 134: 180
Speirs, John 67: 178
Spence, Geraldine 21: 163; 47: 196
Spence, Jim 38: 89; 50: 102
Spencer, Laurie 113: 12
Spencer, Mark 57: 170
Spengler, Kenneth J. 146: 256
Sperling, Andrea 133: 182
Spiegel, Beth 184: 203
Spiegel, Doris 29: 111
Spiegelman, Art 109: 227
Spier, Jo 10: 30
Spier, Peter 3: 155; 4: 200; 7: 61; 11: 78; 38: 106; 54: 120, 121, 122, 123, 124, 125, 126, 127, 128, 129, 130,131, 132, 133, 134

Spilka, Arnold 5: 120; 6: 204; 8: 131
Spirin, Gennady 95: 196, 197; 113: 172; 128: 9; 129: 49; 134: 210; 153: 9
Spivak, I. Howard 8: 10; 13: 172
Spohn, David 72: 233
Spohn, Kate 87: 195; 147: 201, 202
Spollen, Christopher J. 12: 214
Spooner, Malcolm 40: 142
Spowart, Robin 82: 228; 92: 149; 133: 131; 176: 163; 177: 183, 184
Sprague, Kevin 150: 60
Sprattler, Rob 12: 176
Spring, Bob 5: 60
Spring, Ira 5: 60
Springer, Harriet 31: 92
Spudvilas, Anne 110: 74
Spurll, Barbara 78: 199; 88: 141, 142; 99: 215
Spurrier, Steven 28: 198
Spuvilas, Anne 85: 114
Spy
    See Ward, Leslie
Squires, Stuart 127: 74
St. Aubin, Bruno 179: 54
St. John, J. Allen 41: 62
Stabin, Victor 101: 131; 164: 158
Stadler, John 62: 33
Staffan, Alvin E. 11: 56; 12: 187
Stahl, Ben 5: 181; 12: 91; 49: 122; 71: 128; 87: 206; 112: 107
Stair, Gobin 35: 214
Stallwood, Karen 73: 126
Stamaty, Mark Alan 12: 215
Stammen, JoEllen McAllister 113: 14
Stampnick, Ken 51: 142
Stanbridge, Joanne 150: 91
Stanley, Diane 3: 45; 37: 180; 80: 217, 219
Stanley, Sanna 145: 228
Starcke, Helmut 86: 217
Starr, Branka 73: 25
Stasiak, Krystyna 49: 181; 64: 194
Staub, Leslie 103: 54
Staunton, Ted 112: 192
Stawicki, Matt 164: 250
Stead, L. 55: 51, 56
Steadman, Broeck 97: 185, 186; 99: 56; 121: 48
Steadman, Ralph 32: 180; 123: 143, 145
Stearn, Nick 183: 26
Steckler, June 90: 178
Steele, Robert Gantt 169: 174
Steichen, Edward 30: 79
Steig, William 18: 275, 276; 70: 215, 216, 217, 218; 111: 173, 174, 175, 176, 177
Stein, Harve 1: 109
Steinberg, Saul 47: 193
Steinel, William 23: 146
Steiner, Charlotte 45: 196
Steiner, Joan 110: 219
Steirnagel, Michael 80: 56
Stemp, Eric 60: 184
Stephens, Alice Barber 66: 208, 209
Stephens, Charles H. YABC 2: 279
Stephens, Pat 126: 110; 128: 101
Stephens, William M. 21: 165
Steptoe, Javaka 151: 203, 204; 190: 169
Steptoe, John 8: 197; 57: 9; 63: 158, 159, 160, 161,163, 164, 165, 166, 167; 96: 4; 105: 87
Stern, Simon 15: 249, 250; 17: 58; 34: 192, 193
Sterret, Jane 53: 27
Stetsios, Debbie 165: 108, 109
Steven, Kat 158: 237
Stevens, David 62: 44
Stevens, Helen 189: 31
Stevens, Janet 40: 126; 57: 10, 11; 80: 112; 90: 221, 222; 109: 156; 130: 34; 166: 202; 176: 53, 116; 193: 199, 200, 202
Stevens, Mary 11: 193; 13: 129; 43: 95
Stevenson, Harvey 66: 143; 80: 201, 221; 153: 60; 191: 166

Stevenson, James 42: 182, 183; 51: 163; 66: 184; 71: 185, 187, 188; 78: 262; 87: 97; 113: 182, 183,184, 185; 161: 182, 183
Stevenson, Sucie 92: 27; 104: 194, 195; 112: 168; 160: 202
Stewart, April Blair 75: 210
Stewart, Arvis 33: 98; 36: 69; 60: 118; 75: 91; 127: 4
Stewart, Charles 2: 205
Stewart, Joel 151: 205
Stieg, William 172: 58
Stiles, Fran 26: 85; 78: 56; 82: 150
Stillman, Susan 44: 130; 76: 83
Stimpson, Tom 49: 171
Stinemetz, Morgan 40: 151
Stinson, Paul 110: 86
Stirnweis, Shannon 10: 164
Stites, Joe 86: 96
Stobbs, William 1: 48, 49; 3: 68; 6: 20; 17: 117, 217; 24: 150; 29: 250; 60: 179; 87: 204, 205,206
Stock, Catherine 37: 55; 65: 198; 72: 7; 99: 225; 114: 197, 198, 199; 126: 3; 145: 161; 161: 82; 173: 149
Stockman, Jack 113: 24
Stoeke, Janet Morgan 90: 225; 136: 196
Stoerrle, Tom 55: 147
Stolp, Jaap 49: 98
Stolp, Todd 89: 195
Stone, David L. 87: 154
Stone, David 9: 173
Stone, David K. 4: 38; 6: 124; 9: 180; 43: 182; 60: 70
Stone, Helen V. 6: 209
Stone, Helen 44: 121, 122, 126
Stone, Kazuko G. 134: 43
Stone, Phoebe 86: 212; 134: 213; 162: 188
Stone, Steve 166: 213
Stone, Tony 150: 34, 35
Storrings, Michael 191: 108
Stoud, Virginia A. 89: 31
Stover, Jill 82: 234
Stratton, Helen 33: 151
Stratton-Porter, Gene 15: 254, 259, 263, 264, 268, 269
Straub, Matt 192: 176
Streano, Vince 20: 173
Street, Janet Travell 84: 235
Streeter, Clive 121: 2
Stringer, Lauren 129: 187; 154: 172, 173; 161: 127; 183: 187, 188
Strodl, Daniel 47: 95
Strogart, Alexander 63: 139
Stromoski, Rick 111: 179; 124: 161, 190
Strong, Joseph D., Jr. YABC 2: 330
Stroyer, Poul 13: 221
Strugnell, Ann 27: 38
Struzan, Drew 117: 6
Stubbs, William 73: 196
Stubis, Talivaldis 5: 182, 183; 10: 45; 11: 9; 18: 304; 20: 127
Stubley, Trevor 14: 43; 22: 219; 23: 37; 28: 61; 87: 26
Stuck, Marion 104: 44
Stuecklen, Karl W. 8: 34, 65; 23: 103
Stull, Betty 11: 46
Stutzman, Mark 119: 99
Stutzmann, Laura 73: 185
Suarez, Maribel 162: 208
Suba, Susanne 4: 202, 203; 14: 261; 23: 134; 29: 222; 32: 30
Sueling, Barbara 98: 185
Sueling, Gwenn 98: 186
Sugarman, Tracy 3: 76; 8: 199; 37: 181, 182
Sugimoto, Yugo 170: 144
Sugita, Yutaka 36: 180, 181
Suh, John 80: 157
Sullivan, Dorothy 89: 113
Sullivan, Edmund J. 31: 86
Sullivan, James F. 19: 280; 20: 192
Sully, Tom 104: 199, 200; 182: 77

Sumichrast, Jozef *14:* 253; *29:* 168, 213
Sumiko *46:* 57
Summers, Leo *1:* 177; *2:* 273; *13:* 22
Summers, Mark *118:* 144
Summers, Mike *190:* 176
Sutton, Judith *94:* 164
Svarez, Juan *56:* 113
Svendsen, Mark *181:* 176
Svolinsky, Karel *17:* 104
Swain, Carol *172:* 182
Swain, Su Zan Noguchi *21:* 170
Swan, Susan *22:* 220, 221; *37:* 66; *60:* 146; *145:* 205; *181:* 168
Swann, Susan *86:* 55
Swanson, Karl *79:* 65; *89:* 186
Swayne, Sam *53:* 143, 145
Swayne, Zoa *53:* 143, 145
Swearingen, Greg *152:* 56; *165:* 135; *173:* 2
Sweat, Lynn *25:* 206; *57:* 176; *73:* 184; *168:* 178
Sweet, Darrell K. *60:* 9; *69:* 86; *74:* 15; *75:* 215; *76:* 130, 131; *81:* 96, 122; *82:* 253; *83:* 11; *84:* 14; *85:* 37; *89:* 140; *90:* 6; *91:* 137,139; *95:* 160, 161; *126:* 25; *185:* 175
Sweet, Darrell K. *1:* 163; *4:* 136; *164:* 175
Sweet, Melissa *71:* 94; *72:* 172; *111:* 82; *139:* 53, 58; *141:* 88; *142:* 231; *155:* 121; *159:* 121, 122; *172:* 185; *188:* 127
Sweet, Ozzie *31:* 149, 151, 152
Sweetland, Robert *12:* 194
Swiatkowska, Gabi *132:* 43; *175:* 139; *180:* 218; *183:* 176
Swope, Martha *43:* 160; *56:* 86, 87, 89
Sylvada, Peter *154:* 174
Sylvester, Natalie G. *22:* 222
Szafran, Gene *24:* 144
Szasz, Susanne *13:* 55, 226; *14:* 48
Szekeres, Cyndy *2:* 218; *5:* 185; *8:* 85; *11:* 166; *14:* 19; *16:* 57, 159; *26:* 49, 214; *34:* 205; *60:* 150, 151, 152, 153, 154; *73:* 224; *74:* 218; *131:* 213, 215
Szpura, Beata *81:* 68; *119:* 65; *168:* 201

T

Taback, Simms *40:* 207; *52:* 120; *57:* 34; *80:* 241; *104:* 202, 203; *170:* 176, 177
Taber, Patricia *75:* 124
Tabor, Nancy Maria Grande *89:* 210; *161:* 188
Taddei, Richard *112:* 13, 14
Tadgell, Nicole *150:* 77; *161:* 20; *177:* 186
Tadiello, Ed *133:* 200
Tafuri, Nancy *39:* 210; *75:* 199, 200; *92:* 75; *130:* 215, 216, 217
Tailfeathers, Gerald *86:* 85
Tait, Douglas *12:* 220; *74:* 105, 106
Takabayashi, Mari *113:* 112; *130:* 22; *156:* 169
Takahashi, Hideko *136:* 160; *187:* 6
Takakjian, Portia *15:* 274
Takashima, Shizuye *13:* 228
Talarczyk, June *4:* 173
Talbott, Hudson *84:* 240; *163:* 100
Tallarico, Tony *116:* 197
Tallon, Robert *2:* 228; *43:* 200, 201, 202, 203, 204, 205,206, 207, 209
Tamas, Szecsko *29:* 135
Tamburine, Jean *12:* 222
Tandy, H.R. *13:* 69
Tandy, Russell H. *65:* 9; *100:* 30, 131
Tang, Charles *81:* 202; *90:* 192
Tang, Susan *80:* 174; *108:* 158
Tang, You-shan *63:* 100
Tankersley, Paul *69:* 206; *133:* 219
Tannenbaum, Robert *48:* 181
Tanner, Jane *87:* 13; *97:* 37
Tanner, Tim *72:* 192; *84:* 35
Tanobe, Miyuki *23:* 221
Tarabay, Sharif *110:* 149; *113:* 123; *169:* 83
Tarkington, Booth *17:* 224, 225

Tarlow, Phyllis *61:* 198
Tate, Don *159:* 141, 191; *183:* 69; *186:* 120
Tauss, Herbert *95:* 179
Tauss, Marc *117:* 160; *126:* 155; *178:* 221
Tavares, Matt *159:* 192, 193
Taylor, Ann *41:* 226
Taylor, Dahl *129:* 157
Taylor, Geoff *93:* 156
Taylor, Isaac *41:* 228
Taylor, Mike *143:* 99, 100
Teague, Mark *83:* 6; *139:* 241; *170:* 180, 181
Teale, Edwin Way *7:* 196
Teason, James *1:* 14
Teeple, Lyn *33:* 147
Tee-Van, Helen Damrosch *10:* 176; *11:* 182
Teicher, Dick *50:* 211
Teichman, Mary *77:* 220; *124:* 208; *127:* 22
Temertey, Ludmilla *96:* 232; *104:* 43, 45; *109:* 244
Tempest, Margaret *3:* 237, 238; *88:* 200
Temple, Frances *85:* 185, 186, 187
Temple, Herbert *45:* 201
Templeton, Owen *11:* 77
ten Cate, Marijke *183:* 193
Tenggren, Gustaf *18:* 277, 278, 279; *19:* 15; *28:* 86; *YABC2:* 145
Tennent, Julie *81:* 105
Tenneson, Joyce *153:* 166
Tenney, Gordon *24:* 204
Tenniel, John *74:* 234, 235; *100:* 89; *YABC 2:* 99; *153:* 169
Tepper, Matt *116:* 80
Terkel, Ari *103:* 162
Terry, Michael *180:* 209
Terry, Will *131:* 73
Teskey, Donald *71:* 51
Thacher, Mary M. *30:* 72
Thackeray, William Makepeace *23:* 224, 228
Thamer, Katie *42:* 187
Tharlet, Eve *146:* 149
Thelwell, Norman *14:* 201
Theobalds, Prue *40:* 23
Theurer, Marilyn Churchill *39:* 195
Thiesing, Lisa *89:* 134; *95:* 202; *156:* 190; *159:* 195
Thiewes, Sam *133:* 114
Thistlethwaite, Miles *12:* 224
Thollander, Earl *11:* 47; *18:* 112; *22:* 224
Thomas, Allan *22:* 13
Thomas, Art *48:* 217
Thomas, Eric *28:* 49
Thomas, Harold *20:* 98
Thomas, Jacqui *125:* 95
Thomas, Mark *42:* 136
Thomas, Martin *14:* 255
Thomas, Middy *177:* 114
Thompson, Arthur *34:* 107
Thompson, Carol *85:* 189; *95:* 75; *102:* 86; *147:* 166; *189:* 179, 180, 181; *190:* 84
Thompson, Colin *95:* 204
Thompson, Ellen *51:* 88, 151; *60:* 33; *67:* 42; *77:* 148; *78:* 75, 219; *79:* 122, 170; *84:* 219; *85:* 97; *87:* 37; *88:* 192, 194; *89:* 80; *93:* 37; *98:* 59; *132:* 14
Thompson, George W. *22:* 18; *28:* 150; *33:* 135
Thompson, John *58:* 201; *102:* 226; *124:* 154; *128:* 228; *129:* 157; *150:* 49; *185:* 160; *191:* 192
Thompson, Julie *44:* 158
Thompson, Katherine *132:* 146
Thompson, K. Dyble *84:* 6
Thompson, Miles *152:* 77
Thompson, Sharon *74:* 113; *158:* 60; *165:* 87
Thomson, Arline K. *3:* 264
Thomson, Bill *186:* 160
Thomson, Hugh *26:* 88
Thomson, Ross *36:* 179
Thorkelson, Gregg *95:* 183, 184; *98:* 58; *165:* 30, 31
Thorn, Lori *189:* 119

Thornberg, Dan *104:* 125
Thornburgh, Rebecca McKillip *143:* 37
Thorne, Diana *25:* 212
Thornhill, Jan *77:* 213
Thorpe, Peter *58:* 109
Thorvall, Kerstin *13:* 235
Threadgall, Colin *77:* 215
Thurber, James *13:* 239, 242, 243, 245, 248, 249
Thurman, Mark *63:* 173; *168:* 116
Tibbles, Jean-Paul *115:* 200
Tibbles, Paul *45:* 23
Tibo, Gilles *67:* 207; *107:* 199, 201
Tichenor, Tom *14:* 207
Tichnor, Richard *90:* 218
Tiegreen, Alan *36:* 143; *43:* 55, 56, 58; *77:* 200; *94:* 216, 217; *121:* 54, 59
Tierney, Tom *113:* 198, 200, 201
Tilley, Debbie *102:* 134; *133:* 226; *137:* 101; *159:* 96; *190:* 211, 212
Tilney, F.C. *22:* 231
Timbs, Gloria *36:* 90
Timmins, Harry *2:* 171
Tinkelman, Murray *12:* 225; *35:* 44
Titherington, Jeanne *39:* 90; *58:* 138; *75:* 79; *135:* 161
Tobin, Nancy *145:* 197
Toddy, Irving *172:* 144
Tokunbo, Dimitrea *181:* 183; *187:* 182, 183
Tolbert, Jeff *128:* 69
Tolford, Joshua *1:* 221
Tolkien, J.R.R. *2:* 243; *32:* 215
Tolmie, Ken *15:* 292
Tomei, Lorna *47:* 168, 171
Tomes, Jacqueline *2:* 117; *12:* 139
Tomes, Margot *1:* 224; *2:* 120, 121; *16:* 207; *18:* 250; *20:* 7; *25:* 62; *27:* 78, 79; *29:* 81, 199; *33:* 82; *36:* 186, 187, 188, 189, 190; *46:* 129; *56:* 71; *58:* 183; *70:* 228; *75:* 73, 75; *80:* 80; *83:* 97; *90:* 205
Toner, Raymond John *10:* 179
Tong, Gary *66:* 215
Tongier, Stephen *82:* 32
Tooke, Susan *173:* 162
Toothill, Harry *6:* 54; *7:* 49; *25:* 219; *42:* 192
Toothill, Ilse *6:* 54
Topolski, Feliks *44:* 48
Torbert, Floyd James *22:* 226
Torgersen, Don *55:* 157
Torline, Kevin *169:* 171
Tormey, Bertram M. *75:* 3, 4
Torrecilla, Pablo *176:* 207
Torres, Leyla *156:* 199, 201
Torrey, Helen *87:* 41
Torrey, Marjorie *34:* 105
Torrey, Richard *189:* 182
Toschik, Larry *6:* 102
Totten, Bob *13:* 93
Toy, Julie *128:* 112
Trachok, Cathy *131:* 16
Tracy, Libba *82:* 24
Trago, Keith *158:* 253
Trail, Lee *55:* 157
Trang, To Ngoc *167:* 180
Trang, Winson *89:* 151
Trapani, Iza *116:* 202
Travers, Bob *49:* 100; *63:* 145
Treatner, Meryl *95:* 180
Tremain, Ruthven *17:* 238
Tresilian, Stuart *25:* 53; *40:* 212
Trez, Alain *17:* 236
Trezzo, Loretta *86:* 45
Trier, Walter *14:* 96
Trimby, Elisa *47:* 199
Trinkle, Sally *53:* 27
Triplett, Gina *182:* 193; *188:* 100
Tripp, F.J. *24:* 167
Tripp, Wallace *2:* 48; *7:* 28; *8:* 94; *10:* 54,76; *11:* 92; *31:* 170, 171; *34:* 203; *42:* 57; *60:* 157; *73:* 182
Trivas, Irene *53:* 4; *54:* 168; *82:* 46, 101

Trnka, Jiri *22:* 151; *43:* 212, 213, 214, 215; *YABC 1:* 30, 31
Trondheim, Lewis *182:* 183
Troughton, Joanna *37:* 186; *48:* 72
Troyer, Johannes *3:* 16; *7:* 18
Trudeau, G.B. *35:* 220, 221, 222; *48:* 119, 123, 126, 127,128, 129, 133; *168:* 189
Trueman, Matthew *165:* 208; *183:* 191
Truesdell, Sue *55:* 142; *108:* 219, 220
Tryon, Leslie *84:* 7; *139:* 214; *143:* 10; *181:* 10
Tseng, Jean *72:* 195; *94:* 102; *119:* 126; *151:* 106; *173:* 138, 139
Tseng, Mou-sien *72:* 195; *94:* 102; *119:* 126; *151:* 106; *173:* 138, 139
Tsinajinie, Andy *2:* 62
Tsinganos, Jim *180:* 142
Tsugami, Kyuzo *18:* 198, 199
Tucker, Ezra *156:* 31
Tuckwell, Jennifer *17:* 205
Tudor, Bethany *7:* 103
Tudor, Tasha *18:* 227; *20:* 185, 186, 187; *36:* 111; *69:* 196, 198; *100:* 44;
YABC 2: 46, 314; *160:* 234
Tuerk, Hanne *71:* 201
Tulloch, Maurice *24:* 79
Tunis, Edwin *1:* 218, 219; *28:* 209, 210, 211, 212
Tunnicliffe, C.F. *62:* 176; *177;* 178, 179; 181
Turkle, Brinton *1:* 211, 213; *2:* 249; *3:* 226; *11:* 3; *16:* 209; *20:* 22; *50:* 23; *67:* 50; *68:* 65; *79:* 205, 206, 207; *128:* 47; *YABC 1:* 79
Turnbull, Christopher J. *143:* 99, 100
Turner, Gwenda *59:* 195
Turska, Krystyna *12:* 103; *31:* 173, 174, 175; *56:* 32,34; *100:* 66
Tusa, Tricia *72:* 242; *111:* 180, 181; *157:* 165; *164:* 186; *189:* 40
Tusan, Stan *6:* 58; *22:* 236, 237
Tworkov, Jack *47:* 207
Tyers, Jenny *89:* 220
Tylden-Wright, Jenny *114:* 119
Tyrol, Adelaide Murphy *103:* 27
Tyrrell, Frances *107:* 204
Tzimoulis, Paul *12:* 104

U

Uchida, Yoshiko *1:* 220
Uderzo *47:* 88
Udovic, David *189:* 185
Ueno, Noriko *59:* 155
Ulm, Robert *17:* 238
Ulrich, George *73:* 15; *75:* 136, 139; *99:* 150
Ulriksen, Mark *101:* 58; *182:* 43
Unada *84:* 67
See Gliewe, Unada
Underhill, Liz *53:* 159
Underwood, Beck *192:* 36
Underwood, Clarence *40:* 166
Unger, Jim *67:* 208
Ungerer, Tomi *5:* 188; *9:* 40; *18:* 188; *29:* 175; *33:* 221, 222, 223, 225; *71:* 48; *106:* 209, 210, 211, 212
Unwin, Nora S. *3:* 65, 234, 235; *4:* 237; *44:* 173, 174; *YABC 1:* 59; *2:* 301
Upitis, Alvis *145:* 179
Urban, Helle *149:* 243
Urbanovic, Jackie *86:* 86; *189:* 186, 187
Uris, Jill *49:* 188, 197
Ursell, Martin *50:* 51
Utpatel, Frank *18:* 114
Utz, Lois *5:* 190

V

Vagin, Vladimir *66:* 10; *142:* 215
Vaillancourt, Francois *107:* 199
Vainio, Pirkko *123:* 157, 158
Valério, Geraldo *180:* 225
Vallejo, Boris *62:* 130; *72:* 212; *91:* 38; *93:* 61
Van Abbe, S. *16:* 142; *18:* 282; *31:* 90; *YABC 2:* 157, 161
Van Allsburg, Chris *37:* 205, 206; *53:* 161, 162, 163, 165,166, 167, 168, 169, 170, 171; *105:* 215, 216, 217, 218; *156:* 176, 177, 178
Vance, James *65:* 28
Van Der Linde, Henry *99:* 17
van der Meer, Ron *98:* 204, 205
van der Meer, Atie *98:* 204, 205
Vandivert, William *21:* 175
Van Dongen, H.R. *81:* 97
Van Dusen, Chris W. *173:* 169
Van Everen, Jay *13:* 160; *YABC 1:* 121
Van Fleet, John *165:* 12, 13
Van Frankenhuyzen, Gijsbert *145:* 230; *149:* 164; *184:* 151
van Genechten, Guido *165:* 226
van Haeringen, Annemarie *193:* 206
Van Horn, William *43:* 218
van Lawick, Hugo *62:* 76, 79
Van Loon, Hendrik Willem *18:* 285, 289, 291
Van Munching, Paul *83:* 85
van Ommen, Sylvia *186:* 192
Van Patter, Bruce *183:* 195
Van Rynbach, Iris *102:* 192
Van Sciver, Ruth *37:* 162
VanSeveren, Joe *63:* 182
Van Stockum, Hilda *5:* 193
Van Wely, Babs *16:* 50; *79:* 16
Van Wright, Cornelius *72:* 18; *102:* 208; *116:* 107; *152:* 236; *173:* 170, 171
Van Zyle, Jon *103:* 125; *160:* 181, 182; *176:* 199, 200
Vardzigulyants, Ruben *90:* 54
Varga, Judy *29:* 196
Vargo, Kurt *79:* 224
Varley, Susan *61:* 199; *63:* 176, 177; *101:* 148; *134:* 220
Vasconcellos, Daniel *80:* 42
Vasiliu, Mircea *2:* 166, 253; *9:* 166; *13:* 58; *68:* 42
Vaughn, Frank *34:* 157
Vavra, Robert *8:* 206
Vawter, Will *17:* 163
Vayas, Diana *71:* 61
Vazquez, Carlos *125:* 184
Veeder, Larry *18:* 4
Velasquez, Eric *45:* 217; *61:* 45; *63:* 110, 111; *88:* 162; *90:* 34, 144; *94:* 213; *107:* 147; *132:* 192; *138:* 213; *159:* 126; *181:* 184; *184:* 96; *191:* 16; *192:* 234
Velasquez, Jose A. *63:* 73
Velez, Walter *71:* 75; *91:* 154; *121:* 181; *168:* 49
Velthuijs, Max *110:* 228, 229
Vendrell, Carme Sole *42:* 205
Venezia, Mike *54:* 17
Venti, Anthony Bacon *124:* 103; *126:* 26
Venturo, Piero *61:* 194, 195
Ver Beck, Frank *18:* 16, 17
Verkaaik, Ben *110:* 209
Verling, John *71:* 27
Verney, John *14:* 225; *75:* 8
Verrier, Suzanne *5:* 20; *23:* 212
Versace, Marie *2:* 255
Verstraete, Randy *108:* 193
Vestal, H.B. *9:* 134; *11:* 101; *27:* 25; *34:* 158
Vestergaard, Hope *190:* 203
Vicatan *59:* 146
Vickrey, Robert *45:* 59, 64
Victor, Joan Berg *30:* 193
Viereck, Ellen *3:* 242; *14:* 229
Vigna, Judith *15:* 293; *102:* 194, 195, 196, 197

Vilato, Gaspar E. *5:* 41
Villiard, Paul *51:* 178
Vimnera, A. *23:* 154
Vincent, Eric *34:* 98
Vincent, Felix *41:* 237
Vincent, Gabrielle *121:* 175
Vip *45:* 164
Viskupic, Gary *83:* 48
Vitale, Stefano *109:* 71, 107; *114:* 219, 220; *123:* 106; *138:* 232; *180:* 228, 229
Vivas, Julie *51:* 67, 69; *96:* 225
Voake, Charlotte *114:* 221, 222; *180:* 232
Vo-Dinh, Mai *16:* 272; *60:* 191
Vogel, Ilse-Margret *14:* 230
Voigt, Erna *35:* 228
Vojnar, Kamil *95:* 31; *114:* 4; *115:* 62; *121:* 90; *124:* 72; *130:* 31; *141:* 81; *146:* 196; *150:* 123; *158:* 5, 6; *158:* 154; *171:* 119, 188; *179:* 15; *180:* 112
Vojtech, Anna *42:* 190; *108:* 222, 223; *150:* 203; *174:* 173
von Buhler, Cynthia *149:* 237; *162:* 177; *177:* 205; *180:* 77; *185:* 214, 215, 216
von Roehl, Angela *126:* 191
von Schmidt, Eric *8:* 62; *50:* 209, 210
von Schmidt, Harold *30:* 80
Vosburgh, Leonard *1:* 161; *7:* 32; *15:* 295, 296; *23:* 110; *30:* 214; *43:* 181
Voss, Tom *127:* 104
Voter, Thomas W. *19:* 3, 9
Vroman, Tom *10:* 29
Vulliamy, Clara *72:* 65

W

Waber, Bernard *47:* 209, 210, 211, 212, 213, 214; *95:* 215, 216, 217; *156:* 203, 205, 206, 207
Wack, Jeff *95:* 140; *110:* 90
Wagner, John *8:* 200; *52:* 104
Wagner, Ken *2:* 59
Waide, Jan *29:* 225; *36:* 139
Wainwright, Jerry *14:* 85
Waites, Joan C. *171:* 2
Wakeen, Sandra *47:* 97
Wakiyama, Hanako *171:* 96; *192:* 236
Waldherr, Kris *81:* 186
Waldman, Bruce *15:* 297; *43:* 178
Waldman, Neil *35:* 141; *50:* 163; *51:* 180; *54:* 78; *77:* 112; *79:* 162; *82:* 174; *84:* 5, 56, 106; *94:* 232, 233, 234; *96:* 41; *111:* 139; *113:* 9; *118:* 30; *142:* 220, 223
Waldrep, Richard *111:* 147
Walker, Brian *144:* 128
Walker, Charles *1:* 46; *4:* 59; *5:* 177; *11:* 115; *19:* 45; *34:* 74; *62:* 168; *72:* 218
Walker, Dugald Stewart *15:* 47; *32:* 202; *33:* 112
Walker, Gil *8:* 49; *23:* 132; *34:* 42
Walker, Jeff *55:* 154; *123:* 116
Walker, Jim *10:* 94
Walker, Mort *8:* 213
Walker, Norman *41:* 37; *45:* 58
Walker, Stephen *12:* 229; *21:* 174
Wallace, Beverly Dobrin *19:* 259
Wallace, Cly *87:* 93
Wallace, Ian *53:* 176, 177; *56:* 165, 166; *58:* 4; *98:* 4; *101:* 191; *112:* 124; *141:* 197, 198, 199, 200; *151:* 212
Wallace, John *105:* 228
Wallace, Nancy Elizabeth *141:* 204; *186:* 195, 197, 199
Wallenta, Adam *123:* 180
Waller, S.E. *24:* 36
Wallner, Alexandra *15:* 120; *156:* 183
Wallner, John C. *9:* 77; *10:* 188; *11:* 28; *14:* 209; *31:* 56, 118; *37:* 64; *51:* 186, 187, 188, 189, 190, 191,192, 193, 194, 195; *52:* 96; *53:* 23, 26; *71:* 99; *73:* 158; *89:* 215; *141:* 9

Wallner, John *162:* 17
Wallower, Lucille *11:* 226
Walotsky, Ron *93:* 87
Walsh, Ellen Stoll *99:* 209; *147:* 219
Walsh, Rebecca *158:* 193
Walsh, Vivian *149:* 215; *158:* 227
Walters, Audrey *18:* 294
Walther, Tom *31:* 179
Walton, Garry *69:* 149
Walton, Tony *11:* 164; *24:* 209; *153:* 8; *177:* 73
Waltrip, Lela *9:* 195
Waltrip, Mildred *3:* 209; *37:* 211
Waltrip, Rufus *9:* 195
Wan *12:* 76
Wang, Suling *191:* 183
Warburton, Sarah *154:* 187
Wappers, G. *121:* 40
Ward, Fred *52:* 19
Ward, Helen *72:* 244; *144:* 240, 242
Ward, John *42:* 191; *96:* 54; *97:* 110; *123:* 105; *124:* 71; *173:* 66
Ward, Keith *2:* 107; *132:* 69
Ward, Leslie *34:* 126; *36:* 87
Ward, Lynd *1:* 99, 132, 133, 150; *2:* 108, 158, 196, 259; *18:* 86; *27:* 56; *29:* 79, 187, 253, 255; *36:* 199,200, 201, 202, 203, 204, 205, 206, 207, 209; *43:* 34; *56:* 28; *60:* 116; *100:* 65
Ward, Peter *37:* 116
Waring, Geoff *172:* 84
Warhola, James *92:* 5; *115:* 85, 87; *118:* 174, 175, 177; *176:* 84; *187:* 189, 190
Warner, Ben *159:* 171
Warner, Peter *14:* 87
Warnes, Tim *175:* 159
Warnick, Elsa *113:* 223
Warren, Betsy *2:* 101
Warren, Jim *85:* 81
Warren, Marion Cray *14:* 215
Warshaw, Jerry *30:* 197, 198; *42:* 165
Wasden, Kevin *102:* 162
Washington, Nevin *20:* 123
Washington, Phyllis *20:* 123
Wasserman, Amy L. *92:* 110
Waterman, Stan *11:* 76
Watkins-Pitchford, D.J. *6:* 215, 217
Watling, James *67:* 210; *78:* 112; *101:* 81; *117:* 189, 190; *127:* 119, 120
Watson, Aldren A. *2:* 267; *5:* 94; *13:* 71; *19:* 253; *32:* 220; *42:* 193, 194, 195, 196, 197, 198, 199, 200, 201; *YABC 2:* 202
Watson, G. *83:* 162
Watson, Gary *19:* 147; *36:* 68; *41:* 122; *47:* 139
Watson, J.D. *22:* 86
Watson, Karen *11:* 26
Watson, Mary *117:* 193
Watson, Richard Jesse *62:* 188, 189
Watson, Wendy *5:* 197; *13:* 101; *33:* 116; *46:* 163; *64:* 12; *74:* 242, 243; *91:* 21; *142:* 228
Watt, Mélanie *136:* 206; *193:* 211
Wattenberg, Jane *174:* 200; *185:* 46; *187:* 108
Watterson, Bill *66:* 223, 225, 226
Watts, Bernadette *4:* 227; *103:* 182, 183
Watts, James *59:* 197; *74:* 145; *86:* 124
Watts, John *37:* 149
Watts, Leslie Elizabeth *150:* 207; *165:* 106
Watts, Stan *116:* 205
Weatherby, Mark Alan *77:* 141
Webb, Jennifer *110:* 79
Webb, Lanny *142:* 175
Webb, Sophie *135:* 214
Webber, Helen *3:* 141
Webber, Irma E. *14:* 238
Weber, Erik *56:* 19, 20
Weber, Florence *40:* 153
Weber, Jill *127:* 227, 228; *189:* 163
Weber, Roland *61:* 204
Weber, Sam *190:* 227
Weber, William J. *14:* 239

Webster, Jean *17:* 241
Weeks, Sarah *162:* 39
Wegman, William *78:* 243
Wegner, Fritz *14:* 250; *20:* 189; *44:* 165; *86:* 62
Weidenear, Reynold H. *21:* 122
Weigel, Jeff *170:* 193
Weihs, Erika *4:* 21; *15:* 299; *72:* 201; *107:* 207, 208
Weil, Lisl *7:* 203; *10:* 58; *21:* 95; *22:* 188,217; *33:* 193
Weiman, Jon *50:* 162, 165; *52:* 103; *54:* 78, 79, 81; *78:* 80; *82:* 107; *93:* 82; *97:* 69; *105:* 179; *193:* 65
Weiner, Sandra *14:* 240
Weiner, Scott *55:* 27
Weinhaus, Karen Ann *53:* 90; *71:* 50; *86:* 124
Weisgard, Leonard *1:* 65; *2:* 191, 197, 204, 264, 265; *5:* 108; *21:* 42; *30:* 200, 201, 203, 204; *41:* 47; *44:* 125; *53:* 25; *85:* 196, 198, 200, 201; *100:* 139,207; *YABC 2:* 13
Weisman, David *173:* 47
Weiss, Ellen *44:* 202
Weiss, Emil *1:* 168; *7:* 60
Weiss, Harvey *1:* 145, 223; *27:* 224, 227; *68:* 214; *76:* 245, 246, 247
Weiss, Nicki *33:* 229
Weissman, Bari *49:* 72; *90:* 125; *139:* 142
Weitzman, David L. *172:* 199
Welch, Sheila Kelly *130:* 221
Welkes, Allen *68:* 218
Wellington, Monica *99:* 223; *157:* 259, 260, 261
Welliver, Norma *76:* 94
Wellner, Fred *127:* 53
Wells, Frances *1:* 183
Wells, H.G. *20:* 194, 200
Wells, Haru *53:* 120, 121
Wells, Robert E. *184:* 208
Wells, Rosemary *6:* 49; *18:* 297; *60:* 32; *66:* 203; *69:* 215, 216; *114:* 227; *118:* 149, 150; *156:* 188, 189, 190, 191
Wells, Rufus III *56:* 111, 113
Wells, Susan *22:* 43
Wendelin, Rudolph *23:* 234
Wengenroth, Stow *37:* 47
Weninger, Brigitte *189:* 192, 194
Werenskiold, Erik *15:* 6; *62:* 17
Werner, Honi *24:* 110; *33:* 41; *88:* 122
Werth, Kurt *7:* 122; *14:* 157; *20:* 214; *39:* 128
West, Harry A. *124:* 38
Westcott, Nadine Bernard *68:* 46; *84:* 49; *86:* 133; *106:* 199; *111:* 78; *113:* 111; *130:* 224; *139:* 54; *158:* 256
Westerberg, Christine *29:* 226
Westerduin, Anne *105:* 229
Westerman, Johanna *162:* 206
Weston, Martha *29:* 116; *30:* 213; *33:* 85, 100; *53:* 181, 182, 183, 184; *77:* 95; *80:* 152; *119:* 196,197, 198, 199; *127:* 189; *133:* 196
Wetherbee, Margaret *5:* 3
Wexler, Jerome *49:* 73; *150:* 129
Whalley, Peter *50:* 49
Whatley, Bruce *186:* 93, 95
Wheatley, Arabelle *11:* 231; *16:* 276
Wheeler, Cindy *49:* 205
Wheeler, Dora *44:* 179
Wheelright, Rowland *15:* 81; *YABC 2:* 286
Whelan, Michael *56:* 108; *70:* 27, 29, 67, 68, 148; *74:* 18; *84:* 14; *91:* 195, 196; *95:* 147; *98:* 150, 151; *106:* 157; *113:* 218, 220; *116:* 99, 100
Whelan, Patrick *135:* 145
Whistler, Rex *16:* 75; *30:* 207, 208
White, Craig *110:* 130; *119:* 193; *130:* 33; *179:* 31
White, David Omar *5:* 56; *18:* 6
White, Joan *83:* 225
White, Martin *51:* 197; *85:* 127
Whitear *32:* 26
Whitehead, Beck *86:* 171

Whitehead, S.B. *154:* 132
Whithorne, H.S. *7:* 49
Whitney, George Gillett *3:* 24
Whitney, Jean *99:* 53
Whitson, Paul *102:* 161
Whittam, Geoffrey *30:* 191
Whyte, Mary *96:* 127
Wiberg, Harald *38:* 127; *93:* 215
Wick, Walter *77:* 128
Wickstrom, Sylvie *106:* 87; *169:* 180
Widener, Terry *105:* 230; *106:* 7; *163:* 23
Wiese, Kurt *3:* 255; *4:* 206; *14:* 17; *17:* 18, 19; *19:* 47; *24:* 152; *25:* 212; *32:* 184; *36:* 211,213, 214, 215, 216, 217, 218; *45:* 161; *100:* 92
Wiesner, David *33:* 47; *51:* 106; *57:* 67; *58:* 55; *64:* 78, 79, 81; *69:* 233; *72:* 247, 248, 249, 251,252, 253, 254; *83:* 134; *104:* 31; *117:* 197, 199, 200, 202; *139:* 223, 224; *151:* 51; *181:* 189, 190
Wiesner, William *4:* 100; *5:* 200, 201; *14:* 262
Wiggins, George *6:* 133
Wijngaard, Juan *111:* 36; *114:* 124
Wikkelsoe, Otto *45:* 25, 26
Wikland, Ilon *5:* 113; *8:* 150; *38:* 124, 125, 130; *127:* 162
Wikler, Madeline *114:* 233
Wilbur, C. Keith, M.D. *27:* 228
Wilburn, Kathy *53:* 102; *68:* 234
Wilcox, Cathy *105:* 123
Wilcox, J.A.J. *34:* 122
Wilcox, R. Turner *36:* 219
Wild, Jocelyn *46:* 220, 221, 222; *80:* 117
Wilde, George *7:* 139
Wildsmith, Brian *16:* 281, 282; *18:* 170, 171; *66:* 25; *69:* 224, 225, 227; *77:* 103; *83:* 218; *124:* 214,217, 219
Wildsmith, Mike *140:* 229
Wilhelm, Hans *58:* 189, 191; *73:* 157; *77:* 127; *135:* 229, 230, 233, 234
Wilkin, Eloise *36:* 173; *49:* 208, 209, 210
Wilkinson, Barry *50:* 213
Wilkinson, Gerald *3:* 40
Wilkon, Jozef *31:* 183, 184; *71:* 206, 207, 209; *133:* 222
Wilks, Mike *34:* 24; *44:* 203
Willems, Mo *154:* 245, 246, 247; *180:* 236, 237, 239
Willey, Bee *103:* 129; *139:* 159; *173:* 115
Willhoite, Michael A. *71:* 214
William, Maria *168:* 51
Williams, Berkeley, Jr. *64:* 75
Williams, Ferelith Eccles *22:* 238
Williams, Garth *1:* 197; *2:* 49, 270; *4:* 205; *15:* 198, 302, 304, 307; *16:* 34; *18:* 283, 298, 299, 300, 301; *29:* 177, 178, 179, 232, 233, 241, 242, 243, 244, 245, 248; *40:* 106; *66:* 229, 230, 231, 233, 234; *71:* 192; *73:* 218, 219, 220; *78:* 261; *100:* 251, 252, 255; *136:* 117; *YABC 2:* 15, 16, 19
Williams, J. Scott *48:* 28
Williams, Jennifer *102:* 201
Williams, Jenny *60:* 202; *81:* 21; *88:* 71
Williams, Kent *180:* 18
Williams, Kit *44:* 206, 207, 208, 209, 211, 212
Williams, Marcia *97:* 214; *159:* 208, 209
Williams, Maureen *12:* 238
Williams, Patrick *14:* 218
Williams, Richard *44:* 93; *72:* 229; *74:* 133; *78:* 155, 237; *91:* 178; *110:* 212; *136:* 201, 202, 203; *152:* 115
Williams, Sam *124:* 222; *153:* 11; *177:* 201, 202; *180:* 34
Williams, Sophy *135:* 236
Williams, Vera B. *53:* 186, 187, 188, 189; *102:* 201, 202, 203
Williamson, Alex *177:* 180
Williamson, Mel *60:* 9
Willingham, Fred *104:* 206; *154:* 157
Willis, Adam *181:* 75
Willmore, J.T. *54:* 113, 114

Wilsdorf, Anne *180:* 122; *189:* 124; *191:* 195
Wilson, Anne *160:* 114
Wilson, Charles Banks *17:* 92; *43:* 73
Wilson, Connie *113:* 179
Wilson, Dagmar *10:* 47
Wilson, Dawn *67:* 161; *81:* 120; *113:* 158
Wilson, Edward A. *6:* 24; *16:* 149; *20:* 220, 221; *22:* 87; *26:* 67; *38:* 212, 214, 215, 216, 217
Wilson, Forrest *27:* 231
Wilson, Gahan *35:* 234; *41:* 136
Wilson, George *76:* 87
Wilson, Helen Miranda *140:* 61
Wilson, Jack *17:* 139
Wilson, Janet *77:* 154; *96:* 114; *99:* 219, 220; *153:* 64 *106:* 122; *130:* 210; *145:* 178; *173:* 64
Wilson, John *22:* 240
Wilson, Maurice *46:* 224
Wilson, Patten *35:* 61
Wilson, Peggy *15:* 4; *84:* 20
Wilson, Phil *181:* 29
Wilson, Rowland B. *30:* 170
Wilson, Sarah *50:* 215
Wilson, Tom *33:* 232
Wilson, W.N. *22:* 26
Wilson-Max, Ken *170:* 196; *180:* 181
Wilton, Nicholas *103:* 52; *183:* 111
Wilwerding, Walter J. *9:* 202
Wimmer, Mike *63:* 6; *70:* 121; *75:* 186; *76:* 21,22, 23; *91:* 114; *97:* 45, 68; *98:* 28; *107:* 130; *146:* 21; *149:* 47; *173:* 126; *193:* 21, 25
Winborn, Marsha *78:* 34; *99:* 70; *192:* 20
Winch, John *165:* 233
Winchester, Linda *13:* 231
Wind, Betty *28:* 158
Windham, Kathryn Tucker *14:* 260
Windham, Sophie *184:* 212
Winfield, Alison *115:* 78
Winfield, Wayne *72:* 23
Wing, Gary *64:* 147
Wing, Ron *50:* 85
Wingerter, Linda S. *132:* 199; *174:* 181
Winick, Judd *124:* 227, 228, 229
Winslow, Will *21:* 124
Winstead, Rosie *180:* 243
Winsten, Melanie Willa *41:* 41
Winter, Jeanette *151:* 240, 241, 242; *184:* 215, 217, 218, 219
Winter, Milo *15:* 97; *19:* 221; *21:* 181, 203, 204, 205; *64:* 19; *YABC 2:* 144
Winter, Paula *48:* 227
Winter, Susan *163:* 177; *182:* 201
Winters, Greg *70:* 117
Winters, Nina *62:* 194
Wise, Louis *13:* 68
Wiseman, Ann *31:* 187
Wiseman, B. *4:* 233
Wishnefsky, Phillip *3:* 14
Wiskur, Darrell *5:* 72; *10:* 50; *18:* 246
Wisniewski, David *95:* 220, 221
Wisniewski, Robert *95:* 10; *119:* 192
Witschonke, Alan *153:* 149, 150
Witt, Dick *80:* 244
Wittmann, Patrick *162:* 204
Wittman, Sally *30:* 219
Wittner, Dale *99:* 43
Wittwer, Hala *158:* 267
Woehr, Lois *12:* 5
Wohlberg, Meg *12:* 100; *14:* 197; *41:* 255
Wohnoutka, Mike *137:* 68; *190:* 199
Wojtowycz, David *167:* 168
Woldin, Beth Weiner *34:* 211
Wolf, Elizabeth *133:* 151
Wolf, J. *16:* 91
Wolf, Janet *78:* 254
Wolf, Linda *33:* 163
Wolfe, Corey *72:* 213
Wolff, Ashley *50:* 217; *81:* 216; *156:* 216, 217; *170:* 57; *174:* 174; *184:* 72
Wolff, Glenn *178:* 230

Wolfsgruber, Linda *166:* 61
Wondriska, William *6:* 220
Wong, Janet S. *98:* 225; *152:* 43
Wong, Nicole *174:* 13
Wonsetler, John C. *5:* 168
Wood, Audrey *50:* 221, 222, 223; *81:* 219, 221
Wood, Don *50:* 220, 225, 226, 228, 229; *81:* 218, 220; *139:* 239, 240
Wood, Grant *19:* 198
Wood, Heather *133:* 108
Wood, Ivor *58:* 17
Wood, Muriel *36:* 119; *77:* 167; *171:* 55; *187:* 46
Wood, Myron *6:* 220
Wood, Owen *18:* 187; *64:* 202, 204, 205, 206, 208, 210
Wood, Rob *193:* 48
Wood, Ruth *8:* 11
Woodbridge, Curtis *133:* 138
Wooding, Sharon L. *66:* 237
Woodruff, Liza *132:* 239; *182:* 46, 204
Woodruff, Thomas *171:* 73
Woods, John, Jr. *109:* 142
Woodson, Jack *10:* 201
Woodson, Jacqueline *94:* 242
Woodward, Alice *26:* 89; *36:* 81
Wool, David *26:* 27
Woolley, Janet *112:* 75
Woolman, Steven *106:* 47; *163:* 73
Wooten, Vernon *23:* 70; *51:* 170
Worboys, Evelyn *1:* 166, 167
Word, Reagan *103:* 204
Wormell, Christopher *154:* 251
Worth, Jo *34:* 143
Worth, Wendy *4:* 133
Wosmek, Frances *29:* 251
Wrenn, Charles L. *38:* 96; *YABC 1:* 20, 21
Wright, Barbara Mullarney *98:* 161
Wright, Cliff *168:* 203
Wright, Dare *21:* 206
Wright-Frierson, Virginia *58:* 194; *110:* 246
Wright, George *YABC 1:* 268
Wright, Joseph *30:* 160
Wronker, Lili Cassel *3:* 247; *10:* 204; *21:* 10
Wummer, Amy *154:* 181; *168:* 150; *176:* 85
Wyant, Alexander Helwig *110:* 19
Wyatt, David *97:* 9; *101:* 44; *114:* 194; *140:* 20; *167:* 13; *188:* 48
Wyatt, Stanley *46:* 210
Wyeth, Andrew *13:* 40; *YABC 1:* 133, 134
Wyeth, Jamie *41:* 257
Wyeth, N.C. *13:* 41; *17:* 252, 253, 254, 255, 256, 257, 258, 259, 264, 265, 266, 267, 268; *18:* 181; *19:* 80, 191, 200; *21:* 57, 183; *22:* 91; *23:* 152; *24:* 28, 99; *35:* 61; *41:* 65; *100:* 206; *YABC1:* 133, 223; *2:* 53, 75, 171, 187, 317
Wyman, Cherie R. *91:* 42

X

Xuan, YongSheng *119:* 202, 207, 208; *140:* 36; *187:* 21

Y

Yaccarino, Dan *141:* 208, 209; *147:* 171; *192:* 244, 245
Yakovetic, Joe *59:* 202; *75:* 85
Yalowitz, Paul *93:* 33
Yamaguchi, Marianne *85:* 118
Yamasaki, James *167:* 93
Yang, Belle *170:* 198
Yang, Jay *1:* 8; *12:* 239
Yap, Weda *6:* 176

Yaroslava
  See Mills, Yaroslava Surmach
Yashima, Taro *14:* 84
Yates, John *74:* 249, 250
Yayo *178:* 88
Yee, Cora *166:* 233
Yee, Wong Herbert *115:* 216, 217; *172:* 204, 205
Yeo, Brad *135:* 121; *192:* 106
Yerxa, Leo *181:* 195
Yezerski, Thomas F. *162:* 29
Ylla
  See Koffler, Camilla
Yohn, F.C. *23:* 128; *YABC 1:* 269
Yoo, Taeeun *191:* 198
Yorinks, Adrienne *144:* 248
Yorke, David *80:* 178
Yoshida, Toshi *77:* 231
Yoshikawa, Sachiko *168:* 104; *177:* 28; *181:* 196, 197
Youll, Paul *91:* 218
Youll, Stephen *92:* 227; *118:* 136, 137; *164:* 248
Young, Amy L. *185:* 218; *190:* 46
Young, Cybéle *167:* 9
Young, Ed *7:* 205; *10:* 206; *40:* 124; *63:* 142; *74:* 250, 251, 252, 253; *75:* 227; *81:* 159; *83:* 98; *94:* 154; *115:* 160; *137:* 162; *YABC 2:* 242; *173:* 174, 175, 176
Young, Mary O'Keefe *77:* 95; *80:* 247; *134:* 214; *140:* 213
Young, Noela *8:* 221; *89:* 231; *97:* 195
Young, Paul *190:* 222
Young, Selina *153:* 12
Yun, Cheng Mung *60:* 143

Z

Zacharow, Christopher *88:* 98
Zacks, Lewis *10:* 161
Zadig *50:* 58
Zaffo, George *42:* 208
Zagwyn, Deborah Turney *138:* 227
Zahares, Wade *193:* 219
Zaid, Barry *50:* 127; *51:* 201
Zaidenberg, Arthur *34:* 218, 219, 220
Zalben, Jane Breskin *7:* 211; *79:* 230, 231, 233; *170:* 202
Zallinger, Jean *4:* 192; *8:* 8, 129; *14:* 273; *68:* 36; *80:* 254; *115:* 219, 220, 222
Zallinger, Rudolph F. *3:* 245
Zakrajsek, Molly *177:* 146
Zappa, Ahmet *180:* 250
Zebot, George *83:* 214
Zeck, Gerry *40:* 232
Zeff, Joe *181:* 98
Zeifert, Harriet *154:* 265, 267
Zeiring, Bob *42:* 130
Zeldich, Arieh *49:* 124; *62:* 120
Zeldis, Malcah *86:* 239; *94:* 198; *146:* 265, 266
Zelinsky, Paul O. *14:* 269; *43:* 56; *49:* 218-223; *53:* 111; *68:* 195; *102:* 219, 222, 221, 222; *154:* 255, 256, 257; *171:* 141; *185:* 96
Zelvin, Diana *72:* 190; *76:* 101; *93:* 207
Zemach, Kaethe *149:* 250
Zemach, Margot *3:* 270; *8:* 201; *21:* 210, 211; *27:* 204, 205, 210; *28:* 185; *49:* 22, 183, 224; *53:* 151; *56:* 146; *70:* 245, 246; *92:* 74
Zeman, Ludmila *153:* 212
Zemsky, Jessica *10:* 62
Zepelinsky, Paul *35:* 93
Zerbetz, Evon *127:* 34; *158:* 109
Zhang, Ange *101:* 190; *172:* 41
Zhang, Son Nang *163:* 113; *170:* 206
Ziegler, Jack *84:* 134
Zimdars, Berta *129:* 155
Zimet, Jay *147:* 94; *152:* 74

Zimic, Tricia *72:* 95
Zimmer, Dirk *38:* 195; *49:* 71; *56:* 151; *65:* 214; *84:* 159; *89:* 26; *147:* 224
Zimmer, Tracie Vaughn *169:* 183
Zimmerman, Andrea *192:* 49, 50
Zimmermann, H. Werner *101:* 223; *112:* 197
Zimnik, Reiner *36:* 224
Zingone, Robin *180:* 134

Zinkeisen, Anna *13:* 106
Zinn, David *97:* 97
Zoellick, Scott *33:* 231
Zollars, Jaime *190:* 190
Zonia, Dhimitri *20:* 234, 235
Zorn, Peter A., Jr. *142:* 157
Zudeck, Darryl *58:* 129; *63:* 98; *80:* 52
Zug, Mark *88:* 131

Zulewski, Tim *164:* 95
Zuma *99:* 36
Zvorykin, Boris *61:* 155
Zweifel, Francis *14:* 274; *28:* 187
Zwerger, Lisbeth *54:* 176, 178; *66:* 246, 247, 248; *130:* 230, 231, 232, 233; *181:* 92
Zwinger, Herman H. *46:* 227
Zwolak, Paul *67:* 69, 71, 73, 74

Author Index

The following index gives the number of the volume in which an author's biographical sketch, Autobiography Feature, Brief Entry, or Obituary appears.

This index includes references to all entries in the following series, which are also published by The Gale Group.

YABC—*Yesterday's Authors of Books for Children: Facts and Pictures about Authors and Illustrators of Books for Young People from Early Times to 1960*
CLR—*Children's Literature Review: Excerpts from Reviews, Criticism, and Commentary on Books for Children*
SAAS—*Something about the Author Autobiography Series*

A

Aaron, Chester 1923- 74
　Earlier sketch in SATA 9
　See also SAAS 12
Aaseng, Nate
　See Aaseng, Nathan
Aaseng, Nathan 1953- 172
　Brief entry 38
　Earlier sketches in SATA 51, 88
　See also CLR 54
　See also SAAS 12
Abadzis, Nick 1965- 193
Abbas, Jailan 1952- 91
Abbey, Lynn
　See Abbey, Marilyn Lorraine
Abbey, Marilyn Lorraine 1948- 156
Abbott, Alice
　See Borland, Kathryn Kilby
　and Speicher, Helen Ross S(mith)
Abbott, Jacob 1803-1879 22
Abbott, Manager Henry
　See Stratemeyer, Edward L.
Abbott, R(obert) Tucker 1919-1995 61
　Obituary 87
Abbott, Sarah
　See Zolotow, Charlotte
Abbott, Tony 1952- 159
Abdelsayed, Cindy 1962- 123
Abdul, Raoul 1929- 12
Abel, Raymond 1911- 12
Abell, Kathleen 1938- 9
Abelove, Joan 110
Abels, Harriette S(heffer) 1926- 50
Abercrombie, Barbara 1939- 182
　Earlier sketch in SATA 16
Abercrombie, Barbara Mattes
　See Abercrombie, Barbara
Abercrombie, Lynn
　See Sorrells, Walter
Abernethy, Robert G(ordon) 1927- 5
Abisch, Roslyn Kroop 1927- 9
Abisch, Roz
　See Abisch, Roslyn Kroop
Abodaher, David J. (Naiph) 1919- 17
Abolafia, Yossi 1944-
　See Abulafia, Yossi
Abouzeid, Chris 175

Abrahall, Clare Hoskyns
　See Hoskyns-Abrahall, Clare (Constance Drury)
Abrahams, Hilary (Ruth) 1938- 29
Abrahams, Robert David 1905-1998 4
Abrams, Joy 1941- 16
Abrams, Lawrence F. 58
　Brief entry 47
Abrashkin, Raymond 1911-1960 50
Abulafia, Yossi 1944- 177
　Brief entry 46
　Earlier sketch in SATA 60
Acampora, Paul 175
Accardo, Anthony 191
Achebe, Albert Chinualumogu
　See Achebe, Chinua
Achebe, Chinua 1930- 40
　Brief entry 38
　Earlier sketch in SATA 38
　See also CLR 20
Ackerman, Diane 1948- 102
Ackerman, Eugene (Francis) 1888-1974 10
Ackerman, Karen 1951- 126
Ackerman, Susan Yoder 1945- 92
Ackison, Wendy Wassink 1956- 103
Ackley, Peggy Jo 1955- 58
Ackroyd, Peter 1949- 153
Acorn, John (Harrison) 1958- 79
Acredolo, Linda (Potter) 1947- 159
Acs, Laszlo (Bela) 1931- 42
　Brief entry 32
Acuff, Selma Boyd 1924- 45
Ada, Alma Flor 1938- 181
　Earlier sketches in SATA 43, 84, 143
　See also CLR 62
Adair, Gilbert 1944- 98
Adair, Ian 1942- 53
Adair, Margaret Weeks (?)-1971 10
Adam, Cornel
　See Lengyel, Cornel Adam
Adam, Mark
　See Alexander, Marc
Adam, Robert 1948- 93
Adams, Adrienne 1906- 90
　Earlier sketch in SATA 8
　See also CLR 73
Adams, Andy 1859-1935
　See YABC 1
Adams, Barbara Johnston 1943- 60

Adams, Bruin
　See Ellis, Edward S(ylvester)
Adams, Captain Bruin
　See Ellis, Edward S(ylvester)
Adams, Captain J. F. C.
　See Ellis, Edward S(ylvester)
Adams, Dale
　See Quinn, Elisabeth
Adams, Daniel
　See Nicole, Christopher (Robin)
Adams, Debra
　See Speregen, Devra Newberger
Adams, Douglas 1952-2001 116
　Obituary 128
Adams, Douglas Noel
　See Adams, Douglas
Adams, Edith
　See Shine, Deborah
Adams, Florence 1932- 61
Adams, Harriet S(tratemeyer)
　1892(?)-1982 1
　Obituary 29
Adams, Harrison
　See Rathborne, St. George (Henry)
　and Stratemeyer, Edward L.
Adams, Hazard 1926- 6
Adams, Hazard Simeon
　See Adams, Hazard
Adams, John Anthony 1944- 67
Adams, Laurie 1941- 33
Adams, Lowell
　See Joseph, James (Herz)
Adams, Nicholas
　See Pine, Nicholas
Adams, Nicholas
　See Smith, Sherwood
Adams, Nicholas
　See Doyle, Debra
　and Macdonald, James D.
Adams, Pam 1919- 112
Adams, Pamela
　See Adams, Pam
Adams, Richard (George) 1920- 69
　Earlier sketch in SATA 7
　See also CLR 121
Adams, Ruth Joyce 14
Adams, Tricia
　See Kite, Pat
Adams, William Taylor 1822-1897 28

Adam Smith, Janet (Buchanan) 1905-1999 .. *63*
Adamson, Gareth 1925-1982(?) *46*
   Obituary *30*
Adamson, George 1906-1989
   Obituary *63*
Adamson, George (Worsley) 1913-2005 ...... *30*
Adamson, Graham
   See Groom, Arthur William
Adamson, Joy(-Friederike Victoria)
   1910-1980 .... *11*
   Obituary *22*
Adamson, Wendy Writson 1942- *22*
Addison, Kenneth 1949(?)-2005 .... *187*
Addison, Kenneth L.
   See Addison, Kenneth
Addona, Angelo F. 1925- *14*
Addy, Sharon Hart 1943- *192*
   Earlier sketch in SATA *108*
Addy, Ted
   See Winterbotham, R(ussell) R(obert)
Adelberg, Doris
   See Orgel, Doris
Adelson, Leone 1908- *11*
Adinolfi, JoAnn *176*
Adkins, Jan 1944- *144*
   Earlier sketches in SATA *8, 69*
   See also CLR *77*
   See also SAAS *19*
Adler, C(arole) S(chwerdtfeger) 1932- *126*
   Earlier sketches in SATA *26, 63, 102*
   See also CLR *78*
   See also SAAS *15*
Adler, David A. 1947- *178*
   Earlier sketches in SATA *14, 70, 106, 151*
   See also CLR *108*
Adler, Irene
   See Penzler, Otto
   and Storr, Catherine (Cole)
Adler, Irving 1913- *29*
   Autobiography Feature *164*
   Earlier sketch in SATA *1*
   See also CLR *27*
   See also SAAS *15*
Adler, Larry 1939- *36*
Adler, Peggy *22*
Adler, Ruth 1915-1968 .... *1*
Adlerman, Daniel (Ezra) 1963- *163*
   Earlier sketch in SATA *96*
Adlerman, Kim
   See Adlerman, Kimberly M(arie)
Adlerman, Kimberly M(arie) 1964- *163*
   Earlier sketch in SATA *96*
Adoff, Arnold 1935- *96*
   Earlier sketches in SATA *5, 57*
   See also CLR *7*
   See also SAAS *15*
Adoff, Jaime (Levi) *163*
Adorjan, Carol (Madden) 1934- *71*
   Earlier sketch in SATA *10*
Adrian, Frances
   See Polland, Madeleine A(ngela Cahill)
Adrian, Mary
   See Jorgensen, Mary Venn
Adshead, Gladys L(ucy) 1896-1985 .... *3*
Aesop 620(?)B.C.-560(?)B.C. *64*
   See also CLR *14*
Aesop, Abraham
   See Newbery, John
Affabee, Eric
   See Stine, R.L.
Agapida, Fray Antonio
   See Irving, Washington
Agard, John 1949- *138*
Agard, Nadema 1948- *18*
Agarwal, Deepa 1947- *141*
Agee, Jon 1960- *157*
   Earlier sketch in SATA *116*
Agell, Charlotte 1959- *150*
   Earlier sketch in SATA *99*
Agent Orange
   See Moseley, James W(illett)

Aghill, Gordon
   See Garrett, (Gordon) Randall (Phillip)
   and Silverberg, Robert
Agle, Nan Hayden 1905- *3*
   See also SAAS *10*
Agnew, Edith J(osephine) 1897-1988 .... *11*
Agonito, Joseph *177*
Agonito, Rosemary 1937- *177*
Ahern, Margaret McCrohan 1921- *10*
Ahl, Anna Maria 1926- *32*
Ahlberg, Allan 1938- *165*
   Brief entry *35*
   Earlier sketches in SATA *68, 120*
   See also CLR *18*
Ahlberg, Janet 1944-1994 .... *120*
   Brief entry *32*
   Obituary *83*
   Earlier sketch in SATA *68*
   See also CLR *18*
Aichinger, Helga 1937- *4*
Aiken, Clarissa (M.) Lorenz 1899-1992 .... *12*
   Obituary *109*
Aiken, Conrad (Potter) 1889-1973 .... *30*
   Earlier sketch in SATA *3*
Aiken, Joan (Delano) 1924-2004 .... *73*
   Autobiography Feature *109*
   Obituary *152*
   Earlier sketches in SATA *2, 30*
   See also CLR *90*
   See also SAAS *1*
Aillaud, Cindy Lou 1955- *184*
Ainsley, Alix
   See Steiner, Barbara A(nnette)
Ainsworth, Catherine Harris 1910- *56*
Ainsworth, Norma 1911-1987 .... *9*
Ainsworth, Ruth (Gallard) 1908- *73*
   Earlier sketch in SATA *7*
Ainsworth, William Harrison 1805-1882 ..... *24*
Aistrop, Jack 1916- *14*
Aitken, Amy 1952- *54*
   Brief entry *40*
Aitken, Dorothy 1916- *10*
Aitmatov, Chingiz 1928-2008 .... *56*
   See Aytmatov, Chingiz
Aitmatov, Chingiz Torekulovich
   See Aitmatov, Chingiz
Akaba, Suekichi 1910- *46*
Akers, Floyd
   See Baum, L(yman) Frank
Akib, Jamel *181*
Aks, Patricia 1926-1994 .... *68*
Alagoa, Ebiegberi Joe 1933- *108*
Alain
   See Brustlein, Daniel
Alajalov, Constantin 1900-1987
   Obituary *53*
Alan, David
   See Horsfield, Alan
Alan, Robert
   See Silverstein, Robert Alan
Alarcon, Francisco X(avier) 1954- *104*
Albert, Burton 1936- *22*
Albert, Louise 1928- *157*
Albert, Richard E. 1909-1999 .... *82*
Albert, Susan Wittig 1940- *107*
Alberts, Frances Jacobs 1907-1989 .... *14*
Albertson, Susan
   See Wojciechowski, Susan
Albion, Lee Smith *29*
Alborough, Jez 1959- *149*
   Earlier sketch in SATA *86*
Albrecht, Lillie (Vanderveer H.)
   1894-1985 .... *12*
Albyn, Carole Lisa 1955- *83*
Alchemy, Jack
   See Gershator, David
Alcock, Gudrun 1908- *56*
   Brief entry *33*

Alcock, Vivien (Dolores) 1924-2003 .... *76*
   Brief entry *38*
   Obituary *148*
   Earlier sketch in SATA *45*
   See also CLR *26*
Alcorn, John 1935- *31*
   Brief entry *30*
Alcorn, Stephen 1958- *110*
Alcott, Louisa May 1832-1888 .... *100*
   See also YABC *1*
   See also CLR *109*
Alda, Arlene 1933- *158*
   Brief entry *36*
   Earlier sketches in SATA *44, 106*
   See also CLR *93*
Alden, Isabella (Macdonald) 1841-1930 ..... *115*
   See also YABC *2*
Alden, Sue
   See Francis, Dorothy
Alderman, Clifford Lindsey 1902-1988 .... *3*
Alderson, Sue Ann 1940- *59*
   Brief entry *48*
Alding, Peter
   See Jeffries, Roderic
Aldis, Dorothy (Keeley) 1896-1966 .... *2*
Aldiss, Brian W. 1925- *34*
Aldiss, Brian Wilson
   See Aldiss, Brian W.
Aldon, Adair
   See Meigs, Cornelia Lynde
Aldous, Allan (Charles) 1911- *27*
Aldrich, Ann
   See Meaker, Marijane
Aldrich, Bess Streeter 1881-1954
   See CLR *70*
Aldrich, Thomas (Bailey) 1836-1907 .... *114*
   Earlier sketch in SATA *17*
Aldridge, (Harold Edward) James 1918- *87*
Aldridge, Josephine Haskell *14*
Aldridge, Sheila 1974- *192*
Aleas, Richard
   See Appelt, Kathi
Alegria, Malin 1974(?)- *190*
Alegria, Ricardo E(nrique) 1921- *6*
Aleksin, Anatolii Georgievich 1924- *36*
Alenov, Lydia 1948- *61*
Alex, Ben (a pseudonym) 1946- *45*
Alex, Marlee (a pseudonym) 1948- *45*
Alexander, Anna B(arbara Cooke) 1913- *1*
Alexander, Anne
   See Alexander, Anna B(arbara Cooke)
Alexander, Ellen 1938- *91*
Alexander, Frances (Laura) 1888-1979 .... *4*
Alexander, Jocelyn Anne Arundel 1930- *22*
Alexander, Linda 1935- *2*
Alexander, Lloyd 1924-2007 .... *135*
   Obituary *182*
   Earlier sketches in SATA *3, 49, 81, 129*
   See also CLR *48*
   See also SAAS *19*
Alexander, Lloyd Chudley
   See Alexander, Lloyd
Alexander, Marc 1929- *117*
Alexander, Martha 1920- *136*
   Earlier sketches in SATA *11, 70*
Alexander, Rae Pace
   See Alexander, Raymond Pace
Alexander, Raymond Pace 1898-1974 .... *22*
Alexander, Rod
   See Pellowski, Michael (Joseph)
Alexander, Sally Hobart 1943- *84*
Alexander, Sue 1933-2008 .... *136*
   Earlier sketches in SATA *12, 89*
   See also SAAS *15*
Alexander, Vincent Arthur 1925-1980
   Obituary *23*
Alexeieff, Alexandre A. 1901-1979 .... *14*
Alger, Horatio, Jr.
   See Stratemeyer, Edward L.
Alger, Horatio, Jr. 1832-1899 .... *16*
   See also CLR *87*

Alger, Leclaire (Gowans) 1898-1969 .... *15*
Aliki
　See CLR *71*
　See Brandenberg, Aliki (Liacouras)
Alkema, Chester Jay 1932- *12*
Al-Khalili, Jim 1962- *124*
Alkiviades, Alkis 1953- *105*
Alkouatli, Claire *186*
Allaby, John Michael
　See Allaby, Michael
Allaby, Michael 1933- *167*
Allamand, Pascale 1942- *12*
Allan, Mabel Esther 1915-1998 .... *75*
　Earlier sketches in SATA *5, 32*
　See also CLR *43*
　See also SAAS *11*
Allan, Nicholas 1956- *123*
　Earlier sketch in SATA *79*
Allan-Meyer, Kathleen 1918- *51*
　Brief entry *46*
Allard, Harry
　See Allard, Harry G(rover), Jr.
Allard, Harry G(rover), Jr. 1928- *102*
　Earlier sketch in SATA *42*
　See also CLR *85*
Allee, Marjorie Hill 1890-1945 .... *17*
Allen, Adam
　See Epstein, Beryl (M. Williams)
　and Epstein, Samuel
Allen, Alex B.
　See Heide, Florence Parry
Allen, Allyn
　See Eberle, Irmengarde
Allen, Betsy
　See Harrison, Elizabeth (Allen) Cavanna
Allen, Bob 1961- *76*
Allen, Gertrude E(lizabeth) 1888-1984 .... *9*
Allen, Grace
　See Hogarth, Grace (Weston Allen)
Allen, Jeffrey (Yale) 1948- *42*
Allen, John
　See Perry, Ritchie (John Allen)
Allen, Jonathan 1957- *177*
　Earlier sketch in SATA *131*
Allen, Jonathan Dean
　See Allen, Jonathan
Allen, Judy (Christina) 1941- *124*
　Earlier sketch in SATA *80*
Allen, Kenneth S. 1913-1981 .... *56*
Allen, Leroy 1912- *11*
Allen, Linda 1925- *33*
Allen, Marjorie 1931- *22*
Allen, Maury 1932- *26*
Allen, Merritt Parmelee 1892-1954 .... *22*
Allen, Nancy Kelly 1949- *171*
　Earlier sketch in SATA *127*
Allen, Nina (Stroemgren) 1935- *22*
Allen, Pamela (Kay) 1934- *123*
　Earlier sketches in SATA *50, 81*
　See also CLR *44*
Allen, Rodney F. 1938-1999 .... *27*
Allen, Roger MacBride 1957- *105*
Allen, Ruth
　See Peterson, Esther (Allen)
Allen, Samuel W(ashington) 1917- *9*
Allen, T. D.
　See Allen, Terril Diener
Allen, Terril Diener 1908- *35*
　See Allen, T. D.
Allen, Terry D.
　See Allen, Terril Diener
Allen, Thomas B. 1929- *193*
　Earlier sketches in SATA *45, 140*
Allen, Thomas B. 1929- *193*
Allen, Thomas Benton
　See Allen, Thomas B.
Allen, Tom
　See Allen, Thomas B.
Allende, Isabel 1942- *163*
　See also CLR *99*

Allerton, Mary
　See Govan, (Mary) Christine Noble
Alley, Robert W.
　See Alley, R.W.
Alley, R.W. *169*
Alleyn, Ellen
　See Rossetti, Christina
Allington, Richard L(loyd) 1947- *39*
　Brief entry *35*
Allison, Amy 1956- *138*
Allison, Bob *14*
Allison, Diane Worfolk *78*
Allison, Jennifer *173*
Allison, Linda 1948- *43*
Allison, Margaret
　See Klam, Cheryl
Allman, Barbara 1950- *137*
Allmendinger, David F(rederick),
　Jr. 1938- *35*
Allred, Alexandra Powe 1965- *144*
Allred, Gordon T(hatcher) 1930- *10*
Allsop, Kenneth 1920-1973 .... *17*
Allsopp, Sophie *188*
Almedingen, E. M. *3*
　See Almedingen, Martha Edith von
Almon, Russell
　See Clevenger, William R.
　and Downing, David A(lmon)
Almond, David 1951- *158*
　Earlier sketch in SATA *114*
　See also CLR *85*
Almond, Linda Stevens 1881(?)-1987
　Obituary *50*
Almquist, Don 1929- *11*
Alphin, Elaine Marie 1955- *139*
　Autobiography Feature *139*
　Earlier sketches in SATA *80, 130*
Alsenas, Linas 1979- *186*
Alsop, Mary O'Hara 1885-1980 .... *34*
　Obituary *24*
　Earlier sketch in SATA *2*
　See O'Hara, Mary
Alter, Anna 1974- *135*
Alter, Judith (MacBain) 1938- *101*
　Earlier sketch in SATA *52*
Alter, Judy
　See Alter, Judith (MacBain)
Alter, Robert Edmond 1925-1965 .... *9*
Alter, Stephen 1956- *187*
Althea
　See Braithwaite, Althea
Altman, Linda Jacobs 1943- *21*
Altman, Suzanne
　See Orgel, Doris
　and Schecter, Ellen
Alton, Steve *169*
Altschuler, Franz 1923- *45*
Altsheler, Joseph A(lexander) 1862-1919
　See YABC *1*
Alvarez, John
　See del Rey, Lester
Alvarez, Joseph A. 1930- *18*
Alvarez, Julia 1950- *129*
al-Windawi, Thura
　See Windawi, Thura al-
Alyer, Philip A.
　See Stratemeyer, Edward L.
Amado, Elisa *193*
Amann, Janet 1951- *79*
Amato, Carol A. 1942- *92*
Amato, Mary 1961- *178*
　Earlier sketch in SATA *140*
Ambrose, Stephen E. 1936-2002 .... *138*
　Earlier sketch in SATA *40*
Ambrose, Stephen Edward
　See Ambrose, Stephen E.
Ambrus, Gyozo Laszlo 1935- *41*
　See Ambrus, Victor G.
Ambrus, Victor G. *1*
　See also SAAS *4*
　See Ambrus, Gyozo Laszlo

Amend, Bill 1962- *147*
Amerman, Lockhart 1911-1969 .... *3*
Ames, Evelyn 1908-1990 .... *13*
　Obituary *64*
Ames, Gerald 1906-1993 .... *11*
　Obituary *74*
Ames, Lee J(udah) 1921- *151*
　Earlier sketch in SATA *3*
Ames, Mildred 1919-1994 .... *85*
　Earlier sketches in SATA *22, 81*
Amico, Tom 1960(?)- *176*
Ammon, Richard 1942- *124*
Amon, Aline 1928- *9*
Amoss, Berthe 1925- *112*
　Earlier sketch in SATA *5*
Anastasio, Dina 1941- *94*
　Brief entry *30*
　Earlier sketch in SATA *37*
Anaya, Rudolfo A. 1937-
　See CLR *129*
Anaya, Rudolpho Alfonso
　See Anaya, Rudolfo A.
Anckarsvard, Karin Inez
　Maria 1915-1969 .... *6*
Ancona, George 1929- *192*
　Earlier sketches in SATA *12, 85, 145*
　See also SAAS *18*
Anders, C. J.
　See Bennett, Cherie
Anders, Isabel 1946- *101*
Anders, Lou *176*
Andersdatter, Karla M(argaret) 1938- *34*
Andersen, Bethanne 1954- *191*
Andersen, Hans Christian 1805-1875 .... *100*
　See also YABC *1*
　See also CLR *113*
Andersen, Ted
　See Boyd, Waldo T.
Andersen, Yvonne 1932- *27*
Anderson, Bernice G(oudy) 1894-1997 .... *33*
Anderson, Bob 1944- *139*
　Earlier sketch in SATA *136*
Anderson, Brad(ley Jay) 1924- *33*
　Brief entry *31*
Anderson, C. C.
　See Anderson, Catherine Corley
Anderson, C(larence) W(illiam)
　1891-1971 .... *11*
Anderson, Catherine C.
　See Anderson, Catherine Corley
Anderson, Catherine Corley 1909-2001 .... *72*
Anderson, Clifford
　See Gardner, Richard (M.)
Anderson, Daryl Shon 1963- *93*
Anderson, Dave
　See Anderson, David (Poole)
Anderson, David (Poole) 1929- *60*
Anderson, Derek 1969- *169*
Anderson, Eloise Adell 1927- *9*
Anderson, George
　See Groom, Arthur William
Anderson, Grace Fox 1932- *43*
Anderson, J(ohn) R(ichard) L(ane)
　1911-1981 .... *15*
　Obituary *27*
Anderson, Jodi Lynn *182*
Anderson, Joy 1928- *1*
Anderson, Kevin J. 1962- *117*
　Earlier sketch in SATA *74*
Anderson, Kevin James
　See Anderson, Kevin J.
Anderson, Kirsty 1978- *108*
Anderson, K.J.
　See Moesta, Rebecca
Anderson, Laurie Halse 1961- *186*
　Earlier sketches in SATA *95, 132*
　See also CLR *138*
Anderson, LaVere Francis Shoenfelt
　1907-1998 .... *27*
Anderson, Leone Castell 1923- *53*
　Brief entry *49*

Anderson, Lisa G. 1963- 108
Anderson, Lonzo 2
    See Anderson, John L(onzo)
Anderson, Lucia (Lewis) 1922- 10
Anderson, Madelyn Klein 1926-2005 28
Anderson, Margaret J(ean) 1931- 27
    See also SAAS 8
Anderson, Marilyn D. 1943- 144
Anderson, Mary 1939- 82
    Earlier sketch in SATA 7
    See also SAAS 23
Anderson, Matthew Tobin
    See Anderson, M.T.
Anderson, Mona 1910-2004 40
Anderson, Mrs. Melvin
    See Anderson, Catherine Corley
Anderson, M.T. 1968- 182
    Earlier sketches in SATA 97, 146
Anderson, Norman Dean 1928- 22
Anderson, Peggy Perry 1953- 179
    Earlier sketch in SATA 84
Anderson, Poul 1926-2001 90
    Autobiography Feature 106
    Brief entry 39
    See also CLR 58
Anderson, Poul William
    See Anderson, Poul
Anderson, Rachel 1943- 86
    Earlier sketch in SATA 34
    See also SAAS 18
Anderson, Rebecca M.
    See Moesta, Rebecca
Anderson, Rebecca Moesta
    See Moesta, Rebecca
Anderson, Richard
    See Anderson, J(ohn) R(ichard) L(ane)
Anderson, Sara 173
Anderson, (Tom) Scoular 138
Anderson, Susan 1952- 90
Anderson, W. B.
    See Schultz, James Willard
Anderson, Wayne 1946- 147
    Earlier sketch in SATA 56
Andre, Evelyn M(arie) 1924- 27
Andreasen, Dan 186
Andreassen, Karl
    See Boyd, Waldo T.
Andreassi, K. Robert
    See DeCandido, Keith R.A.
Andree, Louise
    See Coury, Louise Andree
Andrew, Ian 1962- 166
    Earlier sketch in SATA 116
Andrew, Ian Peter
    See Andrew, Ian
Andrew, Prudence (Hastings) 1924- 87
Andrews, Benny 1930-2006 31
    Obituary 178
Andrews, Eleanor Lattimore
    See Lattimore, Eleanor Frances
Andrews, Elton V.
    See Pohl, Frederik
Andrews, F(rank) Emerson 1902-1978 22
Andrews, J(ames) S(ydney) 1934- 4
Andrews, Jan 1942- 167
    Brief entry 49
    Earlier sketches in SATA 58, 98
Andrews, Julie 1935- 153
    Earlier sketch in SATA 7
    See also CLR 85
Andrews, Laura
    See Coury, Louise Andree
Andrews, Roy Chapman 1884-1960 19
Andrews, Tamra 1959- 129
Andrews, V(irginia) C(leo) 1924(?)-1986
    Obituary 50
Andrews, Wendy
    See Sharmat, Marjorie Weinman
Andrews, William G(eorge) 1930- 74
Andrezel, Pierre
    See Blixen, Karen (Christentze Dinesen)

Andriani, Renee
    See Williams-Andriani, Renee
Andriola, Alfred J. 1912-1983
    Obituary 34
Andrist, Ralph K. 1914-2004 45
Andronik, Catherine M. 189
Andryszewski, Tricia 1956- 148
    Earlier sketch in SATA 88
Angel, Ann 1952- 192
Angel, Carl 178
Angel, Marie 1923- 47
Angeles, Peter A. 1931- 40
Angeletti, Roberta 1964- 124
Angeli, Marguerite (Lofft) de
    See de Angeli, Marguerite (Lofft)
Angell, Madeline 1919- 18
Angelo, Valenti 1897- 14
Angelou, Maya 1928- 136
    Earlier sketch in SATA 49
    See also CLR 53
Angier, Bradford -1997 12
Angle, Paul M(cClelland) 1900-1975
    Obituary 20
Anglund, Joan Walsh 1926- 2
    See also CLR 94
Ango, Fan D.
    See Longyear, Barry B(rookes)
Angrist, Stanley W(olff) 1933- 4
Anholt, Catherine 1958- 131
    Earlier sketch in SATA 74
Anholt, Laurence 1959- 141
    Earlier sketch in SATA 74
Anita
    See Daniel, Anita
Anmar, Frank
    See Nolan, William F(rancis)
Annett, Cora
    See Scott, Cora Annett (Pipitone)
Annie-Jo
    See Blanchard, Patricia
    and Suhr, Joanne
Annixter, Jane
    See Sturtzel, Jane Levington
Annixter, Paul
    See Sturtzel, Howard A(llison)
Anno, Mitsumasa 1926- 157
    Earlier sketches in SATA 5, 38, 77
    See also CLR 122
Anrooy, Francine Van
    See Van Anrooy, Francine
Ansary, Mir Tamim 1948- 140
Anstey, Caroline 1958- 81
Antell, Will D. 1935- 31
Anthony, Barbara
    See Barber, Antonia
Anthony, C. L.
    See Smith, Dorothy Gladys
Anthony, Edward 1895-1971 21
Anthony, John
    See Beckett, Ronald Brymer
    and Ciardi, John (Anthony)
    and Sabini, John Anthony
Anthony, Joseph Patrick 1964- 103
Anthony, Patricia 1947- 109
Anthony, Piers 1934- 129
    Autobiography Feature 129
    Earlier sketch in SATA 84
    See also CLR 118
    See also SAAS 22
Anthony, Susan C(arol) 1953- 87
Anticaglia, Elizabeth 1939- 12
Antilles, Kem
    See Moesta, Rebecca
Antle, Nancy 1955- 102
Antolini, Margaret Fishback 1904-1985
    Obituary 45
Anton, Michael J(ames) 1940- 12
Antonacci, Robert J(oseph) 1916- 45
    Brief entry 37
Anvil, Christopher
    See Crosby, Harry C., Jr.

Anzaldua, Gloria (Evanjelina) 1942-2004
    Obituary 154
Aoki, Hisako 1942- 45
Apfel, Necia H(alpern) 1930- 51
    Brief entry 41
Aphrodite, J.
    See Livingston, Carole
Apikuni
    See Schultz, James Willard
Apostolina, M. 184
Apostolina, Michael
    See Apostolina, M.
Apostolou, Christine Hale 1955- 128
    Earlier sketch in SATA 82
    See Hale, Christy
Appel, Allen (R.) 1945- 115
Appel, Benjamin 1907-1977 39
    Obituary 21
Appel, Martin 1948- 45
Appel, Martin Eliot
    See Appel, Martin
Appel, Marty
    See Appel, Martin
Appelbaum, Diana Muir Karter 1953- 132
Appelt, Kathi 1954- 190
    Earlier sketches in SATA 83, 129
Apperley, Dawn 1969- 135
Appiah, Peggy 1921-2006 84
    Earlier sketch in SATA 15
    See also SAAS 19
Apple, Margot 152
    Brief entry 42
    Earlier sketch in SATA 64
Applebaum, Stan 1922- 45
Applegate, K. A.
    See CLR 90
    See Applegate, Katherine (Alice)
Applegate, Katherine (Alice) 1956- 162
    Earlier sketch in SATA 109
    See Applegate, K. A.
Appleton, Victor 67
    Earlier sketch in SATA 1
    See Barrett, Neal, Jr.
    and Doyle, Debra
    and Macdonald, James D.
    and Stratemeyer, Edward L.
    and Vardeman, Robert E(dward)
Appleton, Victor II 67
    Earlier sketch in SATA 1
    See Goulart, Ron(ald Joseph)
Apsler, Alfred 1907-1982 10
Aragones, Sergio 1937- 48
    Brief entry 39
Araujo, Frank P. 1937- 86
Arbo, Cris 1950- 103
Arbuckle, Dorothy Fry 1910-1982
    Obituary 33
Arbuthnot, May Hill 1884-1969 2
Archambault, John 163
    Earlier sketches in SATA 67, 112
Archbold, Rick 1950- 97
Archer, Colleen Rutherford 1949- 164
Archer, Frank
    See O'Connor, Richard
Archer, Jules 1915- 85
    Earlier sketch in SATA 4
    See also SAAS 5
Archer, Lily 1981- 193
Archer, Marion Fuller 1917- 11
Archer, Nathan
    See Watt-Evans, Lawrence
Archibald, Joe
    See Archibald, Joseph S(topford)
Archibald, Joseph S(topford) 1898-1986 3
    Obituary 47
Ard, William
    See Jakes, John
Ardagh, Philip 1961- 154
Ardai, Charles 1969- 85
Arden, Barbi
    See Stoutenburg, Adrien (Pearl)

Arden, William
  See Lynds, Dennis
Ardizzone, Edward (Jeffrey Irving)
  1900-1979 28
  Obituary 21
  Earlier sketch in SATA *1*
  See also CLR *3*
Ardley, Neil (Richard) 1937- *121*
  Earlier sketch in SATA *43*
Arehart-Treichel, Joan 1942- 22
Arena, Felice 1968- *151*
Arenella, Roy 1939- 14
Argent, Kerry 1960- *138*
Argueta, Jorge *179*
Arkin, Alan 1934- *59*
  Brief entry 32
Arkin, Alan Wolf
  See Arkin, Alan
Arksey, Neil *158*
Arlen, Leslie
  See Nicole, Christopher (Robin)
Arley, Robert
  See Jackson, Mike
Armer, Alberta (Roller) 1904-1986 9
Armer, Laura Adams 1874-1963 13
Armistead, John 1941- *130*
Armitage, David 1943- *155*
  Brief entry 38
  Earlier sketch in SATA *99*
Armitage, Frank
  See Carpenter, John (Howard)
Armitage, Ronda (Jacqueline) 1943- *155*
  Brief entry 38
  Earlier sketches in SATA *47, 99*
Armour, Richard (Willard) 1906-1989 14
  Obituary 61
Armstrong, Alan 1939- *172*
Armstrong, Alan W.
  See Armstrong, Alan
Armstrong, George D. 1927- *10*
Armstrong, Gerry (Breen) 1929- *10*
Armstrong, Jeannette (C.) 1948- *102*
Armstrong, Jennifer 1961- *165*
  Autobiography Feature *120*
  Earlier sketches in SATA *77, 111*
  See also CLR *66*
  See also SAAS *24*
Armstrong, Louise 43
  Brief entry 33
Armstrong, Martin Donisthorpe
  1882-1974 .... *115*
Armstrong, Matthew 1975- *188*
Armstrong, Matthew S.
  See Armstrong, Matthew
Armstrong, Ralph Richard
  See Armstrong, Richard
Armstrong, Richard 1903-1986 .... *11*
Armstrong, William H(oward)
  1914-1999 4
  Obituary *111*
  See also CLR *117*
  See also SAAS *7*
Armstrong-Ellis, Carey (Fraser) 1956- *145*
Arndt, Ursula (Martha H.) 56
  Brief entry 39
Arneson, D(on) J(on) 1935- 37
Arnett, Caroline
  See Cole, Lois Dwight
Arnett, Jack
  See Goulart, Ron(ald Joseph)
Arnette, Robert
  See Silverberg, Robert
Arno, Enrico 1913-1981 43
  Obituary 28
Arnold, Caroline 1944- *174*
  Brief entry 34
  Earlier sketches in SATA *36, 85, 131*
  See also CLR *61*
  See also SAAS *23*
Arnold, Elizabeth 1944- *164*

Arnold, Elliott 1912-1980 .... *5*
  Obituary 22
Arnold, Emily 1939- 76
  Earlier sketch in SATA *50*
  See McCully, Emily Arnold
Arnold, Katya 1947- *168*
  Earlier sketches in SATA *82, 115*
Arnold, Louise *175*
Arnold, Marsha Diane 1948- *147*
  Earlier sketch in SATA *93*
Arnold, Nick 1961- *113*
Arnold, Oren 1900-1980 .... *4*
Arnold, Susan (Riser) 1951- 58
Arnold, Tedd 1949- *160*
  Earlier sketches in SATA *69, 116*
Arnoldy, Julie
  See Bischoff, Julia Bristol
Arnosky, James Edward 1946- *160*
  Earlier sketch in SATA *22*
  See also CLR *93*
  See Arnosky, Jim
Arnosky, Jim *189*
  Earlier sketches in SATA *70, 118*
  See also CLR *93*
  See Arnosky, James Edward
Arnott, Kathleen 1914- 20
Arnov, Boris, Jr. 1926- 12
Arnow, Harriette (Louisa) Simpson
  1908-1986 42
  Obituary 47
Arnsteen, Katy Keck 1934- 68
Arnstein, Helene S(olomon) 1915- 12
Arntson, Herbert E(dward) 1911-1982 12
Aroner, Miriam 82
Aronin, Ben 1904-1980
  Obituary 25
Aronson, Marc 1950- *189*
  Autobiography Feature *189*
  Earlier sketches in SATA *126, 175*
Aronson, Marc Henry
  See Aronson, Marc
Aronson, Virginia 1954- *122*
Arora, Shirley (Lease) 1930- *2*
Arrasmith, Patrick *176*
Arrigan, Mary 1943- *142*
Arrington, Aileen *183*
Arrington, Stephen L. 1948- 97
Arrington, Stephen Lee
  See Arrington, Stephen L.
Arrley, Richmond
  See Delany, Samuel R., Jr.
Arrowood, (McKendrick Lee) Clinton
  1939- 19
Artell, Mike 1948- *183*
  Earlier sketches in SATA *89, 134*
Arthur, Robert (Andrew) 1909-1969
  See Arthur, Robert, (Jr.)
Arthur, Robert, (Jr.) 1909-1969 .... *118*
  See Arthur, Robert (Andrew)
Arthur, Ruth M(abel) 1905-1979 26
  Earlier sketch in SATA *7*
Artis, Vicki Kimmel 1945- 12
Artzybasheff, Boris (Miklailovich)
  1899-1965 14
Aruego, Ariane
  See Dewey, Ariane
Aruego, Jose 1932- *178*
  Earlier sketches in SATA *6, 68, 125*
  See also CLR *5*
Aruego, Jose Espiritu
  See Aruego, Jose
Arundel, Honor (Morfydd) 1919-1973 .... *4*
  Obituary 24
  See also CLR *35*
Arundel, Jocelyn
  See Alexander, Jocelyn Anne Arundel
Arvey, Michael 1948- 79
Arzoumanian, Alik *177*
Asare, Meshack (Yaw) 1945- *139*
  Earlier sketch in SATA *86*

Asaro, Catherine 1955- *165*
  Earlier sketch in SATA *101*
  See Asaro, Catherine Ann
Asaro, Catherine Ann 1955-
  See Asaro, Catherine
Asay, Donna Day 1945- *127*
Asbjørnsen, Peter Christen 1812-1885 15
  See also CLR *104*
  See Asbjørnsen and Moe
Asch, Frank 1946- *154*
  Earlier sketches in SATA *5, 66, 102*
Ash, Jutta 1942- 38
Ashabranner, Brent 1921- *166*
  Earlier sketches in SATA *1, 67, 130*
  See also CLR *28*
  See also SAAS *14*
Ashabranner, Brent Kenneth
  See Ashabranner, Brent
Ashbless, William
  See Blaylock, James P.
  and Powers, Tim
Ashby, Gil 1958- *146*
Ashby, Gwynneth 1922- 44
Ashby, Ruth *170*
Ashby, Yvonne 1955- *121*
Ashe, Arthur (Robert, Jr.) 1943-1993 65
  Obituary 87
Ashe, Geoffrey (Thomas) 1923- 17
  Autobiography Feature *125*
Ashe, Mary Ann
  See Lewis, Mary (Christianna)
Asher, Sandra Fenichel 71
  Brief entry 34
  Earlier sketch in SATA *36*
  See also SAAS *13*
  See Asher, Sandy
Asher, Sandy 1942- *158*
  Autobiography Feature *158*
  Earlier sketch in SATA *118*
  See Asher, Sandra Fenichel
Asheron, Sara
  See Moore, Lilian
Ashey, Bella
  See Breinburg, Petronella
Ashford, Daisy
  See Ashford, Margaret Mary
Ashford, Jeffrey
  See Jeffries, Roderic
Ashford, Margaret Mary 1881-1972 .... *10*
Ashley, Bernard (John) 1935- *155*
  Brief entry 39
  Earlier sketches in SATA *47, 79*
  See also CLR *4*
Ashley, Elizabeth
  See Salmon, Annie Elizabeth
Ashley, Ray
  See Abrashkin, Raymond
Ashman, Linda 1960- *150*
Ashton, Lorayne
  See Gottfried, Theodore Mark
Ashton, Warren T.
  See Adams, William Taylor
Asimov, Isaac 1920-1992 74
  Earlier sketches in SATA *1, 26*
  See also CLR *79*
Asinof, Eliot 1919-2008 .... *6*
Asinof, Eliot Tager
  See Asinof, Eliot
Aska, Warabe 56
  See Masuda, Takeshi
Asprin, Robert L. 1946-2008 92
Asprin, Robert Lynn
  See Asprin, Robert L.
Asquith, Cynthia Mary Evelyn
  (Charteris) 1887-1960 .... *107*
Asquith, Ros *153*
Astley, Juliet
  See Lofts, Norah (Robinson)
Aston, Dianna Hutts 1964- *176*
Aston, James
  See White, T(erence) H(anbury)

Ata, Te 1895-1995 .... *119*
Atene, Ann
  See Atene, (Rita) Anna
Atene, (Rita) Anna 1922- *12*
Atheling, William, Jr.
  See Blish, James (Benjamin)
Atkins, Catherine *160*
Atkins, Jeannine 1953- *172*
  Earlier sketch in SATA *113*
Atkinson, Allen G. 1953(?)-1987 .... *60*
  Brief entry *46*
  Obituary *55*
Atkinson, M. E.
  See Frankau, Mary Evelyn Atkinson
Atkinson, Margaret Fleming *14*
Atteberry, Kevan J. *186*
Attema, Martha 1949- *156*
  Earlier sketch in SATA *94*
Atticus
  See Davies, Hunter
  and Fleming, Ian
  and Pawle, Gerald Strachan
  and Wilson, (Thomas) Woodrow
Atwater, Florence (Hasseltine Carroll)
  1896-1979 .... *66*
  Earlier sketch in SATA *16*
  See also CLR *19*
Atwater, Montgomery Meigs 1904-1976 ...... *15*
Atwater, Richard (Tupper) 1892-1948 .... *66*
  Brief entry *27*
  Earlier sketch in SATA *54*
  See also CLR *19*
Atwater-Rhodes, Amelia 1984- *170*
  Earlier sketch in SATA *124*
Atwell, Debby 1953- *150*
  Earlier sketch in SATA *87*
Atwood, Ann (Margaret) 1913-1992 .... *7*
Atwood, Margaret 1939- *170*
  Earlier sketch in SATA *50*
Atwood, Margaret Eleanor
  See Atwood, Margaret
Aubrey, Meg Kelleher 1963- *83*
Aubry, Claude B. 1914-1984 .... *29*
  Obituary *40*
Auch, Herm *173*
Auch, Mary Jane *173*
  Earlier sketch in SATA *138*
Auch, M.J.
  See Auch, Mary Jane
Auclair, Joan 1960- *68*
Auel, Jean M(arie) 1936- *91*
Auer, Martin 1951- *77*
Augarde, Steve 1950- *159*
  Earlier sketch in SATA *25*
Augelli, John P(at) 1921- *46*
Augustine, Mildred
  See Benson, Mildred (Augustine Wirt)
Ault, Phil
  See Ault, Phillip H(alliday)
Ault, Phillip H(alliday) 1914- *23*
Ault, Rosalie Sain 1942- *38*
Ault, Roz
  See Ault, Rosalie Sain
Aung, (Maung) Htin 1909- *21*
Auntie Deb
  See Coury, Louise Andree
Auntie Louise
  See Coury, Louise Andree
Aunt Weedy
  See Alcott, Louisa May
Auseon, Andrew 1976- *166*
Austen, Carrie
  See Bennett, Cherie
Austin, Carrie
  See Seuling, Barbara
Austin, Elizabeth S. 1907-1977 .... *5*
Austin, Harry
  See McInerny, Ralph
Austin, Margot 1909(?)-1990 .... *11*
  Obituary *66*
Austin, Michael *178*

Austin, Oliver L(uther), Jr. 1903-1988 .... *7*
  Obituary *59*
Austin, Patricia 1950- *137*
Austin, R. G.
  See Gelman, Rita Golden
  and Lamb, Nancy
Austin, Virginia 1951- *152*
  Earlier sketch in SATA *80*
Auteur, Hillary
  See Gottfried, Theodore Mark
Auth, Tony *192*
  See Auth, William Anthony, Jr.
Auth, William Anthony, Jr. 1942- *51*
  See Auth, Tony
Autry, Gloria Diener
  See Allen, Terril Diener
Auvil, Peggy A 1954- *122*
Auvil, Peggy Appleby
  See Auvil, Peggy A
Aveni, Anthony F. 1938- *181*
Aveni, Anthony Francis
  See Aveni, Anthony F.
Averill, Esther (Holden) 1902-1992 .... *28*
  Obituary *72*
  Earlier sketch in SATA *1*
Avery, A. A.
  See Montgomery, Rutherford George
Avery, Al
  See Montgomery, Rutherford George
Avery, Gillian (Elise) 1926- *137*
  Autobiography Feature *137*
  Earlier sketches in SATA *7, 75*
  See also SAAS *6*
Avery, Kay 1908- *5*
Avery, Lorraine
  See Older, Effin
  and Older, Jules
Avery, Lynn
  See Cole, Lois Dwight
Avi 1937- *190*
  Earlier sketches in SATA *14, 71,*
  108, 156
  See also CLR *68*
Avishai, Susan 1949- *82*
Avril, Francois 1961- *191*
Avril, Lynne
  See Cravath, Lynne W.
Awdry, Christopher Vere 1940- *67*
Awdry, Wilbert Vere 1911-1997 .... *94*
  See also CLR *23*
Axelrod, Amy *131*
Axelsen, Stephen 1953- *165*
Axton, David
  See Koontz, Dean R.
Ayars, James S(terling) 1898-1986 .... *4*
Aye, A. K.
  See Edwards, Hazel (Eileen)
Ayer, Eleanor H. 1947-1998 .... *121*
  Earlier sketch in SATA *78*
Ayer, Jacqueline 1930- *13*
Ayer, Margaret (?)-1981 .... *15*
Aylesworth, Jim 1943- *139*
  Earlier sketches in SATA *38, 89*
  See also CLR *89*
Aylesworth, Thomas G(ibbons)
  1927-1995 .... *88*
  Earlier sketch in SATA *4*
  See also CLR *6*
  See also SAAS *17*
Ayliffe, Alex *190*
Aylward, Marcus
  See Alexander, Marc
Aymar, Brandt 1911- *22*
Ayme, Marcel (Andre) 1902-1967 .... *91*
  See also CLR *25*
Ayres, Becky
  See Hickox, Rebecca (Ayres)
Ayres, Katherine 1947- *187*
Ayres, Pam 1947- *90*
Ayres, Patricia Miller 1923-1985
  Obituary *46*

Aytmatov, Chingiz
  See Aitmatov, Chingiz
Ayto, Russell 1960- *166*
  Earlier sketch in SATA *111*
Azaid
  See Zaidenberg, Arthur
Azar, Penny 1952- *121*
Azarian, Mary 1940- *171*
  Earlier sketch in SATA *112*
Azore, Barbara 1934- *188*

B

Baastad, Babbis Friis
  See Friis-Baastad, Babbis Ellinor
Bab
  See Gilbert, W(illiam) S(chwenck)
Babbis, Eleanor
  See Friis-Baastad, Babbis Ellinor
Babbitt, Lucy Cullyford 1960- *85*
Babbitt, Natalie (Zane Moore) 1932- *106*
  Earlier sketches in SATA *6, 68*
  See also CLR *53*
  See also SAAS *5*
Babcock, Chris 1963- *83*
Babcock, Dennis 1948- *22*
Babcock, Dennis Arthur
  See Babcock, Dennis
Baber, Carolyn Stonnell 1936- *96*
Baca, Ana 1967- *191*
Baca, Maria 1951- *104*
Bach, Alice (Hendricks) 1942- *93*
  Brief entry *27*
  Earlier sketch in SATA *30*
Bach, Bellamy
  See Windling, Terri
Bach, Mary 1960- *125*
Bach, Richard 1936- *13*
Bach, Richard David
  See Bach, Richard
Bache, Ellyn 1942- *124*
Bachel, Beverly K. 1957- *142*
Bachman, Fred 1949- *12*
Bachman, Richard
  See King, Stephen
Bachrach, Deborah *80*
Backus, James Gilmore 1913-1989
  Obituary *63*
Backus, Jim
  See Backus, James Gilmore
Bacmeister, Rhoda W(arner) 1893-1991 .... *11*
Bacon, Betty
  See Bacon, Elizabeth
Bacon, Elizabeth 1914-2001 .... *3*
  Obituary *131*
Bacon, Joan Chase
  See Bowden, Joan Chase
Bacon, Josephine Dodge (Daskam)
  1876-1961 .... *48*
Bacon, Margaret Frances
  Obituary *50*
  See Bacon, Peggy
Bacon, Margaret Hope 1921- *6*
Bacon, Martha Sherman 1917-1981 .... *18*
  Obituary *27*
  See also CLR *3*
Bacon, Melvin 1950- *93*
Bacon, Melvin L.
  See Bacon, Melvin
Bacon, Peggy 1895-1987 .... *2*
  See Bacon, Margaret Frances
Bacon, R(onald) L(eonard) 1924- *84*
  Earlier sketch in SATA *26*
Baden, Robert 1936- *70*
Baden-Powell, Robert (Stephenson
  Smyth) 1857-1941 .... *16*
Badt, Karin L(uisa) 1963- *91*
Bae, Hyun-Joo *186*
Baehr, Kingsley M. 1937- *89*

Baehr, Patricia 1952- *65*
Baehr, Patricia Goehner
  See Baehr, Patricia
Baer, Jill
  See Gilbert, (Agnes) Joan (Sewell)
Baer, Judy 1951- *71*
Baer, Julie 1960- *161*
Baer-Block, Roxanna *172*
Baerg, Harry J(ohn) 1909-1996 .... *12*
Baeten, Lieve 1954- *83*
Bagert, Brod 1947- *191*
  Earlier sketch in SATA *80*
Baggette, Susan K. 1942- *126*
Bagnold, Enid 1889-1981 .... *25*
  Earlier sketch in SATA *1*
Bahlke, Valerie Worth -1994 .... *70*
  Earlier sketch in SATA *8*
  See also CLR *21*
  See Worth, Valerie
Bahous, Sally 1939- *86*
Bahr, Mary (Madelyn) 1946- *95*
Bahr, Robert 1940- *38*
Bahti, Tom 1926-1972 .... *57*
  Brief entry *31*
Baicker-McKee, Carol 1958- *177*
Bailey, Alice Cooper 1890-1978 .... *12*
Bailey, Anne 1958- *71*
Bailey, Bernadine (Freeman) 1901-1995 ..... *14*
Bailey, Carolyn Sherwin 1875-1961 .... *14*
Bailey, Debbie 1954- *123*
Bailey, Donna (Veronica Anne) 1938- *68*
Bailey, Jane H(orton) 1916- *12*
Bailey, John (Robert) 1940- *52*
Bailey, Len *193*
Bailey, Linda 1948- *182*
  Earlier sketch in SATA *107*
Bailey, Maralyn Collins
  (Harrison) 1941- *12*
Bailey, Matilda
  See Radford, Ruby L(orraine)
Bailey, Maurice Charles 1932- *12*
Bailey, Pearl (Mae) 1918-1990 .... *81*
Bailey, Ralph Edgar 1893-1982 .... *11*
Bailey, Sheila (Lucas) 1960- *155*
Baillie, Allan 1943- *151*
  Earlier sketch in SATA *87*
  See also CLR *49*
  See also SAAS *21*
Baillie, Allan Stuart
  See Baillie, Allan
Baines, John (David) 1943- *71*
Bains, Larry
  See Sabin, Louis
Baird, Alison 1963- *138*
Baird, Bil 1904-1987 .... *30*
  Obituary *52*
Baird, Thomas (P.) 1923-1990 .... *45*
  Brief entry *39*
  Obituary *64*
Baird, William Britton
  See Baird, Bil
Baity, Elizabeth Chesley 1907-1989 .... *1*
Baiul, Oksana 1977- *108*
Bajoria, Paul 1964- *187*
Bakeless, John (Edwin) 1894-1978 .... *9*
Bakeless, Katherine Little 1895-1992 .... *9*
Baker, Alan 1951- *146*
  Earlier sketches in SATA *22, 93*
Baker, Augusta 1911-1998 .... *3*
Baker, Barbara 1947- *192*
Baker, Betty Lou 1928-1987 .... *73*
  Obituary *54*
  Earlier sketch in SATA *5*
Baker, Carin Greenberg 1959- *79*
Baker, Charlotte 1910- *2*
Baker, Christina
  See Kline, Christina Baker
Baker, Christopher W. 1952- *144*
Baker, E.D. *190*
Baker, (Mary) Elizabeth (Gillette) 1923- *7*
Baker, Gayle Cunningham 1950- *39*

Baker, James W. 1924- *65*
  Earlier sketch in SATA *22*
Baker, James W. 1926- *122*
Baker, Janice E(dla) 1941- *22*
Baker, Jeanette *178*
Baker, Jeannie 1950- *156*
  Earlier sketches in SATA *23, 88*
  See also CLR *28*
Baker, Jeffrey J(ohn) W(heeler) 1931- *5*
Baker, Jim
  See Baker, James W.
Baker, Keith 1953- *179*
Baker, Ken 1962- *133*
Baker, Laura Nelson 1911- *3*
Baker, Margaret 1890-1965 .... *4*
Baker, Margaret J(oyce) 1918- *12*
  See also SAAS *8*
Baker, Mary Gladys Steel 1892-1974 .... *12*
Baker, (Robert) Michael
  (Graham) 1938- *4*
Baker, Nina (Brown) 1888-1957 .... *15*
Baker, Pamela J. 1947- *66*
Baker, Rachel 1904-1978 .... *2*
  Obituary *26*
Baker, Rosalie F. 1945- *166*
Baker, Samm Sinclair 1909-1997 .... *12*
  Obituary *96*
Baker, Susan (Catherine) 1942-1991 .... *29*
Balaam
  See Lamb, G(eoffrey) F(rederick)
Balan, Bruce 1959- *113*
Balcavage, Dynise 1965- *137*
Balch, Glenn 1902-1989 .... *3*
  Obituary *83*
  See also SAAS *11*
Baldacci, David 1960- *184*
Baldacci, David G.
  See Baldacci, David
  and Baldacci, David
Balderose, Nancy Ward 1952- *93*
Balderson, Margaret 1935- *151*
Baldry, Cherith 1947- *167*
  Earlier sketch in SATA *72*
Balducci, Carolyn 1946- *5*
Balducci, Carolyn Feleppa
  See Balducci, Carolyn
Baldwin, Alex
  See Griffin, W.E.B
Baldwin, Anne Norris 1938- *5*
Baldwin, Clara *11*
Baldwin, Gordo
  See Baldwin, Gordon C(ortis)
Baldwin, Gordon C(ortis) 1908-1983 .... *12*
Baldwin, James 1841-1925 .... *24*
Baldwin, James 1924-1987 .... *9*
  Obituary *54*
Baldwin, Louis 1919- *110*
Baldwin, Margaret
  See Weis, Margaret
Baldwin, Stan(ley C.) 1929- *62*
  Brief entry *28*
Bales, Carol Ann 1940- *57*
  Brief entry *29*
Balet, Jan (Bernard) 1913- *11*
Balgassi, Haemi 1971- *131*
Balian, Lorna 1929- *91*
  Earlier sketch in SATA *9*
Balit, Christina 1961- *159*
  Earlier sketch in SATA *102*
Ball, Duncan 1941- *73*
Ball, Zachary
  See Janas, Frankie-Lee
  and Masters, Kelly R(ay)
Ballantine, Lesley Frost
  See Frost, Lesley
Ballantyne, R(obert)
  M(ichael) 1825-1894 .... *24*
  See also CLR *137*
Ballard, James Graham
  See Ballard, J.G.

Ballard, Jane
  See Gorman, Carol
Ballard, J.G. 1930- *93*
Ballard, John 1945- *110*
Ballard, Lowell C(lyne) 1904-1986 .... *12*
  Obituary *49*
Ballard, (Charles) Martin 1929- *1*
Ballard, Mignon F. 1934- *64*
  Brief entry *49*
Ballard, Mignon Franklin
  See Ballard, Mignon F.
Ballard, Robert D(uane) 1942- *85*
  See also CLR *60*
Ballard, Robin 1965- *126*
Balliett, Blue 1955- *156*
Ballinger, Bryan 1968- *161*
Ballouhey, Pierre 1944- *90*
Balogh, Penelope 1916-1975 .... *1*
  Obituary *34*
Balouch, Kristen *176*
Balow, Tom 1931- *12*
Baltazzi, Evan S(erge) 1921- *90*
Baltimore, J.
  See Catherall, Arthur
Baltzer, Hans (Adolf) 1900- *40*
Bambara, Toni Cade 1939-1995 .... *112*
Bamfylde, Walter
  See Bevan, Tom
Bamman, Henry A. 1918- *12*
Banat, D. R.
  See Bradbury, Ray
Bancroft, Griffing 1907-1999 .... *6*
Bancroft, Laura
  See Baum, L(yman) Frank
Bandel, Betty 1912- *47*
Baner, Skulda Vanadis 1897-1964 .... *10*
Banerjee, Anjali *174*
Banfill, A. Scott 1956- *98*
Bang, Betsy 1912- *48*
  Brief entry *37*
Bang, Garrett
  See Bang, Molly
Bang, Molly 1943- *158*
  Earlier sketches in SATA *24, 69, 111*
  See also CLR *8*
Bang, Molly Garrett
  See Bang, Molly
Bang-Campbell, Monika *140*
Banjo, The
  See Paterson, A(ndrew) B(arton)
Banke, Cecile de
  See de Banke, Cecile
Banks, Kate 1960- *172*
  Earlier sketch in SATA *134*
Banks, Laura Stockton
  Voorhees 1908(?)-1980
  Obituary *23*
Banks, Lynne Reid
  See Reid Banks, Lynne
Banks, Michael A. 1951- *101*
Banks, Paul 1952- *174*
Banks, Sara (Jeanne Gordon Harrell) *26*
  See Harrell, Sara (Jeanne) Gordon
Bannatyne-Cugnet, Elizabeth Jo-Anne
  See Bannatyne-Cugnet, Jo
Bannatyne-Cugnet, Jo 1951- *101*
Banner, Angela
  See CLR *24*
  See Maddison, Angela Mary
Bannerman, Helen (Brodie Cowan
  Watson) 1862(?)-1946 .... *19*
  See also CLR *21*
Banning, Evelyn I. 1903-1993 .... *36*
Bannon, Laura (?)-1963 .... *6*
Bannor, Brett 1959- *143*
Banta, Susan *181*
Bantock, Nick 1950(?)- *95*
Banyai, Istvan *193*
Barakat, Ibtisam 1963- *186*
Barasch, Lynne 1939- *186*
  Earlier sketches in SATA *74, 126*

Barbalet, Margaret 1949- *77*
Barbary, James
  See Beeching, Jack
Barbash, Shepard 1957- *84*
Barbe, Walter Burke 1926- *45*
Barber, Antonia 1932- *163*
  Earlier sketch in SATA 29
Barber, Atiim Kiambu
  See Barber, Tiki
Barber, Lynda
  See Graham-Barber, Lynda
Barber, Lynda Graham
  See Graham-Barber, Lynda
Barber, Richard (William) 1941- *35*
Barber, Ronde 1975- *182*
Barber, Tiki 1975- *182*
Barbera, Joe 1911-2006 .... *51*
  Obituary *179*
Barbera, Joseph
  See Barbera, Joe
Barbera, Joseph Roland
  See Barbera, Joe
Barberis, Juan C(arlos) 1920- *61*
Barbour, Karen 1956- *170*
  Earlier sketches in SATA *63, 121*
Barbour, Ralph Henry 1870-1944 .... *16*
Barclay, Bill
  See Moorcock, Michael
Barclay, Isabel
  See Dobell, I(sabel) M(arian) B(arclay)
Barclay, William Ewert
  See Moorcock, Michael
Bardhan-Quallen, Sudipta *168*
Bardoe, Cheryl *181*
Bare, Arnold Edwin 1920- *16*
Bare, Colleen Stanley *32*
Barenholtz, Bernard 1914-1989
  Obituary *64*
Bargar, Gary W. 1947-1985 .... *63*
Barger, Jan 1948- *147*
Barish, Matthew 1907-2000 .... *12*
Barkan, Joanne *127*
  Earlier sketch in SATA 77
Barker, Albert W. 1900- *8*
Barker, Carol (Minturn) 1938- *31*
Barker, Cicely Mary 1895-1973 .... *49*
  Brief entry *39*
  See also CLR 88
Barker, Melvern 1907-1989 .... *11*
Barker, S(quire) Omar 1894-1985 .... *10*
Barker, Will 1913-1983 .... *8*
Barkin, Carol 1944- *52*
  Earlier sketch in SATA 42
Barklem, Jill 1951- *96*
  See also CLR 31
Barkley, Brad *178*
Barkley, James Edward 1941- *6*
Barks, Carl 1901-2000 .... *37*
Barley, Janet Crane 1934- *95*
Barnaby, Ralph S(tanton) 1893-1986 .... *9*
Barnard, A. M.
  See Alcott, Louisa May
Barnard, Bryn 1956- *169*
  Earlier sketch in SATA 115
Barne, Kitty
  See Barne, Marion Catherine
Barne, Marion Catherine 1883-1957 .... *97*
  See Barne, Kitty
Barner, Bob 1947- *136*
  Earlier sketch in SATA 29
Barnes, Dawn 1957- *175*
Barnes, Derrick *191*
Barnes, Derrick D.
  See Barnes, Derrick
Barnes, (Frank) Eric Wollencott
  1907-1962 .... *22*
Barnes, Joyce Annette 1958- *85*
Barnes, Laura T. 1958- *119*
Barnes, Loutricia
  See Barnes-Svarney, Patricia L(ou)

Barnes, Malcolm 1909(?)-1984
  Obituary *41*
Barnes, Michael 1934- *55*
Barnes-Murphy, Frances 1951- *88*
Barnes-Murphy, Rowan 1952- *88*
Barnes-Svarney, Patricia L(ou) 1953- *67*
Barnet, Nancy 1954- *84*
Barnett, Ivan 1947- *70*
Barnett, Lincoln (Kinnear) 1909-1979 .... *36*
Barnett, Moneta 1922-1976 .... *33*
Barnett, Naomi 1927- *40*
Barney, Maginel Wright 1881(?)-1966 .... *39*
  Brief entry *32*
Barnhart, Clarence L(ewis) 1900-1993 .... *48*
  Obituary *78*
Barnouw, Adriaan Jacob 1877-1968
  Obituary *27*
Barnouw, Victor 1915-1989 .... *43*
  Brief entry *28*
Barnstone, Willis 1927- *20*
Barnum, Jay Hyde 1888(?)-1962 .... *20*
Barnum, P. T., Jr.
  See Stratemeyer, Edward L.
Barnum, Richard *67*
  Earlier sketch in SATA *1*
Barnum, Theodore
  See Stratemeyer, Edward L.
Baron, Kathy 1954- *90*
Baron, Virginia Olsen 1931- *46*
  Brief entry *28*
Barr, Donald 1921-2004 .... *20*
  Obituary *152*
Barr, George 1907-1992 .... *2*
Barr, Jene 1922-1985 .... *16*
  Obituary *42*
  See Cohen, Jene Barr
Barr, Nevada 1952- *126*
  Earlier sketch in SATA *115*
Barrer, Gertrude
  See Barrer-Russell, Gertrude
Barrer-Russell, Gertrude 1921- *27*
Barrett, Angela (Jane) 1955- *145*
  Earlier sketch in SATA *75*
Barrett, Ethel *87*
  Brief entry *44*
Barrett, Joyce Durham 1943- *138*
Barrett, Judi
  See Barrett, Judith
Barrett, Judith 1941- *26*
  See also CLR *98*
Barrett, Robert T(heodore) 1949- *92*
Barrett, Ron 1937- *14*
Barrett, Susan (Mary) 1938- *113*
Barrett, Tracy 1955- *156*
  Earlier sketches in SATA *84, 115*
Barrett, William E(dmund) 1900-1986
  Obituary *49*
Barretta, Gene *176*
Barrie, J(ames) M(atthew) 1860-1937 .... *100*
  See also YABC *1*
  See also CLR *124*
Barringer, William 1940-1996 .... *153*
Barrington, Michael
  See Moorcock, Michael
Barris, George 1925- *47*
Barrol, Grady
  See Bograd, Larry
Barron, Rex 1951- *84*
Barron, T.A. 1952- *192*
  Earlier sketches in SATA *83, 126*
  See also CLR *86*
Barron, Thomas Archibald
  See Barron, T.A.
Barron, Tom
  See Barron, T.A.
Barrow, Lloyd H. 1942- *73*
Barrows, Annie 1962- *180*
Barry, Dan 1958- *177*
Barry, Dana (Marie Malloy) 1949- *139*
Barry, James P(otvin) 1918- *14*
Barry, Katharina Watjen 1936- *4*

Barry, Robert (Everett) 1931- *6*
Barry, Scott 1952- *32*
Barry, Sheila Anne -2003 .... *91*
Bartell, Susan S. *175*
Bartenbach, Jean 1918- *40*
Barth, Edna 1914-1980 .... *7*
  Obituary *24*
Barth, Kelly L. 1964- *152*
Barthelme, Donald 1931-1989 .... *7*
  Obituary *62*
Barth-Grozinger, Inge 1950- *185*
Bartholomew, Barbara 1941- *86*
  Brief entry *42*
Bartholomew, Jean
  See Beatty, Patricia (Robbins)
Bartlett, Alison *153*
Bartlett, Philip A. *1*
Bartlett, Robert Merrill 1899-1995 .... *12*
Bartoletti, Susan Campbell 1958- *173*
  Earlier sketches in SATA *88, 129, 135*
Barton, Byron 1930- *126*
  Earlier sketches in SATA *9, 90*
Barton, Jill(ian) 1940- *75*
Barton, May Hollis *67*
  Earlier sketch in SATA *1*
Barton, Pat *59*
  See Arrowsmith, Pat
Bartos-Hoeppner, Barbara 1923- *5*
Bartram, Simon *156*
Bartsch, Jochen 1906- *39*
Baruch, Dorothy W(alter) 1899-1962 .... *21*
Barunga, Albert 1912(?)-1977 .... *120*
Baryshnikov, Mikhail 1948- *192*
Bas, Rutger
  See Rutgers van der Loeff-Basenau,
  An(na) Maria Margaretha
Base, Graeme (Rowland) 1958- *162*
  Earlier sketches in SATA *67, 101*
  See also CLR 22
Baseman, Gary 1960- *174*
Bash, Barbara 1948- *132*
Bashevis, Isaac
  See Singer, Isaac Bashevis
Bashevis, Yitskhok
  See Singer, Isaac Bashevis
Baskin, Leonard 1922-2000 .... *120*
  Brief entry *27*
  Earlier sketch in SATA 30
Baskin, Nora Raleigh 1961- *189*
  Earlier sketch in SATA *129*
Bason, Lillian 1913- *20*
Bass, L. G.
  See Geringer, Laura
Bassett, Jeni 1959- *64*
  Brief entry *43*
Bassett, John Keith
  See Keating, Lawrence A.
Bassett, Lisa 1958- *61*
Bassil, Andrea
  See Nilsen, Anna
Bastyra, Judy *108*
Bat-Ami, Miriam 1950- *150*
  Autobiography Feature *150*
  Earlier sketches in SATA *82, 122*
Bate, Lucy 1939-1993 .... *18*
Bate, Norman (Arthur) 1916- *5*
Bateman, Colin 1962- *172*
Bateman, Donna M. *190*
Bateman, Teresa 1957- *168*
  Earlier sketch in SATA *112*
Bates, Amy June *189*
Bates, Barbara S(nedeker) 1919- *12*
Bates, Betty *19*
  See Bates, Elizabeth
Bates, Dianne 1948- *147*
Bates, Ivan *175*
Bates, Katharine Lee 1859-1929 .... *113*
  See Lincoln, James
Bates, Martine
  See Leavitt, Martine
Bateson, Catherine 1960- *157*

Batey, Tom 1946- 52
    Brief entry 41
Bath, Kevin P.
    See Bath, K.P.
Bath, K.P. 1959- 171
Batherman, Muriel
    See Sheldon, Muriel
Batson, Larry 1930- 35
Batt, Tanya Robyn 1970- 131
Battaglia, Aurelius 1910- 50
    Brief entry 33
Batten, H(arry) Mortimer 1888-1958 25
Batten, Mary 1937- 162
    Earlier sketches in SATA *5, 102*
Batterberry, Ariane Ruskin 1935- 13
Batterberry, Michael Carver 1932- 32
Battle-Lavert, Gwendolyn 1951- 155
    Earlier sketch in SATA *85*
    See Lavert, Gwendolyn Battle
Battles, (Roxy) Edith 1921- 7
Baudouy, Michel-Aime 1909- 7
Bauer, Caroline Feller 1935- 98
    Brief entry 46
    Earlier sketch in SATA *52*
    See also SAAS *24*
Bauer, Fred 1934- 36
Bauer, Helen 1900-1988 2
Bauer, Joan 1951- 160
    Earlier sketch in SATA *117*
Bauer, Jutta 1955- 150
Bauer, Marion Dane 1938- 192
    Autobiography Feature 144
    Earlier sketches in SATA *20, 69,
    113, 144*
    See also SAAS *9*
Bauer, Michael Gerard 1955(?)- 167
Bauer, Steven 1948- 125
Bauerschmidt, Marjorie 1926- 15
Baughman, Dorothy 1940- 61
Baum, Allyn Z(elton) 1924-1997 98
    Earlier sketch in SATA *20*
Baum, L. Frank
    See Thompson, Ruth Plumly
Baum, L(yman) Frank 1856-1919 100
    Earlier sketch in SATA *18*
    See also CLR *107*
Baum, Louis 1948- 182
    Brief entry 52
    Earlier sketch in SATA *64*
Baum, Louis F.
    See Baum, L(yman) Frank
Baum, Maxie 188
Baum, Willi 1931- 4
Baumann, Amy (Brown)
    Beeching 1922- 10
Baumann, Hans 1914- 2
    See also CLR *35*
Baumann, Kurt 1935- 21
Baumgartner, Barbara 1939- 86
Baurys, Flo(rence) 1938- 122
Bausum, Ann 173
Bawden, Nina 1925- 132
    Earlier sketches in SATA *4, 72*
    See also CLR *51*
    See also SAAS *16*
Bawden, Nina Mary Mabey
    See Bawden, Nina
Baxter, Valerie
    See Meynell, Laurence Walter
Bay, Jeanette Graham 1928- 88
Bayer, Harold
    See Gregg, Andrew K.
Bayer, Jane E. (?)-1985
    Obituary 44
Bayley, Nicola 1949- 129
    Earlier sketches in SATA *41, 69*
Baylor, Byrd 1924- 136
    Earlier sketches in SATA *16, 69*
    See also CLR *3*
Baynes, Pauline 1922-2008 133
    Earlier sketches in SATA *19, 59*

Baynes, Pauline Diana
    See Baynes, Pauline
Bayoc, Cbabi 186
BB
    See Watkins-Pitchford, Denys James
Beach, Charles
    See Reid, (Thomas) Mayne
Beach, Charles Amory 1
Beach, Edward L. 1918-2002 12
    Obituary 140
Beach, Edward Latimer
    See Beach, Edward L.
Beach, Lisa 1957- 111
Beach, Lynn
    See Lance, Kathryn
Beach, Stewart T(aft) 1899-1979 23
Beachcroft, Nina 1931- 18
Beagle, Peter S. 1939- 130
    Earlier sketch in SATA *60*
Beagle, Peter Soyer
    See Beagle, Peter S.
Beaglehole, Helen 1946- 117
Beale, Fleur 107
Bealer, Alex W(inkler III) 1921-1980 8
    Obituary 22
Beales, Valerie 1915- 74
Beals, Carleton 1893-1979 12
Beals, Frank Lee 1881-1972
    Obituary 26
Beam, Matt 1970- 187
Beame, Rona 1934- 12
Beamer, (George) Charles (Jr.) 1942- 43
Bean, Normal
    See Burroughs, Edgar Rice
Beaney, Jan
    See Udall, Jan Beaney
Beaney, Jane
    See Udall, Jan Beaney
Bear, Carolyn
    See Rayban, Chloe
Bear, Greg(ory Dale) 1951- 105
    Earlier sketch in SATA *65*
Bearanger, Marie
    See Messier, Claire
Beard, Charles A(ustin) 1874-1948 18
Beard, Dan(iel Carter) 1850-1941 22
Beard, Darleen Bailey 1961- 96
Bearden, Romare (Howard)
    1914(?)-1988 22
    Obituary 56
Beardmore, Cedric
    See Beardmore, George
Beardmore, George 1908-1979 20
Beardshaw, Rosalind 1969- 190
Beardsley, Martyn R. 1957- 150
Bearman, Jane (Ruth) 1917- 29
Beaton, Clare 1947- 125
Beatty, Elizabeth
    See Holloway, Teresa (Bragunier)
Beatty, Hetty Burlingame 1907-1971 5
Beatty, Jerome, Jr. 1918- 5
Beatty, John (Louis) 1922-1975 6
    Obituary 25
Beatty, Patricia (Robbins) 1922-1991 73
    Obituary 68
    Earlier sketches in SATA *1, 30*
    See also SAAS *4*
Beaty, Andrea 186
Beaty, Mary (T.) 1947- 146
Beccia, Carlyn 189
Bechard, Margaret 1953- 164
    Earlier sketch in SATA *85*
Bechtel, Louise Seaman 1894-1985 4
    Obituary 43
Beck, Barbara L. 1927- 12
Beck, Ian 1947- 190
    Earlier sketch in SATA *138*
    See Beck, Ian Archibald
Beck, Peggy 1949- 171
Becker, Beril 1901-1999 11
Becker, Bonny 184

Becker, Deborah Zimmett 1955- 138
Becker, Helaine 1961- 142
Becker, John (Leonard) 1901- 12
Becker, John E(mil) 1942- 148
Becker, Joyce 1936- 39
Becker, May Lamberton 1873-1958 33
Becker, Neesa 1951- 123
Becker, Shari 174
Beckett, Sheilah 1913- 33
Beckhorn, Susan Williams 1953- 189
Beckman, Delores 1914-1994 51
Beckman, Gunnel 1910- 6
    See also CLR *25*
    See also SAAS *9*
Beckman, Kaj
    See Beckman, Karin
Beckman, Karin 1913- 45
Beckman, Per (Frithiof) 1913- 45
Bedard, Michael 1949- 154
    Earlier sketch in SATA *93*
    See also CLR *35*
Beddows, Eric
    See Nutt, Ken
Bedford, A. N.
    See Watson, Jane Werner
Bedford, Annie North
    See Watson, Jane Werner
Bedford, David 159
Bedoukian, Kerop 1907-1981 53
Bee, Jay
    See Brainerd, John W(hiting)
Bee, William 188
Beebe, B(urdetta) F(aye) 1
    See Johnson, B(urdetta) F(aye)
Beebe, (Charles) William 1877-1962 19
Beeby, Betty 1923- 25
Beech, Mark 1971- 191
Beech, Webb
    See Griffin, W.E.B
Beecham, Jahnna 161
Beechcroft, William
    See Hallstead, William F(inn III)
Beeching, Jack 1922- 14
Beeke, Tiphanie 163
Beeler, Janet
    See Shaw, Janet
Beeler, Nelson F(rederick) 1910-1978 13
Beere, Peter 1951- 97
Beers, Dorothy Sands 1917- 9
Beers, Lorna 1897-1989 14
Beers, V(ictor) Gilbert 1928- 130
    Earlier sketch in SATA *9*
Beeton, Max
    See Redding, Robert Hull
Begay, Shonto 1954- 137
Begaye, Lisa Shook
    See Beach, Lisa
Begin, Maryjane 1963- 82
Begin-Callanan, Maryjane
    See Begin, Maryjane
Begley, Kathleen A. 1948- 21
Begley, Kathleen Anne
    See Begley, Kathleen A.
Behan, Leslie
    See Gottfried, Theodore Mark
Behler, Deborah A. 1947- 145
Behler, John L. 1943-2006 145
    Obituary 173
Behler, John Luther
    See Behler, John L.
Behn, Harry 1898-1973 2
    Obituary 34
Behnke, Frances L. 8
Behr, Joyce 1929- 15
Behrens, June York 1925- 19
Behrman, Carol H(elen) 1925- 144
    Earlier sketch in SATA *14*
Beifuss, John, (Jr.) 1959- 92
Beil, Karen Magnuson 1950- 124
Beiler, Edna 1923- 61
Beinicke, Steve 1956- 69

Beirne, Barbara 1933- *71*
Beiser, Arthur 1931- *22*
Beiser, Germaine 1931- *11*
Belair, Richard L. 1934- *45*
Belaney, Archibald Stansfeld 1888-1938 ...... *24*
    See Grey Owl
Belbin, David 1958- *164*
    Earlier sketch in SATA *106*
Belden, Wilanne Schneider 1925- *56*
Belfrage, Sally 1936-1994 .... *65*
    Obituary *79*
Belknap, B. H.
    See Ellis, Edward S(ylvester)
Belknap, Boynton
    See Ellis, Edward S(ylvester)
Belknap, Boynton M.D.
    See Ellis, Edward S(ylvester)
Bell, Anthea 1936- *148*
    Earlier sketch in SATA *88*
Bell, Clare (Louise) 1952- *99*
Bell, Corydon Whitten 1894-1980 .... *3*
Bell, David Owen 1949- *99*
Bell, Emerson
    See Stratemeyer, Edward L.
Bell, Emily Mary
    See Cason, Mabel Earp
Bell, Frank
    See Benson, Mildred (Augustine Wirt)
Bell, Gertrude (Wood) 1911-1987 .... *12*
Bell, Hilari 1958- *151*
Bell, Jadrien
    See Golden, Christie
Bell, Janet
    See Clymer, Eleanor
Bell, Janet Cheatham 1937- *127*
Bell, Krista (Anne Blakeney) 1950- *126*
Bell, Margaret E(lizabeth) 1898-1990 .... *2*
Bell, Mary Reeves 1946- *88*
Bell, Norman (Edward) 1899- *11*
Bell, Raymond Martin 1907-1999 .... *13*
Bell, Siobhan *177*
Bell, Thelma Harrington 1896-1985 .... *3*
Bell, William 1945- *90*
    See also CLR 91
Bellairs, John (Anthony) 1938-1991 .... *160*
    Obituary *66*
    Earlier sketches in SATA *2, 68*
    See also CLR 37
Beller, Susan Provost 1949- *128*
    Earlier sketch in SATA *84*
    See also CLR 106
Bellingham, Brenda 1931- *99*
    Brief entry *51*
Bello, Rosario de
    See De Bello, Rosario
Belloc, (Joseph) Hilaire (Pierre
    Sebastien Rene Swanton) 1870-1953 .... *112*
    See also YABC 1
    See also CLR 102
Belloc, Joseph Peter Rene Hilaire
    *See Belloc, (Joseph) Hilaire (Pierre
    Sebastien Rene Swanton)*
Belloc, Joseph Pierre Hilaire
    *See Belloc, (Joseph) Hilaire (Pierre
    Sebastien Rene Swanton)*
Belloli, Andrea P. A. 1947- *86*
Bellville, Cheryl Walsh 1944- *54*
    Brief entry *49*
Belpre, Pura 1899-1982 .... *16*
    Obituary *30*
Belting, Natalia Maree 1915-1997 .... *6*
Belton, John Raynor 1931- *22*
Belton, Sandra 1939- *186*
    Earlier sketches in SATA *85, 134*
Belton, Sandra Yvonne
    See Belton, Sandra
Belton, Sandra Yvonne
    See Belton, Sandra
Beltran, Alberto 1923- *43*
Beltran-Hernandez, Irene 1945- *74*

Belvedere, Lee
    See Grayland, Valerie (Merle Spanner)
Bemelmans, Ludwig 1898-1962 .... *100*
    Earlier sketch in SATA *15*
    See also CLR 93
Benander, Carl D. 1941- *74*
Benary, Margot
    See Benary-Isbert, Margot
Benary-Isbert, Margot 1889-1979 .... *2*
    Obituary *21*
    See also CLR 12
Benasutti, Marion 1908-1992 .... *6*
Benatar, Raquel 1955- *167*
Benchley, Nathaniel (Goddard)
    1915-1981 .... *25*
    Obituary *28*
    Earlier sketch in SATA *3*
Benchley, Peter 1940-2006 .... *164*
    Earlier sketches in SATA *3, 89*
Benchley, Peter Bradford
    See Benchley, Peter
Bendall-Brunello, John *185*
Bender, Edna 1941- *92*
Bender, Esther 1942- *88*
Bender, Lucy Ellen 1942- *22*
Bender, Robert 1962- *160*
    Earlier sketch in SATA *79*
Bendick, Jeanne 1919- *135*
    Earlier sketches in SATA *2, 68*
    See also CLR 5
    See also SAAS 4
Bendick, Robert L(ouis) 1917- *11*
Benedetto, William R. 1928- *180*
Benedetto, William Ralph
    See Benedetto, William R.
Benedict, Andrew
    See Arthur, Robert, (Jr.)
Benedict, Dorothy Potter 1889-1979 .... *11*
    Obituary *23*
Benedict, Lois Trimble 1902-1967 .... *12*
Benedict, Rex 1920-1995 .... *8*
Benedict, Stewart H(urd) 1924- *26*
Beneduce, Ann Keay *128*
Benet, Laura 1884-1979 .... *3*
    Obituary *23*
Benet, Stephen Vincent 1898-1943
    See YABC 1
Benet, Sula 1906-1982 .... *21*
    Obituary *33*
Ben-Ezer, Ehud 1936- *122*
Benezra, Barbara (Beardsley) 1921- *10*
Benham, Leslie 1922- *48*
Benham, Lois (Dakin) 1924- *48*
Benham, Mary Lile 1914-1991 .... *55*
Benjamin, E. M. J.
    See Bache, Ellyn
Benjamin, Nora
    See Kubie, Nora Gottheil Benjamin
Benjamin, Saragail Katzman 1953- *86*
Benner, Cheryl 1962- *80*
Benner, Judith Ann 1942- *94*
Bennett, Alice
    See Ziner, Florence
Bennett, Cherie 1960- *158*
    Earlier sketch in SATA *97*
Bennett, Dorothea
    See Young, Dorothea Bennett
Bennett, Holly 1957- *181*
Bennett, Holly 1957- *181*
Bennett, James (W.) 1942- *153*
    Autobiography Feature *153*
    Earlier sketches in SATA *93, 148*
Bennett, Jay 1912- *87*
    Brief entry *27*
    Earlier sketch in SATA *41*
    See also SAAS 4
Bennett, Jill (Crawford) 1934- *41*
Bennett, John 1865-1956
    See YABC 1
Bennett, Penelope (Agnes) 1938- *94*

Bennett, Rachel
    See Hill, Margaret (Ohler)
Bennett, Rainey 1907-1998 .... *15*
    Obituary *111*
Bennett, Richard 1899- *21*
Bennett, Russell H(oradley) 1896- *25*
Bennett, Veronica 1953- *178*
Bennett, William (John) 1943- *102*
Benning, Elizabeth
    See Rice, Bebe Faas
Benson, Elizabeth P(olk) 1924- *65*
Benson, Kathleen 1947- *183*
    Earlier sketches in SATA *62, 111*
Benson, Linda M(aria) 1959- *84*
Benson, Mildred (Augustine Wirt)
    1905-2002 .... *100*
    Obituary *135*
    Earlier sketch in SATA *65*
    See Keene, Carolyn
Benson, Mildred Wirt
    See Benson, Mildred (Augustine Wirt)
Benson, Millie
    See Benson, Mildred (Augustine Wirt)
Benson, Patrick 1956- *147*
Benson, Sally 1900-1972 .... *35*
    Obituary *27*
    Earlier sketch in SATA *1*
Bentley, Judith (McBride) 1945- *89*
    Earlier sketch in SATA *40*
Bentley, Karen
    See Taschek, Karen
Bentley, Nancy (L.) 1946- *78*
Bentley, Nicolas Clerihew 1907-1978
    Obituary *24*
Bentley, Phyllis Eleanor 1894-1977 .... *6*
    Obituary *25*
Bentley, Roy 1947- *46*
Bentley, William (George) 1916- *84*
Benton, Jim 1963- *172*
ben Uzair, Salem
    See Horne, Richard Henry Hengist
Bercaw, Edna Coe 1961- *124*
Berck, Judith 1960- *75*
Berelson, Howard 1940- *5*
Berends, Polly Berrien 1939- *50*
    Brief entry *38*
Berenstain, Jan 1923- *135*
    Earlier sketches in SATA *12, 64, 129*
    See also CLR 19
    See also SAAS 20
Berenstain, Janice
    See Berenstain, Jan
Berenstain, Michael 1951- *45*
Berenstain, Mike
    See Berenstain, Michael
Berenstain, Stan 1923-2005 .... *135*
    Obituary *169*
    Earlier sketches in SATA *12, 64, 129*
    See also CLR 19
    See also SAAS 20
Berenstain, Stanley
    See Berenstain, Stan
Berenzy, Alix 1957- *168*
    Earlier sketch in SATA *65*
Beresford, Elisabeth 1928- *141*
    Earlier sketches in SATA *25, 86*
    See also SAAS 20
Berg, Adriane G(ilda) 1948- *152*
Berg, Dave
    See Berg, David
Berg, David 1920-2002 .... *27*
    Obituary *137*
Berg, Elizabeth 1948- *104*
Berg, Jean Horton 1913-1995 .... *6*
Berg, Joan
    See Victor, Joan Berg
Berg, Ron 1952- *48*
Bergaust, Erik 1925-1978 .... *20*
Bergel, Colin J. 1963- *137*
Bergen, Joyce 1949- *95*
Berger, Barbara (Helen) 1945- *77*

Berger, Carin 185
Berger, Gilda 1935- 88
    Brief entry 42
Berger, Josef 1903-1971 36
Berger, Melvin H. 1927- 158
    Autobiography Feature 124
    Earlier sketches in SATA 5, 88
    See also CLR 32
    See also SAAS 2
Berger, Phil 1942-2001 62
Berger, Samantha (Allison) 1969- 140
Berger, Terry 1933- 8
Bergey, Alyce (Mae) 1934- 45
Bergin, Mark 1961- 160
    Earlier sketch in SATA 114
Berglin, Ruth Marie 1970- 181
Bergman, Donna 1934- 73
Bergman, Tamar 1939- 95
Bergsma, Jody Lynn 163
Bergum, Constance R. 1952- 121
Berkebile, Fred D(onovan) 1900-1978
    Obituary 26
Berkes, Marianne 173
Berkey, Barry Robert 1935- 24
Berkowitz, Freda Pastor 1908-1994 12
Berkus, Clara Widess 1909- 78
Berlan, Kathryn Hook 1946- 78
Berlfein, Judy Reiss 1958- 79
Berliner, Don 1930- 33
Berliner, Franz 1930- 13
Berlitz, Charles (L. Frambach) 1914-2003 ... 32
    Obituary 151
Berman, Linda 1948- 38
Berman, Paul (Lawrence) 1949- 66
Berna, Paul 1910-1994 15
    Obituary 78
    See also CLR 19
Bernadette
    See Watts, (Anna) Bernadette
Bernard, Bruce 1928-2000 78
    Obituary 124
Bernard, George I. 1949- 39
Bernard, Jacqueline (de Sieyes)
    1921-1983 8
    Obituary 45
Bernard, Patricia 1942- 181
    Earlier sketch in SATA 106
Bernard, Trish
    See Bernard, Patricia
Bernardin, James (B.) 1966- 112
Bernardo, Anilu 184
Bernards, Neal 1963- 71
Bernasconi, Pablo 1973- 183
Bernays, Anne 1930- 32
Bernhard, Durga T. 1961- 80
Bernhard, Emery 1950- 80
Bernstein, Daryl (Evan) 1976- 81
Bernstein, Joanne E(ckstein) 1943- 15
Bernstein, Margery 1933- 114
Bernstein, Nina 1949- 180
Bernstein, Theodore M(enline)
    1904-1979 12
    Obituary 27
Berrien, Edith Heal
    See Heal, Edith
Berrill, Jacquelyn (Batsel) 1905- 12
Berrington, John
    See Brownjohn, Alan
Berry, B. J.
    See Berry, Barbara J.
Berry, Barbara J. 1937- 7
Berry, Erick
    See Best, (Evangel) Allena Champlin
Berry, James 1925- 110
    Earlier sketch in SATA 67
    See also CLR 22
Berry, Jane Cobb 1915(?)-1979
    Obituary 22
Berry, Joy
    See Berry, Joy Wilt

Berry, Joy Wilt 1944- 58
    Brief entry 46
Berry, Lynne 190
Berry, William D(avid) 1926- 14
Bersani, Shennen 1961- 164
Berson, Harold 1926- 4
Bertagna, Julie 1962- 151
Bertholf, Bret 189
Bertin, Charles-Francois
    See Berlitz, Charles (L. Frambach)
Bertolet, Paul
    See McLaughlin, Frank
Berton, Pierre (Francis de Marigny)
    1920-2004 99
    Obituary 158
Bertrand, Cecile 1953- 76
Bertrand, Diane Gonzales 1956- 177
    Earlier sketch in SATA 106
Bertrand, Lynne 1963- 164
    Earlier sketch in SATA 81
Beskow, Elsa (Maartman) 1874-1953 20
    See also CLR 17
Bess, Clayton
    See CLR 39
    See Locke, Robert
Best, (Evangel) Allena Champlin
    1892-1974 2
    Obituary 25
Best, Cari 1951- 149
    Earlier sketch in SATA 107
Best, (Oswald) Herbert 1894-1980 2
Bestall, A(lfred) E(dmeades) 1892-1986 97
    Obituary 48
Betancourt, Jeanne 1941- 148
    Brief entry 43
    Earlier sketches in SATA 55, 96
Beth, Mary
    See Miller, Mary Beth
Bethancourt, T. Ernesto 11
    See also CLR 3
    See Paisley, Tom
Bethel, Dell 1929- 52
Bethell, Jean (Frankenberry) 1922- 8
Bethers, Ray 1902-1973 6
Bethke, Bruce Raymond 1955- 114
Bethlen, T.D.
    See Silverberg, Robert
Bethune, J. G.
    See Ellis, Edward S(ylvester)
Bethune, J. H.
    See Ellis, Edward S(ylvester)
Betteridge, Anne
    See Potter, Margaret (Newman)
Bettina
    See Ehrlich, Bettina Bauer
Bettmann, Otto Ludwig 1903-1998 46
Bettoli, Delana 187
Betts, James
    See Haynes, Betsy
Betz, Eva Kelly 1897-1968 10
Bevan, Tom 1868-1930(?)
    See YABC 2
Bewick, Thomas 1753-1828 16
Beyer, Audrey White 1916- 9
Beyer, Paul J. III 1950- 74
Beynon, John
    See Harris, John (Wyndham Parkes
    Lucas) Beynon
Bezencon, Jacqueline (Buxcel) 1924- 48
Bial, Morrison David 1917- 62
Bial, Raymond 1948- 165
    Earlier sketches in SATA 76, 116
Biala
    See Brustlein, Janice Tworkov
Biale, Rachel 1952- 99
Bialk, Elisa
    See Krautter, Elisa (Bialk)
Bianchi, John 1947- 91
Bianchi, Robert S(teven) 1943- 92
Bianco, Margery
    See Bianco, Margery Williams

Bianco, Margery Williams 1881-1944 15
    See also CLR 19
Bianco, Pamela 1906- 28
Bibby, Violet 1908- 24
Bible, Charles 1937- 13
Bibo, Bobette
    See Gugliotta, Bobette
Bice, Clare 1909-1976 22
Bickerstaff, Isaac
    See Swift, Jonathan
Bidner, Jenni 1963- 193
Biegel, Paul 1925- 79
    Earlier sketch in SATA 16
    See also CLR 27
    See also SAAS 18
Biemiller, Carl L(udwig), Jr.) 1912-1979 40
    Obituary 21
Bienenfeld, Florence L(ucille) 1929- 39
Bierhorst, John (William) 1936- 149
    Autobiography Feature 149
    Earlier sketches in SATA 6, 91
    See also SAAS 10
Biggar, Joan R(awlins) 1936- 120
Biggle, Lloyd, Jr. 1923-2002 65
Biggs, Brian 1968- 192
Bilal, Abdel W(ahab) 1970- 92
Bilbrough, Norman 1941- 111
Bildner, Phil 173
Bileck, Marvin 1920- 40
Bilibin, Ivan (Iakolevich) 1876-1942 61
Bill, Alfred Hoyt 1879-1964 44
Billam, Rosemary 1952- 61
Billings, Charlene W(interer) 1941- 41
Billingsley, Franny 1954- 132
Billington, Elizabeth T(hain) 50
    Brief entry 43
Billout, Guy (Rene) 1941- 144
    Earlier sketch in SATA 10
    See also CLR 33
Bilson, Geoffrey 1938-1987 99
Binch, Caroline (Lesley) 1947- 140
    Earlier sketch in SATA 81
Bing, Christopher (H.) 126
Bingham, Caroline 1962- 158
Bingham, Jane M. 1941- 163
Bingham, Jane Marie
    See Bingham, Jane M.
Bingham, Sam(uel A.) 1944- 96
Bingley, Margaret (Jane Kirby) 1947- 72
Binkley, Anne
    See Rand, Ann (Binkley)
Binzen, Bill 24
    See Binzen, William
Birch, David (W.) 1913-1996 89
Birch, Reginald B(athurst) 1856-1943 19
Birchman, David 1949- 72
Birchmore, Daniel A. 1951- 92
Bird, Carmel 1940- 124
Bird, E(lzy) J(ay) 1911- 58
Birdsall, Jeanne 1952(?)- 170
Birdseye, Tom 1951- 148
    Earlier sketches in SATA 66, 98
Birenbaum, Barbara 1941- 65
Birmingham, Lloyd P(aul) 1924- 83
    Earlier sketch in SATA 12
Birmingham, Ruth
    See Sorrells, Walter
Birney, Betty G. 1947- 169
    Earlier sketch in SATA 98
Biro, B.
    See Biro, B(alint) S(tephen)
Biro, B(alint) S(tephen) 1921- 67
    See Biro, Val
Biro, Val 1
    See also CLR 28
    See also SAAS 13
    See Biro, B(alint) S(tephen)
Bischoff, Julia Bristol 1899-1970 12
Bishop, Bonnie 1943- 37

Bishop, Claire Huchet 1899(?)-1993 .... *14*
  Obituary *74*
  See also CLR *80*
Bishop, Courtney
  See Ruemmler, John D(avid)
Bishop, Curtis (Kent) 1912-1967 .... *6*
Bishop, Elizabeth 1911-1979
  Obituary *24*
Bishop, Gavin 1946- *144*
  Earlier sketch in SATA *97*
Bishop, Kathleen Wong 1954- *120*
Bishop, Kathy
  See Bishop, Kathleen Wong
Bishop, Nic 1955- *161*
  Earlier sketch in SATA *107*
Bisset, Donald 1910-1995 .... *86*
  Earlier sketch in SATA *7*
Bisson, Terry 1942- *99*
Bisson, Terry Ballantine
  See Bisson, Terry
Bitter, Gary G(len) 1940- *22*
Bixby, William (Courtney) 1920-1986 .... *6*
  Obituary *47*
Bjoerk, Christina 1938- *99*
  Earlier sketch in SATA *67*
  See also CLR *22*
Bjork, Christina
  See Bjoerk, Christina
Bjorklund, Lorence F. 1913-1978 .... *35*
  Brief entry *32*
Bjorkman, Steve *163*
Black, Algernon David 1900-1993 .... *12*
  Obituary *76*
Black, Holly 1971- *147*
Black, Irma Simonton 1906-1972 .... *2*
  Obituary *25*
Black, Mansell
  See Trevor, Elleston
Black, MaryAnn
  See Easley, MaryAnn
Black, Susan Adams 1953- *40*
Blackall, Bernie 1956- *126*
Blackall, Sophie *182*
Blackburn, Claire
  See Altman, Linda Jacobs
Blackburn, John(ny) Brewton 1952- *15*
Blackburn, Joyce Knight 1920- *29*
Blacker, Tina
  See Louise, Tina
Blackett, Veronica Heath 1927- *12*
Blackie, Jean Cutler 1943- *79*
Blacklin, Malcolm
  See Chambers, Aidan
Blacklock, Dyan 1951- *112*
Blackman, Malorie 1962- *128*
  Earlier sketch in SATA *83*
Blackton, Peter
  See Wilson, Lionel
Blackwood, Alan 1932- *70*
Blackwood, Gary L. 1945- *169*
  Earlier sketches in SATA *72, 118*
Blade, Alexander
  See Garrett, (Gordon) Randall (Phillip)
  and Hamilton, Edmond
  and Silverberg, Robert
Blades, Ann (Sager) 1947- *69*
  Earlier sketch in SATA *16*
  See also CLR *15*
Bladow, Suzanne Wilson 1937- *14*
Blaine, Chris
  See Gardner, Craig Shaw
Blaine, John
  See Goodwin, Harold L(eland)
Blaine, Marge
  See Blaine, Margery Kay
Blaine, Margery Kay 1937- *11*
Blair, Alison
  See Lerangis, Peter
Blair, Anne Denton 1914-1993 .... *46*
Blair, David Nelson 1954- *80*

Blair, Eric (Arthur) 1903-1950 .... *29*
  See Orwell, George
Blair, Jay 1953- *45*
Blair, Lucile
  See Yeakley, Marjory Hall
Blair, Margaret Whitman 1951- *124*
Blair, Pauline Hunter
  See Clarke, Pauline
Blair, Ruth Van Ness 1912-1999 .... *12*
Blair, Shannon
  See Kaye, Marilyn
Blair, Walter 1900-1992 .... *12*
  Obituary *72*
Blaisdell, Bob
  See Blaisdell, Robert
Blaisdell, Robert 1959- *105*
Blake, Bronwyn 1940- *149*
Blake, Jon 1954- *171*
  Earlier sketch in SATA *78*
Blake, Olive
  See Supraner, Robyn
Blake, Quentin (Saxby) 1932- *125*
  Earlier sketches in SATA *9, 52, 96*
  See also CLR *31*
Blake, Robert 1949- *42*
Blake, Robert J. *160*
Blake, Walker E.
  See Griffin, W.E.B
Blake, William 1757-1827 .... *30*
  See also CLR *52*
Blakely, Gloria 1950- *139*
Blakely, Roger K. 1922- *82*
Blakeney, Jay D.
  See Chester, Deborah
Blakey, Nancy 1955- *94*
Blanc, Esther S. 1913-1997 .... *66*
Blanc, Mel 1908-1989
  Obituary *64*
Blanchard, Patricia *125*
Blanchet, M(uriel) Wylie 1891-1961 .... *106*
Blanco, Richard L(idio) 1926- *63*
Bland, E.
  See Nesbit, E.
Bland, Edith Nesbit
  See Nesbit, E.
Bland, Fabian
  See Nesbit, E.
Blane, Gertrude
  See Blumenthal, Gertrude
Blank, Clarissa Mabel 1915-1965 .... *62*
Blankenship, LeeAnn 1944- *181*
Blassingame, Wyatt Rainey 1909-1985 .... *34*
  Obituary *41*
  Earlier sketch in SATA *1*
Blatchford, Claire H. 1944- *94*
Blauer, Ettagale 1940- *49*
Bledsoe, Glen L. 1951- *108*
Bledsoe, Glen Leonard
  See Bledsoe, Glen L.
Bledsoe, Karen E. 1962- *167*
  Earlier sketch in SATA *108*
Bledsoe, Karen Elizabeth
  See Bledsoe, Karen E.
Bledsoe, Lucy Jane 1957- *162*
  Earlier sketch in SATA *97*
Bleeker, Sonia *2*
  Obituary *26*
  See Zim, Sonia Bleeker
Blegen, Daniel M. 1950- *92*
Blegvad, Erik 1923- *132*
  Earlier sketches in SATA *14, 66*
Blegvad, Lenore 1926- *176*
  Earlier sketches in SATA *14, 66*
Bley, Anette 1967- *188*
Blish, James (Benjamin) 1921-1975 .... *66*
Blishen, Edward (William) 1920-1996 .... *66*
  Obituary *93*
  Earlier sketch in SATA *8*
Bliss, Corinne Demas 1947- *37*
  See Demas, Corinne

Bliss, Frederick
  See Card, Orson Scott
Bliss, Gillian
  See Paton Walsh, Jill
Bliss, Harry 1964- *156*
Bliss, Reginald
  See Wells, H(erbert) G(eorge)
Bliss, Ronald G(ene) 1942- *12*
Blitt, Barry *187*
Bliven, Bruce, Jr. 1916-2002 .... *2*
Blixen, Karen (Christentze Dinesen)
  1885-1962 .... *44*
  See Dinesen, Isak
Blizzard, Gladys S. (?)-1992 .... *79*
Blobaum, Cindy 1966- *123*
Bloch, Lucienne 1909-1999 .... *10*
Bloch, Marie Halun 1910-1998 .... *6*
  See also SAAS *9*
Bloch, Robert (Albert) 1917-1994 .... *12*
  Obituary *82*
Blochman, Lawrence G(oldtree)
  1900-1975 .... *22*
Block, Francesca Lia 1962- *158*
  Earlier sketches in SATA *80, 116*
  See also CLR *116*
  See also SAAS *21*
Block, Irvin 1917- *12*
Blomgren, Jennifer (Alice) 1954- *136*
Blood, Charles Lewis 1929- *28*
Bloom, Barbara Lee 1943- *146*
Bloom, Freddy 1914-2000 .... *37*
  Obituary *121*
Bloom, Lloyd 1947- *108*
  Brief entry *43*
Bloom, Suzanne 1950- *172*
Bloomfield, Michaela 1966- *70*
Bloor, Edward 1950- *155*
  Earlier sketch in SATA *98*
Bloor, Edward William
  See Bloor, Edward
Blos, Joan W(insor) 1928- *153*
  Autobiography Feature *153*
  Brief entry *27*
  Earlier sketches in SATA *33, 69, 109*
  See also CLR *18*
  See also SAAS *11*
Blough, Glenn O(rlando) 1907-1995 .... *1*
Blue, Rose 1931- *166*
  Autobiography Feature *117*
  Earlier sketches in SATA *5, 91, 93*
  See also SAAS *24*
Blue, Zachary
  See Stine, R.L.
Bluggage, Oranthy
  See Alcott, Louisa May
Blumberg, Leda 1956- *59*
Blumberg, Rhoda 1917- *123*
  Earlier sketches in SATA *35, 70*
  See also CLR *21*
Blume, Judy (Sussman) 1938- *142*
  Earlier sketches in SATA *2, 31, 79*
  See also CLR *69*
Blume, Lesley M.M. 1975- *180*
Blumenthal, Deborah *161*
Blumenthal, Gertrude 1907-1971
  Obituary *27*
Blumenthal, Shirley 1943- *46*
Blutig, Eduard
  See Gorey, Edward (St. John)
Bly, Janet (Chester) 1945- *43*
Bly, Stephen A(rthur) 1944- *116*
  Earlier sketch in SATA *43*
Blyler, Allison Lee 1966- *74*
Blythe, Gary 1959- *185*
Blyton, Carey 1932-2002 .... *9*
  Obituary *138*
Blyton, Enid 1897-1968 .... *25*
  See also CLR *31*
Blyton, Enid Mary
  See Blyton, Enid

Bo, Ben
  See Richardson, V.A.
Boardman, Fon Wyman, Jr. 1911-2000 6
Boardman, Gwenn R. 12
  See Petersen, Gwenn Boardman
Boase, Wendy 1944-1999 28
  Obituary 110
Boatner, Mark Mayo III 1921- 29
Bobbe, Dorothie de Bear 1905-1975 1
  Obituary 25
Bober, Natalie S. 1930- 134
  Earlier sketch in SATA 87
  See also SAAS 23
Bobette, Bibo
  See Gugliotta, Bobette
Bobritsky, Vladimir 47
  Brief entry 32
  See Bobri, Vladimir V.
Bochak, Grayce 1956- 76
Bock, Hal
  See Bock, Harold I.
Bock, Harold I. 1939- 10
Bock, William Sauts Netamux'we 1939- 14
Bodanis, David 179
Bode, Janet 1943-1999 96
  Obituary 118
  Earlier sketch in SATA 60
Bodecker, N(iels) M(ogens) 1922-1988 73
  Obituary 54
  Earlier sketch in SATA 8
Boden, Hilda
  See Bodenham, Hilda Morris
Bodenham, Hilda Morris 1901- 13
Bodett, Tom 70
  See Bodett, Thomas Edward
Bodie, Idella F(allaw) 1925- 89
  Earlier sketch in SATA 12
Bodker, Cecil 1927- 133
  Earlier sketch in SATA 14
  See also CLR 23
Bodker, Cecil 1927-
  See Bodker, Cecil
Bodsworth, (Charles) Fred(erick) 1918- 27
Boeckman, Charles 1920- 12
Boegehold, Betty (Doyle) 1913-1985
  Obituary 42
Boelts, Maribeth 1964- 163
  Earlier sketch in SATA 78
Boerst, William J. 1939- 170
  Earlier sketch in SATA 121
Boesch, Mark J(oseph) 1917- 12
Boesen, Victor 1908- 16
Bogacki, Tomek 1950- 138
Bogaerts, Gert 1965- 80
Bogan, Paulette 1960- 129
Bogart, Jo Ellen 1945- 92
  See also CLR 59
Boggs, Ralph Steele 1901-1994 7
Bograd, Larry 1953- 89
  Earlier sketch in SATA 33
  See also SAAS 21
Bohdal, Susi 1951- 101
  Earlier sketch in SATA 22
Bohlen, Nina 1931- 58
Bohlmeijer, Arno 1956- 94
Bohner, Charles (Henry) 1927- 62
Bohnhoff, Maya Kaathryn 1954- 88
Boiger, Alexandra 178
Boissard, Janine 1932- 59
Bojunga, Lygia
  See Nunes, Lygia Bojunga
Bojunga-Nunes, Lygia
  See Nunes, Lygia Bojunga
Boland, Janice 98
Bolden, Tonya 1959- 188
  Earlier sketches in SATA 79, 138
Bolden, Tonya Wilyce
  See Bolden, Tonya
Boles, Paul Darcy 1916-1984 9
  Obituary 38
Bolian, Polly 1925- 4

Bollen, Roger 1941(?)- 83
  Brief entry 29
Bolliger, Max 1929- 7
Bollinger, Max 1929- 167
Bollinger, Peter 172
Bolognese, Don(ald Alan) 1934- 129
  Earlier sketches in SATA 24, 71
Bolotin, Norman (Phillip) 1951- 93
Bolton, Carole 1926- 6
Bolton, Elizabeth
  See St. John, Nicole
Bolton, Evelyn
  See Bunting, (Anne) Eve(lyn)
Bonar, Veronica
  See Bailey, Donna (Veronica Anne)
Bond, B. J.
  See Heneghan, James
Bond, Bruce 1939- 61
Bond, Felicia 1954- 126
  Earlier sketch in SATA 49
Bond, Gladys Baker 1912- 14
Bond, Higgins 1951- 177
  Earlier sketch in SATA 83
Bond, J. Harvey
  See Winterbotham, R(ussell) R(obert)
Bond, (Thomas) Michael 1926- 157
  Earlier sketches in SATA 6, 58
  See also CLR 95
  See also SAAS 3
Bond, Nancy 1945- 159
  Autobiography Feature 159
  Earlier sketches in SATA 22, 82
  See also CLR 11
  See also SAAS 13
Bond, Nancy Barbara
  See Bond, Nancy
Bond, Rebecca 1972- 130
Bond, Ruskin 1934- 87
  Earlier sketch in SATA 14
Bondie, J. D.
  See Cunningham, Chet
Bondoux, Anne-Laure 1971- 175
Bone, Ian 1956- 158
  Earlier sketch in SATA 117
Bonehill, Captain Ralph
  See Stratemeyer, Edward L.
Bonestell, Chesley 1888-1986
  Obituary 48
Bonham, Barbara Thomas 1926- 7
Bonham, Frank 1914-1989 49
  Obituary 62
  Earlier sketch in SATA 1
  See also SAAS 3
Boniface, William 1963- 182
  Earlier sketch in SATA 102
Bonino, Louise
  See Williams, Louise Bonino
Bonk, John J. 189
Bonn, Pat
  See Bonn, Patricia Carolyn
Bonn, Patricia Carolyn 1948- 43
Bonner, Mary Graham 1890-1974 19
Bonner, Mike 1951- 121
Bonners, Susan 1947- 85
  Brief entry 48
Bonnett-Rampersaud, Louise 173
Bonning, Tony 1948- 169
Bonsall, Crosby Barbara (Newell)
  1921-1995 23
  Obituary 84
Bonsall, Joseph S. 1948- 119
Bonsignore, Joan 1959- 140
Bontemps, Arna(ud Wendell) 1902-1973 44
  Obituary 24
  Earlier sketch in SATA 2
  See also CLR 6
Bonzon, Paul-Jacques 1908-1978 22
Boock, Paula 1964- 134
Booher, Dianna Daniels 1948- 33
Book, Rick 1949- 119

Book, Rita
  See Holub, Joan
Bookman, Charlotte
  See Zolotow, Charlotte
Boon, Debbie 1960- 103
Boon, Emilie (Laetitia) 1958- 86
Boone, Charles Eugene
  See Boone, Pat
Boone, Pat 1934- 7
Boorman, Linda (Kay) 1940- 46
Boorstin, Daniel J(oseph) 1914-2004 52
Booth, Coe 187
Booth, Ernest Sheldon 1915-1984 43
Booth, George 1926- 191
Booth, Graham (Charles) 1935- 37
Bootman, Colin 159
Borden, Louise 1949- 190
  Autobiography Feature 141
  Earlier sketches in SATA 68, 104, 141
Bordier, Georgette 1924- 16
Borgman, James
  See Borgman, Jim
Borgman, James Mark
  See Borgman, Jim
Borgman, Jim 1954- 122
  See Borgman, James Mark
Boring, Mel 1939- 168
  Earlier sketch in SATA 35
Borja, Corinne 1929- 22
Borja, Robert 1923- 22
Borland, Hal 5
  Obituary 24
  See Borland, Harold Glen
Borland, Kathryn Kilby 1916- 16
Borlenghi, Patricia 1951- 79
Born, Adolf 1930- 49
Bornstein, Ruth Lercher
  Autobiography Feature 107
  See Bornstein-Lercher, Ruth
Bornstein-Lercher, Ruth 1927- 88
  Earlier sketch in SATA 14
  See Bornstein, Ruth Lercher
Borski, Lucia Merecka 18
Borten, Helen Jacobson 1930- 5
Bortolotti, Dan 1969- 157
Borton, Elizabeth
  See Trevino, Elizabeth B(orton) de
Borton, Lady 1942- 98
Borton de Trevino, Elizabeth
  See Trevino, Elizabeth B(orton) de
Bortstein, Larry 1942- 16
Bortz, Alfred B(enjamin) 1944- 139
  Earlier sketch in SATA 74
Bortz, Fred
  See Bortz, Alfred B(enjamin)
Bosco, Jack
  See Holliday, Joseph
Boshell, Gordon 1908- 15
Boshinski, Blanche 1922- 10
Bosman, Paul 1929- 107
Bosse, Malcolm (Joseph, Jr.) 1926-2002 136
  Earlier sketch in SATA 35
Bosserman, (Charles) Phillip 1931- 84
Bossom, Naomi 1933- 35
Bostock, Mike 1962- 114
Boston, L(ucy) M(aria Wood) 1892-1990 19
  Obituary 64
  See also CLR 3
Bostrom, Kathleen (Susan) Long
  1954- 139
Bostrom, Kathy
  See Bostrom, Kathleen (Susan) Long
Bosworth, J. Allan 1925- 19
Bothwell, Jean (?)-1977 2
Botkin, B(enjamin) A(lbert) 1901-1975 40
Botsford, Ward 1927-2004 66
Botting, Douglas (Scott) 1934- 43
Bottner, Barbara 1943- 170
  Autobiography Feature 121
  Earlier sketches in SATA 14, 93
  See also SAAS 26

Bottone, Frank G., Jr. 1969- *141*
Bouchard, David 1952- *117*
Boucher, (Clarence) Carter 1954- *129*
Boudelang, Bob
  See Pell, Ed(ward)
Boughton, Richard 1954- *75*
Boulet, Susan Seddon 1941- *50*
Boulle, Pierre (Francois Marie-Louis)
  1912-1994 .... *22*
  Obituary *78*
Boulton, Jane 1921- *91*
Bouma, Paddy 1947- *128*
Bour, Daniele 1939- *62*
Bourbonniere, Sylvie 1966- *182*
Bourdon, David 1934-1998 .... *46*
Bourgeois, Paulette 1951- *153*
Bourne, Lesley
  See Marshall, Evelyn
Bourne, Miriam Anne 1931-1989 .... *16*
  Obituary *63*
Boutet de Monvel, (Louis) M(aurice)
  1850(?)-1913 .... *30*
  See also CLR *32*
Bova, Ben 1932- *133*
  Earlier sketches in SATA *6, 68*
  See also CLR *96*
Bova, Benjamin William
  See Bova, Ben
Bovaird, Anne E(lizabeth) 1960- *90*
Bow, Patricia 1946- *168*
Bowden, Joan Chase 1925- *51*
  Brief entry *38*
Bowen, Alexandria Russell *97*
Bowen, Andy Russell
  See Bowen, Alexandria Russell
Bowen, Anne 1952- *170*
Bowen, Betty Morgan
  See West, Betty
Bowen, Catherine (Shober) Drinker
  1897-1973 .... *7*
Bowen, David
  See Bowen, Joshua David
Bowen, Fred 1953- *136*
Bowen, Joshua David 1930- *22*
Bowen, Rhys
  See Quin-Harkin, Janet
Bowen, Robert Sydney 1900-1977 .... *52*
  Obituary *21*
Bowermaster, Jon 1954- *135*
  Earlier sketch in SATA *77*
Bowers, Terrell L. 1945- *101*
Bowers, Terry
  See Bowers, Terrell L.
Bowers, Tim *185*
Bowie, C. W.
  See Old, Wendie C(orbin)
  and Wirths, Claudine (Turner) G(ibson)
Bowie, Jim
  See Norwood, Victor G(eorge) C(harles)
  and Stratemeyer, Edward L.
Bowkett, Stephen 1953- *67*
Bowler, Jan Brett
  See Brett, Jan
Bowler, Tim 1953- *149*
Bowman, Crystal 1951- *105*
Bowman, James Cloyd 1880-1961 .... *23*
Bowman, John S(tewart) 1931- *16*
Bowman, Kathleen (Gill) 1942- *52*
  Brief entry *40*
Bowman, Leslie
  See Bowman, Leslie W.
Bowman, Leslie W. *182*
Boxall, Ed *178*
Boyce, Frank Cottrell *182*
Boyce, George A(rthur) 1898- *19*
Boyd, Candy Dawson 1946- *72*
  See also CLR *50*
Boyd, Pauline
  See Schock, Pauline
Boyd, Selma
  See Acuff, Selma Boyd

Boyd, Waldo T. 1918- *18*
Boyden, Linda 1948- *143*
Boyer, Allen B. 1963- *153*
Boyer, Robert E(rnst) 1929- *22*
Boyes, Vivien 1952- *106*
Boyes, Vivien Elizabeth
  See Boyes, Vivien
Boyle, Ann (Peters) 1916- *10*
Boyle, Eleanor Vere (Gordon) 1825-1916 .... *28*
Boyle, Robert H. 1928- *65*
Boylston, Helen Dore 1895-1984 .... *23*
  Obituary *39*
Boyne, John 1971- *181*
Boynton, Sandra (Keith) 1953- *152*
  Brief entry *38*
  Earlier sketches in SATA *57, 107*
  See also CLR *105*
Boz
  See Dickens, Charles (John Huffam)
Bracken, Charles
  See Pellowski, Michael (Joseph)
Brackers de Hugo, Pierre 1960- *115*
Brackett, Dolli Tingle 1911-1993 .... *137*
Brackett, Virginia 1950- *166*
  Earlier sketch in SATA *121*
Brackett, Virginia Roberts Meredith
  See Brackett, Virginia
Bradbury, Bianca (Ryley) 1908-1982 .... *56*
  Earlier sketch in SATA *3*
Bradbury, Edward P.
  See Moorcock, Michael
Bradbury, Ray 1920- *123*
  Earlier sketches in SATA *11, 64*
Bradbury, Ray Douglas
  See Bradbury, Ray
Bradby, Marie *161*
Bradfield, Carl 1942- *91*
Bradford, Ann (Liddell) 1917- *56*
  Brief entry *38*
Bradford, Barbara Taylor 1933- *66*
Bradford, Karleen 1936- *96*
  Earlier sketch in SATA *48*
Bradford, Lois J(ean) 1936- *36*
Bradford, Richard (Roark) 1932-2002 .... *59*
  Obituary *135*
Bradley, Duane
  See Sanborn, Duane
Bradley, Kimberly Brubaker 1967- *179*
Bradley, Marion Zimmer 1930-1999 .... *139*
  Obituary *116*
  Earlier sketch in SATA *90*
  See Chapman, Lee
  and Dexter, John
  and Gardner, Miriam
  and Ives, Morgan
  and Rivers, Elfrida
Bradley, Timothy J. *193*
Bradley, Virginia 1912- *23*
Bradley, Will
  See Strickland, (William) Brad(ley)
Bradman, Tony 1954- *152*
  Earlier sketch in SATA *81*
Bradshaw, Gillian (Joan) 1949- *118*
Bradshaw, Gillian 1956- *127*
Bradshaw, Gillian Marucha
  See Bradshaw, Gillian
Bradstreet, T. J.
  See Thesman, Jean
Brady, Esther Wood 1905-1987 .... *31*
  Obituary *53*
Brady, Irene 1943- *4*
Brady, Kimberley S. 1953- *101*
Brady, Kimberley Smith
  See Brady, Kimberley S.
Brady, Lillian 1902- *28*
Bragdon, Elspeth MacDuffie 1897-1980 .... *6*
Bragdon, Lillian Jacot *24*
Brager, Bruce L. 1949- *146*
Bragg, Mabel Caroline 1870-1945 .... *24*
Bragg, Michael 1948- *46*
Bragg, Ruth Gembicki 1943- *77*

Brahm, Sumishta 1954- *58*
Brailsford, Frances
  See Wosmek, Frances
Brainerd, John W(hiting) 1918- *65*
Braithwaite, Althea 1940- *23*
  Autobiography Feature *119*
  See also SAAS *24*
Bram, Elizabeth 1948- *30*
Brancato, Robin F(idler) 1936- *97*
  See also CLR *32*
  See also SAAS *9*
Branch, Muriel Miller 1943- *152*
  Earlier sketch in SATA *94*
Brand, Christianna
  See Lewis, Mary (Christianna)
Brand, Rebecca
  See Charnas, Suzy McKee
Brandel, Marc 1919- *71*
Brandenberg, Alexa (Demetria) 1966- *97*
Brandenberg, Aliki (Liacouras) 1929- *157*
  Earlier sketches in SATA *2, 35, 75, 113*
  See Aliki
Brandenberg, Franz 1932- *75*
  Earlier sketches in SATA *8, 35*
Brandenburg, Jim 1945- *87*
Brandhorst, Carl T(heodore) 1898-1988 .... *23*
Brandis, Marianne 1938- *149*
  Earlier sketches in SATA *59, 96*
Brandon, Brumsic, Jr. 1927- *9*
Brandon, Curt
  See Bishop, Curtis (Kent)
Brandreth, Gyles 1948- *28*
Brandreth, Gyles Daubeney
  See Brandreth, Gyles
Brandt, Catharine 1905-1997 .... *40*
Brandt, Keith
  See Sabin, Louis
Brandt, Sue R(eading) 1916- *59*
Branfield, John (Charles) 1931- *11*
Branford, Henrietta 1946-1999 .... *106*
Branley, Franklyn M(ansfield)
  1915-2002 .... *136*
  Earlier sketches in SATA *4, 68*
  See also CLR *13*
  See also SAAS *16*
Branscum, Robbie (Tilley) 1937-1997 .... *72*
  Obituary *96*
  Earlier sketch in SATA *23*
  See also SAAS *17*
Bransom, (John) Paul 1885-1979 .... *43*
Brashares, Ann 1967- *188*
  Earlier sketch in SATA *145*
  See also CLR *113*
Brassard, France 1963- *186*
Braswell, E.J.
  See Lynn, Tracy
Braswell, Elizabeth J.
  See Lynn, Tracy
Braswell, Liz
  See Lynn, Tracy
Bratton, Helen 1899-1986 .... *4*
Bratun, Katy 1950- *160*
  Earlier sketch in SATA *83*
Braude, Michael 1936- *23*
Braun, Lilian Jackson 1916(?)- *109*
Brautigan, Richard (Gary) 1935-1984 .... *56*
Bray, Libba *159*
Bray, Martha E.
  See Bray, Libba
Braymer, Marjorie Elizabeth 1911-1988 .... *6*
Breathed, Berke 1957- *161*
  Earlier sketch in SATA *86*
Breathed, Guy Berkeley
  See Breathed, Berke
Brecht, Edith 1895-1975 .... *6*
  Obituary *25*
Breck, Vivian
  See Breckenfeld, Vivian Gurney
Breckenfeld, Vivian Gurney 1895-1992 .... *1*
Breda, Tjalmar
  See DeJong, David C(ornel)

Bredeson, Carmen 1944- *163*
  Earlier sketch in SATA *98*
Breen, Steve 1970- *186*
Breinburg, Petronella 1927- *11*
  See also CLR *31*
Breisky, William J(ohn) 1928- *22*
Brenaman, Miriam *172*
Brennan, Caitlin
  See Tarr, Judith
Brennan, Gale (Patrick) 1927- *64*
  Brief entry *53*
Brennan, Herbie 1940- *183*
  Earlier sketch in SATA *140*
Brennan, James Herbert
  See Brennan, Herbie
Brennan, Jan
  See Brennan, Herbie
Brennan, J.H.
  See Brennan, Herbie
Brennan, Joseph Lomas 1903-2000 .... *6*
Brennan, Linda Crotta 1952- *130*
Brennan, Tim
  See Conroy, John Wesley
Brenner, Anita 1905-1974 .... *56*
Brenner, Barbara (Johnes) 1925- *124*
  Earlier sketches in SATA *4, 42, 76*
  See also SAAS *14*
Brenner, Fred 1920- *36*
  Brief entry *34*
Brent, Hope 1935(?)-1984
  Obituary *39*
Brent, Stuart *14*
Breskin, Jane
  See Zalben, Jane Breskin
Breslin, Theresa *128*
  Autobiography Feature *128*
  Earlier sketch in SATA *70*
Breslow, Maurice 1935- *72*
Breslow, Maurice A
  See Breslow, Maurice
Breslow, Susan 1951- *69*
Brett, Bernard 1925- *22*
Brett, Grace N(eff) 1900-1975 .... *23*
Brett, Jan 1949- *171*
  Earlier sketches in SATA *42, 71, 130*
  See also CLR *27*
Brett, Jan Churchill
  See Brett, Jan
Brett Bowler, Jan
  See Brett, Jan
Brewer, James D. 1951- *108*
Brewer, Sally King 1947- *33*
Brewster, Benjamin
  See Folsom, Franklin (Brewster)
Brewster, Hugh 1950- *191*
  Earlier sketch in SATA *95*
Brewster, Patience 1952- *97*
Brewton, John E(dmund) 1898-1982 .... *5*
Brian, Janeen (Paulette) 1948- *141*
Briant, Ed *180*
Brick, John 1922-1973 .... *10*
Brickman, Robin D. 1954- *155*
Bride, Nadja
  See Nobisso, Josephine
Bridgers, Sue Ellen 1942- *90*
  Autobiography Feature *109*
  Earlier sketch in SATA *22*
  See also CLR *18*
  See also SAAS *1*
Bridges, Laurie
  See Bruck, Lorraine
Bridges, Ruby (Nell) 1954- *131*
Bridges, William (Andrew) 1901-1984 .... *5*
Bridwell, Norman (Ray) 1928- *138*
  Earlier sketches in SATA *4, 68*
  See also CLR *96*
Brier, Howard M(axwell) 1903-1969 .... *8*
Brierley, (Louise) 1958- *59*
Briggs, Katharine Mary 1898-1980 .... *101*
  Obituary *25*

Briggs, Peter 1921-1975 .... *39*
  Obituary *31*
Briggs, Raymond 1934- *184*
  Earlier sketches in SATA *23, 66, 131*
  See also CLR *10*
Briggs, Raymond Redvers
  See Briggs, Raymond
Bright, Paul 1949- *182*
Bright, Robert (Douglas Sr.) 1902-1988 ...... *63*
  Obituary *60*
  Earlier sketch in SATA *24*
Bright, Sarah
  See Shine, Deborah
Brightfield, Richard 1927- *65*
  Brief entry *53*
Brightfield, Rick
  See Brightfield, Richard
Brighton, Catherine 1943- *107*
  Earlier sketch in SATA *65*
Brill, Marlene Targ 1945- *124*
  Earlier sketch in SATA *77*
Brimberg, Stanlee 1947- *9*
Brimner, Larry Dane 1949- *170*
  Autobiography Feature *112*
  Earlier sketch in SATA *79*
Brin, David 1950- *65*
Brin, Ruth Firestone 1921- *22*
Brinckloe, Julie 1950- *13*
Brinckloe, Julie Lorraine
  See Brinckloe, Julie
Brindel, June (Rachuy) 1919- *7*
Brindle, Max
  See Fleischman, Sid
Brindze, Ruth 1903-1984 .... *23*
Brink, Carol Ryrie 1895-1981 .... *100*
  Obituary *27*
  Earlier sketches in SATA *1, 31*
  See also CLR *30*
Brinsmead, H. F.
  See Brinsmead, H(esba) F(ay)
Brinsmead, H. F(ay)
  See Brinsmead, H(esba) F(ay)
Brinsmead, H(esba) F(ay) 1922- *78*
  Earlier sketch in SATA *18*
  See also CLR *47*
  See also SAAS *5*
Briquebec, John
  See Rowland-Entwistle, (Arthur)
  Theodore (Henry)
Brisbane, Henry R.
  See Ellis, Edward S(ylvester)
Brisco, P. A.
  See Matthews, Patricia
Brisco, Patty
  See Matthews, Patricia
  and Matthews, Clayton (Hartley)
Briscoe, Jill (Pauline) 1935- *56*
  Brief entry *47*
Brisley, Joyce Lankester 1896-1978 .... *22*
  Obituary *84*
Brissenden, Connie
  See Brissenden, Constance
Brissenden, Constance 1947- *150*
Brisson, Pat 1951- *177*
  Autobiography Feature *133*
  Earlier sketches in SATA *67, 128, 133*
Britt, Albert 1874-1969
  Obituary *28*
Britt, Dell 1934- *1*
Brittain, Bill
  See SAAS *7*
  See Brittain, William (E.)
Brittain, C. Dale 1948- *82*
Brittain, William (E.) 1930- *76*
  Earlier sketch in SATA *36*
  See Brittain, Bill
Brittingham, Geoffrey (Hugh) 1959- *76*
Britton, Kate *49*
  See Stegeman, Janet Allais
Britton, Louisa
  See McGuire, Leslie (Sarah)

Britton, Rick 1952- *82*
Bro, Margueritte (Harmon) 1894-1977 .... *19*
  Obituary *27*
Broach, Elise 1963- *173*
Broadhead, Helen Cross 1913- *25*
Brochmann, Elizabeth 1938- *41*
Brock, Betty (Carter) 1923-2003 .... *4*
  Obituary *150*
Brock, C(harles) E(dmund) 1870-1938 .... *42*
  Brief entry *32*
Brock, Delia
  See Ephron, Delia
Brock, Emma L(illian) 1886-1974 .... *8*
Brock, H(enry) M(atthew) 1875-1960 .... *42*
Brockett, Eleanor Hall 1913-1967 .... *10*
Brockman, C(hristian) Frank 1902-1985 .... *26*
Brockmeier, Kevin 1972- *176*
Broderick, Dorothy M. 1929- *5*
Brodeur, Ruth Wallace
  See Wallace-Brodeur, Ruth
Brodie, Sally
  See Cavin, Ruth (Brodie)
Brodsky, Beverly
  See McDermott, Beverly Brodsky
Brody, Wendy
  See Staub, Wendy Corsi
Broeger, Achim 1944- *31*
Broekel, Rainer Lothar 1923- *38*
Broekel, Ray
  See Broekel, Rainer Lothar
Broekstra, Lorette 1964- *189*
  Earlier sketch in SATA *124*
Brogden, Sherryl
  See Jordan, Sherryl
Broger, Achim
  See Broeger, Achim
Broida, Marian *154*
Brokamp, Marilyn 1920- *10*
Broman, Fred
  See Moseley, James W(illett)
Bromhall, Winifred *26*
Brommer, Gerald F(rederick) 1927- *28*
Brondfield, Jerome 1913-1998 .... *22*
Brondfield, Jerry
  See Brondfield, Jerome
Bronner, Stephen Eric 1949- *101*
Bronowski, Jacob 1908-1974 .... *55*
Bronson, Alice
  See Watkins, Dawn L.
Bronson, Lynn
  See Lampman, Evelyn Sibley
Bronson, Wilfrid Swancourt 1894-1985
  Obituary *43*
Brook, Judith (Penelope) 1926- *59*
  Brief entry *51*
Brook, Judy
  See Brook, Judith (Penelope)
Brooke, L(eonard) Leslie 1862-1940 .... *17*
  See also CLR *20*
Brooke, William J. 1946- *139*
Brooke-Haven, P.
  See Wodehouse, P(elham) G(renville)
Brookins, Dana 1931- *28*
Brooks, Anita *5*
  See Abramovitz, Anita (Zeltner Brooks)
Brooks, Bill 1939- *59*
Brooks, Bruce 1950- *112*
  Brief entry *53*
  Earlier sketch in SATA *72*
  See also CLR *25*
Brooks, Caryl 1924- *84*
Brooks, Charlotte K(endrick) 1918-1998 ..... *24*
  Obituary *112*
Brooks, Erik 1972- *182*
  Earlier sketch in SATA *152*
Brooks, George
  See Baum, L(yman) Frank
Brooks, Gwendolyn 1917-2000 .... *6*
  Obituary *123*
  See also CLR *27*

Brooks, Gwendolyn Elizabeth
  See Brooks, Gwendolyn
Brooks, Jerome 1931- 23
Brooks, Kevin 1959- 150
Brooks, Kevin M.
  See Brooks, Kevin
Brooks, Lester 1924- 7
Brooks, Martha 1944- 134
  Autobiography Feature 134
  Earlier sketches in SATA *68, 121*
Brooks, Maurice (Graham) 1900- 45
Brooks, Polly Schoyer 1912- 12
Brooks, Ron 1948- 94
  Brief entry 33
Brooks, Ronald George
  See Brooks, Ron
Brooks, Terry 1944- 60
Brooks, Walter R(ollin) 1886-1958 17
Brooks-Hill, Helen (Mason) 1908-1994 59
Broome, Errol 1937- 158
  Earlier sketch in SATA *105*
Brophy, Nannette 1963- 73
Brosnan, James Patrick 1929- 14
Brosnan, Jim
  See Brosnan, James Patrick
Brostoff, Anita 1931- 132
Brothers Grimm
  See Grimm, Jacob Ludwig Karl
  and Grimm, Wilhelm Karl
Brothers Hildebrandt, The
  See Hildebrandt, Greg
  and Hildebrandt, Tim
Broun, Emily
  See Sterne, Emma Gelders
Brouwer, S. W.
  See Brouwer, Sigmund (W.)
Brouwer, Sigmund (W.) 1959- 109
Brow, Thea 1934- 60
Brower, Millicent 8
Brower, Pauline 1929- 22
Browin, Frances Williams 1898-1986 5
Brown, Alexis
  See Baumann, Amy (Brown) Beeching
Brown, Anne Ensign 1937- 61
Brown, Beverly Swerdlow 97
Brown, Bill
  See Brown, William L(ouis)
Brown, Billye Walker
  See Cutchen, Billye Walker
Brown, Bob
  See Brown, Robert Joseph
Brown, Buck 1936- 45
Brown, Calef 179
Brown, Cassie 1919-1986 55
Brown, Charlotte Lewis 181
Brown, Conrad 1922- 31
Brown, Craig McFarland 1947- 73
Brown, David
  See Brown, David A(lan)
  and Myller, Rolf
Brown, Dee 1908-2002 110
  Obituary 141
  Earlier sketch in SATA *5*
Brown, Dee Alexander
  See Brown, Dee
Brown, Don 1949- 172
Brown, Drew T. III 1955- 83
Brown, Drollene P. 1939- 53
Brown, Eleanor Frances 1908-1987 3
Brown, Elizabeth Ferguson 1937- 153
Brown, Elizabeth M(yers) 1915- 43
Brown, Fern G. 1918- 34
Brown, (Robert) Fletch 1923- 42
Brown, Fornan 1901-1996 71
  Obituary 88
Brown, George Earl 1883-1964 11
Brown, George Mackay 1921-1996 35
Brown, Irene Bennett 1932- 3
Brown, Irving
  See Adams, William Taylor

Brown, Ivor (John Carnegie)
  1891-1974 5
  Obituary 26
Brown, Jane Clark 1930- 81
Brown, Janet Mitsui 87
Brown, Jo 1964- 170
Brown, Joanne 1933- 147
Brown, Joe David 1915-1976 44
Brown, Joseph E(dward) 1929- 59
  Brief entry 51
Brown, Judith Gwyn 1933- 20
Brown, Kathryn 1955- 168
  Earlier sketch in SATA *98*
Brown, Kathy
  See Brown, Kathryn
Brown, Ken (James) 129
Brown, Kevin 1960- 101
Brown, Laurene Krasny 1945- 99
  Earlier sketch in SATA *54*
Brown, Laurie Krasny
  See Brown, Laurene Krasny
Brown, Lloyd Arnold 1907-1966 36
Brown, Mahlon A.
  See Ellis, Edward S(ylvester)
Brown, Marc (Tolon) 1946- 145
  Earlier sketches in SATA *10, 53, 80*
  See also CLR *29*
Brown, Marcia (Joan) 1918- 47
  Earlier sketch in SATA *7*
  See also CLR *12*
Brown, Margaret Wise 1910-1952 100
  See also YABC *2*
  See also CLR *107*
Brown, Margery (Wheeler) 78
  Earlier sketch in SATA *5*
Brown, Marion Marsh 1908-2001 6
Brown, Myra Berry 1918- 6
Brown, Palmer 1919- 36
Brown, Pamela (Beatrice) 1924-1989 5
  Obituary 61
Brown, Peter 1979- 178
Brown, Reeve Lindbergh
  See Lindbergh, Reeve
Brown, Richard E. 1946- 61
Brown, Robert Joseph 1907-1989 14
Brown, Roderick (Langmere) Haig-
  See Haig-Brown, Roderick (Langmere)
Brown, Rosalie 9
  See Moore, Rosalie (Gertrude)
Brown, Roswell
  See Webb, Jean Francis (III)
Brown, Roy (Frederick) 1921-1982 51
  Obituary 39
Brown, Ruth 1941- 170
  Earlier sketch in SATA *105*
Brown, Scott 1971- 134
Brown, Sue Ellen 1954- 81
Brown, Tricia 1954- 114
Brown, Vinson 1912-1991 19
Brown, Walter R(eed) 1929- 19
Brown, Will
  See Ainsworth, William Harrison
Brown, William L(ouis) 1910-1964 5
Browne, Anthony 1946- 163
  Brief entry 44
  Earlier sketches in SATA *45, 61, 105*
  See also CLR *19*
Browne, Anthony Edward Tudor
  See Browne, Anthony
Browne, Dik
  See Browne, Richard Arthur Allen
Browne, Hablot Knight 1815-1882 21
Browne, Matthew
  See Rands, William Brighty
Browne, Nicki M.
  See Browne, N.M.
Browne, Nicky Matthews
  See Browne, N.M.
Browne, N.M. 1960- 167

Browne, Richard Arthur Allen
  1917-1989 67
  Brief entry 38
  See Browne, Dik
Browne, Vee F(rances) 1956- 90
Browning, Robert 1812-1889
  See YABC *1*
  See also CLR *97*
Brownjohn, Alan 1931- 6
Brownlee, Walter 1930- 62
Brownlie, Betty 1946- 159
Brownlow, Kevin 1938- 65
Brownlow, Mike 183
Brownridge, William R(oy) 1932- 94
Bruce, Dorita Fairlie 1885-1970
  Obituary 27
Bruce, (William) Harry 1934- 77
Bruce, Mary 1927- 1
Bruchac, Joseph III
  See Bruchac, Joseph
Bruchac, Joseph 1942- 176
  Autobiography Feature 176
  Earlier sketches in SATA *42, 89, 131*
  See also CLR *46*
Bruchac, Margaret M.
  See Bruchac, Marge
Bruchac, Marge 181
Bruck, Lorraine 1921- 55
  Brief entry 46
  See Bridges, Laurie
Bruel, Nick 166
Bruel, Robert O. 1929-2002 189
Bruemmer, Fred 1929- 47
Brugman, Alyssa (F.) 1974- 152
Brumbeau, Jeff 1955- 157
Bruna, Dick 1927- 76
  Brief entry 30
  Earlier sketch in SATA *43*
  See also CLR *7*
Brunhoff, Jean de 1899-1937 24
  See also CLR *116*
Brunhoff, Laurent de 1925- 150
  Earlier sketches in SATA *24, 71*
  See also CLR *116*
Brunskill, Elizabeth Ann Flatt
  See Flatt, Lizann
Brush, Karen A(lexandra) 1960- 85
Brussel-Smith, Bernard 1914- 58
Brust, Steven 1955- 121
  Earlier sketch in SATA *86*
Brust, Steven K. Zoltan
  See Brust, Steven
Brustlein, Daniel 1904- 40
Brustlein, Janice Tworkov -2000 40
  Obituary 126
Brutschy, Jennifer 1960- 84
Bryan, Ashley 1923- 178
  Earlier sketches in SATA *31, 72, 132*
  See also CLR *66*
Bryan, Ashley F.
  See Bryan, Ashley
Bryan, Dorothy M. 1896(?)-1984
  Obituary 39
Bryan, Jennifer 190
Bryan, Sean 192
Bryant, Bernice (Morgan) 1908-1976 11
Bryant, Jen 1960- 175
  Earlier sketch in SATA *94*
Bryant, Jennifer Fisher
  See Bryant, Jen
Bryant, Laura J. 176
Brychta, Alex 1956- 21
Brynie, Faith H. 1946- 113
Brynie, Faith Hickman
  See Brynie, Faith H.
Bryson, Bernarda 1903-2004 9
  See Shahn, Bernarda Bryson
Buba, Joy Flinsch 1904- 44
Buchan, Bryan 1945- 36
Buchan, John 1875-1940
  See YABC *2*

Buchan, Stuart 1942-1987
  Obituary 54
Buchanan, Debby 1952- 82
Buchanan, Deborah Leevonne
  See Buchanan, Debby
Buchanan, Jane 1956- 160
Buchanan, Paul 1959- 116
Buchanan, Sue 1939- 139
Buchheimer, Naomi Barnett
  See Barnett, Naomi
Buchignani, Walter 1965- 84
Buchwald, Art 1925-2007 10
Buchwald, Arthur
  See Buchwald, Art
Buchwald, Emilie 1935- 7
Buck, Gisela 1941- 101
Buck, Lewis 1925- 18
Buck, Margaret Waring 1905-1997 3
Buck, Nola
  See Godwin, Laura
Buck, Pearl S(ydenstricker) 1892-1973 25
  Earlier sketch in SATA *1*
Buck, Siegfried 1941- 101
Buckeridge, Anthony (Malcolm)
  1912-2004 85
  Earlier sketch in SATA *6*
Buckholtz, Eileen (Garber) 1949- 54
  Brief entry 47
Buckler, Ernest 1908-1984 47
Buckless, Andrea K. 1968- 117
Buckley, Helen E(lizabeth) 1918- 90
  Earlier sketch in SATA *2*
Buckley, James, Jr. 1963- 166
  Earlier sketch in SATA *114*
Buckley, Michael 177
Buckley, Susan 184
Buckley, Susan Washburn
  See Buckley, Susan
Buckley-Archer, Linda 185
Buckmaster, Henrietta 6
  See Stephens, Henrietta Henkle
Bucks, Brad
  See Holub, Joan
Budd, E. S.
  See Sirimarco, Elizabeth
Budd, Lillian (Peterson) 1897-1989 7
Budhos, Marina 173
Buehler, Stephanie Jona 1956- 83
Buehner, Caralyn (M.) 1963- 159
  Earlier sketch in SATA *104*
Buehner, Mark 1959- 159
  Earlier sketch in SATA *104*
Buehr, Walter Franklin 1897-1971 3
Buell, Ellen Lewis
  See Cash, Ellen Lewis Buell
Buell, Janet 1952- 185
  Earlier sketch in SATA *106*
Buergel, Paul-Hermann H. 1949- 83
Buettner, Dan 1960- 95
Buff, Conrad 1886-1975 19
Buff, Mary (E. Marsh) 1890-1970 19
Buffett, Jimmy 1946- 110
  Earlier sketch in SATA *76*
Buffie, Margaret 1945- 161
  Earlier sketches in SATA *71, 107*
  See also CLR *39*
Bugbee, Emma 1888(?)-1981
  Obituary 29
Bugni, Alice 1951- 122
Buhhos, Marina Tamar
  See Budhos, Marina
Bujold, Lois McMaster 1949- 136
Bulfinch, Thomas 1796-1867 35
Bulion, Leslie 1958- 161
Bull, Angela (Mary) 1936- 45
Bull, Emma 1954- 190
  Autobiography Feature 103
  Earlier sketch in SATA *99*
Bull, Norman John 1916- 41
Bull, Peter (Cecil) 1912-1984
  Obituary 39

Bull, Schuyler M. 1974- 138
Bulla, Clyde R. 1914-2007 139
  Obituary 182
  Earlier sketches in SATA *2, 41, 91*
  See also SAAS *6*
Bullard, Lisa 1961- 142
Bullock, Kathleen (Mary) 1946- 77
Bullock, Robert (D.) 1947- 92
Bulpin, (Barbara) Vicki 92
Bumstead, Kathleen Mary 1918-1987 53
Bundles, A'Lelia Perry 1952- 76
Bunin, Catherine 1967- 30
Bunin, Sherry 1925- 30
Bunkers, Suzanne L. 1950- 136
Bunting, A. E.
  See Bunting, (Anne) Eve(lyn)
Bunting, Eve
  See Bunting, (Anne) Eve(lyn)
Bunting, (Anne) Eve(lyn) 1928- 158
  Earlier sketches in SATA *18, 64, 110*
  See also CLR *82*
  See Bunting, Eve
Bunting, Glenn (Davison) 1957- 22
Bunyan, John 1628-1688
  See CLR *124*
Burack, Sylvia K. 1916-2003 35
  Obituary 143
Burbank, Addison (Buswell) 1895-1961 37
Burch, Joann J(ohansen) 75
Burch, Robert J(oseph) 1925- 74
  Earlier sketch in SATA *1*
  See also CLR *63*
Burchard, Peter Duncan 1921- 143
  Earlier sketch in SATA *5, 74*
  See also SAAS *13*
Burchard, S. H.
  See Burchard, Sue
Burchard, Sue 1937- 22
Burchardt, Nellie 1921- 7
Burdett, Lois 117
Burdick, Eugene (Leonard) 1918-1965 22
Burford, Eleanor
  See Hibbert, Eleanor Alice Burford
Burgan, Michael 1960- 167
  Earlier sketch in SATA *118*
Burger, Carl 1888-1967 9
Burgess, Ann Marie
  See Gerson, Noel Bertram
Burgess, Barbara Hood 1926- 69
Burgess, Em
  See Burgess, Mary Wyche
Burgess, (Frank) Gelett 1866-1951 32
  Brief entry 30
Burgess, Mark 157
Burgess, Mary Wyche 1916- 18
Burgess, Melvin 1954- 146
  Earlier sketch in SATA *96*
Burgess, Michael
  See Gerson, Noel Bertram
Burgess, Robert F(orrest) 1927- 4
Burgess, Starling
  See Tudor, Tasha
Burgess, Thornton Waldo 1874-1965 17
Burgess, Trevor
  See Trevor, Elleston
Burgwyn, Mebane Holoman 1914-1992 7
Burke, David 1927- 46
Burke, Diana G.
  See Gallagher, Diana G.
Burke, Diana Gallagher
  See Gallagher, Diana G.
Burke, Dianne O'Quinn 1940- 89
Burke, Janine 1952- 139
Burke, Jim 1973- 179
Burke, John
  See O'Connor, Richard
Burke, Katie 1953- 168
Burke, Patrick 1958- 114
Burke, Ralph
  See Garrett, (Gordon) Randall (Phillip)
  and Silverberg, Robert

Burkert, Nancy Ekholm 1933- 24
  See also SAAS *14*
Burke-Weiner, Kimberly 1962- 95
Burks, Brian 1955- 95
Burland, Brian (Berkeley) 1931- 34
Burland, C. A.
  See Burland, Cottie (Arthur)
Burland, Cottie (Arthur) 1905-1983 5
Burleigh, Robert 1936- 193
  Earlier sketches in SATA *55, 98, 146*
Burlingame, (William) Roger 1889-1967 2
Burman, Alice Caddy 1896(?)-1977
  Obituary 24
Burman, Ben Lucien 1896-1984 6
  Obituary 40
Burn, Doris 1923- 1
Burn, Ted
  See Burn, Thomas E.
Burn, Thomas E. 1940- 150
Burnard, Damon 1963- 115
Burnett, Constance Buel 1893-1975 36
Burnett, Frances (Eliza) Hodgson
  1849-1924 100
  See also YABC *2*
  See also CLR *122*
Burnett Bossi, Lisa 193
Burney, Anton
  See Hopkins, (Hector) Kenneth
Burnford, Sheila (Philip Cochrane
  Every) 1918-1984 3
  Obituary 38
  See also CLR *2*
Burnham, Gretchen
  See Sprague, Gretchen
Burnham, Nicole 1970- 161
Burnham, Niki
  See Burnham, Nicole
Burnham, Sophy 1936- 65
Burningham, John 1936- 160
  Earlier sketches in SATA *16, 59, 111*
  See also CLR *9*
Burns, Diane L. 1950- 81
  See also SAAS *24*
Burns, Eloise Wilkin
  See Wilkin, Eloise
Burns, Florence M. 1905-1988 61
Burns, Khephra 1950- 92
Burns, Loree Griffin 193
Burns, Marilyn 1941- 96
  Brief entry 33
Burns, Olive Ann 1924-1990 65
Burns, Paul C. 5
Burns, Ray
  See Burns, Raymond (Howard)
Burns, Raymond (Howard) 1924- 9
Burns, Theresa 1961- 84
Burns, William A. 1909-1999 5
Burr, Dan 1951- 65
Burr, Lonnie 1943- 47
Burrell, Roy E(ric) C(harles) 1923- 72
Burroughs, Edgar Rice 1875-1950 41
Burroughs, Jean Mitchell 1908- 28
Burroughs, Polly 1925- 2
Burroway, Janet (Gay) 1936- 23
Burstein, Chaya M(alamud) 1923- 64
Burstein, Fred 1950- 83
Burstein, John 1949- 54
  Brief entry 40
Burstein, Stanley M.
  See Burstein, Stanley Mayer
Burstein, Stanley Mayer 1941- 175
Bursztynski, Sue 1953- 114
Burt, Jesse Clifton 1921-1976 46
  Obituary 20
Burt, Olive Woolley 1894-1981 4
Burtinshaw, Julie 185
Burton, Gennett 1945- 95
Burton, Hester (Wood-Hill) 1913-2000 74
  Earlier sketch in SATA *7*
  See also CLR *1*
  See also SAAS *8*

Burton, Leslie
  See McGuire, Leslie (Sarah)
Burton, Marilee Robin 1950- 82
  Earlier sketch in SATA *46*
Burton, Maurice 1898-1992 23
Burton, Rebecca 1970- 183
Burton, Robert (Wellesley) 1941- 22
Burton, Virginia Lee 1909-1968 100
  Earlier sketch in SATA *2*
  See also CLR *11*
Burton, William H(enry) 1890-1964 11
Busby, Ailie 192
Busby, Cylin 1970- 118
Busby, Edith (A. Lake) (?)-1964
  Obituary 29
Buscaglia, (Felice) Leo(nardo)
  1924-1998 65
  See Buscaglia, Leo F.
Buscaglia, Leo F.
  See Buscaglia, (Felice) Leo(nardo)
Busch, Phyllis S. 1909- 30
Bush, Anne Kelleher
  See Kelleher, Anne
Bush, Catherine 1961- 128
Bushmiller, Ernie
  Obituary 31
  See Bushmiller, Ernest Paul
Bushnell, Jack 1952- 86
Busoni, Rafaello 1900-1962 16
Buss, Helen M.
  See Clarke, Margaret
Busselle, Rebecca 1941- 80
Bustard, Anne 1951- 173
Butcher, Kristin 1951- 140
Butenko, Bohdan 1931- 90
Butler, Beverly Kathleen 1932- 7
Butler, Bill
  See Butler, William (Arthur) Vivian
  and Butler, Ernest Alton
  and Butler, William Huxford
Butler, Charles 1963- 175
  Earlier sketch in SATA *121*
Butler, Charles Cadman
  See Butler, Charles
Butler, Dori Hillestad 1965- 164
Butler, Dorothy 1925- 73
Butler, Geoff 1945- 94
Butler, M. Christina 1934- 170
  Earlier sketch in SATA *72*
Butler, Octavia E. 1947-2006 84
  See also CLR *65*
Butler, Octavia Estelle
  See Butler, Octavia E.
Butler, Vivian
  See Butler, William (Arthur) Vivian
Butler, William
  See Butler, William (Arthur) Vivian
Butler, William (Arthur) Vivian
  1927-1987 79
  See Marric, J. J.
Butters, Dorothy Gilman 5
  See Gilman, Dorothy
Butterworth, Emma Macalik 1928- 43
Butterworth, Nick 1946- 149
  Earlier sketch in SATA *106*
Butterworth, Oliver 1915-1990 1
  Obituary 66
Butterworth, W.E.
  See Griffin, W.E.B
Butterworth, William E.
  See Griffin, W.E.B
Butterworth, William Edmund III
  See Griffin, W.E.B
Butts, Ed 1951- 177
Butts, Edward P.
  See Butts, Ed
Butts, Ellen R(ubinstein) 1942- 93
Buxton, Ralph
  See Silverstein, Alvin
  and Silverstein, Virginia B(arbara
  Opshelor)

Buzzeo, Toni 1951- 135
Byalick, Marcia 1947- 141
  Earlier sketch in SATA *97*
Byard, Carole (Marie) 1941- 57
Byars, Betsy 1928- 163
  Autobiography Feature 108
  Earlier sketches in SATA *4, 46, 80*
  See also CLR *72*
  See also SAAS *1*
Byars, Betsy Cromer
  See Byars, Betsy
Byfield, Barbara Ninde 1930- 8
Byman, Jeremy 1944- 129
Bynum, Janie 133
Byrd, Elizabeth 1912-1989 34
Byrd, Nicole
  See Zach, Cheryl (Byrd)
Byrd, Robert (John) 1942- 158
  Earlier sketches in SATA *33, 112*
Byrne, Mary Gregg 1951- 162

C

C. 3. 3.
  See Wilde, Oscar
Cabaniss, J(ames) Allen 1911-1997 5
Cabat, Erni 1914- 74
Cabban, Vanessa 1971- 176
Cable, Mary 1920- 9
Cabot, Meg 1967- 175
  Earlier sketch in SATA *127*
  See also CLR *85*
Cabot, Meggin
  See Cabot, Meg
Cabot, Meggin Patricia
  See Cabot, Meg
Cabot, Patricia
  See Cabot, Meg
Cabral, O. M.
  See Cabral, Olga
Cabral, Olga 1909- 46
Cabrera, Cozbi A. 1963- 177
Cabrera, Jane 1968- 182
  Earlier sketches in SATA *103, 152*
Cabrera, Marcela 1966- 90
Caddy, Alice
  See Burman, Alice Caddy
Cade, Toni
  See Bambara, Toni Cade
Cadmus and Harmonia
  See Buchan, John
Cadnum, Michael 1949- 165
  Earlier sketches in SATA *87, 121*
  See also CLR *78*
Caduto, Michael J. 1955- 103
Cadwallader, Sharon 1936- 7
Cady, (Walter) Harrison 1877(?)-1970 19
Caffey, Donna (J.) 1954- 110
Cagle, Malcolm W(infield) 1918- 32
Cahn, Rhoda 1922- 37
Cahn, William 1912-1976 37
Cain, Arthur H(omer) 1913-1981 3
Cain, Christopher
  See Fleming, Thomas
Cain, Sheridan 1952- 186
Caine, Geoffrey
  See Walker, Robert W(ayne)
Caines, Jeannette (Franklin) 1938- 78
  Brief entry 43
  See also CLR *24*
Cairns, Trevor 1922- 14
Calabro, Marian 1954- 79
Caldecott, Moyra 1927- 22
Caldecott, Randolph (J.) 1846-1886 100
  Earlier sketch in SATA *17*
  See also CLR *110*
Calder, Charlotte 1952- 125
Calder, David 1932-1997 105

Calder, Lyn
  See Calmenson, Stephanie
Calder, Marie D(onais) 1948- 96
Calderone-Stewart, Lisa
  See Calderone-Stewart, Lisa-Marie
Calderone-Stewart, Lisa-Marie 1958- 123
Caldwell, Doreen (Mary) 1942- 71
Caldwell, John C(ope) 1913-1984 7
Caletti, Deb 1963- 171
Calhoun, B. B. 1961- 98
Calhoun, Chad
  See Barrett, Neal, Jr.
  and Cunningham, Chet
  and Goulart, Ron(ald Joseph)
Calhoun, Dia 1959- 183
  Earlier sketch in SATA *129*
Calhoun, Mary 2
  See also CLR *42*
  See Wilkins, Mary Huiskamp
Calhoun, T.B.
  See Bisson, Terry
Cali, Davide 1972- 190
Calif, Ruth 1922- 67
Calkins, Franklin
  See Stratemeyer, Edward L.
Call, Hughie Florence 1890-1969 1
Callahan, Dorothy M(onahan) 1934- 39
  Brief entry 35
Callahan, Philip Serna 1923- 25
Callan, Jamie 1954- 59
Callan, Jim 1951- 181
Callaway, Bernice (Anne) 1923- 48
Callaway, Kathy 1943- 36
Callen, Larry
  See Callen, Lawrence Willard, Jr.
Callen, Lawrence Willard, Jr. 1927- 19
Calley, Karin 1965- 92
Calmenson, Stephanie 1952- 139
  Brief entry 37
  Earlier sketches in SATA *51, 84*
Calvert, Elinor H.
  See Lasell, Elinor H.
Calvert, John
  See Leaf, (Wilbur) Munro
Calvert, Patricia 1931- 132
  Earlier sketches in SATA *45, 69*
  See also SAAS *17*
Camburn, Carol A.
  See Camburn-Bracalente, Carol A.
Camburn-Bracalente, Carol A. 1962- 118
Cameron, Ann 1943- 129
  Earlier sketches in SATA *27, 89*
  See also SAAS *20*
Cameron, Edna M. 1905-1999 3
Cameron, Eleanor (Frances) 1912-1996 25
  Obituary 93
  Earlier sketch in SATA *1*
  See also CLR *72*
  See also SAAS *10*
Cameron, Elizabeth
  See Nowell, Elizabeth Cameron
Cameron, Elizabeth Jane 1910-1976 32
  Obituary 30
Cameron, Ian
  See Payne, Donald Gordon
Cameron, M(alcolm) G(ordon) Graham
  See Graham-Cameron, M(alcolm) G(ordon)
Cameron, M. Graham
  See Graham-Cameron, M(alcolm) G(ordon)
Cameron, Mike Graham
  See Graham-Cameron, M(alcolm) G(ordon)
Cameron, Polly 1928- 2
Cameron, Scott 1962- 84
Camp, Charles L. 1893-1975
  Obituary 31
Camp, Lindsay 1957- 133
Camp, Madeleine L'Engle
  See L'Engle, Madeleine
Camp, Walter (Chauncey) 1859-1925
  See YABC *1*
Campbell, (Elizabeth) Andrea 1963- 50

Campbell, Ann R. 1925- *11*
Campbell, Bill 1960- *89*
Campbell, Bruce
  See Epstein, Samuel
Campbell, Camilla 1905-1992 .... *26*
Campbell, Carole R. 1939- *125*
Campbell, Hope 1925- *20*
Campbell, Hugh 1930- *90*
Campbell, Jane
  See Edwards, Jane Campbell
Campbell, Julie
  See Tatham, Julie Campbell
Campbell, Patricia J(ean) 1930- *45*
Campbell, Patty
  See Campbell, Patricia J(ean)
Campbell, Peter A. 1948- *99*
Campbell, R. W.
  See Campbell, Rosemae Wells
Campbell, Robin
  See Strachan, Ian
Campbell, Rod 1945- *98*
  Brief entry *44*
  Earlier sketch in SATA *51*
Campbell, Rosemae Wells 1909- *1*
Camper, Cathy 1956- *170*
Campion, Nardi Reeder 1917-2007 .... *22*
Campling, Elizabeth 1948- *53*
Campoy, F. Isabel 1946- *181*
  Earlier sketch in SATA *143*
Camps, Luis 1928- *66*
Canales, Viola 1957- *141*
Candell, Victor 1903-1977
  Obituary *24*
Canfield, Dorothea F.
  See Fisher, Dorothy (Frances) Canfield
Canfield, Dorothea Frances
  See Fisher, Dorothy (Frances) Canfield
Canfield, Dorothy
  See Fisher, Dorothy (Frances) Canfield
Canfield, Jack 1944- *164*
Canfield, Jane White 1897-1984 .... *32*
  Obituary *38*
Canfield, Muriel 1935- *94*
Caniff, Milton (Arthur) 1907-1988
  Obituary *58*
Cann, Helen 1969- *179*
  Earlier sketch in SATA *124*
Cann, Kate 1954- *152*
  Earlier sketch in SATA *103*
Cannan, Joanna
  See Pullein-Thompson, Joanna Maxwell
Cannon, A(nn) E(dwards) *163*
  Earlier sketch in SATA *93*
Cannon, Bettie (Waddell) 1922- *59*
Cannon, Curt
  See Hunter, Evan
Cannon, Eileen E(mily) 1948- *119*
Cannon, Frank
  See Mayhar, Ardath
Cannon, Janell 1957- *128*
  Earlier sketch in SATA *78*
  See also CLR *120*
Cannon, Marian G. 1923- *85*
Cannon, Taffy
  See Cannon, Eileen E(mily)
Cantone, AnnaLaura *182*
Canusi, Jose
  See Barker, S(quire) Omar
Canyon, Christopher 1966- *150*
  Earlier sketch in SATA *104*
Capek, Michael 1947- *142*
  Earlier sketch in SATA *96*
Capes, Bernard (Edward Joseph)
  1854-1918 .... *116*
Caple, Kathy *193*
Caplin, Alfred Gerald 1909-1979
  Obituary *21*
  See Capp, Al
Caponigro, John Paul 1965- *84*
Capote, Truman 1924-1984 .... *91*

Capp, Al *61*
  See Caplin, Alfred Gerald
Cappel, Constance 1936- *22*
Cappetta, Cynthia 1949- *125*
Cappo, Nan Willard 1955- *143*
Capps, Benjamin (Franklin) 1922- *9*
Cappy Dick
  See Cleveland, George
Captain Kangaroo
  See Keeshan, Robert J.
Captain Wheeler
  See Ellis, Edward S(ylvester)
Captain Young of Yale
  See Stratemeyer, Edward L.
Capucilli, Alyssa Satin 1957- *163*
  Earlier sketch in SATA *115*
Capucine
  See Mazille, Capucine
Caraher, Kim(berley Elizabeth) 1961- *105*
Caraker, Mary 1929- *74*
Caras, Roger A(ndrew) 1928-2001 .... *12*
  Obituary *127*
Caravantes, Peggy 1935- *140*
Caraway, Caren 1939- *57*
Carbone, Elisa 1954- *137*
  Earlier sketch in SATA *81*
  See Carbone, Elisa Lynn
Carbone, Elisa Lynn *173*
  See Carbone, Elisa
Carbonnier, Jeanne 1894-1974 .... *3*
  Obituary *34*
Card, Orson Scott 1951- *127*
  Earlier sketch in SATA *83*
  See also CLR *116*
Care, Felicity
  See Coury, Louise Andree
Carew, Jan 1925- *51*
  Brief entry *40*
Carew, Jan Rynveld
  See Carew, Jan
Carey, Bonnie
  See Marshall, Bonnie C.
Carey, Charles W., Jr. 1951- *170*
Carey, Ernestine Gilbreth 1908-2006 .... *2*
  Obituary *177*
Carey, Janet Lee 1959(?)- *185*
Carey, Lisa *110*
Carey, M. V.
  See Carey, Mary V(irginia)
Carey, Mary V(irginia) 1925-1994 .... *44*
  Brief entry *39*
Carey, Peter 1943- *94*
Carey, Peter Philip
  See Carey, Peter
Carey, Valerie Scho 1949- *60*
Carheden, Goorel Kristina
  See Naaslund, Goorel Kristina
Carigiet, Alois 1902-1985 .... *24*
  Obituary *47*
  See also CLR *38*
Carini, Edward 1923- *9*
Carkeet, David 1946- *75*
Carle, Eric 1929- *163*
  Earlier sketches in SATA *4, 65, 120*
  See also CLR *72*
  See also SAAS *6*
Carleton, Captain L. C.
  See Ellis, Edward S(ylvester)
Carleton, Captain Latham C.
  See Ellis, Edward S(ylvester)
Carleton, Latham C.
  See Ellis, Edward S(ylvester)
Carley, V(an Ness) Royal 1906-1976
  Obituary *20*
Carling, Amelia Lau 1949- *164*
  Earlier sketch in SATA *119*
Carlisle, Carolyn
  See Hawes, Louise
Carlisle, Clark
  See Holding, James (Clark Carlisle, Jr.)
Carlisle, Olga Andreyev 1930- *35*

Carlsen, G(eorge) Robert 1917- *30*
Carlsen, Ruth C(hristoffer) 1918- *2*
Carlson, Bernice Wells 1910- *8*
Carlson, Dale (Bick) 1935- *1*
Carlson, Daniel (Bick) 1960- *27*
Carlson, Kirsten 1968- *192*
Carlson, Kirsten M.
  See Carlson, Kirsten
Carlson, Laurie 1952- *173*
  Earlier sketch in SATA *101*
Carlson, Laurie Winn
  See Carlson, Laurie
Carlson, Melody 1956- *171*
  Earlier sketch in SATA *113*
Carlson, Nancy L.
  See Carlson, Nancy L(ee)
Carlson, Nancy L(ee) 1953- *144*
  Brief entry *45*
  Earlier sketches in SATA *56, 90*
Carlson, Natalie Savage 1906-1997 .... *68*
  Earlier sketch in SATA *2*
  See also SAAS *4*
Carlson, Susan Johnston 1953- *88*
Carlson, Vada F. 1897- *16*
Carlstrom, Nancy White 1948- *156*
  Brief entry *48*
  Earlier sketches in SATA *53, 92*
Carlton, Keith
  See Robertson, Keith (Carlton)
Carlyon, Richard *55*
Carman, Patrick *161*
Carmer, Carl (Lamson) 1893-1976 .... *37*
  Obituary *30*
Carmer, Elizabeth Black 1904- *24*
Carmi, Giora 1944- *149*
  Earlier sketch in SATA *79*
Carmichael, Carrie *40*
  See Carmichael, Harriet
Carmody, Isobelle 1958- *191*
  Earlier sketch in SATA *161*
Carmody, Isobelle Jane
  See Carmody, Isobelle
Carney, Mary Lou 1949- *170*
Carol, Bill J.
  See Knott, William C(ecil, Jr.)
Caron, Romi
  See Caron-Kyselkova', Romana
Caron-Kyselkova', Romana 1967- *94*
Caroselli, Remus F(rancis) 1916- *36*
Carpelan, Bo 1926- *8*
Carpelan, Bo Gustaf Bertelsson
  See Carpelan, Bo
Carpenter, (John) Allan 1917- *81*
  Earlier sketch in SATA *3*
Carpenter, Angelica Shirley 1945- *153*
  Earlier sketch in SATA *71*
Carpenter, Frances 1890-1972 .... *3*
  Obituary *27*
Carpenter, John (Howard) 1948- *58*
Carpenter, Johnny
  See Carpenter, John (Howard)
Carpenter, Patricia (Healy Evans) 1920- *11*
Carr, Glyn
  See Styles, (Frank) Showell
Carr, Harriett H(elen) 1899-1977 .... *3*
Carr, Jan 1953- *132*
  Earlier sketch in SATA *89*
Carr, M. J.
  See Carr, Jan
Carr, Mary Jane 1899-1988 .... *2*
  Obituary *55*
Carr, Philippa
  See Hibbert, Eleanor Alice Burford
Carr, Roger Vaughan 1937- *95*
Carrel, Annette Felder 1929- *90*
Carrick, Carol (Hatfield) 1935- *118*
  Earlier sketches in SATA *7, 63*
  See also SAAS *18*
Carrick, Donald (F.) 1929-1989 .... *63*
  Earlier sketch in SATA *7*
Carrick, Malcolm 1945- *28*

Carrier, Lark 1947- 71
  Brief entry 50
Carrier, Roch 1937- 166
  Earlier sketch in SATA 105
Carrighar, Sally 1898-1985 24
Carrington, G. A.
  See Cunningham, Chet
Carrington, Marsha Gray 1954- 168
  Earlier sketch in SATA 111
Carris, Joan 1938- 182
  Brief entry 42
  Earlier sketch in SATA 44
Carris, Joan Davenport
  See Carris, Joan
Carroll, Curt
  See Bishop, Curtis (Kent)
Carroll, Elizabeth
  See Barkin, Carol
  and James, Elizabeth
Carroll, Jenny
  See Cabot, Meg
Carroll, (Archer) Latrobe 1894-1996 7
Carroll, Laura
  See Parr, Lucy
Carroll, Lewis
  See CLR 108
  See Dodgson, Charles L(utwidge)
Carroll, Raymond 1924- 86
  Brief entry 47
Carruth, Hayden 1921- 47
Carryl, Charles E. 1841-1920 114
Carryl, Charles Edward
  See Carryl, Charles E.
Carse, Robert 1902-1971 5
Carson, J(ohn) Franklin 1920-1981 1
  Obituary 107
Carson, Mary Kay 1964- 150
Carson, Rachel
  See Carson, Rachel Louise
Carson, Rachel Louise 1907-1964 23
  See Carson, Rachel
Carson, Rosalind
  See Chittenden, Margaret
Carson, S. M.
  See Gorsline, (Sally) Marie
Carson, William C. 1928- 154
Carter, Abby 184
Carter, Alden R 1947- 137
  Earlier sketch in SATA 67
  See also CLR 22
  See also SAAS 18
Carter, Alden Richardson
  See Carter, Alden R
Carter, Andy 1948- 134
Carter, Angela 1940-1992 66
  Obituary 70
Carter, Angela Olive
  See Carter, Angela
Carter, Anne Laurel 1953- 135
Carter, Asa Earl
  See Carter, Forrest
Carter, Avis Murton
  See Allen, Kenneth S.
Carter, Bruce
  See Hough, Richard (Alexander)
Carter, Carol S(hadis) 1948- 124
Carter, David A. 1957- 170
  Earlier sketch in SATA 114
Carter, Don 1958- 192
  Earlier sketch in SATA 124
Carter, Dorothy Sharp 1921- 8
Carter, Forrest 1927(?)-1979 32
Carter, Helene 1887-1960 15
Carter, (William) Hodding, Jr. 1907-1972 2
  Obituary 27
Carter, James Earl, Jr.
  See Carter, Jimmy
Carter, Jimmy 1924- 79
Carter, Katharine J(ones) 1905-1984 2
Carter, Lin(wood Vrooman) 1930-1988 91
Carter, Mike 1936- 138

Carter, Nick
  See Avallone, Michael (Angelo, Jr.)
  and Ballard, (Willis) Todhunter
  and Crider, Bill
  and Cassiday, Bruce (Bingham)
  and Chastain, Thomas
  and Dey, Frederic (Merrill) Van Rensselaer
  and Garside, (Clifford) Jack
  and Hayes, Ralph E(ugene)
  and Henderson, M(arilyn) R(uth)
  and Lynds, Dennis
  and Lynds, Gayle (Hallenbeck)
  and Randisi, Robert J.
  and Rasof, Henry
  and Stratemeyer, Edward L.
  and Smith, Martin Cruz
  and Swain, Dwight V(reeland)
  and Vardeman, Robert E(dward)
  and Wallmann, Jeffrey M(iner)
  and White, Lionel
Carter, Peter 1929- 57
Carter, Phyllis Ann
  See Eberle, Irmengarde
Carter, Samuel (Thomson) III 1904-1988 37
  Obituary 60
Carter, William E. 1926-1983 1
  Obituary 35
Cartlidge, Michelle 1950- 96
  Brief entry 37
  Earlier sketch in SATA 49
Cartner, William Carruthers 1910- 11
Cartwright, Ann 1940- 78
Cartwright, Reg(inald Ainsley) 1938- 64
Cartwright, Sally 1923- 9
Carusone, Al 1949- 89
Carvell, Marlene 172
Carver, John
  See Gardner, Richard (M.)
Carwell, L'Ann
  See McKissack, Patricia C.
Cary
  See Cary, Louis F(avreau)
Cary, Barbara Knapp 1912(?)-1975
  Obituary 31
Cary, Kate 1967(?)- 174
Cary, Louis F(avreau) 1915- 9
Caryl, Jean
  See Kaplan, Jean Caryl Korn
Casanova, Mary 1957- 186
  Earlier sketches in SATA 94, 136
Cascone, A.G.
  See Cascone, Annette
  and Cascone, Gina
Cascone, Annette 1960- 103
Cascone, Gina 1955- 103
Case, Marshal T(aylor) 1941- 9
Case, Michael
  See Howard, Robert West
Caseley, Judith 1951- 159
  Brief entry 53
  Earlier sketch in SATA 87
Casewit, Curtis W(erner) 1922-2002 4
Casey, Barbara (Louise) 1944- 147
  Earlier sketch in SATA 79
Casey, Brigid 1950- 9
Casey, Tina 1959- 141
Cash, Ellen Lewis Buell 1905-1989
  Obituary 64
Cash, Megan Montague 160
Casilla, Robert 1959- 146
  Earlier sketch in SATA 75
Cason, Mabel Earp 1892-1965 10
Cass, Joan E(velyn) 1
Cass-Beggs, Barbara 1904- 62
Cassedy, Patrice (Rinaldo) 1953- 149
Cassedy, Sylvia 1930-1989 77
  Obituary 61
  Earlier sketch in SATA 27
  See also CLR 26
Cassel, Lili
  See Wronker, Lili Cassel

Cassels, Jean 173
Cassidy, Anne 1952- 166
Cassidy, Cathy 1962- 183
Casson, Hugh Maxwell 1910-1999 65
  Obituary 115
Cassutt, Michael 1954- 78
Cassutt, Michael Joseph
  See Cassutt, Michael
Castaldo, Nancy Fusco 1962- 151
  Earlier sketch in SATA 93
Castaneda, Omar S. 1954- 71
Castell, Megan
  See Williams, Jeanne
Castellanos, Jane Mollie Robinson
  1913-2001 9
Castellon, Federico 1914-1971 48
Castellucci, Cecil 1969- 176
Castillo, Edmund L. 1924-2005 1
  Obituary 167
Castle, Lee
  See Ogan, George F.
  and Ogan, Margaret E. (Nettles)
Castle, Paul
  See Howard, Vernon (Linwood)
Castle, Robert
  See Hamilton, Edmond
Castrovilla, Selene 1966- 186
Caswell, Brian 1954- 171
  Earlier sketch in SATA 97
Caswell, Helen (Rayburn) 1923- 12
Catalano, Dominic 1956- 163
  Earlier sketch in SATA 76
Catalano, Grace (A.) 1961- 99
Catalanotto, Peter 1959- 159
  Autobiography Feature 113
  Earlier sketches in SATA 70, 114
  See also CLR 68
  See also SAAS 25
Catanese, P.W. 1961- 179
Cate, Dick
  See Cate, Richard Edward Nelson
Cate, Richard Edward Nelson 1932- 28
Cather, Willa (Sibert) 1873-1947 30
  See also CLR 98
Catherall, Arthur 1906-1980 74
  Earlier sketch in SATA 3
  See Ruthin, Margaret
Cathon, Laura E(lizabeth) 1908-1991 27
Catlett, Elizabeth 1919(?)- 82
Catlin, Wynelle 1930- 13
Catlow, Nikalas
  See Catlow, Niki
Catlow, Niki 1975- 193
Cato, Heather 105
Cato, Sheila 114
Catran, Ken 1944- 190
Catrow, David
  See Catrow, David J. III
Catrow, David J. III 152
Catt, Louis
  See French, Vivian
Cattell, James 1954- 123
Catton, (Charles) Bruce 1899-1978 2
  Obituary 24
Catz, Max
  See Glaser, Milton
Caudell, Marian 1930- 52
Caudill, Rebecca 1899-1985 1
  Obituary 44
Cauley, Lorinda Bryan 1951- 46
  Brief entry 43
Caulfield, Peggy F. 1926-1987
  Obituary 53
Cauman, Samuel 1910-1971 48
Causley, Charles (Stanley) 1917-2003 66
  Obituary 149
  Earlier sketch in SATA 3
  See also CLR 30
Cavallaro, Ann (Abelson) 1918- 62
Cavallo, Diana 1931- 7

Cavanagh, Helen (Carol) 1939- 98
  Brief entry 37
  Earlier sketch in SATA 48
Cavanah, Frances 1899-1982 31
  Earlier sketch in SATA 1
Cavanna, Betty 30
  Earlier sketch in SATA 1
  See also SAAS 4
  See Harrison, Elizabeth (Allen) Cavanna
Cavanna, Elizabeth
  See Harrison, Elizabeth (Allen) Cavanna
Cave, Kathryn 1948- 123
  Earlier sketch in SATA 76
Cavendish, Peter
  See Horler, Sydney
Cavin, Ruth (Brodie) 1918- 38
Cavoukian, Raffi 1948- 68
Cawley, Winifred 1915- 13
Caxton, Pisistratus
  See Lytton, Edward G(eorge) E(arle)
  L(ytton) Bulwer-Lytton Baron
Cazeau, Charles J(ay) 1931- 65
Cazet, Denys 1938- 191
  Brief entry 41
  Earlier sketches in SATA 52, 99, 163
Cazzola, Gus 1934- 73
Cebulash, Mel 1937- 91
  Earlier sketch in SATA 10
Ceccoli, Nicoletta 181
Cecil, Randy 1968- 187
Ceder, Georgiana Dorcas -1985 10
Celenza, Anna Harwell 133
Celestino, Martha Laing
  See Laing, Martha
Cepeda, Joe 159
Cerf, Bennett (Alfred) 1898-1971 7
Cerf, Christopher (Bennett) 1941- 2
Cermak, Martin
  See Duchacek, Ivo D(uka)
Cerullo, Mary M. 1949- 145
  Earlier sketch in SATA 86
Cervon, Jacqueline
  See Moussard, Jacqueline
Cetin, Frank Stanley 1921- 2
Chabon, Michael 1963- 145
Chaconas, D.J.
  See Chaconas, Dori
Chaconas, Dori 1938- 175
  Earlier sketch in SATA 145
Chaconas, Doris J.
  See Chaconas, Dori
Chadwick, Lester 67
  Earlier sketch in SATA 1
Chaffee, Allen 3
Chaffin, Lillie D(orton) 1925- 4
Chaikin, Miriam 1924- 152
  Earlier sketches in SATA 24, 102
Chall, Marsha Wilson 150
Challand, Helen J(ean) 1921- 64
Challans, Mary 1905-1983 23
  Obituary 36
  See Renault, Mary
Chalmers, Mary (Eileen) 1927- 6
  See also SAAS 14
Chamberlain, Barbara A.
  See Azore, Barbara
Chamberlain, Margaret 1954- 46
Chamberlin, Kate 1945- 105
Chamberlin, Mary 1960- 177
Chamberlin, Rich 177
Chamberlin, Richard
  See Chamberlin, Rich
Chambers, Aidan 1934- 171
  Earlier sketches in SATA 1, 69, 108
  See also SAAS 12
Chambers, Bradford 1922-1984
  Obituary 39
Chambers, Catherine E.
  See St. John, Nicole
Chambers, John W. 1933- 57
  Brief entry 46

Chambers, Kate
  See St. John, Nicole
Chambers, Margaret Ada Eastwood 1911- 2
Chambers, Peggy
  See Chambers, Margaret Ada Eastwood
Chambers, Robert W(illiam) 1865-1933 107
Chambliss, Maxie 186
Chan, Gillian 1954- 147
  Earlier sketch in SATA 102
Chance, James T.
  See Carpenter, John (Howard)
Chance, John T.
  See Carpenter, John (Howard)
Chance, Stephen
  See Turner, Philip (William)
Chandler, Caroline A(ugusta) 1906-1979 22
  Obituary 24
Chandler, David P(orter) 1933- 28
Chandler, Edna Walker 1908-1982 11
  Obituary 31
Chandler, Jennifer
  See Westwood, Jennifer
Chandler, Karen 1959- 122
Chandler, Linda S(mith) 1929- 39
Chandler, Pauline 175
Chandler, Robert 1953- 40
Chandler, Ruth Forbes 1894-1978 2
  Obituary 26
Chandonnet, Ann F. 1943- 92
Chaney, Jill 1932- 87
Chang, Chih-Wei 1966- 111
Chang, Cindy 1968- 90
Chang, Margaret 1941- 71
Chang, Margaret Scrogin
  See Chang, Margaret
Chang, Raymond 1939- 142
  Earlier sketches in SATA 71, 142 PEN
Chanin, Michael 1952- 84
Channel, A. R.
  See Catherall, Arthur
Chapian, Marie 1938- 29
Chapin, Alene Olsen Dalton 1915(?)-1986
  Obituary 47
Chapin, Tom 1945- 83
Chapman, Allen 67
  Earlier sketch in SATA 1
Chapman, Cheryl O(rth) 1948- 80
Chapman, (Constance) Elizabeth
  (Mann) 1919- 10
Chapman, Gaynor 1935- 32
Chapman, Gillian 1955- 120
Chapman, Jane 1970- 176
  Earlier sketch in SATA 122
Chapman, Jean 104
  Earlier sketch in SATA 34
  See also CLR 65
Chapman, John Stanton Higham 1891-1972
  Obituary 27
Chapman, Lee
  See Bradley, Marion Zimmer
Chapman, Lynne F(erguson) 1963- 150
  Earlier sketch in SATA 94
Chapman, Maristan
  See Chapman, John Stanton Higham
Chapman, Vera (Ivy May) 1898-1996 33
Chapman, Walker
  See Silverberg, Robert
Chappell, Audrey 1954- 72
Chappell, Warren 1904-1991 68
  Obituary 67
  Earlier sketch in SATA 6
  See also SAAS 10
Chapra, Mimi 182
Charbonneau, Eileen 1951- 118
  Earlier sketch in SATA 84
Charbonnet, Gabrielle 1961- 81
Chardiet, Bernice (Kroll) 1927(?)- 27
Charles, Donald
  See Meighan, Donald Charles
Charles, Louis
  See Stratemeyer, Edward L.

Charles, Nicholas J.
  See Kuskin, Karla
Charles, Norma 153
Charles, Veronika Martenova 182
Charlip, Remy 1929- 119
  Earlier sketches in SATA 4, 68
  See also CLR 8
Charlot, Jean 1898-1979 8
  Obituary 31
Charlot, Martin (Day) 1944- 64
Charlton, Michael (Alan) 1923- 34
Charlton-Trujillo, e.E. 189
Charmatz, Bill 1925-2005 7
Charnas, Suzy McKee 1939- 110
  Earlier sketch in SATA 61
Charosh, Mannis 1906- 5
Chartier, Normand L. 1945- 66
Chase, Alice
  See McHargue, Georgess
Chase, Alyssa 1965- 92
Chase, Andra 1942- 91
Chase, Emily
  See Aks, Patricia
  and Garwood, Julie
  and Sachs, Judith
  and White, Carol
Chase, Mary (Coyle) 1907-1981 17
  Obituary 29
Chase, Mary Ellen 1887-1973 10
Chase, Richard 1904-1988 64
  Obituary 56
Chase, Samantha
  See Glick, Ruth (Burtnick)
Chast, Roz 1954- 97
Chastain, Madye Lee 1908-1989 4
Chataway, Carol 1955- 140
Chatterjee, Debjani 1952- 83
Chauncy, Nan(cen Beryl Masterman)
  1900-1970 6
  See also CLR 6
Chaundler, Christine 1887-1972 1
  Obituary 25
Chbosky, Stephen 1972- 164
Cheaney, Janie B.
  See Cheaney, J.B.
Cheaney, J.B. 1950- 188
Chee, Cheng-Khee 1934- 79
Cheese, Chloe 1952- 118
Chekhonte, Antosha
  See Chekhov, Anton (Pavlovich)
Chekhov, Anton (Pavlovich) 1860-1904 90
Chelushkin, Kirill 1968- 186
Chen, Anthony 1929- 6
Chen, Chih-Yuan 1975- 155
Chen, Ju-Hong 1941- 78
Chen, Sara
  See Odgers, Sally Farrell
Chen, Tony
  See Chen, Anthony
Chen, Yong 1963- 183
Chen, Yuan-tsung 1932- 65
Chenault, Nell
  See Smith, Linell Nash
Chenery, Janet (Dai) 1923- 25
Cheney, Cora 1916-1999 3
  Obituary 110
Cheney, Glenn (Alan) 1951- 99
Cheney, Lynne V. 1941- 152
Cheney, Ted
  See Cheney, Theodore Albert
Cheney, Theodore A. Rees
  See Cheney, Theodore Albert
Cheney, Theodore Albert 1928- 11
Cheng, Andrea 1957- 172
  Earlier sketch in SATA 128
Cheng, Christopher 1959- 173
  Earlier sketch in SATA 106
Cheng, Judith 1955- 36
Cheng, Shan
  See Jiang, Cheng An

Cheripko, Jan 1951- 155
  Earlier sketch in SATA *83*
Chermayeff, Ivan 1932- 47
Chernenko, Dan
  See Chernenko, Dan
Chernoff, Dorothy A.
  See Ernst, (Lyman) John
Chernoff, Goldie Taub 1909- 10
Cherry, Carolyn Janice 93
  See Cherryh, C.J.
Cherry, Lynne 1952- 99
  Earlier sketch in SATA *34*
Cherryh, C.J. 1942- 172
  See Cherry, Carolyn Janice
Cherryholmes, Anne
  See Price, Olive
Cheshire, Simon 172
Chesler, Bernice 1932-2002 59
Chess, Victoria (Dickerson) 1939- 92
  Earlier sketch in SATA *33*
Chessa, Francesca 191
Chester, Deborah 1957- 85
Chester, Kate
  See Guccione, Leslie Davis
Chesterton, G(ilbert) K(eith) 1874-1936 27
Chesworth, Michael 160
Chetin, Helen 1922- 6
Chetwin, Grace 86
  Brief entry 50
Chevalier, Christa 1937- 35
Chevalier, Tracy 1962- 128
Chew, Ruth 1920- 7
Chichester Clark, Emma 1955- 156
  Earlier sketch in SATA *117*
  See Clark, Emma Chichester
Chidsey, Donald Barr 1902-1981 3
  Obituary 27
Chiefari, Janet D. 1942- 58
Chien, Catia 193
Chien-min, Lin
  See Rumford, James
Child, L. Maria
  See Child, Lydia Maria
Child, Lauren 1965- 183
  Earlier sketches in SATA *119, 160*
Child, Lincoln 1957- 113
Child, Lincoln B.
  See Child, Lincoln
Child, Lydia Maria 1802-1880 67
Child, Mrs.
  See Child, Lydia Maria
Child, Philip 1898-1978 47
Children's Shepherd, The
  See Westphal, Arnold Carl
Childress, Alice 1920-1994 81
  Earlier sketches in SATA *7, 48*
  See also CLR *14*
Childs, H(alla) Fay (Cochrane)
  1890-1971 1
  Obituary 25
Chilton, Charles (Frederick William)
  1917- 102
Chima, Cinda Williams 192
Chimaera
  See Farjeon, Eleanor
Chin, Richard (M.) 1946- 52
Chinery, Michael 1938- 26
Chin-Lee, Cynthia 1958- 102
Chin-Lee D., Cynthia
  See Chin-Lee, Cynthia
Chippendale, Lisa A. 158
Chipperfield, Joseph Eugene
  1912-1980(?) 87
  Earlier sketch in SATA *2*
Chisholm, P. F.
  See Finney, Patricia
Chislett, Gail (Elaine) 1948- 58
Chittenden, Elizabeth F. 1903-1999 9
Chittenden, Margaret 1935- 28
Chittum, Ida 1918- 7
Chitwood, Suzanne Tanner 1958- 160

Chmielarz, Sharon Lee 1940- 72
Choate, Judith (Newkirk) 1940- 30
Chocolate, Debbi 1954- 96
Chocolate, Deborah M. Newton
  See Chocolate, Debbi
Chodos-Irvine, Margaret 152
Choi, Sook Nyul 1937- 73
  Autobiography Feature 126
  See also CLR *53*
Choi, Yangsook 178
Choldenko, Gennifer 1957- 182
  Earlier sketch in SATA *135*
Chorao, (Ann Mc)Kay (Sproat) 1936- 162
  Earlier sketches in SATA *8, 69*
Choron, Sandra (Zena Samelson) 1950- 146
Chown, Marcus 1959- 137
Choyce, Lesley 1951- 165
  Earlier sketch in SATA *94*
Chrisman, Arthur Bowie 1889-1953 124
  See also YABC *1*
Christelow, Eileen 1943- 184
  Autobiography Feature 120
  Brief entry 35
  Earlier sketches in SATA *38, 90*
Christensen, Bonnie 1951- 157
  Earlier sketch in SATA *110*
Christensen, Gardell Dano 1907-1991 1
Christensen, Laurie
  See Steding, Laurie
Christesen, Barbara 1940- 40
Christgau, Alice Erickson 1902-1977 13
Christian, Mary Blount 1933- 9
Christie, Agatha (Mary Clarissa)
  1890-1976 36
Christie, Ann Philippa
  See Pearce, Philippa
Christie, Gregory
  See Christie, R. Gregory
Christie, Philippa 129
  Earlier sketches in SATA *1, 67*
  See also CLR *9*
  See Pearce, Philippa
Christie, R. Gregory 1971- 185
  Earlier sketch in SATA *127*
Christopher, John
  See CLR *2*
  See Youd, (Christopher) Samuel
Christopher, Louise
  See Hale, Arlene
Christopher, Matt(hew Frederick)
  1917-1997 80
  Obituary 99
  Earlier sketches in SATA *2, 47*
  See also CLR *119*
  See also SAAS *9*
Christopher, Milbourne 1914(?)-1984 46
Christy, Howard Chandler 1873-1952 21
Chrustowski, Rick 176
Chrystie, Frances N(icholson) 1904-1986 60
Chu, Daniel 1933- 11
Chukovsky, Kornei (Ivanovich)
  1882-1969 34
  Earlier sketch in SATA *5*
Church, Caroline Jayne 179
Church, Richard 1893-1972 3
Churchill, E(lmer) Richard 1937- 11
Churchill, Elizabeth
  See Hough, Richard (Alexander)
Chute, B(eatrice) J(oy) 1913-1987 2
  Obituary 53
Chute, Marchette (Gaylord) 1909-1994 1
Chwast, Jacqueline 1932- 6
Chwast, Seymour 1931- 146
  Earlier sketches in SATA *18, 96*
Ciardi, John (Anthony) 1916-1986 65
  Obituary 46
  Earlier sketch in SATA *1*
  See also CLR *19*
  See also SAAS *26*
Ciccone, Madonna Louise Veronica
  See Madonna

Ciment, James D. 1958- 140
Cirrone, Dorian 182
Cisneros, Sandra 1954-
  See CLR *123*
Citra, Becky 1954- 137
Citrin, Michael 1965(?)- 183
Clair, Andree 19
Clampett, Bob 1914(?)-1985
  Obituary 38
  See Clampett, Robert
Clampett, Robert 44
  See Clampett, Bob
Clapp, John 1968- 109
Clapp, Patricia 1912- 74
  Earlier sketch in SATA *4*
  See also SAAS *4*
Clare, Ellen
  See Sinclair, Olga
Clare, Helen
  See Clarke, Pauline
Claremont, Chris 1950- 87
Claremont, Christopher Simon
  See Claremont, Chris
Clark, Ann Nolan 1896-1995 82
  Obituary 87
  Earlier sketch in SATA *4*
  See also CLR *16*
  See also SAAS *16*
Clark, Champ 1923-2002 47
Clark, Christopher (Anthony) Stuart
  See Stuart-Clark, Christopher (Anthony)
Clark, Clara Gillow 1951- 154
  Earlier sketch in SATA *84*
Clark, David
  See Hardcastle, Michael
Clark, David Allen
  See Ernst, (Lyman) John
Clark, Emma Chichester 69
  See Chichester Clark, Emma
Clark, Frank J(ames) 1922- 18
Clark, Garel
  See Garelick, May
Clark, Halsey
  See Deming, Richard
Clark, Joan
  See Benson, Mildred (Augustine Wirt)
Clark, Joan 1934- 182
  Earlier sketches in SATA *59, 96*
Clark, Leonard 1905-1981 30
  Obituary 29
Clark, M. R.
  See Clark, Mavis Thorpe
Clark, Margaret (D.) 1943- 126
Clark, Margaret Goff 1913- 82
  Earlier sketch in SATA *8*
Clark, Mary Higgins 1929- 46
Clark, Mavis Thorpe 1909-1999 74
  Earlier sketch in SATA *8*
  See also CLR *30*
  See also SAAS *5*
Clark, Merle
  See Gessner, Lynne
Clark, Patricia Denise 1921- 117
  See Lorrimer, Claire
Clark, Patricia Finrow 1929- 11
Clark, Ronald William 1916-1987 2
  Obituary 52
Clark, Sherryl 1956- 149
Clark, Van D(eusen) 1909-1974 2
Clark, Virginia
  See Gray, Patricia (Clark)
Clark, Walter Van Tilburg 1909-1971 8
Clarke, Arthur
  See Clarke, Arthur C.
Clarke, Arthur C. 1917-2008 115
  Obituary 191
  Earlier sketches in SATA *13, 70*
  See also CLR *119*
Clarke, Arthur Charles
  See Clarke, Arthur C.
Clarke, Clorinda 1917- 7

Clarke, Gus 1948- *134*
Clarke, J.
  See Clarke, Judith
Clarke, James Hall
  See Rowland-Entwistle, (Arthur) Theodore
    (Henry)
Clarke, Joan B. 1921- *42*
  Brief entry *27*
Clarke, John
  See Laklan, Carli
    and Sontup, Dan(iel)
Clarke, Judith 1943- *164*
  Earlier sketches in SATA *75, 110*
  See also CLR *61*
Clarke, Julia 1950- *138*
Clarke, Kenneth 1957- *107*
Clarke, Lea
  See Rowland-Entwistle, (Arthur)
    Theodore (Henry)
Clarke, Margaret 1941-
  See CLR *99*
Clarke, Mary Stetson 1911-1994 .... *5*
Clarke, Michael
  See Newlon, (Frank) Clarke
Clarke, Pauline 1921- *131*
  See also CLR *28*
  See Clare, Helen
    and Hunter Blair, Pauline
Clarke-Rich, Elizabeth L. 1934- *103*
Clarkson, E(dith) Margaret 1915- *37*
Clarkson, Ewan 1929- *9*
Claudia, Susan
  See Goulart, Ron(ald Joseph)
    and Johnston, William
Claverie, Jean 1946- *38*
Clay, Patrice 1947- *47*
Clayman, Deborah Paula
  See Da Costa, Deborah
Claypool, Jane *103*
  See Miner, Jane Claypool
Clayton, Elaine 1961- *159*
  Earlier sketch in SATA *94*
Clayton, Lawrence (Otto, Jr.) 1945- *75*
Clayton, Sandra 1951- *110*
Cleary, Beverly 1916- *121*
  Earlier sketches in SATA *2, 43, 79*
  See also CLR *72*
  See also SAAS *20*
Cleary, Beverly Atlee Bunn
  See Cleary, Beverly
Cleary, Brian P. 1959- *186*
  Earlier sketches in SATA *93, 132*
Cleaver, Bill *22*
  Obituary *27*
  See also CLR *6*
  See Cleaver, William J(oseph)
Cleaver, Carole 1934- *6*
Cleaver, Elizabeth (Ann Mrazik)
  1939-1985 .... *23*
  Obituary *43*
  See also CLR *13*
Cleaver, Hylton Reginald 1891-1961 .... *49*
Cleaver, Vera (Allen) 1919-1993 .... *76*
  Earlier sketch in SATA *22*
  See also CLR *6*
Cleishbotham, Jebediah
  See Scott, Sir Walter
Cleland, Mabel
  See Widdemer, Mabel Cleland
Clem, Margaret H(ollingsworth) 1923- *90*
Clemens, Samuel Langhorne 1835-1910 .... *100*
  See also YABC *2*
  See Twain, Mark
Clemens, Virginia Phelps 1941- *35*
Clement, Gary *191*
Clement, Janet *182*
Clement, Priscilla Ferguson 1942- *171*
Clement, Rod *97*
Clement-Moore, Rosemary *188*
Clements, Andrew 1949- *158*
  Earlier sketch in SATA *104*

Clements, Bruce 1931- *178*
  Earlier sketches in SATA *27, 94*
Clemesha, David *192*
Clemons, Elizabeth
  See Nowell, Elizabeth Cameron
Clerk, N. W.
  See Lewis, C.S.
Cleveland, Bob
  See Cleveland, George
Cleveland, George 1903(?)-1985
  Obituary *43*
Cleveland-Peck, Patricia *80*
Cleven, Cathrine
  See Cleven, Kathryn Seward
Cleven, Kathryn Seward *2*
Clevenger, William R. 1954- *84*
Clevenger, William Russell
  See Clevenger, William R.
Clevin, Joergen 1920- *7*
Clevin, Jorgen
  See Clevin, Joergen
Clewes, Dorothy (Mary) 1907-2003 .... *86*
  Obituary *138*
  Earlier sketch in SATA *1*
Clifford, David
  See Rosenberg, Eth(el) Clifford
Clifford, Eth *92*
  See also SAAS *22*
  See Rosenberg, Eth(el) Clifford
Clifford, Harold B(urton) 1893-1988 ...... *10*
Clifford, Margaret Cort 1929- *1*
Clifford, Martin
  See Hamilton, Charles (Harold St. John)
Clifford, Mary Louise Beneway 1926- *23*
Clifford, Peggy
  See Clifford, Margaret Cort
Clifford, Rachel Mark
  See Lewis, Brenda Ralph
Clifton, Lucille 1936- *128*
  Earlier sketches in SATA *20, 69*
  See also CLR *5*
Clifton, Thelma Lucille
  See Clifton, Lucille
Climo, Shirley 1928- *166*
  Autobiography Feature *110*
  Brief entry *35*
  Earlier sketches in SATA *39, 77*
  See also CLR *69*
Clinton, Cathryn 1957- *136*
Clinton, Dirk
  See Silverberg, Robert
Clinton, Jon
  See Prince, J(ack) H(arvey)
Clippinger, Carol *193*
Clish, (Lee) Marian 1946- *43*
Clive, Clifford
  See Hamilton, Charles (Harold St. John)
Clokey, Art 1921- *59*
Cloudsley-Thompson, J(ohn)
  L(eonard) 1921- *19*
Clouse, Nancy L. 1938- *78*
Clover, Peter 1952- *152*
Clutha, Janet Paterson Frame
  See Frame, Janet
Clymer, Eleanor 1906-2001 .... *85*
  Obituary *126*
  Earlier sketch in SATA *9*
  See also SAAS *17*
Clyne, Patricia (Edwards) *31*
Coalson, Glo 1946- *94*
  Earlier sketch in SATA *26*
Coates, Anna 1958- *73*
Coates, Belle 1896-1986 .... *2*
Coates, Ruth Allison 1915- *11*
Coats, Alice M(argaret) 1905-1976 .... *11*
Coatsworth, Elizabeth (Jane) 1893-1986 ... *100*
  Obituary *49*
  Earlier sketches in SATA *2, 56*
  See also CLR *2*
Cobalt, Martin
  See Mayne, William (James Carter)

Cobb, Jane
  See Berry, Jane Cobb
Cobb, Mary 1931- *88*
Cobb, Vicki 1938- *136*
  Autobiography Feature *136*
  Earlier sketches in SATA *8, 69, 131*
  See also CLR *2*
  See also SAAS *6*
Cobbett, Richard
  See Pluckrose, Henry (Arthur)
Cober, Alan E(dwin) 1935-1998 .... *7*
  Obituary *101*
Cobham, Sir Alan
  See Hamilton, Charles (Harold St. John)
Coburn, Jake 1978- *155*
Cocagnac, Augustin Maurice(-Jean)
  1924- *7*
Cocca-Leffler, Maryann 1958- *136*
  Earlier sketch in SATA *80*
Cochran, Bill *187*
Cochran, Bobbye A. 1949- *11*
Cockett, Mary *3*
Coddell, Esme Raji
  See Codell, Esme Raji
Codell, Esme Raji 1968- *160*
Cody, C. S.
  See Waller, Leslie
Cody, Jess
  See Cunningham, Chet
Coe, Anne (E.) 1949- *95*
Coe, Douglas
  See Epstein, Beryl (M. Williams)
    and Epstein, Samuel
Coe, Lloyd 1899(?)-1976
  Obituary *30*
Coen, Rena Neumann 1925- *20*
Coerr, Eleanor (Beatrice) 1922- *67*
  Earlier sketch in SATA *1*
Cofer, Judith Ortiz 1952- *164*
  Earlier sketch in SATA *110*
  See Ortiz Cofer, Judith
Coffelt, Nancy 1961- *189*
Coffey, Brian
  See Koontz, Dean R.
Coffin, Geoffrey
  See Mason, F(rancis) van Wyck
Coffin, M. T.
  See Stanley, George Edward
Coffman, Ramon Peyton 1896-1989 .... *4*
Cogan, Karen 1954- *125*
Coggins, Jack (Banham) 1911-2006 .... *2*
Cohen, Barbara 1932-1992 .... *77*
  Obituary *74*
  Earlier sketch in SATA *10*
  See also SAAS *7*
Cohen, Daniel (E.) 1936- *70*
  Earlier sketch in SATA *8*
  See also CLR *43*
  See also SAAS *4*
Cohen, Deborah Bodin 1968- *180*
Cohen, Jan Barger
  See Barger, Jan
Cohen, Jene Barr
  See Barr, Jene
Cohen, Joan Lebold 1932- *4*
Cohen, Judith Love 1933- *78*
Cohen, Miriam 1926-1955 .... *155*
  Earlier sketches in SATA *29, 106*
  See also SAAS *11*
Cohen, Nora *75*
Cohen, Paul S. 1945- *58*
Cohen, Peter Zachary 1931- *150*
  Earlier sketch in SATA *4*
Cohen, Robert Carl 1930- *8*
Cohen, Sholom 1951- *94*
Cohn, Angelo 1914-1997 .... *19*
Cohn, Rachel 1968- *161*
Coit, Margaret Louise 1922-2003 .... *2*
  Obituary *142*
Colato Lainez, Rene 1970- *176*
Colbert, Anthony 1934-2007 .... *15*

Colbert, Nancy A. 1936- *139*
Colby, C(arroll) B(urleigh) 1904-1977 .... *35*
Earlier sketch in SATA *3*
Colby, Jean Poindexter 1909-1993 .... *23*
Cole, Annette
See Steiner, Barbara A(nnette)
Cole, Babette 1949- *155*
Earlier sketches in SATA *61, 96*
Cole, Betsy 1940- *83*
Cole, Brock 1938- *136*
Earlier sketch in SATA *72*
See also CLR *18*
Cole, Davis
See Elting, Mary
Cole, Hannah 1954- *74*
Cole, Henry 1955- *181*
Cole, Jack -1974
See Stewart, John (William)
Cole, Jackson
See Curry, Thomas Albert
and Germano, Peter B.
and Heckelmann, Charles N(ewman)
and Newton, D(wight) B(ennett)
and Schisgall, Oscar
Cole, Jennifer
See Zach, Cheryl (Byrd)
Cole, Joanna 1944- *168*
Brief entry *37*
Earlier sketches in SATA *49, 81, 120*
See also CLR *40*
Cole, Lois Dwight 1903-1979 .... *10*
Obituary *26*
Cole, Michael 1947- *59*
Cole, Sheila R. 1939- *171*
Earlier sketches in SATA *24, 95*
Cole, Sheila Rotenberg
See Cole, Sheila R.
Cole, Stephen 1971- *161*
Cole, William (Rossa) 1919-2000 .... *71*
Earlier sketch in SATA *9*
See also SAAS *9*
Coleman, Andrew
See Pine, Nicholas
Coleman, Clare
See Bell, Clare (Louise)
and Easton, M(alcolm) Coleman
Coleman, Janet Wyman *184*
Coleman, Loren 1947- *164*
Coleman, Loren Elwood, Jr.
See Coleman, Loren
Coleman, Mary Ann 1928- *83*
Coleman, Michael (Lee) 1946- *133*
Autobiography Feature *133*
Earlier sketch in SATA *108*
Coleman, Rowan *187*
Coleman, William L(eRoy) 1938- *49*
Brief entry *34*
Coles, Robert (Martin) 1929- *23*
Colfer, Eoin 1965- *148*
See also CLR *112*
Colin, Ann
See Ure, Jean
Collard, Sneed B. III 1959- *184*
Earlier sketches in SATA *84, 139*
Colledge, Anne 1939- *142*
Collicott, Sharleen 1937- *143*
Earlier sketch in SATA *98*
Collier, Bryan *174*
Earlier sketch in SATA *126*
Collier, Christopher 1930- *70*
Earlier sketch in SATA *16*
See also CLR *126*
Collier, Ethel 1903-1999 .... *22*
Collier, James Lincoln 1928- *166*
Earlier sketches in SATA *8, 70*
See also CLR *126*
See also SAAS *21*
Collier, Jane
See Collier, Zena
Collier, Kristi *182*
Collier, Steven 1942- *61*

Collier, Zena 1926- *23*
See Collier, Jane
Collings, Gillian 1939- *102*
Collington, Peter 1948- *99*
Earlier sketch in SATA *59*
Collins, Ace 1953- *82*
Collins, Andrew J.
See Collins, Ace
Collins, David R(aymond) 1940-2001 .... *121*
Earlier sketch in SATA *7*
Collins, Heather 1946- *81*
Collins, Hunt
See Hunter, Evan
Collins, Michael
See Lynds, Dennis
Collins, Michael 1930- *58*
Collins, Pat(ricia) Lowery 1932- *151*
Earlier sketch in SATA *31*
Collins, Paul 1954- *126*
Collins, Ruth Philpott 1890-1975
Obituary *30*
Collins, Suzanne *180*
Collinson, A. S.
See Collinson, Alan S.
Collinson, Alan S. 1934- *80*
Collinson, Roger (Alfred) 1936- *133*
Collison, Linda 1953- *185*
Collodi, Carlo
See CLR *120*
See Lorenzini, Carlo
Colloms, Brenda 1919- *40*
Colman, Hila *53*
Earlier sketch in SATA *1*
See also SAAS *14*
Colman, Morris 1899(?)-1981
Obituary *25*
Colman, Penny (Morgan) 1944- *160*
Autobiography Feature *160*
Earlier sketches in SATA *77, 114*
Colman, Warren (David) 1944- *67*
Colombo, John Robert 1936- *50*
Colon, Raul *156*
Colonius, Lillian 1911-1992 .... *3*
Colorado, Antonio J.
See Colorado (Capella), Antonio J(ulio)
Colorado (Capella), Antonio J(ulio)
1903-1994 .... *23*
Obituary *79*
Colquhoun, Glenn 1964- *165*
Colston, Fifi E. 1960- *150*
Colt, Martin
See Epstein, Beryl (M. Williams)
and Epstein, Samuel
Colum, Padraic 1881-1972 .... *15*
See also CLR *36*
Columbus, Chris 1959- *97*
Columbus, Christopher
See Columbus, Chris
Columella
See Moore, Clement Clarke
Colver, Anne 1908- *7*
Colvin, James
See Moorcock, Michael
Colwell, Eileen (Hilda) 1904-2002 .... *2*
Colwyn, Stewart
See Pepper, Frank S.
Coman, Carolyn 1951- *127*
Combs, Lisa M.
See McCourt, Lisa
Combs, Robert
See Murray, John
Comfort, Jane Levington
See Sturtzel, Jane Levington
Comfort, Mildred Houghton 1886-1976 .... *3*
Comins, Ethel M(ae) *11*
Comins, Jeremy 1933- *28*
Commager, Henry Steele 1902-1998 .... *23*
Obituary *102*
Comora, Madeleine *190*
Compere, Mickie
See Davidson, Margaret

Compestine, Ying Chang 1963- *187*
Earlier sketch in SATA *140*
Comport, Sally Wern *190*
Compton, Patricia A. 1936- *75*
Comte, The Great
See Hawkesworth, Eric
Comus
See Ballantyne, R(obert) M(ichael)
Comyns, Nance
See Comyns-Toohey, Nantz
Comyns-Toohey, Nantz 1956- *86*
Conan Doyle, Arthur
See Doyle, Sir Arthur Conan
Condit, Martha Olson 1913- *28*
Condon, Bill 1949- *142*
Condon, Judith *83*
Condy, Roy 1942- *96*
Cone, Ferne Geller 1921- *39*
Cone, Molly (Lamken) 1918- *151*
Autobiography Feature *151*
Earlier sketches in SATA *1, 28, 115*
See also SAAS *11*
Cone, Patrick 1954- *89*
Coney, Michael G. 1932-2005 .... *61*
Obituary *170*
Coney, Michael Greatrex
See Coney, Michael G.
Coney, Mike
See Coney, Michael G.
Conford, Ellen 1942- *162*
Earlier sketches in SATA *6, 68, 110*
See also CLR *71*
Conger, Lesley
See Suttles, Shirley (Smith)
Conklin, Gladys Plemon 1903- *2*
Conklin, Paul S. 1929(?)-2003 .... *43*
Brief entry *33*
Obituary *147*
Conkling, Hilda 1910-1986 .... *23*
Conlan, Kathleen Elizabeth 1950- *145*
Conlan, Kathy
See Conlan, Kathleen Elizabeth
Conley-Weaver, Robyn 1963- *125*
Conlon-McKenna, Marita 1956- *71*
Conly, Jane Leslie 1948- *164*
Earlier sketches in SATA *80, 112*
Conly, Robert Leslie 1918(?)-1973 .... *23*
See O'Brien, Robert C.
Connell, Kirk
See Chapman, John Stanton Higham
Connelly, Marc(us Cook) 1890-1980
Obituary *25*
Connolly, Jerome P(atrick) 1931- *8*
Connolly, Pat 1943- *74*
Connolly, Peter 1935- *105*
Earlier sketch in SATA *47*
Conover, Chris 1950- *31*
Conquest, Owen
See Hamilton, Charles (Harold St. John)
Conrad, Joseph 1857-1924 .... *27*
Conrad, Pam 1947-1996 .... *133*
Brief entry *49*
Obituary *90*
Earlier sketches in SATA *52, 80*
See also CLR *18*
See also SAAS *19*
Conroy, Jack *19*
See Conroy, John Wesley
Conroy, John Wesley 1899-1990
Obituary *65*
See Conroy, Jack
Conroy, Robert
See Goldston, Robert (Conroy)
Constable, Kate 1966- *172*
Constant, Alberta Wilson 1908-1981 .... *22*
Obituary *28*
Constantin, Pascale *185*
Conway, Diana C(ohen) 1943- *91*
Conway, Gordon
See Hamilton, Charles (Harold St. John)
Cook, Ande *192*

Cook, Bernadine 1924- *11*
Cook, Fred J(ames) 1911-2003 .... *2*
   Obituary *145*
Cook, Glen 1944- *171*
   Earlier sketch in SATA *108*
Cook, Glen Charles
   See Cook, Glen
Cook, Hugh 1956- *85*
Cook, Hugh, Walter Gilbert
   See Cook, Hugh
Cook, Jean Thor 1930- *94*
Cook, Joel 1934- *79*
Cook, Joseph Jay 1924- *8*
Cook, Lisa Broadie *157*
Cook, Lyn
   See Waddell, Evelyn Margaret
Cook, Roy
   See Silverberg, Robert
Cook, Trish *175*
Cooke, Ann
   See Cole, Joanna
Cooke, Arthur
   See Lowndes, Robert A(ugustine) W(ard)
Cooke, Barbara
   See Alexander, Anna B(arbara Cooke)
Cooke, David Coxe 1917- *2*
Cooke, Donald Ewin 1916-1985 .... *2*
   Obituary *45*
Cooke, Frank E. 1920- *87*
Cooke, Jean (Isobel Esther) 1929- *74*
Cooke, John Estes
   See Baum, L(yman) Frank
Cooke, Trish 1962- *129*
Cookson, Catherine (McMullen)
   1906-1998 .... *9*
   Obituary *116*
Cooley, Regina Francoise 1940- *177*
Coolidge, Olivia E(nsor) 1908- *26*
   Earlier sketch in SATA *1*
Cooling, Wendy *169*
   Earlier sketch in SATA *111*
Coombs, Charles I(ra) 1914-1994 .... *43*
   Earlier sketch in SATA *3*
   See also SAAS *15*
Coombs, Chick
   See Coombs, Charles I(ra)
Coombs, Kate *190*
Coombs, Patricia 1926- *51*
   Earlier sketch in SATA *3*
   See also SAAS *22*
Cooney, Barbara 1917-2000 .... *96*
   Obituary *123*
   Earlier sketches in SATA *6, 59*
   See also CLR *23*
Cooney, Caroline B. 1947- *179*
   Brief entry *41*
   Earlier sketches in SATA *48, 80, 113, 130*
Cooney, Doug *181*
Cooney, Nancy Evans 1932- *42*
Coontz, Otto 1946- *33*
Cooper, Ann (Catharine) 1939- *104*
Cooper, Dutch
   See Kuyper, Sjoerd
Cooper, Elisha 1971- *157*
   Earlier sketch in SATA *99*
Cooper, Elizabeth Keyser -1992 .... *47*
Cooper, Floyd *187*
   Earlier sketches in SATA *96, 144*
   See also CLR *60*
Cooper, Gordon 1932- *23*
Cooper, Helen 1963- *169*
   Earlier sketch in SATA *102*
Cooper, Henry S(potswood)
   F(enimore), Jr. 1933- *65*
Cooper, Ilene 1948- *145*
   Earlier sketches in SATA *66, 97*
Cooper, James Fenimore 1789-1851 .... *19*
   See also CLR *105*
Cooper, John R. *1*
Cooper, Kay 1941- *11*
Cooper, Lee Pelham 1926- *5*

Cooper, Lester (Irving) 1919-1985 .... *32*
   Obituary *43*
Cooper, Lettice (Ulpha) 1897-1994 .... *35*
   Obituary *82*
Cooper, Louise 1952- *152*
Cooper, M.E.
   See Lerangis, Peter
Cooper, M.E.
   See Davis, Maggie S.
Cooper, Melrose
   See Kroll, Virginia L.
Cooper, Michael L. 1950- *181*
   Earlier sketches in SATA *79, 117*
Cooper, Patrick 1949- *134*
Cooper, Susan 1935- *151*
   Earlier sketches in SATA *4, 64, 104*
   See also CLR *67*
   See also SAAS *6*
Cooper, Susan Mary
   See Cooper, Susan
Cope, Jane U(rsula) 1949- *108*
Copeland, Helen 1920- *4*
Copeland, Mark 1956- *180*
Copeland, Paul W. *23*
Coplans, Peta 1951- *84*
Copley (Diana) Heather Pickering 1918- *45*
Coppard, A(lfred) E(dgar) 1878-1957
   See YABC *1*
Copper, Melinda 1952- *172*
Copper, Melinda McConnaughey
   See Copper, Melinda
Coralie
   See Anderson, Catherine Corley
Corbett, Grahame *43*
   Brief entry *36*
Corbett, Scott 1913- *42*
   Earlier sketch in SATA *2*
   See also CLR *1*
   See also SAAS *2*
Corbett, Sue *174*
Corbett, W(illiam) J(esse) 1938- *102*
   Brief entry *44*
   Earlier sketch in SATA *50*
   See also CLR *19*
Corbin, Sabra Lee
   See Malvern, Gladys
Corbin, William
   See McGraw, William Corbin
Corbman, Marjorie 1987- *179*
Corby, Dan
   See Catherall, Arthur
Corcoran, Barbara (Asenath) 1911- *77*
   Autobiography Feature *125*
   Earlier sketch in SATA *3*
   See also CLR *50*
   See also SAAS *20*
Corcos, Lucille 1908-1973 .... *10*
Cordell, Alexander
   See Graber, Alexander
Cordell, Alexander
   See Graber, (George) Alexander
Corder, Zizou
   See Young, Louisa
Corella, Joseph
   See Odgers, Sally Farrell
Coren, Alan 1938-2007 .... *32*
   Obituary *187*
Corey, Dorothy *23*
Corey, Shana 1974- *133*
Corfe, Thomas Howell 1928- *27*
Corfe, Tom
   See Corfe, Thomas Howell
Corfield, Robin Bell 1952- *74*
Corlett, William 1938-2005 .... *46*
   Brief entry *39*
Cormack, M(argaret) Grant 1913- *11*
Cormack, Maribelle B. 1902-1984 .... *39*
Cormier, Robert 1925-2000 .... *83*
   Obituary *122*
   Earlier sketches in SATA *10, 45*
   See also CLR *55*

Cormier, Robert Edmund
   See Cormier, Robert
Cornelius, Carol 1942- *40*
Cornelius, Kay 1933- *157*
Cornell, J.
   See Cornell, Jeffrey
Cornell, James (Clayton, Jr.) 1938- *27*
Cornell, Jean Gay 1920- *23*
Cornell, Jeffrey 1945- *11*
Cornell, Laura *189*
Cornish, D.M. 1972- *185*
Cornish, Sam(uel James) 1935- *23*
Cornwall, Nellie
   See Sloggett, Nellie
Corr, Christopher 1955- *189*
Correy, Lee
   See Stine, G(eorge) Harry
Corrick, James A. 1945- *76*
Corrigan, (Helen) Adeline 1909- *23*
Corrigan, Barbara 1922- *8*
Corrigan, Eireann 1977- *163*
Corrin, Sara 1918- *86*
   Brief entry *48*
Corrin, Stephen *86*
   Brief entry *48*
Corsi, Wendy
   See Staub, Wendy Corsi
Cort, M. C.
   See Clifford, Margaret Cort
Cort, Margaret
   See Clifford, Margaret Cort
Corwin, Judith H(offman) 1946- *10*
Cory, Rowena
   See Lindquist, Rowena Cory
Cosby, Bill
   See Cosby, William Henry, Jr.
Cosby, William Henry, Jr. 1937- *110*
   Earlier sketch in SATA *66*
   See Cosby, Bill
Cosentino, Ralph *169*
Cosgrave, John O'Hara II 1908-1968
   Obituary *21*
Cosgrove, Margaret (Leota) 1926- *47*
Cosgrove, Stephen E(dward) 1945- *53*
   Brief entry *40*
Coskey, Evelyn 1932- *7*
Cosner, Shaaron 1940- *43*
Cossi, Olga 1921- *102*
   Earlier sketch in SATA *67*
Costabel, Eva Deutsch 1924- *45*
Costabel-Deutsch, Eva
   See Costabel, Eva Deutsch
Coste, Marion 1938- *183*
Costello, David *174*
Costello, David F(rancis) 1904-1990 .... *23*
Cte, Genevieve 1964- *184*
Cote, Nancy *182*
Cott, Jonathan 1942- *23*
Cottam, Clarence 1899-1974 .... *25*
Cotten, Cynthia *188*
Cottle, Joan 1960- *135*
Cottler, Joseph 1899-1996 .... *22*
Cottonwood, Joe 1947- *92*
Cottrell, Leonard 1913-1974 .... *24*
Cottringer, Anne 1952- *150*
   Earlier sketch in SATA *97*
Coulman, Valerie 1969- *161*
Couloumbis, Audrey *173*
Counsel, June 1926- *70*
Countryman, The
   See Whitlock, Ralph
Courlander, Harold 1908-1996 .... *6*
   Obituary *88*
Coursen, Valerie 1965(?)- *102*
Curtis, Stuart Appleton 1874-1969
   Obituary *29*
Courtland, Tyler
   See Stevens, Serita
Courtney, Dayle
   See Goldsmith, Howard

Coury, Louise Andree 1895(?)-1983
  Obituary *34*
Cousins, Linda 1946- *90*
Cousins, Lucy 1964- *172*
Cousins, Margaret 1905-1996 .... *2*
  Obituary *92*
Cousteau, Jacques-Yves 1910-1997 ..... *98*
  Earlier sketch in SATA *38*
Couture, Christin 1951- *73*
Coville, Bruce 1950- *155*
  Autobiography Feature *155*
  Earlier sketches in SATA *32, 77, 118*
Covington, Dennis *109*
Covington, Linda
  See Windsor, Linda
Cowan, Catherine *121*
Cowan, Rebecca M.
  See Moesta, Rebecca
Cowan, Rebecca Moesta
  See Moesta, Rebecca
Coward, Fiona 1963- *178*
Cowell, Cressida 1966- *140*
Cowen, Eve
  See Werner, Herma
Cowen, Ida 1898-1993 .... *64*
Cowie, Leonard W(allace) 1919- *4*
Cowles, Kathleen
  See Krull, Kathleen
Cowley, Cassia Joy
  See Cowley, Joy
Cowley, Joy 1936- *164*
Cowley, (Cassia) Joy 1936- *90*
  Autobiography Feature *118*
  Earlier sketch in SATA *4*
  See also CLR *55*
  See also SAAS *26*
Cowley, Marjorie 1925- *111*
Cox, (Christopher) Barry 1931- *62*
Cox, Clinton 1934- *108*
  Earlier sketch in SATA *74*
Cox, David (Dundas) 1933- *56*
Cox, Donald William 1921- *23*
Cox, Jack
  See Cox, John Roberts
Cox, John Roberts 1915-1981 .... *9*
  See Roberts, David
Cox, Judy 1954- *160*
  Earlier sketch in SATA *117*
Cox, Palmer 1840-1924 .... *24*
  See also CLR *24*
Cox, Vic 1942- *88*
Cox, Vicki 1945- *158*
Cox, Victoria
  See Garretson, Victoria Diane
Cox, Wally *25*
  See Cox, Wallace (Maynard)
Cox, William R(obert) 1901-1988 ...... *46*
  Brief entry *31*
  Obituary *57*
  See Ward, Jonas
Coxe, Molly 1959- *101*
  Earlier sketch in SATA *69*
Coxon, Michele 1950- *158*
  Earlier sketch in SATA *76*
Coy, Harold 1902-1986 .... *3*
Coy, John 1958- *171*
  Earlier sketch in SATA *120*
Craats, Rennay 1973- *131*
Crabtree, Judith 1928- *98*
  Earlier sketch in SATA *63*
Cracker, Edward E.B.
  See Odgers, Sally Farrell
Craft, K. Y.
  See Craft, Kinuko Y(amabe)
Craft, Kinuko
  See Craft, Kinuko Y(amabe)
Craft, Kinuko Y(amabe) 1940- *127*
  Earlier sketch in SATA *65*
Craft, Ruth 1935- *87*
  Brief entry *31*

Craig, A. A.
  See Anderson, Poul
Craig, Alisa
  See MacLeod, Charlotte (Matilda)
Craig, Helen 1934- *94*
  Earlier sketches in SATA *46, 49*
Craig, John Eland
  See Chipperfield, Joseph Eugene
Craig, John Ernest 1921- *23*
Craig, Kit
  See Reed, Kit
Craig, M. F.
  See Craig, Mary (Francis) Shura
Craig, M. Jean *17*
Craig, M. S.
  See Craig, Mary (Francis) Shura
Craig, Margaret (Maze) 1911-1964 ..... *9*
Craig, Mary
  See Craig, Mary (Francis) Shura
Craig, Mary Shura
  See Craig, Mary (Francis) Shura
Craig, Mary (Francis) Shura 1923-1991 ...... *86*
  Obituary *65*
  Earlier sketch in SATA *6*
  See also SAAS *7*
Craig, Ruth 1922- *95*
Craik, Mrs.
  See Craik, Dinah Maria (Mulock)
Craik, Dinah Maria (Mulock) 1826-1887 ..... *34*
  See Craik, Mrs.
  and Mulock, Dinah Maria
Crandall, Court 1965- *175*
Crandell, Rachel 1943- *152*
Crane, Barbara (Joyce) 1934- *31*
Crane, Caroline 1930- *11*
Crane, Jordan 1973- *174*
Crane, M. A.
  See Wartski, Maureen (Ann Crane)
Crane, Royston Campbell 1901-1977
  Obituary *22*
Crane, Stephen (Townley) 1871-1900
  See YABC *2*
  See also CLR *132*
Crane, Walter 1845-1915 .... *100*
  Earlier sketch in SATA *18*
  See also CLR *56*
Crane, William D(wight) 1892-1976 ..... *1*
Cranfield, Ingrid 1945- *74*
Cranshaw, Stanley
  See Fisher, Dorothy (Frances) Canfield
Crary, Elizabeth (Ann) 1942- *99*
  Brief entry *43*
Crary, Margaret (Coleman) 1906-1986 ..... *9*
Cravath, Lynne Avril
  See Cravath, Lynne W.
Cravath, Lynne W. 1951- *182*
  Earlier sketches in SATA *98, 148*
Craven, Thomas 1889-1969 .... *22*
Crawford, Charles P. 1945- *28*
Crawford, Deborah 1922- *6*
Crawford, John E(dmund) 1904-1971 ..... *3*
Crawford, K(aren) Michael 1959- *155*
Crawford, Mel 1925- *44*
  Brief entry *33*
Crawford, Phyllis 1899- *3*
Crawley, Dave *177*
Cray, Roberta
  See Emerson, Ru
Crayder, Dorothy *7*
Crayder, Teresa
  See Colman, Hila
Crayon, Geoffrey
  See Irving, Washington
Craz, Albert G. 1926- *24*
Crebbin, June 1938- *169*
  Earlier sketch in SATA *80*
Crecy, Jeanne
  See Williams, Jeanne
Credle, Ellis 1902-1998 .... *1*

Creech, Sharon 1945- *172*
  Earlier sketches in SATA *94, 139*
  See also CLR *89*
Creeden, Sharon 1938- *91*
Creel, Ann Howard 1953- *187*
Creighton, (Mary) Helen 1899-1989
  Obituary *64*
Creighton, Jill 1949- *96*
Crenson, Victoria 1952- *159*
  Earlier sketch in SATA *88*
Cresp, Gael 1954- *119*
Crespo, George 1962- *82*
Cresswell, Helen 1934-2005 .... *79*
  Obituary *168*
  Earlier sketches in SATA *1, 48*
  See also CLR *18*
  See also SAAS *20*
Cressy, Michael 1955- *124*
Cressy, Mike
  See Cressy, Michael
Cretan, Gladys (Yessayan) 1921- *2*
Cretzmeyer, Stacy (Megan) 1959- *124*
Crew, Gary 1947- *163*
  Earlier sketches in SATA *75, 110*
  See also CLR *42*
Crew, Helen (Cecilia) Coale 1866-1941
  See YABC *2*
Crew, Linda (Jean) 1951- *137*
  Earlier sketch in SATA *71*
Crews, Donald 1938- *76*
  Brief entry *30*
  Earlier sketch in SATA *32*
  See also CLR *7*
Crews, Nina 1963- *158*
  Earlier sketch in SATA *97*
Crichton, John Michael
  See Crichton, Michael
Crichton, Michael 1942- *88*
  Earlier sketch in SATA *9*
Crider, Allen Billy
  See Crider, Bill
Crider, Bill 1941- *99*
Crilley, Mark 1966- *148*
  Autobiography Feature *148*
  Earlier sketch in SATA *120*
Crimi, Carolyn 1959- *176*
Cripps, Enid Margaret
  See Appiah, Peggy
Crisler, Curtis L. *188*
Crisman, Ruth 1914- *73*
Crisp, Marta Marie 1947- *128*
Crisp, Marty
  See Crisp, Marta Marie
Crispin, A(nn) C(arol) 1950- *86*
Crist, James J. 1961- *168*
Cristall, Barbara *79*
Crist-Evans, Craig 1954- *153*
Crocker, Carter *193*
Crocker, Nancy 1956- *185*
Crofford, Emily (Ardell) 1927- *61*
Crofut, William E. III 1934- *23*
Croll, Carolyn 1945- *102*
  Brief entry *52*
  Earlier sketch in SATA *56*
Croman, Dorothy Young
  See Rosenberg, Dorothy
Cromie, Alice Hamilton 1914-2000 ..... *24*
Cromie, William J(oseph) 1930- *4*
Crompton, Anne Eliot 1930- *73*
  Earlier sketch in SATA *23*
Crompton, Richmal
  See Lamburn, Richmal Crompton
Cronbach, Abraham 1882-1965 .... *11*
Crone, Ruth 1919-2003 .... *4*
Cronin, A(rchibald) J(oseph) 1896-1981 ...... *47*
  Obituary *25*
Cronin, Doreen (A.) *125*
  See also CLR *105*
Cronin, Doreen 1966(?)- *178*
  See also CLR *136*

Cronin, Doreen A.
  See Cronin, Doreen
Crook, Beverly Courtney 38
  Brief entry 35
Crook, Connie Brummel 1930- 168
  Earlier sketch in SATA 98
Crook, Constance
  See Crook, Connie Brummel
Crosby, Alexander L. 1906-1980 2
  Obituary 23
Crosby, Harry C., Jr. 102
Crosby, Margaret
  See CLR 77
  See Rathmann, Peggy
Crosher, G. R. 14
Cross, Gilbert B. 1939- 60
  Brief entry 51
Cross, Gillian 1945- 178
  Autobiography Feature 178
  Earlier sketches in SATA 38, 71, 110, 165
  See also CLR 28
Cross, Gillian Clare
  See Cross, Gillian
Cross, Helen Reeder
  See Broadhead, Helen Cross
Cross, Peter 1951- 95
Cross, Tom 1954- 146
Cross, Verda 1914- 75
Cross, Wilbur Lucius III 1918- 2
Crossland, Caroline 1964- 83
Crossley-Holland, Kevin 1941- 165
  Earlier sketches in SATA 5, 74, 120
  See also CLR 84
  See also SAAS 20
Crossley-Holland, Kevin John William
  See Crossley-Holland, Kevin
Crouch, Marcus 1913-1996 4
Crout, George C(lement) 1917- 11
Crow, Donna Fletcher 1941- 40
Crow, Francis Luther
  See Luther, Frank
Crowe, Andrew 111
Crowe, John
  See Lynds, Dennis
Crowe, (Bettina) Peter Lum 1911- 6
Crowell, Grace Noll 1877-1969 34
Crowell, Pers 1910-1990 2
Crowell, Robert Leland 1909-2001 63
Crowfield, Christopher
  See Stowe, Harriet (Elizabeth) Beecher
Crowley, Arthur McBlair 1945- 38
Crowley, John 1942- 140
  Earlier sketch in SATA 65
Crownfield, Gertrude 1867-1945
  See YABC 1
Crowther, James Gerald 1899-1983 14
Crowther, Robert 1948- 163
Cruikshank, George 1792-1878 22
  See also CLR 63
Cruise, Robin 1951- 179
Crum, Shutta 192
  Earlier sketch in SATA 134
Crummel, Susan Stevens 1949- 176
  Earlier sketch in SATA 130
Crump, Fred H., Jr. 1931- 76
  Earlier sketch in SATA 11
Crump, J(ames) Irving 1887-1979 57
  Obituary 21
Crump, William D(rake) 1949- 138
Crunden, Reginald
  See Cleaver, Hylton Reginald
Crunk, T.
  See Crunk, Tony
Crunk, Tony 1956- 130
Crutcher, Chris 1946- 153
  Earlier sketches in SATA 52, 99
  See also CLR 28
Crutcher, Christopher C.
  See Crutcher, Chris
Cruz, Ray(mond) 1933- 6
Cruz Martinez, Alejandro (?)-1987 74

Crystal, Billy 1947- 154
Ctvrtek, Vaclav 1911-1976
  Obituary 27
Cuetara, Mittie 1957- 158
  Earlier sketch in SATA 106
Cuffari, Richard 1925-1978 66
  Obituary 25
  Earlier sketch in SATA 6
Cullen, Countee 1903-1946 18
Cullen, Lynn 190
Culliford, Pierre 1928-1992 40
  Obituary 74
Cullinan, Bernice E(llinger) 1926- 135
Culp, Louanna McNary 1901-1965 2
Culper, Felix
  See McCaughrean, Geraldine
Cumbaa, Stephen 1947- 72
Cumming, Peter 1951- 168
Cumming, Primrose Amy 1915- 24
Cumming, Robert 1945- 65
Cummings, Betty Sue 1918- 15
  See also SAAS 9
Cummings, Mary 1951- 185
Cummings, Parke 1902-1987 2
  Obituary 53
Cummings, Pat (Marie) 1950- 107
  Earlier sketches in SATA 42, 71
  See also CLR 48
  See also SAAS 13
Cummings, Phil 1957- 123
  Earlier sketch in SATA 74
Cummings, Priscilla 1951- 170
  Earlier sketch in SATA 129
Cummings, Richard
  See Gardner, Richard (M.)
Cummins, Maria Susanna 1827-1866
  See YABC 1
Cuneo, Mary Louise -2001 85
Cunliffe, John Arthur 1933- 86
  Earlier sketch in SATA 11
Cunliffe, Marcus (Falkner) 1922-1990 37
  Obituary 66
Cunnane, Kelly 175
Cunningham, Bob
  See May, Julian
Cunningham, Captain Frank
  See Glick, Carl (Cannon)
Cunningham, Cathy
  See Cunningham, Chet
Cunningham, Chet 1928- 23
Cunningham, Dale S(peers) 1932- 11
Cunningham, Dru 91
Cunningham, E. V.
  See Fast, Howard
Cunningham, Julia (Woolfolk) 1916- 132
  Earlier sketches in SATA 1, 26
  See also SAAS 2
Cunningham, Lawrence J. 1943- 125
Cunningham, Virginia
  See Holmgren, Virginia C(unningham)
Curiae, Amicus
  See Fuller, Edmund (Maybank)
Curie, Eve 1904-2007 1
  Obituary 188
Curlee, Lynn 1947- 190
  Earlier sketches in SATA 98, 141
Curley, Daniel 1918-1988 23
  Obituary 61
Curley, Marianne 1959- 175
  Earlier sketch in SATA 131
Currie, Robin 1948- 120
Currie, Stephen 1960- 132
  Earlier sketch in SATA 82
Curry, Ann (Gabrielle) 1934- 72
Curry, Jane L(ouise) 1932- 138
  Autobiography Feature 138
  Earlier sketches in SATA 1, 52, 90
  See also CLR 31
  See also SAAS 6
Curry, Peggy Simson 1911-1987 8
  Obituary 50

Curry, Tom 185
Curtis, Bruce (Richard) 1944- 30
Curtis, Chara M(ahar) 1950- 78
Curtis, Christopher Paul 1954(?)- 187
  Earlier sketches in SATA 93, 140
  See also CLR 68
Curtis, Gavin 1965- 107
Curtis, Jamie Lee 1958- 144
  Earlier sketch in SATA 95
  See also CLR 88
Curtis, Jennifer Keats 185
Curtis, Marci 160
Curtis, Patricia 1921- 101
  Earlier sketch in SATA 23
Curtis, Peter
  See Lofts, Norah (Robinson)
Curtis, Philip (Delacourt) 1920- 62
Curtis, Richard (Alan) 1937- 29
Curtis, Richard Hale
  See Deming, Richard
  and Levinson, Leonard
  and Rothweiler, Paul Roger
Curtis, Wade
  See Pournelle, Jerry (Eugene)
Curtiss, A(rlene) B. 1934- 90
Cusack, Margaret 1945- 58
Cushman, Doug 1953- 157
  Earlier sketches in SATA 65, 101
Cushman, Jerome 2
Cushman, Karen 1941- 147
  Earlier sketch in SATA 89
  See also CLR 55
Cusick, Richie Tankersley 1952- 140
  Earlier sketch in SATA 67
Cutchen, Billye Walker 1930- 15
Cutchins, Judy 1947- 59
Cutler, Daniel S(olomon) 1951- 78
Cutler, Ebbitt 1923- 9
Cutler, Ivor 1923-2006 24
  Obituary 174
Cutler, Jane 1936- 162
  Earlier sketches in SATA 75, 118
Cutler, May Ebbitt
  See Cutler, Ebbitt
Cutler, Samuel
  See Folsom, Franklin (Brewster)
Cutlip, Kimbra L(eigh-Ann) 1964- 128
Cutrate, Joe
  See Spiegelman, Art
Cutt, W(illiam) Towrie 1898-1981 16
  Obituary 85
Cuyler, Margery S(tuyvesant) 1948- 156
  Earlier sketches in SATA 39, 99
Cuyler, Stephen
  See Bates, Barbara S(nedeker)
Cyrus, Kurt 1954- 179
  Earlier sketch in SATA 132
Czernecki, Stefan 1946- 178

D

Dabba Smith, Frank 174
Dabcovich, Lydia 99
  Brief entry 47
  Earlier sketch in SATA 58
Dace, Dolores B(oelens) 1929- 89
Da Costa, Deborah 193
Dadey, Debbie 1959- 136
  Earlier sketch in SATA 73
Dahl, Borghild (Margarethe) 1890-1984 7
  Obituary 37
Dahl, Roald 1916-1990 73
  Obituary 65
  Earlier sketches in SATA 1, 26
  See also CLR 111
Dahlberg, Maurine F. 1951- 171
Dahlstedt, Marden (Stewart) 1921-1983 8
  Obituary 110
Dain, Martin J. 1924-2000 35

Dakos, Kalli 1950- 115
Earlier sketch in SATA 80
Dale, Anna 1971- 170
Dale, Gary
See Reece, Colleen L.
Dale, George E.
See Asimov, Isaac
Dale, Jack
See Holliday, Joseph
Dale, Kim 1957- 123
Dale, Margaret J(essy) Miller 1911- 39
Dale, Mitzi
See Hemstock, Gillian
Dale, Norman
See Denny, Norman (George)
Dale, Penny 1954- 151
Earlier sketch in SATA 70
Daley, Michael J. 170
Dalgliesh, Alice 1893-1979 17
Obituary 21
See also CLR 62
Dalkey, Kara 1953- 132
Dalkey, Kara Mia
See Dalkey, Kara
Dallas, Ruth 1919- 86
Dalmas, John
See Jones, John R(obert)
Dalton, Alene
See Chapin, Alene Olsen Dalton
Dalton, Annie 1948- 140
Earlier sketch in SATA 40
Dalton, Kit
See Cunningham, Chet
Dalton, Pamela
See Johnson, Pamela
Dalton, Sean
See Chester, Deborah
Dalton, Sheila 1949- 108
Daly, Jim
See Stratemeyer, Edward L.
Daly, Jude 1951- 177
Daly, Kathleen N(orah) 124
Brief entry 37
Daly, Maureen 1921-2006 129
Obituary 176
Earlier sketch in SATA 2
See also CLR 96
See also SAAS 1
Daly, Nicholas 1946- 164
Earlier sketches in SATA 37, 76, 114
See also CLR 41
See Daly, Niki
Daly, Niki
See SAAS 21
See Daly, Nicholas
D'Amato, Alex 1919- 20
D'Amato, Janet (Potter) 1925- 9
Damerow, Gail 1944- 83
Damerow, Gail Jane
See Damerow, Gail
D'Amico, Carmela 170
D'Amico, Steve 170
Damrell, Liz 1956- 77
Damrosch, Helen
See Tee-Van, Helen Damrosch
Dana, Barbara 1940- 22
Dana, Richard Henry, Jr. 1815-1882 26
Danachair, Caoimhin O
See Danaher, Kevin
Danaher, Kevin 1913-2002 22
Danakas, John 1963- 94
Dandi
See Mackall, Dandi Daley
D'Andrea, Kate
See Steiner, Barbara A(nnette)
Dangerfield, Balfour
See McCloskey, (John) Robert
Daniel, Alan 1939- 76
Brief entry 53
Daniel, Anita 1893(?)-1978 23
Obituary 24

Daniel, Anne
See Steiner, Barbara A(nnette)
Daniel, Becky 1947- 56
Daniel, Claire 1949- 164
Daniel, Colin
See Windsor, Patricia
Daniel, Hawthorne 1890- 8
Daniel, (Donna) Lee 1944- 76
Daniel, Rebecca
See Daniel, Becky
Daniels, Guy 1919-1989 11
Obituary 62
Daniels, Lucy
See Oldfield, Jenny
Daniels, Max
See Gellis, Roberta
Daniels, Olga
See Sinclair, Olga
Daniels, Patricia 1955- 93
Daniels, Zoe
See Laux, Constance
Dank, Gloria Rand 1955- 56
Brief entry 46
Dank, Leonard D(ewey) 1929- 44
Dank, Milton 1920- 31
Dann, Max 1955- 62
Danneberg, Julie 1958- 173
Dantz, William R.
See Philbrick, Rodman
Danziger, Paula 1944-2004 149
Brief entry 30
Obituary 155
Earlier sketches in SATA 36, 63, 102
See also CLR 20
Darby, Gene Kegley
See Darby, Jean (Kegley)
Darby, J. N.
See Govan, (Mary) Christine Noble
Darby, Jean (Kegley) 1921- 68
Darby, Patricia (Paulsen) 14
Darby, Ray(mond) 1912-1982 7
d'Arcy, Willard
See Cox, William R(obert)
Dare, Geena
See McNicoll, Sylvia (Marilyn)
Darian, Shea 1959- 97
Daringer, Helen Fern 1892-1986 1
Darke, Marjorie 1929- 87
Earlier sketch in SATA 16
Darley, F(elix) O(ctavius) C(arr)
1822-1888 35
Darling, David J. 1953- 60
Brief entry 44
Darling, Kathy
See Darling, Mary Kathleen
Darling, Lois (MacIntyre) 1917-1989 3
Obituary 64
Darling, Louis, (Jr.) 1916-1970 3
Obituary 23
Darling, Mary Kathleen 1943- 124
Earlier sketches in SATA 9, 79
Darling, Sandra Louise Woodward
See Day, Alexandra
Darnell, K(athryn) L(ynne) 1955- 150
Darroll, Sally
See Odgers, Sally Farrell
Darrow, Sharon 181
Darrow, Whitney, (Jr.) 1909-1999 13
Obituary 115
Darwin, Len
See Darwin, Leonard
Darwin, Leonard 1916- 24
Dasent, Sir George Webbe 1817-1896 62
Brief entry 29
Dash, Joan 1925- 142
Daskam, Josephine Dodge
See Bacon, Josephine Dodge (Daskam)
D'ath, Justin 1953- 174
Earlier sketch in SATA 106
Dauer, Rosamond 1934- 23
Daugherty, Charles Michael 1914- 16

Daugherty, James (Henry) 1889-1974 13
See also CLR 78
Daugherty, Richard D(eo) 1922- 35
Daugherty, Sonia Medwedeff (?)-1971
Obituary 27
d'Aulaire, Edgar Parin 1898-1986 66
Obituary 47
Earlier sketch in SATA 5
See also CLR 21
d'Aulaire, Ingri (Mortenson Parin)
1904-1980 66
Obituary 24
Earlier sketch in SATA 5
See also CLR 21
Dave, Dave
See Berg, David
Daveluy, Paule Cloutier 1919- 11
Davenier, Christine 1961- 179
Earlier sketch in SATA 127
Davenport, John 1960- 156
Daves, Michael 1938- 40
David, A. R.
See David, A(nn) Rosalie
David, A(nn) Rosalie 1946- 103
David, Jonathan
See Ames, Lee J(udah)
David, Lawrence 1963- 165
Earlier sketch in SATA 111
David, Peter 1956- 72
David, Peter Allen
See David, Peter
David, Rosalie
See David, A(nn) Rosalie
Davidson, Alice Joyce 1932- 54
Brief entry 45
Davidson, Basil 1914- 13
Davidson, (Marie) Diane 1924- 91
Davidson, Hugh
See Hamilton, Edmond
Davidson, Jessica 1915-1986 5
Davidson, Judith 1953- 40
Davidson, Lionel 1922- 87
Davidson, Margaret 1936- 5
Davidson, Marion
See Garis, Howard R(oger)
Davidson, Mary R. 1885-1973 9
Davidson, Mary S. 1940- 61
Davidson, Mickie
See Davidson, Margaret
Davidson, Nicole
See Jensen, Kathryn
Davidson, R.
See Davidson, Raymond
Davidson, Raymond 1926- 32
Davidson, Rosalie 1921- 23
Davie, Helen K(ay) 1952- 148
Earlier sketch in SATA 77
Davies, Andrew (Wynford) 1936- 27
Davies, Bettilu D(onna) 1942- 33
Davies, Hunter 1936- 55
Brief entry 45
Davies, Jacqueline 1962- 186
Earlier sketch in SATA 155
Davies, Joan 1934- 50
Brief entry 47
Davies, Nicola 1958- 182
Earlier sketches in SATA 99, 150
Davies, Peter J(oseph) 1937- 52
Davies, Sumiko 1942- 46
Davis, (A.) Aubrey 1949- 153
Davis, Barbara Steincrohn
See Davis, Maggie S.
Davis, Bette J. 1923- 15
Davis, Burke 1913- 4
Davis, Christopher 1928- 6
Davis, D(elbert) Dwight 1908-1965 33
Davis, Daniel S(heldon) 1936- 12
Davis, David R. 1948- 106
Davis, Donald 1944- 169
Earlier sketch in SATA 93

Davis, Donald D.
See Davis, Donald
Davis, Emma
See Davis, Maggie S.
Davis, Gibbs 1953- 102
Brief entry 41
Earlier sketch in SATA 46
Davis, Grania 1943- 88
Brief entry 50
Davis, H(arold) L(enoir) 1896-1960 114
Davis, Hubert J(ackson) 1904-1997 31
Davis, James Robert 1945- 32
See Davis, Jim
Davis, Jenny 1953- 74
Davis, Jim
See Davis, James Robert
Davis, Julia 1900(?)-1993 6
Obituary 75
Davis, Karen (Elizabeth) 1944- 109
Davis, Katie 1959(?)- 152
Davis, Lambert 176
Davis, Leslie
See Guccione, Leslie Davis
Davis, Louise Littleton 1921- 25
Davis, Maggie S. 1943- 57
Davis, Marguerite 1889- 34
Davis, Mary L(ee) 1935- 9
Davis, Mary Octavia 1901-1976 6
Davis, Nelle 1958- 73
Davis, Ossie 1917-2005 81
See also CLR 56
Davis, Paxton 1925-1994 16
Davis, Robert 1881-1949
See YABC 1
Davis, Robin W(orks) 1962- 87
Davis, Russell Gerard 1922- 3
Davis, Tim(othy N.) 1957- 94
Davis, Verne Theodore 1889-1973 6
Davis, Yvonne 1927- 115
Davol, Marguerite W. 1928- 146
Earlier sketch in SATA 82
DaVolls, Andy (P.) 1967- 85
DaVolls, Linda 1966- 85
Davys, Sarah
See Manning, Rosemary (Joy)
Dawes, Claiborne 1935- 111
Dawson, Elmer A. 67
Earlier sketch in SATA 1
Dawson, Imogen (Zoe) 1948- 126
Earlier sketch in SATA 90
Dawson, Mary 1919- 11
Day, A(rthur) Grove 1904-1994 59
Day, Alexandra 1941- 169
Earlier sketches in SATA 67, 97
See also CLR 22
See also SAAS 19
Day, Beth (Feagles) 1924- 33
Day, Donna
See Asay, Donna Day
Day, Edward C. 1932- 72
Day, Jon 1936(?)- 79
Day, Karen 187
Day, Larry 1956- 181
Day, Nancy 1953- 140
Day, Nancy Raines 1951- 148
Earlier sketch in SATA 93
Day, Shirley 1962- 94
Day, Thomas 1748-1789
See YABC 1
Day, Trevor 1955- 124
Dazey, Agnes J(ohnston) 2
Dazey, Frank M. 2
Deacon, Alexis 1978- 139
Deacon, Eileen
See Geipel, Eileen
Deacon, Richard
See McCormick, (George) Donald (King)
Deadman, Ronald 1919-1988(?)
Obituary 56
Deak, Erzsi 1959- 152
Dean, Anabel 1915- 12

Dean, Carolee 1962- 148
Dean, David 1976- 192
Dean, Karen Strickler 1923- 49
Dean, Ruth (Brigham) 1947- 145
Dean, Zoey
See Bennett, Cherie
de Angeli, Marguerite (Lofft) 1889-1987 ... 100
Obituary 51
Earlier sketches in SATA 1, 27
See also CLR 1
Deans, Sis Boulos 1955- 136
Earlier sketch in SATA 78
DeArmand, Frances Ullmann 1904(?)-1984 . 10
Obituary 38
DeArmond, Dale 1914- 70
DeArmond, Dale Burlison
See DeArmond, Dale
Deary, Terry 1946- 171
Brief entry 41
Earlier sketches in SATA 51, 101
Deaver, Julie Reece 1953- 68
de Banke, Cecile 1889-1965 11
De Bello, Rosario 1923- 89
Debon, Nicolas 186
Earlier sketch in SATA 151
de Bono, Edward 1933- 66
de Brissac, Malcolm
See Dickinson, Peter (Malcolm de Brissac)
de Brunhoff, Jean
See Brunhoff, Jean de
De Brunhoff, Laurent
See Brunhoff, Laurent de
De Bruyn, Monica G. 1952- 13
De Bruyn, Monica Jean Grembowicz
See De Bruyn, Monica G.
DeBry, Roger K. 1942- 91
de Camp, Catherine Crook 1907-2000 83
Earlier sketch in SATA 12
de Camp, L(yon) Sprague 1907-2000 83
Earlier sketch in SATA 9
DeCandido, Keith R.A. 112
Dechausay, Sonia E. 94
Decker, C.B. 172
Decker, Cynthia B.
See Decker, C.B.
Decker, Duane 1910-1964 5
DeClements, Barthe (Faith) 1920- 131
Earlier sketches in SATA 35, 71
See also CLR 23
de Conte, Sieur Louis
See Clemens, Samuel Langhorne
Dedman, Stephen 108
Dee, Catherine 1964- 138
Dee, Ruby 77
See Wallace, Ruby Ann
Deedy, John 1923- 24
Deegan, Paul Joseph 1937- 48
Brief entry 38
Deem, James M. 1950- 191
Autobiography Feature 191
Earlier sketches in SATA 75, 134
Deem, James Morgan
See Deem, James M.
Deeter, Catherine 1947- 137
DeFelice, Cynthia 1951- 165
Earlier sketches in SATA 79, 121
DeFelice, Cynthia C.
See DeFelice, Cynthia
Defoe, Daniel 1660(?)-1731 22
See also CLR 61
DeFord, Deborah H. 123
deFrance, Anthony
See DiFranco, Anthony (Mario)
Degen, Bruce 1945- 147
Brief entry 47
Earlier sketches in SATA 57, 97
DeGering, Etta (Belle) Fowler 1898-1996 7
De Goldi, Kate
See De Goldi, Kathleen Domenica
De Goldi, Kathleen Domenica 1959- 123
de Goursac, Olivier 1959- 184

De Grazia, Ted 39
See De Grazia, Ettore
deGroat, Diane 1947- 169
Earlier sketches in SATA 31, 90
deGros, J. H.
See Villiard, Paul
de Grummond, Lena Young 62
Earlier sketch in SATA 6
de Hamel, Joan Littledale 1924- 86
De Haven, Tom 1949- 72
de Hugo, Pierre
See Brackers de Hugo, Pierre
Deiss, Joseph Jay 1915- 12
de Jenkins, Lyll Becerra 1925-1997 102
DeJong, David C(ornel) 1905-1967 10
de Jong, Dola 1911-2003 7
Obituary 149
See de Jong, Dorothea Rosalie
DeJong, Meindert 1906-1991 2
Obituary 68
See also CLR 73
DeJonge, Joanne E. 1943- 56
Deka, Connie
See Laux, Constance
de Kay, Ormonde (Jr.) 1923-1998 7
Obituary 106
de Kiriline, Louise
See Lawrence, Louise de Kiriline
Dekker, Carl
See Laffin, John (Alfred Charles)
and Lynds, Dennis
deKruif, Paul (Henry) 1890-1971 50
Earlier sketch in SATA 5
Delacre, Lulu 1957- 156
Earlier sketch in SATA 36
DeLaCroix, Alice 1940- 75
de la Cruz, Melissa 1971- 179
De la Garza, Phyllis 1942- 169
De Lage, Ida 1918- 11
de la Mare, Walter (John) 1873-1956 16
See also CLR 23
Delaney, Harry 1932- 3
Delaney, Joseph 1945- 172
Delaney, M.C.
See Delaney, Michael
Delaney, Michael 1955- 180
Earlier sketch in SATA 96
Delaney, Michael Clark
See Delaney, Michael
Delaney, Ned 28
See Delaney, Thomas Nicholas III
Delano, Hugh 1933- 20
Delany, Samuel R., Jr. 1942- 92
Delany, Samuel Ray
See Delany, Samuel R., Jr.
De La Ramee, Marie Louise 1839-1908 20
See Ouida
de la Roche, Mazo 1879-1961 64
De La Roche Saint Andre, Anne 1950- 75
Delaune, (Jewel) Lynn (de Grummond) 7
DeLaurentis, Louise Budde 1920- 12
del Barco, Lucy Salamanca 1900(?)-1989
Obituary 64
Delderfield, Eric R(aymond) 1909-1995 14
Delderfield, Ronald Frederick 1912-1972 20
DeLeeuw, Adele (Louise) 1899-1988 30
Obituary 56
Earlier sketch in SATA 1
De Leon, Nephtali 1945- 97
Delessert, Etienne 1941- 179
Brief entry 27
Earlier sketches in SATA 46, 130
See also CLR 81
Delgado, James P. 1958- 122
de Lint, Charles 1951- 157
Earlier sketch in SATA 115
de Lint, Charles Henri Diederick Hofsmit
See de Lint, Charles
Delmar, Roy
See Wexler, Jerome (LeRoy)

Deloria, Vine, Jr. 1933-2005 .... *21*
   Obituary *171*
Deloria, Vine Victor, Jr.
   See Deloria, Vine, Jr.
del Rey, Lester 1915-1993 .... *22*
   Obituary *76*
Delrio, Martin
   See Doyle, Debra
   and Macdonald, James D.
Delton, Judy 1931-2001 .... *77*
   Obituary *130*
   Earlier sketch in SATA *14*
   See also SAAS *9*
Delulio, John 1938- *15*
Delving, Michael
   See Williams, Jay
de Marcken, Gail *186*
Demarest, Chris L. 1951- *175*
   Brief entry *44*
   Earlier sketches in SATA *45, 82, 128*
Demarest, Christopher Lynn
   See Demarest, Chris L.
Demarest, Doug
   See Barker, Will
De Mari, Silvana 1953- *193*
Demas, Corinne *131*
   See Bliss, Corinne Demas
Demas, Vida 1927- *9*
DeMatteis, J.M. 1953- *180*
DeMatteis, John Marc
   See DeMatteis, J.M.
De Mejo, Oscar 1911-1992 .... *40*
Demers, Dominique 1956- *177*
de Messieres, Nicole 1930- *39*
Demi
   See Hitz, Demi
Demijohn, Thom
   See Disch, Thomas M.
   and Sladek, John
Deming, Richard 1915-1983 .... *24*
   See Queen, Ellery
Deming, Sarah *191*
de Monfreid, Dorothee 1973- *189*
Demuth, Patricia Brennan 1948- *84*
   Brief entry *51*
Dendinger, Roger E. 1952- *158*
Denenberg, Barry *175*
Dengler, Marianna (Herron) 1935- *103*
Dengler, Sandy 1939- *54*
   Brief entry *40*
Denim, Sue
   See Pilkey, Dav
Denise, Christopher 1968- *193*
   Earlier sketch in SATA *147*
Denman, K.L. 1957- *186*
Denmark, Harrison
   See Zelazny, Roger
Dennard, Deborah 1953- *136*
   Earlier sketch in SATA *78*
Denney, Diana 1910-2000 .... *25*
   Obituary *120*
Dennis, Morgan 1891(?)-1960 .... *18*
Dennis, Wesley 1903-1966 .... *18*
Denniston, Elinore 1900-1978
   Obituary *24*
Denny, Norman (George) 1901-1982 .... *43*
Denslow, Sharon Phillips 1947- *142*
   Earlier sketch in SATA *68*
Denslow, W(illiam) W(allace) 1856-1915 .... *16*
   See also CLR *15*
Dent, Grace 1973- *187*
Denton, Kady MacDonald *181*
   Earlier sketches in SATA *66, 110*
   See also CLR *71*
Denton, Terry 1950- *186*
Denver, Walt
   See Redding, Robert Hull
   and Sherman, Jory (Tecumseh)
Denzel, Justin F(rancis) 1917-1999 .... *46*
   Brief entry *38*

Denzer, Ann Wiseman
   See Wiseman, Ann (Sayre)
DePalma, Mary Newell 1961- *185*
   Earlier sketch in SATA *139*
dePaola, Thomas Anthony 1934- *155*
   Earlier sketches in SATA *11, 59, 108*
   See dePaola, Tomie
dePaola, Tomie
   See CLR *81*
   See also SAAS *15*
   See dePaola, Thomas Anthony
deParrie, Paul 1949- *74*
DePauw, Linda Grant 1940- *24*
DeRan, David 1946- *76*
Derby, Ken 1956- *181*
Derby, Kenneth R.
   See Derby, Ken
Derby, Pat 1942- *172*
Derby, Sally 1934- *189*
   Earlier sketches in SATA *89, 132*
de Regniers, Beatrice Schenk
   (Freedman) 1914-2000 .... *68*
   Obituary *123*
   Earlier sketch in SATA *2*
   See also SAAS *6*
Dereske, Jo 1947- *72*
Derleth, August (William) 1909-1971 .... *5*
Derman, Martha (Winn) *74*
Derman, Sarah Audrey 1915- *11*
DeRoberts, Lyndon
   See Silverstein, Robert Alan
de Roo, Anne Louise 1931-1997 .... *84*
   Earlier sketch in SATA *25*
   See also CLR *63*
deRosa, Dee *70*
Derrick, Lionel
   See Cunningham, Chet
Derrickson, Jim 1959- *141*
Derry Down Derry
   See Lear, Edward
Dervaux, Isabelle 1961- *106*
Derwent, Lavinia *14*
Desai, Anita 1937- *126*
   Earlier sketch in SATA *63*
DeSaix, Deborah Durland *188*
De Saulles, Tony 1958- *119*
Desbarats, Peter 1933- *39*
de Selincourt, Aubrey 1894-1962 .... *14*
Deshpande, Chris 1950- *69*
Desimini, Lisa 1964- *148*
   Earlier sketch in SATA *86*
Desjarlais, John 1953- *71*
Desjarlais, John J.
   See Desjarlais, John
Desmoinaux, Christel 1967- *149*
   Earlier sketch in SATA *103*
Desmond, Adrian J(ohn) 1947- *51*
Desmond, Alice Curtis 1897-1990 .... *8*
Desnoettes, Caroline *183*
DeSpain, Pleasant 1943- *87*
Desputeaux, Helene 1959- *95*
Dessen, Sarah 1970- *172*
   Earlier sketch in SATA *120*
Detine, Padre
   See Olsen, Ib Spang
de Trevino, Elizabeth B.
   See Trevino, Elizabeth B(orton) de
de Trevino, Elizabeth Borton
   See Trevino, Elizabeth B(orton) de
Detwiler, Susan Dill 1956- *58*
Deuker, Carl 1950- *150*
   Earlier sketch in SATA *82*
Deutsch, Babette 1895-1982 .... *1*
   Obituary *33*
Deutsch, Eva Costabel
   See Costabel, Eva Deutsch
Deutsch, Helen 1906-1992 .... *76*
Deutsch, Kurt
   See Singer, Kurt D.
De Valera, Sinead 1879(?)-1975
   Obituary *30*

Devaney, John 1926-1994 .... *12*
de Varennes, Monique 1947- *168*
de Varona, Frank J. 1943- *83*
Devereux, Frederick L(eonard), Jr.
   1914-1993 .... *9*
Devi, Nila
   See Woody, Regina Jones
deVinck, Christopher 1951- *85*
DeVito, Cara 1956- *80*
Devlin, Dorothy Wende
   See Devlin, Wende
Devlin, Harry 1918-2001 .... *136*
   Earlier sketches in SATA *11, 74*
Devlin, Wende 1918-2002 .... *74*
   Earlier sketch in SATA *11*
Devon, Paddie 1953- *92*
Devons, Sonia 1974- *72*
Devorah-Leah *111*
de Vos, Gail 1949- *122*
DeVries, Douglas 1933- *122*
De Waard, E(lliott) John 1935- *7*
Dewan, Ted 1961- *157*
   Earlier sketch in SATA *108*
Dewdney, Anna *184*
Dewdney, Selwyn (Hanington)
   1909-1979 .... *64*
DeWeese, Gene
   See DeWeese, Thomas Eugene
DeWeese, Jean
   See DeWeese, Thomas Eugene
DeWeese, Thomas Eugene 1934- *46*
   Brief entry *45*
Dewey, Ariane 1937- *178*
   Earlier sketches in SATA *7, 109*
Dewey, Jennifer (Owings) 1941- *103*
   Brief entry *48*
   Earlier sketch in SATA *58*
Dewey, Kenneth Francis 1940- *39*
De Wire, Elinor 1953- *180*
deWit, Dorothy (May Knowles)
   1916-1980 .... *39*
   Obituary *28*
Dexter, Alison 1966- *125*
Dexter, John
   See Bradley, Marion Zimmer
Deyneka, Anita 1943- *24*
Deyrup, Astrith Johnson 1923- *24*
Dhami, Narinder 1958- *152*
Dhondy, Farrukh 1944- *152*
   Earlier sketch in SATA *65*
   See also CLR *41*
Diakite, Baba Wague 1961- *174*
Diakite, Penda 1993(?)- *174*
Diamond, Arthur 1957- *76*
Diamond, Donna 1950- *69*
   Brief entry *30*
   Earlier sketch in SATA *35*
Diamond, Petra
   See Sachs, Judith
Diamond, Rebecca
   See Sachs, Judith
Dias, Earl Joseph 1916- *41*
Dias, Ron 1937- *71*
Diaz, David 1959(?)- *189*
   Earlier sketches in SATA *96, 150*
   See also CLR *65*
Dibley, Glin *188*
DiCamillo, Kate 1964- *163*
   Earlier sketch in SATA *121*
   See also CLR *117*
Di Certo, J(oseph) J(ohn) 1933- *60*
DiCianni, Ron 1952- *107*
Dick, Trella Lamson 1889-1974 .... *9*
Dickens, Charles (John Huffam)
   1812-1870 .... *15*
   See also CLR *95*
Dickens, Frank
   See Huline-Dickens, Frank William
Dickens, Monica (Enid) 1915-1992 .... *4*
   Obituary *74*

Dickerson, Roy Ernest 1886-1965
  Obituary 26
Dickinson, Emily (Elizabeth) 1830-1886 29
Dickinson, Mary 1949- 48
  Brief entry 41
Dickinson, Mary-Anne
  See Rodda, Emily
Dickinson, Peter (Malcolm de Brissac)
  1927- 150
  Earlier sketches in SATA *5, 62, 95*
  See also CLR *125*
Dickinson, Susan 1931- 8
Dickinson, Terence 1943- 102
Dickinson, W(illiam) Croft 1897-1963 13
Dickson, Gordon R. 1923-2001 77
Dickson, Gordon Rupert
  See Dickson, Gordon R.
Dickson, Helen
  See Reynolds, Helen Mary Greenwood Campbell
Dickson, Naida 1916- 8
Diehn, Gwen 1943- 80
Dierssen, Andreas 1962- 190
Dieterich, Michele M. 1962- 78
Dietz, David H(enry) 1897-1984 10
  Obituary 41
Dietz, Lew 1907-1997 11
  Obituary 95
Diffily, Deborah 159
Di Fiori, Larry
  See Di Fiori, Lawrence
Di Fiori, Lawrence 1934- 130
DiFranco, Anthony (Mario) 1945- 42
Digby, Anne 1935- 72
Digges, Jeremiah
  See Berger, Josef
Digman, Kristina 1959- 176
D'Ignazio, Fred(erick) 1949- 39
  Brief entry 35
Di Grazia, Thomas (?)-1983 32
Dikty, Julian May
  See May, Julian
Dillard, Annie 1945- 140
  Earlier sketch in SATA *10*
Dillard, Kristine 1964- 113
Dillard, Polly Hargis 1916- 24
Diller, Harriett 1953- 78
Dillon, Barbara 1927- 44
  Brief entry 39
Dillon, Diane (Claire) 1933- 106
  Earlier sketches in SATA *15, 51*
  See also CLR *44*
Dillon, Eilis 1920-1994 74
  Autobiography Feature 105
  Obituary 83
  Earlier sketch in SATA *2*
  See also CLR *26*
Dillon, Jana (a pseudonym) 1952- 117
Dillon, Leo 1933- 106
  Earlier sketches in SATA *15, 51*
  See also CLR *44*
Dillon, Sharon Saseen
  See Saseen, Sharon (Dillon)
Dils, Tracey E. 1958- 83
Dilson, Jesse 1914-1988 24
Dinan, Carolyn 59
  Brief entry 47
Dines, Carol 1956- 175
Dines, (Harry) Glen 1925-1996 7
Dinesen, Isak
  See Blixen, Karen (Christentze Dinesen)
Dinessi, Alex
  See Schembri, Jim
Dinneen, Betty 1929- 61
Dinnerstein, Harvey 1928- 42
Dinsdale, Tim(othy Kay) 1924-1987 11
Diop, Birago (Ismael) 1906-1989
  Obituary 64
Diouf, Sylviane A. 168
Diouf, Sylviane Anna
  See Diouf, Sylviane A.

DiPucchio, Kelly 159
Dirk
  See Gringhuis, Richard H.
Dirks, Wilhelmina 1916- 59
Dirks, Willy
  See Dirks, Wilhelmina
Dirtmeister
  See Tomecek, Steve
DiSalvo, DyAnne 1960- 144
  Earlier sketch in SATA *59*
DiSalvo-Ryan, DyAnne
  See DiSalvo, DyAnne
Disch, Thomas M. 1940-2008 92
  See also CLR *18*
  See also SAAS *15*
  See Disch, Tom
Disch, Thomas Michael
  See Disch, Thomas M.
Disch, Tom
  See Disch, Thomas M.
Disher, Garry 1949- 125
  Earlier sketch in SATA *81*
Disney, Walt(er Elias) 1901-1966 28
  Brief entry 27
Ditchfield, Christin 1973- 189
DiTerlizzi, Tony 1969- 154
Divakaruni, Chitra Banerjee 1956- 160
Di Valentin, Maria (Amelia) Messuri
  1911-1985 7
Divine, Arthur Durham 1904-1987
  Obituary 52
Divine, David
  See Divine, Arthur Durham
Dixon, Ann R. 1954- 127
  Earlier sketch in SATA *77*
Dixon, Ann Renee
  See Dixon, Ann R.
Dixon, Dougal 1947- 190
  Earlier sketches in SATA *45, 127*
Dixon, Franklin W. 100
  Earlier sketches in SATA *1, 67*
  See also CLR *61*
  See Barrett, Neal, Jr.
  and Goulart, Ron(ald Joseph)
  and Lantz, Francess L(in)
  and Lerangis, Peter
  and McFarlane, Leslie (Charles)
  and Stanley, George Edward
  and Stratemeyer, Edward L.
Dixon, Jeanne 1936- 31
Dixon, Paige
  See Corcoran, Barbara (Asenath)
Dixon, Peter L(ee) 1931- 6
Dixon, Rachel 1952- 74
Djoleto, (Solomon Alexander) Amu 1929- ... 80
d'lacey, Chris 1949- 165
Doak, Annie
  See Dillard, Annie
Doane, Pelagie 1906-1966 7
Dobell, I(sabel) M(arian) B(arclay)
  1909-1998 11
Dobie, J(ames) Frank 1888-1964 43
Dobkin, Alexander 1908-1975
  Obituary 30
Dobler, Lavinia G. 1910- 6
Dobrin, Arnold 1928- 4
Dobson, Jill 1969- 140
Dobson, Julia 1941- 48
Dobson, Mary 1954- 117
Dockery, Wallene T. 1941- 27
Dockray, Tracy 1962- 139
Dockrey, Karen 1955- 103
Doctor, Bernard
  See Doctor, Bernard Aquina
Doctor, Bernard Aquina 1950- 81
Doctor X
  See Nourse, Alan E(dward)
Dodd, Ed(ward Benton) 1902-1991 4
  Obituary 68

Dodd, Lynley (Stuart) 1941- 132
  Earlier sketches in SATA *35, 86*
  See also CLR *62*
Dodd, Marty 1921- 142
Dodd, Quentin 1972- 137
Dodds, Bill 1952- 78
Dodds, Dayle Ann 1952- 150
  Earlier sketch in SATA *75*
Doder, Joshua
  See Lacey, Josh
Dodge, Bertha S(anford) 1902-1995 8
Dodge, Fremont
  See Grimes, Lee
Dodge, Gil
  See Hano, Arnold
Dodge, Mary (Elizabeth) Mapes
  1831(?)-1905 100
  Earlier sketch in SATA *21*
  See also CLR *62*
Dodgson, Charles L(utwidge) 1832-1898 ... 100
  See also YABC *2*
  See also CLR *2*
  See Carroll, Lewis
Dodson, Kenneth MacKenzie 1907-1999 11
Dodson, Susan 1941- 50
  Brief entry 40
Dogyear, Drew
  See Gorey, Edward (St. John)
Doherty, Berlie 1943- 111
  Earlier sketch in SATA *72*
  See also CLR *21*
  See also SAAS *16*
Doherty, Charles Hugh 1913- 6
Doherty, Craig A. 1951- 169
  Earlier sketch in SATA *83*
Doherty, Katherine M(ann) 1951- 83
Doherty, Kieran 1945- 164
Dokey, Cameron 1956- 97
Dolan, Edward F(rancis), Jr. 1924- 94
  Brief entry 31
  Earlier sketch in SATA *45*
Dolan, Ellen M(eara) 1929-1998 88
Dolan, Sean J. 1958- 74
Dolce, J. Ellen 1948- 75
Dolch, Edward William 1889-1961 50
Dolch, Marguerite Pierce 1891-1978 50
Dollar, Diane (Hills) 1933- 57
Dolson, Hildegarde 5
  See Lockridge, Hildegarde (Dolson)
Domanska, Janina 1913(?)-1995 68
  Obituary 84
  Earlier sketch in SATA *6*
  See also CLR *40*
  See also SAAS *18*
Dominguez, Angel 1953- 76
Domino, John
  See Averill, Esther (Holden)
Domjan, Joseph (Spiri) 1907-1992 25
Domm, Jeffrey C. 1958- 84
Donahue, Dorothy 178
Donald, Rhonda Lucas 1962- 147
Donalds, Gordon
  See Shirreffs, Gordon D(onald)
Donaldson, Bryna
  See Stevens, Bryna
Donaldson, Gordon 1913-1993 64
  Obituary 76
Donaldson, Joan 1953- 78
Donaldson, Julia 1948- 180
  Earlier sketches in SATA *82, 132*
Donaldson, Stephen R. 1947- 121
Donaldson, Stephen Reeder
  See Donaldson, Stephen R.
Doner, Kim 1955- 91
Doney, Todd L. W. 1959- 104
Donkin, Nance (Clare) 1915- 95
Donna, Natalie 1934-1979 9
Donnelly, Elfie 1950-
  See CLR *104*
Donnelly, Jennifer 1963- 154
Donnelly, Matt 1972- 148

Donnio, Sylviane *188*
Donoghue, Emma 1969- *101*
Donoughue, Carol 1935- *139*
Donovan, Frank (Robert) 1906-1975
  Obituary *30*
Donovan, John 1928-1992 .... *72*
  Brief entry *29*
  See also CLR *3*
Donovan, Mary Lee 1961- *86*
Donovan, William
  See Berkebile, Fred D(onovan)
Donze, Mary Terese 1911- *89*
Doob, Leonard W(illiam) 1909-2000 .... *8*
Dooley, Norah 1953- *74*
Dooling, Michael 1958- *105*
Dor, Ana
  See Ceder, Georgiana Dorcas
Dore, (Louis Christophe Paul) Gustave
  1832-1883 .... *19*
Doremus, Robert 1913- *30*
Doren, Marion (Walker) 1928- *57*
Dorenkamp, Michelle 1957- *89*
Dorflinger, Carolyn 1953- *91*
Dorfman, Joaquin 1979- *180*
Dorfman, Joaquin Emiliano
  See Dorfman, Joaquin
Dorian, Edith M(cEwen) 1900-1983 .... *5*
Dorian, Harry
  See Hamilton, Charles (Harold St. John)
Dorian, Marguerite *7*
Dorin, Patrick C(arberry) 1939- *59*
  Brief entry *52*
Dorman, Michael 1932- *7*
Dorman, N. B. 1927- *39*
Dorris, Michael 1945-1997 .... *75*
  Obituary *94*
  See also CLR *58*
Dorris, Michael A.
  See Dorris, Michael
Dorris, Michael Anthony
  See Dorris, Michael
Dorritt, Susan
  See Schlein, Miriam
Dorros, Arthur 1950- *168*
  Earlier sketches in SATA *78, 122*
  See also CLR *42*
  See also SAAS *20*
Dorros, Arthur M.
  See Dorros, Arthur
Dorson, Richard M(ercer) 1916-1981 .... *30*
Doss, Helen (Grigsby) 1918- *20*
Doss, Margot Patterson *6*
Dothers, Anne
  See Chess, Victoria (Dickerson)
Dotlich, Rebecca Kai 1951- *182*
Dottig
  See Grider, Dorothy
Dotts, Maryann J. 1933- *35*
Doty, Jean Slaughter 1929- *28*
Doty, Roy 1922- *28*
Doubtfire, Dianne (Abrams) 1918- *29*
Doucet, Sharon Arms 1951- *144*
  Autobiography Feature *144*
  Earlier sketch in SATA *125*
Dougherty, Charles 1922- *18*
Dougherty, Terri (L.) 1964- *146*
Doughty, Rebecca 1955- *174*
Douglas, Blaise 1960- *101*
Douglas, Carole Nelson 1944- *73*
Douglas, Garry
  See Kilworth, Garry
Douglas, James McM.
  See Griffin, W.E.B
Douglas, Kathryn
  See Ewing, Kathryn
Douglas, Leonard
  See Bradbury, Ray
Douglas, Lola
  See Zeises, Lara M.
Douglas, Marjory Stoneman 1890-1998 .... *10*

Douglas, Michael
  See Bright, Robert (Douglas Sr.)
Douglas, Michael
  See Crichton, Michael
Douglas, Shirley Stewart
  See Tepper, Sheri S.
Douglass, Barbara 1930- *40*
Douglass, Frederick 1817(?)-1895 .... *29*
Douglass, Keith
  See Cunningham, Chet
Douty, Esther M(orris) 1909-1978 .... *8*
  Obituary *23*
Dow, Emily R. 1904-1987 .... *10*
Dow, Vicki
  See McVey, Vicki
Dowd, John David 1945- *78*
Dowdell, Dorothy (Florence) Karns 1910- ... *12*
Dowden, Anne Ophelia Todd 1907-2007 .... *7*
  Obituary *180*
  See also SAAS *10*
Dowdey, Landon Gerald 1923- *11*
Dowdy, Mrs. Regera
  See Gorey, Edward (St. John)
Dowell, Frances O'Roark *157*
Dower, Laura *185*
Dowling, Terry 1947- *101*
Downer, Ann 1960- *155*
Downer, Marion 1892(?)-1971 .... *25*
Downes, Belinda 1962- *180*
Downey, Fairfax D(avis) 1893-1990 .... *3*
  Obituary *66*
Downey, Lynn 1961- *185*
Downham, Jenny *192*
Downie, John 1931- *87*
Downie, Mary Alice 1934- *171*
  Earlier sketches in SATA *13, 87*
Downie, Mary Alice Dawe
  See Downie, Mary Alice
Downing, David A(lmon) 1958- *84*
Downing, Johnette *184*
Downing, Julie 1956- *148*
  Earlier sketch in SATA *81*
Downing, Paula E. 1951- *80*
Downing, Warwick 1931- *138*
Downing, Wick
  See Downing, Warwick
Dowswell, Paul 1957- *184*
Doyle, A. Conan
  See Doyle, Sir Arthur Conan
Doyle, Sir Arthur Conan 1859-1930 .... *24*
  See also CLR *106*
  See Conan Doyle, Arthur
Doyle, Brian 1935- *156*
  Earlier sketches in SATA *67, 104*
  See also CLR *22*
  See also SAAS *16*
Doyle, Charlotte 1937- *178*
  Earlier sketch in SATA *94*
Doyle, Charlotte Lackner
  See Doyle, Charlotte
Doyle, Conan
  See Doyle, Sir Arthur Conan
Doyle, Debra 1952- *165*
  Earlier sketch in SATA *105*
  See Appleton, Victor
Doyle, Donovan
  See Boegehold, Betty (Doyle)
Doyle, John
  See Graves, Robert
Doyle, Malachy 1954- *165*
  Earlier sketch in SATA *120*
  See also CLR *83*
Doyle, Richard 1824-1883 .... *21*
Doyle, Sir A. Conan
  See Doyle, Sir Arthur Conan
Dr. A
  See Asimov, Isaac
  and Silverstein, Alvin
  and Silverstein, Virginia B(arbara Opshelor)
Dr. Alphabet
  See Morice, Dave

Dr. Fred
  See Bortz, Alfred B(enjamin)
Dr. Laura
  See Schlessinger, Laura (Catherine)
Dr. Seuss
  See CLR *100*
  See Geisel, Theodor Seuss
  and LeSieg, Theo.
  and Seuss, Dr.
  and Stone, Rosetta
Dr. Zed
  See Penrose, Gordon
Drabble, Margaret 1939- *48*
Drackett, Phil(ip Arthur) 1922- *53*
Draco, F.
  See Davis, Julia
Dracup, Angela 1943- *74*
Dragisic, Patricia *116*
Dragonwagon, Crescent 1952- *186*
  Autobiography Feature *186*
  Earlier sketches in SATA *11, 41, 75, 133*
  See also SAAS *14*
Drake, David 1945- *85*
Drake, David Allen
  See Drake, David
Drake, Frank
  See Hamilton, Charles (Harold St. John)
Drake, Jane 1954- *82*
Drakeford, Dale B 1952- *113*
Drakeford, Dale Benjamin
  See Drakeford, Dale B
Draper, Hastings
  See Jeffries, Roderic
Draper, Sharon
  See Draper, Sharon M.
Draper, Sharon M. *146*
  Autobiography Feature *146*
  Earlier sketch in SATA *98*
  See also CLR *57*
Draper, Sharon Mills
  See Draper, Sharon M.
Drapier, M. B.
  See Swift, Jonathan
Drawson, Blair 1943- *126*
  Earlier sketch in SATA *17*
Dray, Matt 1967- *177*
Dray, Matthew Frederick
  See Dray, Matt
Dresang, Eliza (Carolyn Timberlake) 1941- . *19*
Drescher, Henrik 1955- *172*
  Earlier sketches in SATA *67, 105*
  See also CLR *20*
Drescher, Joan E(lizabeth) 1939- *137*
  Earlier sketch in SATA *30*
Dressen-McQueen, Stacey *191*
Dreves, Veronica R. 1927-1986
  Obituary *50*
Drew, Patricia (Mary) 1938- *15*
Drewery, Mary 1918- *6*
Drewery, Melanie 1970- *165*
Drewry, Henry N(athaniel) 1924- *138*
Dreyer, Ellen *177*
Drial, J. E.
  See Laird, Jean E(louise)
Drimmer, Frederick 1916-2000 .... *60*
  Obituary *124*
Driskill, J. Lawrence 1920- *90*
Driskill, Larry
  See Driskill, J. Lawrence
Driving Hawk, Virginia
  See Sneve, Virginia Driving Hawk
Dron, Laura
  See Matthews, L.S.
Drucker, Malka 1945- *111*
  Brief entry *29*
  Earlier sketch in SATA *39*
Drucker, Olga Levy 1927- *79*
Drummond, V(iolet) H(ilda) 1911-2000 .... *6*
Drummond, Walter
  See Silverberg, Robert

Drury, Clare Marie
　　See Hoskyns-Abrahall, Clare
　　(Constance Drury)
Drury, Roger W(olcott) 1914-1996 .... *15*
Druse, Eleanor
　　See King, Stephen
Dryden, Pamela
　　See St. John, Nicole
D.T., Hughes
　　See Hughes, Dean
Duane, Diane (Elizabeth) 1952- *145*
　　Brief entry *46*
　　Earlier sketches in SATA *58, 95*
Dubanevich, Arlene 1950- *56*
Dubelaar, Thea 1947- *60*
du Blane, Daphne
　　See Groom, Arthur William
Duble, Kathleen Benner 1958- *164*
Du Bois, Shirley Graham 1907(?)-1977 .... *24*
　　See Graham, Shirley
Du Bois, W(illiam) E(dward)
　　B(urghardt) 1868-1963 .... *42*
du Bois, William Pene
　　See Pene du Bois, William (Sherman)
Duboise, Novella 1911-1999 .... *88*
Dubosarsky, Ursula 1961- *193*
　　Earlier sketches in SATA *107, 147*
DuBose, LaRocque (Russ) 1926- *2*
Dubrovin, Vivian 1931- *139*
　　Earlier sketch in SATA *65*
DuBurke, Randy *172*
Ducey, Jean Sparks 1915- *93*
Duchacek, Ivo D(uka) 1913-1988
　　Obituary *55*
Du Chaillu, Paul (Belloni) 1835(?)-1903 ..... *26*
Ducharme, Dede Fox
　　See Ducharme, Lilian Fox
Ducharme, Lilian Fox 1950- *122*
Ducornet, Erica 1943- *7*
　　See Ducornet, Rikki
Ducornet, Rikki
　　See Ducornet, Erica
Duden, Jane 1947- *136*
Duder, Tessa 1940- *117*
　　Earlier sketch in SATA *80*
　　See also CLR *43*
　　See also SAAS *23*
Dudley, Helen
　　See Hope Simpson, Jacynth
Dudley, Martha Ward 1909(?)-1985
　　Obituary *45*
Dudley, Nancy
　　See Cole, Lois Dwight
Dudley, Robert
　　See Baldwin, James
Dudley, Ruth H(ubbell) 1905-2001 .... *11*
Dudley-Smith, T.
　　See Trevor, Elleston
Due, Linnea A. 1948- *64*
Dueck, Adele 1955- *97*
Dueland, Joy V(ivian) *27*
Duerr, Gisela 1968- *89*
Duey, Kathleen 1950- *132*
Dufault, Joseph Ernest Nephtali
　　See James, Will(iam Roderick)
Duff, Annis (James) 1904(?)-1986
　　Obituary *49*
Duff, Maggie
　　See Duff, Margaret K(app)
Duff, Margaret K(app) 1916-2003 .... *37*
　　Obituary *144*
Duffey, Betsy (Byars) 1953- *131*
　　Earlier sketch in SATA *80*
Duffie, Charles 1960- *144*
Duffield, Katy S. 1961- *147*
Duffy, Carol Ann 1955- *165*
　　Earlier sketch in SATA *95*
Dugan, Jack
　　See Griffin, W.E.B
Dugan, John Kevin
　　See Griffin, W.E.B

Dugan, Michael (Gray) 1947- *15*
Duggan, Alfred Leo 1903-1964 .... *25*
Duggan, Maurice (Noel) 1922-1974 .... *40*
　　Obituary *30*
Duggleby, John 1952- *94*
Dugin, Andrej 1955- *77*
Dugina, Olga 1964- *77*
du Jardin, Rosamond Neal 1902-1963 .... *2*
Duka, Ivo
　　See Duchacek, Ivo D(uka)
Duke, Kate 1956- *192*
　　Earlier sketches in SATA *90, 148*
　　See also CLR *51*
Duke, Will
　　See Gault, William Campbell
Dulac, Edmund 1882-1953 .... *19*
Dumas, Alexandre (pere) 1802-1870 .... *18*
　　See also CLR *134*
Dumas, Jacqueline 1946- *55*
Dumas, Philippe 1940- *119*
　　Earlier sketch in SATA *52*
du Maurier, Daphne 1907-1989 .... *27*
　　Obituary *60*
Dumbleton, Mike 1948- *124*
　　Earlier sketch in SATA *73*
Dunbar, Fiona 1961- *167*
Dunbar, Joyce 1944- *162*
　　Earlier sketches in SATA *76, 112*
Dunbar, Paul Laurence 1872-1906 .... *34*
Dunbar, Polly 1980(?)- *181*
Dunbar, Robert E(verett) 1926- *32*
Duncan, Alexandra
　　See Moore, Ishbel (Lindsay)
Duncan, Alice Faye 1967- *168*
　　Earlier sketch in SATA *95*
Duncan, Gregory
　　See McClintock, Marshall
Duncan, Jane
　　See Cameron, Elizabeth Jane
Duncan, Julia K. *1*
　　See Benson, Mildred (Augustine Wirt)
Duncan, Lois 1934- *141*
　　Autobiography Feature *141*
　　Earlier sketches in SATA *1, 36, 75, 133*
　　See also CLR *129*
　　See also SAAS *2*
Duncan, Norman 1871-1916
　　See YABC *1*
Duncan, Terence
　　See Nolan, William F(rancis)
Duncombe, Frances (Riker) 1900-1994 .... *25*
　　Obituary *82*
Dunham, Montrew 1919- *162*
Dunham, Montrew Goetz
　　See Dunham, Montrew
Dunkle, Clare B. 1964- *155*
Dunlap, Julie 1958- *84*
Dunleavy, Deborah 1951- *133*
Dunlop, Agnes M. R. (?)-1982 .... *87*
　　See Kyle, Elisabeth
Dunlop, Eileen (Rhona) 1938- *76*
　　Earlier sketch in SATA *24*
　　See also SAAS *12*
Dunn, Anne M. 1940- *107*
Dunn, Harvey T(homas) 1884-1952 .... *34*
Dunn, Herb
　　See Gutman, Dan
Dunn, John M. (III) 1949- *93*
Dunn, Judy
　　See Spangenberg, Judith Dunn
Dunn, Mary Lois 1930- *6*
Dunnahoo, Terry Janson 1927- *7*
Dunne, Jeanette 1952- *72*
Dunne, Kathleen 1933- *126*
Dunne, Marie
　　See Clark, Ann Nolan
Dunne, Mary Collins 1914- *11*
Dunne, Mary Jo
　　See Dunne, Mary Collins
Dunnett, Kaitlyn
　　See Emerson, Kathy Lynn

Dunnett, Margaret (Rosalind) 1909-1977 ..... *42*
Dunnick, Regan *178*
Dunrea, Olivier 1953- *160*
　　Brief entry *46*
　　Earlier sketches in SATA *59, 118*
Dunrea, Olivier Jean-Paul Dominique
　　See Dunrea, Olivier
Dunton, Dorothy 1912- *92*
Dupasquier, Philippe 1955- *151*
　　Earlier sketch in SATA *86*
DuPrau, Jeanne 1944- *144*
Dupuy, T(revor) N(evitt) 1916-1995 .... *4*
　　Obituary *86*
DuQuette, Keith 1960- *155*
　　Earlier sketch in SATA *90*
Duran, Gloria 1924- *171*
Duran, Gloria Bradley
　　See Duran, Gloria
Duranceau, Suzanne 1952- *162*
Durango, Julia 1967- *173*
Durant, Alan 1958- *165*
　　Earlier sketch in SATA *121*
Durant, John 1902- *27*
Durbin, William 1951- *174*
　　Earlier sketch in SATA *143*
Durell, Ann 1930- *66*
Durkee, Sarah *173*
Durrant, Lynda 1954- *148*
　　Earlier sketch in SATA *96*
Durrell, Gerald (Malcolm) 1925-1995 .... *8*
　　Obituary *84*
Durrell, Julie 1955- *94*
Durrett, Deanne 1940- *144*
　　Earlier sketch in SATA *92*
Du Soe, Robert C. 1892-1958
　　See YABC *2*
Dussling, Jennifer 1970- *143*
　　Earlier sketch in SATA *96*
DuTemple, Lesley A. 1952- *113*
Dutton, Sandra *191*
Dutz
　　See Davis, Mary Octavia
Duval, Katherine
　　See James, Elizabeth
Duval, Kathy 1946- *181*
Duvall, Aimee
　　See Thurlo, Aimee
　　and Thurlo, David
Duvall, Evelyn Millis 1906- *9*
Duvall, Jill D(onovan) 1932- *102*
Duvoisin, Roger (Antoine) 1904-1980 .... *30*
　　Obituary *23*
　　Earlier sketch in SATA *2*
　　See also CLR *23*
Dwiggins, Don(ald J.) 1913-1988 .... *4*
　　Obituary *60*
Dwight, Allan
　　See Cole, Lois Dwight
Dwyer, Deanna
　　See Koontz, Dean R.
Dwyer, K.R.
　　See Koontz, Dean R.
Dyck, Peter J. 1914- *75*
Dyer, James (Frederick) 1934- *37*
Dyer, Jane *191*
　　Earlier sketch in SATA *147*
Dyess, John (Foster) 1939- *76*
Dygard, Thomas J. 1931-1996 .... *97*
　　Obituary *92*
　　Earlier sketch in SATA *24*
　　See also SAAS *15*
Dyke, John 1935- *35*

　　　　　　　　　　　　　　　E

E. V. L.
　　See Lucas, E(dward) V(errall)

Eagar, Frances (Elisabeth Stuart)
1940-1978 .... *11*
Obituary *55*
Eager, Edward (McMaken) 1911-1964 .... *17*
See also CLR *43*
Eager, George 1921- *56*
See Eager, George B.
Eager, George B.
See Eager, George
Eagle, Ellen 1953- *61*
Eagle, Kin
See Adlerman, Daniel (Ezra)
and Adlerman, Kimberly M(arie)
Eagle, Mike 1942- *11*
Earle, Olive L(ydia) 1888-1982 .... *7*
Earle, William
See Johns, W(illiam) E(arle)
Earls, Nick 1963- *156*
Earlier sketch in SATA *95*
Early, Jack
See Scoppettone, Sandra
Early, Jon
See Johns, W(illiam) E(arle)
Early, Margaret 1951- *72*
Earnshaw, Brian 1929- *17*
Earnshaw, Micky
See Earnshaw, Spencer Wright
Earnshaw, Spencer Wright 1939- *88*
Easley, MaryAnn *94*
Eastman, Charles A(lexander) 1858-1939
See YABC *1*
Eastman, P(hilip) D(ey) 1909-1986 .... *33*
Obituary *46*
Easton, Kelly 1960- *192*
Earlier sketch in SATA *141*
Eastwick, Ivy (Ethel) O(live) *3*
Eaton, Anne T(haxter) 1881-1971 .... *32*
Eaton, Anthony 1971- *167*
Eaton, George L.
See Verral, Charles Spain
Eaton, Janet
See Givens, Janet E(aton)
Eaton, Jeanette 1886-1968 .... *24*
Eaton, Tom 1940- *22*
Ebel, Alex 1927- *11*
Eber, Dorothy (Margaret) Harley 1930- *27*
Eberhart, Sheri S.
See Tepper, Sheri S.
Eberle, Irmengarde 1898-1979 .... *2*
Obituary *23*
Eble, Diane 1956- *74*
Eboch, Chris *113*
Echlin, Kim 1955- *166*
Eckblad, Edith Berven 1923- *23*
Ecke, Wolfgang 1927-1983
Obituary *37*
Eckert, Allan W. 1931- *91*
Brief entry *27*
Earlier sketch in SATA *29*
See also SAAS *21*
Eckert, Horst 1931- *72*
Earlier sketch in SATA *8*
See Janosch
Ecklar, Julia (Marie) 1964- *112*
Eddings, David (Carroll) 1931- *91*
Ede, Janina 1937- *33*
Edell, Celeste *12*
Edelman, Lily (Judith) 1915-1981 .... *22*
Edelson, Edward 1932- *51*
Edens, Cooper 1945- *166*
Earlier sketches in SATA *49, 112*
Edens, (Bishop) David 1926- *39*
Edey, Maitland A(rmstrong) 1910-1992 .... *25*
Obituary *71*
Edgeworth, Maria 1768-1849 .... *21*
Edgy, Wardore
See Gorey, Edward (St. John)
Edison, Theodore
See Stratemeyer, Edward L.
Edler, Tim(othy) 1948- *56*
Edmiston, Jim 1948- *80*

Edmonds, I(vy) G(ordon) 1917- *8*
Edmonds, Walter D(umaux) 1903-1998 .... *27*
Obituary *99*
Earlier sketch in SATA *1*
See also SAAS *4*
Edmund, Sean
See Pringle, Laurence
Edsall, Marian (Stickney) 1920- *8*
Edwards, Al
See Nourse, Alan E(dward)
Edwards, Anne 1927- *35*
Edwards, Audrey 1947- *52*
Brief entry *31*
Edwards, Becky (Jane) 1966- *125*
Edwards, Bertram
See Edwards, Herbert Charles
Edwards, Bronwen Elizabeth
See Rose, Wendy
Edwards, Cecile Pepin 1916- *25*
Edwards, Dorothy 1914-1982 .... *88*
Obituary *31*
Earlier sketch in SATA *4*
Edwards, F. E.
See Nolan, William F(rancis)
Edwards, Frank B. 1952- *93*
Edwards, Gunvor *32*
Edwards, Harvey 1929- *5*
Edwards, Hazel (Eileen) 1945- *135*
Edwards, Herbert Charles 1912- *12*
Edwards, Jane Campbell 1932- *10*
Edwards, Julia
See Stratemeyer, Edward L.
Edwards, Julie
See Andrews, Julie
Edwards, Julie Andrews
See Andrews, Julie
Edwards, Linda Strauss 1948- *49*
Brief entry *42*
Edwards, Margaret (Alexander) 1902-1988
Obituary *56*
Edwards, Michelle 1955- *152*
Earlier sketch in SATA *70*
Edwards, Monica le Doux Newton
1912-1998 .... *12*
Edwards, Olwen
See Gater, Dilys
Edwards, Page (Lawrence, Jr.)
1941-1999 .... *59*
Edwards, Pamela Duncan *189*
Edwards, R. T.
See Goulart, Ron(ald Joseph)
Edwards, Sally (Cary) 1929- *7*
Edwards, Samuel
See Gerson, Noel Bertram
Edwards, Wallace 1957(?)- *170*
Egan, E(dward) W(elstead) 1922- *35*
Egan, Kerry *175*
Egan, Lorraine Hopping 1960- *134*
Earlier sketch in SATA *91*
Egan, Tim 1957- *191*
Earlier sketches in SATA *89, 155*
Egermeier, Elsie E(milie) 1890-1986 .... *65*
Eggenberger, David 1918- *6*
Eggleston, Edward 1837-1902 .... *27*
Egielski, Richard 1952- *163*
Earlier sketches in SATA *11, 49, 106*
Egypt, Ophelia Settle 1903-1984 .... *16*
Obituary *38*
Ehlert, Lois 1934- *172*
Earlier sketches in SATA *35, 69, 128*
See also CLR *28*
Ehlert, Lois Jane
See Ehlert, Lois
Ehling, Katalin Olah 1941- *93*
Ehrenfreund, Norbert 1921- *86*
Ehrenhaft, Daniel 1970- *185*
Ehrhardt, Karen 1963- *184*
Ehrlich, Amy 1942- *132*
Earlier sketches in SATA *25, 65, 96*
Ehrlich, Bettina Bauer 1903-1985 .... *1*

Ehrlich, H. M.
See Ziefert, Harriet
Eichenberg, Fritz 1901-1990 .... *50*
Earlier sketch in SATA *9*
Eichler, Margrit 1942- *35*
Eichner, James A. 1927- *4*
Eidson, Thomas 1944- *112*
Eifert, Virginia (Louise) S(nider)
1911-1966 .... *2*
Eige, (Elizabeth) Lillian 1915- *65*
Eiken, J. Melia 1967- *125*
Einsel, Naiad *10*
Einsel, Walter 1926- *10*
Einzig, Susan 1922- *43*
Eiseman, Alberta 1925- *15*
Eisenberg, Azriel (Louis) 1903-1985 .... *12*
Eisenberg, Lisa 1949- *155*
Brief entry *50*
Earlier sketch in SATA *57*
Eisenberg, Phyllis Rose 1924- *41*
Eisner, Vivienne
See Margolis, Vivienne
Eisner, Will 1917-2005 .... *165*
Earlier sketch in SATA *31*
Eisner, William Erwin
See Eisner, Will
Eitzen, Allan 1928- *9*
Eitzen, Ruth (Carper) 1924- *9*
Ekwensi, C. O. D.
See Ekwensi, Cyprian
Ekwensi, Cyprian 1921-2007 .... *66*
Ekwensi, Cyprian Odiatu Duaka
See Ekwensi, Cyprian
Elam, Richard M(ace, Jr.) 1920- *9*
Elborn, Andrew
See Clements, Andrew
and Clements, Andrew
Elboz, Stephen 1956- *152*
Eldin, Peter 1939- *154*
Eldon, Kathy 1946- *107*
Elfman, Blossom 1925- *8*
Elgin, Kathleen 1923- *39*
Elia
See Lamb, Charles
Eliot, A. D.
See Jewett, (Theodora) Sarah Orne
Eliot, Alice
See Jewett, (Theodora) Sarah Orne
Eliot, Anne
See Cole, Lois Dwight
Eliot, Dan
See Silverberg, Robert
Elish, Dan 1960- *129*
Earlier sketch in SATA *68*
Elisha, Ron 1951- *104*
Elisofon, Eliot 1911-1973
Obituary *21*
Elkeles, Simone *187*
Elkin, Benjamin 1911-1995 .... *3*
Elkins, Dov Peretz 1937- *5*
Ellacott, S(amuel) E(rnest) 1911- *19*
Elleman, Barbara 1934- *147*
Ellen, Jaye
See Nixon, Joan Lowery
Eller, Scott
See Holinger, William (Jacques)
and Shepard, Jim
Ellestad, Myrvin
See Ellestad, Myrvin H.
Ellestad, Myrvin H. 1921- *120*
Elliot, David 1952- *122*
Elliott, Bruce
See Field, Edward
Elliott, David 1952- *163*
Elliott, Don
See Silverberg, Robert
Elliott, Elizabeth Shippen Green
See Green, Elizabeth Shippen
Elliott, Janice 1931-1995 .... *119*
Elliott, Joey
See Houk, Randy

Elliott, Louise *111*
Elliott, Odette 1939- *75*
Elliott, Patricia 1946- *176*
Elliott, Sarah M(cCarn) 1930- *14*
Elliott, (Robert) Scott 1970- *153*
Elliott, William
   See Bradbury, Ray
Ellis, (Mary) Amabel (Nassau Strachey)
  Williams
   See Williams-Ellis, (Mary) Amabel
  (Nassau Strachey)
Ellis, Anyon
   See Rowland-Entwistle, (Arthur)
  Theodore (Henry)
Ellis, Carson 1975- *190*
Ellis, Carson Friedman
   See Ellis, Carson
Ellis, Deborah 1960- *187*
  Earlier sketch in SATA *129*
Ellis, E. S.
   See Ellis, Edward S(ylvester)
Ellis, Edward S(ylvester) 1840-1916
   See YABC *1*
Ellis, Ella Thorp 1928- *127*
  Earlier sketch in SATA *7*
  See also SAAS *9*
Ellis, Harry Bearse 1921-2004 .... *9*
Ellis, Herbert
   See Wilson, Lionel
Ellis, Mel(vin Richard) 1912-1984 .... *7*
  Obituary *39*
Ellis, Richard 1938- *130*
Ellis, Sarah 1952- *179*
  Earlier sketches in SATA *68, 131*
  See also CLR *42*
Ellison, Emily *114*
Ellison, Lucile Watkins 1907(?)-1979 .... *50*
  Obituary *22*
Ellison, Virginia H(owell) 1910- *4*
Ellsberg, Edward 1891-1983 .... *7*
Ellsworth, Mary Ellen (Tressel) 1940- *146*
Elmer, Robert 1958- *154*
  Earlier sketch in SATA *99*
Elmore, (Carolyn) Patricia 1933- *38*
  Brief entry *35*
El-Moslimany, Ann P(axton) 1937- *90*
Elschner, Geraldine 1954- *183*
Elspeth
   See Bragdon, Elspeth MacDuffie
Elster, Jean Alicia 1953- *150*
Elting, Mary 1906- *88*
  Earlier sketch in SATA *2*
  See also SAAS *20*
Elvgren, Jennifer Riesmeyer *179*
Elwart, Joan Potter 1927- *2*
Elwood, Ann 1931- *55*
  Brief entry *52*
Elwood, Roger 1943-2007 .... *58*
Elya, Susan M(iddleton) 1955- *159*
  Earlier sketch in SATA *106*
Elzbieta *88*
Ember, Kathi *190*
Emberley, Barbara A(nne) 1932- *146*
  Earlier sketches in SATA *8, 70*
  See also CLR *5*
Emberley, Ed(ward Randolph) 1931- *146*
  Earlier sketches in SATA *8, 70*
  See also CLR *81*
Emberley, Michael 1960- *189*
  Earlier sketches in SATA *34, 80, 119*
Embry, Margaret Jacob 1919-1975 .... *5*
Emecheta, Buchi 1944- *66*
Emecheta, Florence Onye Buchi
   See Emecheta, Buchi
Emerson, Alice B. *67*
  Earlier sketch in SATA *1*
   See Benson, Mildred (Augustine Wirt)
Emerson, Kathy Lynn 1947- *63*
Emerson, Ru 1944- *107*
  Earlier sketch in SATA *70*
Emerson, Sally 1952- *111*

Emerson, William K(eith) 1925- *25*
Emert, Phyllis R(aybin) 1947- *93*
Emery, Anne (McGuigan) 1907- *33*
  Earlier sketch in SATA *1*
Emmens, Carol Ann 1944- *39*
Emmett, Jonathan 1965- *188*
  Earlier sketch in SATA *138*
Emmons, Della (Florence) Gould 1890-1983
  Obituary *39*
Emory, Jerry 1957- *96*
Emrich, Duncan (Black Macdonald)
  1908-1970(?) *11*
Emshwiller, Carol 1921- *174*
  Autobiography Feature *174*
Emshwiller, Carol Fries
   See Emshwiller, Carol
Emslie, M. L.
   See Simpson, Myrtle L(illias)
Ende, Michael (Andreas Helmuth)
  1929-1995 .... *130*
  Brief entry *42*
  Obituary *86*
  Earlier sketch in SATA *61*
  See also CLR *138*
Enderle, Dotti 1954- *145*
Enderle, Judith (Ann) Ross 1941- *89*
  Autobiography Feature *114*
  Earlier sketch in SATA *38*
  See also SAAS *26*
Enell, Trinka (Gochenour) 1951- *79*
Enfield, Carrie
   See Smith, Susan Vernon
Engdahl, Sylvia Louise 1933- *4*
  Autobiography Feature *122*
  See also CLR *2*
  See also SAAS *5*
Engel, Diana 1947- *70*
Engelbreit, Mary 1952- *169*
Engelhart, Margaret S. 1924- *59*
Engelmann, Kim (V.) 1959- *87*
England, George Allan 1877-1936 .... *102*
Englart, Mindi Rose 1965- *146*
Engle, Eloise *9*
   See Paananen, Eloise (Katherine)
Engle, Margarita 1951- *193*
Englebert, Victor 1933- *8*
English, James W(ilson) 1915- *37*
Engstrom, Elizabeth 1951- *110*
Enright, D(ennis) J(oseph) 1920-2002 .... *25*
  Obituary *140*
Enright, Elizabeth (Wright) 1909-1968 .... *9*
  See also CLR *4*
Ensor, Barbara *180*
Ensor, Robert (T.) 1922- *93*
Enthoven, Sam 1974- *187*
Entwistle, (Arthur) Theodore (Henry)
  Rowland
   See Rowland-Entwistle, (Arthur)
  Theodore (Henry)
Enys, Sarah L.
   See Sloggett, Nellie
Epanya, Christian A(rthur Kingue) 1956- *91*
Ephraim, Shelly S(chonebaum) 1952- *97*
Ephron, Delia 1944- *65*
  Brief entry *50*
Epler, Doris M. 1928- *73*
Epp, Margaret A(gnes) 1913- *20*
Eppenstein, Louise (Kohn) 1892-1987
  Obituary *54*
Epple, Anne Orth 1927- *20*
Epstein, Anne Merrick 1931- *20*
Epstein, Beryl (M. Williams) 1910- *31*
  Earlier sketch in SATA *1*
  See also CLR *26*
  See also SAAS *17*
Epstein, Perle S(herry) 1938- *27*
Epstein, Rachel S. 1941- *102*
Epstein, Samuel 1909-2000 .... *31*
  Earlier sketch in SATA *1*
  See also CLR *26*
  See also SAAS *17*

Erdman, Loula Grace 1905(?)-1976 .... *1*
Erdoes, Richard 1912- *33*
  Brief entry *28*
Erdogan, Buket *187*
Erdrich, Karen Louise
   See Erdrich, Louise
Erdrich, Louise 1954- *141*
  Earlier sketch in SATA *94*
Erickson, Betty J. 1923- *97*
Erickson, Betty Jean
   See Erickson, Betty J.
Erickson, John R. 1943- *136*
  Earlier sketch in SATA *70*
Erickson, Jon 1948- *141*
Erickson, Phoebe *59*
Erickson, Russell E(verett) 1932- *27*
Erickson, Sabra Rollins 1912-1995 .... *35*
Erickson, Walter
   See Fast, Howard
Ericson, Walter
   See Fast, Howard
Ericsson, Jennifer A. *170*
Erikson, Mel 1937- *31*
Ering, Timothy Basil *176*
Erlanger, Baba
   See Trahey, Jane
Erlbach, Arlene 1948- *160*
  Earlier sketches in SATA *78, 115*
Erlbruch, Wolf 1948- *181*
Erlich, Lillian (Feldman) 1910-1983 .... *10*
Ermatinger, James W. 1959- *170*
Ernest, William
   See Berkebile, Fred D(onovan)
Ernst, (Lyman) John 1940- *39*
Ernst, Kathleen
   See Ernst, Kathleen A.
Ernst, Kathleen A. 1959- *162*
Ernst, Kathryn (Fitzgerald) 1942- *25*
Ernst, Lisa Campbell 1957- *154*
  Brief entry *44*
  Earlier sketches in SATA *55, 95*
Erskine, Kathryn *193*
Ervin, Janet Halliday 1923- *4*
Erwin, Will
   See Eisner, Will
Esbaum, Jill *174*
Esbensen, Barbara J(uster) 1925-1996 .... *97*
  Brief entry *53*
  Earlier sketch in SATA *62*
Eschbacher, Roger *160*
Escriva, Vivi *182*
Eseki, Bruno
   See Mphahlele, Ezekiel
Eshmeyer, R. E. *29*
   See Eschmeyer, R(einhart) E(rnst)
Eskridge, Ann E. 1949- *84*
Espeland, Pamela (Lee) 1951- *128*
  Brief entry *38*
  Earlier sketch in SATA *52*
Espriella, Don Manuel Alvarez
   See Southey, Robert
Espy, Willard R(ichardson) 1910-1999 .... *38*
  Obituary *113*
Essrig, Harry 1912- *66*
Estep, Irene Compton *5*
Esterl, Arnica 1933- *77*
Estes, Eleanor (Ruth) 1906-1988 .... *91*
  Obituary *56*
  Earlier sketch in SATA *7*
  See also CLR *70*
Estoril, Jean
   See Allan, Mabel Esther
Estrada, Pau 1961- *74*
Etchemendy, Nancy 1952- *166*
  Earlier sketch in SATA *38*
Etchemendy, Nancy Elise Howell
   See Etchemendy, Nancy
Etchison, Birdie L(ee) 1937- *38*
Etchison, Craig 1945- *133*
Etherington, Frank 1945- *58*

Eton, Robert
   See Meynell, Laurence Walter
Ets, Marie Hall 1893-1984 2
   See also CLR 33
Ettlinger, Doris 1950- 173
Eunson, (John) Dale 1904-2002 5
   Obituary 132
Evan, Frances Y. 1951- 167
Evanoff, Vlad 1916- 59
Evans, Cambria 1981- 178
Evans, Douglas 1953- 144
   Earlier sketch in SATA 93
Evans, Eva (Knox) 1905-1998 27
Evans, Freddi Williams 1957- 134
Evans, Greg 1947- 143
   Earlier sketch in SATA 73
Evans, Hubert Reginald 1892-1986 118
   Obituary 48
Evans, Katherine (Floyd) 1901-1964 5
Evans, Larry
   See Evans, Laurence Chubb
Evans, Laurence Chubb 1939- 88
Evans, Lawrence Watt
   See Watt-Evans, Lawrence
Evans, Lezlie 180
Evans, Mari 1923- 10
Evans, Mark 19
Evans, Nancy 1950- 65
Evans, Patricia Healy
   See Carpenter, Patricia (Healy Evans)
Evans, (Alice) Pearl 1927- 83
Evans, Shane W. 189
Evans, Shirlee 1931- 58
Evans, Tabor
   See Cameron, Lou
   and Knott, William C(ecil, Jr.)
   and Wallmann, Jeffrey M(iner)
   and Whittington, Harry (Benjamin)
Evarts, Esther
   See Benson, Sally
Evarts, Hal G., (Jr.) 1915-1989 6
Everett, Gail
   See Hale, Arlene
Evernden, Margery 1916- 5
Eversole, Robyn 1971- 74
Eversole, Robyn H.
   See Eversole, Robyn
Eversole, Robyn Harbert
   See Eversole, Robyn
Evslin, Bernard 1922-1993 83
   Brief entry 28
   Obituary 77
   Earlier sketch in SATA 45
Ewart, Claire 1958- 145
   Earlier sketch in SATA 76
Ewen, David 1907-1985 4
   Obituary 47
Ewing, Juliana (Horatia Gatty) 1841-1885 ... 16
   See also CLR 78
Ewing, Kathryn 1921- 20
Eyerly, Jeannette (Hyde) 1908-2008 86
   Earlier sketch in SATA 4
   See also SAAS 10
Eyre, Dorothy
   See McGuire, Leslie (Sarah)
Eyre, Frank 1910-1988
   Obituary 62
Eyre, Katherine Wigmore 1901-1970 26
Ezzell, Marilyn 1937- 42
   Brief entry 38

F

Fabe, Maxene 1943- 15
Faber, Doris (Greenberg) 1924- 78
   Earlier sketch in SATA 3
Faber, Harold 1919- 5
Fabre, Jean Henri (Casimir) 1823-1915 22

Facklam, Margery (Metz) 1927- 132
   Earlier sketches in SATA 20, 85
Fadiman, Clifton (Paul) 1904-1999 11
   Obituary 115
Fagan, Cary 1957- 186
Fahs, Sophia Blanche Lyon 1876-1978 102
Failing, Barbara Larmon 182
Fair, David 1952- 96
Fair, Sylvia 1933- 13
Fairfax-Lucy, Brian (Fulke
   Cameron-Ramsay) 1898-1974 6
   Obituary 26
Fairfield, Flora
   See Alcott, Louisa May
Fairlie, Gerard 1899-1983
   Obituary 34
Fairman, Joan A(lexandra) 1935- 10
Faithfull, Gail 1936- 8
Falcone, L(ucy) M. 1951- 155
Falconer, Ian 1959- 179
   Earlier sketch in SATA 125
   See also CLR 90
Falconer, James
   See Kirkup, James
Falconer, Lee N.
   See May, Julian
Falkner, Leonard 1900-1977 12
Fall, Andrew
   See Arthur, Robert, (Jr.)
Fall, Thomas
   See Snow, Donald Clifford
Faller, Regis 1968- 187
Falls, C(harles) B(uckles) 1874-1960 38
   Brief entry 27
Falstein, Louis 1909-1995 37
Fancher, Lou 1960- 177
Fanelli, Sara 1969- 126
   Earlier sketch in SATA 89
Fanning, Leonard M(ulliken) 1888-1967 5
Faralla, Dana 1909- 9
Faralla, Dorothy W.
   See Faralla, Dana
Farb, Peter 1929-1980 12
   Obituary 22
Farber, Norma 1909-1984 75
   Obituary 38
   Earlier sketch in SATA 25
Farish, Terry 1947- 146
   Earlier sketch in SATA 82
Farjeon, (Eve) Annabel 1919-2004 11
   Obituary 153
Farjeon, Eleanor 1881-1965 2
   See also CLR 34
Farley, Carol (J.) 1936- 137
   Earlier sketch in SATA 4
Farley, Terri 165
Farley, Walter (Lorimer) 1915-1989 132
   Earlier sketches in SATA 2, 43
Farlow, James O(rville, Jr.) 1951- 75
Farmer, Nancy 1941- 161
   Earlier sketches in SATA 79, 117
Farmer, Patti 1948- 79
Farmer, Penelope (Jane) 1939- 105
   Brief entry 39
   Earlier sketch in SATA 40
   See also CLR 8
   See also SAAS 22
Farmer, Peter 1950- 38
Farmer, Philip Jose 1918- 93
Farnham, Burt
   See Clifford, Harold B(urton)
Farnsworth, Bill 1958- 186
   Earlier sketches in SATA 84, 135
Farquhar, Margaret C(utting) 1905-1988 13
Farquharson, Alexander 1944- 46
Farquharson, Martha
   See Finley, Martha
Farr, Diana (Pullein-Thompson) 82
   See Pullein-Thompson, Diana
Farr, Finis (King) 1904-1982 10

Farrar, Jill
   See Morris, Jill
Farrar, Susan Clement 1917- 33
Farrell, Ben
   See Cebulash, Mel
Farrell, Patrick
   See Odgers, Sally Farrell
Farrell, Sally
   See Odgers, Sally Farrell
Farrer, Vashti 167
Farrington, Benjamin 1891-1974
   Obituary 20
Farrington, S(elwyn) Kip, Jr. 1904-1983 20
Farshtey, Greg(ory T.) 1965- 148
Farthing, Alison 1936- 45
   Brief entry 36
Farthing-Knight, Catherine 1933- 92
Fassler, Joan (Grace) 1931- 11
Fast, Howard 1914-2003 7
   Autobiography Feature 107
Fast, Howard Melvin
   See Fast, Howard
Fasulo, Michael 1963- 83
Fatchen, Max 1920- 84
   Earlier sketch in SATA 20
   See also SAAS 20
Fate, Marilyn
   See Collins, Paul
Father Goose
   See Ghigna, Charles
Fatigati, (Frances) Evelyn 1948- 24
Fatio, Louise 1904-1993 6
Fatus, Sophie 1957- 182
Faulhaber, Martha 1926- 7
Faulkner, Anne Irvin 1906- 23
Faulkner, Frank
   See Ellis, Edward S(ylvester)
Faulkner, Nancy
   See Faulkner, Anne Irvin
Faulknor, Cliff(ord Vernon) 1913- 86
Favole, Robert J(ames) 1950- 125
Fax, Elton Clay 1909-1993 25
Faxon, Lavinia
   See Russ, Lavinia (Faxon)
Feagles, Anita M(acRae) 1927- 9
Feagles, Elizabeth
   See Day, Beth (Feagles)
Feague, Mildred H. 1915- 14
Fearnley, Jan 1965- 153
Fearrington, Ann (Peyton) 1945- 146
Fecher, Constance
   See Heaven, Constance (Christina)
Feder, Chris Welles 1938- 81
Feder, Harriet K. 1928- 73
Feder, Paula (Kurzband) 1935- 26
Federici, Debbie 1965- 175
Federici, Debbie Tanner
   See Federici, Debbie
Feelings, Muriel (Lavita Grey) 1938- 16
   See also CLR 5
   See also SAAS 8
Feelings, Thomas 1933-2003 8
   Obituary 148
   See Feelings, Tom
Feelings, Tom 69
   See also CLR 58
   See also SAAS 19
   See Feelings, Thomas
Fehler, Gene 1940- 74
Fehrenbach, T(heodore) R(eed, Jr.) 1925- 33
Feiffer, Jules 1929- 157
   Earlier sketches in SATA 8, 61, 111
Feiffer, Jules Ralph
   See Feiffer, Jules
Feiffer, Kate 1964- 170
Feig, Barbara Krane 1937- 34
Feikema, Feike
   See Manfred, Frederick (Feikema)
Feil, Hila 1942- 12
Feilen, John
   See May, Julian

Feinberg, Barbara Jane 1938- *58*
See Feinberg, Barbara Silberdick
Feinberg, Barbara Silberdick *123*
See Feinberg, Barbara Jane
Feinstein, John 1956- *163*
Feldman, Anne (Rodgers) 1939- *19*
Feldman, Elane *79*
Felix
See Vincent, Felix
Fell, Derek 1939- *167*
Fell, Derek John
See Fell, Derek
Fellows, Muriel H. *10*
Fellows, Stan 1957- *177*
Fellows, Stanley
See Fellows, Stan
Felsen, Henry Gregor 1916-1995 .... *1*
See also SAAS 2
Felstead, Cathie 1954- *192*
Feltenstein, Arlene (H.) 1934- *119*
Felton, Harold William 1902-1991 .... *1*
Felton, Ronald Oliver 1909- *3*
Felts, Shirley 1934- *33*
Fenderson, Lewis H., Jr. 1907-1983 .... *47*
Obituary *37*
Fenner, Carol (Elizabeth) 1929-2002 .... *89*
Obituary *132*
Earlier sketch in SATA 7
See also SAAS 24
Fenner, Phyllis R(eid) 1899-1982 .... *1*
Obituary *29*
Fensham, Elizabeth *169*
Fenten, Barbara D(oris) 1935- *26*
Fenten, D(onald) X. 1932- *4*
Fenton, Carroll Lane 1900-1969 .... *5*
Fenton, Edward 1917-1995 .... *7*
Obituary *89*
Fenton, Mildred Adams 1899-1995 .... *21*
Fenwick, Patti
See Grider, Dorothy
Feravolo, Rocco Vincent 1922- *10*
Ferber, Brenda A. 1967- *184*
Ferber, Edna 1887-1968 .... *7*
Fergus, Charles *114*
Ferguson, Alane 1957- *182*
Earlier sketch in SATA 85
Ferguson, Bob
See Ferguson, Robert Bruce
Ferguson, Cecil 1931- *45*
Ferguson, Robert Bruce 1927-2001 .... *13*
Ferguson, Sarah 1959- *180*
Earlier sketches in SATA 66, 110
Ferguson, Sarah Margaret
See Ferguson, Sarah
Ferguson, Walter (W.) 1930- *34*
Fergusson, Erna 1888-1964 .... *5*
Fermi, Laura 1907-1977 .... *6*
Obituary *28*
Fern, Eugene A. 1919-1987 .... *10*
Obituary *54*
Fernandes, Eugenie 1943- *139*
Earlier sketch in SATA 77
Fernandez, Laura 1960- *171*
Ferrari, Maria *123*
Ferreiro, Carmen 1958- *158*
Ferrell, Nancy Warren 1932- *70*
Ferrier, Lucy
See Penzler, Otto
Ferris, Helen Josephine 1890-1969 .... *21*
Ferris, James Cody *1*
See McFarlane, Leslie (Charles)
Ferris, Jean 1939- *149*
Brief entry *50*
Earlier sketches in SATA 56, 105
Ferris, Jeri Chase 1937- *84*
Ferry, Charles 1927- *92*
Earlier sketch in SATA 43
See also CLR 34
See also SAAS 20
Fetz, Ingrid 1915- *30*

Feydy, Anne Lindbergh
Brief entry *32*
See Sapieyevski, Anne Lindbergh
Fiammenghi, Gioia 1929- *66*
Earlier sketch in SATA 9
Fiarotta, Noel *15*
See Ficarotta, Noel
Fiarotta, Phyllis *15*
See Ficarotta, Phyllis
Fichter, George S. 1922-1993 .... *7*
Ficocelli, Elizabeth *189*
Fidler, Kathleen (Annie) 1899-1980 .... *87*
Obituary *45*
Earlier sketch in SATA 3
Fiedler, Jean(nette Feldman) *4*
Fiedler, Joseph Daniel *159*
Fiedler, Lisa *185*
Field, Dorothy 1944- *97*
Field, Edward 1924- *109*
Earlier sketch in SATA 8
Field, Elinor Whitney 1889-1980
Obituary *28*
Field, Eugene 1850-1895 .... *16*
Field, Gans T.
See Wellman, Manly Wade
Field, James 1959- *113*
Field, Peter
See Drago, Harry Sinclair
and Dresser, Davis
and Mann, E(dward) B(everly)
Field, Rachel (Lyman) 1894-1942 .... *15*
See also CLR 21
Fielding, Kate
See Oldfield, Jenny
Fields, Bryan W. 1958(?)- *188*
Fields, Terri 1948- *191*
Fields, T.S.
See Fields, Terri
Fienberg, Anna 1956- *183*
Earlier sketch in SATA 112
Fife, Dale (Odile Hollerbach) 1901- *18*
Fighter Pilot, A
See Johnston, H(ugh) A(nthony) S(tephen)
Figler, Jeanie 1949- *123*
Figley, Marty Rhodes 1948- *158*
Earlier sketch in SATA 88
Figueredo, D(anilo) H. 1951- *155*
Figueroa, Pablo 1938- *9*
Fijan, Carol 1918- *12*
Filderman, Diane E(lizabeth) 1959- *87*
Files, Meg 1946- *107*
Fillmore, Parker H(oysted) 1878-1944
See YABC 1
Filstrup, Chris
See Filstrup, E(dward) Christian
Filstrup, E(dward) Christian 1942- *43*
Filstrup, Janie
See Merrill, Jane
Finchler, Judy 1943- *93*
Finder, Martin
See Salzmann, Siegmund
Findlay, Jamieson 1958- *169*
Findon, Joanne 1957- *161*
Fine, Anne 1947- *160*
Earlier sketches in SATA 29, 72, 111
See also CLR 25
See also SAAS 15
Fine, Edith Hope *169*
Fine, Howard 1961- *181*
Fine, Jane
See Ziefert, Harriet
Finger, Charles J(oseph) 1869(?)-1941 .... *42*
Fink, William B(ertrand) 1916- *22*
Finke, Blythe Foote 1922- *26*
Finkel, George (Irvine) 1909-1975 .... *8*
Finkelstein, Norman H. 1941- *137*
Earlier sketch in SATA 73
Finkelstein, Norman Henry
See Finkelstein, Norman H.
Finlay, Alice Sullivan 1946- *82*

Finlay, Winifred Lindsay Crawford
(McKissack) 1910-1989 .... *23*
Finlayson, Ann 1925- *8*
Finley, Martha 1828-1909 .... *43*
Finley, Mary Peace 1942- *83*
Finney, Jack *109*
See Finney, Walter Braden
Finney, Patricia 1958- *163*
Finney, Shan 1944- *65*
Firer, Ben Zion
See Firer, Benzion
Firer, Benzion 1914- *64*
Fireside, Bryna J. 1932- *73*
Firmin, Charlotte 1954- *29*
Firmin, Peter 1928- *58*
Earlier sketch in SATA 15
Firth, Barbara *179*
Fischbach, Julius 1894-1988 .... *10*
Fischer, John
See Fluke, Joanne
Fischer, R.J.
See Fluke, Joanne
Fischer-Nagel, Andreas 1951- *56*
Fischer-Nagel, Heiderose 1956- *56*
Fischler, Shirley (Walton) *66*
Fischler, Stan(ley I.) *66*
Brief entry *36*
Fishback, Margaret
See Antolini, Margaret Fishback
Fisher, Aileen (Lucia) 1906-2002 .... *73*
Obituary *143*
Earlier sketches in SATA 1, 25
See also CLR 49
Fisher, Barbara 1940- *44*
Brief entry *34*
Fisher, Carolyn 1968- *154*
Fisher, Catherine 1957- *155*
Fisher, Chris 1958- *80*
Fisher, Clavin C(argill) 1912- *24*
Fisher, Dorothy (Frances) Canfield
1879-1958
See YABC 1
See also CLR 71
Fisher, Gary L. 1949- *86*
Fisher, John (Oswald Hamilton) 1909- *15*
Fisher, Laura Harrison 1934- *5*
Fisher, Leonard Everett 1924- *176*
Autobiography Feature *122*
Earlier sketches in SATA 4, 34, 73, 120
See also CLR 18
See also SAAS 1
Fisher, Lois I. 1948- *38*
Brief entry *35*
Fisher, Margery (Turner) 1913-1992 .... *20*
Obituary *74*
Fisher, Marshall Jon 1963- *113*
Fisher, Nikki
See Strachan, Ian
Fisher, Robert (Tempest) 1943- *47*
Fisher, Suzanne
See Staples, Suzanne Fisher
Fisher, Valorie *177*
Fishman, Cathy Goldberg 1951- *106*
Fisk, Nicholas *25*
See Higginbottom, David
Fisk, Pauline 1948- *160*
Earlier sketch in SATA 66
Fiske, Tarleton
See Bloch, Robert (Albert)
Fisscher, Catharina G. M. 1958- *142*
Fisscher, Tiny
See Fisscher, Catharina G. M.
Fitch, Clarke
See Sinclair, Upton
Fitch, John IV
See Cormier, Robert
Fitch, Sheree 1956- *178*
Earlier sketch in SATA 108
Fitschen, Dale 1937- *20*
Fitzalan, Roger
See Trevor, Elleston

Fitzgerald, Captain Hugh
  See Baum, L(yman) Frank
FitzGerald, Cathleen 1932-1987
  Obituary 50
Fitzgerald, Dawn 175
Fitzgerald, Edward Earl 1919-2001 20
Fitzgerald, F(rancis) A(nthony) 1940- 15
Fitzgerald, John D(ennis) 1907(?)-1988 20
  Obituary 56
  See also CLR *1*
Fitzgerald, Merni Ingrassia 1955- 53
Fitzgibbon, Terry 1948- 121
Fitzhardinge, Joan Margaret 1912- 73
  Earlier sketch in SATA *2*
  See Phipson, Joan
Fitzhugh, Louise (Perkins) 1928-1974 45
  Obituary 24
  Earlier sketch in SATA *1*
  See also CLR *72*
Fitzhugh, Percy Keese 1876-1950 65
Fitzpatrick, Marie-Louise 1962- 189
  Earlier sketch in SATA *125*
FitzRalph, Matthew
  See McInerny, Ralph
Fitz-Randolph, Jane (Currens) 1915- 51
Fitzsimons, Cecilia 1952- 97
Fitzsimons, Cecilia A.L.
  See Fitzsimons, Cecilia
Flack, Marjorie 1897-1958 100
  See also YABC *2*
  See also CLR *28*
Flack, Naomi John White -1999 40
  Brief entry 35
Flake, Sharon G. 166
Flanagan, John 1944- 180
Flanagan, John Anthony
  See Flanagan, John
Flannery, Kate
  See De Goldi, Kathleen Domenica
Flatt, Lizann 1966- 88
Fleagle, Gail S(hatto) 1940- 117
Fleetwood, Jenni 1947- 80
Fleischer, Jane
  See Oppenheim, Joanne
Fleischhauer-Hardt, Helga 1936- 30
Fleischman, Albert Sidney
  See Fleischman, Sid
Fleischman, John 1948- 145
Fleischman, Paul 1952- 156
  Brief entry 32
  Earlier sketches in SATA *39, 72, 110*
  See also CLR *66*
  See also SAAS *20*
Fleischman, Sid 1920- 185
  Earlier sketches in SATA *8, 59, 96, 148*
  See also CLR *15*
Fleischner, Jennifer 1956- 188
  Earlier sketch in SATA *93*
Fleisher, Paul 1948- 132
  Earlier sketch in SATA *81*
Fleisher, Robbin 1951-1977 52
  Brief entry 49
Fleishman, Seymour 1918- 66
  Brief entry 32
Fleming, A. A.
  See Arthur, Robert, (Jr.)
Fleming, Alice Mulcahey 1928- 9
Fleming, Candace 1962- 190
  Earlier sketches in SATA *94, 143*
Fleming, Denise 1950- 173
  Earlier sketches in SATA *81, 126*
Fleming, Elizabeth P. 1888-1985
  Obituary 48
Fleming, Ian 1908-1964 9
Fleming, Ian Lancaster
  See Fleming, Ian
Fleming, Ronald Lee 1941- 56
Fleming, Sally
  See Walker, Sally M(acArt)
Fleming, Stuart
  See Knight, Damon (Francis)

Fleming, Susan 1932- 32
Fleming, Thomas 1927- 8
Fleming, Thomas James
  See Fleming, Thomas
Fleming, Virginia (Edwards) 1923- 84
Flesch, Y.
  See Flesch, Yolande (Catarina)
Flesch, Yolande (Catarina) 1950- 55
Fletcher, Charlie May Hogue 1897-1977 3
Fletcher, Colin 1922-2007 28
Fletcher, Dirk
  See Cunningham, Chet
Fletcher, George U.
  See Pratt, (Murray) Fletcher
Fletcher, Helen Jill 1910- 13
Fletcher, Ralph (J.) 1953- 149
  Earlier sketch in SATA *105*
  See also CLR *104*
Fletcher, Richard E. 1917(?)-1983
  Obituary 34
Fletcher, Rick
  See Fletcher, Richard E.
Fletcher, Susan 1951- 181
  Earlier sketches in SATA *70, 110*
Fletcher, Susan Clemens
  See Fletcher, Susan
Fleur, Paul
  See Pohl, Frederik
Flexner, James Thomas 1908-2003 9
Flinn, Alex 1966- 159
Flint, Helen 1952- 102
Flint, Russ 1944- 74
Flitner, David P(erkins), Jr. 1949- 7
Floca, Brian 190
  Earlier sketch in SATA *155*
Floethe, Louise Lee 1913-1988 4
Floethe, Richard 1901-1998 4
Floherty, John Joseph 1882-1964 25
Flood, Bo
  See Flood, Nancy Bo
Flood, Nancy Bo 1945- 130
Flood, Pansie Hart 1964- 140
Flood, William 1942- 129
Flooglebuckle, Al
  See Spiegelman, Art
Flora, James (Royer) 1914-1998 30
  Obituary 103
  Earlier sketch in SATA *1*
  See also SAAS *6*
Flores-Galbis, Enrique 1952- 186
Florian, Douglas 1950- 177
  Earlier sketches in SATA *19, 83, 125*
Flory, Jane Trescott 1917- 22
Flournoy, Valerie 1952- 95
Flournoy, Valerie Rose
  See Flournoy, Valerie
Flowerdew, Phyllis -1994 33
Flowers, Pam 1946- 136
Flowers, Sarah 1952- 98
Floyd, Gareth 1940- 62
  Brief entry 31
Fluchere, Henri 1914-1991 40
Fluke, Joanne 1943- 88
Flutsztejn-Gruda, Ilona 1930- 170
Flynn, Barbara 1928- 9
Flynn, Jackson
  See Bensen, Donald R.
  and Shirreffs, Gordon D(onald)
Flynn, Nicholas
  See Odgers, Sally Farrell
Flynn, Rachel 1953- 171
  Earlier sketch in SATA *109*
Flynn, Warren (G.) 1950- 154
Fodor, R(onald) V(ictor) 1944- 25
Fogelin, Adrian 1951- 175
  Earlier sketch in SATA *129*
Foley, (Anna) Bernice Williams 1902-1987 . 28
Foley, Greg E. 1969- 190
Foley, June 1944- 44

Foley, (Mary) Louise Munro 1933- 106
  Brief entry 40
  Earlier sketch in SATA *54*
Foley, Rae
  See Denniston, Elinore
Folke, Will
  See Bloch, Robert (Albert)
Follett, Helen Thomas 1884(?)-1970
  Obituary 27
Folsom, Franklin (Brewster) 1907-1995 5
  Obituary 88
Folsom, Michael (Brewster) 1938-1990 40
  Obituary 88
Fontenot, Mary Alice 1910- 91
  Earlier sketch in SATA *34*
Fontes, Justine 172
Fontes, Ron 1952- 183
Foon, Dennis 1951- 119
Fooner, Michael 22
Foote, Timothy (Gilson) 1926- 52
Forberg, Ati 22
  See Forberg, Beate Gropius
Forbes, Anna 1954- 101
Forbes, Bryan 1926- 37
Forbes, Cabot L.
  See Hoyt, Edwin P(almer), Jr.
Forbes, Esther 1891-1967 100
  Earlier sketch in SATA *2*
  See also CLR *27*
Forbes, Graham B. 1
Forbes, Kathryn
  See McLean, Kathryn (Anderson)
Forbes, Robert
  See Arthur, Robert, (Jr.)
Ford, Albert Lee
  See Stratemeyer, Edward L.
Ford, Barbara 56
  Brief entry 34
Ford, Brian J(ohn) 1939- 49
Ford, Carolyn (Mott) 1938- 98
Ford, Christine 1953- 176
Ford, David
  See Baldacci, David
  and Baldacci, David
Ford, David B.
  See Baldacci, David
Ford, David Baldacci
  See Baldacci, David
Ford, Elbur
  See Hibbert, Eleanor Alice Burford
Ford, Ellen 1949- 89
Ford, George (Jr.) 31
Ford, Hilary
  See Youd, (Christopher) Samuel
Ford, Hildegarde
  See Morrison, Velma Ford
Ford, Jerome W. 1949- 78
Ford, Jerry
  See Ford, Jerome W.
Ford, Juwanda G(ertrude) 1967- 102
Ford, Marcia
  See Radford, Ruby L(orraine)
Ford, Nancy K(effer) 1906-1961
  Obituary 29
Ford, Peter 1936- 59
Ford, S. M.
  See Uhlig, Susan
Forde, Catherine 1961- 170
Foreman, Michael 1938- 184
  Earlier sketches in SATA *2, 73, 129, 135*
  See also CLR *32*
  See also SAAS *21*
Foreman, Wilmoth 1939- 153
Forest, Dial
  See Gault, William Campbell
Forest, Heather 1948- 185
  Earlier sketch in SATA *120*
Forester, C(ecil) S(cott) 1899-1966 13
Forman, Brenda 1936- 4
Forman, James
  See Forman, James D.

Forman, James D. 1932- 70
   Earlier sketch in SATA 8
Forman, James Douglas
   See Forman, James D.
Forman, Ruth 1970- 186
Forrest, Elizabeth
   See Salsitz, Rhondi Vilott
Forrest, Mary
   See Pausacker, Jenny
Forrest, Sybil
   See Markun, Patricia Maloney
Forrestal, Elaine 1941- 165
   Earlier sketch in SATA 117
Forrester, Frank H. 1919(?)-1986
   Obituary 52
Forrester, Helen 48
   See Bhatia, Jamunadevi
Forrester, Jade
   See Pausacker, Jenny
Forrester, Marian
   See Schachtel, Roger
Forrester, Sandra 1949- 166
   Earlier sketch in SATA 90
Forrester, Victoria 1940- 40
   Brief entry 35
Forsee, (Frances) Aylesa -1986 1
Forsey, Chris 1950- 59
Forshay-Lunsford, Cin 1965- 60
Forster, E(dward) M(organ) 1879-1970 57
Forsyth, Kate 1966- 154
Fort, Paul
   See Stockton, Francis Richard
Forte, Maurizio 1961- 110
Fortey, Richard 1946- 109
Fortey, Richard A.
   See Fortey, Richard
Fortey, Richard Alan
   See Fortey, Richard
Forth, Melissa D(eal) 96
Fortnum, Peggy 26
   See Nuttall-Smith, Margaret Emily Noel
Fortune, Eric 182
Forward, Robert L(ull) 1932-2002 82
Foster, Alan Dean 1946- 70
Foster, Brad W. 1955- 34
Foster, Doris Van Liew 1899-1993 10
Foster, E(lizabeth) C(onnell) 1902- 9
Foster, Elizabeth 1902- 12
Foster, Elizabeth 1905-1963 10
Foster, F. Blanche 1919- 11
Foster, G(eorge) Allen 1907-1969 26
Foster, Genevieve (Stump) 1893-1979 2
   Obituary 23
   See also CLR 7
Foster, Hal
   See Foster, Harold (Rudolf)
Foster, Harold (Rudolf) 1892-1982 31
   See Foster, Hal
Foster, Jeanne
   See Williams, Jeanne
Foster, John
   See Foster, John L(ouis)
   and Furcolo, Foster
Foster, John (Thomas) 1925- 8
Foster, John L(ouis) 1941- 102
Foster, Laura Louise (James) 1918- 6
Foster, Leila Merrell 1929- 73
Foster, Lynne 1937- 74
Foster, Margaret Lesser 1899(?)-1979
   Obituary 21
Foster, Marian Curtis 1909-1978 23
Foster, Sally 58
Foulds, E. V.
   See Foulds, Elfrida Vipont
Foulds, Elfrida Vipont 1902-1992 52
   See Vipont, Elfrida
Fountas, Angela Jane 180
Fourie, Corlia 1944- 91
Fourth Brother, The
   See Aung, (Maung) Htin
Fowke, Edith (Margaret) 1913-1996 14

Fowles, John 1926-2005 22
   Obituary 171
Fowles, John Robert
   See Fowles, John
Fox, Aileen 1907-2005 58
   Obituary 170
Fox, Aileen Mary
   See Fox, Aileen
Fox, Annie 1950- 175
Fox, Charles Philip 1913-2003 12
   Obituary 150
Fox, Christyan 188
Fox, Diane 188
Fox, Eleanor
   See St. John, Wylly Folk
Fox, Fontaine Talbot, Jr. 1884-1964
   Obituary 23
Fox, Fred 1903(?)-1981
   Obituary 27
Fox, Freeman
   See Hamilton, Charles (Harold St. John)
Fox, Geoffrey 1941- 73
Fox, Grace
   See Anderson, Grace Fox
Fox, Helen 1962- 181
Fox, Larry 30
Fox, Lorraine 1922-1976 27
   Earlier sketch in SATA 11
Fox, Louisa
   See Kroll, Virginia L.
Fox, Mary Virginia 1919- 152
   Brief entry 39
   Earlier sketches in SATA 44, 88
Fox, Mem 103
   See also CLR 23
   See Fox, Merrion Frances
Fox, Merrion Frances 1946- 155
   Earlier sketch in SATA 51
   See also CLR 80
   See Fox, Mem
Fox, Michael W(ilson) 1937- 15
Fox, Paula 1923- 167
   Earlier sketches in SATA 17, 60, 120
   See also CLR 96
Fox, Robert J. 1927- 33
Foyt, Victoria 187
Fradin, Dennis
   See Fradin, Dennis Brindell
Fradin, Dennis Brindell 1945- 185
   Earlier sketches in SATA 29, 90, 135
Fradin, Judith Bloom 1945- 185
   Earlier sketches in SATA 90, 152
Frailey, Paige (Menefee) 1965- 82
Frame, Janet 1924-2004 119
Frame, Paul 1913-1994 60
   Brief entry 33
   Obituary 83
Frances, Miss
   See Horwich, Frances R(appaport)
Franchere, Ruth 18
Francis, Charles
   See Holme, Bryan
Francis, Dee
   See Haas, Dorothy F.
Francis, Dorothy 1926- 127
   Earlier sketch in SATA 10
Francis, Dorothy B.
   See Francis, Dorothy
Francis, Dorothy Brenner
   See Francis, Dorothy
Francis, Jaye
   See Pausacker, Jenny
Francis, Pamela (Mary) 1926- 11
Franck, Eddie
   See Cooke, Frank E.
Franco, Betsy 188
   Earlier sketch in SATA 150
Franco, Eloise (Bauder) 1910- 62
Franco, Johan (Henri Gustave) 1908-1988 ... 62
Franco, Marjorie 38
Francois, Andre 1915-2005 25

Francoise
   See Seignobosc, Francoise
Frank, Anne(lies Marie) 1929-1945 87
   Brief entry 42
   See also CLR 101
Frank, Daniel B. 1956- 55
Frank, Emily R.
   See Frank, E.R.
Frank, E.R. 1967- 157
Frank, Helene
   See Vautier, Ghislaine
Frank, Hillary 1976- 148
Frank, Josette 1893-1989 10
   Obituary 63
Frank, Lucy 1947- 166
   Earlier sketch in SATA 94
Frank, Mary 1933- 34
Frank, R., Jr.
   See Ross, Frank (Xavier), Jr.
Frankau, Mary Evelyn Atkinson 1899-1974 .. 4
Frankel, Alona 1937- 66
Frankel, Bernice 9
Frankel, Edward 1910- 44
Frankel, Ellen 1951- 78
Frankel, Julie 1947- 40
   Brief entry 34
Frankenberg, Robert 1911- 22
Franklin, Cheryl J. 1955- 70
Franklin, Harold 1926- 13
Franklin, Kristine L. 1958- 124
   Earlier sketch in SATA 80
Franklin, Lance
   See Lantz, Francess L(in)
Franklin, Madeleine
   See L'Engle, Madeleine
Franklin, Madeleine L'Engle
   See L'Engle, Madeleine
Franklin, Madeleine L'Engle Camp
   See L'Engle, Madeleine
Franklin, Max
   See Deming, Richard
Franklin, Steve
   See Stevens, Franklin
Franson, Leanne R. 1963- 111
Franson, Scott E. 1966- 192
Franzen, Nils-Olof 1916- 10
Frascino, Edward 48
   Brief entry 33
   See also SAAS 9
Frasconi, Antonio 1919- 131
   Earlier sketches in SATA 6, 53
   See also SAAS 11
Fraser, Betty
   See Fraser, Elizabeth Marr
Fraser, Elizabeth Marr 1928- 31
Fraser, Eric (George) 1902-1983 38
Fraser, Mary Ann 1959- 137
   Earlier sketch in SATA 76
   See also SAAS 23
Fraser, Wynnette (McFaddin) 1925- 90
Frasier, Debra 1953- 182
   Earlier sketches in SATA 69, 112
Fraustino, Lisa Rowe 1961- 146
   Autobiography Feature 146
   Earlier sketch in SATA 84
Frazee, Marla 1958- 187
   Earlier sketches in SATA 105, 151
Frazetta, Frank 1928- 58
Frazier, Craig 1955- 177
Frazier, Neta (Osborn) Lohnes 1890-1990 7
Frederic, Mike
   See Cox, William R(obert)
Fredericks, Anthony D. 1947- 113
Freed, Alvyn M. 1913-1993 22
Freedman, Benedict 1919- 27
Freedman, Claire 185
Freedman, Deborah 1960- 191
Freedman, Jeff 1953- 90
Freedman, Nancy 1920- 27

Freedman, Russell 1929- 175
  Earlier sketches in SATA *16, 71, 123*
  See also CLR *71*
Freedman, Russell Bruce
  See Freedman, Russell
Freeman, Barbara C(onstance) 1906- 28
Freeman, Bill
  See Freeman, William Bradford
Freeman, Don 1908-1978 17
  See also CLR *90*
Freeman, Ira Maximilian 1905-1987 21
Freeman, Lucy (Greenbaum) 1916-2004 24
Freeman, Mae (Blacker) 1907- 25
Freeman, Marcia S. 1937- 102
Freeman, Martha 1956- 152
  Earlier sketch in SATA *101*
Freeman, Nancy 1932- 61
Freeman, Peter J.
  See Calvert, Patricia
Freeman, Sarah (Caroline) 1940- 66
Freeman, Tor 1977- 164
Freeman, VicToria
  See Freeman, Tor
Freeman, William Bradford 1938- 58
  Brief entry 48
Fregosi, Claudia (Anne Marie) 1946- 24
French, Allen 1870-1946
  See YABC *1*
French, Dorothy Kayser 1926- 5
French, Fiona 1944- 132
  Earlier sketches in SATA *6, 75*
  See also CLR *37*
  See also SAAS *21*
French, Jackie 186
  Autobiography Feature 139
  Earlier sketches in SATA *108, 139*
  See French, Jackie Anne
  and French, Jacqueline Anne
French, Kathryn
  See Mosesson, Gloria R(ubin)
French, Martin 176
French, Michael 1944- 49
  Brief entry 38
French, Paul
  See Asimov, Isaac
French, Simon 1957- 147
  Earlier sketch in SATA *86*
French, Vivian 165
Frenette, Liza 126
Freschet, Gina 1960- 175
  Earlier sketch in SATA *139*
Frewer, Glyn (M.) 1931- 11
Frey, Darcy 98
Freymann, Saxton 1958(?)- 178
Freymann-Weyr, (Rhoda) Garret
  (Michaela) 1965- 145
Frick, C. H.
  See Irwin, Constance (H.) Frick
Frick, Constance
  See Irwin, Constance (H.) Frick
Fricke, Aaron 1962- 89
Fridell, Ron 1943- 124
Friedlander, Joanne K(ohn) 1930- 9
Friedman, Aimee 1979- 189
Friedman, D. Dina 1957- 180
Friedman, Debra 1955- 150
Friedman, Estelle (Ehrenwald) 1920- 7
Friedman, Frieda 1905- 43
Friedman, Ina R(osen) 1926- 136
  Brief entry 41
  Earlier sketch in SATA *49*
Friedman, Jerrold David
  See Gerrold, David
Friedman, Judi 1935- 59
Friedman, Laurie 1964- 179
  Earlier sketch in SATA *138*
Friedman, Marvin 1930- 42
  Brief entry 33
Friedman, Robin 1968- 162
Friedmann, Stan 1953- 80
Friedrich, Otto (Alva) 1929-1995 33

Friedrich, Priscilla 1927- 39
Friend, Natasha 1972- 184
Friendlich, Dick
  See Friendlich, Richard J.
Friendlich, Richard J. 1909- 11
Friermood, Elisabeth Hamilton 1903-1992 5
Friesen, Bernice (Sarah Anne) 1966- 105
Friesen, Gayle 1960- 109
Friesner, Esther M. 1951- 168
  Earlier sketch in SATA *71*
Friis-Baastad, Babbis Ellinor 1921-1970 7
Frimmer, Steven 1928- 31
Frischmuth, Barbara 1941- 114
Friskey, Margaret (Richards) 1901-1995 5
Fritts, Mary Bahr
  See Bahr, Mary (Madelyn)
Fritz, Jean (Guttery) 1915- 163
  Autobiography Feature 122
  Earlier sketches in SATA *1, 29, 72, 119*
  See also CLR *96*
  See also SAAS *2*
Froehlich, Margaret W(alden) 1930- 56
Frois, Jeanne 1953- 73
Froissart, Jean 1338(?)-1410(?) 28
Froman, Elizabeth Hull 1920-1975 10
Froman, Robert (Winslow) 1917- 8
Fromm, Lilo 1928- 29
Frommer, Harvey 1937- 41
Frost, A(rthur) B(urdett) 1851-1928 19
Frost, Elizabeth
  See Frost-Knappman, Elizabeth
Frost, Erica
  See Supraner, Robyn
Frost, Helen 1949- 183
  Earlier sketch in SATA *157*
Frost, Helen Marie
  See Frost, Helen
Frost, Lesley 1899-1983 14
  Obituary 34
Frost, Robert 1874-1963 14
  See also CLR *67*
Frost, Robert Lee
  See Frost, Robert
Frost, Shelley 1960- 138
Frost-Knappman, Elizabeth 1943- 179
Froud, Brian 1947- 150
Fry, Annette R(iley) 89
Fry, Christopher 1907-2005 66
Fry, Edward Bernard 1925- 35
Fry, Rosalie Kingsmill 1911-1992 3
  See also SAAS *11*
Fry, Virginia Lynn 1952- 95
Frye, Sally
  See Moore, Elaine
Fuchs, Bernie 1932- 162
  Earlier sketch in SATA *95*
Fuchs, Erich 1916- 6
Fuchshuber, Annegert 1940- 43
Fuerst, Jeffrey B. 1956- 143
Fuertes, Gloria 1918-1998 115
Fuge, Charles 1966- 144
  Earlier sketch in SATA *74*
Fujikawa, Gyo 1908-1998 76
  Brief entry 30
  Obituary 110
  Earlier sketch in SATA *39*
  See also CLR *25*
  See also SAAS *16*
Fujita, Tamao 1905-1999 7
Fujiwara, Kim 1957- 81
Fujiwara, Michiko 1946- 15
Fuka, Vladimir 1926-1977
  Obituary 27
Fulcher, Jennifer
  See Westwood, Jennifer
Fuller, Catherine Leuthold 1916- 9
Fuller, Edmund (Maybank) 1914- 21
Fuller, Iola
  See McCoy, Iola Fuller
Fuller, John G(rant, Jr.) 1913-1990 65

Fuller, Kathleen
  See Gottfried, Theodore Mark
Fuller, Lois Hamilton 1915- 11
Fuller, Margaret
  See Ossoli, Sarah Margaret (Fuller)
Fuller, Maud
  See Petersham, Maud (Sylvia Fuller)
Fuller, Roy (Broadbent) 1912-1991 87
Fuller, Sarah Margaret
  See Ossoli, Sarah Margaret (Fuller)
Fuller, Sarah Margaret
  See Ossoli, Sarah Margaret (Fuller)
Fults, John Lee 1932- 33
Funk, Thompson 1911- 7
Funk, Tom
  See Funk, Thompson
Funke, Cornelia 1958- 174
  Earlier sketch in SATA *154*
Funke, Cornelia Caroline
  See Funke, Cornelia
Funke, Lewis 1912-1992 11
Fuqua, Jonathon Scott 1966- 141
Furbee, Mary R.
  See Furbee, Mary Rodd
Furbee, Mary Rodd 1954- 138
Furchgott, Terry 1948- 29
Furlong, Monica (Mavis) 1930-2003 86
  Obituary 142
Furman, Gertrude Lerner Kerman 1909- 21
Furniss, Tim 1948- 49
Furrow, Robert 1985- 172
Furukawa, Toshi 1924- 24
Fusillo, Archimede 1962- 137
Futcher, Jane P. 1947- 76
Futehali, Zahida
  See Whitaker, Zai
Fyleman, Rose (Amy) 1877-1957 21
Fyson, J(enny) G(race) 1904- 42

G

Gaan, Margaret 1914- 65
Gaber, Susan 1956- 169
  Earlier sketch in SATA *115*
Gaberman, Judie Angell 1937- 78
  Earlier sketch in SATA *22*
  See also CLR *33*
Gabhart, Ann
  See Gabhart, Ann H.
Gabhart, Ann H. 1947- 75
Gabler, Mirko 1951- 77
Gabriel, Adriana
  See Rojany, Lisa
Gabrys, Ingrid Schubert
  See Schubert-Gabrys, Ingrid
Gackenbach, Dick 1927- 79
  Brief entry 30
  Earlier sketch in SATA *48*
Gadd, Jeremy 1949- 116
Gaddis, Vincent H. 1913-1997 35
Gadler, Steve J. 1905-1985 36
Gaeddert, Lou Ann (Bigge) 1931- 103
  Earlier sketch in SATA *20*
Gaeddert, Louann
  See Gaeddert, Lou Ann (Bigge)
Gaer, Joseph 1897-1969 118
Gaer, Yossef
  See Gaer, Joseph
Gaetz, Dayle Campbell 1947- 138
Gaffney, Timothy R. 1951- 170
  Earlier sketch in SATA *69*
Gaffron, Norma (Bondeson) 1931- 97
Gag, Flavia 1907-1979
  Obituary 24
Gag, Wanda (Hazel) 1893-1946 100
  See also YABC *1*
  See also CLR *4*
Gage, Brian 162

Gage, Wilson
　See Steele, Mary Q(uintard Govan)
Gagliano, Eugene M. 1946- 150
Gagliardo, Ruth Garver 1895(?)-1980
　Obituary 22
Gagnon, Cecile 1936- 58
Gaiman, Neil 1960- 146
　Earlier sketch in SATA 85
　See also CLR 109
Gaiman, Neil Richard
　See Gaiman, Neil
Gainer, Cindy 1962- 74
Gaines, Ernest J. 1933- 86
　See also CLR 62
Gaines, Ernest James
　See Gaines, Ernest J.
Gaither, Gloria 1942- 127
Gal, Laszlo 1933- 96
　Brief entry 32
　Earlier sketch in SATA 52
　See also CLR 61
Galbraith, Kathryn O(sebold) 1945- 85
Galdone, Paul 1907(?)-1986 66
　Obituary 49
　Earlier sketch in SATA 17
　See also CLR 16
Galinsky, Ellen 1942- 23
Gall, Chris 1961- 176
Gallagher, Diana G. 1946- 153
Gallagher, Lurlene Nora
　See McDaniel, Lurlene
Gallant, Roy A(rthur) 1924- 110
　Earlier sketches in SATA 4, 68
　See also CLR 30
Gallardo, Evelyn 1948- 78
Gallaz, Christophe 1948- 162
　See also CLR 126
Gallego Garcia, Laura 1977- 173
Gallico, Paul (William) 1897-1976 13
Gallo, Donald R. 1938- 112
　Autobiography Feature 104
Gallo, Donald Robert
　See Gallo, Donald R.
Galloway, Owateka (S.) 1981- 121
Galloway, Priscilla 1930- 112
　Earlier sketch in SATA 66
Gallup, Joan 1957- 128
Galouchko, Annouchka Gravel 1960- 95
Galt, Thomas Franklin, Jr. 1908-1989 5
Galt, Tom
　See Galt, Thomas Franklin, Jr.
Galvin, Matthew R. 1950- 93
Galvin, Matthew Reppert
　See Galvin, Matthew R.
Gamble, Kim 1952- 183
　Earlier sketches in SATA 81, 124
Gambrell, Jamey 82
Gamerman, Martha 1941- 15
Gammell, Stephen 1943- 128
　Earlier sketches in SATA 53, 81
　See also CLR 83
Ganly, Helen (Mary) 1940- 56
Gannett, Ruth Chrisman (Arens)
　1896-1979 33
Gannett, Ruth Stiles 1923- 3
Gannon, Robert Haines 1931- 8
Gano, Lila 1949- 76
Gans, Roma 1894-1996 45
　Obituary 93
Gant, Matthew
　See Hano, Arnold
Gantner, Susan (Verble) 1939- 63
Gantos, Jack 1951- 169
　Earlier sketches in SATA 20, 81, 119
　See also CLR 85
Gantos, John Bryan, Jr.
　See Gantos, Jack
Ganz, Yaffa 1938- 61
　Brief entry 52
Garafano, Marie 1942- 84
Garant, Andre J. 1968- 123

Garbe, Ruth Moore
　See Moore, Ruth (Ellen)
Garber, Esther
　See Lee, Tanith
Garcia, Yolanda P. 1952- 113
Garcia, Yolanda Pacheco
　See Garcia, Yolanda P.
Gard, Janice
　See Latham, Jean Lee
Gard, Joyce
　See Reeves, Joyce
Gard, Robert Edward 1910-1992 18
　Obituary 74
Gard, (Sanford) Wayne 1899-1986
　Obituary 49
Gardam, Jane 1928- 130
　Brief entry 28
　Earlier sketches in SATA 39, 76
　See also CLR 12
　See also SAAS 9
Gardam, Jane Mary
　See Gardam, Jane
Gardella, Tricia 1944- 96
Garden, Nancy 1938- 147
　Autobiography Feature 147
　Earlier sketches in SATA 12, 77, 114
　See also CLR 51
　See also SAAS 8
Gardiner, John Reynolds 1944-2006 64
　Obituary 174
Gardiner, Lindsey 1971- 144
Gardner, Craig Shaw 1949- 99
Gardner, Dic
　See Gardner, Richard (M.)
Gardner, Graham 159
Gardner, Hugh 1910-1986
　Obituary 49
Gardner, Jane Mylum 1946- 83
Gardner, Jeanne LeMonnier 1925- 5
Gardner, John, Jr. 1933-1982 40
　Obituary 31
Gardner, John Champlin, Jr.
　See Gardner, John, Jr.
Gardner, Lyn 192
Gardner, Martin 1914- 142
　Earlier sketch in SATA 16
Gardner, Miriam
　See Bradley, Marion Zimmer
Gardner, Richard (M.) 1931- 24
Gardner, Richard A(lan) 1931-2003 13
　Obituary 144
Gardner, Sally 177
Gardner, Sandra 1940- 70
Gardner, Scot 1968- 143
Gardner, Sheldon 1934- 33
Gardner, Ted
　See Gardner, Theodore Roosevelt II
Gardner, Theodore Roosevelt
　See Gardner, Theodore Roosevelt II
Gardner, Theodore Roosevelt II 1934- 84
Garelick, May 1910-1989 19
Garfield, James B. 1881-1984 6
　Obituary 38
Garfield, Leon 1921-1996 76
　Obituary 90
　Earlier sketches in SATA 1, 32
　See also CLR 21
Garfinkle, Debra L.
　See Garfinkle, D.L.
Garfinkle, D.L. 187
Garis, Howard R(oger) 1873-1962 13
Garland, Mark 1953- 79
Garland, Mark A.
　See Garland, Mark
Garland, Michael 1952- 168
Garland, Sarah 1944- 135
　Earlier sketch in SATA 62
Garland, Sherry 1948- 145
　Autobiography Feature 145
　Earlier sketches in SATA 73, 114

Garner, Alan 1934- 69
　Autobiography Feature 108
　Earlier sketch in SATA 18
　See also CLR 130
Garner, David 1958- 78
Garner, Eleanor Ramrath 1930- 122
Garner, James Finn 1960(?)- 92
Garnet, A. H.
　See Slote, Alfred
Garnett, Eve C. R. 1900-1991 3
　Obituary 70
Garofoli, Viviana 1970- 186
Garou, Louis P.
　See Bowkett, Stephen
Garraty, John A. 1920-2007 23
　Obituary 189
Garraty, John Arthur
　See Garraty, John A.
Garren, Devorah-Leah
　See Devorah-Leah
Garret, Maxwell R. 1917- 39
Garretson, Victoria Diane 1945- 44
Garrett, Helen 1895- 21
Garrett, Richard 1920- 82
Garrigue, Sheila 1931- 21
Garrison, Barbara 1931- 163
　Earlier sketch in SATA 19
Garrison, Frederick
　See Sinclair, Upton
Garrison, Mary 1952- 146
Garrison, Peter
　See Gardner, Craig Shaw
Garrison, Webb B(lack) 1919-2000 25
Garrity, Jennifer Johnson 1961- 124
Garrity, Linda K. 1947- 128
Garst, Doris Shannon 1894-1981 1
Garst, Shannon
　See Garst, Doris Shannon
Garth, Will
　See Hamilton, Edmond
　and Kuttner, Henry
Garthwaite, Marion H(ook) 1893-1981 7
Garton, Malinda D(ean) (?)-1976
　Obituary 26
Garvie, Maureen 1944- 175
Garvie, Maureen McCallum
　See Garvie, Maureen
Garza, Carmen Lomas 1948- 182
Garza, Xavier 184
Gascoigne, Bamber 1935- 62
Gaskins, Pearl Fuyo 1957- 134
Gasperini, Jim 1952- 54
　Brief entry 49
Gater, Dilys 1944- 41
Gates, Doris 1901-1987 34
　Obituary 54
　Earlier sketch in SATA 1
　See also SAAS 1
Gates, Frieda 1933- 26
Gates, Susan 1950- 153
Gates, Viola R. 1931- 101
Gathorne-Hardy, Jonathan G. 1933- 124
　Earlier sketch in SATA 26
Gatti, Anne 1952- 103
Gatty, Juliana Horatia
　See Ewing, Juliana (Horatia Gatty)
Gauch, Patricia Lee 1934- 80
　Earlier sketch in SATA 26
　See also CLR 56
　See also SAAS 21
Gaudasinska, Elzbieta 1943- 190
Gaul, Randy 1959- 63
Gault, Clare 1925- 36
Gault, Frank 1926-1982 36
　Brief entry 30
Gault, William Campbell 1910-1995 8
Gauthier, Gail 1953- 160
　Earlier sketch in SATA 118
Gaver, Becky
　See Gaver, Rebecca
Gaver, Rebecca 1952- 20

Gavin, Jamila 1941- *125*
  Earlier sketch in SATA *96*
Gay, Amelia
  See Hogarth, Grace (Weston Allen)
Gay, Francis
  See Gee, H(erbert) L(eslie)
Gay, Kathlyn 1930- *144*
  Earlier sketch in SATA *9*
Gay, Marie-Louise 1952- *179*
  Earlier sketches in SATA *68, 126*
  See also CLR *27*
  See also SAAS *21*
Gay, Michel 1947- *162*
Gay, Zhenya 1906-1978 .... *19*
Gaze, Gillian
  See Barklem, Jill
Gear, Kathleen M. O'Neal
  See Gear, Kathleen O'Neal
Gear, Kathleen O'Neal 1954- *166*
  Earlier sketch in SATA *71*
Gear, W. Michael 1955- *166*
  Earlier sketch in SATA *71*
Geary, Rick 1946- *142*
Geason, Susan 1946- *122*
Gedalof, Robin
  See McGrath, Robin
Gedge, Pauline (Alice) 1945- *101*
Gee, H(erbert) L(eslie) 1901-1977
  Obituary *26*
Gee, Maurice 1931- *101*
  Earlier sketch in SATA *46*
  See also CLR *56*
Gee, Maurice Gough
  See Gee, Maurice
Geehan, Wayne (E.) 1947- *107*
Geer, Charles 1922- *42*
  Brief entry *32*
Geeslin, Campbell 1925- *163*
  Earlier sketch in SATA *107*
Gehman, Mary W. 1923- *86*
Gehr, Mary 1910(?)-1997 .... *32*
  Obituary *99*
Geipel, Eileen 1932- *30*
Geis, Alissa Imre 1976- *189*
Geis, Darlene Stern 1918(?)-1999 .... *7*
  Obituary *111*
Geisel, Helen 1898-1967 .... *26*
Geisel, Theodor Seuss 1904-1991 .... *100*
  Obituary *67*
  Earlier sketches in SATA *1, 28, 75*
  See also CLR *100*
  See Dr. Seuss
Geisert, Arthur 1941- *171*
  Brief entry *52*
  Earlier sketches in SATA *56, 92, 133*
  See also CLR *87*
  See also SAAS *23*
Geisert, Arthur Frederick
  See Geisert, Arthur
Geisert, Bonnie 1942- *165*
  Earlier sketch in SATA *92*
Geist, Ken *191*
Geldart, William 1936- *15*
Gelinas, Paul J. 1904-1996 .... *10*
Gellis, Roberta 1927- *128*
Gellis, Roberta Leah Jacobs
  See Gellis, Roberta
Gellman, Marc *112*
Gelman, Amy 1961- *72*
Gelman, Jan 1963- *58*
Gelman, Rita Golden 1937- *131*
  Brief entry *51*
  Earlier sketch in SATA *84*
Gelman, Steve 1934- *3*
Gemming, Elizabeth 1932- *11*
Gendel, Evelyn W. 1916(?)-1977
  Obituary *27*
Gennaro, Joseph F(rancis), Jr. 1924- *53*
Gentile, Petrina 1969- *91*
Gentle, Mary 1956- *48*
Gentleman, David (William) 1930- *7*

Geoghegan, Adrienne 1962- *143*
George, Barbara
  See Katz, Bobbi
George, Emily
  See Katz, Bobbi
George, Gail
  See Katz, Bobbi
George, Jean
  See George, Jean Craighead
George, Jean Craighead 1919- *170*
  Earlier sketches in SATA *2, 68, 124*
  See also CLR *136*
George, John L(othar) 1916- *2*
George, Kristine O'Connell 1954- *156*
  Earlier sketch in SATA *110*
George, Lindsay Barrett 1952- *155*
  Earlier sketch in SATA *95*
George, S(idney) C(harles) 1898- *11*
George, Sally
  See Orr, Wendy
George, Twig C. 1950- *114*
George, W(illiam) Lloyd 1900(?)-1975
  Obituary *30*
Georgiou, Constantine 1927- *7*
Georgiou, Theo
  See Odgers, Sally Farrell
Geraghty, Paul 1959- *130*
Gerard, Jean Ignace Isidore 1803-1847 .... *45*
Geras, Adele 1944- *180*
  Autobiography Feature *180*
  Earlier sketches in SATA *23, 87, 129, 173*
  See also SAAS *21*
Geras, Adele Daphne Weston
  See Geras, Adele
Gerber, Merrill Joan 1938- *170*
  Autobiography Feature *170*
  Earlier sketches in SATA *64, 127*
Gerber, Perren 1933- *104*
Gerberg, Mort 1931- *64*
Gergely, Tibor 1900-1978 .... *54*
  Obituary *20*
Geringer, Laura 1948- *164*
  Earlier sketches in SATA *29, 94*
Gerler, William R(obert) 1917-1996 .... *47*
Gerrard, Jean 1933- *51*
Gerrard, Roy 1935-1997 .... *90*
  Brief entry *45*
  Obituary *99*
  Earlier sketch in SATA *47*
  See also CLR *23*
Gerritsen, Paula 1956- *177*
Gerrold, David 1944- *144*
  Earlier sketch in SATA *66*
Gershator, David 1937- *180*
Gershator, Phillis 1942- *188*
  Earlier sketches in SATA *90, 158*
Gershon, Dann 1955- *187*
Gershon, Gina 1962- *187*
Gerson, Corinne 1927- *37*
Gerson, Mary-Joan *136*
  Earlier sketch in SATA *79*
Gerson, Noel Bertram 1914-1988 .... *22*
  Obituary *60*
Gerstein, Mordicai 1935- *178*
  Brief entry *36*
  Earlier sketches in SATA *47, 81, 142*
  See also CLR *102*
Gertridge, Allison 1967- *132*
Gervais, Bernadette 1959- *80*
Gervay, Susanne *183*
Gesner, Clark 1938-2002 .... *40*
  Obituary *143*
Gessner, Lynne 1919- *16*
Geter, Tyrone *150*
Getz, David 1957- *91*
Getzinger, Donna 1968- *128*
Gevirtz, Eliezer 1950- *49*
Gevry, Claudine *188*
Gewe, Raddory
  See Gorey, Edward (St. John)
Ghan, Linda (R.) 1947- *77*

Ghent, Natale 1962- *148*
Gherman, Beverly 1934- *123*
  Earlier sketch in SATA *68*
Ghigna, Charles 1946- *153*
  Earlier sketch in SATA *108*
Giacobbe, Beppe 1953- *174*
Giambastiani, Kurt R. A. 1958- *141*
Giannini, Enzo 1946- *68*
Gibbons, Alan 1953- *124*
Gibbons, Faye 1938- *103*
  Earlier sketch in SATA *65*
Gibbons, Gail 1944- *160*
  Earlier sketches in SATA *23, 72, 104*
  See also CLR *8*
  See also SAAS *12*
Gibbons, Gail Gretchen
  See Gibbons, Gail
Gibbons, Kaye 1960- *117*
Gibbs, Adrea 1960- *126*
Gibbs, Alonzo (Lawrence) 1915-1992 .... *5*
Gibbs, (Cecilia) May 1877-1969
  Obituary *27*
Gibbs, Tony
  See Gibbs, Wolcott, Jr.
Gibbs, Wolcott, Jr. 1935- *40*
Giblin, James Cross 1933- *122*
  Earlier sketches in SATA *33, 75*
  See also CLR *29*
  See also SAAS *12*
Gibson, Andrew (William) 1949- *72*
Gibson, Betty 1911- *75*
Gibson, Jo
  See Fluke, Joanne
Gibson, William 1914- *66*
Gibson, William Ford
  See Gibson, William
Gidal, Nachum
  See Gidal, Tim Nachum
Gidal, Sonia (Epstein) 1922- *2*
Gidal, Tim Nachum 1909-1996 .... *2*
Gidalewitsch, Nachum
  See Gidal, Tim Nachum
Gideon, Melanie 1963- *175*
Giegling, John A(llan) 1935- *17*
Gifaldi, David 1950- *76*
Giff, Patricia Reilly 1935- *160*
  Earlier sketches in SATA *33, 70, 121*
Giffard, Hannah 1962- *83*
Gifford, Griselda 1931- *171*
  Earlier sketch in SATA *42*
Gifford, Kerri 1961- *91*
Gifford, Peggy 1952- *191*
Gilbert, Ann
  See Taylor, Ann
Gilbert, Anne Yvonne 1951- *128*
  See Gilbert, Yvonne
Gilbert, Barbara Snow 1954- *97*
Gilbert, Catherine
  See Murdock, Catherine Gilbert
Gilbert, Frances
  See Collings, Gillian
Gilbert, Harriett 1948- *30*
Gilbert, (Agnes) Joan (Sewell) 1931- *10*
Gilbert, John (Raphael) 1926- *36*
Gilbert, Nan
  See Gilbertson, Mildred Geiger
Gilbert, Roby Goodale 1966- *90*
Gilbert, Ruth Gallard Ainsworth
  See Ainsworth, Ruth (Gallard)
Gilbert, Sara (Dulaney) 1943- *82*
  Earlier sketch in SATA *11*
Gilbert, Sheri L. *157*
Gilbert, Suzie 1956- *97*
Gilbert, W(illiam) S(chwenck) 1836-1911 ... *36*
Gilbert, Yvonne *185*
  See Gilbert, Anne Yvonne
Gilbertson, Mildred Geiger 1908-1988 .... *2*
Gilbreath, Alice 1921- *12*
Gilbreth, Frank B(unker), Jr. 1911-2001 .... *2*
Gilchrist, Jan Spivey 1949- *130*
  Earlier sketch in SATA *72*

Gilden, Mel 1947- 97
Giles, Gail 152
Gilfond, Henry 2
Gilge, Jeanette 1924- 22
Gili, Phillida 1944- 70
Gill, Derek (Lewis Theodore) 1919-1997 9
Gill, Margery Jean 1925- 22
Gill, Shelley 176
Gill, Stephen 1932- 63
Gillespie, Carol Ann 1951- 158
Gillett, Mary (Bledsoe) 7
Gillette, Henry Sampson 1915- 14
Gillette, J(an) Lynett 1946- 103
Gilley, Jeremy 1969- 174
Gillham, Bill
    See Gillham, W(illiam) E(dwin) C(harles)
Gillham, W(illiam) E(dwin)
    C(harles) 1936- 42
Gilliam, Stan 1946- 39
    Brief entry 35
Gilliland, Alexis A(rnaldus) 1931- 72
Gilliland, (Cleburne) Hap 1918- 92
Gilliland, Judith Heide 180
Gillmor, Don 1954- 127
Gilman, Esther 1925- 15
Gilman, Laura Anne 178
Gilman, Phoebe 1940-2002 104
    Obituary 141
    Earlier sketch in SATA 58
Gilmore, Iris 1900-1982 22
Gilmore, Kate 1931- 87
Gilmore, Mary (Jean Cameron) 1865-1962 . 49
Gilmore, Susan 1954- 59
Gilpin, Stephen 177
Gilroy, Beryl (Agatha) 1924- 80
Gilson, Barbara
    See Gilson, Charles James Louis
Gilson, Charles James Louis 1878-1943
    See YABC 2
Gilson, Jamie 1933- 176
    Brief entry 34
    Earlier sketches in SATA 37, 91
Ginsburg, Mirra 1909-2000 92
    Earlier sketch in SATA 6
    See also CLR 45
Giovanni, Nikki 1943- 107
    Earlier sketch in SATA 24
    See also CLR 73
Giovanni, Yolanda Cornelia
    See Giovanni, Nikki
Giovanni, Yolande Cornelia
    See Giovanni, Nikki
Giovanni, Yolande Cornelia, Jr.
    See Giovanni, Nikki
Giovanopoulos, Paul (Arthur) 1939- 7
Gipson, Fred(erick Benjamin) 1908-1973 2
    Obituary 24
Girard, Linda (Walvoord) 1942- 41
Girion, Barbara 1937- 78
    Earlier sketch in SATA 26
    See also SAAS 14
Girouard, Patrick 1957- 155
Girzone, Joseph F. 1930- 76
Girzone, Joseph Francis
    See Girzone, Joseph F.
Gise, Joanne
    See Mattern, Joanne
Gittings, Jo (Grenville) Manton 1919- 3
Gittings, Robert (William Victor)
    1911-1992 6
    Obituary 70
Givens, Janet E(aton) 1932- 60
Givner, Joan 1936- 171
Givner, Joan Mary
    See Givner, Joan
Gladstone, Eve
    See Werner, Herma
Gladstone, Gary 1935- 12
Gladstone, M(yron) J. 1923- 37
Glanville, Brian (Lester) 1931- 42
Glanzman, Louis S. 1922- 36

Glaser, Byron 1954- 154
Glaser, Dianne E(lizabeth) 1937- 50
    Brief entry 31
Glaser, Isabel Joshlin 1929- 94
Glaser, Milton 1929- 151
    Earlier sketch in SATA 11
Glaser, Shirley 151
Glaspell, Susan 1882(?)-1948
    See YABC 2
Glass, Andrew 1949- 150
    Brief entry 46
    Earlier sketch in SATA 90
Glass, Linzi 175
Glass, Linzi Alex
    See Glass, Linzi
Glasscock, Amnesia
    See Steinbeck, John (Ernst)
Glassman, Bruce 1961- 76
Glauber, Uta (Heil) 1936- 17
Glazer, Thomas (Zachariah) 1914-2003 9
Glazer, Tom
    See Glazer, Thomas (Zachariah)
Gleasner, Diana (Cottle) 1936- 29
Gleason, Judith 1929- 24
Gleason, Katherine (A.) 1960- 104
Gleeson, Libby 1950- 142
    Autobiography Feature 142
    Earlier sketches in SATA 82, 118
Gleiter, Jan 1947- 111
Gleitzman, Morris 1953- 156
    Earlier sketch in SATA 88
    See also CLR 88
Glen, Maggie 1944- 88
Glendinning, Richard 1917-1988 24
Glendinning, Sally
    See Glendinning, Sara W(ilson)
Glendinning, Sara W(ilson) 1913-1993 24
Glenn, Mel 1943- 93
    Brief entry 45
    Earlier sketch in SATA 51
    See also CLR 51
Glenn, Patricia Brown 1953- 86
Glenn, Sharlee 159
Glenn, Sharlee Mullins
    See Glenn, Sharlee
Glennon, Karen M. 1946- 85
Gles, Margaret Breitmaier 1940- 22
Glick, Carl (Cannon) 1890-1971 14
Glick, Ruth (Burtnick) 1942- 125
Glick, Virginia Kirkus 1893-1980
    Obituary 23
Gliewe, Unada (Grace) 1927- 3
Glimmerveen, Ulco 1958- 85
Glines, Carroll V(ane), Jr. 1920- 19
Gliori, Debi 1959- 189
    Earlier sketches in SATA 72, 138
Globe, Leah Ain 1900- 41
Glori Ann
    See Blakely, Gloria
Glovach, Linda 1947- 105
    Earlier sketch in SATA 7
Glover, Denis (James Matthews) 1912-1980 . 7
Glubok, Shirley (Astor) 146
    Autobiography Feature 146
    Earlier sketches in SATA 6, 68
    See also CLR 1
    See also SAAS 7
Gluck, Felix 1923-1981
    Obituary 25
Glyman, Caroline A. 1967- 103
Glynne-Jones, William 1907-1977 11
Gobbato, Imero 1923- 39
Gobbletree, Richard
    See Quackenbush, Robert M(ead)
Goble, Dorothy 26
Goble, Paul 1933- 131
    Earlier sketches in SATA 25, 69
    See also CLR 21
Goble, Warwick (?)-1943 46

Godden, (Margaret) Rumer 1907-1998 36
    Obituary 109
    Earlier sketch in SATA 3
    See also CLR 20
    See also SAAS 12
Gode, Alexander
    See Gode von Aesch, Alexander
    (Gottfried Friedrich)
Gode von Aesch, Alexander (Gottfried
    Friedrich) 1906-1970 14
Godfrey, Jane
    See Bowden, Joan Chase
Godfrey, Martyn
    See Godfrey, Martyn N.
    and Godfrey, Martyn N.
Godfrey, Martyn N. 1949-2000 95
    See also CLR 57
    See Godfrey, Martyn
Godfrey, William
    See Youd, (Christopher) Samuel
Godkin, Celia (Marilyn) 1948- 145
    Earlier sketch in SATA 66
Godon, Ingrid 1958- 186
Godwin, Laura 1956- 179
Godwin, Sam
    See Pirotta, Saviour
Goedecke, Christopher (John) 1951- 81
Goekler, Susan
    See Wooley, Susan Frelick
Goertzen, Glenda 172
Goettel, Elinor 1930- 12
Goetz, Delia 1898-1996 22
    Obituary 91
Goffe, Toni 1936- 61
Goffstein, Brooke
    See Goffstein, M(arilyn) B(rooke)
Goffstein, M(arilyn) B(rooke) 1940- 70
    Earlier sketch in SATA 8
    See also CLR 3
Goforth, Ellen
    See Francis, Dorothy
Gogol, Sara 1948-2004 80
Goh, Chan Hon 1969- 145
Going, Kelly L.
    See Going, K.L.
Going, Kelly Louise
    See Going, K.L.
Going, K.L. 156
Golann, Cecil Paige 1921-1995 11
Golbin, Andree 1923- 15
Gold, Alison Leslie 1945- 104
Gold, Bernice 150
Gold, Phyllis 21
    See Goldberg, Phyllis
Gold, Robert S(tanley) 1924- 63
Gold, Sharlya 9
Gold, Susan
    See Gold, Susan Dudley
Gold, Susan Dudley 1949- 147
Goldberg, Grace 1956- 78
Goldberg, Herbert S. 1926- 25
Goldberg, Jacob 1943- 94
Goldberg, Jake
    See Goldberg, Jacob
Goldberg, Jan 123
    See Curran, Jan Goldberg
Goldberg, Stan J. 1939- 26
Goldberg, Susan 1948- 71
Goldberg, Whoopi 1955- 119
Goldblatt, Stacey 1969(?)- 191
Golden, Christie 1963- 167
    Earlier sketch in SATA 116
Goldentyer, Debra 1960- 84
Goldfeder, Cheryl
    See Pahz, Cheryl Suzanne
Goldfeder, James
    See Pahz, James Alon
Goldfeder, Jim
    See Pahz, James Alon
Goldfinger, Jennifer P. 1963- 185
Goldfrank, Helen Colodny 1912- 6

Goldin, Augusta 1906-1999 .... *13*
Goldin, Barbara Diamond 1946- *129*
   Autobiography Feature *129*
   Earlier sketch in SATA *92*
   See also SAAS *26*
Goldin, David 1963- *101*
Golding, Julia 1969- *188*
Golding, Theresa Martin 1960- *150*
Golding, William 1911-1993
   See CLR *130*
Golding, William Gerald
   See Golding, William
Goldman, Alex J. 1917- *65*
Goldman, E(leanor) M(aureen) 1943- *103*
Goldman, Elizabeth 1949- *90*
Goldring, Ann 1937- *149*
Goldsborough, June 1923- *19*
Goldsmith, Connie 1945- *147*
Goldsmith, Howard 1943- *108*
   Earlier sketch in SATA *24*
Goldsmith, John Herman Thorburn
   1903-1987
   Obituary *52*
Goldsmith, Oliver 1730(?)-1774 .... *26*
Goldsmith, Ruth M. 1919- *62*
Goldstein, Nathan 1927- *47*
Goldstein, Philip 1910-1997 .... *23*
Goldston, Robert (Conroy) 1927- *6*
Goldstone, Bruce *183*
Goldstone, Lawrence A.
   See Treat, Lawrence
Golembe, Carla 1951- *79*
Golenbock, Peter 1946- *99*
Goll, Reinhold W(eimar) 1897-1993 .... *26*
Gollub, Matthew 1960- *134*
   Earlier sketch in SATA *83*
Gomes, Filomena 1965- *183*
Gomez, Elena *191*
Gomez, Elizabeth *133*
Gomez-Freer, Elizabeth
   See Gomez, Elizabeth
Gomi, Taro 1945- *103*
   Earlier sketch in SATA *64*
   See also CLR *57*
Gondosch, Linda 1944- *58*
Gonzalez, Catherine Troxell 1917-2000 .... *87*
Gonzalez, Christina
   See Gonzalez, Maya Christina
Gonzalez, Gloria 1940- *23*
Gonzalez, Julie 1958- *174*
Gonzalez, Maya
   See Gonzalez, Maya Christina
Gonzalez, Maya Christina 1964- *175*
   Earlier sketch in SATA *115*
Gonzalez, Rigoberto 1970- *147*
Goobie, Beth 1959- *128*
Good, Alice 1950- *73*
Goodall, Daphne Machin
   See Machin Goodall, Daphne (Edith)
Goodall, Jane 1934- *111*
Goodall, John S(trickland) 1908-1996 .... *66*
   Obituary *91*
   Earlier sketch in SATA *4*
   See also CLR *25*
Goodbody, Slim
   See Burstein, John
Goode, Diane 1949- *170*
   Earlier sketches in SATA *15, 84, 114*
Goode, Diane Capuozzo
   See Goode, Diane
Goode, Stephen Ray 1943- *55*
   Brief entry *40*
Goodenow, Earle 1913- *40*
Goodhart, Pippa 1958- *153*
Goodhue, Thomas W. 1949- *143*
Goodin, Sallie (Brown) 1953- *74*
Goodman, Alison 1966- *111*
Goodman, Deborah Lerme 1956- *50*
   Brief entry *49*
Goodman, Elaine 1930- *9*

Goodman, Joan Elizabeth 1950- *162*
   Earlier sketches in SATA *50, 94*
Goodman, Susan E. 1952- *181*
Goodman, Walter 1927-2002 .... *9*
Goodrich, Samuel Griswold 1793-1860 .... *23*
Goodsell, Jane Neuberger 1921(?)-1988
   Obituary *56*
GoodWeather, Hartley
   See King, Thomas
Goodweather, Hartley
   See King, Thomas
Goodwin, Hal
   See Goodwin, Harold L(eland)
Goodwin, Harold L(eland) 1914-1990 .... *51*
   Obituary *65*
   Earlier sketch in SATA *13*
Goodwin, William 1943- *117*
Goor, Nancy (Ruth Miller) 1944- *39*
   Brief entry *34*
Goor, Ron(ald Stephen) 1940- *39*
   Brief entry *34*
Goossen, Agnes
   See Epp, Margaret A(gnes)
Gootman, Marilyn E. 1944- *179*
Gopnik, Adam 1956- *171*
Gorbachev, Valeri 1944- *184*
   Autobiography Feature *143*
   Earlier sketches in SATA *98, 143*
Gordion, Mark
   See Turtledove, Harry
Gordon, Ad
   See Hano, Arnold
Gordon, Amy 1949- *156*
   Earlier sketch in SATA *115*
Gordon, Bernard Ludwig 1931- *27*
Gordon, Colonel H. R.
   See Ellis, Edward S(ylvester)
Gordon, David *180*
   See Garrett, (Gordon) Randall (Phillip)
Gordon, Donald
   See Payne, Donald Gordon
Gordon, Dorothy 1893-1970 .... *20*
Gordon, Esther S(aranga) 1935- *10*
Gordon, Frederick *1*
Gordon, Gaelyn 1939-1997
   See CLR *75*
Gordon, Gary
   See Edmonds, I(vy) G(ordon)
Gordon, Hal
   See Goodwin, Harold L(eland)
Gordon, Jeffie Ross
   See Enderle, Judith (Ann) Ross
   and Gordon, Stephanie Jacob
Gordon, John
   See Gesner, Clark
Gordon, John (William) 1925- *84*
Gordon, Lew
   See Baldwin, Gordon C(ortis)
Gordon, Margaret (Anna) 1939- *9*
Gordon, Mike 1948- *101*
Gordon, Mildred 1912-1979
   Obituary *24*
Gordon, Selma
   See Lanes, Selma Gordon
Gordon, Sheila 1927- *88*
   See also CLR *27*
Gordon, Shirley 1921- *48*
   Brief entry *41*
Gordon, Sol 1923- *11*
Gordon, Stephanie Jacob 1940- *89*
   Autobiography Feature *114*
   Earlier sketch in SATA *64*
   See also SAAS *26*
Gordon, Stewart
   See Shirreffs, Gordon D(onald)
Gordons, The
   See Gordon, Mildred
   and Gordon, Gordon
Gore, Leonid *185*
Gorelick, Molly C(hernow) 1920-2003 .... *9*
   Obituary *153*

Gorey, Edward (St. John) 1925-2000 .... *70*
   Brief entry *27*
   Obituary *118*
   Earlier sketch in SATA *29*
   See also CLR *36*
Gorham, Charles Orson 1868-1936 .... *36*
Gorham, Michael
   See Folsom, Franklin (Brewster)
Gorman, Carol *187*
   Earlier sketch in SATA *150*
Gorman, Jacqueline Laks 1955- *148*
Gormley, Beatrice 1942- *127*
   Brief entry *35*
   Earlier sketch in SATA *39*
Gorog, Judith (Katharine Allen) 1938- *75*
   Earlier sketch in SATA *39*
Gorrell, Gena K. 1946- *170*
Gorsline, Douglas (Warner) 1913-1985 .... *11*
   Obituary *43*
Gorsline, (Sally) Marie 1928- *28*
Gorsline, S. M.
   See Gorsline, (Sally) Marie
Gorton, Kaitlyn
   See Emerson, Kathy Lynn
Goryan, Sirak
   See Saroyan, William
Goscinny, Rene 1926-1977 .... *47*
   Brief entry *39*
   See also CLR *37*
Goss, Clay(ton E.) 1946- *82*
Goss, Gary 1947- *124*
Goss, Mini 1963- *186*
Gottesman, S. D.
   See Kornbluth, C(yril) M.
   and Lowndes, Robert A(ugustine)
   W(ard)
   and Pohl, Frederik
Gottfried, Ted
   See Gottfried, Theodore Mark
Gottfried, Theodore Mark 1928- *150*
   Earlier sketch in SATA *85*
Gottlieb, Gerald 1923- *7*
Gottlieb, William P. 1917-2006 .... *24*
Gottlieb, William Paul
   See Gottlieb, William P.
Goudey, Alice E(dwards) 1898-1993 .... *20*
Goudge, Eileen 1950- *88*
Goudge, Elizabeth (de Beauchamp)
   1900-1984 .... *2*
   Obituary *38*
   See also CLR *94*
Gough, Catherine *24*
   See Mulgan, Catherine
Gough, Philip 1908- *45*
Gough, Sue 1940- *106*
Goulart, Ron(ald Joseph) 1933- *138*
   Earlier sketch in SATA *6*
   See Appleton, Victor II
   and Dixon, Franklin W.
   and Hope, Laura Lee
   and Keene, Carolyn
Gould, Alberta 1945- *96*
Gould, Chester 1900-1985 .... *49*
   Obituary *43*
Gould, Jean R(osalind) 1909-1993 .... *11*
   Obituary *77*
Gould, Lilian *6*
Gould, Marilyn 1928- *76*
   Earlier sketch in SATA *15*
Gould, Robert *154*
Gould, Steven 1955- *95*
Gould, Steven Charles
   See Gould, Steven
Gourley, Catherine 1950- *190*
   Earlier sketch in SATA *95*
Gourse, Leslie 1939-2004 .... *89*
Govan, (Mary) Christine Noble
   1898-1985 .... *9*
Gove, Doris 1944- *72*
Govenar, Alan 1952- *189*

Govenar, Alan Bruce
See Govenar, Alan
Govern, Elaine 1939- 26
Gowen, L. Kris 1968- 156
Graaf, Peter
See Youd, (Christopher) Samuel
Graber, Alexander 1914-1997 98
Earlier sketch in SATA 7
Graber, (George) Alexander 1914-1997 98
Graber, Janet 1942- 170
Graber, Richard (Fredrick) 1927- 26
Grabianski, Janusz 1928-1976 39
Obituary 30
Graboff, Abner 1919-1986 35
Grace, Fran(ces Jane) 45
Grace, Theresa
See Mattern, Joanne
Gracza, Margaret Young 1928- 56
Graduate of Oxford, A
See Ruskin, John
Grady, Denise 1952- 189
Graeber, Charlotte Towner 106
Brief entry 44
Earlier sketch in SATA 56
Graeme, Roderic
See Jeffries, Roderic
Graf, Michael
See Graf, Mike
Graf, Mike 1960- 164
Graff, Lisa 1981- 188
Graff, Polly Anne Colver
See Colver, Anne
Graff, (S.) Stewart 1908- 9
Graham, Ada 1931- 11
Graham, Alastair 1945- 74
Graham, Arthur Kennon
See Harrison, David L.
Graham, Bob 1942- 187
Earlier sketches in SATA 63, 101, 151
See also CLR 31
Graham, Brenda Knight 1942- 32
Graham, Charlotte
See Bowden, Joan Chase
Graham, Eleanor 1896-1984 18
Obituary 38
Graham, Ennis
See Molesworth, Mary Louisa
Graham, Frank, Jr. 1925- 11
Graham, Georgia 1959- 190
Graham, Ian 1953- 112
Graham, John 1926-2007 11
Graham, Kennon
See Harrison, David L.
Graham, Larry
See Graham, Lawrence
Graham, Lawrence 1962- 63
Graham, Lawrence Otis
See Graham, Lawrence
Graham, Linda
See Graham-Barber, Lynda
Graham, Lorenz (Bell) 1902-1989 74
Obituary 63
Earlier sketch in SATA 2
See also CLR 10
See also SAAS 5
Graham, Margaret Bloy 1920- 11
Graham, Robin Lee 1949- 7
Graham, Shirley 1896(?)-1977
See Du Bois, Shirley Graham
Graham-Barber, Lynda 1944- 159
Earlier sketch in SATA 42
Graham-Cameron, M.
See Graham-Cameron, M(alcolm)
G(ordon)
Graham-Cameron, M(alcolm)
G(ordon) 1931- 53
Brief entry 45
Graham-Cameron, Mike
See Graham-Cameron, M(alcolm) G(ordon)

Grahame, Kenneth 1859-1932 100
See also YABC 1
See also CLR 135
Gralley, Jean 166
Gramatky, Hardie 1907-1979 30
Obituary 23
Earlier sketch in SATA 1
See also CLR 22
Grambling, Lois G. 1927- 148
Earlier sketch in SATA 71
Grambo, Rebecca L(ynn) 1963- 109
Grammer, June Amos 1927- 58
Grand, Samuel 1912-1988 42
Grandits, John 1949- 192
GrandPre, Mary 1954- 184
Grandville, J. J.
See Gerard, Jean Ignace Isidore
Grandville, Jean Ignace Isidore Gerard
See Gerard, Jean Ignace Isidore
Granfield, Linda 1950- 160
Earlier sketch in SATA 96
Grange, Peter
See Nicole, Christopher (Robin)
Granger, Margaret Jane 1925(?)-1977
Obituary 27
Granger, Michele 1949- 88
Granger, Peggy
See Granger, Margaret Jane
Granowsky, Alvin 1936- 101
Granstaff, Bill 1925- 10
Granstrom, Brita 1969- 167
Earlier sketch in SATA 111
Grant, Bruce 1893-1977 5
Obituary 25
Grant, Cynthia D. 1950- 147
Earlier sketches in SATA 33, 77
Grant, Eva 1907-1996 7
Grant, Evva H. 1913-1977
Obituary 27
Grant, Gordon 1875-1962 25
Grant, Gwen(doline Ellen) 1940- 47
Grant, Katie M.
See Grant, K.M.
Grant, K.M. 175
Grant, (Alice) Leigh 1947- 10
Grant, Matthew G.
See May, Julian
Grant, Maxwell
See Gibson, Walter B(rown)
and Lynds, Dennis
Grant, Melvyn 183
Grant, Myrna (Lois) 1934- 21
Grant, Neil 1938- 154
Earlier sketch in SATA 14
Grant, Nicholas
See Nicole, Christopher (Robin)
Grant, Richard 1948- 80
Grant, Skeeter
See Spiegelman, Art
Grater, Michael 1923- 57
Gravel, Fern
See Hall, James Norman
Gravelle, Karen 1942- 166
Earlier sketch in SATA 78
Graves, Charles Parlin 1911-1972 4
Graves, Keith 191
Earlier sketch in SATA 156
Graves, Robert 1895-1985 45
Graves, Robert von Ranke
See Graves, Robert
Graves, Valerie
See Bradley, Marion Zimmer
Gravett, Emily 1972(?)- 189
Gray, Betsy
See Poole, Gray Johnson
Gray, Caroline
See Nicole, Christopher (Robin)
Gray, Dianne E. 183
Gray, Elizabeth Janet
See Vining, Elizabeth Gray
Gray, Genevieve S(tuck) 1920-1995 4

Gray, Harold (Lincoln) 1894-1968 33
Brief entry 32
Gray, Jenny
See Gray, Genevieve S(tuck)
Gray, John Lee
See Jakes, John
Gray, Judith A. 1949- 93
Gray, Judith Anne
See Gray, Judith A.
Gray, Keith 151
Gray, Kes 1960- 153
Gray, Les 1929- 82
Gray, Libba Moore 1937- 83
Gray, Luli 1945- 149
Earlier sketch in SATA 90
Gray, Marian
See Pierce, Edith Gray
Gray, Nicholas Stuart 1922-1981 4
Obituary 27
Gray, Nigel 1941- 104
Earlier sketch in SATA 33
Gray, (Lucy) Noel (Clervaux) 1898-1983 47
Gray, Patricia (Clark) 7
Gray, Patsey
See Gray, Patricia (Clark)
Gray, Rita 184
Graydon, Shari 1958- 158
Grayland, V. Merle
See Grayland, Valerie (Merle Spanner)
Grayland, Valerie (Merle Spanner) 7
Grayson, Devin (Kalile) 1970- 119
Grayson, Kristine
See Rusch, Kristine Kathryn
Grayson, Paul 1946- 79
Graystone, Lynn
See Brennan, Joseph Lomas
Great Comte, The
See Hawkesworth, Eric
Greaves, Margaret 1914-1995 87
Earlier sketch in SATA 7
Greaves, Nick 1955- 77
Gree, Alain 1936- 28
Green, Adam
See Weisgard, Leonard (Joseph)
Green, Anne Canevari 1943- 62
Green, Brian
See Card, Orson Scott
Green, Cliff(ord) 1934- 126
Green, Connie Jordan 1938- 80
Green, D.
See Casewit, Curtis W(erner)
Green, Elizabeth Shippen 1871-1954 139
Green, Hannah
See Greenberg, Joanne (Goldenberg)
Green, Jane 1937- 9
Green, John 1977(?)- 170
Green, Mary Moore 1906- 11
Green, Morton 1937- 8
Green, Norma B(erger) 1925- 11
Green, Phyllis 1932- 20
Green, Roger (Gilbert) Lancelyn
1918-1987 2
Obituary 53
Green, (James Le)Roy 1948- 89
Green, Sheila Ellen 1934- 148
Earlier sketches in SATA 8, 87
Green, Timothy 1953- 91
Greenaway, Kate 1846-1901 100
See also YABC 2
See also CLR 111
Greenbank, Anthony Hunt 1933- 39
Greenberg, David 1954- 171
Greenberg, David T.
See Greenberg, David
Greenberg, Harvey R. 1935- 5
Greenberg, Jan 1942- 125
Earlier sketch in SATA 61
Greenberg, Joanne (Goldenberg) 1932- 25
Greenberg, Melanie Hope 1954- 72
Greenberg, Polly 1932- 52
Brief entry 43

Greenblat, Rodney Alan 1960- *106*
Greenburg, Dan 1936- *175*
   Earlier sketch in SATA *102*
Greene, Bette 1934- *161*
   Earlier sketches in SATA *8, 102*
   See also CLR *2*
   See also SAAS *16*
Greene, Carla 1916- *67*
   Earlier sketch in SATA *1*
Greene, Carol *102*
   Brief entry *44*
   Earlier sketch in SATA *66*
Greene, Constance C(larke) 1924- *72*
   Earlier sketch in SATA *11*
   See also CLR *62*
   See also SAAS *11*
Greene, Edgar
   See Papademetriou, Lisa
Greene, Ellin 1927- *23*
Greene, Graham 1904-1991 .... *20*
Greene, Graham Henry
   See Greene, Graham
Greene, Jacqueline Dembar 1946- *131*
   Earlier sketch in SATA *76*
Greene, Laura Offenhartz 1935- *38*
Greene, Meg
   See Malvasi, Meg Greene
Greene, Michele 1962- *178*
Greene, Michele Dominguez
   See Greene, Michele
Greene, Rhonda Gowler 1955- *160*
   Earlier sketch in SATA *101*
Greene, Stephanie 1953- *173*
   Earlier sketch in SATA *127*
Greene, Wade 1933- *11*
Greene, Yvonne
   See Flesch, Yolande (Catarina)
Greenfeld, Howard (Scheinman) 1928- *140*
   Earlier sketch in SATA *19*
Greenfeld, Josh(ua Joseph) 1928- *62*
Greenfield, Eloise 1929- *155*
   Earlier sketches in SATA *19, 61, 105*
   See also CLR *38*
   See also SAAS *16*
Greenhaus, Thelma Nurenberg 1903-1984
   Obituary *45*
Greenhut, Josh
   See Mercer, Sienna
Greening, Hamilton
   See Hamilton, Charles (Harold St. John)
Greenlaw, M. Jean 1941- *107*
Greenleaf, Barbara Kaye 1942- *6*
Greenleaf, Peter 1910-1997 .... *33*
Greenlee, Sharon 1935- *77*
Greeno, Gayle 1949- *81*
Greenseid, Diane 1948- *178*
   Earlier sketch in SATA *93*
Greenspun, Adele Aron 1938- *142*
   Earlier sketch in SATA *76*
Greenstein, Elaine 1959- *150*
   Earlier sketch in SATA *82*
Greenwald, Sheila
   See Green, Sheila Ellen
Greenwood, Barbara 1940- *129*
   Earlier sketch in SATA *90*
Greenwood, Pamela D. 1944- *115*
Greer, Richard
   See Garrett, (Gordon) Randall (Phillip)
   and Silverberg, Robert
Gregg, Andrew K. 1929- *81*
Gregg, Charles T(hornton) 1927- *65*
Gregg, Walter H(arold) 1919- *20*
Gregor, Arthur 1923- *36*
Gregor, Lee
   See Pohl, Frederik
Gregori, Leon 1919- *15*
Gregorian, Joyce Ballou 1946-1991 .... *30*
   Obituary *83*
Gregorich, Barbara 1943- *184*
   Earlier sketch in SATA *66*
Gregorowski, Christopher 1940- *30*

Gregory, Diana (Jean) 1933- *49*
   Brief entry *42*
Gregory, Harry
   See Gottfried, Theodore Mark
Gregory, Jean
   See Ure, Jean
Gregory, Kristiana 1951- *136*
   Earlier sketch in SATA *74*
Gregory, Nan 1944- *192*
   Earlier sketch in SATA *148*
Gregory, Philippa 1954- *122*
Gregory, Stephen
   See Penzler, Otto
Gregory, Valiska 1940- *82*
Greisman, Joan Ruth 1937- *31*
Grendon, Stephen
   See Derleth, August (William)
Grenville, Pelham
   See Wodehouse, P(elham) G(renville)
Gretz, Susanna 1937- *7*
Gretzer, John *18*
Grewdead, Roy
   See Gorey, Edward (St. John)
Grey, Carol
   See Lowndes, Robert A(ugustine) W(ard)
Grey, Christopher *191*
Grey, Christopher Peter
   See Grey, Christopher
Grey, Jerry 1926- *11*
Grey, Mini *166*
Greybeard the Pirate
   See Macintosh, Brownie
Grey Owl
   See CLR *32*
   See Belaney, Archibald Stansfeld
Gri
   See Denney, Diana
Gribbin, John 1946- *159*
Gribbin, John R.
   See Gribbin, John
Grice, Frederick 1910-1983 .... *6*
Grider, Dorothy 1915- *31*
Gridley, Marion E(leanor) 1906-1974 .... *35*
   Obituary *26*
Grieco-Tiso, Pina 1954- *108*
Grieder, Walter 1924- *9*
Griego, Tony A. 1955- *77*
Griese, Arnold A(lfred) 1921- *9*
Griessman, Annette 1962- *170*
   Earlier sketch in SATA *116*
Grieve, James 1934- *146*
Grifalconi, Ann 1929- *133*
   Earlier sketches in SATA *2, 66*
   See also CLR *35*
   See also SAAS *16*
Griffin, Adele 1970- *153*
   Earlier sketch in SATA *105*
Griffin, Elizabeth May 1985- *89*
Griffin, Gillett Good 1928- *26*
Griffin, Judith Berry *34*
Griffin, Kitty 1951- *137*
Griffin, Peni R. 1961- *193*
   Earlier sketches in SATA *67, 99*
Griffin, Peni Rae Robinson
   See Griffin, Peni R.
Griffin, Steven A. 1953- *89*
Griffin, Steven Arthur
   See Griffin, Steven A.
Griffin, W.E.B 1929- *5*
Griffith, Connie 1946- *89*
Griffith, Gershom 1960- *85*
Griffith, Helen V(irginia) 1934- *87*
   Autobiography Feature *107*
   Earlier sketch in SATA *39*
Griffith, Jeannette
   See Eyerly, Jeannette (Hyde)
Griffiths, Andy 1961- *152*
Griffiths, G(ordon) D(ouglas) 1910-1973
   Obituary *20*

Griffiths, Helen 1939- *86*
   Earlier sketch in SATA *5*
   See also CLR *75*
   See also SAAS *5*
Grigson, Jane (McIntire) 1928-1990 .... *63*
Grimes, Lee 1920- *68*
Grimes, Nikki 1950- *174*
   Earlier sketches in SATA *93, 136*
   See also CLR *42*
Grimly, Gris *186*
Grimm, Jacob Ludwig Karl 1785-1863 .... *22*
   See also CLR *112*
   See Grimm Brothers
Grimm, Wilhelm Karl 1786-1859 .... *22*
   See also CLR *112*
   See Grimm Brothers
Grimm, William C(arey) 1907-1992 .... *14*
Grimm and Grim
   See Grimm, Jacob Ludwig Karl
   and Grimm, Wilhelm Karl
Grimm Brothers
   See CLR *112*
   See Grimm, Jacob Ludwig Karl
   and Grimm, Wilhelm Karl
Grimsdell, Jeremy 1942- *83*
Grimshaw, Nigel (Gilroy) 1925- *23*
Grimsley, Gordon
   See Groom, Arthur William
Grindley, (Jane) Sally 1953- *148*
Gringhuis, Dirk
   See Gringhuis, Richard H.
Gringhuis, Richard H. 1918-1974 .... *6*
   Obituary *25*
Grinnell, David
   See Wollheim, Donald A(llen)
Grinnell, George Bird 1849-1938 .... *16*
Grinspoon, David
   See Grinspoon, David H.
Grinspoon, David H. 1959- *156*
Grinspoon, David Harry
   See Grinspoon, David H.
Gripe, Maria 1923- *74*
   Earlier sketch in SATA *2*
   See also CLR *5*
Gripe, Maria Kristina
   See Gripe, Maria
Groch, Judith (Goldstein) 1929- *25*
Grode, Redway
   See Gorey, Edward (St. John)
Groener, Carl
   See Lowndes, Robert A(ugustine)
   W(ard)
Groening, Matt 1954- *116*
   Earlier sketch in SATA *81*
Grohmann, Susan 1948- *84*
Grohskopf, Bernice *7*
Grol, Lini R(icharda) 1913- *9*
Grollman, Earl A. 1925- *22*
Groom, Arthur William 1898-1964 .... *10*
Grooms, Duffy 1964- *169*
Gross, Alan 1947- *54*
   Brief entry *43*
Gross, Ernie 1913- *67*
Gross, Philip 1952- *164*
   Earlier sketch in SATA *84*
Gross, Philip John
   See Gross, Philip
Gross, Ruth Belov 1929- *33*
Gross, Sarah Chokla 1906-1976 .... *9*
   Obituary *26*
Grosser, Morton 1931- *74*
Grosser, Vicky 1958- *83*
Grossman, Bill 1948- *126*
   Earlier sketch in SATA *72*
Grossman, Nancy 1940- *29*
Grossman, Patricia 1951- *73*
Grossman, Robert 1940- *11*
Grote, JoAnn A. 1951- *113*
Groten, Dallas 1951- *64*
Groth, John (August) 1908-1988 .... *21*
   Obituary *56*

Groth-Fleming, Candace
　See Fleming, Candace
Grove, Vicki 1948- *151*
　Autobiography Feature *151*
　Earlier sketch in SATA *122*
Grover, Lorie Ann 1964- *168*
Grover, Wayne 1934- *69*
Groves, Georgina
　See Symons, (Dorothy) Geraldine
Groves, Maketa 1950- *107*
Groves, Seli *77*
Grubb, Lisa *160*
Gruber, Michael 1940- *173*
Gruber, Terry (deRoy) 1953- *66*
Gruelle, John (Barton) 1880-1938 .... *35*
　Brief entry *32*
　See Gruelle, Johnny
Gruelle, Johnny
　See CLR *34*
　See Gruelle, John (Barton)
Gruenberg, Sidonie Matsner 1881-1974 .... *2*
　Obituary *27*
Gruhzit-Hoyt, Olga (Margaret) 1922- *127*
　Earlier sketch in SATA *16*
Grummer, Arnold E(dward) 1923- *49*
Grunewalt, Pine
　See Kunhardt, Edith
Grunwell, Jeanne Marie 1971- *147*
Grupper, Jonathan *137*
Gryski, Camilla 1948- *72*
Guarino, Dagmar
　See Guarino, Deborah
Guarino, Deborah 1954- *68*
Guay, Georgette (Marie Jeanne) 1952- *54*
Guback, Georgia *88*
Guccione, Leslie Davis 1946- *111*
　Earlier sketch in SATA *72*
Guck, Dorothy 1913-2002 .... *27*
Guerny, Gene
　See Gurney, Gene
Guest, Elissa Haden 1953- *125*
Guest, Jacqueline 1952- *135*
Guevara, Susan *167*
　Earlier sketch in SATA *97*
Gugler, Laurel Dee *95*
Gugliotta, Bobette 1918-1994 .... *7*
Guianan, Eve 1965- *102*
Guiberson, Brenda Z. 1946- *124*
　Earlier sketch in SATA *71*
Guibert, Emmanuel 1964- *181*
Guile, Melanie 1949- *152*
　Earlier sketch in SATA *104*
Guillaume, Jeanette G. Flierl 1899-1990 .... *8*
Guillot, Rene 1900-1969 .... *7*
　See also CLR *22*
Guisewite, Cathy (Lee) 1950- *57*
Gulbis, Stephen 1959- *142*
Gulley, Judie 1942- *58*
Gump, P. Q.
　See Card, Orson Scott
Gundrey, Elizabeth 1924- *23*
Gunn, James E. 1923- *35*
Gunn, James Edwin
　See Gunn, James E.
Gunn, Robin Jones 1955- *84*
Gunning, Monica Olwen 1930- *161*
Gunston, Bill
　See Gunston, William Tudor
Gunston, William Tudor 1927- *9*
Gunterman, Bertha Lisette 1886(?)-1975
　Obituary *27*
Gunther, John 1901-1970
Guravich, Dan 1918- *74*
Gurko, Leo 1914- *9*
Gurko, Miriam 1910(?)-1988 .... *9*
　Obituary *58*
Gurney, Gene 1924- *65*
Gurney, James 1958- *120*
　Earlier sketch in SATA *76*
Gurney, John Steven 1962- *143*
　Earlier sketch in SATA *75*

Gustafson, Sarah R.
　See Riedman, Sarah R(egal)
Gustafson, Scott 1956- *34*
Gustavson, Adam *176*
Guthrie, A(lfred) B(ertram), Jr. 1901-1991 .. *62*
　Obituary *67*
Guthrie, Anne 1890-1979 .... *28*
Guthrie, Donna W. 1946- *105*
　Earlier sketch in SATA *63*
Gutierrez, Akemi *172*
Gutman, Bill *128*
　Brief entry *43*
　Earlier sketch in SATA *67*
Gutman, Dan 1955- *188*
　Earlier sketches in SATA *77, 139*
Gutman, Naham 1899(?)-1981
　Obituary *25*
Gutmann, Bessie Pease 1876-1960 .... *73*
Guy, Geoffrey 1942- *153*
Guy, Ginger Foglesong 1954- *171*
Guy, Rosa (Cuthbert) 1925- *122*
　Earlier sketches in SATA *14, 62*
　See also CLR *137*
Guy, Susan 1948- *149*
Guymer, (Wilhelmina) Mary 1909- *50*
Guzman, Lila 1952- *168*
Guzman, Rick 1957- *168*
Gwaltney, Doris 1932- *181*
Gwynne, Fred(erick Hubbard) 1926-1993 .... *41*
　Brief entry *27*
　Obituary *75*
Gwynne, Oscar A.
　See Ellis, Edward S(ylvester)
Gwynne, Oswald A.
　See Ellis, Edward S(ylvester)

H

Haab, Sherri 1964- *169*
　Earlier sketch in SATA *91*
Haar, Jaap ter
　See CLR *15*
　See ter Haar, Jaap
Haarsma, P.J. *183*
Haas, Carolyn Buhai 1926- *43*
Haas, Dan 1957- *105*
Haas, Dorothy F. *46*
　Brief entry *43*
　See also SAAS *17*
Haas, Irene 1929- *96*
　Earlier sketch in SATA *17*
Haas, James E(dward) 1943- *40*
Haas, (Katherine) Jessie 1959- *135*
　Autobiography Feature *135*
　Earlier sketch in SATA *98*
Haas, Merle S. 1896(?)-1985
　Obituary *41*
Habenstreit, Barbara 1937- *5*
Haber, Karen 1955- *78*
Haber, Louis 1910-1988 .... *12*
Hacker, Randi 1951- *185*
Hacker, Randi Dawn
　See Hacker, Randi
Hackett, John Winthrop 1910-1997 .... *65*
Hacks, Peter 1928-2003
　Obituary *151*
Haddix, Margaret Peterson 1964- *187*
　Earlier sketches in SATA *94, 125*
Haddon, Mark 1962- *155*
Hader, Berta (Hoerner) 1891(?)-1976 .... *16*
Hader, Elmer (Stanley) 1889-1973 .... *16*
Hadithi, Mwenye
　See Hobson, Bruce
Hadley, Franklin
　See Winterbotham, R(ussell) R(obert)

Hadley, Lee 1934-1995 .... *89*
　Brief entry *38*
　Obituary *86*
　Earlier sketch in SATA *47*
　See also CLR *40*
　See Irwin, Hadley
Haeffele, Deborah 1954- *76*
Haenel, Wolfram 1956- *89*
　See also CLR *64*
Hafner, Marylin 1925- *179*
　Earlier sketches in SATA *7, 121*
Haft, Erin
　See Ehrenhaft, Daniel
Hager, Alan 1940- *176*
Hager, Alice Rogers 1894-1969
　Obituary *26*
Hager, Betty 1923- *89*
Hager, Sarah *171*
Hager, Thomas 1953- *119*
Hager, Tom
　See Hager, Thomas
Hagerup, Klaus 1946- *186*
Haggard, H(enry) Rider 1856-1925 .... *16*
Haggerty, James J(oseph) 1920- *5*
Hagon, Priscilla
　See Allan, Mabel Esther
Hague, (Susan) Kathleen 1949- *49*
　Brief entry *45*
Hague, Michael 1948- *185*
　Brief entry *32*
　Earlier sketches in SATA *48, 80, 129*
Hague, Michael R.
　See Hague, Michael
Hahn, Emily 1905-1997 .... *3*
　Obituary *96*
Hahn, Hannelore *8*
Hahn, James (Sage) 1947- *9*
Hahn, (Mona) Lynn 1949- *9*
Hahn, Mary Downing 1937- *157*
　Autobiography Feature *157*
　Brief entry *44*
　Earlier sketches in SATA *50, 81, 138*
　See also SAAS *12*
Hahn, Michael T. 1953- *92*
Haig-Brown, Roderick (Langmere)
　1908-1976 .... *12*
　See also CLR *31*
Haight, Anne Lyon 1895-1977
　Obituary *30*
Haight, Rip
　See Carpenter, John (Howard)
Haight, Sandy 1949- *79*
Haij, Vera
　See Jansson, Tove (Marika)
Haines, Gail Kay 1943- *11*
Haines, Margaret Ann Beck
　See Beck, Peggy
Haining, Peter 1940-2007 .... *14*
　Obituary *188*
Haining, Peter Alexander
　See Haining, Peter
Hains, Harriet
　See Watson, Carol
Hajdusiewicz, Babs Bell *163*
Hakim, Joy 1931- *173*
　Earlier sketch in SATA *83*
Halacy, D(aniel) S(tephen), Jr. 1919-2002 ... *36*
　See Halacy, Dan
Halacy, Dan
　See SAAS *8*
　See Halacy, D(aniel) S(tephen), Jr.
Halam, Ann
　See Jones, Gwyneth A(nn)
Haldane, Roger John 1945- *13*
Hale, Arlene 1924-1982 .... *49*
Hale, Bruce 1957- *123*
Hale, Christy *179*
　See Apostolou, Christine Hale
Hale, Edward Everett 1822-1909 .... *16*
Hale, Glenn
　See Walker, Robert W(ayne)

Hale, Helen
    See Mulcahy, Lucille Burnett
Hale, Irina 1932- 26
Hale, Kathleen 1898-2000 66
    Obituary 121
    Earlier sketch in SATA 17
Hale, Linda (Howe) 1929- 6
Hale, Lucretia P.
    See Hale, Lucretia Peabody
Hale, Lucretia Peabody 1820-1900 26
    See also CLR 105
Hale, Nancy 1908-1988 31
    Obituary 57
Hale, Shannon 158
Haley, Gail E(inhart) 1939- 161
    Autobiography Feature 161
    Brief entry 28
    Earlier sketches in SATA 43, 78, 136
    See also CLR 21
    See also SAAS 13
Haley, Neale 52
Hall, Adam
    See Trevor, Elleston
Hall, Adele 1910- 7
Hall, Anna Gertrude 1882-1967 8
Hall, Barbara 1960- 68
Hall, Becky 1950- 186
Hall, Beverly B. 1918- 95
Hall, Borden
    See Yates, Raymond F(rancis)
Hall, Brian P(atrick) 1935- 31
Hall, Cameron
    See del Rey, Lester
Hall, Caryl
    See Hansen, Caryl (Hall)
Hall, Donald 1928- 97
    Earlier sketch in SATA 23
Hall, Donald Andrew, Jr.
    See Hall, Donald
Hall, Douglas 1931- 43
Hall, Elizabeth 1929- 77
Hall, Elvajean 1910-1984 6
Hall, Francie 1940- 166
Hall, James Norman 1887-1951 21
Hall, Jesse
    See Boesen, Victor
Hall, Katy
    See McMullan, Kate
Hall, Kirsten Marie 1974- 67
Hall, Lynn 1937- 79
    Earlier sketches in SATA 2, 47
    See also SAAS 4
Hall, Malcolm 1945- 7
Hall, Marjory
    See Yeakley, Marjory Hall
Hall, Melanie W. 1949- 169
    Earlier sketches in SATA 78, 116
Hall, Patricia 1940- 136
Hall, Rosalys Haskell 1914- 7
Hall, Willis 1929-2005 66
Hallard, Peter
    See Catherall, Arthur
Hallas, Richard
    See Knight, Eric
Hall-Clarke, James
    See Rowland-Entwistle, (Arthur)
    Theodore (Henry)
Hallensleben, Georg 1958- 173
Haller, Dorcas Woodbury 1946- 46
Hallett, Mark 1947- 83
Halliburton, Richard 1900-1939(?) 81
Halliburton, Warren J. 1924- 19
Halliday, Brett
    See Dresser, Davis
    and Johnson, (Walter) Ryerson
    and Terrall, Robert
Halliday, William R(oss) 1926- 52
Hallin, Emily Watson 1916-1995 6
Hallinan, P(atrick) K(enneth) 1944- 39
    Brief entry 37

Hallman, Ruth 1929- 43
    Brief entry 28
Hallowell, Tommy
    See Hill, Thomas
Hall-Quest, (Edna) Olga W(ilbourne)
    1899-1986 11
    Obituary 47
Halls, Kelly Milner 1957- 131
Hallstead, William F(inn III) 1924- 11
Hallward, Michael 1889-1982 12
Halperin, Michael 156
Halperin, Wendy Anderson 1952- 125
    Earlier sketch in SATA 80
Halpin, Brendan 1968- 193
Halpin, Marlene 1927- 88
Halsell, Grace (Eleanor) 1923-2000 13
Halsey, Megan 185
Halsted, Anna Roosevelt 1906-1975
    Obituary 30
Halter, Jon C(harles) 1941- 22
Halvorson, Marilyn 1948- 123
Hamalian, Leo 1920- 41
Hamberger, John 1934- 14
Hamblin, Dora Jane 1920- 36
Hambly, Barbara 1951- 108
Hambly, Barbara Joan
    See Hambly, Barbara
Hamer, Martyn
    See Eldin, Peter
Hamerstrom, Frances 1907-1998 24
Hamil, Thomas Arthur 1928- 14
Hamill, Ethel
    See Webb, Jean Francis (III)
Hamilton, (John) Alan 1943- 66
Hamilton, Alice
    See Cromie, Alice Hamilton
Hamilton, Anita 1919- 92
Hamilton, Buzz
    See Hemming, Roy G.
Hamilton, Carol (Jean Barber) 1935- 94
Hamilton, Charles (Harold St. John)
    1876-1961 13
Hamilton, Charles 1913-1996 65
    Obituary 93
Hamilton, Clive
    See Lewis, C.S.
Hamilton, Dorothy (Drumm) 1906-1983 12
    Obituary 35
Hamilton, Edith 1867-1963 20
Hamilton, Edmond 1904-1977 118
Hamilton, (Muriel) Elizabeth (Mollie)
    1906- 23
Hamilton, Emma Walton 1962- 177
Hamilton, Franklin
    See Silverberg, Robert
Hamilton, Gail
    See Corcoran, Barbara (Asenath)
    and Dodge, Mary Abigail
Hamilton, Kersten 1958- 134
Hamilton, Martha 1953- 183
    Earlier sketch in SATA 123
Hamilton, Mary (E.) 1927- 55
Hamilton, Mollie
    See Kaye, M.M.
Hamilton, Morse 1943-1998 101
    Earlier sketch in SATA 35
Hamilton, Peter F. 1960- 109
Hamilton, Priscilla
    See Gellis, Roberta
Hamilton, Ralph
    See Stratemeyer, Edward L.
Hamilton, Virginia 1936-2002 123
    Obituary 132
    Earlier sketches in SATA 4, 56, 79
    See also CLR 127
Hamilton, Virginia Esther
    See Hamilton, Virginia
Hamilton-Paterson, James 1941- 82
Hamlet, Ova
    See Lupoff, Richard A(llen)

Hamley, Dennis 1935- 69
    Earlier sketch in SATA 39
    See also CLR 47
    See also SAAS 22
Hamlin, Peter J. 1970- 84
Hamm, Diane Johnston 1949- 78
Hammer, Charles 1934- 58
Hammer, Richard 1928- 6
Hammerman, Gay M(orenus) 1926- 9
Hammond, Andrew 1970- 181
Hammond, Ralph
    See Hammond Innes, Ralph
Hammond, Winifred G(raham) 1899-1992 ... 29
    Obituary 107
Hammond Innes, Ralph 1913-1998 116
Hammontree, Marie (Gertrude) 1913- 13
Hample, Zack 1977- 161
Hampshire, Joyce Gregorian
    See Gregorian, Joyce Ballou
Hampshire, Susan 1942- 98
Hampson, (Richard) Denman 1929- 15
Hampson, Frank 1918(?)-1985
    Obituary 46
Hampton, Wilborn 156
Hamre, Leif 1914- 5
Hamsa, Bobbie 1944- 52
    Brief entry 38
Han, Jenny 1981- 175
Han, Lu
    See Stickler, Soma Han
Han, Soma
    See Stickler, Soma Han
Han, Suzanne Crowder 1953- 89
Hancock, Mary A. 1923- 31
Hancock, Sibyl 1940- 9
Hand, Elizabeth 1957- 167
    Earlier sketch in SATA 118
Handford, Martin (John) 1956- 64
    See also CLR 22
Handforth, Thomas (Schofield) 1897-1948 .. 42
Handler, Daniel
    See Snicket, Lemony
Handville, Robert (Tompkins) 1924- 45
Hane, Roger 1940-1974
    Obituary 20
Hanel, Wolfram
    See Haenel, Wolfram
Haney, Lynn 1941- 23
Hanff, Helene 1916-1997 97
    Earlier sketch in SATA 11
Hanley, Boniface Francis 1924- 65
Hanlon, Emily 1945- 15
Hann, Jacquie 1951- 19
Hann, Judith 1942- 77
Hanna, Bill
    See Hanna, William (Denby)
Hanna, Cheryl 1951- 84
Hanna, Jack (Bushnell) 1947- 74
Hanna, Nell(ie L.) 1908- 55
Hanna, Paul R(obert) 1902-1988 9
Hanna, William (Denby) 1910-2001 51
    Obituary 126
Hannam, Charles 1925- 50
Hannan, Peter 1954- 187
Hannigan, Katherine 170
Hannon, Ezra
    See Hunter, Evan
Hann-Syme, Marguerite 127
Hano, Arnold 1922- 12
Hano, Renee Roth
    See Roth-Hano, Renee
Hanover, Terri
    See Huff, Tanya
Hansen, Ann Larkin 1958- 96
Hansen, Brooks 1965- 104
Hansen, Caryl (Hall) 1929- 39
Hansen, Ian V. 1929- 113
Hansen, Jennifer 1972- 156

Hansen, Joyce 1942- 172
    Autobiography Feature 172
    Brief entry 39
    Earlier sketches in SATA *46, 101*
    See also CLR *21*
    See also SAAS *15*
Hansen, Joyce Viola
    See Hansen, Joyce
Hansen, Mark Victor 112
Hansen, Ron(ald Thomas) 1947- 56
Hanser, Richard (Frederick) 1909-1981 13
Hanson, Joan 1938- 8
Hanson, Joseph E. 1894(?)-1971
    Obituary 27
Hanson, Mary Elizabeth 188
Hanson, Warren 1949- 155
Hansson, Gunilla 1939- 64
Harald, Eric
    See Boesen, Victor
Harcourt, Ellen Knowles 1890(?)-1984
    Obituary 36
Hard, Charlotte (Ann) 1969- 98
Hardcastle, Michael 1933- 47
    Brief entry 38
Harding, Lee 1937- 32
    Brief entry 31
Hardt, Helga Fleischhauer
    See Fleischhauer-Hardt, Helga
Hardwick, Richard Holmes, Jr. 1923- 12
Hardy, Alice Dale 67
    Earlier sketch in SATA *1*
Hardy, David A(ndrews) 1936- 9
Hardy, Jon 1958- 53
Hardy, LeAnne 1951- 154
Hardy, Stuart
    See Schisgall, Oscar
Hare, Norma Q(uarles) 1924- 46
    Brief entry 41
Harel, Nira 1936- 154
Harford, Henry
    See Hudson, W(illiam) H(enry)
Hargrave, Leonie
    See Disch, Thomas M.
Hargreaves, (Charles) Roger 1935-1988
    Obituary 56
Hargrove, James 1947- 57
    Brief entry 50
Hargrove, Jim
    See Hargrove, James
Hariton, Anca I. 1955- 79
Hark, Mildred
    See McQueen, Mildred Hark
Harkaway, Hal
    See Stratemeyer, Edward L.
Harkins, Philip 1912-1997 6
    Obituary 129
Harlan, Elizabeth 1945- 41
    Brief entry 35
Harlan, Glen
    See Cebulash, Mel
Harlan, Judith 1949- 135
    Earlier sketch in SATA *74*
    See also CLR *81*
Harland, Richard 1947- 152
Harlee, J. V.
    See Leese, Jennifer L.B.
Harler, Ann
    See Van Steenwyk, Elizabeth (Ann)
Harley, Avis 183
Harley, Bill 1954- 87
Harlow, Joan Hiatt 1932- 157
Harman, Fred 1902(?)-1982
    Obituary 30
Harman, Hugh 1903-1982
    Obituary 33
Harmelink, Barbara (Mary) 9
Harmer, Mabel 1894-1992 45
Harmon, Dan
    See Harmon, Daniel E(lton)
Harmon, Daniel E(lton) 1949- 157
Harmon, Margaret 1906- 20

Harmon, Michael 1969- 189
Harmon, William (Ruth) 1938- 65
Harnan, Terry 1920- 12
Harness, Cheryl 1951- 178
    Earlier sketch in SATA *131*
Harnett, Cynthia (Mary) 1893-1981 5
    Obituary 32
Harper, Anita 1943- 41
Harper, Betty 1946- 126
Harper, Charise
    See Harper, Charise Mericle
Harper, Charise Mericle 179
Harper, Elaine
    See Hallin, Emily Watson
Harper, Ellen
    See Noble, Marty
Harper, Jamie 174
Harper, Jessica (R.) 1949- 148
Harper, Jo 1932- 169
    Earlier sketch in SATA *97*
Harper, Mary Wood
    See Dixon, Jeanne
Harper, Piers 1966- 161
    Earlier sketch in SATA *105*
Harper, Wilhelmina 1884-1973 4
    Obituary 26
Harrah, Madge 1931- 154
Harrah, Michael 1940- 41
Harrah, Monique
    See Harrah, Madge
Harrar, George E. 1949- 124
Harrell, Beatrice Orcutt 1943- 93
Harrell, Janice 1945- 70
Harries, Joan 1922- 39
Harrill, Ronald 1950- 90
Harrington, Denis J(ames) 1932- 88
Harrington, Janice N. 1956- 187
Harrington, Lyn 5
    See Harrington, Evelyn Davis
Harris, Alan 1944- 71
Harris, Aurand 1915-1996 37
    Obituary 91
Harris, Carol Flynn 1933- 135
Harris, Catherine
    See Ainsworth, Catherine Harris
Harris, Christie
    See Harris, Christie (Lucy) Irwin
Harris, Christie (Lucy) Irwin 1907-2002 74
    Autobiography Feature 116
    Earlier sketch in SATA *6*
    See also CLR *47*
    See also SAAS *10*
Harris, Christine 1955- 105
Harris, Colver
    See Colver, Anne
Harris, David 1942- 118
Harris, David William
    See Harris, David
Harris, Dorothy Joan 1931- 153
    Earlier sketch in SATA *13*
Harris, Geraldine (Rachel) 1951- 54
Harris, Jacqueline L. 1929- 62
Harris, Janet 1932-1979 4
    Obituary 23
Harris, Jesse
    See Standiford, Natalie
Harris, Joan 1946- 146
Harris, Joel Chandler 1848-1908 100
    See also YABC *1*
    See also CLR *128*
Harris, John (Wyndham Parkes Lucas) Beynon
    1903-1969 118
    See Wyndham, John
Harris, Johnson
    See Harris, John (Wyndham Parkes Lucas)
    Beynon
Harris, Jonathan 1921-1997 52
Harris, Larry Vincent 1939- 59
Harris, Lavinia
    See St. John, Nicole
Harris, Leon A., Jr. 1926-2000 4

Harris, Lorle K(empe) 1912-2001 22
Harris, Marilyn
    See Springer, Marilyn Harris
Harris, Mark Jonathan 1941- 84
    Earlier sketch in SATA *32*
Harris, Mary K(athleen) 1905-1966 119
Harris, Robie H. 1940- 147
    Brief entry 53
    Earlier sketch in SATA *90*
Harris, Robin
    See Shine, Deborah
Harris, Rosemary (Jeanne) 82
    Earlier sketch in SATA *4*
    See also CLR *30*
    See also SAAS *7*
Harris, Ruth Elwin 1935- 164
Harris, Sherwood 1932- 25
Harris, Steven Michael 1957- 55
Harris, Trudy 1949- 191
    Earlier sketch in SATA *128*
Harris-Filderman, Diane
    See Filderman, Diane E(lizabeth)
Harrison, C(hester) William 1913-1994 35
Harrison, Carol
    See Harrison, Carol Thompson
Harrison, Carol Thompson 113
Harrison, David L. 1937- 186
    Earlier sketches in SATA *26, 92, 150*
Harrison, Deloris 1938- 9
Harrison, Edward Hardy 1926- 56
Harrison, Elizabeth (Allen) Cavanna
    1909-2001 142
    See Cavanna, Betty
Harrison, Harry 1925- 4
Harrison, Harry Max
    See Harrison, Harry
Harrison, Mette Ivie 1970- 149
Harrison, Michael 1939- 106
Harrison, Molly (Hodgett) 1909-2002 41
Harrison, Sarah 1946- 63
Harrison, Ted
    See Harrison, Edward Hardy
Harsh, Fred (T.) 1925- 72
Harshaw, Ruth H(etzel) 1890-1968 27
Harshman, Marc 1950- 109
    Earlier sketch in SATA *71*
Hart, Alison
    See Leonhardt, Alice
Hart, Bruce 1938-2006 57
    Brief entry 39
Hart, Carole 1943- 57
    Brief entry 39
Hart, Carolyn 1936- 74
Hart, Carolyn G.
    See Hart, Carolyn
Hart, Carolyn Gimpel
    See Hart, Carolyn
Hart, Jan Siegel 1940- 79
Hart, Joyce 1954- 148
Hart, Karen 185
Hart, Lenore 171
Hart, Philip S. 1944- 180
Hart, Virginia 1949- 83
Harte, (Francis) Bret(t) 1836(?)-1902 26
Harter, Debbie 1963- 107
Hartfield, Claire 1957- 147
Hartinger, Brent 1964- 174
    Earlier sketch in SATA *145*
Hartland, Jessie 171
Hartley, Ellen (Raphael) 1915-1980 23
Hartley, Fred Allan III 1953- 41
Hartley, William B(rown) 1913-1980 23
Hartling, Peter
    See CLR *29*
    See Hartling, Peter
Hartling, Peter 1933- 66
    See Hartling, Peter
Hartman, Evert 1937- 38
    Brief entry 35
Hartman, Jane E(vangeline) 1928- 47
Hartman, Louis F(rancis) 1901-1970 22

Hartman, Rachel *174*
Hartman, Victoria 1942- *91*
Hartnett, Sonya 1968- *176*
　Earlier sketches in SATA *93, 130*
Hartshorn, Ruth M. 1928- *11*
Hartung, Susan Kathleen *192*
　Earlier sketch in SATA *150*
Hartwig, Manfred 1950- *81*
Harvey, Brett 1936- *61*
Harvey, Edith 1908(?)-1972
　Obituary *27*
Harvey, Gill *189*
Harvey, Karen D. 1935- *88*
Harvey, Roland 1945- *179*
　Earlier sketches in SATA *71, 123*
Harvey-Fitzhenry, Alyxandra 1974- *189*
Harwick, B. L.
　See Keller, Beverly L(ou)
Harwin, Brian
　See Henderson, LeGrand
Harwood, Pearl Augusta (Bragdon)
　1903-1998 .... *9*
Haseley, Dennis 1950- *157*
　Brief entry *44*
　Earlier sketches in SATA *57, 105*
Hashmi, Kerri 1955- *108*
Haskell, Arnold L(ionel) 1903-1981(?) *6*
Haskins, James
　See Haskins, James S.
Haskins, James S. 1941-2005 .... *132*
　Autobiography Feature *132*
　Earlier sketches in SATA *9, 69, 105*
　See also CLR *39*
　See Haskins, Jim
Haskins, Jim
　See SAAS *4*
　See Haskins, James S.
Hasler, Eveline 1933- *181*
Hasler, Joan 1931- *28*
Hass, Robert 1941- *94*
Hassall, Joan 1906-1988 .... *43*
　Obituary *56*
Hassett, Ann 1958- *162*
Hassett, John *162*
Hassler, Jon 1933-2008 .... *19*
　Obituary *191*
Hassler, Jon Francis
　See Hassler, Jon
Hastings, Beverly
　See Barkin, Carol
　and James, Elizabeth
Hastings, Graham
　See Jeffries, Roderic
Hastings, Ian 1912- *62*
Hatch, Lynda S. 1950- *90*
Hathaway, Barbara *164*
Hathorn, Libby 1943- *156*
　Autobiography Feature *156*
　Earlier sketches in SATA *74, 120*
　See Hathorn, Elizabeth Helen
Hatkoff, Craig 1954- *192*
Hatlo, Jimmy 1898-1963
　Obituary *23*
Haugaard, Erik Christian 1923- *68*
　Earlier sketch in SATA *4*
　See also CLR *11*
　See also SAAS *12*
Haugaard, Kay *117*
Haugen, Hayley Mitchell 1968- *172*
Haugen, Tormod 1945- *66*
Hauman, Doris 1898-1984 .... *32*
Hauman, George 1890-1961 .... *32*
Hauptly, Denis J(ames) 1945- *57*
Hauser, Jill Frankel 1950- *127*
Hauser, Margaret L(ouise) 1909- *10*
Hausherr, Rosmarie 1943- *86*
Hausman, Gerald 1945- *180*
　Earlier sketches in SATA *13, 90, 132*
　See also CLR *89*
Hausman, Gerry
　See Hausman, Gerald

Hauth, Katherine B. 1940- *99*
Hautman, Pete 1952- *173*
　Earlier sketches in SATA *82, 128*
Hautman, Peter Murray
　See Hautman, Pete
Hautzig, Deborah 1956- *106*
　Earlier sketch in SATA *31*
Hautzig, Esther Rudomin 1930- *148*
　Earlier sketches in SATA *4, 68*
　See also CLR *22*
　See also SAAS *15*
Havel, Geoff 1955- *152*
Havel, Jennifer
　See Havill, Juanita
Havelin, Kate 1961- *143*
Havighurst, Walter (Edwin) 1901-1994 .... *1*
　Obituary *79*
Haviland, Virginia 1911-1988 .... *6*
　Obituary *54*
Havill, Juanita 1949- *155*
　Earlier sketch in SATA *74*
Hawes, Judy 1913- *4*
Hawes, Louise 1943- *180*
　Earlier sketch in SATA *60*
Hawke, Rosanne 1953- *165*
　Earlier sketch in SATA *124*
Hawke, Rosanne Joy
　See Hawke, Rosanne
Hawkes, Kevin (Cliff) 1959- *150*
　Earlier sketch in SATA *78*
Hawkes, Nigel 1943- *119*
Hawkesworth, Eric 1921- *13*
Hawkins, Arthur 1903-1985 .... *19*
Hawkins, Colin 1945- *162*
　Earlier sketch in SATA *112*
Hawkins, Jacqui *162*
　Earlier sketch in SATA *112*
Hawkins, Jimmy 1941- *188*
Hawkins, Laura 1951- *74*
Hawkins, (Helena Ann) Quail 1905-2002 .... *6*
　Obituary *141*
Hawkinson, John (Samuel) 1912-1994 .... *4*
Hawkinson, Lucy (Ozone) 1924-1971 .... *21*
Hawks, Robert 1961- *85*
Hawley, Mabel C. *67*
　Earlier sketch in SATA *1*
Hawthorne, Captain R. M.
　See Ellis, Edward S(ylvester)
Hawthorne, Nathaniel 1804-1864
　See YABC *2*
　See also CLR *103*
Hay, Jeff T. *154*
Hay, John 1915- *13*
Hay, Timothy
　See Brown, Margaret Wise
Hayashi, Leslie Ann 1954- *115*
Hayashi, Nancy 1939- *186*
　Earlier sketch in SATA *80*
Haycak, Cara 1961- *180*
Haycock, Kate 1962- *77*
Haycraft, Howard 1905-1991 .... *6*
　Obituary *70*
Haycraft, Molly Costain 1911- *6*
Hayden, Gwendolen Lampshire 1904- *35*
Hayden, Robert C(arter), Jr. 1937- *47*
　Brief entry *28*
Hayden, Robert E(arl) 1913-1980 .... *19*
　Obituary *26*
Hayden, Torey L. 1951- *163*
　Earlier sketch in SATA *65*
Hayden, Torey Lynn
　See Hayden, Torey L.
Hayes, Carlton J(oseph) H(untley)
　1882-1964 .... *11*
Hayes, Daniel 1952- *109*
　Earlier sketch in SATA *73*
Hayes, Geoffrey 1947- *91*
　Earlier sketch in SATA *26*
Hayes, Joe 1945- *131*
　Earlier sketch in SATA *88*
Hayes, John F. 1904-1980 .... *11*

Hayes, Rosemary *158*
Hayes, Sheila 1937- *51*
　Brief entry *50*
Hayes, Will *7*
Hayes, William D(imitt) 1913-1976 .... *8*
Haynes, Betsy 1937- *94*
　Brief entry *37*
　Earlier sketch in SATA *48*
　See also CLR *90*
Haynes, David 1955- *97*
Haynes, Linda
　See Swinford, Betty (June Wells)
Haynes, Mary 1938- *65*
Haynes, Max 1956- *72*
Hays, H(offmann) R(eynolds) 1904-1980 .... *26*
Hays, Thomas Anthony 1957- *84*
Hays, Tony
　See Hays, Thomas Anthony
Hays, Wilma Pitchford 1909- *28*
　Earlier sketch in SATA *1*
　See also CLR *59*
　See also SAAS *3*
Hayward, Linda 1943- *185*
　Brief entry *39*
　Earlier sketch in SATA *101*
Haywood, Carolyn 1898-1990 .... *75*
　Obituary *64*
　Earlier sketches in SATA *1, 29*
　See also CLR *22*
Hazell, Rebecca (Eileen) 1947- *141*
Hazen, Barbara Shook 1930- *178*
　Earlier sketches in SATA *27, 90*
Head, Gay
　See Hauser, Margaret L(ouise)
Head, Tom 1978- *167*
Headley, Elizabeth
　See Harrison, Elizabeth (Allen) Cavanna
Headley, Justina Chen 1968- *176*
Headstrom, (Birger) Richard 1902-1985 .... *8*
Heady, Eleanor B(utler) 1917-1979 .... *8*
Heagy, William D. 1964- *76*
Heal, Edith 1903-1995 .... *7*
Heal, Gillian 1934- *89*
Heale, Jay (Jeremy Peter Wingfield) 1937- .. *84*
Healey, Brooks
　See Albert, Burton
Healey, Larry 1927- *44*
　Brief entry *42*
Heap, Sue 1954- *187*
　Earlier sketch in SATA *150*
Heaps, Willard A(llison) 1908-1987 .... *26*
Hearn, Diane Dawson 1952- *79*
Hearn, Emily
　See Valleau, Emily
Hearn, Julie 1958- *152*
Hearn, Lian
　See Rubinstein, Gillian
Hearn, Sneed
　See Gregg, Andrew K.
Hearne, Betsy Gould 1942- *146*
　Earlier sketches in SATA *38, 95*
Heath, Charles D(ickinson) 1941- *46*
Heath, Veronica
　See Blackett, Veronica Heath
Heaven, Constance (Christina) 1911- *7*
Hebert-Collins, Sheila 1948- *111*
Hecht, George J(oseph) 1895-1980
　Obituary *22*
Hecht, Henri Joseph 1922- *9*
Hechtkopf, Henryk 1910- *17*
Heck, Bessie (Mildred) Holland 1911-1995 . *26*
Heck, Ed 1963- *173*
Heckert, Connie K(aye Delp) 1948- *82*
Hedderwick, Mairi 1939- *145*
　Earlier sketches in SATA *30, 77*
Hedges, Sid(ney) G(eorge) 1897-1974 .... *28*
Hedrick, Irene Hope 1920- *175*
Heelan, Jamee Riggio 1965- *146*
Heerboth, Sharon
　See Leon, Sharon

Heffernan, John 1949- 168
Earlier sketch in SATA 121
Heffron, Dorris 1944- 68
Hefter, Richard 1942- 31
Hegarty, Reginald Beaton 1906-1973 10
Hehenberger, Shelly 1968- 126
Heidbreder, Robert K. 1947- 130
Heide, Florence Parry 1919- 192
Earlier sketches in SATA 32, 69, 118
See also CLR 60
See also SAAS 6
Heiderstadt, Dorothy 1907-2001 6
Heidi Louise
See Erdrich, Louise
Heidler, David S(tephen) 1955- 132
Heidler, Jeanne T. 1956- 132
Heilbroner, Joan Knapp 1922- 63
Heilbrun, Lois Hussey 1922(?)-1987
Obituary 54
Heiligman, Deborah 1958- 193
Earlier sketches in SATA 90, 144
Heilman, Joan Rattner 50
Heimann, Rolf 1940- 164
Earlier sketch in SATA 120
Hein, Lucille Eleanor 1915-1994 20
Heine, Helme 1941- 135
Earlier sketch in SATA 67
See also CLR 18
Heinlein, Robert A. 1907-1988 69
Obituary 56
Earlier sketch in SATA 9
See also CLR 75
Heinlein, Robert Anson
See Heinlein, Robert A.
Heins, Ethel L(eah) 1918-1997 101
Heins, Paul 1909- 13
Heintze, Carl 1922- 26
Heinz, Bill
See Heinz, W.C.
Heinz, Brian J. 1946- 181
Earlier sketch in SATA 95
Heinz, Brian James
See Heinz, Brian J.
Heinz, W.C. 1915-2008 26
Heinz, Wilfred Charles
See Heinz, W.C.
Heinzen, Mildred
See Masters, Mildred
Heisel, Sharon E(laine) 1941- 125
Earlier sketch in SATA 84
Heitzmann, William Ray 1948- 73
Heitzmann, Wm. Ray
See Heitzmann, William Ray
Helakoski, Leslie 178
Helberg, Shirley Adelaide Holden 1919- ... 138
Helfer, Andrew 187
Helfer, Ralph 1937- 177
Helfman, Elizabeth S(eaver) 1911-2001 3
Helfman, Harry Carmozin 1910-1995 3
Helgerson, Joseph 1950- 181
Hellard, Susan 182
Hellberg, Hans-Eric 1927- 38
Heller, Linda 1944- 46
Brief entry 40
Heller, Mike
See Hano, Arnold
Heller, Ruth M. 1924- 112
Earlier sketch in SATA 66
Hellman, Hal
See Hellman, Harold
Hellman, Harold 1927- 4
Helman, Andrea (Jean) 1946- 160
Earlier sketch in SATA 107
Helmer, Diana Star 1962- 86
Helmer, Marilyn 160
Earlier sketch in SATA 112
Helps, Racey 1913-1971 2
Obituary 25
Helquist, Brett 187
Earlier sketch in SATA 146

Helweg, Hans H. 1917- 50
Brief entry 33
Helyar, Jane Penelope Josephine 1933- 138
Autobiography Feature 138
Earlier sketch in SATA 82
See Poole, Josephine
Hemmant, Lynette 1938- 69
Hemming, Roy G. 1928-1995 11
Obituary 86
Hemphill, Helen 1955- 179
Hemphill, Kris (Harrison) 1963- 118
Hemphill, Martha Locke 1904-1973 37
Hemphill, Stephanie 190
Hemstock, Gillian 1956- 173
Henba, Bobbie 1926- 87
Henbest, Nigel 1951- 55
Brief entry 52
Henderley, Brooks 1
Henderson, Aileen Kilgore 1921- 178
Henderson, Aileen Mary
See Fox, Aileen
Henderson, Gordon 1950- 53
Henderson, Kathy 1949- 155
Brief entry 53
Earlier sketches in SATA 55, 95
Henderson, LeGrand 1901-1965 9
Henderson, Nancy Wallace 1916- 22
Henderson, Zenna (Chlarson) 1917-1983 5
Hendrickson, Walter Brookfield, Jr. 1936- 9
Hendry, Diana 1941- 106
Earlier sketch in SATA 68
Hendry, Frances Mary 1941- 171
Earlier sketch in SATA 110
Hendry, Linda (Gail) 1961- 83
Heneghan, James 1930- 160
Earlier sketches in SATA 53, 97
Henkes, Kevin 1960- 154
Earlier sketches in SATA 43, 76, 108
See also CLR 108
Hennessy, Barbara G.
See Hennessy, B.G.
Hennessy, Barbara Gulbrandsen
See Hennessy, B.G.
Hennessy, B.G. 1951- 175
Henney, Carolee Wells 1928- 102
Henriod, Lorraine 1925- 26
Henriquez, Emile F. 1937- 170
Earlier sketch in SATA 89
Henry, April 1959- 174
Henry, Ernest 1948- 107
Henry, Joanne Landers 1927- 6
Henry, Maeve 1960- 75
Henry, Marguerite 1902-1997 100
Obituary 99
See also CLR 4
See also SAAS 7
Henry, Marie H. 1935- 65
Henry, Marilyn 1939- 117
Henry, Marion
See del Rey, Lester
Henry, O.
See Porter, William Sydney
Henry, Oliver
See Porter, William Sydney
Henry, T. E.
See Rowland-Entwistle, (Arthur) Theodore
(Henry)
Henschel, Elizabeth Georgie 56
Henson, James Maury
See Henson, Jim
Henson, Jim 1936-1990 43
Obituary 65
Henstra, Friso 1928- 73
Earlier sketch in SATA 8
See also SAAS 14
Hentoff, Nat(han Irving) 1925- 133
Brief entry 27
Earlier sketches in SATA 42, 69
See also CLR 52
Henty, G(eorge) A(lfred) 1832-1902 64
See also CLR 76

Heo, Yumi 1964- 146
Earlier sketch in SATA 94
Hepler, Heather 177
Herald, Kathleen
See Peyton, Kathleen Wendy (Herald)
Herb, Angela M. 1970- 92
Herbert, Cecil
See Hamilton, Charles (Harold St. John)
Herbert, Don 1917-2007 2
Obituary 184
Herbert, Donald Jeffrey
See Herbert, Don
Herbert, Frank 1920-1986 37
Obituary 47
Earlier sketch in SATA 9
Herbert, Frank Patrick
See Herbert, Frank
Herbert, Helen (Jean) 1947- 57
Herbert, Janis 1956- 139
Herbert, Wally 1934-2007 23
Herbert, Walter William
See Herbert, Wally
Herbst, Judith 1947- 74
Herda, D.J. 1948- 80
Herge
See CLR 114
See Remi, Georges
Heritage, Martin
See Horler, Sydney
Herkimer, L(awrence) R(ussell) 1925(?)- 42
Herlihy, Dirlie Anne 1935- 73
Herman, Charlotte 1937- 99
Earlier sketch in SATA 20
Hermanson, Dennis (Everett) 1947- 10
Hermes, Jules 1962- 92
Hermes, Patricia 1936- 191
Earlier sketches in SATA 31, 78, 141
Hermes, Patricia Mary
See Hermes, Patricia
Hernandez, Natalie Nelson 1929- 123
Herndon, Ernest 91
Herold, Ann Bixby 1937- 72
Herrera, Juan Felipe 1948- 127
Herrick, Steven 1958- 156
Earlier sketch in SATA 103
Herriman, George (Joseph) 1880-1944 140
Herriot, James 1916-1995 135
Earlier sketch in SATA 86
See also CLR 80
See Wight, James Alfred
Herrmanns, Ralph 1933- 11
Herrold, Tracey
See Dils, Tracey E.
Herron, Edward A(lbert) 1912- 4
Herschler, Mildred Barger 130
Hersey, John 1914-1993 25
Obituary 76
Hersey, John Richard
See Hersey, John
and Hersey, John
Hershberger, Priscilla (Gorman) 1951- 81
Hershenhorn, Esther 1945- 151
Hershey, Kathleen M. 1934- 80
Hershey, Mary 173
Hersom, Kathleen 1911- 73
Hertz, Grete Janus 1915- 23
Herzig, Alison Cragin 1935- 87
Herzog, Brad 1968- 131
Heslewood, Juliet 1951- 82
Hess, Lilo 1916- 4
Hess, Paul 1961- 134
Hesse, Hermann 1877-1962 50
Hesse, Karen 1952- 158
Autobiography Feature 113
Earlier sketches in SATA 74, 103
See also CLR 54
See also SAAS 25
Hest, Amy 1950- 193
Earlier sketches in SATA 55, 82, 129
Heuer, Kenneth John 1927- 44
Heuman, William 1912-1971 21

Heuston, Kimberley 1960- *167*
Heuston, Kimberley Burton
  See Heuston, Kimberley
Hewes, Agnes Danforth 1874-1963 .... *35*
Hewett, Anita 1918-1989 .... *13*
Hewett, Joan 1930- *140*
  Earlier sketch in SATA *81*
Hewett, Richard 1929- *81*
Hewitson, Jennifer 1961- *97*
Hewitt, Margaret 1961- *84*
Hewitt, Sally 1949- *127*
Hext, Harrington
  See Phillpotts, Eden
Hey, Nigel S(tewart) 1936- *20*
Heyduck-Huth, Hilde 1929- *8*
Heyer, Carol 1950- *130*
  Earlier sketch in SATA *74*
Heyer, Marilee 1942- *102*
  Earlier sketch in SATA *64*
Heyerdahl, Thor 1914-2002 .... *52*
  Earlier sketch in SATA *2*
Heyes, (Nancy) Eileen 1956- *150*
  Earlier sketch in SATA *80*
Heyliger, William 1884-1955
  See YABC *1*
Heyman, Ken(neth Louis) 1930- *114*
  Earlier sketch in SATA *34*
Heyward, (Edwin) DuBose 1885-1940 .... *21*
Heywood, Karen 1946- *48*
Hezlep, William (Earl) 1936- *88*
Hibbert, Christopher 1924- *4*
Hibbert, Eleanor Alice Burford 1906-1993 .... *2*
  Obituary *74*
  See Holt, Victoria
Hickman, Estella (Lee) 1942- *111*
Hickman, Janet 1940- *127*
  Earlier sketch in SATA *12*
Hickman, Martha Whitmore 1925- *26*
Hickman, Pamela 1958- *186*
  Earlier sketch in SATA *128*
Hickock, Will
  See Harrison, C(hester) William
Hickok, Lorena A. 1893-1968 .... *20*
Hickox, Rebecca (Ayres) *116*
Hicks, Barbara Jean 1953- *165*
Hicks, Betty *191*
Hicks, Clifford B. 1920- *50*
Hicks, Eleanor B.
  See Coerr, Eleanor (Beatrice)
Hicks, Harvey
  See Stratemeyer, Edward L.
Hicks, Peter 1952- *111*
Hicyilmaz, Gaye 1947- *157*
  Earlier sketch in SATA *77*
Hieatt, Constance B(artlett) 1928- *4*
Hiebert, Ray Eldon 1932- *13*
Higdon, Hal 1931- *4*
Higginbottom, David 1923- *87*
  See Fisk, Nicholas
Higginbottom, J(effrey) Winslow 1945- *29*
Higgins, Joanna 1945- *125*
Higgins, Simon (Richard) 1958- *105*
Higginsen, Vy *79*
High, Linda Oatman 1958- *188*
  Autobiography Feature *188*
  Earlier sketches in SATA *94, 145*
High, Philip E. 1914- *119*
High, Philip Empson
  See High, Philip E.
Higham, David (Michael) 1949- *50*
Higham, Jon Atlas
  See Higham, Jonathan Huw
Higham, Jonathan Huw 1960- *59*
Highet, Helen
  See MacInnes, Helen (Clark)
Hightman, Jason 1971(?)- *189*
Hightman, J.P.
  See Hightman, Jason
Hightower, Florence Cole 1916-1981 .... *4*
  Obituary *27*

Highwater, Jamake (Mamake)
  1942(?)-2001 .... *69*
  Brief entry *30*
  Earlier sketch in SATA *32*
  See also CLR *17*
Hilb, Nora 1953- *178*
Hildebrandt, Greg 1939- *172*
  Brief entry *33*
  Earlier sketch in SATA *55*
Hildebrandt, Tim 1939-2006 .... *55*
  Brief entry *33*
Hildebrandt, Timothy
  See Hildebrandt, Tim
Hildebrandts, The
  See Hildebrandt, Greg
  and Hildebrandt, Tim
Hilder, Rowland 1905-1993 .... *36*
  Obituary *77*
Hildick, E. W.
  See SAAS *6*
  See Hildick, (Edmund) Wallace
Hildick, (Edmund) Wallace 1925-2001 .... *68*
  Earlier sketch in SATA *2*
  See Hildick, E. W.
Hilgartner, Beth 1957- *58*
Hill, Alexis
  See Craig, Mary (Francis) Shura
  and Glick, Ruth (Burtnick)
Hill, Anthony R. 1942- *164*
  Earlier sketch in SATA *91*
Hill, Anthony Robert
  See Hill, Anthony R.
Hill, David 1942- *152*
  Earlier sketch in SATA *103*
Hill, Donna (Marie) 1921- *124*
  Earlier sketch in SATA *24*
Hill, Douglas 1935-2007 .... *78*
  Earlier sketch in SATA *39*
Hill, Douglas Arthur
  See Hill, Douglas
Hill, Elizabeth Starr 1925- *143*
  Earlier sketch in SATA *24*
Hill, Eric 1927- *133*
  Brief entry *53*
  Earlier sketch in SATA *66*
  See also CLR *13*
Hill, Gordon
  See Eldin, Peter
Hill, Grace Brooks *67*
  Earlier sketch in SATA *1*
Hill, Grace Livingston 1865-1947
  See YABC *2*
Hill, Helen M(orey) 1915- *27*
Hill, John
  See Koontz, Dean R.
Hill, Johnson
  See Kunhardt, Edith
Hill, Judy I. R.
  See Roberts, Judy I.
Hill, Kathleen Louise 1917- *4*
Hill, Kay
  See Hill, Kathleen Louise
Hill, Kirkpatrick 1938- *188*
  Earlier sketches in SATA *72, 126*
Hill, Laban Carrick *170*
Hill, Lee Sullivan 1958- *96*
Hill, Lorna 1902-1991 .... *12*
Hill, Margaret (Ohler) 1915- *36*
Hill, Meg
  See Hill, Margaret (Ohler)
Hill, Meredith
  See Craig, Mary (Francis) Shura
Hill, Monica
  See Watson, Jane Werner
Hill, Pamela Smith 1954- *112*
Hill, Ralph Nading 1917-1987 .... *65*
Hill, Robert W(hite) 1919-1982 .... *12*
  Obituary *31*
Hill, Ruth A.
  See Viguers, Ruth Hill

Hill, Ruth Livingston
  See Munce, Ruth Hill
Hill, Stuart 1958- *186*
Hill, Susan 1942- *183*
Hill, Susan Elizabeth
  See Hill, Susan
Hill, Susanna Leonard 1965- *193*
Hill, Thomas 1960- *82*
Hillcourt, William 1900-1992 .... *27*
Hillenbrand, Will 1960- *147*
  Earlier sketch in SATA *84*
Hiller, Ilo (Ann) 1938- *59*
Hillerman, Tony 1925-2008 .... *6*
Hillert, Margaret 1920- *91*
  Earlier sketch in SATA *8*
Hilliard, Richard *183*
Hillman, Elizabeth 1942- *75*
Hillman, John 1952- *120*
Hillman, Martin
  See Hill, Douglas
Hillman, Priscilla 1940- *48*
  Brief entry *39*
Hills, C.A.R. 1955- *39*
Hills, Charles Albert Reis
  See Hills, C.A.R.
Hills, Tad *173*
Hilton, Irene Pothus -1979 .... *7*
Hilton, James 1900-1954 .... *34*
Hilton, Margaret Lynette 1946- *105*
  Earlier sketch in SATA *68*
  See Hilton, Nette
Hilton, Nette
  See CLR *25*
  See also SAAS *21*
  See Hilton, Margaret Lynette
Hilton, Ralph 1907-1982 .... *8*
Hilton, Suzanne 1922- *4*
Hilton-Bruce, Anne
  See Hilton, Margaret Lynette
Him, George 1937-1982
  Obituary *30*
Himelblau, Linda -2005 .... *179*
Himelstein, Shmuel 1940- *83*
Himler, Ann 1946- *8*
Himler, Ronald 1937- *183*
  Earlier sketches in SATA *6, 92, 137*
Himler, Ronald Norbert
  See Himler, Ronald
Himmelman, John C(arl) 1959- *159*
  Earlier sketches in SATA *47, 94*
Hinckley, Helen
  See Jones, Helen Hinckley
Hind, Dolores (Ellen) 1931- *53*
  Brief entry *49*
Hindin, Nathan
  See Bloch, Robert (Albert)
Hindley, Judy 1940- *179*
  Earlier sketch in SATA *120*
Hinds, P(atricia) Mignon *98*
Hines, Anna Grossnickle 1946- *141*
  Brief entry *45*
  Earlier sketches in SATA *51, 95*
  See also SAAS *16*
Hines, Gary (Roger) 1944- *136*
  Earlier sketch in SATA *74*
Hinojosa, Maria (de Lourdes) 1961- *88*
Hinton, Nigel 1941- *166*
Hinton, Sam 1917- *43*
Hinton, S.E. 1950- *160*
  Earlier sketches in SATA *19, 58, 115*
  See also CLR *23*
Hinton, Susan Eloise
  See Hinton, S.E.
Hintz, Martin 1945- *128*
  Brief entry *39*
  Earlier sketch in SATA *47*
Hintz, Stephen V. 1975- *129*
Hippopotamus, Eugene H.
  See Kraus, (Herman) Robert
Hirano, Cathy 1957- *68*
Hirsch, Karen 1941- *61*

Hirsch, Odo *157*
  Earlier sketch in SATA *111*
Hirsch, Phil 1926- *35*
Hirsch, S. Carl 1913-1990 .... *2*
  See also SAAS *7*
Hirschfelder, Arlene B. 1943- *138*
  Earlier sketch in SATA *80*
Hirschi, Ron 1948- *192*
  Earlier sketches in SATA *56, 95*
Hirsh, Marilyn 1944-1988 .... *7*
  Obituary *58*
Hirshberg, Al(bert Simon) 1909-1973 .... *38*
Hiscock, Bruce 1940- *137*
  Earlier sketch in SATA *57*
Hiser, Constance 1950- *71*
Hiser, Iona Seibert -1998 .... *4*
Hislop, Julia Rose Catherine 1962- *74*
Hissey, Jane 1952- *130*
  Autobiography Feature *130*
  Earlier sketches in SATA *58, 103*
Hissey, Jane Elizabeth
  See Hissey, Jane
Hitchcock, Alfred (Joseph) 1899-1980 .... *27*
  Obituary *24*
Hite, Sid 1954- *175*
  Earlier sketches in SATA *75, 136*
Hitte, Kathryn 1919- *16*
Hitz, Demi 1942- *152*
  Earlier sketches in SATA *11, 66, 102*
  See also CLR *58*
  See Demi
Hitzeroth, Deborah L. 1961- *78*
Hnizdovsky, Jacques 1915- *32*
Ho, Louise *185*
Ho, Minfong 1951- *151*
  Earlier sketches in SATA *15, 94*
  See also CLR *28*
Hoagland, Edward (Morley) 1932- *51*
Hoare, Robert J(ohn) 1921-1975 .... *38*
Hoban, Lillian 1925-1998 .... *69*
  Obituary *104*
  Earlier sketch in SATA *22*
  See also CLR *67*
Hoban, Russell 1925- *136*
  Earlier sketches in SATA *1, 40, 78*
  See also CLR *139*
Hoban, Russell Conwell
  See Hoban, Russell
Hoban, Tana 1917(?)-2006 .... *104*
  Obituary *173*
  Earlier sketches in SATA *22, 70*
  See also CLR *76*
  See also SAAS *12*
Hobart, Lois (Elaine) *7*
Hobbie, Holly 1944- *178*
  See also CLR *88*
Hobbie, Jocelyn *190*
Hobbs, Leigh 1953- *166*
Hobbs, Valerie 1941- *193*
  Autobiography Feature *145*
  Earlier sketches in SATA *93, 145*
Hobbs, Will 1947- *177*
  Autobiography Feature *127*
  Earlier sketches in SATA *72, 110*
  See also CLR *59*
Hobbs, William Carl
  See Hobbs, Will
Hoberman, Mary Ann 1930- *158*
  Earlier sketches in SATA *5, 72, 111*
  See also CLR *22*
  See also SAAS *18*
Hobson, Bruce 1950- *62*
Hobson, Burton (Harold) 1933- *28*
Hobson, Laura Z(ametkin) 1900-1986 .... *52*
Hobson, Sally 1967- *172*
  Earlier sketch in SATA *84*
Hoce, Charley E. *174*
Hochschild, Arlie Russell 1940- *11*
Hockaby, Stephen
  See Mitchell, Gladys (Maude Winifred)

Hockenberry, Hope
  See Newell, Hope Hockenberry
Hodge, Deborah 1954- *163*
  Earlier sketch in SATA *122*
Hodge, P. W.
  See Hodge, Paul W(illiam)
Hodge, Paul W(illiam) 1934- *12*
Hodgell, P(atricia) C(hristine) 1951- *42*
Hodges, C. Walter 1909-2004 .... *2*
  Obituary *158*
Hodges, Carl G. 1902-1964 .... *10*
Hodges, Cyril Walter
  See Hodges, C. Walter
Hodges, Elizabeth Jamison *1*
Hodges, Margaret 1911-2005 .... *167*
  Obituary *172*
  Earlier sketches in SATA *1, 33, 75, 117*
  See also SAAS *9*
Hodges, Margaret Moore
  See Hodges, Margaret
Hodgetts, Blake Christopher 1967- *43*
Hodgson, Harriet (W.) 1935- *84*
Hoehne, Marcia 1951- *89*
Hoellwarth, Cathryn Clinton
  See Clinton, Cathryn
Hoestlandt, Jo 1948- *94*
Hoestlandt, Jocelyne
  See Hoestlandt, Jo
Hoexter, Corinne K. 1927- *6*
Hoeye, Michael 1947- *136*
Hoff, Carol 1900-1979 .... *11*
Hoff, Mary (King) 1956- *157*
  Earlier sketch in SATA *74*
Hoff, Syd(ney) 1912-2004 .... *138*
  Obituary *154*
  Earlier sketches in SATA *9, 72*
  See also CLR *83*
  See also SAAS *4*
Hoffman, Edwin D. *49*
Hoffman, Elizabeth P(arkinson) 1921-2003
  Obituary *153*
Hoffman, Mary (Margaret) 1945- *144*
  Earlier sketches in SATA *59, 97*
  See also SAAS *24*
  See Lassiter, Mary
Hoffman, Mat 1972- *150*
Hoffman, Nina Kiriki 1955- *160*
Hoffman, Phyllis M(iriam) 1944- *4*
Hoffman, Rosekrans 1926- *15*
Hoffmann, E(rnst) T(heodor) A(madeus)
  1776-1822 .... *27*
  See also CLR *133*
Hoffmann, Felix 1911-1975 .... *9*
Hoffmann, Heinrich 1809-1894
  See CLR *122*
Hoffmann, Margaret Jones 1910- *48*
Hoffmann, Peggy
  See Hoffmann, Margaret Jones
Hofher, Catherine Baxley 1954- *130*
Hofher, Cathy
  See Hofher, Catherine Baxley
Hofmeyr, Dianne (Louise) *138*
Hofsepian, Sylvia A. 1932- *74*
Hofsinde, Robert 1902-1973 .... *21*
Hogan, Bernice Harris 1929- *12*
Hogan, Inez 1895-1973 .... *2*
Hogan, James P(atrick) 1941- *81*
Hogan, Jamie *192*
Hogan, Linda 1947- *132*
Hogarth, Burne 1911-1996 .... *89*
  Earlier sketch in SATA *63*
Hogarth, Grace (Weston Allen) 1905-1995 .. *91*
Hogarth, Jr.
  See Kent, Rockwell
Hogarth, (Arthur) Paul 1917-2001 .... *41*
Hogg, Garry 1902-1976 .... *2*
Hogg, Gary 1957- *172*
  Earlier sketch in SATA *105*
Hogner, Dorothy Childs *4*
Hogner, Nils 1893-1970 .... *25*

Hogrogian, Nonny 1932- *74*
  Autobiography Feature *127*
  Earlier sketch in SATA *7*
  See also CLR *95*
  See also SAAS *1*
Hoh, Diane 1937- *102*
  Brief entry *48*
  Earlier sketch in SATA *52*
Hoke, Helen
  Obituary *65*
  See Watts, Helen L. Hoke
Hoke, John (Lindsay) 1925- *7*
Hokenson, Terry 1948- *193*
Hol, Coby 1943- *126*
Holabird, Katharine 1948- *135*
  Earlier sketch in SATA *62*
Holaday, Bobbie 1922- *153*
Holbeach, Henry
  See Rands, William Brighty
Holberg, Ruth L(angland) 1889-1984 .... *1*
Holbrook, Kathy 1963- *107*
Holbrook, Peter
  See Glick, Carl (Cannon)
Holbrook, Sabra
  See Erickson, Sabra Rollins
Holbrook, Sara *131*
Holbrook, Stewart Hall 1893-1964 .... *2*
Holcomb, Jerry (Leona) Kimble 1927- *113*
Holcomb, Nan
  See McPhee, Norma H.
Holden, Elizabeth Rhoda
  See Lawrence, Louise
Holding, James (Clark Carlisle, Jr.)
  1907-1997 .... *3*
  See Queen, Ellery
Holeman, Linda 1949- *136*
  Autobiography Feature *136*
  Earlier sketch in SATA *102*
Holinger, William (Jacques) 1944- *90*
Holisher, Desider 1901-1972 .... *6*
Holl, Adelaide Hinkle 1910- *8*
Holl, Kristi D(iane) 1951- *51*
Holland, Gay W. 1941- *128*
Holland, Isabelle (Christian) 1920-2002 .... *70*
  Autobiography Feature *103*
  Obituary *132*
  Earlier sketch in SATA *8*
  See also CLR *57*
Holland, Janice 1913-1962 .... *18*
Holland, John L(ewis) 1919- *20*
Holland, Joyce
  See Morice, Dave
Holland, Julia 1954- *106*
Holland, Lynda (H.) 1959- *77*
Holland, Lys
  See Gater, Dilys
Holland, Marion 1908-1989 .... *6*
  Obituary *61*
Hollander, John 1929- *13*
Hollander, Nicole 1940(?)- *101*
Hollander, Paul
  See Silverberg, Robert
Hollander, Phyllis 1928- *39*
Hollander, Zander 1923- *63*
Holldobler, Turid 1939- *26*
Holliday, Joe
  See Holliday, Joseph
Holliday, Joseph 1910- *11*
Holling, Holling C(lancy) 1900-1973 .... *15*
  Obituary *26*
  See also CLR *50*
Hollingsworth, Alvin C(arl) 1930- *39*
Hollingsworth, Mary 1947- *166*
  Earlier sketch in SATA *91*
Holloway, Teresa (Bragunier) 1906- *26*
Holm, (Else) Anne (Lise) 1922-1998 .... *1*
  See also CLR *75*
  See also SAAS *7*
Holm, Jennifer L. 1968(?)- *183*
  Earlier sketches in SATA *120, 163*
Holm, Matthew 1974- *174*

Holm, Sharon Lane 1955- 114
  Earlier sketch in SATA 78
Holman, Felice 1919- 82
  Earlier sketch in SATA 7
  See also SAAS 17
Holm and Hamel
  See Holm, Jennifer L.
Holme, Bryan 1913-1990 26
  Obituary 66
Holmes, Barbara Ware 1945- 127
  Earlier sketch in SATA 65
Holmes, Elizabeth 1957- 191
Holmes, Elizabeth Ann
  See Holmes, Elizabeth
Holmes, John
  See Souster, (Holmes) Raymond
Holmes, Marjorie (Rose) 1910-2002 43
Holmes, Martha 1961- 72
Holmes, Mary Z(astrow) 1943- 80
Holmes, Oliver Wendell 1809-1894 34
Holmes, Peggy 1898- 60
Holmes, Raymond
  See Souster, (Holmes) Raymond
Holmes, Rick
  See Hardwick, Richard Holmes, Jr.
Holmes, Sara Lewis 186
Holmgren, Helen Jean 1930- 45
Holmgren, Sister George Ellen
  See Holmgren, Helen Jean
Holmgren, Virginia C(unningham) 1909- 26
Holmquist, Eve 1921- 11
Holt, Kimberly Willis 1960- 179
  Earlier sketch in SATA 122
Holt, Margaret 1937- 4
Holt, Margaret Van Vechten (Saunders)
  1899-1963 32
Holt, Michael (Paul) 1929- 13
Holt, Rackham
  See Holt, Margaret Van Vechten (Saunders)
Holt, Rochelle L. 41
  See DuBois, Rochelle (Lynn) Holt
Holt, Stephen
  See Thompson, Harlan (Howard)
Holt, Victoria
  See Hibbert, Eleanor Alice Burford
Holton, Leonard
  See Wibberley, Leonard (Patrick
  O'Connor)
Holtze, Sally Holmes 1952- 64
Holtzman, Jerome 1926-2008 57
Holub, Joan 1956- 149
  Earlier sketch in SATA 99
Holub, Josef 1926- 175
Holubitsky, Katherine 1955- 165
  Earlier sketch in SATA 121
Holyer, Erna Maria 1925- 22
Holyer, Ernie
  See Holyer, Erna Maria
Holz, Loretta (Marie) 1943- 17
Homel, David 1952- 97
Homze, Alma C. 1932- 17
Honey, Elizabeth 1947- 137
  Autobiography Feature 137
  Earlier sketch in SATA 112
Honeycutt, Natalie 1945- 97
Hong, Lily Toy 1958- 76
Hong, Maxine Ting Ting
  See Kingston, Maxine Hong
Honig, Donald 1931- 18
Honness, Elizabeth H. 1904- 2
Hoobler, Dorothy 1941- 161
  Earlier sketches in SATA 28, 109
Hoobler, Thomas 161
  Earlier sketches in SATA 28, 109
Hood, Joseph F. 1925- 4
Hood, Robert E. 1926- 21
Hood, Sarah
  See Killough, (Karen) Lee
Hook, Brendan 1963- 105
Hook, Frances 1912-1983 27
Hook, Geoffrey R(aynor) 1928- 103

Hook, Jeff
  See Hook, Geoffrey R(aynor)
Hook, Martha 1936- 27
Hooker, Richard
  See Heinz, W.C.
Hooker, Ruth 1920-1998 21
hooks, bell 1952(?)- 170
  Earlier sketch in SATA 115
Hooks, William H(arris) 1921- 94
  Earlier sketch in SATA 16
Hoon, Patricia Easterly 1954- 90
Hooper, Byrd
  See St. Clair, Byrd Hooper
Hooper, Mary 1944- 160
Hooper, Maureen Brett 1927- 76
Hooper, Meredith 1939- 159
  Earlier sketches in SATA 28, 101
Hooper, Meredith Jean
  See Hooper, Meredith
Hooper, Patricia 1941- 95
Hoopes, Lyn Littlefield 1953- 49
  Brief entry 44
Hoopes, Ned E(dward) 1932- 21
Hoopes, Roy 1922- 11
Hoose, Phillip M. 1947- 137
Hoover, H(elen) M(ary) 1935- 132
  Brief entry 33
  Earlier sketches in SATA 44, 83
  See also SAAS 8
Hoover, Helen (Drusilla Blackburn)
  1910-1984 12
  Obituary 39
Hope, Christopher 1944- 62
Hope, Christopher David Tully
  See Hope, Christopher
Hope, Laura Lee 67
  Earlier sketch in SATA 1
  See Goulart, Ron(ald Joseph)
  and Stanley, George Edward
Hope Simpson, Jacynth 1930- 12
Hopf, Alice (Martha) L(ightner) 1904-1988 ... 5
  Obituary 55
Hopkins, A. T.
  See Turngren, Annette
Hopkins, C. M.
  See Hopkins, Cathy
Hopkins, Cathy 1953- 165
Hopkins, Cathy M.
  See Hopkins, Cathy
Hopkins, Clark 1895-1976
  Obituary 34
Hopkins, Ellen L. 1955- 128
Hopkins, Jackie
  See Hopkins, Jackie Mims
Hopkins, Jackie Mims 1952- 178
  Earlier sketch in SATA 92
Hopkins, Joseph G(erard) E(dward) 1909- ... 11
Hopkins, (Hector) Kenneth 1914-1988
  Obituary 58
Hopkins, Lee Bennett 1938- 168
  Earlier sketches in SATA 3, 68, 125
  See also CLR 44
  See also SAAS 4
Hopkins, Lyman
  See Folsom, Franklin (Brewster)
Hopkins, Marjorie 1911-1999 9
Hopkins, Mary R(ice) 1956- 97
Hopkinson, Amanda 1948- 84
Hopkinson, Deborah 1952- 180
  Autobiography Feature 180
  Earlier sketches in SATA 76, 108, 159
  See also CLR 118
Hopman, Philip 1961- 177
Hoppe, Joanne 1932- 42
Hoppe, Matthias 1952- 76
Hopper, Nancy J. 1937- 38
  Brief entry 35
Hopping, Lorraine Jean
  See Egan, Lorraine Hopping
Horacek, Petr 163
Horenstein, Henry 1947- 108

Horgan, Paul (George Vincent
  O'Shaughnessy) 1903-1995 13
  Obituary 84
Horlak, E.E.
  See Tepper, Sheri S.
Horler, Sydney 1888-1954 102
Horn, Sandra Ann 1944- 154
Hornblow, Arthur, Jr. 1893-1976 15
Hornblow, Leonora 1920-2005 18
  Obituary 171
Hornblow, Leonora Schinasi
  See Hornblow, Leonora
Horne, Constance 1927- 149
Horne, Richard 1960-2007 169
  Obituary 180
  Earlier sketch in SATA 111
Horne, Richard Henry Hengist
  1802(?)-1884 29
Horner, Althea (Jane) 1926- 36
Horner, Dave 1934- 12
Horner, Jack
  See Horner, John R(obert)
Horner, John R(obert) 1946- 106
Hornik, Laurie Miller 159
Horniman, Joanne 1951- 167
  Earlier sketch in SATA 98
Hornos, Axel 1907-1994 20
Hornstein, Reuben Aaron 1912- 64
Horowitz, Anthony 1955- 137
Horowitz, Dave 1973(?)- 172
Horowitz, Ruth 1957- 136
Horrocks, Anita 1958- 169
Horse, Harry
  See Horne, Richard
Horsfield, Alan 1939- 153
Hort, Lenny 179
Horton, James O. 1943- 173
Horton, James Oliver
  See Horton, James O.
Horton, Madelyn (Stacey) 1962- 77
Horvath, Betty 1927- 4
Horvath, David 1972(?)- 192
Horvath, Polly 1957- 140
  Earlier sketch in SATA 85
  See also CLR 90
Horwich, Frances R(appaport) 1908-2001 11
  Obituary 130
Horwitz, Elinor Lander 45
  Brief entry 33
Horwood, William 1944- 85
Hosford, Dorothy (Grant) 1900-1952 22
Hosford, Jessie 1892-1990 5
Hoshi, Shin'ichi 1926- 101
Hoshino, Felicia 1968- 189
Hoskyns-Abrahall, Clare (Constance
  Drury) 13
Hosler, Danamarie 1978- 184
Hossack, Sylvia 1939- 83
Hossack, Sylvie Adams
  See Hossack, Sylvia
Hosseini, Khaled 1965- 156
Hossell, Karen Price
  See Price, Karen
Hosta, Dar 192
Hostetler, Marian 1932- 91
Houck, Carter 1924- 22
Hough, (Helen) Charlotte 1924- 9
Hough, Judy Taylor 1932- 63
  Brief entry 51
  Earlier sketch in SATA 56
Hough, Richard (Alexander) 1922-1999 17
Houghton, Eric 1930- 7
Houk, Randy 1944- 97
Houlehen, Robert J. 1918- 18
Household, Geoffrey (Edward West)
  1900-1988 14
  Obituary 59
Housman, Laurence 1865-1959 25
Houston, Dick 1943- 74

Houston, Gloria *138*
  Autobiography Feature *138*
  Earlier sketch in SATA *81*
Houston, James A(rchibald) 1921-2005 .... *74*
  Obituary *163*
  Earlier sketch in SATA *13*
  See also CLR *3*
  See also SAAS *17*
Houston, James D. 1933- *78*
Houston, Jeanne Toyo Wakatsuki
  See Houston, Jeanne Wakatsuki
Houston, Jeanne Wakatsuki 1934- *168*
  Autobiography Feature *168*
  Earlier sketch in SATA *78*
Houston, Juanita C. 1921- *129*
Houton, Kathleen
  See Kilgore, Kathleen
Houts, Amy F. *164*
Hovey, Kate *158*
Howard, Alan 1922- *45*
Howard, Alyssa
  See Buckholtz, Eileen (Garber)
  and Glick, Ruth (Burtnick)
  and Titchener, Louise
Howard, Arthur 1948- *165*
Howard, Arthur Charles
  See Howard, Arthur
Howard, Elizabeth Fitzgerald 1927- *119*
  Earlier sketch in SATA *74*
Howard, Ellen 1943- *184*
  Earlier sketches in SATA *67, 99*
Howard, Jane R(uble) 1924- *87*
Howard, Norman Barry 1949- *90*
Howard, P. M.
  See Howard, Pauline Rodriguez
Howard, Paul 1967- *190*
  Earlier sketch in SATA *118*
Howard, Pauline Rodriguez 1951- *124*
Howard, Prosper
  See Hamilton, Charles (Harold St. John)
Howard, Robert West 1908-1988 .... *5*
Howard, Todd 1964- *135*
Howard, Tristan
  See Currie, Stephen
Howard, Vernon (Linwood) 1918-1992 .... *40*
  Obituary *73*
Howard, Warren F.
  See Pohl, Frederik
Howarth, Daniel *188*
Howarth, David (Armine) 1912-1991 .... *6*
  Obituary *68*
Howarth, Lesley 1952- *94*
Howe, Deborah 1946-1978 .... *29*
Howe, James 1946- *161*
  Earlier sketches in SATA *29, 71, 111*
  See also CLR *9*
Howe, John F. 1957- *79*
Howe, Norma 1930- *126*
Howell, Pat 1947- *15*
Howell, S.
  See Styles, (Frank) Showell
Howell, Virginia
  See Ellison, Virginia H(owell)
Howes, Barbara 1914-1996 .... *5*
Howie, Diana 1945- *122*
Howie, Diana Melson
  See Howie, Diana
Howker, Janni 1957- *72*
  Brief entry *46*
  See also CLR *14*
  See also SAAS *13*
Howland, Ethan 1963- *131*
Hoy, Linda 1946- *65*
Hoy, Nina
  See Roth, Arthur J(oseph)
Hoyle, Geoffrey 1942- *18*
Hoyt, Ard *190*
Hoyt, Edwin P(almer), Jr. 1923- *28*
Hoyt, Erich 1950- *140*
  Earlier sketch in SATA *65*

Hoyt, Olga
  See Gruhzit-Hoyt, Olga (Margaret)
Hrdlitschka, Shelley 1956- *167*
  Earlier sketch in SATA *111*
Hrdlitschka, Shelley Joanne
  See Hrdlitschka, Shelley
Htin Aung, U.
  See Aung, (Maung) Htin
Hu, Ying-Hwa *173*
Huang, Benrei 1959- *86*
Hubalek, Linda K. 1954- *111*
Hubbard, Margaret Ann
  See Priley, Margaret (Ann) Hubbard
Hubbard, Michelle Calabro 1953- *122*
Hubbard, Patricia 1945- *124*
Hubbard, Woodleigh Marx *160*
  Earlier sketch in SATA *98*
Hubbell, Patricia 1928- *186*
  Earlier sketches in SATA *8, 132*
Hubley, Faith Elliot 1924-2001 .... *48*
  Obituary *133*
Hubley, John 1914-1977 .... *48*
  Obituary *24*
Huck, Charlotte S. 1922- *136*
  Earlier sketch in SATA *82*
Hudak, Michal 1956- *143*
Hudson, Cheryl Willis 1948- *160*
  Earlier sketch in SATA *81*
Hudson, Jan 1954-1990 .... *77*
  See also CLR *40*
Hudson, Jeffrey
  See Crichton, Michael
Hudson, (Margaret) Kirsty 1947- *32*
Hudson, Margaret
  See Shuter, Jane (Margaret)
Hudson, W(illiam) H(enry) 1841-1922 .... *35*
Hudson, Wade 1946- *162*
  Earlier sketch in SATA *74*
Huelsmann, Eva 1928- *16*
Huff, Barbara A. 1929- *67*
Huff, Tanya 1957- *171*
  Earlier sketch in SATA *85*
Huff, Tanya Sue
  See Huff, Tanya
Huff, T.S.
  See Huff, Tanya
Huff, Vivian 1948- *59*
Huffaker, Sandy 1943- *10*
Huffman, Tom *24*
Huggins, Nathan Irvin 1927-1989 .... *63*
Huggins, Peter *178*
Hughes, Carol 1955- *108*
Hughes, Dean 1943- *139*
  Earlier sketches in SATA *33, 77*
  See also CLR *76*
Hughes, Eden
  See Griffin, W.E.B
Hughes, Edward James
  See Hughes, Ted
Hughes, (James Mercer) Langston
  1902-1967 .... *33*
  Earlier sketch in SATA *4*
  See also CLR *17*
Hughes, Libby *71*
Hughes, Matilda
  See MacLeod, Charlotte (Matilda)
Hughes, Monica 1925-2003 .... *162*
  Earlier sketches in SATA *15, 70, 119*
  See also CLR *60*
  See also SAAS *11*
Hughes, Monica Ince
  See Hughes, Monica
Hughes, Richard (Arthur Warren)
  1900-1976 .... *8*
  Obituary *25*
Hughes, Sara
  See Saunders, Susan
Hughes, Shirley 1927- *159*
  Earlier sketches in SATA *16, 70, 110*
  See also CLR *15*

Hughes, Ted 1930-1998 .... *49*
  Brief entry *27*
  Obituary *107*
  See also CLR *131*
  See Hughes, Edward James
Hughes, Thomas 1822-1896 .... *31*
Hughes, Virginia
  See Campbell, Hope
Hughes, Walter (Llewellyn) 1910-1993 .... *26*
Hughey, Roberta 1942- *61*
Hugo, Pierre Brackers de
  See Brackers de Hugo, Pierre
Hugo, Victor (Marie) 1802-1885 .... *47*
Huline-Dickens, Frank William 1931- *34*
Huling, Jan *172*
Huliska-Beith, Laura *175*
Hull, Eleanor (Means) 1913- *21*
Hull, Eric Traviss
  See Harnan, Terry
Hull, H. Braxton
  See Jacobs, Helen Hull
Hull, Jesse Redding
  See Hull, Jessie Redding
Hull, Jessie Redding 1932- *51*
Hull, Katharine 1921-1977 .... *23*
Hull, Lise (E.) 1954- *148*
Hull, Maureen 1949- *142*
Hulme, Joy N. 1922- *161*
  Earlier sketches in SATA *74, 112*
Hults, Dorothy Niebrugge 1898-2000 .... *6*
Humble, Richard 1945- *60*
Hume, Lachie *189*
Hume, Lotta Carswell *7*
Hume, Ruth Fox 1922-1980 .... *26*
  Obituary *22*
Hume, Stephen Eaton 1947- *136*
Hummel, Berta 1909-1946 .... *43*
Hummel, Sister Maria Innocentia
  See Hummel, Berta
Humphrey, Carol Sue 1956- *167*
Humphrey, Henry (III) 1930- *16*
Humphrey, Kate
  See Forsyth, Kate
Humphrey, Sandra McLeod 1936- *95*
Humphreys, Martha 1943- *71*
Humphreys, Susan L.
  See Lowell, Susan
Hundal, Nancy 1957- *128*
Huneck, Stephen 1949- *183*
  Earlier sketch in SATA *129*
Hungerford, Hesba Fay
  See Brinsmead, H(esba) F(ay)
Hungerford, Pixie
  See Brinsmead, H(esba) F(ay)
Hunkin, Timothy Mark Trelawney 1950- *53*
Hunt, Angela Elwell 1957- *159*
  Earlier sketch in SATA *75*
Hunt, Francesca
  See Holland, Isabelle (Christian)
Hunt, Irene 1907-2001 .... *91*
  Earlier sketch in SATA *2*
  See also CLR *1*
Hunt, Janie Louise 1963- *102*
Hunt, Jonathan 1966- *84*
Hunt, Joyce 1927- *31*
Hunt, Linda 1940- *39*
Hunt, Lisa B(ehnke) 1967- *84*
Hunt, Mabel Leigh 1892-1971 .... *1*
  Obituary *26*
Hunt, Morton M(agill) 1920- *22*
Hunt, Nigel
  See Greenbank, Anthony Hunt
Hunt, Peter (Leonard) 1945- *76*
Hunter, Anne B. 1966- *118*
Hunter, Bernice Thurman 1922-2002 .... *85*
  Brief entry *45*
Hunter, Bobbi Dooley 1945- *89*
Hunter, Captain Marcy
  See Ellis, Edward S(ylvester)
Hunter, Chris
  See Fluke, Joanne

Hunter, Clingham M.D.
  See Adams, William Taylor
Hunter, Edith Fisher 1919- 31
Hunter, Erin
  See Cary, Kate
Hunter, Evan 1926-2005 25
  Obituary 167
  See McBain, Ed
Hunter, George E.
  See Ellis, Edward S(ylvester)
Hunter, Hilda 1921- 7
Hunter, Jana
  See Hunter, Jana Novotny
Hunter, Jana Novotny 190
Hunter, Jim 1939- 65
Hunter, Kristin
  See Lattany, Kristin (Elaine Eggleston)
  Hunter
Hunter, Leigh
  See Etchison, Birdie L(ee)
Hunter, Lieutenant Ned
  See Ellis, Edward S(ylvester)
Hunter, Mel 1927-2004 39
Hunter, Mollie 1922- 139
  Autobiography Feature 139
  Earlier sketches in SATA 54, 106
  See also CLR 25
  See also SAAS 7
  See McIlwraith, Maureen Mollie Hunter
Hunter, Ned
  See Ellis, Edward S(ylvester)
Hunter, Norman (George Lorimer)
  1899-1995 84
  Earlier sketch in SATA 26
Hunter, Ryan Ann
  See Greenwood, Pamela D.
  and Macalaster, Elizabeth G.
Hunter, Sara Hoagland 1954- 98
Hunter Blair, Pauline 3
  See Clarke, Pauline
Huntington, Amy 1956- 180
  Earlier sketch in SATA 138
Huntington, Geoffrey 145
Huntington, Harriet E(lizabeth) 1909- 1
Huntsberry, William E(mery) 1916- 5
Hurd, Clement (G.) 1908-1988 64
  Obituary 54
  Earlier sketch in SATA 2
  See also CLR 49
Hurd, Edith Thacher 1910-1997 64
  Obituary 95
  Earlier sketch in SATA 2
  See also CLR 49
  See also SAAS 13
Hurd, (John) Thacher 1949- 94
  Autobiography Feature 123
  Brief entry 45
  Earlier sketch in SATA 46
Hurley, Jo
  See Dower, Laura
Hurlimann, Bettina 39
  Obituary 34
  See Huerlimann, Bettina
Hurlimann, Ruth 32
  Brief entry 31
  See Huerlimann, Ruth
Hurmence, Belinda 1921- 77
  See also CLR 25
  See also SAAS 20
Hurst, Carol Otis 1933-2007 185
  Earlier sketch in SATA 130
Hurt-Newton, Tania 1968- 84
Hurwin, Davida Wills 1950- 180
Hurwitz, Johanna 1937- 175
  Earlier sketches in SATA 20, 71, 113
  See also SAAS 18
Hurwood, Bernhardt J. 1926-1987 12
  Obituary 50
Husain, Shahrukh 1950- 108
Huser, Glen 1943- 151
Hutchens, Paul 1902-1977 31

Hutchins, Carleen Maley 1911- 9
Hutchins, Hazel J. 1952- 175
  Brief entry 51
  Earlier sketch in SATA 81, 135
  See also SAAS 24
Hutchins, Pat 1942- 178
  Earlier sketches in SATA 15, 70, 111
  See also CLR 20
  See also SAAS 16
Hutchins, Ross Elliott 1906- 4
Hutchison, Linda 1942- 152
Huthmacher, J. Joseph 1929- 5
Hutto, Nelson (Allen) 1904-1985 20
Hutton, Kathryn 1915- 89
Hutton, Warwick 1939-1994 20
  Obituary 83
  See also SAAS 17
Huxley, Aldous (Leonard) 1894-1963 63
Huxley, Elspeth (Josceline Grant)
  1907-1997 62
  Obituary 95
Hyde, Catherine R.
  See Hyde, Catherine Ryan
Hyde, Catherine Ryan 1955- 141
Hyde, Dayton O(gden) 9
Hyde, Hawk
  See Hyde, Dayton O(gden)
Hyde, Margaret O. 1917- 139
  Earlier sketches in SATA 1, 42, 76
  See also CLR 23
  See also SAAS 8
Hyde, Margaret Oldroyd
  See Hyde, Margaret O.
Hyde, Shelley
  See Reed, Kit
Hyde, Wayne Frederick 1922- 7
Hylander, Clarence J(ohn) 1897-1964 7
Hyman, Robin P(hilip) 1931- 12
Hyman, Trina Schart 1939-2004 95
  Obituary 158
  Earlier sketches in SATA 7, 46
  See also CLR 50
Hymes, Lucia M(anley) 1907-1998 7
Hyndman, Jane Andrews Lee 1912-1978 46
  Obituary 23
  Earlier sketch in SATA 1
Hyndman, Robert Utley 1906-1973 18
Hynes, Pat 98

I

Iannone, Jeanne 7
  See Balzano, Jeanne (Koppel)
Ibatoulline, Bagram 1965(?)- 174
Ibbitson, John Perrie 1955- 102
Ibbotson, Eva 1925- 156
  Earlier sketches in SATA 13, 103
Ibbotson, M. C(hristine) 1930- 5
Icenoggle, Jodi 1967- 168
Icenoggle, Jodi O.
  See Icenoggle, Jodi
Ichikawa, Satomi 1949- 146
  Brief entry 36
  Earlier sketches in SATA 47, 78
  See also CLR 62
Ignoffo, Matthew 1945- 92
Igus, Toyomi 1953- 112
  Earlier sketch in SATA 76
Ihimaera, Witi (Tame) 1944- 148
Ikeda, Daisaku 1928- 77
Ilowite, Sheldon A. 1931- 27
Ilsey, Dent
  See Chapman, John Stanton Higham
Ilsley, Dent
  See Chapman, John Stanton Higham
Ilsley, Velma (Elizabeth) 1918- 12
Imai, Ayano 1980- 190
Imai, Miko 1963- 90
Imershein, Betsy 1953- 62

Immel, Mary Blair 1930- 28
Immell, Myra H. 1941- 92
Impey, Rose 1947- 152
  Earlier sketch in SATA 69
Ingelow, Jean 1820-1897 33
Ingermanson, Randall 1958- 134
Ingermanson, Randy
  See Ingermanson, Randall
Ingersoll, Norman 1928- 79
Ingham, Colonel Frederic
  See Hale, Edward Everett
Ingman, Bruce 1963- 182
  Earlier sketch in SATA 134
Ingman, Nicholas 1948- 52
Ingold, Jeanette 128
Ingpen, Robert 1936- 166
  Earlier sketch in SATA 109
Ingpen, Robert Roger
  See Ingpen, Robert
Ingraham, Erick 1950- 145
Ingraham, Leonard W(illiam) 1913-2003 4
Ingram, Scott 1948- 167
  Earlier sketch in SATA 92
Ingram, W. Scott
  See Ingram, Scott
Ingrams, Doreen 1906-1997 97
  Earlier sketch in SATA 20
Ingrid, Charles
  See Salsitz, Rhondi Vilott
Ingves, Gunilla (Anna Maria
  Folkesdotter) 1939- 101
Inkpen, Mick 1952- 154
  Earlier sketch in SATA 99
Innes, (Ralph) Hammond
  See Hammond Innes, Ralph
Innes, Ralph Hammond
  See Hammond Innes, Ralph
Innocenti, Roberto 1940- 159
  Earlier sketch in SATA 96
  See also CLR 126
Innocenti and Gallaz
  See Gallaz, Christophe
  and Innocenti, Roberto
Inyart, Gene 6
  See Namovicz, Gene Inyart
Ionesco, Eugene 1912-1994 7
  Obituary 79
Ipcar, Dahlov (Zorach) 1917- 147
  Autobiography Feature 147
  Earlier sketches in SATA 1, 49
  See also SAAS 8
Ireland, Karin 151
  Earlier sketch in SATA 101
Ironside, Jetske 1940- 60
Irvin, Fred 1914- 15
Irvine, Georgeanne 1955- 72
Irvine, Joan 1951- 80
Irving, Alexander
  See Hume, Ruth Fox
Irving, Robert
  See Adler, Irving
Irving, Washington 1783-1859
  See YABC 2
  See also CLR 97
Irwin, Ann(abelle Bowen) 1915-1998 89
  Brief entry 38
  Obituary 106
  Earlier sketch in SATA 44
  See also CLR 40
  See Irwin, Hadley
Irwin, Constance (H.) Frick 1913-1995 6
Irwin, Hadley
  See CLR 40
  See also SAAS 14
  See Hadley, Lee
  and Irwin, Ann(abelle Bowen)
Irwin, Keith Gordon 1885-1964 11
Isaac, Joanne 1934- 21
Isaacs, Anne 1949- 185
  Earlier sketch in SATA 90

Isaacs, Jacob
  See Kranzler, George G(ershon)
Isaacson, Philip M(arshal) 1924- 87
Isadora, Rachel 1953(?)- 165
  Brief entry 32
  Earlier sketches in SATA 54, 79, 121
  See also CLR 7
Isbell, Rebecca T(emple) 1942- 125
Isham, Charlotte H(ickock) 1912- 21
Ishida, Jui 176
Ish-Kishor, Judith 1892-1972 11
Ish-Kishor, Sulamith 1896-1977 17
Ishmael, Woodi 1914-1995 31
  Obituary 109
Isle, Sue 1963- 105
Israel, Elaine 1945- 12
Israel, Marion Louise 1882-1973
  Obituary 26
Iterson, S(iny) R(ose) Van
  See Van Iterson, S(iny) R(ose)
Ivanko, John D. 1966- 111
Ivanko, John Duane
  See Ivanko, John D.
Iversen, Jeremy 1980(?)- 174
Iversen, Jeremy Watt
  See Iversen, Jeremy
Iverson, Carol (L.) 1941- 145
Iverson, Diane 1950- 122
Iverson, Eric G.
  See Turtledove, Harry
Ivery, Martha M. 1948- 124
Ives, David 1951- 173
Ives, Morgan
  See Bradley, Marion Zimmer
Iwai, Melissa 183
Iwamatsu, Jun Atsushi 1908-1994 81
  Earlier sketch in SATA 14
  See Yashima, Taro
Iwasaki (Matsumoto), Chihiro 1918-1974
  See CLR 18

J

Jablonski, Carla 184
Jac, Lee
  See Morton, Lee Jack, Jr.
Jacka, Martin 1943- 72
Jackson, Alison 1953- 160
  Earlier sketches in SATA 73, 108
Jackson, Anne 1896(?)-1984
  Obituary 37
Jackson, C(aary) Paul 1902-1991 6
Jackson, Caary
  See Jackson, C(aary) Paul
Jackson, Charlotte E. (Cobden)
  1903(?)-1989
  Obituary 62
Jackson, Dave
  See Jackson, J. David
Jackson, Ellen B. 1943- 167
  Earlier sketches in SATA 75, 115
Jackson, Garnet Nelson 1944- 87
Jackson, Geoffrey (Holt Seymour)
  1915-1987
  Obituary 53
Jackson, Gina
  See Fluke, Joanne
Jackson, Guida M. 1930- 71
Jackson, J. David 1944- 91
Jackson, Jacqueline 1928- 65
Jackson, Jacqueline Dougan
  See Jackson, Jacqueline
Jackson, Jesse 1908-1983 29
  Obituary 48
  Earlier sketch in SATA 2
  See also CLR 28
Jackson, Marjorie 1928- 127
Jackson, Melanie 1956- 141
Jackson, Mike 1946- 91

Jackson, Neta J. 1944- 91
Jackson, O. B.
  See Jackson, C(aary) Paul
Jackson, Rob 1961- 176
Jackson, Robert B(lake) 1926- 8
Jackson, Robert Bradley
  See Jackson, Rob
Jackson, Sally
  See Kellogg, Jean (Defrees)
Jackson, Shirley 1919-1965 2
Jackson, Woody 1948- 92
Jacob, Helen Pierce 1927- 21
Jacobin
  See Bisson, Terry
Jacobs, Deborah Lynn 187
Jacobs, Flora Gill 1918-2006 5
  Obituary 178
Jacobs, Francine 1935- 150
  Brief entry 42
  Earlier sketch in SATA 43
Jacobs, Frank 1929- 30
Jacobs, Helen Hull 1908-1997 12
Jacobs, Joseph 1854-1916 25
Jacobs, Judy 1952- 69
Jacobs, Laurie A. 1956- 89
Jacobs, Leah
  See Gellis, Roberta
Jacobs, Leland Blair 1907-1992 20
  Obituary 71
Jacobs, Linda
  See Altman, Linda Jacobs
Jacobs, Lou(is), Jr. 1921- 2
Jacobs, Shannon K. 1947- 77
Jacobs, Susan 30
  See Quinn, Susan
Jacobs, William Jay 1933- 89
  Earlier sketch in SATA 28
Jacobsen, Laura 177
Jacobsen, Daniel 1923- 12
Jacobson, Jennifer
  See Jacobson, Jennifer Richard
Jacobson, Jennifer Richard 1958- 170
Jacobson, Morris K(arl) 1906- 21
Jacobson, Rick 170
Jacopetti, Alexandra 14
  See Hart, Alexandra
Jacques, Brian 1939- 176
  Earlier sketches in SATA 62, 95, 138
  See also CLR 21
Jacques, Robin 1920-1995 32
  Brief entry 30
  Obituary 86
  See also SAAS 5
Jaekel, Susan M. 1948- 89
Jaffe, Michele 179
Jaffe, Michele Sharon
  See Jaffe, Michele
Jaffee, Al(lan) 1921- 66
  Earlier sketch in SATA 37
Jagendorf, Moritz (Adolf) 1888-1981 2
  Obituary 24
Jahn, Michael
  See Jahn, (Joseph) Michael
Jahn, (Joseph) Michael 1943- 28
Jahn, Mike
  See Jahn, (Joseph) Michael
Jahn-Clough, Lisa 1967- 193
  Earlier sketches in SATA 88, 152
Jahsmann, Allan Hart 1916- 28
Jakes, John 1932- 62
Jakes, John William
  See Jakes, John
James, Andrew
  See Kirkup, James
James, Ann 1952- 168
  Earlier sketches in SATA 82, 117
James, Betsy 183
James, Brian 1976- 140
James, Bronte
  See Nash, Renea Denise

James, Captain Lew
  See Stratemeyer, Edward L.
James, Charlie 1961- 185
James, Curtis E. 182
James, Dynely
  See Mayne, William (James Carter)
James, Edwin
  See Gunn, James E.
James, Elizabeth 1942- 97
  Earlier sketches in SATA 39, 45, 52
James, Emily
  See Standiford, Natalie
James, Harry Clebourne 1896-1978 11
James, J. Alison 1962- 146
  Earlier sketch in SATA 83
James, Josephine
  See Sterne, Emma Gelders
James, Mary
  See Meaker, Marijane
James, Philip
  See del Rey, Lester
  and Moorcock, Michael
James, Robin 1953- 50
James, Robin Irene
  See James, Robin
James, Tegan
  See Odgers, Sally Farrell
James, T.F.
  See Fleming, Thomas
James, Will(iam Roderick) 1892-1942 19
Jameson, W. C. 1942- 93
Jamieson, Ian R.
  See Goulart, Ron(ald Joseph)
Jamiolkowski, Raymond M. 1953- 81
Jane, Mary Childs 1909- 6
Jane, Pamela 158
Janeczko, Paul B(ryan) 1945- 155
  Earlier sketches in SATA 53, 98
  See also CLR 47
  See also SAAS 18
Janes, Edward C. 1908- 25
Janes, J(oseph) Robert 1935- 148
  Brief entry 50
  Earlier sketch in SATA 101
Janeway, Elizabeth (Hall) 1913-2005 19
Janger, Kathleen N. 1940- 66
Janice
  See Brustlein, Janice Tworkov
Janisch, Heinz 1960- 181
Janosch
  See CLR 26
  See Eckert, Horst
Janover, Caroline (Davis) 1943- 141
  Earlier sketch in SATA 89
Jansen, Jared
  See Cebulash, Mel
Janson, Dora Jane (Heineberg) 1916- 31
Janson, H(orst) W(oldemar) 1913-1982 9
Jansson, Tove (Marika) 1914-2001 41
  Earlier sketch in SATA 3
  See also CLR 125
Janus, Grete
  See Hertz, Grete Janus
Jaques, Faith 1923-1997 97
  Earlier sketches in SATA 21, 69
Jaquith, Priscilla 1908- 51
Jaramillo, Mari-Luci 1928- 139
Jarman, Julia 1946- 133
Jarman, Rosemary Hawley 1935- 7
Jarrell, Mary Von Schrader 1914- 35
Jarrell, Randall 1914-1965 7
  See also CLR 111
Jarrett, Roxanne
  See Werner, Herma
Jarrow, Gail 1952- 185
  Earlier sketch in SATA 84
Jarvis, E.K.
  See Ellison, Harlan
  and Silverberg, Robert
Jarvis, Robin 1963- 181
Jaskol, Julie 1958- 127

Jasner, W. K.
  See Watson, Jane Werner
Jassem, Kate
  See Oppenheim, Joanne
Jauss, Anne Marie 1902(?)-1991 .... *10*
  Obituary *69*
Javernick, Ellen 1938- *89*
Jayne, Lieutenant R. H.
  See Ellis, Edward S(ylvester)
Jaynes, Clare
  See Mayer, Jane Rothschild
Jeake, Samuel, Jr.
  See Aiken, Conrad (Potter)
Jean-Bart, Leslie 1954- *121*
Jeapes, Ben 1965- *174*
Jefferds, Vincent H(arris) 1916- *59*
  Brief entry *49*
Jefferies, (John) Richard 1848-1887 .... *16*
Jeffers, Dawn *189*
Jeffers, Oliver 1977- *175*
Jeffers, Susan 1942- *137*
  Earlier sketches in SATA *17, 70, 129*
  See also CLR *30*
Jefferson, Sarah
  See Farjeon, (Eve) Annabel
Jeffries, Roderic 1926- *4*
Jeffries, Roderic Graeme
  See Jeffries, Roderic
Jenkin-Pearce, Susie 1943- *80*
Jenkins, A.M. *174*
Jenkins, Amanda McRaney
  See Jenkins, A.M.
Jenkins, Debra Reid
  See Reid Jenkins, Debra
Jenkins, Emily 1967- *174*
  Earlier sketch in SATA *144*
Jenkins, Jean *98*
Jenkins, Jerry B. 1949- *149*
Jenkins, Jerry Bruce
  See Jenkins, Jerry B.
Jenkins, Leonard *189*
Jenkins, Marie M(agdalen) 1909- *7*
Jenkins, Patrick 1955- *72*
Jenkins, Steve 1952- *188*
  Earlier sketch in SATA *154*
Jenkins, William A(twell) 1922-1998 .... *9*
Jenkyns, Chris 1924- *51*
Jennings, Coleman A(lonzo) 1933- *64*
Jennings, Dana Andrew 1957- *93*
Jennings, Elizabeth (Joan) 1926-2001 .... *66*
Jennings, Gary 1928-1999 .... *9*
  Obituary *117*
Jennings, Gary Gayne
  See Jennings, Gary
Jennings, Patrick 1962- *160*
  Earlier sketch in SATA *96*
Jennings, Paul 1943- *165*
  Earlier sketch in SATA *88*
  See also CLR *40*
Jennings, Richard W. 1945- *185*
  Earlier sketch in SATA *136*
Jennings, Robert
  See Hamilton, Charles (Harold St. John)
Jennings, S. M.
  See Meyer, Jerome Sydney
Jennings, Sharon 1954- *95*
Jennings, Sharon Elizabeth
  See Jennings, Sharon
Jennison, C. S.
  See Starbird, Kaye
Jennison, Keith Warren 1911-1995 .... *14*
Jensen, Kathryn 1949- *81*
Jensen, Kristine Mary 1961- *78*
Jensen, Niels 1927- *25*
Jensen, Vickie (Dee) 1946- *81*
Jensen, Virginia Allen 1927- *8*
Jenson-Elliott, Cynthia L(ouise) 1962- *143*
Jeram, Anita 1965- *154*
  Earlier sketches in SATA *71, 102*
Jerman, Jerry 1949- *89*
Jernigan, E. Wesley 1940- *85*

Jernigan, Gisela (Evelyn) 1948- *85*
Jeschke, Susan 1942- *42*
  Brief entry *27*
Jessel, Camilla (Ruth) 1937- *143*
  Earlier sketch in SATA *29*
Jessell, Tim *177*
Jessey, Cornelia
  See Sussman, Cornelia Silver
Jewel
  See Kilcher, Jewel
Jewell, Nancy 1940- *109*
  Brief entry *41*
Jewett, Eleanore Myers 1890-1967 .... *5*
Jewett, (Theodora) Sarah Orne 1849-1909 ... *15*
Jezard, Alison 1919- *57*
  Brief entry *34*
Jiang, Cheng An 1943- *109*
Jiang, Ji-li 1954- *101*
Jiang, Zheng An
  See Jiang, Cheng An
Jiler, John 1946- *42*
  Brief entry *35*
Jimenez, Francisco 1943- *108*
Jinks, Catherine 1963- *155*
  Earlier sketch in SATA *94*
Jobb, Jamie 1945- *29*
Jobling, Curtis *131*
Jocelyn, Ann Henning 1948- *92*
Jocelyn, Marthe 1956- *163*
  Earlier sketch in SATA *118*
Joerns, Consuelo *44*
  Brief entry *33*
Joey D
  See Macaulay, Teresa (E.)
Johansen, Krista V.
  See Johansen, K.V.
Johansen, K.V 1968- *186*
Johansen, K.V. 1968- *186*
  Earlier sketch in SATA *129*
Johansson, Philip *163*
John, Joyce *59*
Johns, Avery
  See Cousins, Margaret
Johns, Elizabeth 1943- *88*
Johns, Janetta
  See Quin-Harkin, Janet
Johns, Linda 1945- *173*
Johns, W(illiam) E(arle) 1893-1968 .... *55*
Johns, Captain W. E.
  See Johns, W(illiam) E(arle)
Johnson, A.
  See Johnson, Annabell (Jones)
Johnson, A. E.
  See Johnson, Annabell (Jones)
  and Johnson, Edgar (Raymond)
Johnson, Angela 1961- *188*
  Earlier sketches in SATA *69, 102, 150*
  See also CLR *33*
Johnson, Annabel
  See Johnson, Annabell (Jones)
Johnson, Annabell (Jones) 1921- *72*
  Earlier sketch in SATA *2*
  See Johnson, Annabel
Johnson, Art 1946- *123*
Johnson, Benjamin F., of Boone
  See Riley, James Whitcomb
Johnson, Bettye 1858-1919
  See Rogers, Bettye
Johnson, Caryn
  See Goldberg, Whoopi
Johnson, Caryn E.
  See Goldberg, Whoopi
Johnson, Caryn Elaine
  See Goldberg, Whoopi
Johnson, Charles R. 1925- *11*
Johnson, Charlotte Buel *46*
  See von Wodtke, Charlotte Buel Johnson
Johnson, Chuck
  See Johnson, Charles R.

Johnson, Crockett
  See CLR *98*
  See Leisk, David (Johnson)
Johnson, D(ana) William 1945- *23*
Johnson, Daniel Shahid 1954- *73*
Johnson, David
  See Johnson, David A.
Johnson, David A. 1951- *191*
Johnson, D.B. 1944- *183*
  Earlier sketch in SATA *146*
Johnson, Dinah *130*
  See Johnson, Dianne
Johnson, Dolores 1949- *69*
Johnson, Donald B.
  See Johnson, D.B.
Johnson, Dorothy M(arie) 1905-1984 .... *6*
  Obituary *40*
Johnson, E(ugene) Harper *44*
Johnson, Edgar (Raymond) 1912-1990 .... *72*
  Earlier sketch in SATA *2*
Johnson, Eleanor Murdock 1892-1987
  Obituary *54*
Johnson, Elizabeth 1911-1984 .... *7*
  Obituary *39*
Johnson, Eric W(arner) 1918-1994 ....
  Obituary *82*
  Earlier sketch in SATA *8*
Johnson, Evelyne 1922- *20*
Johnson, Fred 19(?)-1982 .... *63*
Johnson, Gaylord 1884-1972 .... *7*
Johnson, Gerald White 1890-1980 .... *19*
  Obituary *28*
Johnson, Harper
  See Johnson, E(ugene) Harper
Johnson, Harriett 1908-1987
  Obituary *53*
Johnson, James Ralph 1922- *1*
Johnson, James Weldon 1871-1938 .... *31*
  See also CLR *32*
Johnson, Jane 1951- *48*
Johnson, Joan J. 1942- *59*
Johnson, John E(mil) 1929- *34*
Johnson, Johnny 1901-1995
  See Johnson, (Walter) Ryerson
Johnson, Kathleen Jeffrie 1950- *186*
Johnson, La Verne B(ravo) 1925- *13*
Johnson, Layne *187*
Johnson, Lee Kaiser 1962- *78*
Johnson, Lissa H(alls) 1955- *65*
Johnson, Lois Smith 1894-1993 .... *6*
Johnson, Lois Walfrid 1936- *130*
  Earlier sketches in SATA *22, 91*
Johnson, Margaret S(weet) 1893-1964 .... *35*
Johnson, Marguerite Annie
  See Angelou, Maya
Johnson, Mary Frances K. 1929(?)-1979
  Obituary *27*
Johnson, Maud Battle 1918(?)-1985
  Obituary *46*
Johnson, Meredith Merrell 1952- *104*
Johnson, Milton 1932- *31*
Johnson, Neil 1954- *135*
  Earlier sketch in SATA *73*
Johnson, Pamela 1949- *71*
Johnson, Patricia Polin 1956- *84*
Johnson, Paul Brett 1947- *132*
  Earlier sketch in SATA *83*
Johnson, Rebecca L. 1956- *147*
  Earlier sketch in SATA *67*
Johnson, Rick L. 1954- *79*
Johnson, (Walter) Ryerson 1901-1995 .... *10*
  Obituary *106*
  See Halliday, Brett
Johnson, Scott 1952- *119*
  Earlier sketch in SATA *76*
Johnson, Sherrie 1948- *87*
Johnson, Shirley K(ing) 1927- *10*
Johnson, Siddie Joe 1905-1977
  Obituary *20*
Johnson, Spencer 1938- *145*
  Brief entry *38*

Johnson, Stacie
See Myers, Walter Dean
Johnson, Stephen T. 1964- 189
Earlier sketches in SATA *84, 141*
Johnson, Steve 1960- 177
Johnson, Sue Kaiser 1963- 78
Johnson, Sylvia A. 166
Brief entry 52
Earlier sketch in SATA *104*
Johnson, William R. 38
Johnson, William Weber 1909-1992 7
Johnston, Agnes Christine
See Dazey, Agnes J(ohnston)
Johnston, Annie Fellows 1863-1931 37
Johnston, Dorothy Grunbock 1915-1979 54
Johnston, Ginny 1946- 60
Johnston, H(ugh) A(nthony) S(tephen)
1913-1967 14
Johnston, Janet 1944- 71
Johnston, Jeffry W. 188
Johnston, Johanna 1914(?)-1982 12
Obituary 33
Johnston, Julie 1941- 110
Autobiography Feature 128
Earlier sketch in SATA *78*
See also CLR *41*
See also SAAS *24*
Johnston, Lynn 1947- 118
Johnston, Lynn Beverley
See Johnston, Lynn
Johnston, Norma 29
See St. John, Nicole
Johnston, Portia
See Takakjian, Portia
Johnston, Susan Taylor 1942- 128
Earlier sketch in SATA *83*
See Johnston, Tony
Johnston, Tim(othy Patrick) 1962- 146
Johnston, Tony 180
Earlier sketch in SATA *8*
See Johnston, Susan Taylor
Joinson, Carla 160
Jolin, Paula 186
Jonas, Ann 1932- 135
Brief entry 42
Earlier sketch in SATA *50*
See also CLR *74*
Jonell, Lynne 109
Jones, Adrienne 1915-2000 82
Earlier sketch in SATA *7*
See also SAAS *10*
Jones, Annabel
See Lewis, Mary (Christianna)
Jones, Betty Millsaps 1940- 54
Jones, Carol 1942- 153
Earlier sketch in SATA *79*
Jones, Carrie 1971- 191
Jones, Charles M(artin) 1912-2002 53
Obituary 133
See Jones, Chuck
Jones, Charlotte Foltz 1945- 122
Earlier sketch in SATA *77*
Jones, Chuck
See Jones, Charles M(artin)
Jones, Constance 112
Jones, Constance A.
See Jones, Constance
Jones, Diana Wynne 1934- 160
Earlier sketches in SATA *9, 70, 108*
See also CLR *120*
See also SAAS *7*
Jones, Douglas C(lyde) 1924-1998 52
Jones, Elizabeth McDavid 155
Jones, Elizabeth Orton 1910-2005 18
Obituary 164
Jones, Evan 1915-1996 3
Jones, Geraldine
See McCaughrean, Geraldine
Jones, Gillingham
See Hamilton, Charles (Harold St. John)
Jones, Gwyneth A(nn) 1952- 159

Jones, Harold 1904-1992 14
Obituary 72
Jones, Helen Hinckley 1903-1991 26
Jones, Helen L(ouise) 1903-1973
Obituary 22
Jones, Hettie 1934- 42
Brief entry 27
Jones, Hortense P. 1918- 9
Jones, J. Sydney 1948- 101
Jones, Jasmine
See Papademetriou, Lisa
Jones, Jennifer (Berry) 1947- 90
Jones, Jessie Mae Orton 1887(?)-1983
Obituary 37
Jones, John R(obert) 1926- 76
Jones, Jon Sydney
See Jones, J. Sydney
Jones, Kimberly K. 1957- 187
Jones, Marcia Thornton 1958- 115
Earlier sketch in SATA *73*
Jones, Martha T(annery) 1931- 130
Jones, Mary Alice 1898(?)-1980 6
Jones, McClure 34
Jones, Noah Z. 182
Jones, Patrick 1961- 136
Jones, Penelope 1938- 31
Jones, Rebecca C(astaldi) 1947- 99
Earlier sketch in SATA *33*
Jones, Robin D(orothy) 1959- 80
Jones, Sanford W.
See Thorn, John
Jones, Sylvie 185
Jones, Sylvie Michelle
See Jones, Sylvie
Jones, Terence Graham Parry 1942- 127
See Jones, Terry
and Monty Python
Jones, Terry 67
Brief entry 51
See Jones, Terence Graham Parry
Jones, Tim Wynne
See Wynne-Jones, Tim
Jones, Traci L. 186
Jones, V(ictoria) M(ary) 1958- 147
Jones, Veda Boyd 1948- 119
Jones, Volcano
See Mitchell, Adrian
Jones, Weyman (B.) 1928- 4
See also SAAS *11*
Jones, William Glynne
See Glynne-Jones, William
Jonk, Clarence 1906-1987 10
Jonsberg, Barry 1951- 168
Joos, Francoise 1956- 78
Joos, Frederic 1953- 78
Joosse, Barbara M. 1949- 164
Earlier sketches in SATA *52, 96*
Joosse, Barbara Monnot
See Joosse, Barbara M.
Jordan, Alexis Hill
See Glick, Ruth (Burtnick)
and Titchener, Louise
Jordan, Anne Devereaux 1943- 80
Jordan, Chris
See Philbrick, Rodman
Jordan, Deloris 191
Jordan, Don
See Howard, Vernon (Linwood)
Jordan, Hope Dahle 1905-1995 15
Jordan, Jael (Michal) 1949- 30
Jordan, June 1936-2002 136
Earlier sketch in SATA *4*
See also CLR *10*
Jordan, June Meyer
See Jordan, June
Jordan, Lee
See Scholefield, Alan
Jordan, Martin George 1944- 84
Jordan, Robert 1948-2007 95
See Rigney, James Oliver, Jr.

Jordan, Robert K.
See Jordan, Robert
Jordan, Rosa 1939- 191
Jordan, Roslyn M. 189
Jordan, Sherryl 1949- 122
Earlier sketch in SATA *71*
See also SAAS *23*
Jordan, Shirley 1930- 154
Jordan, Tanis 1946- 84
Jorgensen, Mary Venn -1995 36
Jorgensen, Norman 1954- 157
Jorgenson, Ivar
See Silverberg, Robert
Jorisch, Stephane 178
Joseph, Anne
See Coates, Anna
Joseph, James (Herz) 1924- 53
Joseph, Joan 1939- 34
Joseph, Joseph M(aron) 1903-1979 22
Joseph, Patrick
See O'Malley, Kevin
Josephs, Rebecca
See Talbot, Toby
Josh
See Clemens, Samuel Langhorne
Joshua, Peter
See Stone, Peter
Joslin, Mary 1953- 176
Joslin, Sesyle 2
See Hine, Sesyle Joslin
Joyce, Bill
See Joyce, William
Joyce, J(ames) Avery 1902-1987 11
Obituary 50
Joyce, Peter 1937- 127
Joyce, William 1957- 118
Brief entry 46
Earlier sketch in SATA *72*
See also CLR *26*
Joyner, Jerry 1938- 34
Juan, Ana 1961- 179
Jubert, Herve 185
Juby, Susan 1969- 156
Jucker, Sita 1921- 5
Judah, Aaron 1923- 118
Judd, Cyril
See Kornbluth, C(yril) M.
and Merril, Judith
and Pohl, Frederik
Judd, Denis (O'Nan) 1938- 33
Judd, Frances K. 1
See Benson, Mildred (Augustine Wirt)
Jude, Conny 81
Judge, Lita 192
Judson, Clara Ingram 1879-1960 38
Brief entry 27
Judy, Stephen
See Tchudi, Stephen N.
Judy, Stephen N.
See Tchudi, Stephen N.
Juhasz, Victor 1954- 177
Jukes, Mavis 1947- 111
Brief entry 43
Earlier sketch in SATA *72*
See also SAAS *12*
Jules, Jacqueline 1956- 183
Earlier sketch in SATA *148*
Julian, Jane
See Wiseman, David
Jumpp, Hugo
See MacPeek, Walter G.
Jungman, Ann 165
Jupo, Frank J. 1904-1981 7
Jurmain, Suzanne 1945- 169
Earlier sketch in SATA *72*
Jurmain, Suzanne Tripp
See Jurmain, Suzanne
Juster, Norton 1929- 132
Earlier sketch in SATA *3*
See also CLR *112*

Justus, May 1898-1989 .... *1*
  Obituary *106*
Juvenilia
  See Taylor, Ann

K

Kaaberbol, Lene
  See Kaaberbol, Lene
Kaaberbol, Lene 1960- *159*
Kabdebo, Tamas
  See Kabdebo, Thomas
Kabdebo, Thomas 1934- *10*
Kabibble, Osh
  See Jobb, Jamie
Kacer, Kathy 1954- *184*
  Earlier sketch in SATA *142*
Kaczman, James *156*
Kadair, Deborah Ousley *184*
Kadesch, Robert R(udstone) 1922- *31*
Kadohata, Cynthia 1956(?)- *180*
  Earlier sketch in SATA *155*
  See also CLR *121*
Kaempfert, Wade
  See del Rey, Lester
Kaestner, Erich 1899-1974 .... *14*
  See also CLR *4*
  See Kastner, Erich
Kahl, Jonathan (D.) 1959- *77*
Kahl, M(arvin) P(hilip) 1934- *37*
Kahl, Virginia (Caroline) 1919-2004 .... *48*
  Brief entry *38*
  Obituary *158*
Kahn, Joan 1914-1994 .... *48*
  Obituary *82*
Kahn, Katherine Janus 1942- *167*
  Earlier sketch in SATA *90*
Kahn, Peggy
  See Katz, Bobbi
Kahn, Roger 1927- *37*
Kahukiwa, Robyn 1940- *134*
Kains, Josephine
  See Goulart, Ron(ald Joseph)
Kaizuki, Kiyonori 1950- *72*
Kakimoto, Kozo 1915- *11*
Kalashnikoff, Nicholas 1888-1961 .... *16*
Kalb, Jonah 1926- *23*
Kalbacken, Joan 1925- *96*
Kalechofsky, Roberta 1931- *92*
Kaler, James Otis 1848-1912 .... *15*
Kalish, Claire M. 1947- *92*
Kallen, Stuart A(rnold) 1955- *126*
  Earlier sketch in SATA *86*
Kallevig, Christine Petrell 1955- *164*
Kalman, Bobbie 1947- *63*
Kalman, Maira 1949- *137*
  Earlier sketch in SATA *96*
  See also CLR *32*
Kalnay, Francis 1899-1992 .... *7*
Kaloustian, Rosanne 1955- *93*
Kalow, Gisela 1946- *32*
Kalstein, Dave *175*
Kamen, Gloria 1923- *98*
  Earlier sketch in SATA *9*
Kamerman, Sylvia E.
  See Burack, Sylvia K.
Kamm, Josephine (Hart) 1905-1989 .... *24*
Kammerman, Sylvia K.
  See Burack, Sylvia K.
Kandel, Michael 1941- *93*
Kandell, Alice S. 1938- *35*
Kane, Bob 1916-1998 .... *120*
Kane, Henry Bugbee 1902-1971 .... *14*
Kane, L. A.
  See Mannetti, Lisa
Kane, Robert W. 1910- *18*
Kane, Wilson
  See Bloch, Robert (Albert)
Kanefield, Teri 1960- *135*

Kaner, Etta 1947- *126*
Kanetzke, Howard W(illiam) 1932- *38*
Kann, Elizabeth *180*
Kann, Victoria *180*
Kanoza, Muriel Canfield
  See Canfield, Muriel
Kantner, Seth 1965- *179*
Kanzawa, Toshiko
  See Furukawa, Toshi
Kanzler, John 1963- *188*
Kaplan, Andrew 1960- *78*
Kaplan, Anne Bernays
  See Bernays, Anne
Kaplan, Bess 1927- *22*
Kaplan, Boche 1926- *24*
Kaplan, Elizabeth 1956- *83*
Kaplan, Elizabeth A.
  See Kaplan, Elizabeth
Kaplan, Irma 1900- *10*
Kaplan, Jean Caryl Korn 1926- *10*
Kaplow, Robert 1954- *70*
Karageorge, Michael
  See Anderson, Poul
Karas, G. Brian 1957- *178*
Karas, George Brian
  See Karas, G. Brian
Karasz, Ilonka 1896-1981
  Obituary *29*
Karen, Ruth 1922-1987 .... *9*
  Obituary *54*
Kark, Nina Mary
  See Bawden, Nina
Karl, Herb 1938- *73*
Karl, Jean E(dna) 1927-2000 .... *122*
  Earlier sketch in SATA *34*
  See also SAAS *10*
Karlin, Bernie 1927- *68*
Karlin, Eugene 1918- *10*
Karlin, Nurit *103*
  Earlier sketch in SATA *63*
Karnes, Frances A. 1937- *110*
Karp, Naomi J. 1926- *16*
Karpinski, J. Rick
  See Karpinski, John Eric
Karpinski, John Eric 1952- *81*
Karpinski, Rick
  See Karpinski, John Eric
Karr, Kathleen 1946- *127*
  Earlier sketch in SATA *82*
Karr, Phyllis Ann 1944- *119*
Karwoski, Gail 1949- *127*
Karwoski, Gail Langer
  See Karwoski, Gail
Kashiwagi, Isami 1925- *10*
Kaslik, Ibi *185*
  See Kaslik, Ibolya Emma
Kassem, Lou 1931- *62*
  Brief entry *51*
Kastel, Warren
  See Silverberg, Robert
Kastner, Erich
  See Kaestner, Erich
Kastner, Jill (Marie) 1964- *117*
  Earlier sketch in SATA *70*
Kasuya, Masahiro 1937- *51*
Kasza, Keiko 1951- *191*
  Earlier sketch in SATA *124*
Kataphusin
  See Ruskin, John
Katchen, Carole 1944- *9*
Kathryn
  See Searle, Kathryn Adrienne
Katona, Robert 1949- *21*
Katsarakis, Joan Harries
  See Harries, Joan
Katz, Alan *185*
Katz, Avner 1939- *103*
Katz, Bobbi 1933- *179*
  Earlier sketch in SATA *12*
Katz, Fred(eric Phillip) 1938- *6*
Katz, Jane B(resler) 1934- *33*

Katz, Karen 1947- *158*
Katz, Marjorie P.
  See Weiser, Marjorie P(hillis) K(atz)
Katz, Susan 1945- *156*
Katz, Welwyn Wilton 1948- *96*
  Autobiography Feature *118*
  Earlier sketch in SATA *62*
  See also CLR *45*
Katz, William 1940- *98*
Katz, William Loren 1927- *13*
Kaufman, Bel *57*
Kaufman, Jeff 1955- *84*
Kaufman, Joe 1911-2001 .... *33*
Kaufman, Joseph
  See Kaufman, Joe
Kaufman, Mervyn D. 1932- *4*
Kaufmann, Angelika 1935- *15*
Kaufmann, John 1931- *18*
Kaula, Edna Mason 1906-1987 .... *13*
Kaur Khalsa, Dayal
  See Khalsa, Dayal Kaur
Kavaler, Lucy 1930- *23*
Kavanagh, Jack 1920- *85*
Kavanagh, P(atrick) J(oseph
  Gregory) 1931- *122*
Kavanaugh, Ian
  See Webb, Jean Francis (III)
Kay, Alan N. 1965- *144*
Kay, Elizabeth 1949- *165*
Kay, Guy Gavriel 1954- *167*
  Earlier sketch in SATA *121*
Kay, Helen
  See Goldfrank, Helen Colodny
Kay, Jackie 1961- *165*
  Earlier sketch in SATA *97*
Kay, Jacqueline Margaret
  See Kay, Jackie
Kay, Mara *13*
Kay, Verla 1946- *120*
Kaye, Danny 1913-1987
  Obituary *50*
Kaye, Geraldine (Hughesdon) 1925- *85*
  Earlier sketch in SATA *10*
Kaye, Judy
  See Baer, Judy
Kaye, Marilyn 1949- *110*
  Earlier sketch in SATA *56*
Kaye, Mary Margaret
  See Kaye, M.M.
Kaye, M.M. 1908-2004 .... *62*
  Obituary *152*
Kaye, Mollie
  See Kaye, M.M.
Kaye, Peggy 1948- *143*
Keach, James P. 1950- *125*
Keams, Geri 1951- *117*
Keane, Bil 1922- *4*
Keaney, Brian 1954- *188*
  Earlier sketch in SATA *106*
Kearney, Meg 1964- *178*
Kearny, Jillian
  See Goulart, Ron(ald Joseph)
Keating, Bern
  See Keating, Leo Bernard
Keating, Frank 1944- *143*
Keating, Lawrence A. 1903-1966 .... *23*
Keating, Leo Bernard 1915- *10*
Keats, Emma 1899(?)-1979(?) *68*
Keats, Ezra Jack 1916-1983 .... *57*
  Obituary *34*
  Earlier sketch in SATA *14*
  See also CLR *35*
Keefer, Catherine
  See Ogan, George F.
  and Ogan, Margaret E. (Nettles)
Keefer, Janice Kulyk *132*
  See Kulyk Keefer, Janice
Keegan, Marcia 1943- *104*
  Earlier sketch in SATA *9*
Keehn, Sally M. 1947- *165*
  Earlier sketch in SATA *87*

Keel, Frank
  See Keeler, Ronald F(ranklin)
Keeler, Patricia 183
Keeler, Patricia A.
  See Keeler, Patricia
Keeler, Ronald F(ranklin) 1913-1983 47
Keely, Jack 1951- 119
Keen, Martin L. 1913-1992 4
Keenan, Sheila 1953- 95
Keene, Ann T(odd) 1940- 86
Keene, Carolyn 100
  Earlier sketch in SATA 65
  See also CLR 118
  See Benson, Mildred (Augustine Wirt)
  and Goulart, Ron(ald Joseph)
  and Lerangis, Peter
  and McFarlane, Leslie (Charles)
  and Stanley, George Edward
  and Stratemeyer, Edward L.
Keens-Douglas, Richardo 1953- 154
  Earlier sketch in SATA 95
Keep, Linda Lowery
  See Lowery, Linda
Keep, Richard 1949- 170
Keep, Richard Cleminson
  See Keep, Richard
Keeping, Charles (William James)
  1924-1988 69
  Obituary 56
  Earlier sketch in SATA 9
  See also CLR 34
Keeshan, Robert J. 1927-2004 32
  Obituary 151
Kehlenbeck, Angela 1959- 186
Kehret, Peg 1936- 149
  Autobiography Feature 149
  Earlier sketches in SATA 73, 108
Keillor, Garrison 1942- 58
Keillor, Gary Edward
  See Keillor, Garrison
Keir, Christine
  See Pullein-Thompson, Christine
Keister, Douglas 1948- 88
Keith, Doug 1952- 81
Keith, Eros 1942- 52
Keith, Hal 1934- 36
Keith, Harold (Verne) 1903-1998 74
  Earlier sketch in SATA 2
Keith, Robert
  See Applebaum, Stan
Keleinikov, Andrei 1924- 65
Kelemen, Julie 1959- 78
Kelen, Emery 1896-1978 13
  Obituary 26
Kelleam, Joseph E(veridge) 1913-1975 31
Kelleher, Anne 1959- 97
Kelleher, Annette 1950- 122
Kelleher, Daria Valerian 1955- 79
Kelleher, Victor (Michael Kitchener)
  1939- 129
  Brief entry 52
  Earlier sketch in SATA 75
  See also CLR 36
Keller, Beverly L(ou) 91
  Earlier sketch in SATA 13
Keller, Charles 1942- 82
  Earlier sketch in SATA 8
Keller, Debra 1958- 94
Keller, Dick 1923- 36
Keller, Emily 96
Keller, Gail Faithfull
  See Faithfull, Gail
Keller, Holly 1942- 157
  Brief entry 42
  Earlier sketches in SATA 76, 108
  See also CLR 45
Keller, Irene (Barron) 1927-2002 36
  Obituary 139
Kelley, Ellen A. 185
Kelley, Ellen Chavez
  See Kelley, Ellen A.

Kelley, Gary 1945- 183
Kelley, Leo P(atrick) 1928- 32
  Brief entry 31
Kelley, Patrick (G.) 1963- 129
Kelley, Patte 1947- 93
Kelley, True 1946- 179
Kelley, True (Adelaide) 1946- 130
  Brief entry 39
  Earlier sketches in SATA 41, 92
Kelley, True Adelaide
  See Kelley, True
Kellin, Sally Moffet 1932- 9
Kelling, Furn L. 1914-2000 37
Kellogg, Gene
  See Kellogg, Jean (Defrees)
Kellogg, Jean (Defrees) 1916-1978 10
Kellogg, Steven 1941- 177
  Earlier sketches in SATA 8, 57, 130
  See also CLR 6
Kellogg, Steven Castle
  See Kellogg, Steven
Kellow, Kathleen
  See Hibbert, Eleanor Alice Burford
Kelly, C. M. O.
  See Gibbs, (Cecilia) May
Kelly, Clint 1950- 140
Kelly, Eric P(hilbrook) 1884-1960
  See YABC 1
Kelly, Fiona
  See Coleman, Michael (Lee)
  and Hendry, Frances Mary
  and Oldfield, Jenny
  and Welford, Sue
Kelly, Irene 1957- 147
Kelly, Jeff
  See Kelly, Jeffrey
Kelly, Jeffrey 1946- 65
Kelly, Joanne (W.) 1934- 87
Kelly, Kate 1958- 91
Kelly, Kathleen M. 1964- 71
Kelly, Katy 1955- 169
Kelly, Lauren
  See Oates, Joyce Carol
Kelly, Laurene 1954- 123
Kelly, Martha Rose 1914-1983 37
Kelly, Marty
  See Kelly, Martha Rose
Kelly, Mij 166
Kelly, Ralph
  See Geis, Darlene Stern
Kelly, Regina Z(immerman) 1898-1986 5
Kelly, Rosalie (Ruth) 43
Kelly, Tom 1961- 191
Kelly, Walt(er Crawford) 1913-1973 18
Kelsey, Alice Geer 1896-1982 1
Kelsey, Elin 159
Kemnitz, Thomas Milton, Jr. 1984- 152
Kemnitz, Tom, Jr.
  See Kemnitz, Thomas Milton, Jr.
Kemp, Gene 1926- 75
  Earlier sketch in SATA 25
  See also CLR 29
Kempner, Mary Jean 1913-1969 10
Kempter, Christa 1945- 187
Kempton, Jean Welch 1914- 10
Kenah, Katharine 1949- 182
Kenda, Margaret 1942- 71
Kendall, Carol (Seeger) 1917- 74
  Earlier sketch in SATA 11
  See also SAAS 7
Kendall, Katherine
  See Applegate, Katherine (Alice)
Kendall, Lace
  See Stoutenburg, Adrien (Pearl)
Kendall, Martha E. 87
Kendall, Russ 1957- 83
Kenealy, James P. 1927- 52
  Brief entry 29
Kenealy, Jim
  See Kenealy, James P.

Kennaway, Adrienne 1945- 171
  Earlier sketch in SATA 60
Kennedy, Brendan 1970- 57
Kennedy, Dana Forrest 1917- 74
Kennedy, Dorothy M(intzlaff) 1931- 53
Kennedy, Doug 1963- 189
  Earlier sketch in SATA 122
Kennedy, Frances 1937- 192
Kennedy, John Fitzgerald 1917-1963 11
Kennedy, Joseph Charles 1929- 130
  Autobiography Feature 130
  Earlier sketches in SATA 14, 86
  See Kennedy, X. J.
Kennedy, Kim 189
Kennedy, Pamela (J.) 1946- 87
Kennedy, Paul E(dward) 1929- 113
  Earlier sketch in SATA 33
Kennedy, Richard (Pitt) 1910-1989
  Obituary 60
Kennedy, (Jerome) Richard 1932- 22
Kennedy, Robert 1938- 63
Kennedy, T.A. 1953- 42
  Brief entry 35
Kennedy, Teresa
  See Kennedy, T.A.
Kennedy, Teresa A.
  See Kennedy, T.A.
Kennedy, William 1928- 57
Kennedy, William Joseph
  See Kennedy, William
Kennedy, X. J.
  See CLR 27
  See also SAAS 22
  See Kennedy, Joseph Charles
Kennell, Ruth Epperson 1893-1977 6
  Obituary 25
Kennemore, Tim 1957- 133
Kennen, Ally 190
Kennett, David 1959- 121
Kenny, Ellsworth Newcomb 1909-1971
  Obituary 26
Kenny, Herbert Andrew 1912-2002 13
Kenny, Jude
  See Daly, Jude
Kenny, Kathryn
  See Bowden, Joan Chase
  and Krull, Kathleen
  and Sanderlin, Owenita (Harrah)
  and Stack, Nicolete Meredith
Kenny, Kevin
  See Krull, Kathleen
Kensinger, George
  See Fichter, George S.
Kensington, Kathryn Wesley
  See Rusch, Kristine Kathryn
Kent, Alexander
  See Reeman, Douglas Edward
Kent, David
  See Lambert, David (Compton)
Kent, Deborah Ann 1948- 155
  Brief entry 41
  Earlier sketches in SATA 47, 104
Kent, Jack
  See Kent, John Wellington
Kent, John Wellington 1920-1985 24
  Obituary 45
Kent, Lisa 1942- 90
Kent, Mallory
  See Lowndes, Robert A(ugustine) W(ard)
Kent, Margaret 1894- 2
Kent, Rockwell 1882-1971 6
Kent, Rose 188
Kent, Sherman 1903-1986 20
  Obituary 47
Kenward, Jean 1920- 42
Kenworthy, Leonard S. 1912-1991 6
Kenyon, Karen (Smith) 1938- 145
Kenyon, Kate
  See Adorjan, Carol (Madden)
  and Ransom, Candice F.
Kenyon, Ley 1913-1990 6

Keown, Elizabeth 78
Kepes, Juliet A(ppleby) 1919-1999 13
Kerby, Mona 1951- 75
Kerigan, Florence 1896-1984 12
Kerley, Barbara 1960- 191
  Earlier sketch in SATA 138
Kerman, Gertrude
  See Furman, Gertrude Lerner Kerman
Kerns, Thelma 1929- 116
Kerr, Anne Louise
  See Mackey, Weezie Kerr
Kerr, Bob 1951- 120
Kerr, Jessica 1901-1991 13
Kerr, (Anne-)Judith 1923-1970 24
Kerr, M. E.
  See Meaker, Marijane
Kerr, P.B.
  See Kerr, Philip
Kerr, Philip 1956- 168
Kerr, Phyllis Forbes 1942- 72
Kerr, Tom 1950- 77
Kerrin, Jessica Scott 174
Kerry, Frances
  See Kerigan, Florence
Kerry, Lois
  See Duncan, Lois
Kershen, (L.) Michael 1982- 82
Kerven, Rosalind 1954- 83
Ker Wilson, Barbara 1929- 121
  Earlier sketches in SATA 20, 70
  See also SAAS 18
Keselman, Gabriela 1953- 128
Kesey, Ken 1935-2001 66
  Obituary 131
Kesey, Ken Elton
  See Kesey, Ken
Kesler, Jay 1935- 65
Kessel, Joyce Karen 1937- 41
Kessler, Cristina 190
Kessler, Ethel 1922- 44
  Brief entry 37
Kessler, Leonard P. 1921- 14
Kest, Kristin 1967- 168
  Earlier sketch in SATA 118
Kesteven, G. R.
  See Crosher, G. R.
Ketcham, Hank
  See Ketcham, Henry King
Ketcham, Henry King 1920-2001 28
  Brief entry 27
  Obituary 128
Ketcham, Sallie 1963- 124
Ketchum, Liza 1946- 132
  See Murrow, Liza Ketchum
Ketner, Mary Grace 1946- 75
Kettelkamp, Larry (Dale) 1933- 2
  See also SAAS 3
Ketteman, Helen 1945- 167
  Earlier sketches in SATA 73, 115
Kettle, Peter
  See Glover, Denis (James Matthews)
Kevles, Bettyann Holtzmann 1938- 23
Key, Alexander (Hill) 1904-1979 8
  Obituary 23
Key, Samuel M.
  See de Lint, Charles
Key, Watt 1970- 189
Keyes, Daniel 1927- 37
Keyes, Fenton 1915-1999 34
Keyes, Greg 1963- 116
Keyes, J. Gregory
  See Keyes, Greg
Keyser, Marcia 1933- 42
Keyser, Sarah
  See McGuire, Leslie (Sarah)
Khalsa, Dayal Kaur 1943-1989 62
  See also CLR 30
  See Kaur Khalsa, Dayal
Khan, Rukhsana 1962- 165
  Earlier sketch in SATA 118

Khanshendel, Chiron
  See Rose, Wendy
Kheirabadi, Masoud 1951- 158
Khemir, Sabiha 87
Kherdian, David 1931- 74
  Autobiography Feature 125
  Earlier sketch in SATA 16
  See also CLR 24
Khing, T.T. 1933- 192
Kibbe, Pat (Hosley) 60
Kidd, Diana 1933-2000 150
Kidd, Richard 1952-2008 152
Kidd, Ronald 1948- 173
  Earlier sketches in SATA 42, 92
Kiddell, John 1922- 3
Kiddell-Monroe, Joan 1908-1972 55
Kidwell, Carl 1910- 43
Kiefer, Irene 1926- 21
Kiefer, Kathleen Balmes 1957- 142
Kierstead, Vera M.
  See Kierstead-Farber, Vera M.
Kierstead-Farber, Vera M. 1913- 121
Kierstead-Farber, Vera May
  See Kierstead-Farber, Vera M.
Kiesel, Stanley 1925- 35
Kiesler, Kate (A.) 1971- 152
  Earlier sketch in SATA 90
Kihn, Greg 1952- 110
Kikukawa, Cecily H(arder) 1919- 44
  Brief entry 35
Kilcher, Jewel 1974- 109
Kile, Joan 1940- 78
Kilgore, Kathleen 1946- 42
Kilian, Crawford 1941- 35
Killdeer, John
  See Mayhar, Ardath
Killien, Christi 1956- 73
Killilea, Marie (Lyons) 1913-1991 2
Killingback, Julia 1944- 63
Killough, (Karen) Lee 1942- 64
Kilreon, Beth
  See Walker, Barbara (Jeanne) K(erlin)
Kilworth, Garry 1941- 94
Kilworth, Garry D.
  See Kilworth, Garry
Kilworth, Garry Douglas
  See Kilworth, Garry
Kim, Helen 1899-1970 98
Kimball, Gayle 1943- 90
Kimball, Violet T(ew) 1932- 126
Kimball, Yeffe 1914-1978 37
Kimber, Murray 1964- 171
Kimble, Warren 176
Kimbrough, Emily 1899-1989 2
  Obituary 59
Kimeldorf, Martin 1948- 121
Kimeldorf, Martin R.
  See Kimeldorf, Martin
Kimenye, Barbara 1940(?)- 121
Kimmel, Elizabeth Cody 170
Kimmel, Eric A. 1946- 176
  Earlier sketches in SATA 13, 80, 125
Kimmel, Margaret Mary 1938- 43
  Brief entry 33
Kimmelman, Burt 1947- 180
Kimmelman, Leslie (Grodinsky) 1958- 156
  Earlier sketch in SATA 85
Kincaid, Jamaica 1949-
  See CLR 63
Kincher, Jonni 1949- 79
Kindl, Patrice 1951- 128
  Earlier sketch in SATA 82
  See also CLR 132
Kindred, Wendy (Good) 1937- 7
Kines, Pat Decker 1937- 12
King, Adam
  See Hoare, Robert J(ohn)
King, Alison
  See Martini, Teri
King, (Maria) Anna 1964- 72
King, Billie Jean 1943- 12

King, Christopher (L.) 1945- 84
King, (David) Clive 1924- 144
  Earlier sketch in SATA 28
King, Colin 1943- 76
King, Cynthia 1925- 7
King, Daniel (John) 1963- 130
King, Elizabeth 1953- 83
King, Frank O. 1883-1969
  Obituary 22
King, Frank R. 1904-1999 127
King, Jane
  See Currie, Stephen
King, Jeanette (Margaret) 1959- 105
King, Larry L. 1929- 66
King, Laurie R. 1952- 88
King, Marian 1900(?)-1986 23
  Obituary 47
King, Martin Luther, Jr. 1929-1968 14
King, Mary Ellen 1958- 93
King, Paul
  See Drackett, Phil(ip Arthur)
King, Paula
  See Downing, Paula E.
King, Stephen 1947- 161
  Earlier sketches in SATA 9, 55
  See also CLR 124
King, Stephen Edwin
  See King, Stephen
King, Stephen Michael 157
King, Steve
  See King, Stephen
King, Thomas 1943- 96
King, Thomas Hunt
  See King, Thomas
King, Tony 1947- 39
Kingman, Dong (Moy Shu) 1911-2000 44
Kingman, Lee 67
  Earlier sketch in SATA 1
  See also SAAS 3
  See Natti, (Mary) Lee
Kingsland, Leslie William 1912- 13
Kingsley, Charles 1819-1875
  See YABC 2
  See also CLR 77
Kingsley, Emily Perl 1940- 33
Kingsley, Kaza 193
King-Smith, Dick 1922- 192
  Brief entry 38
  Earlier sketches in SATA 47, 80, 135
  See also CLR 40
Kingston, Maxine Hong 1940- 53
Kingston, Maxine Ting Ting Hong
  See Kingston, Maxine Hong
Kinney, C. Cle(land) 1915- 6
Kinney, Harrison 1921- 13
Kinney, Jean Stout 1912- 12
Kinney, Jeff 1971- 187
Kinsey, Elizabeth
  See Clymer, Eleanor
Kinsey, Helen 1948- 82
Kinsey-Warnock, Natalie 1956- 167
  Earlier sketches in SATA 71, 116
Kinzel, Dorothy 1950- 57
Kinzel, Dottie
  See Kinzel, Dorothy
Kipling, (Joseph) Rudyard 1865-1936 100
  See also YABC 2
  See also CLR 65
Kippax, Frank
  See Needle, Jan
Kirby, David K. 1944- 78
Kirby, David Kirk
  See Kirby, David K.
Kirby, Margaret
  See Bingley, Margaret (Jane Kirby)
Kirby, Susan E. 1949- 62
Kirk, Connie Ann 1957- 167
Kirk, Daniel 1952- 153
  Earlier sketch in SATA 107
Kirk, David 1955- 161
  Earlier sketch in SATA 117

Kirk, Heather 1949- *166*
Kirk, Ruth (Kratz) 1925- 5
Kirkham, Dinah
   See Card, Orson Scott
Kirkland, Will
   See Hale, Arlene
Kirkpatrick, Katherine (Anne) 1964- *113*
Kirkup, James 1918- *12*
Kirkus, Virginia
   See Glick, Virginia Kirkus
Kirkwood, Kathryn
   See Fluke, Joanne
Kirshenbaum, Binnie 79
Kirshner, David S. 1958- *123*
Kish, Eleanor M(ary) 1924- 73
Kish, Ely
   See Kish, Eleanor M(ary)
Kishida, Eriko 1929- *12*
Kisinger, Grace Gelvin (Maze) 1913-1965 .. *10*
Kissin, Eva H. 1923- *10*
Kissinger, Rosemary K.
   See Updyke, Rosemary K.
Kistler, John M. 1967- *160*
Kitamura, Satoshi 1956- *143*
   Earlier sketches in SATA *62, 98*
   See also CLR *60*
Kitchen, Bert
   See Kitchen, Herbert Thomas
Kitchen, Herbert Thomas 1940- 70
Kite, L. Patricia
   See Kite, Pat
Kite, Pat 1940- 78
Kitt, Tamara
   See de Regniers, Beatrice Schenk (Freedman)
Kittinger, Jo S(usenbach) 1955- *148*
   Earlier sketch in SATA *96*
Kituomba
   See Odaga, Asenath (Bole)
Kitzinger, Sheila 1929- 57
Kiwak, Barbara 1966- *103*
Kjelgaard, James Arthur 1910-1959 .... *17*
   See also CLR *81*
   See Kjelgaard, Jim
Kjelgaard, Jim
   See Kjelgaard, James Arthur
Kjelle, Marylou Morano 1954- *146*
Klagsbrun, Francine (Lifton) 36
Klaits, Barrie 1944- 52
Klam, Cheryl *191*
Klaperman, Gilbert 1921- 33
Klaperman, Libby Mindlin 1921-1982 33
   Obituary 31
Klass, David 1960- *142*
   Earlier sketch in SATA *88*
Klass, Morton 1927-2001 .... *11*
Klass, Sheila Solomon 1927- 99
   Autobiography Feature *126*
   Earlier sketch in SATA *45*
   See also SAAS *26*
Klause, Annette Curtis 1953- *175*
   Earlier sketch in SATA *79*
   See also CLR *104*
Klaveness, Jan O'Donnell 1939- 86
Kleberger, Ilse 1921- 5
Kleeberg, Irene (Flitner)
   Cumming 1932- 65
Klein, Aaron E. 1930-1998 45
   Brief entry 28
Klein, Bill 1945- 89
Klein, David 1919-2001 59
Klein, Frederick C. 1938- *154*
Klein, Gerda Weissmann 1924- 44
Klein, H(erbert) Arthur 8
Klein, James 1932- *115*
Klein, Leonore (Glotzer) 1916- 6
Klein, Mina C(ooper) 1906-1979 8
Klein, Norma 1938-1989 57
   Earlier sketch in SATA *7*
   See also CLR *19*
   See also SAAS *1*
Klein, Rachel S. 1953- *105*

Klein, Robin 1936- *164*
   Brief entry 45
   Earlier sketches in SATA *55, 80*
   See also CLR *21*
Klemin, Diana 65
Klemm, Barry 1945- *104*
Klemm, Edward G., Jr. 1910-2001 30
Klemm, Roberta K(ohnhorst) 1884-1975 30
Kleven, Elisa 1958- *173*
   Earlier sketch in SATA *76*
   See also CLR *85*
Klevin, Jill Ross 1935- 39
   Brief entry 38
Kliban, B(ernard) 1935-1990 35
   Obituary 66
Klimowicz, Barbara 1927- *10*
Kline, Christina Baker 1964- *101*
Kline, James
   See Klein, James
Kline, Jim
   See Kline, Jim
Kline, Lisa Williams 1954- *143*
Kline, Suzy 1943- *193*
   Autobiography Feature *193*
   Brief entry 48
   Earlier sketches in SATA *67, 99, 152*
Kliros, Thea 1935- *106*
Klise, Kate *181*
Klise, M. Sarah 1961- *180*
   Earlier sketch in SATA *128*
Klots, Alexander Barrett 1903-1989
   Obituary 62
Klug, Ron(ald) 1939- 31
Knaak, Richard A. 1961- *166*
   Earlier sketch in SATA *86*
Knaak, Richard Allen
   See Knaak, Richard A.
Knapp, Edward
   See Kunhardt, Edith
Knapp, Ron 1952- 34
Knebel, Fletcher 1911-1993 36
   Obituary 75
Kneeland, Linda Clarke 1947- 94
Knickerbocker, Diedrich
   See Irving, Washington
Knifesmith
   See Cutler, Ivor
Knigge, Robert (R.) 1921(?)-1987 50
Knight, Anne (Katherine) 1946- 34
Knight, Brenda *112*
Knight, Christopher G. 1943- 96
Knight, Damon (Francis) 1922-2002 9
   Obituary *139*
Knight, David C(arpenter) 1925-1984 .... *14*
   See also CLR *38*
Knight, Eric 1897-1943 .... *18*
Knight, Eric Mowbray
   See Knight, Eric
Knight, Francis Edgar 1905- *14*
Knight, Frank
   See Knight, Francis Edgar
Knight, Hilary 1926- *132*
   Earlier sketches in SATA *15, 69*
Knight, Joan (MacPhail) *159*
   Earlier sketch in SATA *82*
Knight, Joan
   See Knight, Joan (MacPhail)
Knight, Kathryn Lasky
   See Lasky, Kathryn
Knight, Mallory T.
   See Hurwood, Bernhardt J.
Knight, Ruth Adams 1898-1974
   Obituary 20
Knight, Theodore O. 1946- 77
Knobloch, Dorothea 1951- 88
Knoepfle, John (Ignatius) 1923- 66
Knott, Bill
   See Knott, William C(ecil, Jr.)

Knott, William C(ecil, Jr.) 1927- 3
   See Knott, Bill
   and Mitchum, Hank
   and Sharpe, Jon
Knotts, Howard (Clayton, Jr.) 1922- 25
Knowles, Anne 1933- 37
Knowles, John 1926-2001 89
   Obituary *134*
   Earlier sketch in SATA *8*
   See also CLR *98*
Knox, Calvin M.
   See Silverberg, Robert
Knox, (Mary) Eleanor Jessie 1909-2000 59
   Earlier sketch in SATA *30*
Knox, Elizabeth 1959- *176*
Knox, Elizabeth Fiona
   See Knox, Elizabeth
Knox, James
   See Brittain, William (E.)
Knox, Jolyne 1937- 76
Knudsen, James 1950- 42
Knudsen, Michelle *171*
Knudson, R. R.
   See SAAS *18*
   See Knudson, Rozanne
Knudson, Richard L(ewis) 1930- 34
Knudson, Rozanne 1932-2008 79
   Earlier sketch in SATA *7*
   See Knudson, R. R.
Knutson, Barbara 1959-2005 .... *166*
Knutson, Kimberley *115*
Knye, Cassandra
   See Disch, Thomas M.
Koch, Dorothy Clarke 1924- 6
Koch, Kenneth 1925-2002 65
Koch, Kenneth Jay
   See Koch, Kenneth
Koch, Phyllis (Mae) McCallum 1911- *10*
Kocsis, J. C.
   See Paul, James
Koda-Callan, Elizabeth 1944- *140*
   Earlier sketch in SATA *67*
Koehler, Phoebe 1955- 85
Koehler-Pentacoff, Elizabeth 1957- *160*
   Earlier sketch in SATA *96*
Koehn, Ilse
   See Van Zwienen, Ilse Charlotte Koehn
Koeller, Carol *192*
Koenig, Viviane 1950- 80
Koering, Ursula 1921-1976 64
Koerner, W(illiam) H(enry) D(avid)
   1878-1938 .... *21*
Koertge, Ronald 1940- *131*
   Earlier sketches in SATA *53, 92*
Koestler-Grack, Rachel A. 1973- *156*
Koff, Richard Myram 1926- 62
Koffinke, Carol 1949- 82
Kogan, Deborah 50
   See Kogan Ray, Deborah
Kogan Ray, Deborah 1940- *161*
   See Kogan, Deborah
   and Ray, Deborah
Kogawa, Joy Nozomi 1935- 99
Kogler, Jennifer Anne 1982(?)- *174*
Kohl, Herbert 1937- 47
Kohl, Herbert R.
   See Kohl, Herbert
Kohl, MaryAnn F(aubion) 1947- *144*
   Earlier sketch in SATA *74*
Kohler, Julilly H(ouse) 1908-1976
   Obituary 20
Kohn, Bernice 4
   See Hunt, Bernice (Kohn)
Kohn, Rita (T.) 1933- 89
Kohner, Frederick 1905-1986 .... *10*
   Obituary 48
Koide, Tan 1938-1986 50
Koike, Kay 1940- 72
Koja, Kathe 1960- *155*
Kolb, Larry J. 1953- *175*
Kolba, St. Tamara 22

Kolibalova, Marketa
  See Kolibalova, Marketa
Kolibalova, Marketa 1953- 126
Koller, Jackie French 1948- 157
  Earlier sketches in SATA 72, 109
  See also CLR 68
Kolodny, Nancy J. 1946- 76
Komaiko, Leah 1954- 164
  Earlier sketch in SATA 97
Komisar, Lucy 1942- 9
Komoda, Beverly 1939- 25
Komoda, Kiyo 1937- 9
Kompaneyets, Marc 1974- 169
Komroff, Manuel 1890-1974 2
  Obituary 20
Konigsburg, E.L. 1930- 126
  Earlier sketches in SATA 4, 48, 94
  See also CLR 81
Konigsburg, Elaine Lobl
  See Konigsburg, E.L.
Koning, Hans 1921-2007
  Obituary 182
  See Koningsberger, Hans
Koningsberger, Hans 5
  See Koning, Hans
Konkle, Janet Everest 1917- 12
Kono, Erin Eitter 1973- 177
Konzak, Burt 1946- 151
Koob, Theodora (J. Foth) 1918- 23
Kooiker, Leonie
  See Kooyker-Romijn, Johanna Maria
Koons, James
  See Pernu, Dennis
Koontz, Dean
  See Koontz, Dean R.
Koontz, Dean R. 1945- 165
  Earlier sketch in SATA 92
Koontz, Dean Ray
  See Koontz, Dean R.
Koontz, Robin Michal 1954- 136
  Earlier sketch in SATA 70
Kooyker, Leonie
  See Kooyker-Romijn, Johanna Maria
Kooyker-Romijn, Johanna Maria 1927- 48
  See Kooyker, Leonie
Kooyker-Romyn, Johanna Maria
  See Kooyker-Romijn, Johanna Maria
Kopelke, Lisa 1963- 154
Kopper, Lisa (Esther) 1950- 105
  Brief entry 51
Koppes, Steven N. 1957- 169
Koppes, Steven Nelson
  See Koppes, Steven N.
Korach, Mimi 1922- 9
Koralek, Jenny 1934- 140
  Earlier sketch in SATA 71
Korczak, Janusz 65
  See Goldszmit, Henryk
Koren, Edward (Benjamin) 1935- 148
  Earlier sketch in SATA 5
Korinets, Iurii Iosifovich
  See Korinetz, Yuri (Iosifovich)
Korinetz, Yuri (Iosifovich) 1923- 9
  See also CLR 4
Korman, Bernice 1937- 78
Korman, Gordon 1963- 167
  Brief entry 41
  Earlier sketches in SATA 49, 81, 119
  See also CLR 25
Korman, Gordon Richard
  See Korman, Gordon
Korman, Justine 1958- 70
Kornblatt, Marc 1954- 147
  Earlier sketch in SATA 84
Kornprobst, Jacques 1937- 177
Korte, Gene J. 1950- 74
Korty, Carol 1937- 15
Koscielniak, Bruce 1947- 153
  Earlier sketches in SATA 67, 99
Koshin, Alexander (A.) 1952- 86
Kositsky, Lynne 1947- 158

Koskenmaki, Rosalie
  See Maggio, Rosalie
Koss, Amy Goldman 1954- 158
  Earlier sketch in SATA 115
Kossin, Sandy (Sanford) 1926- 10
Kossman, Nina 1959- 84
Kostick, Conor 1964- 186
Kotzwinkle, William 1938- 146
  Earlier sketches in SATA 24, 70
  See also CLR 6
Kouhi, Elizabeth 1917- 54
  Brief entry 49
Kouts, Anne 1945- 8
Koutsky, Jan Dale 1955- 146
Kovacs, Deborah 1954- 132
  Earlier sketch in SATA 79
Kovalski, Maryann 1951- 175
  Earlier sketches in SATA 58, 97
  See also CLR 34
  See also SAAS 21
Kowalski, Kathiann M. 1955- 151
  Earlier sketch in SATA 96
Kraft, Betsy Harvey 1937- 157
Kraft, Erik P. 193
Krahn, Fernando 1935- 49
  Brief entry 31
  See also CLR 3
Krakauer, Hoong Yee Lee 1955- 86
Krakauer, Jon 1954- 108
Kramer, George
  See Heuman, William
Kramer, Nora 1896(?)-1984 26
  Obituary 39
Kramer, Remi (Thomas) 1935- 90
Krantz, Hazel (Newman) 12
Kranzler, George G(ershon) 1916- 28
Kranzler, Gershon
  See Kranzler, George G(ershon)
Krasilovsky, Phyllis 1926- 38
  Earlier sketch in SATA 1
  See also CLR 83
  See also SAAS 5
Krasne, Betty
  See Levine, Betty K(rasne)
Krasner, Steven 1953- 154
Krasno, Rena 1923- 104
Kratman, Tom 175
Kraus, Joanna Halpert 1937- 87
Kraus, (Herman) Robert 1925-2001 93
  Obituary 130
  Earlier sketches in SATA 4, 65
  See also SAAS 11
Krauss, Ruth (Ida) 1911-1993 30
  Obituary 75
  Earlier sketch in SATA 1
  See also CLR 42
Krautter, Elisa (Bialk) 1912(?)-1990 1
  Obituary 65
Krautwurst, Terry 1946- 79
Kray, Robert Clement 1930- 82
Krech, Bob 1956- 185
Krech, Robert
  See Krech, Bob
Kredel, Fritz 1900-1973 17
Kreikemeier, Gregory Scott 1965- 85
Kreloff, Elliot 189
Krementz, Jill 1940- 134
  Earlier sketches in SATA 17, 71
  See also CLR 5
  See also SAAS 8
Kremer, Marcie
  See Sorenson, Margo
Krenina, Katya 1968- 101
Krensky, Stephen 1953- 188
  Brief entry 41
  Earlier sketches in SATA 47, 93, 136
Krensky, Stephen Alan
  See Krensky, Stephen
Kresh, Paul 1919-1997 61
  Obituary 94

Kress, Nancy 1948- 147
  Autobiography Feature 147
  Earlier sketch in SATA 85
Kricher, John C. 1944- 113
Krieger, Melanie 96
Kripke, Dorothy Karp 30
Krisher, Trudy 1946- 160
  Earlier sketch in SATA 86
Krisher, Trudy B.
  See Krisher, Trudy
Krishnaswami, Uma 1956- 182
  Earlier sketch in SATA 144
Kristof, Jane 1932- 8
Kroeber, Theodora (Kracaw) 1897-1979 1
Kroeger, Mary Kay 1950- 92
Krohn, Katherine E(lizabeth) 1961- 125
  Earlier sketch in SATA 84
Kroll, Francis Lynde 1904-1973 10
Kroll, Steven 1941- 135
  Autobiography Feature 135
  Earlier sketches in SATA 19, 66, 125
  See also SAAS 7
Kroll, Virginia L. 1948- 168
  Earlier sketches in SATA 76, 114
Kroll, Virginia Louisa
  See Kroll, Virginia L.
Kromhout, Rindert 1958- 189
Krommes, Beth 1956- 181
  Earlier sketch in SATA 128
Kronenwetter, Michael 1943- 62
Kroniuk, Lisa
  See Berton, Pierre (Francis de Marigny)
Kropp, Paul (Stephan) 1948- 38
  Brief entry 34
  See also CLR 96
Krosoczka, Jarrett J. 1977- 155
Krovatin, Christopher 1985- 171
Kruess, James
  See CLR 9
  See Kruss, James
Kruglik, Gerald 187
Krull, Kathleen 1952- 184
  Autobiography Feature 106
  Brief entry 39
  Earlier sketches in SATA 52, 80, 149
  See also CLR 44
Krumgold, Joseph (Quincy) 1908-1980 48
  Obituary 23
  Earlier sketch in SATA 1
Krupinski, Loretta 1940- 161
  Earlier sketches in SATA 67, 102
Krupnick, Karen 1947- 89
Krupp, E(dwin) C(harles) 1944- 123
  Earlier sketch in SATA 53
Krupp, Robin Rector 1946- 53
Krush, Beth 1918- 18
Krush, Joe 1918- 18
  See Krush, Joseph P.
Kruss, James 1926-1997 8
  See Kruess, James
Krykorka, Vladyana 1945- 96
Kubie, Eleanor Gottheil
  See Kubie, Nora Gottheil Benjamin
Kubie, Nora Benjamin
  See Kubie, Nora Gottheil Benjamin
Kubie, Nora Gottheil Benjamin
  1899-1988 39
  Obituary 59
Kubinyi, Laszlo 1937- 94
  Earlier sketch in SATA 17
Kudlinski, Kathleen V. 1950- 150
Kuenstler, Morton 1927- 10
Kuh, Charlotte 1892(?)-1985
  Obituary 43
Kuharski, Janice 1947- 128
Kuijer, Guus 1942- 179
Kujoth, Jean Spealman 1935-1975
  Obituary 30
Kuklin, Susan 1941- 163
  Earlier sketches in SATA 63, 95
  See also CLR 51

Kulikov, Boris 1966- *170*
Kulka, Joe *188*
Kulling, Monica 1952- *89*
Kullman, Harry 1919-1982 .... *35*
Kumin, Maxine 1925- *12*
Kumin, Maxine Winokur
   See Kumin, Maxine
Kunhardt, Dorothy (Meserve) 1901-1979 .... *53*
   Obituary *22*
Kunhardt, Edith 1937- *67*
Kunjufu, Jawanza 1953- *73*
Kunstler, Morton
   See Kuenstler, Morton
Kuntz, J(ohn) L. 1947- *91*
Kuntz, Jerry 1956- *133*
Kupferberg, Herbert 1918-2001 .... *19*
Kuratomi, Chizuko 1939- *12*
   See also CLR 32
Kurczok, Belinda 1978- *121*
Kurelek, William 1927-1977 .... *8*
   Obituary *27*
   See also CLR 2
Kurian, George 1928- *65*
Kurjian, Judi(th M.) 1944- *127*
Kurland, Gerald 1942- *13*
Kurland, Michael 1938- *118*
   Earlier sketch in SATA 48
Kurland, Michael Joseph
   See Kurland, Michael
Kuroi, Ken 1947- *120*
Kurokawa, Mitsuhiro 1954- *88*
Kurten, Bjorn (Olof) 1924-1988 .... *64*
Kurtz, Jane 1952- *139*
   Earlier sketch in SATA 91
   See also CLR 123
Kurtz, Katherine 1944- *182*
   Earlier sketches in SATA 76, 126
Kurtz, Katherine Irene
   See Kurtz, Katherine
Kurz, Rudolf 1952- *95*
Kushner, Donn (J.) 1927- *52*
   See also CLR 55
Kushner, Ellen 1955- *98*
Kushner, Ellen Ruth
   See Kushner, Ellen
Kushner, Jill Menkes 1951- *62*
Kushner, Lawrence 1943- *169*
   Earlier sketch in SATA 83
Kushner, Tony 1956- *160*
Kuskin, Karla 1932- *164*
   Earlier sketches in SATA 2, 68, 111
   See also CLR 4
   See also SAAS 3
Kuskin, Karla Seidman
   See Kuskin, Karla
Kusugak, Michael (Arvaaluk) 1948- *143*
Kuttner, Paul 1922- *18*
Kuyper, Sjoerd 1952- *177*
Kuzma, Kay 1941- *39*
Kvale, Velma R(uth) 1898-1979 .... *8*
Kvasnosky, Laura McGee 1951- *182*
   Earlier sketches in SATA 93, 142
Kwasney, Michelle D. 1960- *162*
Kyle, Benjamin
   See Gottfried, Theodore Mark
Kyle, Elisabeth
   See Dunlop, Agnes M. R.
Kyte, Kathy S. 1946- *50*
   Brief entry *44*

L

L., Barry
   See Longyear, Barry B(rookes)
L., Tommy
   See Lorkowski, Thomas V(incent)
Labouisse, Eve Curie
   See Curie, Eve

Labouisse, Eve Denise
   See Curie, Eve
Lace, William W. 1942- *126*
Lacey, Josh 1968- *187*
Lachner, Dorothea
   See Knobloch, Dorothea
Lachtman, Ofelia Dumas 1919- *179*
Lackey, Mercedes R. 1950- *127*
   Earlier sketch in SATA 81
Lackey, Mercedes Ritchie
   See Lackey, Mercedes R.
Lacoe, Addie *78*
Lacome, Julie 1961- *174*
   Earlier sketch in SATA 80
Lacy, Leslie Alexander 1937- *6*
Ladd, Cheryl (Jean) 1951- *113*
Ladd, Louise 1943- *97*
Ladd, Veronica
   See Miner, Jane Claypool
Laden, Nina 1962- *148*
   Earlier sketch in SATA 85
Lader, Lawrence 1919-2006 .... *6*
   Obituary *178*
LaDoux, Rita C. 1951- *74*
Lady, A
   See Taylor, Ann
Lady Mears
   See Tempest, Margaret Mary
Lady of Quality, A
   See Bagnold, Enid
La Farge, Oliver 1901-1963 .... *19*
La Farge, Oliver Hazard Perry
   See La Farge, Oliver
La Farge, Phyllis *14*
LaFaye, A. 1970- *156*
   Earlier sketch in SATA 105
LaFaye, Alexandria R.T.
   See LaFaye, A.
LaFevers, R.L. *191*
LaFevers, Robin L.
   See LaFevers, R.L.
Laffin, John (Alfred Charles) 1922- *31*
LaFontaine, Bruce 1948- *176*
   Earlier sketch in SATA 114
La Fontaine, Jean de 1621-1695 .... *18*
Lager, Claude
   See Lapp, Christiane (Germain)
Lager, Marilyn 1939- *52*
Lagercrantz, Rose (Elsa) 1947- *39*
Lagerloef, Selma (Ottiliana Lovisa)
   See Lagerlof, Selma (Ottiliana Lovisa)
Lagerlof, Selma (Ottiliana Lovisa)
   1858-1940 .... *15*
   See also CLR 7
   See Lagerloef, Selma (Ottiliana Lovisa)
Laguna, Sofie 1968- *158*
LaHaye, Tim F. 1926- *149*
LaHaye, Timothy F.
   See LaHaye, Tim F.
Laiken, Deirdre S(usan) 1948- *48*
   Brief entry *40*
Laimgruber, Monika 1946- *11*
Lain, Anna
   See Lamb, Nancy
Laing, Alexander (Kinnan) 1903-1976 .... *117*
Laing, Martha 1951- *39*
Laird, Christa 1944- *108*
   Autobiography Feature *120*
   See also SAAS 26
Laird, Elizabeth (Mary Risk) 1943- *159*
   Earlier sketches in SATA 77, 114
   See also CLR 65
Laird, Jean E(louise) 1930- *38*
Laite, Gordon 1925- *31*
Lake, Harriet
   See Taylor, Paula (Wright)
Lakin, Patricia 1944- *190*
Laklan, Carli 1907-1988 .... *5*
Laliberte, Louise-Andree 1958- *169*
Lalicki, Barbara *61*
Lalicki, Tom 1949- *186*

Lally, Soinbhe 1945- *119*
LaMarche, Jim *162*
Lamb, Albert *187*
Lamb, Beatrice Pitney 1904-1997 .... *21*
Lamb, Charles 1775-1834 .... *17*
Lamb, Elizabeth Searle 1917- *31*
Lamb, G(eoffrey) F(rederick) *10*
Lamb, Harold (Albert) 1892-1962 .... *53*
Lamb, Lynton (Harold) 1907-1977 .... *10*
Lamb, Mary Ann 1764-1847 .... *17*
Lamb, Nancy 1939- *80*
Lamb, Robert (Boyden) 1941- *13*
Lambert, David (Compton) 1932- *84*
   Brief entry *49*
Lambert, Janet 1895(?)-1973 .... *25*
Lambert, Martha L. *113*
Lambert, Saul 1928- *23*
Lambert, Stephen *174*
Lamburn, Richmal Crompton 1890-1969 .... *5*
   See Crompton, Richmal
Lamensdorf, Len 1930- *120*
Lamensdorf, Leonard
   See Lamensdorf, Len
Laminack, Lester L. 1956- *163*
   Earlier sketch in SATA 120
Lamorisse, Albert (Emmanuel) 1922-1970 ... *23*
Lampert, Emily 1951- *52*
   Brief entry *49*
Lamplugh, Lois 1921- *17*
Lampman, Evelyn Sibley 1907-1980 .... *87*
   Obituary *23*
   Earlier sketch in SATA 4
Lamprey, Louise 1869-1951
   See YABC 2
Lampton, Chris
   See Lampton, Christopher F.
Lampton, Christopher
   See Lampton, Christopher F.
Lampton, Christopher F. *67*
   Brief entry *47*
Lamstein, Sarah 1943- *174*
   Earlier sketch in SATA 126
Lamstein, Sarah Marwil
   See Lamstein, Sarah
Lanagan, Margo 1960- *163*
Lancaster, Bruce 1896-1963 .... *9*
Lancaster, Matthew 1973(?)-1983
   Obituary *45*
Lance, Kathryn 1943- *76*
Land, Barbara (Neblett) 1923- *16*
Land, Jane
   See Borland, Kathryn Kilby
   and Speicher, Helen Ross S(mith)
Land, Myrick (Ebben) 1922-1998 .... *15*
Land, Ross
   See Borland, Kathryn Kilby
   and Speicher, Helen Ross S(mith)
Landau, Elaine 1948- *141*
   Earlier sketches in SATA 10, 94
Landau, Jacob 1917- *38*
Landeck, Beatrice 1904-1978 .... *15*
Landin, Les 1923- *2*
Landis, J(ames) D(avid) 1942- *60*
   Brief entry *52*
Landis, James D.
   See Landis, J(ames) D(avid)
Landis, Jill Marie 1948- *101*
Landmann, Bimba 1968- *176*
Landon, Dena 1978(?)- *168*
Landon, Lucinda 1950- *56*
   Brief entry *51*
Landon, Margaret (Dorothea
   Mortenson) 1903-1993 .... *50*
Landshoff, Ursula 1908-1989 .... *13*
Landstrom, Lena 1943- *146*
Landstrom, Olof 1943- *146*
Lane, Carolyn 1926-1993 .... *10*
Lane, Connie
   See Laux, Constance
Lane, Dakota 1959- *166*
   Earlier sketch in SATA 105

Lane, Jerry
  See Martin, Patricia Miles
Lane, John (Richard) 1932- *15*
Lane, Margaret 1907-1994 .... *65*
  Brief entry *38*
  Obituary *79*
Lane, Rose Wilder 1887-1968 .... *29*
  Brief entry *28*
Lanes, Selma Gordon 1929- *3*
Lanfredi, Judy 1964- *83*
Lang, Andrew 1844-1912 .... *16*
  See also CLR *101*
Lang, Aubrey *169*
Lang, Paul 1948- *83*
Lang, Susan S. 1950- *68*
Lang, T.T.
  See Taylor, Theodore
Langdo, Bryan 1973- *191*
  Earlier sketch in SATA *138*
Lange, John
  See Crichton, Michael
Lange, Karen E. *190*
Lange, Suzanne 1945- *5*
Langley, Andrew 1949- *166*
  Earlier sketch in SATA *104*
Langley, Charles P(itman) III 1949- *103*
Langley, Jonathan 1952- *122*
Langley, Noel 1911-1980
  Obituary *25*
Langley, Wanda *173*
Langner, Nola *8*
  See Malone, Nola Langner
Langone, John (Michael) 1929- *46*
  Brief entry *38*
Langreuter, Jutta 1944- *122*
Langrish, Katherine *177*
Langsen, Richard C. 1953- *95*
Langstaff, John 1920-2005 .... *68*
  Obituary *172*
  Earlier sketch in SATA *6*
  See also CLR *3*
Langstaff, John Meredith
  See Langstaff, John
Langstaff, Launcelot
  See Irving, Washington
Langston, Laura 1958- *186*
Langton, Jane (Gillson) 1922- *140*
  Autobiography Feature *140*
  Earlier sketches in SATA *3, 68, 129*
  See also CLR *33*
  See also SAAS *5*
Lanier, Sidney 1842-1881 .... *18*
Lanier, Sterling E. 1927-2007 .... *109*
Lanier, Sterling Edmund
  See Lanier, Sterling E.
Lanino, Deborah 1964- *123*
Lankford, Mary D. 1932- *112*
  Earlier sketch in SATA *77*
Lannin, Joanne 1951- *121*
Lannin, Joanne A.
  See Lannin, Joanne
Lansdale, Joe R. 1951- *116*
Lansdale, Joe Richard
  See Lansdale, Joe R.
Lansing, Alfred 1921-1975 .... *35*
Lansing, Karen E. 1954- *71*
Lansky, Vicki 1942- *177*
Lantier-Sampon, Patricia 1952- *92*
Lantz, Fran
  See Lantz, Francess L(in)
Lantz, Francess L(in) 1952-2004 .... *153*
  Autobiography Feature *153*
  Obituary *159*
  Earlier sketches in SATA *63, 109*
  See Dixon, Franklin W.
Lantz, Paul 1908- *45*
Lantz, Walter 1900-1994 .... *37*
  Obituary *79*
Lanza, Barbara 1945- *101*
Lapp, Christiane (Germain) 1948- *74*
Lappin, Peter 1911-1999 .... *32*

Larbalestier, Justine *178*
Lardy, Philippe 1963- *168*
LaReau, Jenna *181*
LaReau, Kara *181*
Larios, Julie 1949- *178*
Larios, Julie Hofstrand
  See Larios, Julie
Larkin, Amy
  See Burns, Olive Ann
Larkin, Maia
  See Wojciechowska, Maia (Teresa)
Laroche, Giles 1956- *126*
  Earlier sketch in SATA *71*
LaRochelle, David 1960- *171*
  Earlier sketch in SATA *115*
Larom, Henry V. 1903(?)-1975
  Obituary *30*
LaRose, Linda *125*
Larrabee, Lisa 1947- *84*
Larrecq, John M(aurice) 1926-1980 .... *44*
  Obituary *25*
Larrick (Crosby), Nancy 1910-2004 .... *4*
Larsen, Anita 1942- *78*
Larsen, Egon 1904- *14*
Larsen, Rebecca 1944- *54*
Larson, Eve
  See St. John, Wylly Folk
Larson, Gary 1950- *57*
Larson, Ingrid D(ana) 1965- *92*
Larson, Jean Russell 1930- *121*
Larson, Kirby 1954- *181*
  Earlier sketch in SATA *96*
Larson, Norita D(ittberner) 1944- *29*
Larson, William H. 1938- *10*
Larsson, Carl (Olof) 1853-1919 .... *35*
LaSalle, Charles A.
  See Ellis, Edward S(ylvester)
LaSalle, Charles E.
  See Ellis, Edward S(ylvester)
Lasell, Elinor H. 1929- *19*
Lasell, Fen H.
  See Lasell, Elinor H.
Lasenby, Jack 1931- *172*
  Earlier sketches in SATA *65, 103*
Laser, Michael 1954- *117*
Lash, Joseph P. 1909-1987 .... *43*
Lasher, Faith B. 1921- *12*
Lasker, David 1950- *38*
Lasker, Joe *83*
  See also SAAS *17*
  See Lasker, Joseph Leon
Lasker, Joseph Leon 1919- *9*
  See Lasker, Joe
Laski, Marghanita 1915-1988 .... *55*
Laskin, Pamela L. 1954- *75*
Lasky, Kathryn 1944- *157*
  Earlier sketches in SATA *13, 69, 112*
  See also CLR *11*
Lasky Knight, Kathryn
  See Lasky, Kathryn
Lass, Bonnie *131*
Lassalle, C. E.
  See Ellis, Edward S(ylvester)
Lassiter, Mary *59*
  See Hoffman, Mary (Margaret)
Lassiter, Rhiannon 1977- *157*
Latham, Barbara 1896- *16*
Latham, Frank B(rown) 1910-2000 .... *6*
Latham, Jean Lee 1902-1995 .... *68*
  Earlier sketch in SATA *2*
  See also CLR *50*
Latham, Mavis
  See Clark, Mavis Thorpe
Latham, Philip
  See Richardson, Robert S(hirley)
Lathrop, Dorothy P(ulis) 1891-1980 .... *14*
  Obituary *24*
Lathrop, Francis
  See Leiber, Fritz (Reuter, Jr.)
Latimer, Jim 1943- *80*

Latta, Rich
  See Latta, Richard
Latta, Richard 1946- *113*
Latta, Sara L. 1960- *174*
Lattany, Kristin
  See Lattany, Kristin (Elaine Eggleston)
  Hunter
Lattany, Kristin (Eggleston)
  Hunter 1931- *154*
  Autobiography Feature *154*
  Earlier sketch in SATA *132*
Lattany, Kristin (Elaine Eggleston)
  Hunter 1931- *132*
  Earlier sketch in SATA *12*
  See also CLR *3*
  See also SAAS *10*
  See Hunter, Kristin
Lattimore, Eleanor Frances 1904-1986 .... *7*
  Obituary *48*
Lattin, Ann
  See Cole, Lois Dwight
Lauber, Patricia (Grace) 1924- *138*
  Earlier sketches in SATA *1, 33, 75*
  See also CLR *16*
Laugesen, Mary E(akin) 1906-1995 .... *5*
Laughbaum, Steve 1945- *12*
Laughlin, Florence Young 1910-2001 .... *3*
Laughlin, Rosemary 1941- *123*
Laure, Ettagale
  See Blauer, Ettagale
Laure, Jason 1940- *50*
  Brief entry *44*
Laurence, Ester Hauser 1935- *7*
Laurence, Jean Margaret Wemyss
  See Laurence, Margaret
Laurence, Margaret 1926-1987
  Obituary *50*
Laurie, Rona 1916- *55*
Laurin, Anne
  See McLaurin, Anne
Lauritzen, Jonreed 1902-1979 .... *13*
Lauscher, Hermann
  See Hesse, Hermann
Lauture, Denize 1946- *86*
Laux, Connie
  See Laux, Constance
Laux, Constance 1952- *97*
Laux, Dorothy 1920- *49*
Lavallee, Barbara 1941- *166*
  Earlier sketch in SATA *74*
Lavender, David (Sievert) 1910-2003 .... *97*
  Obituary *145*
  Earlier sketch in SATA *64*
Lavender, William D. 1921- *143*
Laverne, Christine *175*
Lavert, Gwendolyn Battle 1951- *131*
  See Battle-Lavert, Gwendolyn
Laverty, Donald
  See Blish, James (Benjamin)
  and Knight, Damon (Francis)
Lavigne, Louis-Dominique *107*
Lavine, David 1928- *31*
Lavine, Sigmund Arnold 1908-1986 .... *82*
  Earlier sketch in SATA *3*
  See also CLR *35*
Lavond, Paul Dennis
  See Kornbluth, C(yril) M.
  and Lowndes, Robert A(ugustine) W(ard)
  and Pohl, Frederik
Lawhead, Stephen R. 1950- *109*
Lawhead, Steve
  See Lawhead, Stephen R.
Lawlor, Laurie 1953- *137*
  Earlier sketch in SATA *80*
Lawlor, William
  See Lawlor, William T.
Lawlor, William T. 1951- *183*
Lawrence, Ann (Margaret) 1942-1987 .... *41*
  Obituary *54*
Lawrence, Iain 1955- *183*
  Earlier sketch in SATA *135*

Lawrence, J. T.
   See Rowland-Entwistle, (Arthur)
   Theodore (Henry)
Lawrence, Jerome 1915-2004 65
Lawrence, John 1933- 30
Lawrence, Josephine 1890(?)-1978
   Obituary 24
Lawrence, Louise 1943- 119
   Earlier sketches in SATA *38, 78*
Lawrence, Louise de Kiriline 1894-1992 ..... *13*
Lawrence, Lynn
   See Garland, Sherry
Lawrence, Margery H. 1889-1969 .... *120*
Lawrence, Michael 1943- *132*
Lawrence, Mildred Elwood 1907-1997 3
Lawrence, R(onald) D(ouglas) 1921- 55
Lawrinson, Julia 1969- *141*
Lawson, Amy
   See Gordon, Amy
Lawson, Carol (Antell) 1946- 42
Lawson, Don(ald Elmer) 1917-1990 9
Lawson, Joan 1906- 55
Lawson, Julie 1947- *126*
   Earlier sketch in SATA *79*
   See also CLR *89*
Lawson, Marion Tubbs 1896-1994 22
Lawson, Robert 1892-1957 .... *100*
   See also YABC *2*
   See also CLR *73*
Lawton, Clive A. 1951- *145*
Laxdal, Vivienne 1962- *112*
Laybourn, Emma *193*
Laycock, George (Edwin) 1921- 5
Layne, Laura
   See Knott, William C(ecil, Jr.)
Layne, Steven L. *171*
Layton, Neal 1971- *187*
   Earlier sketch in SATA *152*
Layton, Neal Andrew
   See Layton, Neal
Lazare, Gerald John 1927- 44
Lazare, Jerry
   See Lazare, Gerald John
Lazarevich, Mila 1942- *17*
Lazarus, Keo Felker 1913-1993 21
   Obituary *129*
Lea, Alec 1907- *19*
Lea, Joan
   See Neufeld, John (Arthur)
Leach, Maria 1892-1977 .... *39*
   Brief entry 28
Leacock, Elspeth 1946- *131*
Leacroft, Helen (Mabel Beal) 1919- 6
Leacroft, Richard (Vallance Becher) 1914- 6
Leaf, Margaret P. 1909(?)-1988
   Obituary 55
Leaf, (Wilbur) Munro 1905-1976 20
   See also CLR *25*
Leaf, VaDonna Jean 1929- 26
Leah, Devorah
   See Devorah-Leah
Leakey, Richard E(rskine Frere) 1944- 42
Leander, Ed
   See Richelson, Geraldine
Lear, Edward 1812-1888 .... *100*
   Earlier sketch in SATA *18*
   See also CLR *75*
Lears, Laurie 1955- *127*
Leasor, James 1923-2007 54
Leasor, Thomas James
   See Leasor, James
Leavitt, Jerome E(dward) 1916- 23
Leavitt, Martine 1953- *170*
LeBar, Mary E(velyn) 1910-1982 35
LeBlanc, Annette M. 1965- 68
LeBlanc, L(ee) 1913- 54
LeBox, Annette 1943- *145*
Lebrun, Claude 1929- 66
Le Cain, Errol (John) 1941-1989 68
   Obituary 60
   Earlier sketch in SATA *6*

Lecourt, Nancy (Hoyt) 1951- *73*
Ledbetter, Suzann 1953- *119*
Leder, Jane Mersky 1945- *61*
   Brief entry 51
Lederer, Muriel 1929- 48
Lederer, William J(ulius) 1912- 62
Lee, Amanda
   See Baggett, Nancy
   and Buckholtz, Eileen (Garber)
   and Glick, Ruth (Burtnick)
Lee, Benjamin 1921- 27
Lee, Betsy 1949- 37
Lee, Carol
   See Fletcher, Helen Jill
Lee, Carol Ann 1969- *185*
Lee, Chinlun *182*
Lee, Cora
   See Anderson, Catherine Corley
Lee, Dennis (Beynon) 1939- *102*
   Earlier sketch in SATA *14*
   See also CLR *3*
Lee, Dom 1959- *146*
   Autobiography Feature *121*
   Earlier sketch in SATA *83*
   See also SAAS *26*
Lee, Doris Emrick 1905-1983 44
   Obituary 35
Lee, Edward
   See Lee, J. Edward
Lee, Elizabeth Rogers 1940- 90
Lee, Harper 1926- 11
Lee, Hector Viveros 1962- *115*
Lee, Howard N.
   See Goulart, Ron(ald Joseph)
Lee, Huy Voun 1969- *129*
Lee, J. Edward 1953- *130*
Lee, Jeanne M. 1943- *138*
Lee, John R(obert) 1923-1976 27
Lee, Jordan
   See Scholefield, Alan
Lee, Joseph Edward
   See Lee, J. Edward
Lee, Julian
   See Latham, Jean Lee
Lee, Liz
   See Lee, Elizabeth Rogers
Lee, Lucy
   See Talbot, Charlene Joy
Lee, Lyn 1953- *128*
Lee, Manning de Villeneuve 1894-1980 37
   Obituary 22
Lee, Marian
   See Clish, (Lee) Marian
Lee, Marie G. 1964- *178*
   Earlier sketches in SATA *81, 130*
Lee, Marie Myung-Ok
   See Lee, Marie G.
Lee, Mary Price 1934- 82
   Earlier sketch in SATA *8*
Lee, Mildred 6
   See also SAAS *12*
   See Scudder, Mildred Lee
Lee, Nelle Harper
   See Lee, Harper
Lee, Richard S. 1927- 82
Lee, Robert C. 1931- 20
Lee, Robert E(dwin) 1918-1994 65
   Obituary 82
Lee, Robert J. 1921- 10
Lee, Roy
   See Hopkins, Clark
Lee, Sally 1943- 67
Lee, Suzy *193*
Lee, Tammie
   See Townsend, Thomas L.
Lee, Tanith 1947- *185*
   Earlier sketches in SATA *8, 88, 134*
Leech, Ben
   See Bowkett, Stephen
Leeds, Constance *188*

Leedy, Loreen 1959- *175*
   Brief entry 50
   Earlier sketches in SATA *54, 84, 128*
Leedy, Loreen Janelle
   See Leedy, Loreen
Lee-Hostetler, Jeri 1940- 63
Leekley, Thomas B(riggs) 1910-2001 23
Leeming, Jo Ann
   See Leeming, Joseph
Leeming, Joseph 1897-1968 26
Leemis, Ralph B. 1954- 72
Leese, Jennifer L.B. 1970- *163*
Leeson, Muriel 1920- 54
Leeson, R. A.
   See Leeson, Robert (Arthur)
Leeson, Robert (Arthur) 1928- 76
   Earlier sketch in SATA *42*
Lee-Tai, Amy 1964- *189*
Leffland, Ella 1931- 65
Lefler, Irene (Whitney) 1917- *12*
LeFrak, Karen *182*
Le Gallienne, Eva 1899-1991 9
   Obituary 68
Legg, Gerald 1947- *143*
Legg, Sarah Martha Ross
   Bruggeman (?)-1982
   Obituary 40
LeGrand
   See Henderson, LeGrand
Le Guin, Ursula K. 1929- *149*
   Earlier sketches in SATA *4, 52, 99*
   See also CLR *91*
Le Guin, Ursula Kroeber
   See Le Guin, Ursula K.
Legum, Colin 1919-2003 10
Lehman, Barbara 1963- *170*
   Earlier sketch in SATA *115*
Lehman, Bob 91
Lehman, Elaine 91
Lehmann, Debra Lynn
   See Vanasse, Deb
Lehn, Cornelia 1920- 46
Lehne, Judith Logan 1947- 93
Lehr, Delores 1920- 10
Lehr, Norma 1930- 71
Leiber, Fritz (Reuter, Jr.) 1910-1992 45
   Obituary 73
Leibold, Jay 1957- 57
   Brief entry 52
Leichman, Seymour 1933- 5
Leigh, Nila K. 1981- 81
Leigh, Tom 1947- 46
Leigh-Pemberton, John 1911-1997 35
Leighton, Clare (Veronica Hope)
   1899-1989 37
Leighton, Margaret (Carver) 1896-1987 1
   Obituary 52
Leiner, Al(an) 1938- 83
Leiner, Katherine 1949- 93
Leipold, L. Edmond 1902-1983 16
Leisk, David (Johnson) 1906-1975 30
   Obituary 26
   Earlier sketch in SATA *1*
   See also CLR *98*
   See Johnson, Crockett
Leister, Mary 1917- 29
Leitch, Patricia 1933- 98
   Earlier sketch in SATA *11*
Leitner, Isabella 1924- 86
Leland, Bob 1956- 92
Leland, Robert E.
   See Leland, Bob
Lematre, Pascal 1967- *176*
Lember, Barbara Hirsch 1941- 92
LeMieux, A.C. 1954- *125*
   Earlier sketch in SATA *90*
   See LeMieux, Anne
LeMieux, Anne
   See LeMieux, A.C.
LeMieux, Anne Connelly
   See LeMieux, A.C.

Lemieux, Michele 1955- 139
Lemke, Horst 1922- 38
Lenanton, Carola Mary Anima Oman
    See Oman, Carola (Mary Anima)
Lenard, Alexander 1910-1972
    Obituary 21
L'Engle, Madeleine 1918-2007 128
    Obituary 186
    Earlier sketches in SATA 1, 27, 75
    See also CLR 57
    See also SAAS 15
L'Engle, Madeleine Camp Franklin
    See L'Engle, Madeleine
Lengyel, Cornel Adam 1915- 27
Lengyel, Emil 1895-1985 3
    Obituary 42
Lennon, John (Ono) 1940-1980 114
Leno, Jay 1950- 154
LeNoir, Janice 1941- 89
Lens, Sidney 1912-1986 13
    Obituary 48
Lenski, Lois 1893-1974 100
    Earlier sketches in SATA 1, 26
    See also CLR 26
Lent, Blair 133
    Earlier sketch in SATA 2
Lent, Henry Bolles 1901-1973 17
Lent, John 1948- 108
Leodhas, Sorche Nic
    See Alger, Leclaire (Gowans)
Leokum, Arkady 1916(?)- 45
Leon, Sharon 1959- 79
Leonard, Alison 1944- 70
Leonard, Constance (Brink) 1923- 42
    Brief entry 40
Leonard, Dutch
    See Leonard, Elmore
Leonard, Elmore 1925- 163
Leonard, Elmore John, Jr.
    See Leonard, Elmore
Leonard, Jonathan N(orton) 1903-1975 36
Leonard, Laura 1923- 75
Leong, Gor Yun
    See Ellison, Virginia H(owell)
Leonhardt, Alice 1950- 152
Lerangis, Peter 1955- 171
    Earlier sketch in SATA 72
    See Dixon, Franklin W.
    and Keene, Carolyn
Lerner, Aaron 1920-2007 35
    Obituary 179
Lerner, Aaron Bunsen
    See Lerner, Aaron
Lerner, Carol 1927- 86
    Earlier sketch in SATA 33
    See also CLR 34
    See also SAAS 12
Lerner, Gerda 1920- 65
Lerner, Harriet 1944- 101
Lerner, Marguerite Rush 1924-1987 11
    Obituary 51
Lerner, Sharon (Ruth) 1938-1982 11
    Obituary 29
Leroe, Ellen W(hitney) 1949- 99
    Brief entry 51
    Earlier sketch in SATA 61
Leroux, Gaston 1868-1927 65
Leroux-Hugon, Helene 1955- 132
LeRoy, Gen 52
    Brief entry 36
Lerrigo, Marion Olive 1898-1968
    Obituary 29
LeShan, Eda J(oan) 1922-2002 21
    See also CLR 6
LeSieg, Theo.
    See Dr. Seuss
    and Geisel, Theodor Seuss
    and Seuss, Dr.
    and Stone, Rosetta
Lesinski, Jeanne M. 1960- 120
Leslie, Robert Franklin 1911-1990 7

Leslie, Roger 1961- 168
Leslie, Roger James
    See Leslie, Roger
Leslie, Sarah
    See McGuire, Leslie (Sarah)
LeSourd, Catherine
    See Marshall, (Sarah) Catherine (Wood)
Lessac, Frane
    See Lessac, Frane
Lessac, Frane 1954- 148
    Earlier sketch in SATA 61
Lessem, Dino Don
    See Lessem, Don
Lessem, Don 1951- 182
    Earlier sketches in SATA 97, 155
Lesser, Margaret 1899(?)-1979
    Obituary 22
Lesser, Rika 1953- 53
Lester, Alison 1952- 129
    Earlier sketches in SATA 50, 90
Lester, Helen 1936- 189
    Earlier sketches in SATA 46, 92, 145
Lester, Julius 1939- 157
    Earlier sketches in SATA 12, 74, 112
    See also CLR 41
Lester, Julius Bernard
    See Lester, Julius
Lester, Mike 1955- 131
Le Sueur, Meridel 1900-1996 6
Lethcoe, Jason 191
Le Tord, Bijou 1945- 95
    Earlier sketch in SATA 49
Letts, Billie 1938- 121
Leuck, Laura 1962- 192
    Earlier sketches in SATA 85, 146
Leutscher, Alfred (George) 1913- 23
Levai, Blaise 1919- 39
Levenkron, Steven 1941- 86
Leverich, Kathleen 1948- 103
LeVert, (William) John 1946- 55
Levete, Sarah 1961- 153
Levin, Betty 1927- 137
    Earlier sketches in SATA 19, 84
    See also SAAS 11
Levin, Ira 1929-2007 66
    Obituary 187
Levin, Ira Marvin
    See Levin, Ira
Levin, Ira Marvin
    See Levin, Ira
Levin, Marcia Obrasky 1918- 13
Levin, Meyer 1905-1981 21
    Obituary 27
Levin, Miriam (Ramsfelder) 1962- 97
Levine, Abby 1943- 54
    Brief entry 52
Levine, Betty K(rasne) 1933- 66
Levine, David 1926- 43
    Brief entry 35
Levine, Edna S(imon) 35
Levine, Ellen 1939- 190
Levine, Evan 1962- 77
    Earlier sketch in SATA 74
Levine, Gail Carson 1947- 161
    Earlier sketch in SATA 98
    See also CLR 85
Levine, I(srael) E. 1923-2003 12
    Obituary 146
Levine, Joan Goldman 11
Levine, Joseph 1910- 33
Levine, Marge 1934- 81
Levine, Rhoda 14
Levine, Sarah 1970- 57
Levine, Shar 1953- 131
Levine-Freidus, Gail
    See Provost, Gail Levine
Levinson, Nancy Smiler 1938- 140
    Earlier sketches in SATA 33, 80
Levinson, Riki 99
    Brief entry 49
    Earlier sketch in SATA 52

Levithan, David 1972- 166
Levitin, Sonia 1934- 192
    Autobiography Feature 131
    Earlier sketches in SATA 4, 68, 119, 131
    See also CLR 53
    See also SAAS 2
Levitt, Sidney (Mark) 1947- 68
Levon, O. U.
    See Kesey, Ken
Levoy, Myron 49
    Brief entry 37
Levy, Barrie 112
Levy, Constance 1931- 140
    Earlier sketch in SATA 73
    See also SAAS 22
Levy, Elizabeth 1942- 169
    Earlier sketches in SATA 31, 69, 107
    See also SAAS 18
Levy, Janice 172
Levy, Marilyn 1937- 67
Levy, Nathan 1945- 63
Levy, Robert 1945- 82
Lewees, John
    See Stockton, Francis Richard
Lewin, Betsy 1937- 169
    Autobiography Feature 115
    Earlier sketches in SATA 32, 90
Lewin, Hugh 1939- 72
    Brief entry 40
    See also CLR 9
Lewin, Ted 1935- 165
    Autobiography Feature 115
    Earlier sketches in SATA 21, 76, 119
Lewis, Alice C. 1936- 46
Lewis, Alice Hudson 1895(?)-1971
    Obituary 29
Lewis, Amanda 1955- 80
Lewis, Anthony 1927- 27
Lewis, Anthony 1966- 120
Lewis, Barbara A. 1943- 73
Lewis, Beverly 1949- 80
Lewis, Brenda Ralph 1932- 72
Lewis, Brian 1963- 128
Lewis, Claudia (Louise) 1907-2001 5
Lewis, Clive Staples
    See Lewis, C.S.
Lewis, C.S. 1898-1963 100
    Earlier sketch in SATA 13
    See also CLR 109
Lewis, Cynthia Copeland 1960- 111
Lewis, E. M. 123
    Earlier sketch in SATA 20
Lewis, Earl Bradley
    See Lewis, E.B.
Lewis, E.B. 1956- 168
    Earlier sketches in SATA 93, 124
Lewis, Elizabeth Foreman 1892-1958 121
    See also YABC 2
Lewis, Francine
    See Wells, Helen
Lewis, Hilda (Winifred) 1896-1974
    Obituary 20
Lewis, J. Patrick 1942- 162
    Earlier sketches in SATA 69, 104
Lewis, Jack P(earl) 1919- 65
Lewis, Jean 1924- 61
Lewis, Joseph Anthony
    See Lewis, Anthony
Lewis, Julinda
    See Lewis-Ferguson, Julinda
Lewis, Kevin 173
Lewis, Kim 1951- 136
    Earlier sketch in SATA 84
Lewis, Linda (Joy) 1946- 67
Lewis, Lucia Z.
    See Anderson, Lucia (Lewis)
Lewis, Marjorie 1929- 40
    Brief entry 35
Lewis, Mary (Christianna) 1907(?)-1988 64
    Obituary 56
    See Brand, Christianna

Lewis, Mervyn
    See Frewer, Glyn (M.)
Lewis, Michael
    See Untermeyer, Louis
Lewis, Naomi 144
    Earlier sketch in SATA 76
Lewis, Paeony 1960- 173
Lewis, Paul
    See Gerson, Noel Bertram
Lewis, Richard 1935- 3
Lewis, Rob 1962- 72
Lewis, Roger
    See Zarchy, Harry
Lewis, Shannon
    See Llywelyn, Morgan
Lewis, Shari 1934-1998 35
    Brief entry 30
    Obituary 104
Lewis, Sylvan R.
    See Aronson, Virginia
Lewis, Thomas P(arker) 1936- 27
Lewis, Wendy A. 1966- 150
Lewis-Ferguson, Julinda 1955- 85
Lewison, Wendy Cheyette 177
Lewiton, Mina 1904-1970 2
Lew-Vriethoff, Joanne 186
Lexau, Joan M. 130
    Earlier sketches in SATA 1, 36
Ley, Willy 1906-1969 2
Leydon, Rita (Floden) 1949- 21
Leyland, Eric (Arthur) 1911- 37
L'Hommedieu, Dorothy Keasley
    1885-1961
    Obituary 29
Li, Xiao Jun 1952- 86
Liatsos, Sandra Olson 1942- 103
Libby, Alisa M. 189
Libby, Barbara M. 153
Libby, Bill
    See Libby, William M.
Libby, William M. 1927-1984 5
    Obituary 39
Liberty, Gene 1924- 3
Lichtenheld, Tom 152
Lichtman, Wendy 1946- 193
Liddell, Kenneth 1912-1975 63
Lidz, Jane 120
Lieberman, E(dwin) James 1934- 62
Liebers, Arthur 1913-1984 12
Lieblich, Irene 1923- 22
Liers, Emil E(rnest) 1890-1975 37
Lies, Brian 1963- 190
    Earlier sketch in SATA 131
Liestman, Vicki 1961- 72
Lietz, Gerald S. 1918- 11
Life, Kay (Guinn) 1930- 83
Lifton, Betty Jean 118
    Earlier sketch in SATA 6
Lifton, Robert Jay 1926- 66
Lightburn, Ron 1954- 91
Lightburn, Sandra 1955- 91
Lightner, A. M.
    See Hopf, Alice (Martha) L(ightner)
Lightner, Alice
    See Hopf, Alice (Martha) L(ightner)
Lignell, Lois 1911- 37
Liles, Maurine Walpole 1935- 81
Lillegard, Dee 184
Lilley, Stephen R. 1950- 97
Lilley, Stephen Ray
    See Lilley, Stephen R.
Lillington, Kenneth (James) 1916-1998 39
Lilly, Nate 182
Lilly, Ray
    See Curtis, Richard (Alan)
Lim, John 1932- 43
Liman, Ellen (Fogelson) 1936- 22
Limb, Sue 1946- 158
Limburg, Peter R(ichard) 1929- 13
Lin, Grace 1974- 162
    Earlier sketch in SATA 111

Lincoln, C(harles) Eric 1924-2000 5
Lincoln, Hazel 187
Lincoln, James
    See Bates, Katharine Lee
Lindbergh, Anne 81
    See Sapieyevski, Anne Lindbergh
Lindbergh, Anne Morrow 1906-2001 33
    Obituary 125
Lindbergh, Anne Spencer Morrow
    See Lindbergh, Anne Morrow
Lindbergh, Charles A(ugustus, Jr.)
    1902-1974 33
Lindbergh, Reeve 1945- 163
    Earlier sketch in SATA 116
Lindblom, Steven (Winther) 1946- 94
    Brief entry 39
    Earlier sketch in SATA 42
Linde, Gunnel 1924- 5
Lindenbaum, Pija 1955- 183
    Earlier sketches in SATA 77, 144
Lindgren, Astrid (Anna Emilia Ericsson)
    1907-2002 38
    Obituary 128
    Earlier sketch in SATA 2
    See also CLR 119
Lindgren, Barbro 1937- 120
    Brief entry 46
    Earlier sketch in SATA 63
    See also CLR 86
Lindman, Maj (Jan) 1886-1972 43
Lindop, Edmund 1925- 5
Lindquist, Jennie Dorothea 1899-1977 13
Lindquist, Rowena Cory 1958- 98
Lindquist, Willis 1908-1988 20
Lindsay, Norman Alfred William
    1879-1969 67
    See also CLR 8
Lindsay, (Nicholas) Vachel 1879-1931 40
Lindsey, Kathleen D(orothy) 1949- 153
Line, David
    See Davidson, Lionel
Line, Les 1935- 27
Lines, Kathleen Mary 1902-1988
    Obituary 61
Linfield, Esther 40
Lingard, Joan (Amelia) 1932- 130
    Autobiography Feature 130
    Earlier sketches in SATA 8, 74, 114
    See also CLR 89
    See also SAAS 5
Link, Martin 1934- 28
Linn, Margot
    See Ziefert, Harriet
Linnea, Sharon 1956- 82
Lion, Melissa 1976- 176
Lionni, Leo(nard) 1910-1999 72
    Obituary 118
    Earlier sketch in SATA 8
    See also CLR 71
Lipinsky de Orlov, Lino S. 1908- 22
Lipkind, William 1904-1974 15
Lipman, David 1931-2008 21
Lipman, Matthew 1923- 14
Lippincott, Bertram 1898(?)-1985
    Obituary 42
Lippincott, Gary A. 1953- 119
    Earlier sketch in SATA 73
Lippincott, Joseph W(harton) 1887-1976 17
Lippincott, Sarah Lee 1920- 22
Lippman, Peter J. 1936- 31
Lipsyte, Robert 1938- 161
    Earlier sketches in SATA 5, 68, 113
    See also CLR 76
Lipsyte, Robert Michael
    See Lipsyte, Robert
Lisandrelli, Elaine Slivinski 1951- 94
Lisker, Sonia O. 1933- 44
Lisle, Holly 1960- 98

Lisle, Janet Taylor 1947- 150
    Brief entry 47
    Earlier sketches in SATA 59, 96
    See also SAAS 14
Lisle, Rebecca 162
Lisle, Seward D.
    See Ellis, Edward S(ylvester)
Lisowski, Gabriel 1946- 47
    Brief entry 31
Liss, Howard 1922-1995 4
    Obituary 84
Lisson, Deborah 1941- 110
    Earlier sketch in SATA 71
List, Ilka Katherine 1935- 6
Liston, Robert A. 1927- 5
Litchfield, Ada B(assett) 1916-1999 5
Litchfield, Jo 1973- 116
Lithgow, John (Arthur) 1945- 145
Litowinsky, Olga (Jean) 1936- 26
Littke, Lael J. 1929- 140
    Earlier sketches in SATA 51, 83
Little, A. Edward
    See Klein, Aaron E.
Little, Douglas 1942- 96
Little, (Flora) Jean 1932- 149
    Earlier sketches in SATA 2, 68, 106
    See also CLR 4
    See also SAAS 17
Little, Lessie Jones 1906-1986 60
    Obituary 50
Little, Mary E. 1912-1999 28
Littlechild, George 1958- 85
Littledale, Freya (Lota) 1929-1992 74
    Earlier sketch in SATA 2
Littlefield, Bill 1948- 83
Littlefield, Holly 1963- 97
Littlesugar, Amy 1953- 176
    Earlier sketch in SATA 122
Littleton, Mark R. 1950- 142
    Earlier sketch in SATA 89
Littman, Sarah Darer 175
Litty, Julie 1971- 181
Lively, Penelope 1933- 164
    Earlier sketches in SATA 7, 60, 101
    See also CLR 7
Lively, Penelope Margaret
    See Lively, Penelope
Liverakos, L.A.
    See Gilman, Laura Anne
Liversidge, (Henry) Douglas 1913- 8
Livesey, Claire (Warner) 1927- 127
Livingston, Carole 1941- 42
Livingston, (M.) Irene 1932- 150
Livingston, Myra Cohn 1926-1996 68
    Obituary 92
    Earlier sketch in SATA 5
    See also CLR 7
    See also SAAS 1
Livingston, Richard R(oland) 1922- 8
Livo, Norma J. 1929- 76
Ljungkvist, Laura 180
Llerena Aguirre, Carlos 1952- 19
Llerena Aguirre, Carlos Antonio
    See Llerena Aguirre, Carlos
Llewellyn, Claire 1954- 143
    Earlier sketch in SATA 77
Llewellyn, Grace 1964- 110
Llewellyn, Richard
    See Llewellyn Lloyd, Richard
    Dafydd Vivian
Llewellyn, Sam 1948- 185
    Earlier sketch in SATA 95
Llewellyn Lloyd, Richard Dafydd Vivian
    1906-1983 11
    Obituary 37
    See Llewellyn, Richard
Llewelyn, T. Harcourt
    See Hamilton, Charles (Harold St. John)
Lloyd, Alan
    See Lloyd, A.R.

Lloyd, Alan Richard
    See Lloyd, A.R.
Lloyd, A.R. 1927- *168*
    Earlier sketch in SATA *97*
Lloyd, David
    See Lloyd, David T.
Lloyd, David T. 1954- *167*
Lloyd, E. James
    See James, Elizabeth
Lloyd, Errol 1943- *22*
Lloyd, Hugh
    See Fitzhugh, Percy Keese
Lloyd, James
    See James, Elizabeth
Lloyd, Megan 1958- *189*
    Earlier sketches in SATA *77, 117*
Lloyd, Norman 1909-1980
    Obituary *23*
Lloyd, (Mary) Norris 1908-1993 .... *10*
    Obituary *75*
Lloyd, Sam *183*
Lloyd-Jones, Sally 1960- *179*
Lloyd Webber, Andrew 1948- *56*
    See Webber, Andrew Lloyd
Llywelyn, Morgan 1937- *109*
Lo, Ginnie *165*
Lo, Virginia M.
    See Lo, Ginnie
Lobato, Jose Bento Monteiro 1882-1948 ... *114*
Lobel, Anita (Kempler) 1934- *162*
    Earlier sketches in SATA *6, 55, 96*
Lobel, Arnold (Stark) 1933-1987 .... *55*
    Obituary *54*
    Earlier sketch in SATA *6*
    See also CLR *5*
Lobel, Gillian *181*
Lobsenz, Amelia *12*
Lobsenz, Norman M(itchell) 1919- *6*
Lochak, Michele 1936- *39*
Lochlons, Colin
    See Jackson, C(aary) Paul
Locke, Clinton W. *1*
Locke, Elsie (Violet) 1912-2001 .... *87*
Locke, Lucie 1904-1989 .... *10*
Locke, Robert 1944- *63*
    See Bess, Clayton
Locker, Thomas 1937- *109*
    Earlier sketch in SATA *59*
    See also CLR *14*
Lockhart, E.
    See Jenkins, Emily
Lockridge, Hildegarde (Dolson)
    1908-1981 .... *121*
    See Dolson, Hildegarde
Lockwood, Mary
    See Spelman, Mary
Lodge, Bernard 1933- *107*
    Earlier sketch in SATA *33*
Lodge, Jo 1966- *173*
    Earlier sketch in SATA *112*
Loeb, Jeffrey 1946- *57*
Loeb, Robert H., Jr. 1917- *21*
Loefgren, Ulf 1931- *3*
Loehfelm, Bill 1969- *153*
Loehr, Mallory *184*
Loeper, John J(oseph) 1929- *118*
    Earlier sketch in SATA *10*
Loescher, Ann Dull 1942- *20*
Loescher, Gil(burt Damian) 1945- *20*
Loewer, Jean Jenkins
    See Jenkins, Jean
Loewer, (Henry) Peter 1934- *98*
LoFaro, Jerry 1959- *77*
Lofo
    See Heimann, Rolf
Lofting, Hugh (John) 1886-1947 .... *100*
    Earlier sketch in SATA *15*
    See also CLR *19*
Lofts, Norah (Robinson) 1904-1983 .... *8*
    Obituary *36*

Logan, Jake
    See Knott, William C(ecil, Jr.)
    and Krepps, Robert W(ilson)
    and Pearl, Jacques Bain
    and Riefe, Alan
    and Rifkin, Shepard
    and Smith, Martin Cruz
Logan, Mark
    See Nicole, Christopher (Robin)
Logan, Rochelle 1954- *169*
Logston, Anne 1962- *112*
Logue, Christopher 1926- *23*
Logue, Mary 1952- *161*
    Earlier sketch in SATA *112*
Logue, Mary Louise
    See Logue, Mary
Loh, Morag 1935- *73*
Lohans, Alison 1949- *101*
Loizeaux, William *185*
Loken, Newton Clayton 1919- *26*
Lomas, Steve
    See Brennan, Joseph Lomas
Lomask, Milton (Nachman) 1909-1991 .... *20*
Lombard, Jenny *178*
Lombino, Salvatore
    See Hunter, Evan
LoMonaco, Palmyra 1932- *102*
London, Jack 1876-1916 .... *18*
    See also CLR *108*
    See London, John Griffith
London, Jane
    See Geis, Darlene Stern
London, Jonathan (Paul) 1947- *157*
    Earlier sketches in SATA *74, 113*
Lonergan, (Pauline) Joy (MacLean) 1909- ... *10*
Lonette, Reisie (Dominee) 1924- *43*
Long, Cathryn J. 1946- *89*
Long, Earlene (Roberta) 1938- *50*
Long, Emmett
    See Leonard, Elmore
Long, Ethan 1968(?)- *182*
Long, Helen Beecher *1*
Long, Judith Elaine 1953- *20*
Long, Judy
    See Long, Judith Elaine
Long, Kim 1949- *69*
Long, Laura Mooney 1892-1967
    Obituary *29*
Long, Loren 1966(?)- *188*
    Earlier sketch in SATA *151*
Long, Melinda 1960- *152*
Long, Sylvia 1948- *179*
    Earlier sketch in SATA *120*
Longbeard, Frederick
    See Longyear, Barry B(rookes)
Longfellow, Henry Wadsworth 1807-1882 ... *19*
    See also CLR *99*
Longfellow, Layne (A.) 1937- *102*
Longman, Harold S. 1919- *5*
Longsworth, Polly 1933- *28*
Longtemps, Kenneth 1933- *17*
Longway, A. Hugh
    See Lang, Andrew
Longyear, Barry B(rookes) 1942- *117*
Look, Lenore *180*
Loomans, Diane 1955- *90*
Loomis, Christine *160*
    Earlier sketch in SATA *113*
Loomis, Jennifer A. 1942- *101*
Loomis, Robert D. *5*
Lopez, Angelo (Cayas) 1967- *83*
Lopez, Barry (Holstun) 1945- *67*
Lopez, Jack 1950- *178*
Lopez, Loretta 1963- *190*
Lopez, Lorraine M. 1956- *181*
Lopshire, Robert M(artin) 1927- *6*
Loraine, Connie
    See Reece, Colleen L.
Lorbiecki, Marybeth 1959- *172*
    Earlier sketch in SATA *121*
Lord, Athena V. 1932- *39*

Lord, Beman 1924-1991 .... *5*
    Obituary *69*
Lord, Bette Bao 1938- *58*
Lord, Cynthia *182*
Lord, (Doreen Mildred) Douglas 1904- *12*
Lord, John Vernon 1939- *21*
Lord, Nancy
    See Titus, Eve
Lord, Patricia C. 1927-1988
    Obituary *58*
Lord, Walter 1917-2002 .... *3*
Lorde, Diana
    See Reno, Dawn E(laine)
Lorenz, Albert 1941- *115*
Lorenzini, Carlo 1826-1890 .... *100*
    Earlier sketch in SATA *29*
    See Collodi, Carlo
Lorey, Dean 1967- *193*
Lorimer, Janet 1941- *60*
Loring, Emilie (Baker) 1864(?)-1951 .... *51*
Lorkowski, Thomas V(incent) 1950- *92*
Lorkowski, Tom
    See Lorkowski, Thomas V(incent)
Lorraine, Walter (Henry) 1929- *16*
Lorrimer, Claire
    See Clark, Patricia Denise
Loss, Joan 1933- *11*
Lothrop, Harriet Mulford Stone
    1844-1924 .... *20*
Lottridge, Celia Barker 1936- *157*
    Earlier sketch in SATA *112*
LoTurco, Laura 1963- *84*
Lotz, Wolfgang 1912-1981 .... *65*
Louie, Ai-Ling 1949- *40*
    Brief entry *34*
Louis, Catherine 1963- *186*
Louis, Pat
    See Francis, Dorothy
Louisburgh, Sheila Burnford
    See Burnford, Sheila (Philip Cochrane
    Every)
Louise, Anita
    See Riggio, Anita
Louise, Tina 1934- *191*
Lourie, Helen
    See Storr, Catherine (Cole)
Lourie, Peter 1952- *183*
    Earlier sketches in SATA *82, 142*
Lourie, Peter King
    See Lourie, Peter
Love, Ann 1947- *168*
    Earlier sketch in SATA *79*
Love, D. Anne 1949- *180*
    Earlier sketches in SATA *96, 145*
Love, Douglas 1967- *92*
Love, Judith Dufour
    See Love, Judy
Love, Judy *188*
Love, Katherine (Isabel) 1907- *3*
Love, Kathleen Ann
    See Love, Ann
Love, Sandra (Weller) 1940- *26*
Lovejoy, Jack 1937- *116*
Lovelace, Delos Wheeler 1894-1967 .... *7*
Lovelace, Maud Hart 1892-1980 .... *2*
    Obituary *23*
Lovell, Ingraham
    See Bacon, Josephine Dodge (Daskam)
Loverseed, Amanda (Jane) 1965- *75*
Lovett, Margaret (Rose) 1915- *22*
Low, Alice 1926- *156*
    Earlier sketches in SATA *11, 76*
Low, Elizabeth Hammond 1898-1991 .... *5*
Low, Joseph 1911-2007 .... *14*
Low, Penelope Margaret
    See Lively, Penelope
Low, William *177*
Lowe, Jay, Jr.
    See Loeper, John J(oseph)
Lowell, Pamela *187*

Lowell, Susan 1950- 127
  Earlier sketch in SATA 81
Lowenstein, Dyno 1914-1996 6
Lowenstein, Sallie 1949- 116
Lowery, Linda 1949- 151
  Earlier sketch in SATA 74
Lowitz, Anson C. 1901(?)-1978 18
Lowitz, Sadyebeth Heath 1901-1969 17
Lowndes, Robert A(ugustine) W(ard)
  1916-1998 117
Lowrey, Janette Sebring 1892-1986 43
Lowry, Lois 1937- 177
  Autobiography Feature 127
  Earlier sketches in SATA 23, 70, 111
  See also CLR 72
  See also SAAS 3
Lowry, Lois Hammersberg
  See Lowry, Lois
Lowry, Peter 1953- 7
Lowther, George F. 1913-1975
  Obituary 30
Loyie, Larry 1933- 150
Lozansky, Edward D. 1941- 62
Lozier, Herbert 1915- 26
Lubar, David 1954- 190
  Earlier sketch in SATA 133
Lubell, Cecil 1912-2000 6
Lubell, Winifred (A. Milius) 1914- 6
Lubin, Leonard
  See Lubin, Leonard B.
Lubin, Leonard B. 1943-1994 45
  Brief entry 37
Lubka, S. Ruth 1948- 154
Lubner, Susan 185
Luby, Thia 1954- 124
Lucado, Max (Lee) 1955- 104
Lucas, Cedric 1962- 101
Lucas, E(dward) V(errall) 1868-1938 20
Lucas, Eileen 1956- 113
  Earlier sketch in SATA 76
Lucas, George 1944- 56
Lucas, Jerry 1940- 33
Lucas, Margeaux 186
Lucas, Victoria
  See Plath, Sylvia
Lucashenko, Melissa 1967- 104
Luccarelli, Vincent 1923- 90
Luce, Celia (Geneva Larsen) 1914- 38
Luce, Willard (Ray) 1914-1990 38
Lucht, Irmgard 1937- 82
Luckett, Dave 1951- 167
  Earlier sketch in SATA 106
Luckhardt, Mildred Corell 1898-1990 5
Ludden, Allen (Ellsworth) 1918(?)-1981
  Obituary 27
Ludel, Jacqueline 1945- 64
Ludlow, Geoffrey
  See Meynell, Laurence Walter
Ludlum, Mabel Cleland
  See Widdemer, Mabel Cleland
Ludwig, Helen 33
Ludwig, Lyndell 1923- 63
Ludwig, Trudy 1959- 166
Lueders, Edward (George) 1923- 14
Luenn, Nancy 1954- 79
  Earlier sketch in SATA 51
Lufkin, Raymond H. 1897- 38
Lugard, Flora Louisa Shaw 1852-1929 21
Luger, Harriett Mandelay 1914- 23
Luhrmann, Winifred B(ruce) 1934- 11
Luis, Earlene W. 1929- 11
Luke, Pauline 178
Luke, Pauline R.
  See Luke, Pauline
Lum, Peter
  See Crowe, (Bettina) Peter Lum
Lumry, Amanda (R.) 159
Lund, Deb 157
Lund, Doris Herold 1919- 12
Lung, Chang
  See Jordan, Robert

Lunge-Larsen, Lise 1955- 184
  Earlier sketch in SATA 138
Lunn, Carolyn (Kowalczyk) 1960- 67
Lunn, Janet (Louise Swoboda) 1928- 110
  Earlier sketches in SATA 4, 68
  See also CLR 18
  See also SAAS 12
Lunsford, Cin Forshay
  See Forshay-Lunsford, Cin
Lupica, Mike 177
  See Lupica, Michael
Lupoff, Dick
  See Lupoff, Richard A(llen)
Lupoff, Richard A(llen) 1935- 60
Lurie, Alison 1926- 112
  Earlier sketch in SATA 46
Lurie, Morris 1938- 72
Lussert, Anneliese 1929- 101
Lusted, Marcia Amidon 1962- 143
Lustig, Arnost 1926- 56
Lustig, Loretta 1944- 46
Luthardt, Kevin 1973- 172
Luther, Frank 1905-1980
  Obituary 25
Luther, Rebekah (Lyn) S(tiles) 1960- 90
Luttmann, Gail
  See Damerow, Gail
Luttrell, Guy L. 1938- 22
Luttrell, Ida (Alleene) 1934- 91
  Brief entry 35
  Earlier sketch in SATA 40
Luttrell, William (J. III) 1954- 149
Lutz, John 1939- 180
Lutz, John Thomas
  See Lutz, John
Lutz, Norma Jean 1943- 122
Lutzeier, Elizabeth 1952- 72
Lutzker, Edythe 1904-1991 5
Luxbacher, Irene M. 1970- 153
Luzadder, Patrick 1954- 89
Luzzati, Emanuele 1921-2007 7
Luzzatto, Paola Caboara 1938- 38
Lybbert, Tyler 1970- 88
Lydon, Michael 1942- 11
Lyfick, Warren
  See Reeves, Lawrence F.
Lyle, Katie Letcher 1938- 8
Lynch, Chris 1962- 171
  Earlier sketches in SATA 95, 131
  See also CLR 58
Lynch, Lorenzo 1932- 7
Lynch, Marietta 1947- 29
Lynch, P(atrick) J(ames) 1962- 122
  Earlier sketch in SATA 79
Lynch, Patricia (Nora) 1898-1972 9
Lynds, Dennis 1924-2005 47
  Brief entry 37
Lyne, Alison Davis 188
Lyngseth, Joan
  See Davies, Joan
Lynn, Elizabeth A(nne) 1946- 99
Lynn, Mary
  See Brokamp, Marilyn
Lynn, Patricia
  See Watts, Mabel Pizzey
Lynn, Tracy 175
Lyon, Elinor 1921-2008 6
  Obituary 192
Lyon, Elinor Bruce
  See Lyon, Elinor
Lyon, George Ella 1949- 148
  Autobiography Feature 148
  Earlier sketches in SATA 68, 119
Lyon, Lyman R.
  See de Camp, L(yon) Sprague
Lyons, Dorothy M(arawee) 1907-1997 3
Lyons, Grant 1941- 30
Lyons, Marcus
  See Blish, James (Benjamin)
Lyons, Mary E. 1947- 142
  Earlier sketch in SATA 93

Lyons, Mary Evelyn
  See Lyons, Mary E.
Lystad, Mary (Hanemann) 1928- 11
Lytle, Elizabeth Stewart 1949- 79
Lytle, Robert A. 1944- 119
Lyttle, Richard B(ard) 1927- 23
Lytton, Edward G(eorge) E(arle) L(ytton)
  Bulwer-Lytton Baron 1803-1873 23

M

Ma, Wenhai 1954- 84
Maar, Leonard (Frank, Jr.) 1927- 30
Maartens, Maretha 1945- 73
Maas, Selve -1997 14
Mabie, Grace
  See Mattern, Joanne
Mac
  See MacManus, Seumas
  and Maccari, Ruggero
Macalaster, Elizabeth G. 1951- 115
MacAlister, Katie 159
MacAllan, Andrew
  See Leasor, James
MacAodhagain, Eamon
  See Egan, E(dward) W(elstead)
MacArthur-Onslow, Annette Rosemary
  1933- 26
Macaulay, David (Alexander) 1946- 137
  Brief entry 27
  Earlier sketches in SATA 46, 72
  See also CLR 14
Macaulay, Teresa (E.) 1947- 95
Macavinta, Courtney 176
MacBeth, George (Mann) 1932-1992 4
  Obituary 70
MacBride, Roger Lea 1929-1995 85
MacCarter, Don 1944- 91
MacClintock, Dorcas 1932- 8
MacCready, Robin Merrow 1959(?)- 190
MacCullough, Carolyn 174
MacDonald, Alan 1958- 192
MacDonald, Amy 1951- 156
  Autobiography Feature 156
  Earlier sketches in SATA 76, 136
MacDonald, Anne Elizabeth Campbell Bard
  -1958
  See MacDonald, Betty
MacDonald, Anson
  See Heinlein, Robert A.
MacDonald, Betty 1908-1958
  See YABC 1
  See MacDonald, Anne Elizabeth
  Campbell Bard
Macdonald, Blackie
  See Emrich, Duncan (Black Macdonald)
Macdonald, Caroline 1948- 86
  Obituary 111
  See also CLR 60
Macdonald, Dwight 1906-1982 29
  Obituary 33
MacDonald, George 1824-1905 100
  Earlier sketch in SATA 33
  See also CLR 67
MacDonald, Golden
  See Brown, Margaret Wise
Macdonald, James D. 1954- 165
  Earlier sketches in SATA 81, 114
  See Appleton, Victor
Macdonald, Marcia
  See Hill, Grace Livingston
MacDonald, Margaret Read 1940- 164
  Earlier sketch in SATA 94
Macdonald, Marianne 1934- 113
Macdonald, Mary
  See Gifford, Griselda
Macdonald, Maryann 1947- 189
  Earlier sketch in SATA 72
Macdonald, Shelagh 1937- 25

MacDonald, Suse 1940- *193*
    Brief entry *52*
    Earlier sketches in SATA *54, 109*
Macdonald, Zillah K(atherine)
    1885-1979 .... *11*
MacDonnell, Megan
    See Stevens, Serita
MacDougal, John
    See Blish, James (Benjamin)
Mace, Elisabeth 1933- *27*
Mace, Varian 1938- *49*
MacEwen, Gwendolyn (Margaret)
    1941-1987 .... *50*
    Obituary *55*
Macfarlan, Allan A. 1892-1982 .... *35*
MacFarlane, Iris 1922- *11*
MacGill-Callahan, Sheila 1926-2000 .... *78*
MacGregor, Carol Lynn *153*
MacGregor, Ellen 1906-1954 .... *39*
    Brief entry *27*
MacGregor-Hastie, Roy (Alasdhair
    Niall) 1929- *3*
MacGrory, Yvonne 1948- *142*
Machado, Ana Maria 1941- *150*
MacHale, D.J. 1956- *175*
MacHale, Donald James
    See MacHale, D.J.
Machetanz, Frederick 1908- *34*
Machin Goodall, Daphne (Edith) *37*
Macht, Norman L(ee) 1929- *122*
MacInnes, Helen (Clark) 1907-1985 .... *22*
    Obituary *44*
Macintosh, Brownie 1950- *98*
MacIntyre, Elisabeth 1916- *17*
Mack, L.V.
    See Kimmelman, Burt
Mack, Stan(ley) *17*
Mack, Todd *168*
Mack, Tracy 1968- *183*
    Earlier sketch in SATA *128*
Mackall, Dandi D.
    See Mackall, Dandi Daley
Mackall, Dandi Daley 1949- *182*
    Earlier sketches in SATA *118, 177*
Mackay, Claire 1930- *97*
    Autobiography Feature *124*
    Earlier sketch in SATA *40*
    See also CLR *43*
Mackay, Constance D'Arcy (?)-1966 .... *125*
Mackay, Donald 1914-2005 .... *81*
    Obituary *173*
Mackay, Donald Alexander
    See Mackay, Donald
MacKaye, Percy (Wallace) 1875-1956 .... *32*
Mackel, Kathryn 1950- *162*
Mackel, Kathy
    See Mackel, Kathryn
MacKellar, William 1914- *4*
Macken, Walter 1915-1967 .... *36*
MacKenzie, Jill (Kelly) 1947- *75*
Mackey, Ernan
    See McInerny, Ralph
Mackey, Weezie Kerr *188*
Mackie, Maron
    See McNeely, Jeannette
Mackin, Edward
    See McInerny, Ralph
MacKinnon, Bernie 1957- *69*
MacKinnon Groomer, Vera 1915- *57*
MacKinstry, Elizabeth 1879-1956 .... *42*
Mackler, Carolyn 1973- *156*
MacLachlan, Patricia 1938- *168*
    Brief entry *42*
    Earlier sketches in SATA *62, 107*
    See also CLR *14*
MacLane, Jack
    See Crider, Bill
MacLean, Alistair (Stuart) 1922(?)-1987 ...... *23*
    Obituary *50*
Maclean, Art
    See Shirreffs, Gordon D(onald)

MacLean, Christine Kole *177*
MacLean, Glynne 1964- *150*
MacLeod, Beatrice 1910- *162*
    Earlier sketch in SATA *10*
MacLeod, Beatrice Beach
    See MacLeod, Beatrice
MacLeod, Charlotte (Matilda) 1922-2005 .... *28*
    Obituary *160*
MacLeod, Doug 1959- *60*
MacLeod, Elizabeth *184*
    Earlier sketch in SATA *158*
MacLeod, Ellen Jane (Anderson) 1916- *14*
MacManus, James
    See MacManus, Seumas
MacManus, Seumas 1869-1960 .... *25*
MacMaster, Eve (Ruth) B(owers) 1942- *46*
MacMillan, Annabelle
    See Quick, Annabelle
MacMillan, Dianne M(arie) 1943- *125*
    Earlier sketch in SATA *84*
Macnaughton, Tina *182*
Macneill, Janet
    See McNeely, Jeannette
MacPeek, Walter G. 1902-1973 .... *4*
    Obituary *25*
MacPhail, Catherine 1946- *130*
MacPherson, Margaret 1908-2001 .... *9*
    See also SAAS *4*
MacPherson, Thomas George 1915-1976
    Obituary *30*
MacPherson, Winnie 1930- *107*
MacRae, Tom 1980- *181*
Macrae, Travis
    See Feagles, Anita M(acRae)
MacRaois, Cormac 1944- *72*
Macumber, Mari
    See Sandoz, Mari(e Susette)
Macy, Sue 1954- *134*
    Earlier sketch in SATA *88*
Madaras, Lynda 1947- *151*
Madden, Don 1927- *3*
Madden, Kerry 1961- *168*
Madden-Lunsford, Kerry
    See Madden, Kerry
Maddern, Eric 1950- *166*
Maddigan, Beth 1967- *174*
Maddison, Angela Mary 1923- *10*
    See Banner, Angela
Maddock, Reginald (Bertram) 1912-1994 .... *15*
Madenski, Melissa (Ann) 1949- *77*
Madian, Jon 1941- *9*
Madison, Alan *182*
Madison, Arnold 1937- *6*
Madison, Winifred *5*
Madonna 1958- *149*
Madsen, Gunnar *171*
Madsen, Ross Martin 1946- *82*
Madsen, Susan A. 1954- *90*
Madsen, Susan Arrington
    See Madsen, Susan A.
Maestro, Betsy (Crippen) 1944- *106*
    Brief entry *30*
    Earlier sketch in SATA *59*
    See also CLR *45*
Maestro, Giulio 1942- *106*
    Earlier sketches in SATA *8, 59*
    See also CLR *45*
Maeterlinck, Maurice 1862-1949 .... *66*
Magee, Doug 1947- *78*
Magee, Wes 1939- *64*
Maggio, Rosalie 1943- *69*
Magid, Ken(neth Marshall) *65*
Magnus, Erica 1946- *77*
Magoon, Scott *182*
Magorian, James 1942- *92*
    Earlier sketch in SATA *32*
Magorian, Michelle 1947- *128*
    Earlier sketch in SATA *67*
Magorian, Michelle Jane
    See Magorian, Michelle
Magovern, Peg *103*

Maguire, Anne
    See Nearing, Penny
Maguire, Gregory 1954- *129*
    Earlier sketches in SATA *28, 84*
    See also SAAS *22*
Maguire, Gregory Peter
    See Maguire, Gregory
Maguire, Jack 1920-2000 .... *74*
Maguire, Jesse
    See Smith, Sherwood
Maguire, Jessie
    See Smith, Sherwood
Maher, Ramona 1934- *13*
Mahlqvist, (Karl) Stefan *30*
    See Maehlqvist, (Karl) Stefan
Mahon, Julia C(unha) 1916- *11*
Mahood, Kenneth 1930- *24*
Mahy, Margaret 1936- *171*
    Earlier sketches in SATA *14, 69, 119*
    See also CLR *78*
Mahy, Margaret May
    See Mahy, Margaret
Maiden, Cecil (Edward) 1902-1981 .... *52*
Maidoff, Ilka
    See List, Ilka Katherine
Maifair, Linda Lee 1947- *83*
Maik, Henri
    See Hecht, Henri Joseph
Maillu, David G(ian) 1939- *111*
Maine, Trevor
    See Catherall, Arthur
Mains, Randolph P. 1946- *80*
Maione, Heather *189*
Maiorano, Robert 1946- *43*
Maisner, Heather 1947- *89*
Maison, Della
    See Katz, Bobbi
Maitland, Antony Jasper 1935- *25*
Maitland, Barbara *102*
Mai-Wyss, Tatjana 1972- *187*
Major, Kevin (Gerald) 1949- *134*
    Earlier sketches in SATA *32, 82*
    See also CLR *11*
Majure, Janet 1954- *96*
Makhijani, Pooja *188*
Makie, Pam 1943- *37*
Makowski, Silk
    See Makowski, Silvia Ann
Makowski, Silvia Ann 1940- *101*
Malam, John 1957- *152*
    Earlier sketch in SATA *89*
Malcolm, Dan
    See Silverberg, Robert
Malcolm, Jahnna N.
    See Beecham, Jahnna
Malcolmson, Anne
    See von Storch, Anne B.
Malcolmson, David 1899-1978 .... *6*
Maletta, Dr. Arlene
    See Feltenstein, Arlene (H.)
Mali, Jane Lawrence 1937-1995 .... *51*
    Brief entry *44*
    Obituary *86*
Malkin, Nina 1959(?)- *179*
Mallett, Jerry J. 1939- *76*
Mallory, Kenneth 1945- *185*
    Earlier sketch in SATA *128*
Mallowan, Agatha Christie
    See Christie, Agatha (Mary Clarissa)
Malmberg, Carl 1904-1979 .... *9*
Malmgren, Dallin 1949- *65*
Malo, John W. 1911-2000 .... *4*
Malone, James Hiram 1930- *84*
Malone, Nola Langner 1930-2003
    Obituary *151*
    See Langner, Nola
Malone, Patricia 1932- *155*
Malone, Peter 1953- *191*
Maloney, Pat
    See Markun, Patricia Maloney

Malory, Sir Thomas 1410(?)-1471(?) *59*
  Brief entry *33*
Maltese, Michael 1909(?)-1981
  Obituary *24*
Malvasi, Meg Greene *143*
Malvern, Corinne 1905-1956 .... *34*
Malvern, Gladys (?)-1962 .... *23*
Mama G.
  See Davis, Grania
Mammano, Julie (Lynn) 1962- *107*
Mamonova, Tatyana 1943- *93*
Manchel, Frank 1935- *10*
Manchester, William (Raymond)
  1922-2004 .... *65*
Mandel, Brett H. 1969- *108*
Mandel, Peter 1957- *87*
Mandel, Sally (Elizabeth) 1944- *64*
Mandell, Muriel (Hortense Levin) 1921- *63*
Manders, John 1957- *175*
Manes, Stephen 1949- *99*
  Brief entry *40*
  Earlier sketch in SATA *42*
Manfred, Frederick (Feikema) 1912-1994 .... *30*
Mangin, Marie France 1940- *59*
Mangione, Jerre *6*
  Obituary *104*
  See Mangione, Gerlando
Mango, Karin N. 1936- *52*
Mangurian, David 1938- *14*
Mania, Cathy 1950- *102*
Mania, Robert 1952- *102*
Mania, Robert C., Jr.
  See Mania, Robert
Maniatty, Taramesha 1978- *92*
Maniscalco, Joseph 1926- *10*
Manley, Deborah 1932- *28*
Manley, Seon 1921- *15*
  See also CLR *3*
  See also SAAS *2*
Mann, Elizabeth 1948- *153*
Mann, Josephine
  See Pullein-Thompson, Josephine
  (Mary Wedderburn)
Mann, Kenny 1946- *91*
Mann, Pamela 1946- *91*
Mann, Patrick
  See Waller, Leslie
Mann, Peggy *6*
  See Houlton, Peggy Mann
Mannetti, Lisa 1953- *57*
  Brief entry *51*
Mannheim, Grete (Salomon) 1909-1986 ...... *10*
Manniche, Lise 1943- *31*
Manning, Jane K. *185*
Manning, Mick 1959- *176*
Manning, Rosemary (Joy) 1911-1988 .... *10*
  See Davys, Sarah
  and Voyle, Mary
Manning, Sarra *162*
Manning-Sanders, Ruth (Vernon)
  1895(?)-1988 .... *73*
  Obituary *57*
  Earlier sketch in SATA *15*
Mannion, Diane
  See Paterson, Diane
Mannis, Celeste Davidson *173*
Mannon, Warwick
  See Hopkins, (Hector) Kenneth
Mansir, A. Richard 1932- *170*
Manson, Ainslie Kertland 1938- *115*
Manson, Beverlie 1945- *57*
  Brief entry *44*
Manthorpe, Helen 1958- *122*
Mantinband, Gerda (B.) 1917- *74*
Manton, Jo
  See Gittings, Jo (Grenville) Manton
Manuel, Lynn 1948- *179*
  Earlier sketch in SATA *99*
Manushkin, Fran 1942- *166*
  Earlier sketches in SATA *7, 54, 93*

Manushkin, Frances
  See Manushkin, Fran
Man Without a Spleen, A
  See Chekhov, Anton (Pavlovich)
Manzano, Sonia 1950- *167*
Mapes, Mary A.
  See Ellison, Virginia H(owell)
Maple, Marilyn 1931- *80*
Mappin, Strephyn 1956- *109*
Mara, Barney
  See Roth, Arthur J(oseph)
Mara, Jeanette
  See Cebulash, Mel
Marais, Josef 1905-1978
  Obituary *24*
Marasmus, Seymour
  See Rivoli, Mario
Marbach, Ethel
  See Pochocki, Ethel (Frances)
Marcal, Annette B.
  See Callaway, Bernice (Anne)
Marcelino
  See Agnew, Edith J(osephine)
Marcellino, Fred 1939-2001 .... *118*
  Obituary *127*
  Earlier sketch in SATA *68*
March, Carl
  See Fleischman, Sid
Marchant, Bessie 1862-1941
  See YABC *2*
Marchant, Catherine
  See Cookson, Catherine (McMullen)
Marcher, Marion Walden 1890-1987 .... *10*
Marchesi, Stephen 1951- *114*
Marchesi, Steve
  See Marchesi, Stephen
  and Older, Effin
  and Older, Jules
Marchetta, Melina 1965- *170*
Marciano, John Bemelmans 1970- *167*
  Earlier sketch in SATA *118*
  See also CLR *93*
Marco, Lou
  See Gottfried, Theodore Mark
Marcus, Leonard S. 1950- *187*
  Earlier sketch in SATA *133*
Marcus, Paul 1953- *82*
Marcus, Rebecca B(rian) 1907- *9*
Marcuse, Aida E. 1934- *89*
Marek, Margot L. 1934(?)-1987
  Obituary *54*
Margaret, Karla
  See Andersdatter, Karla M(argaret)
Margolin, Harriet
  See Ziefert, Harriet
Margolis, Jeffrey A. 1948- *108*
Margolis, Leslie *187*
Margolis, Richard J(ules) 1929-1991 .... *86*
  Obituary *67*
  Earlier sketch in SATA *4*
Margolis, Vivienne 1922- *46*
Mariana
  See Foster, Marian Curtis
Marie, Geraldine 1949- *61*
Mariner, Scott
  See Pohl, Frederik
Marino, Dorothy Bronson 1912- *14*
Marino, Jan 1936- *114*
Marino, Nick
  See Deming, Richard
Marino, Peter 1960- *179*
Mario, Anna
  See Odgers, Sally Farrell
Marion, Henry
  See del Rey, Lester
Maris, Ron *71*
  Brief entry *45*
Mark, Jan 1943-2006 .... *164*
  Obituary *173*
  Earlier sketches in SATA *22, 69, 114*
  See also CLR *11*

Mark, Janet Marjorie
  See Mark, Jan
Mark, Joan T. 1937- *122*
Mark, Pauline (Dahlin) 1913-1997 .... *14*
Mark, Polly
  See Mark, Pauline (Dahlin)
Mark, Ted
  See Gottfried, Theodore Mark
Markel, Michelle *169*
Marker, Sherry 1941- *76*
Markert, Jennifer 1965- *83*
Markert, Jenny
  See Markert, Jennifer
Markham, Lynne 1947- *102*
Markham, Marion M. 1929- *60*
Markham, Wendy
  See Staub, Wendy Corsi
Markins, W. S.
  See Jenkins, Marie M(agdalen)
Markle, Sandra L. 1946- *185*
  Brief entry *41*
  Earlier sketches in SATA *57, 92, 148*
Markle, Sandra Lee
  See Markle, Sandra L.
Marko, Katherine D(olores) *28*
Markoosie
  See Patsauq, Markoosie
Marks, Alan 1957- *187*
  Earlier sketches in SATA *77, 151*
Marks, Burton 1930- *47*
  Brief entry *43*
Marks, Graham *158*
Marks, Hannah K.
  See Trivelpiece, Laurel
Marks, J.
  See Highwater, Jamake (Mamake)
Marks, J(ames) M(acdonald) 1921- *13*
Marks, Laurie J. 1957- *68*
Marks, Margaret L. 1911(?)-1980
  Obituary *23*
Marks, Mickey Klar -1986 .... *12*
Marks, Peter
  See Smith, Robert Kimmel
Marks, Rita 1938- *47*
Marks, Stan(ley) *14*
Marks-Highwater, J.
  See Highwater, Jamake (Mamake)
Markun, Patricia Maloney 1924- *15*
Markusen, Bruce (Stanley Rodriguez)
  1965- *141*
Marley, Louise 1952- *173*
  Earlier sketch in SATA *120*
Marlin, Hilda
  See Van Stockum, Hilda
Marlow, Max
  See Nicole, Christopher (Robin)
Marlow, Susan K. 1953- *178*
Marlowe, Amy Bell *67*
  Earlier sketch in SATA *1*
Marlowe, Jack
  See Deary, Terry
Marney, Dean 1952- *90*
Marokvia, Artur 1909- *31*
Marokvia, Mireille 1908-2008 .... *5*
Marokvia, Mireille Journet
  See Marokvia, Mireille
Marol, Jean-Claude 1946- *125*
Marr, John S(tuart) 1940- *48*
Marr, Melissa 1972- *189*
Marric, J. J.
  See Butler, William (Arthur) Vivian
  and Creasey, John
Marrin, Albert 1936- *193*
  Brief entry *43*
  Earlier sketches in SATA *53, 90, 126*
  See also CLR *53*
Marriott, Alice Lee 1910-1992 .... *31*
  Obituary *71*
Marriott, Janice 1946- *134*
Marriott, Pat(ricia) 1920- *35*

Marroquin, Patricio
　See Markun, Patricia Maloney
Mars, W. T.
　See Mars, Witold Tadeusz J.
Mars, Witold Tadeusz J. 1912-1985 3
Marsden, Carolyn 1950- 175
　Earlier sketch in SATA *140*
Marsden, John 1950- 146
　Earlier sketches in SATA *66, 97*
　See also CLR *34*
　See also SAAS *22*
Marsh, Carole 1946- 127
Marsh, Dave 1950- 66
Marsh, J. E.
　See Marshall, Evelyn
Marsh, James 1946- 73
Marsh, Jean
　See Marshall, Evelyn
Marsh, Joan F. 1923- 83
Marsh, Paul
　See Hopkins, (Hector) Kenneth
Marsh, Valerie 1954- 89
Marshall, Anthony D(ryden) 1924- 18
Marshall, Bonnie C. 1941- 141
　Earlier sketch in SATA *18*
Marshall, Bridget M(ary) 1974- 103
Marshall, (Sarah) Catherine (Wood)
　1914-1983 2
　Obituary 34
Marshall, Douglas
　See McClintock, Marshall
Marshall, Edmund
　See Hopkins, (Hector) Kenneth
Marshall, Edward
　See Marshall, James
Marshall, Evelyn 1897-1991 11
Marshall, Felicity 1950- 116
Marshall, Garry 1934- 60
Marshall, H. H.
　See Jahn, (Joseph) Michael
Marshall, James 1942-1992 75
　Earlier sketches in SATA *6, 51*
　See also CLR *21*
Marshall, James Edward
　See Marshall, James
Marshall, James Vance
　See Payne, Donald Gordon
Marshall, Janet (Perry) 1938- 97
Marshall, Jeff
　See Laycock, George (Edwin)
Marshall, Kim
　See Marshall, Michael (Kimbrough)
Marshall, Michael (Kimbrough) 1948- 37
Marshall, Percy
　See Young, Percy M(arshall)
Marshall, S(amuel) L(yman) A(twood)
　1900-1977 21
Marsoli, Lisa Ann 1958- 101
　Brief entry 53
Marsten, Richard
　See Hunter, Evan
Marston, Elsa 1933- 156
Marston, Hope Irvin 1935- 127
　Earlier sketch in SATA *31*
Marszalek, John F. 1939- 167
Marszalek, John Francis, Jr.
　See Marszalek, John F.
Marszalek, John Francis 1939-
　See Marszalek, John F.
Martchenko, Michael 1942- 154
　Earlier sketches in SATA *50, 95*
Martel, Aimee
　See Thurlo, Aimee
　and Thurlo, David
Martel, Suzanne 1924- 99
Martignoni, Margaret E. 1908(?)-1974
　Obituary 27
Martin, Ann M. 1955- 192
　Brief entry 41
　Earlier sketches in SATA *44, 70, 126*
　See also CLR *32*

Martin, Bill, Jr. 67
　Brief entry 40
　See also CLR *97*
　See Martin, William Ivan, Jr.
Martin, Charles E(lmer) 70
　Earlier sketch in SATA *69*
　See Mastrangelo, Charles E(lmer)
Martin, Christopher
　See Hoyt, Edwin P(almer), Jr.
Martin, Claire 1933- 76
Martin, David Stone 1913-1992 39
Martin, Donald
　See Honig, Donald
Martin, Dorothy 1921- 47
Martin, Eugene 1
Martin, Eva M. 1939- 65
Martin, Frances M(cEntee) 1906-1998 36
Martin, Francesca 1947- 101
Martin, Fred 1948- 119
Martin, Fredric
　See Christopher, Matt(hew Frederick)
Martin, George Raymond Richard
　See Martin, George R.R.
Martin, George R.R. 1948- 118
Martin, J(ohn) P(ercival) 1880(?)-1966 15
Martin, Jacqueline Briggs 1945- 188
　Earlier sketches in SATA *98, 149*
Martin, Jane Read 1957- 84
Martin, Jeremy
　See Levin, Marcia Obrasky
Martin, Les
　See Schulman, L(ester) M(artin)
Martin, Linda 1961- 82
Martin, Lynne 1923- 21
Martin, Marcia
　See Levin, Marcia Obrasky
Martin, Marvin 1926- 126
Martin, Melanie
　See Pellowski, Michael (Joseph)
Martin, Nancy
　See Salmon, Annie Elizabeth
Martin, Patricia Miles 1899-1986 43
　Obituary 48
　Earlier sketch in SATA *1*
Martin, Peter
　See Chaundler, Christine
Martin, Rafe 1946- 175
Martin, Rene 1891-1977 42
　Obituary 20
Martin, Rupert (Claude) 1905- 31
Martin, S. R.
　See Mappin, Strephyn
Martin, Stefan 1936- 32
Martin, Vicky
　See Storey, Victoria Carolyn
Martin, Webber
　See Silverberg, Robert
Martin, Wendy
　See Martini, Teri
Martin, William Ivan, Jr. 1916-2004 145
　Earlier sketch in SATA *40*
　See Martin, Bill, Jr.
Martineau, Diane 1940- 178
Martineau, Harriet 1802-1876
　See YABC *2*
Martinet, Jeanne 1958- 80
Martinez, Agnes 167
Martinez, Arturo O. 1933- 192
Martinez, Ed(ward) 1954- 98
Martinez, Elizabeth Coonrod 1954- 85
Martinez, Victor 1954- 95
Martini, Teri 1930- 3
Martini, Therese
　See Martini, Teri
Martino, Alfred C. 1964- 174
Martinson, Janis
　See Herbert, Janis
Marton, Jirina 1946- 144
　Earlier sketch in SATA *95*
Marton, Pierre
　See Stone, Peter

Martson, Del
　See Lupoff, Richard A(llen)
Martyr, Paula (Jane) 57
　See Lawford, Paula Jane
Maruki, Toshi 1912-2000 112
　See also CLR *19*
Marvin, Isabel R(idout) 1924- 84
Marx, Patricia Windschill 1948- 160
　Earlier sketch in SATA *112*
Marx, Robert F(rank) 1936- 24
Marx, Trish
　See Marx, Patricia Windschill
Marzani, Carl (Aldo) 1912-1994 12
Marzollo, Jean 1942- 190
　Autobiography Feature 190
　Earlier sketches in SATA *29, 77, 130*
　See also SAAS *15*
Masefield, John (Edward) 1878-1967 19
Masoff, Joy 1951- 118
Mason, Adrienne 1962- 163
Mason, Cherie 170
Mason, Edwin A. 1905-1979
　Obituary 32
Mason, Ernst
　See Pohl, Frederik
Mason, F(rancis) van Wyck 1901-1978 3
　Obituary 26
Mason, Frank W.
　See Mason, F(rancis) van Wyck
Mason, George Frederick 1904-2000 14
Mason, Miriam E(vangeline) 1900-1973 2
　Obituary 26
Mason, Simon 1962- 178
Mason, Tally
　See Derleth, August (William)
Mason, Van Wyck
　See Mason, F(rancis) van Wyck
Mass, Wendy 1967- 158
Mass, William
　See Gibson, William
Masselman, George 1897-1971 19
Massie, Dianne Redfield 1938- 125
　Earlier sketch in SATA *16*
Massie, Elizabeth 108
Masson, Sophie 1959- 179
　Earlier sketch in SATA *133*
Masters, Anthony (Richard) 1940-2003 112
　Obituary 145
Masters, Kelly R(ay) 1897-1987 3
Masters, Mildred 1932- 42
Masters, William
　See Cousins, Margaret
Masters, Zeke
　See Bensen, Donald R.
　and Goulart, Ron(ald Joseph)
Matas, Carol 1949- 93
　Autobiography Feature 112
　See also CLR *52*
Matchette, Katharine E. 1941- 38
Math, Irwin 1940- 42
Mathabane, Mark 1960- 123
Mather, Kirtley F(letcher) 1888-1978 65
Mathers, Petra 1945- 176
　Earlier sketch in SATA *119*
　See also CLR *76*
Matheson, Richard (Christian) 1953- 119
Matheson, Shirlee Smith 1942- 155
Mathews, Ellie 1946(?)- 193
Mathews, Janet 1914-1992 41
Mathews, Judith 80
　See Goldberger, Judith M.
Mathews, Louise
　See Tooke, Louise Mathews
Mathiesen, Egon 1907-1976
　Obituary 28
Mathieu, Joe 1949- 185
　Brief entry 36
　Earlier sketches in SATA *43, 94*
Mathieu, Joseph P.
　See Mathieu, Joe

Mathis, Sharon Bell 1937- 58
  Earlier sketch in SATA 7
  See also CLR 3
  See also SAAS 3
Matlin, Marlee 1965- 181
Matlin, Marlee Beth
  See Matlin, Marlee
Matloff, Gregory 1945- 73
Matott, Justin 1961- 109
Matranga, Frances Carfi 1922- 78
Matray, James I. 1948- 161
Matray, James Irving
  See Matray, James I.
Matson, Emerson N(els) 1926- 12
Matsui, Tadashi 1926- 8
Matsuno, Masako 6
  See Kobayashi, Masako Matsuno
Matsuoka, Mei 1981- 192
Matte, (Encarnacion) L'Enc 1936- 22
Mattern, Joanne 1963- 122
Matthesson, Jenny 180
Matthews, Aline
  See De Wire, Elinor
Matthews, Andrew 1948- 138
Matthews, Caitlin 1952- 122
Matthews, Downs 1925- 71
Matthews, Ellen
  See Bache, Ellyn
Matthews, Ellen 1950- 28
Matthews, Harold Downs
  See Matthews, Downs
Matthews, Jacklyn Meek
  See Meek, Jacklyn O'Hanlon
Matthews, John (Kentigern) 1948- 116
Matthews, Laura S.
  See Matthews, L.S.
Matthews, Liz
  See Pellowski, Michael (Joseph)
Matthews, L.S. 183
Matthews, Morgan
  See Pellowski, Michael (Joseph)
Matthews, Nicola
  See Browne, N.M.
Matthews, Patricia 1927-2006 28
Matthews, Patricia Anne
  See Matthews, Patricia
Matthews, Tina 1961- 190
Matthews, Tom L.
  See Lalicki, Tom
Matthews, William Henry III 1919- 45
  Brief entry 28
Matthiessen, Peter 1927- 27
Mattingley, Christobel (Rosemary) 1931- 85
  Earlier sketch in SATA 37
  See also CLR 24
  See also SAAS 18
Matulay, Laszlo 1912- 43
Matus, Greta 1938- 12
Maugham, W. S.
  See Maugham, W(illiam) Somerset
Maugham, W(illiam) Somerset 1874-1965 .. 54
Maugham, William Somerset
  See Maugham, W(illiam) Somerset
Maurer, Diane Philippoff
  See Maurer-Mathison, Diane V(ogel)
Maurer, Diane Vogel
  See Maurer-Mathison, Diane V(ogel)
Maurer-Mathison, Diane V(ogel) 1944- 89
Mauser, Pat Rhoads
  See McCord, Patricia
Mauser, Patricia Rhoads 37
  See McCord, Patricia
Maves, Mary Carolyn 1916- 10
Maves, Paul B(enjamin) 1913-1994 10
Mavor, Salley 1955- 125
Mawicke, Tran 1911- 15
Max 1906-1989
  See Diop, Birago (Ismael)
Max, Peter 1939- 45
Maxon, Anne
  See Best, (Evangel) Allena Champlin

Maxwell, Arthur S. 1896-1970 11
Maxwell, Edith 1923- 7
Maxwell, Gavin 1914-1969 65
Maxwell, Katie
  See MacAlister, Katie
Maxwell, William (Keepers, Jr.) 1908-2000
  Obituary 128
Maxwell-Hyslop, Miranda 1968- 154
May, Charles Paul 1920- 4
May, Elaine Tyler 1947- 120
May, J. C.
  See May, Julian
May, Julian 1931- 11
May, Robert Lewis 1905-1976
  Obituary 27
May, Robert Stephen 1929-1996 46
May, Robin
  See May, Robert Stephen
Mayall, Beth 171
Mayberry, Florence V(irginia) Wilson 10
Maybury, Richard J. 1946- 72
Maybury, Rick
  See Maybury, Richard J.
Mayer, Agatha
  See Maher, Ramona
Mayer, Albert Ignatius, Jr. 1906-1994
  Obituary 29
Mayer, Ann M(argaret) 1938- 14
Mayer, Danuta 1958- 117
Mayer, Jane Rothschild 1903-2001 38
Mayer, Marianna 1945- 132
  Earlier sketches in SATA 32, 83
Mayer, Mercer 1943- 137
  Earlier sketches in SATA 16, 32, 73, 129
  See also CLR 11
Mayerson, Charlotte Leon 36
Mayerson, Evelyn Wilde 1935- 55
Mayfield, Katherine 1958- 118
Mayfield, Sue 1963- 146
  Earlier sketch in SATA 72
Mayhar, Ardath 1930- 38
Mayhew, James (John) 1964- 149
  Earlier sketch in SATA 85
Maynard, Olga 1920- 40
Mayne, William (James Carter) 1928- 122
  Earlier sketches in SATA 6, 68
  See also CLR 123
  See also SAAS 11
Maynes, J. O. Rocky, Jr.
  See Maynes, J. Oscar, Jr.
Maynes, J. Oscar, Jr. 1929- 38
Mayo, Gretchen Will 1936- 163
  Earlier sketch in SATA 84
Mayo, Margaret 1935- 165
  Earlier sketches in SATA 38, 96
Mayo, Margaret Mary
  See Mayo, Margaret
Mays, Lucinda L(a Bella) 1924- 49
Mays, (Lewis) Victor (Jr.) 1927- 5
Mazer, Anne 1953- 192
  Earlier sketches in SATA 67, 105
Mazer, Harry 1925- 167
  Earlier sketches in SATA 31, 67, 105
  See also CLR 16
  See also SAAS 11
Mazer, Norma Fox 1931- 168
  Earlier sketches in SATA 24, 67, 105
  See also CLR 23
  See also SAAS 1
Mazille, Capucine 1953- 96
Mazza, Adriana 1928- 19
Mazzio, Joann 1926- 74
Mbugua, Kioi Wa 1962- 83
McAfee, Carol 1955- 81
McAllister, Amanda
  See Dowdell, Dorothy (Florence) Karns
  and Hager, Jean
  and Meaker, Eloise
McAllister, Angela 182
McAllister, Margaret I. 1956- 169
  Earlier sketch in SATA 117

McAllister, M.I.
  See McAllister, Margaret I.
McArthur, Nancy 96
McAvoy, Jim 1972- 142
McBain, Ed
  See Hunter, Evan
McBain, Georgina 189
McBratney, Sam 1943- 164
  Earlier sketch in SATA 89
  See also CLR 44
McBrier, Michael
  See Older, Effin
  and Older, Jules
McCafferty, Jim 1954- 84
McCaffery, Janet 1936- 38
McCaffrey, Anne 1926- 152
  Autobiography Feature 152
  Earlier sketches in SATA 8, 70, 116
  See also CLR 130
  See also SAAS 11
McCaffrey, Anne Inez
  See McCaffrey, Anne
McCaffrey, Mary
  See Szudek, Agnes S(usan) P(hilomena)
McCain, Becky Ray 1954- 138
McCain, Murray (David, Jr.) 1926-1981 7
  Obituary 29
McCall, Edith (Sansom) 1911- 6
McCall, Virginia Nielsen 1909-2000 13
McCall, Wendell
  See Pearson, Ridley
McCallum, Phyllis
  See Koch, Phyllis (Mae) McCallum
McCallum, Stephen 1960- 91
McCampbell, Darlene Z. 1942- 83
McCann, Edson
  See del Rey, Lester
  and Pohl, Frederik
McCann, Gerald 1916- 41
McCann, Helen 1948- 75
McCannon, Dindga 41
McCants, William D. 1961- 82
McCarter, Neely Dixon 1929- 47
McCarthy, Agnes 1933- 4
McCarthy, Colin (John) 1951- 77
McCarthy, Meghan 168
McCarthy, Ralph F. 1950- 139
McCarthy-Tucker, Sherri N. 1958- 83
McCarty, Peter 1966- 182
McCarty, Rega Kramer 1904-1986 10
McCaslin, Nellie 1914-2005 12
McCaughrean, Geraldine 1951- 173
  Earlier sketches in SATA 87, 139
  See also CLR 38
McCaughren, Tom 1936- 75
McCauley, Adam 1965- 128
McCay, (Zenas) Winsor 1869-1934 134
  Earlier sketch in SATA 41
McClafferty, Carla Killough 1958- 137
McClary, Jane Stevenson 1919-1990
  Obituary 64
McCleery, Patsy R. 1925- 133
  Earlier sketch in SATA 88
McClintock, Barbara 1955- 146
  Earlier sketches in SATA 57, 95
McClintock, Marshall 1906-1967 3
McClintock, May Garelick
  See Garelick, May
McClintock, Mike
  See McClintock, Marshall
McClintock, Norah 178
McClintock, Theodore 1902-1971 14
McClinton, Leon 1933- 11
McCloskey, Kevin 1951- 79
McCloskey, (John) Robert 1914-2003 100
  Obituary 146
  Earlier sketches in SATA 2, 39
  See also CLR 7
McCloy, James F(loyd) 1941- 59

McClung, Robert M(arshall) 1916- 135
  Earlier sketches in SATA 2, 68
  See also CLR 11
  See also SAAS 15
McClure, Gillian Mary 1948- 31
McColley, Kevin 1961- 80
  See also SAAS 23
McConduit, Denise Walter 1950- 89
McConnell, James Douglas Rutherford
  1915-1988 40
  Obituary 56
McCord, Anne 1942- 41
McCord, David (Thompson Watson)
  1897-1997 18
  Obituary 96
  See also CLR 9
McCord, Jean 1924- 34
McCord, Pat Mauser
  See McCord, Patricia
McCord, Patricia 1943- 159
  See Mauser, Patricia Rhoads
McCord, Patricia Sue Rhoads Mauser
  See McCord, Patricia
McCormick, Brooks
  See Adams, William Taylor
McCormick, Dell J. 1892-1949 19
McCormick, (George) Donald (King)
  1911-1998 14
McCormick, Edith (Joan) 1934- 30
McCormick, Kimberly A. 1960- 153
McCormick, Patricia 1956- 181
  Earlier sketch in SATA 128
McCourt, Edward (Alexander) 1907-1972
  Obituary 28
McCourt, Lisa 1964- 159
  Earlier sketch in SATA 117
McCourt, Malachy 1931- 126
McCoy, Iola Fuller 3
McCoy, J(oseph) J(erome) 1917- 8
McCoy, Karen Kawamoto 1953- 82
McCoy, Lois (Rich) 1941- 38
McCrady, Lady 1951- 16
McCrea, James (Craig, Jr.) 1920- 3
McCrea, Ruth (Pirman) 1921- 3
McCreigh, James
  See Pohl, Frederick
McCrumb, Sharyn 1948- 109
McCue, Lisa 1959- 177
  Earlier sketch in SATA 65
McCue, Lisa Emiline
  See McCue, Lisa
McCullen, Andrew
  See Arthur, Robert, (Jr.)
McCullers, (Lula) Carson (Smith)
  1917-1967 27
McCulloch, Derek (Ivor Breashur) 1897-1967
  Obituary 29
McCulloch, John Tyler
  See Burroughs, Edgar Rice
McCulloch, Sarah
  See Ure, Jean
McCullough, David 1933- 62
McCullough, David Gaub
  See McCullough, David
McCullough, Frances Monson 1938- 8
McCullough, Sharon Pierce 1943- 131
McCully, Emily Arnold 134
  Autobiography Feature 134
  Earlier sketches in SATA 5, 110
  See also CLR 46
  See also SAAS 7
  See Arnold, Emily
McCune, Dan
  See Haas, Dorothy F.
McCunn, Ruthanne Lum 1946- 63
McCurdy, Michael (Charles) 1942- 147
  Earlier sketches in SATA 13, 82
McCutcheon, Elsie (Mary Jackson) 1937- ... 60
McCutcheon, John 1952- 97
McDaniel, Becky Bring 1953- 61

McDaniel, Lurlene 1944- 146
  Earlier sketch in SATA 71
McDaniels, Pellom III 1968- 121
McDaniels, Preston 1952- 192
McDearmon, Kay 20
McDermott, Beverly Brodsky 1941- 11
McDermott, Eleni 156
McDermott, Gerald (Edward) 1941- 163
  Earlier sketches in SATA 16, 74
  See also CLR 9
McDermott, Michael 1962- 76
McDevitt, Jack 1935- 155
  Earlier sketch in SATA 94
McDevitt, John Charles
  See McDevitt, Jack
McDole, Carol
  See Farley, Carol (J.)
McDonald, Collin 1943- 79
McDonald, Gerald D(oan) 1905-1970 3
McDonald, Jamie
  See Heide, Florence Parry
McDonald, Janet 1953- 148
McDonald, Jill (Masefield) 1927-1982 13
  Obituary 29
McDonald, Joyce 1946- 164
  Earlier sketch in SATA 101
McDonald, Lucile Saunders 1898-1992 10
McDonald, Mary Ann 1956- 84
McDonald, Megan 1959- 151
  Autobiography Feature 151
  Earlier sketches in SATA 67, 99, 148
  See also CLR 94
McDonald, Meme 1954- 112
McDonald, Mercedes 1956- 169
  Earlier sketch in SATA 97
McDonell, Chris 1960- 138
McDonnell, Christine 1949- 115
  Earlier sketch in SATA 34
McDonnell, Flora (Mary) 1963- 146
  Earlier sketch in SATA 90
McDonnell, Kathleen 1947- 186
McDonnell, Lois Eddy 1914-2001 10
McDonnell, Patrick 1956- 179
McDonough, Yona Zeldis 1957- 73
McElligott, Matt(hew) 1968- 135
McElmeel, Sharron L. 1942- 128
McElmurry, Jill 159
McElrath, William N. 1932- 65
McElrath-Eslick, Lori 1960- 96
McEntee, Dorothy (Layng) 1902- 37
McEwen, Katherine 183
McEwen, Robert (Lindley) 1926-1980
  Obituary 23
McFadden, Kevin Christopher
  See Pike, Christopher
McFall, Christie 1918- 12
McFall, Gardner 1952- 183
McFarlan, Donald M(aitland) 1915- 59
McFarland, Henry "Hammer"
  See McFarland, Henry O.
McFarland, Henry O. 1934- 143
McFarland, Kenton D(ean) 1920- 11
McFarland, Martha
  See Smith-Ankrom, M. E.
McFarlane, Leslie (Charles) 1902-1977 31
  See Dixon, Franklin W.
  and Ferris, James Cody
  and Keene, Carolyn
  and Rockwood, Roy
McFarlane, Peter (William) 1940- 95
McFarlane, Sheryl P. 1954- 86
McFarlane, Todd 1961- 117
McGaw, Jessie Brewer 1913-1997 10
McGee, Barbara 1943- 6
McGee, Marni 163
McGiffin, (Lewis) Lee (Shaffer) 1908-1978 ... 1
McGill, Alice 159
McGill, Ormond 1913- 92
McGinley, Jerry 1948- 116

McGinley, Phyllis 1905-1978 44
  Obituary 24
  Earlier sketch in SATA 2
McGinnis, Lila S(prague) 1924- 44
McGinty, Alice B. 1963- 134
McGivern, Justin 1985- 129
McGivern, Maureen Daly
  See Daly, Maureen
McGivern, Maureen Patricia Daly
  See Daly, Maureen
McGough, Elizabeth (Hemmes) 1934- 33
McGovern, Ann 1930- 132
  Earlier sketches in SATA 8, 69, 70
  See also CLR 50
  See also SAAS 17
McGowen, Thomas E. 1927- 109
  Earlier sketch in SATA 2
McGowen, Tom
  See McGowen, Thomas E.
McGrady, Mike 1933- 6
McGrath, Barbara Barbieri 1953- 169
  Earlier sketch in SATA 108
McGrath, Robin 1949- 121
McGrath, Thomas (Matthew) 1916-1990 41
  Obituary 66
McGraw, Eloise Jarvis 1915-2000 67
  Obituary 123
  Earlier sketch in SATA 1
  See also SAAS 6
McGraw, William Corbin 1916-1999 3
McGreal, Elizabeth
  See Yates, Elizabeth
McGregor, Barbara 1959- 82
McGregor, Craig 1933- 8
McGregor, Iona 1929- 25
McGrory, Anik 193
McGuffey, Alexander Hamilton 1816-1896 . 60
McGuigan, Mary Ann 1949- 106
McGuire, Edna 1899- 13
McGuire, Leslie (Sarah) 1945- 94
  Brief entry 45
  Earlier sketch in SATA 52
McGuire, Robert 187
McGuirk, Leslie (A.) 1960- 152
McGurk, Slater
  See Roth, Arthur J(oseph)
McHargue, Georgess 1941- 77
  Earlier sketch in SATA 4
  See also CLR 2
  See also SAAS 5
McHenry, E.B. 1963(?)- 193
McHugh, (Berit) Elisabet 1941- 55
  Brief entry 44
McIlvaine, Jane
  See McClary, Jane Stevenson
McIlwraith, Maureen Mollie Hunter 2
  See Hunter, Mollie
McInerney, Judith W(hitelock) 1945- 49
  Brief entry 46
McInerny, Ralph 1929- 93
McInerny, Ralph Matthew
  See McInerny, Ralph
McKaughan, Larry (Scott) 1941- 75
McKay, Donald 1895- 45
McKay, Hilary (Jane) 1959- 145
  Earlier sketch in SATA 92
  See also SAAS 23
McKay, Lawrence, Jr. 1948- 114
McKay, Robert W. 1921- 15
McKay, Sharon E. 1954- 165
McKay, Simon
  See Nicole, Christopher (Robin)
McKeating, Eileen 1957- 81
McKee, David (John) 1935- 158
  Earlier sketches in SATA 70, 107
  See also CLR 38
McKee, Tim 1970- 111
McKeever, Marcia
  See Laird, Jean E(louise)
McKelvey, Carole A. 1942- 78
McKelvy, Charles 1950- 124

McKendrick, Melveena (Christine) 1941- *55*
McKendry, Joe 1972- *170*
McKenna, Colleen O'Shaughnessy 1948- .. *136*
  Earlier sketch in SATA *76*
McKenzie, Dorothy Clayton 1910-1981
  Obituary *28*
McKenzie, Ellen Kindt 1928- *80*
McKernan, Victoria 1957- *171*
McKie, Robin *112*
McKillip, Patricia A. 1948- *174*
  Earlier sketches in SATA *30, 80, 126*
McKillip, Patricia Anne
  See McKillip, Patricia A.
McKim, Audrey Margaret 1909-1999 .... *47*
McKinley, Jennifer Carolyn Robin
  See McKinley, Robin
McKinley, Robin 1952- *130*
  Brief entry *32*
  Earlier sketches in SATA *50, 89*
  See also CLR *127*
McKinney, Barbara Shaw 1951- *116*
McKinney, Nadine 1938- *91*
McKinty, Adrian *186*
McKissack, Fredrick L. 1939- *162*
  Brief entry *53*
  Earlier sketches in SATA *73, 117*
  See also CLR *55*
McKissack, Fredrick Lemuel
  See McKissack, Fredrick L.
McKissack, Patricia C. 1944- *162*
  Earlier sketches in SATA *51, 73, 117*
  See also CLR *129*
McKissack, Patricia L'Ann Carwell
  See McKissack, Patricia C.
McKissack and McKissack
  See McKissack, Fredrick L.
  and McKissack, Patricia C.
McKown, Robin (?)-1976 .... *6*
McKy, Katie 1956- *184*
McLaren, Clemence 1938- *158*
  Earlier sketch in SATA *105*
McLaughlin, Frank 1934- *73*
McLaurin, Anne 1953- *27*
McLean, Andrew 1946- *172*
  Earlier sketch in SATA *113*
McLean, J. Sloan
  See Gillette, Virginia M(ary)
  and Wunsch, Josephine (McLean)
McLean, Janet 1946- *113*
McLean, Kathryn (Anderson) 1909-1966 .... *9*
McLean, Virginia Overton 1946- *90*
McLean-Carr, Carol 1948- *122*
McLeish, Kenneth 1940-1997 .... *35*
McLenighan, Valjean 1947- *46*
  Brief entry *40*
McLennan, Connie *171*
McLennan, Will
  See Wisler, G(ary) Clifton
McLeod, Bob 1951- *173*
McLeod, Chum 1955- *95*
McLeod, Emilie Warren 1926-1982 .... *23*
  Obituary *31*
McLeod, Kirsty
  See Hudson, (Margaret) Kirsty
McLeod, Margaret Vail
  See Holloway, Teresa (Bragunier)
McLerran, Alice 1933- *137*
  Earlier sketch in SATA *68*
McLimans, David 1949- *182*
McLoughlin, John C. 1949- *47*
McManus, Patrick F. 1933- *46*
McManus, Patrick Francis
  See McManus, Patrick F.
McMeekin, Clark
  See McMeekin, Isabel McLennan
McMeekin, Isabel McLennan 1895-1973 .... *3*
McMenemy, Sarah 1965- *156*
McMillan, Bruce 1947- *192*
  Earlier sketches in SATA *22, 70, 129*
  See also CLR *47*

McMillan, Naomi
  See Grimes, Nikki
McMorey, James L.
  See Moyer, Terry J.
McMorrow, Annalisa 1969- *104*
McMullan, Jim 1934- *150*
  Earlier sketch in SATA *87*
McMullan, K. H.
  See McMullan, Kate
McMullan, Kate 1947- *189*
  Brief entry *48*
  Earlier sketches in SATA *52, 87, 132*
McMullan, Kate Hall
  See McMullan, Kate
McMurtrey, Martin A(loysias) 1921- *21*
McNabb, Linda 1963- *147*
McNair, Kate *3*
McNair, Sylvia 1924-2002 .... *74*
McNamara, Margaret C(raig) 1915-1981
  Obituary *24*
McNaught, Harry *32*
McNaughton, Colin 1951- *134*
  Earlier sketches in SATA *39, 92*
  See also CLR *54*
McNaughton, Janet 1953- *162*
  Earlier sketch in SATA *110*
McNeely, Jeannette 1918- *25*
McNeer, May (Yonge) 1902-1994 .... *81*
  Earlier sketch in SATA *1*
McNeese, Tim 1953- *139*
McNeill, Janet *97*
  Earlier sketch in SATA *1*
  See Alexander, Janet
McNicholas, Shelagh *191*
McNickle, (William) D'Arcy 1904-1977
  Obituary *22*
McNicoll, Sylvia (Marilyn) 1954- *113*
  See also CLR *99*
McNulty, Faith 1918-2005 .... *168*
  Earlier sketches in SATA *12, 84, 139*
McPhail, David 1940- *183*
  Brief entry *32*
  Earlier sketches in SATA *47, 81, 140*
McPhail, David M.
  See McPhail, David
McPhail, David Michael
  See McPhail, David
McPhee, Norma H. 1928- *95*
McPhee, Richard B(yron) 1934- *41*
McPherson, James M. 1936- *141*
  Earlier sketch in SATA *16*
McPherson, James Munro
  See McPherson, James M.
McQueen, Lucinda 1950- *58*
  Brief entry *48*
McQueen, Mildred Hark 1908-1978 .... *12*
McRae, Russell (William) 1934- *63*
McShean, Gordon 1936- *41*
Mc Swigan, Marie 1907-1962 .... *24*
McVeity, Jen *148*
McVey, Vicki 1946- *80*
McVicker, Charles (Taggart) 1930- *39*
McVicker, Chuck
  See McVicker, Charles (Taggart)
McWhirter, A(lan) Ross 1925-1975 .... *37*
  Obituary *31*
McWhirter, Norris (Dewar) 1925-2004 .... *37*
McWilliams, Karen 1943- *65*
Mdurvwa, Hajara E. 1962- *92*
Meacham, Margaret 1952- *95*
Meachum, Virginia 1918- *133*
  Earlier sketch in SATA *87*
Mead, Alice 1952- *146*
  Earlier sketch in SATA *94*
Mead, Margaret 1901-1978
  Obituary *20*
Mead, Russell (M., Jr.) 1935- *10*
Mead, Stella (?)-1981
  Obituary *27*
Meade, Ellen *5*
  See Roddick, Ellen

Meade, Marion 1934- *127*
  Earlier sketch in SATA *23*
Meader, Stephen W(arren) 1892-1977 .... *1*
Meadmore, Susan
  See Sallis, Susan (Diana)
Meadow, Charles T(roub) 1929- *23*
Meadowcroft, Enid LaMonte
  See Wright, Enid Meadowcroft (LaMonte)
Meadows, Graham (W.) 1934- *161*
Meaker, M. J.
  See Meaker, Marijane
Meaker, Marijane 1927- *160*
  Autobiography Feature *111*
  Earlier sketches in SATA *20, 61, 99*
  See also CLR *29*
  See also SAAS *1*
Meaker, Marijane Agnes
  See Meaker, Marijane
Means, Florence Crannell 1891-1980 .... *1*
  Obituary *25*
  See also CLR *56*
Mearian, Judy Frank 1936- *49*
Mecca, Judy Truesdell 1955- *127*
Medary, Marjorie 1890-1980 .... *14*
Meddaugh, Susan 1944- *176*
  Earlier sketches in SATA *29, 84, 125*
Medearis, Angela Shelf 1956- *123*
  Earlier sketch in SATA *72*
Medearis, Mary 1915- *5*
Medina, Jane 1953- *167*
  Earlier sketch in SATA *122*
Medina, Nico 1982- *193*
Medlicott, Mary 1946- *88*
Mee, Charles L., Jr. 1938- *72*
  Earlier sketch in SATA *8*
Meek, Jacklyn O'Hanlon 1933- *51*
  Brief entry *34*
Meek, S(terner St.) P(aul) 1894-1972
  Obituary *28*
Meeker, Clare Hodgson 1952- *96*
Meeker, Oden 1919(?)-1976 .... *14*
Meeker, Richard
  See Brown, Fornan
Meeks, Esther MacBain *1*
Meggs, Libby Phillips 1943- *130*
Mehdevi, Alexander (Sinclair) 1947- *7*
Mehdevi, Anne (Marie) Sinclair 1947- *8*
Meidell, Sherry 1951- *73*
Meier, Minta 1906- *55*
Meighan, Donald Charles 1929- *30*
Meigs, Cornelia Lynde 1884-1973 .... *6*
  See also CLR *55*
Meilach, Dona Z(weigoron) 1926- *34*
Meilman, Philip W(arren) 1951- *79*
Meinstereifel, Ronald L. 1960- *134*
Meisel, Paul *184*
Melcher, Daniel 1912-1985
  Obituary *43*
Melcher, Frederic Gershom 1879-1963
  Obituary *22*
Melcher, Marguerite Fellows 1879-1969 ...... *10*
Melendez, Francisco 1964- *72*
Melin, Grace Hathaway 1892-1973 .... *10*
Mellersh, H(arold) E(dward) L(eslie)
  1897- *10*
Melling, David *186*
Melmoth, Sebastian
  See Wilde, Oscar
Melnikoff, Pamela (Rita) *97*
Meltzer, Milton 1915- *128*
  Autobiography Feature *124*
  Earlier sketches in SATA *1, 50, 80*
  See also CLR *13*
  See also SAAS *1*
Melville, Anne
  See Potter, Margaret (Newman)
Melville, Herman 1819-1891 .... *59*
Melwood, Mary
  See Lewis, E. M.
Melzack, Ronald 1929- *5*
Memling, Carl 1918-1969 .... *6*

Menchin, Scott 188
Mendel, Jo
  See Bond, Gladys Baker
  and Gilbertson, Mildred Geiger
Mendelson, Steven T. 1958-1995 86
Mendelson-Stevens, Serita Deborah
  See Stevens, Serita
Mendes, Valerie 1939- 157
Mendez, Raymond A. 1947- 66
Mendonca, Susan
  Brief entry 45
  See Smith, Susan Vernon
Mendoza, George 1934- 41
  Brief entry 39
  See also SAAS 7
Menendez, Shirley (C.) 1937- 146
Meng, Heinz (Karl) 1924- 13
Mennen, Ingrid 1954- 85
Menotti, Gian Carlo 1911-2007 29
  Obituary 180
Menuhin, Sir Yehudi 1916-1999 40
  Obituary 113
Menville, Douglas 1935- 64
Menzel, Barbara Jean 1946- 63
Mercati, Cynthia 164
Mercati, Cynthia J.
  See Mercati, Cynthia
Mercer, Charles (Edward) 1917-1988 16
  Obituary 61
Mercer, Sienna 192
Meredith, Arnold
  See Hopkins, (Hector) Kenneth
Meredith, David William
  See Miers, Earl Schenck
Meringoff, Laurene Krasny
  See Brown, Laurene Krasny
Meriwether, Louise 1923- 52
  Brief entry 31
Merlin, Arthur
  See Blish, James (Benjamin)
Merlin, Christina
  See Heaven, Constance (Christina)
Merriam, Eve 1916-1992 73
  Earlier sketches in SATA *3, 40*
  See also CLR *14*
Merrill, Jane 1946- 42
Merrill, Jane Merrill
  See Merrill, Jane
Merrill, Jean (Fairbanks) 1923- 82
  Earlier sketch in SATA *1*
  See also CLR *52*
Merrill, Phil
  See Merrill, Jane
Merriman, Alex
  See Silverberg, Robert
Merriman, Rachel 1971- 149
  Earlier sketch in SATA *98*
Merrit, Elizabeth
  See Goudge, Eileen
Merski, Patricia K.
  See Merski, P.K.
Merski, P.K. 172
Mertz, Barbara
  See Peters, Elizabeth
Mertz, Barbara Gross
  See Peters, Elizabeth
Meschel, Susan V. 1936- 83
Messenger, Charles (Rynd Milles) 1942- 59
Messick, Dale 1906-2005 64
  Brief entry 48
Messier, Claire 1956- 103
Messieres, Nicole de
  See de Messieres, Nicole
Messmer, Otto 1892(?)-1983 37
Mesta, Gabriel
  See Moesta, Rebecca
Metcalf, Doris H(unter) 91
Metcalf, Suzanne
  See Baum, L(yman) Frank
Metos, Thomas H(arry) 1932- 37
Metter, Bert(ram Milton) 1927- 56

Metzenthen, David 1958- 167
  Earlier sketch in SATA *106*
Meyer, Barbara 1939- 77
Meyer, Carolyn 1935- 142
  Autobiography Feature 142
  Earlier sketches in SATA *9, 70, 118*
  See also SAAS *9*
Meyer, Carolyn Mae
  See Meyer, Carolyn
Meyer, Edith Patterson 1895-1993 5
Meyer, F(ranklyn) E(dward) 1932- 9
Meyer, Jean Shepherd 11
Meyer, Jerome Sydney 1895-1975 3
  Obituary 25
Meyer, June
  See Jordan, June
Meyer, Kerstin 1966- 190
Meyer, L. A.
  See Meyer, Louis A(lbert), Jr.
Meyer, Louis A(lbert), Jr. 1942- 144
  Earlier sketch in SATA *12*
Meyer, Renate 1930- 6
Meyer, Stephenie 1973- 193
Meyer, Susan E. 1940- 64
Meyers, Susan 1942- 164
  Earlier sketches in SATA *19, 108*
Meynell, Laurence Walter 1899-1989
  Obituary 61
Meynier, Yvonne (Pollet) 1908- 14
Mezey, Robert 1935- 33
Micale, Albert 1913- 22
Michael, James
  See Scagnetti, Jack
Michael, Livi 1960- 172
Michael, Manfred
  See Winterfeld, Henry
Michael, Olivia
  See Michael, Livi
Michaels, Barbara
  See Peters, Elizabeth
Michaels, Joanne Louise
  See Teitelbaum, Michael
Michaels, Kristin
  See Williams, Jeanne
Michaels, Molly
  See Untermeyer, Louis
Michaels, Neal
  See Teitelbaum, Michael
Michaels, Ski
  See Pellowski, Michael (Joseph)
Michaels, Steve 1955- 71
Michaels, William M. 1917- 77
Michel, Anna 1943- 49
  Brief entry 40
Michel, Francois 1948- 82
Michelin, Linda 183
Michelson, Richard 173
Micich, Paul 74
Micklish, Rita 1931- 12
Micklos, John, Jr. 1956- 173
  Earlier sketch in SATA *129*
Micklos J., John, Jr. 1956-
  See Micklos, John, Jr.
Micucci, Charles (Patrick, Jr.) 1959- 144
  Earlier sketch in SATA *82*
Middleton, Haydn 1955- 152
  Earlier sketch in SATA *85*
Miers, Earl Schenck 1910-1972 1
  Obituary 26
Migdale, Lawrence 1951- 89
Mikaelsen, Ben 1952- 173
  Earlier sketches in SATA *73, 107*
Mikaelsen, Benjamin John
  See Mikaelsen, Ben
Miklowitz, Gloria D. 1927- 129
  Earlier sketches in SATA *4, 68*
  See also SAAS *17*
Mikolaycak, Charles 1937-1993 78
  Obituary 75
  Earlier sketch in SATA *9*
  See also SAAS *4*

Mild, Warren (Paul) 1922- 41
Milelli, Pascal 1965- 135
Miles, Betty 1928- 78
  Earlier sketch in SATA *8*
  See also SAAS *9*
Miles, Miska
  See Martin, Patricia Miles
Miles, (Mary) Patricia 1930- 29
Miles, Patricia A.
  See Martin, Patricia Miles
Miles, Victoria 1966- 188
Milgrim, David 187
  Earlier sketch in SATA *158*
Milgrom, Harry 1912-1978 25
Milhous, Katherine 1894-1977 15
Milich, Zoran 174
Milios, Rita 1949- 79
Militant
  See Sandburg, Carl (August)
Millais, Raoul 1901- 77
Millar, Barbara F. 1924- 12
Millar, Margaret (Ellis Sturm) 1915-1994 61
  Obituary 79
Millbank, Captain H. R.
  See Ellis, Edward S(ylvester)
Millen, C(ynthia) M. 1955- 114
Miller, Albert G(riffith) 1905-1982 12
  Obituary 31
Miller, Alice Ann 1958- 150
Miller, Alice P(atricia McCarthy) 22
Miller, Debbie 1951- 160
  Earlier sketch in SATA *103*
Miller, Debbie S.
  See Miller, Debbie
Miller, Deborah Uchill 1944- 61
Miller, Don 1923- 15
Miller, Doris R.
  See Mosesson, Gloria R(ubin)
Miller, Eddie
  See Miller, Edward
Miller, Edna Anita 1920- 29
Miller, Edward 1905-1974 8
Miller, Edward 1964- 183
Miller, Elizabeth 1933- 41
Miller, Ellanita 1957- 87
Miller, Eugene 1925- 33
Miller, Frances A. 1937- 52
  Brief entry 46
Miller, Helen M(arkley) -1984 5
Miller, Helen Topping 1884-1960
  Obituary 29
Miller, Jane (Judith) 1925-1989 15
Miller, Jewel 1956- 73
Miller, John
  See Samachson, Joseph
Miller, Judi 117
Miller, Kate 1948- 193
Miller, Kirsten 1973- 185
Miller, Louise (Rolfe) 1940- 76
Miller, M. L. 85
Miller, Madge 1918- 63
Miller, Margaret J.
  See Dale, Margaret J(essy) Miller
Miller, Marilyn (Jean) 1925- 33
Miller, Marvin 65
Miller, Mary
  See Northcott, (William) Cecil
Miller, Mary Beth 1942- 9
Miller, Mary Beth 1964- 185
Miller, Maryann 1943- 73
Miller, Natalie 1917-1976 35
Miller, Robert H. 1944- 91
Miller, Ron 1947- 185
Miller, Ruth White
  See White, Ruth C.
Miller, Sandra
  See Miller, Sandy
Miller, Sandra Peden
  See Miller, Sandy
Miller, Sandy 1948- 41
  Brief entry 35

Miller, Sarah 1969- *175*
Miller, Virginia
   See Austin, Virginia
Miller, William R. 1959- *116*
Milligan, Bryce 1953- *170*
Milligan, Spike
   See CLR *92*
   See Milligan, Terence Alan
Milligan, Terence Alan 1918-2002 .... *29*
   Obituary *134*
   See Milligan, Spike
Millington, Ada
   See Deyneka, Anita
Millman, Isaac 1933- *140*
Mills, Adam
   See Stanley, George Edward
Mills, Claudia 1954- *191*
   Brief entry *41*
   Earlier sketches in SATA *44, 89, 145*
Mills, Elaine (Rosemary) 1941- *72*
Mills, Joyce C. 1944- *102*
Mills, Judith Christine 1956- *130*
Mills, Yaroslava Surmach 1925- *35*
Millspaugh, Ben P. 1936- *77*
Millstead, Thomas E. *30*
Milne, A. A. 1882-1956 .... *100*
   See also YABC *1*
   See also CLR *108*
Milne, Alan Alexander
   See Milne, A. A.
Milne, Lorus J. *5*
   See also CLR *22*
   See also SAAS *18*
Milne, Margery *5*
   See also CLR *22*
   See also SAAS *18*
Milne, Terry
   See Milne, Theresa Ann
Milne, Theresa Ann 1964- *84*
Milnes, Irma McDonough 1924- *101*
Milonas, Rolf
   See Myller, Rolf
Milord, Susan 1954- *147*
   Earlier sketch in SATA *74*
Milotte, Alfred G(eorge) 1904-1989 .... *11*
   Obituary *62*
Milstein, Linda 1954- *80*
Milton, Ann *134*
Milton, Hilary (Herbert) 1920- *23*
Milton, John R(onald) 1924- *24*
Milton, Joyce 1946- *101*
   Brief entry *41*
   Earlier sketch in SATA *52*
Milverton, Charles A.
   See Penzler, Otto
Minahan, John A. 1956- *92*
Minar, Barbra (Goodyear) 1940- *79*
Minard, Rosemary 1939- *63*
Minarik, Else Holmelund 1920- *127*
   Earlier sketch in SATA *15*
   See also CLR *33*
Miner, Jane Claypool 1933- *38*
   Brief entry *37*
   See Claypool, Jane
Miner, Lewis S. 1909-1971 .... *11*
Mines, Jeanette 1948- *61*
Mines, Jeanette Marie
   See Mines, Jeanette
Minier, Nelson
   See Stoutenburg, Adrien (Pearl)
Minnitt, Ronda Jacqueline
   See Armitage, David
Minor, Wendell G. 1944- *164*
   Earlier sketches in SATA *78, 109*
Minter, Daniel 1961- *176*
Mintonye, Grace *4*
Miranda, Anne 1954- *109*
   Earlier sketch in SATA *71*
Mirocha, Paul *192*
Mirsky, Jeannette 1903-1987 .... *8*
   Obituary *51*

Mirsky, Reba Paeff 1902-1966 .... *1*
Misako Rocks! *192*
Mishica, Clare 1960- *91*
Miskovits, Christine 1939- *10*
Miss Frances
   See Horwich, Frances R(appaport)
Miss Read
   See Saint, Dora Jessie
Mister Rogers
   See Rogers, Fred McFeely
Mitchard, Jacquelyn 1956- *168*
   Earlier sketch in SATA *98*
Mitchell, Adrian 1932- *166*
   Earlier sketch in SATA *104*
Mitchell, Allison
   See Griffin, W.E.B
Mitchell, Betty Jo
   See Mitchell, B.J.
Mitchell, B.J. 1931- *120*
Mitchell, Clyde
   See Ellison, Harlan
   and Silverberg, Robert
Mitchell, Cynthia 1922- *29*
Mitchell, (Sibyl) Elyne (Keith) 1913- *10*
Mitchell, Gladys (Maude Winifred)
   1901-1983 .... *46*
   Obituary *35*
Mitchell, Jay
   See Roberson, Jennifer
Mitchell, Joyce Slayton 1933- *142*
   Brief entry *43*
   Earlier sketch in SATA *46*
Mitchell, K. L.
   See Lamb, Elizabeth Searle
Mitchell, Kathy 1948- *59*
Mitchell, Lori 1961- *128*
Mitchell, Margaree King 1953- *84*
Mitchell, Marianne 1947- *145*
Mitchell, Rhonda *89*
Mitchell, Todd 1974- *191*
Mitchell, Yvonne 1925-1979
   Obituary *24*
Mitchelson, Mitch
   See Mitchelson, Peter Richard
Mitchelson, Peter Richard 1950- *104*
Mitchison, Naomi (Margaret Haldane)
   1897-1999 .... *24*
   Obituary *112*
Mitchnik, Helen 1901-1982 .... *41*
   Brief entry *35*
Mitchum, Hank
   See Knott, William C(ecil, Jr.)
   and Murray, Stuart A. P.
   and Newton, D(wight) B(ennett)
   and Sherman, Jory (Tecumseh)
Mitgutsch, Ali 1935- *76*
Mitsuhashi, Yoko *45*
   Brief entry *33*
Mitton, Jacqueline 1948- *162*
   Earlier sketches in SATA *66, 115*
Mitton, Simon 1946- *66*
Mitton, Tony 1951- *149*
   Earlier sketch in SATA *104*
Miura, Taro 1968- *181*
Mizner, Elizabeth Howard 1907- *27*
Mizumura, Kazue *18*
Mlynowski, Sarah 1977(?)- *180*
Mobin-Uddin, Asma *172*
Mobley, Joe A. 1945- *91*
Moche, Dinah (Rachel) L(evine) 1936- *44*
   Brief entry *40*
Mochi, Ugo (A.) 1889-1977 .... *38*
Mochizuki, Ken 1954- *146*
   Earlier sketch in SATA *81*
   See also SAAS *22*
Modarressi, Mitra 1967- *126*
Modell, Frank B. 1917- *39*
   Brief entry *36*
Modesitt, Jeanne 1953- *143*
   Earlier sketch in SATA *92*

Modesitt, L.E., Jr. 1943- *164*
   Earlier sketch in SATA *91*
Modesitt, Leland Exton, Jr.
   See Modesitt, L.E., Jr.
Modrell, Dolores 1933- *72*
Moe, Barbara 1937- *20*
Moe, Jorgen (Ingebretsen) 1813-1882
   See CLR *104*
   See Asbjornsen and Moe
Moed-Kass, Pnina *169*
Moerbeek, Kees 1955- *98*
Moeri, Louise 1924- *93*
   Earlier sketch in SATA *24*
   See also SAAS *10*
Moesta, Rebecca 1956- *182*
Moffett, Jami 1952- *84*
Moffett, Martha (Leatherwood) 1934- *8*
Mogensen, Suzanne A(ncher) 1946- *129*
Mohn, Peter B(urnet) 1934- *28*
Mohn, Viola Kohl 1914- *8*
Mohr, Nicholasa 1938- *97*
   Autobiography Feature *113*
   Earlier sketch in SATA *8*
   See also CLR *22*
   See also SAAS *8*
Mok, Esther 1953- *93*
Molan, Christine 1943- *84*
Molarsky, Osmond 1909- *16*
Moldon, Peter L(eonard) 1937- *49*
Mole, John 1941- *103*
   Earlier sketch in SATA *36*
   See also CLR *61*
Molesworth, Mary Louisa 1839-1921 .... *98*
Molin, Charles
   See Mayne, William (James Carter)
Molina, Silvia 1946- *97*
Molk, Laurel 1957- *162*
   Earlier sketch in SATA *92*
Mollel, Tololwa M. 1952- *88*
Molloy, Anne Baker 1907-1999 .... *32*
Molloy, Michael (John) 1940- *162*
Molloy, Paul (George) 1924- *5*
Moloney, James 1954- *144*
   Autobiography Feature *144*
   Earlier sketch in SATA *94*
Momaday, N. Scott 1934- *48*
   Brief entry *30*
Momaday, Navarre Scott
   See Momaday, N. Scott
Monaco, Octavia 1963- *169*
Monagle, Bernie 1957- *121*
Moncure, Jane Belk 1926- *23*
Monjo, F(erdinand) N(icholas III)
   1924-1978 .... *16*
   See also CLR *2*
Monk, Isabell 1952- *136*
Monks, Lydia *189*
Monroe, Lyle
   See Heinlein, Robert A.
Monroe, Marion
   Obituary *34*
   See Cox, Marion Monroe
Monsell, Helen Albee 1895-1971 .... *24*
Monson-Burton, Marianne 1975- *139*
Montana, Bob 1920-1975
   Obituary *21*
Montecalvo, Janet *177*
Montenegro, Laura Nyman 1953- *95*
Montero, Gloria 1933- *109*
Montes, Marisa 1951- *144*
Montgomerie, Norah (Mary) 1913- *26*
Montgomery, Constance
   See Cappel, Constance
Montgomery, Elizabeth Rider *34*
   Obituary *41*
   Earlier sketch in SATA *3*
   See Julesberg, Elizabeth Rider
   Montgomery
Montgomery, Hugh (Edward) 1962- *146*

Montgomery, L(ucy) M(aud) 1874-1942 .... *100*
 See also YABC *1*
 See also CLR *91*
Montgomery, Raymond A. (Jr.) 1936- *39*
Montgomery, Rutherford George 1894-1985 . *3*
Montgomery, Sy 1958- *184*
 Autobiography Feature *132*
 Earlier sketches in SATA *114, 132*
Montgomery, Vivian *36*
Monthei, Betty *179*
Montijo, Rhode *179*
Montileaux, Donald F. 1948- *183*
Montpetit, Charles 1958- *101*
Montresor, Beni 1926-2001 .... *38*
 Earlier sketch in SATA *3*
 See also SAAS *4*
Montserrat, Pep *181*
Monty Python
 See Chapman, Graham
 and Cleese, John (Marwood)
 and Gilliam, Terry
 and Idle, Eric
 and Jones, Terence Graham Parry
 and Palin, Michael
Moodie, Craig 1956- *172*
Moodie, Fiona 1952- *133*
Moody, Minerva
 See Alcott, Louisa May
Moody, Ralph Owen 1898-1982 .... *1*
Moon, Carl 1879(?)-1948 .... *25*
Moon, Grace (Purdie) 1877(?)-1947 .... *25*
Moon, Lily
 See Warnes, Tim
Moon, Nicola 1952- *147*
 Earlier sketch in SATA *96*
Moon, Pat 1946- *113*
Moon, Sheila 1910-1991 .... *5*
 Obituary *114*
Moon, Sheila Elizabeth
 See Moon, Sheila
Mooney, Bel 1946- *95*
Mooney, Bill 1936- *122*
Mooney, Elizabeth C(omstock) 1918-1986
 Obituary *48*
Mooney, William
 See Mooney, Bill
Moor, Emily
 See Deming, Richard
Moorcock, Michael 1939- *166*
 Earlier sketch in SATA *93*
 See Bradbury, Edward P.
Moorcock, Michael John
 See Moorcock, Michael
Moore, Anne Carroll 1871-1961 .... *13*
Moore, Cheri
 See Ladd, Cheryl (Jean)
Moore, Clement Clarke 1779-1863 .... *18*
Moore, Cyd 1957- *186*
 Earlier sketches in SATA *83, 133*
Moore, Don W. 1905(?)-1986
 Obituary *48*
Moore, Elaine 1944- *86*
Moore, Eva 1942- *103*
 Earlier sketch in SATA *20*
Moore, Ishbel (Lindsay) 1954- *140*
Moore, Jack (William) 1941- *46*
 Brief entry *32*
Moore, Janet Gaylord 1905-1992 .... *18*
Moore, Jim 1946- *42*
Moore, John Travers 1908- *12*
Moore, Lilian 1909-2004 .... *137*
 Obituary *155*
 Earlier sketch in SATA *52*
 See also CLR *15*
Moore, Liz
 See Moore, M. Elizabeth
Moore, M. Elizabeth 1959- *156*
Moore, Margaret R(umberger) 1903- *12*
Moore, Margie *176*
Moore, Marianne (Craig) 1887-1972 .... *20*

Moore, Patrick (Alfred Caldwell) 1923- *49*
 Brief entry *39*
 See also SAAS *8*
Moore, Patrick 1959- *184*
Moore, Perry *193*
Moore, Peter 1963- *175*
Moore, Peter G.
 See Moore, Peter
Moore, Ray (S.) 1905(?)-1984
 Obituary *37*
Moore, Regina
 See Dunne, Mary Collins
Moore, Ruth (Ellen) 1908-1989 .... *23*
Moore, Ruth Nulton 1923- *38*
Moore, S(arah) E. *23*
Moore, Sarah Margaret
 See Hodges, Margaret
Moore, Tara 1950- *61*
Moore, Yvette 1958- *154*
 Earlier sketches in SATA *69, 70*
Moores, Dick
 See Moores, Richard (Arnold)
Moores, Richard (Arnold) 1909-1986
 Obituary *48*
Mooser, Stephen 1941- *75*
 Earlier sketch in SATA *28*
Mora, Francisco X(avier) 1952- *90*
Mora, Pat 1942- *186*
 Earlier sketches in SATA *92, 134*
 See also CLR *58*
Mora, Patricia
 See Mora, Pat
Morales, Yuyi *180*
 Earlier sketch in SATA *154*
Moran, Tom 1943- *60*
Moranville, Sharelle Byars *152*
Moray Williams, Ursula 1911-2006 .... *142*
 Obituary *177*
 Earlier sketch in SATA *73*
 See also SAAS *9*
 See Williams, Ursula Moray
Mordvinoff, Nicolas 1911-1973 .... *17*
More, Caroline
 See Cone, Molly (Lamken)
 and Strachan, Margaret Pitcairn
Moreno, Rene King *190*
Moreton, Andrew Esq.
 See Defoe, Daniel
Morey, Charles
 See Fletcher, Helen Jill
Morey, Walt(er Nelson) 1907-1992 .... *51*
 Obituary *70*
 Earlier sketch in SATA *3*
 See also SAAS *9*
Morgan, Alfred P(owell) 1889-1972 .... *33*
Morgan, Alison (Mary) 1930- *85*
 Earlier sketch in SATA *30*
Morgan, Anne 1954- *121*
Morgan, Douglas
 See Macdonald, James D.
Morgan, Ellen
 See Bumstead, Kathleen Mary
Morgan, Geoffrey 1916- *46*
Morgan, Helen (Gertrude Louise)
 1921-1990 .... *29*
Morgan, Jane
 See Cooper, James Fenimore
 and Franklin, Jane (Morgan)
 and Moren, Sally M(oore)
Morgan, Lenore H. 1908-1976 .... *8*
Morgan, Mary 1957- *114*
 Earlier sketch in SATA *81*
Morgan, Michaela *180*
 See Basile, Gloria Vitanza
Morgan, Nicola 1961- *161*
Morgan, Nina 1953- *110*
Morgan, Pierr 1952- *122*
 Earlier sketch in SATA *77*
Morgan, Robin (Evonne) 1941- *80*
Morgan, Roxanne
 See Gentle, Mary

Morgan, Sarah (Nicola) 1959- *68*
Morgan, Shirley *10*
 See Kiepper, Shirley Morgan
Morgan, Stacy T(owle) 1959- *104*
Morgan, Stevie
 See Davies, Nicola
Morgan, Tom 1942- *42*
Morgan, Wendy
 See Staub, Wendy Corsi
Morgan-Vanroyen, Mary
 See Morgan, Mary
Morgenstern, Susie Hoch 1945- *133*
Mori, Hana 1909-1990(?) *88*
Mori, Kyoko 1957- *122*
 Autobiography Feature *126*
 See also CLR *64*
 See also SAAS *26*
Moriarty, Jaclyn *162*
Moriarty, William J. 1930- *127*
Morice, Dave 1946- *93*
Morin, Isobel V. 1928- *110*
Morine, Hoder
 See Conroy, John Wesley
Morley, Wilfred Owen
 See Lowndes, Robert A(ugustine) W(ard)
Morningstar, Mildred (Whaley) 1912-1997 .. *61*
 Obituary *114*
Morozumi, Atsuko *110*
Morpurgo, Michael 1943- *184*
 Earlier sketches in SATA *93, 143*
 See also CLR *51*
Morrah, Dave
 See Morrah, David Wardlaw, Jr.
Morrah, David Wardlaw, Jr. 1914-1991 .... *10*
Morreale-de la Garza, Phyllis
 See De la Garza, Phyllis
Morressy, John 1930-2006 .... *23*
Morrill, Leslie H(olt) 1934-2003 .... *48*
 Brief entry *33*
 Obituary *148*
 See also SAAS *22*
Morris, Chris(topher Crosby) 1946- *66*
Morris, Deborah 1956- *91*
Morris, Desmond 1928- *14*
Morris, Desmond John
 See Morris, Desmond
Morris, Don 1954- *83*
Morris, Gerald 1963- *150*
 Earlier sketch in SATA *107*
Morris, Gerald Paul
 See Morris, Gerald
Morris, Gilbert (Leslie) 1929- *104*
Morris, Jackie *151*
Morris, Janet (Ellen) 1946- *66*
Morris, Jay
 See Tatham, Julie Campbell
Morris, (Margaret) Jean 1924- *98*
Morris, Jeffrey B(randon) 1941- *92*
Morris, Jennifer E. 1969- *179*
Morris, Jill 1936- *165*
 Earlier sketch in SATA *119*
Morris, Juddi *85*
Morris, Judy K. 1936- *61*
Morris, Oradel Nolen *128*
Morris, Robert A(da) 1933- *7*
Morris, William 1913-1994 .... *29*
Morrison, Bill 1935- *66*
 Brief entry *37*
Morrison, Chloe Anthony Wofford
 See Morrison, Toni
Morrison, Dorothy Nafus *29*
Morrison, Frank 1971- *185*
Morrison, Gordon 1944- *183*
 Earlier sketches in SATA *87, 128*
Morrison, Joan 1922- *65*
Morrison, Lillian 1917- *108*
 Earlier sketch in SATA *3*
Morrison, Lucile Phillips 1896- *17*
Morrison, Martha A. 1948- *77*
Morrison, Meighan 1966- *90*

Morrison, Richard
  See Lowndes, Robert A(ugustine) W(ard)
Morrison, Robert
  See Lowndes, Robert A(ugustine) W(ard)
Morrison, Roberta
  See Webb, Jean Francis (III)
Morrison, Susan Dudley
  See Gold, Susan Dudley
Morrison, Taylor 1971- *187*
  Earlier sketches in SATA *95, 159*
Morrison, Toni 1931- *144*
  Earlier sketch in SATA *57*
  See also CLR *99*
Morrison, Velma Ford 1909- *21*
Morrison, Wilbur Howard 1915- *64*
Morrison, William
  See Samachson, Joseph
Morriss, James E(dward) 1932- *8*
Morrissey, Dean *183*
Morrow, Barbara Olenyik 1952- *167*
Morrow, Betty
  See Bacon, Elizabeth
Morse, Carol
  See Yeakley, Marjory Hall
Morse, Dorothy B(ayley) 1906-1979
  Obituary *24*
Morse, Flo 1921- *30*
Morse, Tony 1953- *129*
Mort, Vivian
  See Cromie, Alice Hamilton
Mortensen, Denise Dowling *179*
Mortimer, Anne 1958- *116*
Mortimer, Mary H.
  See Coury, Louise Andree
Morton, Alexandra (Hubbard) 1957- *144*
Morton, Anthony
  See Arthur, Robert, (Jr.)
Morton, Jane 1931- *50*
Morton, Joseph C. 1932- *156*
Morton, Lee Jack, Jr. 1928- *32*
Morton, Miriam 1918(?)-1985 .... *9*
  Obituary *46*
Mosatche, Harriet (S.) 1949- *122*
Moscow, Alvin 1925- *3*
Mosel, Arlene (Tichy) 1921-1996 .... *7*
Moseley, James W(illett) 1931- *139*
Moseng, Elisabeth 1967- *90*
Moser, Barry 1940- *185*
  Earlier sketches in SATA *56, 79, 138*
  See also CLR *49*
  See also SAAS *15*
Moser, Don(ald Bruce) 1932- *31*
Moser, Lisa *192*
Moses, Sheila P. 1961- *168*
Moses, Will 1956- *178*
  Earlier sketch in SATA *120*
Mosesson, Gloria R(ubin) *24*
Mosher, Richard 1949- *120*
Moskin, Marietta D(unston) 1928- *23*
Moskof, Martin Stephen 1930- *27*
Mosley, Francis 1957- *57*
Moss, Don(ald) 1920- *11*
Moss, Elaine (Dora) 1924- *57*
  Brief entry *31*
Moss, Jeff(rey) 1942-1998 .... *73*
  Obituary *106*
Moss, Marissa 1959- *163*
  Earlier sketches in SATA *71, 104*
  See also CLR *134*
Moss, Miriam 1955- *140*
  Earlier sketch in SATA *76*
Moss, Thylias 1954- *108*
Moss, Thylias Rebecca Brasier
  See Moss, Thylias
Most, Bernard 1937- *134*
  Brief entry *40*
  Earlier sketches in SATA *48, 91*
Mott, Evelyn Clarke 1962- *133*
  Earlier sketch in SATA *75*
Motz, Lloyd 1909-2004 .... *20*

Mould, Edwin
  See Whitlock, Ralph
Mouly, Francoise *155*
Mountain, Robert
  See Montgomery, Raymond A. (Jr.)
Mountfield, David
  See Grant, Neil
Mourlevat, Jean-Claude 1952- *187*
Moussard, Jacqueline 1924- *24*
Mowat, Claire 1933- *123*
Mowat, Claire Angel Wheeler
  See Mowat, Claire
Mowat, Farley 1921- *55*
  Earlier sketch in SATA *3*
  See also CLR *20*
Mowat, Farley McGill
  See Mowat, Farley
Mowll, Joshua 1970(?)- *188*
Mowry, Jess 1960- *131*
  Autobiography Feature *131*
  Earlier sketch in SATA *109*
  See also CLR *65*
Moxley, Sheila 1966- *96*
Moyer, Terry J. 1937- *94*
Moyes, Patricia *63*
  See Haszard, Patricia Moyes
Moyler, Alan (Frank Powell) 1926- *36*
Mozelle, Shirley *179*
Mozley, Charles 1915- *43*
  Brief entry *32*
Mphahlele, Es'kia
  See Mphahlele, Ezekiel
Mphahlele, Ezekiel 1919- *119*
  See Mphahlele, Es'kia
Mr. McGillicuddy
  See Abisch, Roslyn Kroop
Mr. Sniff
  See Abisch, Roslyn Kroop
Mr. Tivil
  See Lorkowski, Thomas V(incent)
Mr. Wizard
  See Herbert, Don
Mrs. Fairstar
  See Horne, Richard Henry Hengist
Muchamore, Robert 1972- *175*
Muchmore, Jo Ann 1937- *103*
Mude, O.
  See Gorey, Edward (St. John)
Mudgeon, Apeman
  See Mitchell, Adrian
Mueller, Jorg 1942- *67*
  See also CLR *43*
Mueller, Virginia 1924- *28*
Muggs
  See Watkins, Lois
Muir, Diana
  See Appelbaum, Diana Muir Karter
Muir, Frank (Herbert) 1920-1998 .... *30*
Muir, Helen 1937- *65*
Mukerji, Dhan Gopal 1890-1936 .... *40*
  See also CLR *10*
Mulcahy, Lucille Burnett *12*
Mulford, Philippa G. 1948- *112*
  Earlier sketch in SATA *43*
Mulford, Philippa Greene
  See Mulford, Philippa G.
Mulila, Vigad G.
  See Maillu, David G(ian)
Mull, Brandon 1974- *190*
Mullen, Michael 1937- *122*
Muller, Billex
  See Ellis, Edward S(ylvester)
Muller, Jorg
  See Mueller, Jorg
Muller, (Lester) Robin 1953- *86*
Mullin, Caryl Cude 1969- *130*
Mullins, Edward S(wift) 1922- *10*
Mullins, Hilary 1962- *84*
Mulock, Dinah Maria
  See Craik, Dinah Maria (Mulock)
Mulvihill, William Patrick 1923- *8*

Mumford, Ruth
  See Dallas, Ruth
Mumy, Bill 1954- *112*
Mun
  See Leaf, (Wilbur) Munro
Munari, Bruno 1907-1998 .... *15*
  See also CLR *9*
Munce, Ruth Hill 1898- *12*
Mundy, Simon 1954- *64*
Mundy, Simon Andrew James Hainault
  See Mundy, Simon
Munger, Nancy *170*
Munowitz, Ken 1935-1977 .... *14*
Munoz, William 1949- *92*
  Earlier sketch in SATA *42*
Munro, Alice 1931- *29*
Munro, Alice Anne
  See Munro, Alice
Munro, Eleanor 1928- *37*
Munro, Roxie 1945- *184*
  Earlier sketches in SATA *58, 136*
Munsch, Bob
  See Munsch, Robert (Norman)
Munsch, Robert (Norman) 1945- *120*
  Brief entry *48*
  Earlier sketches in SATA *50, 83*
  See also CLR *19*
Munsinger, Lynn 1951- *177*
  Earlier sketches in SATA *33, 94*
Munson, Derek 1970- *139*
Munson, R. W.
  See Karl, Jean E(dna)
Munson-Benson, Tunie 1946- *15*
Munsterberg, Peggy 1921- *102*
Muntean, Michaela *182*
Munthe, Nelly 1947- *53*
Munves, James (Albert) 1922- *30*
Munzer, Martha E. 1899-1999 .... *4*
Murawski, Darlyne A. *193*
Murch, Mel
  See Manes, Stephen
Murdoch, David H(amilton) 1937- *96*
Murdoch, Patricia 1957- *192*
Murdock, Catherine Gilbert *185*
Murhall, J(acqueline) J(ane) 1964- *143*
Murphy, Barbara Beasley 1933- *130*
  Earlier sketch in SATA *5*
Murphy, Claire Rudolf 1951- *137*
  Earlier sketch in SATA *76*
Murphy, E(mmett) Jefferson 1926- *4*
Murphy, Jill (Frances) 1949- *142*
  Earlier sketches in SATA *37, 70*
  See also CLR *39*
Murphy, Jim 1947- *185*
  Brief entry *32*
  Earlier sketches in SATA *37, 77, 124*
  See also CLR *53*
Murphy, Joseph E., Jr. 1930- *65*
Murphy, Kelly 1977- *190*
  Earlier sketch in SATA *143*
Murphy, Louise 1943- *155*
Murphy, Pat
  See Murphy, E(mmett) Jefferson
Murphy, Patricia J. 1963- *132*
Murphy, Rita *180*
Murphy, Robert (William) 1902-1971 .... *10*
Murphy, Shirley Rousseau 1928- *126*
  Earlier sketches in SATA *36, 71*
  See also SAAS *18*
Murphy, Stuart J. 1942- *157*
  Earlier sketch in SATA *115*
Murphy, Tim
  See Murphy, Jim
Murphy, Tom *191*
  See Murphy, Thomas Basil, Jr.
Murray, John 1923- *39*
Murray, Kirsty 1960- *165*
  Earlier sketch in SATA *108*
Murray, Marguerite 1917- *63*
Murray, Marian *5*
Murray, Martine 1965- *125*

Murray, (Judith) Michele (Freedman)
1933-1974 7
Murray, Ossie 1938- 43
Murray, Peter
See Hautman, Pete
Murrow, Liza Ketchum 1946- 78
See Ketchum, Liza
Musgrave, Florence 1902-1999 3
Musgrove, Margaret W(ynkoop) 1943- 124
Earlier sketch in SATA 26
Mussey, Virginia Howell
See Ellison, Virginia H(owell)
Mussey, Virginia T.H.
See Ellison, Virginia H(owell)
Mutel, Cornelia F. 1947- 74
Muth, Jon J. 165
Mutz
See Kuenstler, Morton
Mwangi, Meja 1948- 174
My Brother's Brother
See Chekhov, Anton (Pavlovich)
Myers, Anna 160
Myers, Arthur 1917- 91
Earlier sketch in SATA 35
Myers, Bernice 81
Earlier sketch in SATA 9
Myers, Caroline Elizabeth Clark
1887-1980 28
Myers, Christopher 1975- 183
See also CLR 97
Myers, Edward 1950- 172
Earlier sketch in SATA 96
Myers, Elisabeth P(erkins) 1918- 36
Myers, (Mary) Hortense (Powner)
1913-1987 10
Myers, Jack 1913-2006 83
Obituary 178
Myers, Jack Edgar
See Myers, Jack
Myers, Lou 1915-2005 81
Obituary 171
Myers, Louis
See Myers, Lou
Myers, R.E. 1924- 119
Myers, Robert Eugene
See Myers, R.E.
Myers, Tim 1953- 176
Earlier sketch in SATA 147
Myers, Timothy Joseph
See Myers, Tim
Myers, Walter Dean 1937- 193
Brief entry 27
Earlier sketches in SATA 41, 71, 109, 157
See also CLR 110
See also SAAS 2
See Myers, Walter M.
Myers, Walter M.
See Myers, Walter Dean
Myller, Rolf 1926-2006 27
Obituary 175
Myra, Harold L(awrence) 1939- 46
Brief entry 42
Myracle, Lauren 1969- 162
Myrus, Donald (Richard) 1927- 23
Mysterious Traveler, The
See Arthur, Robert, (Jr.)

N

Na, An 149
Naaslund, Goorel Kristina 1940- 170
Nadel, Laurie 1948- 74
Naden, Corinne J. 1930- 166
Earlier sketch in SATA 79
Nadimi, Suzan 188
Nagel, Andreas Fischer
See Fischer-Nagel, Andreas
Nagel, Heiderose Fischer
See Fischer-Nagel, Heiderose

Nagle, Shane 176
Naidoo, Beverley 1943- 180
Earlier sketches in SATA 63, 135
See also CLR 29
Naipaul, Shivadhar Srinivasa
See Naipaul, Shiva
Nakae, Noriko 1940- 59
Nakatani, Chiyoko 1930-1981 55
Brief entry 40
See also CLR 30
Nally, Susan W. 1947- 90
Namioka, Lensey 1929- 157
Autobiography Feature 116
Earlier sketches in SATA 27, 89
See also CLR 48
See also SAAS 24
Nanji, Shenaaz 1954- 131
Nanogak Agnes 1925- 61
Napier, Mark
See Laffin, John (Alfred Charles)
Napoli, Donna Jo 1948- 190
Earlier sketches in SATA 92, 137
See also CLR 51
See also SAAS 23
Narahashi, Keiko 1959- 115
Earlier sketch in SATA 79
Narayan, Rasipuram Krishnaswami
See Narayan, R.K.
Narayan, R.K. 1906-2001 62
Nascimbene, Yan 1949- 173
Earlier sketch in SATA 133
Nash, Bruce M(itchell) 1947- 34
Nash, Linell
See Smith, Linell Nash
Nash, Mary (Hughes) 1925- 41
Nash, (Fredric) Ogden 1902-1971 46
Earlier sketch in SATA 2
Nash, Renea Denise 1963- 81
Nast, Elsa Ruth
See Watson, Jane Werner
Nast, Thomas 1840-1902 51
Brief entry 33
Nastick, Sharon 1954- 41
Natarajan, Srividya 187
Nathan, Adele (Gutman) 1900(?)-1986
Obituary 48
Nathan, Amy 155
Earlier sketch in SATA 104
Nathan, Dorothy (Goldeen) (?)-1966 15
Nathan, Robert (Gruntal) 1894-1985 6
Obituary 43
Nathanson, Laura Walther 1941- 57
Natti, Susanna 1948- 125
Earlier sketch in SATA 32
Nau, Thomas 186
Naughtie, Eleanor
See Updale, Eleanor
Naughton, Bill
See Naughton, William John (Francis)
Naughton, James Franklin 1957- 85
Naughton, Jim
See Naughton, James Franklin
Naughton, William John (Francis)
1910-1992 86
See Naughton, Bill
Navarra, John Gabriel 1927- 8
Naylor, Penelope 1941- 10
Naylor, Phyllis 1933- 152
Autobiography Feature 152
Earlier sketches in SATA 12, 66, 102
See also CLR 135
See also SAAS 10
Naylor, Phyllis Reynolds 1933-
See Naylor, Phyllis
Nazarian, Nikki
See Nichols, Cecilia Fawn
Nazaroff, Alexander I(vanovich) 1898-1981 .. 4
Neal, Harry Edward 1906-1993 5
Obituary 76
Neal, Michael
See Teitelbaum, Michael

Nearing, Penny 1916- 47
Brief entry 42
Nebel, Gustave E. 45
Brief entry 33
Nebel, Mimouca
See Nebel, Gustave E.
Nee, Kay Bonner 10
Needham, Kate 1962- 95
Needle, Jan 1943- 98
Earlier sketch in SATA 30
See also CLR 43
See also SAAS 23
Needleman, Jacob 1934- 6
Neel, David 1960- 82
Neel, Preston 1959- 93
Negri, Rocco 1932- 12
Negrin, Fabian 1963- 189
Neier, Aryeh 1937- 59
Neigoff, Anne 13
Neigoff, Mike 1920- 13
Neilson, Frances Fullerton (Jones)
1910-2001 14
Neimark, Anne E. 1935- 145
Earlier sketch in SATA 4
Neimark, Paul G. 1934- 80
Brief entry 37
Neitzel, Shirley 1941- 134
Earlier sketch in SATA 77
Nell
See Hanna, Nell(ie L.)
Nelscott, Kris
See Rusch, Kristine Kathryn
Nelson, Blake 1960- 177
Nelson, Catherine Chadwick 1926- 87
Nelson, Cordner (Bruce) 1918- 54
Brief entry 29
Nelson, Drew 1952- 77
Nelson, Esther L. 1928- 13
Nelson, Jim A.
See Stotter, Mike
Nelson, Julie L. 1970- 117
Nelson, Kadir 181
Earlier sketch in SATA 154
Nelson, Kris
See Rusch, Kristine Kathryn
Nelson, Lawrence E(rnest) 1928-1977
Obituary 28
Nelson, Marilyn 1946- 180
Autobiography Feature 180
Earlier sketch in SATA 151
See Waniek, Marilyn Nelson
Nelson, Mary Carroll 1929- 23
Nelson, O. Terry 1941- 62
Nelson, Peter N. 1953- 73
Nelson, Richard K(ing) 1941- 65
Nelson, Robin Laura 1971- 141
Nelson, Roy Paul 1923- 59
Nelson, S.D. 181
Nelson, Sharlene (P.) 1933- 96
Nelson, Suzanne 1976- 184
Nelson, Ted (W.) 1931- 96
Nelson, Theresa 1948- 143
Autobiography Feature 143
Earlier sketch in SATA 79
Nemeth, Sally 187
Nerlove, Miriam 1959- 53
Brief entry 49
Nesbit, E. 1858-1924 100
See also YABC 1
See also CLR 70
Nesbit, Edith
See Nesbit, E.
Nesbit, Troy
See Folsom, Franklin (Brewster)
Nespojohn, Katherine V(eronica) 1912-1975 . 7
Ness, Evaline (Michelow) 1911-1986 26
Obituary 49
Earlier sketch in SATA 1
See also CLR 6
See also SAAS 1
Nestor, Larry 1940- 149

Nestor, William P(rodromos) 1947- *49*
Nethery, Mary *93*
Neubecker, Robert *170*
Neuberger, Julia (Babette Sarah) 1950- *142*
  Earlier sketch in SATA *78*
Neufeld, John (Arthur) 1938- *131*
  Autobiography Feature *131*
  Earlier sketches in SATA *6, 81*
  See also CLR *52*
  See also SAAS *3*
Neuhaus, David 1958- *83*
Neumeyer, Peter F(lorian) 1929- *13*
Neurath, Marie (Reidemeister) 1898-1986 ..... *1*
Neuschwander, Cindy 1953- *157*
  Earlier sketch in SATA *107*
Neusner, Jacob 1932- *38*
Neville, Charles
  See Bodsworth, (Charles) Fred(erick)
Neville, Emily Cheney 1919- *1*
  See also SAAS *2*
Neville, Mary
  See Woodrich, Mary Neville
Nevins, Albert (Francis) J(erome)
  1915-1997 .... *20*
Nevius, Carol 1955- *186*
Newberger, Devra
  See Speregen, Devra Newberger
Newberry, Clare Turlay 1903-1970 .... *1*
  Obituary *26*
Newbery, John 1713-1767 .... *20*
Newbery, Linda 1952- *184*
  Earlier sketch in SATA *142*
Newcomb, Ellsworth
  See Kenny, Ellsworth Newcomb
Newcombe, Jack *45*
  Brief entry *33*
  See Newcombe, Eugene A.
Newcome, Robert 1955- *91*
Newcome, Zita 1959- *88*
Newell, Crosby
  See Bonsall, Crosby Barbara (Newell)
Newell, Edythe W(eatherford) 1910-1989 .... *11*
Newell, Hope Hockenberry 1896-1965 .... *24*
Newfeld, Frank 1928- *26*
Newlon, (Frank) Clarke 1905(?)-1982 .... *6*
  Obituary *33*
Newman, Barbara Johansen *191*
Newman, Daisy 1904-1994 .... *27*
  Obituary *78*
Newman, Gerald 1939- *46*
  Brief entry *42*
Newman, Jerry 1935- *82*
Newman, Leslea 1955- *134*
  Earlier sketches in SATA *71, 128*
Newman, Margaret
  See Potter, Margaret (Newman)
Newman, Marjorie *146*
Newman, Matthew (Harrison) 1955- *56*
Newman, Nanette 1934- *162*
Newman, Robert (Howard) 1909-1988 .... *87*
  Obituary *60*
  Earlier sketch in SATA *4*
Newman, Shirlee P(etkin) *144*
  Earlier sketches in SATA *10, 90*
Newsom, Carol 1948- *92*
  Earlier sketch in SATA *40*
Newsom, Tom 1944- *80*
Newth, Mette 1942- *140*
Newton, David E(dward) 1933- *67*
Newton, James R(obert) 1935- *23*
Newton, Robert 1965- *191*
Newton, Suzanne 1936- *77*
  Earlier sketch in SATA *5*
Ney, John 1923- *43*
  Brief entry *33*
Nez, John *155*
Ng, Franklin *82*
Nguyen, Vincent *187*
Nichol, B(arrie) P(hillip) 1944-1988 .... *66*
Nicholas, Louise D.
  See Watkins, Dawn L.

Nicholls, Judith (Ann) 1941- *61*
Nichols, Cecilia Fawn 1906-1987 .... *12*
Nichols, Grace 1950- *164*
  Earlier sketch in SATA *98*
Nichols, Janet (Louise) 1952- *67*
Nichols, Judy 1947- *124*
Nichols, Leigh
  See Koontz, Dean R.
Nichols, Paul
  See Hawks, Robert
Nichols, Peter
  See Youd, (Christopher) Samuel
Nichols, (Joanna) Ruth 1948- *15*
Nicholson, C. R.
  See Nicole, Christopher (Robin)
Nicholson, Christina
  See Nicole, Christopher (Robin)
Nicholson, Joyce Thorpe 1919- *35*
Nicholson, Lois P. 1949- *88*
Nicholson, Robin
  See Nicole, Christopher (Robin)
Nicholson, William *180*
Nicholson, William 1872-1949
  See CLR *76*
Nickel, Barbara 1966- *188*
Nickell, Joe 1944- *167*
  Earlier sketch in SATA *73*
Nickelsburg, Janet 1893-1983 .... *11*
Nickerson, Elizabeth *14*
  See Nickerson, Betty
Nickl, Barbara (Elisabeth) 1939- *56*
Nicklaus, Carol *62*
  Brief entry *33*
Nickle, John *181*
Nickless, Will 1902-1979(?) *66*
Nic Leodhas, Sorche
  See Alger, Leclaire (Gowans)
Nicol, Ann
  See Turnbull, Ann
Nicolas
  See Mordvinoff, Nicolas
Nicolay, Helen 1866-1954
  See YABC *1*
Nicole, Christopher (Robin) 1930- *5*
Nicoll, Helen 1937- *87*
Nicolson, Cynthia Pratt 1949- *141*
Ni Dhuibhne, Eilis 1954- *91*
Niehaus, Paddy Bouma
  See Bouma, Paddy
Nields, Nerissa 1967- *166*
Nielsen, Kay (Rasmus) 1886-1957 .... *16*
  See also CLR *16*
Nielsen, Laura F(arnsworth) 1960- *93*
Nielsen, Nancy J. 1951- *77*
Nielsen, Virginia
  See McCall, Virginia Nielsen
Niemann, Christoph 1970- *191*
Nieuwsma, Milton J(ohn) 1941- *142*
Nightingale, Sandy 1953- *76*
Nikolajeva, Maria 1952- *127*
Nikola-Lisa, W. 1951- *180*
  Earlier sketch in SATA *71*
Niland, Deborah 1951- *172*
  Earlier sketch in SATA *27*
Niland, Kilmeny *75*
Nilsen, Anna 1948- *174*
  Earlier sketch in SATA *96*
Nilsson, Eleanor 1939- *117*
  Earlier sketch in SATA *81*
  See also SAAS *23*
Nilsson, Per 1954- *159*
Nimmo, Jenny 1944- *144*
  Earlier sketch in SATA *87*
  See also CLR *44*
Niven, Larry 1938- *171*
  Earlier sketch in SATA *95*
  See Niven, Laurence VanCott
Niven, Laurence VanCott
  See Niven, Larry
Nivola, Claire A. 1947- *140*
  Earlier sketch in SATA *84*

Nix, Garth 1963- *143*
  Earlier sketch in SATA *97*
  See also CLR *68*
Nixon, Hershell Howard 1923- *42*
Nixon, Joan Lowery 1927-2003 .... *115*
  Obituary *146*
  Earlier sketches in SATA *8, 44, 78*
  See also CLR *24*
  See also SAAS *9*
Nixon, K.
  See Nixon, Kathleen Irene (Blundell)
Nixon, Kathleen Irene (Blundell)
  1894-1988(?) *14*
  Obituary *59*
Nobisso, Josephine 1953- *121*
  Earlier sketch in SATA *78*
Noble, Iris (Davis) 1922-1986 .... *5*
  Obituary *49*
Noble, Marty 1947- *125*
  Earlier sketch in SATA *97*
Noble, Trinka Hakes 1944- *123*
  Brief entry *37*
Noda, Takayo 1961- *168*
Nodelman, Perry 1942- *101*
Nodset, Joan L.
  See Lexau, Joan M.
Noel Hume, Ivor 1927- *65*
Noestlinger, Christine
  See Nostlinger, Christine
Noguere, Suzanne 1947- *34*
Nolan, Dennis 1945- *166*
  Brief entry *34*
  Earlier sketches in SATA *42, 92*
Nolan, Han 1956- *157*
  Earlier sketch in SATA *109*
Nolan, Janet 1956- *191*
  Earlier sketch in SATA *145*
Nolan, Jeannette Covert 1897-1974 .... *2*
  Obituary *27*
Nolan, Paul T(homas) 1919- *48*
Nolan, William F(rancis) 1928- *88*
  Brief entry *28*
Nolen, Jerdine 1953- *157*
  Earlier sketch in SATA *105*
Noll, Sally 1946- *82*
Noonan, Brandon 1979- *184*
Noonan, Diana 1960- *146*
Noonan, Julia 1946- *148*
  Earlier sketches in SATA *4, 95*
Norac, Carl 1960- *166*
Norcross, John
  See Conroy, John Wesley
Nordan, Robert W(arren) 1934-2004 .... *133*
Nordhoff, Charles Bernard 1887-1947 .... *23*
Nordlicht, Lillian *29*
Nordstrom, Ursula 1910-1988 .... *3*
  Obituary *57*
Nordtvedt, Matilda 1926- *67*
Norling, Beth 1969- *149*
Norman, Charles 1904-1996 .... *38*
  Obituary *92*
Norman, Howard
  See Norman, Howard A.
Norman, Howard A. 1949- *81*
Norman, James
  See Schmidt, James Norman
Norman, Jay
  See Arthur, Robert, (Jr.)
Norman, Lilith 1927- *120*
  Earlier sketch in SATA *86*
Norman, Mary 1931- *36*
Norman, Steve
  See Pashko, Stanley
Norment, Lisa 1966- *91*
Norris, Gunilla Brodde 1939- *20*
North, Andrew
  See Norton, Andre
North, Anthony
  See Koontz, Dean R.
North, Captain George
  See Stevenson, Robert Louis (Balfour)

North, Captain George
  See Stevenson, Robert Louis (Balfour)
North, Howard
  See Trevor, Elleston
North, Joan 1920- *16*
North, Milou
  See Erdrich, Louise
North, Robert
  See Withers, Carl A.
North, Sara
  See Bonham, Barbara Thomas
  and Hager, Jean
North, Sterling 1906-1974 .... *45*
  Obituary *26*
  Earlier sketch in SATA *1*
Northcott, (William) Cecil 1902-1987
  Obituary *55*
Northeast, Brenda V(ictoria) 1948- *106*
Northmore, Elizabeth Florence 1906-1974 . *122*
Norton, Alice Mary *43*
  Earlier sketch in SATA *1*
  See Norton, Andre
Norton, Andre 1912-2005 .... *91*
  See also CLR *50*
  See Norton, Alice Mary
Norton, Browning
  See Norton, Frank R. B(rowning)
Norton, Frank R. B(rowning) 1909-1989 ..... *10*
Norton, Mary 1903-1992 .... *60*
  Obituary *72*
  Earlier sketch in SATA *18*
  See also CLR *6*
Nosredna, Trebor
  See Anderson, Bob
Nostlinger, Christine 1936- *162*
  Brief entry *37*
  Earlier sketch in SATA *64*
  See also CLR *12*
Nourse, Alan E(dward) 1928-1992 .... *48*
  See also CLR *33*
Novak, Matt 1962- *165*
  Brief entry *52*
  Earlier sketches in SATA *60, 104*
Novelli, Luca 1947- *61*
Nowell, Elizabeth Cameron *12*
Noyes, Deborah
  See Wayshak, Deborah Noyes
Nugent, Nicholas 1949- *73*
Numeroff, Laura Joffe 1953- *142*
  Earlier sketches in SATA *28, 90*
  See also CLR *85*
Nunes, Lygia Bojunga 1932- *154*
  Earlier sketch in SATA *75*
  See Bojunga, Lygia
Nunn, Laura (Donna) Silverstein 1968- *124*
Nurenberg, Thelma
  See Greenhaus, Thelma Nurenberg
Nurnberg, Maxwell 1897-1984 .... *27*
  Obituary *41*
Nussbaumer, Paul (Edmund) 1934- *16*
Nutt, Ken 1951- *163*
  Earlier sketch in SATA *97*
Nuygen, Mathieu 1967- *80*
Nyberg, (Everett Wayne) Morgan 1944- *87*
Nyce, (Nellie) Helene von Strecker
  1885-1969 .... *19*
Nyce, Vera 1862-1925 .... *19*
Nye, Naomi Shihab 1952- *147*
  Earlier sketch in SATA *86*
  See also CLR *59*
Nye, Robert 1939- *6*
Nyikos, Stacy A. 1969- *164*
Nystrom, Carolyn 1940- *130*
  Earlier sketch in SATA *67*

O

Oakes, Elizabeth H. 1964- *132*
Oakes, Vanya 1909-1983 .... *6*
  Obituary *37*
Oakley, Don(ald G.) 1927- *8*
Oakley, Graham 1929- *84*
  Earlier sketch in SATA *30*
  See also CLR *7*
Oakley, Helen (McKelvey) 1906- *10*
Oana, Katherine 1929- *53*
  Brief entry *37*
Oates, Eddie H. 1943- *88*
Oates, Joyce Carol 1938- *159*
Oates, Stephen B(aery) 1936- *59*
Obed, Ellen Bryan 1944- *74*
Oberle, Joseph 1958- *69*
Oberman, Sheldon 1949-2004 .... *85*
  Autobiography Feature *114*
  Obituary *153*
  See also CLR *54*
  See also SAAS *26*
Obligado, Lilian (Isabel) 1931- *61*
  Brief entry *45*
Obrant, Susan 1946- *11*
O'Brian, E.G.
  See Clarke, Arthur C.
O'Brien, Anne Sibley 1952- *80*
  Brief entry *48*
  Earlier sketch in SATA *53*
O'Brien, E.G.
  See Clarke, Arthur C.
O'Brien, Esse Forrester 1895(?)-1975
  Obituary *30*
O'Brien, Patrick 1960- *193*
O'Brien, Robert C.
  See CLR *2*
  See Conly, Robert Leslie
O'Brien, Thomas C(lement) 1938- *29*
O'Callaghan, Julie 1954- *113*
O'Callahan, Jay 1938- *88*
O'Carroll, Ryan
  See Markun, Patricia Maloney
Ochiltree, Dianne 1953- *117*
Ockham, Joan Price
  See Price, Joan
O'Connell, Margaret F(orster) 1935-1977 .... *30*
  Obituary *30*
O'Connell, Peg
  See Ahern, Margaret McCrohan
O'Connell, Rebecca 1968- *130*
O'Connor, Barbara 1950- *193*
  Earlier sketch in SATA *154*
O'Connor, Francine M(arie) 1930- *90*
O'Connor, Genevieve A. 1914- *75*
O'Connor, George *183*
O'connor, Ian 1965- *188*
O'Connor, Jane 1947- *186*
  Brief entry *47*
  Earlier sketches in SATA *59, 103, 150*
O'Connor, Karen 1938- *89*
  Earlier sketch in SATA *34*
O'Connor, Patrick
  See Wibberley, Leonard (Patrick O'Connor)
O'Connor, Richard 1915-1975
  Obituary *21*
O'Conor, Jane 1958- *78*
Odaga, Asenath (Bole) 1937- *130*
  Earlier sketch in SATA *67*
  See also SAAS *19*
O Danachair, Caoimhin
  See Danaher, Kevin
Odanaka, Barbara *159*
O'Daniel, Janet 1921- *24*
O'Day, Cathy
  See Crane, Barbara (Joyce)
O'Dell, Scott 1898-1989 .... *134*
  Earlier sketches in SATA *12, 60*
  See also CLR *126*
Odenwald, Robert P(aul) 1899-1965 ...... *11*

Odgers, Sally
  See Odgers, Sally Farrell
Odgers, Sally Farrell 1957- *139*
  Earlier sketch in SATA *72*
O'Donnell, Dick
  See Lupoff, Richard A(llen)
  and Thompson, Don(ald Arthur)
Odriozola, Elena *186*
Oechsli, Kelly 1918-1999 .... *5*
Oesterle, Virginia Rorby
  See Rorby, Ginny
Ofek, Uriel 1926- *36*
  See also CLR *28*
Offenbacher, Ami 1958- *91*
Offit, Sidney 1928- *10*
Ofosu-Appiah, L(awrence) H(enry) 1920- ... *13*
Ogan, George F. 1912-1983 .... *13*
Ogan, M. G.
  See Ogan, George F.
  and Ogan, Margaret E. (Nettles)
Ogan, Margaret E. (Nettles) 1923-1979 ... *13*
Ogburn, Charlton (Jr.) 1911-1998 .... *3*
  Obituary *109*
Ogburn, Jacqueline K. *162*
Ogilvie, Elisabeth May 1917-2006 .... *40*
  Brief entry *29*
  Obituary *176*
Ogilvy, Gavin
  See Barrie, J(ames) M(atthew)
Ogilvy, Ian 1943- *177*
Ogilvy, Ian Raymond
  See Ogilvy, Ian
Ogle, Lucille Edith 1904-1988
  Obituary *59*
Ogletree, Charles J. 1952- *175*
O'Green, Jennifer
  See Roberson, Jennifer
O'Green, Jennifer Roberson
  See Roberson, Jennifer
O'Hagan, Caroline 1946- *38*
O'Hanlon, Jacklyn
  See Meek, Jacklyn O'Hanlon
O'Hara, Elizabeth
  See Ni Dhuibhne, Eilis
O'Hara, Kenneth
  See Morris, (Margaret) Jean
O'Hara, Mary
  See Alsop, Mary O'Hara
O'Hara (Alsop), Mary
  See Alsop, Mary O'Hara
O'Hare, Jeff(rey A.) 1958- *105*
Ohi, Ruth 1964- *95*
Ohiyesa
  See Eastman, Charles A(lexander)
Ohlsson, Ib 1935- *7*
Ohmi, Ayano 1959- *115*
Ohtomo, Yasuo 1946- *37*
o huigin, sean 1942- *138*
  See also CLR *75*
Oiseau
  See Moseley, James W(illett)
Oke, Janette 1935- *97*
O'Keefe, Susan Heyboer *176*
  Earlier sketch in SATA *133*
O'Keeffe, Frank 1938- *99*
O'Kelley, Mattie Lou 1908-1997 .... *97*
  Earlier sketch in SATA *36*
Okimoto, Jean Davies 1942- *103*
  Earlier sketch in SATA *34*
Okomfo, Amasewa
  See Cousins, Linda
Olaleye, Isaac O. 1941- *96*
  See also SAAS *23*
Olcott, Frances Jenkins 1872(?)-1963 .... *19*
Old, Wendie C(orbin) 1943- *154*
Old Boy
  See Hughes, Thomas
Oldenburg, E(gbert) William 1936-1974 ... *35*
Older, Effin 1942- *114*
Older, Jules 1940- *156*
  Earlier sketch in SATA *114*

Oldfield, Jenny 1949- *140*
Oldfield, Margaret J(ean) 1932- *56*
Oldfield, Pamela 1931- *86*
Oldham, June *70*
Oldham, Mary 1944- *65*
Olds, Elizabeth 1896-1991 .... *3*
  Obituary *66*
Olds, Helen Diehl 1895-1981 .... *9*
  Obituary *25*
Oldstyle, Jonathan
  See Irving, Washington
O'Leary, Brian (Todd) 1940- *6*
O'Leary, Patsy B(aker) 1937- *97*
Oliphant, B.J.
  See Tepper, Sheri S.
Oliver, Burton
  See Burt, Olive Woolley
Oliver, Chad
  See Oliver, Symmes C(hadwick)
Oliver, John Edward 1933- *21*
Oliver, Marilyn Tower 1935- *89*
Oliver, Narelle 1960- *152*
Oliver, Shirley (Louise Dawkins) 1958- *74*
Oliver, Symmes C(hadwick) 1928-1993 .... *101*
  See Oliver, Chad
Oliviero, Jamie 1950- *84*
Olmsted, Lorena Ann 1890-1989 .... *13*
Olney, Ross R. 1929- *13*
Olschewski, Alfred (Erich) 1920- *7*
Olsen, Barbara *148*
Olsen, Carol 1945- *89*
Olsen, Ib Spang 1921- *81*
  Earlier sketch in SATA *6*
Olsen, Violet (Mae) 1922-1991 .... *58*
Olson, Arielle North 1932- *67*
Olson, Gene 1922- *32*
Olson, Gretchen *187*
Olson, Helen Kronberg *48*
Olson, Kay Melchisedech 1948- *175*
Olson, Marianne
  See Mitchell, Marianne
Olson-Brown, Ellen 1967- *183*
Olugebefola, Ademole 1941- *15*
Oluonye, Mary N(kechi) 1955- *111*
Om
  See Gorey, Edward (St. John)
O'Malley, Kevin 1961- *191*
  Earlier sketch in SATA *157*
Oman, Carola (Mary Anima) 1897-1978 ..... *35*
O'Mara, Carmel 1965- *166*
O'Mara-Horwitz, Carmel
  See O'Mara, Carmel
O'Meara, Walter (Andrew) 1897-1989 .... *65*
Ommanney, F(rancis) D(ownes) 1903-1980 . *23*
O Mude
  See Gorey, Edward (St. John)
Oneal, Elizabeth 1934- *82*
  Earlier sketch in SATA *30*
  See Oneal, Zibby
O'Neal, Reagan
  See Jordan, Robert
O'Neal, Regan
  See Jordan, Robert
Oneal, Zibby
  See CLR *13*
  See Oneal, Elizabeth
O'Neill, Amanda 1951- *111*
O'Neill, Gerard K(itchen) 1927-1992 .... *65*
O'Neill, Judith (Beatrice) 1930- *34*
O'Neill, Mary L(e Duc) 1908(?)-1990 .... *2*
  Obituary *64*
O'Neill, Reagan
  See Jordan, Robert
Onslow, Annette Rosemary MacArthur
  See MacArthur-Onslow, Annette Rosemary
Onslow, John 1906-1985
  Obituary *47*
Onyefulu, Ifeoma 1959- *157*
  Earlier sketches in SATA *81, 115*

Opie, Iona (Margaret Balfour) 1923- *118*
  Earlier sketches in SATA *3, 63*
  See also SAAS 6
Opie, Peter (Mason) 1918-1982 .... *118*
  Obituary *28*
  Earlier sketches in SATA *3, 63*
Oppel, Kenneth 1967- *153*
  Earlier sketch in SATA *99*
Oppenheim, Joanne 1934- *174*
  Earlier sketches in SATA *5, 82, 136*
Oppenheim, Shulamith Levey 1928- *177*
Oppenheimer, Joan L(etson) 1925- *28*
Oppong, Joseph Ransford 1953- *160*
Optic, Oliver
  See Adams, William Taylor
  and Stratemeyer, Edward L.
Oram, Hiawyn 1946- *101*
  Earlier sketch in SATA *56*
Orbach, Ruth Gary 1941- *21*
Orczy, Emma
  See Orczy, Baroness Emmuska
Orczy, Emma Magdalena Rosalia Maria Josefa
  See Orczy, Baroness Emmuska
Orczy, Emmuska
  See Orczy, Baroness Emmuska
Orczy, Baroness Emmuska 1865-1947 .... *40*
  See Orczy, Emma
Orde, A.J.
  See Tepper, Sheri S.
O'Reilly, Jackson
  See Jordan, Robert
Orenstein, Denise Gosliner 1950- *157*
Orgel, Doris 1929- *148*
  Earlier sketches in SATA *7, 85*
  See also CLR *48*
  See also SAAS *19*
Oriolo, Joe
  See Oriolo, Joseph D.
Oriolo, Joseph D. 1913-1985
  Obituary *46*
Orleans, Ilo 1897-1962 .... *10*
Orlev, Uri 1931- *135*
  Earlier sketch in SATA *58*
  See also CLR *30*
  See also SAAS *19*
Ormai, Stella *57*
  Brief entry *48*
Ormerod, Jan 1946- *132*
  Brief entry *44*
  Earlier sketches in SATA *55, 70*
  See also CLR *20*
Ormes, Jackie
  See Ormes, Zelda J.
Ormes, Zelda J. 1914-1986
  Obituary *47*
Ormondroyd, Edward 1925- *14*
Ormsby, Virginia H(aire) 1906-1990 .... *11*
Orona-Ramirez, Kristy 1964- *189*
Orozco, Jose-Luis 1948- *179*
Orr, Katherine S(helley) 1950- *72*
Orr, Wendy 1953- *141*
  Earlier sketch in SATA *90*
Orris
  See Ingelow, Jean
Orth, Richard
  See Gardner, Richard (M.)
Ortiz Cofer, Judith
  See Cofer, Judith Ortiz
Orwell, George
  See CLR *68*
  See Blair, Eric (Arthur)
Orwin, Joanna 1944- *141*
Osborn, Elinor 1939- *145*
Osborn, Lois D(orothy) 1915- *61*
Osborne, Charles 1927- *59*
Osborne, Chester G(orham) 1915-1987 .... *11*
Osborne, David
  See Silverberg, Robert
Osborne, George
  See Silverberg, Robert
Osborne, Leone Neal 1914-1996 .... *2*

Osborne, Mary Pope 1949- *144*
  Earlier sketches in SATA *41, 55, 98*
  See also CLR *88*
Osceola
  See Blixen, Karen (Christentze Dinesen)
Osgood, William E(dward) 1926- *37*
O'Shaughnessy, Darren
  See Shan, Darren
O'Shaughnessy, Ellen Cassels 1937- *78*
O'Shea, Catherine Patricia Shiels
  See O'Shea, Pat
O'Shea, Pat 1931-2007 .... *87*
  See also CLR *18*
Osmond, Edward 1900- *10*
Ossoli, Sarah Margaret (Fuller) 1810-1850 .. *25*
  See Fuller, Margaret
Ostendorf, (Arthur) Lloyd, (Jr.) 1921-2000 .. *65*
  Obituary *125*
Ostow, Micol 1976- *170*
Otfinoski, Steven 1949- *116*
  Earlier sketch in SATA *56*
Otis, James
  See Kaler, James Otis
O'Toole, Thomas 1941- *71*
O'Trigger, Sir Lucius
  See Horne, Richard Henry Hengist
Otten, Charlotte
  See Otten, Charlotte F.
Otten, Charlotte F. 1926- *98*
Otten, Charlotte Fennema
  See Otten, Charlotte F.
Ottley, Matt 1962- *171*
  Earlier sketch in SATA *102*
Ottley, Reginald Leslie 1909-1985 .... *26*
  See also CLR *16*
Otto, Margaret Glover 1909-1976
  Obituary *30*
Otto, Svend
  See Soerensen, Svend Otto
Oughton, Jerrie (Preston) 1937- *131*
  Earlier sketch in SATA *76*
Oughton, (William) Taylor 1925- *104*
Ouida
  See De La Ramee, Marie Louise
Ousley, Odille 1896-1976 .... *10*
Outcalt, Todd 1960- *123*
Overmyer, James E. 1946- *88*
Overton, Jenny (Margaret Mary) 1942- *52*
  Brief entry *36*
Owen, Ann
  See Qualey, Marsha
Owen, Annie 1949- *75*
Owen, Caroline Dale
  See Snedeker, Caroline Dale (Parke)
Owen, Clifford
  See Hamilton, Charles (Harold St. John)
Owen, Dilys
  See Gater, Dilys
Owen, (Benjamin) Evan 1918-1984 .... *38*
Owen, (John) Gareth 1936-2002 .... *162*
  Earlier sketch in SATA *83*
  See also CLR *31*
  See also SAAS *14*
Owen, James A. *185*
Owens, Bryant 1968- *116*
Owens, Dana Elaine
  See Queen Latifah
Owens, Gail 1939- *54*
Owens, Mary Beth *191*
Owens, Thomas S(heldon) 1960- *86*
Owens, Tom
  See Owens, Thomas S(heldon)
Oxenbury, Helen 1938- *149*
  Earlier sketches in SATA *3, 68*
  See also CLR *70*
Oxendine, Bess Holland 1933- *90*
Oz, Frank (Richard) 1944- *60*
Ozer, Jerome S. 1927- *59*

P

Pace, Lorenzo 1943- *131*
Pace, Mildred Mastin 1907- *46*
    Brief entry *29*
Pachter, Hedwig (?)-1988 .... *63*
Pack, Janet 1952- *77*
Pack, Robert 1929- *118*
Packard, Edward 1931- *148*
    Earlier sketches in SATA *47, 90*
Packer, Kenneth L. 1946- *116*
Packer, Vin
    See Meaker, Marijane
Pad, Peter
    See Stratemeyer, Edward L.
Page, Eileen
    See Heal, Edith
Page, Eleanor
    See Coerr, Eleanor (Beatrice)
Page, Jake 1936- *81*
Page, James Keena, Jr.
    See Page, Jake
Page, Lou Williams 1912-1997 .... *38*
Page, Mary
    See Heal, Edith
Page, Robin 1943- *154*
Pagnucci, Susan 1944- *90*
Pahlen, Kurt 1907-2003
    Obituary *147*
Pahz, Cheryl
    See Pahz, Cheryl Suzanne
Pahz, Cheryl Suzanne 1949- *11*
Pahz, James Alon 1943- *11*
Paice, Margaret 1920- *10*
Paige, Harry W(orthington) 1922- *41*
    Brief entry *35*
Paige, Richard
    See Koontz, Dean R.
Paige, Robin
    See Albert, Susan Wittig
Paine, Penelope Colville 1946- *87*
Paine, Roberta M. 1925- *13*
Paisley, Tom 1932- *78*
    See Bethancourt, T. Ernesto
Palatini, Margie *174*
    Earlier sketch in SATA *134*
Palazzo, Anthony D.
    See Palazzo, Tony
Palazzo, Tony 1905-1970 .... *3*
Palder, Edward L. 1922- *5*
Palecek, Josef 1932- *56*
Palecek, Libuse 1937- *89*
Palin, Michael 1943- *67*
    See Monty Python
Palin, Michael Edward
    See Palin, Michael
Palladini, David (Mario) 1946- *40*
    Brief entry *32*
Pallas, Norvin 1918-1983 .... *23*
Pallister, John C(lare) 1891-1980
    Obituary *26*
Pallotta, Gerard Larry
    See Pallotta, Jerry
Pallotta, Jerry 1953- *186*
Pallotta-Chiarolli, Maria 1960- *117*
Palmer, Bernard (Alvin) 1914-1998 .... *26*
Palmer, C. Everard 1930- *14*
Palmer, (Ruth) Candida 1926- *11*
Palmer, Cyril Everard
    See Palmer, C. Everard
Palmer, Don
    See Benson, Mildred (Augustine Wirt)
Palmer, Hap 1942- *68*
Palmer, Heidi 1948- *15*
Palmer, Helen Marion
    See Geisel, Helen
Palmer, Jessica 1953- *120*
Palmer, Judd 1972- *153*
Palmer, Juliette 1930- *15*
Palmer, Kate Salley 1946- *97*

Palmer, Maria
    See Strachan, Ian
Palmer, Maria
    See Brennan, Herbie
Palmer, Robin 1909-2000 .... *43*
Paltrowitz, Donna 1950- *61*
    Brief entry *50*
Paltrowitz, Donna Milman
    See Paltrowitz, Donna
Paltrowitz, Stuart 1946- *61*
    Brief entry *50*
Pamintuan, Macky *178*
Panagopoulos, Janie Lynn *149*
Panati, Charles 1943- *65*
Panchyk, Richard 1970- *138*
Panetta, George 1915-1969 .... *15*
Panetta, Joseph N. 1953- *96*
Panik, Sharon 1952- *82*
Panowski, Eileen Thompson 1920- *49*
Pansy
    See Alden, Isabella (Macdonald)
Pantell, Dora (Fuchs) *39*
Panter, Carol 1936- *9*
Paolini, Christopher 1983- *157*
    See also CLR *102*
Papademetriou, Lisa *175*
Paparone, Pam *185*
Paparone, Pamela
    See Paparone, Pam
Papas, Bill
    See Papas, William
Papas, William 1927-2000 .... *50*
Papashvily, George 1898-1978 .... *17*
Papashvily, Helen (Waite) 1906-1996 .... *17*
Pape, D. L.
    See Pape, Donna (Lugg)
Pape, Donna (Lugg) 1930- *82*
    Earlier sketch in SATA *2*
Paperny, Myra (Green) 1932- *51*
    Brief entry *33*
Paradis, Adrian A(lexis) 1912- *67*
    Earlier sketch in SATA *1*
    See also SAAS *8*
Paradis, Marjorie Bartholomew
    1886(?)-1970 .... *17*
Paradiz, Valerie 1963- *176*
Parenteau, Shirley Laurolyn 1935- *47*
    Brief entry *40*
Parish, Margaret (Cecile) 1927-1988 .... *73*
    See Parish, Peggy
Parish, Margaret Holt
    See Holt, Margaret
Parish, Peggy *17*
    Obituary *59*
    See also CLR *22*
    See Parish, Margaret (Cecile)
Park, Barbara 1947- *123*
    Brief entry *35*
    Earlier sketches in SATA *40, 78*
    See also CLR *34*
Park, Bill
    See Park, W(illiam) B(ryan)
Park, Frances 1955- *171*
Park, Ginger *173*
Park, Janie Jaehyun *150*
Park, Jordan
    See Kornbluth, C(yril) M.
    and Pohl, Frederik
Park, Linda Sue 1960- *173*
    Earlier sketch in SATA *127*
    See also CLR *84*
Park, Nick 1958- *113*
Park, (Rosina) Ruth (Lucia) 1923(?)- *93*
    Earlier sketch in SATA *25*
    See also CLR *51*
Park, W(illiam) B(ryan) 1936- *22*
Parke, Marilyn 1928- *82*
Parker, Barbara Keevil 1938- *157*
Parker, Daniel
    See Ehrenhaft, Daniel
Parker, Elinor Milnor 1906- *3*

Parker, Julie F. 1961- *92*
Parker, Kim 1963- *174*
Parker, Kristy 1957- *59*
Parker, Lois M(ay) 1912-1996 .... *30*
Parker, Margot M. 1937- *52*
Parker, Marjorie Blain 1960- *145*
Parker, Mary Jessie 1948- *71*
Parker, Nancy Winslow 1930- *132*
    Earlier sketches in SATA *10, 69*
    See also SAAS *20*
Parker, Richard 1915-1990 .... *14*
Parker, Robert
    See Boyd, Waldo T.
Parker, Toni Trent 1947-2005 .... *142*
    Obituary *169*
Parker-Rees, Guy *193*
Parkes, Lucas
    See Harris, John (Wyndham Parkes
    Lucas) Beynon
Parkhill, John
    See Cox, William R(obert)
Parkins, David 1955- *176*
Parkinson, Ethelyn M(inerva) 1906-1999 ..... *11*
Parkinson, Kathy *71*
    See Parkinson, Kathryn N.
Parkinson, Siobhan
    See Parkinson, Siobhan
Parkinson, Siobhan 1954- *178*
Parks, Deborah A. 1948- *133*
    Earlier sketch in SATA *91*
Parks, Edd Winfield 1906-1968 .... *10*
Parks, Gordon 1912-2006 .... *108*
    Obituary *175*
    Earlier sketch in SATA *8*
Parks, Gordon Roger Alexander
    See Parks, Gordon
Parks, Peggy J. 1951- *143*
Parks, PJ
    See Parks, Peggy J.
Parks, Rosa 1913-2005 .... *83*
    Obituary *169*
Parks, Rosa Louise Lee
    See Parks, Rosa
Parks, Van Dyke 1943- *62*
Parley, Peter
    See Goodrich, Samuel Griswold
Parlin, John
    See Graves, Charles Parlin
Parme, Fabrice 1966- *191*
Parnall, Peter 1936- *69*
    Earlier sketch in SATA *16*
    See also SAAS *11*
Parotti, Phillip (Elliott) 1941- *109*
Parr, Ann 1943- *144*
Parr, Danny
    See Parr, Ann
Parr, Letitia (Evelyn) 1906-1985(?) *37*
Parr, Lucy 1924- *10*
Parr, Todd *179*
    Earlier sketch in SATA *134*
Parrish, Anne 1888-1957 .... *27*
Parrish, Mary
    See Cousins, Margaret
Parrish, Maxfield
    See Parrish, (Frederick) Maxfield
Parrish, (Frederick) Maxfield 1870-1966 ..... *14*
Parry, Marian 1924- *13*
Parson Lot
    See Kingsley, Charles
Parsons, Alexandra 1947- *92*
Parsons, Ellen
    See Dragonwagon, Crescent
Parsons, Martin 1951- *116*
Parsons, Martin Leslie
    See Parsons, Martin
Parsons, Tom
    See MacPherson, Thomas George
Parsons-Yazzi, Evangeline *172*
Partch, Virgil Franklin II 1916-1984 .... *39*
    Obituary *39*
Parton, Dolly 1946- *94*

Parton, Dolly Rebecca
  See Parton, Dolly
Partridge, Benjamin W., Jr. 1915-2005 28
  Obituary *163*
Partridge, Benjamin Waring, Jr.
  See Partridge, Benjamin W., Jr.
Partridge, Cora Cheney
  See Cheney, Cora
Partridge, Elizabeth 134
Partridge, Jenny (Lilian) 1947- 52
  Brief entry 37
Pasachoff, Naomi 1947- 147
Pascal, David 1918- 14
Pascal, Francine 1938- 143
  Brief entry 37
  Earlier sketches in SATA *51, 80*
  See also CLR 25
Paschal, Nancy
  See Trotter, Grace V(iolet)
Paschkis, Julie 1957- 177
Pascudniak, Pascal
  See Lupoff, Richard A(llen)
Pashko, Stanley 1913-1982 29
Passailaigue, Thomas E.
  See Paisley, Tom
Pateman, Robert 1954- 84
Patent, Dorothy Hinshaw 1940- 162
  Autobiography Feature 162
  Earlier sketches in SATA *22, 69, 120*
  See also CLR 19
  See also SAAS 13
Paterson, A(ndrew) B(arton) 1864-1941 97
Paterson, Banjo
  See Paterson, A(ndrew) B(arton)
Paterson, Diane 1946- 177
  Brief entry 33
  Earlier sketch in SATA *59*
Paterson, John (Barstow) 1932- 114
Paterson, Katherine 1932- 133
  Earlier sketches in SATA *13, 53, 92*
  See also CLR 127
Paterson, Katherine Womeldorf
  See Paterson, Katherine
Patience, John 1949- 90
Patneaude, David 1944- 159
  Earlier sketch in SATA *85*
Paton, Alan 1903-1988 11
  Obituary 56
Paton, Alan Stewart
  See Paton, Alan
Paton, Jane (Elizabeth) 1934- 35
Paton, Priscilla 1952- 98
Paton Walsh, Gillian
  See Paton Walsh, Jill
Paton Walsh, Jill 1937- 190
  Autobiography Feature 190
  Earlier sketches in SATA *4, 72, 109*
  See also CLR 65
  See also SAAS 3
  See Paton Walsh, Gillian
  and Walsh, Jill Paton
Patrick, Susan
  See Clark, Patricia Denise
Patron, Susan 1948- 182
  Earlier sketch in SATA *76*
Patsauq, Markoosie 1942-
  See CLR 23
Patschke, Steve 1955- 125
Patten, Brian 1946- 152
  Earlier sketch in SATA *29*
Patterson, Charles 1935- 59
Patterson, Geoffrey 1943- 54
  Brief entry 44
Patterson, James 1947- 164
Patterson, James B.
  See Patterson, James
Patterson, Lillie G. -1999 88
  Earlier sketch in SATA *14*
Patterson, Nancy Ruth 1944- 148
  Earlier sketch in SATA *72*

Pattison, Darcy (S.) 1954- 126
  Earlier sketch in SATA *72*
Pattou, Edith 164
Patz (Blaustein), Nancy 154
Paul, Aileen 1917- 12
Paul, Ann Whitford 1941- 168
  Earlier sketches in SATA *76, 110*
Paul, David (Tyler) 1934-1988
  Obituary 56
Paul, Dominique 1973- 184
Paul, Elizabeth
  See Crow, Donna Fletcher
Paul, Hamish Vigne Christie 1951- 151
  See also CLR 87
Paul, James 1936- 23
Paul, Korky
  See Paul, Hamish Vigne Christie
Paul, Robert
  See Roberts, John G(aither)
Paul, Tessa 1944- 103
Pauli, Hertha (Ernestine) 1909-1973 3
  Obituary 26
Paull, Grace A. 1898- 24
Paulsen, Gary 1939- 189
  Earlier sketches in SATA *22, 50, 54,
  79, 111, 158*
  See also CLR 82
Paulson, Jack
  See Jackson, C(aary) Paul
Pauquet, Gina Ruck
  See Ruck-Pauquet, Gina
Pausacker, Jenny 1948- 72
  See also SAAS 23
Pausewang, Gudrun 1928- 165
  Earlier sketch in SATA *104*
Pavel, Frances 1907- 10
Paver, Michelle 170
Paxton, Tom 70
Paxton, Thomas R.
  See Paxton, Tom
Paye, Won-Ldy 185
Payne, Alan
  See Jakes, John
Payne, Bernal C., Jr. 1941- 60
Payne, C. Douglas
  See Payne, C.D.
Payne, C.D. 1949- 133
Payne, C.F. 1956- 179
Payne, Chris Fox
  See Payne, C.F.
Payne, Donald Gordon 1924- 37
Payne, Emmy
  See West, Emily Govan
Payne, Nina 135
Payne, Rachel Ann
  See Jakes, John
Payson, Dale 1943- 9
Payzant, Charles 18
Paz, A.
  See Pahz, James Alon
Paz, Zan
  See Pahz, Cheryl Suzanne
Peace, Mary
  See Finley, Mary Peace
Peacock, Shane 1957- 192
Peake, Mervyn 1911-1968 23
Peale, Norman Vincent 1898-1993 20
  Obituary 78
Pearce, Ann Philippa
  See Pearce, Philippa
Pearce, Jacqueline 1962- 146
Pearce, Margaret 104
Pearce, Philippa 1920-2006
  Obituary 179
  See Christie, Philippa
Peare, Catherine Owens 1911- 9
Pearsall, Shelley 1966- 190
Pearson, Gayle 1947- 119
  Earlier sketch in SATA *53*
Pearson, Jean Mary
  See Gardam, Jane

Pearson, Kit 1947- 77
  Autobiography Feature 117
  See also CLR 26
Pearson, Mary E. 1955- 134
Pearson, Ridley 1953- 182
Pearson, Susan 1946- 166
  Brief entry 27
  Earlier sketches in SATA *39, 91*
Pearson, Tracey Campbell 1956- 155
  Earlier sketch in SATA *64*
Pease, (Clarence) Howard 1894-1974 2
  Obituary 25
Peavy, Linda 1943- 54
Peck, Anne Merriman 1884-1976 18
Peck, Beth 1957- 190
  Earlier sketch in SATA *79*
Peck, Jan 159
Peck, Jeanie J. 1967- 147
Peck, Marshall III 1951- 92
Peck, Richard 1934- 190
  Autobiography Feature 110
  Earlier sketches in SATA *18, 55, 97, 110, 158*
  See also CLR 15
  See also SAAS 2
Peck, Richard Wayne
  See Peck, Richard
Peck, Robert Newton 1928- 156
  Autobiography Feature 108
  Earlier sketches in SATA *21, 62, 111*
  See also CLR 45
  See also SAAS 1
Peck, Sylvia 1953- 133
Peck-Whiting, Jeanie J.
  See Peck, Jeanie J.
Pedersen, Janet 193
Pederson, Sharleen
  See Collicott, Sharleen
Peebles, Anne
  See Galloway, Priscilla
Peek, Merle 1938- 39
Peel, John 1954- 79
Peel, Norman Lemon
  See Hirsch, Phil
Peeples, Edwin A(ugustus, Jr.) 1915-1994 6
Peers, Judi 1956- 119
Peers, Judith May West
  See Peers, Judi
Peet, Bill
  See CLR 12
  See Peet, William Bartlett
Peet, Creighton B. 1899-1977 30
Peet, Mal 171
Peet, Malcolm
  See Peet, Mal
Peet, William Bartlett 1915-2002 78
  Obituary 137
  Earlier sketches in SATA *2, 41*
  See Peet, Bill
Peguero, Leone 116
Pelaez, Jill 1924- 12
Pelham, David 1938- 70
Pell, Ed(ward) 1950- 157
Pellowski, Anne 1933- 20
Pellowski, Michael (Joseph) 1949- 151
  Brief entry 48
  Earlier sketch in SATA *88*
Pellowski, Michael Morgan
  See Pellowski, Michael (Joseph)
Pelta, Kathy 1928- 18
Peltier, Leslie C(opus) 1900-1980 13
Pemberton, Bonnie 191
Pemberton, John Leigh
  See Leigh-Pemberton, John
Pembury, Bill
  See Groom, Arthur William
Pemsteen, Hans
  See Manes, Stephen
Pendennis, Arthur Esquir
  See Thackeray, William Makepeace
Pender, Lydia Podger 1907- 61
Pendery, Rosemary (Schmitz) 7

Pendle, Alexy 1943- 29
Pendle, George 1906-1977
    Obituary 28
Pendleton, Don
    See Cunningham, Chet
    and Garside, (Clifford) Jack
    and Jagninski, Tom
    and Krauzer, Steven M(ark)
    and Obstfeld, Raymond
Pendziwol, Jean E. 1965- 177
Pene du Bois, William (Sherman)
    1916-1993 68
    Obituary 74
    Earlier sketch in SATA 4
    See also CLR 1
Penn, Ruth Bonn
    See Rosenberg, Eth(el) Clifford
Pennac, Daniel 1944- 155
Pennage, E. M.
    See Finkel, George (Irvine)
Penner, Fred 1946- 169
    Earlier sketch in SATA 67
Penner, Frederick Ralph Cornelius
    See Penner, Fred
Penney, Grace Jackson 1904-2000 35
Penney, Ian 1960- 76
Penney, Sue 1957- 152
    Earlier sketch in SATA 102
Pennington, Eunice 1923- 27
Pennington, Lillian Boyer 1904- 45
Pennypacker, Sara 1951- 187
Penrose, Gordon 1925- 66
Penson, Mary E. 1917- 78
Penzler, Otto 1942- 38
Pepe, Phil 1935- 20
Pepe, Philip
    See Pepe, Phil
Peppe, Rodney (Darrell) 1934- 74
    Earlier sketch in SATA 4
    See also SAAS 10
Pepper, Frank S. 1910-1988
    Obituary 61
Percy, Charles Henry
    See Smith, Dorothy Gladys
Percy, Rachel 1930- 63
Perdrizet, Marie-Pierre 1952- 79
Perenyi, Constance 1954- 93
Perenyi, Constance Marie
    See Perenyi, Constance
Perera, Hilda 1926- 105
Perera, Thomas Biddle 1938- 13
Peretti, Frank E. 1951- 141
    Earlier sketch in SATA 80
Perez, Lana
    See Perez, Marlene
Perez, Lucia Angela 1973- 182
Perez, Marlene 170
Pericoli, Matteo 1968- 178
Perkins, Al(bert Rogers) 1904-1975 30
Perkins, Lucy Fitch 1865-1937 72
Perkins, Lynne Rae 172
    Earlier sketch in SATA 131
Perkins, (Richard) Marlin 1905-1986 21
    Obituary 48
Perkins, Mitali 1963- 188
    Earlier sketch in SATA 88
Perks, Anne-Marie 1955- 122
Perl, Erica S. 188
Perl, Lila 72
    Earlier sketch in SATA 6
Perl, Susan 1922-1983 22
    Obituary 34
Perlman, Rhea 1948- 183
Perlmutter, O(scar) William 1920-1975 8
Pernu, Dennis 1970- 87
Perrault, Charles 1628-1703 25
    See also CLR 134
Perret, Delphine 1980- 190
Perret, Gene (Richard) 1937- 76
Perrine, Mary 1913-1976 2
Perrins, Lesley 1953- 56

Perrow, Angeli 1954- 121
Perry, Andrea 1956- 190
    Earlier sketch in SATA 148
Perry, Barbara Fisher
    See Fisher, Barbara
Perry, Elizabeth 1959- 174
Perry, Elizabeth Goodwin
    See Perry, Elizabeth
Perry, Marie Fritz 165
Perry, Patricia 1949- 30
Perry, Phyllis J(ean) 1933- 152
    Earlier sketches in SATA 60, 101
Perry, Ritchie (John Allen) 1942- 105
Perry, Roger 1933- 27
Perry, Steve(n Carl) 1947- 76
Pershall, Mary K. 1951- 172
    Earlier sketch in SATA 70
Pershing, Marie
    See Schultz, Pearle Henriksen
Perske, Robert 1927- 57
Persun, Morgan Reed
    See Watkins, Dawn L.
Petach, Heidi 149
Peter
    See Stratemeyer, Edward L.
Peters, Alexander
    See Hollander, Zander
Peters, Andrew Fusek 1965- 169
    Earlier sketch in SATA 107
Peters, Caroline
    See Betz, Eva Kelly
Peters, David
    See David, Peter
Peters, Elizabeth 1927- 49
Peters, Emma
    See Price, Karen
Peters, Gabriel
    See Matott, Justin
Peters, Julie Anne 1952- 128
    Earlier sketch in SATA 82
Peters, Linda
    See Catherall, Arthur
Peters, Lisa Westberg 1951- 161
    Earlier sketches in SATA 74, 115
Peters, Patricia 1953- 84
Peters, Russell M. 1929- 78
Peters, S. H.
    See Porter, William Sydney
    and Proffitt, Nicholas
Petersen, David 1946- 109
    Earlier sketch in SATA 62
Petersen, Gwenn Boardman 1924- 61
    See Boardman, Gwenn R.
Petersen, P(eter) J(ames) 1941- 118
    Brief entry 43
    Earlier sketches in SATA 48, 83
Petersen, Palle 1943- 85
Petersham, Maud (Sylvia Fuller)
    1890-1971 17
    See also CLR 24
Petersham, Miska 1888-1960 17
    See also CLR 24
Peterson, Cris 1952- 174
    Earlier sketches in SATA 84, 145
Peterson, Dawn 1934- 86
Peterson, Esther (Allen) 1934- 35
Peterson, Hans 1922- 8
Peterson, Harold L(eslie) 1922-1978 8
Peterson, Helen Stone 1910- 8
Peterson, Jean Sunde 1941- 108
Peterson, Jeanne Whitehouse 1939- 159
    See Whitehouse, Jeanne
Peterson, Kathleen B. 1951- 119
Peterson, Lorraine 1940- 56
    Brief entry 44
Peterson, Shelley 1952- 146
Petie, Haris 10
    See Petty, Roberta
Petricic, Dusan 1946- 176
Petrides, Heidrun 1944- 19

Petrie, Catherine 1947- 52
    Brief entry 41
Petrone, Valeria 186
Petrosino, Tamara 193
Petroski, Catherine (Ann Groom) 1939- 48
Petrovich, Michael B(oro) 1922- 40
Petrovskaya, Kyra
    See Wayne, Kyra Petrovskaya
Petruccio, Steven James 1961- 67
Petry, Ann (Lane) 1908-1997 5
    Obituary 94
    See also CLR 12
Pettit, Jayne 1932- 108
Petty, J.T. 1977- 189
Pevsner, Stella 131
    Earlier sketches in SATA 8, 77
    See also SAAS 14
Peyo
    See Culliford, Pierre
Peyton, K. M.
    See CLR 3
    See also SAAS 17
    See Peyton, Kathleen Wendy (Herald)
Peyton, Kathleen Wendy (Herald) 1929- 157
    Earlier sketches in SATA 15, 62
    See Peyton, K. M.
Pfanner, (Anne) Louise 1955- 68
Pfeffer, Susan Beth 1948- 180
    Earlier sketches in SATA 4, 83
    See also CLR 11
    See also SAAS 17
Pfeffer, Wendy 1929- 142
    Earlier sketch in SATA 78
Pfeiffer, Janet (B.) 1949- 96
Pfister, Marcus 150
    Earlier sketch in SATA 83
    See also CLR 42
Pfitsch, Patricia Curtis 1948- 148
Pflieger, Pat 1955- 84
Pham, LeUyen 1973- 175
Phelan, Mary Kay 1914- 3
Phelan, Matt 1970- 172
Phelan, Terry Wolfe 1941- 56
Phelps, Ethel Johnston 1914-1984 35
Philbrick, Rodman 1951- 163
    Earlier sketch in SATA 122
    See Philbrick, W. R.
Philbrick, W. R. 163
    See Philbrick, Rodman
Philbrick, W. Rodman
    See Philbrick, Rodman
Philbrook, Clem(ent E.) 1917- 24
Phillips, Aileen Paul
    See Paul, Aileen
Phillips, Betty Lou
    See Phillips, Elizabeth Louise
Phillips, Bob 1940- 95
Phillips, Douglas A. 1949- 161
Phillips, Elizabeth Louise 58
    Brief entry 48
Phillips, Irv(ing W.) 1905-2000 11
    Obituary 125
Phillips, Jack
    See Sandburg, Carl (August)
Phillips, Leon
    See Gerson, Noel Bertram
Phillips, Loretta (Hosey) 1893-1987 10
Phillips, Louis 1942- 102
    Earlier sketch in SATA 8
Phillips, Mary Geisler 1881-1964 10
Phillips, Michael
    See Nolan, William F(rancis)
Phillips, (Woodward) Prentice 1894-1981 10
Phillips, Suzanne 192
Phillpotts, Eden 1862-1960 24
Phin
    See Thayer, Ernest Lawrence
Phipson, Joan
    See CLR 5
    See also SAAS 3
    See Fitzhardinge, Joan Margaret

Phiz
  See Browne, Hablot Knight
Phleger, Fred B. 1909-1993 34
Phleger, Marjorie Temple 1908(?)-1986 1
  Obituary 47
Piaget, Jean 1896-1980
  Obituary 23
Piatti, Celestino 1922- 16
Picard, Barbara Leonie 1917- 89
  Earlier sketch in SATA 2
  See also SAAS 10
Pichon, Liz 174
Pickard, Charles 1932- 36
Pickering, James Sayre 1897-1969 36
  Obituary 28
Pickering, Robert B. 1950- 93
Pielichaty, Helena 1955- 142
Pienkowski, Jan (Michal) 1936- 131
  Earlier sketches in SATA 6, 58
  See also CLR 6
Pierce, Edith Gray 1893-1977 45
Pierce, Katherine
  See St. John, Wylly Folk
Pierce, Meredith Ann 1958- 127
  Brief entry 48
  Earlier sketch in SATA 67
  See also CLR 20
Pierce, Ruth (Ireland) 1936- 5
Pierce, Sharon
  See McCullough, Sharon Pierce
Pierce, Tamora 1954- 187
  Brief entry 49
  Earlier sketches in SATA 51, 96, 153
Pierce, Terry 178
Pierik, Robert 1921- 13
Piers, Robert
  See Anthony, Piers
Pig, Edward
  See Gorey, Edward (St. John)
Pike, Bob
  See Pike, Robert W(ilson)
Pike, Christopher 1961(?)- 156
  Earlier sketch in SATA 68
  See also CLR 29
Pike, Deborah 1951- 89
Pike, E(dgar) Royston 1896-1980 22
  Obituary 56
Pike, R. William 1956- 92
Pike, Robert W(ilson) 1931- 102
Pilarski, Laura 1926- 13
Pilgrim, Anne
  See Allan, Mabel Esther
Pilkey, Dav 1966- 166
  Earlier sketches in SATA 68, 115
  See also CLR 48
Pilkey, David Murray, Jr.
  See Pilkey, Dav
Pilkington, Francis Meredyth 1907- 4
Pilkington, Roger (Windle) 1915-2003 10
  Obituary 144
Pin, Isabel 1975- 183
Pinchot, David 1914(?)-1983
  Obituary 34
Pincus, Harriet 1938- 27
Pinczes, Elinor J(ane) 1940- 81
Pine, Nicholas 1951- 91
Pine, Tillie S(chloss) 1896-1999 13
Pini, Richard (Alan) 1950- 89
Pini, Wendy 1951- 89
Pinkerton, Kathrene Sutherland (Gedney)
  1887-1967
  Obituary 26
Pinkett, Jada
  See Smith, Jada Pinkett
Pinkney, Andrea Davis 1963- 160
  Earlier sketch in SATA 113
Pinkney, (Jerry) Brian 1961- 148
  Earlier sketch in SATA 74
  See also CLR 54
Pinkney, Gloria Jean 1941- 85

Pinkney, J. Brian
  See Pinkney, (Jerry) Brian
Pinkney, Jerry 1939- 151
  Brief entry 32
  Earlier sketches in SATA 41, 71, 107
  See also CLR 43
  See also SAAS 12
Pinkney, John 97
Pinkney, Sandra L. 193
  Earlier sketch in SATA 128
Pinkwater, D. Manus
  See Pinkwater, Daniel Manus
Pinkwater, Daniel
  See Pinkwater, Daniel Manus
Pinkwater, Daniel M.
  See Pinkwater, Daniel Manus
Pinkwater, Daniel Manus 1941- 158
  Earlier sketches in SATA 8, 46, 76, 114
  See also CLR 4
  See also SAAS 3
Pinkwater, Jill 188
Pinkwater, Manus
  See Pinkwater, Daniel Manus
Pinner, Joma
  See Werner, Herma
Pioneer
  See Yates, Raymond F(rancis)
Piowaty, Kim Kennelly 1957- 49
Piper, Roger
  See Fisher, John (Oswald Hamilton)
Pirner, Connie White 1955- 72
Piro, Richard 1934- 7
Pirot, Alison Lohans
  See Lohans, Alison
Pirotta, Saviour 184
Pirsig, Robert M(aynard) 1928- 39
Pita
  See Rendon, Maria
Pitcher, Caroline (Nell) 1948- 128
Pitman, (Isaac) James 1901-1985
  Obituary 46
Pitre, Felix 1949- 84
Pitrone, Jean Maddern 1920- 4
Pittman, Helena Clare 1945- 71
Pitz, Henry C(larence) 1895-1976 4
  Obituary 24
Pitzer, Susanna 1958- 181
Piven, Hanoch 1963- 173
Pizer, Vernon 1918- 21
Place, Marian T(empleton) 1910- 3
Place, Robin (Mary) 1926- 71
Plaidy, Jean
  See Hibbert, Eleanor Alice Burford
Plain, Belva 1919- 62
Plaine, Alfred R. 1898(?)-1981
  Obituary 29
Plath, Sylvia 1932-1963 96
Platt, Chris 1959- 185
Platt, Kin 1911- 86
  Earlier sketch in SATA 21
  See also SAAS 17
Platt, Randall 1948- 95
Platt, Randall Beth
  See Platt, Randall
Platt, Richard 1953- 166
  Earlier sketch in SATA 120
Playfellow, Robin
  See Ellis, Edward S(ylvester)
Playsted, James
  See Wood, James Playsted
Plecas, Jennifer 1966- 149
  Earlier sketch in SATA 84
Plimpton, George 1927-2003 10
  Obituary 150
Plimpton, George Ames
  See Plimpton, George
Plomer, William Charles Franklin
  1903-1973 24
Plotz, Helen Ratnoff 1913-2000 38
Plourde, Lynn 1955- 168
  Earlier sketch in SATA 122

Plowden, David 1932- 52
Plowden, Martha Ward 1948- 98
Plowhead, Ruth Gipson 1877-1967 43
Plowman, Stephanie 1922- 6
Pluckrose, Henry (Arthur) 1931- 141
  Earlier sketch in SATA 13
Plum, J.
  See Wodehouse, P(elham) G(renville)
Plum, Jennifer
  See Kurland, Michael
Plumb, Charles P. 1900(?)-1982
  Obituary 29
Plume, Ilse 170
  Brief entry 43
Plumme, Don E.
  See Katz, Bobbi
Plummer, Margaret 1911- 2
Plum-Ucci, Carol 184
Pochocki, Ethel (Frances) 1925- 76
Podendorf, Illa (E.) 1903(?)-1983 18
  Obituary 35
Podwal, Mark 1945- 160
  Earlier sketch in SATA 101
Podwal, Mark H.
  See Podwal, Mark
Poe, Edgar Allan 1809-1849 23
Poe, Ty (Christopher) 1975- 94
Pogany, William Andrew 1882-1955 44
  See Pogany, Willy
Pogany, Willy
  Brief entry 30
  See Pogany, William Andrew
Pohl, Frederik 1919- 24
Pohlmann, Lillian (Grenfell) 1902-1997 11
Pohrt, Tom 1953- 152
  Earlier sketch in SATA 67
Pointon, Robert
  See Rooke, Daphne (Marie)
Points, Larry G. 1945- 177
  Earlier sketch in SATA 133
Points, Larry Gene
  See Points, Larry G.
Pokeberry, P.J.
  See Mitchell, B.J.
POLA
  See Watson, Pauline
Polacco, Patricia 1944- 180
  Earlier sketches in SATA 74, 123
  See also CLR 40
Polacco, Patricia Ann
  See Polacco, Patricia
Polak, Monique 1960- 178
Polatnick, Florence T. 1923- 5
Polder, Markus
  See Kruss, James
Polese, Carolyn 1947- 58
Polese, James 1914- 87
Polette, Nancy (Jane) 1930- 42
Polhamus, Jean Burt 1928- 21
Policoff, Stephen Phillip 1948- 77
Polikoff, Barbara G. 1929- 162
  Earlier sketch in SATA 77
Polikoff, Barbara Garland
  See Polikoff, Barbara G.
Polisar, Barry Louis 1954- 134
  Earlier sketch in SATA 77
Politi, Leo 1908-1996 47
  Obituary 88
  Earlier sketch in SATA 1
  See also CLR 29
Polking, Kirk 1925- 5
Pollack, Jill S. 1963- 88
Pollack, Merrill S. 1924-1988
  Obituary 55
Polland, Barbara K(ay) 1939- 44
Polland, Madeleine A(ngela Cahill) 1918- ... 68
  Earlier sketch in SATA 6
  See also SAAS 8
Pollema-Cahill, Phyllis 1958- 123
Pollock, Bruce 1945- 46

Pollock, Mary
    See Blyton, Enid
Pollock, Penny 1935- 137
    Brief entry 42
    Earlier sketch in SATA 44
Pollowitz, Melinda Kilborn 1944- 26
Polner, Murray 1928- 64
Polonsky, Arthur 1925- 34
Polseno, Jo 17
Pomaska, Anna 1946- 117
Pomerantz, Charlotte 1930- 177
    Earlier sketches in SATA 20, 80
Pomeroy, Pete
    See Roth, Arthur J(oseph)
Pond, Alonzo W(illiam) 1894-1986 5
Pontiflet, Ted 1932- 32
Poole, Gray Johnson 1906- 1
Poole, Josephine 5
    See also SAAS 2
    See Helyar, Jane Penelope Josephine
Poole, (Jane Penelope) Josephine
    See Helyar, Jane Penelope Josephine
Poole, Lynn 1910-1969 1
Poole, Peggy 1925- 39
Poortvliet, Rien 1932- 65
    Brief entry 37
Pope, Elizabeth Marie 1917-1992 38
    Brief entry 36
Pope, Kevin 1958- 183
Popescu, Christine
    See Pullein-Thompson, Christine
Poploff, Michelle 1956- 67
Popp, K. Wendy 91
Poppel, Hans 1942- 71
Portal, Colette 1936- 6
Porte, Barbara Ann 1943- 152
    Brief entry 45
    Earlier sketches in SATA 57, 93
Porter, A(nthony) P(eyton) 1945- 68
Porter, Connie (Rose) 1959(?)- 129
    Earlier sketch in SATA 81
Porter, Donald Clayton
    See Gerson, Noel Bertram
Porter, Eleanor H(odgman) 1868-1920
    See CLR 110
Porter, Gene(va Grace) Stratton
    See Stratton-Porter, Gene(va Grace)
Porter, Janice Lee 1953- 108
    Earlier sketch in SATA 68
Porter, Katherine Anne 1890-1980 39
    Obituary 23
Porter, Kathryn
    See Swinford, Betty (June Wells)
Porter, Pamela 1956- 193
Porter, Sheena 1935- 24
    See also SAAS 10
Porter, Sue
    See Limb, Sue
Porter, Sue 1951- 76
Porter, Tracey 191
Porter, William Sydney 1862-1910
    See YABC 2
    See Henry, O.
Portis, Antoinette 189
Porto, Tony 1960- 153
Portteus, Eleanora Marie Manthei (?)-1983
    Obituary 36
Posada, Mia 187
Posell, Elsa Z(eigerman) -1995 3
Posten, Margaret L(ois) 1915- 10
Posthuma, Sieb 1960- 150
Potok, Chaim 1929-2002 106
    Obituary 134
    Earlier sketch in SATA 33
    See also CLR 92
Potok, Herbert Harold -2002
    See Potok, Chaim
Potok, Herman Harold
    See Potok, Chaim

Potter, Beatrix 1866-1943 132
    Earlier sketch in SATA 100
    See also YABC 1
    See also CLR 73
Potter, Giselle 187
    Earlier sketch in SATA 150
Potter, Helen Beatrix
    See Potter, Beatrix
Potter, Margaret (Newman) 1926-1998 21
    Obituary 104
    See Betteridge, Anne
Potter, Marian 1915- 9
Potter, Miriam Clark 1886-1965 3
Poulin, Stephane 1961- 98
    See also CLR 28
Poulton, Kimberly 1957(?)- 136
Pournelle, Jerry (Eugene) 1933- 161
    Earlier sketches in SATA 26, 91
Povelite, Kay 1955- 102
Pow, Tom 1950- 163
Powe-Allred, Alexandra
    See Allred, Alexandra Powe
Powell, A. M.
    See Morgan, Alfred P(owell)
Powell, Consie 174
Powell, E. Sandy 1947- 72
Powell, E.S.
    See Powell, E. Sandy
Powell, Pamela 1960- 78
Powell, Patricia Hruby 1951- 136
Powell, Randy 1956- 118
Powell, Richard Stillman
    See Barbour, Ralph Henry
Powell, Robert (Stephenson Smyth) Baden
    See Baden-Powell, Robert
        (Stephenson Smyth)
Powell, Stephanie 1953- 93
Power, Margaret (M.) 1945- 125
    Earlier sketch in SATA 75
Powers, Anne
    See Schwartz, Anne Powers
Powers, Bill 1931- 52
    Brief entry 31
Powers, Daniel 1959- 164
Powers, Margaret
    See Heal, Edith
Powers, Tim 1952- 107
Powers, Timothy Thomas
    See Powers, Tim
Powledge, Fred 1935- 37
Poydar, Nancy 190
Poynter, Margaret 1927- 27
Prachaticka, Marketa
    See Kolibalova, Marketa
Prachatika, Marketa
    See Kolibalova, Marketa
Prager, Arthur 44
Prager, Ellen J. 1962- 136
Prange, Beckie 172
Prap, Lila 1955- 177
Praprotnik-Zupancic, Lilijana
    See Prap, Lila
Pratchett, Terence David John
    See Pratchett, Terry
Pratchett, Terry 1948- 185
    Earlier sketches in SATA 82, 139
    See also CLR 64
Prater, John 1947- 149
    Earlier sketches in SATA 72, 103
Prato, Rodica 184
Pratt, (Murray) Fletcher 1897-1956 102
Pratt, Kristin Joy 1976- 87
Pratt, Pierre 1962- 166
    Earlier sketch in SATA 95
Preiss, Byron 1953-2005 166
    Brief entry 42
    Earlier sketch in SATA 47
Preiss, Byron Cary
    See Preiss, Byron
Preller, James 1961- 88

Prelutsky, Jack 1940- 171
    Earlier sketches in SATA 22, 66, 118
    See also CLR 115
Prentice, Amy
    See Kaler, James Otis
Prescott, Casey
    See Morris, Chris(topher Crosby)
Presnall, Judith (Ann) Janda 1943- 96
Pressler, Mirjam 1940- 155
Preston, Douglas 1956- 113
Preston, Edna Mitchell 40
Preston, Lillian Elvira 1918- 47
Preussler, Otfried 1923- 24
Prevert, Jacques (Henri Marie) 1900-1977
    Obituary 30
Prevost, Guillaume 1964- 192
Price, Beverley Joan 1931- 98
Price, Charlie 187
Price, Christine (Hilda) 1928-1980 3
    Obituary 23
Price, Garrett 1896-1979
    Obituary 22
Price, Jennifer
    See Hoover, Helen (Drusilla Blackburn)
Price, Joan 1931- 124
Price, Jonathan (Reeve) 1941- 46
Price, Karen 1957- 125
Price, Kathy Z. 1957- 172
Price, Lucie Locke
    See Locke, Lucie
Price, Olive 1903-1991 8
Price, Susan 1955- 128
    Earlier sketches in SATA 25, 85
Price, Willard 1887-1983 48
    Brief entry 38
Price-Groff, Claire 127
Priceman, Marjorie 1958- 168
    Earlier sketches in SATA 81, 120
Prichard, Katharine Susannah 1883-1969 66
Prideaux, Tom 1908-1993 37
    Obituary 76
Priestley, Alice 1962- 95
Priestley, Lee (Shore) 1904-1999 27
Priestly, Doug 1954- 122
Priestly, Douglas Michael
    See Priestly, Doug
Prieto, Mariana Beeching 1912-1999 8
Priley, Margaret (Ann) Hubbard 1909-1992
    Obituary 130
Primavera, Elise 1954- 185
    Brief entry 48
    Earlier sketches in SATA 58, 109
Prime, Derek (James) 1931- 34
Prince, Alison (Mary) 1931- 86
    Earlier sketch in SATA 28
Prince, April Jones 1975- 180
Prince, J(ack) H(arvey) 1908- 17
Prince, Joshua 188
Prince, Maggie 102
Pringle, Eric 138
Pringle, Laurence 1935- 154
    Earlier sketches in SATA 4, 68, 104
    See also CLR 57
    See also SAAS 6
Pringle, Laurence Patrick
    See Pringle, Laurence
Prinz, Yvonne 1960- 175
Prior, Natalie Jane 1963- 106
Pritchett, Elaine H(illyer) 1920- 36
Pritchett, Laura 1971- 178
Pritchett, Laura Rose
    See Pritchett, Laura
Pritts, Kim Derek 1953- 83
Prochazkova, Iva 1953- 68
Proctor, Everitt
    See Montgomery, Rutherford George
Proeysen, Alf 1914-1970
    See CLR 24
    See Proysen, Alf
Professor Scribbler
    See Hollingsworth, Mary

Proimos, James 1955- *173*
Prose, Francine 1947- *149*
  Earlier sketch in SATA *101*
Protopopescu, Orel *186*
Protopopescu, Orel Odinov
  See Protopopescu, Orel
Provensen, Alice 1918- *147*
  Earlier sketches in SATA *9, 70*
  See also CLR *11*
Provensen, Martin (Elias) 1916-1987 .... *70*
  Obituary *51*
  Earlier sketch in SATA *9*
  See also CLR *11*
Provenzo, Eugene (F., Jr.) 1949- *142*
  Earlier sketch in SATA *78*
Provist, d'Alain 1906-1989
  See Diop, Birago (Ismael)
Provost, Gail Levine 1944- *65*
Provost, Gary (Richard) 1944-1995 .... *66*
Proysen, Alf *67*
  See Proeysen, Alf
Pruett, Candace (J.) 1968- *157*
Pryor, Bonnie H. 1942- *69*
Pryor, Boori (Monty) 1950- *112*
Pryor, Helen Brenton 1897-1972 .... *4*
Pryor, Michael 1957- *153*
Pucci, Albert John 1920- *44*
Pudney, John (Sleigh) 1909-1977 .... *24*
Pugh, Ellen (Tiffany) 1920- *7*
Pullein-Thompson, Christine 1925-2005 ...... *82*
  Obituary *172*
  Earlier sketch in SATA *3*
Pullein-Thompson, Diana *3*
  See Farr, Diana (Pullein-Thompson)
Pullein-Thompson, Josephine (Mary
  Wedderburn) *82*
  Earlier sketch in SATA *3*
Pullen, Zachary *189*
Pullman, Philip 1946- *150*
  Earlier sketches in SATA *65, 103*
  See also CLR *84*
  See also SAAS *17*
Pullman, Philip Nicholas
  See Pullman, Philip
Pulver, Harry, Jr. 1960- *129*
Pulver, Robin 1945- *133*
  Earlier sketch in SATA *76*
Puner, Helen W(alker) 1915-1989 .... *37*
  Obituary *63*
Purdy, Carol 1943- *120*
  Earlier sketch in SATA *66*
Purdy, Susan G(old) 1939- *8*
Purmell, Ann 1953- *147*
Purnell, Idella 1901-1982 .... *120*
Purscell, Phyllis 1934- *7*
Purtill, Richard L. 1931- *53*
Pushker, Gloria 1927- *162*
  Earlier sketch in SATA *75*
Pushker, Gloria Teles
  See Pushker, Gloria
Pushkin, Aleksandr Sergeevich
  See Pushkin, Alexander (Sergeyevich)
Pushkin, Alexander (Sergeyevich)
  1799-1837 .... *61*
  See Pushkin, Aleksandr Sergeevich
Putnam, Alice 1916- *61*
Putnam, Arthur Lee
  See Alger, Horatio, Jr.
Putnam, Peter B(rock) 1920-1998 .... *30*
  Obituary *106*
Puttock, Simon *178*
Pyle, Howard 1853-1911 .... *100*
  Earlier sketch in SATA *16*
  See also CLR *117*
Pyle, Katharine 1863-1938 .... *66*
Pyne, Mable Mandeville 1903-1969 .... *9*
Pyrnelle, Louise-Clarke 1850-1907 .... *114*

Q

Quackenbush, Robert M(ead) 1929- *133*
  Autobiography Feature *133*
  Earlier sketches in SATA *7, 70*
  See also CLR *122*
  See also SAAS *7*
Qualey, Marsha 1953- *124*
  Earlier sketch in SATA *79*
Qualls, Sean *177*
Quammen, David 1948- *7*
Quark, Jason
  See Eldin, Peter
Quarles, Benjamin (Arthur) 1904-1996 .... *12*
Quatermass, Martin
  See Carpenter, John (Howard)
Quattlebaum, Mary 1958- *185*
  Earlier sketches in SATA *88, 134*
Quay, Emma *173*
  Earlier sketch in SATA *119*
Queen, Ellery
  See Deming, Richard
  and Dannay, Frederic
  and Davidson, Avram (James)
  and Fairman, Paul W.
  and Flora, Fletcher
  and Holding, James (Clark Carlisle, Jr.)
  and Hoch, Edward D.
  and Kane, Henry
  and Lee, Manfred B.
  and Marlowe, Stephen
  and Powell, (Oval) Talmage
  and Sheldon, Walter J(ames)
  and Sturgeon, Theodore (Hamilton)
  and Tracy, Don(ald Fiske)
  and Vance, Jack
Queen Latifah 1970- *185*
Quennell, Marjorie Courtney 1884-1972 ...... *29*
Quentin
  See Sheldon, David
Quentin, Brad
  See Bisson, Terry
Quest, (Edna) Olga W(ilbourne) Hall
  See Hall-Quest, (Edna) Olga W(ilbourne)
Quick, Annabelle 1922-1986 .... *2*
Quigg, Jane (Hulda) (?)-1986
  Obituary *49*
Quill, Monica
  See McInerny, Ralph
Quin-Harkin, Janet 1941- *165*
  Earlier sketches in SATA *18, 90, 119*
Quin-Harkin, Janet Elizabeth
  See Quin-Harkin, Janet
Quinlan, Susan E. 1954- *88*
Quinlan, Susan Elizabeth
  See Quinlan, Susan E.
Quinn, Elisabeth 1881-1962 .... *22*
Quinn, Pat 1947- *130*
Quinn, Patrick 1950- *73*
Quinn, Rob 1972- *138*
Quinn, Theodora K.
  See Kroeber, Theodora (Kracaw)
Quinn, Vernon
  See Quinn, Elisabeth
Quintano, D.M.
  See Sheldon, Dyan
Quirk, Anne (E.) 1956- *99*
Quixley, Jim 1931- *56*
Quyth, Gabriel
  See Jennings, Gary

R

Ra, Carol F. 1939- *76*
Raab, Evelyn 1951- *129*
Rabb, Margo 1972- *188*
Rabb, M.E.
  See Rabb, Margo

Rabe, Berniece (Louise) 1928- *148*
  Autobiography Feature *148*
  Earlier sketches in SATA *7, 77*
  See also SAAS *10*
Rabe, Olive H(anson) (?)-1968 .... *13*
Rabin, Staton 1958- *162*
  Earlier sketch in SATA *84*
Rabinowich, Ellen 1946- *29*
Rabinowitz, Sandy 1954- *52*
  Brief entry *39*
Rachlin, Carol K(ing) 1919- *64*
Rachlin, Harvey 1951- *47*
Rachlin, Harvey Brant
  See Rachlin, Harvey
Rachlin, Nahid *64*
Rachlis, Eugene (Jacob) 1920-1986
  Obituary *50*
Rackham, Arthur 1867-1939 .... *100*
  Earlier sketch in SATA *15*
  See also CLR *57*
Raczka, Bob 1963- *191*
  Earlier sketch in SATA *163*
Radencich, Marguerite C. 1952-1998 .... *79*
Radford, Ruby L(orraine) 1891-1971 .... *6*
Radin, Ruth Yaffe 1938- *107*
  Brief entry *52*
  Earlier sketch in SATA *56*
Radlauer, David 1952- *28*
Radlauer, Edward 1921- *15*
Radlauer, Ruth Shaw 1926- *98*
  Earlier sketch in SATA *15*
Radley, Gail 1951- *112*
  Earlier sketch in SATA *25*
Radunsky, Vladimir *177*
Rae, Gwynedd 1892-1977 .... *37*
Raebeck, Lois 1921- *5*
Rael, Elsa Okon 1927-
  See CLR *84*
Raffi
  See Cavoukian, Raffi
Raftery, Gerald (Bransfield) 1905-1986 .... *11*
Ragan-Reid, Gale 1956- *90*
Rahaman, Vashanti 1953- *98*
Rahn, Joan Elma 1929- *27*
Rai, Bali 1971- *152*
Raible, Alton (Robert) 1918- *35*
Raiff, Stan 1930- *11*
Raines, Shirley C(arol) 1945- *128*
Rainey, W. B.
  See Blassingame, Wyatt Rainey
Rake, Jody 1961- *157*
Rallison, Janette 1966- *183*
Ralston, Jan
  See Dunlop, Agnes M. R.
Rama, Sue *190*
Ramal, Walter
  See de la Mare, Walter (John)
Ramanujan, A(ttipat) K(rishnaswami)
  1929-1993 .... *86*
Rame, David
  See Divine, Arthur Durham
Ramstad, Ralph L. 1919- *115*
Rana, Indi
  See Rana, Indira Higham
Rana, Indira Higham 1944- *82*
Ranadive, Gail 1944- *10*
Rand, Ann (Binkley) *30*
Rand, Gloria 1925- *156*
  Earlier sketch in SATA *101*
Rand, Paul 1914-1996 .... *6*
Randall, Carrie
  See Ransom, Candice F.
Randall, David 1972- *167*
Randall, Florence Engel 1917-1997 .... *5*
Randall, Janet
  See Young, Janet Randall
  and Young, Robert W(illiam)
Randall, Robert
  See Garrett, (Gordon) Randall (Phillip)
  and Silverberg, Robert
Randall, Ruth (Elaine) Painter 1892-1971 ..... *3*

Randell, Beverley
See Price, Beverley Joan
Randle, Kristen D. 1952- 92
Autobiography Feature 119
See also SAAS 24
Randle, Kristen Downey
See Randle, Kristen D.
Randolph, Boynton M.D.
See Ellis, Edward S(ylvester)
Randolph, Ellen
See Rawn, Melanie
Randolph, Geoffrey
See Ellis, Edward S(ylvester)
Randolph, J. H.
See Ellis, Edward S(ylvester)
Randolph, Lieutenant J. H.
See Ellis, Edward S(ylvester)
Rands, William Brighty 1823-1882 17
Raney, Ken 1953- 74
Rankin, Joan 1940- 148
Earlier sketch in SATA 88
Rankin, Laura 1953(?)- 176
Ranney, Agnes V. 1916-1985 6
Ransom, Candice F. 1952- 183
Brief entry 49
Earlier sketches in SATA 52, 89, 135
Ransom, Jeanie Franz 1957- 187
Ransome, Arthur (Michell) 1884-1967 22
See also CLR 8
Ransome, James E. 1961- 178
Earlier sketches in SATA 76, 123
See also CLR 86
Rant, Tol E.
See Longyear, Barry B(rookes)
Raphael, Elaine 23
See Bolognese, Elaine (Raphael Chionchio)
Raposo, Joseph Guilherme 1938-1989
Obituary 61
Rapp, Adam 1968(?)- 148
Rappaport, Doreen 151
Rappaport, Eva 1924- 6
Rappoport, Ken 1935- 167
Earlier sketch in SATA 89
Rarick, Carrie 1911-2002 41
Raschka, Chris 1959- 166
Earlier sketches in SATA 80, 117
Raschka, Christopher
See Raschka, Chris
Rascol, Sabina I. 159
Rash, Andy 162
Raskin, Edith Lefkowitz 1908-1987 9
Raskin, Ellen 1928-1984 139
Earlier sketches in SATA 2, 38
See also CLR 12
Raskin, Joseph 1897-1982 12
Obituary 29
Rathjen, Carl Henry 1909-1984 11
Rathmann, Peggy 1953- 157
Earlier sketch in SATA 94
See Crosby, Margaret
Ratliff, Thomas M. 1948- 118
Rattigan, Jama Kim 1951- 99
Ratto, Linda Lee 1952- 79
Rattray, Simon
See Trevor, Elleston
Ratz de Tagyos, Paul 1958- 76
Rau, Dana Meachen 1971- 167
Earlier sketch in SATA 94
Rau, Margaret 1913- 168
Earlier sketch in SATA 9
See also CLR 8
Rauch, Mabel Thompson 1888-1972
Obituary 26
Raucher, Herman 1928- 8
Raum, Elizabeth 1949- 155
Raven, Margot Theis 184
RavenWolf, Silver 1956- 155
Ravielli, Anthony 1916-1997 3
Obituary 95
Ravilious, Robin 1944- 77
Rawding, F(rederick) W(illiam) 1930- 55

Rawlings, Marjorie Kinnan 1896-1953 100
See also YABC 1
See also CLR 63
Rawlinson, Julia 175
Rawls, (Woodrow) Wilson 1913-1984 22
See also CLR 81
Rawlyk, George Alexander 1935- 64
Rawn, Melanie 1954- 98
Rawn, Melanie Robin
See Rawn, Melanie
Rawson, Katherine 1955- 190
Ray, Carl 1943-1978 63
Ray, Deborah 8
See Kogan Ray, Deborah
Ray, Delia 1963- 179
Earlier sketch in SATA 70
Ray, Irene
See Sutton, Margaret Beebe
Ray, Jane 1960- 152
Earlier sketch in SATA 72
Ray, JoAnne 1935- 9
Ray, Mary (Eva Pedder) 1932- 127
Earlier sketch in SATA 2
Ray, Mary Lyn 1946- 154
Earlier sketch in SATA 90
Rayban, Chloe 1944- 167
Rayevsky, Robert 1955- 190
Earlier sketch in SATA 81
Raymond, James Crossley 1917-1981
Obituary 29
Raymond, Robert
See Alter, Robert Edmond
Rayner, Hugh 151
Rayner, Mary 1933- 87
Earlier sketch in SATA 22
See also CLR 41
Rayner, Shoo
See Rayner, Hugh
Rayner, William 1929- 55
Brief entry 36
Raynor, Dorka 28
Rayson, Steven 1932- 30
Razzell, Arthur (George) 1925- 11
Razzell, Mary (Catherine) 1930- 102
Razzi, James 1931- 10
Read, Elfreida 1920- 2
Read, Nicholas 1956- 146
Read, Piers Paul 1941- 21
Reade, Deborah 1949- 69
Reader, Dennis 1929- 71
Reading, Richard P(atrick) 1962- 161
Readman, Jo 1958- 89
Ready, Kirk L(ewis) 1943- 39
Reaney, James 1926-2008 43
Reaney, James Crerar
See Reaney, James
Reardon, Joyce
See Pearson, Ridley
Reaver, Chap 1935-1993 69
Obituary 77
Reaver, Herbert R.
See Reaver, Chap
Reaves, J. Michael
See Reaves, (James) Michael
Reaves, (James) Michael 1950- 99
Reber, Deborah 189
Recorvits, Helen 191
Redding, Robert Hull 1919- 2
Redekopp, Elsa 61
Redlich, Ben 1977- 181
Redsand, Anna 1948- 184
Redway, Ralph
See Hamilton, Charles (Harold St. John)
Redway, Ridley
See Hamilton, Charles (Harold St. John)
Reece, Colleen L. 1935- 116
Reece, Gabrielle 1970- 108
Reed, Betty Jane 1921- 4
Reed, E.
See Evans, Mari
Reed, Gwendolyn E(lizabeth) 1932- 21

Reed, Kit 1932- 184
Autobiography Feature 184
Earlier sketches in SATA 34, 116
Reed, Lynn Rowe 171
Reed, Neil 1961- 99
Reed, Talbot Baines 1852-1893
See CLR 76
Reed, Thomas (James) 1947- 34
Reed, William Maxwell 1871-1962 15
Reeder, Carolyn 1937- 97
Earlier sketch in SATA 66
See also CLR 69
Reeder, Colin (Dawson) 1938- 74
Reeder, Colonel Red
See Reeder, Russell P(otter), Jr.
Reeder, Russell P(otter), Jr. 1902-1998 4
Obituary 101
Reeder, Stephanie Owen 1951- 102
Reed-Jones, Carol 1955- 112
Reef, Catherine 1951- 189
Earlier sketches in SATA 73, 128
Reekie, Jocelyn (Margaret) 1947- 145
Reeman, Douglas Edward 1924- 63
Brief entry 28
Rees, Celia 1949- 124
Rees, David (Bartlett) 1936-1993 69
Obituary 76
Earlier sketch in SATA 36
See also SAAS 5
Rees, Douglas 1947- 169
Rees, Ennis (Samuel, Jr.) 1925- 3
Rees, (George) Leslie (Clarence)
1905-2000 105
Obituary 135
Reese, Bob
See Reese, Robert A.
Reese, Della 1931(?)- 114
Reese, Lyn
See Reese, Carolyn Johnson
Reese, Robert A. 1938- 60
Brief entry 53
Reese, (John) Terence 1913-1996 59
Reeve, Joel
See Cox, William R(obert)
Reeve, Kirk 1934- 117
Reeve, Philip 170
Reeve, Rosie 188
Reeve, Rosie 186
Reeves, Faye Couch 1953- 76
Reeves, James 15
See Reeves, John Morris
Reeves, Jeni 1947- 111
Reeves, John Morris 1909-1978 87
See Reeves, James
Reeves, Joyce 1911- 17
Reeves, Lawrence F. 1926- 29
Reeves, Ruth Ellen
See Ranney, Agnes V.
Regan, Dian Curtis 1950- 149
Autobiography Feature 149
Earlier sketches in SATA 75, 133
Regehr, Lydia 1903-1991 37
Reger, James P. 1952- 106
Reggiani, Renee 1925- 18
Rehm, Karl M. 1935- 72
Reich, Ali
See Katz, Bobbi
Reich, Susanna 1954- 113
Reiche, Dietlof 1941- 159
Reichert, Edwin C(lark) 1909-1988
Obituary 57
Reichert, Mickey Zucker
See Reichert, Miriam Zucker
Reichert, Miriam Zucker 1962- 85
Reichert, Renee 172
Reichhold, Jane(t E.) 1937- 147
Reid, Alastair 1926- 46
Reid, Barbara 1922- 21
Reid, Barbara (Jane) 1957- 93
See also CLR 64

Reid, Desmond
  See Moorcock, Michael
  and McNeilly, Wilfred (Glassford)
Reid, Eugenie Chazal 1924- 12
Reid, John Calvin 21
Reid, (Thomas) Mayne 1818-1883 24
Reid, Meta Mayne 1905-1991 58
  Brief entry 36
Reid, Robin (Nicole) 1969- 145
Reid Banks, Lynne 1929- 165
  Earlier sketches in SATA 22, 75, 111
  See also CLR 86
  See Banks, Lynne Reid
Reider, Katja 1960- 126
Reid Jenkins, Debra 1955- 87
Reiff, Stephanie Ann 1948- 47
  Brief entry 28
Reig, June 1933- 30
Reigot, Betty Polisar 1924- 55
  Brief entry 41
Reim, Melanie (K.) 1956- 104
Reinach, Jacquelyn (Krasne) 1930-2000 28
Reiner, Carl 1922- 151
Reiner, William B(uck) 1910-1976 46
  Obituary 30
Reinfeld, Fred 1910-1964 3
Reinhardt, Dana 1971- 175
Reinhart, Matthew 1971- 161
Reiniger, Lotte 1899-1981 40
  Obituary 33
Reinsma, Carol 1949- 91
Reinstedt, Randall A. 1935- 101
Reinstedt, Randy
  See Reinstedt, Randall A.
Reisberg, Mira 1955- 82
Reisberg, Veg
  See Reisberg, Mira
Reiser, Lynn 1944- 180
  Earlier sketches in SATA 81, 138
Reiser, Lynn Whisnant
  See Reiser, Lynn
Reisgies, Teresa (Maria) 1966- 74
Reiss, Johanna (de Leeuw) 1929(?)- 18
  See also CLR 19
Reiss, John J. 23
Reiss, Kathryn 1957- 144
  Earlier sketch in SATA 76
Reit, Seymour Victory 1918-2001 21
  Obituary 133
Reit, Sy
  See Reit, Seymour Victory
Relf, Patricia 1954- 134
  Earlier sketch in SATA 71
Remi, Georges 1907-1983 13
  Obituary 32
  See Herge
Remington, Frederic S(ackrider)
  1861-1909 41
Remkiewicz, Frank 1939- 152
  Earlier sketch in SATA 77
Remy, Georges
  See Remi, Georges
Renaud, Bernadette 1945- 66
Renault, Mary
  See Challans, Mary
Rendell, Joan 28
Rendina, Laura (Jones) Cooper 1902- 10
Rendon, Marcie R. 1952- 97
Rendon, Maria 1965- 116
Renee, Janina 1956- 140
Renfro, Ed 1924- 79
Renick, Marion (Lewis) 1905-1983 1
Renken, Aleda 1907- 27
Renlie, Frank H. 1936- 11
Rennert, Richard Scott 1956- 67
Rennison, Louise 1951- 149
Reno, Dawn E(laine) 1953- 130
Rensie, Willis
  See Eisner, Will
Renton, Cam
  See Armstrong, Richard

Renvoize, Jean 5
Resau, Laura 1973- 190
Resciniti, Angelo G. 1952- 75
Resnick, Michael David
  See Resnick, Mike
Resnick, Mike 1942- 159
  Earlier sketches in SATA 38, 106
Resnick, Seymour 1920- 23
Retla, Robert
  See Alter, Robert Edmond
Reuter, Bjarne (B.) 1950- 142
  Earlier sketch in SATA 68
Reuter, Carol (Joan) 1931- 2
Revena
  See Wright, Betty Ren
Revsbech, Vicki
  See Liestman, Vicki
Rex, Adam 186
Rex, Michael 191
Rey, H(ans) A(ugusto) 1898-1977 100
  Earlier sketches in SATA 1, 26, 69
  See also CLR 93
Rey, Margret (Elisabeth) 1906-1996 86
  Obituary 93
  Earlier sketch in SATA 26
  See also CLR 93
Reyher, Becky
  See Reyher, Rebecca Hourwich
Reyher, Rebecca Hourwich 1897-1987 18
  Obituary 50
Reynold, Ann
  See Bernardo, Anilu
Reynolds, Adrian 1963- 192
Reynolds, C. Buck 1957- 107
Reynolds, Dickson
  See Reynolds, Helen Mary
  Greenwood Campbell
Reynolds, Helen Mary Greenwood
  Campbell 1884-1969
  Obituary 26
Reynolds, Jan 1956- 180
Reynolds, John
  See Whitlock, Ralph
Reynolds, Madge
  See Whitlock, Ralph
Reynolds, Malvina 1900-1978 44
  Obituary 24
Reynolds, Marilyn 1935- 121
  See also SAAS 23
Reynolds, Marilyn M.
  See Reynolds, Marilyn
Reynolds, Marilynn 1940- 141
  Earlier sketch in SATA 80
Reynolds, Pamela 1923- 34
Reynolds, Peter H. 1961- 128
Reynolds, Peter J. 1961- 179
Reynolds, Susan 179
Rhine, Richard
  See Silverstein, Alvin
  and Silverstein, Virginia B(arbara
  Opshelor)
Rhoades, Diane 1952- 90
Rhodes, Bennie (Loran) 1927- 35
Rhodes, Donna McKee 1962- 87
Rhodes, Frank Harold Trevor 1926- 37
Rhue, Morton
  See Strasser, Todd
Rhyne, Nancy 1926- 66
Rhynes, Martha E. 1939- 141
Ribbons, Ian 1924- 37
  Brief entry 30
  See also SAAS 3
Ricciuti, Edward R(aphael) 1938- 10
Rice, Alice (Caldwell) Hegan 1870-1942 63
Rice, Bebe Faas 1932- 89
Rice, Charles D(uane) 1910-1971
  Obituary 27
Rice, Dale R. 1948- 42
Rice, Dale Richard
  See Rice, Dale R.

Rice, Dick
  See Rice, R. Hugh
Rice, Earle (Wilmont), Jr. 1928- 151
  Earlier sketch in SATA 92
Rice, Edward 1918-2001 47
  Brief entry 42
Rice, Elizabeth 1913-1976 2
Rice, Eve 1951- 91
  Earlier sketch in SATA 34
Rice, Eve Hart
  See Rice, Eve
Rice, Inez 1907- 13
Rice, James 1934- 93
  Earlier sketch in SATA 22
Rice, John F. 1958- 82
Rice, R. Hugh 1929- 115
Rice, Richard H.
  See Rice, R. Hugh
Rich, Barbara
  See Graves, Robert
Rich, Elaine Sommers 1926- 6
Rich, Josephine Bouchard 1912- 10
Rich, Louise Dickinson 1903-1991 54
  Obituary 67
Richard, Adrienne 1921- 5
  See also SAAS 9
Richard, James Robert
  See Bowen, Robert Sydney
Richards, Chuck 1957- 170
Richards, Frank
  See Hamilton, Charles (Harold St. John)
Richards, Hilda
  See Hamilton, Charles (Harold St. John)
Richards, Jackie 1925- 102
Richards, Jean 1940- 135
Richards, Justin 169
Richards, Kay
  See Baker, Susan (Catherine)
Richards, Laura E(lizabeth Howe)
  1850-1943
  See YABC 1
  See also CLR 54
Richards, Leigh
  See King, Laurie R.
Richards, Marlee
  See Brill, Marlene Targ
Richards, Norman 1932- 48
Richards, R(onald) C(harles) W(illiam)
  1923- 59
  Brief entry 43
Richards, Walter Alden (Jr.) 1907-1988
  Obituary 56
Richardson, Andrew (William) 1986- 120
Richardson, Carol 1932- 58
Richardson, Frank Howard 1882-1970
  Obituary 27
Richardson, Grace Lee
  See Dickson, Naida
Richardson, Jean (Mary) 59
Richardson, Judith Benet 1941- 77
Richardson, Nigel 1957- 187
Richardson, Robert S(hirley) 1902-1981 8
Richardson, Sandy 1949- 116
Richardson, V.A. 189
Richardson, Willis 1889-1977 60
Richelson, Geraldine 1922- 29
Richemont, Enid 1940- 82
Richler, Mordecai 1931-2001 98
  Brief entry 27
  Earlier sketch in SATA 44
  See also CLR 17
Richman, Sophia 1941- 142
Rich-McCoy, Lois
  See McCoy, Lois (Rich)
Richmond, Robin 1951- 75
Richoux, Pat(ricia) 1927- 7
Richter, Alice 1941- 30
Richter, Conrad (Michael) 1890-1968 3
Richter, Hans Peter 1925-1993 6
  See also CLR 21
  See also SAAS 11

Richter, Jutta 1955- *184*
Rickard, Graham 1949- *71*
Rico, Don(ato) 1917-1985
  Obituary *43*
Riddell, Chris 1962- *166*
  Earlier sketch in SATA *114*
Riddell, Christopher Barry
  See Riddell, Chris
Riddell, Edwina 1955- *82*
Ridden, Brian (John) 1934- *123*
Riddle, Tohby 1965- *151*
  Earlier sketch in SATA *74*
Riddles, Libby 1956- *140*
Ridge, Antonia (Florence) (?)-1981 .... *7*
  Obituary *27*
Ridge, Martin 1923-2003 .... *43*
Ridley, Philip *171*
  Earlier sketch in SATA *88*
Ridlon, Marci *22*
  See Balterman, Marcia Ridlon
Riedman, Sarah R(egal) 1902-1995 .... *1*
Riehecky, Janet 1953- *164*
Ries, Lori *185*
Riesenberg, Felix, Jr. 1913-1962 .... *23*
Rieu, E(mile) V(ictor) 1887-1972 .... *46*
  Obituary *26*
Riffenburgh, Beau 1955- *175*
Rigg, Sharon
  See Creech, Sharon
Riggio, Anita 1952- *148*
  Earlier sketch in SATA *73*
Riggs, Shannon *190*
Riggs, Sidney Noyes 1892-1975
  Obituary *28*
Riggs, Stephanie 1964- *138*
Riglietti, Serena 1969- *189*
Rigney, James Oliver, Jr.
  See Jordan, Robert
Rikhoff, Jean 1928- *9*
Rikki
  See Ducornet, Erica
Riley, James A. 1939- *97*
Riley, James Whitcomb 1849-1916 .... *17*
Riley, Jocelyn 1949- *60*
  Brief entry *50*
Riley, Jocelyn Carol
  See Riley, Jocelyn
Riley, Linda Capus 1950- *85*
Riley, Martin 1948- *81*
Rimbauer, Steven
  See Pearson, Ridley
Rimes, (Margaret) LeAnn 1982- *154*
Rinaldi, Ann 1934- *161*
  Brief entry *50*
  Earlier sketches in SATA *51, 78, 117*
  See also CLR *46*
Rinard, Judith E(llen) 1947- *140*
  Earlier sketch in SATA *44*
Rinder, Lenore 1949- *92*
Ring, Elizabeth 1920- *79*
Ringdahl, Mark
  See Longyear, Barry B(rookes)
Ringgold, Faith 1930- *187*
  Earlier sketches in SATA *71, 114*
  See also CLR *30*
Ringi, Kjell (Arne Soerensen) 1939- *12*
Rinkoff, Barbara Jean (Rich) 1923-1975 .... *4*
  Obituary *27*
Rinn, Miriam 1946- *127*
Riordan, James 1936- *95*
Riordan, Rick *174*
Rios, Tere
  See Versace, Marie Teresa Rios
Ripken, Cal, Jr. 1960- *114*
Ripken, Calvin Edward, Jr.
  See Ripken, Cal, Jr.
Ripley, Catherine 1957- *82*
Ripley, Elizabeth Blake 1906-1969 .... *5*
Ripper, Charles L(ewis) 1929- *3*
Ripper, Chuck
  See Ripper, Charles L(ewis)

Riq
  See Atwater, Richard (Tupper)
Rish, David 1955- *110*
Riskind, Mary 1944- *60*
Rissinger, Matt 1956- *93*
Rissman, Art
  See Sussman, Susan
Rissman, Susan
  See Sussman, Susan
Ritchie, Barbara Gibbons *14*
Ritter, Felix
  See Kruss, James
Ritter, John H. 1951- *137*
  Earlier sketch in SATA *129*
Ritter, Lawrence S(tanley) 1922-2004 .... *58*
  Obituary *152*
Ritthaler, Shelly 1955- *91*
Ritts, Paul 1920(?)-1980
  Obituary *25*
Ritz, Karen 1957- *80*
Rivera, Geraldo (Miguel) 1943- *54*
  Brief entry *28*
Rivers, Elfrida
  See Bradley, Marion Zimmer
Rivers, Karen 1970- *131*
Riverside, John
  See Heinlein, Robert A.
Rivkin, Ann 1920- *41*
Rivoli, Mario 1943- *10*
Roach, Marilynne K. 1946- *9*
Roach, Marilynne Kathleen
  See Roach, Marilynne K.
Roach, Portia
  See Takakjian, Portia
Robb, Laura 1937- *95*
Robberecht, Thierry 1960- *182*
Robbins, Frank 1917-1994(?) *42*
  Brief entry *32*
Robbins, Ken 1945- *147*
  Brief entry *53*
  Earlier sketch in SATA *94*
Robbins, Raleigh
  See Hamilton, Charles (Harold St. John)
Robbins, Ruth 1917(?)- *14*
Robbins, Tony
  See Pashko, Stanley
Robbins, Wayne
  See Cox, William R(obert)
Robel, S. L.
  See Fraustino, Lisa Rowe
Roberson, Jennifer 1953- *72*
Roberson, John R(oyster) 1930- *53*
Robert, Adrian
  See St. John, Nicole
Roberts, Bethany *133*
Roberts, Bruce (Stuart) 1930- *47*
  Brief entry *39*
Roberts, Charles G(eorge) D(ouglas)
  1860-1943 .... *88*
  Brief entry *29*
  See also CLR *33*
Roberts, David *191*
  See Cox, John Roberts
Roberts, Diane 1937- *184*
Roberts, Elizabeth 1944- *80*
Roberts, Elizabeth Madox 1886-1941 .... *33*
  Brief entry *27*
  See also CLR *100*
Roberts, Jim
  See Bates, Barbara S(nedeker)
Roberts, John G(aither) 1913-1993 .... *27*
Roberts, Judy I. 1957- *93*
Roberts, Katherine 1962- *152*
Roberts, M. L.
  See Mattern, Joanne
Roberts, Nancy Correll 1924- *52*
  Brief entry *28*
Roberts, Priscilla 1955- *184*
Roberts, Terence
  See Sanderson, Ivan T(erence)

Roberts, Willo Davis 1928-2004 .... *150*
  Autobiography Feature *150*
  Obituary *160*
  Earlier sketches in SATA *21, 70, 133*
  See also CLR *95*
  See also SAAS *8*
Robertson, Barbara (Anne) 1931- *12*
Robertson, Don 1929-1999 .... *8*
  Obituary *113*
Robertson, Dorothy Lewis 1912- *12*
Robertson, Ellis
  See Ellison, Harlan
  and Silverberg, Robert
Robertson, James I., Jr. 1930- *182*
Robertson, James Irvin
  See Robertson, James I., Jr.
Robertson, Janet (E.) 1935- *68*
Robertson, Jennifer Sinclair 1942-1998 .... *12*
Robertson, Jenny
  See Robertson, Jennifer Sinclair
Robertson, Keith (Carlton) 1914-1991 .... *85*
  Obituary *69*
  Earlier sketch in SATA *1*
  See also SAAS *15*
Robertson, Stephen
  See Walker, Robert W(ayne)
Robertus, Polly M. 1948- *73*
Robeson, Kenneth
  See Dent, Lester
  and Goulart, Ron(ald Joseph)
Robeson, Kenneth
  See Johnson, (Walter) Ryerson
Robinet, Harriette Gillem 1931- *104*
  Earlier sketch in SATA *27*
  See also CLR *64*
Robins, Deri 1958- *166*
  Earlier sketch in SATA *117*
Robins, Patricia
  See Clark, Patricia Denise
Robins, Rollo, Jr.
  See Ellis, Edward S(ylvester)
Robins, Seelin
  See Ellis, Edward S(ylvester)
Robinson, Adjai 1932- *8*
Robinson, Aminah Brenda Lynn 1940- *159*
  Earlier sketch in SATA *77*
Robinson, Barbara (Webb) 1927- *84*
  Earlier sketch in SATA *8*
Robinson, C(harles) A(lexander), Jr.
  1900-1965 .... *36*
Robinson, Charles 1870-1937 .... *17*
Robinson, Charles 1931- *6*
Robinson, Dorothy W. 1929- *54*
Robinson, Eve
  See Tanselle, Eve
Robinson, Glen 1953- *92*
Robinson, Glendal P.
  See Robinson, Glen
Robinson, Jan M. 1933- *6*
Robinson, Jean O. 1934- *7*
Robinson, Joan (Mary) G(ale Thomas)
  1910-1988 .... *7*
Robinson, Kim Stanley 1952- *109*
Robinson, Lee 1948- *110*
Robinson, Lloyd
  See Silverberg, Robert
Robinson, Lynda S(uzanne) 1951- *107*
Robinson, Marileta 1942- *32*
Robinson, Maudie Millian Oller 1914- *11*
Robinson, Maurice R(ichard) 1895-1982
  Obituary *29*
Robinson, Nancy K(onheim) 1942-1994 ..... *91*
  Brief entry *31*
  Obituary *79*
  Earlier sketch in SATA *32*
Robinson, Ray(mond Kenneth) 1920- *23*
Robinson, Shari
  See McGuire, Leslie (Sarah)
Robinson, Sharon 1950- *162*
Robinson, Spider 1948- *118*

Robinson, Sue
  See Robinson, Susan Maria
Robinson, Susan Maria 1955- 105
Robinson, Suzanne
  See Robinson, Lynda S(uzanne)
Robinson, T(homas) H(eath) 1869-1950 17
Robinson, (Wanda) Veronica 1926- 30
Robinson, W(illiam) Heath 1872-1944 17
Robison, Bonnie 1924- 12
Robison, Nancy L(ouise) 1934- 32
Robles, Harold E. 1948- 87
Robottom, John 1934- 7
Robson, Eric 1939- 82
Rocco, John 1967- 188
Roche, A. K.
  See Abisch, Roslyn Kroop
  and Kaplan, Boche
Roche, Denis (Mary) 1967- 99
Roche, Luane 1937- 170
Roche, P(atricia) K. 1935- 57
  Brief entry 34
Roche, Terry
  See Poole, Peggy
Rochman, Hazel 1938- 105
Rock, Lois
  See Joslin, Mary
Rock, Maxine 1940- 108
Rocker, Fermin 1907- 40
Rocklin, Joanne 1946- 134
  Earlier sketch in SATA 86
Rockwell, Anne F. 1934- 162
  Earlier sketches in SATA 33, 71, 114
  See also SAAS 19
Rockwell, Anne Foote
  See Rockwell, Anne F.
Rockwell, Bart
  See Pellowski, Michael (Joseph)
Rockwell, Harlow 1910-1988 33
  Obituary 56
Rockwell, Lizzy 1961- 185
Rockwell, Norman (Percevel) 1894-1978 23
Rockwell, Thomas 1933- 70
  Earlier sketch in SATA 7
  See also CLR 6
Rockwood, Joyce 1947- 39
Rockwood, Roy 67
  Earlier sketch in SATA 1
  See McFarlane, Leslie (Charles)
  and Stratemeyer, Edward L.
Rodanas, Kristina 1952- 155
Rodari, Gianni 1920-1980
  See CLR 24
Rodd, Kathleen Tennant 57
  Obituary 55
  See Rodd, Kylie Tennant
Rodda, Emily 1948- 146
  Earlier sketch in SATA 97
  See also CLR 32
Roddenberry, Eugene Wesley 1921-1991 45
  Obituary 69
  See Roddenberry, Gene
Roddenberry, Gene
  Obituary 69
  See Roddenberry, Eugene Wesley
Roddie, Shen 153
Roddy, Lee 1921- 57
Rodenas, Paula 73
Rodgers, Frank 1944- 69
Rodgers, Mary 1931- 130
  Earlier sketch in SATA 8
  See also CLR 20
Rodman, Emerson
  See Ellis, Edward S(ylvester)
Rodman, Eric
  See Silverberg, Robert
Rodman, Maia
  See Wojciechowska, Maia (Teresa)
Rodman, Mary Ann 185
Rodman, (Cary) Selden 1909-2002 9

Rodowsky, Colby 1932- 164
  Earlier sketches in SATA 21, 77, 120
  See also SAAS 22
Rodowsky, Colby F.
  See Rodowsky, Colby
Rodriguez, Alejo 1941- 83
Rodriguez, Alex 1975- 189
Rodriguez, Christina 1981- 177
Rodriguez, Luis J. 1954- 125
Rodriguez, Rachel 180
Rodriguez, Rachel Victoria
  See Rodriguez, Rachel
Roeder, Virginia Marsh 1926- 98
Roehrig, Catharine H. 1949- 67
Roennfeldt, Robert 1953- 78
Roessel-Waugh, C. C.
  See Waugh, Carol-Lynn Rossel
  and Waugh, Charles G(ordon)
Roets, Lois F. 1937- 91
Roever, J(oan) M(arilyn) 1935- 26
Rofes, Eric 1954-2006 52
Rofes, Eric Edward 1954-2006
  See Rofes, Eric
Roffey, Maureen 1936- 33
Rogak, Lisa 1962- 80
Rogak, Lisa Angowski
  See Rogak, Lisa
Rogasky, Barbara 1933- 144
  Earlier sketch in SATA 86
Rogers, (Thomas) Alan (Stinchcombe)
  1937- 81
  Earlier sketch in SATA 2
Rogers, Bettye 1858-1919 103
Rogers, Cindy 1950- 89
Rogers, Emma 1951- 74
Rogers, Frances 1888-1974 10
Rogers, Fred McFeely 1928-2003 33
  Obituary 138
Rogers, Hal
  See Sirimarco, Elizabeth
Rogers, Jean 1919- 55
  Brief entry 47
Rogers, Matilda 1894-1976 5
  Obituary 34
Rogers, Pamela 1927- 9
Rogers, Paul 1950- 98
  Earlier sketch in SATA 54
Rogers, Robert
  See Hamilton, Charles (Harold St. John)
Rogers, Sherry 193
Rogers, W(illiam) G(arland) 1896-1978 23
Rohan, M. S.
  See Rohan, Michael Scott
Rohan, Michael Scott 1951- 98
Rohan, Mike Scott
  See Rohan, Michael Scott
Rohmann, Eric 1957- 171
  See also CLR 100
Rohmer, Harriet 1938- 56
Rohrer, Doug 1962- 89
Rojan
  See Rojankovsky, Feodor (Stepanovich)
Rojankovsky, Feodor (Stepanovich)
  1891-1970 21
Rojany, Lisa 94
Rokeby-Thomas, Anna E(lma) 1911- 15
Roland, Albert 1925-2002 11
Roland, Mary
  See Lewis, Mary (Christianna)
Roleff, Tamara L. 1959- 143
Rolerson, Darrell A(llen) 1946- 8
Roll, Winifred 1909-1998 6
Rollins, Charlemae Hill 1897-1979 3
  Obituary 26
Rollock, Barbara T(herese) 1924- 64
Romack, Janice Reed
  See LeNoir, Janice
Romain, Trevor 134
Romanenko, Vitaliy 1962- 101
Romano, Louis G. 1921- 35
Romano, Melora A. 1966- 118

Romano, Ray 1957- 170
Romano, Raymond
  See Romano, Ray
Romijn, Johanna Maria Kooyker
  See Kooyker-Romijn, Johanna Maria
Romyn, Johanna Maria Kooyker
  See Kooyker-Romijn, Johanna Maria
Rong, Yu 1970- 174
Rongen, Bjoern 1906- 10
Rongen, Bjorn
  See Rongen, Bjoern
Ronson, Mark
  See Alexander, Marc
Rood, Ronald (N.) 1920- 12
Rook, Sebastian
  See Jeapes, Ben
Rooke, Daphne (Marie) 1914- 12
Roop, Connie 1951- 167
  Brief entry 49
  Earlier sketches in SATA 54, 116
Roop, Constance Betzer
  See Roop, Connie
Roop, Peter 1951- 167
  Brief entry 49
  Earlier sketches in SATA 54, 116
Roop, Peter G.
  See Roop, Peter
Roop, Peter Geiger
  See Roop, Peter
Roos, Stephen 1945- 128
  Brief entry 41
  Earlier sketches in SATA 47, 77
Roose-Evans, James 1927- 65
Roosevelt, (Anna) Eleanor 1884-1962 50
Root, Barry 182
Root, Betty 84
Root, Kimberly Bulcken 192
Root, Phyllis 1949- 184
  Brief entry 48
  Earlier sketches in SATA 55, 94, 145
Root, Shelton L., Jr. 1923-1986
  Obituary 51
Roper, Laura (Newbold) Wood 1911-2003 .. 34
  Obituary 150
Roper, Robert 1946- 142
  Earlier sketch in SATA 78
Roraback, Robin (Ellan) 1964- 111
Rorby, Ginny 1944- 94
Rorer, Abigail 1949- 85
Rosamel, Godeleine de 1968- 151
Roscoe, D(onald) T(homas) 1934- 42
Rose, Anne 8
Rose, Deborah Lee 1955- 185
  Earlier sketches in SATA 71, 124
Rose, Elizabeth (Jane Pretty) 1933- 68
  Brief entry 28
Rose, Florella
  See Carlson, Vada F.
Rose, Gerald (Hembdon Seymour) 1935- 68
  Brief entry 30
Rose, Malcolm 1953- 168
  Earlier sketch in SATA 107
Rose, Nancy A.
  See Sweetland, Nancy A(nn)
Rose, Ted 1940- 93
Rose, Wendy 1948- 12
Rosen, Lillian (Diamond) 1928- 63
Rosen, Marvin 1933- 161
Rosen, Michael 1946- 181
  Brief entry 40
  Earlier sketches in SATA 48, 84, 137
  See also CLR 45
Rosen, Michael J(oel) 1954- 86
Rosen, Michael Wayne
  See Rosen, Michael
Rosen, Sidney 1916- 1
Rosen, Winifred 1943- 8
Rosenbaum, Maurice 1907- 6
Rosenberg, Amye 1950- 74
Rosenberg, Dorothy 1906- 40

Rosenberg, Eth(el) Clifford 1915- *3*
  See Clifford, Eth
Rosenberg, Jane 1949- *58*
Rosenberg, Liz 1958- *129*
  Earlier sketch in SATA *75*
Rosenberg, Maxine B(erta) 1939- *93*
  Brief entry *47*
  Earlier sketch in SATA *55*
Rosenberg, Nancy (Sherman) 1931- *4*
Rosenberg, Sharon 1942- *8*
Rosenberry, Vera 1948- *144*
  Earlier sketch in SATA *83*
Rosenblatt, Arthur
  See Rosenblatt, Arthur S.
Rosenblatt, Arthur S. 1938- *68*
  Brief entry *45*
Rosenblatt, Lily 1956- *90*
Rosenbloom, Joseph 1928- *21*
Rosenblum, Richard 1928- *11*
Rosenburg, John M. 1918- *6*
Rosenfeld, Dina 1962- *99*
Rosenthal, Amy Krouse 1965- *177*
Rosenthal, Betsy R. 1957- *178*
Rosenthal, Harold 1914-1999 .... *35*
Rosenthal, M(acha) L(ouis) 1917-1996 .... *59*
Rosenthal, Marc 1949- *193*
Rosenthal, Mark A(lan) 1946- *64*
Rosman, Steven M 1956- *81*
Rosman, Steven Michael
  See Rosman, Steven M
Rosoff, Meg 1956- *160*
Ross, Alan
  See Warwick, Alan R(oss)
Ross, Christine 1950- *172*
  Earlier sketch in SATA *83*
Ross, Clare *111*
  Earlier sketch in SATA *48*
  See Romano, Clare
Ross, Dana Fuller
  See Cockrell, Amanda
  and Gerson, Noel Bertram
Ross, Dave *32*
  See Ross, David
Ross, David 1896-1975 .... *49*
  Obituary *20*
Ross, David 1949- *133*
  See Ross, Dave
Ross, Diana
  See Denney, Diana
Ross, Edward S(hearman) 1915- *85*
Ross, Eileen 1950- *115*
Ross, Frank (Xavier), Jr. 1914- *28*
Ross, Jane 1961- *79*
Ross, John 1921- *45*
Ross, Judy 1942- *54*
Ross, Katharine Reynolds
  See Ross, Kathy
Ross, Kathy 1948- *169*
  Earlier sketch in SATA *89*
Ross, Kent 1956- *91*
Ross, Lillian Hammer 1925- *72*
Ross, Michael Elsohn 1952- *170*
  Earlier sketches in SATA *80, 127*
Ross, Pat(ricia Kienzle) 1943- *53*
  Brief entry *48*
Ross, Ramon R(oyal) 1930- *62*
Ross, Stewart 1947- *134*
  Earlier sketch in SATA *92*
  See also SAAS *23*
Ross, Tom 1958- *84*
Ross, Tony 1938- *176*
  Earlier sketches in SATA *17, 65, 130*
Ross, Wilda 1915- *51*
  Brief entry *39*
Rossel, Seymour 1945- *28*
Rossell, Judith 1953- *187*
Rossel-Waugh, C. C.
  See Waugh, Carol-Lynn Rossel
Rossetti, Christina 1830-1894 .... *20*
  See also CLR *115*

Rossetti, Christina Georgina
  See Rossetti, Christina
Rossi, Joyce 1943- *116*
Rossotti, Hazel Swaine 1930- *95*
Rostkowski, Margaret I. 1945- *59*
Roth, Arnold 1929- *21*
Roth, Arthur J(oseph) 1925-1993 .... *43*
  Brief entry *28*
  Obituary *75*
  See also SAAS *11*
Roth, David 1940- *36*
Roth, Julie Jersild *180*
Roth, Matthue 1978(?)- *174*
Roth, Roger *190*
Roth, Susan L. *181*
  Earlier sketch in SATA *134*
Rothberg, Abraham 1922- *59*
Roth-Hano, Renee 1931- *85*
Rothkopf, Carol Z. 1929- *4*
Rothman, Joel 1938- *7*
Rotner, Shelley 1951- *169*
  Earlier sketch in SATA *76*
Rottman, S(usan) L(ynn) 1970- *157*
  Earlier sketch in SATA *106*
Roueche, Berton 1911-1994 .... *28*
Roughsey, Dick 1921(?)-1985 .... *35*
  See also CLR *41*
Roughsey, Goobalathaldin
  See Roughsey, Dick
Rounds, Glen (Harold) 1906-2002 .... *112*
  Obituary *141*
  Earlier sketches in SATA *8, 70*
Rourke, Constance Mayfield 1885-1941
  See YABC *1*
Rowan, Deirdre
  See Williams, Jeanne
Rowe, Jennifer
  See Rodda, Emily
Rowe, John A. 1949- *146*
Rowe, Viola Carson 1903-1969
  Obituary *26*
Rowh, Mark 1952- *90*
Rowland, Florence Wightman 1900-1997 ...... *8*
  Obituary *108*
Rowland-Entwistle, (Arthur)
  Theodore (Henry) 1925- *94*
  Earlier sketch in SATA *31*
Rowling, J.K. 1965- *174*
  Earlier sketch in SATA *109*
  See also CLR *112*
Rowling, Joanne Kathleen
  See Rowling, J.K.
Rowsome, Frank (Howard), Jr. 1914-1983 .. *36*
Roy, Gabrielle 1909-1983 .... *104*
Roy, Jacqueline 1954- *74*
Roy, Jennifer
  See Roy, Jennifer Rozines
Roy, Jennifer Rozines 1967- *178*
Roy, Jessie Hailstalk 1895-1986
  Obituary *51*
Roy, Liam
  See Scarry, Patricia (Murphy)
Roy, Ron(ald) 1940- *110*
  Brief entry *35*
  Earlier sketch in SATA *40*
Roybal, Laura 1956- *85*
Roybal, Laura Husby
  See Roybal, Laura
Royds, Caroline 1953- *55*
Royston, Angela 1945- *169*
  Earlier sketch in SATA *120*
Rozakis, Laurie E. 1952- *84*
Rubel, Nicole 1953- *181*
  Earlier sketches in SATA *18, 95, 135*
Rubin, Eva Johanna 1925- *38*
Rubin, Susan Goldman 1939- *182*
  Earlier sketches in SATA *84, 132*
Rubin, Vicky 1964- *193*
Rubinetti, Donald 1947- *92*

Rubinstein, Gillian 1942- *158*
  Autobiography Feature *116*
  Earlier sketches in SATA *68, 105*
  See also CLR *35*
  See also SAAS *25*
Rubinstein, Gillian Margaret
  See Rubinstein, Gillian
Rubinstein, Patricia (Giulia Caulfield
  Kate) -2003 .... *29*
  Obituary *149*
  See Forest, Antonia
Rubinstein, Robert E(dward) 1943- *49*
Rublowsky, John M(artin) 1928- *62*
Rubright, Lynn 1936- *171*
Ruby, Laura *181*
  Earlier sketch in SATA *155*
Ruby, Lois 1942- *184*
  Autobiography Feature *105*
  Brief entry *34*
  Earlier sketches in SATA *35, 95*
Ruby, Lois F.
  See Ruby, Lois
Ruchlis, Hy(man) 1913-1992 .... *3*
  Obituary *72*
Rucker, Mike 1940- *91*
Ruckman, Ivy 1931- *93*
  Earlier sketch in SATA *37*
Ruck-Pauquet, Gina 1931- *40*
  Brief entry *37*
Ruditis, Paul *190*
Rudley, Stephen 1946- *30*
Rudolph, Marguerita 1908- *21*
Rudomin, Esther
  See Hautzig, Esther Rudomin
Rue, Leonard Lee III 1926- *142*
  Earlier sketch in SATA *37*
Rueda, Claudia *183*
Ruedi, Norma Paul
  See Ainsworth, Norma
Ruelle, Karen Gray 1957- *126*
  Earlier sketch in SATA *84*
Ruemmler, John D(avid) 1948- *78*
Ruepp, Krista 1947- *143*
Ruffell, Ann 1941- *30*
Ruffins, Reynold 1930- *125*
  Earlier sketch in SATA *41*
Rugoff, Milton 1913- *30*
Ruhen, Olaf 1911-1989 .... *17*
Rukeyser, Muriel 1913-1980
  Obituary *22*
Rumbaut, Hendle 1949- *84*
Rumford, James 1948- *193*
  Earlier sketch in SATA *116*
Rumsey, Marian (Barritt) 1928- *16*
Rumstuckle, Cornelius
  See Brennan, Herbie
Runnerstroem, Bengt Arne 1944- *75*
Runyan, John
  See Palmer, Bernard (Alvin)
Runyon, Catherine 1947- *62*
Ruoff, A. LaVonne Brown 1930- *76*
Rupp, Rebecca *185*
Rusch, Kris
  See Rusch, Kristine Kathryn
Rusch, Kristine Kathryn 1960- *113*
Rush, Alison 1951- *41*
Rush, Peter 1937- *32*
Rushdie, Ahmed Salman
  See Rushdie, Salman
Rushdie, Salman 1947-
  See CLR *125*
Rushford, Patricia H(elen) 1943- *134*
Rushmore, Helen 1898-1994 .... *3*
Rushmore, Robert (William) 1926-1986 .... *8*
  Obituary *49*
Ruskin, Ariane
  See Batterberry, Ariane Ruskin
Ruskin, John 1819-1900 .... *24*
Russ, Lavinia (Faxon) 1904-1992 .... *74*
Russell, Charlotte
  See Rathjen, Carl Henry

Russell, Ching Yeung 1946- *107*
Russell, Don(ald Bert) 1899-1986
  Obituary *47*
Russell, Franklin (Alexander) 1926- *11*
Russell, Gertrude Barrer
  See Barrer-Russell, Gertrude
Russell, Helen Ross 1915- *8*
Russell, James 1933- *53*
Russell, Jim
  See Russell, James
Russell, Joan Plummer 1930- *139*
Russell, P(hilip) Craig 1951- *162*
  Earlier sketch in SATA *80*
Russell, Patrick
  See Sammis, John
Russell, Paul (Gary) 1942- *57*
Russell, Sarah
  See Laski, Marghanita
Russell, Sharman Apt 1954- *123*
Russell, Solveig Paulson 1904-1985 .... *3*
Russo, Marisabina 1950- *188*
  Earlier sketches in SATA *106, 151*
Russo, Monica J. 1950- *83*
Russo, Susan 1947- *30*
Russon, Penni 1974- *179*
Rutgers van der Loeff, An
  See Rutgers van der Loeff-Basenau,
  An(na) Maria Margaretha
Rutgers van der Loeff-Basenau, An(na)
  Maria Margaretha 1910- *22*
Ruth, Rod 1912-1987 .... *9*
Rutherford, Douglas
  See McConnell, James Douglas
  Rutherford
Rutherford, Meg 1932- *34*
Ruthin, Margaret *4*
  See Catherall, Arthur
Rutledge, Jill Zimmerman 1951- *155*
Rutz, Viola Larkin 1932- *12*
Ruurs, Margriet 1952- *147*
  Earlier sketch in SATA *97*
Ruzicka, Rudolph 1883-1978
  Obituary *24*
Ruzzier, Sergio 1966- *159*
Ryan, Betsy
  See Ryan, Elizabeth (Anne)
Ryan, Cheli Duran *20*
Ryan, Darlene 1958- *176*
Ryan, Elizabeth (Anne) 1943- *30*
Ryan, Jeanette
  See Mines, Jeanette
Ryan, John (Gerald Christopher) 1921- *22*
Ryan, Margaret 1950- *166*
  Earlier sketch in SATA *78*
Ryan, Mary E. 1953- *61*
Ryan, Mary Elizabeth
  See Ryan, Mary E.
Ryan, Pam Munoz 1951- *134*
Ryan, Patrick 1957- *138*
Ryan, Peter (Charles) 1939- *15*
Ryan-Lush, Geraldine 1949- *89*
Rybakov, Anatoli (Naumovich) 1911-1998 .. *79*
  Obituary *108*
  See Rybakov, Anatolii (Naumovich)
Rybakov, Anatolii (Naumovich)
  See Rybakov, Anatoli (Naumovich)
Rybolt, Thomas R. 1954- *62*
Rybolt, Thomas Roy
  See Rybolt, Thomas R.
Rybolt, Tom
  See Rybolt, Thomas R.
Rydberg, Ernest E(mil) 1901-1993 .... *21*
Rydberg, Lou(isa Hampton) 1908- *27*
Rydell, Katy 1942- *91*
Rydell, Wendell
  See Rydell, Wendy
Rydell, Wendy *4*
Ryden, Hope *91*
  Earlier sketch in SATA *8*

Ryder, Joanne (Rose) 1946- *163*
  Brief entry *34*
  Earlier sketches in SATA *65, 122*
  See also CLR *37*
Ryder, Pamela
  See Lamb, Nancy
Rye, Anthony
  See Youd, (Christopher) Samuel
Rylant, Cynthia 1954- *160*
  Brief entry *44*
  Earlier sketches in SATA *50, 76, 112*
  See also CLR *86*
  See also SAAS *13*
Rymer, Alta May 1925- *34*

S

S. L. C.
  See Clemens, Samuel Langhorne
S., Svend Otto
  See Soerensen, Svend Otto
Saaf, Donald W(illiam) 1961- *124*
Saal, Jocelyn
  See Sachs, Judith
Sabbeth, Carol (Landstrom) 1957- *125*
Saberhagen, Fred 1930-2007 .... *89*
  Obituary *184*
  Earlier sketch in SATA *37*
Saberhagen, Fred T.
  See Saberhagen, Fred
Saberhagen, Fred Thomas
  See Saberhagen, Fred
Saberhagen, Frederick Thomas
  See Saberhagen, Fred
Sabin, Edwin L(egrand) 1870-1952
  See YABC *2*
Sabin, Francene *27*
Sabin, Lou
  See Sabin, Louis
Sabin, Louis 1930- *27*
Sabre, Dirk
  See Laffin, John (Alfred Charles)
Sabuda, Robert (James) 1965- *120*
  Earlier sketch in SATA *81*
Sabuda, Robert 1965- *170*
Sabuda, Robert James
  See Sabuda, Robert
Sachar, Louis 1954- *154*
  Brief entry *50*
  Earlier sketches in SATA *63, 104*
  See also CLR *79*
Sachs, Elizabeth-Ann 1946- *48*
Sachs, Judith 1947- *52*
  Brief entry *51*
Sachs, Marilyn 1927- *164*
  Autobiography Feature *110*
  Earlier sketches in SATA *3, 68*
  See also CLR *2*
  See also SAAS *2*
Sachs, Marilyn Stickle
  See Sachs, Marilyn
Sackett, S(amuel) J(ohn) 1928- *12*
Sackson, Sid 1920- *16*
Sacre, Antonio 1968- *152*
Saddler, Allen
  See Richards, R(onald) C(harles)
  W(illiam)
Saddler, K. Allen
  See Richards, R(onald) C(harles)
  W(illiam)
Sadie, Stanley 1930-2005 .... *14*
Sadie, Stanley John
  See Sadie, Stanley
Sadiq, Nazneen 1944- *101*
Sadler, Catherine Edwards 1952- *60*
  Brief entry *45*
Sadler, Marilyn (June) 1950- *79*
Sadler, Mark
  See Lynds, Dennis

Saffer, Barbara *144*
Sagan, Carl 1934-1996 .... *58*
  Obituary *94*
Sagan, Carl Edward
  See Sagan, Carl
Sage, Juniper
  See Brown, Margaret Wise
  and Hurd, Edith Thacher
Sagsoorian, Paul 1923- *12*
Said, S.F. 1967- *174*
Saidman, Anne 1952- *75*
Saint, Dora Jessie 1913- *10*
St. Anthony, Jane *175*
St. Antoine, Sara L. 1966- *84*
St. Clair, Byrd Hooper 1905-1976
  Obituary *28*
Saint-Exupery, Antoine de 1900-1944 .... *20*
  See also CLR *10*
Saint-Exupery, Antoine Jean Baptiste
  Marie Roger de
  See Saint-Exupery, Antoine de
St. George, Judith 1931- *161*
  Earlier sketches in SATA *13, 99*
  See also CLR *57*
  See also SAAS *12*
St. James, Blakely
  See Gottfried, Theodore Mark
  and Platt, Charles
St. James, Blakely
  See Griffin, W.E.B
St. James, Sierra
  See Rallison, Janette
Saint James, Synthia 1949- *152*
  Earlier sketch in SATA *84*
St. John, Nicole *143*
  Autobiography Feature *143*
  Earlier sketch in SATA *89*
  See also CLR *46*
  See also SAAS *7*
  See Johnston, Norma
St. John, Patricia Mary 1919-1993
  Obituary *79*
St. John, Philip
  See del Rey, Lester
St. John, Wylly Folk 1908-1985 .... *10*
  Obituary *45*
St. Max, E. S.
  See Ellis, Edward S(ylvester)
St. Meyer, Ned
  See Stratemeyer, Edward L.
St. Mox, E. A.
  See Ellis, Edward S(ylvester)
St. Myer, Ned
  See Stratemeyer, Edward L.
St. Tamara
  See Kolba, St. Tamara
Saito, Michiko
  See Fujiwara, Michiko
Sakaki, Ichiro 1969- *192*
Sakers, Don 1958- *72*
Sakharnov, S.
  See Sakharnov, Svyatoslav
Sakharnov, Svyatoslav 1923- *65*
Sakharnov, Svyatoslav Vladimirovich
  See Sakharnov, Svyatoslav
Saksena, Kate *148*
Sakurai, Gail 1952- *153*
  Earlier sketch in SATA *87*
Salamanca, Lucy
  See del Barco, Lucy Salamanca
Salassi, Otto R(ussell) 1939-1993 .... *38*
  Obituary *77*
Salat, Cristina *82*
Saldana, Rene, Jr. *186*
Saldutti, Denise 1953- *39*
Sale, Tim 1956- *153*
Salem, Kay 1952- *92*
Salerno, Steven *176*
Salinger, J.D. 1919- *67*
  See also CLR *18*

Salinger, Jerome David
  See Salinger, J.D.
Salisbury, Graham 1944- *161*
  Earlier sketches in SATA *76, 108*
Salisbury, Joyce E(llen) 1944- *138*
Salkey, (Felix) Andrew (Alexander)
  1928-1995 .... *118*
  Earlier sketch in SATA *35*
Salley, Coleen *166*
Sallis, Susan (Diana) 1929- *55*
Salmon, Annie Elizabeth 1899- *13*
Salonen, Roxane Beauclair 1968- *184*
Salsi, Lynn 1947- *130*
Salsitz, R. A. V.
  See Salsitz, Rhondi Vilott
Salsitz, Rhondi Vilott *115*
  See Salsitz, R. A. V.
Salten, Felix
  See Salzmann, Siegmund
Salter, Cedric
  See Knight, Francis Edgar
Saltman, Judith 1947- *64*
Saltzberg, Barney 1955- *135*
Saltzman, David (Charles Laertes)
  1967-1990 .... *86*
Salvadori, Mario (George) 1907-1997 .... *97*
  Earlier sketch in SATA *40*
Salwood, F.K.
  See Kilworth, Garry
Salzer, L. E.
  See Wilson, Lionel
Salzman, Marian 1959- *77*
Salzmann, Siegmund 1869-1945 .... *25*
  See Salten, Felix
Samachson, Dorothy (Mirkin) 1914-1997 ...... *3*
Samachson, Joseph 1906-1980 .... *3*
  Obituary *52*
Sammis, John 1942- *4*
Sampson, Emma (Keats) Speed
  1868-1947 .... *68*
Sampson, Fay (Elizabeth) 1935- *151*
  Brief entry *40*
  Earlier sketch in SATA *42*
Sampson, Michael 1952- *143*
  Earlier sketch in SATA *95*
Samson, Anne S(tringer) 1933- *2*
Samson, Joan 1937-1976 .... *13*
Samson, Suzanne M. 1959- *91*
Samuels, Charles 1902-1982 .... *12*
Samuels, Cynthia K(alish) 1946- *79*
Samuels, Gertrude 1910(?)-2003 .... *17*
  Obituary *147*
Sanborn, Duane 1914-1996 .... *38*
Sancha, Sheila 1924- *38*
Sanchez, Alex 1957- *151*
Sanchez, Sonia 1934- *136*
  Earlier sketch in SATA *22*
  See also CLR *18*
Sanchez-Silva, Jose Maria 1911- *132*
  Earlier sketch in SATA *16*
  See also CLR *12*
Sand, George X. *45*
Sandak, Cass R(obert) 1950-2001 .... *51*
  Brief entry *37*
Sandberg, (Karin) Inger 1930- *15*
Sandberg, Karl C. 1931- *35*
Sandberg, Lasse (E. M.) 1924- *15*
Sandburg, Carl (August) 1878-1967 .... *8*
  See also CLR *67*
Sandburg, Charles
  See Sandburg, Carl (August)
Sandburg, Charles A.
  See Sandburg, Carl (August)
Sandburg, Helga 1918- *3*
  See also SAAS *10*
Sandell, Lisa Ann 1977- *175*
Sander, Heather L. 1947- *157*
Sanderlin, George 1915- *4*
Sanderlin, Owenita (Harrah) 1916- *11*
Sanders, Betty Jane
  See Monthei, Betty

Sanders, Nancy I. 1960- *141*
  Earlier sketch in SATA *90*
Sanders, Scott Russell 1945- *109*
  Earlier sketch in SATA *56*
Sanders, Winston P.
  See Anderson, Poul
Sanderson, Irma 1912- *66*
Sanderson, Ivan T(erence) 1911-1973 .... *6*
Sanderson, Margaret Love
  See Keats, Emma
  and Sampson, Emma (Keats) Speed
Sanderson, Ruth 1951- *172*
  Earlier sketches in SATA *41, 109*
Sanderson, Ruth L.
  See Sanderson, Ruth
Sandin, Joan 1942- *153*
  Earlier sketches in SATA *12, 94*
Sandison, Janet
  See Cameron, Elizabeth Jane
Sandler, Martin W. *160*
Sandom, J. Gregory
  See Welsh, T.K.
Sandom, J.G.
  See Welsh, T.K.
Sandoz, Mari(e Susette) 1900-1966 .... *5*
Sanford, Agnes (White) 1897-1976 .... *61*
Sanford, Doris 1937- *69*
Sanger, Marjory Bartlett 1920- *8*
San Jose, Christine 1929- *167*
Sankey, Alice (Ann-Susan) 1910- *27*
San Souci, Daniel *192*
  Earlier sketch in SATA *96*
San Souci, Robert D. 1946- *158*
  Earlier sketches in SATA *40, 81, 117*
  See also CLR *43*
Santamaria, Benjamin 1955- *184*
Santat, Dan *188*
Santesson, Hans Stefan 1914(?)-1975
  Obituary *30*
Santiago, Esmeralda 1948- *129*
Santos, Helen
  See Griffiths, Helen
Santrey, Louis
  See Sabin, Louis
Santucci, Barbara 1948- *130*
Sapergia, Barbara 1943- *181*
Sapieyevski, Anne Lindbergh 1940-1993 ..... *78*
  Earlier sketch in SATA *35*
  See Feydy, Anne Lindbergh
  and Lindbergh, Anne
Saport, Linda 1954- *123*
Sapp, Allen 1929- *151*
Sarac, Roger
  See Caras, Roger A(ndrew)
Sarah, Duchess of York
  See Ferguson, Sarah
Sarasin, Jennifer
  See Sachs, Judith
Sardinha, Rick *192*
Sarg, Anthony Frederick
  See Sarg, Tony
Sarg, Tony 1882-1942
  See YABC *1*
Sargent, Pamela 1948- *78*
  Earlier sketch in SATA *29*
Sargent, Robert 1933- *2*
Sargent, Sarah 1937- *44*
  Brief entry *41*
Sargent, Shirley 1927-2004 .... *11*
Sarnoff, Jane 1937- *10*
Saroyan, William 1908-1981 .... *23*
  Obituary *24*
Sarton, Eleanor May
  See Sarton, May
Sarton, May 1912-1995 .... *36*
  Obituary *86*
Sasaki, Chris *182*
Saseen, Sharon (Dillon) 1949- *59*
Sasek, Miroslav 1916-1980 .... *16*
  Obituary *23*
  See also CLR *4*

Sasso, Sandy Eisenberg 1947- *162*
  Earlier sketches in SATA *86, 116*
Sathre, Vivian 1952- *133*
  Earlier sketch in SATA *79*
Satterfield, Charles
  See del Rey, Lester
  and Pohl, Frederik
Sattgast, L. J.
  See Sattgast, Linda J.
Sattgast, Linda J. 1953- *91*
Sattler, Helen Roney 1921-1992 .... *74*
  Earlier sketch in SATA *4*
  See also CLR *24*
Sauer, Julia Lina 1891-1983 .... *32*
  Obituary *36*
Sauerwein, Leigh 1944- *155*
Saul, Carol P. 1947- *117*
  Earlier sketch in SATA *78*
Saul, John III
  See Saul, John
Saul, John 1942- *98*
Saul, John W.
  See Saul, John
Saul, John W. III
  See Saul, John
Saul, John Woodruff III
  See Saul, John
Saul, (Ellen) Wendy 1946- *42*
Saulnier, Karen Luczak 1940- *80*
Saunders, Caleb
  See Heinlein, Robert A.
Saunders, Dave 1939- *85*
Saunders, Julie 1939- *85*
Saunders, (William) Keith 1910-1994 .... *12*
Saunders, Rubie (Agnes) 1929- *21*
Saunders, Susan 1945- *96*
  Brief entry *41*
  Earlier sketch in SATA *46*
Saunders-Smith, Gail 1952- *169*
Sauvain, Philip Arthur 1933- *111*
Savadier, Elivia 1950- *164*
  Earlier sketch in SATA *79*
Savage, Alan
  See Nicole, Christopher (Robin)
Savage, Blake
  See Goodwin, Harold L(eland)
Savage, Candace (M.) 1949- *142*
Savage, Deborah 1955- *76*
Savage, Jeff 1961- *97*
Savage, Katharine James 1905-1989
  Obituary *61*
Savage, Thomas 1915-2003
  Obituary *147*
Savageau, Cheryl 1950- *96*
Savery, Constance (Winifred) 1897-1999 .... *1*
Saville, Andrew
  See Taylor, Andrew
Saville, (Leonard) Malcolm 1901-1982 .... *23*
  Obituary *31*
Saviozzi, Adriana
  See Mazza, Adriana
Savitt, Sam 1917(?)-2000 .... *8*
  Obituary *126*
Savitz, Harriet May 1933- *72*
  Earlier sketch in SATA *5*
  See also SAAS *26*
Sawicki, Mary 1950- *90*
Sawyer, (Frederick) Don(ald) 1947- *72*
Sawyer, Kem Knapp 1953- *84*
Sawyer, Robert J. 1960- *149*
  Earlier sketch in SATA *81*
Sawyer, Robert James
  See Sawyer, Robert J.
Sawyer, Ruth 1880-1970 .... *17*
  See also CLR *36*
Saxby, H.M.
  See Saxby, (Henry) Maurice
Saxby, (Henry) Maurice 1924- *71*
Saxon, Andrew
  See Arthur, Robert, (Jr.)

Saxon, Antonia
  See Sachs, Judith
Say, Allen 1937- *161*
  Earlier sketches in SATA *28, 69, 110*
  See also CLR *135*
Sayers, Frances Clarke 1897-1989 .... *3*
  Obituary *62*
Sayles, Elizabeth 1956- *163*
  Earlier sketch in SATA *108*
Saylor-Marchant, Linda 1963- *82*
Sayre, April Pulley 1966- *191*
  Earlier sketches in SATA *88, 131*
Sazer, Nina 1949- *13*
Scabrini, Janet 1953- *13*
Scagell, Robin 1946- *107*
Scagnetti, Jack 1924- *7*
Scamander, Newt
  See Rowling, J.K.
Scamell, Ragnhild 1940- *180*
  Earlier sketch in SATA *77*
Scanlon, Marion Stephany *11*
Scannel, John Vernon
  See Scannell, Vernon
Scannell, Vernon 1922-2007 .... *59*
  Obituary *188*
Scarborough, Elizabeth *171*
  See Scarborough, Elizabeth Ann
Scarborough, Elizabeth Ann 1947- *171*
  Earlier sketch in SATA *98*
  See Scarborough, Elizabeth
Scarf, Maggi
  See Scarf, Maggie
Scarf, Maggie 1932- *5*
Scariano, Margaret M. 1924- *86*
Scarlett, Susan
  See Streatfeild, Noel
Scarry, Huck
  See Scarry, Richard McClure, Jr.
Scarry, Patricia (Murphy) 1924- *2*
Scarry, Patsy
  See Scarry, Patricia (Murphy)
Scarry, Richard (McClure) 1919-1994 .... *75*
  Obituary *90*
  Earlier sketches in SATA *2, 35*
  See also CLR *41*
Scarry, Richard McClure, Jr. 1953- *35*
Schachner, Judith Byron 1951- *178*
  Earlier sketch in SATA *88*
Schachner, Judy
  See Schachner, Judith Byron
Schachtel, Roger 1949- *38*
Schachtel, Roger Bernard
  See Schachtel, Roger
Schade, Susan *189*
Schaedler, Sally *116*
Schaefer, Carole Lexa *173*
Schaefer, Jack (Warner) 1907-1991 .... *66*
  Obituary *65*
  Earlier sketch in SATA *3*
Schaefer, Lola M. 1950- *183*
  Earlier sketches in SATA *91, 144*
Schaeffer, Mead 1898- *21*
Schaeffer, Susan Fromberg 1941- *22*
Schaer, Brigitte 1958- *112*
Schaller, George
  See Schaller, George B.
Schaller, George B. 1933- *30*
Schaller, George Beals
  See Schaller, George B.
Schanzer, Rosalyn (Good) 1942- *138*
  Earlier sketch in SATA *77*
Schatell, Brian *66*
  Brief entry *47*
Schechter, Betty (Goodstein) 1921- *5*
Schechter, Simone
  See Elkeles, Simone
Schecter, Ellen 1944- *85*
Scheeder, Louis 1946- *141*
Scheer, Julian (Weisel) 1926-2001 .... *8*
Scheffer, Victor B(lanchard) 1906- *6*
Scheffler, Axel 1957- *180*

Scheffler, Ursel 1938- *81*
Scheffrin-Falk, Gladys 1928- *76*
Scheidl, Gerda Marie 1913- *85*
Scheier, Michael 1943- *40*
  Brief entry *36*
Schell, Mildred 1922- *41*
Schell, Orville (Hickok) 1940- *10*
Scheller, Melanie 1953- *77*
Schellie, Don 1932- *29*
Schembri, Jim 1962- *124*
Schemm, Mildred Walker 1905-1998 .... *21*
  Obituary *103*
  See Walker, Mildred
Schenker, Dona 1947- *133*
  Earlier sketch in SATA *68*
Scher, Paula 1948- *47*
Scherf, Margaret 1908-1979 .... *10*
Schermer, Judith (Denise) 1941- *30*
Schertle, Alice 1941- *192*
  Earlier sketches in SATA *36, 90, 145*
Schick, Alice 1946- *27*
Schick, Eleanor 1942- *144*
  Earlier sketches in SATA *9, 82*
Schick, Joel 1945- *31*
  Brief entry *30*
Schields, Gretchen 1948- *75*
Schiff, Ken(neth Roy) 1942- *7*
Schiller, Andrew 1919- *21*
Schiller, Barbara (Heyman) 1928- *21*
Schiller, Pamela (Byrne) *127*
Schindel, John 1955- *115*
  Earlier sketch in SATA *77*
Schindelman, Joseph 1923- *67*
  Brief entry *32*
Schindler, S.D. 1952- *171*
  Brief entry *50*
  Earlier sketches in SATA *75, 118*
Schindler, Steven D.
  See Schindler, S.D.
Schinto, Jeanne 1951- *93*
Schisgall, Oscar 1901-1984 .... *12*
  Obituary *38*
Schlaepfer, Gloria G. 1931- *154*
Schlee, Ann 1934- *44*
  Brief entry *36*
Schleichert, Elizabeth 1945- *77*
Schlein, Miriam 1926-2004 .... *130*
  Obituary *159*
  Earlier sketches in SATA *2, 87*
  See also CLR *41*
Schlesinger, Arthur M., Jr. 1917-2007 .... *61*
  Obituary *181*
  See Schlesinger, Arthur Meier
Schlesinger, Arthur Meier 1888-1965
Schlessinger, Laura (Catherine) 1947- *160*
  Earlier sketch in SATA *110*
Schlitz, Laura Amy *184*
Schloat, G. Warren, Jr. 1914-2000 .... *4*
Schmid, Eleonore 1939- *126*
  Earlier sketches in SATA *12, 84*
Schmiderer, Dorothy 1940- *19*
Schmidt, Annie M. G. 1911-1995 .... *67*
  Obituary *91*
  See also CLR *22*
Schmidt, Diane 1953- *70*
Schmidt, Elizabeth 1915- *15*
Schmidt, Gary D. 1957- *193*
  Earlier sketches in SATA *93, 135*
Schmidt, James Norman 1912-1983 .... *21*
Schmidt, Karen Lee 1953- *185*
  Earlier sketch in SATA *94*
Schmidt, Lynette 1952- *76*
Schneider, Antonie 1954- *167*
  Earlier sketch in SATA *89*
Schneider, Christine M. 1972(?)- *171*
  Earlier sketch in SATA *120*
Schneider, Dick
  See Schneider, Richard H.
Schneider, Elisa
  See Kleven, Elisa

Schneider, Herman 1905-2003 .... *7*
  Obituary *148*
Schneider, Howie -2007 .... *181*
Schneider, Laurie
  See Adams, Laurie
Schneider, Nina 1913-2007 .... *2*
  Obituary *186*
Schneider, Nina Zimet
  See Schneider, Nina
Schneider, Rex 1937- *44*
Schneider, Richard H. 1922- *171*
Schneider, Richard Henry
  See Schneider, Richard H.
Schneider, Robyn 1986- *187*
Schnirel, James R. 1931- *14*
Schnitter, Jane T. 1958- *88*
Schnitzlein, Danny *134*
Schnur, Steven 1952- *144*
  Earlier sketch in SATA *95*
Schnurre, Wolfdietrich 1920-1989
  Obituary *63*
Schoberle, Cecile 1949- *80*
Schock, Pauline 1928- *45*
Schoell, William 1951- *160*
Schoen, Barbara (Taylor) 1924-1993 .... *13*
Schoenherr, Ian *177*
Schoenherr, John (Carl) 1935- *66*
  Earlier sketch in SATA *37*
  See also SAAS *13*
Schofield, Sandy
  See Rusch, Kristine Kathryn
Scholastica, Sister Mary
  See Jenkins, Marie M(agdalen)
Scholefield, A. T.
  See Scholefield, Alan
Scholefield, Alan 1931- *66*
Scholefield, Edmund O.
  See Griffin, W.E.B
Scholey, Arthur 1932- *28*
Scholz, Jackson Volney 1897-1986
  Obituary *49*
Schone, Virginia *22*
Schongut, Emanuel 1936- *184*
  Brief entry *36*
  Earlier sketch in SATA *52*
Schoonover, Frank (Earle) 1877-1972 .... *24*
Schoor, Gene 1921- *3*
Schories, Pat 1952- *164*
  Earlier sketch in SATA *116*
Schott, Jane A. 1946- *172*
Schotter, Roni *190*
  Earlier sketches in SATA *105, 149*
Schraff, Anne E(laine) 1939- *92*
  Earlier sketch in SATA *27*
Schram, Peninnah 1934- *119*
Schrank, Joseph 1900-1984
  Obituary *38*
Schrecengost, Maity 1938- *118*
Schrecengost, S. Maitland
  See Schrecengost, Maity
Schreck, Karen
  See Schreck, Karen Halvorsen
Schreck, Karen Halvorsen 1962- *185*
Schrecker, Judie 1954- *90*
Schreiber, Elizabeth Anne (Ferguson)
  1947- *13*
Schreiber, Ralph W(alter) 1942- *13*
Schreiner, Samuel A(gnew), Jr. 1921- *70*
Schroeder, Alan 1961- *98*
  Earlier sketch in SATA *66*
Schroeder, Binette
  See Nickl, Barbara (Elisabeth)
Schroeder, Russell (K.) 1943- *146*
Schroeder, Ted 1931(?)-1973
  Obituary *20*
Schubert, Dieter 1947- *101*
  Earlier sketch in SATA *62*
Schubert, Leda 1950(?)- *181*
Schubert-Gabrys, Ingrid 1953- *101*
  Earlier sketch in SATA *62*

Schuelein-Steel, Danielle
  See Steel, Danielle
Schuelein-Steel, Danielle Fernande
  See Steel, Danielle
Schuerger, Michele R. *110*
Schuett, Stacey 1960- *168*
  Earlier sketch in SATA *75*
Schulke, Flip Phelps Graeme 1930- *57*
Schulman, Arlene 1961- *105*
Schulman, Janet 1933- *137*
  Earlier sketch in SATA *22*
Schulman, L(ester) M(artin) 1934- *13*
Schulte, Elaine L(ouise) 1934- *36*
Schultz, Betty K(epka) 1932- *125*
Schultz, Gwendolyn *21*
Schultz, James Willard 1859-1947
  See YABC *1*
Schultz, Pearle Henriksen 1918- *21*
Schulz, Charles M. 1922-2000 .... *10*
  Obituary *118*
Schulz, Charles Monroe
  See Schulz, Charles M.
Schumacher, Julie 1958- *191*
Schumaker, Ward 1943- *96*
Schuman, Michael A. 1953- *134*
  Earlier sketch in SATA *85*
Schur, Maxine
  See Schur, Maxine Rose
Schur, Maxine Rose 1948- *135*
  Autobiography Feature *135*
  Brief entry *49*
  Earlier sketches in SATA *53, 98*
Schurfranz, Vivian 1925- *13*
Schutzer, A. I. 1922- *13*
Schuyler, Pamela R. 1948- *30*
Schwabach, Karen *185*
Schwager, Tina 1964- *110*
Schwandt, Stephen (William) 1947- *61*
Schwark, Mary Beth 1954- *51*
Schwartz, Alvin 1927-1992 .... *56*
  Obituary *71*
  Earlier sketch in SATA *4*
  See also CLR *89*
Schwartz, Amy 1954- *189*
  Brief entry *41*
  Earlier sketches in SATA *47, 83, 131*
  See also CLR *25*
  See also SAAS *18*
Schwartz, Anne Powers 1913-1987 .... *10*
Schwartz, Carol 1954- *77*
Schwartz, Charles W(alsh) 1914- *8*
Schwartz, David M. 1951- *110*
  Earlier sketch in SATA *59*
Schwartz, David Martin
  See Schwartz, David M.
Schwartz, Elizabeth Reeder 1912- *8*
Schwartz, Ellen 1949- *117*
Schwartz, Jerome L.
  See Lawrence, Jerome
Schwartz, Joel L. 1940- *54*
  Brief entry *51*
Schwartz, Joyce R. 1950- *93*
Schwartz, Julius 1907-2004 .... *45*
Schwartz, Perry 1942- *75*
Schwartz, Sheila (Ruth) 1929- *27*
Schwartz, Stephen (Lawrence) 1948- *19*
Schwartz, Virginia Frances 1950- *184*
  Earlier sketch in SATA *131*
Schwarz, (Silvia Tessa) Viviane 1977- *141*
Schweitzer, Byrd Baylor
  See Baylor, Byrd
Schweitzer, Iris *59*
  Brief entry *36*
Schweninger, Ann 1951- *168*
  Earlier sketches in SATA *29, 98*
Schwerin, Doris H(alpern) 1922- *64*
Scieszka, Jon 1954- *160*
  Earlier sketches in SATA *68, 105*
  See also CLR *107*
Scillian, Devin *128*
Scioscia, Mary (Hershey) 1926- *63*

Scofield, Penrod 1933- *62*
  Obituary *78*
Scoggin, Margaret C(lara) 1905-1968 .... *47*
  Brief entry *28*
Scoltock, Jack 1942- *141*
  Earlier sketch in SATA *72*
Scoppettone, Sandra 1936- *92*
  Earlier sketch in SATA *9*
  See Early, Jack
Scot, Michael
  See Rohan, Michael Scott
Scot-Bernard, P.
  See Bernard, Patricia
Scotland, Jay
  See Jakes, John
Scott, Alastair
  See Allen, Kenneth S.
Scott, Ann Herbert 1926- *140*
  Autobiography Feature *140*
  Brief entry *29*
  Earlier sketches in SATA *56, 94*
Scott, Bill
  See Scott, William N(eville)
Scott, Bill 1920(?)-1985
  Obituary *46*
Scott, Cora Annett (Pipitone) 1931- *11*
Scott, Dan
  See Barker, S(quire) Omar
Scott, Elaine 1940- *164*
  Earlier sketches in SATA *36, 90*
Scott, Jack Denton 1915-1995 .... *83*
  Earlier sketch in SATA *31*
  See also CLR *20*
  See also SAAS *14*
Scott, Jane (Harrington) 1931- *55*
Scott, Jessica
  See De Wire, Elinor
Scott, John 1912-1976 .... *14*
Scott, John Anthony 1916- *23*
Scott, John M(artin) 1913- *12*
Scott, Mary
  See Mattern, Joanne
Scott, Melissa 1960- *109*
Scott, Richard
  See Rennert, Richard Scott
Scott, Roney
  See Gault, William Campbell
Scott, Sally 1909-1978 .... *43*
Scott, Sally 1948- *44*
Scott, Sally Elisabeth
  See Scott, Sally
Scott, W. N.
  See Scott, William N(eville)
Scott, Sir Walter 1771-1832
  See YABC *2*
Scott, Warwick
  See Trevor, Elleston
Scott, William N(eville) 1923- *87*
Scotti, Anna
  See Coates, Anna
Scotton, Rob 1960- *177*
Scribner, Charles, Jr. 1921-1995 .... *13*
  Obituary *87*
Scribner, Joanne L. 1949- *33*
Scribner, Kimball 1917- *63*
Scrimger, Richard 1957- *164*
  Earlier sketch in SATA *119*
Scrimsher, Lila Gravatt 1897-1974
  Obituary *28*
Scroder, Walter K. 1928- *82*
Scroggs, Kirk *187*
Scruggs, Sandy 1961- *89*
Scudder, Brooke 1959- *154*
Scull, Marie-Louise 1943-1993 .... *77*
Scuro, Vincent 1951- *21*
Seabrooke, Brenda 1941- *148*
  Earlier sketches in SATA *30, 88*
Seaman, Augusta Huiell 1879-1950 .... *31*
Seamands, Ruth 1916- *9*
Searcy, Margaret Zehmer 1926- *54*
  Brief entry *39*

Searight, Mary W(illiams) 1918- *17*
Searle, Kathryn Adrienne 1942- *10*
Searle, Ronald (William Fordham) 1920- *70*
  Earlier sketch in SATA *42*
Sears, Stephen W. 1932- *4*
Sebastian, Lee
  See Silverberg, Robert
Sebestyen, Igen
  See Sebestyen, Ouida
Sebestyen, Ouida 1924- *140*
  Earlier sketch in SATA *39*
  See also CLR *17*
  See also SAAS *10*
Sebrey, Mary Ann 1951- *62*
Sechrist, Elizabeth Hough 1903-1991 .... *2*
Sedges, John
  See Buck, Pearl S(ydenstricker)
Sedgwick, Marcus 1968- *160*
Seed, Cecile Eugenie 1930- *86*
  See Seed, Jenny
Seed, Jenny *8*
  See also CLR *76*
  See Seed, Cecile Eugenie
Seed, Sheila Turner 1937(?)-1979
  Obituary *23*
Seeger, Elizabeth 1889-1973
  Obituary *20*
Seeger, Laura Vaccaro *172*
Seeger, Pete 1919- *139*
  Earlier sketch in SATA *13*
Seeger, Peter R.
  See Seeger, Pete
Seeley, Laura L. 1958- *71*
Seever, R.
  See Reeves, Lawrence F.
Sefozo, Mary 1925- *82*
Sefton, Catherine
  See Waddell, Martin
Segal, John *178*
Segal, Joyce 1940- *35*
Segal, Lore 1928- *163*
  Earlier sketches in SATA *4, 66*
  See also SAAS *11*
Segal, Lore Groszmann
  See Segal, Lore
Segar, E(lzie) C(risler) 1894-1938 .... *61*
Segovia, Andres 1893(?)-1987
  Obituary *52*
Seguin, Marilyn W(eymouth) 1951- *91*
Seguin-Fontes, Marthe 1924- *109*
Seibold, J. Otto 1960- *149*
  Earlier sketch in SATA *83*
  See also SAAS *22*
Seidel, Ross *95*
Seidelman, James Edward 1926- *6*
Seiden, Art(hur) *107*
  Brief entry *42*
Seidler, Ann (G.) 1925- *131*
Seidler, Tor 1952- *149*
  Brief entry *46*
  Earlier sketches in SATA *52, 98*
Seidman, Laurence Ivan 1925- *15*
Seigel, Kalman 1917-1998 .... *12*
  Obituary *103*
Seignobosc, Francoise 1897-1961 .... *21*
Seinfeld, Jerry 1954- *146*
Seitz, Jacqueline 1931- *50*
Seixas, Judith S. 1922- *17*
Sejima, Yoshimasa 1913- *8*
Selberg, Ingrid (Maria) 1950- *68*
Selden, George
  See CLR *8*
  See Thompson, George Selden
Selden, Neil R(oy) 1931- *61*
Self, Margaret Cabell 1902-1996 .... *24*
Selfors, Suzanne 1963- *193*
Selick, Henry 1952- *183*
Selig, Sylvie 1942- *13*
Selkirk, Jane
  See Chapman, John Stanton Higham

Sellers, Naomi
  See Flack, Naomi John White
Selman, LaRue W. 1927- 55
Selsam, Millicent E(llis) 1912-1996 29
  Obituary 92
  Earlier sketch in SATA *1*
  See also CLR *1*
Seltzer, Meyer 1932- 17
Seltzer, Richard 1946- 41
Seltzer, Richard Warren, Jr.
  See Seltzer, Richard
Selvadurai, Shyam 1965(?)- 171
Selway, Martina 1940- 169
  Earlier sketch in SATA *74*
Selzer, Adam 1980- 192
Selznick, Brian 1966- 171
  Earlier sketches in SATA *79, 117*
Semel, Nava 1954- 107
Semloh
  See Holmes, Peggy
Sendak, Jack 1924(?)-1995 28
Sendak, Maurice 1928- 165
  Earlier sketches in SATA *1, 27, 113*
  See also CLR *131*
Sendak, Maurice Bernard
  See Sendak, Maurice
Sender, Ruth M(insky) 1926- 62
Sengler, Johanna 1924- 18
Senisi, Ellen B. 1951- 116
Senisi, Ellen Babinec
  See Senisi, Ellen B.
Senn, J(oyce) A(nn) 1941- 115
Senn, Steve 1950- 60
  Brief entry 48
Serage, Nancy 1924- 10
Seredy, Kate 1899-1975 1
  Obituary 24
  See also CLR *10*
Seroff, Victor I(lyitch) 1902-1979 12
  Obituary 26
Serraillier, Ian (Lucien) 1912-1994 73
  Obituary 83
  Earlier sketch in SATA *1*
  See also CLR *2*
  See also SAAS *3*
Serros, Michele 175
Serros, Michele M.
  See Serros, Michele
Servello, Joe 1932- 10
Service, Pamela F. 1945- 64
Service, Robert
  See Service, Robert W(illiam)
Service, Robert W(illiam) 1874(?)-1958 20
  See Service, Robert
Serwadda, W(illiam) Moses 1931- 27
Serwer-Bernstein, Blanche L(uria)
  1910-1997 10
Sescoe, Vincent E. 1938- 123
Seth, Mary
  See Lexau, Joan M.
Seton, Anya 1904(?)-1990 3
  Obituary 66
Seton, Ernest (Evan) Thompson
  1860-1946 18
  See also CLR *59*
Seton-Thompson, Ernest
  See Seton, Ernest (Evan) Thompson
Seuling, Barbara 1937- 193
  Earlier sketches in SATA *10, 98, 145*
  See also SAAS *24*
Seuss, Dr.
  See Dr. Seuss
  and Geisel, Theodor Seuss
  and LeSieg, Theo.
  and Stone, Rosetta
Severn, Bill
  See Severn, William Irving
Severn, David
  See Unwin, David S(torr)
Severn, William Irving 1914- 1

Sewall, Marcia 1935- 119
  Earlier sketches in SATA *37, 69*
Seward, Prudence 1926- 16
Sewell, Anna 1820-1878 100
  Earlier sketch in SATA *24*
  See also CLR *17*
Sewell, Helen (Moore) 1896-1957 38
Sexton, Anne (Harvey) 1928-1974 10
Seymour, Alta Halverson 10
Seymour, Jane 1951- 139
Seymour, Tres 1966- 164
  Earlier sketch in SATA *82*
Sfar, Joann 1971- 182
Shachtman, Tom 1942- 49
Shackleton, C.C.
  See Aldiss, Brian W.
Shader, Rachel
  See Sofer, Barbara
Shadow, Jak
  See Sutherland, Jon
Shadyland, Sal
  See Cooper, Louise
Shafer, Audrey 183
Shafer, Robert E(ugene) 1925- 9
Shaffer, Terea 1968- 79
Shahan, Sherry 1949- 134
  Earlier sketch in SATA *92*
Shahn, Ben(jamin) 1898-1969
  Obituary 21
Shahn, Bernarda Bryson
  See Bryson, Bernarda
Shaik, Fatima 114
Shalant, Phyllis 1949- 150
Shan, Darren 1972- 168
  Earlier sketch in SATA *129*
Shanberg, Karen
  See Shragg, Karen (I.)
Shane, Harold Gray 1914-1993 36
  Obituary 76
Shange, Ntozake 1948- 157
Shanks, Ann Zane (Kushner) 10
Shannon, David 1959- 152
  Earlier sketch in SATA *107*
  See also CLR *87*
Shannon, George (William Bones) 1952- ... 143
  Earlier sketches in SATA *35, 94*
Shannon, Jacqueline 63
Shannon, Margaret
  See Silverwood, Margaret Shannon
Shannon, Monica 1905(?)-1965 28
Shannon, Terry 21
  See Mercer, Jessie
Shannon, Terry Miller 1951- 148
Shapiro, Irwin 1911-1981 32
Shapiro, Jody Fickes 1940- 193
Shapiro, Karen Jo 1964- 186
Shapiro, Milton J. 1926- 32
Shapiro, Tricia
  See Andryszewski, Tricia
Shapp, Charles M(orris) 1906-1989
  Obituary 61
Shapp, Martha Glauber 1910- 3
Sharenow, Robert 193
Sharfman, Amalie 14
Sharma, Partap 1939- 15
Sharma, Rashmi
  See Singh, Rashmi Sharma
Sharman, Alison
  See Leonard, Alison
Sharmat, Marjorie Weinman 1928- 133
  Earlier sketches in SATA *4, 33, 74*
Sharmat, Mitchell 1927- 127
  Earlier sketch in SATA *33*
Sharp, Anne Wallace 1947- 144
Sharp, Luke
  See Alkiviades, Alkis
Sharp, Margery 1905-1991 29
  Obituary 67
  Earlier sketch in SATA *1*
  See also CLR *27*

Sharp, Zerna A. 1889-1981
  Obituary 27
Sharpe, Jon
  See Duncan, Alice
  and Knott, William C(ecil, Jr.)
  and Messman, Jon
Sharpe, Mitchell R(aymond) 1924- 12
Sharpe, Susan 1946- 71
Sharratt, Nick 1962- 153
  Earlier sketch in SATA *104*
Shasha, Mark 1961- 80
Shattuck, Roger 1923-2005 64
  Obituary 174
Shattuck, Roger Whitney
  See Shattuck, Roger
Shaw, Arnold 1909-1989 4
  Obituary 63
Shaw, Carolyn V. 1934- 91
Shaw, Charles (Green) 1892-1974 13
Shaw, Evelyn S. 1927- 28
Shaw, Flora Louisa
  See Lugard, Flora Louisa Shaw
Shaw, Janet 1937- 146
  Earlier sketch in SATA *61*
  See also CLR *96*
Shaw, Janet Beeler
  See Shaw, Janet
Shaw, Lisa
  See Rogak, Lisa
Shaw, Margret 1940- 68
Shaw, Mary 1965- 180
Shaw, Nancy 1946- 162
  Earlier sketch in SATA *71*
Shaw, Ray 7
Shaw, Richard 1923- 12
Shawn, Frank S.
  See Goulart, Ron(ald Joseph)
Shay, Art
  See Shay, Arthur
Shay, Arthur 1922- 4
Shay, Lacey
  See Shebar, Sharon Sigmond
Shea, Bob 188
Shea, George 1940- 54
  Brief entry 42
Shea, Pegi Deitz 1960- 172
  Earlier sketches in SATA *77, 137*
Shearer, John 1947- 43
  Brief entry 27
  See also CLR *34*
Shearer, Ted 1919- 43
Shearing, Leonie 1972- 184
Sheban, Chris 182
Shebar, Sharon Sigmond 1945- 36
Shecter, Ben 1935- 16
Shedd, Warner 1934- 147
  Earlier sketch in SATA *87*
Sheedy, Alexandra Elizabeth 1962- 39
  Earlier sketch in SATA *19*
Sheehan, Ethna 1908-2000 9
Sheehan, Patty 1945- 77
Sheehan, Sean 1951- 154
  Earlier sketch in SATA *86*
Sheen, Barbara 1949- 143
Shefelman, Janice Jordan 1930- 129
  Earlier sketch in SATA *58*
Shefelman, Tom (Whitehead) 1927- 58
Sheffer, H. R.
  See Abels, Harriette S(heffer)
Sheffield, Charles 1935-2002 109
Sheffield, Janet N. 1926- 26
Sheikh, Nazneen
  See Sadiq, Nazneen
Shekerjian, Regina Tor 16
Shelby, Anne 1948- 85
  Autobiography Feature 121
  See also SAAS *26*
Sheldon, Ann
  See Antle, Nancy
Sheldon, Ann 67
  Earlier sketch in SATA *1*

Sheldon, Aure 1917-1976 12
Sheldon, David 185
Sheldon, Dyan 181
Sheldon, John
  See Bloch, Robert (Albert)
Sheldon, Muriel 1926- 45
  Brief entry 39
Shell, Barry 1951- 176
Shelley, Frances
  See Wees, Frances Shelley
Shelley, Mary Wollstonecraft
  (Godwin) 1797-1851 29
  See also CLR 133
Shelton, William Roy 1919-1995 5
  Obituary 129
Shemie, Bonnie (Jean Brenner) 1949- 96
Shemin, Margaretha (Hoeneveld) 1928- 4
Shen, Michele 1953- 173
Shenker, Michele
  See Shen, Michele
Shenton, Edward 1895-1977 45
Shepard, Aaron 1950- 187
  Earlier sketches in SATA 75, 113
Shepard, Ernest Howard 1879-1976 100
  Obituary 24
  Earlier sketches in SATA 3, 33
  See also CLR 27
Shepard, James R.
  See Shepard, Jim
Shepard, Jim 1956- 164
  Earlier sketch in SATA 90
Shepard, Mary
  See Knox, (Mary) Eleanor Jessie
Shephard, Esther 1891-1975 5
  Obituary 26
Shepherd, Donna Walsh
  See Walsh Shepherd, Donna
Shepherd, Elizabeth 4
Shepherd, Irana 173
Shepherd, Roni
  See Shepherd, Irana
Shepperson, Rob 178
Sherburne, Zoa (Lillian Morin) 1912-1995 3
  See also SAAS 18
Sherlock, Patti 71
Sherman, D(enis) R(onald) 1934- 48
  Brief entry 29
Sherman, Diane (Finn) 1928- 12
Sherman, Elizabeth
  See Friskey, Margaret (Richards)
Sherman, Harold (Morrow) 1898-1987 37
  Obituary 137
Sherman, Josepha 163
  Earlier sketch in SATA 75
Sherman, Michael
  See Lowndes, Robert A(ugustine) W(ard)
Sherman, Nancy
  See Rosenberg, Nancy (Sherman)
Sherman, Pat 174
Sherman, Peter Michael
  See Lowndes, Robert A(ugustine) W(ard)
Sherrard, Valerie (Anne) 1957- 141
Sherrod, Jane
  See Singer, Jane Sherrod
Sherry, Clifford J. 1943- 84
Sherry, (Dulcie) Sylvia 1932- 122
  Earlier sketch in SATA 8
Sherwan, Earl 1917- 3
Sherwood, Jonathan
  See London, Jonathan (Paul)
Sheth, Kashmira 186
Shetterly, Will 1955- 78
  Autobiography Feature 106
Shetterly, William Howard
  See Shetterly, Will
Shiefman, Vicky 1942- 22
Shields, Brenda Desmond
  (Armstrong) 1914- 37
Shields, Carol Diggory 174
Shields, Charles 1944- 10

Shiels, Barbara
  See Adams, Barbara Johnston
Shiffman, Lena 1957- 101
Shiina, Makoto 1944- 83
Shimin, Symeon 1902-1984 13
Shimko, Bonnie 1941- 191
Shine, Andrea 1955- 104
Shine, Deborah 1932- 71
Shinn, Everett 1876-1953 21
Shinn, Sharon 1957- 164
  Earlier sketch in SATA 110
Shippen, Katherine B(inney) 1892-1980 1
  Obituary 23
  See also CLR 36
Shippey, T. A. 1943- 143
Shippey, Thomas Alan
  See Shippey, T. A.
Shipton, Eric Earle 1907-1977 10
Shiraz, Yasmin 173
Shirer, William L(awrence) 1904-1993 45
  Obituary 78
Shirley, Gayle C 1955- 96
Shirley, Gayle Corbett
  See Shirley, Gayle C
Shirley, Jean 1919- 70
Shirreffs, Gordon D(onald) 1914-1996 11
Shirts, Morris A(lpine) 1922- 63
Shlichta, Joe 1968- 84
Shmurak, Carole B. 1944- 118
Sholokhov, Mikhail (Aleksandrovich)
  1905-1984
  Obituary 36
Shore, Diane Z. 179
Shore, Diane ZuHone
  See Shore, Diane Z.
Shore, June Lewis 30
Shore, Nancy 1960- 124
Shore, Robert 1924- 39
Short, Michael 1937- 65
Short, Roger
  See Arkin, Alan
Shortall, Leonard W. 19
Shortt, Tim(othy Donald) 1961- 96
Shotwell, Louisa Rossiter 1902-1993 3
Shoup, Barbara 1947- 156
  Earlier sketch in SATA 86
  See also SAAS 24
Shoveller, Herb 184
Showalter, Jean B(reckinridge) 12
Showell, Ellen Harvey 1934- 33
Showers, Paul C. 1910-1999 92
  Obituary 114
  Earlier sketch in SATA 21
  See also CLR 6
  See also SAAS 7
Shpakow, Tanya 1959(?)- 94
Shpitalnik, Vladimir 1964- 83
Shragg, Karen (I.) 1954- 142
Shreeve, Elizabeth 1956- 156
Shreve, Susan
  See Shreve, Susan Richards
Shreve, Susan Richards 1939- 152
  Brief entry 41
  Earlier sketches in SATA 46, 95
Shriver, Jean Adair 1932- 75
Shriver, Maria 1955- 134
Shriver, Maria Owings
  See Shriver, Maria
Shrode, Mary
  See Hollingsworth, Mary
Shtainmets, Leon 32
Shub, Elizabeth 1915(?)-2004 5
Shuken, Julia 1948- 84
Shulevitz, Uri 1935- 165
  Earlier sketches in SATA 3, 50, 106
  See also CLR 61
Shulman, Alix Kates 1932- 7
Shulman, Dee 1957- 146
Shulman, Irving 1913-1995 13
Shulman, Mark 1962- 184

Shulman, Max 1919-1988
  Obituary 59
Shulman, Milton 1913-2004
  Obituary 154
Shulman, Neil B(arnett) 1945- 89
Shumsky, Zena
  See Collier, Zena
Shura, Mary Francis
  See Craig, Mary (Francis) Shura
Shusterman, Neal 1962- 140
  Autobiography Feature 140
  Earlier sketches in SATA 85, 121
Shuter, Jane (Margaret) 1955- 151
  Earlier sketch in SATA 90
Shuttlesworth, Dorothy Edwards 3
Shwartz, Susan (Martha) 1949- 94
Shyer, Christopher 1961- 98
Shyer, Marlene Fanta 13
Siberell, Anne 29
Sibley, Don 1922- 12
Siburt, Ruth 1951- 121
Siculan, Daniel 1922- 12
Siddon, Barbara
  See Bradford, Barbara Taylor
Sidgwick, Ethel 1877-1970 116
Sidjakov, Nicolas 1924- 18
Sidman, Joyce 1956- 181
  Earlier sketch in SATA 145
Sidney, Frank
  See Warwick, Alan R(oss)
Sidney, Margaret
  See Lothrop, Harriet Mulford Stone
Siebert, Diane 1948- 189
Siegal, Aranka 1930- 88
  Brief entry 37
Siegel, Beatrice 36
Siegel, Helen
  See Siegl, Helen
Siegel, Robert 1939- 39
Siegel, Robert Harold
  See Siegel, Robert
Siegel, Siena Cherson 1967(?)- 185
Siegelson, Kim L. 1962- 114
Sieger, Ted 1958- 189
Siegl, Helen 1924- 34
Siepmann, Mary Aline
  See Wesley, Mary (Aline)
Sierra, Judy 1945- 162
  Earlier sketch in SATA 104
Sieswerda, Paul L. 1942- 147
Sievert, Terri
  See Dougherty, Terri (L.)
Silas
  See McCay, (Zenas) Winsor
Silcock, Sara Lesley 1947- 12
Silin-Palmer, Pamela 184
Sill, Cathryn 1953- 141
  Earlier sketch in SATA 74
Sill, John 1947- 140
  Earlier sketch in SATA 74
Sillitoe, Alan 1928- 61
Sills, Leslie (Elka) 1948- 129
Silly, E. S.
  See Kraus, (Herman) Robert
Silsbe, Brenda 1953- 73
Silva, Joseph
  See Goulart, Ron(ald Joseph)
Silver, Ruth
  See Chew, Ruth
Silverberg, Robert 1935- 91
  Autobiography Feature 104
  Earlier sketch in SATA 13
  See also CLR 59
Silverman, Erica 1955- 165
  Earlier sketches in SATA 78, 112
Silverman, Janis L. 1946- 127
Silverman, Mel(vin Frank) 1931-1966 9
Silverman, Robin L. 1954- 96
Silverman, Robin Landew
  See Silverman, Robin L.

Silverstein, Alvin 1933- *124*
  Earlier sketches in SATA *8, 69*
  See also CLR *25*
Silverstein, Herma 1945- *106*
Silverstein, Robert Alan 1959- *124*
  Earlier sketch in SATA *77*
Silverstein, Shel 1932-1999 .... *92*
  Brief entry *27*
  Obituary *116*
  Earlier sketch in SATA *33*
  See also CLR *96*
Silverstein, Sheldon Allan
  See Silverstein, Shel
Silverstein, Virginia B(arbara
  Opshelor) 1937- *124*
  Earlier sketches in SATA *8, 69*
  See also CLR *25*
Silverthorne, Elizabeth 1930- *35*
Silverwood, Margaret Shannon 1966- *137*
  Earlier sketch in SATA *83*
Silvey, Diane F. 1946- *135*
Sim, David 1953- *162*
Sim, Dorrith M. 1931- *96*
Simak, Clifford D(onald) 1904-1988
  Obituary *56*
Simard, Remy 1959- *168*
Simmie, Lois (Ann) 1932- *106*
Simmonds, Posy 1945- *130*
  See also CLR *23*
Simmons, Andra 1939- *141*
Simmons, Elly 1955- *134*
Simmons, Michael 1970- *185*
Simms, Laura 1947- *117*
Simner, Janni Lee *113*
Simon, Charlie May
  See Fletcher, Charlie May Hogue
Simon, Francesca 1955- *111*
Simon, Gabriel 1972- *118*
Simon, Hilda Rita 1921- *28*
  See also CLR *39*
Simon, Howard 1903-1979 .... *32*
  Obituary *21*
Simon, Joe
  See Simon, Joseph H.
Simon, Joseph H. 1913- *7*
Simon, Martin P(aul William) 1903-1969 .... *12*
Simon, Mina Lewiton
  See Lewiton, Mina
Simon, Norma (Feldstein) 1927- *129*
  Earlier sketches in SATA *3, 68*
Simon, Seymour 1931- *138*
  Earlier sketches in SATA *4, 73*
  See also CLR *63*
Simon, Shirley (Schwartz) 1921- *11*
Simon, Solomon 1895-1970 .... *40*
Simonetta, Linda 1948- *14*
Simonetta, Sam 1936- *14*
Simons, Barbara B(rooks) 1934- *41*
Simont, Marc 1915- *126*
  Earlier sketches in SATA *9, 73*
Simpson, Colin 1908-1983 .... *14*
Simpson, Harriette
  See Arnow, Harriette (Louisa) Simpson
Simpson, Jacynth Hope
  See Hope Simpson, Jacynth
Simpson, Lesley 1963- *150*
Simpson, Margaret 1943- *128*
Simpson, Myrtle L(illias) 1931- *14*
Sims, Blanche *168*
  Earlier sketch in SATA *75*
Sims, Blanche L.
  See Sims, Blanche
Simundsson, Elva 1950- *63*
Sinclair, Clover
  See Gater, Dilys
Sinclair, Emil
  See Hesse, Hermann
Sinclair, Jeff 1958- *77*
Sinclair, Olga 1923- *121*
Sinclair, Rose
  See Smith, Susan Vernon

Sinclair, Upton 1878-1968 .... *9*
Sinclair, Upton Beall
  See Sinclair, Upton
Singer, A.L.
  See Lerangis, Peter
Singer, Arthur 1917-1990 .... *64*
Singer, Isaac
  See Singer, Isaac Bashevis
Singer, Isaac Bashevis 1904-1991 .... *27*
  Obituary *68*
  Earlier sketch in SATA *3*
  See also CLR *1*
Singer, Jane Sherrod 1917-1985 .... *4*
  Obituary *42*
Singer, Julia 1917- *28*
Singer, Kurt D. 1911-2005 .... *38*
  Obituary *172*
Singer, Marilyn 1948- *158*
  Autobiography Feature *158*
  Brief entry *38*
  Earlier sketches in SATA *48, 80, 125*
  See also CLR *48*
  See also SAAS *13*
Singer, Muff 1942-2005 .... *104*
  Obituary *160*
Singer, Susan (Mahler) 1941- *9*
Singh, Rashmi Sharma 1952- *90*
Singleton, Linda Joy 1957- *166*
  Earlier sketch in SATA *88*
Singleton, L.J.
  See Singleton, Linda Joy
Sinykin, Sheri(l Terri) Cooper 1950- *142*
  Autobiography Feature *142*
  Earlier sketches in SATA *72, 133*
Sipiera, Paul P., (Jr.) 1948- *144*
  Earlier sketch in SATA *89*
Siracusa, Catherine (Jane) 1947- *82*
Sirett, Dawn (Karen) 1966- *88*
Sirimarco, Elizabeth 1966- *158*
Sirof, Harriet 1930- *94*
  Earlier sketch in SATA *37*
Sirois, Allen L. 1950- *76*
Sirvaitis (Chernyaev), Karen (Ann) 1961- ... *79*
Sis, Peter 1949- *192*
  Earlier sketch in SATA *149*
  See also CLR *110*
Sisson, Rosemary Anne 1923- *11*
Sister Mary Terese
  See Donze, Mary Terese
Sita, Lisa 1962- *87*
Sitomer, Alan Lawrence *174*
Sitomer, Harry 1903-1985 .... *31*
Sitomer, Mindel 1903-1987 .... *31*
Sittenfeld, Curtis 1976(?)- *164*
Sive, Helen R(obinson) 1951- *30*
Sivulich, Sandra (Jeanne) Stroner 1941- *9*
Siy, Alexandra *193*
Skarmeta, Antonio 1940- *57*
Skelly, James R(ichard) 1927- *17*
Skelton, Matthew 1971- *185*
Skinner, Constance Lindsay 1877-1939
  See YABC *1*
Skinner, Cornelia Otis 1901-1979 .... *2*
Skipper, G. C. 1939- *46*
  Brief entry *38*
Sklansky, Amy E(dgar) 1971- *145*
Skofield, James *95*
  Brief entry *44*
Skold, Betty Westrom 1923- *41*
Skorpen, Liesel Moak 1935- *3*
Skott, Maria
  See Nikolajeva, Maria
Skrypuch, Marsha Forchuk 1954- *134*
Skultety, Nancy Laney 1960- *175*
Skurzynski, Gloria 1930- *145*
  Autobiography Feature *145*
  Earlier sketches in SATA *8, 74, 122*
  See also SAAS *9*
Skurzynski, Gloria Joan
  See Skurzynski, Gloria
Skutch, Robert 1925- *89*

Skye, Maggie
  See Werner, Herma
Skye, Obert *170*
Slack, Michael 1969- *189*
Slackman, Charles B. 1934- *12*
Slade, Arthur G. 1967- *149*
  Earlier sketch in SATA *106*
Slade, Arthur Gregory
  See Slade, Arthur G.
Slade, Christian 1974- *193*
Slade, Richard 1910-1971 .... *9*
Slangerup, Erik Jon 1969- *130*
Slate, Joseph 1928- *174*
  Earlier sketches in SATA *38, 122*
Slate, Joseph Frank
  See Slate, Joseph
Slater, Dashka 1963- *179*
Slater, Ray
  See Lansdale, Joe R.
Slaughter, Hope 1940- *84*
Slaughter, Jean
  See Doty, Jean Slaughter
Slaughter, Tom 1955- *152*
Slavicek, Louise Chipley 1956- *144*
Slavin, Bill 1959- *148*
  Earlier sketch in SATA *76*
Slaymaker, Melissa Eskridge 1958- *158*
Sleator, William 1945- *161*
  Earlier sketches in SATA *3, 68, 118*
  See also CLR *128*
Sleator, William Warner III
  See Sleator, William
Slegers, Liesbet 1975- *154*
Sleigh, Barbara 1906-1982 .... *86*
  Obituary *30*
  Earlier sketch in SATA *3*
Slepian, Jan 1921- *85*
  Brief entry *45*
  Earlier sketch in SATA *51*
  See also SAAS *8*
Slepian, Janice B.
  See Slepian, Jan
Slicer, Margaret O. 1920- *4*
Slier, Debby
  See Shine, Deborah
Sloan, Brian 1966- *172*
Sloan, Carolyn 1937- *116*
  Earlier sketch in SATA *58*
Sloan, Glenna (Davis) 1930- *120*
Sloane, Eric 1910(?)-1985 .... *52*
  Obituary *42*
Sloane, Todd 1955- *88*
Sloat, Teri 1948- *164*
  Earlier sketches in SATA *70, 106*
Slobodkin, Florence Gersh 1905-1994 .... *5*
  Obituary *107*
Slobodkin, Louis 1903-1975 .... *26*
  Earlier sketch in SATA *1*
Slobodkina, Esphyr 1908-2002 .... *1*
  Obituary *135*
  See also SAAS *8*
Sloggett, Nellie 1851-1923 .... *44*
Sloss, Lesley Lord 1965- *72*
Slote, Alfred 1926- *72*
  Earlier sketch in SATA *8*
  See also CLR *4*
  See also SAAS *21*
Slote, Elizabeth 1956- *80*
Small, David 1945- *183*
  Brief entry *46*
  Earlier sketches in SATA *50, 95, 126*
  See also CLR *53*
Small, Ernest
  See Lent, Blair
Small, Mary 1932- *165*
Small, Terry 1942- *75*
Smallcomb, Pam 1954- *159*
Smalls, Irene
  See Smalls-Hector, Irene

Smalls-Hector, Irene 1950- *146*
  Earlier sketch in SATA *73*
  See also CLR *103*
Smallwood, Norah (Evelyn) 1910(?)-1984
  Obituary *41*
Smaridge, Norah (Antoinette) 1903-1994 ...... *6*
Smee, Nicola 1948- *167*
  Earlier sketch in SATA *76*
Smiley, Virginia Kester 1923- *2*
Smith, Alexander McCall 1948- *179*
  Earlier sketch in SATA *73*
Smith, Anne Warren 1938- *41*
  Brief entry *34*
Smith, Barry (Edward Jervis) 1943- *75*
Smith, Beatrice S(chillinger) *12*
Smith, Betsy Covington 1937- *55*
  Earlier sketch in SATA *43*
Smith, Betty (Wehner) 1904-1972 .... *6*
Smith, Bradford 1909-1964 .... *5*
Smith, Brenda 1946- *82*
Smith, C. Pritchard
  See Hoyt, Edwin P(almer), Jr.
Smith, Caesar
  See Trevor, Elleston
Smith, Charles R., (Jr.) 1969- *159*
Smith, Craig 1955- *172*
  Earlier sketches in SATA *81, 117*
Smith, Cynthia Leitich 1967- *152*
Smith, Datus C(lifford), Jr. 1907-1999 .... *13*
  Obituary *116*
Smith, Debra 1955- *89*
Smith, Derek 1943- *141*
Smith, Dick King
  See King-Smith, Dick
Smith, Dodie
  See Smith, Dorothy Gladys
Smith, Doris Buchanan 1934-2002 .... *75*
  Obituary *140*
  Earlier sketch in SATA *28*
  See also SAAS *10*
Smith, Dorothy Gladys 1896-1990 .... *82*
  Obituary *65*
  See Smith, Dodie
Smith, Dorothy Stafford 1905- *6*
Smith, E(lmer) Boyd 1860-1943
  See YABC *1*
Smith, E(dric) Brooks 1917- *40*
Smith, Emma 1923- *52*
  Brief entry *36*
Smith, (Katherine) Eunice (Young)
  1902-1993 .... *5*
Smith, Frances C(hristine) 1904-1986 .... *3*
Smith, Gary R. 1932- *14*
Smith, Geof 1969- *102*
Smith, George Harmon 1920- *5*
Smith, Gordon 1951- *184*
Smith, Greg Leitich *152*
Smith, H(arry) Allen 1907-1976
  Obituary *20*
Smith, Helene 1937- *142*
Smith, Howard E(verett), Jr. 1927- *12*
Smith, Hugh L(etcher) 1921-1968 .... *5*
Smith, Imogene Henderson 1922- *12*
Smith, Jacqueline B. 1937- *39*
Smith, Jada Pinkett 1971- *161*
Smith, James D. 1955- *176*
Smith, James Noel 1950- *193*
Smith, Janet (Buchanan) Adam
  See Adam Smith, Janet (Buchanan)
Smith, Janice Lee 1949- *155*
  Earlier sketch in SATA *54*
Smith, Jean
  See Smith, Frances C(hristine)
Smith, Jean Pajot 1945- *10*
Smith, Jeff(rey Alan) 1960- *161*
  Earlier sketch in SATA *93*
Smith, Jeff Allen
  See Smith, Jeff(rey Alan)
Smith, Jenny 1963- *90*
Smith, Jessie
  See Kunhardt, Edith

Smith, Jessie Willcox 1863-1935 .... *21*
  See also CLR *59*
Smith, Joan (Mary) 1933- *54*
  Brief entry *46*
Smith, Johnston
  See Crane, Stephen (Townley)
Smith, Jos A. 1936- *181*
  Earlier sketches in SATA *73, 120*
Smith, Joseph Arthur
  See Smith, Jos A.
Smith, Judie R. 1936- *80*
Smith, Lafayette
  See Higdon, Hal
Smith, Lane 1959- *179*
  Earlier sketches in SATA *76, 131*
  See also CLR *47*
Smith, Lee
  See Albion, Lee Smith
Smith, Lendon H(oward) 1921- *64*
Smith, Lillian H(elena) 1887-1983
  Obituary *32*
Smith, Linda 1949- *177*
Smith, Linell Nash 1932- *2*
Smith, Lucia B. 1943- *30*
Smith, Maggie 1965- *190*
Smith, Marion Hagens 1913- *12*
Smith, Marion Jaques 1899-1987 .... *13*
Smith, Mary Ellen *10*
Smith, Marya 1945- *78*
Smith, Mike
  See Smith, Mary Ellen
Smith, Nancy Covert 1935- *12*
Smith, Norman F. 1920- *70*
  Earlier sketch in SATA *5*
Smith, Patricia Clark 1943- *96*
Smith, Pauline C.
  See Arthur, Robert, (Jr.)
Smith, Pauline C(oggeshall) 1908-1994 .... *27*
Smith, Philip Warren 1936- *46*
Smith, R. Alexander McCall
  See Smith, Alexander McCall
Smith, Rebecca 1946- *123*
Smith, Robert Kimmel 1930- *77*
  Earlier sketch in SATA *12*
Smith, Robert Paul 1915-1977 .... *52*
  Obituary *30*
Smith, Roland 1951- *193*
  Earlier sketches in SATA *115, 161*
Smith, Rosamond
  See Oates, Joyce Carol
Smith, Ruth Leslie 1902- *2*
Smith, Samantha 1972-1985
  Obituary *45*
Smith, Sandra Lee 1945- *75*
Smith, Sarah Stafford
  See Smith, Dorothy Stafford
Smith, Sharon 1947- *82*
Smith, Sherri L. 1971- *156*
Smith, Sherwood 1951- *140*
  Earlier sketch in SATA *82*
Smith, Shirley Raines
  See Raines, Shirley C(arol)
Smith, Susan Carlton 1923- *12*
Smith, Susan Mathias 1950- *43*
  Brief entry *35*
Smith, Susan Vernon 1950- *48*
  See Mendonca, Susan
Smith, Tim(othy R.) 1945- *151*
Smith, Ursula 1934- *54*
Smith, Vian (Crocker) 1920-1969 .... *11*
Smith, Wanda VanHoy 1926- *65*
Smith, Ward
  See Goldsmith, Howard
Smith, William A. 1918- *10*
Smith, William Jay 1918- *154*
  Autobiography Feature *154*
  Earlier sketches in SATA *2, 68*
  See also SAAS *22*
Smith, Winsome 1935- *45*
Smith, Z.Z.
  See Westheimer, David

Smith-Ankrom, M. E. 1942- *130*
Smith-Griswold, Wendy 1955- *88*
Smith-Rex, Susan J. 1950- *94*
Smithsen, Richard
  See Pellowski, Michael (Joseph)
Smits, Teo
  See Smits, Theodore R(ichard)
Smits, Theodore R(ichard) 1905-1996 .... *45*
  Brief entry *28*
Smolinski, Dick 1932- *86*
Smothers, Ethel Footman 1944- *149*
  Earlier sketch in SATA *76*
Smucker, Barbara 1915-2003 .... *130*
  Earlier sketches in SATA *29, 76*
  See also CLR *10*
  See also SAAS *11*
Smucker, Barbara Claassen
  See Smucker, Barbara
Smyth, Iain 1959- *105*
Snedeker, Caroline Dale (Parke) 1871-1956
  See YABC *2*
Sneed, Brad *191*
Snell, Nigel (Edward Creagh) 1936- *57*
  Brief entry *40*
Snellgrove, L(aurence) E(rnest) 1928- *53*
Snelling, Dennis (Wayne) 1958- *84*
Sneve, Virginia Driving Hawk 1933- *95*
  Earlier sketch in SATA *8*
  See also CLR *2*
Snicket, Lemony 1970- *187*
  Earlier sketch in SATA *126*
  See also CLR *79*
Snodgrass, Mary Ellen 1944- *75*
Snodgrass, Quentin Curtius
  See Clemens, Samuel Langhorne
Snodgrass, Thomas Jefferson
  See Clemens, Samuel Langhorne
Snook, Barbara (Lillian) 1913-1976 .... *34*
Snow, Alan 1959- *190*
Snow, Donald Clifford 1917-1979 .... *16*
Snow, Dorothea J(ohnston) 1909- *9*
Snow, Richard F(olger) 1947- *52*
  Brief entry *37*
Snyder, Anne 1922-2001 .... *4*
  Obituary *125*
Snyder, Bernadette McCarver 1930- *97*
Snyder, Carol 1941- *35*
Snyder, Gerald S(eymour) 1933- *48*
  Brief entry *34*
Snyder, Jerome 1916-1976
  Obituary *20*
Snyder, Midori 1954- *106*
Snyder, Paul A. 1946- *125*
Snyder, Zilpha Keatley 1927- *163*
  Autobiography Feature *163*
  Earlier sketches in SATA *1, 28, 75, 110*
  See also CLR *121*
  See also SAAS *2*
Snyderman, Reuven K. 1922- *5*
So, Meilo *162*
Sobel, June 1950- *149*
Soble, Jennie
  See Cavin, Ruth (Brodie)
Sobol, Donald J. 1924- *132*
  Earlier sketches in SATA *1, 31, 73*
  See also CLR *4*
Sobol, Harriet Langsam 1936- *47*
  Brief entry *34*
Sobol, Rose 1931- *76*
Sobott-Mogwe, Gaele 1956- *97*
Soderlind, Arthur E(dwin) 1920- *14*
Soentpiet, Chris K. 1970- *159*
  Earlier sketch in SATA *97*
Soerensen, Svend Otto 1916- *67*
Sofer, Barbara 1949- *109*
Sofer, Rachel
  See Sofer, Barbara
Softly, Barbara Frewin 1924- *12*
Soglow, Otto 1900-1975
  Obituary *30*
Sohl, Frederic J(ohn) 1916- *10*

Sohr, Daniel 1973- *190*
Sokol, Bill
  See Sokol, William
Sokol, William 1923- *37*
Sokolov, Kirill 1930- *34*
Solbert, Romaine G. 1925- *2*
Solbert, Ronni
  See Solbert, Romaine G.
Solheim, James *133*
Solomon, Heather M. *188*
Solomon, Joan 1930- *51*
  Brief entry *40*
Solomons, Ikey Esquir
  See Thackeray, William Makepeace
Solonevich, George 1915-2003 .... *15*
Solot, Mary Lynn 1939- *12*
Somerlott, Robert 1928-2001 .... *62*
Somervill, Barbara A(nn) 1948- *140*
Sommer, Angela
  See Sommer-Bodenburg, Angela
Sommer, Carl 1930- *175*
  Earlier sketch in SATA *126*
Sommer, Elyse 1929- *7*
Sommer, Robert 1929- *12*
Sommer-Bodenburg, Angela 1948- *113*
  Earlier sketch in SATA *63*
Sommerdorf, Norma 1926- *131*
Sommerdorf, Norma Jean
  See Sommerdorf, Norma
Sommerfelt, Aimee 1892-1975 .... *5*
Son, John *160*
Sones, Sonya *131*
Sonneborn, Ruth (Cantor) 1899-1974 .... *4*
  Obituary *27*
Sonnenblick, Jordan 1969- *185*
Sonnenmark, Laura A. 1958- *73*
Sopko, Eugen 1949- *58*
Sorel, Edward 1929- *126*
  Brief entry *37*
  Earlier sketch in SATA *65*
Sorensen, Henri 1950- *115*
  Earlier sketch in SATA *77*
Sorensen, Svend Otto
  See Soerensen, Svend Otto
Sorensen, Virginia 1912-1991 .... *2*
  Obituary *72*
  See also SAAS *15*
Sorenson, Jane 1926- *63*
Sorenson, Margo 1946- *96*
Sorley Walker, Kathrine *41*
Sorra, Kristin *185*
Sorrells, Walter *177*
Sorrentino, Joseph N. 1937- *6*
Sortor, June Elizabeth 1939- *12*
Sortor, Toni
  See Sortor, June Elizabeth
Soskin, V. H.
  See Ellison, Virginia H(owell)
Soto, Gary 1952- *174*
  Earlier sketches in SATA *80, 120*
  See also CLR *38*
Sotomayor, Antonio 1902-1985 .... *11*
Souci, Robert D. San
  See San Souci, Robert D.
Soudley, Henry
  See Wood, James Playsted
Souhami, Jessica *176*
Soule, Gardner (Bosworth) 1913-2000 .... *14*
Soule, Jean Conder 1919- *10*
Souster, (Holmes) Raymond 1921- *63*
South, Sheri Cobb 1959- *82*
Southall, Ivan (Francis) 1921- *134*
  Autobiography Feature *134*
  Earlier sketches in SATA *3, 68*
  See also CLR *2*
  See also SAAS *3*
Southey, Robert 1774-1843 .... *54*
Southgate, Vera *54*
Sovak, Jan 1953- *115*
Sowden, Celeste
  See Walters, Celeste

Sowter, Nita *69*
Spafford, Suzy 1945- *160*
Spagnoli, Cathy 1950- *134*
  Earlier sketch in SATA *79*
Spain, Sahara Sunday 1991- *133*
Spain, Susan Rosson *185*
Spalding, Andrea 1944- *150*
  Earlier sketch in SATA *101*
Spanfeller, James J(ohn) 1930- *19*
  See Spanfeller, Jim
Spanfeller, Jim
  See SAAS *8*
  See Spanfeller, James J(ohn)
Spangenberg, Judith Dunn 1942- *5*
Spanyol, Jessica 1965- *137*
Spar, Jerome 1918- *10*
Sparks, Barbara 1942- *78*
Sparks, Beatrice (Mathews) 1918- *44*
  Brief entry *28*
  See also CLR *139*
Sparks, Mary W. 1920- *15*
Spaulding, Douglas
  See Bradbury, Ray
Spaulding, Leonard
  See Bradbury, Ray
Spaulding, Norma *107*
Speare, Elizabeth George 1908-1994 .... *62*
  Obituary *83*
  Earlier sketch in SATA *5*
  See also CLR *8*
Spearing, Judith (Mary Harlow) 1922- *9*
Spears, Rick *182*
Speck, Nancy 1959- *104*
Specking, Inez 1890-1960(?) *11*
Speed, Nell
  See Keats, Emma
  and Sampson, Emma (Keats) Speed
Speed, Nell (Ewing) 1878-1913 .... *68*
Speer, Bonnie Stahlman 1929- *113*
Speer-Lyon, Tammie L. 1965- *89*
Speicher, Helen Ross S(mith) 1915- *8*
Speir, Nancy 1958- *81*
Spellman, John W(illard) 1934- *14*
Spellman, Roger G.
  See Cox, William R(obert)
Spelman, Cornelia Maude 1946- *144*
  Earlier sketch in SATA *96*
Spelman, Mary 1934- *28*
Spelvin, George
  See Lerangis, Peter
  and Phillips, David Atlee
Spence, Cynthia
  See Eble, Diane
Spence, Eleanor (Rachel) 1928- *21*
  See also CLR *26*
Spence, Geraldine 1931- *47*
Spencer, Ann 1918- *10*
Spencer, Cornelia
  See Yaukey, Grace S(ydenstricker)
Spencer, Donald D(ean) 1931- *41*
Spencer, Elizabeth 1921- *14*
Spencer, Leonard G.
  See Garrett, (Gordon) Randall (Phillip)
  and Silverberg, Robert
Spencer, William 1922- *9*
Spencer, Zane A(nn) 1935- *35*
Sper, Emily 1957- *142*
Speregen, Devra Newberger 1964- *84*
Sperling, Dan(iel Lee) 1949- *65*
Sperry, Armstrong W. 1897-1976 .... *1*
  Obituary *27*
Sperry, Raymond
  See Garis, Howard R(oger)
Sperry, Raymond, Jr. *1*
Spetter, Jung-Hee 1969- *134*
Spicer, Dorothy Gladys -1975 .... *32*
Spiegel, Beth *184*
Spiegelman, Art 1948- *158*
  Earlier sketch in SATA *109*
Spiegelman, Judith M. *5*
Spielberg, Steven 1947- *32*

Spier, Peter (Edward) 1927- *54*
  Earlier sketch in SATA *4*
  See also CLR *5*
Spilhaus, Athelstan (Frederick) 1911-1998 .. *13*
  Obituary *102*
Spilka, Arnold 1917- *6*
Spillane, Frank Morrison
  See Spillane, Mickey
Spillane, Mickey 1918-2006 .... *66*
  Obituary *176*
  See Spillane, Frank Morrison
Spinelli, Eileen 1942- *186*
  Earlier sketches in SATA *38, 101, 150*
Spinelli, Jerry 1941- *158*
  Earlier sketches in SATA *39, 71, 110*
  See also CLR *82*
Spink, Reginald (William) 1905-1994 .... *11*
Spinka, Penina Keen 1945- *72*
Spinner, Stephanie 1943- *132*
  Earlier sketches in SATA *38, 91*
Spinossimus
  See White, William, Jr.
Spiotta-DiMare, Loren *173*
Spires, Ashley 1978- *183*
Spires, Elizabeth 1952- *111*
  Earlier sketch in SATA *71*
Spirin, Gennadii
  See Spirin, Gennady
Spirin, Gennadij
  See Spirin, Gennady
Spirin, Gennady 1948- *134*
  Earlier sketch in SATA *95*
  See also CLR *88*
Spivak, Dawnine *101*
Spohn, David 1948- *72*
Spohn, Kate 1962- *147*
  Earlier sketch in SATA *87*
Spollen, Christopher 1952- *12*
Spooner, Michael (Tim) 1954- *92*
Spowart, Robin 1947- *177*
  Earlier sketch in SATA *82*
Sprague, Gretchen 1926-2003 .... *27*
Sprengel, Artie
  See Lerangis, Peter
Sprigge, Elizabeth (Miriam Squire)
  1900-1974 .... *10*
Spring, (Robert) Howard 1889-1965 .... *28*
Springer, Margaret 1941- *78*
Springer, Marilyn Harris 1931- *47*
Springer, Nancy 1948- *172*
  Earlier sketches in SATA *65, 110*
Springstubb, Tricia 1950- *78*
  Brief entry *40*
  Earlier sketch in SATA *46*
Spudvilas, Anne 1951- *94*
Spurll, Barbara 1952- *78*
Spurr, Elizabeth *172*
Spykman, E(lizabeth) C(hoate) 1896-1965 .. *10*
  See also CLR *35*
Spyri, Johanna (Heusser) 1827-1901 .... *100*
  Earlier sketch in SATA *19*
  See also CLR *115*
Squires, Phil
  See Barker, S(quire) Omar
Srba, Lynne *98*
Sreenivasan, Jyotsna 1964- *101*
S-Ringi, Kjell
  See Ringi, Kjell (Arne Soerensen)
Stacey, Cherylyn 1945- *96*
Stacy, Donald
  See Pohl, Frederik
Stadtler, Bea 1921- *17*
Stafford, Jean 1915-1979
  Obituary *22*
Stafford, Liliana 1950- *141*
Stafford, Paul 1966- *116*
Stahl, Ben(jamin) 1910-1987 .... *5*
  Obituary *54*
Stahl, Hilda 1938-1993 .... *48*
  Obituary *77*
Stahler, David, Jr. *162*

Stainton, Sue 187
Stair, Gobin (John) 1912- 35
Stalder, Valerie 27
Stamaty, Mark Alan 1947- 12
Stambler, Irwin 1924- 5
Standiford, Natalie 1961- 169
    Earlier sketch in SATA 81
Stanek, Lou Willett 1931- 63
Stang, Judit 1921-1977 29
Stang, Judy
    See Stang, Judit
Stangl, (Mary) Jean 1928- 67
Stanhope, Eric
    See Hamilton, Charles (Harold St. John)
Stankevich, Boris 1928- 2
Stanley, Diane 1943- 164
    Brief entry 32
    Earlier sketches in SATA 37, 80, 115
    See also CLR 46
    See also SAAS 15
Stanley, George Edward 1942- 157
    Earlier sketches in SATA 53, 111
    See Dixon, Franklin W.
    and Hope, Laura Lee
    and Keene, Carolyn
Stanley, Jerry 1941- 127
    Earlier sketch in SATA 79
Stanley, Mandy 165
Stanley, Robert
    See Hamilton, Charles (Harold St. John)
Stanley, Sanna 1962- 145
Stanli, Sue
    See Meilach, Dona Z(weigoron)
Stanstead, John
    See Groom, Arthur William
Stanton, Karen 1960- 190
Stanton, Schuyler
    See Baum, L(yman) Frank
Staples, Suzanne Fisher 1945- 151
    Earlier sketches in SATA 70, 105
    See also CLR 137
Stapleton, Marjorie (Winifred) 1932- 28
Stapp, Arthur D(onald) 1906-1972 4
Starbird, Kaye 1916- 6
    See also CLR 60
Stark, Evan 1942- 78
Stark, James
    See Goldston, Robert (Conroy)
Stark, Ulf 1944- 124
Starke, Ruth (Elaine) 1946- 129
Starkey, Marion L(ena) 1901-1991 13
Starr, Ward
    See Manes, Stephen
Starret, William
    See McClintock, Marshall
Starr Taylor, Bridget 1959- 99
Stasiak, Krystyna 49
Staub, Frank 1949- 116
Staub, Frank Jacob
    See Staub, Frank
Staub, Wendy Corsi 1964- 114
Stauffacher, Sue 1961- 155
Stauffer, Don
    See Berkebile, Fred D(onovan)
Staunton, Schuyler
    See Baum, L(yman) Frank
Staunton, Ted 1956- 167
    Earlier sketch in SATA 112
Stead, Rebecca 1968(?)- 188
Steadman, Ralph 1936- 123
    Earlier sketch in SATA 32
Steadman, Ralph Idris
    See Steadman, Ralph
Stearman, Kaye 1951- 118
Stearns, Monroe (Mather) 1913-1987 5
    Obituary 55
Steckler, Arthur 1921-1985 65
Steding, Laurie 1953- 119
Steel, Danielle 1947- 66
Steel, Danielle Fernande
    See Steel, Danielle

Steele, Addison II
    See Lupoff, Richard A(llen)
Steele, Alexander 1958- 116
Steele, Henry Maxwell
    See Steele, Max
Steele, Mary 1930- 94
Steele, Mary Q(uintard Govan) 1922-1992 .. 51
    Obituary 72
    Earlier sketch in SATA 3
Steele, Max 1922-2005 168
    Earlier sketch in SATA 10
Steele, Philip 1948- 140
    Earlier sketch in SATA 81
Steele, William O(wen) 1917-1979 51
    Obituary 27
    Earlier sketch in SATA 1
Steelhammer, Ilona 1952- 98
Steelsmith, Shari 1962- 72
Stefanik, Alfred T. 1939- 55
Steffanson, Con
    See Cassiday, Bruce (Bingham)
    and Goulart, Ron(ald Joseph)
Steffens, Bradley 1955- 166
    Earlier sketch in SATA 77
Stegeman, Janet Allais 1923- 53
    Brief entry 49
    See Britton, Kate
Steggall, Susan 1967- 182
Steig, William 1907-2003 111
    Obituary 149
    Earlier sketches in SATA 18, 70
    See also CLR 103
Steig, William H.
    See Steig, William
Stein, David Ezra 180
Stein, M(eyer) L(ewis) 1920- 6
Stein, Mini 2
Stein, R(ichard) Conrad 1937- 154
    Earlier sketches in SATA 31, 82
Stein, Wendy 1951- 77
Steinbeck, John (Ernst) 1902-1968 9
Steinberg, Alfred 1917-1995 9
Steinberg, Fannie 1899-1990 43
Steinberg, Fred J. 1933- 4
Steinberg, Phillip Orso 1921- 34
Steinberg, Rafael (Mark) 1927- 45
Steinberg, Saul 1914-1999 67
Steincrohn, Maggie
    See Davis, Maggie S.
Steiner, Barbara A(nnette) 1934- 83
    Earlier sketch in SATA 13
    See also SAAS 13
Steiner, Charlotte 1900-1981 45
Steiner, George 1929- 62
Steiner, Joan 110
Steiner, Jorg
    See Steiner, Jorg
Steiner, Jorg 1930- 35
Steiner, K. Leslie
    See Delany, Samuel R., Jr.
Steiner, Stan(ley) 1925-1987 14
    Obituary 50
Steinhardt, Bernice 193
Steins, Richard 1942- 79
Stem, Jacqueline 1931- 110
Stemple, Jason 179
Steneman, Shep 1945- 132
Stengel, Joyce A. 1938- 158
Stephanie, Gordon
    See Gordon, Stephanie Jacob
Stephens, Alice Barber 1858-1932 66
Stephens, Casey
    See Wagner, Sharon B.
Stephens, J.B.
    See Lynn, Tracy
Stephens, Mary Jo 1935- 8
Stephens, Rebecca 1961- 141
Stephens, Reed
    See Donaldson, Stephen R.
Stephens, Suzanne
    See Kirby, Susan E.

Stephens, William M(cLain) 1925- 21
Stephensen, A. M.
    See Manes, Stephen
Stephenson, Lynda 1941- 179
Stephenson, Lynda A.
    See Stephenson, Lynda
Stepp, Ann 1935- 29
Stepto, Michele 1946- 61
Steptoe, Javaka 1971- 151
Steptoe, John (Lewis) 1950-1989 63
    Earlier sketch in SATA 8
    See also CLR 12
Sterling, Brett
    See Bradbury, Ray
    and Hamilton, Edmond
    and Samachson, Joseph
Sterling, Dorothy 1913- 83
    Autobiography Feature 127
    Earlier sketch in SATA 1
    See also CLR 1
    See also SAAS 2
Sterling, Philip 1907-1989 8
    Obituary 63
Sterling, Shirley (Anne) 1948- 101
Stern, Ellen Norman 1927- 26
Stern, Judith M. 1951- 75
Stern, Madeleine
    See Stern, Madeleine B.
Stern, Madeleine B. 1912-2007 14
Stern, Madeleine Bettina
    See Stern, Madeleine B.
Stern, Maggie 1953- 156
Stern, Philip Van Doren 1900-1984 13
    Obituary 39
Stern, Simon 1943- 15
Sterne, Emma Gelders 1894- 6
Steurt, Marjorie Rankin 1888-1978 10
Stevens, Bryna 1924- 65
Stevens, Carla M(cBride) 1928- 13
Stevens, Chambers 1968- 128
Stevens, Diane 1939- 94
Stevens, Franklin 1933- 6
Stevens, Greg
    See Cook, Glen
Stevens, Gwendolyn 1944- 33
Stevens, Jan Romero 1953- 95
Stevens, Janet 1953- 193
    Earlier sketches in SATA 90, 148
Stevens, Kathleen 1936- 49
Stevens, Leonard A. 1920- 67
Stevens, Lucile Vernon 1899-1994 59
Stevens, Margaret Dean
    See Aldrich, Bess Streeter
Stevens, Patricia Bunning 1931- 27
Stevens, Peter
    See Geis, Darlene Stern
Stevens, Serita 1949- 70
Stevens, Serita Deborah
    See Stevens, Serita
Stevens, Serita Mendelson
    See Stevens, Serita
Stevens, Shira
    See Stevens, Serita
Stevenson, Anna (M.) 1905- 12
Stevenson, Augusta 1869(?)-1976 2
    Obituary 26
Stevenson, Burton Egbert 1872-1962 25
Stevenson, Drew 1947- 60
Stevenson, Harvey 1960- 148
    Earlier sketch in SATA 80
Stevenson, James 1929- 161
    Brief entry 34
    Earlier sketches in SATA 42, 71, 113
    See also CLR 17
Stevenson, Janet 1913- 8
Stevenson, Robert Louis (Balfour)
    1850-1894 100
    See also YABC 2
    See also CLR 107
Stevenson, Sucie 1956- 104
Stewart, A(gnes) C(harlotte) 15

Stewart, Amber *181*
Stewart, Chantal 1945- *173*
   Earlier sketch in SATA *121*
Stewart, Charles
   See Zurhorst, Charles (Stewart, Jr.)
Stewart, Eleanor
   See Porter, Eleanor H(odgman)
Stewart, Elisabeth J(ane) 1927- *93*
Stewart, Elizabeth Laing 1907- *6*
Stewart, Gail B. 1949- *141*
Stewart, George Rippey 1895-1980 .... *3*
   Obituary *23*
Stewart, Jennifer J(enkins) 1960- *128*
Stewart, Joel *151*
Stewart, John (William) 1920- *14*
   See Cole, Jack
Stewart, Mary (Florence Elinor) 1916- *12*
Stewart, Mary Rainbow
   See Stewart, Mary (Florence Elinor)
Stewart, Melissa 1968- *167*
   Earlier sketch in SATA *111*
Stewart, Paul 1955- *163*
   Earlier sketch in SATA *114*
Stewart, Robert Neil 1891-1972 .... *7*
Stewart, Sarah *143*
Stewart, Scott
   See Zaffo, George J.
Stewart, W(alter) P. 1924- *53*
Stewart, Whitney 1959- *167*
   Earlier sketch in SATA *92*
Stewig, John Warren 1937- *162*
   Earlier sketches in SATA *26, 110*
Stickler, Soma Han 1942- *128*
Stidworthy, John 1943- *63*
Stiegemeyer, Julie *180*
Stiles, Martha Bennett *108*
   Earlier sketch in SATA *6*
Still, James 1906-2001 .... *29*
   Obituary *127*
Stille, Darlene R. 1942- *170*
   Earlier sketch in SATA *126*
Stille, Darlene Ruth
   See Stille, Darlene R.
Stillerman, Marci *104*
Stillerman, Robbie 1947- *12*
Stilley, Frank 1918- *29*
Stilton, Geronimo *158*
Stimpson, Gerald
   See Mitchell, Adrian
Stine, Catherine *165*
Stine, G(eorge) Harry 1928-1997 .... *136*
   Earlier sketch in SATA *10*
Stine, Jovial Bob
   See Stine, R.L.
Stine, R.L. 1943- *129*
   Earlier sketches in SATA *31, 76*
   See also CLR *111*
Stine, Robert Lawrence
   See Stine, R.L.
Stinetorf, Louise (Allender) 1900-1992 .... *10*
Stinson, Kathy 1952- *98*
Stirling, Arthur
   See Sinclair, Upton
Stirling, Ian 1941- *77*
Stirling, Nora B(romley) 1900-1997 .... *3*
Stirnweis, Shannon 1931- *10*
Stobbs, William 1914-2000 .... *17*
   Obituary *120*
Stock, Carolmarie 1951- *75*
Stock, Catherine 1952- *158*
   Earlier sketches in SATA *65, 114*
Stockdale, Susan 1954- *98*
Stockham, Peter (Alan) 1928- *57*
Stockton, Francis Richard 1834-1902 .... *44*
   See Stockton, Frank R.
Stockton, Frank R.
   Brief entry *32*
   See Stockton, Francis Richard
Stockwell-Moniz, Marc J. 1954- *164*
Stoddard, Edward G. 1923- *10*
Stoddard, Hope 1900-1987 .... *6*

Stoddard, Sandol 1927- *98*
   See Warburg, Sandol Stoddard
Stoehr, Shelley 1969- *107*
Stoeke, Janet Morgan 1957- *136*
   Earlier sketch in SATA *90*
Stohner, Anu 1952- *179*
Stoiko, Michael 1919- *14*
Stojic, Manya 1967- *156*
Stoker, Abraham 1847-1912 .... *29*
   See Stoker, Bram
Stoker, Bram
   See Stoker, Abraham
Stokes, Cedric
   See Beardmore, George
Stokes, Jack (Tilden) 1923- *13*
Stokes, Olivia Pearl 1916- *32*
Stolz, Mary 1920-2006 .... *133*
   Obituary *180*
   Earlier sketches in SATA *10, 71*
   See also SAAS *3*
Stolz, Mary Slattery
   See Stolz, Mary
Stone, Alan
   See Svenson, Andrew E(dward)
Stone, David K(arl) 1922- *9*
Stone, David Lee 1978- *166*
Stone, Eugenia 1879-1971 .... *7*
Stone, Gene
   See Stone, Eugenia
Stone, Helen V(irginia) *6*
Stone, Idella Purnell
   See Purnell, Idella
Stone, Ikey
   See Purnell, Idella
Stone, Irving 1903-1989 .... *3*
   Obituary *64*
Stone, Jeff *178*
Stone, Jon 1931-1997 .... *39*
   Obituary *95*
Stone, Josephine Rector
   See Dixon, Jeanne
Stone, Lesley
   See Trevor, Elleston
Stone, Peter 1930-2003 .... *65*
   Obituary *143*
Stone, Phoebe *134*
Stone, Raymond *1*
Stone, Rosetta
   See Dr. Seuss
   and Geisel, Theodor Seuss
   and LeSieg, Theo.
   and Seuss, Dr.
Stone, Tanya Lee *182*
Stonehouse, Bernard 1926- *140*
   Earlier sketches in SATA *13, 80*
Stones, (Cyril) Anthony 1934- *72*
Stong, Phil(ip Duffield) 1899-1957 .... *32*
Stoops, Erik D(aniel) 1966- *142*
   Earlier sketch in SATA *78*
Stoppelmoore, Cheryl Jean
   See Ladd, Cheryl (Jean)
Stops, Sue 1936- *86*
Storace, Patricia *193*
Storad, Conrad J. 1957- *119*
Storey, Margaret 1926- *9*
Storey, Victoria Carolyn 1945- *16*
Storme, Peter
   See Stern, Philip Van Doren
Storr, Catherine (Cole) 1913-2001 .... *87*
   Obituary *122*
   Earlier sketch in SATA *9*
Story, Josephine
   See Loring, Emilie (Baker)
Stotko, Mary-Ann 1960- *154*
Stott, Dorothy (M.) 1958- *99*
   Earlier sketch in SATA *67*
Stott, Dot
   See Stott, Dorothy (M.)
Stotter, Mike 1957- *108*
Stout, William 1949- *132*
Stoutenburg, Adrien (Pearl) 1916-1982 .... *3*

Stoutland, Allison 1963- *130*
Stover, Allan C(arl) 1938- *14*
Stover, Jill (Griffin) 1958- *82*
Stover, Marjorie Filley 1914- *9*
Stowe, Harriet (Elizabeth) Beecher
   1811-1896
   See YABC *1*
   See also CLR *131*
Stowe, Leland 1899-1994 .... *60*
   Obituary *78*
Stowe, Rosetta
   See Ogan, George F.
   and Ogan, Margaret E. (Nettles)
Strachan, Ian 1938- *85*
Strachan, Linda *167*
Strachan, Margaret Pitcairn 1908-1998 .... *14*
Strahinich, H. C.
   See Strahinich, Helen C.
Strahinich, Helen C. 1949- *78*
Strait, Treva Adams 1909-2002 .... *35*
Strand, Mark 1934- *41*
Strange, Philippa
   See Coury, Louise Andree
Stranger, Joyce
   See SAAS *24*
   See Wilson, Joyce M(uriel Judson)
Strangis, Joel 1948- *124*
Strannigan, Shawn 1956- *93*
Strannigan, Shawn Alyne
   See Strannigan, Shawn
Strasser, Todd 1950- *153*
   Earlier sketches in SATA *41, 45, 71, 107*
   See also CLR *11*
Stratemeyer, Edward L. 1862-1930 .... *100*
   Earlier sketches in SATA *1, 67*
   See Adams, Harrison
   and Appleton, Victor
   and Dixon, Franklin W.
   and Keene, Carolyn
   and Rockwood, Roy
   and Young, Clarence
Stratford, Philip 1927- *47*
Stratton, Allan 1951- *178*
Stratton, J. M.
   See Whitlock, Ralph
Stratton, Thomas
   See Coulson, Robert S(tratton)
   and DeWeese, Thomas Eugene
Stratton-Porter, Gene(va Grace) 1863-1924 . *15*
   See also CLR *87*
   See Porter, Gene(va Grace) Stratton
Strauss, Gwen 1963- *77*
Strauss, Joyce 1936- *53*
Strauss, Linda Leopold 1942- *127*
Strauss, Susan (Elizabeth) 1954- *75*
Strayer, E. Ward
   See Stratemeyer, Edward L.
Streano, Vince(nt Catello) 1945- *20*
Streatfeild, Mary Noel
   See Streatfeild, Noel
Streatfeild, Noel 1897(?)-1986 .... *20*
   Obituary *48*
   See also CLR *83*
Street, Janet Travell 1959- *84*
Street, Julia Montgomery 1898-1993 .... *11*
Streissguth, Thomas 1958- *116*
Strelkoff, Tatiana 1957- *89*
Stren, Patti 1949- *88*
   Brief entry *41*
   See also CLR *5*
Strete, Craig Kee 1950- *96*
   Earlier sketch in SATA *44*
Stretton, Barbara (Humphrey) 1936- *43*
   Brief entry *35*
Strickland, (William) Brad(ley) 1947- *142*
   Earlier sketches in SATA *83, 137*
Strickland, Craig (A.) 1956- *102*
Strickland, Dorothy S(alley) 1933- *89*
Strickland, Michael R. 1965- *144*
   Earlier sketch in SATA *83*
Strickland, Tessa *173*

Striegel, Jana 1955- 140
Striegel-Wilson, Jana
  See Striegel, Jana
Striker, Lee
  See Clark, Margaret (D.)
Striker, Susan 1942- 63
Stringer, Lauren 1957- 183
  Earlier sketch in SATA 129
Stroeyer, Poul 1923- 13
Stromoski, Rick 1958- 111
Strong, Charles
  See Epstein, Beryl (M. Williams)
  and Epstein, Samuel
Strong, David
  See McGuire, Leslie (Sarah)
Strong, Jeremy 1949- 175
  Earlier sketches in SATA 36, 105
Strong, J.J.
  See Strong, Jeremy
Strong, Pat
  See Hough, Richard (Alexander)
Strong, Stacie 1965- 74
Stroud, Bettye 1939- 165
  Earlier sketch in SATA 96
Stroud, Jonathan 1970- 159
  Earlier sketch in SATA 102
  See also CLR 134
Stroyer, Poul
  See Stroeyer, Poul
Strug, Kerri 1977- 108
Stryer, Andrea Stenn 1938- 192
Stryker, Daniel
  See Morris, Chris(topher Crosby)
  and Stump, Jane Barr
Stuart, David
  See Hoyt, Edwin P(almer), Jr.
Stuart, Derek
  See Foster, John L(ouis)
Stuart, Forbes 1924- 13
Stuart, Ian
  See MacLean, Alistair (Stuart)
Stuart, Jesse (Hilton) 1906-1984 2
  Obituary 36
Stuart, Ruth McEnery 1849(?)-1917 116
Stuart, Sheila
  See Baker, Mary Gladys Steel
Stuart-Clark, Christopher (Anthony) 1940- .. 32
Stubis, Talivaldis 1926- 5
Stubley, Trevor (Hugh) 1932- 22
Stucky, Naomi R. 1922- 72
Stucley, Elizabeth
  See Northmore, Elizabeth Florence
Stultifer, Morton
  See Curtis, Richard (Alan)
Sture-Vasa, Mary
  See Alsop, Mary O'Hara
Sturges, Philemon 174
Sturtevant, Katherine 1950- 180
  Earlier sketch in SATA 130
Sturton, Hugh
  See Johnston, H(ugh) A(nthony) S(tephen)
Sturtzel, Howard A(llison) 1894-1985 1
Sturtzel, Jane Levington 1903-1996 1
Stutley, D(oris) J(ean) 1959- 142
Stutson, Caroline 1940- 104
Stuve-Bodeen, Stephanie 1965- 158
  Earlier sketch in SATA 114
Stux, Erica 1929- 140
Styles, (Frank) Showell 1908- 10
Stynes, Barbara White 133
Suba, Susanne 4
Subond, Valerie
  See Grayland, Valerie (Merle Spanner)
Sudbery, Rodie 1943- 42
Suen, Anastasia 1956(?)- 157
Sufrin, Mark 1925- 76
Sugarman, Joan G. 1917- 64
Sugarman, Tracy 1921- 37
Sugita, Yutaka 1930- 36

Suhl, Yuri (Menachem) 1908-1986 8
  Obituary 50
  See also CLR 2
  See also SAAS 1
Suhr, Joanne 129
Suid, Murray 1942- 27
Sullivan, George (Edward) 1927- 147
  Earlier sketches in SATA 4, 89
Sullivan, Jody
  See Rake, Jody
Sullivan, Kathryn A. 1954- 141
Sullivan, Mary Ann 1954- 63
Sullivan, Mary W(ilson) 1907- 13
Sullivan, Pat
  See Messmer, Otto
Sullivan, Paul 1939- 106
Sullivan, Sarah G. 1953- 179
Sullivan, Silky
  See Makowski, Silvia Ann
Sullivan, Sue
  See Sullivan, Susan E.
Sullivan, Susan E. 1962- 123
Sullivan, Thomas Joseph, Jr. 1947- 16
Sullivan, Tom
  See Sullivan, Thomas Joseph, Jr.
Sully, Tom 1959- 104
Sumichrast, Jozef 1948- 29
Sumiko
  See Davies, Sumiko
Summerforest, Ivy B.
  See Kirkup, James
Summers, Barbara 1944- 182
Summers, James L(evingston) 1910-1973 57
  Brief entry 28
Summertree, Katonah
  See Windsor, Patricia
Sun, Chyng Feng 1959- 90
Sunderlin, Sylvia (S.) 1911-1997 28
  Obituary 99
Sung, Betty Lee 26
Supeene, Shelagh Lynne 1952- 153
Supraner, Robyn 1930- 101
  Earlier sketch in SATA 20
Supree, Burt(on) 1941-1992 73
Surface, Mary Hall 1958- 126
Surge, Frank 1931- 13
Susac, Andrew 1929- 5
Susi, Geraldine Lee 1942- 98
Sussman, Cornelia Silver 1914-1999 59
Sussman, Irving 1908-1996 59
Sussman, Susan 1942- 48
Sutcliff, Rosemary 1920-1992 78
  Obituary 73
  Earlier sketches in SATA 6, 44
  See also CLR 138
Sutcliffe, Jane 1957- 138
Sutherland, Colleen 1944- 79
Sutherland, Efua (Theodora Morgue)
  1924-1996 25
Sutherland, Jon 1958- 167
Sutherland, Jonathan D.
  See Sutherland, Jon
Sutherland, Jonathan David
  See Sutherland, Jon
Sutherland, Margaret 1941- 15
Sutherland, Zena Bailey 1915-2002 37
  Obituary 137
Suttles, Shirley (Smith) 1922- 21
Sutton, Ann (Livesay) 1923- 31
Sutton, Eve(lyn Mary) 1906-1992 26
Sutton, Felix 1910(?)-1973 31
Sutton, Jane 1950- 52
  Brief entry 43
Sutton, Larry M(atthew) 1931- 29
Sutton, Margaret Beebe 1903-2001 1
  Obituary 131
Sutton, Myron Daniel 1925- 31
Sutton, Roger 1956- 93

Suzanne, Jamie
  See Hawes, Louise
  and Lantz, Francess L(in)
  and Singleton, Linda Joy
  and Zach, Cheryl (Byrd)
Suzuki, David T(akayoshi) 1936- 138
Svendsen, Mark 1962- 181
  Earlier sketch in SATA 120
Svendsen, Mark Nestor
  See Svendsen, Mark
Svenson, Andrew E(dward) 1910-1975 2
  Obituary 26
Swaab, Neil 1978- 191
Swain, Carol 1962- 172
Swain, Gwenyth 1961- 134
  Earlier sketch in SATA 84
Swain, Ruth
  See Swain, Ruth Freeman
Swain, Ruth Freeman 1951- 161
  Earlier sketch in SATA 119
Swain, Su Zan (Noguchi) 1916- 21
Swallow, Pamela Curtis 178
Swamp, Jake 1941- 98
Swan, Susan 1944- 108
  Earlier sketch in SATA 22
Swann, Brian (Stanley Frank) 1940- 116
Swann, E. L.
  See Lasky, Kathryn
Swann, Ruth Rice 1920- 84
Swanson, Helen M(cKendry) 1919- 94
Swanson, June 1931- 76
Swanson, Wayne 1942- 167
Swarthout, Glendon (Fred) 1918-1992 26
Swarthout, Kathryn 1919- 7
Swayne, Sam(uel F.) 1907- 53
Swayne, Zoa (Lourana) 1905- 53
Sweat, Lynn 1934- 168
  Earlier sketch in SATA 57
Swede, George 1940- 67
Sweeney, James B(artholomew)
  1910-1999 21
Sweeney, Joyce 1955- 167
  Earlier sketches in SATA 65, 68, 108
Sweeney, Joyce Kay
  See Sweeney, Joyce
Sweeney, Karen O'Connor
  See O'Connor, Karen
Sweeney, Matthew (Gerard) 1952- 156
Sweet, Melissa 1956- 172
Sweet, Sarah C.
  See Jewett, (Theodora) Sarah Orne
Sweetland, Nancy A(nn) 1934- 48
Swenson, Allan A(rmstrong) 1933- 21
Swenson, May 1919-1989 15
Swentzell, Rina 1939- 79
Swiatkowska, Gabi 1971(?)- 180
Swift, Bryan
  See Knott, William C(ecil, Jr.)
Swift, David
  See Kaufmann, John
Swift, Hildegarde Hoyt 1890(?)-1977
  Obituary 20
Swift, Jonathan 1667-1745 19
  See also CLR 53
Swift, Merlin
  See Leeming, Joseph
Swiger, Elinor Porter 1927- 8
Swinburne, Laurence (Joseph) 1924- 9
Swinburne, Stephen R. 1952- 188
  Earlier sketch in SATA 150
Swinburne, Steve
  See Swinburne, Stephen R.
Swindells, Robert (Edward) 1939- 150
  Brief entry 34
  Earlier sketches in SATA 50, 80
  See also SAAS 14
Swinford, Betty (June Wells) 1927- 58
Swinford, Bob
  See Swinford, Betty (June Wells)
Swithen, John
  See King, Stephen

Switzer, Ellen 1923- *48*
Swope, Sam *156*
Swope, Samuel
　See Swope, Sam
Sybesma, Jetske
　See Ironside, Jetske
Sydney, Frank
　See Warwick, Alan R(oss)
Sylvester, Natalie G(abry) 1922- *22*
Syme, (Neville) Ronald 1913-1992 .... *87*
　Earlier sketch in SATA *2*
Symes, R. F. *77*
Symes, Ruth Louise 1962- *179*
Symons, (Dorothy) Geraldine 1909- *33*
Symons, Stuart
　See Stanley, George Edward
Symynkywicz, Jeffrey B. 1954- *87*
Symynkywicz, Jeffrey Bruce
　See Symynkywicz, Jeffrey B.
Synge, (Phyllis) Ursula 1930- *9*
Sypher, Lucy Johnston 1907- *7*
Szasz, Suzanne (Shorr) 1915-1997 .... *13*
　Obituary *99*
Szekeres, Cyndy 1933- *157*
　Autobiography Feature *157*
　Earlier sketches in SATA *5, 60, 131*
　See also SAAS *13*
Szekessy, Tanja *98*
Szpura, Beata 1961- *93*
Szudek, Agnes S(usan) P(hilomena) *57*
　Brief entry *49*
Szulc, Tad 1926-2001 .... *26*
Szydlow, Jarl
　See Szydlowski, Mary Vigliante
Szydlowski, Mary Vigliante 1946- *94*
Szymanski, Lois 1957- *91*

T

Taback, Simms 1932- *170*
　Brief entry *36*
　Earlier sketches in SATA *40, 104*
　See also CLR *100*
Taber, Gladys (Bagg) 1899-1980
　Obituary *22*
Tabor, Nancy Maria Grande 1949- *161*
　Earlier sketch in SATA *89*
Tabrah, Ruth Milander 1921- *14*
Tackach, James 1953- *123*
Tackach, James M.
　See Tackach, James
Tadgell, Nicole 1969- *177*
Tafuri, Nancy 1946- *192*
　Autobiography Feature *192*
　Earlier sketches in SATA *39, 75, 130*
　See also CLR *74*
　See also SAAS *14*
Tagg, Christine Elizabeth 1962- *138*
Tagliaferro, Linda *173*
Taha, Karen T(erry) 1942- *156*
　Earlier sketch in SATA *71*
Tai, Sharon O. 1963- *153*
Tait, Douglas 1944- *12*
Takabayashi, Mari 1960- *156*
　Earlier sketch in SATA *115*
Takahashi, Rumiko 1957- *163*
Takakjian, Portia 1930- *15*
Takashima, Misako
　See Misako Rocks!
Takashima, Shizuye 1928- *13*
Takayama, Sandi 1962- *106*
Takeda, Pete(r M.) 1964- *148*
Tal, Eve 1947- *176*
Talbert, Marc (Alan) 1953- *154*
　Autobiography Feature *154*
　Earlier sketches in SATA *68, 99*
Talbot, Charlene Joy 1928- *10*
Talbot, Toby 1928- *14*

Talbott, Hudson 1949- *131*
　Earlier sketch in SATA *84*
Talifero, Gerald 1950- *75*
Talker, T.
　See Rands, William Brighty
Tallarico, Tony 1933- *116*
Tallcott, Emogene *10*
Tallis, Robyn
　See Coville, Bruce
　and Doyle, Debra
　and Macdonald, James D.
　and Smith, Sherwood
　and Zambreno, Mary Frances
Tallon, Robert 1939- *43*
　Brief entry *28*
Talmadge, Marian *14*
Tamar, Erika 1934- *150*
　Earlier sketches in SATA *62, 101*
Tamarin, Alfred H. 1913-1980 .... *13*
Tamburine, Jean 1930- *12*
Tames, Richard (Lawrence) 1946- *102*
　Earlier sketch in SATA *67*
Tamminga, Frederick W(illiam) 1934- *66*
Tammuz, Benjamin 1919-1989
　Obituary *63*
Tan, Amy 1952- *75*
Tan, Amy Ruth
　See Tan, Amy
Tanaka, Beatrice 1932- *76*
Tanaka, Shelley *136*
Tang, Charles 1948- *81*
Tang, Greg *172*
Tang, You-Shan 1946- *53*
Tania B.
　See Blixen, Karen (Christentze Dinesen)
Tankard, Jeremy 1973- *191*
Tannen, Mary 1943- *37*
Tannenbaum, Beulah Goldstein 1916- *3*
Tannenbaum, D(onald) Leb 1948- *42*
Tanner, Jane 1946- *74*
Tanner, Louise S(tickney) 1922-2000 .... *9*
Tanobe, Miyuki 1937- *23*
Tanselle, Eve 1933- *125*
Tapio, Pat Decker
　See Kines, Pat Decker
Tapp, Kathy Kennedy 1949- *88*
　Brief entry *50*
Tarbescu, Edith 1939- *107*
Tarkington, (Newton) Booth 1869-1946 .... *17*
Tarpley, Natasha A(nastasia) 1971- *147*
Tarr, Judith 1955- *149*
　Earlier sketch in SATA *64*
Tarry, Ellen 1906- *16*
　See also CLR *26*
　See also SAAS *16*
Tarshis, Jerome 1936- *9*
Tarshis, Lauren *187*
Tarsky, Sue 1946- *41*
Taschek, Karen 1956- *185*
Tashjian, Janet 1956- *151*
　Earlier sketch in SATA *102*
Tashjian, Virginia A. 1921-2008 .... *3*
Tasker, James 1908- *9*
Tate, Don(ald E.) *159*
Tate, Eleanora E. 1948- *191*
　Earlier sketches in SATA *38, 94*
　See also CLR *37*
Tate, Eleanora Elaine
　See Tate, Eleanora E.
Tate, Ellalice
　See Hibbert, Eleanor Alice Burford
Tate, Joan 1922- *86*
　Earlier sketch in SATA *9*
　See also SAAS *20*
Tate, Mary Anne
　See Hale, Arlene
Tate, Nikki *134*
Tate, Richard
　See Masters, Anthony (Richard)
Tate, Suzanne 1930- *91*
Tatham, Betty *142*

Tatham, Campbell
　See Elting, Mary
Tatham, Julie
　See Tatham, Julie Campbell
Tatham, Julie Campbell 1908-1999 .... *80*
Tavares, Matt *159*
Tavares, Victor 1971- *176*
Taves, Isabella 1915- *27*
Taylor, Alastair 1959- *130*
Taylor, Andrew 1951- *70*
Taylor, Andrew John Robert
　See Taylor, Andrew
Taylor, Ann 1782-1866 .... *41*
　Brief entry *35*
Taylor, Audilee Boyd 1931- *59*
Taylor, Barbara J. 1927- *10*
Taylor, Ben
　See Strachan, Ian
Taylor, Carl 1937- *14*
Taylor, Cheryl Munro 1957- *96*
Taylor, Cora (Lorraine) 1936- *103*
　Earlier sketch in SATA *64*
　See also CLR *63*
Taylor, Dave 1948- *78*
Taylor, David
　See Taylor, Dave
Taylor, David 1900-1965 .... *10*
Taylor, Debbie A. 1955- *169*
Taylor, Elizabeth 1912-1975 .... *13*
Taylor, Florance Walton *9*
Taylor, Florence M(arian Tompkins)
　1892-1983 .... *9*
Taylor, G(raham) P(eter) 1959(?)- *156*
Taylor, Gage 1942-2000 .... *87*
Taylor, Graham
　See Taylor, G(raham) P(eter)
Taylor, Herb(ert Norman, Jr.) 1942-1987 ..... *22*
　Obituary *54*
Taylor, J. David
　See Taylor, Dave
Taylor, Jane 1783-1824 .... *41*
　Brief entry *35*
Taylor, Jerry D(uncan) 1938- *47*
Taylor, John Robert
　See Taylor, Andrew
Taylor, Judy
　See Hough, Judy Taylor
Taylor, Kenneth N. 1917-2005 .... *26*
Taylor, Kenneth Nathaniel
　See Taylor, Kenneth N.
Taylor, Kim *180*
Taylor, L(ester) B(arbour), Jr. 1932- *27*
Taylor, Lois Dwight Cole
　See Cole, Lois Dwight
Taylor, Louise Todd 1939- *47*
Taylor, Margaret 1950- *106*
Taylor, Mark 1927- *32*
　Brief entry *28*
Taylor, Mildred D. 1943- *135*
　See also CLR *90*
　See also SAAS *5*
Taylor, Mildred Delois
　See Taylor, Mildred D.
Taylor, Paula (Wright) 1942- *48*
　Brief entry *33*
Taylor, Robert Lewis 1912-1998 .... *10*
Taylor, Sean 1965- *192*
Taylor, Sydney (Brenner) 1904(?)-1978 .... *28*
　Obituary *26*
　Earlier sketch in SATA *1*
Taylor, Theodore 1921-2006 .... *128*
　Obituary *177*
　Earlier sketches in SATA *5, 54, 83*
　See also CLR *30*
　See also SAAS *4*
Taylor, William 1938- *164*
　Earlier sketches in SATA *78, 113*
　See also CLR *63*
Tazewell, Charles 1900-1972 .... *74*
Tchana, Katrin
　See Tchana, Katrin Hyman

Tchana, Katrin H.
See Tchana, Katrin Hyman
Tchana, Katrin Hyman 1963- 177
Earlier sketch in SATA 125
Tchekhov, Anton
See Chekhov, Anton (Pavlovich)
Tchen, Richard 120
Tchudi, Stephen N. 1942- 55
Teague, Bob
See Teague, Robert
Teague, Mark 1963- 170
Earlier sketches in SATA 68, 99
Teague, Mark Christopher
See Teague, Mark
Teague, Robert 1929- 32
Brief entry 31
Teal, Val 1902-1997 10
Obituary 114
Teal, Valentine M.
See Teal, Val
Teale, Edwin Way 1899-1980 7
Obituary 25
Teasdale, Sara 1884-1933 32
Tebbel, John (William) 1912-2004 26
Teensma, Lynne Bertrand
See Bertrand, Lynne
Tee-Van, Helen Damrosch 1893-1976 10
Obituary 27
Tegner, Bruce 1928- 62
Teitelbaum, Michael 1953- 116
Earlier sketch in SATA 59
Tejima
See Tejima, Keizaburo
Tejima, Keizaburo 1931- 139
See also CLR 20
Telander, Todd (G.) 1967- 88
Teleki, Geza 1943- 45
Telemaque, Eleanor Wong 1934- 43
Telescope, Tom
See Newbery, John
Tellis, Annabel 1967- 191
Temkin, Sara Anne Schlossberg 1913-1996 . 26
Temko, Florence 13
Tempest, Margaret Mary 1892-1982
Obituary 33
Templar, Maurice
See Groom, Arthur William
Temple, Arthur
See Northcott, (William) Cecil
Temple, Charles 1947- 79
Temple, Frances (Nolting) 1945-1995 85
Temple, Herbert 1919- 45
Temple, Paul
See McConnell, James Douglas Rutherford
Temple, William F(rederick) 1914-1989 107
Tenggren, Gustaf 1896-1970 18
Obituary 26
Tennant, Kylie 6
See Rodd, Kylie Tennant
Tennant, Veronica 1947- 36
Tenneshaw, S.M.
See Beaumont, Charles
and Garrett, (Gordon) Randall (Phillip)
and Silverberg, Robert
Tenniel, John 1820-1914 74
Brief entry 27
See also CLR 18
Tepper, Sheri S. 1929- 113
Terada, Alice M. 1928- 90
Terban, Marvin 1940- 54
Brief entry 45
ter Haar, Jaap 1922- 6
See Haar, Jaap ter
Terhune, Albert Payson 1872-1942 15
Terkel, Susan N(eiburg) 1948- 103
Earlier sketch in SATA 59
Terlouw, Jan (Cornelis) 1931- 30
Terrell, John Upton 1900-1988
Obituary 60
Terris, Susan 1937- 77
Earlier sketch in SATA 3

Terry, Luther L(eonidas) 1911-1985 11
Obituary 42
Terry, Margaret
See Dunnahoo, Terry Janson
Terry, Walter 1913-1982 14
Terzian, James P. 1915- 14
Tessendorf, K(enneth) C(harles)
1925-2003 75
Obituary 142
Tessler, Stephanie Gordon
See Gordon, Stephanie Jacob
Tester, Sylvia Root 1939- 64
Brief entry 37
Tether, (Cynthia) Graham 1950- 46
Brief entry 36
Tetzner, Lisa 1894-1963 169
Thacher, Mary McGrath 1933- 9
Thackeray, William Makepeace
1811-1863 23
Thaler, Michael C.
See Thaler, Mike
Thaler, Mike 1936- 93
Brief entry 47
Earlier sketch in SATA 56
Thaler, Shmuel 1958- 126
Earlier sketch in SATA 72
Thamer, Katie 1955- 42
Thane, Elswyth 1900-1984(?) 32
Tharp, Louise (Marshall) Hall 1898-1992 3
Obituary 129
Tharp, Tim 1957- 189
Thayer, Ernest Lawrence 1863-1940 60
Thayer, Jane
See Woolley, Catherine
Thayer, Marjorie 1908-1992 74
Brief entry 37
Thayer, Peter
See Wyler, Rose
Thelwell, Norman 1923-2004 14
Themerson, Stefan 1910-1988 65
Thermes, Jennifer 1966- 155
Theroux, Paul 1941- 109
Earlier sketch in SATA 44
Theroux, Paul Edward
See Theroux, Paul
Thesman, Jean 124
Earlier sketch in SATA 74
The Tjong-Khing
See Khing, T.T.
Thieda, Shirley Ann 1943- 13
Thiele, Colin 1920-2006 125
Earlier sketches in SATA 14, 72
See also CLR 27
See also SAAS 2
Thiele, Colin Milton
See Thiele, Colin
Thiesing, Lisa 1958- 159
Earlier sketch in SATA 95
Thimmesh, Catherine 189
Thiry, Joan (Marie) 1926- 45
Thistlethwaite, Miles 1945- 12
Thollander, Earl 1922- 22
Thomas, Abigail 1941- 112
Thomas, Andrea
See Hill, Margaret (Ohler)
Thomas, Art(hur Lawrence) 1952- 48
Brief entry 38
Thomas, Carroll
See Ratliff, Thomas M.
and Shmurak, Carole B.
Thomas, Dylan (Marlais) 1914-1953 60
Thomas, Egbert S.
See Ellis, Edward S(ylvester)
Thomas, Estelle Webb 1899-1982 26
Thomas, Frances 1943- 171
Earlier sketch in SATA 92
Thomas, H. C.
See Keating, Lawrence A.
Thomas, Ianthe 1951- 139
Brief entry 42
See also CLR 8

Thomas, Jane Resh 1936- 171
Earlier sketches in SATA 38, 90
Thomas, Jerry D. 1959- 91
Thomas, J.F.
See Fleming, Thomas
Thomas, Joan Gale
See Robinson, Joan (Mary)
G(ale Thomas)
Thomas, Joyce Carol 1938- 137
Autobiography Feature 137
Earlier sketches in SATA 40, 78, 123
See also CLR 19
See also SAAS 7
Thomas, Lowell Jackson, Jr. 1923- 15
Thomas, Margaret
See Thomas, Peggy
Thomas, Meredith 1963- 119
Thomas, Michael
See Wilks, Michael Thomas
Thomas, Middy 1931- 191
Thomas, Patricia J. 1934- 51
Thomas, Peggy 174
Thomas, Rob 1965- 97
Thomas, Scott 1959- 147
Thomas, Velma Maia 1955- 171
Thomas, Vernon (Arthur) 1934- 56
Thomas, Victoria
See DeWeese, Thomas Eugene
and Kugi, Constance Todd
Thomasma, Kenneth R. 1930- 90
Thomassie, Tynia 1959- 92
Thompson, Brenda 1935- 34
Thompson, Carol 1951- 189
Earlier sketch in SATA 85
Thompson, China
See Lewis, Mary (Christianna)
Thompson, Colin (Edward) 1942- 163
Earlier sketch in SATA 95
Thompson, David H(ugh) 1941- 17
Thompson, Eileen
See Panowski, Eileen Thompson
Thompson, George Selden 1929-1989 73
Obituary 63
Earlier sketch in SATA 4
See Selden, George
Thompson, Harlan (Howard) 1894-1987 10
Obituary 53
See Holt, Stephen
Thompson, Hilary 1943- 56
Brief entry 49
Thompson, Julian F(rancis) 1927- 155
Brief entry 40
Earlier sketches in SATA 55, 99
See also CLR 24
See also SAAS 13
Thompson, K(athryn Carolyn) Dyble
1952- 82
Thompson, Kay 1912(?)-1998 16
See also CLR 22
Thompson, Lauren 1962- 174
Earlier sketch in SATA 132
Thompson, Lauren Stevens
See Thompson, Lauren
Thompson, Megan Lloyd
See Lloyd, Megan
Thompson, Richard 1951- 184
Thompson, Ruth Plumly 1891-1976 66
Thompson, Sharon 1952- 119
Thompson, Sharon Elaine
See Thompson, Sharon
Thompson, Stith 1885-1976 57
Obituary 20
Thompson, Vivian L(aubach) 1911- 3
Thomson, Bill 1963- 187
Thomson, Celia
See Lynn, Tracy
Thomson, David (Robert Alexander)
1914-1988 40
Obituary 55
Thomson, Pat 1939- 122
Earlier sketch in SATA 77

Thomson, Peggy 1922- *31*
Thomson, Sarah L. 178
Thon, Melanie Rae 1957- *132*
Thong, Roseanne 174
Thorburn, John
  See Goldsmith, John Herman Thorburn
Thorn, John 1947- *59*
Thorndyke, Helen Louise 67
  Earlier sketch in SATA *1*
  See Benson, Mildred (Augustine Wirt)
Thorne, Ian
  See May, Julian
Thorne, Jean Wright
  See May, Julian
Thornhill, Jan 1955- *148*
  Earlier sketch in SATA *77*
Thornton, Hall
  See Silverberg, Robert
Thornton, W. B.
  See Burgess, Thornton Waldo
Thornton, Yvonne S(hirley) 1947- 96
Thorpe, E(ustace) G(eorge) 1916- 21
Thorpe, J. K.
  See Nathanson, Laura Walther
Thorvall, Kerstin 1925- 13
Thorvall-Falk, Kerstin
  See Thorvall, Kerstin
Thrasher, Crystal (Faye) 1921- 27
Threadgall, Colin 1941- 77
Three Little Pigs
  See Lantz, Francess L(in)
Thum, Gladys 1920- 26
Thum, Marcella 28
  Earlier sketch in SATA *3*
Thundercloud, Katherine
  See Witt, Shirley Hill
Thurber, James (Grover) 1894-1961 .... *13*
Thurlo, Aimee *161*
Thurlo, David *161*
Thurman, Judith 1946- 33
Thurman, Mark (Gordon Ian) 1948- 63
Thwaite, Ann (Barbara Harrop) 1932- 14
Tibbetts, Peggy 127
Tibbles, Jean-Paul 1958- 115
Tibo, Gilles 1951- *107*
  Earlier sketch in SATA *67*
Tiburzi, Bonnie 1948- 65
Ticheburn, Cheviot
  See Ainsworth, William Harrison
Tichenor, Tom 1923-1992 14
Tichnor, Richard 1959- 90
Tichy, William 1924- 31
Tickle, Jack
  See Chapman, Jane
Tiegreen, Alan F. 1935- 94
  Brief entry 36
Tierney, Frank M. 1930- 54
Tierney, Tom 1928- *113*
Tiffault, Benette W. 1955- 77
Tiller, Ruth L. 1949- 83
Tilley, Debbie *190*
Tilly, Nancy 1935- *62*
Tilton, Madonna Elaine 1929- *41*
Tilton, Rafael
  See Tilton, Madonna Elaine
Timberlake, Amy 156
Timberlake, Carolyn
  See Dresang, Eliza (Carolyn Timberlake)
Timmers, Leo 1970- *190*
Timmins, William F(rederick) 10
Tinbergen, Niko(laas) 1907-1988
  Obituary 60
Tiner, John Hudson 1944- 32
Tingle, Dolli (?)-
  See Brackett, Dolli Tingle
Tingle, Rebecca 174
Tingum, Janice 1958- *91*
Tinkelman, Murray 1933- *12*
Tinkham, Kelly A. 188
Tinkle, (Julien) Lon 1906-1980 36
Tinling, Marion (Rose) 1904- *140*

Tipene, Tim 1972- *141*
Tippett, James S(terling) 1885-1958 66
Tirone Smith, Mary-Ann 1944- 143
Titler, Dale M(ilton) 1926- 35
  Brief entry 28
Titmarsh, Michael Angelo
  See Thackeray, William Makepeace
Titus, Eve 1922- 2
Tjong Khing, The 1933- 76
Tobias, Katherine
  See Gottfried, Theodore Mark
Tobias, Tobi 1938- 82
  Earlier sketch in SATA *5*
  See also CLR 4
Todd, Anne Ophelia
  See Dowden, Anne Ophelia Todd
Todd, Barbara 1961- 173
Todd, Barbara K(eith) 1917- *10*
Todd, H(erbert) E(atton) 1908-1988 84
  Earlier sketch in SATA *11*
Todd, Loreto 1942- 30
Todd, Pamela 1950- *124*
Todd, Peter
  See Hamilton, Charles (Harold St. John)
Toews, Miriam 1964- *165*
Tofel, Richard J. 1957- *140*
Toft, Kim Michelle 1960- *170*
Tokunbo, Dimitrea 187
Tolan, Stephanie S. 1942- *142*
  Earlier sketches in SATA *38, 78*
Toland, John (Willard) 1912-2004 38
Tolbert, Steve 1944- *143*
Tolkien, John Ronald Reuel
  See Tolkien, J.R.R
Tolkien, J.R.R 1892-1973 .... *100*
  Obituary 24
  Earlier sketches in SATA *2, 32*
  See also CLR 56
Toll, Emily
  See Cannon, Eileen E(mily)
Toll, Nelly S. 1935- 78
Tolland, W. R.
  See Heitzmann, William Ray
Tolles, Martha 1921- 76
  Earlier sketch in SATA *8*
Tolliver, Ruby C(hangos) 1922- *110*
  Brief entry 41
  Earlier sketch in SATA *55*
Tolmie, Kenneth Donald 1941- 15
Tolstoi, Lev
  See Tolstoy, Leo (Nikolaevich)
Tolstoy, Leo (Nikolaevich) 1828-1910 26
  See Tolstoi, Lev
Tolstoy, Count Leo
  See Tolstoy, Leo (Nikolaevich)
Tomalin, Ruth 29
Tomaselli, Rosa
  See Pausacker, Jenny
Tomecek, Steve 172
Tomes, Margot (Ladd) 1917-1991 70
  Brief entry 27
  Obituary 69
  Earlier sketch in SATA *36*
Tomey, Ingrid 1943- 77
Tomfool
  See Farjeon, Eleanor
Tomkins, Jasper
  See Batey, Tom
Tomline, F. Latour
  See Gilbert, W(illiam) S(chwenck)
Tomlinson, Heather 192
Tomlinson, Jill 1931-1976 3
  Obituary 24
Tomlinson, Reginald R(obert) 1885-1979(?)
  Obituary 27
Tomlinson, Theresa 1946- 165
  Earlier sketch in SATA *103*
  See also CLR 60
Tompert, Ann 1918- *139*
  Earlier sketches in SATA *14, 89*
Toner, Raymond John 1908-1986 10

Tong, Gary S. 1942- 66
Tong, Paul 188
Took, Belladonna
  See Chapman, Vera (Ivy May)
Tooke, Louise Mathews 1950- 38
Tooke, Susan 173
Toonder, Martin
  See Groom, Arthur William
Toothaker, Roy Eugene 1928- 18
Tooze, Ruth (Anderson) 1892-1972 4
Topek, Susan Remick 1955- 78
Topping, Audrey R(onning) 1928- 14
Tor, Regina
  See Shekerjian, Regina Tor
Torbert, Floyd James 1922- 22
Torgersen, Don Arthur 1934- 55
  Brief entry 41
Torley, Luke
  See Blish, James (Benjamin)
Torres, Andres Segovia
  See Segovia, Andres
Torres, Daniel 1958- *102*
Torres, John A. 1965- *163*
  Earlier sketch in SATA *94*
Torres, John Albert
  See Torres, John A.
Torres, Laura 1967- *146*
  Earlier sketch in SATA *87*
Torres, Leyla 1960- *155*
Torrey, Rich
  See Torrey, Richard
Torrey, Richard *189*
Torrie, Malcolm
  See Mitchell, Gladys (Maude Winifred)
Toten, Teresa 1955- *99*
Totham, Mary
  See Breinburg, Petronella
Touponce, William F. 1948- *114*
Tournier, Michel 1924- 23
Tournier, Michel Edouard
  See Tournier, Michel
Towle, Wendy 1963- 79
Towne, Mary
  See Spelman, Mary
Townley, Rod
  See Townley, Roderick
Townley, Roderick 1942- *177*
Townsend, Brad W. 1962- *91*
Townsend, John Rowe 1922- *132*
  Autobiography Feature *132*
  Earlier sketches in SATA *4, 68*
  See also CLR 2
  See also SAAS 2
Townsend, Sue *93*
  Brief entry 48
  Earlier sketch in SATA *55*
  See Townsend, Susan Lilian
Townsend, Thomas L. 1944- 59
Townsend, Tom
  See Townsend, Thomas L.
Townson, Hazel 134
Toye, William Eldred 1926- 8
Traherne, Michael
  See Watkins-Pitchford, Denys James
Trahey, Jane 1923-2000 36
  Obituary 120
Trapani, Iza 1954- *116*
  Earlier sketch in SATA *80*
Trapp, Maria Augusta von 16
  See von Trapp, Maria Augusta
Travers, P(amela) L(yndon) 1899-1996 ...... *100*
  Obituary 90
  Earlier sketches in SATA *4, 54*
  See also CLR 93
  See also SAAS 2
Travis, Lucille *133*
  Earlier sketch in SATA *88*
Treadgold, Mary 1910- 49

Trease, (Robert) Geoffrey 1909-1998 .... *60*
  Obituary *101*
  Earlier sketch in SATA *2*
  See also CLR *42*
  See also SAAS *6*
Treat, Lawrence 1903-1998 .... *59*
Tredez, Alain 1926- *17*
Tredez, Denise 1930- *50*
Treece, Henry 1912-1966 .... *2*
  See also CLR *2*
Tregarthen, Enys
  See Sloggett, Nellie
Tregaskis, Richard 1916-1973 .... *3*
  Obituary *26*
Treherne, Katie Thamer 1955- *76*
Trell, Max 1900-1996 .... *14*
  Obituary *108*
Tremain, Ruthven 1922- *17*
Trembath, Don 1963- *168*
  Earlier sketch in SATA *96*
Tremens, Del
  See MacDonald, Amy
Trent, Robbie 1894-1988 .... *26*
Trent, Timothy
  See Malmberg, Carl
Treseder, Terry Walton 1956- *68*
Tresilian, (Cecil) Stuart 1891-(?) *40*
Tresselt, Alvin 1916-2000 .... *7*
  See also CLR *30*
Trevino, Elizabeth B(orton) de 1904- *29*
  Earlier sketch in SATA *1*
  See also SAAS *5*
Trevor, Elleston 1920-1995 .... *28*
  See Hall, Adam
Trevor, Frances
  See Teasdale, Sara
Trevor, Glen
  See Hilton, James
Trevor, (Lucy) Meriol 1919-2000 .... *113*
  Obituary *122*
  Earlier sketch in SATA *10*
Trez, Alain
  See Tredez, Alain
Trez, Denise
  See Tredez, Denise
Trezise, Percy (James) 1923-
  See CLR *41*
Triggs, Tony D. 1946- *70*
Trimble, Marshall I(ra) 1939- *93*
Trimby, Elisa 1948- *47*
  Brief entry *40*
Tring, A. Stephen
  See Meynell, Laurence Walter
Tripp, Eleanor B(aldwin) 1936- *4*
Tripp, Janet 1942- *108*
Tripp, Jenny *188*
Tripp, John
  See Moore, John Travers
Tripp, Nathaniel 1944- *101*
Tripp, Paul 1916-2002 .... *8*
  Obituary *139*
Tripp, Valerie 1951- *168*
  Earlier sketch in SATA *78*
Tripp, Wallace (Whitney) 1940- *31*
Trivelpiece, Laurel 1926- *56*
  Brief entry *46*
Trivett, Daphne Harwood 1940- *22*
Trivizas, Eugene 1946- *84*
Trnka, Jiri 1912-1969 .... *43*
  Brief entry *32*
Trollope, Anthony 1815-1882 .... *22*
Trost, Lucille W(ood) 1938- *149*
  Earlier sketch in SATA *12*
Trott, Betty 1933- *91*
Trotter, Deborah W. *184*
Trotter, Grace V(iolet) 1900-1991 .... *10*
Trottier, Maxine 1950- *175*
  Earlier sketch in SATA *131*
Troughton, Joanna (Margaret) 1947- *37*
Trout, Kilgore
  See Farmer, Philip Jose

Trout, Richard E. *123*
Trudeau, Garretson Beekman
  See Trudeau, G.B.
Trudeau, Garry
  See Trudeau, G.B.
Trudeau, Garry B.
  See Trudeau, G.B.
Trudeau, G.B. 1948- *168*
  Earlier sketch in SATA *35*
  See Trudeau, Garry B.
Trueit, Trudi
  See Trueit, Trudi Strain
Trueit, Trudi Strain 1963- *179*
Trueman, Matthew *183*
Trueman, Terry 1947- *178*
  Earlier sketch in SATA *132*
Truesdell, Judy
  See Mecca, Judy Truesdell
Truesdell, Sue
  See Truesdell, Susan G.
Truesdell, Susan G. *108*
  Brief entry *45*
Trumbauer, Lisa (Trutkoff) 1963- *149*
Truss, Jan 1925- *35*
Tryon, Leslie *139*
Tubb, Jonathan N. 1951- *78*
Tubby, I. M.
  See Kraus, (Herman) Robert
Tucker, Caroline
  See Nolan, Jeannette Covert
Tudor, Edward
  See Browne, Anthony
Tudor, Tasha 1915-2008 .... *160*
  Earlier sketches in SATA *20, 69*
  See also CLR *13*
Tuerk, Hanne 1951- *71*
Tulloch, Richard 1949- *180*
  Earlier sketch in SATA *76*
Tulloch, Richard George
  See Tulloch, Richard
Tulloch, Shirley *169*
Tully, John (Kimberley) 1923- *14*
Tumanov, Vladimir A. 1961- *138*
Tung, Angela 1972- *109*
Tunis, Edwin (Burdett) 1897-1973 .... *28*
  Obituary *24*
  Earlier sketch in SATA *1*
  See also CLR *2*
Tunis, John R(oberts) 1889-1975 .... *37*
  Brief entry *30*
Tunnell, Michael
  See Tunnell, Michael O('Grady)
Tunnell, Michael O('Grady) 1950- *157*
  Earlier sketch in SATA *103*
Tunnicliffe, C(harles) F(rederick)
  1901-1979 .... *62*
Turck, Mary C. 1950- *144*
Turk, Hanne
  See Tuerk, Hanne
Turk, Ruth 1917- *82*
Turkle, Brinton 1915- *79*
  Earlier sketch in SATA *2*
Turlington, Bayly 1919-1977 .... *5*
  Obituary *52*
Turnbull, Agnes Sligh 1888-1982 .... *14*
Turnbull, Ann 1943- *160*
  Earlier sketch in SATA *18*
Turnbull, Ann Christine
  See Turnbull, Ann
Turner, Alice K. 1940- *10*
Turner, Ann 1945- *188*
  Autobiography Feature *188*
  Earlier sketches in SATA *14, 77, 113, 178*
Turner, Ann Warren
  See Turner, Ann
Turner, Bonnie 1932- *75*
Turner, Elizabeth 1774-1846
  See YABC *2*
Turner, Glennette Tilley 1933- *183*
  Earlier sketch in SATA *71*

Turner, Josie
  See Crawford, Phyllis
Turner, Megan Whalen 1965- *174*
  Earlier sketch in SATA *94*
Turner, Philip (William) 1925- *83*
  Earlier sketch in SATA *11*
  See also CLR *89*
  See also SAAS *6*
Turner, Robyn 1947- *77*
Turner, Sheila R.
  See Seed, Sheila Turner
Turngren, Annette 1902(?)-1980
  Obituary *23*
Turngren, Ellen (?)-1964 .... *3*
Turska, Krystyna (Zofia) 1933- *31*
  Brief entry *27*
Turteltaub, H.N.
  See Turtledove, Harry
Turtledove, Harry 1949- *166*
  Earlier sketch in SATA *116*
Turtledove, Harry Norman
  See Turtledove, Harry
Tusa, Tricia 1960- *111*
  Earlier sketch in SATA *72*
Tusiani, Joseph 1924- *45*
Twain, Mark
  See CLR *66*
  See Clemens, Samuel Langhorne
Tweit, Susan J 1956- *94*
Tweit, Susan Joan
  See Tweit, Susan J
Tweton, D. Jerome 1933- *48*
Twinem, Neecy 1958- *92*
Tworkov, Jack 1900-1982 .... *47*
  Obituary *31*
Tyche
  See Papademetriou, Lisa
Tyers, Jenny 1969- *89*
Tyers, Kathy 1952- *82*
Tyler, Anne 1941- *173*
  Earlier sketches in SATA *7, 90*
Tyler, Linda
  See Tyler, Linda W(agner)
Tyler, Linda W(agner) 1952- *65*
Tyler, Vicki 1952- *64*
Tyne, Joel
  See Schembri, Jim
Tyrrell, Frances 1959- *107*

U

Ubell, Earl 1926-2007 .... *4*
  Obituary *182*
Uchida, Yoshiko 1921-1992 .... *53*
  Obituary *72*
  Earlier sketch in SATA *1*
  See also CLR *56*
  See also SAAS *1*
Udall, Jan Beaney 1938- *10*
Uden, (Bernard Gilbert) Grant 1910- *26*
Uderzo, Albert 1927-
  See CLR *37*
Udovic, David 1950- *189*
Udry, Janice May 1928- *152*
  Earlier sketch in SATA *4*
Uegaki, Chieri 1969- *153*
Ueno, Noriko
  See Nakae, Noriko
Uhlberg, Myron *174*
Uhlig, Susan 1955- *129*
Ulam, S(tanislaw) M(arcin) 1909-1984 .... *51*
Ullman, James Ramsey 1907-1971 .... *7*
Ulm, Robert 1934-1977 .... *17*
Ulmer, Louise 1943- *53*
Ulyatt, Kenneth 1920- *14*
Umansky, Kaye 1946- *188*
  Earlier sketch in SATA *158*
Unada
  See Gliewe, Unada (Grace)

Uncle Carter
  See Boucher, (Clarence) Carter
Uncle Eric
  See Maybury, Richard J.
Uncle Gus
  See Rey, H(ans) A(ugusto)
Uncle Mac
  See McCulloch, Derek (Ivor Breashur)
Uncle Ray
  See Coffman, Ramon Peyton
Uncle Shelby
  See Silverstein, Shel
Underhill, Alice Mertie (Waterman)
  1900-1971 .... *10*
Underhill, Liz 1948- *53*
  Brief entry *49*
Unger, Harlow G. 1931- *75*
Unger, Jim 1937- *67*
Ungerer, (Jean) Thomas 1931- *106*
  Earlier sketches in SATA *5, 33*
  See Ungerer, Tomi
Ungerer, Tomi 1931-
  See CLR *77*
  See Ungerer, (Jean) Thomas
Unkelbach, Kurt 1913-1992 .... *4*
Unnerstad, Edith (Totterman) 1900-1982 .... *3*
  See also CLR *36*
Unobagha, Uzo *139*
Unrau, Ruth 1922- *9*
Unstead, R(obert) J(ohn) 1915-1988 .... *12*
  Obituary *56*
Unsworth, Walt(er) 1928- *4*
Untermeyer, Bryna Ivens 1909-1985 .... *61*
Untermeyer, Louis 1885-1977 .... *37*
  Obituary *26*
  Earlier sketch in SATA *2*
Unwin, David S(torr) 1918- *14*
Unwin, Nora S(picer) 1907-1982 .... *3*
  Obituary *49*
Unzner, Christa 1958- *141*
  Earlier sketch in SATA *80*
Unzner-Fischer, Christa
  See Unzner, Christa
Updale, Eleanor 1953- *175*
Updyke, Rosemary K. 1924- *103*
Upitis, Alvis *109*
Urban, Helle (Denise) 1957- *149*
Urbanovic, Jackie *189*
Ure, Jean 1943- *192*
  Autobiography Feature *192*
  Earlier sketches in SATA *48, 78, 129*
  See also CLR *34*
  See also SAAS *14*
U'Ren, Andrea 1968- *142*
Uris, Leon 1924-2003 .... *49*
  Obituary *146*
Uris, Leon Marcus
  See Uris, Leon
Ursu, Anne *177*
Ury, Allen B. 1954- *98*
Uschan, Michael V. 1948- *129*
Usher, Margo Scegge
  See McHargue, Georgess
Uslan, Michael E. 1951- *169*
Uston, Ken(neth Senzo) 1935-1987 .... *65*
Uttley, Alice Jane (Taylor) 1884-1976 .... *88*
  Obituary *26*
  Earlier sketch in SATA *3*
  See Uttley, Alison
Uttley, Alison
  See Uttley, Alice Jane (Taylor)
Utz, Lois (Marie) 1932-1986 .... *5*
  Obituary *50*

V

Vaeth, J(oseph) Gordon 1921- *17*
Vagin, Vladimir (Vasilevich) 1937- *142*
Vail, Rachel 1966- *163*
  Earlier sketch in SATA *94*
Vainio, Pirkko 1957- *123*
  Earlier sketch in SATA *76*
Valen, Nanine 1950- *21*
Valencak, Hannelore *42*
  See Mayer, Hannelore Valencak
Valens, Amy 1946- *70*
Valens, E(vans) G(ladstone), Jr. 1920-1992 ... *1*
Valentine, Johnny *72*
Valerio, Geraldo 1970- *180*
Valgardson, W(illiam) D(empsey) 1939- *151*
  Earlier sketch in SATA *101*
Valleau, Emily 1925- *51*
Van Abbe, Salaman 1883-1955 .... *18*
Van Allsburg, Chris 1949- *156*
  Earlier sketches in SATA *37, 53, 105*
  See also CLR *113*
Van Anrooy, Francine 1924- *2*
Van Anrooy, Frans
  See Van Anrooy, Francine
Vanasse, Deb 1957- *170*
Vance, Eleanor Graham 1908-1985 .... *11*
Vance, Gerald
  See Garrett, (Gordon) Randall (Phillip)
  and Silverberg, Robert
Vance, Marguerite 1889-1965 .... *29*
VanCleave, Janice 1942- *116*
  Autobiography Feature *123*
  Earlier sketch in SATA *75*
Vandenburg, Mary Lou 1943- *17*
Vander Boom, Mae M. *14*
Vander-Els, Betty 1936- *9*
van der Heide, Iris 1970- *183*
van der Linde, Laurel 1952- *78*
van der Meer, Ron 1945- *98*
Van der Veer, Judy 1912-1982 .... *4*
  Obituary *33*
Vanderwerff, Corrine 1939- *117*
Vander Zee, Ruth *159*
Vande Velde, Vivian 1951- *141*
  Earlier sketches in SATA *62, 95*
Vandivert, Rita (Andre) 1905-1986 .... *21*
Van Draanen, Wendelin *122*
Van Dusen, Chris *173*
Van Duyn, Janet 1910- *18*
Van Dyne, Edith
  See Baum, L(yman) Frank
  and Sampson, Emma (Keats) Speed
  and van Zantwijk, Rudolf
  (Alexander Marinus)
Vane, Mitch
  See Vane, Mitchelle
Vane, Mitchelle *176*
van Frankenhuyzen, Gijsbert 1951- *132*
Van Genechten, Guido 1957- *165*
van Haeringen, Annemarie *193*
Van Hook, Beverly H. 1941- *99*
Van Horn, William 1939- *43*
van Hout, Mies 1962- *178*
Van Iterson, S(iny) R(ose) *26*
Van Kampen, Vlasta 1943- *163*
  Earlier sketch in SATA *54*
Van Laan, Nancy 1939- *105*
van Lawick-Goodall, Jane
  See Goodall, Jane
Van Leeuwen, Jean 1937- *141*
  Autobiography Feature *141*
  Earlier sketches in SATA *6, 82, 132*
  See also SAAS *8*
van Lhin, Erik
  See del Rey, Lester
Van Loon, Hendrik Willem 1882-1944 .... *18*
van Ommen, Sylvia 1978- *186*
VanOosting, James 1951- *170*
Van Orden, M(erton) D(ick) 1921- *4*
Van Patter, Bruce *183*

Van Rensselaer, Alexander (Taylor
  Mason) 1892-1962 .... *14*
Van Riper, Guernsey, Jr. 1909-1995 .... *3*
van Rossum, Heleen 1962- *174*
Van Rynbach, Iris 1952- *102*
Vansant, Rhonda Joy Edwards 1950- *92*
Van Steenwyk, Elizabeth (Ann) 1928- *89*
  Earlier sketch in SATA *34*
Van Stockum, Hilda 1908-2006 .... *5*
  Obituary *179*
Van Tuyl, Barbara 1940- *11*
van Vogt, A(lfred) E(lton) 1912-2000 .... *14*
  Obituary *124*
Van Woerkom, Dorothy (O'Brien)
  1924-1996 .... *21*
Van Wormer, Joe
  See Van Wormer, Joseph Edward
Van Wormer, Joseph Edward 1913-1998 ...... *35*
Van Wright, Cornelius *173*
Van Zwienen, Ilse Charlotte Koehn
  1929-1991 .... *34*
  Brief entry *28*
  Obituary *67*
Van Zyle, Jon 1942- *176*
  Earlier sketch in SATA *84*
Varela, Barry *180*
Varga, Judy
  See Stang, Judit
Varley, Dimitry V. 1906-1984 .... *10*
Varley, Susan 1961- *134*
  Earlier sketch in SATA *63*
Vasileva, Tatiana
  See Wassiljewa, Tatjana
Vasiliev, Valery 1949- *80*
Vasilieva, Tatiana
  See Wassiljewa, Tatjana
Vasiliu, Mircea 1920- *2*
Vass, George 1927- *57*
  Brief entry *31*
Vaughan, Carter A.
  See Gerson, Noel Bertram
Vaughan, Harold Cecil 1923- *14*
Vaughan, Marcia (K.) 1951- *159*
  Earlier sketches in SATA *60, 95*
Vaughan, Richard 1947- *87*
Vaughan, Sam(uel) 1928- *14*
Vaughn, Ruth 1935- *14*
Vautier, Ghislaine 1932- *53*
Vavra, Robert James 1935- *8*
Vecsey, George Spencer 1939- *9*
Vedral, Joyce L(auretta) 1943- *65*
Vega, Denise B. *174*
  See Vega, Denise
Veglahn, Nancy (Crary) 1937- *5*
Vejjajiva, Jane 1963- *189*
Velasquez, Eric *192*
Velasquez, Gloria (Louise) 1949- *113*
  See Velasquez(-Trevino), Gloria
  (Louise)
Velthuijs, Max 1923-2005 .... *110*
  Obituary *160*
  Earlier sketch in SATA *53*
Venable, Alan (Hudson) 1944- *8*
Venezia, Mike 1945- *150*
Ventura, Anthony
  See Pellowski, Michael (Joseph)
Ventura, Piero (Luigi) 1937- *61*
  Brief entry *43*
  See also CLR *16*
Vequin, Capini
  See Quinn, Elisabeth
Verba, Joan Marie 1953- *78*
Verboven, Agnes 1951- *103*
verDorn, Bethea (Stewart) 1952- *76*
Verissimo, Erico (Lopes) 1905-1975 .... *113*
Verne, Jules (Gabriel) 1828-1905 .... *21*
  See also CLR *88*
Verner, Gerald 1897(?)-1980
  Obituary *25*
Verney, John 1913-1993 .... *14*
  Obituary *75*

Verniero, Joan C. 1949- *181*
Vernon, (Elda) Louise A(nderson) 1914- *14*
Vernon, Rosemary
  See Smith, Susan Vernon
Vernor, D.
  See Casewit, Curtis W(erner)
Verr, Harry Coe
  See Kunhardt, Edith
Verral, Charles Spain 1904-1990 .... *11*
  Obituary *65*
Verrone, Robert J. 1935(?)-1984
  Obituary *39*
Versace, Marie Teresa Rios 1917- *2*
Vertreace, Martha M(odena) 1945- *78*
Vesey, A(manda) 1939- *62*
Vesey, Mark (David) 1958- *123*
Vesey, Paul
  See Allen, Samuel W(ashington)
Vestergaard, Hope *178*
Vestly, Anne-Cath(arina) 1920- *14*
  See also CLR 99
Vevers, (Henry) Gwynne 1916-1988 .... *45*
  Obituary *57*
Viator, Vacuus
  See Hughes, Thomas
Vicar, Henry
  See Felsen, Henry Gregor
Vick, Helen Hughes 1950- *88*
Vicker, Angus
  See Felsen, Henry Gregor
Vickers, Sheena 1960- *94*
Vickery, Kate
  See Kennedy, T.A.
Victor, Edward 1914- *3*
Victor, Joan Berg 1942- *30*
Vidrine, Beverly Barras 1938- *188*
  Earlier sketch in SATA 103
Viereck, Ellen K. 1928- *14*
Viereck, Phillip 1925- *3*
Viertel, Janet 1915- *10*
Vigliante, Mary
  See Szydlowski, Mary Vigliante
Vigna, Judith 1936- *102*
  Earlier sketch in SATA 15
Viguers, Ruth Hill 1903-1971 .... *6*
Villareal, Ray *187*
Villasenor, Edmundo
  See Villasenor, Victor
Villasenor, Victor 1940- *171*
Villasenor, Victor E. 1940-
  See Villasenor, Victor
Villasenor, Victor Edmundo
  See Villasenor, Victor
Villiard, Paul 1910-1974 .... *51*
  Obituary *20*
Villiers, Alan (John) 1903-1982 .... *10*
Vilott, Rhondi
  See Salsitz, Rhondi Vilott
Vincent, Eric Douglas 1953- *40*
Vincent, Erin 1969- *188*
Vincent, Felix 1946- *41*
Vincent, Gabrielle 1928-2000 .... *121*
  Earlier sketch in SATA 61
  See also CLR 13
Vincent, Mary Keith
  See St. John, Wylly Folk
Vincent, William R.
  See Heitzmann, William Ray
Vinegar, Tom
  See Gregg, Andrew K.
Vinest, Shaw
  See Longyear, Barry B(rookes)
Vinge, Joan (Carol) D(ennison) 1948- *113*
  Earlier sketch in SATA 36
Vining, Elizabeth Gray 1902-1999 .... *6*
  Obituary *117*
  See Gray, Elizabeth Janet
Vinson, Kathryn 1911-1995 .... *21*
Vinton, Iris 1906(?)-1988 .... *24*
  Obituary *55*
Viola, Herman J(oseph) 1938- *126*

Viorst, Judith 1931- *172*
  Earlier sketches in SATA 7, 70, 123
  See also CLR 90
Vip
  See Partch, Virgil Franklin II
Vipont, Charles
  See Foulds, Elfrida Vipont
Vipont, Elfrida
  See Foulds, Elfrida Vipont
Viscott, David S(teven) 1938-1996 .... *65*
Visser, W(illem) F(rederik) H(endrik)
  1900-1968 .... *10*
Vitale, Stefano 1958- *180*
  Earlier sketch in SATA 114
Vivas, Julie 1947- *96*
Vivelo, Jackie 1943- *63*
Vivelo, Jacqueline J.
  See Vivelo, Jackie
Vivelo, Jacqueline Jean
  See Vivelo, Jackie
Vizzini, Ned 1981- *179*
  Earlier sketch in SATA 125
Vlahos, Olivia 1924- *31*
Vlasic, Bob
  See Hirsch, Phil
Voake, Charlotte *180*
  Earlier sketch in SATA 114
Voake, Steve 1961- *178*
Vo-Dinh, Mai 1933- *16*
Vogel, Carole Garbuny 1951- *105*
  Earlier sketch in SATA 70
Vogel, Ilse-Margret 1918- *14*
Vogel, John H., Jr. 1950- *18*
Vogt, Esther Loewen 1915-1999 .... *14*
Vogt, Gregory L. *94*
Vogt, Marie Bollinger 1921- *45*
Voight, Virginia Frances 1909-1989 .... *8*
Voigt, Cynthia 1942- *160*
  Brief entry *33*
  Earlier sketches in SATA 48, 79, 116
  See also CLR 48
Voigt, Erna 1925- *35*
Voigt-Rother, Erna
  See Voigt, Erna
Vojtech, Anna 1946- *108*
  Earlier sketch in SATA 42
Vollstadt, Elizabeth Weiss 1942- *121*
Volponi, Paul *175*
Volting, Dr. R.E.
  See Lerangis, Peter
Von Ahnen, Katherine 1922- *93*
von Buhler, Cynthia *185*
Vondra, J. Gert
  See Vondra, Josef
Vondra, Josef 1941- *121*
Vondra, Josef Gert
  See Vondra, Josef
Von Gunden, Kenneth 1946- *113*
Von Hagen, Victor Wolfgang 1908-1985 ...... *29*
von Klopp, Vahrah
  See Malvern, Gladys
von Schmidt, Eric 1931-2007 .... *50*
  Brief entry *36*
  Obituary *181*
von Storch, Anne B. 1910- *1*
von Ziegesar, Cecily 1970- *161*
Vos, Ida 1931-2006 .... *121*
  Earlier sketch in SATA 69
  See also CLR 85
Vosburgh, Leonard (W.) 1912- *15*
Voyle, Mary
  See Manning, Rosemary (Joy)
Vrettos, Adrienne Maria *187*
Vriens, Jacques 1946- *151*
Vugteveen, Verna Aardema *107*
  Obituary *119*
  Earlier sketches in SATA 4, 68
  See also CLR 17
  See also SAAS 8
  See Aardema, Verna

Vulture, Elizabeth T.
  See Gilbert, Suzie
Vuong, Lynette Dyer 1938- *110*
  Earlier sketch in SATA 60

W

Waas, Uli
  See Waas-Pommer, Ulrike
Waas-Pommer, Ulrike 1949- *85*
Waber, Bernard 1924- *155*
  Brief entry *40*
  Earlier sketches in SATA 47, 95
  See also CLR 55
Wachtel, Shirley Russak 1951- *88*
Wachter, Oralee (Roberts) 1935- *61*
  Brief entry *51*
Waddell, Evelyn Margaret 1918- *10*
Waddell, Martin 1941- *129*
  Autobiography Feature *129*
  Earlier sketches in SATA 43, 81, 127
  See also CLR 31
  See also SAAS 15
Waddy, Lawrence (Heber) 1914- *91*
Wade, Mary Dodson 1930- *151*
  Earlier sketch in SATA 79
Wade, Suzanne
  See Kirby, Susan E.
Wade, Theodore E., Jr. 1936- *37*
Wademan, Peter John 1946- *122*
Wademan, Spike
  See Wademan, Peter John
Wadsworth, Ginger 1945- *157*
  Earlier sketch in SATA 103
Wagenheim, Kal 1935- *21*
Wagner, Michele R. 1975- *157*
Wagner, Sharon B. 1936- *4*
Wagoner, David (Russell) 1926- *14*
Wahl, Jan (Boyer) 1933- *132*
  Earlier sketches in SATA 2, 34, 73
  See also SAAS 3
Wahl, Mats 1945- *186*
Waide, Jan 1952- *29*
Wainscott, John Milton 1910-1981 .... *53*
Wainwright, Richard M. 1935- *91*
Wainwright, Ruth
  See Symes, Ruth Louise
Wait, Lea 1946- *137*
Waite, Judy *174*
Waite, Judy Bernard
  See Bernard, Patricia
Waite, Michael P(hillip) 1960- *101*
Waite, P(eter) B(usby) 1922- *64*
Waites, Joan C. *187*
Waitley, Douglas 1927- *30*
Wakefield, Jean L.
  See Laird, Jean E(louise)
Wakin, Daniel (Joseph) 1961- *84*
Wakin, Edward 1927- *37*
Wakiyama, Hanako 1966- *192*
Walck, Henry Z. 1908(?)-1984
  Obituary *40*
Walden, Amelia Elizabeth *3*
Walden, Mark *188*
Waldherr, Kris 1963- *76*
Waldman, Bruce 1949- *15*
Waldman, Neil 1947- *142*
  Earlier sketches in SATA 51, 94
Waldron, Ann Wood 1924- *16*
Waldron, Kathleen Cook *176*
Walgren, Judy 1963- *118*
Walker, Addison
  See Walker, (Addison) Mort
Walker, Alice 1944- *31*
Walker, Alice Malsenior
  See Walker, Alice
Walker, Barbara (Jeanne) K(erlin) 1921- *80*
  Earlier sketch in SATA 4
Walker, Barbara M(uhs) 1928- *57*

Walker, (James) Braz(elton) 1934-1983 45
Walker, David G(ordon) 1926- 60
Walker, David Harry 1911-1992 8
    Obituary 71
Walker, Diana 1925- 9
Walker, Diane Marie Catherine
    See Walker, Kate
Walker, Dick
    See Pellowski, Michael (Joseph)
Walker, Frank 1931-2000 36
Walker, Holly Beth
    See Bond, Gladys Baker
Walker, Kate 1950- 165
    Earlier sketch in SATA 82
Walker, Kathrine Sorley
    See Sorley Walker, Kathrine
Walker, Lou Ann 1952- 66
    Brief entry 53
Walker, Louise Jean 1891-1976
    Obituary 35
Walker, Mary Alexander 1927- 61
Walker, Mildred
    See Schemm, Mildred Walker
Walker, (Addison) Mort 1923- 8
Walker, Pamela 1948- 142
    Earlier sketch in SATA 24
Walker, Paul Robert 1953- 154
Walker, Robert W(ayne) 1948- 66
Walker, Sally M(acArt) 1954- 135
Walker, Stephen J. 1951- 12
Walker-Blondell, Becky 1951- 89
Wallace, Barbara Brooks 1922- 136
    Earlier sketches in SATA 4, 78
    See also SAAS 17
Wallace, Beverly Dobrin 1921- 19
Wallace, Bill 1947- 169
    Brief entry 47
    Earlier sketches in SATA 53, 101
Wallace, Daisy
    See Cuyler, Margery S(tuyvesant)
Wallace, Ian 1950- 141
    Earlier sketches in SATA 53, 56
    See also CLR 37
Wallace, John 1966- 155
    Earlier sketch in SATA 105
Wallace, John A(dam) 1915-2004 3
    Obituary 155
Wallace, Karen 1951- 188
    Earlier sketches in SATA 83, 139
Wallace, Nancy Elizabeth 1948- 186
    Earlier sketch in SATA 141
Wallace, Nigel
    See Hamilton, Charles (Harold St. John)
Wallace, Paula S. 153
Wallace, Rich 1957- 158
    Earlier sketch in SATA 117
Wallace, Robert 1932-1999 47
    Brief entry 37
Wallace, William Keith
    See Wallace, Bill
Wallace-Brodeur, Ruth 1941- 169
    Brief entry 41
    Earlier sketches in SATA 51, 88
Wallenta, Adam 1974- 123
Waller, Leslie 1923-2007 20
Walley, Byron
    See Card, Orson Scott
Wallis, Diz 1949- 77
Wallis, G. McDonald
    See Campbell, Hope
Wallner, Alexandra 1946- 156
    Brief entry 41
    Earlier sketches in SATA 51, 98
Wallner, John C. 1945- 133
    Earlier sketches in SATA 10, 51
Wallower, Lucille 11
Walrod, Amy 1973(?)- 182
Walsh, Ann 1942- 176
    Earlier sketch in SATA 62
Walsh, Ellen Stoll 1942- 147
    Earlier sketches in SATA 49, 99

Walsh, George Johnston 1889-1981 53
Walsh, Gillian Paton
    See Paton Walsh, Jill
Walsh, Jill Paton
    See CLR 128
    See Paton Walsh, Jill
Walsh, Joanna 1970- 182
Walsh, Lawrence 1942- 170
Walsh, Mary Caswell 1949- 118
Walsh, Suella 170
Walsh, V. L.
    See Walsh, Vivian
Walsh, Vivian 1960- 120
Walsh Shepherd, Donna 1948- 78
Walter, Frances V. 1923- 71
Walter, Mildred Pitts 1922- 133
    Brief entry 45
    Earlier sketch in SATA 69
    See also CLR 61
    See also SAAS 12
Walter, Villiam Christian
    See Andersen, Hans Christian
Walter, Virginia 134
    See Walter, Virginia A.
Walters, Audrey 1929- 18
Walters, Celeste 1938- 126
Walters, Eric (Robert) 1957- 155
    Earlier sketch in SATA 99
Walters, Helen B. (?)-1987
    Obituary 50
Walters, Hugh
    See Hughes, Walter (Llewellyn)
Walther, Thomas A. 1950- 31
Walther, Tom
    See Walther, Thomas A.
Waltner, Elma 1912-1987 40
Waltner, Willard H. 1909- 40
Walton, Darwin McBeth 1926- 119
Walton, Fiona L. M. 1959- 89
Walton, Richard J. 1928- 4
Walton, Rick 1957- 151
    Earlier sketch in SATA 101
Waltrip, Lela (Kingston) 1904-1995 9
Waltrip, Mildred 1911- 37
Waltrip, Rufus (Charles) 1898-1988 9
Walworth, Nancy Zinsser 1917- 14
Wangerin, Walter, Jr. 1944- 98
    Brief entry 37
    Earlier sketch in SATA 45
Waniek, Marilyn Nelson 1946- 60
    See Nelson, Marilyn
Wannamaker, Bruce
    See Moncure, Jane Belk
Warbler, J. M.
    See Cocagnac, Augustin Maurice(-Jean)
Warburg, Sandol Stoddard 14
    See Stoddard, Sandol
Ward, E. D.
    See Gorey, Edward (St. John)
    and Lucas, E(dward) V(errall)
Ward, Ed
    See Stratemeyer, Edward L.
Ward, Helen 1962- 144
    Earlier sketch in SATA 72
Ward, Jay 1920-1989
    Obituary 63
Ward, Jennifer 1963- 146
Ward, John (Stanton) 1917- 42
Ward, Jonas
    See Ard, William (Thomas)
    and Cox, William R(obert)
    and Garfield, Brian (Francis Wynne)
Ward, Lynd (Kendall) 1905-1985 36
    Obituary 42
    Earlier sketch in SATA 2
Ward, Martha (Eads) 5
Ward, Melanie
    See Curtis, Richard (Alan)
    and Lynch, Marilyn
Ward, Nick 190

Ward, Tom
    See Stratemeyer, Edward L.
Wardell, Dean
    See Prince, J(ack) H(arvey)
Wardlaw, Lee 1955- 115
    Earlier sketch in SATA 79
Ware, Cheryl 1963- 101
Ware, Chris 1967- 140
Ware, Leon (Vernon) 1909-1976 4
Wargin, Kathy-jo 1965- 145
Warhola, James 1955- 187
Warner, Frank A. 67
    Earlier sketch in SATA 1
Warner, Gertrude Chandler 1890-1979 9
    Obituary 73
Warner, J(ohn) F. 1929- 75
Warner, Lucille Schulberg 30
Warner, Matt
    See Fichter, George S.
Warner, Oliver (Martin Wilson) 1903-1976 . 29
Warner, Sally 1946- 131
Warner, Sunny (B.) 1931- 108
Warnes, Tim 1971- 166
    Earlier sketch in SATA 116
Warnes, Timothy
    See Warnes, Tim
Warnick, Elsa 1942- 113
Warren, Andrea 1946- 98
Warren, Betsy
    See Warren, Elizabeth Avery
Warren, Billy
    See Warren, William Stephen
Warren, Cathy 1951- 62
    Brief entry 46
Warren, Elizabeth
    See Supraner, Robyn
Warren, Elizabeth Avery 1916- 46
    Brief entry 38
Warren, Jackie M. 1953- 135
Warren, Joshua P(aul) 1976- 107
Warren, Joyce W(illiams) 1935- 18
Warren, Mary Phraner 1929- 10
Warren, Robert Penn 1905-1989 46
    Obituary 63
Warren, Scott S. 1957- 79
Warren, William Stephen 1882-1968 9
Warrick, Patricia Scott 1925- 35
Warriner, John 1907(?)-1987
    Obituary 53
Warsh
    See Warshaw, Jerry
Warshaw, Jerry 1929- 30
Warshaw, Mary 1931- 89
Warshofsky, Fred 1931- 24
Warshofsky, Isaac
    See Singer, Isaac Bashevis
Wartski, Maureen (Ann Crane) 1940- 50
    Brief entry 37
Warwick, Alan R(oss) 1900-1973 42
Wa-sha-quon-asin
    See Belaney, Archibald Stansfeld
Wa-Sha-Quon-Asin
    See Belaney, Archibald Stansfeld
Washburn, Bradford 1910-2007 38
    Obituary 181
Washburn, Henry Bradford, Jr.
    See Washburn, Bradford
Washburn, Jan(ice) 1926- 63
Washburn, Lucia 193
Washburne, Carolyn Kott 1944- 86
Washburne, Heluiz Chandler 1892-1970 10
    Obituary 26
Washington, Booker T(aliaferro)
    1856-1915 28
Washington, Donna L. 1967- 159
    Earlier sketch in SATA 98
Wasserstein, Wendy 1950-2006 94
    Obituary 174
Wassiljewa, Tatjana 1928- 106

Watanabe, Shigeo 1928- *131*
    Brief entry *32*
    Earlier sketch in SATA *39*
    See also CLR 8
Waters, John F(rederick) 1930- *4*
Waters, Tony 1958- *75*
Waterton, Betty (Marie) 1923- *99*
    Brief entry *34*
    Earlier sketch in SATA *37*
Watkins, Dawn L. *126*
Watkins, Gloria Jean
    See hooks, bell
Watkins, Lois 1930- *88*
Watkins, Peter 1934- *66*
Watkins, Yoko Kawashima 1933- *93*
Watkins-Pitchford, Denys James
    1905-1990 .... *87*
    Obituary *66*
    Earlier sketch in SATA *6*
    See also SAAS 4
Watling, James 1933- *117*
    Earlier sketch in SATA *67*
Watson, Aldren A(uld) 1917- *42*
    Brief entry *36*
Watson, Amy Zakrzewski 1965- *76*
Watson, B. S.
    See Teitelbaum, Michael
Watson, Carol 1949- *78*
Watson, C.G. *193*
Watson, Clyde 1947- *68*
    Earlier sketch in SATA *5*
    See also CLR 3
Watson, Helen Orr 1892-1978
    Obituary *24*
Watson, James 1936- *106*
    Earlier sketch in SATA *10*
Watson, Jane Werner 1915- *54*
    Earlier sketch in SATA *3*
Watson, John H.
    See Farmer, Philip Jose
Watson, Mary 1953- *117*
Watson, N. Cameron 1955- *81*
Watson, Nancy Dingman *32*
Watson, Pauline 1925- *14*
Watson, Richard F.
    See Silverberg, Robert
Watson, Richard Jesse 1951- *62*
Watson, Sally (Lou) 1924- *3*
Watson, Wendy (McLeod) 1942- *142*
    Earlier sketches in SATA *5, 74*
Watson Taylor, Elizabeth 1915- *41*
Watt, Melanie 1975- *193*
Watt, Thomas 1935- *4*
    Earlier sketch in SATA *136*
Wattenberg, Jane *174*
Watterson, Bill 1958- *66*
Watt-Evans, Lawrence 1954- *121*
Watts, (Anna) Bernadette 1942- *103*
    Earlier sketch in SATA *4*
Watts, Ephraim
    See Horne, Richard Henry Hengist
Watts, Franklin (Mowry) 1904-1978 .... *46*
    Obituary *21*
Watts, Irene N(aemi) 1931- *111*
    Earlier sketch in SATA *56*
Watts, Isaac 1674-1748 .... *52*
Watts, James K(ennedy) M(offitt) 1955- *59*
Watts, Jeri Hanel 1957- *170*
Watts, Julia 1969- *103*
Watts, Leander 1956- *146*
Watts, Leslie Elizabeth 1961- *168*
Watts, Mabel Pizzey 1906-1994 .... *11*
Watts, Nigel 1957-1999 .... *121*
Waugh, C. C. Roessel
    See Waugh, Carol-Lynn Rossel
    and Waugh, Charles G(ordon)
Waugh, Carol-Lynn Rossel 1947- *41*
Waugh, Dorothy -1996 .... *11*
Waugh, Sylvia 1935- *169*
Waugh, Virginia
    See Sorensen, Virginia

Wax, Wendy A. 1963- *163*
    Earlier sketch in SATA *73*
Wayland, April Halprin 1954- *143*
    Earlier sketch in SATA *78*
    See also SAAS 26
Wayland, Patrick
    See O'Connor, Richard
Wayne, (Anne) Jenifer 1917-1982 .... *32*
Wayne, Kyra Petrovskaya 1918- *8*
Wayne, Richard
    See Decker, Duane
Wayshak, Deborah Noyes 1965- *145*
Waystaff, Simon
    See Swift, Jonathan
Weales, Gerald (Clifford) 1925- *11*
Weary, Ogdred
    See Gorey, Edward (St. John)
Weatherford, Carole Boston 1956- *181*
    Earlier sketch in SATA *138*
Weatherly, Lee 1967- *192*
Weatherly, Myra 1926- *130*
Weatherly, Myra S.
    See Weatherly, Myra
Weaver, Harriett E. 1908-1993 .... *65*
Weaver, John L. 1949- *42*
Weaver, Robyn
    See Conley-Weaver, Robyn
Weaver, Robyn M.
    See Conley-Weaver, Robyn
Weaver, Ward
    See Mason, F(rancis) van Wyck
Weaver, Will 1950- *161*
    Earlier sketches in SATA *88, 109*
Weaver, William Weller
    See Weaver, Will
Weaver-Gelzer, Charlotte 1950- *79*
Webb, Christopher
    See Wibberley, Leonard (Patrick O'Connor)
Webb, Jacqueline
    See Pearce, Margaret
Webb, Jacquelyn
    See Pearce, Margaret
    and Pearce, Margaret
Webb, Jean Francis (III) 1910-1991 .... *35*
Webb, Kaye 1914- *60*
Webb, Lois Sinaiko 1922- *82*
Webb, Margot 1934- *67*
Webb, Sharon 1936- *41*
Webb, Sophie 1958- *135*
Webber, Andrew Lloyd
    See Lloyd Webber, Andrew
Webber, Desiree Morrison 1956- *170*
Webber, Irma E(leanor Schmidt)
    1904-1995 .... *14*
Weber, Alfons 1921- *8*
Weber, Bruce 1942- *120*
    Earlier sketch in SATA *73*
Weber, Debora 1955- *58*
Weber, EdNah New Rider 1919(?)- *168*
Weber, Jill 1950- *127*
Weber, Judith E(ichler) 1938- *64*
Weber, Ken(neth J.) 1940- *90*
Weber, Lenora Mattingly 1895-1971 .... *2*
    Obituary *26*
Weber, Michael 1945- *87*
Weber, Sandra 1961- *158*
Weber, William J(ohn) 1927- *14*
Webster, Alice Jane Chandler 1876-1916 ..... *17*
Webster, David 1930- *11*
Webster, Frank V. *67*
    Earlier sketch in SATA *1*
Webster, Gary
    See Garrison, Webb B(lack)
Webster, James 1925-1981 .... *17*
    Obituary *27*
Webster, Jean
    See Webster, Alice Jane Chandler
Wechsler, Doug *189*
Wechsler, Herman J. 1904-1976
    Obituary *20*

Wechter, Nell (Carolyn) Wise 1913-1989 .. *127*
    Earlier sketch in SATA *60*
Weck, Thomas L. 1942- *62*
Wedd, Kate
    See Gregory, Philippa
Weddle, Ethel Harshbarger 1897-1996 .... *11*
Weeks, Sarah *158*
Weems, David B(urnola) 1922- *80*
Wees, Frances Shelley 1902-1982 .... *58*
Weevers, Peter 1944- *59*
Wegen, Ronald 1946-1985 .... *99*
Wegman, William (George) 1943- *135*
    Earlier sketches in SATA *78, 129*
Wegner, Fritz 1924- *20*
Weidhorn, Manfred 1931- *60*
Weidt, Maryann N. 1944- *85*
Weigel, Jeff 1958- *170*
Weigelt, Udo 1960- *168*
Weihs, Erika 1917- *107*
    Earlier sketch in SATA *15*
Weik, Mary Hays 1898(?)-1979 .... *3*
    Obituary *23*
Weil, Ann Yezner 1908-1969 .... *9*
Weil, Lisl 1910- *7*
Weilerstein, Sadie Rose 1894-1993 .... *3*
    Obituary *75*
Weill, Cynthia 1959- *167*
Wein, Elizabeth E(ve) 1964- *151*
    Earlier sketch in SATA *82*
Weinberg, Larry
    See Weinberg, Lawrence (E.)
Weinberg, Lawrence (E.) *92*
    Brief entry *48*
Weinberger, Tanya 1939- *84*
Weiner, Sandra 1922- *14*
Weingarten, Violet (Brown) 1915-1976 .... *3*
    Obituary *27*
Weingartner, Charles 1922- *5*
Weinheimer, Beckie 1958- *186*
Weinstein, Nina 1951- *73*
Weir, Bob 1947- *76*
Weir, Diana (R.) Loiewski 1958- *111*
Weir, Joan S(herman) 1928- *99*
Weir, LaVada *2*
Weir, Rosemary (Green) 1905-1994 .... *21*
Weir, Wendy 1949- *76*
Weis, Margaret 1948- *164*
    Earlier sketches in SATA *38, 92*
Weisberger, Bernard A(llen) 1922- *21*
Weiser, Marjorie P(hillis) K(atz) 1934- *33*
Weisgard, Leonard (Joseph) 1916-2000 .... *85*
    Obituary *122*
    Earlier sketches in SATA *2, 30*
    See also SAAS 19
Weiss, Adelle 1920- *18*
Weiss, Ann E(dwards) 1943- *69*
    Earlier sketch in SATA *30*
    See also SAAS 13
Weiss, Edna
    See Barth, Edna
Weiss, Ellen 1953- *44*
Weiss, Harvey 1922- *76*
    Earlier sketches in SATA *1, 27*
    See also CLR 4
    See also SAAS 19
Weiss, Jaqueline Shachter 1926- *65*
Weiss, Malcolm E. 1928- *3*
Weiss, Margaret Edith
    See Weis, Margaret
Weiss, Miriam
    See Schlein, Miriam
Weiss, Mitch 1951- *183*
    Earlier sketch in SATA *123*
Weiss, Nicki 1954- *86*
    Earlier sketch in SATA *33*
Weiss, Renee Karol 1923- *5*
Weissberger, Ela 1930- *181*
Weissberger, Ela Stein
    See Weissberger, Ela
Weissenborn, Hellmuth 1898-1982
    Obituary *31*

Weitzman, David L. 1936- *172*
  Earlier sketch in SATA *122*
Wekesser, Carol A. 1963- *76*
Welber, Robert *26*
Welch, Amanda (Jane) 1945- *75*
Welch, D'Alte Aldridge 1907-1970
  Obituary *27*
Welch, Jean-Louise
  See Kempton, Jean Welch
Welch, Pauline
  See Bodenham, Hilda Morris
Welch, Ronald
  See Felton, Ronald Oliver
Welch, Sheila Kelly 1945- *130*
Welch, Willy 1952- *93*
Weldin, Frauke 1969- *188*
Welford, Sue 1942- *75*
Weller, George 1907-2002 .... *31*
  Obituary *140*
Weller, George Anthony
  See Weller, George
Welling, Peter J. 1947- *135*
Wellington, Monica 1957- *157*
  Earlier sketches in SATA *67, 99*
Wellman, Alice 1900-1984 .... *51*
  Brief entry *36*
Wellman, Manly Wade 1903-1986 .... *6*
  Obituary *47*
Wellman, Paul I. 1898-1966 .... *3*
Wellman, Paul Iselin
  See Wellman, Paul I.
Wellman, Sam(uel) 1939- *122*
Wells, H(erbert) G(eorge) 1866-1946 .... *20*
  See also CLR *133*
Wells, Helen
  See Campbell, Hope
Wells, Helen 1910-1986 .... *49*
  Earlier sketch in SATA *2*
Wells, J. Wellington
  See de Camp, L(yon) Sprague
Wells, June
  See Swinford, Betty (June Wells)
Wells, Robert
  See Welsch, Roger L(ee)
Wells, Robert E. *184*
Wells, Rosemary 1943- *156*
  Earlier sketches in SATA *18, 69, 114*
  See also CLR *69*
  See also SAAS *1*
Wells, Susan (Mary) 1951- *78*
Wels, Byron G(erald) 1924-1993 .... *9*
Welsbacher, Anne 1955- *89*
Welsch, Roger L(ee) 1936- *82*
Welsh, David
  See Hills, C.A.R.
Welsh, Mary Flynn 1910(?)-1984
  Obituary *38*
Welsh, T.K. 1956- *184*
Weltner, Linda R(iverly) 1938- *38*
Welton, Jude 1955- *143*
  Earlier sketch in SATA *79*
Welty, S. F.
  See Welty, Susan F.
Welty, Susan F. 1905- *9*
Wemmlinger, Raymond *190*
Wendelin, Rudolph 1910-2000 .... *23*
Weninger, Brigitte 1960- *189*
Wentworth, Robert
  See Hamilton, Edmond
Werlin, Nancy 1961- *161*
  Earlier sketches in SATA *87, 119*
Werner, Elsa Jane
  See Watson, Jane Werner
Werner, Herma 1926- *47*
  Brief entry *41*
Werner, Jane
  See Watson, Jane Werner
Werner, K.
  See Casewit, Curtis W(erner)

Wersba, Barbara 1932- *58*
  Autobiography Feature *103*
  Earlier sketch in SATA *1*
  See also CLR *78*
  See also SAAS *2*
Werstein, Irving 1914(?)-1971 .... *14*
Werth, Kurt 1896-1983 .... *20*
Wesley, Alison
  See Barnes, Michael
Wesley, Kathryn
  See Rusch, Kristine Kathryn
Wesley, Mary (Aline) 1912-2002 .... *66*
Wesley, Valerie Wilson 1947- *168*
  Earlier sketch in SATA *106*
West, Andrew
  See Arthur, Robert, (Jr.)
West, Anna 1938- *40*
West, Barbara
  See Price, Olive
West, Betty 1921- *11*
West, Bruce 1951- *63*
West, C. P.
  See Wodehouse, P(elham) G(renville)
West, Dorothy
  See Benson, Mildred (Augustine Wirt)
West, Emily Govan 1919- *38*
West, Emmy
  See West, Emily Govan
West, James
  See Withers, Carl A.
West, Jerry
  See Svenson, Andrew E(dward)
West, (Mary) Jessamyn 1902-1984
  Obituary *37*
West, John
  See Arthur, Robert, (Jr.)
West, Owen
  See Koontz, Dean R.
Westall, Robert (Atkinson) 1929-1993 .... *69*
  Obituary *75*
  Earlier sketch in SATA *23*
  See also CLR *13*
  See also SAAS *2*
Westaway, Jane 1948- *121*
Westcott, Nadine Bernard 1949- *130*
Westera, Marleen 1962- *187*
Westerberg, Christine 1950- *29*
Westerduin, Anne 1945- *105*
Westerfeld, Scott *161*
Westervelt, Virginia Veeder 1914-2005 .... *10*
Westheimer, David 1917-2005 .... *14*
  Obituary *170*
Westheimer, David Kaplan
  See Westheimer, David
Westmacott, Mary
  See Christie, Agatha (Mary Clarissa)
Westman, Barbara *70*
Westman, Paul (Wendell) 1956- *39*
Westmoreland, William C. 1914-2005 .... *63*
Westmoreland, William Childs
  See Westmoreland, William C.
Weston, Allen
  See Hogarth, Grace (Weston Allen)
  and Norton, Andre
Weston, Carol 1956- *135*
Weston, Carrie *190*
Weston, John (Harrison) 1932- *21*
Weston, Martha 1947- *119*
  Earlier sketch in SATA *53*
Westphal, Arnold Carl 1897- *57*
Westrup, Hugh *102*
Westwood, Jennifer 1940-2008 .... *10*
  Obituary *192*
Wexler, Jerome (LeRoy) 1923- *14*
Weyland, Jack 1940- *81*
Weyn, Suzanne 1955- *164*
  Earlier sketches in SATA *63, 101*
Weyr, Garret
  See Freymann-Weyr, (Rhoda)
  Garret (Michaela)
Wezyk, Joanna 1966- *82*

Whaley, Joyce Irene 1923- *61*
Whalin, W. Terry 1953- *93*
Wharf, Michael
  See Weller, George
Wharmby, Margot *63*
Wharton, Edith (Newbold Jones) 1862-1937
  See CLR *136*
Whatley, Bruce 1954- *177*
Wheatley, Arabelle 1921- *16*
Wheatley, Nadia 1949- *147*
Wheeler, Cindy 1955- *49*
  Brief entry *40*
Wheeler, Deborah (Jean Ross) 1947- *83*
Wheeler, Janet D. *1*
Wheeler, Jill C. 1964- *136*
  Earlier sketch in SATA *86*
Wheeler, Jody 1952- *148*
  Earlier sketch in SATA *84*
Wheeler, Lisa 1963- *162*
Wheeler, Opal 1898- *23*
Whelan, Elizabeth M(urphy) 1943- *14*
Whelan, Gloria 1923- *178*
  Earlier sketches in SATA *85, 128*
  See also CLR *90*
Whelan, Gloria Ann
  See Whelan, Gloria
Whipple, A(ddison) B(eecher) C(olvin)
  1918- *64*
Whipple, Cal
  See Whipple, A(ddison) B(eecher) C(olvin)
Whisp, Kennilworthy
  See Rowling, J.K.
Whistler, Reginald John 1905-1944 .... *30*
Whistler, Rex
  See Whistler, Reginald John
Whitaker, Zai *183*
Whitcher, Susan (Godsil) 1952- *96*
Whitcomb, Jon 1906-1988 .... *10*
  Obituary *56*
Whitcomb, Laura *171*
White, Anne Terry 1896-1980 .... *2*
White, Bessie (Felstiner) 1892(?)-1986
  Obituary *50*
White, Carolyn 1948- *130*
White, Dale
  See Place, Marian T(empleton)
White, Dori 1919- *10*
White, E. B. 1899-1985 .... *100*
  Obituary *44*
  Earlier sketches in SATA *2, 29*
  See also CLR *107*
White, Eliza Orne 1856-1947
  See YABC *2*
White, Elwyn Brooks
  See White, E. B.
White, Florence M(eiman) 1910- *14*
White, Laurence B(arton), Jr. 1935- *10*
White, Lee *176*
White, Martin 1943- *51*
White, Nancy 1942- *126*
White, Ramy Allison *67*
  Earlier sketch in SATA *1*
White, Robb 1909-1990 .... *83*
  Earlier sketch in SATA *1*
  See also CLR *3*
  See also SAAS *1*
White, Ruth C. 1942- *186*
  Autobiography Feature *186*
  Earlier sketches in SATA *39, 117, 165*
White, T(erence) H(anbury) 1906-1964 .... *12*
  See also CLR *139*
White, Tekla N. 1934- *115*
White, Timothy (Thomas Anthony)
  1952-2002 .... *60*
White, Tom 1923- *148*
White, William, Jr. 1934- *16*
Whitehead, Don(ald) F. 1908-1981 .... *4*
Whitehead, Jenny 1964- *191*
Whitehead, Kathy 1957- *176*
Whitehouse, Arch
  See Whitehouse, Arthur George Joseph

Whitehouse, Arthur George Joseph
  1895-1979 .... *14*
  Obituary *23*
Whitehouse, Elizabeth S(cott) 1893-1968 .... *35*
Whitehouse, Jeanne *29*
  See Peterson, Jeanne Whitehouse
Whitelaw, Nancy 1933- *166*
  Earlier sketch in SATA *76*
Whitesel, Cheryl Aylward *162*
Whitinger, R. D.
  See Place, Marian T(empleton)
Whitley, Mary Ann
  See Sebrey, Mary Ann
Whitley, Peggy 1938- *140*
Whitlock, Pamela 1921(?)-1982
  Obituary *31*
Whitlock, Ralph 1914-1995 .... *35*
Whitman, Alice
  See Marker, Sherry
Whitman, Sylvia (Choate) 1961- *135*
  Earlier sketch in SATA *85*
Whitman, Walt(er) 1819-1892 .... *20*
Whitmore, Arvella 1922- *125*
Whitney, Alex(andra) 1922- *14*
Whitney, David C(harles) 1921- *48*
  Brief entry *29*
Whitney, Kim Ablon *162*
Whitney, Phyllis A. 1903-2008 .... *30*
  Obituary *189*
  Earlier sketch in SATA *1*
  See also CLR *59*
Whitney, Phyllis Ayame
  See Whitney, Phyllis A.
Whitney, Phyllis Ayame
  See Whitney, Phyllis A.
Whitney, Sharon 1937- *63*
Whitney, Thomas P. 1917-2007 .... *25*
  Obituary *189*
Whitney, Thomas Porter
  See Whitney, Thomas P.
Whittington, Mary K(athrine) 1941- *75*
Whitworth, John 1945- *123*
Whybrow, Ian *132*
Whyte, Mal(colm Kenneth, Jr.) 1933- *62*
Whyte, Mary 1953- *148*
  Earlier sketch in SATA *94*
Whyte, Ron 1942(?)-1989
  Obituary *63*
Whytock, Cherry *177*
Wiater, Stanley 1953- *84*
Wibbelsman, Charles J(oseph) 1945- *59*
Wibberley, Leonard (Patrick O'Connor)
  1915-1983 .... *45*
  Obituary *36*
  Earlier sketch in SATA *2*
  See also CLR *3*
  See Holton, Leonard
Wiberg, Harald (Albin) 1908- *93*
  Brief entry *40*
Wick, Walter 1953- *148*
Wickens, Elaine *86*
Wicker, Ireene 1905(?)-1987
  Obituary *55*
Wickstrom, Sylvie 1960- *169*
Widdemer, Mabel Cleland 1902-1964 .... *5*
Widener, Terry 1950- *105*
Widerberg, Siv 1931- *10*
Wiebe, Rudy 1934- *156*
Wiebe, Rudy Henry
  See Wiebe, Rudy
Wieler, Diana (Jean) 1961- *109*
Wiener, Lori 1956- *84*
Wier, Ester (Alberti) 1910-2000 .... *3*
Wiese, Kurt 1887-1974 .... *36*
  Obituary *24*
  Earlier sketch in SATA *3*
  See also CLR *86*
Wiesel, Elie 1928- *56*
Wiesel, Eliezer
  See Wiesel, Elie

Wiesner, David 1956- *181*
  Earlier sketches in SATA *72, 117, 139*
  See also CLR *84*
Wiesner, Portia
  See Takakjian, Portia
Wiesner, William 1899-1984 .... *5*
Wiggers, Raymond 1952- *82*
Wiggin, Eric E. 1939- *167*
  Earlier sketch in SATA *88*
Wiggin, Eric Ellsworth 1939-
  See Wiggin, Eric E.
Wiggin (Riggs), Kate Douglas (Smith)
  1856-1923
  See YABC *1*
  See also CLR *52*
Wiggins, VeraLee (Chesnut) 1928-1995 .... *89*
Wight, James Alfred 1916-1995 .... *55*
  Brief entry *44*
  See Herriot, James
Wignell, Edel 1936- *69*
Wijnberg, Ellen *85*
Wikland, Ilon 1930- *93*
  Brief entry *32*
Wikler, Madeline 1943- *114*
Wilber, Donald N(ewton) 1907-1997 .... *35*
Wilbur, C. Keith 1923- *27*
Wilbur, Frances 1921- *107*
Wilbur, Richard 1921- *108*
  Earlier sketch in SATA *9*
Wilbur, Richard Purdy
  See Wilbur, Richard
Wilburn, Kathy 1948- *68*
Wilcox, Charlotte 1948- *72*
Wilcox, R(uth) Turner 1888-1970 .... *36*
Wilcox, Roger
  See Collins, Paul
Wild, Jocelyn 1941- *46*
Wild, Kate 1954- *192*
Wild, Margaret 1948- *151*
Wild, Robin (Evans) 1936- *46*
Wild, Robyn 1947- *117*
Wilde, D. Gunther
  See Hurwood, Bernhardt J.
Wilde, Oscar 1854(?)-1900 .... *24*
  See also CLR *114*
Wilde, Oscar Fingal O'Flahertie Willis
  See Wilde, Oscar
Wilder, Buck
  See Smith, Tim(othy R.)
Wilder, Laura (Elizabeth) Ingalls
  1867-1957 .... *100*
  Earlier sketches in SATA *15, 29*
  See also CLR *111*
Wildsmith, Brian 1930- *124*
  Earlier sketches in SATA *16, 69*
  See also CLR *52*
  See also SAAS *5*
Wiles, Deborah *171*
Wilhelm, Doug 1952- *190*
Wilhelm, Hans 1945- *135*
  Earlier sketch in SATA *58*
  See also CLR *46*
  See also SAAS *21*
Wilkie, Katharine E(lliott) 1904-1980 .... *31*
Wilkin, Eloise 1904-1987 .... *49*
  Obituary *54*
Wilkins, Frances 1923- *14*
Wilkins, Kim *147*
Wilkins, Marilyn (Ruth) 1926- *30*
Wilkins, Marne
  See Wilkins, Marilyn (Ruth)
Wilkins, Mary Huiskamp 1926- *139*
  Earlier sketch in SATA *84*
  See Calhoun, Mary
Wilkins, Mary Huiskamp Calhoun
  See Wilkins, Mary Huiskamp
Wilkins, Rose *180*
Wilkinson, (Thomas) Barry 1923- *50*
  Brief entry *32*
Wilkinson, Beth 1925- *80*

Wilkinson, Brenda 1946- *91*
  Earlier sketch in SATA *14*
  See also CLR *20*
Wilkinson, (John) Burke 1913-2000 .... *4*
Wilkinson, Sylvia 1940- *56*
  Brief entry *39*
Wilkon, Jozef 1930- *133*
  Earlier sketches in SATA *31, 71*
Wilkowski, Sue *193*
Wilks, Michael Thomas 1947- *44*
Wilks, Mike
  See Wilks, Michael Thomas
Will
  See Lipkind, William
Willard, Barbara (Mary) 1909-1994 .... *74*
  Earlier sketch in SATA *17*
  See also CLR *2*
  See also SAAS *5*
Willard, Mildred Wilds 1911-1978 .... *14*
Willard, Nancy 1936- *191*
  Brief entry *30*
  Earlier sketches in SATA *37, 71, 127*
  See also CLR *5*
Willcox, Isobel 1907-1996 .... *42*
Willems, Mo *180*
  Earlier sketch in SATA *154*
  See also CLR *114*
Willett, Edward (C.) 1959- *115*
Willey, Bee *184*
Willey, Margaret 1950- *86*
Willey, Robert
  See Ley, Willy
Willhoite, Michael A. 1946- *71*
William, Kate
  See Armstrong, Jennifer
Williams, Arlene *171*
Williams, Barbara 1925- *107*
  Earlier sketch in SATA *11*
  See also CLR *48*
  See also SAAS *16*
Williams, Barbara 1937- *62*
Williams, Beryl
  See Epstein, Beryl (M. Williams)
Williams, Brian (Peter) 1943- *54*
Williams, Carol Lynch 1959- *110*
Williams, Charles
  See Collier, James Lincoln
Williams, Clyde C. 1881-1974 .... *8*
  Obituary *27*
Williams, Coe
  See Harrison, C(hester) William
Williams, Colleen Madonna Flood 1963- .. *156*
Williams, Cynthia G. 1958- *123*
Williams, Dar 1967- *168*
Williams, Donna Reilly 1945- *83*
Williams, (Marcia) Dorothy *71*
  See Williams, Marcia (Dorothy)
Williams, Dorothy
  See Williams, Marcia (Dorothy)
Williams, Dorothy Snowden
  See Williams, Dar
Williams, Eric (Ernest) 1911-1983 .... *14*
  Obituary *38*
Williams, Ferelith Eccles *22*
  See Eccles Williams, Ferelith
Williams, Frances B.
  See Browin, Frances Williams
Williams, Garth (Montgomery) 1912-1996 .. *66*
  Obituary *90*
  Earlier sketch in SATA *18*
  See also CLR *57*
  See also SAAS *7*
Williams, Guy R(ichard) 1920- *11*
Williams, Hawley
  See Heyliger, William
Williams, Helen 1948- *77*
Williams, J. R.
  See Williams, Jeanne
Williams, J. Walker
  See Wodehouse, P(elham) G(renville)

Williams, Jay 1914-1978 41
  Obituary 24
  Earlier sketch in SATA 3
  See also CLR 8
Williams, Jeanne 1930- 5
Williams, Jenny 1939- 60
Williams, Karen Lynn 1952- 99
  Earlier sketch in SATA 66
Williams, Kit 1946(?)- 44
  See also CLR 4
Williams, Laura E. 180
Williams, Laura Ellen
  See Williams, Laura E.
Williams, L.E.
  See Williams, Laura Ellen
Williams, Leslie 1941- 42
Williams, Linda 1948- 59
Williams, Louise Bonino 1904(?)-1984
  Obituary 39
Williams, Lynn
  See Hale, Arlene
Williams, Marcia (Dorothy) 1945- 159
  Earlier sketch in SATA 97
  See Williams, (Marcia) Dorothy
Williams, Margery
  See Bianco, Margery Williams
Williams, Mark
  See Arthur, Robert, (Jr.)
Williams, Mark London 1959- 140
Williams, Maureen 1951- 12
Williams, Michael
  See St. John, Wylly Folk
Williams, Patrick J.
  See Griffin, W.E.B
Williams, Pete
  See Faulknor, Cliff(ord Vernon)
Williams, S. P.
  See Hart, Virginia
Williams, Sam 177
  Earlier sketch in SATA 124
Williams, Selma R(uth) 1925- 14
Williams, Sherley Anne 1944-1999 78
  Obituary 116
Williams, Sheron 1955- 77
Williams, Shirley
  See Williams, Sherley Anne
Williams, Slim
  See Williams, Clyde C.
Williams, Sophy 1965- 135
Williams, Susan
  See Beckhorn, Susan Williams
Williams, Suzanne (Bullock) 1953- 71
Williams, Ursula Moray 3
  See Moray Williams, Ursula
Williams, Vera B(aker) 1927- 102
  Brief entry 33
  Earlier sketch in SATA 53
  See also CLR 9
Williams-Andriani, Renee 1963- 98
Williams-Ellis, (Mary) Amabel (Nassau
  Strachey) 1894-1984 29
  Obituary 41
Williams-Garcia, Rita 1957- 160
  Earlier sketch in SATA 98
  See also CLR 36
Williamson, Gwyneth 1965- 109
Williamson, Henry (William) 1895-1977 37
  Obituary 30
Williamson, Joanne S(mall) 1926- 122
  Earlier sketch in SATA 3
Willis, Charles
  See Clarke, Arthur C.
Willis, Connie 1945- 110
  See also CLR 66
Willis, Jeanne 1959- 123
  Earlier sketch in SATA 61
Willis, Jeanne Mary
  See Willis, Jeanne
Willis, Meredith Sue 1946- 101
Willis, Nancy Carol 1952- 139
  Earlier sketch in SATA 93

Willis, Paul J. 1955- 113
Willms, Russ 95
Willoughby, Lee Davis
  See Avallone, Michael (Angelo, Jr.)
  and Brandner, Gary (Phil)
  and Deming, Richard
  and DeAndrea, William L(ouis)
  and Laymon, Richard (Carl)
  and Streib, Dan(iel Thomas)
  and Toombs, John
  and Webb, Jean Francis (III)
Willson, Robina Beckles 27
  See Beckles Willson, Robina (Elizabeth)
Wilma, Dana
  See Faralla, Dana
Wilsdorf, Anne 1954- 191
Wilson, April 80
Wilson, Barbara Ker
  See Ker Wilson, Barbara
Wilson, Beth P(ierre) 8
Wilson, Budge 1927- 55
  See Wilson, Marjorie
Wilson, Carletta 1951- 81
Wilson, Carter 1941- 6
Wilson, Charles Morrow 1905-1977 30
Wilson, Christopher B. 1910(?)-1985
  Obituary 46
Wilson, Darryl B(abe) 1939- 90
Wilson, Diane Lee 172
Wilson, Dirk
  See Pohl, Frederik
Wilson, Dorothy Clarke 1904-2003 16
Wilson, Edward A(rthur) 1886-1970 38
Wilson, Ellen (Janet Cameron) (?)-1976 9
  Obituary 26
Wilson, Eric (H.) 1940- 34
  Brief entry 32
Wilson, Erica 51
Wilson, Forrest 1918- 27
Wilson, Gahan 1930- 35
  Brief entry 27
Wilson, Gina 1943- 85
  Brief entry 34
  Earlier sketch in SATA 36
Wilson, (Leslie) Granville 1912- 14
Wilson, Hazel (Hutchins) 1898-1992 3
  Obituary 73
Wilson, J(erry) M. 1964- 121
Wilson, Jacqueline 1945- 153
  Brief entry 52
  Earlier sketches in SATA 61, 102
Wilson, John 1922- 22
Wilson, John 1951- 182
Wilson, John Alexander
  See Wilson, John
Wilson, Johnniece Marshall 1944- 75
Wilson, Jonathan 1950- 181
Wilson, Joyce M(uriel Judson) 84
  Earlier sketch in SATA 21
  See Stranger, Joyce
Wilson, Karma 174
Wilson, Leslie 1952- 166
Wilson, Linda Miller 1936- 116
Wilson, Lionel 1924-2003 33
  Brief entry 31
  Obituary 144
Wilson, Marjorie
  Brief entry 51
  See Wilson, Budge
Wilson, Maurice (Charles John) 1914- 46
Wilson, Nancy Hope 1947- 138
  Earlier sketch in SATA 81
Wilson, Nick
  See Ellis, Edward S(ylvester)
Wilson, Phil 1948- 181
Wilson, Ron(ald William) 1941- 38
Wilson, Sarah 1934- 142
  Earlier sketch in SATA 50
Wilson, Tom 1931- 33
  Brief entry 30
Wilson, Troy 1970- 169

Wilson, Walt(er N.) 1939- 14
Wilson-Max, Ken 1965- 170
  Earlier sketch in SATA 93
Wilton, Elizabeth 1937- 14
Wilton, Hal
  See Pepper, Frank S.
Wilwerding, Walter Joseph 1891-1966 9
Wimmer, Mike 1961- 70
Winborn, Marsha (Lynn) 1947- 75
Winch, John 1944- 165
  Earlier sketch in SATA 117
Winchester, James H(ugh) 1917-1985 30
  Obituary 45
Winchester, Stanley
  See Youd, (Christopher) Samuel
Windawi, Thura al- 1983(?)- 165
Winders, Gertrude Hecker -1987 3
Windham, Basil
  See Wodehouse, P(elham) G(renville)
Windham, Kathryn T(ucker) 1918- 14
Windham, Sophie 184
Windling, Terri 1958- 151
Windrow, Martin
  See Windrow, Martin Clive
Windrow, Martin C.
  See Windrow, Martin Clive
Windrow, Martin Clive 1944- 68
Windsor, Claire
  See Hamerstrom, Frances
Windsor, Linda 1950- 124
Windsor, Patricia 1938- 78
  Earlier sketch in SATA 30
  See also SAAS 19
Wineman-Marcus, Irene 1952- 81
Winer, Yvonne 1934- 120
Winerip, Michael 175
Winfield, Arthur M.
  See Stratemeyer, Edward L.
Winfield, Edna
  See Stratemeyer, Edward L.
Winfield, Julia
  See Armstrong, Jennifer
Wing, Natasha (Lazutin) 1960- 82
Winick, Judd 1970- 124
Winks, Robin William 1930-2003 61
Winn, Alison
  See Wharmby, Margot
Winn, Chris 1952- 42
Winn, Janet Bruce 1928- 43
Winn, Marie 1936(?)- 38
Winnick, Karen B(eth) B(inkoff) 1946- 51
Winslow, Barbara 1947- 91
Winstead, Rosie 180
Winston, Clara 1921-1983 54
  Obituary 39
Winston, Richard 1917-1979 54
Winter, Janet 1926- 126
Winter, Jeanette 1939- 184
  Earlier sketch in SATA 151
Winter, Jonah 1962- 179
Winter, Milo (Kendall) 1888-1956 21
Winter, Paula Cecelia 1929- 48
Winter, R. R.
  See Winterbotham, R(ussell) R(obert)
Winter, Susan 182
Winterbotham, R(ussell) R(obert)
  1904-1971 10
Winterbotham, Russ
  See Winterbotham, R(ussell) R(obert)
Winterfeld, Henry 1901-1990 55
Winters, J. C.
  See Cross, Gilbert B.
Winters, Jon
  See Cross, Gilbert B.
Winters, Katherine 1936- 153
  Earlier sketch in SATA 103
Winters, Kay
  See Winters, Katherine
Winters, Nina 1944- 62
Winters, Paul A. 1965- 106
Winterson, Jeanette 1959- 190

Winterton, Gayle
  See Adams, William Taylor
Winthrop, Elizabeth *164*
  Autobiography Feature *116*
  Earlier sketches in SATA *8, 76*
  See also CLR *89*
  See Mahony, Elizabeth Winthrop
Winton, Ian (Kenneth) 1960- *76*
Winton, Tim 1960- *98*
Wintz-Litty, Julie
  See Litty, Julie
Wirt, Ann
  See Benson, Mildred (Augustine Wirt)
Wirt, Mildred A.
  See Benson, Mildred (Augustine Wirt)
Wirtenberg, Patricia Z. 1932-2007 .... *10*
Wirtenberg, Patricia Zarrella
  See Wirtenberg, Patricia Z.
Wirth, Beverly 1938- *63*
Wirths, Claudine (Turner) G(ibson)
  1926-2000 .... *104*
  Earlier sketch in SATA *64*
Wise, Bill 1958- *191*
Wise, Lenny
  See Wise, Leonard
Wise, Leonard 1940- *167*
Wise, Leonard A.
  See Wise, Leonard
Wise, Leonard Allan
  See Wise, Leonard
Wise, William 1923- *163*
  Earlier sketch in SATA *4*
Wise, Winifred E. *2*
Wiseman, Ann (Sayre) 1926- *31*
Wiseman, B(ernard) 1922-1995 .... *4*
Wiseman, David 1916- *43*
  Brief entry *40*
Wishinsky, Frieda 1948- *166*
  Earlier sketches in SATA *70, 112*
Wisler, G(ary) Clifton 1950- *103*
  Brief entry *46*
  Earlier sketch in SATA *58*
Wismer, Donald (Richard) 1946- *59*
Wisner, Bill
  See Wisner, William L.
Wisner, William L. 1914(?)-1983 .... *42*
Wisnewski, David 1953-2002
  See Wisniewski, David
Wisniewski, David 1953-2002 .... *95*
  Obituary *139*
  See also CLR *51*
Wister, Owen 1860-1938 .... *62*
Witham, (Phillip) Ross 1917- *37*
Withers, Carl A. 1900-1970 .... *14*
Withers, Pam 1956- *182*
Withrow, Sarah 1966- *124*
Witt, Dick 1948- *80*
Witt, Shirley Hill 1934- *17*
Wittanen, Etolin 1907- *55*
Wittels, Harriet Joan 1938- *31*
Wittig, Susan
  See Albert, Susan Wittig
Wittlinger, Ellen 1948- *189*
  Autobiography Feature *128*
  Earlier sketches in SATA *83, 122*
Wittman, Sally (Anne Christensen) 1941- *30*
Witty, Paul 1898-1976 .... *50*
  Obituary *30*
Wodehouse, P(elham) G(renville)
  1881-1975 .... *22*
Wodge, Dreary
  See Gorey, Edward (St. John)
Woelfle, Gretchen 1945- *145*
Wohlberg, Meg 1905-1990 .... *41*
  Obituary *66*
Wohlrabe, Raymond A. 1900-1977 .... *4*

Wojciechowska, Maia (Teresa) 1927-2002 ... *83*
  Autobiography Feature *104*
  Obituary *134*
  Earlier sketches in SATA *1, 28*
  See also CLR *1*
  See also SAAS *1*
Wojciechowski, Susan *126*
  Earlier sketch in SATA *78*
Wojnarowski, Adrian 1970- *190*
Wolcott, Patty 1929- *14*
Wold, Allen L. 1943- *64*
Wold, Jo Anne 1938- *30*
Woldin, Beth Weiner 1955- *34*
Wolf, Allan 1963- *192*
Wolf, Bernard 1930- *102*
  Brief entry *37*
Wolf, Erica (Van Varick) 1978- *156*
Wolf, Gita 1956- *101*
Wolf, Janet 1957- *78*
Wolf, J.M.
  See Wolf, Joan M.
Wolf, Joan M. 1966- *193*
Wolf, Sallie 1950- *80*
Wolfe, Art 1952- *76*
Wolfe, Burton H. 1932- *5*
Wolfe, Gene 1931- *165*
  Earlier sketch in SATA *118*
Wolfe, Gene Rodman
  See Wolfe, Gene
Wolfe, Louis 1905-1985 .... *8*
  Obituary *133*
Wolfe, Rinna (Evelyn) 1925- *38*
Wolfenden, George
  See Beardmore, George
Wolfer, Dianne 1961- *167*
  Autobiography Feature *117*
  Earlier sketch in SATA *104*
Wolff, Alexander (Nikolaus) 1957- *137*
  Earlier sketch in SATA *63*
Wolff, Ashley 1956- *155*
  Earlier sketches in SATA *50, 81*
Wolff, Diane 1945- *27*
Wolff, Ferida 1946- *164*
  Earlier sketch in SATA *79*
Wolff, Jennifer Ashley
  See Wolff, Ashley
Wolff, Robert Jay 1905-1977 .... *10*
Wolff, Sonia
  See Levitin, Sonia
Wolff, Virginia Euwer 1937- *137*
  Earlier sketch in SATA *78*
  See also CLR *62*
Wolfman, Judy 1933- *138*
Wolfson, Evelyn 1937- *62*
Wolitzer, Hilma 1930- *31*
Wolkoff, Judie (Edwards) *93*
  Brief entry *37*
Wolkstein, Diane 1942- *138*
  Earlier sketches in SATA *7, 82*
Wollheim, Donald A(llen) 1914-1990
  Obituary *69*
Wolny, P.
  See Janeczko, Paul B(ryan)
Wolters, Richard A. 1920-1993 .... *35*
Wondriska, William 1931- *6*
Wong, Jade Snow 1922-2006 .... *112*
  Obituary *175*
Wong, Janet S. 1962- *148*
  Earlier sketch in SATA *98*
  See also CLR *94*
Wood, Anne (Savage) 1937- *64*
Wood, Audrey *139*
  Brief entry *44*
  Earlier sketches in SATA *50, 81*
  See also CLR *26*
Wood, Catherine
  See Etchison, Birdie L(ee)
Wood, David 1944- *87*
Wood, Don 1945- *50*
  Brief entry *44*
  See also CLR *26*

Wood, Douglas 1951- *180*
  Earlier sketches in SATA *81, 132*
Wood, Douglas Eric
  See Wood, Douglas
Wood, Edgar A(llardyce) 1907-1998 .... *14*
Wood, Esther
  See Brady, Esther Wood
Wood, Frances Elizabeth *34*
Wood, Frances M. 1951- *97*
Wood, James Playsted 1905- *1*
Wood, Jenny 1955- *88*
Wood, John Norris 1930- *85*
Wood, June Rae 1946- *120*
  Earlier sketch in SATA *79*
  See also CLR *82*
Wood, Kerry
  See Wood, Edgar A(llardyce)
Wood, Kim Marie *134*
Wood, Laura N.
  See Roper, Laura (Newbold) Wood
Wood, Linda C(arol) 1945- *59*
Wood, Marcia 1956- *80*
Wood, Marcia Mae
  See Wood, Marcia
Wood, Nancy
  See Wood, Nancy C.
Wood, Nancy C. 1936- *178*
  Earlier sketch in SATA *6*
Wood, Nuria
  See Nobisso, Josephine
Wood, Owen 1929- *64*
Wood, Phyllis Anderson 1923- *33*
  Brief entry *30*
Wood, Richard 1949- *110*
Wood, Tim(othy William Russell) 1946- *88*
Wood, Wallace 1927-1981
  Obituary *33*
Woodard, Carol 1929- *14*
Woodburn, John Henry 1914- *11*
Woodbury, David Oakes 1896-1981 .... *62*
Woodford, Peggy 1937- *25*
Woodhouse, Barbara (Blackburn)
  1910-1988 .... *63*
Wooding, Chris 1977- *166*
Wooding, Sharon
  See Wooding, Sharon L(ouise)
Wooding, Sharon L(ouise) 1943- *66*
Woodman, Allen 1954- *76*
Woodrich, Mary Neville 1915- *2*
Woodruff, Elvira 1951- *162*
  Earlier sketches in SATA *70, 106*
Woodruff, Joan Leslie 1953- *104*
Woodruff, Liza 1971(?)- *182*
Woodruff, Marian
  See Goudge, Eileen
Woodruff, Noah 1977- *86*
Woods, George A(llan) 1926-1988 .... *30*
  Obituary *57*
Woods, Geraldine 1948- *111*
  Brief entry *42*
  Earlier sketch in SATA *56*
Woods, Harold 1945- *56*
  Brief entry *42*
Woods, Lawrence
  See Lowndes, Robert A(ugustine) W(ard)
Woods, Margaret 1921- *2*
Woods, Nat
  See Stratemeyer, Edward L.
Woodson, Jack
  See Woodson, John Waddie Jr.
Woodson, Jacqueline 1964- *189*
  Earlier sketches in SATA *94, 139*
  See also CLR *49*
Woodson, Jacqueline Amanda
  See Woodson, Jacqueline
Woodson, John Waddie Jr. 1913- *10*
Woodtor, Dee
  See Woodtor, Delores Parmer
Woodtor, Dee Parmer 1945(?)-2002
  See Woodtor, Delores Parmer
Woodtor, Delores Parmer 1945-2002 .... *93*

Wood-Trost, Lucille
  See Trost, Lucille W(ood)
Woodward, (Landon) Cleveland 1900-1986 . *10*
  Obituary *48*
Woodworth, Chris 1957- *168*
Woodworth, Viki 1952- *127*
Woody, Regina Jones 1894-1983 .... *3*
Woog, Adam 1953- *125*
  Earlier sketch in SATA *84*
Wooldridge, Connie Nordhielm 1950- *143*
  Earlier sketch in SATA *92*
Wooldridge, Frosty 1947- *140*
Wooldridge, Rhoda 1906-1988 .... *22*
Wooley, Susan Frelick 1945- *113*
Woolf, Paula 1950- *104*
Woolfe, Angela 1976- *169*
Woolley, Catherine 1904-2005 .... *3*
  Obituary *166*
Woolman, Steven 1969-2004 .... *163*
  Earlier sketch in SATA *90*
Woolsey, Janette 1904-1989 .... *3*
  Obituary *131*
Worcester, Donald E(mmet) 1915- *18*
Word, Reagan 1944- *103*
Work, Virginia 1946- *57*
  Brief entry *45*
Worline, Bonnie Bess 1914- *14*
Wormell, Christopher 1955- *154*
  Earlier sketch in SATA *103*
Wormell, Mary 1959- *96*
Wormser, Richard 1933- *106*
  Autobiography Feature *118*
  See also SAAS *26*
Wormser, Sophie 1897-1979 .... *22*
Worth, Richard 1945- *59*
  Brief entry *46*
Worth, Valerie 1933-1994 .... *81*
  See Bahlke, Valerie Worth
Wortis, Avi
  See Avi
Wortis, Edward Irving
  See Avi
Wosmek, Frances 1917- *29*
Woychuk, Denis 1953- *71*
Wrede, Patricia C(ollins) 1953- *146*
  Earlier sketch in SATA *67*
Wriggins, Sally Hovey 1922- *17*
Wright, Alexandra 1979- *103*
Wright, Betty Ren *109*
  Brief entry *48*
  Earlier sketch in SATA *63*
Wright, Cliff 1963- *168*
  Earlier sketch in SATA *76*
Wright, Courtni
  See Wright, Courtni C(rump)
Wright, Courtni C(rump) 1950- *84*
Wright, Courtni Crump
  See Wright, Courtni C(rump)
Wright, Dare 1914(?)-2001 .... *21*
  Obituary *124*
Wright, David K. 1943- *112*
  Earlier sketch in SATA *73*
Wright, Elinor
  See Lyon, Elinor
Wright, Enid Meadowcroft (LaMonte)
  1898-1966 .... *3*
Wright, Esmond 1915-2003 .... *10*
Wright, Frances Fitzpatrick 1897-1982 .... *10*
Wright, J. B.
  See Barkan, Joanne
Wright, Judith 1915-2000 .... *14*
  Obituary *121*
Wright, Judith Arundell
  See Wright, Judith
Wright, Katrina
  See Gater, Dilys
Wright, Kenneth
  See del Rey, Lester
Wright, Kit 1944- *87*
Wright, Leslie B(ailey) 1959- *91*
Wright, Nancy Means *38*

Wright, R(obert) H(amilton) 1906- *6*
Wright, Rachel *134*
Wright, Susan Kimmel 1950- *97*
Wrightfrierson
  See Wright-Frierson, Virginia (Marguerite)
Wright-Frierson, Virginia (Marguerite)
  1949- *110*
  Earlier sketch in SATA *58*
Wrightson, (Alice) Patricia 1921- *112*
  Earlier sketches in SATA *8, 66*
  See also CLR *14*
  See also SAAS *4*
Wroble, Lisa A. 1963- *134*
Wrongo, I.B.
  See Katz, Alan
Wronker, Lili
  See Wronker, Lili Cassel
Wronker, Lili Cassel 1924- *10*
Wryde, Dogear
  See Gorey, Edward (St. John)
Wu, Elizabeth
  See Wu, Liz
Wu, Liz *184*
Wu, Norbert 1961- *155*
  Earlier sketch in SATA *101*
Wulffson, Don 1943- *155*
  Earlier sketches in SATA *32, 88*
Wulffson, Don L.
  See Wulffson, Don
Wunderli, Stephen 1958- *79*
Wunsch, Josephine (McLean) 1914- *64*
Wuorio, Eva-Lis 1918- *34*
  Brief entry *28*
Wurts, Janny 1953- *98*
Wyatt, B. D.
  See Robinson, Spider
Wyatt, David 1968- *185*
Wyatt, Jane
  See Bradbury, Bianca (Ryley)
Wyatt, Melissa 1963- *177*
Wyeth, Betsy James 1921- *41*
Wyeth, N(ewell) C(onvers) 1882-1945 .... *17*
  See also CLR *106*
Wyler, Rose 1909-2000 .... *18*
  Obituary *121*
Wylie, Betty Jane *48*
Wylie, Laura
  See Matthews, Patricia
Wylie, Laurie
  See Matthews, Patricia
Wyllie, Stephen *86*
Wyman, Andrea *75*
Wyman, Carolyn 1956- *83*
Wymer, Norman (George) 1911- *25*
Wynard, Talbot
  See Hamilton, Charles (Harold St. John)
Wyndham, John
  See Harris, John (Wyndham Parkes
  Lucas) Beynon
Wyndham, Lee
  See Hyndman, Jane Andrews Lee
Wyndham, Robert
  See Hyndman, Robert Utley
Wynne-Jones, Tim 1948- *186*
  Autobiography Feature *136*
  Earlier sketches in SATA *67, 96, 136*
  See also CLR *58*
Wynne-Jones, Timothy
  See Wynne-Jones, Tim
Wynter, Edward (John) 1914- *14*
Wynyard, Talbot
  See Hamilton, Charles (Harold St. John)
Wyss, Johann David Von 1743-1818 .... *29*
  Brief entry *27*
  See also CLR *92*
Wyss, Thelma Hatch 1934- *140*
  Earlier sketch in SATA *10*

X

Xavier, Father
  See Hurwood, Bernhardt J.
Xuan, YongSheng 1952- *116*
  Autobiography Feature *119*

Y

Yaccarino, Dan *192*
  Earlier sketch in SATA *141*
Yadin, (Rav-Aloof) Yigael 1917-1984 .... *55*
Yaffe, Alan
  See Yorinks, Arthur
Yagher, Kevin 1962- *143*
Yakovetic, (Joseph Sandy) 1952- *59*
Yakovetic, Joe
  See Yakovetic, (Joseph Sandy)
Yamada, Utako 1963- *188*
Yamaguchi, Marianne (Illenberger) 1936- *7*
Yamaka, Sara 1978- *92*
Yamanaka, Lois-Ann 1961- *166*
Yancey, Diane 1951- *138*
  Earlier sketch in SATA *81*
Yancey, Richard *193*
Yancey, Rick
  See Yancey, Richard
Yang, Belle 1960- *170*
Yang, James 1960- *190*
Yang, Jay 1941- *12*
Yang, Mingyi 1943- *72*
Yarbrough, Camille 1938- *79*
  See also CLR *29*
Yarbrough, Ira 1910(?)-1983
  Obituary *35*
Yaroslava
  See Mills, Yaroslava Surmach
Yashima, Taro
  See CLR *4*
  See Iwamatsu, Jun Atsushi
Yates, Elizabeth 1905-2001 .... *68*
  Obituary *128*
  Earlier sketch in SATA *4*
  See also SAAS *6*
Yates, Janelle K(aye) 1957- *77*
Yates, John 1939- *74*
Yates, Philip 1958- *149*
  Earlier sketch in SATA *92*
Yates, Raymond F(rancis) 1895-1966 .... *31*
Yaukey, Grace S(ydenstricker)
  1899-1994 .... *80*
  Earlier sketch in SATA *5*
Ye, Ting-xing 1952- *106*
Yeahpau, Thomas M. 1975- *187*
Yeakley, Marjory Hall 1908- *21*
Yeatman, Linda 1938- *42*
Yee, Brenda Shannon *133*
Yee, Lisa 1959- *160*
Yee, Paul (R.) 1956- *143*
  Earlier sketches in SATA *67, 96*
  See also CLR *44*
Yee, Wong Herbert 1953- *172*
  Earlier sketches in SATA *78, 115*
Yeh, Chun-Chan 1914- *79*
  See Ye Junjian
Ye Junjian
  See Yeh, Chun-Chan
Yenawine, Philip 1942- *85*
Yensid, Retlaw
  See Disney, Walt(er Elias)
Yeo, Wilma (Lethem) 1918-1994 .... *81*
  Earlier sketch in SATA *24*
Yeoman, John 1934- *80*
  Earlier sketch in SATA *28*
  See also CLR *46*
Yep, Laurence 1948- *176*
  Earlier sketches in SATA *7, 69, 123*
  See also CLR *132*

Author Index

Yep, Laurence Michael
  See Yep, Laurence
Yepsen, Roger B(ennet), Jr. 1947- 59
Yerian, Cameron John 21
Yerian, Margaret A. 21
Yerxa, Leo 1947- 181
Yetska
  See Ironside, Jetske
Yezerski, Thomas F. 1969- 190
Ylvisaker, Anne 1965(?)- 172
Yoder, Carolyn P(atricia) 1953- 149
Yoder, Dorothy Meenen 1921- 96
Yoder, Dot
  See Yoder, Dorothy Meenen
Yoder, Walter D. 1933- 88
Yolen, Jane 1939- 158
  Autobiography Feature 111
  Earlier sketches in SATA *4, 40, 75, 112*
  See also CLR *44*
  See also SAAS *1*
Yolen, Jane Hyatt
  See Yolen, Jane
Yonge, Charlotte (Mary) 1823-1901 17
Yoo, Paula 1969(?)- 174
Yoo, Taeeun 191
Yorinks, Adrienne 1956- 171
Yorinks, Arthur 1953- 144
  Earlier sketches in SATA *33, 49, 85*
  See also CLR *20*
York, Alison
  See Nicole, Christopher (Robin)
York, Andrew
  See Nicole, Christopher (Robin)
York, Carol Beach 1928- 77
  Earlier sketch in SATA *6*
York, Rebecca
  See Buckholtz, Eileen (Garber)
  and Glick, Ruth (Burtnick)
York, Simon
  See Heinlein, Robert A.
Yoshida, Toshi 1911- 77
Yoshikawa, Sachiko 181
Yost, Edna 1889-1971
  Obituary 26
Youd, C. S.
  See SAAS *6*
  See Youd, (Christopher) Samuel
Youd, (Christopher) Samuel 1922- 135
  Brief entry 30
  Earlier sketch in SATA *47*
  See Christopher, John
  and Youd, C. S.
Young, Amy L. 185
Young, Bob
  See Young, Robert W(illiam)
  and Young, James Robert
Young, Carol 1945- 102
Young, Catherine
  See Olds, Helen Diehl
Young, Clarence 67
  Earlier sketch in SATA *1*
  See Stratemeyer, Edward L.
Young, Collier
  See Bloch, Robert (Albert)
Young, Dan 1952- 126
Young, Dianne 1959- 88
Young, Dorothea Bennett 1924- 31
Young, Ed 1931- 173
  Earlier sketches in SATA *10, 74, 122*
  See also CLR *27*
Young, Ed Tse-chun
  See Young, Ed
Young, Edward
  See Reinfeld, Fred
Young, Elaine L.
  See Schulte, Elaine L(ouise)
Young, James
  See Graham, Ian
Young, Jan
  See Young, Janet Randall
Young, Janet 1957- 188

Young, Janet Randall 1919-1994 3
Young, Janet Ruth
  See Young, Janet
Young, Jeff C. 1948- 132
Young, John
  See Macintosh, Brownie
Young, Judy 1956- 155
Young, Judy (Elaine) Dockrey 1949- 72
Young, Karen Romano 1959- 168
  Earlier sketch in SATA *116*
Young, Ken 1956- 86
Young, Lois Horton 1911-1981 26
Young, Louisa 161
Young, Louise B. 1919- 64
Young, Margaret B(uckner) 1922- 2
Young, Mary 1940- 89
Young, Miriam 1913-1974 7
Young, Noela 1930- 89
Young, (Rodney Lee) Patrick (Jr.) 1937- 22
Young, Percy M(arshall) 1912-2004 31
  Obituary 154
Young, Richard Alan 1946- 72
Young, Robert W(illiam) 1916-1969 3
Young, Ross B. 1955- 150
Young, Ruth 1946- 67
Young, Sara
  See Pennypacker, Sara
Young, Scott A. 1918-2005 5
Young, Scott Alexander
  See Young, Scott A.
Young, Vivien
  See Gater, Dilys
Younger, Barbara 1954- 108
Youngs, Betty 1934-1985 53
  Obituary 42
Younkin, Paula 1942- 77
Yount, Lisa (Ann) 1944- 124
  Earlier sketch in SATA *74*
Yourgrau, Barry 179
Yuditskaya, Tatyana 1964- 75
Yumoto, Kazumi 1959- 153

Z

Zach, Cheryl (Byrd) 1947- 98
  Brief entry 51
  Earlier sketch in SATA *58*
  See also SAAS *24*
Zacharias, Gary L. 1946- 153
Zaffo, George J. (?)-1984 42
Zagarenski, Pamela 1969(?)- 183
Zagwyn, Deborah Turney 1953- 138
  Earlier sketch in SATA *78*
Zahares, Wade 193
Zahn, Timothy 1951- 156
  Earlier sketch in SATA *91*
Zaid, Barry 1938- 51
Zaidenberg, Arthur 1908(?)-1990 34
  Obituary 66
Zalben, Jane Breskin 1950- 170
  Earlier sketches in SATA *7, 79, 120*
  See also CLR *84*
Zallinger, Jean (Day) 1918- 115
  Earlier sketches in SATA *14, 80*
Zallinger, Peter Franz 1943- 49
Zambreno, Mary Frances 1954- 140
  Earlier sketch in SATA *75*
Zanderbergen, George
  See May, Julian
Zappa, Ahmet 1974- 180
Zappa, Ahmet Emuukha Rodan
  See Zappa, Ahmet
Zappler, Lisbeth 1930- 10
Zarchy, Harry 1912-1987 34
Zarin, Cynthia 1959- 192
  Earlier sketch in SATA *108*
Zaring, Jane (Thomas) 1936- 40
Zarins, Joyce Audy 57
  See dos Santos, Joyce Audy

Zaslavsky, Claudia 1917- 36
Zaugg, Sandra L. 1938- 118
Zaugg, Sandy
  See Zaugg, Sandra L.
Zaunders, Bo 1939- 137
Zawadzki, Marek 1958- 97
Zebra, A.
  See Scoltock, Jack
Zebrowski, George 1945- 67
Zebrowski, George T.
  See Zebrowski, George
Zeck, Gerald Anthony 1939- 40
Zeck, Gerry
  See Zeck, Gerald Anthony
Zed, Dr.
  See Penrose, Gordon
Zei, Alki 1925- 24
  See also CLR *6*
Zeier, Joan T(heresa) 1931- 81
Zeinert, Karen 1942-2002 137
  Earlier sketch in SATA *79*
Zeises, Lara M. 1976- 184
  Earlier sketch in SATA *145*
Zelazny, Roger 1937-1995 57
  Brief entry 39
Zelazny, Roger Joseph
  See Zelazny, Roger
Zeldis, Malcah 1931- 146
  Earlier sketch in SATA *86*
Zelinsky, Paul O. 1953- 154
  Brief entry 33
  Earlier sketches in SATA *49, 102*
  See also CLR *55*
Zellan, Audrey Penn 22
  See Penn, Audrey
Zemach, Harve 3
  See Fischtrom, Harvey
Zemach, Kaethe 1958- 149
  Brief entry 39
  Earlier sketch in SATA *49*
Zemach, Margot 1931-1989 70
  Obituary 59
  Earlier sketch in SATA *21*
Zemach-Bersin, Kaethe
  See Zemach, Kaethe
Zeman, Ludmila 1947- 153
Zephaniah, Benjamin 1958- 189
  Earlier sketches in SATA *86, 140*
Zephaniah, Benjamin Obadiah Iqbal
  See Zephaniah, Benjamin
Zephaniah, Benjamin Pbadiah Iqubal
  See Zephaniah, Benjamin
Zephaniah, Benjamin Pbadiah Iqubal
  See Zephaniah, Benjamin
Zerman, Melvyn Bernard 1930- 46
Zettner, Pat 1940- 70
Zevin, Gabrielle 176
Zhang, Christopher Zhong-Yuan 1954- 91
Zhang, Song Nan 1942- 170
  Earlier sketch in SATA *85*
Ziefert, Harriet 1941- 154
  Earlier sketch in SATA *101*
Ziegler, Jack (Denmore) 1942- 60
Ziemienski, Dennis (Theodore) 1947- 10
Ziliox, Marc
  See Fichter, George S.
Zillah
  See Macdonald, Zillah K(atherine)
Zim, Herbert S(pencer) 1909-1994 30
  Obituary 85
  Earlier sketch in SATA *1*
  See also CLR *2*
  See also SAAS *2*
Zima, Gordon 1920- 90
Zimelman, Nathan 1921- 65
  Brief entry 37
Zimmer, Dirk 1943- 147
  Earlier sketch in SATA *65*
Zimmer, Tracie Vaughn 169
Zimmerman, Andrea 1950- 192
  Earlier sketch in SATA *123*

Zimmerman, Andrea Griffing
  See Zimmerman, Andrea
Zimmerman, H. Werner 1951- *101*
Zimmerman, Heinz Werner
  See Zimmerman, H. Werner
Zimmerman, Naoma 1914-2004 .... *10*
Zimmermann, Arnold E. 1909- *58*
Zimmett, Debbie
  See Becker, Deborah Zimmett
Zimmy
  See Stratemeyer, Edward L.
Zimnik, Reiner 1930- *36*
  See also CLR 3
Zindel, Bonnie 1943- *34*
Zindel, Lizabeth *187*
Zindel, Paul 1936-2003 .... *102*
  Obituary *142*
  Earlier sketches in SATA *16, 58*
  See also CLR 85
Ziner, Feenie
  See Ziner, Florence
Ziner, Florence 1921- *5*
Zingara, Professor
  See Leeming, Joseph

Zinger, Yitskhok
  See Singer, Isaac Bashevis
Zion, Eugene 1913-1975 .... *18*
Zion, Gene
  See Zion, Eugene
Zoehfeld, Kathleen Weidner 1954- *193*
Zohorsky, Janet R. 1958- *148*
Zolkower, Edie Stoltz *171*
Zolkowski, Cathy (A.) 1969- *121*
Zollars, Jaime *191*
Zolotow, Charlotte 1915- *138*
  Earlier sketches in SATA *1, 35, 78*
  See also CLR 77
Zolotow, Charlotte Gertrude Shapiro
  See Zolotow, Charlotte
Zolotow, Ellen
  See Dragonwagon, Crescent
Zonderman, Jon 1957- *92*
Zonia, Dhimitri 1921- *20*
Zonta, Pat 1951- *143*
Zubrowski, Bernard 1939- *90*
  Earlier sketch in SATA *35*
Zubrowski, Bernie
  See Zubrowski, Bernard

Zucker, Miriam S.
  See Reichert, Miriam Zucker
Zuckerman, Linda *190*
Zudeck, Darryl 1961- *61*
Zupa, G. Anthony
  See Zeck, Gerald Anthony
Zupancic, Lilijana Praprotnik
  See Prap, Lila
Zurbo, Matt(hew) 1967- *98*
Zurhorst, Charles (Stewart, Jr.) 1913-1989 .. *12*
Zurlo, Tony 1941- *145*
Zuromskis, Diane
  See Stanley, Diane
Zuromskis, Diane Stanley
  See Stanley, Diane
Zusak, Markus 1975- *149*
Zwahlen, Diana 1947- *88*
Zweifel, Frances W. 1931- *14*
Zwerger, Lisbeth 1954- *130*
  Earlier sketch in SATA *66*
  See also CLR 46
  See also SAAS 13
Zwinger, Ann (H.) 1925- *46*
Zymet, Cathy Alter 1965- *121*